Essentials of Managerial Finance

Tenth Edition

Essentials of Managerial Finance

Tenth Edition

J. FRED WESTON

Anderson Graduate School of Management
University of California, Los Angeles

EUGENE F. BRIGHAM

University of Florida

THE DRYDEN PRESS
Harcourt Brace College Publishers

Fort Worth   Philadelphia   San Diego   New York   Orlando   Austin   San Antonio
Toronto   Montreal   London   Sydney   Tokyo

Acquisitions Editor: Michael P. Roche
Developmental Editor: Barbara J. C. Rosenberg
Marketing Manager: Ted Barnett
Manager of Production: Lynne Bush

Project Management: Elm Street Publishing Services, Inc.
Project Editor: Karen Hill
Cover Designer: Rebecca Lemna
Copy Editor: Susan Nodine
Compositor: The Clarinda Company
Text Type: 10/12 ITC Garamond Book

ISBN: 0-03-075474-7

Library of Congress Catalog Number: 92-20736

Printed in the United States of America
3456789012 036 98765432

Cover Source: © 1992 Don Leavitt/The Image Bank

The Dryden Press Series in Finance

Amling and Droms
Investment Fundamentals

Berry and Young
**Managing Investments:
A Case Approach**

Boyet
**Security Analysis for
Investment Decisions:
Text and Software**

Brigham
**Fundamentals of Financial
Management**
Sixth Edition

Brigham and Gapenski
Cases in Financial Management
Second Edition

Brigham and Gapenski
**Cases in Financial
Management: Module A**
Second Edition

Brigham and Gapenski
**Cases in Financial
Management: Module B**

Brigham and Gapenski
**Cases in Financial
Management: Module C**

Brigham and Gapenski
**Financial Management:
Theory and Practice**
Sixth Edition

Brigham and Gapenski
Intermediate Financial Management
Fourth Edition

Brigham, Aberwald, and Gapenski
**Finance with Lotus 1-2-3:
Text and Models**
Second Edition

Campsey and Brigham
**Introduction to
Financial Management**
Third Edition

Chance
**An Introduction to
Options and Futures**
Second Edition

Clauretie and Webb
**The Theory and Practice of
Real Estate Finance**

Cooley
**Advances in Business
Financial Management:
A Collection of Readings**

Cooley and Roden
Business Financial Management
Second Edition

Curran
Principles of Corporate Finance

Evans
**International Finance:
A Markets Approach**

Fama and Miller
The Theory of Finance

Gardner and Mills
**Managing Financial Institutions:
An Asset/Liability Approach**
Second Edition

Gitman and Joehnk
Personal Financial Planning
Sixth Edition

Harrington
**Case Studies in Financial
Decision Making**
Third Edition

Hayes and Meerschwam
**Financial Institutions:
Contemporary Cases in the
Financial Services Industry**

Johnson
**Issues and Readings in
Managerial Finance**
Third Edition

Kidwell, Peterson, and Blackwell
**Financial Institutions,
Markets, and Money**
Fifth Edition

Koch
Bank Management
Second Edition

Kohn
**Money, Banking, and
Financial Markets**
Second Edition

Lee and Finnerty
**Corporate Finance: Theory,
Method, and Application**

Maisel
Real Estate Finance
Second Edition

Martin, Cox, and MacMinn
**The Theory of Finance:
Evidence and Applications**

Mayo
Finance: An Introduction
Fourth Edition

Mayo
Investments: An Introduction
Third Edition

Pettijohn
PROFIT +

Reilly
Investment Analysis and
Portfolio Management
Third Edition

Reilly
Investments
Third Edition

Sears and Trennepohl
Investment Management

Seitz
Capital Budgeting and Long-
Term Financing Decisions

Siegel and Siegel
Futures Markets

Smith and Spudeck
Interest Rates:
Principles and Applications

Stickney
Financial Statement Analysis:
A Strategic Perspective
Second Edition

Turnbull
Option Valuation

Weston and Brigham
Essentials of Managerial Finance
Tenth Edition

Weston and Copeland
Managerial Finance
Ninth Edition

Wood and Wood
Financial Markets

The HBJ College Outline Series

Baker
Financial Management

Preface

Essentials of Managerial Finance is intended for use in the introductory finance course. The book begins with a discussion of basic concepts, including accounting statements, security markets, interest rates, taxes, risk analysis, time value of money, and the basics of security valuation. Subsequent chapters explain how financial managers can help maximize their firms' values by improving decisions in such areas as working capital management, capital budgeting, and choice of capital structure. This organization has three important advantages:

1. Explaining early in the book how accounting data are used, how financial markets operate, and how security prices are determined helps students understand how managerial finance can affect the value of the firm. Also, early coverage of such key concepts as risk analysis, time value, and valuation techniques permits their use and reinforcement throughout the remainder of the book.

2. Structuring the book around markets and valuation enhances continuity because this organization helps students see how the various topics relate to one another.

3. Most students — even those who do not plan to major in finance — are generally interested in stock and bond valuation, rates of return, and the like. Since people's ability to learn a subject is a function of their interest and motivation, and since *Essentials* begins by showing the relationships between security markets, stock values, and managerial finance, this organization is good from a pedagogic standpoint.

RELATIONSHIP WITH OUR OTHER BOOKS

As the body of knowledge expanded, it first became difficult, then impossible, to provide everything one needs to know about managerial finance in one text, especially an undergraduate text. This recognition has led us to limit the scope of this book and also to write other texts to deal with the materials that cannot be included in *Essentials*. Thus, Fred Weston has coauthored a theory text with Tom Copeland *(Financial Theory and Corporate Policy),* and Weston and Copeland have also coauthored the ninth edtion of *Managerial Finance,* a very comprehensive text designed primarily for the MBA market. Lou Gapenski and Gene Brigham have coauthored both an intermediate undergraduate text (*Intermediate Financial Management,* fourth edition) and a comprehensive book aimed primarily at MBAs (*Financial Management: Theory and Practice,* sixth edition).

The relationship between *Essentials* and these more advanced books deserves special comment. First, we recognize that the advanced books are often used by students who have used *Essentials* in the introductory undergraduate course, so we wanted to avoid excessive overlap but also to be sure to expose students to alternative points of view on controversial subjects. To avoid unnecessary overlap, both we and our reviewers were on the alert to eliminate excessive duplications. We should note, though, that our students in advanced courses invariably tell us that they find it helpful to have the more difficult materials repeated—they need the review. Students also say they like the fact that the style and notation used in our upper-level books are consistent with those in the introductory text, as this makes learning easier. Regarding alternative points of view, we have made every effort to take a moderate, middle-of-the-road approach, and where serious controversy exists, we have tried to present the alternative points of view. Reviewers were asked to consider this point, and their comments have helped us eliminate potential biases.

INTENDED MARKET AND USE

As noted above, *Essentials* is intended for use as an introductory text. The key chapters can be covered in a one-term course, and, supplemented with cases and some outside readings, the book can also be used in a two-term course. If it is used in a one-term course, the instructor will probably cover only selected chapters, leaving the others for students either to examine on their own or to use as references in conjunction with work in later courses. Also, we have made every effort to write the chapters in a flexible, modular format, which helps instructors cover the material in a different sequence should they choose to do so.

MAJOR CHANGES IN THE TENTH EDITION

The theory and practice of finance are dynamic, and as new developments occur, they should be incorporated into a textbook such as this one. Also, working with a team of reviewers, we are constantly looking for ways to improve the book in terms of clarity and student understanding. As a result, several important changes were made in this edition, the most important of which are discussed below.

Combination/Deletion of Chapters

The organization of the ninth edition was generally well received, but reviewers made two suggestions which led to significant structural changes. First, financial statements and ratio analysis were moved forward to Chapter 2 and used to show how financial decisions discussed in the balance of the book affect the operations of the firm, and hence the value of its stock. Second, multinational managerial finance was both integrated throughout the text and included as a separate chapter in recognition of the increasing importance of globalization.

Time Line and Solutions Approach to TVM Analysis

Chapter 5, "Time Value of Money," has been completely rewritten. We now begin each major section with a verbal discussion of a time value issue, then we present a time line to show graphically the cash flows that are involved, after which we give the equation that must be solved to obtain the required answer. Finally, we present three methods which can be used to solve the equation: (1) a numerical solution, (2) a solution based on the time value tables, and (3) a financial calculator solution. The time line helps students visualize the problem at hand and see how to set it up for solution, the equation helps them understand the mathematics, and the three-pronged solution approach helps them see that time value problems can be solved in alternative ways. Each student will focus on the particular solution technique he or she will actually use, which increasingly calls for using a financial calculator. One advantage of our new approach is that with it financial calculators are no longer seen as a "black box," but, rather, as an efficient way to solve a particular time value equation.

The same approach is used in subsequent chapters, especially in the chapters dealing with stock and bond valuation, with aspects of working capital management, and with capital budgeting.

Globalization

The movement toward the globalization of financial markets and institutions is continuing ever more rapidly. A Japanese commercial bank is now the largest in the world, and Japanese and European commercial and investment bankers are aggressively moving into areas that have traditionally been dominated by U.S. firms. This situation is subjecting U.S. banks and investment bankers to increasing competition, but it is also giving U.S. companies access to additional sources of funds. All of this means that U.S. financial managers must know more about foreign capital markets and securities, as well as more about the ways foreign firms affect domestic U.S. markets of all kinds.

Successful firms are recognizing that it is becoming increasingly difficult to remain competitive without becoming a global player. New technological developments have led to increasingly complex products, and hence to higher developmental costs for autos, computers, aircraft, prescription drugs, and the like. Huge developmental costs require huge sales volumes, which in turn make it necessary for firms to sell globally. At the same time, improvements in air freight and other types of transportation, and in communications, are making it increasingly feasible to manufacture products virtually anywhere, and strong competitive pressures from multinational companies make it imperative that businesses manufacture wherever costs are lowest. Service companies, including banks, advertising agencies, and accounting firms, must follow their customers, so they too are "going global." However, even if a firm operates only domestically, international events influence domestic interest rates and economic activity, so no one is immune to global pressures. All of this means that financial managers must think globally about many decisions.

Because of these trends, we have incorporated a "think globally" theme into this tenth edition. Throughout the text, we have woven global threads in an effort to make students recognize that success in today's world requires a multinational perspective. In addition, we have added a separate chapter on multinational managerial finance. We are not attempting to make multinational finance experts out of introductory finance students, but even introductory students should understand that successful firms must make decisions within a global context.

Computerization

Personal computers are changing the way financial managers think about financial analysis. Cash flows through time are thought of as cells across a row in a spreadsheet, and factors which determine the cash flows, such as sales price, unit sales, variable costs, and taxes, can be visualized as cells running down a spreadsheet column. Since real-world analyses will be done using PCs, it is important that textbooks be structured to make the transition from the classroom to the real world as easy as possible. Students must recognize that computers are capable of providing answers to questions that were not even asked a few years ago, and it helps if textbook problems are structured so that students can see how the power of computers can be brought to bear on the issues at hand.

With these thoughts in mind, parts of *Essentials* have been restructured to reflect computerization. For example, certain tables have been recast to reflect spreadsheet formats, and text discussions have been revised to enable students to visualize computer solutions. Note, though, that it is not necessary for students using the text to be proficient (or even literate) in computer usage. However, students who do continue their studies in finance and who later use spreadsheets such as *Lotus 1-2-3* (either to analyze cases or in real-world applications) will benefit greatly from the changes. For students who do have access to computers and *Lotus 1-2-3* while they are taking the course, and for instructors who want their students to explore the power of the computer for analyzing financial problems, the book contains a computer-related problem for most chapters, and a diskette containing the models is available to adopting instructors.

OTHER CHANGES

As always, we have updated and clarified the text and end-of-chapter problems, and we have made numerous improvements in the pedagogy. Particular emphasis has been placed on including the latest tax laws, updating the real-world examples, and including the latest changes in the financial environment and in financial theory. Here is a sampling of the changes we made:

1. Additional "exam-type" end-of-chapter problems have been added to give students practice with problems similar to some of the more difficult ones in the *Test Bank*. This addition is especially useful for students in large classes, where exams are necessarily in a multiple-choice format.

2. A table summarizing the major market instruments, market participants, and security characteristics has been added to Chapter 3, "The Financial Environment." This information provides an overview for students while they are reading the chapter material.

3. Graphs which illustrate the relationships between business risk, financial risk, and debt levels were added to Chapter 17, "Capital Structure and Leverage."

4. An illustration of the effects of dividend policy on stock prices and cost of equity was added to Chapter 18, "Dividend Policy."

5. We have improved the integrative problems that appear in each chapter after the regular end-of-chapter problems. The integrative problems cover, in a comprehensive manner, all of the major concepts discussed in the chapters. We use these problems as the basis for our lectures, but other instructors assign them as comprehensive study problems.

6. To facilitate the use of the integrative problems as lecture problems, we wrote the *Instructor's Manual* solutions in a lecture note format, and we also developed a set of transparency masters/acetates to go with the solutions. In addition, since students often get left behind when instructors use overheads, we have changed the *Blueprints* ancillary to make it much easier for students to take notes. Specifically, more information, and less blank space, is provided in *Blueprints,* and it is in a larger (8½″ × 11″) format. Also, rather than being packaged with the text, a copy of *Blueprints* is made available to instructors, who can, if they choose to, have it copied in an off-campus copy center. In any event, *Blueprints* restates the integrative problem, provides partially completed answers, and leaves room for additional notes. Using *Blueprints* as a guide, students will be able to take good notes and still have time to follow the lecture.

ANCILLARY MATERIALS

A number of items are available free of charge to adopting instructors:

1. **Instructor's Manual.** A comprehensive manual is available to instructors who adopt the book. The manual contains answers to all text questions and problems, a detailed set of lecture notes (including suggestions for using the transparency acetates described below), detailed solutions to integrative problems, sample exams, and suggested course outlines.

2. **Transparencies.** A comprehensive set of transparency masters and acetates, including approximately 40 color acetates, is available.

3. **Test Bank.** A revised and enlarged *Test Bank,* with more than 1,200 class-tested questions and problems in objective format, is available both in book form and on IBM and Macintosh computer diskettes. The diskettes come either in the regular computerized test bank format or in *WordPerfect* files for easy editing. New questions, which are more challenging than those in many test banks, have been added. Also, information regarding the topics covered, the degree of difficulty, and the correct answer are provided in the margin for each question. Complete solutions are given for all numerical problems, and explanations for many conceptual questions are also provided. Those questions which require the use of a financial calculator are grouped together in a separate section at the end of each chapter. Finally, it is worth noting that a new, easy-to-use system makes it

extremely easy to construct exams, which come with keys automatically generated by the test bank program.

4. **Supplemental Problems.** Another set of additional problems, organized according to topic and level of difficulty, will be provided to instructors who request it.

5. **Problem Diskette.** A diskette containing *Lotus 1-2-3* models for the computer-related end-of-chapter problems is also available. To obtain the diskette, complete the order form found at the front of the *Instructor's Manual.*

6. **Blueprints and "Course-Pack."** The *Blueprints* supplement is provided to instructors free of charge, and it (or selected parts of it) can be copied in an off-campus copy center and sold to students for only the copying cost. We do this with the chapters we cover in our course, and we add some items such as the syllabus, several old exams, instructions on the use of financial calculators, and other course-specific materials. Other instructors have only the transparencies copied or some transparencies plus the solutions to some of the end-of-chapter problems. In any event, we encourage instructors to construct their own "course-packs," drawing from materials we have provided, to facilitate their students' learning.

A number of additional items are available for purchase by students:

1. **Study Guide.** This supplement outlines the key sections of each chapter, provides students with self-test questions, and also provides a set of problems and solutions similar to those in the text and in the *Test Bank.* Since many instructors are now using multiple-choice exams, we have increased coverage of exam-type questions and problems in the new study guide.

2. **Casebook.** A new casebook, *Cases in Financial Management,* second edition, by Eugene F. Brigham and Louis C. Gapenski, is well suited for use with this text. The cases provide real-world applications of the methodologies and concepts developed in the text. Subsets of this casebook, designated "Module A," "Module B," and so forth, which contain 12 cases each, are also available. The modules are a perfect supplement for professors seeking a limited number of cases to use with *Essentials.*

3. **Readings Books.** A readings book, *Issues and Readings in Managerial Finance* (Dryden Press, 1987), edited by Ramon E. Johnson, provides an excellent mix of theoretical and practical articles which can be used to supplement the text. Another supplemental reader is *Advances in Business Financial Management: A Collection of Readings* (Dryden Press, 1989), edited by Philip L. Cooley, which provides a broader selection of articles from which to choose.

4. **Finance with Lotus 1-2-3: Text and Models.** In its second edition, this text by Eugene F. Brigham, Dana A. Aberwald, and Louis C. Gapenski (Dryden Press, 1992) enables students to learn, on their own, how to use *Lotus 1-2-3* and apply it to financial decisions.

5. **PROFIT+.** This software supplement by James Pettijohn of Southwest Missouri State University contains 18 user-friendly programs that include the time value of money, forecasting, and capital budgeting. The package includes a user's manual, and it is available for the IBM PC.

ACKNOWLEDGMENTS

This book reflects the efforts of a great many people over a number of years. First, we extend our gratitude to Scott Besley, University of South Florida, who reviewed the manuscript and also worked through the end-of-chapter questions, problems, integrative problems, and computer-related problems to ensure their accuracy, clarity, and consistency with the text.

Next, we would like to thank the following professors, whose reviews and comments have helped this and prior editions and our companion books: Mike Adler, Syed Ahmad, Ed Altman, Bruce Anderson, Ron Anderson, Bob Angell, Vince Apilado, Henry Arnold, Bob Aubey, Gil Babcock, Peter Bacon, Kent Baker, Robert Balik, Tom Bankston, Les Barenbaum, Charles Barngrover, Bill Beedles, Moshe Ben-Horim, Bill Beranek, Tom Berry, Will Bertin, Dan Best, Roger Bey, Dalton Bigbee, John Bildersee, Russ Boisjoly, Keith Boles, Geof Booth, Jerry Boswell, Kenneth Boudreaux, Helen Bowers, Oswald Bowlin, Don Boyd, G. Michael Boyd, Pat Boyer, Joe Brandt, Elizabeth Brannigan, Greg Brauer, Mary Broske, Dave Brown, Kate Brown, Bill Brueggeman, Stephen G. Buell, Ted Byrley, Bill Campsey, Bob Carlson, Severin Carlson, David Cary, Steve Celec, Don Chance, Antony Chang, Susan Chaplinsky, Jay Choi, S. K. Choudhary, Lal Chugh, Maclyn Clouse, Margaret Considine, Phil Cooley, Joe Copeland, David Cordell, Marcia Cornett, M. P. Corrigan, John Cotner, Charles Cox, David Crary, John Crockett, Jr., Roy Crum, Brent Dalrymple, Bill Damon, Joel Dauten, Steve Dawson, Sankar De, Fred Dellva, James Desreumaux, Bodie Dickerson, Bernard Dill, J. David Diltz, Gregg Dimkoff, Les Dlabay, Mark Dorfman, Gene Drzycimski, Dean Dudley, David Durst, Ed Dyl, Richard Edelman, Charles Edwards, John Ellis, Dave Ewert, John Ezzell, Michael Ferri, Jim Filkins, John Finnerty, Susan Fischer, Steven Flint, Russ Fogler, Dan French, Michael Garlington, David Garraty, Jim Garven, Adam Gehr, Jr., Jim Gentry, Philip Glasgo, Rudyard Goode, Walt Goulet, Bernie Grablowsky, Theoharry Grammatikos, Reynold Griffith, Ed Grossnickle, John Groth, Alan Grunewald, Manak Gupta, Sam Hadaway, Don Hakala, Paul Halpern, Gerald Hamsmith, William Hardin, John Harris, Paul Hastings, Bob Haugen, Steve Hawke, Del Hawley, Robert Hehre, George Hettenhouse, Hans Heymann, Kendall Hill, Roger Hill, Tom Hindelang, Linda Hittle, Ralph Hocking, J. Ronald Hoffmeister, Robert Hollinger, Jim Horrigan, John Houston, John Howe, Keith Howe, Steve Isberg, Jim Jackson, Kose John, Craig Johnson, Keith Johnson, Ramon Johnson, Ray Jones, Frank Jordan, Manual Jose, Alfred Kahl, Gus Kalogeras, Mike Keenan, Bill Kennedy, James Keys, Carol Kiefer, Joe Kiernan, Rick Kish, Don Knight, Dorothy Koehl, Jaroslaw Komarynsky, Duncan Kretovich, Harold Krogh, Charles Kroncke, Don Kummer, Joan Lamm, Larry Lang, P. Lange, Howard Lanser, John Lasik, Edward Lawrence, Martin Lawrence, Wayne Lee, Jim LePage, Jules Levine, John Lewis, Jason Lin, Chuck Linke, Bill Lloyd, Susan Long, Judy Maese, Bob Magee, Ileen Malitz, Phil Malone, Lewis Mandell, Terry Maness, Chris Manning, S. K. Mansinghka, Terry Martell, D. J. Masson, John Mathys, John McAlhany, Andy McCollough, Ambrose McCoy, Thomas McCue, Bill McDaniel, John McDowell, Charles McKinney, Robyn McLaughlin, Jamshid Mehran, Larry Merville, Rick Meyer, Jim Millar, Ed Miller, John Mitchell, Carol Moerdyk, Bob Moore, Barry Morris, Gene Morris, Fred Morrissey, Chris Muscarella, David Nachman, Tim Nantell, Don Nast, Bill Nelson, Bob Nelson, Bob Niendorf, Tom O'Brien, Dennis O'Connor, John O'Donnell, Jim

Olsen, Robert Olsen, Jim Pappas, Stephen Parrish, Glenn Petry, Jim Pettijohn, Rich Pettit, Dick Pettway, Hugo Phillips, H. R. Pickett, John Pinkerton, Gerald Pogue, Eugene Poindexter, R. Potter, Franklin Potts, R. Powell, Chris Prestopino, Jerry Prock, Howard Puckett, Herbert Quigley, George Racette, Bob Radcliffe, Bill Rentz, Ken Riener, Charles Rini, John Ritchie, Pietra Rivoli, Antonio Rodriguez, James Rosenfeld, E. N. Roussakis, Dexter Rowell, Jim Sachlis, Abdul Sadik, Thomas Scampini, Kevin Scanlon, Frederick Schadler, Mary Jane Scheuer, Carl Schweser, David Scott, John Settle, Alan Severn, Sol Shalit, Frederic Shipley, Dilip Shome, Ron Shrieves, Neil Sicherman, J. B. Silvers, Clay Singleton, Joe Sinkey, Stacy Sirmans, Jaye Smith, Patricia Smith, Patrick Smith, Steve Smith, Don Sorensen, David Speairs, Ken Stanly, Ed Stendardi, Alan Stephens, Don Stevens, Jerry Stevens, Glen Strasburg, Philip Swensen, Ernest Swift, Paul Swink, Gary Tallman, Dular Talukdar, Dennis Tanner, Craig Tapley, Russ Taussig, Richard Teweles, Ted Teweles, Francis C. Thomas, Andrew Thompson, John Thompson, Dogan Tirtiroglu, Marco Tonietti, William Tozer, George Trivoli, George Tsetsekos, Ricardo Ulivi, David Upton, Howard Van Auken, Pretorious Van den Dool, Pieter Vandenberg, Paul Vanderheiden, JoAnn Vaughan, Jim Verbrugge, Patrick Vincent, Steve Vinson, Susan Visscher, John Wachowicz, Mike Walker, Sam Weaver, Kuo-Chiang Wei, Bill Welch, Robert J. Wiley, Norm Williams, Tony Wingler, Ed Wolfe, Don Woods, Michael Yonan, Dennis Zocco, and Kent Zumwalt.

Special thanks are due to Chris Barry, Texas Christian University, who wrote many of the small business sections; to Dilip Shome, Virginia Polytechnic Institute, who helped greatly with the capital structure chapter; to Roy Crum, University of Florida, who coauthored the multinational finance chapter; and to Art Herrmann, University of Hartford, who coauthored the bankruptcy appendix. Dana Aberwald worked closely with us at every stage of the revision; her assistance was absolutely invaluable. Also, Louis Gapenski worked closely with us on the integrative problems and offered advice on many other parts of the book. In addition, Steve Bouchard and Chad Hamilton of the University of Florida worked through and/or discussed with us all or major parts of the book and ancillaries to help eliminate errors and confusing sections. Carol Stanton and Bob Karp typed and helped proof the various manuscripts. Finally, the Dryden Press and Elm Street Publishing Services staffs helped greatly with all phases of the text development and production: Ted Barnett, Lynne Bush, Guy Jacobs, Sheryl McMaster, Mike Roche, and Barbara Rosenberg of Dryden and Barb Bahnsen, Karen Hill, Suzanne Martiradonna, Sue Nodine, Jane Perkins, Cate Rzasa, and David Talley of Elm Street.

ERRORS IN THE TEXT

At this point, most authors make a statement like this: "We appreciate all the help we received from the people listed above, but any remaining errors are, of course, our own responsibility." And generally there are more than enough remaining errors. As a part of our quest for clarity, we resolved to avoid this problem in *Essentials,* and as a result of our error-detection procedures, we are convinced that it is virtually free of mistakes.

Some of our colleagues suggested that if we are so confident about the book's accuracy, we should offer a reward to people who find errors. With this in mind, but primarily because we want to detect any remaining errors and correct them in subsequent printings, we hereby offer a reward of $10.00 per error to the first person who reports it to us. (Any error that has follow-through effects is counted as two errors only.) Two accounting students have set up a foolproof audit system to make sure we pay—accounting students tend to be skeptics! Please report any errors to Eugene Brigham at the address below.

CONCLUSION

Finance is, in a real sense, the cornerstone of the enterprise system—good financial management is vitally important to the economic health of business firms, and hence to the nation and the world. Because of its importance, finance should be widely and thoroughly understood, but this is easier said than done. The field is relatively complex, and it is undergoing constant change in response to shifts in economic conditions. All of this makes finance stimulating and exciting but also challenging and sometimes perplexing. We sincerely hope that *Essentials* will meet its own challenge by contributing to a better understanding of our financial system.

J. Fred Weston
Anderson Graduate School of Management
University of California, Los Angeles
Los Angeles, California 90024

Eugene F. Brigham
College of Business
University of Florida
Gainesville, Florida 32611-2017

October 1992

Brief Contents

Part I **Introduction to Managerial Finance 1**

Chapter 1   An Overview of Managerial Finance 3

Chapter 2   Analysis of Financial Statements 31

    Appendix 2A   Statement of Cash Flows 81

Chapter 3   The Financial Environment: Markets, Institutions, Interest Rates, and Taxes 85

Part II **Essential Concepts in Managerial Finance 139**

Chapter 4   Risk and Rates of Return 141

    Appendix 4A   Calculating Beta Coefficients 182

Chapter 5   Time Value of Money 187

    Appendix 5A   Continuous Compounding and Discounting 232

Chapter 6   Bond and Stock Valuation 235

Part III **Financial Forecasting, Planning, and Control 287**

Chapter 7   Financial Forecasting 289

Chapter 8   Financial Planning and Control 323

Part IV **Working Capital Management 355**

Chapter 9   Working Capital Policy 357

Chapter 10   Cash and Marketable Securities 381

Chapter 11   Credit Management 409

Chapter 12   Inventory Management 431

Chapter 13   Short-Term Financing 455

Part V   **Strategic Long-Term Investment Decisions: Capital Budgeting**   493

Chapter 14   Capital Budgeting Techniques   495

Chapter 15   Project Cash Flows and Risk   531

           Appendix 15A   Depreciation   576

Part VI   **The Cost of Capital, Leverage, and Dividend Policy**   581

Chapter 16   The Cost of Capital   583

Chapter 17   Capital Structure and Leverage   621

Chapter 18   Dividend Policy   665

Part VII   **Strategic Long-Term Financing Decisions**   703

Chapter 19   Common Stock and the Investment Banking Process   705

Chapter 20   Long-Term Debt   739

           Appendix 20A   Bankruptcy and Reorganization   773

           Appendix 20B   Refunding Operations   780

Chapter 21   Hybrid Financing: Preferred Stock, Leasing, and Option Securities   787

Chapter 22   Mergers, Divestitures, Holding Companies, and LBOs   829

Chapter 23   Multinational Managerial Finance   861

Appendix A   Mathematical Tables   A-1

Appendix B   Solutions to Self-Test Problems   B-1

Appendix C   Answers to End-of-Chapter Problems   C-1

Appendix D   Selected Equations and Data   D-1

Contents

Part I   **Introduction to Managerial Finance 1**

Chapter 1   An Overview of Managerial Finance 3

A Managerial Perspective 3   Career Opportunities in Finance 5   Managerial Finance in the 1990s 6   Increasing Importance of Managerial Finance 8   The Financial Manager's Responsibility 9   Alternative Forms of Business Organization 10   Finance in the Organizational Structure of the Firm 13   The Goals of the Corporation 14   Business Ethics 16   Agency Relationships 17   *Industry Practice   How Important is the Shareholder's Proxy? 21*   Managerial Actions to Maximize Shareholder Wealth 23   The External Environment 25   Organization of the Book 25   *Small Business   Goals and Resources in the Small Firm 27*   Summary 28

Chapter 2   Analysis of Financial Statements 31

A Managerial Perspective 31   Financial Statements and Reports 33   *Industry Practice   Creative Accounting and Cooking the Books Hollywood Style 46*   Ratio Analysis 48   Comparative Ratios 64   Uses and Limitations of Ratio Analysis 66   *Small Business   Financial Analysis in the Small Firm 68*   Summary 69

Appendix 2A   Statement of Cash Flows 81

Chapter 3   The Financial Environment: Markets, Institutions, Interest Rates, and Taxes 85

A Managerial Perspective 85   The Financial Markets 87   Financial Institutions 91   The Stock Market 94   *Industry Practice   The New Banking Law Gets Tough with Banks 95*   The Cost of Money 98   Interest Rate Levels 100   The Determinants of Market Interest Rates 104   The Term Structure of Interest Rates 109   Other Factors That Influence Interest Rate Levels 113   Interest Rate Levels and Stock Prices 116   Interest Rates and Business Decisions 116   The Federal Income Tax System 118   Depreciation 127   *Small Business   Building a Banking Relationship 127*   Summary 129

Part II   **Essential Concepts in Managerial Finance 139**

Chapter 4   Risk and Rates of Return 141

A Managerial Perspective 141   Defining and Measuring Risk 143   Expected Rate of Return 145   Portfolio Risk and the Capital Asset Pricing Model 154

The Relationship between Risk and Rates of Return 167   Physical Assets versus
Securities 173   A Word of Caution 173   Risk in a Global Context 174
Summary 174

Appendix 4A   Calculating Beta Coefficients 182

Chapter 5   Time Value of Money 187

A Managerial Perspective 187   Time Lines 188   Future Value 189   Present
Value 195   Solving for Time and Interest Rates 198   Future Value of an
Annuity 200   Present Value of an Annuity 203   Perpetuities 206   Uneven
Cash Flow Streams 207   Semiannual and Other Compounding Periods 210
Fractional Time Periods 215   Amortized Loans 215   Comparison of Different
Types of Interest Rates 217   Summary 220

Appendix 5A   Continuous Compounding and Discounting 232

Chapter 6   Bond and Stock Valuation 235

A Managerial Perspective 235   Bond Valuation 236   Preferred Stock
Valuation 253   Common Stock Valuation 254   Stock Market Equilibrium 266
Small Business   Valuation of Small Firms 275   Summary 276

Part III   **Financial Forecasting, Planning, and Control 287**

Chapter 7   Financial Forecasting 289

A Managerial Perspective 289   Sales Forecasts 290   The Projected Balance Sheet
Method 293   The Formula Method for Forecasting AFN 301   Forecasting
Financial Requirements When the Balance Sheet Ratios Are Subject to Change 304
Other Forecasting Techniques 307   Computerized Financial Planning Models 309
Summary 310

Chapter 8   Financial Planning and Control 323

A Managerial Perspective 323   Financial Planning and Control Processes 324
Breakeven Analysis 326   Operating Leverage 331   Cash Breakeven Analysis 336
The Cash Budget 338   Control in Multidivisional Companies 343   Summary 346

Part IV   **Working Capital Management 355**

Chapter 9   Working Capital Policy 357

A Managerial Perspective 357   Working Capital Terminology 358   The
Requirement for External Working Capital Financing 360   The Cash Conversion
Cycle 361   Working Capital Investment and Financing Policies 364   Advantages
and Disadvantages of Short-Term Financing 369   *Small Business   Growth and
Working Capital Needs 371*   Summary 372

Chapter 10   Cash and Marketable Securities Management 381

A Managerial Perspective 381   Cash Management 382   Cash Management
Techniques 384   *Industry Practice   Where to Stash the Cash? 391*

Compensating Banks for Services 392   Matching the Costs and Benefits of Cash Management 393   Marketable Securities 394   The Baumol Model for Balancing Cash and Marketable Securities 400   Summary 403

Chapter 11   Credit Management 409

A Managerial Perspective 409   Receivables Management 410   *Industry Practice Trade Credit and Bankruptcy 415*   Credit Policy 416   Setting the Credit Period and Standards 416   Setting the Collection Policy 420   Cash Discounts 420   Other Factors Influencing Credit Policy 421   Analyzing Proposed Changes in Credit Policy 423   Summary 426

Chapter 12   Inventory Management 431

A Managerial Perspective 431   Inventories 432   Inventory Management 434   Inventory Costs 434   The Economic Ordering Quantity (EOQ) Model 438   EOQ Model Extensions 442   Inventory Control Systems 445   Monitoring Inventory Levels 448   Summary 448

Chapter 13   Short-Term Financing 455

A Managerial Perspective 455   Sources of Short-Term Financing 457   Accruals 457   Accounts Payable (Trade Credit) 457   Short-Term Bank Loans 463   The Cost of Bank Loans 465   Choosing a Bank 472   Commerical Paper 474   Use of Security in Short-Term Financing 475   *Small Business Receivables Financing by a Small Firm 482*   Summary 483

Part V   **Strategic Long-Term Investment Decisions: Capital Budgeting 493**

Chapter 14   Capital Budgeting Techniques 495

A Managerial Perspective 495   Importance of Capital Budgeting 497   Generating Ideas for Capital Projects 498   Project Classifications 499   Similarities between Capital Budgeting and Security Valuation 500   Capital Budgeting Evaluation Techniques 501   Comparison of the NPV and IRR Methods 509   Modified Internal Rate of Return (MIRR) 516   Conclusions on the Capital Budgeting Decision Methods 518   The Post-Audit 519   *Small Business Capital Budgeting in the Small Firm 520*   Summary 522

Chapter 15   Project Cash Flows and Risk 531

A Managerial Perspective 531   Cash Flow Estimation 532   Identifying the Relevant Cash Flows 533   Changes in Net Working Capital 536   Capital Budgeting Project Evaluation 536   Comparing Projects with Unequal Lives 543   Dealing with Inflation 547   Introduction to Project Risk Analysis 547   Techniques for Measuring Stand-Alone Risk 549   Beta (or Market) Risk 555   Techniques for Measuring Beta Risk 558   Should Firms Diversify to Reduce Risk? 560   Project Risk Conclusions 560   Incorporating Project Risk and Capital Structure into Capital Budgeting 561   Capital Rationing 563   Summary 563

Appendix 15A   Depreciation 576

Part VI   **The Cost of Capital, Leverage, and Dividend Policy   581**

Chapter 16   The Cost of Capital   583

A Managerial Perspective   583   The Logic of the Weighted Average Cost of
Capital   584   Basic Definitions   585   Cost of Debt, $k_d(1 - T)$ 586   Cost of
Preferred Stock, k_p 588   Cost of Retained Earnings, k_s 588   Cost of Newly Issued
Common Stock, or External Equity, k_e 593   Weighted Average, or Composite, Cost
of Capital, WACC   595   The Marginal Cost of Capital, MCC   596   Combining the
MCC and Investment Opportunity Schedules   604   Some Problem Areas in Cost of
Capital   607   *Small Business   The Cost of Equity Capital for Small Firms   608*
Summary   609

Chapter 17   Capital Structure and Leverage   621

A Managerial Perspective   621   The Target Capital Structure   622   Business and
Financial Risk   623   *Industry Practice   Too Much Debt Hurts Company with Sound
Basic Operations   627*   Determining the Optimal Capital Structure   628   Degree
of Leverage   638   Liquidity and Cash Flow Analysis   644   Capital Structure
Theory   646   Capital Structure and Mergers   651   Checklist for Capital Structure
Decisions   651   Variations in Capital Structures among Firms   654   Summary   655

Chapter 18   Dividend Policy   665

A Managerial Perspective   665   Dividend Policy Theories   667   Tests of the
Dividend Theories   671   Other Dividend Policy Issues   672   *Industry Practice
The Tax Bite on Dividends   674*   Dividend Policy in Practice   675   Summary of
Factors Influencing Dividend Policy   684   Stock Dividends and Stock Splits   686
Stock Repurchases   689   *Small Business   Dividend Policy for Small
Businesses   693*   Summary   693

Part VII   **Strategic Long-Term Financing Decisions   703**

Chapter 19   Common Stock and the Investment Banking Process   705

A Managerial Perspective   705   Balance Sheet Accounts and Definitions   707
Legal Rights and Privileges of Common Stockholders   709   Types of Common
Stock   711   Evaluation of Common Stock as a Source of Funds   711   The Market
for Common Stock   714   *Industry Practice   SCOR Aids Small Firms in Going
Public   720*   The Investment Banking Process   721   IBM's Initial Debt
Offering   728   Emerging Trends   730   *Small Business   Why Go Public for Less
Than You're Worth?   732*   Summary   733

Chapter 20   Long-Term Debt   739

A Managerial Perspective   739   Traditional Debt Instruments   741   Specific Debt
Contract Features   745   Recent Innovations   748   Bond Ratings   754   Rationale
for Using Different Types of Securities   759   Factors Influencing Long-Term
Financing Decisions   759   Bankruptcy and Reorganization   763   *Industry
Practice   Fast-Track Bankruptcies for Small Businesses   764*   Refunding
Operations   765   Summary   767

Appendix 20A   Bankruptcy and Reorganization   773

Appendix 20B   Refunding Operations   780

Chapter 21   Hybrid Financing: Preferred Stock, Leasing, and Option Securities 787

A Managerial Perspective 787   Preferred Stock 789   Leasing 794
Options 802   *Industry Practice   Are the Futures Markets Too Risky for Pension
Funds? 807*   Warrants 808   Convertibles 811   Reporting Earnings when
Warrants or Convertibles Are Outstanding 817   *Small Business   Lease Financing
for Small Businesses 817*   Summary 818

Chapter 22   Mergers, Divestitures, Holding Companies, and LBOs 829

A Managerial Perspective 829   Rationale for Mergers 831   Types of
Mergers 834   Level of Merger Activity 834   Procedures for Combining
Firms 838   Merger Analysis 839   Valuing the Target Firm 842   The Role of
Investment Bankers 844   Corporate Alliances 846   Divestitures 847   Holding
Companies 850   *Industry Practice   Are LBOs on Their Way Out? 853*
Leveraged Buyouts (LBOs) 853   Summary 854

Chapter 23   Multinational Managerial Finance 861

A Managerial Perspective 861   Multinational Corporations 862   Multinational
versus Domestic Managerial Finance 864   *Industry Practice   Learning a New
Vocabulary 866*   Exchange Rates 868   The International Monetary System 870
Trading in Foreign Exchange 875   Inflation, Interest Rates, and Exchange
Rates 877   International Capital Markets 878   Multinational Capital
Budgeting 881   International Capital Structures 883   Multinational Working
Capital Management 884   Summary 888

Appendix A   Mathematical Tables A-1

Appendix B   Solutions to Self-Test Problems B-1

Appendix C   Answers to End-of-Chapter Problems C-1

Appendix D   Selected Equations and Data D-1

Index   I-1

Introduction to Managerial Finance

Chapter 1   An Overview of Managerial Finance

Chapter 2   Analysis of Financial Statements
            Appendix 2A   Statement of Cash Flows

Chapter 3   The Financial Environment: Markets,
            Institutions, Interest Rates, and Taxes

An Overview of Managerial Finance

In the early 1990s, NCR Corporation (formerly the National Cash Register Company) was doing well. Its management had transformed a stodgy company into a leading player in the computer game, one that was beating out IBM and other world-class firms in automatic bank teller machines and other rapidly growing high-tech markets. In the words of Value Line, *a leading investment advisory service, "This is shaping up as the ninth consecutive year of earnings growth for NCR. We're looking for continued gains out to 1995. These good quality shares are ranked to outpace the year-ahead markets." NCR's stock was selling for $65, up from $9 in 1982, so its stockholders had benefitted from management's good performance. NCR's workers had also been well served and were happy, as were its customers.*

AT&T, meanwhile, had been raking in huge cash flows from its quasi-monopolistic telephone business, but it had failed in its efforts to become a major player in the computer industry, and it was losing lots of money there. Then AT&T's Chairman, Bob Allen, decided to buy NCR. Allen approached NCR's management and suggested a price of $90 per share, or $6.2 billion in total, and he indicated a willingness to "negotiate," i.e., to go higher.

NCR's Chairman, Charles Exley, responded that "the company is not for sale." He felt, justifiably, that his team had done a good job, and he wanted to continue to control a dynamic, growing entity, not just become one part of a huge conglomerate. Exley commented, after his talk with Allen, that AT&T ought to change its advertising slogan from "Reach out and touch someone" to "Reach out and grab someone."

NCR's labor force, by and large, agreed with Chairman Exley—they were well aware that in most mergers quite a few workers lose their jobs as tasks are consolidated. Further, the higher the worker in the hierarchy, the more likely he or she is to be tossed out. Exley would no longer be chief executive of a major company, and his top managers would, if they were retained at all, be subordinates of AT&T's senior executives. NCR's customers were also concerned—the company had been turning out good, attractively priced products. Would the same situation hold under AT&T's control? Customers like having as many potential suppliers as possible, and, if the merger occurred, there would be one less firm in the computer industry. Further, NCR is headquartered in Dayton, Ohio, but if AT&T acquired it, many headquarter functions would be moved to New York. This would have an adverse effect on Dayton, so the city fathers were not happy about the prospects for the merger.

NCR's stockholders, meanwhile, had mixed feelings. On the one hand, thoughtful investors recognized that the company had been run well, that management deserved a chance to remain in control, and that investors might be better off in the long run if Exley and his team remained in charge. On the other hand, the stock had been selling for only $65, yet AT&T had offered $90 and held out the chance for more, and a quick 40 percent profit is nothing to sneeze at. Further, almost 70 percent of NCR's stock was owned by institutional investors such as pension funds, mutual funds, and insurance companies, whose owners like to see rapidly rising values such as the buyout would provide.

As you read this chapter, think about these issues: To what extent should NCR's managers let their own personal positions (versus those of NCR's stockholders) influence their decision to resist AT&T's advances; e.g., should the fact that Charles Exley would no longer be chief executive influence his actions? Would you, as an outside stockholder, feel more "comfortable" that your interests were well represented if NCR's managers were themselves large stockholders? To what extent should consideration be given to the views of NCR's nonmanagement labor force? Its customers? Residents of Dayton? If you were an NCR stockholder, would you vote for the merger? As an AT&T stockholder, what would your reaction be? On balance, would the merger be good or bad for America?

The purpose of this chapter is to give you an overview of managerial finance. After you finish the chapter, you should have a reasonably good idea of what finance majors might do after graduation. You should also have a better understanding of (1) some of the forces that will affect managerial finance in the future; (2) the way businesses are organized; (3) the place finance has in a firm's organization; (4) the relationships of financial managers with their counterparts in accounting, marketing, production, and personnel departments; and (5) the goals of a firm and the way financial managers can contribute to the attainment of these goals.

CAREER OPPORTUNITIES IN FINANCE

Finance consists of three interrelated areas: (1) *money and capital markets,* which deals with many of the topics covered in macroeconomics; (2) *investments,* which focuses on the decisions of individuals and financial and other institutions as they choose securities for their investment portfolios; and (3) *managerial finance,* or "business finance," which involves the actual management of the firm. The career opportunities within each field are many and varied, but financial managers must have a knowledge of all three areas if they are to do their jobs well.

Money and Capital Markets

Many finance majors go to work for financial institutions, including banks, insurance companies, savings and loans, and credit unions. For success here one needs a knowledge of the factors that cause interest rates to rise and fall, the regulations to which financial institutions are subject, and the various types of financial instruments (mortgages, auto loans, certificates of deposit, and so on). One also needs a general knowledge of all aspects of business administration, because the management of a financial institution involves accounting, marketing, personnel, and computer systems, as well as managerial finance. An ability to communicate, both orally and in writing, is important, and "people skills," or the ability to get others to do their jobs, is critical.

The most common initial job in this area is a bank officer trainee, where you go into bank operations and learn about the business, from tellers' work, to cash management, to making loans. You could expect to spend a year or so being rotated among these different areas, after which you would settle into a department, often as an assistant manager in a branch. Alternatively, you might become a specialist in some area such as real estate, and be authorized to make loans going into the millions of dollars, or in the management of trusts, estates, and pension funds. Similar career paths are available with insurance companies, credit unions, and consumer loan companies.

Investments

Finance graduates who go into investments generally work for a brokerage house such as Merrill Lynch, either in sales or as a security analyst. Others work for a bank, a mutual fund, or an insurance company in the management of their investment portfolios or for a financial consulting firm which advises individual investors or pension funds on how to invest their funds. The three main functions in the investments area are (1) sales, (2) the analysis of individual securities, and (3) determining the optimal mix of securities for a given investor.

Managerial Finance

Managerial finance is the broadest of the three areas, and the one with the greatest number of job opportunities. Managerial finance is important in all types of businesses, including banks and other financial institutions, as well as industrial and retail firms. Managerial finance is also important in governmental operations, from schools to hospitals to highway departments. The types of jobs one encounters in managerial finance range from decisions regarding plant expansions to choosing what types of securities to issue to finance expansion. Financial managers also have the responsibility for deciding the credit terms under which customers may buy, how much inventory the firm should carry, how much cash to keep on hand, whether to acquire other firms (merger analysis), and how much of the firm's earnings to plow back into the business versus pay out as dividends.

Regardless of which area you go into, you will need a knowledge of all three areas. For example, a banker lending to businesses cannot do his or her job well without a good understanding of managerial finance, because he or she must be able to judge how well a business is operated. The same thing holds for one of Merrill Lynch's security analysts, and even stockbrokers must have an understanding of general financial principles if they are to give intelligent advice to their customers. At the same time, corporate financial managers need to know what their bankers are thinking about, and how investors are likely to judge their corporations' performances and thus determine their stock prices. So, if you decide to make finance your career, you will need to know something about all three areas.

Self-Test Questions

What are the three main areas of finance?

If you have definite plans to go into one area, why is it necessary that you know something about the other areas?

MANAGERIAL FINANCE IN THE 1990s

When managerial finance emerged as a separate field of study in the early 1900s, the emphasis was on the legal aspects of mergers, the formation of new firms, and the various types of securities firms could issue to raise capital. During the Depression era of the 1930s, the emphasis shifted to bankruptcy and reorganization, to corporate liquidity, and to regulation of security markets. During the 1940s and early 1950s, finance continued to be taught as a descriptive, institutional subject, viewed more from the standpoint of an outsider rather than from that of management. However, a movement toward theoretical analysis began during the 1960s, and the focus of managerial finance shifted to managerial decisions regarding the choice of assets and liabilities so as to maximize the value of the firm. The focus on valuation continued on through the 1980s, but the analysis was expanded to include (1) *inflation* and its effects on business decisions;

(2) *deregulation* of financial institutions and the resulting trend toward large, broadly diversified financial services companies; (3) the dramatic increase in both the use of *computers* for analysis and the electronic transfer of information; and (4) the increased importance of *global* markets and business operations. The two most important trends during the 1990s are likely to be the continued globalization of business and a further increase in the use of computer technology.

The Globalization of Business

Four factors have made the trend toward globalization mandatory for many businesses: (1) Improvements in transportation and communications have lowered shipping costs and made international trade more feasible. (2) The political clout of consumers who desire low-cost, high-quality products has helped lower trade barriers designed to protect inefficient, high-cost domestic manufacturers. (3) As technology has become more advanced, the cost of developing new products has increased, and, as development costs rise, so must unit sales if the firm is to be competitive. (4) In a world populated with multinational firms able to shift production to wherever costs are lowest, a firm whose manufacturing operations are restricted to one country cannot compete unless costs in its home country happen to be low, a condition that does not necessarily exist for many U.S. corporations. As a result of these four factors, survival requires that most manufacturers produce and sell globally.

Service companies, including banks, advertising agencies, and accounting firms, are also being forced to "go global," because such firms can better serve their multinational clients if they have worldwide operations. There will, of course, always be some purely domestic companies, but you should keep in mind that the most dynamic growth, and the best opportunities, are often with companies that operate worldwide.

Computer Technology

The 1990s will see continued advances in computer and communications technology, and this technology will revolutionize the way financial decisions are made. Companies will have networks of personal computers linked to one another, to the firm's own mainframe computers, and to their customers' and suppliers' computers. Thus, financial managers will be able to share data and programs and to have "face-to-face" meetings with distant colleagues through video teleconferencing. The ability to access and analyze data on a real-time basis will also mean that quantitative analyses will be used routinely to "test out" alternative courses of action. As a result, the next generation of financial managers will need stronger computer and quantitative skills than were required in the past.

Self-Test Questions

How has managerial finance changed from the early 1900s to the 1990s?

How might a person become better prepared for a career in managerial finance?

INCREASING IMPORTANCE
OF MANAGERIAL FINANCE

The historical trends discussed in the previous section have greatly increased the importance of managerial finance. In earlier times the marketing manager would project sales, the engineering and production staffs would determine the assets necessary to meet those demands, and the financial manager's job was simply to raise the money needed to purchase the required plant, equipment, and inventories. That situation no longer exists—decisions are now made in a much more coordinated manner, and the financial manager generally has direct responsibility for the control process.

Eastern Airlines and Delta can be used to illustrate both the importance of managerial finance and the effects of financial decisions. In the 1960s, Eastern's stock sold for more than $60 per share while Delta's sold for $10. By the early 1990s, Delta had become one of the world's strongest airlines, and its stock was selling for more than $60 per share. Eastern, on the other hand, had gone bankrupt and was no longer in existence. Although many factors combined to produce these divergent results, financial decisions exerted a major influence. Because Eastern had traditionally used a great deal of debt while Delta had not, Eastern's costs increased significantly, and its profits were lowered, when interest rates rose during the 1980s. Rising rates had only a minor effect on Delta. Further, when fuel price increases made it imperative for the airlines to buy new, fuel-efficient planes, Delta was able to do so, but Eastern was not. Finally, when the airlines were deregulated, Delta was strong enough to expand into developing markets and to cut prices as necessary to attract business, but Eastern was not.

The Delta-Eastern story, and others like it, are now well known, so all companies today are greatly concerned with financial planning, and this has increased the importance of corporate financial staffs. Indeed, the value of managerial finance is reflected in the fact that more chief executive officers (CEOs) in the top 1,000 U.S. companies started their careers in finance than in any other functional area.

It is also becoming increasingly important for people in marketing, accounting, production, personnel, and other areas to understand finance in order to do a good job in their own fields. Marketing people, for instance, must understand how marketing decisions affect and are affected by funds availability, by inventory levels, by excess plant capacity, and so on. Similarly, accountants must understand how accounting data are used in corporate planning and are viewed by investors.

Thus, there are financial implications in virtually all business decisions, and nonfinancial executives simply must know enough finance to work these implications into their own specialized analyses.[1] Because of this, every student of business, regardless of major, should be concerned with finance.

---

[1] It is an interesting fact that the course "Managerial Finance for Nonfinancial Executives" has the highest enrollment in most executive development programs.

? *Self-Test Questions*

Explain why financial planning is important to today's chief executives.

Why do marketing people need to know something about managerial finance?

THE FINANCIAL MANAGER'S RESPONSIBILITIES

The financial manager's task is to acquire and use funds so as to maximize the value of the firm. Here are some specific activities which are involved:

1. **Forecasting and planning.** The financial manager must interact with other executives as they look ahead and lay the plans which will shape the firm's future position.

2. **Major investment and financing decisions.** A successful firm usually has rapid growth in sales, which requires investments in plant, equipment, and inventory. The financial manager must help determine the optimal sales growth rate, and he or she must help decide on the specific assets to acquire and the best way to finance those assets. For example, should the firm finance with debt or equity, and if debt is used, should it be long term or short term?

3. **Coordination and control.** The financial manager must interact with other executives to insure that the firm is operated as efficiently as possible. All business decisions have financial implications, and all managers — financial and otherwise — need to take this into account. For example, marketing decisions affect sales growth, which in turn influences investment requirements. Thus, marketing decision makers must take account of how their actions affect (and are affected by) such factors as the availability of funds, inventory policies, and plant capacity utilization.

4. **Dealing with the financial markets.** The financial manager must deal with the money and capital markets. As we shall see in Chapter 3, each firm affects and is affected by the general financial markets where funds are raised, where the firm's securities are traded, and where its investors are either rewarded or penalized.

In summary, financial managers make decisions regarding which assets their firms should acquire, how those assets should be financed, and how the firm should manage its existing resources. If these responsibilities are performed optimally, financial managers will help to maximize the values of their firms, and this will also maximize the long-run welfare of those who buy from or work for the company.

? *Self-Test Question*

What are four specific activities with which financial managers are involved?

ALTERNATIVE FORMS OF BUSINESS ORGANIZATION

There are three main forms of business organization: (1) sole proprietorships, (2) partnerships, and (3) corporations. In terms of numbers, about 80 percent of businesses are operated as sole proprietorships, while the remainder are divided equally between partnerships and corporations. Based on dollar value of sales, however, about 80 percent of all business is conducted by corporations, about 13 percent by sole proprietorships, and about 7 percent by partnerships. Because most business is conducted by corporations, we will concentrate on them in this book. However, it is important to understand the differences among the three forms.

Sole Proprietorship

sole proprietorship
An unincorporated business owned by one individual.

A **sole proprietorship** is an unincorporated business owned by one individual. Going into business as a single proprietor is easy—one merely begins business operations. However, even the smallest establishments must be licensed by a governmental unit.

The proprietorship has three important advantages: (1) It is easily and inexpensively formed, (2) it is subject to few government regulations, and (3) the business pays no corporate income taxes.

The proprietorship also has three important limitations: (1) It is difficult for a proprietorship to obtain large sums of capital; (2) the proprietor has unlimited personal liability for business debts, which can result in losses which exceed the money he or she invested in the company; and (3) the life of a business organized as a proprietorship is limited to the life of the individual who created it. For these three reasons, individual proprietorships are restricted primarily to small business operations. However, businesses are frequently started as proprietorships and then converted to corporations when their growth causes the disadvantages of being a proprietorship to outweigh the advantages.

Partnership

partnership
An unincorporated business owned by two or more persons.

A **partnership** exists whenever two or more persons associate to conduct a noncorporate business. Partnerships may operate under different degrees of formality, ranging from informal, oral understandings to formal agreements filed with the secretary of the state in which the partnership does business. The major advantage of a partnership is its low cost and ease of formation. The disadvantages are similar to those associated with proprietorships: (1) unlimited liability, (2) limited life of the organization, (3) difficulty of transferring ownership, and (4) difficulty of raising large amounts of capital. The tax treatment of a partnership is similar to that for proprietorships, which is generally an advantage, as we demonstrate in Chapter 3.

Regarding liability, the partners can potentially lose all of their personal assets, even those assets not invested in the business, because under partnership law each partner is liable for the business's debts. Therefore, if any partner is unable to meet his or her pro rata claim in the event the partnership goes bankrupt, the remaining partners must make good on the unsatisfied claims, drawing on their personal assets if necessary. The partners of the national accounting firm Laventhol and Horwath, a huge partnership which went bankrupt recently as a result of suits filed by investors who relied on faulty audit statements, are learning all about the perils of doing business as a partnership. Thus, a Texas partner who audits a savings and loan which goes under can bring ruin to a millionaire New York partner who never went near the S&L.[2]

The first three disadvantages — unlimited liability, impermanence of the organization, and difficulty of transferring ownership — lead to the fourth, the difficulty partnerships have in attracting substantial amounts of capital. This is no particular problem for a slow-growing business, but if a business's products really catch on, and if it needs to raise large amounts of capital in order to capitalize on its opportunities, the difficulty in attracting capital becomes a real drawback. Thus, growth companies such as Hewlett-Packard and Apple Computer generally begin life as a proprietorship or partnership, but at some point they find it necessary to convert to a corporation.

Corporation

corporation

A legal entity created by a state, separate and distinct from its owners and managers, having unlimited life, easy transferability of ownership, and limited liability.

A **corporation** is a legal entity created by a state. It is separate and distinct from its owners and managers. This separateness gives the corporation three major advantages: (1) *Unlimited life* — A corporation can continue after its original owners and managers are deceased. (2) *Easy transferability of ownership interest* — Ownership interests can be divided into shares of stock, which in turn can be transferred far more easily than can proprietorship or partnership interests. (3) *Limited liability* — To illustrate the concept of limited liability, suppose you invested $10,000 in a partnership which then went bankrupt owing $1 million. Because the owners are liable for the debts of a partnership, you could be assessed for a share of the company's debt, and you could be held liable for the entire $1 million if your partners could not pay their shares. Thus, an investor in a partnership is exposed to unlimited liability. On the other hand, if you invested $10,000 in the stock of a corporation which then went bankrupt, your potential loss on the investment would be limited to your $10,000 investment.[3] These three factors — unlimited life, easy transferability of ownership interest, and limited liability — make it much easier for corporations than for proprietorships or partnerships to raise money in the general capital markets.

The corporate form offers significant advantages over proprietorships and partnerships, but it does have two primary disadvantages: (1) Corporate earnings are subject to double taxation — the earnings of the corporation are taxed, and then any earnings paid out as dividends are taxed again as income to the stockholders. (2) Setting up a corporation, and filing required state and federal reports, is more complex and time-consuming than for a proprietorship or a partnership.

---

[2]However, it is possible to limit the liabilities of some of the partners by establishing a *limited partnership,* wherein one partner is designated the *general partner* and others *limited partners.* Limited partnerships are quite common in the area of real estate investment, but they do not work well with most types of businesses, including accounting firms, because one partner is rarely willing to assume all of the business's risk.

[3]In the case of small corporations, the limited liability feature is often a fiction, since bankers and credit managers frequently require personal guarantees from the stockholders of small, weak businesses.

Although a proprietorship or a partnership can commence operations without much paperwork, setting up a corporation requires that the incorporators hire a lawyer to prepare a charter and a set of bylaws. The *charter* includes the following information: (1) name of the proposed corporation, (2) types of activities it will pursue, (3) amount of capital stock, (4) number of directors, and (5) names and addresses of directors. The charter is filed with the secretary of the state in which the firm will be incorporated, and, when it is approved, the corporation is officially in existence.[4] Then, after the corporation is in operation, quarterly and annual financial and tax reports must be filed with state and federal authorities.

The *bylaws* are a set of rules drawn up by the founders of the corporation to aid in governing the internal management of the company. Included are such points as (1) how directors are to be elected (all elected each year, or perhaps one-third each year for three-year terms); (2) whether the existing stockholders will have the first right to buy any new shares the firm issues; and (3) procedures for changing the bylaws themselves, should conditions require it.

The value of any business other than a very small one will probably be maximized if it is organized as a corporation for these reasons:

1. Limited liability reduces the risks borne by investors, and, other things held constant, *the lower the firm's risk, the higher its value*.

2. A firm's value is dependent on its *growth opportunities*, which in turn are dependent on the firm's ability to attract capital. Since corporations can attract capital more easily than can unincorporated businesses, they have superior growth opportunities.

3. The value of an asset also depends on its *liquidity,* which means the ease of selling the asset and converting it to cash at a "fair market value." Since an investment in the stock of a corporation is much more liquid than a similar investment in a proprietorship or partnership, this too means that the corporate form of organization can enhance the value of a business.

4. Corporations are taxed differently than proprietorships and partnerships; generally, businesses must pay more taxes if they are incorporated, but under certain conditions the tax burden is the same. This point is discussed in detail in Chapter 3.

As we will see later in the chapter, most firms are managed with value maximization in mind, and this, in turn, has caused most large businesses to be organized as corporations.

Self-Test Questions

What are the key differences between sole proprietorships, partnerships, and corporations?

Explain why the value of any business other than a very small one will probably be maximized if it is organized as a corporation.

---

[4]Note that over 60 percent of major U.S. corporations are chartered in Delaware, which has, over the years, provided a favorable legal environment for corporations. It is not necessary for a firm to be headquartered, or even to conduct operations, in its state of incorporation.

Figure 1-1   ▪   **Place of Finance in a Typical Business Organization**

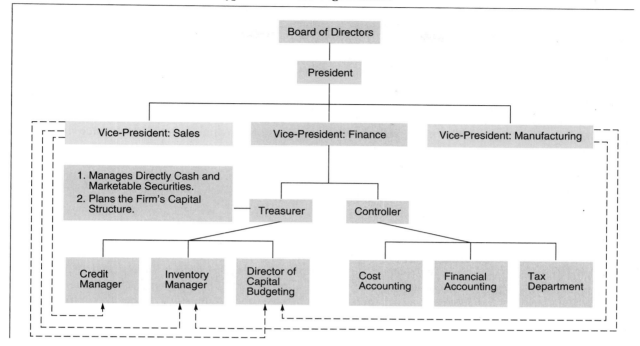

FINANCE IN THE ORGANIZATIONAL STRUCTURE OF THE FIRM

Organizational structures vary from firm to firm, but Figure 1-1 presents a fairly typical picture of the role of finance within a corporation. The chief financial officer—who has the title of vice-president: finance—reports to the president. The financial vice-president's key subordinates are the treasurer and the controller. In most firms the treasurer has direct responsibility for managing the firm's cash and marketable securities, for planning its capital structure, for selling stocks and bonds to raise capital, and for overseeing the corporate pension fund. The treasurer also supervises the credit manager, the inventory manager, and the director of capital budgeting (who analyzes decisions related to investments in fixed assets). The controller is responsible for the activities of the accounting and tax departments.

?   *Self-Test Question*

Identify the two subordinates who report to the firm's chief financial officer, and indicate the primary responsibilities of each.

THE GOALS OF THE CORPORATION

stockholder wealth maximization

The appropriate goal for management decisions; considers the risk and timing associated with expected earnings per share in order to maximize the price of the firm's common stock.

Business decisions are not made in a vacuum—decision makers have some objective in mind. *Throughout this book we operate on the assumption that management's primary goal is* **stockholder wealth maximization**, which, as we shall see, translates into *maximizing the price of the firm's common stock.* Firms do, of course, have other objectives—in particular, managers, who make the actual decisions, are interested in their own personal satisfaction, in their employees' welfare, and in the good of the community and of society at large. Still, for the reasons set forth in the following sections, *stock price maximization is the most important goal of most corporations.*

Managerial Incentives to Maximize Shareholder Wealth

Stockholders own the firm and elect the management team. Management, in turn, is supposed to operate in the best interests of the stockholders. We know, however, that because the stock of most large firms is widely held, the managers of large corporations have a great deal of autonomy. This being the case, might not managers pursue goals other than stock price maximization? For example, some have argued that the managers of a large, well-entrenched corporation could work just hard enough to keep stockholder returns at a "reasonable" level and then devote the remainder of their efforts and resources to public service activities, to employee benefits, to higher executive salaries, or to golf.

It is almost impossible to determine whether a particular management team is trying to maximize shareholder wealth or is merely attempting to keep stockholders satisfied while pursuing other goals. For example, how can we tell whether employee or community benefit programs are in the long-run best interests of the stockholders? Similarly, are relatively high executive salaries really necessary to attract and retain excellent managers or just another example of managers' taking advantage of stockholders?

It is impossible to give definitive answers to these questions. However, we do know that the managers of a firm operating in a competitive market will be forced to undertake actions that are reasonably consistent with shareholder wealth maximization. If they depart from this goal, they run the risk of being removed from their jobs through a hostile takeover or a proxy fight.

hostile takeover

The acquisition of a company over the opposition of its management.

proxy fight

An attempt to gain control of a firm by soliciting stockholders to vote for a new management team.

A **hostile takeover** is the purchase by one company of the stock of another over the opposition of its management, whereas a **proxy fight** involves an attempt to gain control by getting stockholders to vote a new management group into place. Both actions are facilitated by low stock prices, so for the sake of self-preservation, management will try to keep its stock value as high as possible. Therefore, while some managers may be more interested in their own personal positions than in maximizing shareholder wealth, the threat of losing their jobs still motivates them to try to maximize stock prices. We will have more to say about the conflict between managers and shareholders later in the chapter.

Social Responsibility

social responsibility
The concept that businesses should be actively concerned with the welfare of society at large.

Another issue that deserves consideration is **social responsibility:** Should businesses operate strictly in their stockholders' best interests, or are firms also responsible for the welfare of their employees, customers, and the communities in which they operate? Certainly firms have an ethical responsibility to provide a safe working environment, to avoid polluting the air or water, and to produce safe products. However, socially responsible actions have costs, and it is questionable whether businesses would incur these costs voluntarily. If some firms do act in a socially responsible manner while others do not, then the socially responsible firms will be at a disadvantage in attracting capital. To illustrate, suppose the firms in a given industry have **profits** and **rates of return on investment** that are close to **normal,** that is, close to the average for all firms and just sufficient to attract capital. If one company attempts to exercise social responsibility, it will have to raise prices to cover the added costs. If the other businesses in its industry do not follow suit, their costs and prices will be lower. The socially responsible firm will not be able to compete, and it will be forced to abandon its efforts. Thus, any voluntary socially responsible acts that raise costs will be difficult, if not impossible, in industries that are subject to keen competition.

**normal profits/
rates of return**
Those profits and rates of return that are close to the average for all firms and are just sufficient to attract capital.

What about oligopolistic firms with profits above normal levels — cannot such firms devote resources to social projects? Undoubtedly they can, and many large, successful firms do engage in community projects, employee benefit programs, and the like to a greater degree than would appear to be called for by pure profit or wealth maximization goals.[5] Still, publicly owned firms are constrained in such actions by capital market factors. To illustrate, suppose a saver who has funds to invest is considering two alternative firms. One firm devotes a substantial part of its resources to social actions, while the other concentrates on profits and stock prices. Most investors are likely to shun the socially oriented firm, thus putting it at a disadvantage in the capital market. After all, why should the stockholders of one corporation subsidize society to a greater extent than those of other businesses? For this reason, even highly profitable firms (unless they are closely held rather than publicly owned) are generally constrained against taking unilateral cost-increasing social actions.

Does all this mean that firms should not exercise social responsibility? Not at all, but it does mean that most significant cost-increasing actions will have to be put on a *mandatory* rather than a voluntary basis, at least initially, to insure that the burden falls uniformly on all businesses. Thus, such social benefit programs as fair hiring practices, minority training, product safety, pollution abatement, and antitrust actions are most likely to be effective if realistic rules are established initially and then enforced by government agencies. Of course, it is critical that industry and government cooperate in establishing the rules of corporate behavior, that the costs as well as the benefits of such actions be accurately estimated and taken into account, and that firms follow the spirit as well as the letter of the law in their actions.

---

[5]Even firms like these often find it necessary to justify such projects at stockholder meetings by stating that these programs will contribute to long-run profit maximization.

Stock Price Maximization and Social Welfare

If a firm attempts to maximize its stock price, is this good or bad for society? In general, it is good. Aside from such illegal actions as attempting to form monopolies, violating safety codes, and failing to meet pollution control requirements, *the same actions that maximize stock prices also benefit society.* First, note that stock price maximization requires efficient, low-cost plants that produce high-quality goods and services at the lowest possible cost. Second, stock price maximization requires the development of products that consumers want and need, so the profit motive leads to new technology, to new products, and to new jobs. Finally, stock price maximization necessitates efficient and courteous service, adequate stocks of merchandise, and well-located business establishments — these factors are all necessary to make sales, and sales are necessary for profits. Therefore, actions which help a firm increase the price of its stock are also beneficial to society at large. This is why profit-motivated, free-enterprise economies have been so much more successful than socialistic and communistic economic systems. Since managerial finance plays a crucial role in the operation of successful firms, and since successful firms are absolutely necessary for a healthy, productive economy, it is easy to see why finance is important from a social standpoint.[6]

? *Self-Test Questions*

What is management's primary goal?

What actions could be taken to remove management if it departed from the goal of maximizing shareholder wealth?

Explain the difference between a hostile takeover and a proxy fight. How does a firm's stock price influence the likelihood of those actions?

What would happen if one firm attempted to exercise costly social responsibility, while its competitors did *not* exercise social responsibility?

How does the goal of stock price maximization benefit society at large?

BUSINESS ETHICS

The word *ethics* is defined in Webster's dictionary as "standards of conduct or moral behavior." Business ethics can be thought of as a company's attitude and conduct toward its employees, customers, community, and stockholders. High standards of ethical behavior demand that a firm treat each party that it deals

---

[6]People sometimes argue that firms, in their efforts to raise profits and stock prices, increase product prices and gouge the public. In a reasonably competitive economy, which we have, prices are constrained by competition and consumer resistance. If a firm raises its prices beyond reasonable levels, it will simply lose its market share. Even giant firms like General Motors lose business to the Japanese and Germans, as well as to Ford and Chrysler, if they set prices above levels necessary to cover production costs plus a "normal" profit. Of course, firms *want* to earn more, and they constantly try to cut costs, to develop new products, and so on, and thereby to earn above-normal profits. Note, though, that if they are indeed successful and do earn above-normal profits, those very profits will attract competition which will eventually drive prices down, so again the main long-term beneficiary is the consumer.

with in a fair and honest manner. A firm's commitment to business ethics can be measured by the tendency of the firm and its employees to adhere to laws and regulations relating to such factors as product safety and quality, fair employment practices, fair marketing and selling practices, the use of confidential information for personal gain, community involvement, bribery, and illegal payments to foreign governments to obtain business.

There are many instances of firms engaging in unethical behavior. For example, in recent years the employees of several prominent Wall Street investment banking houses have been sentenced to prison for illegally using insider information on proposed mergers for their own personal gain, and E. F. Hutton, a large brokerage firm, lost its independence through a forced merger after it was convicted of cheating its banks out of millions of dollars in a check kiting scheme. Drexel Burnham Lambert, one of the largest investment banking firms, went bankrupt, and its "junk bond king," Michael Milken, who had earned $550 million in just one year, was sentenced to 10 years in prison plus charged a huge fine for securities-law violations. Recently, Salomon Brothers Inc. was implicated in a Treasury-auction bidding scandal which has resulted in the removal of key officers and a significant reorganization of the firm.

In spite of all this, the results of a recent study indicate that the executives of most major firms in the United States believe that their firms should, and do, try to maintain high ethical standards in all of their business dealings. Further, most executives believe that there is a positive correlation between ethics and long-run profitability. For example, Chemical Bank suggested that ethical behavior has increased its profitability because such behavior (1) avoids fines and legal expenses, (2) builds public trust, (3) attracts business from customers who appreciate and support its policies, (4) attracts and keeps employees of the highest caliber, and (5) supports the economic viability of the communities in which it operates.

Most firms today have in place strong codes of ethical behavior, and they conduct training programs designed to ensure that all employees understand the correct behavior in different business situations. However, it is imperative that top management—the chairman, president, and vice-presidents—be openly committed to ethical behavior, and that they communicate this commitment through their own personal actions as well as through company policies, directives, and punishment/reward systems.

 Self-Test Questions

How would you define "business ethics"?

Is "being ethical" good for profits in the long run? In the short run?

AGENCY RELATIONSHIPS

An *agency relationship* exists when one or more people (the principals) hire another person (the agent) to perform a service and then delegate decision-making authority to that agent. Important agency relationships exist (1) between stockholders and managers and (2) between stockholders and creditors (debtholders).

Stockholders versus Managers

agency problem

A potential conflict of interest between (1) the principals (outside shareholders) and the agent (manager) or (2) stockholders and creditors (debtholders).

A potential **agency problem** arises whenever the manager of a firm owns less than 100 percent of the firm's common stock. If a firm is a proprietorship managed by the owner, the owner-manager will presumably operate so as to improve his or her own welfare, with welfare measured in the form of increased personal wealth, more leisure, or perquisites.[7] However, if the owner-manager incorporates and sells some of the firm's stock to outsiders, a potential conflict of interests immediately arises. For example, the owner-manager may now decide not to work as hard to maximize shareholder wealth because less of this wealth will go to him or her, or to take a higher salary or enjoy more perquisites because part of those costs will fall on the outside stockholders. This potential conflict between two parties, the principals (outside shareholders) and the agent (manager), is an agency problem.

leveraged buyout (LBO)

A situation in which a group, often the firm's management, uses credit to purchase the outstanding shares of the company's stock.

tender offer

An offer to buy the stock of a firm directly from its shareholders.

Another potential conflict between management and stockholders arises in a **leveraged buyout (LBO),** a term used to describe the situation in which management itself (1) arranges a line of credit; (2) makes an offer, called a **tender offer,** to buy the stock not already owned by the management group; and then (3) "takes the company private." Dozens of such buyouts of major corporations have occurred recently, and a potential conflict clearly exists whenever one is contemplated. For example, RJR Nabisco's President, Ross Johnson, recently attempted to take the company private in an LBO. If he had been successful, Johnson and several other RJR executives would have ended up owning about 20 percent of the company, worth over a billion dollars. Management tried to pave the way for the LBO in various ways that were questionable from the stockholders' point of view. Management argued that its bid was in all stockholders' interests, but many disagreed: If management itself was buying the stock, would it not be in management's own best interest to keep the price down until the deal was completed, and thus didn't a clear conflict of interest exist?

In general, if a conflict of interest exists, what can be done to insure that management treats the outside stockholders fairly? For one thing, the U.S. Securities and Exchange Commission (SEC), which regulates our securities markets, now requires that management disclose all material information relating to a proposed deal, and that a committee of outside (i.e., nonofficer) directors be established (1) to seek other bids for the company, (2) to evaluate and compare any other bids with that of management, and (3) then to recommend the best bid to stockholders. Further, the outside directors' committee members cannot have any interest in the reorganized company; this requirement is designed to insure their independence, and lawsuits would quickly be filed if a conflicting situation developed.

In RJR's case, the outside directors' committee received bids from several groups, including one from Kohlberg Kravis Roberts (KKR), an investment company that specializes in LBOs using pension funds as its primary source of equity capital. (KKR generally finances with about 10 percent equity and 90 percent debt, with the debt divided between short-term bank loans and longer-term

---

[7]*Perquisites* are executive fringe benefits such as luxurious offices, use of corporate planes and yachts, personal assistants, and general use of business assets for personal purposes.

junk bonds.) A bidding war ensued, and in the end KKR beat out the management group with a bid of $109 per share, up from management's original $75 offer. The final management and KKR bids were similar, but the outside directors recommended KKR in part because of the widespread feeling that management had tried to "steal" the company. This whole episode is a good example of the fact that leveraged buyouts constitute an important type of agency problem between stockholders and managers.

Several mechanisms are used to motivate managers to act in the shareholders' best interests. These include (1) the threat of firing, (2) the threat of takeover, and (3) managerial compensation.

1. **The threat of firing.** Until recently, the probability of a large firm's management being ousted by its stockholders was so remote that it posed little threat. This situation existed because ownership of most firms was so widely distributed, and management's control over the proxy (voting) mechanism was so strong, that it was almost impossible for dissident stockholders to gain enough votes to overthrow the managers. However, today 55 percent of the stock of an average large corporation is owned by a relatively few large institutions rather than by thousands of individual investors, and the institutional money managers have the clout to influence a firm's operations. Examples of major corporations whose managements have been ousted include United Airlines, Disney, and Bank of America.

2. **The threat of takeover.** Hostile takeovers (where management does not want the firm to be taken over) are most likely to occur when a firm's stock is undervalued relative to its potential. In a hostile takeover, the managers of the acquired firm are generally fired, and any who are able to stay on lose the autonomy they had prior to the acquisition. Thus, managers have a strong incentive to take actions which maximize stock prices. In the words of one company president, "If you want to keep control, don't let your company's stock sell at a bargain price."

    Actions to increase the firm's stock price and to keep it from being a bargain are obviously good from the standpoint of the stockholders, but other tactics that managers can use to ward off a hostile takeover may not be. Two examples of questionable tactics are *poison pills* and *greenmail.* A **poison pill** is an action that a firm can take which practically kills it and thus makes it unattractive to potential suitors. Examples include Disney's plan to sell large blocks of its stock at low prices to "friendly" parties, Scott Industries' decision to make all of its debt immediately payable if its management changed, and Carleton Corporation's decision to give huge retirement bonuses, which represented a large part of the company's wealth, to its managers if the firm was taken over (such payments are called *golden parachutes*).

    Greenmail, which is like blackmail, occurs when (1) a potential acquirer (firm or individual) buys a block of stock in a company, (2) the target company's management becomes frightened that the acquirer will make a tender offer and gain control of the company, and (3) to head off a possible takeover, management offers to pay greenmail, buying the stock owned by the potential raider at a price above the existing market price without offering the same deal to other stockholders. A good example of

poison pill

An action taken by management to make a firm unattractive to potential buyers and thus to avoid a hostile takeover.

greenmail

A situation in which a firm, in trying to avoid a takeover, buys back stock from a raider at a price above the existing market price.

greenmail was Disney's buy-back of 11.1 percent of its stock from Saul Steinberg's Reliance Group, giving Steinberg a quick $60 million profit. A group of stockholders sued, and Steinberg and the Disney directors were forced to pay $45 million to Disney stockholders.

3. **Structuring managerial incentives.** Firms are increasingly tying managers' compensation to the company's performance, and this motivates managers to operate in a manner consistent with stock price maximization.

In the 1950s and 1960s, most performance-based incentive plans involved **executive stock options,** which allowed managers to purchase stock at some future time at a given price. Since the value of the options was tied directly to the price of the stock, it was assumed that granting options would provide an incentive for managers to take actions which would maximize the stock's price. This type of managerial incentive lost favor in the 1970s, however, because the general stock market declined, and stock prices did not necessarily reflect companies' earnings growth. Incentive plans ought to be based on those factors over which managers have control, and since they cannot control the general stock market, stock option plans were not good incentive devices. Therefore, whereas 61 of the 100 largest U.S. firms used stock options as their sole incentive compensation in 1970, not even one of the largest 100 companies relied exclusively on such plans in 1992.

An important incentive plan now is **performance shares,** which are shares of stock given to executives on the basis of performance as measured by earnings per share, return on assets, return on equity, and so on. For example, Honeywell uses growth in earnings per share as its primary performance measure. The firm has two overlapping four-year performance periods, beginning two years apart. At the start of each period, the participating executives are allocated a certain number of performance shares, say 10,000 shares for the president down to 1,000 shares for a low-ranking manager. If the company achieves a targeted 13 percent annual average growth in earnings per share, the managers will earn 100 percent of their shares. If the corporate performance is above the target, Honeywell's managers can earn even more shares, up to a maximum of 130 percent, which requires a 16 percent growth rate. However, if growth is below 13 percent, they get less than 100 percent of the shares, and below a 9 percent growth rate, they get zero. Executives must remain with Honeywell through the performance period (four years) in order to receive the performance shares.

All incentive compensation plans — executive stock options, performance shares, profit-based bonuses, and so forth — are designed to accomplish two things. First, these plans provide inducements to executives to act on those factors under their control in a manner that will contribute to stock price maximization. Second, the existence of such performance plans helps companies attract and retain top-level executives. Well-designed plans can accomplish both goals.

executive stock option

A type of incentive plan that allows managers to purchase stock at some future time at a given price.

performance shares

A type of incentive plan in which managers are awarded shares of stock on the basis of the firm's performance over given intervals with respect to earnings per share or other measures.

INDUSTRY PRACTICE | How Important Is the Shareholder's Proxy?

The shareholder's proxy is important, especially when outsiders try to gain control of a corporation. And management looks at proxy votes in other matters very seriously, too. Two years ago, shareholder votes forced Honeywell to trim costs and to abandon its unprofitable defense operations.

The latest evidence that shareholders are taking their roles as firm owners quite seriously is the growing number of shareholder-sponsored proposals. A proposal can be sponsored by anyone who has owned at least $1,000 of a company's stock for a year or more. These proposals are nonbinding and are limited to issues that are outside the firm's day-to-day operations; however, the votes on these proposals do reach the firm's top executives. In 1991, there were 123 shareholder proposals on proxy ballots, which was 28 percent higher than the 1990 number and double the 1989 total. The success of these proposals is increasing, too. In 1987, none of the proposals was successful; however, in 1989, 13 of the proposals carried at least 50 percent of shareholder votes cast. Current shareholder proposals are directed toward executive salaries, poison pills, confidentiality of shareholder votes, golden parachutes, management-dominated boards of directors, and social issues (such as the environment and South African investment). A few of the pending proposals are discussed here.

Poison pills are measures used by management in their efforts to defeat takeovers. One currently popular pill dilutes a would-be purchaser's current holdings by letting all shareholders, except the would-be purchaser, buy stock at a discount. Thirty-eight companies, including International Paper and Chevron, have proxy proposals pending directed toward constraining the use of poison pills. These proposals either call for the rescission of poison pills or require that they be

put to a shareholder vote. Generally, management has been able to convince stockholders that poison pills are beneficial by using the arguments (1) that poison pills screen out all but the most serious suitors and (2) that they force hostile bidders to offer the best possible price. However, stockholder support for poison pills has been declining recently. In 1990, 29 percent of shareholders voted to rescind poison pills, up from 20 percent in 1987.

Shareholder proposals also have been directed toward the confidentiality of shareholder votes. Currently, companies can easily identify and pressure institutional investors because (1) most proxy ballots are signed and (2) votes can be changed right up to the annual meeting. A 1990 survey done by the Investor Responsibility Research Center indicated that 15 percent of institutional investors encountered management arm twisting. Thirty-nine companies, including Raytheon and Dow Chemical, have shareholder proposals pending that ask for votes to be confidential.

Twenty-five companies, including Eastman Kodak, currently have shareholder proposals that call for throwing out golden parachutes (lucrative severance packages for top managers) or for putting these packages to a shareholder vote. An increasingly popular shareholder proposal calls for the majority of a firm's directors, and its entire compensation committee, to have no other tie to the company. It is believed that directors with no ties to a company will represent shareholder interests without having to worry about losing their jobs or perks.

Shareholders are just beginning to flex their muscles, and they are showing no signs of backing off anytime soon.

Source: *U.S. News & World Report,* April 22, 1991.

Stockholders versus Creditors

A second agency problem involves conflicts between stockholders and creditors (debtholders). Creditors lend funds to the firm at rates that are based on (1) the riskiness of the firm's existing assets, (2) expectations concerning the riskiness of future asset additions, (3) the firm's existing capital structure (that is, the amount of debt financing it uses), and (4) expectations concerning future capital structure changes. These are the factors that determine the riskiness of the firm's debt, so creditors base the interest rate they charge on expectations regarding these factors.

Now suppose the stockholders, acting through management, cause the firm to take on new ventures that have much greater risk than was anticipated by the creditors. This increased risk will cause the value of the outstanding debt to fall. If the risky ventures turn out to be successful, all of the benefits will go to the stockholders because the creditors get only a fixed return. However, if things go sour, the bondholders will have to share the losses. What this amounts to, from the stockholders' point of view, is a game of "heads I win, tails you lose," which is obviously not a good game for the bondholders.

Similarly, if the firm increases its use of debt in an effort to boost the return to stockholders, the value of the old debt will decrease, so we have another "heads I win, tails you lose" situation. To illustrate, consider what happened to RJR Nabisco's bondholders when RJR's CEO announced his plan to take the company private in an LBO. Stockholders saw their shares jump in value from $56 to over $90 in just a few days, but RJR's bondholders suffered losses of approximately 20 percent. Investors immediately realized that the LBO would cause the amount of RJR's debt to rise dramatically, and thus its riskiness would soar. This, in turn, led to a huge decline in the price of RJR's outstanding bonds.

The entire industrial bond market was shaken by the RJR announcement because bond investors realized that virtually any company could become an LBO target. Indeed, the state of Ohio's pension fund administrator announced that he was liquidating the fund's entire industrial bond portfolio and switching to Treasury bonds because of the danger of other LBOs.

The bond market's disarray caught many experts by surprise. Even though bond investors had been stung many times in recent years by LBOs and restructurings, the gargantuan size of the RJR Nabisco deal made investors realize that no firm is too large to be a target. "Now, bond investors are going to have to pay much closer attention to the fine print in the credit agreements," said one analyst. He went on to say that "anybody who holds an industrial bond that is not protected against something like this is sitting on a credit toxic waste site."

The RJR situation increased the use of "poison puts." A *put* is an option which gives the holder the right to sell something at a stipulated price, and a *poison put* is a provision in a bond agreement which permits the holder of the bond to sell it back to the issuer at par in the event of an LBO or some similar corporate action. We anticipate a continued increase in the use of poison puts as a result of the RJR deal.

Can and should stockholders, through their managers/agents, try to expropriate wealth from the firm's creditors? In general, the answer is no. First, because such attempts have been made in the past, creditors today protect themselves reasonably well against stockholder actions through restrictions in credit agreements. Second, if potential creditors perceive that a firm will try to take advantage of them in unethical ways, they will either refuse to deal with the firm or else will require a much higher than normal rate of interest to compensate for the risks of such "sneaky" actions. Thus, firms which try to deal unfairly with creditors either lose access to the debt markets or are saddled with higher interest rates, both of which decrease the long-run value of the stock.

In view of these constraints, it follows that the goal of maximizing shareholder wealth requires fair play with creditors: Stockholder wealth depends on continued access to capital markets, and access depends on fair play and abiding by both the letter and the spirit of credit agreements. Managers, as agents of both the creditors and the shareholders, must act in a manner which is fairly balanced between the interests of these two classes of security holders. Similarly, because of other constraints and sanctions, management actions which would expropriate wealth from any of the firm's *stakeholders* (employees, customers, suppliers, and so on) will ultimately be to the detriment of shareholders. Therefore, maximizing shareholder wealth requires the fair treatment of all stakeholders.

Self-Test Questions

What is an agency relationship, and what two major agency relationships affect managerial finance?

Give some examples of potential agency problems between stockholders and managers.

List several factors which motivate managers to act in the shareholders' interests.

Give an example of how an agency problem might arise between stockholders and creditors.

MANAGERIAL ACTIONS TO MAXIMIZE SHAREHOLDER WEALTH

profit maximization

The maximization of the firm's net income.

earnings per share (EPS)

Net income divided by the number of shares of common stock outstanding.

To maximize the price of a firm's stock, what types of actions should its management take? First, consider the question of stock prices versus profits: Will **profit maximization** also result in stock price maximization? In answering this question, we must consider the matter of total corporate profits versus **earnings per share (EPS).**

For example, suppose Xerox had 100 million shares outstanding and earned $400 million, or $4 per share. If you owned 100 shares of the stock, your share of the total profits would be $400. Now suppose Xerox sold another 100 million shares and invested the funds received in assets which produced $100 million of income. Total income would rise to $500 million, but earnings per share would decline from $4 to $500/200 = $2.50. Now your share of the firm's earnings would be only $250, down from $400. You (and other current stockholders) would have suffered an earnings dilution, even though total corporate profits had risen. Therefore, other things held constant, *if management is interested in the well-being of its current stockholders, it should concentrate on earnings per share rather than on total corporate profits.*

Will maximization of expected earnings per share always maximize stockholder welfare, or should other factors be considered? Think about the *timing of the earnings.* Suppose Xerox had one project that would cause earnings per share to rise by $0.20 per year for 5 years, or $1 in total, while another project would have no effect on earnings for 4 years but would increase earnings by

$1.25 in the fifth year. Which project is better—in other words, is $0.20 per year for 5 years better or worse than $1.25 in Year 5? The answer depends on which project adds the most to the value of the stock, which in turn depends on the time value of money to investors. Thus, timing is an important reason to concentrate on wealth as measured by the price of the stock rather than on earnings alone.

Another issue relates to *risk*. Suppose one project is expected to increase earnings per share by $1, while another is expected to raise earnings by $1.20 per share. The first project is not very risky—if it is undertaken, earnings will almost certainly rise by about $1 per share. However, the other project is quite risky, so, although our best guess is that earnings will rise by $1.20 per share, we must recognize the possibility that there may be no increase whatsoever, or even a loss. Depending on how averse stockholders are to risk, the first project might be preferable to the second.

The riskiness inherent in projected earnings per share (EPS) also depends on *how the firm is financed.* As we shall see, many firms go bankrupt every year, and the greater the use of debt, the greater the threat of bankruptcy. *Consequently, while the use of debt financing may increase projected EPS, debt also increases the riskiness of projected future earnings.*

Another issue is the matter of paying dividends to stockholders versus retaining earnings and reinvesting them in the firm, thereby causing the earnings stream to grow over time. Stockholders like cash dividends, but they also like the growth in EPS that results from plowing earnings back into the business. The financial manager must decide exactly how much of the current earnings to pay out as dividends rather than to retain and reinvest—this is called the **dividend policy decision.** The optimal dividend policy is the one that maximizes the firm's stock price.

dividend policy decision
The decision as to how much of current earnings to pay out as dividends rather than to retain for reinvestment in the firm.

We see, then, that the firm's stock price is dependent on the following factors:

1. Projected earnings per share
2. Timing of the earnings stream
3. Riskiness of the projected earnings
4. Use of debt
5. Dividend policy

Every significant corporate decision should be analyzed in terms of its effect on these factors and hence on the price of the firm's stock. For example, suppose Occidental Petroleum's coal division is considering opening a new mine. If this is done, can it be expected to increase EPS? Is there a chance that costs will exceed estimates, that prices and output will fall below projections, and that EPS will be reduced because the new mine was opened? How long will it take for the new mine to show a profit? How should the capital required to open the mine be raised? If debt is used, by how much will this increase Occidental's riskiness? Should Occidental reduce its current dividends and use the cash thus saved to finance the project, or should it maintain its dividends and finance the mine with external capital? Managerial finance is designed to help answer questions like these, plus many more.

Figure 1-2   ▪   **Summary of Major Factors Affecting Stock Prices**

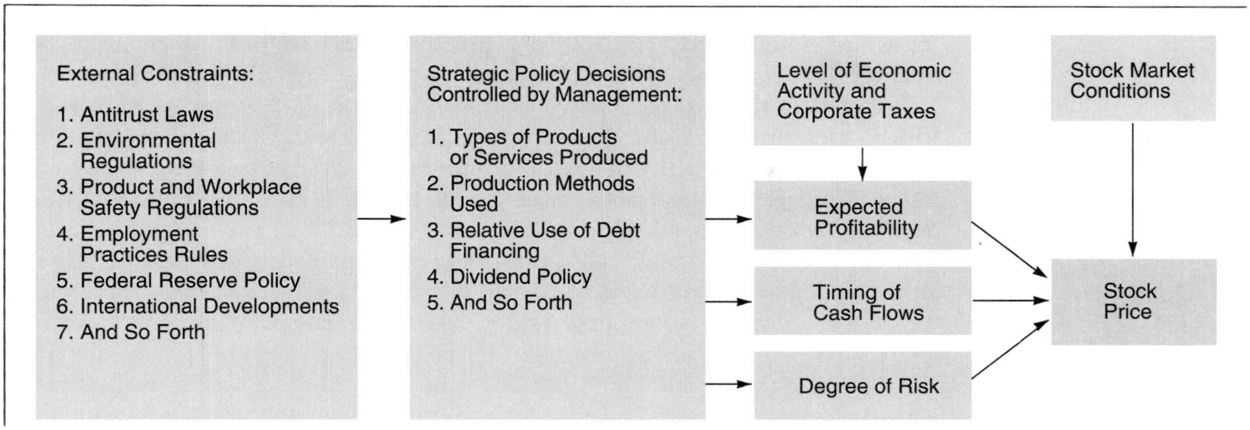

External Constraints:

1. Antitrust Laws
2. Environmental Regulations
3. Product and Workplace Safety Regulations
4. Employment Practices Rules
5. Federal Reserve Policy
6. International Developments
7. And So Forth

Strategic Policy Decisions Controlled by Management:

1. Types of Products or Services Produced
2. Production Methods Used
3. Relative Use of Debt Financing
4. Dividend Policy
5. And So Forth

Level of Economic Activity and Corporate Taxes

Stock Market Conditions

Expected Profitability

Timing of Cash Flows

Degree of Risk

Stock Price

Self-Test Questions

Will profit maximization always result in stock price maximization?

Identify five factors which affect the firm's stock price, and explain the effects of each of them.

THE EXTERNAL ENVIRONMENT

Although managerial actions affect the value of a firm's stock, external factors also influence stock prices. Included among these factors are legal constraints, the general level of economic activity, the tax laws, and conditions in the stock market. Figure 1-2 diagrams these general relationships. Working within the set of external constraints shown in the box at the extreme left, management makes a set of long-run strategic policy decisions which chart a future course for the firm. These policy decisions, along with the general level of economic activity and the level of corporate income taxes, influence the firm's expected profitability, the timing of its cash flows, their eventual transfer to stockholders in the form of dividends, and the degree of risk inherent in projected earnings and dividends. Profitability, timing, and risk all affect the price of the firm's stock, but so does another factor, conditions in the stock market as a whole, because all stock prices tend to move up and down together to some extent.

Self-Test Question

Identify some factors beyond a firm's control which influence its stock price.

ORGANIZATION OF THE BOOK

Part I consists of three background chapters. In Chapter 1 we discussed the goals of the firm and the "philosophy" of managerial finance. Chapter 2 describes the key financial statements, shows how analysts appraise a firm's performance, and explains how the various aspects of managerial finance relate to one another. Chapter 3 then discusses how financial markets operate, how interest rates are determined, and how our tax system affects both stock prices and managerial decisions.

Part II deals with the theory of valuation. First, in Chapter 4, we see how risk is measured and how it affects security prices and rates of return. Then, Chapter 5 discusses the time value of money and its effects on asset values and rates of return. Finally, Chapter 6 explains how risk and time value jointly determine stock and bond values in the marketplace.

Part III, which includes Chapters 7 and 8, examines financial forecasting and financial planning and control. In these two chapters, we focus on projecting future financial statements under different strategic plans and operating conditions.

Beginning with Part IV (Chapters 9 through 13), we examine short-term, day-to-day operating decisions. From accounting, we know that assets which are expected to be converted to cash within a year, such as inventories and accounts receivable, are called *current assets,* and that liabilities which must be paid off within a year are called *current liabilities.* The management of current assets and current liabilities is known as *working capital management.* In Chapters 9 through 13, we see how the proper amounts of cash, inventories, and accounts receivable are determined, and how these current assets should be financed.

Part V, "Strategic Long-Term Investment Decisions: Capital Budgeting," applies the concepts covered in Parts I and II to long-term, fixed asset decisions. Here we move into the execution phase of the long-range strategic planning process, considering the vital subject of *capital budgeting.* Because major capital expenditures take years to plan and implement, and since decisions in this area are generally not reversible and hence affect the firm's operations for many years, their effect on the firm's value is significant.

Parts VI and VII focus on long-term financial decisions: What are the principal sources and forms of long-term capital, how much does each type of capital cost, and how does the method of financing affect the value of the firm? These sections use most of the valuation concepts developed earlier in the book, and here we analyze such key issues as the optimal debt/equity mix and dividend policy. Part VII serves to integrate the long-term strategic aspects of the book and to show how the parts fit together. Part VII also includes a chapter on "International Managerial Finance." It was added because of the increasing importance of the globalization of businesses.

It is worth noting that some instructors may choose to cover the chapters in a different sequence from their order in the book. The chapters are written in a modular, self-contained manner, so such a reordering will present no major difficulties.

SMALL BUSINESS | Goals and Resources in the Small Firm

The Small Business Administration (SBA) reports that more than 98 percent of all businesses are considered small by SBA standards. Further, these small businesses provide approximately 60 percent of U.S. business employment, plus almost 100 percent of the *new* jobs in American industry. The SBA also reports that more than half of all product and service innovations developed in the United States since World War II have been developed by independent small business entrepreneurs.[8]

Although small business is a vital contributor to the financial health of our economy, the businesses themselves are often fragile and susceptible to failure because of poor management, particularly financial management.

Significant differences exist between small and big businesses regarding the way they are owned, the way they are managed, and the financial and managerial resources at their disposal. These differences make it necessary to modify managerial finance principles for application in the small business area. Two especially important differences are resource shortages and goal conflicts.

Resource Shortages.   Circuit Products Corporation is a small but growing manufacturer of semiconductor components. Sam Edwards owns 75 percent of the stock, and the remainder is owned by his friends and relatives. The company began operations with $250,000 in cash, and it has now developed a promising line of products. However, nearly all of the original capital has been used up.

In addition to Edwards, the company has 12 employees; 10 are engineers or technicians involved in the development and testing of new products, and the other two are clerical/secretarial personnel. Edwards uses the services of an outside accounting firm to produce the company's monthly statements, which typically are completed approximately six weeks after the end of the month.

Edwards has full responsibility for all phases of management except for product development, which is handled by Vice President Craig Settle. Settle is a technical whiz with no interest or background in business management, but he does have impressive technical credentials. He recently left a senior engineering position at a large electronics company to join Edwards's company.

Edwards's responsibilities include making contacts with potential customers, handling all personnel decisions, giving final approval to all proposed new products recommended by the technical staff, overseeing investor relations, handling legal issues both in the patent area and in the issuance of securities, managing the firm's relations with its bank, and managing the firm's cash. He has not taken a day off in six months, and he does not expect to do so for several more months.

Edwards is not unusual. Management in small firms is often spread very thin, with one or two key individuals taking on far more responsibility than they can handle properly. Edwards, for example, believes that other priorities in the business are too important to let him spend time putting together a budget or checking regularly to see how well the company is doing against such a budget. He argues, "I have a pretty good feel for how we're doing cash-wise, and I simply don't have the time to go into any more detail. Making budgets doesn't make money."

Given a request by the technical staff for some new and expensive equipment for testing new products, Edwards would make the decision to buy or not to buy the equipment with little or no formal analysis, proceeding on the basis of his "gut feelings." He sees formal analysis as being too time-consuming in view of the fact that this week he must put together a presentation for a potential customer and talk with a venture capital firm about providing Circuit Products with the capital needed to get its products into new markets, in addition to his normal duties.

Not only is management often spread thin in small firms, but such firms have great difficulty acquiring the new funds needed for expansion. Until Circuit Products achieves a fairly substantial size, say $15 million or so in sales, the company cannot sell stock or bonds to the general public. Further, if the company does have a public stock offering at the first opportunity, its costs will be quite high in comparison to larger firms' costs of issuing stock. Thus, Circuit Products currently has almost no access to public capital markets. Access to nonpublic markets is also limited. For example, its bank is reluctant to lend Circuit Products substantial amounts of money because of the firm's lack of financial history.

---

[8]Small Business Administration, *Facts about Small Business and the U.S. Small Business Administration* (Washington, D.C.: U.S. Government Printing Office, published annually).

Small firms thus have constraints both on their managerial talent and on their ability to obtain adequate capital. It is no wonder small firms often fail, given their poor (or overworked) management and lack of capital.

Goal Conflicts.   Small businesses also differ from large firms with regard to corporate goals. Earlier in the chapter we pointed out that share price maximization is taken to be the goal of all firms. Edwards, however, is a good example of an owner whose life is tied up in his company. He depends on the firm for his livelihood, and he has bet his future on the company's success. His personal wealth portfolio is not at all diversified: he has put everything he owns into the business. Given his level of commitment and his lack of a fall-back position, Edwards takes a very different posture toward risk-taking than would a typical investor in a public company. Most public investors hold a well-diversified portfolio of assets, and their employment incomes generally come from jobs in altogether separate industries. On the other hand, both Edwards's salary and his investment income are dependent on the success of one company, Circuit Products. This makes his risk exposure quite high.

The owner-managers of small firms are keenly interested in the value of their firms, even if this value cannot be observed in the market. Edwards and others in similar positions generally have in mind either "taking the firm public" or having it acquired by a larger firm at some future date—at the highest possible price. But the motives of small business owners are complex. Some owners are motivated primarily by such considerations as the desire to be their "own boss," even if this means not letting the firm grow at the fastest rate possible or be as profitable as it could be. In other words, there is value to being in control, and that value is not easily measurable. As a result, we often observe small businesses taking actions, such as refusing to bring in new stockholders even when they badly need new capital, that do not make sense when judged on the basis of value maximization but that do make sense when seen in the light of the personal objectives of the owners.

To the extent that the goals of the small firm differ from value maximization, some of the prescriptions in this text may not be entirely applicable. However, most of the tools we develop will be useful for small businesses, even though the tools may have to be modified somewhat. In any event, brief "Small Business" sections in various chapters will serve as our vehicle for discussing issues of special importance to small firms.

SUMMARY

This chapter has provided an overview of managerial finance. The key concepts covered are listed below.

- Finance consists of three interrelated areas: (1) **money and capital markets,** (2) **investments,** and (3) **managerial finance.**

- Managerial finance has undergone significant changes over time, but four issues have received the most emphasis in recent years: (1) **inflation** and its effects on interest rates, (2) **deregulation of financial institutions,** (3) a dramatic increase in the **use of telecommunications** for transmitting information **and of computers** for analyzing the effects of alternative financial decisions, and (4) the increased importance of **global financial markets and business operations.**

- **Financial managers** are responsible for **obtaining and using funds** in a way that will **maximize the value of their firms.**

- The three main forms of business organization are the **sole proprietorship,** the **partnership,** and the **corporation.**

- Although each form of organization offers some advantages and disadvantages, **most business is conducted by corporations because this organizational form maximizes most firms' values.**

▪ The primary goal of management should be to **maximize stockholders' wealth,** and this means **maximizing the price of the firm's stock.** Further, actions which maximize stock prices also increase social welfare.

▪ An **agency problem** is a potential conflict of interests that can arise between (1) the owners of the firm and its management or (2) the stockholders and the creditors (debtholders).

▪ There are a number of ways to **motivate managers to act in the best interests of stockholders,** including (1) the **threat of firing,** (2) the **threat of takeovers,** and (3) properly structured **managerial incentives.**

▪ The **price of the firm's stock** depends on the firm's **projected earnings per share,** the **timing of its earnings,** the **riskiness of the projected earnings,** its **use of debt,** and its **dividend policy.**

▪ **Small businesses** are quite important in the aggregate, so we shall discuss small business issues throughout the text.

Questions

1-1   What are the three principal forms of business organization? What are the advantages and disadvantages of each?

1-2   Would the "normal" rate of return on investment be the same in all industries? Would "normal" rates of return change over time? Explain.

1-3   Would the role of the financial manager be likely to increase or decrease in importance relative to other executives if the rate of inflation increased? Explain.

1-4   Should stockholder wealth maximization be thought of as a long-term or a short-term goal—for example, if one action would probably increase the firm's stock price from a current level of $20 to $25 in 6 months and then to $30 in 5 years, but another action would probably keep the stock at $20 for several years but then increase it to $40 in 5 years, which action would be better? Can you think of some specific corporate actions which might have these general tendencies?

1-5   Drawing on your background in accounting, can you think of any accounting procedure differences that might make it difficult to compare the relative performance of different firms?

1-6   Would the management of a firm in an oligopolistic or in a competitive industry be more likely to engage in what might be called "socially conscious" practices? Explain your reasoning.

1-7   What is the difference between stock price maximization and profit maximization? Under what conditions might profit maximization not lead to stock price maximization?

1-8   If you were the president of a large, publicly owned corporation, would you make decisions to maximize stockholders' welfare or your own personal interests? What are some actions stockholders could take to insure that management's interests and those of stockholders coincided? What are some other factors that might influence management's actions?

1-9   The president of United Semiconductor Corporation made this statement in the company's annual report: "United's primary goal is to increase the value of the common stockholders' equity over time." Later on in the report, the following announcements were made:

a. The company contributed $1.5 million to the symphony orchestra in San Francisco, its headquarters city.

b. The company is spending $500 million to open a new plant in Mexico. No revenues will be produced by the plant for 4 years, so earnings will be depressed during this period versus what they would have been had the decision not been made to open the new plant.

c. The company is increasing its relative use of debt. Whereas assets were formerly financed with 35 percent debt and 65 percent equity, henceforth the financing mix will be 50-50.

d. The company uses a great deal of electricity in its manufacturing operations, and it generates most of this power itself. Plans are to utilize nuclear fuel rather than coal to produce electricity in the future.

e. The company has been paying out half of its earnings as dividends and retaining the other half. Henceforth, it will pay out only 30 percent as dividends.

Discuss how each of these actions would be reacted to by United's stockholders, customers, and labor force, and then how each action might affect United's stock price.

Self-Test Problem   *(Solution Appears in Appendix B)*

ST-1 Define each of the following terms:

Key terms

a. Proprietorship; partnership; corporation
b. Stockholder wealth maximization
c. Hostile takeover; proxy fight; tender offer
d. Social responsibility; business ethics
e. Normal profits; normal rate of return
f. Agency problem; agency costs
g. Leveraged buyout (LBO)
h. Poison pill; greenmail
i. Performance shares; executive stock option
j. Profit maximization
k. Earnings per share
l. Dividend policy decision
m. Small business versus large business

Analysis of Financial Statements

A MANAGERIAL PERSPECTIVE

Of all the documents that large companies publish, none receives as much attention as the annual report to shareholders. At some companies, top executives begin work on the report as much as six months before its publication, and most hire professional designers and writers to ensure that the final product looks sharp and reads well.

Obviously, so much fuss would hardly be necessary if the only goal of an annual report were to inform shareholders about financial results. But, in fact, most big companies have turned their annual reports into flashy management showcases. In slick magazine format, using four-color photos, feature stories, and elaborate graphics, each firm tells the story its chairman would like to see told. Indeed, to get the desired results, most annual reports are now produced by the director of public relations instead of the chief financial officer.

Because of their puffery, annual reports have lost credibility with serious seekers of financial information. Instead, Wall Street analysts and other sophisticated investors prefer more straightforward financial disclosure documents, such as 10-Ks, which contain more detailed and unadorned information and which must by law be filed with the Securities and Exchange Commission.

Of course, a company's philosophy and personality do count, and few other documents can offer better insight into these intangibles than an annual report. Most financial analysts believe, however, that companies owe it to their investors to distinguish between the fanfare and the facts. They want to see annual reports that realistically examine the firm's business affairs and that factually discuss projects which will affect corporate welfare in the future. Indeed, they would like to see annual reports become the equivalent of management report cards, detailing strengths and weaknesses and plans for improvement. Given such information, shareholders would be better equipped to make intelligent investment decisions.

One chief executive who agrees with the financial analysts is Warren Buffett, legendary Chairman of Berkshire Hathaway and Interim Chaiman of Salomon Brothers Inc. Describing his attitude toward his readers, Buffett says, "I assume I have a very intelligent partner who has been away for a year and needs to be filled in on all that's happened." Consequently, in his letters he often admits mistakes and emphasizes the negative. For example, in one recent report he wrote, "We continue to look for ways to expand our insurance operation, but your reaction to this intent should not be unrestrained joy. Some of our expansion efforts — largely initiated by your chairman — have been lackluster, while others have been expensive failures."

Buffett also uses his letters to educate his shareholders and to help them interpret the data presented in the rest of the report. In one letter he lamented the complexities of accounting and observed, "The Yãnomamö Indians employ only three numbers: one, two, and more than two. Maybe their time will come."

Buffett's letters, although probably a bit too subjective for financial reporting purists, represent a giant step in the desired direction. In fact, Berkshire Hathaway's annual reports contain no photographs, colored ink, bar charts, or graphs, freeing readers to focus on the company's financial statements and Buffett's interpretation of them. Some CEOs might contend that such a barebones approach is too dull for the average stockholder and, further, that some readers may actually be intimidated by the information overload. But Buffett would no doubt counter that, whatever its shortcomings, his approach shows much greater respect for shareholders' intelligence and capacity to understand than does the average annual report.

A. A. Sommer, Jr., who chaired an SEC panel which studied disclosure practices, says that his group agreed that letters like Buffett's were important. But, he says, "Warren's letters are unique. Few CEOs are as smart in as many ways as Warren. It would be awfully hard to require that kind of discussion from all CEOs." In other words, it takes a chairman with interesting ideas to write an interesting chairman's letter.

As you read this chapter, think about the kinds of information that corporations provide their stockholders. Do the basic financial statements provide adequate data for investment decisions? What other information might be helpful? Also, consider the pros and cons of Chairman Buffett's decision to include long, frank, and frequently self-critical letters in his company's annual reports. Would you suggest that other companies follow suit?

If management is to maximize a firm's value, it must take advantage of the firm's strengths and correct its weaknesses. Financial statement analysis involves a comparison of the firm's performance with that of other firms in the same industry. This helps management identify deficiencies and then take actions to improve performance. In this chapter, we discuss how financial managers (and investors) evaluate the firm's current position. Then, in the remaining chapters, we will examine the types of actions that a financial manager can take to improve his or her company's position in the future, and thus to increase the price of its stock.

The chapter should, for the most part, be a review of things you learned in accounting. However, accounting focuses on how financial statements are *made,* whereas our focus is on how they are *used* by management to improve the firm's performance and by investors to set a value on the firm's stock.

FINANCIAL STATEMENTS AND REPORTS

annual report

A report issued annually by a corporation to its stockholders. It contains basic financial statements, as well as management's opinion of the past year's operations and the firm's future prospects.

Of the various reports corporations issue to their stockholders, the **annual report** is probably the most important. Two types of information are given in this report. First, there is a verbal section, often presented as a letter from the chairman, that describes the firm's operating results during the past year and then discusses new developments that will affect future operations. Second, the annual report presents four basic financial statements—the *income statement,* the *balance sheet,* the *statement of retained earnings,* and the *statement of cash flows.* Taken together, these statements give an accounting picture of the firm's operations and financial position. Detailed data are provided for the two most recent years, along with historical summaries of key operating statistics for the past five or ten years.[1]

The quantitative and verbal information are equally important. The financial statements report *what has actually happened* to earnings and dividends over the past few years, whereas the verbal statements attempt to explain why things turned out the way they did. For example, Allied Food Products' earnings dropped sharply in 1992, to $113.5 million versus $118 million in 1991. Management reported that the drop resulted from losses associated with a drought and from increased costs due to a 3-month strike. However, management then went on to paint a more optimistic picture for the future, stating that full operations had been resumed, that several unprofitable businesses had been eliminated, and that 1993 profits were expected to rise sharply. Of course, an increase in profitability may not occur, and analysts should compare management's past statements with subsequent results. In any event, *the information contained in an annual report is used by investors to form expectations about future earnings and dividends.* Therefore, the annual report is obviously of great interest to investors.

---

[1]Firms also provide quarterly reports, but these are much less comprehensive than the annual reports. In addition, larger firms file even more detailed statements, giving breakdowns for each major division or subsidiary, with the Securities and Exchange Commission (SEC). These reports, called *10-K reports,* are made available to stockholders upon request to a company's corporate secretary. Finally, many larger firms also publish *statistical supplements,* which give financial statement data and key ratios going back 10 to 20 years.

Table 2-1 ▪ **Allied Food Products: Income Statements for Years Ending December 31 (Millions of Dollars, Except for Per-Share Data)**

	1992	1991
Net sales	$3,000.0	$2,850
Costs excluding depreciation	2,616.2	2,497
Depreciation	100.0	90
Total operating costs	$2,716.2	$2,587
Earnings before interest and taxes (EBIT)	$ 283.8	$ 263
Less interest	88.0	60
Earnings before taxes (EBT)	$ 195.8	$ 203
Taxes (40%)	78.3	81
Net income before preferred dividends	$ 117.5	$ 122
Preferred dividends	4.0	4
Net income available to common stockholders	$ 113.5	$ 118
Common dividends	$ 57.5	$ 53
Addition to retained earnings	$ 56.0	$ 65
Per-share data:		
Common stock price	$23.00	$24.00
Earnings per share (EPS)[a]	$ 2.27	$ 2.36
Dividends per share (DPS)[a]	$ 1.15	$ 1.06

[a]There are 50,000,000 shares of common stock outstanding. Note that EPS is based on earnings after preferred dividends—that is, on net income available to common stockholders. Calculations of EPS and DPS for 1992 are as follows:

$$EPS = \frac{\text{Net income}}{\text{Common shares outstanding}} = \frac{\$113,500,000}{50,000,000} = \$2.27.$$

$$DPS = \frac{\text{Dividends paid to common stockholders}}{\text{Common shares outstanding}} = \frac{\$57,500,000}{50,000,000} = \$1.15.$$

For illustrative purposes, we shall use data taken from Allied Food Products, a processor and distributor of a wide variety of staple foods. Formed in 1977 when several regional firms merged, Allied has grown steadily and has earned a reputation for being one of the best firms in its industry.

The Income Statement

income statement

A statement summarizing the firm's revenues and expenses over an accounting period, generally a quarter or a year.

Table 2-1 gives the 1991 and 1992 **income statements** for Allied Food Products. Net sales are shown at the top of each statement, after which various costs, including income taxes, are subtracted to obtain the net income available to common stockholders. A report on earnings and dividends per share is given at the bottom of the statement. In managerial finance, earnings per share (EPS) is called "the bottom line," denoting that of all the items on the income statement, EPS is the most important. Allied earned $2.27 per share in 1992, down from $2.36 in 1991, but it still raised the dividend from $1.06 to $1.15.

Table 2-2 ▪ Allied Food Products: December 31 Balance Sheets (Millions of Dollars)

Assets	1992	1991	Liabilities and Equity	1992	1991
Cash and marketable securities	$ 10	$ 80	Accounts payable	$ 60	$ 30
Accounts receivable	375	315	Notes payable	110	60
Inventories	615	415	Accruals	140	130
Total current assets	$1,000	$ 810	Total current liabilities	$ 310	$ 220
Net plant and equipment	1,000	870	Long-term bonds	754	580
			Total debt	$1,064	$ 800
			Preferred stock (400,000 shares)	40	40
			Common stock (50,000,000 shares)	130	130
			Retained earnings	766	710
			Common equity	$ 896	$ 840
Total assets	$2,000	$1,680	Total liabilities and equity	$2,000	$1,680

Note: The bonds have a sinking fund requirement of $20 million a year. Sinking funds are discussed in Chapter 20, but in brief, a sinking fund simply involves the repayment of long-term debt. Thus, Allied was required to pay off $20 million of its mortgage bonds during 1992. The current portion of the long-term debt is included in notes payable here, although in a more detailed balance sheet it would be shown as a separate item under current liabilities.

The Balance Sheet

balance sheet

A statement of the firm's financial position at a specific point in time.

The left-hand side of Allied's year-end 1991 and 1992 **balance sheets,** which are given in Table 2-2, shows the firm's assets, while the right-hand side shows the liabilities and equity, or the claims against these assets. The assets are listed in order of their "liquidity," or the length of time it typically takes to convert them to cash. The claims are listed in the order in which they must be paid: Accounts payable must generally be paid within 30 days, notes are payable within 90 days, and so on, down to the stockholders' equity accounts, which represent ownership and need never be "paid off."

Some additional points about the balance sheet are worth noting:

1. **Cash versus other assets.** Although the assets are all stated in terms of dollars, only cash represents actual money. Receivables are bills others owe Allied; inventories show the dollars the company has invested in raw materials, work-in-process, and finished goods available for sale; and fixed assets reflect the amount of money Allied paid for its plant and equipment when it acquired those assets at some time in the past. Allied can write checks at present for a total of $10 million (versus current liabilities of $310 million due within a year). The noncash assets should produce cash over time, but they do not represent cash in hand, and the amount of cash they would bring if they were sold today could be higher or lower than the values at which they are carried on the books.

2. **Liabilities versus stockholders' equity.** The claims against assets are of two types—liabilities (or money the company owes) and the stockhold-

common stockholders' equity (net worth)

The capital supplied by common stockholders—capital stock, paid-in capital, retained earnings, and, occasionally, certain reserves. *Total equity* is common equity plus preferred stock.

ers' ownership position.[2] The **common stockholders' equity,** or **net worth,** is a residual:

Assets   −   Liabilities   − Preferred stock = Common stockholders' equity.

$2,000,000,000 − $1,064,000,000 − $40,000,000   = $896,000,000.

Suppose assets decline in value—for example, suppose some of the accounts receivable are written off as bad debts. Liabilities and preferred stock remain constant, so the value of the common stockholders' equity must decline. Therefore, the risk of asset value fluctuations is borne by the common stockholders. Note, however, that if asset values rise (perhaps because of inflation), these benefits will accrue exclusively to the common stockholders.

3. **Preferred versus common stock.** As we will see in Chapter 21, preferred stock is a hybrid, or a cross between common stock and debt. In the event of bankruptcy, preferred stock ranks below debt but above common stock. Also, the preferred dividend is fixed, so preferred stockholders do not benefit if the company's earnings grow. Finally, many firms do not use any preferred stock, and those that do generally do not use very much of it. Therefore, when the term "equity" is used in finance, we generally mean "common equity" unless the word "total" is included.

4. **Breakdown of the common equity account.** A detailed discussion of the common equity accounts is given in Chapter 19, "Common Stock and the Investment Banking Process," but a brief preview of that discussion is useful here. First, note that the common equity section is divided into three accounts—common stock, paid-in capital, and retained earnings. The **retained earnings** account is built up over time as the firm "saves" a part of its earnings rather than paying all earnings out as dividends. The other two common equity accounts arise from the issuance of stock to raise capital.

retained earnings

That portion of the firm's earnings that has been saved rather than paid out as dividends.

The breakdown of the common equity accounts is important for some purposes but not for others. For example, a potential stockholder would want to know whether the company actually earned the funds reported in its equity accounts or whether the funds came mainly from selling stock. A potential creditor, on the other hand, would be more interested in the amount of money the owners put up than in the form in which the money was put up. In the remainder of this chapter, we generally aggregate the three common equity accounts and call this sum *common equity* or *net worth.*

5. **Inventory accounting.** Allied uses the FIFO (first-in, first-out) method to determine the inventory value shown on its balance sheet ($615 million).

---

[2]One could divide liabilities into (1) debts owed to someone and (2) other items, such as deferred taxes, reserves, and so on. Because we do not make this distinction, the terms *debt* and *liabilities* are used synonymously. It should be noted that firms occasionally set up reserves for certain contingencies, such as the potential costs involved in a lawsuit currently in the courts. These reserves represent an accounting transfer from retained earnings to the reserve account. If the company wins the suit, retained earnings will be credited, and the reserve will be eliminated. If it loses, a loss will be recorded, cash will be reduced, and the reserve will be eliminated.

It could have used the LIFO (last-in, first-out) method. During a period of rising prices, compared to LIFO, FIFO will produce a higher balance sheet inventory value but a lower cost of goods sold on the income statement. For example, if costs are rising at an annual rate of 10 percent, inventory items that were just acquired would cost 10 percent more than identical items that were acquired a year ago. Since Allied uses FIFO, and since inflation has been occurring, (a) its cost of goods sold is lower than it would have been under LIFO, (b) its reported profits are therefore higher, and (c) its balance sheet inventories are higher than they would have been had it used LIFO. In Allied's case, had the company elected to switch to LIFO in 1992, EPS would have been lowered by 36 cents, to $1.91, and its balance sheet figure for inventories would have been $585,000,000 rather than $615,000,000. Thus, the inventory valuation method used can have a significant effect on the financial statements.

6. **Depreciation methods.** Companies often use the most accelerated method permissible to calculate depreciation for tax purposes but use straight line, which results in a lower depreciation charge, for stockholder reporting. However, Allied has elected to use rapid depreciation for both stockholder reporting and tax purposes. Had Allied elected to use straight line depreciation for stockholder reporting, its depreciation expense would have been almost $25,000,000 less, so its net income would have been higher, as would its EPS. The $1 billion shown for "net plant" on its balance sheet, and hence its retained earnings, would also have been approximately $25,000,000 higher.

7. **The time dimension.** The balance sheet may be thought of as a snapshot of the firm's financial position *at a point in time*—for example, on December 31, 1991. Thus, on December 31, 1991, Allied had $80 million of cash and marketable securities, but this account had been reduced to $10 million by the end of 1992. The income statement, on the other hand, reports on operations *over a period of time*—for example, during the calendar year 1992. Allied had sales of $3 billion, and its net income available to common stockholders was $113.5 million. The balance sheet changes every day as inventories are increased or decreased, as fixed assets are added or retired, as bank loans are increased or decreased, and so on. Companies whose businesses are seasonal have especially large changes in their balance sheets. Allied's inventories are low just before the harvest season and high after the fall crops have been brought in and processed. Similarly, most retailers have large inventories just before Christmas but low inventories and high accounts receivable just after Christmas. Therefore, firms' balance sheets will change over the year, depending on the date on which the statement is constructed.

statement of retained earnings

A statement reporting how much of the firm's earnings were not paid out in dividends. The figure for retained earnings that appears here is the sum of the annual retained earnings for each year of the firm's history.

Statement of Retained Earnings

Changes in the common equity accounts between balance sheet dates are reported in the **statement of retained earnings.** Allied's statement is shown in Table 2-3. The company earned $113.5 million during 1992, it paid out $57.5 million in common dividends, and it plowed $56 million back into the business.

Table 2-3 ▪ **Allied Food Products: Statement of Retained Earnings for Year Ending December 31, 1992 (Millions of Dollars)**

Balance of retained earnings, December 31, 1991	$710.0
Add: Net income, 1992	113.5
Less: Dividends to common stockholders	(57.5)[a]
Balance of retained earnings, December 31, 1992	$766.0

[a]Here, and throughout the book, parentheses are used to denote negative numbers.

Thus, the balance sheet item "Retained earnings" increased from $710,000,000 at the end of 1991 to $766,000,000 at the end of 1992.

Note that the balance sheet account "Retained earnings" represents a *claim against assets,* not assets per se. Further, firms retain earnings primarily to expand the business, and this means investing in plant and equipment, in inventories, and so on, *not* in a bank account. Changes in retained earnings represent the recognition that income generated by the firm during the accounting period has been invested in assets. In other words, changes in retained earnings result because common stockholders allow the firm to reinvest in itself funds that otherwise could be distributed as dividends. *Thus, retained earnings as reported on the balance sheet do not represent cash and are not "available" for the payment of dividends or anything else.*[3]

Accounting Income versus Cash Flow

When you studied income statements in accounting, the emphasis was probably on determining the net income of the firm. In finance, however, we focus on **cash flows.** The value of an asset (or a whole firm) is determined by the cash flows it generates. The firm's net income is important, but cash flows are even more important, because dividends must be paid in cash and because cash is necessary to purchase the assets required to continue operations.

As we discussed in Chapter 1, the goal of the firm should be to maximize the price of its stock. Since the value of any asset, including a share of stock, depends on the cash flows produced by the asset, managers should strive to maximize cash flows available to investors over the long run. A business's cash flows are generally equal to cash from sales, minus cash operating costs, minus interest charges, and minus taxes. Before we go any further though, we need to discuss depreciation, which is an operating cost.

Recall from your accounting course that depreciation is an annual charge against income which reflects the estimated dollar cost of the capital equipment

cash flows

The actual net cash, as opposed to accounting net income, that a firm generates during some specified period.

---

[3]The amount reported in the retained earnings account is *not* an indication of the amount of cash the firm has. Cash (as of the balance sheet date) is found in the cash account—an asset account. A positive number in the retained earnings account indicates only that in the past, according to generally accepted accounting principles, the firm has earned an income, but its dividends have been less than its reported income. Even though a company reports record earnings and shows an increase in the retained earnings account, it still may be short of cash.

The same situation holds for individuals. You might own a new BMW (no loan), lots of clothes, and an expensive stereo, and, hence, have a high net worth, but if you had only 23 cents in your pocket plus $5 in your checking account, you would still be short of cash.

used up in the production process. For example, suppose a machine with a life of 5 years and a zero expected salvage value was purchased in 1991 for $100,000. This $100,000 cost is not expensed in the purchase year; rather, it is charged against production over the machine's 5-year depreciable life. If the depreciation expense were not taken, profits would be overstated, and taxes would be too high. The annual depreciation charge is deducted from sales revenues, along with such other costs as labor and raw materials, to determine income. However, because funds were expended back in 1991, the depreciation charged against income in 1992 through 1996 is not a cash outlay, as are labor or raw materials charges. *Depreciation is a noncash charge, so it must be added back to net income to obtain an estimate of the cash flow from operations.*

To see how depreciation affects cash flows, consider the following simplified income statement (Column 1) and cash flow statement (Column 2). Here we assume that all sales revenues were received in cash during the year and that all costs except depreciation were paid in cash during the year. Cash flows are seen to equal net income plus depreciation:

	Income Statement (1)	Cash Flows (2)	
Sales revenues	$1,500	$1,500	
Costs except depreciation	1,050	1,050	
Depreciation (DEP)	150	—	
Total costs	$1,200	$1,050	(Cash costs)
Earnings before taxes	$ 300	$ 450	(Pretax cash flow)
Taxes (40%)	120	120	(From Column 1)
Net income (NI)	$ 180		
Add back depreciation	150		
Net cash flow = NI + DEP	$ 330	$ 330	

As we shall see in Chapter 6, a stock's value is based on the *present value of the cash flows* which investors expect it to provide in the future. Although any individual investor could sell the stock and receive cash for it, the *cash flow* provided by the stock itself is the expected future dividend stream, and that expected dividend stream provides the fundamental basis for the stock's value.

accounting profit
A firm's net income as reported on its income statement.

Because dividends are paid in cash, a company's ability to pay dividends depends on its cash flows. Cash flows are generally related to **accounting profit,** which is simply net income as reported on the income statement. Although companies with relatively high accounting profits generally have relatively high cash flows, the relationship is not precise. Therefore, investors are concerned about cash flow projections as well as profit projections.

Firms can be thought of as having two separate but related bases of value: *existing assets,* which provide profits and cash flows, and *growth opportunities,* which represent opportunities to make new investments that will increase future profits and cash flows. The ability to take advantage of growth opportunities often depends on the availability of the cash needed to buy new assets, and the cash flows from existing assets are often the primary source of the funds used

operating cash flows
Those cash flows that arise from normal operations; the difference between sales revenues and cash expenses.

to make profitable new investments. This is another reason why both investors and managers are concerned with cash flows as well as profits.

For our purposes, it is useful to divide cash flows into two classes: (1) *operating cash flows* and (2) *other cash flows*. **Operating cash flows** are those that arise from normal operations, and they are, in essence, the difference between sales revenues and cash expenses, including taxes paid. Other cash flows arise from the issuance of stock, from borrowing, or from the sale of fixed assets. Our focus here is on operating cash flows.

Operating cash flows can differ from accounting profits (or net income) for two primary reasons:

1. All the taxes reported on the income statement may not have to be paid during the current year, or, under certain circumstances, the actual cash payments for taxes may exceed the tax figure deducted from sales to calculate net income. The reasons for these tax cash flow differentials are discussed in detail in accounting courses.

2. Sales may be on credit, hence not represent cash, and some of the expenses (or costs) deducted from sales to determine profits may not be cash costs. Most important, depreciation is not a cash cost.

Thus, operating cash flows could be larger or smaller than accounting profits during any given year. The effect of the major noncash expense, depreciation, was discussed above, and we shall consider the cash flow implications of credit sales as opposed to sales for cash in a later chapter.

The Cash Flow Cycle

As a company like Allied goes about its business, it makes sales, which lead (1) to a reduction of inventories, (2) to an increase in cash, and, (3) if the sales price exceeds the cost of the item sold, to a profit. These transactions cause the balance sheet to change, and they are also reflected in the income statement. It is critical that you understand (1) that businesses deal with *physical* units like autos, computers, or aluminum, (2) that physical transactions are translated into dollar terms through the accounting system, and (3) that the purpose of financial analysis is to examine the accounting numbers in order to determine how efficiently the firm is making and selling physical goods and services.

Several factors make financial analysis difficult. One of them is the variations that exist in accounting methods among firms. As was discussed previously, different methods of inventory valuation and depreciation can lead to differences in reported profits for otherwise identical firms, and a good financial analyst must be able to adjust for these differences if he or she is to make valid comparisons among companies. Another factor involves timing—an action is taken at one point in time, but its full effects cannot be accurately measured until some later period.

cash flow cycle
The way in which actual net cash, as opposed to accounting net income, flows into or out of the firm during some specified period.

To understand how timing influences the financial statements, one must understand the **cash flow cycle** as set forth in Figure 2-1. Rectangles represent balance sheet accounts—assets and claims against assets—whereas circles represent income statement items. Each rectangle may be thought of as a reservoir, and there is a certain amount of the asset or liability in the reservoir (account) on each balance sheet date. Various transactions cause changes in the accounts, just as adding or subtracting water changes the level in a reservoir. For example,

Figure 2-1 ▪ **Cash and Materials Flows within the Firm**

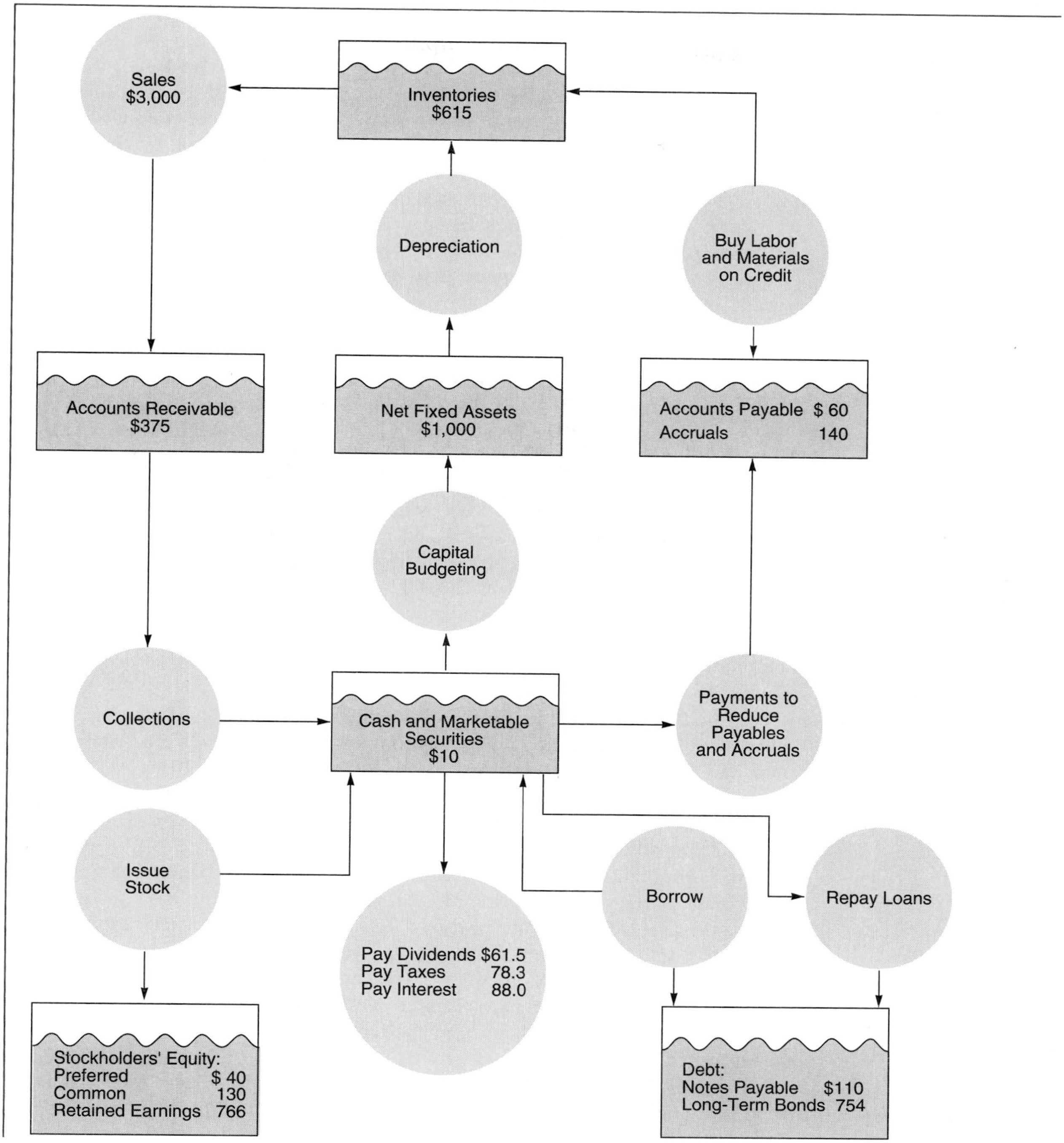

collecting an account receivable reduces the receivables reservoir but increases the cash reservoir.

The cash account is the focal point of the figure. Certain events, such as collecting accounts receivable or borrowing money from the bank, will cause the cash account to increase, while the payment of taxes, interest, dividends, and accounts payable will cause it to decline. Similar comments could be made about all the balance sheet accounts—their balances rise, fall, or remain constant depending on events that occur during the period under study, which for Allied is January 1, 1992, through December 31, 1992.

Projected increases in sales may require the firm to raise cash by borrowing from its bank or by selling new stock. For example, if Allied anticipates an increase in sales, it will (1) expend cash to buy or build fixed assets through the capital budgeting process; (2) step up purchases of raw materials, thereby increasing both raw materials inventories and accounts payable; (3) increase production, which will lead to an increase in both accrued wages and work-in-process; and (4) eventually build up its finished goods inventory. Some cash will have been expended and hence removed from the cash account, and the firm will have obligated itself to expend still more cash within a few weeks to pay off its accounts payable and its accrued wages. These cash-using events will have occurred *before* any new cash has been generated from sales. Even when the expected sales do occur, there will still be a lag in the generation of cash until receivables are collected—because Allied grants credit for 30 days, it will have to wait 30 days after a sale is made before cash comes in. Depending on how much cash the firm had at the beginning of the build-up, on the length of its production-sales-collection cycle, and on how long it can delay payment of its own payables and accrued wages, Allied may have to obtain substantial amounts of additional cash by selling stock or bonds, or by borrowing from the bank.

If the firm is profitable, its sales revenues will exceed its costs, and its cash inflows will eventually exceed its cash outlays. However, even a profitable business can experience a cash shortage if it is growing rapidly. It may have to pay for plant, materials, and labor before cash from the expanded sales starts flowing in. For this reason, rapidly growing firms generally require large bank loans or capital from other sources.

An unprofitable firm such as Eastern Airlines before its bankruptcy will have larger cash outlays than inflows. This, in turn, will lower the cash account and also cause a slowdown in the payment of accrued wages and accounts payable, and it may also lead to heavy borrowings. Accordingly, liabilities rise to excessive levels in unprofitable firms. Similarly, an overly ambitious expansion plan will result in excessive inventories and fixed assets, while too lenient a credit/collection policy will result in high accounts receivable, which eventually will result in bad debts and reduced profits.

If a firm runs out of cash and cannot obtain enough to meet its obligations, then it cannot operate, and it will have to declare bankruptcy. In fact, Eastern Airlines and thousands of other companies have been forced to do just that. Therefore, an accurate cash flow forecast is a critical element in managerial finance. Financial analysts are well aware of all this, and they use the analytical techniques discussed in the remainder of this chapter to help discover cash flow problems before they become serious.

Table 2-4 ▪ **Allied Food Products: Statement of Cash Flows
for 1992 (Millions of Dollars)**

Operating Activities:	
Net income	$117.5
Other additions (sources of cash)	
Depreciation[a]	100.0
Increase in accounts payable	30.0
Increase in accruals	10.0
Subtractions (uses of cash)	
Increase in accounts receivable	(60.0)
Increase in inventories	(200.0)
Net cash flow from operations	($ 2.5)
Long-Term Investing Activities:	
Acquisition of fixed assets[b]	($230.0)
Financing Activities:	
Increase in notes payable	$ 50.0
Increase in bonds	174.0
Payment of common and preferred dividends	(61.5)
Net cash flow from financing	$162.5
Net reduction in cash and marketable securities	($ 70.0)
Cash at beginning of year	80.0
Cash at end of year	$ 10.0

[a]Depreciation is a noncash expense that was deducted when calculating net income. It must be added back to show the correct cash flow from operations.

[b]The net increase in fixed assets is $130 million; however, this net amount includes a deduction for the year's depreciation expense. Depreciation expense should be added back to show the increase in gross fixed assets. From the company's income statement, we see that 1992 depreciation expense is $100 million; thus, the acquisition of fixed assets equals $230 million.

Statement of Cash Flows

statement of cash flows

A statement reporting the impact of a firm's operating, investing, and financing activities on cash flows over an accounting period.

The graphic cash flow analysis set forth in Figure 2-1 is converted into numerical form and reported in annual reports as the **statement of cash flows.** This statement is designed to show how the firm's operations have affected its cash position and to help answer questions such as these: Is the firm generating the cash needed to purchase additional fixed assets for growth? Is growth so rapid that external financing is required both to maintain operations and for investment in new fixed assets? Does the firm have excess cash flows that can be used to repay debt or to invest in new products? This information is useful both for financial managers and investors, so the statement of cash flows is an important part of the annual report. A detailed discussion of how to create the statement of cash flows is presented in Appendix 2A. At this point, we are concerned with the interpretation of the statement of cash flows rather than its construction. Table 2-4 is Allied's statement of cash flows as it would appear in the company's annual report.

The top part of Table 2-4 shows cash flows generated by and used in operations—for Allied, operations provided net cash flows of *minus* $2.5 million. The operating cash flows are generated principally from the day-to-day operations of the firm, and this amount can be determined by adjusting the net income figure to account for noncash items. The day-to-day operations of Allied in 1992 provided $257.5 million of funds; however, the increase in inventories during the year accounted for a use of funds almost equal to this amount. The second section shows long-term investing activities. Allied purchased fixed assets totaling $230 million; this was its only investment activity during 1992. Allied's financing activities, shown in the lower section of Table 2-4, included borrowing from banks (notes payable), selling new bonds, and paying dividends on its common and preferred stock. Allied raised $224 million by borrowing, but it paid $61.5 million in preferred and common dividends, so its net inflow of funds from financing activities during 1992 was $162.5 million.

When all of these sources and uses of cash are totaled, we see that Allied had a $70 million cash shortfall during 1992. It met that shortfall by drawing down its cash and marketable securities holdings by $70 million, as shown in Table 2-2, the firm's balance sheet.

Allied's statement of cash flows should be of some concern to the financial manager and to outside analysts. The company had a $2.5 million cash shortfall from operations, it spent an additional $230 million on new fixed assets, and it paid out another $61.5 million in dividends. It covered these cash outlays by borrowing heavily, by selling off marketable securities, and by drawing down its bank account. Obviously, this situation cannot continue year after year, so something will have to be done. We will consider some of the actions the financial manager might recommend, but first we must examine the financial statements in more depth.

Earnings and Dividends

In addition to the four statements described above, most annual reports also give a summary of earnings and dividends over the last few years. For Allied, these data are analyzed in Figure 2-2. Earnings have been variable, but there was a definite upward trend over the period. In 1984–85 a strike caused earnings to drop sharply, but that was merely a temporary break in the long-run growth trend.

Although dividends and dividend policy are discussed in detail in Chapter 18, we can make several comments about dividends at this point:

1. Dividends per share (DPS) represent the basic cash flows passed from the firm to its stockholders. As such, dividends are a key element in the stock price models which we will develop in Chapter 6.

2. DPS in any given year can exceed EPS, but in the long run dividends are paid from earnings, so DPS normally is smaller than EPS. The percentage of earnings paid out in dividends, or the ratio of DPS to EPS, is called the *dividend payout ratio*. Allied's payout ratio has varied from year to year, but it has averaged about 55 percent.

3. In a graph such as that in Figure 2-2, the DPS line is typically below the EPS line, but the two lines generally have about the same slope, indicating

Figure 2-2 ▪ **Allied Food Products: Earnings and Dividends 1981–1992**

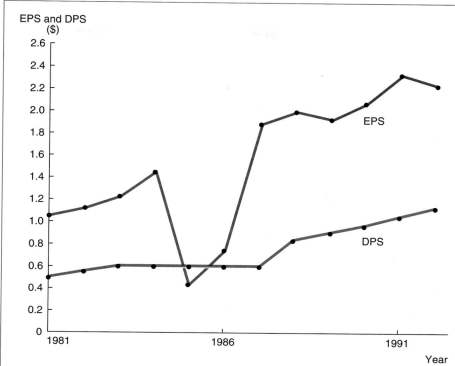

Year	Earnings per Share	Dividends per Share	Payout Ratio
1981	$1.05	$0.49	46.7%
1982	1.12	0.55	49.1
1983	1.23	0.60	48.8
1984	1.45	0.60	41.4
1985	0.45	0.60	133.3
1986	0.75	0.60	80.0
1987	1.91	0.60	31.4
1988	2.01	0.85	42.3
1989	1.95	0.91	46.7
1990	2.10	0.99	47.1
1991	2.36	1.06	44.9
1992	2.27	1.15	50.7
11-year growth rate	7.26%	8.06%	55.2% (Average)

Note: The growth rates shown here are based on the beginning and ending figures and are calculated using procedures discussed in Chapter 5.

that EPS and DPS generally grow at approximately the same rate. As the data in Figure 2-2 indicate, Allied's earnings and dividends have both been growing at an average rate of 7 to 8 percent per year.

? Self-Test Questions

Identify the two types of information given in the annual report.

Describe these four basic financial statements: (1) the income statement, (2) the balance sheet, (3) the statement of retained earnings, and (4) the statement of cash flows.

Explain the following statement: "Retained earnings as reported on the balance sheet do not represent cash and are not 'available' for the payment of dividends or anything else."

Differentiate between operating cash flows and other cash flows.

List two reasons why operating cash flows can differ from net income.

In accounting, the emphasis is on the determination of net income. What is emphasized in finance, and why is that emphasis important?

Assuming that depreciation is the only noncash cost, how can someone calculate a business's cash flow?

INDUSTRY PRACTICE | Creative Accounting and Cooking the Books Hollywood Style

Orion Pictures, a small publicly traded company founded in 1982, with a reputation for making high-quality movies with low levels of corporate interference, is filing for bankruptcy protection. Last spring the studio was forced to sell four partially completed films, including its sure-fire hit *The Addams Family,* to rival studios for needed cash, and one of its leading film makers, Woody Allen, had at least temporarily left the studio because of Orion's inability to finance the scheduled November production of his next film. By mid-October 1991, Orion had defaulted on loan payments of $70 million, was expected to report a substantial loss for its second fiscal quarter, and was in the process of negotiating for payment extensions on $52 million of movie-production financing obligations. To avoid a bankruptcy filing, Orion had hoped to swap $285 million of subordinated debt for equity in a restructuring plan. However, those hopes were quashed when five months of bondholder negotiations suddenly collapsed. How did Orion get in this situation? Aggressive accounting practices in an industry where accounting rules are vague killed the company.

Until April 1991, Orion's 81-year-old founder, Arthur B. Krim, ran the company as a committee of one. Then, Orion's principal stockholder, John Kluge,

the founder of Metromedia Company, seized direct control of Orion and its board of directors. Mr. Kluge had watched the value of his 15.3 million shares, representing a 70 percent stake in the company, dwindle from $240 million to less than $69 million. Whether Mr. Krim violated generally accepted accounting principles to disguise Orion's mounting losses will be decided by the courts; however, his ambition may have proved fatal for the company.

At the start, Orion was undercapitalized. Its management hoped to make films in the $15 to $17 million range (in an industry where the average cost of a film is $25 million) and to skimp on marketing. Orion was not able to keep up with the increasing sums of money offered by its competitors; despite Orion's attempt to keep costs down, the company spent more money than it took in, believing that a hit would save them from disaster. Early on its stock performed well, partly due to its existing management team, which had worked well together for years.

After Orion's fall 1982 hit, *First Blood,* its luck at the box office faded, but somehow its earnings kept rising, and the stock was pushed by industry analysts and kept performing well. With hindsight, it is apparent that Orion's success resulted less from concrete results than from a legal but highly unusual "book-keeping exercise that created the impression of a dramatic turnaround." Management revalued assets on the books so as to transform a negative net worth of $45 million to a positive net worth of $21.5 million.

Melvin F. Woods, Orion's former chief financial officer, said, "It's easy to say they cooked the books, and you may be able to make a case for that. But at the end of the day, accounting doesn't change how much money you bring in. The bottom line is that their movies didn't perform."

Between 1983 and 1990, Mr. Krim was determined to show increased quarterly earnings, and a pattern began to emerge in the company's financial disclosures. During this period, as the company had more bad years than good and many planned hits proved to be flops, Orion recorded profits in every year but 1986. It was also showing rising assets, but a growing proportion of assets were actually failed films that had not been written down. The accounting directions came right from the top. Instead of writing off failed films, Orion was carrying many of them as assets. Between 1985 and 1990, the value Orion placed on its film inventory grew at an annual rate of $89 million. For the year ending February 1991, the company had an unamortized film inventory of $766 million compared with revenues of $584 million. One example of Orion's mistakes was its valuation of 125 episodes of the hit television series "Cagney and Lacey." The company had counted on receiving $100 million for the episodes but received only $25 million. The error was partly due to a radical change in the TV syndication market, which fell apart for one-hour dramas in the late 1980s. To make matters worse, the company had borrowed against the series's inflated value. In 1987, the SEC investigated Orion's write-down policy, but it found nothing illegal.

However, in February and March 1990, Orion was so desperate for cash to meet its debt obligations and to boost earnings that it entered into a deal which raised even more serious accounting questions. Columbia Pictures agreed to pay Orion a $175 million advance against future revenue to be earned from distributing abroad some of the films Orion would make over the next six years, plus for 50 future videocassettes and an unspecified quantity of the company's pre-1982 film and TV shows. The deal raised immediate cash for Orion, but it mortgaged part of the company's future profits. Because the deal reflected the sale of future products, the revenue should have been treated as deferred earnings; however, Orion recorded more than $50 million in profits immediately for the foreign distribution of its pre-1982 movies and TV shows. This recognition of the $50 million allowed Orion to show a 1990 profit of $20 million before taxes rather than a $30 million loss.

The inclusion of the $50 million in profits was questionable; Orion's foreign revenue from the same properties in the prior year was only $5 million. If these properties were not worth $50 million, it was materially misleading for Orion to say that they were. Also, it is a violation of generally accepted accounting principles to record revenue prematurely. Orion's CEO, Bill Bernstein, will not comment on the firm's accounting but says that it is in compliance with the law. Columbia executives involved with the deal say they got what they wanted and that it was not up to them to tell Orion how to account for the deal.

While misgivings about Orion's financial stability multiplied, Orion's 1990 annual report presented a very rosy picture. In addition, at the June 1990 stockholders' meeting, Orion referred to the company's "good health" in a letter to the stockholders.

The first indications of problems occurred in a January 1991 third-quarter financial filing, when the company showed a net loss of $15 million for the quarter, a negative cash flow of $173.4 million for the previous nine months, and an unamortized film inventory of $807.5 million. The bubble finally burst in May when the company announced fourth-quarter losses of $48 million, which included a $32.8 million write down for its films. Orion's bond price fell from $100 to $15, and its stock fell through the floor even as its new films were leading at the box office and receiving Academy Awards. At the same time, the company announced a restructuring plan, which it hoped would save it from bankruptcy.

According to an entertainment industry analyst, the company's aggressive accounting methods disguised its weaknesses. Mr. Kluge and Metromedia had hoped that the restructuring would go through so that they could sell their Orion shares and get out of the film business. However, in December 1991, the news broke that Orion Pictures was filing for bankruptcy. Currently, its stock is selling for $1.875, and its bonds are selling at 15 percent of their par value. Obviously, the wisdom of Columbia's deal with Orion is now questionable; Orion and its legendary founder will never be viewed in the same light as they were before the company's financial difficulties, and the need for truthful financial statements and careful financial statement analysis has been vividly demonstrated.

Source: *The Wall Street Journal,* October 16, 1991, and December 12, 1991.

RATIO ANALYSIS

Financial statements report both on a firm's position at a point in time and on its operations over some past period. However, the real value of financial statements lies in the fact that they can be used to help predict the firm's future earnings and dividends. From an investor's standpoint, *predicting the future is what financial statement analysis is all about*, while from management's standpoint, *financial statement analysis is useful both as a way to anticipate future conditions and, more important, as a starting point for planning actions that will influence the future course of events.*

An analysis of the firm's ratios is generally the first step in a financial analysis. The ratios are designed to show relationships between financial statement accounts. For example, Firm A might have debt of $5,248,760 and interest charges of $419,900, while Firm B might have debt of $52,647,980 and interest charges of $3,948,600. Which company is stronger? The true burden of these debts, and the companies' ability to repay them, can be ascertained (1) by comparing each firm's debt to its assets and (2) by comparing the interest it must pay to the income it has available for payment of interest. Such comparisons are made by *ratio analysis*.

In the paragraphs which follow, we will calculate the 1992 financial ratios for Allied Food Products and then evaluate those ratios in relation to the industry averages.[4] Note that all dollar amounts in the ratio calculations are in millions.

Liquidity Ratios

liquid asset
An asset that can be easily converted to cash at a "fair market value."

liquidity ratios
Ratios that show the relationship of a firm's cash and other current assets to its current liabilities.

current ratio
This ratio is calculated by dividing current assets by current liabilities. It indicates the extent to which current liabilities are covered by assets expected to be converted to cash in the near future.

A **liquid asset** is one that can be easily converted to cash at a "fair market value," and a firm's "liquidity position" deals with this question: Will the firm be able to meet its current obligations? Allied has debts totaling $310 million that must be paid off within the coming year. Will it have trouble satisfying those obligations? A full liquidity analysis requires the use of cash budgets (described in Chapter 8), but by relating the amount of cash and other current assets to the firm's current obligations, ratio analysis provides a quick, easy-to-use measure of liquidity. Two commonly used **liquidity ratios** are discussed in this section.

Current Ratio. The **current ratio** is calculated by dividing current assets by current liabilities:

$$\text{Current ratio} = \frac{\text{Current assets}}{\text{Current liabilities}}$$

[4]In addition to the ratios discussed in this section, financial analysts also employ a tool known as *common size* balance sheets and income statements. To form a common size balance sheet, one simply divides each asset and liability item by total assets and then expresses the result as a percentage. The resultant percentage statement can be compared with statements of larger or smaller firms, or with those of the same firm over time. To form a common size income statement, one simply divides each income statement item by sales.

$$= \frac{\$1,000}{\$310} = 3.2 \text{ times.}$$

Industry average $= 4.2$ times.

Current assets normally include cash, marketable securities, accounts receivable, and inventories. Current liabilities consist of accounts payable, short-term notes payable, current maturities of long-term debt, accrued income taxes, and other accrued expenses (principally wages).

If a company is getting into financial difficulty, it begins paying its bills (accounts payable) more slowly, borrowing from its bank, and so on. If current liabilities are rising faster than current assets, the current ratio will fall, and this could spell trouble. Because the current ratio provides the best single indicator of the extent to which the claims of short-term creditors are covered by assets that are expected to be converted to cash fairly quickly, it is the most commonly used measure of short-term solvency.

Allied's current ratio is well below the average for its industry, 4.2, so its liquidity position is relatively weak. Still, since current assets are scheduled to be converted to cash in the near future, it is highly probable that they could be liquidated at close to their stated value. With a current ratio of 3.2, Allied could liquidate current assets at only 31 percent of book value and still pay off current creditors in full.[5]

Although industry average figures are discussed later in some detail, it should be noted at this point that an industry average is not a magic number that all firms should strive to maintain — in fact, some very well-managed firms will be above the average while other good firms will be below it. However, if a firm's ratios are far removed from the average for its industry, an analyst should be concerned about why this variance occurs. Thus, a deviation from the industry average should signal the analyst (or management) to check further.

quick (acid test) ratio
This ratio is calculated by deducting inventories from current assets and dividing the remainder by current liabilities.

Quick, or Acid Test, Ratio.   The **quick,** or **acid test, ratio** is calculated by deducting inventories from current assets and then dividing the remainder by current liabilities:

$$\text{Quick, or acid test, ratio} = \frac{\text{Current assets} - \text{Inventories}}{\text{Current liabilities}}$$

$$= \frac{\$385}{\$310} = 1.2 \text{ times.}$$

Industry average $= 2.1$ times.

Inventories are typically the least liquid of a firm's current assets, hence they are the assets on which losses are most likely to occur in the event of liquidation. Therefore, a measure of the firm's ability to pay off short-term obligations without relying on the sale of inventories is important.

---

[5]$1/3.2 = 0.31$, or 31 percent. Note that $0.31(\$1,000) = \$310$, the amount of current liabilities.

The industry average quick ratio is 2.1, so Allied's 1.2 ratio is low in comparison with the ratios of other firms in its industry. Still, if the accounts receivable can be collected, the company can pay off its current liabilities even without having to liquidate its inventory.

Asset Management Ratios

asset management ratios
A set of ratios which measures how effectively a firm is managing its assets.

The second group of ratios, the **asset management ratios,** measures how effectively the firm is managing its assets. These ratios are designed to answer this question: Does the total amount of each type of asset as reported on the balance sheet seem reasonable, too high, or too low in view of current and projected sales levels? Allied and other companies must borrow or obtain capital from other sources to acquire assets. If they have too many assets, their interest expenses will be too high, hence their profits will be depressed. On the other hand, if assets are too low, profitable sales may be lost.

inventory turnover ratio
The ratio calculated by dividing sales by inventories.

Inventory Turnover.   The **inventory turnover ratio** is defined as sales divided by inventories:

$$\text{Inventory turnover ratio} = \frac{\text{Sales}}{\text{Inventories}}$$

$$= \frac{\$3,000}{\$615} = 4.9 \text{ times.}$$

Industry average = 9.0 times.

As a rough approximation, each item of Allied's inventory is sold out and restocked, or "turned over," 4.9 times per year.[6]

Allied's turnover of 4.9 times is much lower than the industry average of 9 times. This suggests that Allied is holding excessive stocks of inventory; excess stocks are, of course, unproductive and represent an investment with a low or zero rate of return. Allied's low inventory turnover ratio makes us question the current ratio. With such a low turnover, we must wonder whether the firm is holding damaged or obsolete goods not actually worth their stated value.

Two problems arise in calculating and analyzing the inventory turnover ratio. First, sales are stated at market prices, so if inventories are carried at cost, as they generally are, the calculated turnover overstates the true turnover ratio. Therefore, it would be more appropriate to use cost of goods sold in place of sales in the numerator of the formula. However, established compilers of financial ratio statistics, such as Dun & Bradstreet, use the ratio of sales to inventories carried at cost. To develop a figure that can be compared with those published

---

[6]"Turnover" is a term that originated many years ago with the old Yankee peddler, who would load up his wagon with goods, then go off on his route to peddle his wares. The merchandise was his "working capital," because it was what he actually sold, or "turned over," to produce his profits, whereas his "turnover" was the number of trips he took each year. Annual sales divided by inventory equaled turnover, or trips per year. If he made 10 trips per year, stocked 100 pans, and made a gross profit of $5 per pan, his annual gross profit would be $(100)(\$5)(10) = \$5,000$. If he went faster and made 20 trips per year, his gross profit would double, other things held constant.

by Dun & Bradstreet and similar organizations, it is necessary to measure inventory turnover with sales in the numerator, as we do here.

The second problem lies in the fact that sales occur over the entire year, whereas the inventory figure is for one point in time. For this reason, it is better to use an average inventory measure.[7] If the firm's business is highly seasonal, or if there has been a strong upward or downward sales trend during the year, it is essential to make some such adjustment. To maintain comparability with industry averages, however, we did not use the average inventory figure.

days sales outstanding (DSO)

The ratio calculated by dividing accounts receivable by average sales per day; indicates the average length of time the firm must wait after making a sale before receiving payment.

Days Sales Outstanding. **Days sales outstanding (DSO)**, also called the "average collection period" (ACP), is used to appraise accounts receivable, and it is calculated by dividing average daily sales into accounts receivable to find the number of days' sales that are tied up in receivables. Thus, the DSO represents the average length of time that the firm must wait after making a sale before receiving cash, which is the average collection period. Allied has 45 days' sales outstanding, well above the 36-day industry average.[8]

$$\text{DSO} = \frac{\text{Days}}{\text{sales}} = \frac{\text{Receivables}}{\text{Average sales per day}} = \frac{\text{Receivables}}{\text{Annual sales/360}}$$

$$= \frac{\$375}{\$3,000/360} = \frac{\$375}{\$8.333} = 45 \text{ days}.$$

$$\text{Industry average} = 36 \text{ days}.$$

The DSO can also be evaluated by comparison with the terms on which the firm sells its goods. For example, Allied's sales terms call for payment within 30 days, so the fact that 45 days' sales, not 30 days', are outstanding indicates that customers, on the average, are not paying their bills on time. If the trend in DSO over the past few years has been rising, but the credit policy has not been changed, this would be even stronger evidence that steps should be taken to expedite the collection of accounts receivable.

fixed assets turnover ratio

The ratio of sales to net fixed assets.

Fixed Assets Turnover. The **fixed assets turnover ratio** measures how effectively the firm uses its plant and equipment. It is the ratio of sales to net fixed assets:

---

[7]Preferably, the average inventory value should be calculated by summing the monthly figures during the year and dividing by 12. If monthly data are not available, one can add the beginning and ending figures and divide by 2; this will adjust for growth but not for seasonal effects.

[8]Because information on credit sales is generally unavailable, total sales must be used. Since all firms do not have the same percentage of credit sales, there is a chance that the days sales outstanding will be somewhat in error. Also, note that by convention the financial community generally uses 360 rather than 365 as the number of days in the year for purposes such as this. Finally, it would be better to use *average* receivables, either an average of the monthly figures or (beginning receivables + ending receivables)/2 = ($315 + $375)/2 = $345 in the formula. Had the annual average receivables been used, Allied's DSO would have been $345.00/$8.333 = 41 days. The 41-day figure is the more accurate one, but because the industry average was based on year-end receivables, we used 45 days for our comparison. The DSO is discussed further in Chapter 11.

$$\text{Fixed assets turnover ratio} = \frac{\text{Sales}}{\text{Net fixed assets}}$$

$$= \frac{\$3,000}{\$1,000} = 3.0 \text{ times.}$$

$$\text{Industry average} = 3.0 \text{ times.}$$

Allied's ratio of 3.0 times is equal to the industry average, indicating that the firm is using its fixed assets about as intensively as are the other firms in the industry. Allied seems to have neither too much nor too few fixed assets in relation to other firms.

A major potential problem can exist when the fixed assets turnover ratio is used to compare different firms. Recall from accounting that all assets except cash and accounts receivable reflect the historical costs of the assets. Inflation has caused the value of many assets that were purchased in the past to be seriously understated. Therefore, if we were comparing an old firm which had acquired many of its fixed assets years ago at low prices with a new company which had acquired its fixed assets only recently, we probably would find that the old firm had a higher fixed assets turnover. However, this would be more reflective of the inability of accountants to deal with inflation than of any inefficiency on the part of the new firm. The accounting profession is trying to devise ways of making financial statements reflect current values rather than historical values. If balance sheets were actually stated on a current value basis, this would eliminate the problem of comparisons, but at the moment the problem still exists. Since financial analysts typically do not have the data necessary to make adjustments, they must simply recognize that a problem exists and deal with it judgmentally. In Allied's case, the issue is not a serious one because all firms in the industry have been expanding at about the same rate; thus, the balance sheets of the comparison firms are indeed comparable.[9]

total assets turnover ratio

The ratio calculated by dividing sales by total assets.

Total Assets Turnover.   The final asset management ratio, the **total assets turnover ratio**, measures the turnover of all of the firm's assets; it is calculated by dividing sales by total assets:

$$\text{Total assets turnover ratio} = \frac{\text{Sales}}{\text{Total assets}}$$

$$= \frac{\$3,000}{\$2,000} = 1.5 \text{ times.}$$

$$\text{Industry average} = 1.8 \text{ times.}$$

Allied's ratio is somewhat below the industry average, indicating that the company is not generating a sufficient volume of business given its total asset in-

[9]See FASB #33, *Financial Reporting and Changing Prices* (September 1979), for a discussion of the effects of inflation on financial statements and what the accounting profession is trying to do to provide better and more useful balance sheets and income statements.

vestment. Sales should be increased, some assets should be disposed of, or a combination of these steps should be taken.

Debt Management Ratios

financial leverage

The use of debt financing.

The extent to which a firm uses debt financing, or **financial leverage**, has three important implications: (1) By raising funds through debt, stockholders can maintain control of a firm with a limited investment. (2) Creditors look to the equity, or owner-supplied funds, to provide a margin of safety; if the stockholders have provided only a small proportion of the total financing, the risks of the enterprise are borne mainly by its creditors. (3) If the firm earns more on investments financed with borrowed funds than it pays in interest, the return on the owners' capital is magnified, or "leveraged."

To understand better how the use of debt, or financial leverage, affects risk and return, consider Table 2-5. Here we are analyzing two companies that are identical except for the way they are financed. Firm U (for "unleveraged") has no debt, whereas Firm L (for "leveraged") is financed half with equity and half with debt that bears an interest rate of 15 percent. Both companies have $100 of assets and $100 of sales. Their expected ratio of operating income (also called earnings before interest and taxes, or EBIT) to assets, or the *basic earning power (BEP) ratio*, is EBIT/Total assets = $30/$100 = 0.30 = 30%. Thus, both firms expect to earn 30 percent, before taxes, on their assets. Of course, things could turn out badly, in which case the basic earning power ratio would be lower; in the table, we show the earning power ratio declining from 30 percent to 2.5 percent under bad conditions.

Even though both companies' assets have the same expected earning power, under normal conditions Firm L should provide its stockholders with a return on equity of 27 percent versus only 18 percent for Firm U. This difference is caused by Firm L's use of debt. Financial leverage raises the expected rate of return to stockholders for two reasons: (1) Since interest is deductible, the use of debt financing lowers the tax bill and leaves more of the firm's operating income available to its investors. (2) If the expected rate of return on assets (EBIT/Total assets) exceeds the interest rate on debt, as it generally does, then a company can use debt to finance assets, pay the interest on the debt, and have something left over as a "bonus" for its stockholders. For our hypothetical firms, these two effects have combined to push Firm L's expected rate of return on equity up far above that of Firm U. Thus, debt can be used to "leverage up" the rate of return on equity.

However, financial leverage can cut both ways. As we show in Column 2 of the income statements, if sales are lower and costs are higher than were expected, the return on assets will be lower than was expected. Under these conditions, the leveraged firm's return on equity falls especially sharply, and losses occur. For example, under the "bad conditions" in Table 2-5, the unleveraged firm still shows a profit, but the firm which uses debt shows a loss, and a negative return on equity. This occurs because Firm L needs cash to service its debt, while Firm U does not. Firm U, because of its strong balance sheet, could ride out the recession and be ready for the next boom. Firm L, on the other hand, must pay interest of $7.50 regardless of its level of sales. Consequently, when day-to-day operations do not generate operating income sufficient to provide

Table 2-5 ▪ Effects of Financial Leverage on Stockholders' Returns

Firm U (Unleveraged)

Current assets	$ 50	Debt	$ 0
Fixed assets	50	Common equity	100
Total assets	$100	Total liabilities and equity	$100

	Expected Conditions (1)	Bad Conditions (2)
Sales	$100.00	$82.50
Operating costs	70.00	80.00
Operating income (EBIT)	$ 30.00	$ 2.50
Interest	0.00	0.00
Earnings before taxes (EBT)	$ 30.00	$ 2.50
Taxes (40%)	12.00	1.00
Net income (NI)	$ 18.00	$ 1.50
ROE_U = NI/Common equity = NI/$100 =	18.00%	1.50%

Firm L (Leveraged)

Current assets	$ 50	Debt (interest = 15%)	$ 50
Fixed assets	50	Common equity	50
Total assets	$100	Total liabilities and equity	$100

	Expected Conditions (1)	Bad Conditions (2)
Sales	$100.00	$82.50
Operating costs	70.00	80.00
Operating income (EBIT)	$ 30.00	$ 2.50
Interest	7.50	7.50
Earnings before taxes (EBT)	$ 22.50	($ 5.00)
Taxes (40%)	9.00	(2.00)
Net income (NI)	$ 13.50	($ 3.00)
ROE_L = NI/Common equity = NI/$50 =	27.00%	(6.00%)

cash to meet the interest payments, cash would be depleted and the firm probably would need to raise additional funds. This situation is evident for Firm L when bad economic conditions exist, because only $2.50 in operating income is generated but the interest payment for debt is three times this amount. Because it would be running a loss, Firm L would have a hard time selling stock to raise capital, and the losses would cause lenders to raise the interest rate, increasing L's problems still further. As a final result, Firm L just might not survive to enjoy the next boom.

We see, then, that firms with relatively high debt ratios have higher expected returns when the economy is normal, but they are exposed to risk of loss when the economy is in a recession. Thus, firms with low debt ratios are less risky, but they also forgo the opportunity to leverage up their return on equity. The prospects of high returns are desirable, but investors are averse to risk. Therefore, decisions about the use of debt require firms to balance higher expected returns against increased risk. Determining the optimal amount of debt for a given firm is a complicated process, and we defer a discussion of this topic until Chapter 17. For now we will simply look at two procedures analysts use to examine the firm's debt in a financial statement analysis: (1) They check balance sheet ratios to determine the extent to which borrowed funds have been used to finance assets, and (2) they review income statement ratios to determine the number of times fixed charges are covered by operating profits. These two sets of ratios are complementary, so analysts use both types.

debt ratio

The ratio of total debt to total assets.

Total Debt to Total Assets. The ratio of total debt to total assets, generally called the **debt ratio**, measures the percentage of funds provided by creditors:

$$\text{Debt ratio} = \frac{\text{Total debt}}{\text{Total assets}}$$

$$= \frac{\$310 + \$754}{\$2,000} = \frac{\$1,064}{\$2,000} = 53.2\%.$$

$$\text{Industry average} = 40.0\%.$$

Total debt includes both current liabilities and long-term debt. Creditors prefer low debt ratios, because the lower the ratio, the greater the cushion against creditors' losses in the event of liquidation. The owners, on the other hand, can benefit from leverage because it magnifies earnings.

Allied's debt ratio is 53.2 percent; this means that its creditors have supplied more than half the firm's total financing. Since the average debt ratio for this industry — and for manufacturers generally — is about 40 percent, Allied would find it difficult to borrow additional funds without first raising more equity capital. Creditors would be reluctant to lend the firm more money, and management would probably be subjecting the firm to the risk of bankruptcy if it sought to increase the debt ratio any further by borrowing additional funds.[10]

times-interest-earned (TIE) ratio

The ratio of earnings before interest and taxes (EBIT) to interest charges; measures the ability of the firm to meet its annual interest payments.

Times Interest Earned. The **times-interest-earned (TIE) ratio** is determined by dividing earnings before interest and taxes (EBIT in Table 2-1) by the interest charges:

---

[10]The ratio of debt to equity is also used in financial analysis. The debt to assets (D/A) and debt to equity (D/E) ratios are simply transformations of each other:

$$D/E = \frac{D/A}{1 - D/A}, \text{ and } D/A = \frac{D/E}{1 + D/E}.$$

$$\text{Times-interest-earned (TIE) ratio} = \frac{\text{EBIT}}{\text{Interest charges}}$$

$$= \frac{\$283.8}{\$88} = 3.2 \text{ times.}$$

$$\text{Industry average} = 6.0 \text{ times.}$$

The TIE ratio measures the extent to which operating income can decline before the firm is unable to meet its annual interest costs. Failure to meet this obligation can bring legal action by the firm's creditors, possibly resulting in bankruptcy. Note that earnings before interest and taxes, rather than net income, is used in the numerator. Because interest is paid with pre-tax dollars, the firm's ability to pay current interest is not affected by taxes.

Allied's interest is covered 3.2 times. Since the industry average is 6 times, Allied is covering its interest charges by a relatively low margin of safety. Thus, the TIE ratio reinforces our conclusion based on the debt ratio that Allied would face difficulties if it attempted to borrow additional funds.

fixed charge coverage ratio

This ratio expands upon the TIE ratio to include the firm's annual long-term lease and sinking fund obligations.

Fixed Charge Coverage.   The **fixed charge coverage ratio** is similar to the times-interest-earned ratio, but it is more inclusive because it recognizes that many firms lease assets and also must make sinking fund payments.[11] Leasing has become widespread in certain industries in recent years, making this ratio preferable to the times-interest-earned ratio for many purposes. Allied's annual long-term lease payments are $28 million, and it must make an annual $20 million sinking fund payment to help retire its debt. Because sinking fund payments must be paid with after-tax dollars, whereas interest and lease payments are paid with pre-tax dollars, the sinking fund payment must be divided by (1 − Tax rate) to find the before-tax income required to pay taxes and still have enough left to make the sinking fund payment.[12]

Fixed charges include interest, annual long-term lease obligations, and sinking fund payments, and the fixed charge coverage ratio is defined as follows:

$$\text{Fixed charge coverage ratio} = \frac{\text{EBIT} + \text{Lease payments}}{\text{Interest charges} + \text{Lease payments} + \dfrac{\text{Sinking fund payments}}{(1 - \text{Tax rate})}}$$

$$= \frac{\$283.8 + \$28}{\$88 + \$28 + \dfrac{\$20}{0.6}} = 2.1 \text{ times.}$$

$$\text{Industry average} = 5.5 \text{ times.}$$

---

[11]Generally, a long-term lease is defined as one that extends for more than 1 year. Thus, rent incurred under a 6-month lease would not be included in the fixed charge coverage ratio, but rental payments under a 1-year or longer lease would be defined as a fixed charge and would be included. A sinking fund is a required annual payment designed to reduce the balance of a bond or preferred stock issue. Sinking funds will be discussed in Chapter 20.

[12]Note that $20/0.6 = $33.33. Therefore, if the company had pre-tax income of $33.33, it could pay taxes at a 40 percent rate and have exactly $20 left with which to make the sinking fund payment. Thus, a $20 sinking fund requirement requires $20/0.6 = $33.33 of pre-tax income. Dividing by (1 − T) is called "grossing up" an after-tax value to find the corresponding pre-tax value.

Allied's fixed charges are covered only 2.1 times, as opposed to an industry average of 5.5 times. Again, this indicates that the firm is weaker than average, and this points out the difficulties Allied would probably encounter if it attempted to increase its debt.

Profitability Ratios

profitability ratios
A group of ratios showing the combined effects of liquidity, asset management, and debt management on operating results.

Profitability is the net result of a number of policies and decisions. The ratios examined thus far provide some information about the way the firm is operating, but the **profitability ratios** show the combined effects of liquidity, asset management, and debt management on operating results.

Profit Margin on Sales.   The **profit margin on sales,** calculated by dividing net income by sales, gives the profit per dollar of sales:

profit margin on sales
This ratio measures income per dollar of sales; it is calculated by dividing net income by sales.

$$\text{Profit margin on sales} = \frac{\text{NI}}{\text{Sales}}$$

$$= \frac{\$113.5}{\$3,000} = 3.8\%.$$
$$\text{Industry average} = 5.0\%.$$

Allied's profit margin is below the industry average of 5 percent, indicating that its sales are too low, its costs are too high, or both.

Basic Earning Power (BEP).   The **basic earning power (BEP) ratio,** which we discussed earlier, is calculated by dividing earnings before interest and taxes (EBIT) by total assets:

basic earning power (BEP) ratio
This ratio indicates the ability of the firm's assets to generate operating income; calculated by dividing EBIT by total assets.

$$\text{Basic earning power ratio} = \text{BEP} = \frac{\text{EBIT}}{\text{Total assets}}$$

$$= \frac{\$283.8}{\$2,000} = 14.2\%.$$
$$\text{Industry average} = 17.2\%.$$

This ratio shows the raw earning power of the firm's assets, before the influence of taxes and leverage, and it is useful for comparing firms with different tax situations and different degrees of financial leverage. Because of its low turnover ratios and low profit margin on sales, Allied is not getting as high a return on its assets as is the average food processing company.[13]

---

[13]Notice that EBIT is earned throughout the year, whereas the total assets figure is an end of the year number. Therefore, it would be conceptually better to calculate this ratio as EBIT/Average assets = EBIT/[(Beginning assets + Ending assets)/2]. We have not made this adjustment because the published ratios used for comparative purposes do not include it, but when we construct our own comparative ratios, we do make the adjustment. Incidentally, the same adjustment would also be appropriate for the next two ratios, ROA and ROE.

Return on Total Assets.   The ratio of net income to total assets measures the **return on total assets (ROA)** after interest and taxes:

return on total assets (ROA)
The ratio of net income to total assets.

$$\begin{array}{c} \text{Return on} \\ \text{total assets} \\ (\text{ROA}) \end{array} = \dfrac{\text{Net income available to}}{\text{common stockholders}} \Big/ \text{Total assets}$$

$$= \frac{\$113.5}{\$2,000} = 5.7\%.$$
Industry average $= 9.0\%$.

Allied's 5.7 percent return is well below the 9 percent average for the industry. This low return results from the company's low basic earning power plus its above-average use of debt, both of which cause its net income to be relatively low.

return on common equity (ROE)
The ratio of net income to common equity; measures the rate of return on common stockholders' investment.

Return on Common Equity.   The ratio of net income to common equity measures the **return on common equity (ROE),** or the *rate of return on stockholders' investment*:

$$\begin{array}{c} \text{Return on} \\ \text{common equity} \\ (\text{ROE}) \end{array} = \dfrac{\text{Net income available to}}{\text{common stockholders}} \Big/ \text{Common equity}$$

$$= \frac{\$113.5}{\$896} = 12.7\%.$$
Industry average $= 15.0\%$.

Allied's 12.7 percent return is below the 15 percent industry average, but it is not as far below as the return on total assets. This somewhat better result is due to the company's greater use of debt, a point that is analyzed in detail later in the chapter.

Market Value Ratios

market value ratios
A set of ratios that relate the firm's stock price to its earnings and book value per share.

A final group of ratios, the **market value ratios,** relates the firm's stock price to its earnings and book value per share. These ratios give management an indication of what investors think of the company's past performance and future prospects. If the firm's liquidity, asset management, debt management, and profitability ratios are all good, then its market value ratios will be high, and its stock price will probably be as high as can be expected.

price/earnings (P/E) ratio
The ratio of the price per share to earnings per share; shows the dollar amount investors will pay for $1 of current earnings.

Price/Earnings Ratio.   The **price/earnings (P/E) ratio** shows how much investors are willing to pay per dollar of reported profits. Allied's stock sells for $23, so with an EPS of $2.27 its P/E ratio is 10.1:

$$\text{Price/earnings (P/E) ratio} = \frac{\text{Price per share}}{\text{Earnings per share}}$$

$$= \frac{\$23.00}{\$2.27} = 10.1 \text{ times.}$$

$$\text{Industry average} = 12.5 \text{ times.}$$

As we will see in Chapter 6, P/E ratios are higher for firms with high growth prospects, other things held constant, but they are lower for riskier firms. Since Allied's P/E ratio is below those of other food processors, this suggests that the company is regarded as being somewhat riskier than most, as having poorer growth prospects, or both.

Market/Book Ratio. The ratio of a stock's market price to its book value gives another indication of how investors regard the company. Companies with relatively high rates of return on equity generally sell at higher multiples of book value than those with low returns. First, we find Allied's book value per share:

$$\text{Book value per share} = \frac{\text{Common equity}}{\text{Shares outstanding}}$$

$$= \frac{\$896}{50} = \$17.92.$$

market/book (M/B) ratio
The ratio of a stock's market price to its book value.

Now we divide the market price per share by the book value to get a **market/book (M/B) ratio** of 1.3 times:

$$\text{Market/book ratio} = \frac{\text{Market price per share}}{\text{Book value per share}}$$

$$= \frac{\$23.00}{\$17.92} = 1.3 \text{ times.}$$

$$\text{Industry average} = 1.7 \text{ times.}$$

Investors are willing to pay less for Allied's book value than for that of an average food processing company.

The typical railroad, which has a very low rate of return on assets, has a market/book value ratio of less than 0.5. On the other hand, very successful firms such as Microsoft (which makes the operating system for virtually all PCs) achieve high rates of return on their assets, and their market values are well in excess of their book values. In 1991, Microsoft's book value per share was $7.50 versus a market price of $75, so its market/book ratio was $75/$7.50 = 10 times.

Figure 2-3   ▪   **Rate of Return on Common Equity, 1988–1992**

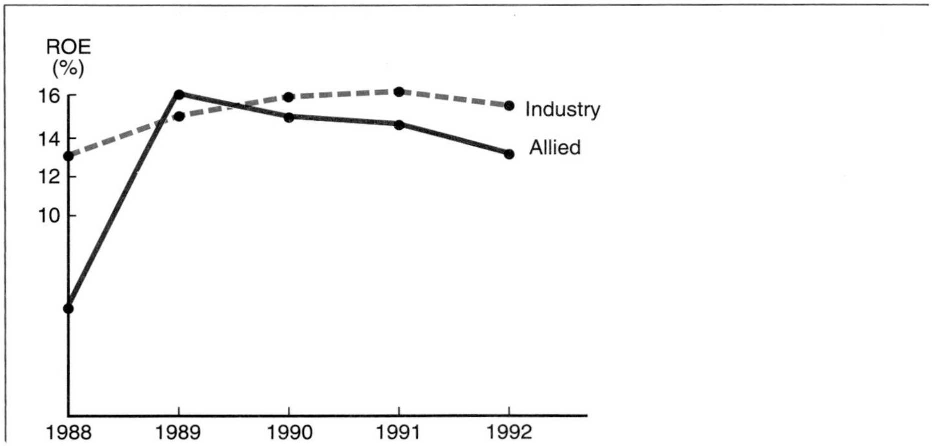

Trend Analysis

trend analysis

An analysis of a firm's financial ratios over time; used to determine the improvement or deterioration in its financial situation.

It is important to analyze trends in ratios as well as their absolute levels, for trends give clues as to whether the financial situation is likely to improve or to deteriorate. To do a **trend analysis**, one simply graphs a ratio against years, as shown in Figure 2-3. This graph shows that Allied's rate of return on common equity has been declining since 1989, even though the industry average has been relatively stable. Other ratios could be analyzed similarly.

Summary of Ratio Analysis: The Du Pont Chart

Du Pont chart

A chart designed to show the relationships among return on investment, asset turnover, the profit margin, and leverage.

Table 2-6 summarizes Allied's ratios, and Figure 2-4, which is called a modified **Du Pont chart** because that company's managers developed the general approach, shows the relationships between return on investment, asset turnover, the profit margin, and leverage. The left-hand side of the chart develops the *profit margin on sales*. The various expense items are listed and then summed to obtain Allied's total costs, which are subtracted from sales to obtain the company's net income. When we divide net income by sales, we find that 3.8 percent of each sales dollar is left over for stockholders. If the profit margin is low or trending down, one can examine the individual expense items to identify and then correct problems.

Du Pont equation

A formula that gives the rate of return on assets by multiplying the profit margin by the total assets turnover.

The right-hand side of Figure 2-4 lists the various categories of assets, totals them, and then divides sales by total assets to find the number of times Allied "turns its assets over" each year. The company's total assets turnover ratio is 1.5 times.

The profit margin times the total assets turnover is called the **Du Pont equation**, and it gives the rate of return on assets (ROA):

Table 2-6 ▪ Allied Food Products: Summary of Financial Ratios (Millions of Dollars)

Ratio	Formula for Calculation	Calculation	Ratio	Industry Average	Comment
Liquidity					
Current	$\dfrac{\text{Current assets}}{\text{Current liabilities}}$	$\dfrac{\$1{,}000}{\$310}$	= 3.2 ×	4.2 ×	Poor
Quick, or acid, test	$\dfrac{\text{Current assets} - \text{Inventories}}{\text{Current liabilities}}$	$\dfrac{\$385}{\$310}$	= 1.2 ×	2.1 ×	Poor
Asset Management					
Inventory turnover	$\dfrac{\text{Sales}}{\text{Inventories}}$	$\dfrac{\$3{,}000}{\$615}$	= 4.9 ×	9.0 ×	Poor
Days sales outstanding (DSO)	$\dfrac{\text{Receivables}}{\text{Annual sales}/360}$	$\dfrac{\$375}{\$8.333}$	= 45 days	36 days	Poor
Fixed assets turnover	$\dfrac{\text{Sales}}{\text{Net fixed assets}}$	$\dfrac{\$3{,}000}{\$1{,}000}$	= 3.0 ×	3.0 ×	OK
Total assets turnover	$\dfrac{\text{Sales}}{\text{Total assets}}$	$\dfrac{\$3{,}000}{\$2{,}000}$	= 1.5 ×	1.8 ×	Somewhat low
Debt Management					
Total debt to total assets	$\dfrac{\text{Total debt}}{\text{Total assets}}$	$\dfrac{\$1{,}064}{\$2{,}000}$	= 53.2%	40.0%	High (risky)
Times-interest-earned (TIE)	$\dfrac{\text{Earnings before interest and taxes (EBIT)}}{\text{Interest charges}}$	$\dfrac{\$283.8}{\$88}$	= 3.2 ×	6.0 ×	Low (risky)
Fixed charge coverage	$\dfrac{\text{Earnings before interest and taxes} + \text{Lease payments}}{\text{Interest charges} + \text{Lease payments} + \dfrac{\text{SF payments}}{(1 - T)}}$	$\dfrac{\$311.8}{\$149.3}$	= 2.1 ×	5.5 ×	Low (risky)
Profitability					
Profit margin on sales	$\dfrac{\text{Net income available to common stockholders}}{\text{Sales}}$	$\dfrac{\$113.5}{\$3{,}000}$	= 3.8%	5.0%	Poor
Basic earning power	$\dfrac{\text{Earnings before interest and taxes (EBIT)}}{\text{Total assets}}$	$\dfrac{\$283.8}{\$2{,}000}$	= 14.2%	17.2%	Poor
Return on total assets (ROA)	$\dfrac{\text{Net income available to common stockholders}}{\text{Total assets}}$	$\dfrac{\$113.5}{\$2{,}000}$	= 5.7%	9.0%	Poor
Return on common equity (ROE)	$\dfrac{\text{Net income available to common stockholders}}{\text{Common equity}}$	$\dfrac{\$113.5}{\$896}$	= 12.7%	15.0%	Poor
Market Value					
Price/earnings (P/E)	$\dfrac{\text{Price per share}}{\text{Earnings per share}}$	$\dfrac{\$23.00}{\$2.27}$	= 10.1 ×	12.5 ×	Low
Market/book	$\dfrac{\text{Market price per share}}{\text{Book value per share}}$	$\dfrac{\$23.00}{\$17.92}$	= 1.3 ×	1.7 ×	Low

Figure 2-4 ▪ Modified Du Pont Chart Applied to Allied Food Products (Millions of Dollars)

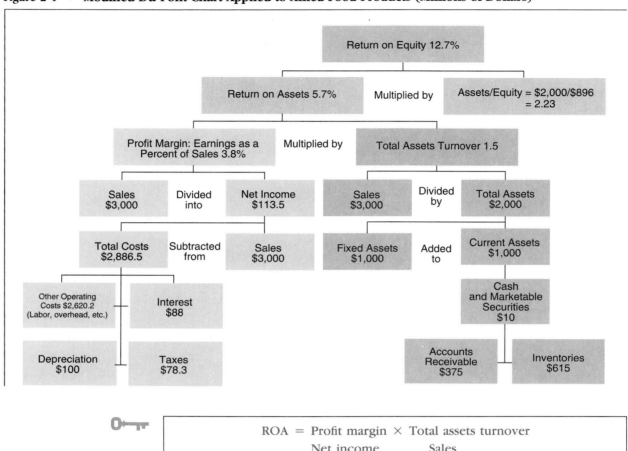

$$
\begin{aligned}
\text{ROA} &= \text{Profit margin} \times \text{Total assets turnover} \\
&= \frac{\text{Net income}}{\text{Sales}} \times \frac{\text{Sales}}{\text{Total assets}}
\end{aligned}
\qquad (2\text{-}1)
$$

$$= 3.8\% \times 1.5 = 5.7\%.$$

Allied made 3.8 percent, or 3.8 cents, on each dollar of sales, and assets were "turned over" 1.5 times during the year, so the company earned a return of 5.7 percent on its assets.

If the company were financed only with common equity, the rate of return on assets (ROA) and the return on equity (ROE) would be the same because the total assets would equal the amount of common equity. But, only 44.8 percent of the capital for Allied Foods is common equity, so the ROA and the ROE are not equal. Instead, because the ROA is defined as the net income *available to common shareholders* (not the amount available to pay interest and preferred dividends) divided by total assets, the ROA of 5.7 percent earned by Allied all goes to the common stockholders. The common equity represents less than 50 percent of Allied's capital, so the return to the common stockholders (ROE) must be greater than twice the ROA of 5.7 percent. Specifically, the rate of return on assets (ROA) must be multiplied by the *equity multiplier*, which is the ratio of assets to common equity, to obtain the rate of return on equity (ROE):[14]

$$\boxed{\begin{aligned} \text{ROE} &= \text{ROA} \times \text{Equity multiplier} \\ &= \frac{\text{Net income}}{\text{Total assets}} \times \frac{\text{Total assets}}{\text{Common equity}} \end{aligned}} \qquad (2\text{-}2)$$

$$\begin{aligned} &= \quad 5.7\% \quad \times \quad \$2{,}000/\$896 \\ &= \quad 5.7\% \quad \times \quad 2.23 \\ &= \quad 12.7\%. \end{aligned}$$

We can combine Equations 2-1 and 2-2 to form the extended Du Pont equation:

$$\boxed{\begin{aligned} \text{ROE} &= (\text{Profit margin})(\text{Total assets turnover})(\text{Equity multiplier}) \\ &= \frac{\text{Net income}}{\text{Sales}} \times \frac{\text{Sales}}{\text{Total assets}} \times \frac{\text{Total assets}}{\text{Common equity}} \end{aligned}} \qquad (2\text{-}3)$$

Thus, for Allied, we have

$$\begin{aligned} \text{ROE} &= (3.8\%)(1.5)(2.23) \\ &= 12.7\%. \end{aligned}$$

The 12.7 percent rate of return could, of course, be calculated directly: Net income/Common equity = $113.5/$896 = 12.7%. However, the Du Pont equation shows how the profit margin, the total assets turnover ratio, and the use of debt interact to determine the return on equity.[15]

Allied's management can use the Du Pont system to analyze ways of improving the firm's performance. Focusing on the left, or "profit margin," side of its modified Du Pont chart, Allied's marketing people can study the effects of raising sales prices (or lowering them to increase volume), of moving into new

---

[14]The equity multiplier can also be written as $\dfrac{1}{1 - \text{D/A}}$, where D/A is the debt ratio. Note that this equation can only be used if the firm has no preferred stock. Because Allied has preferred stock, we use the equation for the equity multiplier as given in Equation 2-2.

Note that we could also find the ROE by "grossing up" the ROA, by dividing the ROA by the common equity fraction: ROE = ROA/Equity fraction = 5.7%/0.448 = 12.7%. The two procedures are algebraically equivalent.

[15]Another ratio that is frequently used is the following:

$$\text{Rate of return on investors' capital} = \frac{\text{Net income} + \text{Interest}}{\text{Debt} + \text{Equity}}$$

The numerator shows the dollar returns to investors, the denominator shows the total amount of money investors have put up, and the ratio itself shows the rate of return on all investors' capital. This ratio is especially important in the public utility industries, where regulators are concerned about the companies' using their monopoly positions to earn excessive returns on investors' capital. In fact, regulators try to set utility prices (service rates) at levels that will force the return on investors' capital to equal a company's cost of capital as defined in Chapter 16.

products or markets with higher margins, and so on. The company's cost accountants can study various expense items and, working with engineers, purchasing agents, and other operating personnel, seek ways of holding down costs. On the "turnover" side, Allied's financial analysts, working with both production and marketing people, can investigate ways of minimizing the investment in various types of assets. At the same time, the treasury staff can analyze the effects of alternative financing strategies, seeking to hold down interest expense and the risk of debt while still using leverage to increase the rate of return on equity.

As a result of such an analysis, Al Jackson, Allied's president, recently announced a series of moves designed to cut operating costs by more than 20 percent per year. Jackson also announced that the company intended to concentrate its capital in markets where profit margins are reasonably high, and that if competition increases in certain of its product markets (such as the low-price end of the canned fruit market), Allied will withdraw from those markets. Allied is seeking a high return on equity, and Jackson recognizes that if competition drives profit margins too low in a particular market, it then becomes impossible to earn high returns on the capital invested to serve that market. Therefore, if it is to achieve a high ROE, Allied may have to develop new products and shift capital into new areas. The company's future depends on this type of analysis, and if it succeeds in the future, then the Du Pont system will have helped it achieve that success.

Self-Test Questions

Identify two ratios that are used to analyze a firm's liquidity position, and write out their equations.

Identify four ratios that are used to measure how effectively a firm is managing its assets, and write out their equations.

Identify three ratios that are used to measure the extent to which a firm uses debt financing, and write out their equations.

Identify four ratios that show the combined effects of liquidity, asset management, and debt management on profitability, and write out their equations.

Identify two ratios that relate a firm's stock price to its earnings and book value per share, and write out their equations.

Explain how the modified Du Pont equation and chart combine several ratios to reveal the basic determinants of ROE.

COMPARATIVE RATIOS

comparative ratio analysis

An analysis based on a comparison of a firm's ratios with those of other firms in the same industry.

The preceding analysis of Allied Food Products involved a **comparative ratio analysis** because the ratios calculated for Allied were compared with those of other firms in the same industry. Comparative ratios are available from a number of sources. One useful set is compiled by Dun & Bradstreet (D&B), which provides various ratios calculated for a large number of industries; nine of these ratios are shown for a small sample of industries in Table 2-7. Useful ratios can also be found in the *Annual Statement Studies* published by Robert Morris Associates, which is the national association of bank loan officers. The U.S. Com-

Table 2-7 ■ Dun & Bradstreet Ratios for Selected Industries: Upper Quartile, Median, and Lower Quartile[a]

SIC Codes, Line of Business, and Number of Concerns Reporting	Quick Ratio	Current Ratio	Total Liabilities to Net Worth	Days Sales Outstanding	Net Sales to Inventory	Total Assets to Net Sales	Return on Net Sales	Return on Total Assets	Return on Net Worth
	×	×	%	Days	×	%	%	%	%
2879 Agricultural chemicals (61)	1.7	3.0	47.4	29.8	16.8	37.7	11.3	16.6	31.3
	1.0	1.9	98.1	47.3	8.0	55.6	3.5	4.4	9.0
	0.5	1.4	172.9	61.5	5.0	102.3	(1.0)	(0.8)	(3.0)
3724 Aircraft parts, including engines (97)	1.6	3.9	31.3	41.4	8.2	44.2	7.2	8.6	23.8
	0.9	2.1	95.1	50.0	4.5	66.2	3.8	5.6	12.6
	0.6	1.3	235.3	68.0	3.0	96.1	1.6	2.4	4.9
2051 Bakery products (203)	2.3	3.3	35.7	15.3	58.2	22.4	6.1	16.6	42.9
	1.1	1.5	92.6	23.4	36.1	33.4	2.8	7.6	20.5
	0.6	0.9	207.4	35.8	18.4	46.5	0.7	1.9	5.9
2086 Beverages (144)	3.2	4.7	18.2	17.5	30.8	30.5	6.3	10.7	16.8
	1.3	2.5	47.9	28.1	18.1	43.3	2.9	5.0	7.9
	0.6	1.4	140.5	37.2	11.5	75.4	0.6	1.2	2.3
3312 Blast furnaces and steel mills (302)	1.9	2.8	58.4	31.4	28.0	31.4	8.7	15.4	44.2
	1.1	1.8	122.0	42.7	10.9	43.9	4.4	7.2	17.4
	0.6	1.2	231.4	60.6	6.3	71.9	1.9	2.1	7.1
2731 Book publishing (399)	2.6	5.4	24.1	32.5	8.5	45.0	12.5	13.2	30.0
	1.2	2.6	60.7	49.6	4.9	68.1	4.4	5.3	12.3
	0.7	1.6	150.4	79.9	3.0	105.7	0.8	0.7	1.8

Source: Industry Norms and Key Business Ratios, 1990–91 Edition, Dun & Bradstreet Credit Services.

[a]The median and quartile ratios can be illustrated by an example. The median quick ratio for agricultural chemical manufacturers, as shown in this table, is 1.0. To obtain this figure, the ratios of current assets less inventories to current debt for each of the 61 concerns were arranged in a graduated series, with the largest ratio at the top and the smallest at the bottom. The median ratio of 1.0 is the ratio halfway between the top and the bottom. The ratio of 1.7, representing the upper quartile, is one-quarter of the way down from the top (or halfway between the top and the median). The ratio 0.5, representing the lower quartile, is one-quarter of the way up from the bottom (or halfway between the median and the bottom). SIC codes are "Standard Industrial Classification" codes used by the U.S. government to classify companies.

merce Department's *Quarterly Financial Report*, which is found in most librar-ies, gives a set of ratios for manufacturing firms by industry group and size of firm. Trade associations and individual firms' credit departments also compile industry average financial ratios. Finally, financial statement data for thousands of publicly owned corporations are available on magnetic tapes and diskettes, and since brokerage houses, banks, and other financial institutions have access to these data, security analysts can and do generate comparative ratios tailored to their specific needs.

Each of the data-supplying organizations uses a somewhat different set of ratios designed for its own purposes. For example, D&B deals mainly with small firms, many of which are proprietorships, and it sells its services primarily to banks and other lenders. Therefore, D&B is concerned largely with the credi-tor's viewpoint, and its ratios emphasize current assets and liabilities, not market value ratios. Therefore, when you select a comparative data source, you should be sure that your emphasis is similar to that of the agency whose ratios you plan to use. Additionally, there are often definitional differences in the ratios presented by different sources, so before using a source, be sure to verify the exact definitions of the ratios to insure consistency with your past work.

Self-Test Questions

Differentiate between trend analysis and comparative ratio analysis.

Why is it necessary to conduct both trend and comparative ratio analyses?

USES AND LIMITATIONS OF RATIO ANALYSIS

As noted earlier, ratio analysis is used by three main groups: (1) *managers*, who employ ratios to help analyze, control, and thus improve the firm's operations; (2) *credit analysts*, such as bank loan officers or bond rating analysts, who an-alyze ratios to help ascertain a company's ability to pay its debts; and (3) *secu-rity analysts*, including both stock analysts, who are interested in a company's efficiency and growth prospects, and bond analysts, who are concerned with a company's ability to pay interest on its bonds as well as with the liquidating value of the assets in the event the company went bankrupt. In later chapters we will look more closely at the basic factors which underlie each ratio, and at that point you will get a better idea about how to interpret and use ratios.

We should also note that while ratio analysis can provide useful information concerning a company's operations and financial condition, it does have inher-ent problems and limitations that necessitate care and judgment. Some potential problems are listed below:

1. Many large firms operate a number of different divisions in quite different industries, and in such cases it is difficult to develop a meaningful set of industry averages for comparative purposes. This tends to make ratio anal-ysis more useful for small, narrowly focused firms than for large, multidivi-sional ones.

2. Most firms want to be better than average, so merely attaining average per-formance is not necessarily good. As a target for high-level performance, it is best to focus on the industry leaders' ratios.

3. Inflation has badly distorted firms' balance sheets—recorded values are often substantially different from "true" values. Further, since inflation affects both depreciation charges and inventory costs, profits are also affected. Thus, a ratio analysis for one firm over time, or a comparative analysis of firms of different ages, must be interpreted with judgment.

4. Seasonal factors can also distort a ratio analysis. For example, the inventory turnover ratio for a food processor will be radically different if the balance sheet figure used for inventory is the one just before versus the one just after the close of the canning season. This problem can be minimized by using monthly averages for inventory (and receivables) when calculating ratios such as turnover.

"window dressing" techniques

Techniques employed by firms to make their financial statements look better than they really are.

5. Firms can employ **"window dressing" techniques** to make their financial statements look stronger. To illustrate, a Chicago builder borrowed on a two-year basis on December 28, 1992, held the proceeds of the loan as cash for a few days, and then paid off the loan ahead of time on January 2, 1993. This improved his current and quick ratios, and made his year-end 1992 balance sheet look good. However, the improvement was strictly window dressing; a week later the balance sheet was back at the old level.

6. Different accounting practices can distort comparisons. As noted earlier, inventory valuation and depreciation methods can affect financial statements and thus distort comparisons among firms. Also, if one firm leases a substantial amount of its productive equipment, then its assets may appear low relative to sales, because leased assets often do not appear on the balance sheet. At the same time, the lease liability may not be shown as a debt. Therefore, leasing can artificially improve both the turnover and the debt ratios. However, the accounting profession has taken steps to reduce this problem, as we discuss in Chapter 21.

7. It is difficult to generalize about whether a particular ratio is "good" or "bad." For example, a high current ratio may indicate a strong liquidity position, which is good, or excessive cash, which is bad (because excess cash in the bank is a nonearning asset). Similarly, a high fixed assets turnover ratio may denote either a firm that uses its assets efficiently or one that is undercapitalized and cannot afford to buy enough assets.

8. A firm may have some ratios which look "good" and others which look "bad," making it difficult to tell whether the company is, on balance, strong or weak. However, statistical procedures can be used to analyze the *net effects* of a set of ratios. Many banks and other lending organizations use statistical procedures to analyze firms' financial ratios, and, on the basis of their analyses, classify companies according to their probability of getting into financial trouble.[16]

Ratio analysis is useful, but analysts should be aware of these problems and make adjustments as necessary. Ratio analysis conducted in a mechanical, un-

---

[16]The technique used is discriminant analysis. For a discussion, see Edward I. Altman, "Financial Ratios, Discriminant Analysis, and the Prediction of Corporate Bankruptcy," *Journal of Finance,* September 1968, 589–609, or Eugene F. Brigham and Louis C. Gapenski, *Intermediate Financial Management,* 4th ed., 1993, Chapter 26.

thinking manner is dangerous, but, used intelligently and with good judgment, it can provide useful insights into a firm's operations. Your judgment in interpreting a set of ratios is necessarily weak at this point, but it will improve as you go through the remainder of the book.

 Self-Test Questions

Name three types of users of ratio analysis. What type of ratios does each group emphasize?

List several potential problems with ratio analysis.

SMALL BUSINESS   Financial Analysis in the Small Firm

Financial ratio analysis is especially useful for small businesses, and readily available sources provide comparative data by size of firm. For example, Robert Morris Associates provides comparative ratios for a number of small-firm classes, including the size range of zero to $250,000 in annual sales. Nevertheless, analyzing a small firm's statements presents some unique problems. We examine here some of those problems from the standpoint of a bank loan officer, one of the most frequent users of ratio analysis.

When examining a small-business credit prospect, a banker is essentially making a prediction about the ability of the company to repay its debt. In making this prediction, the banker will be especially concerned about indicators of liquidity and about continuing prospects for profitability. Bankers like to do business with a new customer if it appears that loans can be paid off on a timely basis and that the company will remain in business and therefore be a customer of the bank for some years to come. Thus, both short-run and long-run viability are of interest to the banker. At the same time, the banker's perceptions about the business are important to the owner-manager, because the bank will probably be the firm's primary source of funds.

The first problem the banker is likely to encounter is that, unlike the bank's bigger customers, the small firm may not have audited financial statements. Further, the statements that are available may have been produced on an irregular basis (for example, in some months or quarters but not in others). If the firm is young, it may have historical financial statements for only one year, or perhaps none at all. Also, the financial statements may not have been produced by a reputable accounting firm but by the owner's brother-in-law.

The quality of its financial data may therefore be a problem for a small business that is attempting to establish a banking relationship. This could keep the firm from getting credit even though it is really on solid financial ground. Therefore, it is in the owner's interest to make sure that the firm's financial data are credible, even if it is more expensive to do so. Furthermore, if the banker is uncomfortable with the data, the firm's management should also be uncomfortable: Because many managerial decisions depend on the numbers in the firm's accounting statements, those numbers should be as accurate as possible.

For a given set of financial ratios, a small firm may be riskier than a larger one. Small firms often produce a single product or rely heavily on a single customer, or both. For example, several years ago a company called Yard Man Inc. manufactured and sold lawn equipment. Most of Yard Man's sales were to Sears, so most of its revenues and profits were due to its Sears account. When Sears decided to drop Yard Man as a supplier, the company was left without its most important customer. Yard Man is no longer in business. Because large firms typically have a broad customer base, they are not as exposed to a loss of a large portion of their business.

A similar danger applies to a single-product company. Just as the loss of a key customer can be disastrous for a small business, so can a shift in the tides of consumer interest in a particular fad. For example, Coleco manufactured and sold the extremely popular Cabbage Patch dolls. The phenomenal popularity of the dolls was a great boon for Coleco, but the public is fickle. One can never predict when such a fad will die out, leaving the company with a great deal of capacity to make a product that no one will buy, and with a large amount of overvalued inventory. Exactly that situation hit Coleco, and it was forced into bankruptcy.

The extension of credit to a small company, and especially to a small owner-managed company, often involves yet another risk that is less of a problem for larger firms — namely, dependence on the leadership of a single key individual whose unexpected death could cause the company to fail. Similarly, if the company is family owned and managed, there is typically one key decision maker, even though several other family members may be involved in helping to manage the company. In the case of the family business, the loss of the top person may not wipe out the company, but it often creates the equally serious problem of who will assume the leadership role. The loss of a key family member is often a highly emotional event, and it is not at all unusual for it to be followed by an ugly and prolonged struggle for control of the business. It is in the family's interest, and certainly in the creditors' interests, to see that a plan of management succession is clearly specified before trouble arises. If no good plan can be worked out, perhaps the firm should be forced to carry "key person insurance," payable to the bank and used to retire the loan in the event of the key person's death.

In summary, to determine the creditworthiness of a small firm, the financial analyst must "look beyond the ratios" and analyze the viability of the firm's products, customers, management, and market. Ratio analysis is only the first step in a sound credit analysis.

SUMMARY

The primary purposes of this chapter were (1) to describe the basic financial statements and (2) to discuss techniques used by investors and managers to analyze the statements. The key concepts covered are listed below.

- The four basic statements contained in the annual report are the **balance sheet**, the **income statement**, the **statement of retained earnings**, and the **statement of cash flows.** Investors use the information provided in these statements to form expectations about the future levels of earnings and dividends, and about the firm's riskiness.

- **Operating cash flows** differ from reported **accounting income.** Investors should be more interested in a firm's projected cash flows than in reported earnings, because it is cash, not paper profits, that is paid out as dividends and plowed back into the business to produce growth.

- **Financial statement analysis** generally begins with the calculation of a set of **financial ratios** designed to reveal the relative strengths and weaknesses of a company as compared to other companies in the same industry, and to show whether the firm's position has been improving or deteriorating over time.

- **Liquidity ratios** show the relationship of a firm's current assets to its current liabilities, and thus indicate the firm's ability to meet its maturing debts.

- **Asset management ratios** measure how effectively a firm is managing its assets.

- **Debt management ratios** reveal (1) the extent to which the firm is financed with debt and (2) its likelihood of defaulting on its debt obligations.

- **Profitability ratios** show the combined effects of liquidity, asset management, and debt management policies on operating results.

▪ **Market value ratios** relate the firm's stock price to its earnings and book value per share.

▪ **Trend analysis** is important, because it reveals whether the firm's ratios are improving or deteriorating over time.

▪ The **Du Pont chart** is designed to show how the profit margin on sales, the assets turnover ratio, and the use of debt interact to determine the rate of return on equity.

▪ In analyzing a small firm's financial position, ratio analysis is a useful starting point. However, the analyst must also (1) examine the quality of the financial data, (2) insure that the firm is sufficiently diversified to withstand shifts in customers' buying habits, and (3) insure that the firm has a plan for the succession of its management.

Ratio analysis has limitations, but used with care and judgment, it can be very helpful.

Questions

2-1 What four statements are contained in most annual reports?

2-2 If a "typical" firm reports $20 million of retained earnings on its balance sheet, could its directors declare a $20 million cash dividend without any qualms whatsoever?

2-3 Financial ratio analysis is conducted by four groups of analysts: managers, equity investors, long-term creditors, and short-term creditors. What is the primary emphasis of each of these groups in evaluating ratios?

2-4 Why would the inventory turnover ratio be more important when analyzing a grocery chain than an insurance company?

2-5 Profit margins and turnover ratios vary from one industry to another. What differences would you expect to find between a grocery chain like Safeway and a steel company? Think particularly about the turnover ratios and the profit margin, and think about the Du Pont equation.

2-6 How does inflation distort ratio analysis comparisons, both for one company over time (trend analysis) and when different companies are compared? Are only balance sheet items or both balance sheet and income statement items affected?

2-7 If a firm's ROE is low and management wants to improve it, explain how using more debt might help.

2-8 How might (a) seasonal factors and (b) different growth rates distort a comparative ratio analysis? Give some examples. How might these problems be alleviated?

2-9 Indicate the effects of the transactions listed in the following table on total current assets, current ratio, and net income. Use (+) to indicate an increase, (−) to indicate a decrease, and (0) to indicate either no effect or an indeterminate effect. Be prepared to state any necessary assumptions, and assume an initial current ratio of more than 1.0. (Note: A good accounting background is necessary to answer some of these questions; if yours is not strong, just answer the questions you can handle.)

	Total Current Assets	Current Ratio	Effect on Net Income
a. Cash is acquired through issuance of additional common stock.	_____	_____	_____
b. Merchandise is sold for cash.	_____	_____	_____
c. Federal income tax due for the previous year is paid.	_____	_____	_____
d. A fixed asset is sold for less than book value.	_____	_____	_____
e. A fixed asset is sold for more than book value.	_____	_____	_____
f. Merchandise is sold on credit.	_____	_____	_____
g. Payment is made to trade creditors for previous purchases.	_____	_____	_____
h. A cash dividend is declared and paid.	_____	_____	_____
i. Cash is obtained through short-term bank loans.	_____	_____	_____
j. Short-term notes receivable are sold at a discount.	_____	_____	_____
k. Marketable securities are sold below cost.	_____	_____	_____
l. Advances are made to employees.	_____	_____	_____
m. Current operating expenses are paid.	_____	_____	_____
n. Short-term promissory notes are issued to trade creditors in exchange for past due accounts payable.	_____	_____	_____
o. Ten-year notes are issued to pay off accounts payable.	_____	_____	_____
p. A fully depreciated asset is retired.	_____	_____	_____
q. Accounts receivable are collected.	_____	_____	_____
r. Equipment is purchased with short-term notes.	_____	_____	_____
s. Merchandise is purchased on credit.	_____	_____	_____
t. The estimated taxes payable are increased.	_____	_____	_____

Self-Test Problems   *(Solutions Appear in Appendix B)*

ST-1

Key terms

Define each of the following terms:

a.   Annual report; income statement; balance sheet
b.   Equity, or net worth; paid-in capital; retained earnings
c.   Cash flow cycle
d.   Statement of retained earnings; statement of cash flows
e.   Depreciation; inventory valuation methods
f.   Liquidity ratios: current ratio; quick, or acid test, ratio
g.   Asset management ratios: inventory turnover ratio; days sales outstanding (DSO); fixed assets turnover ratio; total assets turnover ratio
h.   Financial leverage: debt ratio; times-interest-earned (TIE) ratio; fixed charge coverage ratio
i.   Profitability ratios: profit margin on sales; basic earning power (BEP) ratio; return on total assets (ROA); return on common equity (ROE)
j.   Market value ratios: price/earnings (P/E) ratio; market/book (M/B) ratio; dividend payout ratio; book value per share
k.   Trend analysis; comparative ratio analysis
l.   Du Pont chart; Du Pont equation
m.   "Window dressing"; seasonal effects on ratios

Debt ratio

K. Billingsworth & Co. had earnings per share of $4 last year, and it paid a $2 dividend. Total retained earnings increased by $12 million during the year, while book value per share at year-end was $40. Billingsworth has no preferred stock, and no new common stock was issued during the year. If Billingsworth's year-end debt (which equals its total liabilities) was $120 million, what was the company's year-end debt/assets ratio?

ST-3   The following data apply to A.L. Kaiser & Company (millions of dollars):

Ratio analysis

Cash and marketable securities	$100.00
Fixed assets	$283.50
Sales	$1,000.00
Net income	$50.00
Quick ratio	2.0×
Current ratio	3.0×
DSO	40 days
ROE	12%

Kaiser has no preferred stock—only common equity, current liabilities, and long-term debt.

a. Find Kaiser's (1) accounts receivable (A/R), (2) current liabilities, (3) current assets, (4) total assets, (5) ROA, (6) common equity, and (7) long-term debt.

b. In Part a, you should have found Kaiser's accounts receivable (A/R) = $111.1 million. If Kaiser could reduce its DSO from 40 days to 30 days while holding other things constant, how much cash would it generate? If this cash were used to buy back common stock (at book value) and thus reduced the amount of common equity, how would this affect (1) the ROE, (2) the ROA, and (3) the total debt/total assets ratio?

Problems

2-1   Data for Campsey Computer Company and its industry averages follow.

Ratio analysis

a. Calculate the indicated ratios for Campsey.

b. Construct the extended Du Pont equation for both Campsey and the industry.

c. Outline Campsey's strengths and weaknesses as revealed by your analysis.

d. Suppose Campsey had doubled its sales as well as its inventories, accounts receivable, and common equity during 1992. How would that information affect the validity of your ratio analysis? (Hint: Think about averages and the effects of rapid growth on ratios if averages are not used. No calculations are needed.)

Campsey Computer Company: Balance Sheet as of December 31, 1992

Cash	$ 77,500	Accounts payable	$ 129,000
Receivables	336,000	Notes payable	84,000
Inventories	241,500	Other current liabilities	117,000
Total current assets	$ 655,000	Total current liabilities	$ 330,000
Net fixed assets	292,500	Long-term debt	256,500
		Common equity	361,000
Total assets	$ 947,500	Total liabilities and equity	$ 947,500

**Campsey Computer Company: Income Statement
for Year Ended December 31, 1992**

Sales		$1,607,500
Cost of goods sold		
Materials	$717,000	
Labor	453,000	
Heat, light, and power	68,000	
Indirect labor	113,000	
Depreciation	41,500	1,392,500
Gross profit		$ 215,000
Selling expenses		115,000
General and administrative expenses		30,000
Earnings before interest and taxes (EBIT)		$ 70,000
Interest expense		24,500
Earnings before taxes (EBT)		$ 45,500
Federal and state income taxes (40%)		18,200
Net income		$ 27,300

Ratio	Campsey	Industry Average
Current assets/current liabilities	————	2.0 ×
Days sales outstanding	————	35 days
Sales/inventories	————	6.7 ×
Sales/total assets	————	3.0 ×
Net income/sales	————	1.2%
Net income/total assets	————	3.6%
Net income/equity	————	9.0%
Total debt/total assets	————	60.0%

2-2

Balance sheet analysis

Complete the balance sheet and sales information in the table that follows for Isberg Industries using the following financial data:

Debt ratio: 50%
Quick ratio: 0.80 ×
Total assets turnover: 1.5 ×
Days sales outstanding: 36 days
Gross profit margin on sales: (Sales − Cost of goods sold)/Sales = 25%
Inventory turnover ratio: 5 ×

Balance Sheet

Cash	————	Accounts payable	———
Accounts receivable	————	Long-term debt	60,000
Inventories	————	Common stock	———
Fixed assets	————	Retained earnings	97,500
Total assets	$300,000	Total liabilities and equity	———
Sales	————	Cost of goods sold	———

2-3

Du Pont analysis

The Finnerty Furniture Company, a manufacturer and wholesaler of high-quality home furnishings, has been experiencing low profitability in recent years. As a result, the board of directors has replaced the president of the firm with a new president, Elizabeth Brannigan, who has asked you to make an analysis of the firm's financial position using the Du Pont chart. The most recent industry average ratios, and Finnerty's financial statements, are as follows:

Industry Average Ratios

Current ratio	2×	Sales/fixed assets	6×
Debt/total assets	30%	Sales/total assets	3×
Times-interest-earned	7×	Profit margin on sales	3%
Sales/inventory	10×	Return on total assets	9%
Days sales outstanding	24 days	Return on common equity	12.9%

Finnerty Furniture Company: Balance Sheet as of December 31, 1992 (Millions of Dollars)

Cash	$ 45	Accounts payable	$ 45
Marketable securities	33	Notes payable	45
Net receivables	66	Other current liabilities	21
Inventories	159	Total current liabilities	$111
Total current assets	$303	Long-term debt	24
		Total liabilities	$135
Gross fixed assets	225		
Less depreciation	78	Common stock	114
Net fixed assets	$147	Retained earnings	201
		Total stockholders' equity	$315
Total assets	$450	Total liabilities and equity	$450

Finnerty Furniture Company: Income Statement for Year Ended December 31, 1992 (Millions of Dollars)

Net sales	$795.0
Cost of goods sold	660.0
Gross profit	$135.0
Selling expenses	73.5
Depreciation expense	12.0
Earnings before interest and taxes	$ 49.5
Interest expense	4.5
Earnings before taxes (EBT)	45.0
Taxes (40%)	18.0
Net income	$ 27.0

a. Calculate those ratios that you think would be useful in this analysis.
b. Construct an extended Du Pont equation for Finnerty, and compare the company's ratios to the industry average ratios.

c. Do the balance sheet accounts or the income statement figures seem to be primarily responsible for the low profits?

d. Which specific accounts seem to be most out of line in relation to other firms in the industry?

e. If Finnerty had a pronounced seasonal sales pattern, or if it grew rapidly during the year, how might that affect the validity of your ratio analysis? How might you correct for such potential problems?

2-4

Ratio analysis

The Cary Corporation's forecasted 1993 financial statements follow, along with some industry average ratios.

a. Calculate Cary's 1993 forecasted ratios, compare them with the industry average data, and comment briefly on Cary's projected strengths and weaknesses.

b. What do you think would happen to Cary's ratios if the company initiated cost-cutting measures that allowed it to hold lower levels of inventory and substantially decreased the cost of goods sold? No calculations are necessary. Think about which ratios would be affected by changes in these two accounts.

Cary Corporation: Forecasted Balance Sheet as of December 31, 1993

Cash	$ 72,000
Accounts receivable	439,000
Inventories	894,000
Total current assets	$1,405,000
Land and building	238,000
Machinery	132,000
Other fixed assets	61,000
Total assets	$1,836,000
Accounts and notes payable	$ 432,000
Accruals	170,000
Total current liabilities	$ 602,000
Long-term debt	404,290
Common stock	575,000
Retained earnings	254,710
Total liabilities and equity	$1,836,000

Cary Corporation: Forecasted Income Statement for 1993

Sales	$4,290,000
Cost of goods sold	3,580,000
Gross operating profit	$ 710,000
General administrative and selling expenses	236,320
Depreciation	159,000
Miscellaneous	134,000
Earnings before taxes (EBT)	$ 180,680
Taxes (40%)	72,272
Net income	$ 108,408
Number of shares outstanding	23,000

Per-Share Data

EPS	$4.71
Cash dividends	$0.95
P/E ratio	5×
Market price (average)	$23.57

Industry Financial Ratios (1993)[a]

Quick ratio	1.0×
Current ratio	2.7×
Inventory turnover[b]	7.0×
Days sales outstanding	32 days
Fixed assets turnover[b]	13.0×
Total assets turnover[b]	2.6×
Return on assets	9.1%
Return on equity	18.2%
Debt ratio	50.0%
Profit margin on sales	3.5%
P/E ratio	6.0×

[a]Industry average ratios have been constant for the past four years.

[b]Based on year-end balance sheet figures.

EXAM-TYPE PROBLEMS

The problems included in this section are set up in such a way that they could be used as multiple-choice exam problems.

2-5
Ratio calculation

Assume you are given the following relationships for The Zumwalt Corporation:

Sales/total assets	1.5×
Return on assets (ROA)	3%
Return on equity (ROE)	5%

Calculate Zumwalt's profit margin and debt ratio.

2-6
Liquidity ratios

The Hindelang Company has $1,312,500 in current assets and $525,000 in current liabilities. Its initial inventory level is $375,000, and it will raise funds as additional notes payable and use them to increase inventory. How much can Hindelang's short-term debt (notes payable) increase without pushing its current ratio below 2.0? What will be the firm's quick ratio after Hindelang has raised the maximum amount of short-term funds?

2-7
Ratio calculations

The Edelman Company had a quick ratio of 1.4, a current ratio of 3.0, an inventory turnover of 6 times, total current assets of $810,000, and cash and marketable securities of $120,000 in 1992. What were Edelman's annual sales and its DSO for that year?

2-8
Times-interest-earned ratio

Wolken Corporation has $500,000 of debt outstanding, and it pays an interest rate of 10 percent annually. Wolken's annual sales are $2 million; its average tax rate is 20 percent; and its net profit margin on sales is 5 percent. If the company does not maintain a TIE ratio of at least 5 times, its bank will refuse to renew the loan, and bankruptcy will result. What is Wolken's TIE ratio?

2-9

Return on equity

Coastal Packaging's ROE last year was only 3 percent, but its management has developed a new operating plan designed to improve things. The new plan calls for a total debt ratio of 60 percent, which will result in interest charges of $300 per year. Management projects an EBIT of $1,000 on sales of $10,000, and it expects to have a total assets turnover ratio of 2.0. Under these conditions, the average tax rate will be 30 percent. If the changes are made, what return on equity will Coastal earn?

2-10

Return on equity

Central City Construction Company, which is just being formed, needs $1 million of assets, and it expects to have a basic earning power ratio of 20 percent. Central City will own no securities, so all of its income will be operating income. If it chooses to, Central City can finance up to 50 percent of its assets with debt which will have an 8 percent interest rate. Assuming a 40 percent tax rate on all taxable income, what is the *difference* between its expected ROE if Central City finances with 50 percent debt versus its expected ROE if it finances entirely with common stock?

2-11

Conceptual: Return on equity

Which of the following statements is most correct? (Hint: Work Problem 2-10 before answering 2-11, and consider the solution setup for 2-10 as you think about 2-11.)

a. If a firm's expected basic earning power (BEP) is constant for all of its assets and exceeds the interest rate on its debt, then adding assets and financing them with debt will raise the firm's expected rate of return on common equity (ROE).

b. The higher its tax rate, the lower a firm's BEP ratio will be, other things held constant.

c. The higher the interest rate on its debt, the lower a firm's BEP ratio will be, other things held constant.

d. The higher its debt ratio, the lower a firm's BEP ratio will be, other things held constant.

e. Statement a is false, but b, c, and d are all true.

2-12

Return on equity

Earth's Best Company has sales of $200,000, a net income of $15,000, and the following balance sheet:

Cash	$ 10,000	Accounts payable	$ 30,000
Receivables	50,000	Other current liabilities	20,000
Inventories	150,000	Long-term debt	50,000
Net fixed assets	90,000	Common equity	200,000
Total assets	$300,000	Total liabilities and equity	$300,000

a. The company's new owner thinks that inventories are excessive and can be lowered to the point where the current ratio is equal to the industry average, 2.5×, without affecting either sales or net income. If inventories are sold off and not replaced so as to reduce the current ratio to 2.5×, if the funds generated are used to reduce common equity (stock can be repurchased at book value), and if no other changes occur, by how much will the ROE change?

b. Now suppose we wanted to take this problem and modify it for use on an exam, that is, to create a new problem which you have not seen to test your knowledge of this type of problem. How would your answer change if (1) We doubled all the dollar amounts? (2) We stated that the target current ratio was 3.0×? (3) We stated that the target was to achieve an inventory turnover ratio of 2× rather than a current ratio of 2.5×? (Hint: Compare the ROE obtained with an inventory turnover ratio of 2× to the original ROE obtained before any changes are considered.) (4) We said that the company had 10,000 shares of stock outstanding, and we asked how much the change in Part a would increase EPS? (5) What would your answer to (4) be if we changed the original problem to state that the stock was selling for twice book value, so common equity would not be reduced on a dollar-for-dollar basis?

c. Now explain how we could have set the problem up to have you focus on changing accounts receivable, or fixed assets, or using the funds generated to retire debt (we would give you the interest rate on outstanding debt), or how the original problem could have stated that the company needed *more* inventories and it would finance them with new common equity or with new debt.

INTEGRATIVE PROBLEM

2-13

Financial statement analysis

Donna Jamison was recently hired as a financial analyst by Computron Industries, a manufacturer of electronic components. Her first task was to conduct a financial analysis of the firm covering the last two years. To begin, she gathered the following financial statements and other data.

BALANCE SHEETS	1992	1991
Assets		
Cash	$ 52,000	$ 57,600
Accounts receivable	402,000	351,200
Inventories	836,000	715,200
Total current assets	$1,290,000	$1,124,000
Gross fixed assets	$ 527,000	$ 491,000
Less accumulated depreciation	166,200	146,200
Net fixed assets	$ 360,800	$ 344,800
Total assets	$1,650,800	$1,468,800
Liabilities and Equity		
Accounts payable	$ 175,200	$ 145,600
Notes payable	225,000	200,000
Accruals	140,000	136,000
Total current liabilities	$ 540,200	$ 481,600
Long-term debt	$ 424,612	$ 323,432
Common stock (100,000 shares)	$ 460,000	$ 460,000
Retained earnings	225,988	203,768
Total equity	$ 685,988	$ 663,768
Total liabilities and equity	$1,650,800	$1,468,800
INCOME STATEMENTS		
Sales	$3,850,000	$3,432,000
Cost of goods sold	3,250,000	2,864,000
Other expenses	430,300	340,000
Depreciation	20,000	18,900
Total operating costs	$3,700,300	$3,222,900
EBIT	$ 149,700	$ 209,100
Interest expense	76,000	62,500
EBT	$ 73,700	$ 146,600
Taxes (40%)	29,480	58,640
Net income	$ 44,220	$ 87,960
EPS	$0.442	$0.880

STATEMENT OF CASH FLOWS (1992):

Operating Activities:

Net income		$ 44,220

Other additions (Sources of cash):

Depreciation		20,000
Increase in accounts payable		29,600
Increase in accruals		4,000

Subtractions (Uses of cash):

Increase in accounts receivable		(50,800)
Increase in inventories		(120,800)
Net cash flow from operations		($ 73,780)

Long-Term Investing Activities:

Investment in fixed assets		($ 36,000)

Financing Activities:

Increase in notes payable		$ 25,000
Increase in long-term debt		101,180
Payment of cash dividends		(22,000)
Net cash flow from financing		104,180
Net reduction in cash account		($ 5,600)
Cash at beginning of year		57,600
Cash at end of year		$ 52,000

Other Data

December 31 stock price	$ 6.00	$ 8.50
Number of shares	100,000	100,000
Dividends per share	$ 0.22	$ 0.22
Lease payments	$ 40,000	$ 40,000

Industry average data for 1992:

Ratio	Industry Average
Current	2.7×
Quick	1.0×
Inventory turnover	7.0×
Days sales outstanding (DSO)	32.0 days
Fixed assets turnover	10.7×
Total assets turnover	2.6×
Debt ratio	50.0%
TIE	2.5×
Fixed charge coverage	2.1×
Profit margin	3.5%
Basic earning power	19.1%
ROA	9.1%
ROE	18.2%
Price/earnings	14.2×
Market/book	1.4×

Assume that you are Donna Jamison's assistant, and that she has asked you to help her prepare a report which evaluates the company's financial condition. Then answer the following questions.

a. What can you conclude about the company's financial condition from its statement of cash flows?

b. What is the purpose of financial ratio analysis, and what are the five major categories of ratios?

c. What are Computron's current and quick ratios? What do they tell you about the company's liquidity position?

d. What are Computron's inventory turnover, days sales outstanding, fixed assets turnover, and total assets turnover ratios? How does the firm's utilization of assets stack up against that of the industry?

e. What are the firm's debt, times-interest-earned, and fixed charge coverage ratios? How does Computron compare to the industry with respect to financial leverage? What conclusions can you draw from these ratios?

f. Calculate and discuss the firm's profitability ratios — that is, its profit margin, basic earning power (BEP), return on assets (ROA), and return on equity (ROE).

g. Calculate Computron's market value ratios — that is, its price/earnings ratio and its market/book ratio. What do these ratios tell you about investors' opinions of the company?

h. Use the extended Du Pont equation to provide a summary and overview of Computron's financial condition. What are the firm's major strengths and weaknesses?

i. Use the following simplified 1992 balance sheet to show, in general terms, how an improvement in one of the ratios, say the DSO, would affect the stock price. For example, if the company could improve its collection procedures and thereby lower the DSO from 37.6 days to 27.6 days, how would that change "ripple through" the financial statements (shown in thousands below) and influence the stock price?

Accounts receivable	$ 402	Debt	$ 965
Other current assets	888		
Net fixed assets	361	Equity	686
Total asssets	$1,651	Total liabilities and equity	$1,651

j. Although financial statement analysis can provide useful information about a company's operations and its financial condition, this type of analysis does have some potential problems and limitations, and it must be used with care and judgment. What are some problems and limitations?

COMPUTER-RELATED PROBLEM

Work the problem in this section only if you are using the computer problem diskette.

2-14
Ratio analysis

Use the computerized model in the File C2 to solve this problem.

a. Refer back to Problem 2-4. Suppose Cary Corporation is considering installing a new computer system which would provide tighter control of inventories, accounts receivable, and accounts payable. If the new system is installed, the following data are projected (rather than the data given in Problem 2-4) for the indicated balance sheet and income statement accounts:

Accounts receivable	$ 395,000
Inventories	700,000
Other fixed assets	150,000
Accounts and notes payable	275,000
Accruals	120,000
Cost of goods sold	3,450,000
Administrative and selling expenses	248,775
P/E ratio	6 $\times$

How do these changes affect the projected ratios and the comparison with the industry averages? (Note that any changes to the income statement will change the amount of retained earnings; therefore, the model is set up to calculate 1993 retained earnings as 1992 retained earnings plus net income minus dividends paid. The model also adjusts the cash balance so that the balance sheet balances.)

b. If the new computer were even more efficient than Cary's management had estimated and thus caused the cost of goods sold to decrease by $125,000 from the projections in Part a, what effect would that have on the company's financial position?

c. If the new computer were less efficient than Cary's management had estimated and caused the cost of goods sold to increase by $125,000 from the projections in Part a, what effect would that have on the company's financial position?

d. Change, one by one, the other items in Part a to see how each change affects the ratio analysis. Then think about, and write a paragraph describing, how computer models like this one can be used to help make better decisions about the purchase of such things as a new computer system.

Appendix 2A

Statement of Cash Flows

In Chapter 2 we presented Allied Food Products' 1992 statement of cash flows as it would appear in its annual report, and we discussed its interpretation. In this appendix we explain its construction.

Preparing the Statement of Cash Flows

The first step in preparing a statement of cash flows is to identify which balance sheet items provided cash and which used cash during the year. This is done with a sources and uses of funds statement. The change in each balance sheet account is determined, and this change is recorded as either a source or use of funds in accordance with the following rules:

Sources:

1. **Any increase in a liability or equity account.** Borrowing from the bank is an example of a source of funds.

2. **Any decrease in an asset account.** Selling some fixed assets and reducing inventories are other examples of sources of funds.

Table 2A-1   ▪   **Allied Food Products: Changes in Balance Sheet Accounts during 1992 (Millions of Dollars)**

			Change	
	12/31/92	**12/31/91**	**Sources**	**Uses**
Cash and marketable securities	$ 10	$ 80	$ 70	
Accounts receivable	375	315		$ 60
Inventories	615	415		200
Net plant and equipment[a]	1,000	870		130
Accounts payable	60	30	30	
Notes payable	110	60	50	
Accruals	140	130	10	
Long-term bonds	754	580	174	
Preferred stock	40	40		
Common stock	130	130		
Retained earnings	766	710	56	
Totals			$390	$390

[a]This line really represents two accounts: gross fixed assets and accumulated depreciation. Typically, the sources and uses worksheet would show this line as two separate lines. Due to Allied's simplified balance sheet, we show net plant and equipment as one line. As explained in the note to Table 2-4 in the text, 1992 depreciation expense is $100 million; therefore, gross fixed assets increased by $230 million. Alternatively, Δ Net fixed assets = Δ Gross fixed assets − Δ Accumulated depreciation, where Δ means "change in." By definition, Δ Accumulated depreciation = 1992 depreciation expense = $100 million; therefore,

$$\$130 \text{ million} = \Delta GFA - \$100 \text{ million}$$
$$\$230 \text{ million} = \Delta GFA.$$

Uses:

1. **Any decrease in a liability or equity account.** Paying off a loan is an example of a use of funds.

2. **Any increase in an asset account.** Buying fixed assets and building up inventories are other examples of uses of funds.

Thus, sources of funds include bank loans and retained earnings, as well as money generated by selling assets, by collecting receivables, and even by drawing down the cash account. Uses include acquiring fixed assets, building up receivables or inventories, and paying off debts.

Table 2A-1 shows the changes that occurred in Allied's balance sheet accounts during 1992 using the balance sheet information in Table 2-2 presented earlier in the chapter, with each change designated as a source or a use. Sources and uses each total $390 million.[1] Note that the table does not contain any summary accounts such as total current assets. If we included summary accounts in Table 2A-1 and then used these accounts to prepare the statement of cash flows, we would be "double counting."

---

[1]Adjustments would have to be made if fixed assets were sold during the year. Allied had no sales of assets during 1992.

Table 2A-2   ▪   **Allied Food Products: Statement of Cash Flows
for 1992 (Millions of Dollars)**

Operating Activities:	
Net income	$117.5
Other additions (sources of cash)	
Depreciation[a]	100.0
Increase in accounts payable	30.0
Increase in accruals	10.0
Subtractions (uses of cash)	
Increase in accounts receivable	(60.0)
Increase in inventories	(200.0)
Net cash flow from operations	($ 2.5)
Long-Term Investing Activities:	
Acquisition of fixed assets[b]	($230.0)
Financing Activities:	
Increase in notes payable	$ 50.0
Increase in bonds	174.0
Payment of common and preferred dividends	(61.5)
Net cash flow from financing	$162.5
Net reduction in cash and marketable securities	($ 70.0)
Cash at beginning of year	80.0
Cash at end of year	$10.0

[a]Depreciation is a noncash expense that was deducted when calculating net income. It must be added back to show the correct cash flow from operations.

[b]The net increase in fixed assets is $130 million; however, this net amount includes a deduction for the year's depreciation expense. Depreciation expense should be added back to show the increase in gross fixed assets. From the company's income statement, we see that 1992 depreciation expense is $100 million; thus, the acquisition of fixed assets equals $230 million.

The data in Table 2A-1 are used to prepare the formal statement of cash flows. We again show the statement of cash flows contained in Allied's annual report in Table 2A-2.[2] Each balance sheet change in Table 2A-1 is classified as resulting from (1) operations, (2) long-term investments, or (3) financing activities. Operating cash flows are those associated with the production and sale of goods and services. Net income is the primary operating cash flow, but changes in accounts payable, accounts receivable, inventories, and accruals are also classified as operating cash flows. Investment cash flows arise from the purchase or sale of plant, property, and equipment. Financing cash inflows result from issuing debt or common stock, while financing outflows occur when the firm pays dividends or repays debt. The cash inflows and outflows from these three activities

---

[2]There are two different formats for presenting the cash flow statement. The method we present here is called the *indirect method.* Cash flows from operations are calculated by starting with net income, adding back expenses not paid out of cash, and subtracting revenues that do not provide cash. Using the *direct method,* operating cash flows are found by summing all revenues that provide cash and then subtracting all expenses that are paid in cash. Both formats produce the same result, and both are accepted by the Financial Accounting Standards Board.

are summed to determine their impact on the firm's liquidity position, which is measured by the change in the cash and marketable securities accounts.

Note that every item in the "change" columns of Table 2A-1 is carried over to Table 2A-2 except retained earnings. Table 2A-2 shows net income as the first line item in the "Operating Activities" section, while dividends paid are shown as a negative cash flow in the "Financing Activities" section, rather than netting these items out and simply reporting the increase in retained earnings. Table 2A-2 shows the sources as positive numbers and the uses as negative numbers with regard to their effects on Allied's cash and marketable securities. Also, note that the last 3 lines in the Statement of Cash Flows show the reconciliation of the cash account and give the ending cash balance for the year. Like most companies, Allied considers its marketable securities to be cash equivalents, so with regard to financial position, they are treated as being equivalent to cash.

Problem

2A-1

Statement of cash flows

The consolidated balance sheets for the Lloyd Lumber Company at the beginning and end of 1992 follow. The company bought $50 million worth of fixed assets. The charge for depreciation in 1992 was $10 million. Net income was $33 million, and the company paid out $5 million in dividends.

a. Fill in the amount of the source or use in the appropriate column.

Lloyd Lumber Company: Balance Sheets at Beginning and End of 1992 (Millions of Dollars)

			Change	
	Jan. 1	Dec. 31	Source	Use
Cash	$ 7	$ 15	_____	_____
Marketable securities	0	11	_____	_____
Net receivables	30	22	_____	_____
Inventories	53	75	_____	_____
Total current assets	$ 90	$123	_____	_____
Gross fixed assets	75	125	_____	_____
Less accumulated depreciation	25	35	_____	_____
Net fixed assets	$ 50	$ 90	_____	_____
Total assets	$140	$213	_____	_____
Accounts payable	$ 18	$ 15	_____	_____
Notes payable	3	15	_____	_____
Other current liabilities	15	7	_____	_____
Long-term debt	8	24	_____	_____
Common stock	29	57	_____	_____
Retained earnings	67	95	_____	_____
Total liabilities and equity	$140	$213	_____	_____

Note: Total sources must equal total uses.

b. Prepare a statement of cash flows.
c. Briefly summarize your findings.

The Financial Environment: Markets, Institutions, Interest Rates, and Taxes

A M A N A G E R I A L P E R S P E C T I V E

In December 1991, after 17 months of recession, Chairman Alan Greenspan of the Federal Reserve Board took two drastic actions in an attempt to halt the recession: He announced that the Fed (1) was cutting the discount rate that it charges on loans to banks from 4.5 percent to 3.5 percent, its lowest level in 27 years, and (2) was lowering the federal funds rate (the interest rate charged on overnight loans between banks) from 4.5 percent to 4 percent. The announcement came as a surprise—this was the biggest interest-rate cut in a decade. Previous Fed actions had been small, cautious quarter-point reductions which had been announced with minimum fanfare to keep the financial markets convinced of the Fed's commitment to fight inflation.

Mr. Greenspan's announcement came in response to growing criticism from the White House, Congress, and private economists, who accused the Fed of worrying too much about bond-market psychology and too little about the rapidly deteriorating confidence of both consumers and business executives. In addition, new forecasts by the Fed's economists (who had earlier been confident that the economy was recovering) showed an economy "dead in the water." Their revised forecasts predicted no growth, or even negative growth, for both the fourth quarter of 1991 and the first quarter of 1992. Finally, a survey of manufacturers revealed that manufacturing activity had fallen to its lowest level of the year.

The financial system responded immediately to Mr. Greenspan's announcement. Morgan Guaranty Trust Co. cut its prime lending rate from 7.5 percent to 6.5 percent, and other large banks followed Morgan's ac-

tions. Long-term rates in the bond market decreased to levels not seen in years.

What do these actions mean for the economy? On the one hand, lower rates will almost immediately cut the interest payments of heavily indebted businesses and homeowners. Home mortgage refinancings alone will put billions of dollars into consumers' pockets, and more quickly than through a tax cut. Lower rates should also encourage businesses to borrow for investment, provide new life for the housing market, and help exporters by decreasing the value of the dollar relative to other currencies, which will make U.S. goods less expensive overseas. On the other hand, lower interest rates will take income away from elderly Americans who live on the income they receive from their bond investments and savings accounts. (Overall, U.S. households will receive $76 billion more in interest income than they pay out in interest expense.) While the reduction of income to elderly Americans will limit the favorable effect of lower interest rates to some extent, it is not likely to offset the rate cut because (1) this $76 billion excess of interest income over interest expense represents less than 2 percent of all personal income and (2) many of those individuals with substantial interest income are wealthy, so their day-to-day spending is not affected very much by their interest income.

What are the responses of the critics? Martin Feldstein, a Harvard economist and former Reagan adviser, made this statement about interest rates: "Although they've come down a number of times, interest rates are still very high in real [inflation-adjusted] terms, relative to where they've been in previous business cycles." Economist Robert Brusca of Nikko Securities International, who had been criticizing the Fed for months for not doing more, said, "People think monetary policy has been used and it's not effective. Monetary policy works. It's just not been used aggressively to fight this recession." Thus, if Greenspan's move does not work, economists believe the Fed still has room to cut rates further.

As you read this chapter, think about (1) all the factors the Fed must have considered before deciding to cut rates to stimulate the economy and (2) the repercussions lower interest rates might have on inflation, on the financial markets, and on the economy as a whole.

Source: "Changing Its Course, The Fed Boldly Tries to Bolster Economy," *The Wall Street Journal,* December 23, 1991, and subsequent news releases.

Financial managers must understand the environment and markets within which businesses operate. Therefore, this chapter examines the markets where capital is raised, securities are traded, and stock prices are established, as well as the institutions which operate in these markets. In the process, we shall see how money costs are determined, and we shall explore the principal factors that determine the level of interest rates in the economy. In addition, since taxes are critically important in financial decisions, we also discuss the key features of the U.S. tax laws.

THE FINANCIAL MARKETS

Business firms, individuals, and government units often need to raise capital. For example, suppose Carolina Power & Light (CP&L) forecasts an increase in the demand for electricity in North Carolina, and the company decides to build a new power plant. Because CP&L almost certainly will not have the $2 billion or so necessary to pay for the plant, the company will have to raise this capital in the financial markets. Or suppose Mr. Fong, the proprietor of a San Francisco hardware store, decides to expand into appliances. Where will he get the money to buy the initial inventory of TV sets, washers, and freezers? Similarly, if the Johnson family wants to buy a home that costs $100,000, but they have only $20,000 in savings, how can they raise the additional $80,000? If the city of New York wants to borrow $200 million to finance a new sewer plant, or if the federal government needs over $300 billion to cover its projected 1993 deficit, they too need access to the capital markets.

On the other hand, some individuals and firms have incomes which are greater than their current expenditures, so they have funds available to invest. For example, Carol Hawk has an income of $36,000, but her expenses are only $30,000, while Ford Motor Company recently had accumulated over $17 billion of excess cash, which it wanted to invest.

People and organizations wanting to borrow money are brought together with those having surplus funds in the *financial markets.* Note that "markets" is plural—there are a great many different financial markets, each one consisting of many institutions, in a developed economy such as ours. Each market deals with a somewhat different type of instrument in terms of the instrument's maturity and the assets backing it. Also, different markets serve different types of customers, or operate in different parts of the country. Here are some of the major types of markets:

1. *Physical asset markets* (also called "tangible" or "real" asset markets) are those for such products as wheat, autos, real estate, computers, and machinery. *Financial asset markets* deal with stocks, bonds, notes, mortgages, and other *claims on real assets.*

2. *Spot markets* and *futures markets* are terms that refer to whether the assets are being bought or sold for "on the spot" delivery (literally, within a few days) or for delivery at some future date, such as six months or a year into the future. The futures markets are growing in importance, but we shall not discuss them until Chapter 21.

money markets

The financial markets in which funds are borrowed or loaned for short periods (less than one year).

capital markets

The financial markets for stocks and for long-term debt (one year or longer).

primary markets

Markets in which corporations raise capital by issuing new securities.

secondary markets

Markets in which securities and other financial assets are traded among investors after they have been issued by corporations.

3. **Money markets** are the markets for debt securities with maturities of less than one year. The New York and London money markets have long been the world's largest, but Tokyo is rising rapidly. **Capital markets** are the markets for long-term debt and corporate stocks. The New York Stock Exchange, which handles the stocks of the largest U.S. corporations, is a prime example of a capital market.

4. *Mortgage markets* deal with loans on residential, commercial, and industrial real estate, and on farmland, while *consumer credit markets* involve loans on autos and appliances, as well as loans for education, vacations, and so on.

5. *World, national, regional,* and *local markets* also exist. Thus, depending on an organization's size and scope of operations, it may be able to borrow all around the world, or it may be confined to a strictly local, even neighborhood, market.

6. **Primary markets** are the markets in which corporations raise new capital. If GE were to sell a new issue of common stock to raise capital, this would be a primary market transaction. The corporation selling the newly created stock receives the proceeds from the sale in a primary market transaction. **Secondary markets** are markets in which existing, already outstanding, securities are traded among investors. Thus, if Edgar Rice decided to buy 1,000 shares of IBM stock, the purchase would occur in the secondary market. The New York Stock Exchange is a secondary market, since it deals in outstanding as opposed to newly issued stocks and bonds. Secondary markets also exist for mortgages, various other types of loans, and other financial assets. The corporation whose securities are being traded is not involved in a secondary market transaction and, thus, does not receive any funds from such a sale.

Other classifications could be made, but this breakdown is sufficient to show that there are many types of financial markets.

A healthy economy is dependent on efficient transfers of funds from people who are net savers to firms and individuals who need capital. Without efficient transfers, the economy simply could not function: Carolina Power & Light could not raise capital, so Raleigh's citizens would have no electricity; the Johnson family would not have adequate housing; Carol Hawk would have no place to invest her savings; and so on. Obviously, the level of employment and productivity, hence our standard of living, would be much lower. Therefore, it is absolutely essential that our financial markets function efficiently — not only quickly, but also at a low cost.[1]

Table 3-1 gives a listing of the most important instruments traded in the various financial markets. The instruments are arranged from top to bottom in ascending order of typical length of maturity. As we go through the book, we will look in much more detail at many of these instruments. For example, we

---

[1] As the Commonwealth of Independent States (the former Soviet Union) and the Eastern European nations move toward capitalism, just as much attention must be paid to the establishment of cost-efficient financial markets as to electrical power, transportation, communications, and other infrastructure systems. Economic efficiency is simply impossible without a good system for allocating capital within the economy.

Table 3-1   ▪   **Summary of Major Market Instruments, Market Participants, and Security Characteristics**

Instrument (1)	Market (2)	Major Participants (3)	Security Characteristics		
			Riskiness (4)	Maturity (5)	Interest Rate on 1/13/92[a] (6)
U.S. Treasury bills	Money	Sold by U.S. Treasury to finance federal expenditures to institutional investors	Default-free	91 days to 1 year	3.8%
Banker's acceptances	Money	Firm's promise to pay, guaranteed by bank	Low degree of risk if guaranteed by a strong bank	Up to 180 days	3.9
Commercial paper	Money	Issued by financially secure firms to large investors	Low default risk	Up to 270 days	4.0
Negotiable certificates of deposit (CDs)	Money	Issued by major money-center commercial banks to large investors	Riskier than Treasury bills	Up to 1 year	3.6
Money market mutual funds	Money	Invest in Treasury bills, CDs, and commercial paper; held by individuals and businesses	Low degree of risk	No specific maturity (instant liquidity)	4.5
Eurodollar market time deposits	Money	Issued by banks outside U.S.	Default risk is a function of issuing bank	Up to 1 year	4.1
U.S. Treasury notes and bonds	Capital	Issued by U.S. government	No default risk, but price can decline if interest rates rise	1 to 30 years	7.6
Consumer credit loans	Money	Issued by banks/credit unions/finance companies to individuals	Risk is variable	Variable	Variable
Mortgages	Capital	Borrowings from commercial banks and S&Ls by individuals and businesses	Risk is variable	Up to 30 years	8.0%
State and local government bonds	Capital	Issued by state and local governments to individuals and institutional investors	Riskier than U.S. government securities, but exempt from most taxes	Up to 30 years	6.6

[a]Interest rates are for longest maturity securities of the type and for the strongest securities of a given type. Thus, the 8.4% interest rate shown for corporate bonds reflects the rate on 30-year, Aaa bonds. Lower-rated bonds had higher interest rates.

(continued)

Table 3-1 ▪ *continued*

| Instrument (1) | Market (2) | Major Participants (3) | Security Characteristics | | |
			Riskiness (4)	Maturity (5)	Interest Rate on 1/13/92[a] (6)
Corporate bonds	Capital	Issued by corporations to individuals and institutional investors	Riskier than U.S. government securities, but less risky than preferred and common stocks; varying degree of risk within bonds depending on strength of issuer	Up to 40 years	8.4
Leases	Capital	Similar to debt in that firms can lease assets rather than borrow and then buy the assets	Risk similar to corporate bonds	Generally 3 to 20 years	Similar to bond yields
Preferred stocks	Capital	Issued by corporations to individuals and institutional investors	Riskier than corporate bonds, but less risky than common stock	Unlimited	8 to 10%
Common stocks[b]	Capital	Issued by corporations to individuals and institutional investors	Risky	Unlimited	10 to 15%

[b]Common stocks are expected to provide a "return" in the form of dividends and capital gains rather than interest. Of course, if you buy a stock, while you may *expect* to earn 10 percent on your money, the stock's price may decline and cause you to experience a 100 percent loss.

will see that there are actually many varieties of corporate bonds, ranging from "plain vanilla flavored" bonds, to bonds that are convertible into common stocks, and to bonds whose interest payments vary depending on the rate of inflation. Still, the table gives an idea of the characteristics and costs of the instruments traded in the major financial markets.

❓ *Self-Test Questions*

Distinguish between physical asset markets and financial asset markets.

What is the difference between spot and futures markets?

Distinguish between money and capital markets.

What is the difference between primary and secondary markets?

Why are financial markets essential for a healthy economy?

Figure 3-1   ▪   **Diagram of the Capital Formation Process**

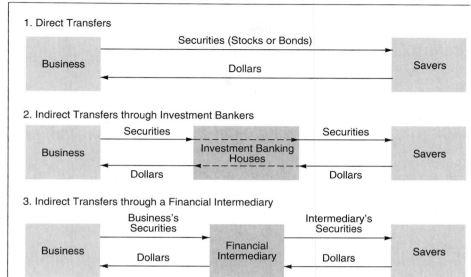

FINANCIAL INSTITUTIONS

Transfers of capital between savers and those who need capital take place in the three different ways diagrammed in Figure 3-1:

1. *Direct transfers* of money and securities, as shown in the top section, occur when a business sells its stocks or bonds directly to savers, without going through any type of financial institution. The business delivers its securities to savers, who in turn give the firm the money it needs.

2. As shown in the middle section, transfers may also go through an *investment banking house* such as Morgan Stanley, which serves as a middleman and facilitates the issuance of securities. The company sells its stocks or bonds to the investment bank, which in turn sells these same securities to savers. The businesses' securities and the savers' money merely "pass through" the investment banking house. However, the investment bank does buy and hold the securities for a period of time, so it is taking a chance — it may not be able to resell them to savers for as much as it paid. Because new securities are involved and the corporation receives money from the sale, this is a primary market transaction.

3. Transfers can also be made through a *financial intermediary* such as a bank or mutual fund. Here the intermediary obtains funds from savers, issuing its own securities in exchange, and then it uses the money to purchase and then hold a business's securities. For example, a saver might give dollars to a bank, receiving from it a certificate of deposit, and then the bank might lend the money to a small business in the form of a mortgage loan. Thus, intermediaries literally create new forms of capital — in this case, certificates of deposit, which are both safer and more liquid than

mortgages and thus are better securities for most savers to hold. The existence of intermediaries greatly increases the efficiency of money and capital markets.

For simplicity, we assumed that the entity which needs capital is a business, and specifically a corporation, but it is easy to visualize the demander of capital as a home purchaser, a government unit, and so on.

Direct transfers of funds from savers to businesses are possible and do occur on occasion, but it is generally more efficient for a business to enlist the services of an **investment banking house.** Merrill Lynch, Salomon Brothers, Dean Witter, and Goldman Sachs are examples of financial service corporations which offer investment banking services. Such organizations (1) help corporations design securities with the features that are currently most attractive to investors, (2) buy these securities from the corporation, and (3) then resell them to savers. Although the securities are sold twice, this process is really one primary market transaction, with the investment banker acting as a middleman as capital is transferred from savers to businesses.

The **financial intermediaries** shown in the third section of Figure 3-1 do more than simply transfer money and securities between firms and savers—they literally create new financial products. Since the intermediaries are generally large, they gain economies of scale in analyzing the creditworthiness of potential borrowers, in processing and collecting loans, and in pooling risks and thus helping individual savers diversify, i.e., "not put all their financial eggs in one basket." Further, a system of specialized intermediaries can enable savings to do more than just draw interest. For example, individuals can put money into banks and get both interest income and a convenient way of making payments (checking), or put money into life insurance companies and get both interest income and protection for their beneficiaries.

In the United States and other developed nations, a large set of specialized, highly efficient financial intermediaries has evolved. The situation is changing rapidly, however, and different types of institutions are performing services that were formerly reserved for others, causing institutional distinctions to become blurred. Still, there is a degree of institutional identity, and here are the major classes of intermediaries:

investment banking house

An organization that underwrites and distributes new investment securities and helps businesses obtain financing.

financial intermediaries

Specialized financial firms that facilitate the transfer of funds from savers to demanders of capital.

1. *Commercial banks,* which are the traditional "department stores of finance," serve a wide variety of savers and those with needs for funds. Historically, the commercial banks were the major institutions which handled checking accounts and through which the Federal Reserve System expanded or contracted the money supply. Today, however, several other institutions also provide checking services and significantly influence the effective money supply. Conversely, commercial banks are providing an ever-widening range of services, including stock brokerage services and insurance.

   Note that commercial banks are quite different from investment banks. Commercial banks lend money, whereas investment banks help companies raise capital from other parties. Prior to 1933, commercial banks offered investment banking services, but the Glass-Steagall Act, which was passed in that year, prohibited commercial banks from engaging in investment banking. Thus, the Morgan Bank was broken up into two separate organizations, one of which is now the Morgan Guaranty Trust Company, a commercial bank, while the other is Morgan Stanley, a major investment banking house. Note also that Japanese and European banks can offer both commercial and investment banking services. This severely hinders U.S. banks in global competition, so efforts are being made to get Glass-Steagall repealed.

2. *Savings and loan associations (S&Ls),* which have traditionally served individual savers and residential and commercial mortgage borrowers, take the funds of many small savers and then lend this money to home buyers and other types of borrowers. Because the savers obtain a degree of liquidity that would be absent if they bought the mortgages or other securities directly, perhaps the most significant economic function of the S&Ls is to "create liquidity" which would otherwise be lacking. Also, the S&Ls have more expertise in analyzing credit, setting up loans, and making collections than individual savers, so they reduce the cost and increase the availability of real estate loans. Finally, the S&Ls hold large, diversified portfolios of loans and other assets and thus spread risks in a manner that would be impossible if small savers were making mortgage loans directly. Because of these factors, savers benefit by being able to invest their savings in more liquid, better managed, and less risky accounts, whereas borrowers benefit by being able to obtain more capital, and at lower costs, than would otherwise be possible.

3. *Mutual savings banks,* which are similar to S&Ls, operate primarily in the northeastern states, accept savings primarily from individuals, and lend mainly on a long-term basis to home buyers and consumers.

4. *Credit unions* are cooperative associations whose members have a common bond, such as being employees of the same firm. Members' savings are loaned only to other members, generally for auto purchases, home improvements, and the like. Credit unions often are the cheapest source of funds available to individual borrowers.

5. *Pension funds* are retirement plans funded by corporations or government agencies for their workers and administered primarily by the trust departments of commercial banks or by life insurance companies. Pension funds invest primarily in bonds, stocks, mortgages, and real estate.

6. *Life insurance companies* take savings in the form of annual premiums, then invest these funds in stocks, bonds, real estate, and mortgages, and finally make payments to the beneficiaries of the insured parties. In recent years life insurance companies have also offered a variety of tax-deferred savings plans designed to provide benefits to the participants when they retire.

7. *Mutual funds* are corporations which accept money from savers and then use these funds to buy stocks, long-term bonds, or short-term debt instruments issued by businesses or government units. These organizations pool funds and thus reduce risks by diversification. They also achieve economies of scale, which lower the costs of analyzing securities, managing portfolios, and buying and selling securities. Different funds are designed to meet the objectives of different types of savers. Hence, there are bond funds for

money market fund

A mutual fund that invests in short-term, low-risk securities and allows investors to write checks against their accounts.

those who desire safety, stock funds for savers who are willing to accept significant risks in the hope of higher returns, and still other funds that are used as interest-bearing checking accounts (the **money market funds**). There are literally hundreds of different mutual funds with dozens of different goals and purposes.

Financial institutions have historically been heavily regulated, with the primary purpose of this regulation being to insure the safety of the institutions and thus to protect depositors. However, these regulations—which have taken the form of prohibitions on nationwide branch banking, restrictions on the types of assets the institutions can buy, ceilings on the interest rates they can pay, and limitations on the types of services they can provide—have tended to impede the free flow of capital from surplus to deficit areas, and thus have hurt the efficiency of our capital markets. Recognizing this fact, Congress has authorized some major changes, and more will be forthcoming.

financial service corporation

A firm which offers a wide range of financial services, including investment banking, brokerage operations, insurance, and commercial banking.

The result of the ongoing regulatory changes has been a blurring of the distinctions between the different types of institutions. Indeed, the trend in the United States today is toward huge **financial service corporations,** which own banks, S&Ls, investment banking houses, insurance companies, pension plan operations, and mutual funds, and which have branches across the country and even around the world. Sears, Roebuck is, interestingly, one of the largest financial service corporations. It owns Allstate Insurance, Dean Witter (a leading brokerage and investment banking firm), Coldwell Banker (the largest real estate brokerage firm), a huge credit card business, and a host of other related businesses. Other financial service corporations, most of which started in one area and have now diversified to cover most of the financial spectrum, include Transamerica, Merrill Lynch, American Express, Citicorp, Fidelity, and Prudential.

 Self-Test Questions

Identify the three different ways capital is transferred between savers and borrowers.

What is the difference between a commercial bank and an investment bank?

Distinguish between investment banking houses and financial intermediaries.

List the major types of intermediaries and briefly describe each one's function.

THE STOCK MARKET

As noted earlier, secondary markets are those in which outstanding, previously issued securities are traded. By far the most active secondary market, and the most important one to financial managers, is the *stock market*. It is here that the prices of firms' stocks are established, and, since the primary goal of managerial finance is to maximize the firm's stock price, a knowledge of this market is essential for anyone involved in managing a business.

INDUSTRY PRACTICE	The New Banking Law Gets Tough with Banks

In late 1991, Congress passed a new banking law which created a much tougher regulatory system for banks. The Bush administration had proposed to modernize the banking system by allowing well-capitalized banks to establish nationwide branch systems and to become financial supermarkets which could offer a broad range of insurance, securities, and financial services. The Bush package was designed to strengthen the U.S. banking system by expanding banking's horizons. However, the legislation passed by Congress rejected most of Bush's proposals and even imposed new restrictions on banks. Congress had recently been forced to authorize the expenditure of over $200 billion to bail out the savings and loan industry, and banking regulators were seeking another $70 billion to keep the Bank Insurance Fund solvent. Congress reasoned that the bank and S&L problems had been caused by granting these institutions too much leeway and by regulation that was too loose, so it was reluctant to let banks go into new business areas. Now, though, many bankers and industry analysts fear that Congress went too far with its legislation—they think the new banking law will undermine banks further by keeping them out of profitable businesses, so rules designed to prevent banks from failing will mainly keep them from prospering.

The new legislation (1) will require regulators to move more quickly to correct problems and to close banks before they become insolvent rather than working with them to correct developing problems, (2) will limit the Federal Reserve Board's ability to keep ailing banks open with long-term loans from its discount window, and (3) will end the Federal Deposit Insurance Corporation's authority to pay off uninsured deposits (those over $100,000) when banks fail.

Bush was forced to accept the tougher regulation in a political compromise to get the $70 billion needed to support the Bank Insurance Fund, which had been depleted by more than 1,100 bank failures since 1984.

Many bankers believe that the new legislation will make it more difficult for them to lend money at a time when the administration is urging them to stimulate the economy with easier credit. They also worry that, if many more banks fail, the premiums the surviving banks must pay for deposit insurance will rise sharply. Then, consumers might have to pay much of the premium increases through increases in loan charges and reductions in rates paid on deposit accounts. This situation could hurt both the banks and the economy.

Robert Litan of the Brookings Institution argued that in the long run the legislation will strengthen banks but that in the short run it may well exacerbate the credit squeeze. Thus, while the Fed is easing credit, legislation is being passed which requires banks to tighten it. Still, Mr. Litan believes that this is "modest good news" for taxpayers because money has been provided for deposit insurance, and new regulations are in place which will lead to sounder banking.

The new regulation is tied closely to banks' capital—when a bank's capital declines, regulators will be required to take prompt action to make the bank restrict its growth, to force reductions or suspensions of dividends, to require the sale of stock to raise capital, and in extreme cases to change the management team. Also, regulators can force banks to close when their ratio of capital to assets falls to 2 percent; this provision alone could close down at least 100 small and medium-sized banks. Thus, the new law will require many banks to boost their capital at a time when they are already suffering from low earnings and low stock prices. De facto, this will force many weaker banks to merge with stronger banks.

Both bank shareholders and borrowers could be hurt by the new legislation. Due to the higher capital requirements, some banks will have to sell more stock to raise capital, diluting the wealth of current stockholders. Also, if a bank's capital falls to the threshold level and if regulators then close the bank even though it is not insolvent, then stockholders will be wiped out before the bank has a chance to get back on sound footing. All this will make weakly capitalized banks reluctant to lend to all but their strongest customers, which will compound the difficulty smaller firms and those in financial difficulty are having in rolling over exisiting loans or getting new credit. Finally, banks will think a little more about whether they want to fund high-risk ventures, which the nation needs if we are to grow and prosper.

The new legislation signaled an end to the "too big to fail" doctrine. Under this doctrine large banks, whose failure might have brought down the banking system, were either given loans by the Fed sufficient to keep them afloat or were merged with healthy banks under terms whereby the government reimbursed the acquiring bank for any losses it incurred.

This doctrine meant that all depositors were protected, even those with accounts greater than the $100,000 deposit insurance limit. Therefore, depositors did not "shop" for strong banks, and weak banks could get almost unlimited funds at artificially low costs to lend at high rates to risky borrowers. If the loans were paid off, the banks would do well, but if they went into default, the insurance fund (or taxpayers) would pick up the bill. Thus, banks were able to play a game of "heads I win, tails you lose" with U.S. taxpayers.

During the recent wave of bank failures, the insurance fund was further depleted by reimbursements to uninsured depositors, and this led to a need to increase banks' insurance premiums. These premiums tripled from 1990 to 1991, and they will be increased again if failures continue at their recent pace. Banks are anxious to slow this increase, because every one-cent rise in premiums per $100 of domestic deposits costs the banking industry $250 million a year.

Some experts believe that the Fed will be tougher on banks because of these changes—since the Fed now has less flexibility to help the banks once they get into trouble, it will work harder to keep them out of trouble in the first place. Also, it is likely that banks will benefit eventually as the new law reduces bank failures and as payments from the insurance fund slow, easing pressure for insurance premium increases. The new regulatory plan is designed to encourage banks to operate safely and to maintain ample capital as a cushion against failure. As taxpayers, we can only hope that this goal will be accomplished.

Source: "Cracking Down—The New Banking Law Toughens Regulation, Some Say Too Much," *The Wall Street Journal,* November 29, 1991, and subsequent news releases.

The Stock Exchanges

There are two basic types of stock markets: (1) *organized exchanges,* which include the New York Stock Exchange (NYSE), the American Stock Exchange (AMEX), and several regional exchanges and (2) the less formal *over-the-counter market.* Since the organized exchanges have actual physical market locations and are easier to describe and understand, we shall consider them first.

organized security exchanges

Formal organizations having tangible physical locations that conduct auction markets in designated ("listed") securities. The two major U.S. stock exchanges are the New York Stock Exchange (NYSE) and the American Stock Exchange (AMEX).

The **organized security exchanges** are tangible physical entities. Each of the larger ones occupies its own building, has specifically designated members, and has an elected governing body—its board of governors. Members are said to have "seats" on the exchange, although everybody stands up. These seats, which are bought and sold, give the holder the right to trade on the exchange. There are 1,366 seats on the New York Stock Exchange, and in February 1992, NYSE seats were selling for about $600,000.

Most of the larger investment banking houses operate *brokerage departments,* which own seats on the exchanges and designate one or more of their officers as members. The exchanges are open on all normal working days, with the members meeting in a large room equipped with telephones and other electronic equipment that enable each member to communicate with his or her firm's offices throughout the country.

Like other markets, security exchanges facilitate communication between buyers and sellers. For example, Merrill Lynch (the largest brokerage firm) might receive an order in its Atlanta office from a customer who wants to buy 100 shares of IBM stock. Simultaneously, Dean Witter's Denver office might receive an order from a customer wishing to sell 100 shares of IBM. Each broker communicates by wire with the firm's representative on the NYSE. Other brokers throughout the country are also communicating with their own exchange members. The exchange members with *sell orders* offer the shares for sale, and they are bid for by the members with *buy orders*. Thus, the exchanges operate as *auction markets*.[2]

The Over-the-Counter Market

over-the-counter market

A large collection of brokers and dealers, connected electronically by telephones and computers, that provides for trading in unlisted securities.

In contrast to the organized security exchanges, the **over-the-counter market** is a nebulous, intangible organization. An explanation of the term "over-the-counter" will help clarify exactly what this market is. The exchanges operate as auction markets—buy and sell orders come in more or less simultaneously, and exchange members match these orders. If a stock is traded less frequently, perhaps because it is the stock of a new or a small firm, few buy and sell orders come in, and matching them within a reasonable length of time would be difficult. To avoid this problem, some brokerage firms maintain an inventory of such stocks—they buy when individual investors want to sell and sell when investors want to buy. At one time the inventory of securities was kept in a safe, and the stocks, when bought and sold, were literally passed over the counter.

Today, the over-the-counter market is defined to include all facilities that are needed to conduct security transactions not conducted on the organized exchanges. These facilities consist of (1) the relatively few *dealers* who hold inventories of over-the-counter securities and who are said to "make a market" in these securities, (2) the thousands of brokers who act as *agents* in bringing these dealers together with investors, and (3) the computers, terminals, and electronic networks that provide a communications link between dealers and brokers. The dealers who make a market in a particular stock continuously quote a price at which they are willing to buy the stock (the *bid price*) and a price at which they will sell shares (the *asked price*). Each dealer's prices, which are adjusted as supply and demand conditions change, can be read off computer screens all across the country. The spread between bid and asked prices represents the dealer's markup, or profit.

---

[2]The NYSE is actually a modified auction market, wherein people (through their brokers) bid for stocks. Originally—about two hundred years ago—brokers would literally shout, "I have 100 shares of Union Pacific for sale; how much am I offered?" and then sell to the highest bidder. If a broker had a buy order, he or she would shout, "I want to buy 100 shares of Union Pacific; who'll sell at the best price?" The same general situation still exists, although the exchanges now have members known as *specialists* who facilitate the trading process by keeping an inventory of shares of the stocks in which they specialize. If a buy order comes in at a time when no sell order arrives, the specialist will sell off some inventory. Similarly, if a sell order comes in, the specialist will buy and add to inventory. The specialist sets a *bid price* (the price the specialist will pay for the stock) and an *asked price* (the price at which shares will be sold out of inventory). The bid and asked prices are set at levels designed to keep the inventory in balance. If many buy orders start coming in because of favorable developments or sell orders come in because of unfavorable events, the specialist will raise or lower prices to keep supply and demand in balance. Bid prices are somewhat lower than asked prices, with the difference, or *spread*, representing the specialist's profit margin.

Special facilities are available to help institutional investors such as mutual funds or pension funds sell large blocks of stock without depressing their prices. In essence, brokerage houses which cater to institutional clients will purchase blocks (defined as 10,000 or more shares) and then resell the stock to other institutions or individuals. Also, when a firm has a major announcement which is likely to cause its stock price to change sharply, it will ask the exchanges to halt trading in its stock until the announcement has been made and digested by investors. Thus, when Texaco announced that it planned to acquire Getty Oil, trading was halted for one day in both Texaco and Getty stocks.

Brokers and dealers who make up the over-the-counter market are members of a self-regulating body known as the *National Association of Security Dealers (NASD),* which licenses brokers and oversees trading practices. The computerized trading network used by NASD is known as the NASD Automated Quotation System (NASDAQ), and *The Wall Street Journal* and other newspapers contain information on NASDAQ transactions.

In terms of numbers of issues, the majority of stocks are traded over the counter. However, because the stocks of larger companies are listed on the exchanges, about two-thirds of the dollar volume of stock trading takes place on the exchanges.

Some Trends in Security Trading Procedures

From the NYSE's inception in 1792 until the 1970s, the vast majority of all stock trading occurred on the Exchange and was conducted by member firms. The NYSE established a set of minimum brokerage commission rates, and no member firm could charge a commission lower than the set rate. This was a monopoly, pure and simple. However, on May 1, 1975, the Securities and Exchange Commission (SEC), with strong prodding from the Antitrust Division of the Justice Department, forced the NYSE to abandon its fixed commissions. Commission rates declined dramatically, falling in some cases as much as 90 percent from former levels.

These changes were a boon to the investing public, but not to the brokerage industry. A number of "full-service" brokerage houses went bankrupt, and others were forced to merge with stronger firms. The number of brokerage houses has declined from literally thousands in the 1960s to a much smaller number of large, strong, nationwide companies, many of which are units of diversified financial service corporations. Deregulation has also spawned a number of "discount brokers," some of which are affiliated with commercial banks; several of these are growing quite rapidly.[3]

 ### Self-Test Questions

What are the two basic types of stock markets, and how do they differ?

How has deregulation changed security trading procedures?

THE COST OF MONEY

Capital in a free economy is allocated through the price system. *The interest rate is the price paid to borrow debt capital, whereas in the case of equity capital, investors expect to receive dividends and capital gains.* The factors which affect the supply of and demand for investment capital, and hence the cost of money, are discussed in this section.

---

[3]Full-service brokers give investors information on different stocks and make recommendations as to which stocks to buy. Discount brokers do not give advice—they merely execute orders. Some brokerage houses (institutional houses) cater primarily to institutional investors such as pension funds and insurance companies, while others cater to individual investors and are called "retail houses." Large firms such as Merrill Lynch generally have both retail and institutional brokerage operations.

production opportunities

The returns available within an economy from investment in productive (cash-generating) assets.

time preferences for consumption

The preferences of consumers for current consumption as opposed to saving for future consumption.

risk

In a financial market context, the chance that a loan will not be repaid as promised.

inflation

The tendency of prices to increase over time.

The four most fundamental factors affecting the cost of money are (1) **production opportunities,** (2) **time preferences for consumption,** (3) **risk,** and (4) **inflation.** To see how these factors operate, visualize an isolated island community where the people live on fish. They have a stock of fishing gear which permits them to survive reasonably well, but they would like to have more fish. Now suppose Mr. Crusoe had a bright idea for a new type of fishnet that would enable him to double his daily catch. However, it would take him a year to perfect his design, to build his net, and to learn how to use it efficiently, and Mr. Crusoe would probably starve before he could put his new net into operation. Therefore, he might suggest to Ms. Robinson, Mr. Friday, and several others that if they would give him one fish each day for a year, he would return two fish a day during all of the next year. If someone accepted the offer, then the fish which Ms. Robinson or one of the others gave to Mr. Crusoe would constitute *savings;* these savings would be *invested* in the fishnet; and the extra fish the net produced would constitute a *return on the investment.*

Obviously, the more productive Mr. Crusoe thought the new fishnet would be, the higher his expected return on the investment would be and the more he could afford to offer potential investors for their savings. In this example we assume that Mr. Crusoe thought he would be able to pay, and thus he offered, a 100 percent rate of return—he offered to give back two fish for every one he received. He might have tried to attract savings for less—for example, he might have decided to offer only 1.5 fish next year for every one he received this year, which would represent a 50 percent rate of return to Ms. Robinson and the other potential savers.

How attractive Mr. Crusoe's offer appeared to a potential saver would depend in large part on the saver's *time preference for consumption.* For example, Ms. Robinson might be thinking of retirement, and she might be willing to trade fish today for fish in the future on a one-for-one basis. On the other hand, Mr. Friday might have a wife and several young children and need his current fish, so he might be unwilling to "lend" a fish today for anything less than three fish next year. Mr. Friday would be said to have a high time preference for consumption and Ms. Robinson a low time preference. Note also that if the entire population were living right at the subsistence level, time preferences for current consumption would necessarily be high, aggregate savings would be low, interest rates would be high, and capital formation would be difficult.

The *risk* inherent in the fishnet project, and thus in Mr. Crusoe's ability to repay the loan, would also affect the return investors would require: The higher the perceived risk, the higher the required rate of return. Also, in a more complex society there are many businesses like Mr. Crusoe's, many goods other than fish, and many savers like Ms. Robinson and Mr. Friday. Further, people use money as a medium of exchange rather than barter with fish. When money is used, rather than fish, its value in the future, which is affected by *inflation,* comes into play: The higher the expected rate of inflation, the larger the required return.

Thus, we see that the interest rate paid to savers depends in a basic way (1) on the rate of return producers expect to earn on invested capital, (2) on savers' time preferences for current versus future consumption, (3) on the riskiness of the loan, and (4) on the expected future rate of inflation. Producers' expected returns on their business investments set an upper limit on how much they can pay for savings, while consumers' time preferences for consumption establish how much consumption they are willing to defer, hence how much they will save at different levels of interest offered by producers.[4] Higher risk and higher inflation also lead to higher interest rates.

 Self-Test Questions

What is the price paid to borrow money called?

What is the "price" of equity capital?

What four fundamental factors affect the cost of money?

INTEREST RATE LEVELS

Capital is allocated among borrowers by interest rates: Firms with the most profitable investment opportunities are willing and able to pay the most for capital, so they tend to attract it away from inefficient firms or from those whose products are not in demand. Of course, our economy is not completely free in the sense of being influenced only by market forces. Thus, the federal government has agencies which help designated individuals or groups obtain credit on favorable terms. Among those eligible for this kind of assistance are small businesses, certain minorities, and firms willing to build plants in areas with high unemployment. Still, most capital in the U.S. economy is allocated through the price system.

Figure 3-2 shows how supply and demand interact to determine interest rates in two capital markets. Markets A and B represent two of the many capital markets in existence. The going interest rate, which can be designated as either k or i, but for purposes of the discussion here is designated as k, is initially 10 percent for the low-risk securities in Market A.[5] Borrowers whose credit is strong enough to qualify for this market can obtain funds at a cost of 10 percent, and investors who want to put their money to work without much risk can obtain a 10 percent return. Riskier borrowers must obtain higher-cost funds in Market B. Investors who are more willing to take risks invest in Market B expecting to earn a 12 percent return but also realizing that they might actually receive much less.

If the demand for funds declines, as it typically does during business recessions, the demand curves will shift to the left, as shown in Curve D_2 in Market A. The market-clearing, or equilibrium, interest rate in this example declines to 8 percent. Similarly, you should be able to visualize what would happen if the Federal Reserve tightened credit: The supply curve, S_1, would shift to the left, and this would raise interest rates and lower the level of borrowing in the economy.

---

[4]The term "producers" is really too narrow. A better word might be "borrowers," which would include corporations, home purchasers, people borrowing to go to college, or even people borrowing to buy autos or to pay for vacations. Also, the wealth of a society influences its people's ability to save and thus their time preferences for current versus future consumption.

[5]In Chapter 5, when the time value of money is discussed, the term i for interest rate will be used because this term corresponds to the interest rate key on most financial calculators.

Figure 3-2   ▪   **Interest Rates as a Function of Supply and Demand for Funds**

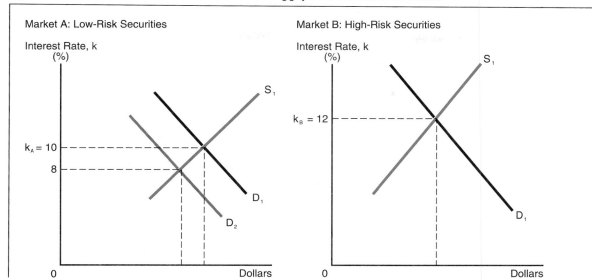

Capital markets are interdependent. For example, if Markets A and B were in equilibrium before the demand shift to D_2 in Market A, this means that investors were willing to accept the higher risk in Market B in exchange for a *risk premium* of $12\% - 10\% = 2\%$. After the shift to D_2, the risk premium would initially increase to $12\% - 8\% = 4\%$. In all likelihood, this much larger premium would induce some of the lenders in Market A to shift to Market B; this, in turn, would cause the supply curve in Market A to shift to the left (or up) and that in Market B to shift to the right. The transfer of capital between markets would raise the interest rate in Market A and lower it in Market B, thus bringing the risk premium back closer to the original level, 2 percent.

There are many capital markets in the United States. U.S. firms also invest and raise capital throughout the world, and foreigners both borrow and lend capital in the United States. There are markets in the United States for home loans; farm loans; business loans; federal, state, and local government loans; and consumer loans. Within each category, there are regional markets as well as different types of submarkets. For example, in real estate there are separate markets for first and second mortgages and for loans on single-family homes, apartments, office buildings, shopping centers, vacant land, and so on. Within the business sector, there are dozens of types of debt and also several different markets for common stocks.

There is a price for each type of capital, and these prices change over time as shifts occur in supply and demand conditions. Figure 3-3 shows how long- and short-term interest rates to business borrowers have varied since the 1950s. Notice that short-term interest rates are especially prone to rise during booms and then fall during recessions. (The shaded areas of the chart indicate recessions.) When the economy is expanding, firms need capital, and this demand for capital pushes rates up. Also, inflationary pressures are strongest during business booms, and that also exerts upward pressure on rates. Conditions are reversed

Figure 3-3   ▪   **Long- and Short-Term Interest Rates, 1955–1992**

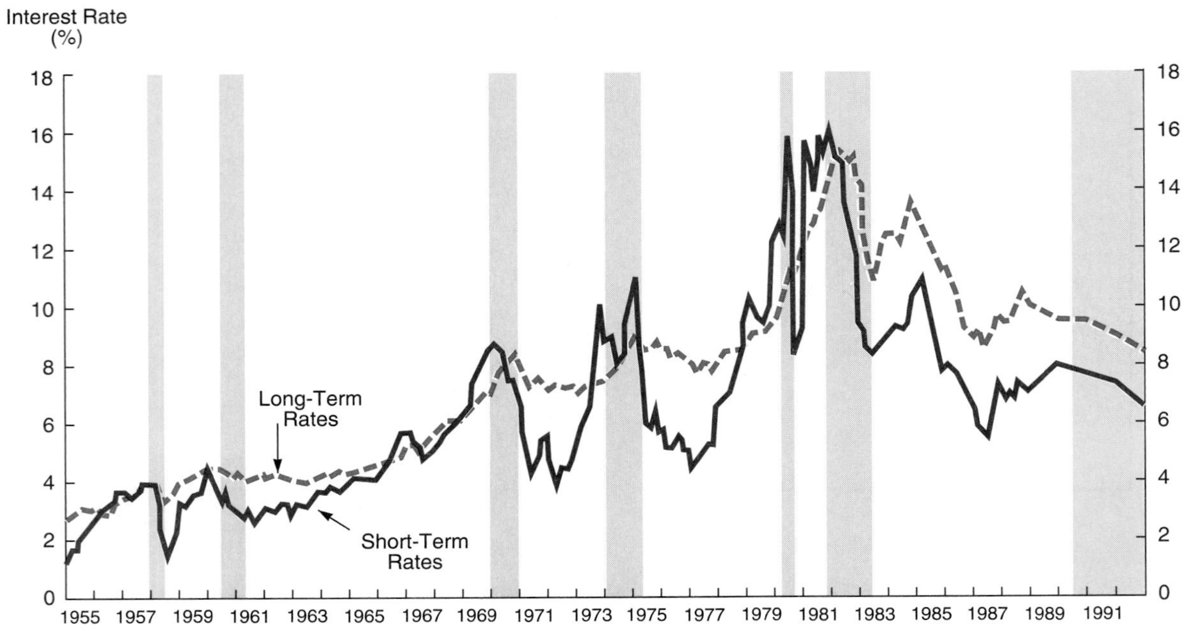

Notes:

a. The shaded areas designate business recessions.

b. Short-term rates are measured by four- to six-month loans to very large, strong corporations, and long-term rates are measured by AAA corporate bonds.

Source: *Federal Reserve Bulletin.*

during recessions such as the one in 1991 and 1992. Slack business reduces the demand for credit, the rate of inflation falls, and the result is a drop in interest rates.

These tendencies do not hold exactly—the period after 1984 is a case in point. The price of oil fell dramatically in 1985 and 1986, reducing inflationary pressures on other prices and easing fears of serious long-term inflation. Earlier, these fears had pushed interest rates to record levels. The economy from 1984 to 1987 was fairly strong, but the declining fears about inflation more than offset the normal tendency of interest rates to rise during good economic times, and the net result was lower interest rates.[6]

The relationship between inflation and long-term interest rates is highlighted in Figure 3-4, which plots rates of inflation along with long-term interest rates. Prior to 1965, when the average rate of inflation was about 1 percent, interest rates on AAA-rated bonds generally ranged from 4 to 5 percent. As the

---

[6]Short-term rates are responsive to current economic conditions, whereas long-term rates primarily reflect long-run expectations for inflation. As a result, short-term rates are sometimes above and sometimes below long-term rates. The relationship between long-term and short-term rates is called the *term structure of interest rates.* This topic is discussed later in the chapter.

Figure 3-4 ▪ Relationship between Annual Inflation Rates and Long-Term Interest Rates, 1955–1992

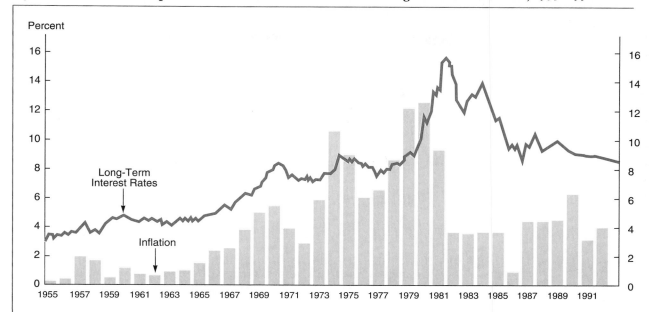

Notes:

a. Interest rates are those on AAA long-term corporate bonds.

b. Inflation is measured as the annual rate of change in the Consumer Price Index (CPI).

c. The 1992 figure is an estimate.

Source: *Federal Reserve Bulletin.*

war in Vietnam accelerated in the late 1960s, the rate of inflation increased, and interest rates began to rise. The rate of inflation dropped after 1970 and so did long-term interest rates. However, the 1973 Arab oil embargo was followed by a quadrupling of oil prices in 1974, which caused a spurt in inflation, which in turn drove interest rates to new record highs in 1974 and 1975. Inflationary pressures eased in late 1975 and 1976 but then rose again after 1976. In 1980, inflation rates hit the highest level on record, and fears of continued double-digit inflation pushed interest rates up to historic highs. From 1981 through 1986, the inflation rate dropped sharply, and in 1986 inflation was only 1.1 percent, the lowest level in 25 years. Currently (1992), inflation is in the 3½ to 4 percent range, and interest rates to strong corporations have declined to about 8.4 percent.

❔ *Self-Test Questions*

How are interest rates used to allocate capital among firms?

What happens to market-clearing, or equilibrium, interest rates in a capital market when the demand for funds declines? What happens when inflation increases or decreases?

Why does the price of capital change during booms and recessions?

How does risk affect interest rates?

THE DETERMINANTS OF MARKET INTEREST RATES

In general, the quoted (or nominal) interest rate on a debt security, k, is composed of a real risk-free rate of interest, k*, plus several premiums that reflect inflation, the riskiness of the security, and the security's marketability (or liquidity). This relationship can be expressed as follows:

$$\text{Quoted interest rate} = k = k^* + IP + DRP + LP + MRP. \quad (3\text{-}1)$$

Here

k = the quoted, or nominal, rate of interest on a given security.[7] There are many different securities, hence many different quoted interest rates.

k^* = the real risk-free rate of interest; k^* is pronounced "k-star," and it is the rate that would exist on a riskless security if zero inflation were expected.

k_{RF} = the quoted risk-free rate of interest. This is the quoted interest rate on a security such as a U.S. Treasury bill which is very liquid and free of most risks. Note that k_{RF} does include a premium for expected inflation, as $k_{RF} = k^* + IP$.

IP = inflation premium. IP is equal to the average expected inflation rate over the life of the security.

DRP = default risk premium. This premium reflects the possibility that the issuer will not pay interest or principal on a security at the stated time and in the stated amount. DRP is zero for U.S. Treasury securities, but it rises as the riskiness of issuers increases.

LP = liquidity, or marketability, premium. This is a premium charged by lenders to reflect the fact that some securities cannot be converted to cash on short notice at a "reasonable" price. LP is very low for Treasury securities, but it is relatively high on securities issued by very small firms.

MRP = maturity risk premium. As we will explain later, longer-term bonds are exposed to a significant risk of price declines, and a maturity risk premium is charged by lenders to reflect this risk.

If we combine $k^* + IP$ and let this sum equal k_{RF}, then we have this expression:

$$k = k_{RF} + DRP + LP + MRP. \quad (3\text{-}2)$$

---

[7]The term *nominal* as it is used here means the *stated* rate as opposed to the *real* rate, which is adjusted to remove the effects of inflation. If you bought a 10-year Treasury bond in January 1992, the quoted, or nominal, rate would be about 7 percent, but if inflation averages 5 percent over the next 10 years, the real rate would be about 7% − 5% = 2%. In Chapter 5 we will use the term nominal in yet another way: to distinguish between quoted rates and effective annual rates when compounding occurs more frequently than once a year.

We discuss the components whose sum makes up the quoted, or nominal, rate on a given security in the following sections.

The Real Risk-Free Rate of Interest, k*

real risk-free rate of interest, k*

The rate of interest that would exist on default-free U.S. Treasury securities if no inflation were expected.

The **real risk-free rate of interest, k***, is defined as the interest rate that would exist on a riskless security if no inflation were expected, and it may be thought of as the rate of interest that would exist on short-term U.S. Treasury securities in an inflation-free world. The real risk-free rate is not static — it changes over time depending on economic conditions, especially (1) on the rate of return corporations and other borrowers can expect to earn on productive assets and (2) on people's time preferences for current versus future consumption. Borrowers' expected returns on real asset investments set an upper limit on how much they can afford to pay for borrowed funds, while savers' time preferences for consumption establish how much consumption they are willing to defer, and hence the amount of funds they will lend at different levels of interest. It is difficult to measure the real risk-free rate precisely, but most experts think that in the United States k* has fluctuated in the range of 1 to 4 percent in recent years.

The Nominal, or Quoted, Risk-Free Rate of Interest, k_{RF}

nominal (quoted) risk-free rate, k_{RF}

The rate of interest on a security that is free of all risk; k_{RF} is proxied by the T-bill rate or the T-bond rate. k_{RF} includes an inflation premium.

The **nominal,** or **quoted, risk-free rate, k_{RF}**, is the real risk-free rate plus a premium for expected inflation: $k_{RF} = k^* + IP$. To be strictly correct, the risk-free rate should mean the interest rate on a totally risk-free security — one that has no risk of default, no maturity risk, no liquidity risk, and no risk of loss if inflation increases. There is no such security, hence there is no observable truly risk-free rate. However, there is one security that is free of most risks — a U.S. Treasury bill (T-bill), which is a short-term security issued by the U.S. government. Treasury bonds (T-bonds), which are longer-term government securities, are free of default and liquidity risks, but T-bonds are exposed to some risk due to changes in the general level of interest rates.

If the term "risk-free rate" is used without either the modifier "real" or the modifier "nominal," people generally mean the quoted (nominal) rate, and we will follow that convention in this book. Therefore, when we use the term risk-free rate, k_{RF}, we mean the nominal risk-free rate, which includes an inflation premium equal to the average expected inflation rate over the life of the security. In general, we use the T-bill rate to approximate the short-term risk-free rate, and the T-bond rate to approximate the long-term risk-free rate. So, whenever you see the term "risk-free rate," assume that we are referring either to the quoted U.S. T-bill rate or to the quoted T-bond rate.

Inflation Premium (IP)

Inflation has a major impact on interest rates because it erodes the purchasing power of the dollar and lowers the real rate of return on investments. To illustrate, suppose you saved $1,000 and invested it in a Treasury bill that matures in 1 year and will pay 5 percent interest. At the end of the year you will receive $1,050 — your original $1,000 plus $50 of interest. Now suppose the inflation rate during the year is 10 percent, and it affects all items equally. If beer had cost $1 per bottle at the beginning of the year, it would cost $1.10 at the end of the year. Therefore, your $1,000 would have bought $1,000/$1 = 1,000 bottles at the beginning of the year but only $1,050/$1.10 = 955 bottles at the end. Thus, in *real terms,* you would be worse off—you would receive $50 of interest, but it would not be sufficient to offset inflation. You would thus be better off buying 1,000 bottles of beer (or some other storable asset such as land, timber, apartment buildings, wheat, or gold) than buying the Treasury bill.

inflation premium (IP)

A premium for expected inflation that investors add to the real risk-free rate of return.

Investors are well aware of all this, so when they lend money, they build in an **inflation premium (IP)** equal to the expected inflation rate over the life of the security. As discussed previously, for a short-term, default-free U.S. Treasury bill, the actual interest rate charged, k_{T-bill}, would be the real risk-free rate, k^*, plus the inflation premium (IP):

$$k_{T-bill} = k_{RF} = k^* + IP.$$

Therefore, if the real risk-free rate of interest were $k^* = 3\%$, and if inflation were expected to be 4 percent (and hence IP = 4%) during the next year, then the quoted rate of interest on 1-year T-bills would be 7 percent. In early January of 1992, the expected 1-year inflation rate was about 3.5 percent, and the yield on 1-year T-bills was about 4.2 percent. This implies that the real risk-free rate on short-term securities at that time was about 0.7 percent.

It is important to note that the rate of inflation built into interest rates is the *rate of inflation expected in the future,* not the rate experienced in the past. Thus, the latest reported figures might show an annual inflation rate of 3 percent, but that is for a past period. If people on the average expect a 6 percent inflation rate in the future, then 6 percent would be built into the current rate of interest. Note also that the inflation rate reflected in the quoted interest rate on any security is the *average rate of inflation expected over the security's life.* Thus, the inflation rate built into a 1-year bond is the expected inflation rate for the next year, but the inflation rate built into a 30-year bond is the average rate of inflation expected over the next 30 years.[8]

Expectations for future inflation are closely, but not perfectly, correlated with rates experienced in the recent past. Therefore, if the inflation rate reported for last month increased, people would tend to raise their expectations for future inflation, and this change in expectations would cause an increase in interest rates.

Default Risk Premium (DRP)

The risk that a borrower will *default* on a loan, which means not to pay the interest or the principal, also affects the market interest rate on a security: the greater the default risk, the higher the interest rate lenders charge. Treasury

---

[8]To be theoretically precise, we should use a *geometric average.* Also, since millions of investors are active in the market, it is impossible to determine exactly the consensus expected inflation rate. Survey data are available, however, which give us a reasonably good idea of what investors expect over the next few years. For example, in 1980 the University of Michigan's Survey Research Center reported that people expected inflation during the next year to be 11.9 percent and that the average rate of inflation expected over the next 5 to 10 years was 10.5 percent. Those expectations led to record high interest rates. However, the economy cooled in 1981 and 1982 and, as Figure 3-4 showed, actual inflation dropped sharply after 1980. This led to gradual reductions in the *expected future* inflation rate. In 1992, as we write this, the expected future inflation rate is about 3.5 percent. As inflationary expectations dropped, so did quoted market rates of interest.

securities have no default risk; thus, they carry the lowest interest rates on taxable securities in the United States. For corporate bonds, the higher the bond's rating, the lower its default risk, and, consequently, the lower its interest rate.[9] Here are some representative interest rates on long-term bonds during early January 1992:

	Rate	DRP
U.S. Treasury	7.4%	—
AAA	8.2	0.8%
AA	8.4	1.0
A	8.7	1.3

default risk premium (DRP)

The difference between the interest rate on a U.S. Treasury bond and a corporate bond of equal maturity and marketability.

The difference between the quoted interest rate on a T-bond and that on a corporate bond with similar maturity, liquidity, and other features is the **default risk premium (DRP).** Therefore, if the bonds listed above were otherwise similar, the default risk premium would be DRP = 8.2% − 7.4% = 0.8 percentage points for AAA corporate bonds, 8.4% − 7.4% = 1.0 percentage point for AA, and 8.7% − 7.4% = 1.3 percentage points for A corporate bonds. Default risk premiums vary somewhat over time, but the January 1992 figures are representative of levels in recent years.

Liquidity Premium (LP)

Liquidity generally is defined as the ability to convert an asset to cash at a "fair market value." Assets have varying degrees of liquidity, depending on the characteristics of the market in which they are traded. For instance, there exist very active and easily accessible secondary markets for financial assets such as government notes and bonds and the stocks and bonds of large corporations, but the markets for real estate are limited because they are geographically constrained. Therefore, most financial assets are considered more liquid than real assets. Of course, the most liquid asset of all is cash, and the more easily an asset can be converted to cash at a "fair market value," the more liquid it is considered. Consequently, short-term financial assets generally are more liquid than long-term financial assets. Because liquidity is important, investors evaluate liquidity and include **liquidity premiums (LP)** when market rates of securities are established. Although it is very difficult to accurately measure liquidity premiums, a differential of at least two and probably four or five percentage points exists between the least liquid and the most liquid financial assets of similar default risk and maturity.

liquidity premium (LP)

A premium added to the equilibrium interest rate on a security if that security cannot be converted to cash on short notice and at close to the original cost.

Maturity Risk Premium (MRP)

U.S. Treasury securities are free of default risk in the sense that one can be virtually certain that the federal government will pay interest on its bonds and will also pay them off when they mature. Therefore, the default risk premium

---

[9]Bond ratings, and bonds' riskiness in general, will be discussed in detail in Chapter 20. For now, merely note that bonds rated AAA are judged to have less default risk than bonds rated AA, AA bonds are less risky than A bonds, and so on. Ratings are designated AAA or Aaa, AA or Aa, and so forth, depending on the rating agency. In this book the designations are used interchangeably.

interest rate risk

The risk of capital losses to which investors are exposed because of changing interest rates.

maturity risk premium (MRP)

A premium which reflects interest rate risk.

reinvestment rate risk

The risk that a decline in interest rates will lead to lower income when bonds mature and funds are reinvested.

on Treasury securities is essentially zero. Further, active markets exist for Treasury securities, so their liquidity premiums are also close to zero. Thus, as a first approximation, the rate of interest on a Treasury bond should be the risk-free rate, k_{RF}, which is equal to the real risk-free rate, k^*, plus an inflation premium, IP. However, an adjustment is needed for long-term Treasury bonds. The prices of long-term bonds decline sharply whenever interest rates rise, and since interest rates can and do occasionally rise, all long-term bonds, even Treasury bonds, have an element of risk called **interest rate risk.** As a general rule, the bonds of any organization, from the U.S. government to Continental Airlines, have more interest rate risk the longer the maturity of the bond.[10] Therefore, a **maturity risk premium (MRP),** which is higher the longer the years to maturity, must be included in the required interest rate.

The effect of maturity risk premiums is to raise interest rates on long-term bonds relative to those on short-term bonds. This premium, like the others, is extremely difficult to measure, but (1) it seems to vary over time, rising when interest rates are more volatile and uncertain, then falling when interest rates are more stable, and (2) in recent years, the maturity risk premium on 30-year T-bonds appears to have generally been in the range of one or two percentage points.[11]

We should mention that although long-term bonds are heavily exposed to interest rate risk, short-term bills are heavily exposed to **reinvestment rate risk.** When short-term bills mature and the funds are reinvested, or "rolled over," a decline in interest rates would necessitate reinvestment at a lower rate, and hence would lead to a decline in interest income. To illustrate, suppose you had $100,000 invested in 1-year T-bills, and you lived on the income. In 1981, short-term rates were about 15 percent, so your income would have been about $15,000. However, your income would have declined to about $9,000 by 1983, and to just $4,200 by 1992. Had you invested your money in long-term T-bonds, your income (but not the value of the principal) would have been stable.[12] Thus, although "investing short" preserves one's principal, the interest income provided by short-term T-bills varies from year to year, depending on reinvestment rates.

---

[10]For example, if someone had bought a 30-year Treasury bond for $1,000 in 1972, when the long-term interest rate was 7 percent, and held it until 1981, when long-term T-bond rates were about 14.5 percent, the value of the bond would have declined to about $514. That would represent a loss of almost half the money, and it demonstrates that long-term bonds, even U.S. Treasury bonds, are not riskless. However, had the investor purchased short-term T-bills in 1972 and subsequently reinvested the principal each time the bills matured, he or she would still have had $1,000. This point will be discussed in detail in Chapter 6.

[11]The MRP has averaged 1.3 percentage points over the last 65 years. See *Stocks, Bonds, Bills, and Inflation: 1992 Yearbook* (Chicago: Ibbotson Associates, 1992).

[12]Long-term bonds also have some reinvestment rate risk. To actually earn the quoted rate on a long-term bond, the interest payments must be reinvested at the quoted rate. However, if interest rates fall, the interest payments must be reinvested at a lower rate; thus, the realized return would be less than the quoted rate. Note, though, that the reinvestment rate risk is lower on a long-term bond than on a short-term bond because only the interest payments (rather than interest plus principal) on the long-term bond are exposed to reinvestment rate risk. Only zero coupon bonds, discussed in Chapters 6 and 20, are completely free of reinvestment rate risk.

Self-Test Questions

Write out an equation for the nominal interest rate on any debt security.

Distinguish between the *real* risk-free rate of interest, k*, and the *nominal,* or *quoted,* risk-free rate of interest, k_{RF}.

How is inflation considered when interest rates are determined by investors in the financial markets? Explain.

Does the interest rate on a T-bond include a default risk premium? Explain.

Distinguish between liquid and illiquid assets, and identify some assets that are liquid and some that are illiquid.

Briefly explain the following statement: "Although long-term bonds are heavily exposed to interest rate risk, short-term bills are heavily exposed to reinvestment rate risk."

THE TERM STRUCTURE OF INTEREST RATES

term structure of interest rates
The relationship between yields and maturities of securities.

A study of Figure 3-3 reveals that at certain times, such as in 1992, short-term interest rates are lower than long-term rates, whereas at other times, such as in 1980 and 1981, short-term rates were higher than long-term rates. The relationship between long- and short-term rates, which is known as the **term structure of interest rates,** is important to corporate treasurers, who must decide whether to borrow by issuing long- or short-term debt, and to investors, who must decide whether to buy long- or short-term bonds. Thus, it is important to understand (1) how long- and short-term rates are related to each other and (2) what causes shifts in their relative positions.

To begin, we can look up in a source such as *The Wall Street Journal* or the *Federal Reserve Bulletin* the interest rates on Treasury bonds of various maturities at a given point in time. For example, the tabular section of Figure 3-5 presents interest rates for different maturities on two dates. The set of data for a given date, when plotted on a graph such as that in Figure 3-5, is called the **yield curve** for that date. The yield curve changes both in position and in slope over time. In March of 1980, all rates were relatively high, and short-term rates were higher than long-term rates, so the yield curve on that date was *downward sloping.* However, in January of 1992, all rates had fallen, and short-term rates were lower than long-term rates, so the yield curve at that time was *upward sloping.* Had we drawn the yield curve during January of 1982, it would have been essentially horizontal, for long-term and short-term bonds on that date had about the same rate of interest. (See Figure 3-3.)

yield curve
A graph showing the relationship between yields and maturities of securities.

Figure 3-5 shows yield curves for U.S. Treasury securities, but we could have constructed them for corporate bonds; for example, we could have developed yield curves for IBM, General Motors, Chrysler, or any other company that borrows money over a range of maturities. Had we constructed such curves and plotted them on Figure 3-5, the corporate yield curves would have been above those for Treasury securities on the same date because the corporate yields would include default risk premiums, but they would have had the same general shape as the Treasury curves. Also, the riskier the corporation, the higher its

Figure 3-5 ■ **U.S. Treasury Bond Interest Rates on Different Dates**

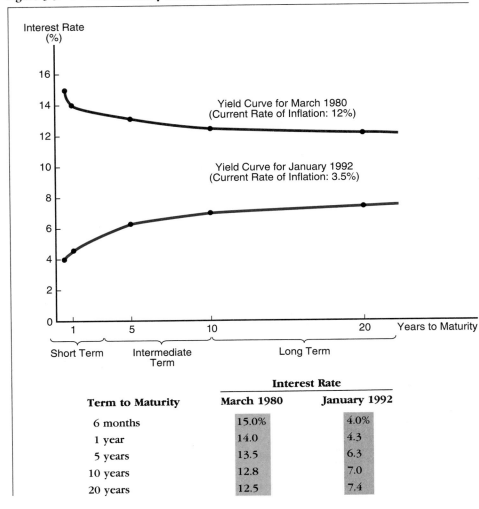

Term to Maturity	Interest Rate	
	March 1980	**January 1992**
6 months	15.0%	4.0%
1 year	14.0	4.3
5 years	13.5	6.3
10 years	12.8	7.0
20 years	12.5	7.4

yield curve; thus, Chrysler, which is in a relatively weak financial position, would have had a yield curve substantially higher than that of IBM, which is rated an AAA company.

Historically, in most years long-term rates have been above short-term rates, so usually the yield curve has been upward sloping. For this reason, people often call an upward-sloping yield curve a **"normal" yield curve** and a yield curve which slopes downward an **inverted,** or **"abnormal," yield curve.** Thus, in Figure 3-5 the yield curve for March 1980 was inverted, but the one for January 1992 was normal. We explain in the next section why an upward slope is the normal situation, but, briefly, the reason is that short-term securities are less risky than longer-term securities, hence short-term rates are normally lower than long-term rates.

"normal" yield curve

An upward-sloping yield curve.

inverted ("abnormal") yield curve

A downward-sloping yield curve.

Term Structure Theories

Several theories have been proposed to explain the shape of the yield curve. The three major ones are (1) the market segmentation theory, (2) the liquidity preference theory, and (3) the expectations theory.

market segmentation theory

The theory that each borrower and lender has a preferred maturity and that the slope of the yield curve depends on the supply of and demand for funds in the long-term market relative to the short-term market.

Market Segmentation Theory.   Briefly, the **market segmentation theory** states that each lender and each borrower has a preferred maturity. For example, a person borrowing to buy a long-term asset like a house, or an electric utility borrowing to build a power plant, would want a long-term loan. However, a retailer borrowing in September to build its inventories for Christmas would prefer a short-term loan. Similar differences exist among savers—for example, a person saving up to take a vacation next summer would want to lend in the short-term market, but someone saving for retirement 20 years hence would probably buy long-term securities.

The thrust of the market segmentation theory is that the slope of the yield curve depends on supply/demand conditions in the long-term and short-term markets. Thus, according to this theory, the yield curve could at any given time be either flat, upward sloping, or downward sloping. An upward-sloping yield curve would occur when there was a large supply of short-term funds relative to demand, but a shortage of long-term funds. Similarly, a downward-sloping curve would indicate relatively strong demand in the short-term market compared to that in the long-term market. A flat curve would indicate balance between the two markets.

liquidity preference theory

The theory that lenders prefer to make short-term loans rather than long-term loans; hence, they will lend short-term funds at lower rates than long-term funds.

Liquidity Preference Theory.   The **liquidity preference theory** states that long-term bonds normally yield more than short-term bonds for two reasons: (1) Investors generally prefer to hold short-term securities, because such securities are more liquid in the sense that they can be converted to cash with little danger of loss of principal. Investors will, therefore, generally accept lower yields on short-term securities, and this leads to relatively low short-term rates. (2) Borrowers, on the other hand, generally prefer long-term debt, because short-term debt exposes them to the risk of having to repay the debt under adverse conditions. Accordingly, borrowers are willing to pay a higher rate, other things held constant, for long-term funds than for short-term funds, and this also leads to relatively low short-term rates. Thus, lender and borrower preferences both operate to cause short-term rates to be lower than long-term rates. Taken together, these two sets of preferences—and hence the liquidity preference theory—imply that under normal conditions, a positive maturity risk premium (MRP) exists, and the MRP increases with years to maturity, causing the yield curve to be upward sloping.

expectations theory

The theory that the shape of the yield curve depends on investors' expectations about future inflation rates.

Expectations Theory.   The **expectations theory** states that the yield curve depends on expectations about future inflation rates. Specifically, k_t, the nominal interest rate on a U.S. Treasury bond that matures in t years, is found as follows under the expectations theory:

$$k_t = k^* + IP_t.$$

Here k* is the real risk-free interest rate, and IP_t is an inflation premium which is equal to the average expected rate of inflation over the t years until the bond matures. Under the pure expectations theory, the maturity risk premium (MRP) is assumed to be zero, and, for Treasury securities, the default risk premium (DRP) and liquidity premium (LP) are also zero.

To illustrate, suppose that in late December of 1992 the real risk-free rate of interest was k* = 3% and expected inflation rates for the next 3 years were as follows:[13]

	Expected Annual (1-Year) Inflation Rate	Expected Average Inflation Rate from 1992 to Indicated Year
1993	4%	4%/1 = 4.0%
1994	6%	(4% + 6%)/2 = 5.0%
1995	8%	(4% + 6% + 8%)/3 = 6.0%

Given these expectations, the following pattern of interest rates should exist:

	Real Risk-free Rate (k*)		Inflation Premium, Which Is Equal to the Average Expected Inflation Rate (IP_t)		Nominal Treasury Bond Rate for Each Maturity ($k_{T\text{-bond}}$)
1-year bond	3%	+	4.0%	=	7.0%
2-year bond	3%	+	5.0%	=	8.0%
3-year bond	3%	+	6.0%	=	9.0%

Had the pattern of expected inflation rates been reversed, with inflation expected to fall from 8 percent to 6 percent and then to 4 percent, the following situation would have existed:

	Real Risk-free Rate		Average Expected Inflation Rate		Treasury Bond Rate for Each Maturity
1-year bond	3%	+	8.0%	=	11.0%
2-year bond	3%	+	7.0%	=	10.0%
3-year bond	3%	+	6.0%	=	9.0%

These hypothetical data are plotted in Figure 3-6. According to the expectations theory, whenever the annual rate of inflation is expected to decline, the yield curve must be downward sloping, whereas it must be upward sloping if inflation is expected to increase.

---

[13]Technically, we should be using geometric averages rather than arithmetic averages, but the differences are not material in this example. For a discussion of this point, see Robert C. Radcliffe, *Investment: Concepts, Analysis, and Strategy,* 3rd ed. (Glenview, Ill.: Scott, Foresman, 1990), Chapter 6.

Figure 3-6 ▪ **Hypothetical Example of the Term Structure of Interest Rates**

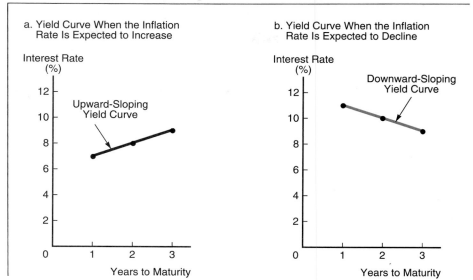

Various tests of the theories have been conducted, and these tests indicate that all three theories have some validity. Thus, the shape of the yield curve at any given time is affected (1) by supply/demand conditions in long- and short-term markets, (2) by liquidity preferences, and (3) by expectations about future inflation. One factor may dominate at one time, another at another time, but all three affect the term structure of interest rates.

 Self-Test Questions

What is a yield curve, and what information would you need to draw this curve?

Discuss each of the following theories: (1) market segmentation theory, (2) liquidity preference theory, and (3) expectations theory.

Distinguish between the shapes of a "normal" yield curve and an "abnormal" yield curve, and explain when each might exist.

OTHER FACTORS THAT INFLUENCE INTEREST RATE LEVELS

In addition to inflationary expectations, liquidity preferences, and the supply/demand situation, other factors also influence both the general level of interest rates and the shape of the yield curve. The four most important factors are (1) Federal Reserve policy, (2) the level of the federal budget deficit, (3) the foreign trade balance, and (4) the level of business activity.

Federal Reserve Policy

As you probably learned in your economics courses, (1) the money supply has a major effect on both the level of economic activity and the rate of inflation, and (2) in the United States, the Federal Reserve Board controls the money supply. If the Fed wants to stimulate the economy, as it did in 1991 and 1992, it increases growth in the money supply. The initial effect of such an action is to cause interest rates to decline. However, a larger money supply may also lead to an increase in the expected rate of inflation, which in turn could push interest rates up. The reverse holds if the Fed tightens the money supply.

To illustrate, in 1981 inflation was quite high, so the Fed tightened up the money supply. The Fed deals primarily in the short-term end of the market, so this tightening had the direct effect of pushing short-term interest rates up sharply. At the same time, the very fact that the Fed was taking strong action to reduce inflation led to a decline in expectations for long-run inflation, which led to a drop in long-term bond yields. Short-term rates decreased shortly thereafter.

In 1991, the situation was just the reverse. To combat the recession, the Fed took steps to reduce interest rates. Short-term rates first fell, and later long-term rates also dropped, but not as sharply. These lower rates will benefit heavily indebted businesses and individual borrowers, and home mortgage refinancings will put additional billions of dollars into consumers' pockets. Savers will of course lose out, but the net effect will benefit the economy. In time, lower rates will encourage businesses to borrow for investment, give new life to the housing market, and bring down the value of the dollar relative to other currencies, which will help U.S. exporters and lower the trade deficit.

During periods when the Fed is actively intervening in the markets, the yield curve will be distorted. Short-term rates will be temporarily "too low" if the Fed is easing credit, and "too high" if it is tightening credit. Long-term rates are not affected as much by Fed intervention.

Federal Deficits

If the federal government spends more than it takes in from tax revenues, it runs a deficit, and that deficit must be covered either by borrowing or by printing money. If the government borrows, this added demand for funds pushes up interest rates. If it prints money, this increases expectations for future inflation, which also drives up interest rates. Thus, the larger the federal deficit, other things held constant, the higher the level of interest rates. Whether long- or short-term rates are more affected depends on how the deficit is financed, so we cannot state, in general, how deficits will affect the slope of the yield curve.

Foreign Trade Balance

Businesses and individuals in the United States buy from and sell to people and firms in other countries. If we buy more than we sell (that is, if we import more than we export), we are said to be running a *foreign trade deficit*. When trade deficits occur, they must be financed, and the main source of financing is debt. In other words, if we import $200 billion of goods but export only $100 billion, we run a trade deficit of $100 billion, and we must borrow the $100 billion.[14] Therefore, the larger our trade deficit, the more we must borrow, and as we increase our borrowing, this drives up interest rates. Also, foreigners are willing to hold U.S. debt if and only if the interest on this debt is competitive with interest rates in other countries. Therefore, if the Federal Reserve attempts to lower interest rates in the United States, causing our rates to fall below rates abroad, then foreigners will sell U.S. bonds, those sales will depress bond prices, and the result will be higher U.S. rates. Thus, the existence of a deficit trade balance hinders the Fed's ability to combat a recession by lowering interest rates.

The United States has been running annual trade deficits since the mid-1970s, and the cumulative effect of these deficits is that the United States is by far the largest debtor nation of all time. As a result, our interest rates are very much influenced by interest rate trends in other countries around the world (higher rates abroad lead to higher U.S. rates). Because of all this, U.S. corporate treasurers—and anyone else who is affected by interest rates—must keep up with developments in the world economy.

Business Activity

Figure 3-3, presented earlier, can be examined to see how business conditions influence interest rates. Here are the key points revealed by the graph:

1. Because inflation increased from 1955 to 1981, the general tendency during this period was toward higher interest rates. However, since the 1981 peak, the trend has generally been downward.

2. Until 1966, short-term rates were almost always below long-term rates. Thus, in those years the yield curve was almost always "normal" in the sense that it was upward sloping.

3. The shaded areas in the graph represent recessions, during which both the demand for money and the rate of inflation tend to fall, and, at the same time, the Federal Reserve tends to increase the money supply in an effort to stimulate the economy. As a result, there is a tendency for interest rates to decline during recessions. Currently, in early 1992, we are in the midst of a recession. The Fed's actions to lower interest rates are efforts to stimulate the economy. Lower interest rates should stimulate business investment and consumer spending and, consequently, bring an end to the recession.

4. During recessions, short-term rates decline more sharply than long-term rates. This occurs because (1) the Fed operates mainly in the short-term sector, so its intervention has the strongest effect here, and (2) long-term rates reflect the average expected inflation rate over the next 20 to 30 years, and this expectation generally does not change much, even when the current rate of inflation is low because of a recession.

---

[14]The deficit could also be financed by selling assets, including gold, corporate stocks, entire companies, and real estate. The United States has financed its massive trade deficits by all of these means in recent years, but the primary method has been by borrowing.

Self-Test Questions

Other than inflationary expectations, liquidity preferences, and normal supply/demand fluctuations, name four additional factors which influence interest rates, and explain their effects.

How does the Fed stimulate the economy? How does the Fed affect interest rates?

INTEREST RATE LEVELS AND STOCK PRICES

Interest rates have two effects on corporate profits: (1) First, because interest is a cost, the higher the rate of interest, the lower a firm's profits, other things held constant. (2) Second, interest rates affect the level of economic activity, and economic activity affects corporate profits. Interest rates obviously affect stock prices because of their effects on profits, but, perhaps even more important, they have an effect due to competition in the marketplace between stocks and bonds. If interest rates rise sharply, investors can get higher returns in the bond market, which induces them to sell stocks and to transfer funds from the stock market to the bond market. Stock sales in response to rising interest rates obviously depress stock prices. Of course, the reverse occurs if interest rates decline. Indeed, the bull market of December 1991, when the Dow Jones Industrial Index rose 10 percent in less than a month, was caused almost entirely by the sharp drop in long-term interest rates.

The experience of Commonwealth Edison, the electric utility serving the Chicago area, can be used to illustrate the effects of interest rates on stock prices. In 1984 Edison's stock sold for $21 per share, and, since the company paid a $3 dividend, the dividend yield was $3/$21 = 14.3%. Edison's bonds at the time also yielded about 14.3 percent. Thus, if someone had saved $100,000 and invested it in either the stock or the bonds, his or her annual income would have been about $14,300. (The investor might also have expected the stock price to grow over time, providing some capital gains, but that point is not relevant for the example.)

By 1992, all interest rates were lower, and Edison's bonds were yielding only 8.5 percent. If the stock still yielded 14.3 percent, investors could switch $100,000 out of Edison's bonds and into its stock and, in the process, increase their annual income from $8,500 to $14,300. Many people did exactly that—as interest rates dropped, orders poured in for the stock, and its price was bid up. In January 1992, Edison's stock sold for $37, up about 76 percent over the 1984 level, and the dividend yield (8.1%) was close to the bond yield (8.5%).

Self-Test Question

In what two ways do changes in interest rates affect stock prices?

INTEREST RATES AND BUSINESS DECISIONS

The yield curve for January 1992, shown earlier in Figure 3-5, indicates how much the U.S. government had to pay in 1992 to borrow money for 1 year, 5 years, 10 years, and so on. A business borrower would have had to pay somewhat more, but assume for the moment that we are back in 1992 and that the yield curve for that year also applies to your company. Now suppose your company has decided (1) to build a new plant with a 20-year life which will cost $1 million and (2) to raise the $1 million by selling an issue of debt (or borrowing) rather than by selling stock. If you borrowed in 1992 on a short-term basis—say for one year—your interest cost for that year would be only 4.3 percent, or $43,000, whereas if you used long-term (20-year) financing, your cost would be 7.4 percent, or $74,000. Therefore, at first glance, it would seem that you should use short-term debt.

However, this could prove to be a horrible mistake. If you use short-term debt, you will have to renew your loan every year, and the rate charged on each new loan will reflect the then-current short-term rate. Interest rates could return to their March 1980 levels, so by 1993 you could be paying 14 percent, or $140,000, per year. These high interest payments would cut into and perhaps eliminate your profits. Your reduced profitability could easily increase your firm's risk to the point where its bond rating would be lowered, causing lenders to increase the risk premium built into the interest rates they charge, which in turn would force you to pay even higher rates. These very high interest rates would further reduce your profitability, worrying lenders even more, and making them reluctant to renew your loan. If your lenders refused to renew the loan and demanded payment, as they have every right to do, you might have trouble raising the cash. If you had to make price cuts to convert physical assets to cash, you might incur heavy operating losses, or even bankruptcy.

On the other hand, if you used long-term financing in 1992, your interest costs would remain constant at $74,000 per year, so an increase in interest rates in the economy would not hurt you. You might even be able to buy up some of your bankrupt competitors at bargain prices—bankruptcies increase dramatically when interest rates rise, primarily because many firms do use short-term debt.

Does all this suggest that firms should always avoid short-term debt? Not necessarily. If inflation falls in the next few years, so will interest rates. If you had borrowed on a long-term basis for 7.4 percent in January 1992, your company would be at a major disadvantage if its debt were locked in at 7.4 percent while its competitors (who used short-term debt in 1992 and thus rode interest rates down in subsequent years) had a borrowing cost of only 5 or 6 percent. On the other hand, large federal deficits might drive inflation and interest rates up to new record levels. In that case, you would wish you had borrowed on a long-term basis in 1992.

Financing decisions would be easy if we could develop accurate forecasts of future interest rates. Unfortunately, predicting future interest rates with consistent accuracy is somewhere between difficult and impossible—people who make a living by selling interest rate forecasts say it is difficult, but many others say it is impossible.

Even if it is difficult to predict future interest rate *levels*, it is easy to predict that interest rates will *fluctuate*—they always have, and they always will. This being the case, sound financial policy calls for using a mix of long- and short-term debt, as well as equity, in such a manner that the firm can survive in most interest rate environments. Further, the optimal financial policy depends in an important way on the nature of the firm's assets—the easier it is to sell off assets and thus to pay off debts, the more feasible it is to use large amounts of short-term debt. This makes it more feasible to finance current assets than fixed assets with short-term debt. We will return to this issue later in the book, when we discuss working capital policy.

Self-Test Questions

If short-term interest rates are lower than long-term rates, why might a firm still choose to finance with long-term debt?

Explain the following statement: "The optimal financial policy depends in an important way on the nature of the firm's assets."

THE FEDERAL INCOME TAX SYSTEM

The value of any financial asset, including stocks, bonds, and mortgages, as well as the values of most real assets such as plants or even entire firms, depends on the stream of cash flows produced by the asset. Cash flows from an asset consist of *usable* income plus depreciation, and usable income means income *after taxes.*

Our tax laws can be changed by Congress, and in recent years changes have occurred almost every year. Indeed, a major change has occurred, on average, every 3 to 4 years since 1913, when our federal income tax system began. Further, certain parts of our tax system are tied to the rate of inflation, so changes occur automatically each year, depending on the rate of inflation during the previous year. Therefore, although this chapter will give you a good background on the basic nature of our tax system, you should consult current rate schedules and other data published by the Internal Revenue Service (and available in U.S. post offices) before you file your personal or business tax return.

Currently (1992), federal income tax rates for individuals go up to almost 35 percent, and, when state and city income taxes are included, the marginal tax rate on an individual's income can exceed 40 percent. Business income is also taxed heavily. The income from partnerships and proprietorships is reported by the individual owners as personal income and, consequently, is taxed at rates going up to 40 percent or more. Corporate profits are subject to federal income tax rates of up to 39 percent, in addition to state income taxes. Because of the magnitude of the tax bite, taxes play an important role in many financial decisions.

As we write this, Congress and the administration are debating the merits of different changes in the tax laws. There is pressure to raise taxes to reduce our huge deficits and to help rebuild our inner cities. Yet, there is pressure to reduce taxes to help stimulate the economy and pull it out of the recession. Many experts are guessing that politics in the 1992 election year will result in few tax law changes, but larger changes will probably occur in coming years. At some point, depreciation schedules may be liberalized, and capital gains may be taxed at a lower rate. Even in the unlikely event that Congress does not change the tax laws, changes will still occur because certain aspects of the tax calculation are tied to the rate of inflation. Thus, by the time you read this chapter, tax rates and other factors may well be different from those we pro-

Table 3-2   ▪   **Individual Tax Rates for 1992**

Single Individuals

If Your Taxable Income Is	You Pay This Amount on the Base of the Bracket	Plus This Percentage on the Excess over the Base	Average Tax Rate at Top of Bracket
Up to $21,450	$ 0	15%	15.0%
$21,450–$51,900	3,218	28	22.6
Over $51,900	11,744	31	31.0

Married Couples Filing Joint Returns

If Your Taxable Income Is	You Pay This Amount on the Base of the Bracket	Plus This Percentage on the Excess over the Base	Average Tax Rate at Top of Bracket
Up to $35,800	$ 0	15%	15.0%
$35,800–$86,500	5,370	28	22.6
Over $86,500	19,566	31	31.0

Notes:

a. These are estimated tax rates for 1992 and beyond. The income ranges at which the 31 percent rate takes effect, as well as the ranges for the additional taxes discussed below, are indexed with inflation each year, so they will change from those shown in the table.

b. A *personal exemption* of $2,300 in 1992 per person or dependent can be deducted from gross income to determine taxable income. Thus, a husband and wife, with two children, would have a 1992 exemption of 4 × $2,300 = $9,200. The amount of the exemption is scheduled to increase with inflation. However, if the gross income exceeds certain limits (generally, $157,900 for joint returns and $105,250 for single individuals), the exemption is phased out, and this has the effect of raising the effective tax rate on incomes over the specified limit by about 0.5 percent per family member, or 2.0 percent for a family of four. In addition, taxpayers can claim *itemized deductions* for charitable contributions and certain other items, but these deductions are reduced if the gross income exceeds $105,250, and this has the effect of raising the effective tax rate on most high-income taxpayers by about 0.93 percent. The combined effect of the loss of exemptions and reduction of itemized deductions is thus about 3 percent, so the marginal tax rate for high income individuals goes up to about 34 percent.

In addition, high-income taxpayers who have "earned income" (as opposed to income from capital such as dividends) are hit with an additional 1.45 percent tax that goes into the medicare fund, thus increasing their marginal tax rate to over 35 percent. Also, there is the social security tax, which for a self-employed person amounts to about 12.4 percent of income up to $55,500. Finally, high-income older taxpayers who are eligible for social security payments lose those payments; this amounts to yet another tax. All of this can push the effective marginal tax rate up close to 50 percent.

The Tax Code is extremely complex with respect to the items covered in this note, so we make no attempt to get specific and exact.

vide. Still, if you understand the chapter, you will also understand the basics of our tax system, and you will know how to operate under the revised tax code.

Taxes are so complicated that university law schools offer master's degrees in taxation to practicing lawyers, many of whom also have CPA certification. In a field complicated enough to warrant such detailed study, we can cover only the highlights. This is really enough, though, because business managers and investors should and do rely on tax specialists rather than trusting their own limited knowledge. Still, it is important to know the basic elements of the tax system as a starting point for discussions with tax experts.

Individual Income Taxes

progressive tax
A tax that requires a higher percentage payment on higher incomes. The personal income tax in the United States, which goes from a rate of 0 percent on the lowest increments of income to almost 35 percent, is progressive.

Individuals pay taxes on wages and salaries, on investment income (dividends, interest, and profits from the sale of securities), and on the profits of proprietorships and partnerships. Our tax rates are **progressive** — that is, the higher one's income, the larger the percentage paid in taxes. Table 3-2 gives the tax rates for single individuals and married couples filing joint returns under the rate schedules in effect in 1992.

taxable income

Gross income minus exemptions and allowable deductions as set forth in the Tax Code.

1. **Taxable income** is defined as gross income less a set of exemptions and deductions which are spelled out in the instructions to the tax forms individuals must file. When filing a tax return in 1993 for the tax year 1992, each taxpayer will receive an exemption of $2,300 for each dependent, including the taxpayer, which reduces taxable income. However, this exemption is indexed to rise with inflation, and the exemption is phased out for high-income taxpayers. Also, certain expenses, such as mortgage interest paid, state and local income taxes paid, and charitable contributions, can be deducted and thus be used to reduce taxable income, but again, high-income taxpayers lose some of this benefit.

marginal tax rate

The tax applicable to the last unit of income.

2. The **marginal tax rate** is defined as the tax on the last unit of income. Marginal rates begin at 15 percent, rise to 28 and then to 31 percent. Note, though, that when consideration is given to the phase-out of exemptions and deductions, plus social security, the marginal tax rate actually goes up to well over 35 percent.

average tax rate

Taxes paid divided by taxable income.

3. One can calculate **average tax rates** from the data in Table 3-2. For example, if Jill Smith, a single individual, had taxable income of $35,000, her tax bill would be $3,218 + ($35,000 − $21,450)(0.28) = $3,218 + $3,794 = $7,012. Her *average tax rate* would be $7,012/$35,000 = 20.0% versus a *marginal rate* of 28 percent. If Jill received a raise of $1,000, bringing her income to $36,000, she would have to pay $280 of it as taxes, so her after-tax raise would be $720. In addition, her social security taxes would also increase.

bracket creep

A situation that occurs when progressive tax rates combine with inflation to cause a greater portion of each taxpayer's real income to be paid as taxes.

4. As indicated in the notes to the table, current legislation provides for tax brackets to be indexed to inflation to avoid the **bracket creep** that occurred during the 1970s and that in reality raised tax rates substantially.[15]

Taxes on Dividend and Interest Income.   Dividend and interest income received by individuals from corporate securities is added to other income and thus is taxed at rates going up to about 35 percent. Since corporations pay dividends out of earnings that have already been taxed, there is *double taxation* of corporate income.

---

[15]For example, if you were single and had a taxable income of $21,450, your tax bill would be $3,218. Now suppose inflation caused prices to double and your income, being tied to a cost-of-living index, rose to $42,900. Because our tax rates are progressive, if tax brackets were not indexed, your taxes would jump to $9,224. Your after-tax income would thus increase from $18,232 to $33,676, but, because prices have doubled, your real income would *decline* from $18,232 to $16,838 (calculated as one-half of $33,676). You would be in a higher tax bracket, so you would be paying a higher percentage of your real income in taxes. If this happened to everyone, and if Congress failed to change tax rates sufficiently, real disposable incomes would decline because the federal government would be taking a larger share of the national product. This is called the federal government's "inflation dividend." However, since tax brackets are now indexed, if your income doubled due to inflation, your tax bill would double, but your after-tax real income would remain constant at $18,232. Bracket creep was a real problem during the 1970s and early 1980s, but indexing—if it stays in the law—will put an end to it.

It should be noted that under U.S. tax laws, interest on most state and local government bonds, called *municipals* or *"munis,"* is not subject to federal income taxes. Thus, investors get to keep all of the interest received from most municipal bonds but only a fraction of the interest received from bonds issued by corporations or by the U.S. government. This means that a lower-yielding muni can provide the same after-tax return as a higher-yielding corporate bond. For example, a taxpayer in the 31 percent marginal tax bracket who could buy a muni that yielded 10 percent would have to receive a before-tax yield of 14.49 percent on a corporate or U.S. Treasury bond to have the same after-tax income:

$$\text{Equivalent pretax yield on taxable bond} = \frac{\text{Yield on muni}}{1 - \text{Marginal tax rate}}$$

$$= \frac{10\%}{1 - 0.31} = 14.49\%.$$

If we know the yield on the taxable bond, we can use the following equation to find the equivalent yield on a muni:

$$\text{Yield on muni} = \left(\begin{array}{c} \text{Pretax yield} \\ \text{on taxable} \\ \text{bond} \end{array} \right) (1 - \text{Marginal tax rate})$$

$$= 14.49\% (1 - 0.31) = 14.49\% (0.69) = 10.0\%.$$

The exemption from federal taxes stems from the separation of federal and state powers, and its primary effect is to help state and local governments borrow at lower rates than would otherwise be available to them.

Capital Gains versus Ordinary Income.   Assets such as stocks, bonds, and real estate are defined as *capital assets.* If you buy a capital asset and later sell it for more than your purchase price, the profit is called a **capital gain;** if you suffer a loss, it is called a **capital loss.** An asset sold within one year of the time it was purchased produces a *short-term gain or loss,* whereas one held for more than one year produces a *long-term gain or loss.* Thus, if you buy 100 shares of Disney stock for $127 per share and sell it for $137 per share, you make a capital gain of 100 × $10, or $1,000. However, if you sell the stock for $117 per share, you will have a $1,000 capital loss. If you hold the stock for more than one year, the gain or loss is long-term; otherwise, it is short-term. If you sell the stock for exactly $127 per share, you make neither a gain nor a loss; you simply get your $12,700 back, and no tax is due.

From 1921 through 1986, long-term capital gains were taxed at substantially lower rates than ordinary income. For example, in 1986 long-term capital gains were taxed at only 40 percent of the tax rate on ordinary income. The tax law changes which took effect in 1987 eliminated this differential, and from 1987 through 1990 all capital gains income (both long-term and short-term)

capital gain or loss
The profit (loss) from the sale of a capital asset for more (less) than its purchase price.

was taxed as if it were ordinary income. However, beginning in 1991, the maximum tax rate on long-term capital gains was capped at 28 percent.

There has been a great deal of controversy over the proper tax rate for capital gains. It has been argued that lower tax rates on capital gains (1) stimulate the flow of venture capital to new, start-up businesses (which generally provide capital gains as opposed to dividend income) and (2) cause companies to retain and reinvest a high percentage of their earnings in order to provide their stockholders with lightly taxed capital gains as opposed to highly taxed dividend income. Thus, it was argued that elimination of the favorable rates on capital gains retarded investment and economic growth. The proponents of preferential capital gains tax rates lost the argument in 1986, but in 1990 they did succeed in getting the rate capped at 28 percent versus the top marginal rate of about 35 percent. You should not be surprised if the capital gains differential is changed again in the future.

Since capital gains are taxed at lower rates, this has implications for dividend policy—it favors lower payouts, hence higher earnings retention. Favorable treatment of capital gains also favors stock investments over bond investments, because part of the income from stock normally comes from capital gains. We will discuss this issue in Chapter 6.

Corporate Income Taxes

The corporate tax structure, shown in Table 3-3, is relatively simple. To illustrate, if a firm had $75,000 of taxable income, its tax bill would be

$$\text{Taxes} = \$7,500 + 0.25(\$25,000)$$
$$= \$7,500 + \$6,250 = \$13,750,$$

and its average tax rate would be $13,750/$75,000 = 18.3\%$. Note that for all income over $335,000, one can simply calculate the corporate tax as 34 percent of all taxable income. Thus, the corporate tax is progressive up to $335,000 of income, but it is constant thereafter.[16]

---

[16]Prior to 1987, many large, profitable corporations such as General Electric and Boeing paid no income taxes. The reasons for this were as follows: (1) expenses, especially depreciation, were defined differently for calculating taxable income than for reporting earnings to stockholders, so some companies reported positive profits to stockholders but losses—hence no taxes—to the Internal Revenue Service; and (2) some companies which did have tax liabilities used various tax credits to offset taxes that would otherwise have been payable. This situation was effectively eliminated in 1987.

The principal method used to eliminate this situation is the Alternative Minimum Tax (AMT). Under the AMT, both corporate and individual taxpayers must figure their taxes in two ways, the "regular" way and the AMT way, and then pay the higher of the two. The AMT is calculated as follows: (1) Figure your regular taxes. (2) Take your taxable income under the regular method and then add back certain items, especially income on certain municipal bonds, depreciation in excess of straight line depreciation, certain research and drilling costs, itemized or standard deductions (for individuals), and a number of other items. (3) The income determined in (2) is defined as AMT income, and it must then be multiplied by the AMT tax rate (24% in 1992) to determine the tax due under the AMT system. An individual or corporation must then pay the higher of the regular tax or the AMT tax.

Table 3-3 ▪ **Corporate Tax Rates**

If a Corporation's Taxable Income Is	It Pays This Amount on the Base of the Bracket	Plus This Percentage on the Excess over the Base	Average Tax Rate at Top of Bracket
Up to $50,000	$ 0	15%	15.0%
$50,000 to $75,000	7,500	25	18.3
$75,000 to $100,000	13,750	34	22.3
$100,000 to $335,000	22,250	39	34.0
Over $335,000	113,900	34	34.0

Note:

For income in the range of $100,000 to $335,000, a surtax of 5% is added to the base rate of 34%. This surtax, which eliminates the effects of the lower rates on income below $75,000, results in a marginal tax rate of 39% for income in the $100,000 to $335,000 range.

Interest and Dividend Income Received by a Corporation.   Interest income received by a corporation is taxed as ordinary income at regular corporate tax rates. However, 70 percent of the dividends received by one corporation from another is excluded from taxable income, while the remaining 30 percent is taxed at the ordinary tax rate.[17] Thus, a corporation earning over $335,000 and paying a 34 percent marginal tax rate would pay only $(0.30)(0.34) = 0.102 = 10.2\%$ of its dividend income as taxes, so its effective tax rate on intercorporate dividends would be 10.2 percent. If this firm had $10,000 in pretax dividend income, its after-tax dividend income would be $8,980:

$$
\begin{aligned}
\text{After-tax income} &= \text{Before-tax income} - \text{Taxes} \\
&= \text{Before-tax income} - (\text{Before-tax income})(\text{Effective tax rate}) \\
&= \text{Before-tax income}(1 - \text{Effective tax rate}) \\
&= \$10,000\,[1 - (0.30)(0.34)] \\
&= \$10,000(1 - 0.102) = \$10,000(0.898) = \$8,980.
\end{aligned}
$$

If the corporation pays its own after-tax income out to its stockholders as dividends, the income is ultimately subjected to *triple taxation:* (1) the original corporation is first taxed, (2) the second corporation is then taxed on the dividends it received, and (3) the individuals who receive the final dividends are taxed again. This is the reason for the 70 percent exclusion on intercorporate dividends.

_____

[17]The size of the dividend exclusion actually depends on the degree of ownership. Corporations that own less than 20 percent of the stock of the dividend-paying company can exclude 70 percent of the dividends received; firms that own over 20 percent but less than 80 percent can exclude 80 percent of the dividends; and firms that own over 80 percent can exclude the entire dividend payment. Since most companies own less than 20 percent of other companies, we will, in general, assume a 70 percent dividend exclusion.

If a corporation has surplus funds that can be invested in marketable securities, the tax factor favors investment in stocks, which pay dividends, rather than in bonds, which pay interest. For example, suppose GE had $100,000 to invest, and it could buy either bonds that paid interest of $8,000 per year or preferred stock that paid dividends of $7,000. GE is in the 34 percent tax bracket; therefore, its tax on the interest, if it bought bonds, would be $0.34($8,000) = $2,720$, and its after-tax income would be $5,280. If it bought preferred stock, its tax would be $0.34[(0.30)($7,000)] = 714, and its after-tax income would be $6,286. Other factors might lead GE to invest in bonds, but the tax factor certainly favors stock investments when the investor is a corporation.[18]

Interest and Dividends Paid by a Corporation.   A firm's operations can be financed with either debt or equity capital. If it uses debt, it must pay interest on this debt, whereas if it uses equity, it will pay dividends to the equity investors (stockholders). The interest paid by a corporation is deducted from its operating income to obtain its taxable income, but dividends paid are not deductible. Therefore, a firm needs $1 of pretax income to pay $1 of interest, but if it is in the 40 percent federal-plus-state tax bracket, it needs $1.67 of pretax income to pay $1 of dividends:

$$\frac{\text{Pretax income needed}}{\text{to pay \$1 of dividends}} = \frac{\$1}{1 - \text{Tax rate}} = \frac{\$1}{0.60} = \$1.67.$$

To illustrate, Table 3-4 shows the situation for a firm with $1.5 million of earnings before interest and taxes (EBIT). As shown in Column 1, if the firm were financed entirely by bonds, and if it made interest payments of $1.5 million, its taxable income would be zero, taxes would be zero, and its investors would receive the entire $1.5 million. (The term *investors* includes both stockholders and bondholders.) As shown in Column 2, if the firm had no debt and was therefore financed only by stock, all of the $1.5 million of EBIT would be taxable income to the corporation, the tax would be $1,500,000(0.40) = $600,000, and investors would receive only $0.9 million versus $1.5 million under debt financing.

Of course, it is generally not possible to finance exclusively with debt capital, and the risk of doing so would offset the benefits of the higher expected income. *Still, the fact that interest is a deductible expense has a profound effect on the way businesses are financed — our tax system favors debt financing over equity financing.* This point is discussed in more detail in Chapters 16 and 17.

---

[18]This illustration demonstrates why corporations favor investing in lower-yielding preferred stocks over higher-yielding bonds. When tax consequences are considered, the yield on the preferred stock, $[1 - 0.34(0.30)](7.0\%) = 6.286\%$, is higher than the yield on the bond, $(1 - 0.34)(8.0\%) = 5.280\%$. Also, note that corporations are restricted in their use of borrowed funds to purchase other firms' preferred or common stocks. Without such restrictions, firms could engage in *tax arbitrage,* whereby the interest on borrowed funds reduces taxable income on a dollar-for-dollar basis, but taxable income is increased by only $0.30 per dollar of dividend income. Thus, current tax laws reduce the 70 percent dividend exclusion in proportion to the amount of borrowed funds used to purchase the stock.

Table 3-4   ▪   **Cash Flows to Investors under Bond and Stock Financing**

	Use Bonds (1)	Use Stock (2)
Earnings before interest and taxes (EBIT)	$1,500,000	$1,500,000
Interest	1,500,000	0
Taxable income	$ 0	$1,500,000
Federal-plus-state taxes (40%)	0	600,000
After-tax income	$ 0	$ 900,000
Income to investors	$1,500,000	$ 900,000
Advantage to bonds		$ 600,000

Corporate Capital Gains.   Before 1987, corporate long-term capital gains were taxed at lower rates than ordinary income, as is true for individuals. Under current law, however, corporations' capital gains are taxed at the same rates as their operating income.

tax loss carry-back and carry-forward
Losses that can be carried backward or forward in time to offset taxable income in a given year.

Corporate Loss Carry-Back and Carry-Forward.   Ordinary corporate operating losses can be carried back (**carry-back**) to each of the preceding 3 years and forward (**carry-forward**) for the next 15 years in the future to offset taxable income in those years. For example, an operating loss in 1993 could be carried back and used to reduce taxable income in 1990, 1991, and 1992, and forward, if necessary, and used in 1994, 1995, and so on, to the year 2008. The loss is typically applied first to the earliest year, then to the next earliest year, and so on, until losses have been used up or the 15-year carry-forward limit has been reached.

To illustrate, suppose Apex Corporation had a $2 million *pretax* profit (taxable income) in 1990, 1991, and 1992, and then, in 1993, Apex lost $12 million as shown in Table 3-5. Also, assume that Apex's tax rate is 40 percent. The company would use the carry-back feature to recompute its taxes for 1990, using $2 million of the 1993 operating losses to reduce the 1990 pretax profit to zero. This would permit it to recover the amount of taxes paid in 1990. Therefore, in 1994 Apex would receive a refund of its 1990 taxes because of the loss experienced in 1993. Because $10 million of the unrecovered losses would still be available, Apex would repeat this procedure for 1991 and 1992. Thus, in 1994 the company would pay zero taxes for 1993 and also would receive a refund for taxes paid from 1990 through 1992. Apex would still have $6 million of unrecovered losses to carry forward, subject to the 15-year limit, until the entire $12 million loss had been used to offset taxable income. The purpose of permitting this loss treatment is, of course, to avoid penalizing corporations whose incomes fluctuate substantially from year to year.

improper accumulation
Retention of earnings by a business for the purpose of enabling stockholders to avoid personal income taxes.

Improper Accumulation to Avoid Payment of Dividends.   Corporations could refrain from paying dividends to permit their stockholders to avoid personal income taxes on dividends. To prevent this, the Tax Code contains an **improper accumulation** provision which states that earnings accumulated by a corporation are subject to penalty rates *if the purpose of the accumulation*

Table 3-5 ▪ **Apex Corporation: Calculation of Loss Carry-Back and Carry-Forward for 1990–1992 Using a $12 Million 1993 Loss**

	1990	1991	1992
Original taxable income	$2,000,000	$2,000,000	$2,000,000
Carry-back credit	− 2,000,000	− 2,000,000	− 2,000,000
Adjusted profit	$ 0	$ 0	$ 0
Taxes previously paid (40%)	800,000	800,000	800,000
Difference = Tax refund	$ 800,000	$ 800,000	$ 800,000

Total refund check received in 1994: $800,000 + $800,000 + $800,000 = $2,400,000.

Amount of loss carry-forward available for use in 1994–2008:

1993 loss	$12,000,000
Carry-back losses used	6,000,000
Carry-forward losses still available	$ 6,000,000

is to enable stockholders to avoid personal income taxes. A cumulative total of $250,000 (the balance sheet item "retained earnings") is by law exempted from the improper accumulation tax for most corporations. This is a benefit primarily to small corporations.

The improper accumulation penalty applies only if the retained earnings in excess of $250,000 are *shown to be unnecessary to meet the reasonable needs of the business.* A great many companies do indeed have legitimate reasons for retaining more than $250,000 of earnings. For example, earnings may be retained and used to pay off debt, to finance growth, or to provide the corporation with a cushion against possible cash drains caused by losses. How much a firm should properly accumulate for uncertain contingencies is a matter of judgment. We shall consider this matter again in Chapter 18, which deals with corporate dividend policy.

Consolidated Corporate Tax Returns.   If a corporation owns 80 percent or more of another corporation's stock, it can aggregate income and file one consolidated tax return; thus, the losses of one company can be used to offset the profits of another. (Similarly, one division's losses can be used to offset another division's profits.) No business ever wants to incur losses (you can go broke losing $1 to save 34¢ in taxes), but tax offsets do make it more feasible for large, multidivisional corporations to undertake risky new ventures or ventures that will suffer losses during a developmental period.

Taxation of Small Businesses: S Corporations

S corporation

A small corporation which, under Subchapter S of the Internal Revenue Code, elects to be taxed as a proprietorship or a partnership yet retains limited liability and other benefits of the corporate form of organization.

The Internal Revenue Code provides that small businesses which meet certain restrictions as spelled out in the code may be set up as corporations and thus receive the benefits of the corporate form of organization—especially limited liability—yet still be taxed as proprietorships or partnerships rather than as corporations. These corporations are called **S corporations.** For a corporation that elects S corporation status for tax purposes, all of the income of the business is reported as personal income by the owners, and it is taxed at the rates that apply to individuals. This would be preferred by owners of small corporations in which all or most of the income earned each year is distributed as dividends because the income would be taxed only once at the individual level.

 Self-Test Questions

Explain what is meant by the statement: "Our tax rates are progressive."

Are tax rates progressive for all income ranges?

Explain the difference between marginal tax rates and average tax rates.

What is "bracket creep," and how did the government avoid it in the late 1980s?

What are capital gains and losses, and how are they differentiated from ordinary income?

How does the federal income tax system tax corporate dividends received by a corporation and those received by an individual? Why is this distinction made?

Briefly explain how tax loss carry-back and carry-forward procedures work.

DEPRECIATION

Depreciation plays an important role in income tax calculations. Congress specifies, in the tax code, the life over which assets can be depreciated for tax purposes and the methods of depreciation which can be used. Since these factors have a major influence on the amount of depreciation a firm can take in a given year, and thus on the firm's taxable income, depreciation has an important effect on taxes paid and cash flows from operations. We will discuss in detail how depreciation is calculated, and how it affects income and cash flows, when we take up capital budgeting in Chapters 14 and 15.

SMALL BUSINESS   Building a Banking Relationship

Building a good banking relationship is important for a small business for two reasons. The most obvious reason is that the firm may need money for working capital, expansion, equipment, and so on. A less obvious reason is that the banker may be a valuable source of financial advice for an inexperienced small-business owner. Once the bank has loaned the business money, it is in both the bank's and the business's best interest for the company to survive. Thus, a good banker will take a genuine interest in the firm and will care about how it is doing.

Even though the bank is interested in the firm's survival, it is likely to be more risk averse than the

business, because the bank shares in the firm's negative risk but not in its positive potential. If the firm fails, the entrepreneur and the bank both lose their investment. If things go well, the banker gets back only the loan money plus the interest, but the entrepreneur has the potential for huge profits. The entrepreneur, therefore, may be willing to take great risks in the hopes of great rewards, whereas the banker will want to avoid risks.

There is a possibility, then, of a conflict of interest between the banker and the entrepreneur. Because of that potential conflict, the bank will often impose restrictions on how the firm can use its revenues or profits, on how much the firm can pay the entrepreneur in salary, and so on. The bank probably will require some or all of the business's assets as collateral to safeguard the loan. The banker will be concerned about and be watchful for the one thing the entrepreneur most wants to avoid — the failure of the business. To that end, the banker will follow the firm's financial progress very closely, and that watchful eye can be of great benefit to the entrepreneur.

The 1980s saw major changes in the nature of commercial banks. As a result of innovations in financial services and of competition, a growing business today can expect to find a wider array of options than in the past. For the most part, the stereotypical image of the banker — overweight, cigar-smoking, grumpy, and stuck behind a desk — is dead. Today's bankers are generally aggressive, bright, involved, and probably belong to a health club! A small business today should be able to find a knowledgeable banker who will get involved in the business and who can offer valuable advice. But, as when buying a car, always seek out more than one offer. Exert a significant effort toward finding the *right* banker.

Finding the Right Banker.   Often the small business owner may not know how to go about finding the right banker. Looking for funds, he or she might go to the nearest bank and ask for money to fund an idea or proposal. If the bank is largely a retail bank with little expertise in commercial accounts, one of two negative events may occur:

1.   The banker may turn down the loan, failing to see that the proposal is, in fact, a good one; or

2.   The banker may make a loan that should not have been made. Then, if the project cannot return the funds, the entrepreneur might end up with worse credit than before the loan was made.

Both of these events are avoidable.

The right banker should satisfy at least three conditions: (1) The banker should understand the entrepreneur's business. (2) The banker should be interested in the business and commit to follow it closely. (3) The banker should be experienced and understand the pitfalls that wipe out small firms. In addition, the bank itself should be adequately capitalized and able to offer funds at the level the business needs, and it should also provide other services (such as cash management) that businesses need. Also, the banker and entrepreneur must have rapport. If they can't communicate candidly and easily with one another, things may go wrong that might have been avoided.

The Approach.   The first meeting between the banker and the entrepreneur should not involve a detailed discussion of the firm's financial statements. Rather, it should be a "get-acquainted" session in which the banker learns about the business and the entrepreneur learns about the bank and banker. At that first meeting, the entrepreneur should leave the business's historical financial statements with the banker for review.

By not immediately delving into problems and projections, the two parties will have an opportunity to become acquainted without pressure. Also, at such a meeting, the entrepreneur has the chance to convey the impression that he or she is in control of the business, rather than appearing excessively anxious to resolve some financial crisis.

The second meeting (if there is one) should begin with a discussion of the historical financial statements, which should then be followed by a presentation of projections. Together, the banker and entrepreneur should discuss the business's financing needs. If the banker is effective, he or she will have some suggestions for improving the projections, or perhaps he or she will anticipate some potential problems.

What the Banker Evaluates.   Bankers are trained to use the following "five Cs" when evaluating a loan proposal:

- Character
- Capacity (to manage)
- Capital
- Collateral
- Conditions

Character refers to the reputation of the firm. Will the firm try to honor the loan agreement even if difficult financial times arise? The second factor, *capacity,* is the firm's ability to repay the debt. Can the firm honor the loan agreement even in difficult times? Will sufficient cash flows be generated to service the debt?

Capital is a measure of the worth, or financial position, of the firm. *Collateral* refers to specific assets that might be pledged as security for the debt. Certain assets, such as receivables and inventory, make very good collateral for short-term debt, while other assets, such as plant and equipment, make good collateral for long-term debt. *Conditions* refer to the economic conditions expected during the time the debt is outstanding. How will the economic conditions affect the firm's ability to generate the cash needed to service the debt? Some firms are very cyclical in nature, and their cash flows fluctuate closely with the economy. For such firms, when the economy is bad, so are the cash flows generated. In the Oil Belt, for example, bankers have been reluctant to lend funds against oil revenues because such revenues have been especially unpredictable.

Tips from a Senior Loan Officer.   The senior loan officer of a large commercial bank was interviewed to obtain his point of view about establishing a banking relationship with a small business. He summarized the points he teaches new officers to consider when reviewing a proposal to grant credit.

First, he tells officers to simply ask, "Why do you need the money?" He wants to know not only how the funds will be used, but also why the company cannot generate funds itself. This is not to imply that the bank is taking the arrogant view that "We only lend money to people who don't need it." Rather, the loan officer needs to be sure that the entrepreneur understands the business well enough to know the answers.

Next, he tells junior loan officers to carefully investigate how the loan will be repaid. If the funds will come from operating cash flows, how realistic are the projections? If it is a seasonal working capital loan, what is the company's track record for managing inventories and receivables? If the business is not seasonal, is the firm sufficiently profitable to meet payments on the debt from operating profits?

Loan officers should realize that some working capital in a growing business is essentially permanent. Therefore, the next concern is whether management is truly in control of the business and whether the financing can be supported by assets.

The final question the senior loan officer asks, which is the most important of all, is: "What are your biggest problems?" A loan officer should explain that he or she isn't looking for firms that have no problems, because every firm has problems. What the banker is really trying to find out is whether the entrepreneur is

1.   perceptive, and in control of the business, and
2.   frank and candid, and willing to talk honestly about the business's problems.

The senior officer explained that a good small-business owner-manager will perceive problems. If the entrepreneur isn't aware of them, they can lead to business failure. If they are recognized, the problems perhaps can be solved. It is especially important that the entrepreneur understand all this.

Frankness is the key to success. The business owner's willingness to share concerns is viewed by the senior loan officer as the bank's greatest protection against "surprises."

Conclusion.   For a small business, a good banking relationship can mean the difference between success and failure. Establishing that relationship is important. Both sides are better off if the relationship is an open one, where the banker and the business owner understand each other and communicate honestly when dealing with the various problems of the small, but growing, firm.

SUMMARY

In this chapter we discussed the nature of financial markets, the types of institutions that operate in these markets, how interest rates are determined, some of the ways in which interest rates affect business decisions, and the Federal income tax system. The key concepts covered are listed below.

▪ There are many different types of **financial markets.** Each market serves a different region or deals with a different type of security.

▪ Transfers of capital between borrowers and savers take place (1) by **direct transfers** of money and securities; (2) by transfers through **investment banking houses,** which act as middlemen; and (3) by transfers through **financial intermediaries,** which create new securities.

▮ The **stock market** is an especially important market because this is where stock prices (which are used to "grade" managers' performances) are established.

▮ There are two basic types of stock markets—the **organized exchanges** and the **over-the-counter market.**

▮ Capital is allocated through the price system—a price must be paid to "rent" money. Lenders charge **interest** on funds they lend, while equity investors receive dividends and capital gains in return for letting firms use their money.

▮ Four fundamental factors affect the cost of money: (1) **production opportunities**, (2) **time preferences for consumption**, (3) **risk**, and (4) **inflation**.

▮ The **risk-free rate of interest, k_{RF},** is defined as the real risk-free rate, k^*, plus an inflation premium (IP): $k_{RF} = k^* + IP$.

▮ The **nominal** (or **quoted**) **interest rate** on a debt security, **k,** is composed of the real risk-free rate, k^*, plus premiums that reflect inflation (IP), default risk (DRP), liquidity (LP), and maturity risk (MRP):

$$k = k^* + IP + DRP + LP + MRP.$$

▮ If the **real risk-free rate of interest and the various premiums were constant over time,** interest rates in the economy would be stable. However, both the real rate and the premiums—especially the premium for expected inflation—**do change over time, causing market interest rates to change.** Also, Federal Reserve intervention to increase or decrease the money supply, as well as international currency flows, lead to fluctuations in interest rates.

▮ The relationship between the yields on securities and the securities' maturities is known as the **term structure of interest rates,** and the **yield curve** is a graph of this relationship.

▮ The yield curve is normally **upward sloping**—this is called a **normal yield curve**—but the curve can slope downward (an **inverted yield curve**) if the demand for short-term funds is relatively strong or if the rate of inflation is expected to decline.

▮ **Interest rate levels have a profound effect on stock prices.** Higher interest rates (1) slow down the economy, (2) increase interest expenses and thus lower corporate profits, and (3) cause investors to sell stocks and transfer funds to the bond market. Each of these factors tends to depress stock prices.

▮ Interest rate levels have a significant influence on **corporate financial policy.** Because interest rate levels are difficult if not impossible to predict, sound financial policy calls for using a mix of short- and long-term debt, and also for positioning the firm to survive in any future interest rate environment.

▮ The value of any asset depends on the stream of **after-tax cash flows** it produces. Tax rates and other aspects of our tax system are changed by Congress every year or so.

▪ In the United States, income tax rates are **progressive**—the higher one's income, the larger the percentage paid in taxes, up to a point.

▪ Assets such as stocks, bonds, and real estate are defined as **capital assets.** If a capital asset is sold for more than the purchase price, the profit is called a **capital gain.** If the capital asset is sold for a loss, it is called a **capital loss.**

▪ Operating income paid out as dividends is subject to **double taxation:** the income is first taxed at the corporate level, and then shareholders must pay personal taxes on their dividends.

▪ **Interest income** received by a corporation is taxed as **ordinary income;** however, 70 percent of the dividends received by one corporation from another are excluded from **taxable income.** The reason for this exclusion is because corporate dividend income is ultimately subjected to **triple taxation.**

▪ Because interest paid by a corporation is a **deductible** expense while dividends are not, our tax system favors debt financing over equity financing.

▪ Ordinary corporate operating losses can be **carried back** to each of the preceding 3 years and **carried forward** for the next 15 years to offset taxable income in those years.

▪ **S corporations** are small businesses which have the limited-liability benefits of the corporate form of organization yet obtain the benefits of being taxed as a partnership or a proprietorship.

▪ For a small business, a good **banking relationship** can mean the difference between success and failure. Establishing that relationship is important.

Questions

3-1   What are financial intermediaries, and what economic functions do they perform?

3-2   Suppose interest rates on residential mortgages of equal risk were 8 percent in California and 10 percent in New York. Could this differential persist? What forces might tend to equalize rates? Would differentials in borrowing costs for businesses of equal risk located in California and New York be more or less likely to exist than differentials in residential mortgage rates? Would differentials in the cost of money for New York and California firms be more likely to exist if the firms being compared were very large or if they were very small? What are the implications of all this for the pressure now being put on Congress to permit banks to engage in nationwide branching?

3-3   What would happen to the standard of living in the United States if people lost faith in the safety of our financial institutions? Why?

3-4   How does a cost-efficient capital market help to reduce the prices of goods and services?

3-5   Which fluctuate more, long-term or short-term interest rates? Why?

3-6   Suppose you believe that the economy is just entering a recession. Your firm must raise capital immediately, and debt will be used. Should you borrow on a long-term or a short-term basis? Why?

3-7   Suppose the population of Area Y is relatively young while that of Area O is relatively old, but everything else about the two areas is equal.
   a. Would interest rates likely be the same or different in the two areas? Explain.
   b. Would a trend toward nationwide branching by banks and savings and loans, and the development of nationwide diversified financial corporations, affect your answer to Part a?

3-8   Suppose a new process was developed which could be used to make oil out of seawater. The equipment required is quite expensive but it would, in time, lead to very low prices for gasoline, electricity, and other types of energy. What effect would this have on interest rates?

3-9   Suppose a new and much more liberal Congress and administration were elected, and their first order of business was to take away the independence of the Federal Reserve System and to force the Fed to greatly expand the money supply. What effect would this have
   a. On the level and slope of the yield curve immediately after the announcement?
   b. On the level and slope of the yield curve that would exist two or three years in the future?

3-10   It is a fact that the federal government (1) encouraged the development of the savings and loan industry; (2) virtually forced the industry to make long-term, fixed-interest-rate mortgages; and (3) forced the savings and loans to obtain most of their capital as deposits that were withdrawable on demand.
   a. Would the savings and loans be better off in a world with a "normal" or an inverted yield curve?
   b. Would the savings and loan industry be better off if the individual institutions sold their mortgages to federal agencies and then collected servicing fees or if the institutions held the mortgages that they originated?

3-11   Suppose interest rates on Treasury bonds rose from 7 to 14 percent as a result of higher interest rates in Europe. What effect would this have on the price of an average company's common stock?

3-12   Suppose you owned 100 shares of General Motors stock, and the company earned $6 per share during the last reporting period. Suppose further that GM could either pay all its earnings out as dividends (in which case you would receive $600) or retain the earnings in the business, buy more assets, and cause the price of the stock to go up by $6 per share (in which case the value of your stock would rise by $600).
   a. How would the tax laws influence what you, as a typical stockholder, would want the company to do?
   b. Would your choice be influenced by how much other income you had? Why might the desires of a 45-year-old doctor differ with respect to corporate dividend policy from those of a pension fund manager or a retiree living on a small income?
   c. How might the corporation's decision with regard to dividend policy influence the price of its stock?

3-13   What does *double taxation of corporate income* mean?

3-14   If you were starting a business, what tax considerations might cause you to prefer to set it up as a proprietorship or a partnership rather than as a corporation?

3-15   Explain how the federal income tax structure affects the choice of financing (use of debt versus equity) of U.S. business firms.

3-16   For someone planning to start a new business, is the average or the marginal tax rate more relevant?

Self-Test Problems   *(Solutions Appear in Appendix B)*

ST-1
Key terms

Define each of the following terms:
a. Money market; capital market
b. Primary market; secondary market
c. Investment banker; financial service corporation
d. Financial intermediary
e. Mutual fund; money market fund
f. Organized security exchanges; over-the-counter market
g. Production opportunities; time preferences for consumption
h. Real risk-free rate of interest, k*; nominal risk-free rate of interest, k_{RF}
i. Inflation premium (IP)
j. Default risk premium (DRP)
k. Liquidity; liquidity premium (LP)
l. Interest rate risk; maturity risk premium (MRP)
m. Reinvestment rate risk
n. Term structure of interest rates; yield curve
o. "Normal" yield curve; inverted ("abnormal") yield curve
p. Market segmentation theory; liquidity preference theory
q. Expectations theory
r. Progressive tax
s. Marginal and average tax rates
t. Bracket creep
u. Capital gain or loss
v. Tax loss carry-back and carry-forward
w. Improper accumulation
x. S corporation

ST-2
Inflation rates

Assume that it is now January 1, 1993. The rate of inflation is expected to be 6 percent throughout 1993. However, increased government deficits and renewed vigor in the economy are then expected to push inflation rates higher. Investors expect the inflation rate to be 7 percent in 1994, 8 percent in 1995, and 9 percent in 1996. The real risk-free rate, k*, is currently 3 percent. Assume that no maturity risk premiums are required on bonds with 5 years or less to maturity. The current interest rate on 5-year T-bonds is 11 percent.
a. What is the average expected inflation rate over the next 4 years?
b. What should be the prevailing interest rate on 4-year T-bonds?
c. What is the implied expected inflation rate in 1997, or Year 5, given that bonds which mature in that year yield 11 percent?

ST-3
Effect of form of organization on taxes

John Thompson is planning to start a new business, JT Enterprises, and he must decide whether to incorporate or to do business as a sole proprietorship. Under either form, Thompson will initially own 100 percent of the firm, and tax considerations are important to him. He plans to finance the firm's expected growth by drawing a salary just sufficient for his family living expenses, which he estimates will be about $40,000, and by retaining all other income in the business. Assume that as a married man with one child, Thompson has income tax exemptions of 3 × $2,300 = $6,900, and he estimates that his itemized deductions for each of the three years will be $8,750. He expects JT Enterprises to grow and to earn income of $60,000 in 1993, $90,000 in 1994, and $110,000 in 1995. Which form of business organization will allow Thompson to pay the lowest taxes (and retain the most income) during the period from 1993 to 1995? Assume that the tax rates given in the chapter are applicable for all future years. (Social security taxes would also have to be paid, but ignore them.)

Problems

(Note: By the time this book is published, Congress may have changed rates and/or other provisions of current tax law — as noted in the chapter, such changes occur fairly often. Work all problems on the assumption that the information in the chapter is still current.)

3-1
Yield curves

Suppose you and most other investors expect the rate of inflation to be 7 percent next year, to fall to 5 percent during the following year, and then to remain at a rate of 3 percent thereafter. Assume that the real risk-free rate, k*, is 2 percent and that maturity risk premiums on Treasury securities rise from zero on very short-term bonds (those that mature in a few days) by 0.2 percentage points for each year to maturity, up to a limit of 1.0 percentage point on 5-year or longer-term T-bonds.

a. Calculate the interest rate on 1-, 2-, 3-, 4-, 5-, 10-, and 20-year Treasury securities, and plot the yield curve.

b. Now suppose Exxon, an AAA-rated company, had bonds with the same maturities as the Treasury bonds. As an approximation, plot an Exxon yield curve on the same graph with the Treasury bond yield curve. (Hint: Think about the default risk premium on Exxon's long-term versus its short-term bonds.)

c. Now plot the approximate yield curve of Long Island Lighting Company, a risky nuclear utility.

3-2
Yield curves

The following yields on U.S. Treasury securities were taken from *The Wall Street Journal* of January 15, 1992:

Term	Rate
6 months	3.9%
1 year	4.3
2 years	5.0
3 years	5.6
4 years	6.2
5 years	6.5
10 years	7.1
20 years	7.5
30 years	7.6

Plot a yield curve based on these data. (Note: If you looked the data up in the *Journal,* you would find that some of the bonds — for example, the 3 percent issue which matures in February 1995 — will show very low yields. These are "flower bonds," which are generally owned by older people and are associated with funerals because they can be turned in and used at par value to pay estate taxes. Thus, flower bonds always sell at close to par and have a yield which is close to the coupon yield, irrespective of the "going rate of interest." "Flower" bonds no longer are issued; the last one was issued in 1971 with a coupon of 3.5 percent and a maturity of 1998. Also, the yields quoted in the *Journal* are not for the same point in time for all bonds, so random variations will appear. An interest rate series that is purged of flower bonds and random variations, and hence provides a better picture of the true yield curve, is known as the "constant maturity series"; this series can be obtained from the *Federal Reserve Bulletin.*)

3-3
Inflation and interest rates

In late 1980 the U.S. Commerce Department released new figures which showed that inflation was running at an annual rate of close to 15 percent. However, many investors expected the new Reagan administration to be more effective in controlling inflation than the Carter administration had been. At the time the prime rate of interest was 21 percent, a record high. However, many observers believed that the extremely high interest rates and generally tight credit, which resulted from the Federal Reserve System's attempts to curb the inflation rate, would shortly bring about a recession, which in turn would lead to a decline in the inflation rate and also in the rate of interest. Assume that at the beginning of 1981 the expected rate of inflation for 1981 was 13 percent; for 1982, 9 percent; for 1983, 7 percent; and for 1984 and thereafter, 6 percent.

a. What was the average expected inflation rate over the 5-year period 1981–1985? (Use the arithmetic average.)

b. What average *nominal* interest rate would, over the 5-year period, be expected to produce a 2 percent real risk-free rate of return on 5-year Treasury securities?

c. Assuming a real risk-free rate of 2 percent and a maturity risk premium which starts at 0.1 percent and increases by 0.1 percent each year, estimate the interest rate in January 1981 on bonds that mature in 1, 2, 5, 10, and 20 years, and draw a yield curve based on these data.

d. Describe the general economic conditions that could be expected to produce an upward-sloping yield curve.

e. If the consensus among investors in early 1981 had been that the expected rate of inflation for every future year was 10 percent (that is, $I_t = I_{t+1} = 10\%$ for $t = 1$ to ∞), what do you think the yield curve would have looked like? Consider all the factors that are likely to affect the curve. Does your answer here make you question the yield curve you drew in Part c?

3-4
Loss carry-back, carry-forward

The Angell Company has made $150,000 before taxes during each of the last 15 years, and it expects to make $150,000 a year before taxes in the future. However, in 1992 the firm incurred a loss of $650,000. The firm will claim a tax credit at the time it files its 1992 income tax return, and it will receive a check from the U.S. Treasury. Show how it calculates this credit, and then indicate the firm's tax liability for each of the next 5 years. Assume a 30 percent tax rate on *all* income to ease the calculations.

3-5
Loss carry-back, carry-forward

The projected taxable income of the Glasgo Corporation, formed in 1993, is indicated in the table below. (Losses are shown in parentheses.) What is the corporate tax liability for each year? Use tax rates as shown in the text.

Year	Taxable Income
1993	($ 95,000)
1994	70,000
1995	55,000
1996	80,000
1997	(150,000)

3-6
Form of organization

Kate Brown has operated her small repair shop as a sole proprietorship for several years, but projected changes in her business's income have led her to consider incorporating.

Brown is married and has two children. Her family's only income, an annual salary of $45,000, is from operating the business. (The business actually earns more than $45,000, but Kate reinvests the additional earnings in the business.) She itemizes deductions, and she is able to deduct $6,000. These deductions, combined with her four personal exemptions for $4 \times \$2,300 = \$9,200$, give her a taxable income of $45,000 − $6,000 − $9,200. (Assume the personal exemption remains at $2,300.) Of course, her actual taxable income, if she does not incorporate, would be higher by the amount of reinvested income. Brown estimates that her business earnings before salary and taxes for the period 1993 to 1995 will be:

Year	Earnings before Salary and Taxes
1993	$65,000
1994	85,000
1995	95,000

   a. What would her total taxes (corporate plus personal) be in each year under
     (1) A non-S corporate form of organization? (1993 tax = $7,470.)
     (2) A proprietorship? (1993 tax = $9,290.)
   b. Should Brown incorporate? Discuss.

3-7
Personal taxes

Margaret Considine has this situation for the year 1992: salary of $60,000; dividend income of $10,000; interest on IBM bonds of $5,000; interest on state of Florida municipal bonds of $10,000; proceeds of $22,000 from the sale of IBM stock purchased in 1984 at a cost of $9,000; and proceeds of $22,000 from the November 1992 sale of IBM stock purchased in October 1992 at a cost of $21,000. Margaret gets one exemption ($2,300), and she has allowable itemized deductions of $5,000; these amounts will be deducted from her gross income to determine her taxable income.

   a. What is Margaret's federal tax liability for 1992?
   b. What are her marginal and average tax rates?
   c. If she had some money to invest and was offered a choice of either state of Florida bonds with a yield of 9 percent or more IBM bonds with a yield of 11 percent, which should she choose, and why?
   d. At what marginal tax rate would Margaret be indifferent in her choice between the Florida and IBM bonds?

EXAM-TYPE PROBLEMS

The problems included in this section are set up in such a way that they could be used as multiple-choice exam problems.

3-8
Expected rate
of interest

Suppose the annual yield on a 2-year Treasury bond is 11.5 percent, while that on a 1-year bond is 10 percent. k* is 3%, and the maturity risk premium is zero.

   a. Using the expectations theory, forecast the interest rate on a 1-year bond during the second year. (Hint: Under the expectations theory, the yield on a 2-year bond is equal to the average yield on 1-year bonds in Years 1 and 2.)
   b. What is the expected inflation rate in Year 1? Year 2?

3-9
Expected rate
of interest

Assume that the real risk-free rate is 4 percent and that the maturity risk premium is zero. If the nominal rate of interest on 1-year bonds is 11 percent and that on comparable-risk 2-year bonds is 13 percent, what is the 1-year interest rate that is expected for Year 2? What inflation rate is expected during Year 2? Comment on why the average interest rate during the 2-year period differs from the 1-year interest rate expected for Year 2.

3-10
Corporate tax
liability

The Zocco Corporation had a 1992 taxable income of $365,000 from operations after all operating costs but before (1) interest charges of $50,000, (2) dividends received of $15,000, (3) dividends paid of $25,000, and (4) income taxes. What is the firm's income tax liability and its after-tax income? What are the company's marginal and average tax rates on taxable income?

3-11
Corporate tax
liability

The Schweser Corporation had $200,000 of taxable income from operations in 1992.
   a. What is the company's federal income tax bill for the year?
   b. Assume the firm receives an additional $40,000 of interest income from some bonds it owns. What is the tax on this interest income?

c. Now assume that Schweser does not receive the interest income but does receive an additional $40,000 as dividends on some stock it owns. What is the tax on this dividend income?

3-12
Maturity risk premium

Assume that the real risk-free rate, k*, is 3 percent and that inflation is expected to be 8% in Year 1, 5% in Year 2, and 4% thereafter. Assume also that all Treasury bonds are highly liquid and free of default risk. If 2-year and 5-year Treasury bonds both yield 10%, what is the difference in the maturity risk premiums (MRPs) on the two bonds, i.e., what is MRP_5 minus MRP_2?

3-13
After-tax yield

Carver Corporation has $10,000 which it plans to invest in marketable securities. It is choosing between AT&T bonds, which yield 11%, state of Florida muni bonds, which yield 8%, and AT&T preferred stock, with a dividend yield of 9%. Carver's corporate tax rate is 20%, and 70% of the dividends received are tax exempt. Assuming that the investments are equally risky and that Carver chooses strictly on the basis of after-tax returns, which security should be selected? What is the after-tax rate of return on the highest yielding security?

3-14
Interest rates

Due to the recession, the rate of inflation expected for the coming year is only 3 percent. However, the rate of inflation in Year 2 and thereafter is expected to be constant at some level above 3 percent. Assume that the real risk-free rate is k* = 2% for all maturities and that the expectations theory fully explains the yield curve, so there are no maturity premiums. If 3-year Treasury bonds yield 2 percentage points more than 1-year bonds, what rate of inflation is expected after Year 1?

INTEGRATIVE PROBLEM

3-15
Financial markets, institutions, and taxes

Assume that you recently graduated with a degree in finance and have just reported to work as an investment advisor at the firm of Balik and Kiefer Inc. Your first assignment is to explain the nature of the U.S. financial markets and institutions to Michelle Dela-Torre, a professional tennis player who has just come to the United States from Chile. DelaTorre is a highly ranked tennis player who expects to invest substantial amounts of money through Balik and Kiefer. She is also very bright, and, therefore, she would like to understand in general terms what will happen to her money. Your boss has developed the following set of questions, which you must ask and answer to explain the U.S. financial system to DelaTorre.

a. What is a financial market? How are financial markets differentiated from markets for physical assets?

b. Differentiate between money markets and capital markets.

c. Differentiate between a primary market and a secondary market. If Apple Computer decided to issue additional common stock, and DelaTorre purchased 100 shares of this stock from Merrill Lynch, the underwriter, would this transaction be a primary market transaction or a secondary market transaction? Would it make a difference if DelaTorre purchased previously outstanding Apple stock in the over-the-counter market?

d. Describe the three primary ways in which capital is transferred between savers and borrowers.

e. Securities can be traded on organized exchanges or in the over-the-counter market. Define each of these markets, and describe how stocks are traded in each of them.

f. What do we call the price that a borrower must pay for debt capital? What is the price of equity capital? What are the four most fundamental factors that affect the cost of money, or the general level of interest rates, in the economy?

g. What is the real risk-free rate of interest (k*) and the nominal risk-free rate (k_{RF})? How are these two rates measured?

h. Define the terms inflation premium (IP), default risk premium (DRP), liquidity premium (LP), and maturity risk premium (MRP). Which of these premiums is included when determining the interest rate on (1) short-term U.S. Treasury securities, (2) long-term U.S. Treasury securities, (3) short-term corporate securities, and (4) long-term corporate securities? Explain how the premiums would vary over time and among the different securities listed above.

i. What is the term structure of interest rates? What is a yield curve? At any given time, how would the yield curve facing a given company such as AT&T or Chrysler (whose bonds are classified as "junk bonds") compare with the yield curve for U.S. Treasury securities? Draw a graph to illustrate your answer.

j. Several theories have been advanced to explain the shape of the yield curve. The three major ones are (1) the market segmentation theory, (2) the liquidity preference theory, and (3) the expectations theory. Briefly describe each of these theories. Do economists regard one as being "true"?

k. Suppose most investors expect the rate of inflation to be 5 percent next year, 6 percent the following year, and 8 percent thereafter. The real risk-free rate is 3 percent. The maturity risk premium is zero for bonds that mature in 1 year or less, 0.1 percent for 2-year bonds, and the MRP increases by 0.1 percent per year thereafter for 20 years, after which it is stable. What is the interest rate on 1-year, 10-year, and 20-year Treasury bonds? Draw a yield curve with these data. Is your yield curve consistent with the three term structure theories?

l. Working with DelaTorre has required you to put in a lot of overtime, so you have had very little time to spend on your private finances. It's now April 1, and you have only two weeks left to file your income tax return. You have managed to get all the information together that you will need to complete your return. Balik and Kiefer Inc. paid you a salary of $45,000, and you received $3,000 in dividends from common stock that you own. You are single, so your personal exemption is $2,300, and your itemized deductions are $4,650.

    (1) On the basis of the information above and the 1992 individual tax rate schedule, what is your tax liability?

    (2) What are your marginal and average tax rates?

m. Assume that a corporation has $100,000 of taxable income from operations plus $5,000 of interest income and $10,000 of dividend income. What is the company's tax liability?

n. Assume that after paying your personal income tax, as calculated in Part l, you have $5,000 to invest. You have narrowed your investment choice down to California bonds with a yield of 7 percent or IBM bonds with a yield of 10 percent. Which one should you choose, and why? At what marginal tax rate would you be indifferent to the choice between California and IBM bonds?

COMPUTER-RELATED PROBLEM

Work the problem in this section only if you are using the computer problem diskette.

3-16
Effect of form of organization on taxes

The problem requires you to rework Problem 3-6, using the data given below. Use File C3 on the computer problem diskette.

a. Suppose Brown decides to pay out (1) 50 percent or (2) 100 percent of the after-salary corporate income in each year as dividends. Would such dividend policy changes affect her decision about whether or not to incorporate?

b. Suppose business improves, and actual earnings before salary and taxes in each year are twice the original estimate. Assume that if Brown chooses to incorporate she will continue to receive a salary of $45,000 and to reinvest additional earnings in the business. (No dividends would be paid.) What would be the effect of this increase in business income on Brown's decision to incorporate or not incorporate?

P A R T

II

Essential Concepts in Managerial Finance

Chapter 4   Risk and Rates of Return

     Appendix 4A   **Calculating Beta Coefficients**

Chapter 5   Time Value of Money

     Appendix 5A   **Continuous Compounding and Discounting**

Chapter 6   Bond and Stock Valuation

Risk and Rates of Return

A MANAGERIAL PERSPECTIVE

For an individual, watching savings grow and deciding how to invest them can be very satisfying, but it can also entail a lot of anxiety, so most people study past returns and strategies to best position themselves for the future. They know that well-diversified portfolios — those containing a mix of bonds, stocks, Treasury bills, money funds, and other types of investments — are less risky than nondiversified portfolios. Furthermore, studies show that by holding portfolios investors can reduce risk without sacrificing very much return. The question is, What mix should each individual choose to achieve this goal in the future?

Laurence B. Siegel, managing director of Ibbotson Associates Inc., an investment research firm based in Chicago, suggests that if you have a long time horizon — that is, if you are sure you will not need to liquidate your investments for cash for many years — and are interested in making the most money possible, you should invest 100 percent in stocks. However, most people are unsure of their time horizons, and for these individuals, Siegel advises that a "diversified mix of U.S. and international stocks, bonds, and other assets — certainly including real estate — is a better approach."

Depending on the time horizon and the types of investments chosen, returns can vary greatly. For most of the 1980s, stocks were the investment to own because they generally offered the highest returns, but the 1990s have also shown how volatile stock prices can be. Bonds have long been perceived as being much safer than stocks, but that perception has changed in the last 10 years. Investment advisers now say that a bond portfolio can be just as risky, and occasionally riskier, than an all-stock portfolio because in a period of rising inflation, and subsequently rising interest rates, bond prices fall, while stocks are a better hedge against inflation. Data provided by Shearson Lehman Hutton, a leading brokerage firm, show that total annual returns on government and corporate bonds during the 1980s ranged from a low of 2.29 percent in 1987 to a high of 31.09 percent in 1982.

Many investors hedge their portfolios by including some near-cash investments such as Treasury bills or money-market mutual funds. According to one consulting firm, an "ideal" investment portfolio for most individuals would contain 60 percent stocks, 35 percent bonds, and 5 percent cash. Such a strategy would have produced an average annual return of 9.4 percent, with relatively little volatility, if it had been started in 1966.

A lesson learned from the 1980s is that foreign stocks should be included in diversified portfolios. During that time, foreign stocks performed better than any other asset group, and many investment managers predict that the 1990s will be the "Decade of Europe and Asia." Unfortunately, it is more difficult for American investors to become knowledgeable about foreign stocks, and currency exchange rates may affect returns.

One simple diversification strategy that has worked well during the past few decades is the "fixed-mix" approach, which involves holding equal percentages of five types of investments: U.S. stocks, bonds, real estate, and near-cash, and foreign stocks. The actual investing can be done through no-load mutual funds, which would reduce transactions costs while obtaining expert diversification within each of the five sectors. At the end of each year, the investor should adjust his or her holdings so they are again evenly balanced among the five groups, although this is likely to involve selling holdings that have done well enough to increase as a percentage of the portfolio and buying kinds of securities that have not done as well, which can be psychologically difficult. However, according to one investment advisor, one should think of portfolio rebalancing as buying an all-risk insurance policy, for, if used over the past 25 years, this strategy would have had an average annual return of approximately 10.5 percent as compared with 10.1 percent for the Standard & Poor's 500, and with less risk.

Critics of the fixed-mix approach say it is mechanistic, lazy, and "dangerous to your wealth." They have likened it to a pilot's putting the airplane on automatic pilot and leaving it on, even when a big storm is approaching. Another criticism of this approach is that it forces investors to put large sums of their money into areas they know very little about. However, proponents of the technique argue that investors who use it do not need to "time the market," which is extraordinarily difficult, and that, by using mutual funds, they do not need to be experts on the securities in each sector.

As times change, strategies and portfolio mixes may need to be changed to meet new situations, but it is important for you to understand the basic concepts of risk and return and the ways a portfolio can reduce risk without reducing your return. After reading this chapter, you should have a better understanding of the risk and return concepts discussed above.

Source: "What's Wall Street's First Rule? Diversify," *The Wall Street Journal*, January 25, 1990, and other publications.

In this chapter we take an in-depth look at how investment risk should be measured and how it affects security prices and rates of return. Recall that in Chapter 3, when we examined the determinants of interest rates, we defined the real risk-free rate, k*, to be the rate of interest on a risk-free security in the absence of inflation. The actual interest rate on a particular debt security was shown to be equal to the real risk-free rate plus several premiums which reflect both inflation and the riskiness of the security in question. In this chapter we define more precisely what the term *risk* means as it relates to securities, we examine procedures managers use for measuring risk, and we discuss the relationship between risk and return. Then, in Chapters 5 and 6, we extend these relationships to show how they interact to determine security prices in the financial markets. Business executives should understand these concepts and use them as they plan the actions which will shape their firms' futures.

We will demonstrate in this chapter that each investment — each stock, bond, or physical asset — has two different types of risk: (1) *diversifiable risk* and (2) *nondiversifiable risk.* The sum of these two components is the investment's *total risk.* Diversifiable risk is not important to rational, informed investors, because they will eliminate its effects by diversifying it away. The really significant risk is nondiversifiable risk — this risk is bad in the sense that it cannot be eliminated, and if you invest in anything other than riskless assets such as short-term Treasury bills, you will be exposed to it. In the balance of the chapter we will explain these risk concepts and show you how risk enters into the decision process.

DEFINING AND MEASURING RISK

risk

The chance that some unfavorable event will occur.

Risk is defined in *Webster's* as "a hazard; a peril; exposure to loss or injury." Thus, risk refers to the chance that some unfavorable event will occur. If you engage in skydiving, you are taking a chance with your life — skydiving is risky. If you bet on the horses, you are risking your money. If you invest in speculative stocks (or, really, *any* stock), you are taking a risk in the hope of making an appreciable return.

To illustrate the riskiness of financial assets, suppose an investor buys $100,000 of short-term government bonds with an expected return of 10 percent. In this case, the rate of return on the investment, 10 percent, can be estimated quite precisely, and the investment is defined as being risk-free. However, if the $100,000 were invested in the stock of a company just being organized to prospect for oil in the mid-Atlantic, then the investment's return could not be estimated precisely. One might analyze the situation and conclude that the *expected* rate of return, in a statistical sense, is 20 percent, but the investor should also recognize that the *actual* rate of return could range from, say, +1,000 percent to −100 percent. Because there is a significant danger of actually earning considerably less than the expected return, the stock would be described as being relatively risky.

Investment risk, then, is related to the probability of actually earning less than the expected return—the greater the chance of low or negative returns, the riskier the investment. However, we can define risk more precisely, and it is useful to do so.

Probability Distributions

An event's *probability* is defined as the chance that the event will occur. For example, a weather forecaster might state, "There is a 40 percent chance of rain today and a 60 percent chance that it will not rain." If all possible events, or outcomes, are listed, and if a probability is assigned to each event, the listing is called a **probability distribution.** For our weather forecast, we could set up the following probability distribution:

probability distribution

A listing of all possible outcomes, or events, with a probability (chance of occurrence) assigned to each outcome.

Outcome (1)	Probability (2)
Rain	0.4 = 40%
No rain	0.6 = 60
	1.0 = 100%

The possible outcomes are listed in Column 1, while the probabilities of these outcomes, expressed both as decimals and as percentages, are given in Column 2. Notice that the probabilities must sum to 1.0, or 100 percent.

Probabilities can also be assigned to the possible outcomes (or returns) from an investment. If you buy a bond, you expect to receive interest on the bond, and those interest payments will provide you with a rate of return on your investment. The possible outcomes from this investment are (1) that the issuer will make the interest payments or (2) that the issuer will fail to make the interest payments. The higher the probability of default on the interest payments, the riskier the bond, and the higher the risk, the higher your required rate of return on the bond. If instead of buying a bond you invest in a stock, you will again expect to earn a return on your money. A stock's return will come from dividends plus capital gains. Again, the riskier the stock—which means the higher the probability that the firm will fail to pay expected dividends or that the stock price will not increase as much as you expected—the higher the expected return must be to induce you to invest in it.

Table 4-1   ▪   **Probability Distributions for Martin Products and U.S. Electric**

State of the Economy	Probability of This State Occurring	Rate of Return on Stock if This State Occurs	
		Martin Products	U.S. Electric
Boom	0.3	100%	20%
Normal	0.4	15	15
Recession	0.3	(70)	10
	1.0		

With this in mind, consider the possible rates of return (dividend yield plus capital gain or loss) that you might earn next year on a $10,000 investment in the stock of either Martin Products Inc. or U.S. Electric Company. Martin manufactures and distributes computer terminals and equipment for the rapidly growing data transmission industry. Because its sales are cyclical, its profits rise and fall with the business cycle. Further, its market is extremely competitive, and some new company could develop better products which could literally bankrupt Martin. U.S. Electric, on the other hand, supplies an essential service, and because it has city franchises which protect it from competition, its sales and profits are relatively stable and predictable.

The rate-of-return probability distributions for the two companies are shown in Table 4-1. Here we see that there is a 30 percent chance of a boom, in which case both companies will have high earnings, pay high dividends, and enjoy capital gains; there is a 40 percent probability of a normal economy and moderate returns; and there is a 30 percent probability of a recession, which will mean low earnings and dividends as well as capital losses. Notice, however, that Martin Products' rate of return could vary far more widely than that of U.S. Electric. There is a fairly high probability that the value of Martin's stock will drop substantially, resulting in a loss of 70 percent, while there is no chance of a loss for U.S. Electric.[1]

 Self-Test Questions

What does "investment risk" mean?

Set up illustrative probability distributions for (1) a bond investment and (2) a stock investment.

EXPECTED RATE OF RETURN

If we multiply each possible outcome by its probability of occurrence and then sum these products, as in Table 4-2, we have a *weighted average* of outcomes.

---

[1]It is, of course, completely unrealistic to think that any stock has no chance of a loss. Only in hypothetical examples could this occur. To illustrate, the price of Columbia Gas's stock dropped from $34.50 to $20.00 in just three hours on June 19, 1991. All investors were reminded that any stock is exposed to some risk of loss, and those investors who bought Columbia Gas learned this lesson the hard way.

Table 4-2 ▪ **Calculation of Expected Rates of Return: Payoff Matrix**

State of the Economy (1)	Probability of This State Occurring (2)	Martin Products Rate of Return If This State Occurs (3)	Product: (2) × (3) = (4)	U.S. Electric Rate of Return If This State Occurs (5)	Product: (2) × (5) = (6)
Boom	0.3	100%	30%	20%	6%
Normal	0.4	15	6	15	6
Recession	0.3	(70)	(21)	10	3
	1.0		$\hat{k}$ = 15%		$\hat{k}$ = 15%

expected rate of return, k̂

The rate of return expected to be realized from an investment; the mean value of the probability distribution of possible results.

The weights are the probabilities, and the weighted average is the **expected rate of return, k̂,** called "k-hat."[2] The expected rates of return for both Martin Products and U.S. Electric are shown in Table 4-2 to be 15 percent. This type of table is known as a *payoff matrix.*

The expected rate of return calculation can also be expressed as an equation which does the same thing as the payoff matrix table:[3]

$$\text{Expected rate of return} = \hat{k} = P_1k_1 + P_2k_2 + \cdots + P_nk_n$$

$$= \sum_{i=1}^{n} P_ik_i. \qquad (4\text{-}1)$$

Here k_i is the *i*th possible outcome, P_i is the probability of the *i*th outcome, and n is the number of possible outcomes. Thus, $\hat{k}$ is a weighted average of the possible outcomes (the k_i values), with each outcome's weight being its probability of occurrence. Using the data for Martin Products, we obtain its expected rate of return as follows:

$$\hat{k} = P_1(k_1) + P_2(k_2) + P_3(k_3)$$
$$= 0.3(100\%) + 0.4(15\%) + 0.3(-70\%)$$
$$= 15\%.$$

U.S. Electric's expected rate of return is also 15 percent:

$$\hat{k} = 0.3(20\%) + 0.4(15\%) + 0.3(10\%)$$
$$= 15\%.$$

---

[2]In Chapter 6, we will use k_d to signify the return on a debt instrument and k_s to signify the return on a stock. In this section, however, we discuss only returns on stocks; thus, the subscript s is unnecessary, and we use the term $\hat{k}$ rather than $\hat{k}_s$.

[3]The second form of the equation is simply a shorthand expression in which sigma (Σ) means "sum up," or add the values of n factors. If i = 1, then $P_ik_i = P_1k_1$; if i = 2, then $P_ik_i = P_2k_2$; and so on until i = n, the last possible outcome. The symbol $\sum_{i=1}^{n}$ simply says, "Go through the following process: First, let i = 1 and find the first product; then let i = 2 and find the second product; then continue until each individual product up to i = n has been found, and then add these individual products to find the expected rate of return."

Figure 4-1   ▪   **Probability Distributions of Martin Products' and U.S. Electric's Rates of Return**

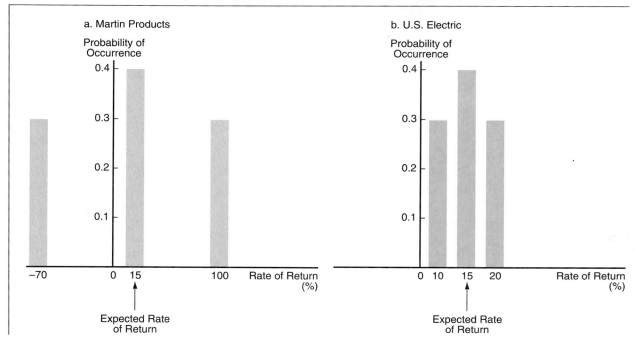

We can graph the rates of return to obtain a picture of the variability of possible outcomes; this is shown in the Figure 4-1 bar charts. The height of each bar signifies the probability that a given outcome will occur. The range of probable returns for Martin Products is from + 100 to − 70 percent, with an expected return of 15 percent. The expected return for U.S. Electric is also 15 percent, but its range is much narrower.

Continuous Probability Distributions

Thus far we have assumed that only three states of the economy can exist: recession, normal, and boom. Actually, of course, the state of the economy could range from a deep depression to a fantastic boom, and there are an unlimited number of possibilities in between. Suppose we had the time and patience to assign a probability to each possible state of the economy (with the sum of the probabilities still equaling 1.0), and to assign a rate of return to each stock for each state of the economy. We would have a table similar to Table 4-2, except that it would have many more entries in each column. This table could be used to calculate expected rates of return as shown previously, and the probabilities and outcomes could be approximated by continuous curves such as those presented in Figure 4-2. Here we have changed the assumptions so that there is essentially a zero probability that Martin Products' return will be less than − 70 percent or more than 100 percent, or that U.S. Electric's return will be less than 10 percent or more than 20 percent, but virtually any return within these limits is possible.

Figure 4-2 ▪ **Continuous Probability Distributions of Martin Products' and U.S. Electric's Rates of Return**

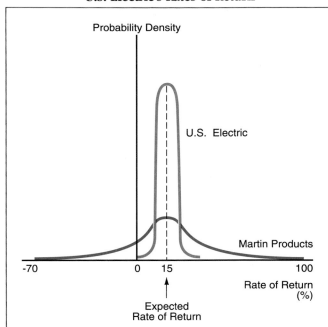

Note: The assumptions regarding the probabilities of various outcomes have been changed from those in Figure 4-1. There the probability of obtaining exactly 15 percent was 40 percent; here it is *much smaller*, because there are many possible outcomes instead of just three. With continuous distributions, it is more appropriate to ask what the probability is of obtaining at least some specified rate of return than to ask what the probability is of obtaining exactly that rate. This topic is covered in detail in statistics courses.

The tighter, or more peaked, the probability distribution, the more likely it is that the actual outcome will be close to the expected value, and, consequently, the less likely it is that the actual return will end up far below the expected return. Thus, the tighter the probability distribution, the lower the risk assigned to a stock. Since U.S. Electric has a relatively tight probability distribution, its *actual return* is likely to be closer to its 15 percent *expected return* than is that of Martin Products.

Measuring Risk: The Standard Deviation

Risk is a difficult concept to grasp, and a great deal of controversy has surrounded attempts to define and measure it. However, a common definition, and one that is satisfactory for many purposes, is stated in terms of probability distributions such as those presented in Figure 4-2: *The tighter the probability distribution of expected future returns, the smaller the risk of a given investment.* According to this definition, U.S. Electric is less risky than Martin Products, because there is a smaller chance that the actual return will end up far below the expected return for U.S. Electric than for Martin Products.

To be most useful, any measure of risk should have a definite value—we need a measure of the tightness of the probability distribution. One such mea-

Table 4-3 ▪ **Calculating Martin Products' Standard Deviation**

$k_i - \hat{k}$ (1)		$(k_i - \hat{k})^2$ (2)	$(k_i - \hat{k})^2 P_i$ (3)
$100 - 15 =$	85	$7{,}225$	$(7{,}225)(0.3) = 2{,}167.5$
$15 - 15 =$	0	0	$(0)(0.4) = 0.0$
$-70 - 15 =$	-85	$7{,}225$	$(7{,}225)(0.3) = \underline{2{,}167.5}$
			Variance $= \sigma^2 = \underline{4{,}335.0}$

$$\text{Standard deviation} = \sigma = \sqrt{\sigma^2} = \sqrt{4{,}335} = 65.84\%.$$

standard deviation, σ

A statistical measure of the variability of a set of observations.

sure is the **standard deviation,** the symbol for which is **σ,** pronounced "sigma." The smaller the standard deviation, the tighter the probability distribution, and, accordingly, the lower the riskiness of the stock. To calculate the standard deviation, we proceed as shown in Table 4-3, taking the following steps:

1. We calculate the expected rate of return:

$$\text{Expected rate of return} = \hat{k} = \sum_{i=1}^{n} P_i k_i.$$

For Martin, we previously found $\hat{k} = 15\%$.

2. In Column 1 of Table 4-3, we subtract the expected rate of return $(\hat{k})$ from each possible outcome (k_i) to obtain a set of deviations about $\hat{k}$:

$$\text{Deviation}_i = k_i - \hat{k}.$$

3. In Columns 2 and 3 of the table, we square each deviation, then multiply the result by the probability of occurrence for its related outcome, and then sum these products to obtain the **variance** of the probability distribution:

variance, σ²

The square of the standard deviation.

$$\text{Variance} = \sigma^2 = \sum_{i=1}^{n} (k_i - \hat{k})^2 P_i. \tag{4-2}$$

4. Finally, we take the square root of the variance to obtain the standard deviation:

$$\text{Standard deviation} = \sigma = \sqrt{\sum_{i=1}^{n} (k_i - \hat{k})^2 P_i}. \tag{4-3}$$

Thus, the standard deviation is a probability-weighted average deviation from the expected value, and it provides an idea of how far above or below the expected value the actual value is likely to be. Martin's standard deviation is seen in Table 4-3 to be $\sigma = 65.84\%$, and using these same procedures, we find U.S. Electric's standard deviation to be 3.87 percent. The larger standard deviation of Martin Products indicates a greater variation of returns, thus a greater chance that the expected return will not be realized; therefore, Martin Products would be considered a riskier investment than U.S. Electric, according to this measure of risk.

If a probability distribution is normal, the *actual* return will be within ± 1 standard deviation of the *expected* return 68.26 percent of the time. Figure 4-3 illustrates this point, and it also shows the situation for $\pm 2\sigma$ and $\pm 3\sigma$. For Martin Products, $\hat{k} = 15\%$ and $\sigma = 65.84\%$, whereas $\hat{k} = 15\%$ and $\sigma = 3.87\%$ for U.S. Electric. Thus, there is a 68.26 percent probability that the actual return for Martin Products will be in the range of 15 ± 65.84 percent, or from -50.84 to 80.84 percent. For U.S. Electric, the 68.26 percent range is 15 ± 3.87 percent, or from 11.13 to 18.87 percent. With such a small σ, there is only a small probability that U.S. Electric's return will be significantly less than expected, so the stock is not very risky. For the average firm listed on the New York Stock Exchange, σ has been close to 30 percent in recent years.[4]

Another useful measure of risk is the **coefficient of variation (CV),** which is the standard deviation divided by the expected return:

coefficient of variation (CV)

Standardized measure of the risk per unit of return; calculated as the standard deviation divided by the expected return.

$$\text{Coefficient of variation} = \text{CV} = \frac{\sigma}{\hat{k}}. \qquad (4\text{-}4)$$

The coefficient of variation shows the risk per unit of return, and it provides a more meaningful basis for comparison when the expected returns on two alter-

---

[4]In the example we described the procedure for finding the mean and standard deviation when the data are in the form of a known probability distribution. If only sample returns data over some past period are available, the standard deviation of returns can be estimated using this formula:

$$\text{Estimated } \sigma = S = \sqrt{\frac{\sum_{t=1}^{n} (\bar{k}_t - \bar{k}_{Avg})^2}{n - 1}}. \qquad (4\text{-}3a)$$

Here $\bar{k}_t$ ("k bar t") denotes the past realized rate of return in Period t, and $\bar{k}_{Avg}$ is the average annual return earned during the last n years. Here is an example:

Year	$\bar{k}_t$
1990	15%
1991	-5
1992	20

$$\bar{k}_{Avg} = \frac{(15 - 5 + 20)}{3} = 10.0\%.$$

$$\text{Estimated } \sigma \text{ (or S)} = \sqrt{\frac{(15 - 10)^2 + (-5 - 10)^2 + (20 - 10)^2}{3 - 1}}$$

$$= \sqrt{\frac{350}{2}} = 13.2\%.$$

The historical σ is often used as an estimate of the future σ. Much less often, and generally incorrectly, $\bar{k}_{Avg}$ for some past period is used as an estimate of $\hat{k}$, the expected future return. Because past variability is likely to be repeated, σ may be a good estimate of future risk, but it is much less reasonable to expect that the past *level* of return (which could have been as high as $+100\%$ or as low as -50%) is the best expectation of what investors think will happen in the future.

Figure 4-3 ▪ **Probability Ranges for a Normal Distribution**

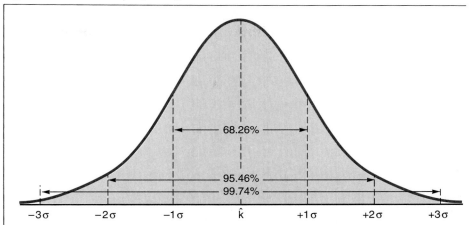

Notes:

a. The area under the normal curve equals 1.0, or 100 percent. *Thus, the areas under any pair of normal curves drawn on the same scale, whether they are peaked or flat, must be equal.*

b. Half of the area under a normal curve is to the left of the mean, indicating that there is a 50 percent probability that the actual outcome will be less than the mean, and half is to the right of $\hat{k}$, indicating a 50 percent probability that it will be greater than the mean.

c. Of the area under the curve, 68.26 percent is within $\pm 1\sigma$ of the mean, indicating that the probability is 68.26 percent that the actual outcome will be within the range $\hat{k} - 1\sigma$ to $\hat{k} + 1\sigma$.

d. Procedures exist for finding the probability of other ranges. These procedures are covered in statistics courses.

e. For a normal distribution, the larger the value of σ, the greater the probability that the actual outcome will vary widely from, and hence perhaps be far below, the expected, or most likely, outcome. *Since the probability of having the actual result turn out to be far below the expected result is one definition of risk, and since σ measures this probability, we can use σ as a measure of risk.* This definition may not be a good one, however, if we are dealing with an asset held in a diversified portfolio. This point is covered later in the chapter.

natives are not the same. Since U.S. Electric and Martin Products have the same expected return, the coefficient of variation is not really necessary in this case. The firm with the larger standard deviation, Martin, must have the larger coefficient of variation when the means are equal. In fact, the coefficient of variation for Martin is 65.84/15 = 4.39 and that for U.S. Electric is 3.87/15 = 0.26. Thus, Martin is almost 17 times riskier than U.S. Electric on the basis of this criterion.

For a case where the coefficient of variation is necessary, consider two projects, X and Y, which have different expected rates of return and different standard deviations. Project X has a 45 percent expected rate of return and a 15 percent standard deviation, while Project Y has an 8 percent expected return and a 4 percent standard deviation. Is Project X riskier, on a relative basis, because it has the larger standard deviation? If we calculate the coefficients of variation for these two projects, we find that Project X has a coefficient of variation of 15/45 = 0.33, and Project Y has a coefficient of variation of 4/8 = 0.50. Thus, we see that Project Y actually has more risk per unit of return than Project X, in spite of the fact that X's standard deviation is larger. Therefore, even though Project Y has the lower standard deviation, according to the coefficient

Figure 4-4 ▪ **Comparison of Probability Distributions
and Rates of Return for Projects X and Y**

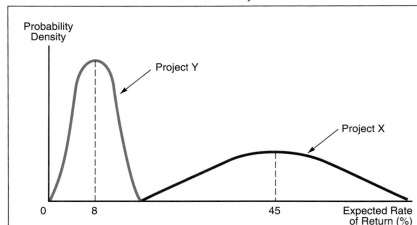

of variation measure it is not preferred because its risk/return relationship is not as favorable as that of Project X.

The situation with Projects X and Y is graphed in Figure 4-4. Project Y has the smaller standard deviation, hence the more peaked probability distribution, but it is clear from the graph that the chances of a really low return are higher for Y than for X, because X's expected return is so high. Because the coefficient of variation captures the effects of both risk and return, it is a better measure for evaluating risk in situations where investments differ with respect to both their amounts of total risk and their expected returns.

Risk Aversion and Required Returns

Suppose you have worked hard and saved $1 million, which you now plan to invest. You can buy a 10 percent U.S. Treasury note, and at the end of 1 year you will have a sure $1.1 million, which is your original investment plus $100,000 in interest. Alternatively, you can buy stock in R&D Enterprises. If R&D's research programs are successful, your stock will increase in value to $2.2 million; however, if the research is a failure, the value of your stock will go to zero, and you will be penniless. You regard R&D's chances of success or failure as being 50-50, so the expected value of the stock investment is $0.5(\$0) + 0.5(\$2,200,000) = \$1,100,000$. Subtracting the $1 million cost of the stock leaves an expected profit of $100,000, or an expected (but risky) 10 percent rate of return:

$$\begin{aligned} \text{Expected rate} \atop \text{of return} &= \frac{\text{Expected ending value} - \text{Cost}}{\text{Cost}} \\ &= \frac{\$1,100,000 - \$1,000,000}{\$1,000,000} \\ &= \frac{\$100,000}{\$1,000,000} = 10\%. \end{aligned}$$

risk aversion

Risk-averse investors require higher rates of return on higher-risk securities.

Thus, you have a choice between a sure $100,000 profit (representing a 10 percent rate of return) on the Treasury note and a risky expected $100,000 profit (also representing a 10 percent expected rate of return) on the R&D Enterprises stock. Which one would you choose? *If you choose the less risky investment, you are risk averse. Most investors are indeed risk averse, and certainly the average investor is risk averse, at least with regard to his or her "serious money." Because this is a well-documented fact, we shall assume* **risk aversion** *throughout the remainder of the book.*

What are the implications of risk aversion for security prices and rates of return? The answer is that, other things held constant, the higher a security's risk, the lower its price and the higher its required return. To see how risk aversion affects security prices, we can analyze the situation with U.S. Electric and Martin Products stocks. Suppose each stock sold for $100 per share and each had an expected rate of return of 15 percent. Investors are averse to risk, so there would be a general preference for U.S. Electric. People with money to invest would bid for U.S. Electric rather than Martin stock, and Martin's stockholders would start selling their stock and using the money to buy U.S. Electric stock. Buying pressure would drive up the price of U.S. Electric's stock, and selling pressure would simultaneously cause Martin's price to decline.

These price changes, in turn, would cause changes in the expected rates of return on the two securities. Suppose, for example, that the price of U.S. Electric stock was bid up from $100 to $150, whereas the price of Martin's stock declined from $100 to $75. This would cause U.S. Electric's expected return to fall to 10 percent, while Martin's expected return would rise to 20 percent. The difference in returns, 20% − 10% = 10%, is a **risk premium, RP,** which represents the compensation investors require for assuming the additional risk of Martin stock.

risk premium, RP

The difference between the expected rate of return on a given risky asset and that on a less risky asset.

This example demonstrates a very important principle: *In a market dominated by risk-averse investors, riskier securities must have higher expected returns, as estimated by the average investor, than less risky securities, for if this situation does not hold, stock prices will change in the market to force it to occur.* We will consider the question of how much higher the returns on risky securities must be later in the chapter, after we see how diversification affects the way risk should be measured. Then, in Chapter 6, we will see how risk-adjusted rates of return affect the price investors are willing to pay for a security.

Self-Test Questions

What is a payoff matrix?

Which of the two stocks graphed in Figure 4-2 is less risky? Why?

How does one calculate the standard deviation?

Which is a better measure of risk: (1) standard deviation or (2) coefficient of variation? Explain.

What is meant by the following statement: "Most investors are risk averse"?

How does risk aversion affect relative rates of return?

PORTFOLIO RISK AND THE CAPITAL ASSET PRICING MODEL

In the preceding section we considered the riskiness of stocks held in isolation. Now we analyze the riskiness of stocks held in portfolios.[5] As we shall see, a stock held as part of a portfolio is less risky than the same stock held in isolation. This fact has been incorporated into a procedure used to analyze the relationship between risk and rates of return, the **Capital Asset Pricing Model,** or **CAPM.** The CAPM is an extremely important analytical tool in both managerial finance and investment analysis. Indeed, the 1990 Nobel Prize was awarded to the developers of the CAPM, Professors Harry Markowitz and William F. Sharpe. In the following sections we discuss the elements of the CAPM.[6]

Capital Asset Pricing Model (CAPM)

A model based on the proposition that any stock's required rate of return is equal to the risk-free rate of return plus a risk premium, where risk reflects diversification.

Portfolio Risk and Return

Most financial assets are not held in isolation; rather, they are held as parts of portfolios. Banks, pension funds, insurance companies, mutual funds, and other financial institutions are required by law to hold diversified portfolios. Even individual investors — at least those whose security holdings constitute a significant part of their total wealth — generally hold stock portfolios, not the stock of only one firm. This being the case, from an investor's standpoint the fact that a particular stock goes up or down is not very important; *what is important is the return on his or her portfolio, and the portfolio's risk. Logically, then, the risk and return of an individual security should be analyzed in terms of how that security affects the risk and return of the portfolio in which it is held.*

To illustrate, Payco American is a collection agency company which operates nationwide through 37 offices. The company is not well known, its stock is not very liquid, its earnings have fluctuated quite a bit in the past, and it doesn't even pay a dividend. All this suggests that Payco is risky and that its required rate of return, k, should be relatively high. However, Payco's k in 1992, and all other years, was quite low in relation to those of most other companies. This indicates that investors regard Payco as being a low-risk company in spite of its uncertain profits and its nonexistent dividend stream. The reason for this somewhat counterintuitive fact has to do with diversification and its effect on risk. Payco's stock price rises during recessions, whereas other stocks tend to decline when the economy slumps. Therefore, holding Payco in a portfolio of "normal" stocks tends to stabilize returns on the entire portfolio.

expected return on a portfolio, $\hat{k}_p$

The weighted average expected return on the stocks held in the portfolio.

Portfolio Returns. The **expected return on a portfolio, $\hat{k}_p$,** is simply the weighted average of the expected returns on the individual stocks in the portfolio, with the weights being the fraction of the total portfolio invested in each stock:

---

[5]A *portfolio* is a collection of investment securities. If you owned some General Motors stock, some Exxon stock, and some IBM stock, you would be holding a three-stock portfolio. For the reasons set forth in this section, the majority of all stocks are held as parts of portfolios.

[6]The CAPM is a relatively complex subject, and we present only its basic elements in this text. For a more detailed discussion, see any standard investments textbook.

$$\hat{k}_p = w_1\hat{k}_1 + w_2\hat{k}_2 + \ldots + w_n\hat{k}_n$$

$$= \sum_{i=1}^{n} w_i\hat{k}_i. \qquad (4\text{-}5)$$

Here the $\hat{k}_i$'s are the expected returns on the individual stocks, the w_i's are the weights, and there are n stocks in the portfolio. Note (1) that w_i is the proportion of the portfolio's dollar value invested in Stock i (that is, the value of the investment in Stock i divided by the total value of the portfolio) and (2) that the w_i's must sum to 1.0.

In January 1992, a security analyst estimated that the following returns could be expected on four large companies:

	Expected Return, $\hat{k}$
Lotus Development	14%
General Electric	13%
Artic Oil	20%
Citicorp	18%

If we formed a $100,000 portfolio, investing $25,000 in each stock, the expected portfolio return would be 16.25%:

$$\hat{k}_p = w_1\hat{k}_1 + w_2\hat{k}_2 + w_3\hat{k}_3 + w_4\hat{k}_4$$

$$= 0.25(14\%) + 0.25(13\%) + 0.25(20\%) + 0.25(18\%)$$

$$= 16.25\%.$$

realized rate of return, $\bar{k}$

The return that is actually earned. The actual return ($\bar{k}$) is usually different from the expected return ($\hat{k}$).

Of course, after the fact and a year later, the actual **realized rates of return, $\bar{k}$,** on the individual stocks—the $\bar{k}_i$, or "k-bar," values—will almost certainly be different from their expected values, so $\bar{k}_p$ will be somewhat different from $\hat{k}_p = 16.25\%$. For example, Lotus stock might double in price and provide a return of $+100\%$, whereas Citicorp stock might have a terrible year, fall sharply, and have a return of -75%. Note, though, that those two events would be somewhat offsetting, so the portfolio's return might still be close to its expected return, even though the individual stocks' actual returns were far from their expected returns.

Portfolio Risk.   As we just saw, the expected return on a portfolio is simply a weighted average of the expected returns on the individual stocks in the portfolio. However, unlike returns, the riskiness of a portfolio, σ_p, is generally *not* a weighted average of the standard deviations of the individual securities in the portfolio; the portfolio's risk will be *smaller* than the weighted average of the stocks' σs. In fact, it may even be theoretically possible to combine two stocks which are individually quite risky as measured by their standard deviations and to form a portfolio which is completely riskless, with $\sigma_p = 0$.

To illustrate the effect of combining securities, consider the situation in Figure 4-5. The bottom section gives data on rates of return for Stocks W and M individually, and also for a portfolio invested 50 percent in each stock. The three top graphs show plots of the data in a time series format, and the lower

Figure 4-5 ▮ **Rate of Return Distributions for Two Perfectly Negatively Correlated Stocks (r = −1.0) and for Portfolio WM**

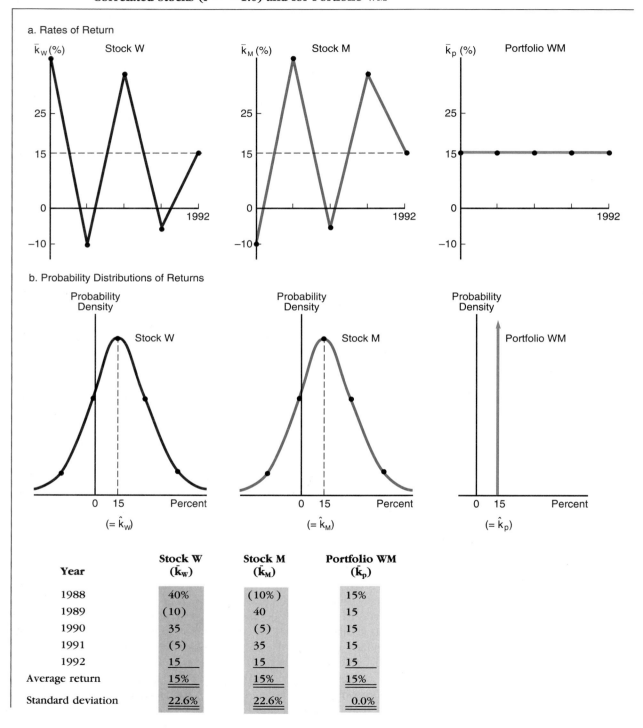

Year	Stock W ($\bar{k}_W$)	Stock M ($\bar{k}_M$)	Portfolio WM ($\bar{k}_p$)
1988	40%	(10%)	15%
1989	(10)	40	15
1990	35	(5)	15
1991	(5)	35	15
1992	15	15	15
Average return	15%	15%	15%
Standard deviation	22.6%	22.6%	0.0%

graphs show the probability distributions of returns, assuming that the future is expected to be like the past. The two stocks would be quite risky if they were held in isolation, but when they are combined to form Portfolio WM, they are not risky at all. (Note: These stocks are called W and M because their returns graphs in Figure 4-5 resemble a W and an M.)

The reason Stocks W and M can be combined to form a riskless portfolio is that their returns move countercyclically to each other—when W's returns fall, those of M rise, and vice versa. The tendency of two variables to move together is called *correlation,* and the **correlation coefficient, r,** measures this tendency.[7] In statistical terms, we say that the returns on Stocks W and M are *perfectly negatively correlated,* with r = −1.0.

correlation coefficient, r
A measure of the degree of relationship between two variables.

The opposite of perfect negative correlation, with r = −1.0, is *perfect positive correlation,* with r = +1.0. Returns on two perfectly positively correlated stocks would move up and down together, and a portfolio consisting of two such stocks would be exactly as risky as the individual stocks. This point is illustrated in Figure 4-6, where we see that the portfolio's standard deviation is equal to that of the individual stocks. Thus, diversification does nothing to reduce risk if the portfolio consists of perfectly positively correlated stocks.

Figures 4-5 and 4-6 demonstrate that when stocks are perfectly negatively correlated (r = −1.0), all risk can be diversified away, but when stocks are perfectly positively correlated (r = +1.0), diversification does no good whatsoever. In reality, most stocks are positively correlated, but not perfectly so. On average, the correlation coefficient for the returns on two randomly selected stocks would be about +0.6, and for most pairs of stocks, r would lie in the range of +0.5 to +0.7. *Under such conditions, combining stocks into portfolios reduces risk but does not eliminate it completely.* Figure 4-7 illustrates this point with two stocks whose correlation coefficient is r = +0.67. The portfolio's average return is 15.0 percent, which is exactly the same as the average return for each of the two stocks, but its standard deviation is 20.6 percent, which is less than the standard deviation of either stock. Thus, the portfolio's risk is *not* an average of the risks of its individual stocks—diversification has reduced, but not eliminated, risk.

From these two-stock portfolio examples, we have seen that in one extreme case (r = −1.0), risk can be completely eliminated, while in the other extreme case (r = +1.0), diversification does no good whatever. In between these extremes, combining two stocks into a portfolio reduces, but does not eliminate, the riskiness inherent in the individual stocks.

What would happen if we included more than two stocks in the portfolio? *As a rule, the riskiness of a portfolio will be reduced as the number of stocks in the portfolio increases.* If we added enough partially correlated stocks, could we completely eliminate risk? In general, the answer is no, but the extent to which adding stocks to a portfolio reduces its risk depends on the *degree of correlation* among the stocks: The smaller the positive correlation coefficient, the lower the risk in a large portfolio. If we could find a set of stocks whose

---

[7]The *correlation coefficient, r,* can range from +1.0, denoting that the two variables move up and down in perfect synchronization, to −1.0, denoting that the variables always move in exactly opposite directions. A correlation coefficient of zero suggests that the two variables are not related to each other—that is, changes in one variable are *independent* of changes in the other.

Figure 4-6 ▪ Rate of Return Distributions for Two Perfectly Positively
Correlated Stocks (r = +1.0) and for Portfolio MM′

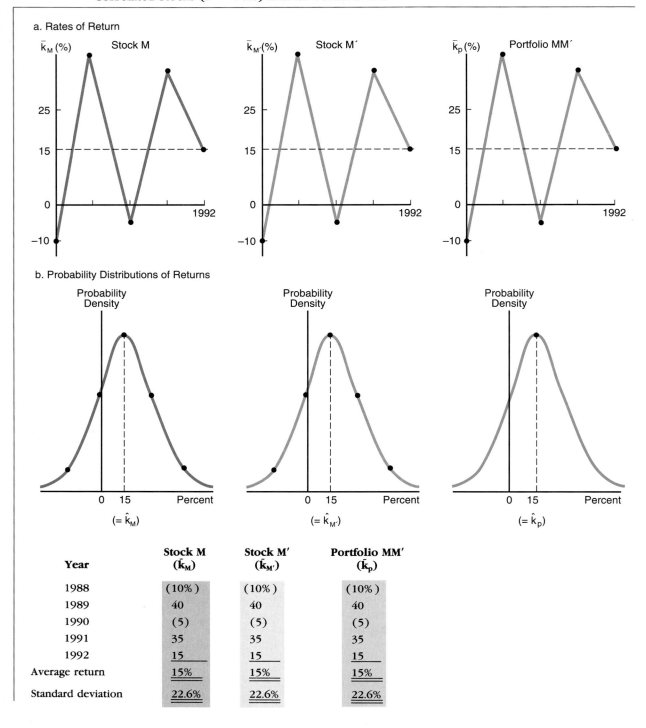

a. Rates of Return

b. Probability Distributions of Returns

Year	Stock M $(\bar{k}_M)$	Stock M′ $(\bar{k}_{M'})$	Portfolio MM′ $(\bar{k}_p)$
1988	(10%)	(10%)	(10%)
1989	40	40	40
1990	(5)	(5)	(5)
1991	35	35	35
1992	15	15	15
Average return	15%	15%	15%
Standard deviation	22.6%	22.6%	22.6%

Figure 4-7 ▪ **Rate of Return Distributions for Two Partially Correlated Stocks**
                (r = +0.67) and for Portfolio WY

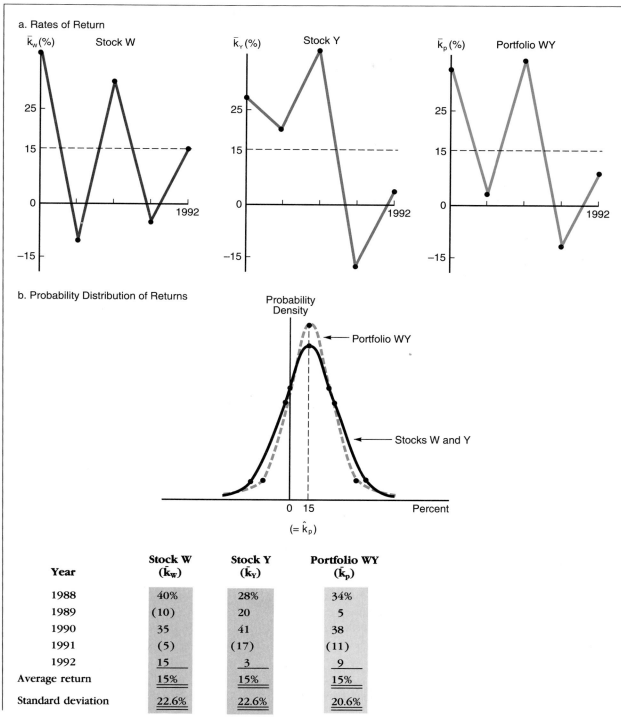

a. Rates of Return

b. Probability Distribution of Returns

Year	Stock W $(\bar{k}_W)$	Stock Y $(\bar{k}_Y)$	Portfolio WY $(\bar{k}_p)$
1988	40%	28%	34%
1989	(10)	20	5
1990	35	41	38
1991	(5)	(17)	(11)
1992	15	3	9
Average return	15%	15%	15%
Standard deviation	22.6%	22.6%	20.6%

correlations were zero or negative, all risk could be eliminated. *In the typical case, where the correlations among the individual stocks are positive but less than + 1.0, some, but not all, risk can be eliminated.*

To test your understanding, would you expect to find higher correlations between the returns on two companies in the same or in different industries? For example, would the correlation of returns on Ford's and General Motors' stocks be higher, or would the correlation coefficient be higher between either Ford or GM and IBM, and how would those correlations affect the risk of portfolios containing them?

Answer: Ford's and GM's returns have a correlation coefficient of about 0.9 with one another because both are affected by auto sales, but only about 0.6 with those of IBM.

Implications: A two-stock portfolio consisting of Ford and GM would be riskier than a two-stock portfolio consisting of Ford or GM, plus IBM. Thus, to minimize risk, portfolios should be diversified across industries.

Company-Specific Risk versus Market Risk.   As noted earlier, it is very difficult, if not impossible, to find stocks whose expected returns are not positively correlated—most stocks tend to do well when the national economy is strong and badly when it is weak.[8] Thus, even very large portfolios end up with a substantial amount of risk, but not as much risk as if all the money were invested in only one stock.

To see more precisely how portfolio size affects portfolio risk, consider Figure 4-8, which shows how portfolio risk is affected by forming larger and larger portfolios of randomly selected NYSE stocks. Standard deviations are plotted for an average one-stock portfolio, a two-stock portfolio, and so on, up to a portfolio consisting of all 1,500-plus common stocks that were listed on the NYSE at the time the data were graphed. The graph illustrates that, in general, the riskiness of a portfolio consisting of average NYSE stocks tends to decline and to approach some limit as the size of the portfolio increases. According to data accumulated in recent years, σ_1, the standard deviation of a one-stock portfolio (or an average stock), is approximately 28 percent. A portfolio consisting of all stocks, which is called the *market portfolio,* would have a standard deviation, σ_M, of about 15.1 percent, which is shown as the horizontal dashed line in Figure 4-8.

Thus, almost half of the riskiness inherent in an average individual stock can be eliminated if the stock is held in a reasonably well-diversified portfolio, which is one containing 40 or more stocks. Some risk always remains, however, so it is virtually impossible to diversify away the effects of broad stock market movements that affect almost all stocks.

That part of the risk of a stock which can be eliminated is called *diversifiable,* or *company-specific,* or *unsystematic, risk;* that part which cannot be eliminated is called *nondiversifiable,* or *market,* or *systematic, risk.* The name

---

[8]It is not too hard to find a few stocks that happened to rise because of a particular set of circumstances in the past while most other stocks were declining; it is much harder to find stocks that could logically be *expected* to go up in the future when other stocks are falling. Payco American, the collection agency discussed earlier, is one of those rare exceptions.

Figure 4-8 ▪ Effects of Portfolio Size on Portfolio Risk for Average Stocks

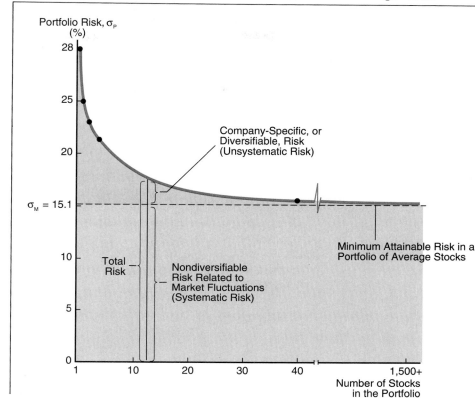

is not especially important, but the fact that a large part of the riskiness of any individual stock can be eliminated is vitally important.

 Company-specific risk is caused by such things as lawsuits, strikes, successful and unsuccessful marketing programs, the winning and losing of major contracts, and other events that are unique to a particular firm. Since these events are essentially random, their effects on a portfolio can be eliminated by diversification—bad events in one firm will be offset by good events in another. **Market risk,** on the other hand, stems from factors which systematically affect most firms, such as war, inflation, recessions, and high interest rates. Since most stocks will tend to be negatively affected by these factors, systematic risk cannot be eliminated by diversification.

 We know that investors demand a premium for bearing risk; that is, the higher the riskiness of a security, the higher the expected return required to induce investors to buy (or to hold) it. However, if investors are primarily concerned with *portfolio risk* rather than the risk of the individual securities in the portfolio, how should the riskiness of an individual stock be measured? The answer, as provided by the Capital Asset Pricing Model (CAPM), is this: *The relevant riskiness of an individual stock is its contribution to the riskiness of a well-diversified portfolio.* In other words, the riskiness of General Electric's stock to a doctor who has a portfolio of 40 stocks or to a trust officer managing

relevant risk

The risk of a security that cannot be diversified away, or its *market risk*. This reflects a security's contribution to the risk of a portfolio.

a 150-stock portfolio, is the contribution that the GE stock makes to the portfolio's riskiness. The stock might be quite risky if held by itself, but if most of its risk can be eliminated by diversification, then its **relevant risk,** which is its *contribution to the portfolio's risk,* may be small.

A simple example will help make this point clear. Suppose you are offered the chance to flip a coin once; if a head comes up, you win $20,000, but if it comes up tails, you lose $16,000. This is a good bet — the expected return is $0.5(\$20,000) + 0.5(-\$16,000) = \$2,000$. However, it is a highly risky proposition, because you have a 50 percent chance of losing $16,000. Thus, you might well refuse to make the bet. Alternatively, suppose you were offered the chance to flip a coin 100 times, and you would win $200 for each head but lose $160 for each tail. It is possible that you would flip all heads and win $20,000, and it is also possible that you would flip all tails and lose $16,000, but the chances are very high that you would actually flip about 50 heads and about 50 tails, winning a net of about $2,000. Although each individual flip is a risky bet, collectively you have a low-risk proposition, because most of the risk has been diversified away. This is the idea behind holding portfolios of stocks rather than just one stock, except that with stocks all of the risk cannot be eliminated by diversification — those risks related to broad, systematic changes in the stock market will remain.

Are all stocks equally risky in the sense that adding them to a well-diversified portfolio would have the same effect on the portfolio's riskiness? The answer is no. Different stocks will affect the portfolio differently, so different securities have different degrees of relevant risk. How can the relevant risk of an individual stock be measured? As we have seen, all risk except that related to broad market movements can, and presumably will, be diversified away. After all, why accept risk that can easily be eliminated? *The risk that remains after diversifying is market risk, or risk that is inherent in the market, and it can be measured by the degree to which a given stock tends to move up and down with the market.* In the next section, we develop a measure of a stock's market risk, and then, in a later section, we introduce an equation for determining the required rate of return on a stock, given its market risk.

The Concept of Beta

beta coefficient, b

A measure of the extent to which the returns on a given stock move with the stock market.

The tendency of a stock to move with the market is reflected in its **beta coefficient, b,** which is a measure of the stock's volatility relative to that of an average stock. Beta is a key element of the CAPM.

An *average-risk stock* is defined as one that tends to move up and down in step with the general market as measured by some index, such as the Dow Jones Industrials, the S&P 500, or the New York Stock Exchange Index. Such a stock will, *by definition,* have a beta, b, of 1.0, which indicates that, in general, if the market moves up by 10 percent, the stock will also move up by 10 percent, while if the market falls by 10 percent, the stock will likewise fall by 10 percent. A portfolio of such b = 1.0 stocks will move up and down with the broad market averages, and it will be just as risky as the averages. If b = 0.5, the stock is only half as volatile as the market — it will rise and fall only half as much — and a portfolio of such stocks will be half as risky as a portfolio of b = 1.0 stocks. On the other hand, if b = 2.0, the stock is twice as volatile as an average

Figure 4-9 ▪ **Relative Volatility of Stocks H, A, and L**

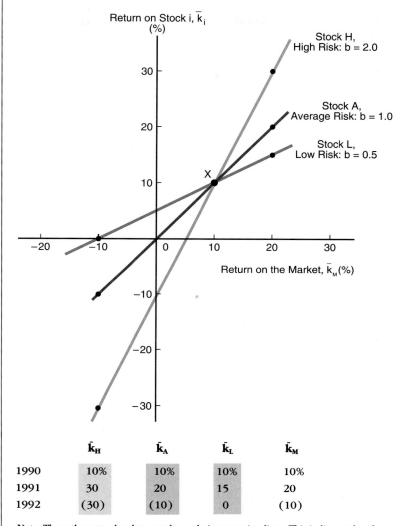

	$\bar{k}_H$	$\bar{k}_A$	$\bar{k}_L$	$\bar{k}_M$
1990	10%	10%	10%	10%
1991	30	20	15	20
1992	(30)	(10)	0	(10)

Note: These three stocks plot exactly on their regression lines. This indicates that they are exposed only to market risk. Mutual funds which concentrate on stocks with a specific degree of market risk would have patterns similar to those shown in the graph.

stock, so a portfolio of such stocks will be twice as risky as an average portfolio. The value of such a portfolio could double — or halve — in a short time, and if you held such a portfolio, you could quickly become a millionaire — or a pauper.

Figure 4-9 graphs the relative volatility of three stocks. The data below the graph assume that in 1990 the "market," defined as a portfolio consisting of all stocks, had a total return (dividend yield plus capital gains yield) of $k_M = 10\%$, and Stocks H, A, and L (for High, Average, and Low risk) also had returns of 10 percent. In 1991 the market went up sharply, and the return on the market portfolio was $\bar{k}_M = 20\%$. Returns on the three stocks also went up: H soared to

Table 4-4   ∎   **Illustrative List of Beta Coefficients**

Stock	Beta
Apple Computer	1.25
General Electric	1.10
Johnson & Johnson	1.05
Heinz	1.00
Anheuser Busch	1.00
Procter & Gamble	1.00
IBM	0.95
Pacific Gas & Electric	0.70
Energen Corp.[a]	0.65

Source: *Value Line,* January 10, 1992.

[a]Energen is a gas distribution company. It has a monopoly in much of Alabama, and its rates are adjusted every 3 months so as to keep its profits relatively constant.

30 percent; A went up to 20 percent, the same as the market; and L only went up to 15 percent. Now suppose that the market dropped in 1992, and the market return was $\bar{k}_M = -10\%$. The three stocks' returns also fell, H plunging to −30 percent, A falling to −10 percent, and L going down only to $\bar{k}_L = 0\%$. Thus, the three stocks all moved in the same direction as the market, but H was by far the most volatile; A was just as volatile as the market; and L was less volatile.

Beta measures a stock's volatility relative to an average stock, which has b = 1.0, and a stock's beta can be calculated by plotting a line like those in Figure 4-9. The slopes of the lines show how each stock moves in response to a movement in the general market—*indeed, the slope coefficient of such a "regression line" is defined as a beta coefficient.* (Procedures for actually calculating betas are described in Appendix 4A.) Betas for literally thousands of companies are calculated and published by Merrill Lynch, Value Line, and numerous other organizations. The beta coefficients of some well-known companies are shown in Table 4-4. Most stocks have betas in the range of 0.50 to 1.50, and the average for all stocks is 1.0 by definition.[9]

If a higher-beta-than-average stock (one whose beta is greater than 1.0) is added to an average-beta (b = 1.0) portfolio, then the beta, and consequently the riskiness, of the portfolio will increase. Conversely, if a lower-beta-than-average stock (one whose beta is less than 1.0) is added to an average-risk portfolio, the portfolio's beta and risk will decline. *Thus, since a stock's beta measures its contribution to the riskiness of a portfolio, beta is the theoretically correct measure of the stock's riskiness.*

---

[9]Betas can, in theory, be negative—if a stock's returns tend to rise when those of other stocks decline, and vice versa, then the regression line in a graph such as Figure 4-9 will have a downward slope, and the beta will be negative. Note though, that *Value Line* follows 1,700 stocks, and none have negative betas. Payco American, the collection agency company, might have a negative beta, but it is too small to be followed by *Value Line* and most other services which calculate and report betas.

The preceding analysis of risk in a portfolio setting is part of the Capital Asset Pricing Model (CAPM), and we can summarize our discussion to this point as follows:

1. A stock's risk consists of two components, market risk and company-specific risk.

2. Company-specific risk can be eliminated by diversification, and most investors do indeed diversify, either by holding large portfolios or by purchasing shares in a mutual fund. We are left, then, with market risk, which is caused by general movements in the stock market and which reflects the fact that most stocks are systematically affected by certain overall economic events like war, recessions, and inflation. Market risk is the only relevant risk to a rational, diversified investor, because he or she should have already eliminated company-specific risk.

3. Investors must be compensated for bearing risk—the greater the riskiness of a stock, the higher its required return. However, compensation is required only for risk which cannot be eliminated by diversification. If risk premiums existed on stock with high diversifiable risk, well-diversified investors would start buying these securities and bidding up their prices, and their final (equilibrium) expected returns would reflect only nondiversifiable market risk.

    If this point is not clear, an example may help clarify it. Suppose half of Stock A's risk is market risk (it occurs because Stock A moves up and down with the market, and the market can go down). The other half of A's risk is diversifiable. You hold only Stock A, so you are exposed to all of its risk. As compensation for bearing so much risk, you want a risk premium of 8 percent over the 10 percent T-bond rate. Thus, your required return is $k_A = 10\% + 8\% = 18\%$. But suppose other investors, including your professor, are well diversified; they also hold Stock A, but they have eliminated its diversifiable risk and thus are exposed to only half as much risk as you. Therefore, their risk premium will be only half as large as yours, and their required rate of return will be $k_A = 10\% + 4\% = 14\%$.

    If the stock were yielding more than 14 percent in the market, others, including your professor, would buy it. If it were yielding 18 percent, you would be willing to buy it, but well-diversified investors would bid its price up and its yield down, and keep you from getting it. In the end, you would have to accept a 14 percent return or else keep your money in the bank. Thus, risk premiums in a market populated with rational investors will reflect only market risk.

4. The market risk of a stock is measured by its beta coefficient, which is an index of the stock's relative volatility. Some benchmark betas follow:

    $b = 0.5$: Stock is only half as volatile, or risky, as the average stock.
    $b = 1.0$: Stock is of average risk.
    $b = 2.0$: Stock is twice as risky as the average stock.

5. *Since a stock's beta coefficient determines how the stock affects the riskiness of a diversified portfolio, beta is the most relevant measure of a stock's risk.*

Portfolio Beta Coefficients

A portfolio consisting of low-beta securities will itself have a low beta, because the beta of any set of securities is a weighted average of the individual securities' betas:

$$b_p = w_1 b_1 + w_2 b_2 + \cdots + w_n b_n$$

$$= \sum_{i=1}^{n} w_i b_i. \qquad (4\text{-}6)$$

Here b_p is the beta of the portfolio, and it reflects how volatile the portfolio is in relation to the market; w_i is the fraction of the portfolio invested in the *i*th stock; and b_i is the beta coefficient of the *i*th stock. For example, if an investor holds a $100,000 portfolio consisting of $33,333.33 invested in each of 3 stocks, and each of the stocks has a beta of 0.7, then the portfolio's beta will be $b_p = 0.7$:

$$b_p = 0.3333(0.7) + 0.3333(0.7) + 0.3333(0.7) = 0.7.$$

Such a portfolio will be less risky than the market: it should experience relatively narrow price swings and have relatively small rate-of-return fluctuations. In terms of Figure 4-9, the slope of its regression line would be 0.7, which is less than that for a portfolio of average stocks.

Now suppose one of the existing stocks is sold and replaced by a stock with $b_i = 2.0$. This action will increase the riskiness of the portfolio from $b_{p1} = 0.7$ to $b_{p2} = 1.13$:

$$b_{p2} = 0.3333(0.7) + 0.3333(0.7) + 0.3333(2.0)$$

$$= 1.13.$$

Had a stock with $b_i = 0.2$ been added, the portfolio beta would have declined from 0.7 to 0.53. Adding a low-beta stock, therefore, would reduce the riskiness of the portfolio.

Self-Test Questions

Explain the following statement: "A stock held as part of a portfolio is generally less risky than the same stock held in isolation."

What is meant by perfect positive correlation, by perfect negative correlation, and by zero correlation?

In general, can the riskiness of a portfolio be reduced to zero by increasing the number of stocks in the portfolio? Explain.

What is an average-risk stock?

Why is beta the theoretically correct measure of a stock's riskiness?

If you plotted the returns on a particular stock versus those on the Dow Jones Index over the past 5 years, what would the slope of the line you obtained indicate about the stock's risk?

THE RELATIONSHIP BETWEEN RISK AND RATES OF RETURN

In the preceding section we saw that under the CAPM theory, beta is the appropriate measure of a stock's relevant risk. Now we must specify the relationship between risk and return: For a given level of beta, what rate of return will investors require on a stock in order to compensate them for assuming the risk? To begin, let us define the following terms:

$\hat{k}_i$ = expected rate of return on the ith stock.

k_i = required rate of return on the ith stock. Note that if $\hat{k}_i$ is less than k_i, you would not purchase this stock, or you would sell it if you owned it. If $\hat{k}_i$ were greater than k_i, you would want to buy the stock, and you would be indifferent if $\hat{k}_i = k_i$.

k_{RF} = risk-free rate of return. In this context, k_{RF} is generally measured by the return on long-term U.S. Treasury bonds.

b_i = beta coefficient of the ith stock. The beta of an average stock is $b_A = 1.0$.

k_M = required rate of return on a portfolio consisting of all stocks, which is the market portfolio. k_M is also the required rate of return on an average ($b_A = 1.0$) stock.

$RP_M = (k_M - k_{RF})$ = market risk premium. This is the additional return over the risk-free rate required to compensate an average investor for assuming an average amount of risk. Average risk means $b_A = 1.0$.

$RP_i = (k_M - k_{RF})b_i$ = risk premium on the ith stock. The stock's risk premium is less than, equal to, or greater than the premium on an average stock, depending on whether its beta is less than, equal to, or greater than 1.0. If $b_i = b_A = 1.0$, then $RP_i = RP_M$.

market risk premium, RP_M

The additional return over the risk-free rate needed to compensate investors for assuming an average amount of risk.

The **market risk premium, RP_M,** depends on the degree of aversion that investors on average have to risk.[10] Let us assume that at the current time,

---

[10]This concept, as well as other aspects of CAPM, is discussed in more detail in Chapter 3 of Brigham and Gapenski, *Intermediate Financial Management*. It should be noted that the risk premium of an average stock, $k_M - k_{RF}$, cannot be measured with great precision because it is impossible to obtain precise values for the expected future return on the market, k_M. However, empirical studies suggest that where long-term U.S. Treasury bonds are used to measure k_{RF} and where k_M is an estimate of the expected return on the S&P 400 Industrial Stocks, the market risk premium varies somewhat from year to year, and it has generally ranged from 4 to 8 percent during the last 20 years.

Chapter 3 of *Intermediate Financial Management* also discusses the assumptions embodied in the CAPM framework. Some of the assumptions of the CAPM theory are unrealistic, and, because of this, the theory does not hold exactly.

Treasury bonds yield $k_{RF} = 9\%$ and an average share of stock has a required return of $k_M = 13\%$. Therefore, the market risk premium is 4 percent:

$$RP_M = k_M - k_{RF} = 13\% - 9\% = 4\%.$$

It follows that if one stock were twice as risky as another, its risk premium would be twice as high, and, conversely, if its risk were only half as much, its risk premium would be half as large. Further, we can measure a stock's relative riskiness by its beta coefficient. Therefore, if we know the market risk premium, RP_M, and the stock's risk as measured by its beta coefficient, b_i, we can find its risk premium as the product $(RP_M)b_i$. For example, if $b_i = 0.5$ and $RP_M = 4\%$, then RP_i is 2 percent:

$$\text{Risk premium for Stock i} = RP_i = (RP_M)b_i \qquad (4\text{-}7)$$

$$= (4\%)(0.5)$$
$$= 2.0\%.$$

As the discussion in Chapter 3 implies, the required return for any investment can be expressed in general terms as

$$\text{Required return} = \text{Risk-free return} + \text{Premium for risk.}$$

According to the discussion presented above, then, the required return for Stock i can be written as

$$\text{SML Equation: } k_i = k_{RF} + (k_M - k_{RF})b_i \qquad (4\text{-}8)$$

$$= k_{RF} + (RP_M)b_i$$
$$= 9\% + (13\% - 9\%)(0.5)$$
$$= 9\% + 4\%(0.5)$$
$$= 11\%.$$

Equation 4-8 is the equation for CAPM equilibrium pricing, and it generally is called the **Security Market Line (SML).**

Security Market Line (SML)

The line that shows the relationship between risk as measured by beta and the required rate of return for individual securities. SML = Equation 4-8.

If some other stock, j, were riskier than Stock i and had $b_j = 2.0$, then its required rate of return would be 17 percent:

$$k_j = 9\% + (4\%)2.0 = 17\%.$$

An average stock, with $b = 1.0$, would have a required return of 13 percent, the same as the market return:

$$k_A = 9\% + (4\%)1.0 = 13\% = k_M.$$

As noted above, Equation 4-8 is called the Security Market Line (SML) equation, and it is often expressed in graph form, as in Figure 4-10, which shows the SML when $k_{RF} = 9\%$ and $k_M = 13\%$. Note the following points:

1. Required rates of return are shown on the vertical axis, while risk as measured by beta is shown on the horizontal axis. This graph is quite different from the one shown in Figure 4-9, where the returns on individual stocks

Figure 4-10   ▪   The Security Market Line (SML)

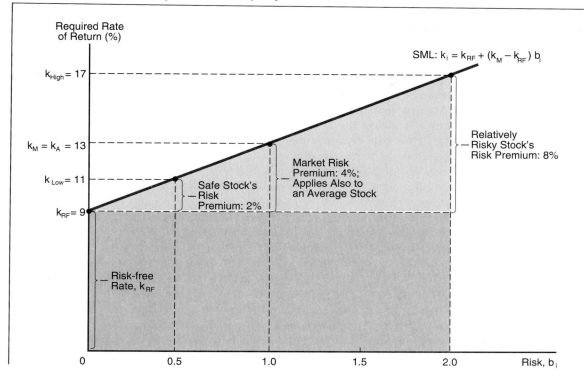

were plotted on the vertical axis and returns on the market index were shown on the horizontal axis. The slopes of the three lines in Figure 4-9 represented the three stocks' betas, and these three betas are now plotted as points on the horizontal axis in Figure 4-10.

2. Riskless securities have $b_i = 0$; therefore, k_{RF} appears as the vertical axis intercept in Figure 4-10.

3. The slope of the SML reflects the degree of risk aversion in the economy; the greater the average investor's aversion to risk, (1) the steeper the slope of the line, (2) the greater the risk premium for any stock, and (3) the higher the required rate of return on stocks.[11] These points are discussed further in a later section.

4. The values we worked out for stocks with $b_i = 0.5$, $b_i = 1.0$, and $b_i = 2.0$ agree with the values shown on the graph for k_{Low}, k_A, and k_{High}.

---

[11]Students sometimes confuse beta with the slope of the SML. This is a mistake. The slope of any line is equal to the "rise" divided by the "run," or $(Y_1 - Y_0)/(X_1 - X_0)$. Consider Figure 4-10. If we let $Y = k$ and $X = $ beta, and we go from the origin to $b = 1.0$, we see that the slope is $(k_M - k_{RF})/(beta_M - beta_{RF}) = (13 - 9)/(1 - 0) = 4$. Thus, the slope of the SML is equal to $(k_M - k_{RF})$, the market risk premium. In Figure 4-10, $k_i = 9\% + 4b_i$, so a doubling of beta (for example, from 1.0 to 2.0) would produce a 4 percentage point increase in k_i.

Both the Security Market Line and a company's position on it change over time due to changes in interest rates, investors' risk aversion, and individual companies' betas. Such changes are discussed in the following sections.

The Impact of Inflation

As we learned in Chapter 3, interest amounts to "rent" on borrowed money, or the price of money; thus, k_{RF} is the price of money to a riskless borrower. We also learned that the risk-free rate as measured by the rate on U.S. Treasury securities is called the *nominal, or quoted, rate,* and it consists of two elements: (1) a *real inflation-free rate of return, k*,* and (2) an *inflation premium, IP,* equal to the anticipated rate of inflation.[12] Thus, $k_{RF} = k^* + IP$. The real rate on long-term Treasury bonds has historically ranged from 2 to 4 percent, with a mean of about 3 percent. Therefore, if no inflation were expected, long-term Treasury bonds would yield about 3 percent. However, as the expected rate of inflation increases, a premium must be added to the real risk-free rate of return to compensate investors for the loss of purchasing power that results from inflation. Therefore, the 9 percent k_{RF} shown in Figure 4-10 might be thought of as consisting of a 3 percent real risk-free rate of return plus a 6 percent inflation premium: $k_{RF} = k^* + IP = 3\% + 6\% = 9\%$.

If the expected rate of inflation rose by 2 percent, to $6\% + 2\% = 8\%$, this would cause k_{RF} to rise to 11 percent. Such a change is shown in Figure 4-11. Notice that under the CAPM, the increase in k_{RF} also causes an *equal* increase in the rate of return on all risky assets because the inflation premium is built into the required rate of return of both riskless and risky assets.[13] For example, the rate of return on an average stock, k_M, increases from 13 to 15 percent. Other risky securities' returns also rise by two percentage points.

Changes in Risk Aversion

The slope of the Security Market Line reflects the extent to which investors are averse to risk—the steeper the slope of the line, the greater the average investor's risk aversion. If investors were indifferent to risk, and if k_{RF} were 9 percent, then risky assets would also provide an expected return of 9 percent: If there were no risk aversion, there would be no risk premium, so the SML would be horizontal. As risk aversion increases, so does the risk premium and, thus, the slope of the SML.

Figure 4-12 illustrates an increase in risk aversion. The market risk premium rises from 4 to 6 percent, and k_M rises from $k_{M1} = 13\%$ to $k_{M2} = 15\%$. The

---

[12]Long-term Treasury bonds also contain a maturity risk premium, MRP. Here we include the MRP in k^* to simplify the discussion.

[13]Recall that the inflation premium for any asset is equal to the average expected rate of inflation over the life of the asset. Thus, in this analysis we must assume either that all securities plotted on the SML graph have the same life or else that the expected rate of future inflation is constant.

It should also be noted that k_{RF} in a CAPM analysis can be proxied by either a long-term rate (the T-bond rate) or a short-term rate (the T-bill rate). Traditionally, the T-bill rate was used, but in recent years there has been a movement toward use of the T-bond rate because there is a closer relationship between T-bond yields and stocks than between T-bill yields and stocks. See Ibbotson and Sinquefield, *Stocks, Bonds, Bills, and Inflation; 1992, Yearbook* (Chicago: Ibbotson & Associates, 1992), for a discussion.

Figure 4-11 ▪ Shift in the SML Caused by an Increase in Inflation

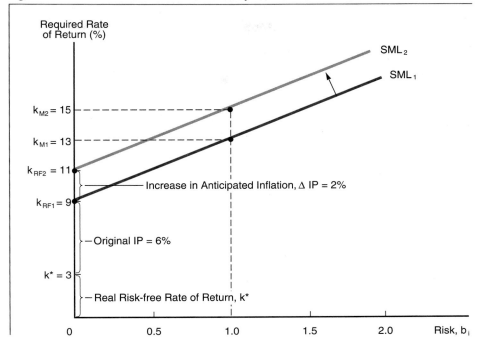

Figure 4-12 ▪ Shift in the SML Caused by Increased Risk Aversion

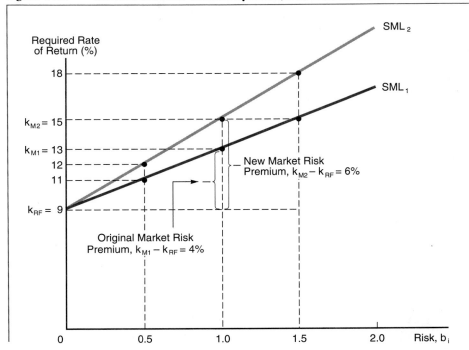

returns on other risky assets also rise, with the effect of this shift in risk aversion being more pronounced on riskier securities. For example, the required return on a stock with $b_i = 0.5$ increases by only one percentage point, from 11 to 12 percent, whereas that on a stock with $b_i = 1.5$ increases by three percentage points, from 15 to 18 percent.

Changes in a Stock's Beta Coefficient

As we shall see later in the book, a firm can affect its beta risk through changes in the composition of its assets as well as through its use of debt financing. A company's beta can also change as a result of external factors such as increased competition in its industry, the expiration of basic patents, and the like. When such changes occur, the required rate of return also changes, and, as we shall see in Chapter 6, this will affect the price of the firm's stock. For example, consider Allied Food Products, with a beta equal to 1.0. Now suppose some action occurred that caused Allied's beta to increase from 1.0 to 1.5. If the conditions depicted in Figure 4-10 held, Allied's required rate of return would increase from

$$
\begin{aligned}
k_1 &= k_{RF} + (k_M - k_{RF})b_i \\
&= 9\% + (13\% - 9\%)1.0 \\
&= 13\%
\end{aligned}
$$

to

$$
\begin{aligned}
k_2 &= 9\% + (13\% - 9\%)1.5 \\
&= 15\%.
\end{aligned}
$$

Any change which affects the required rate of return on a security, such as a change in its beta coefficient or in expected inflation, will have an impact on the price of the security. We will examine in detail the relationship between a security's required rate of return and its stock price in Chapter 6.

Self-Test Questions

Differentiate between the expected rate of return ($\hat{k}$) and the required rate of return (k) on a stock. Which would have to be larger to get you to buy the stock?

What are the differences between the relative volatility graph (Figure 4-9), where "betas are made," and the SML graph (Figure 4-10), where "betas are used"? Consider both how the graphs are constructed and the purpose for which they were developed.

What happens to the SML graph (1) when inflation increases or (2) when it decreases?

What happens to the SML graph (1) when risk aversion increases or (2) when it decreases? What would the SML look like if investors were indifferent to risk, i.e., had zero risk aversion?

How can a firm influence its market, or beta, risk?

PHYSICAL ASSETS VERSUS SECURITIES

In a book on managerial finance for business firms, why do we spend so much time on the riskiness of stocks? Why not begin by looking at the riskiness of such business assets as plant and equipment? *The reason is that, for a management whose goal is stock price maximization, the overriding consideration is the riskiness of the firm's stock, and the relevant risk of any physical asset must be measured in terms of its effect on the stock's risk.* For example, suppose Goodyear Tire Company is considering a major investment in a new product, recapped tires. Sales of recaps and hence earnings on the new operation are highly uncertain, so it would appear that the new venture is quite risky. However, suppose returns on the recap business are negatively correlated with Goodyear's regular operations — when times are good and people have plenty of money, they buy new tires, but when times are bad, they tend to buy more recaps. Therefore, returns would be high on regular operations and low on the recap division during good times, but the opposite situation would occur during recessions. The result might be a pattern like that shown in Figure 4-5 earlier in the chapter for Stocks W and M. Thus, what appears to be a risky investment when viewed on a stand-alone basis might not be very risky when viewed within the context of the company as a whole.

This analysis can be extended to the corporation's owners, the stockholders. Because the stock of Goodyear is owned by diversified stockholders, the real issue each time the company makes a major asset investment is this: How does this investment affect the risk of our stockholders? Again, the stand-alone risk of an individual project may look quite high, but viewed in the context of the project's effect on stockholders' risk, it may not be very large. We will address this subject again in Chapter 15, where we will examine the effects of capital budgeting projects on companies' beta coefficients and thus on their risk to stockholders.

Self-Test Questions

Explain the following statement: "The stand-alone risk of an individual project may look quite high, but viewed in the context of a project's effect on stockholders' risk, the project's risk may not be very large."

How would the correlation between returns on the project and other assets' returns affect the preceding statement?

A WORD OF CAUTION

A word of caution about betas and the Capital Asset Pricing Model (CAPM) is in order. Although these concepts are logical, the entire theory is based on *ex ante,* or expected, conditions, yet we have available only *ex post,* or past, data. Thus, the betas we calculate show how volatile a stock has been in the *past,* but conditions may change, and the stock's *future volatility,* which is the item of real concern to investors, might be quite different from its past volatility. Although the CAPM represents a significant step forward in security pricing theory, it does have some potentially serious deficiencies when applied in practice, so estimates of k_i found through use of the SML may be subject to considerable error.

RISK IN A GLOBAL CONTEXT

It seems reasonable to think that investments outside the United States are, for a U.S. citizen or company, riskier than investments in U.S. assets. However, this is not necessarily true — because returns on foreign investments are not perfectly positively correlated with returns on U.S. assets, it has been argued that multinational corporations may be less risky than companies which operate strictly within the boundaries of any one country. Similarly, portfolio managers have argued that to minimize risk investors should diversify not only across stocks but also across countries. We will address these issues in more depth in Chapter 23, "Multinational Managerial Finance," but you should understand the logic behind the case for global diversification.

SUMMARY

The primary goals of this chapter were (1) to show how risk is measured in financial analysis and (2) to explain how risk affects rates of return. The key concepts covered are listed below.

- **Risk** can be defined as the chance that some unfavorable event will occur.
- Most rational investors hold **portfolios of stocks,** and they are more concerned with the risks of their portfolios than with the risks of individual stocks.
- The **expected return** on an investment is the mean value of its probability distribution of possible returns.
- The **higher the probability** that the actual return will be far below the expected return, the **greater the risk** associated with owning an asset.
- The average investor is **risk averse,** which means that he or she must be compensated for holding risky securities; therefore, riskier securities must have higher expected returns than less risky securities.
- A stock's risk consists of (1) **company-specific risk,** which can be eliminated by diversification, plus (2) **market,** or **beta, risk,** which cannot be eliminated by diversification.
- The **relevant risk** of an individual security is its contribution to the riskiness of a well-diversified **portfolio,** which is the security's **market risk.** Since market risk cannot be eliminated by diversification, investors must be compensated for it.
- A stock's **beta coefficient, b,** is a measure of the stock's market risk. Beta measures the extent to which the stock's returns move with the market.

▪ A **high-beta stock** is more volatile than an average stock, while a **low-beta stock** is less volatile than an average stock. An **average stock** has b = 1.0.

▪ The **beta of a portfolio** is a **weighted average** of the betas of the individual securities in the portfolio.

▪ The **Security Market Line (SML)** equation shows the relationship between a security's risk and its required rate of return. The return required for any security i is equal to the **risk-free rate** plus the **market risk premium** times the **security's beta:** $k_i = k_{RF} + (k_M - k_{RF})b_i$.

▪ Even though the expected rate of return on a stock is generally equal to its required return, a number of things can happen to cause the required rate of return to change: (1) **the risk-free rate can change** because of changes in anticipated inflation, (2) **a stock's beta can change,** or (3) **investors' aversion to risk can change**.

▪ Because returns on assets in different countries are not perfectly correlated, **global diversification** may result in lower risk and lower required rates of return for multinational companies.

In the next two chapters, we will see how a security's rate of return affects its value. Then, in the remainder of the book, we will examine the ways in which a firm's management can influence a stock's riskiness and hence its price.

Questions

4-1 The probability distribution of a less risky expected return is more peaked than that of a riskier return. What shape would the probability distribution have for (a) completely certain returns and (b) completely uncertain returns?

4-2 Security A has an expected return of 7 percent, a standard deviation of expected returns of 35 percent, a correlation coefficient with the market of −0.3, and a beta coefficient of −0.5. Security B has an expected return of 12 percent, a standard deviation of returns of 10 percent, a correlation with the market of 0.7, and a beta coefficient of 1.0. Which security is riskier? Why?

4-3 Suppose you owned a portfolio consisting of $250,000 worth of long-term U.S. government bonds.
a. Would your portfolio be riskless?
b. Now suppose you hold a portfolio consisting of $250,000 worth of 30-day Treasury bills. Every 30 days your bills mature and you reinvest the principal ($250,000) in a new batch of bills. Assume that you live on the investment income from your portfolio and that you want to maintain a constant standard of living. Is your portfolio truly riskless?
c. Can you think of any asset that would be completely riskless? Could someone develop such an asset? Explain.

4-4 A life insurance policy is a financial asset. The premiums paid represent the investment's cost.
a. How would you calculate the expected return on a life insurance policy?
b. Suppose the owner of a life insurance policy has no other financial assets — the person's only other asset is "human capital," or lifetime earnings capacity. What is the correlation coefficient between returns on the insurance policy and returns on the policyholder's human capital?

c. Life insurance companies have to pay administrative costs and sales representatives' commissions; hence, the expected rate of return on insurance premiums is generally low, or even negative. Use the portfolio concept to explain why people buy life insurance in spite of negative expected returns.

4-5 If investors' aversion to risk increased, would the risk premium on a high-beta stock increase more or less than that on a low-beta stock? Explain.

Self-Test Problems *(Solutions Appear in Appendix B)*

ST-1
Key terms

Define the following terms, using graphs or equations to illustrate your answers wherever feasible:
a. Risk; probability distribution
b. Expected rate of return, $\hat{k}$
c. Continuous probability distribution
d. Standard deviation, σ; variance, σ^2; coefficient of variation, CV
e. Risk aversion; realized rate of return, $\bar{k}$
f. Risk premium for Stock i, RP_i; market risk premium, RP_M
g. Capital Asset Pricing Model (CAPM)
h. Expected return on a portfolio, $\hat{k}_p$
i. Correlation coefficient, r
j. Market risk; company-specific risk; relevant risk
k. Beta coefficient, b; average stock's beta, b_A
l. Security Market Line (SML); SML equation
m. Slope of SML as a measure of risk aversion

ST-2
Realized rates of return

Stocks A and B have the following historical returns:

Year	Stock A's Returns, k_A	Stock B's Returns, k_B
1988	(10.00%)	(3.00%)
1989	18.50	21.29
1990	38.67	44.25
1991	14.33	3.67
1992	33.00	28.30

a. Calculate the average rate of return for each stock during the period 1988 through 1992. Assume that someone held a portfolio consisting of 50 percent of Stock A and 50 percent of Stock B. What would have been the realized rate of return on the portfolio in each year from 1988 through 1992? What would have been the average return on the portfolio during this period?
b. Now calculate the standard deviation of returns for each stock and for the portfolio. Use Equation 4-3a in Footnote 4.
c. Looking at the annual returns data on the two stocks, would you guess that the correlation coefficient between returns on the two stocks is closer to 0.9 or to -0.9?
d. If you added more stocks at random to the portfolio, which of the following is the most accurate statement of what would happen to σ_p?
(1) σ_p would remain constant.
(2) σ_p would decline to somewhere in the vicinity of 15 percent.
(3) σ_p would decline to zero if enough stocks were included.

Problems

4-1
Expected returns

Suppose you won the Florida lottery and were offered (1) $0.5 million or (2) a gamble in which you would get $1 million if a head were flipped but zero if a tail came up.

a. What is the expected value of the gamble?

b. Would you take the sure $0.5 million or the gamble?

c. If you choose the sure $0.5 million, are you a risk averter or a risk seeker?

d. Suppose you actually take the sure $0.5 million. You can invest it in either a U.S. Treasury bond that will return $537,500 at the end of a year or a common stock that has a 50-50 chance of being either worthless or worth $1,150,000 at the end of the year.

   (1) What is the expected dollar profit on the stock investment? (The expected profit on the T-bond investment is $37,500.)

   (2) What is the expected rate of return on the stock investment? (The expected rate of return on the T-bond investment is 7.5 percent.)

   (3) Would you invest in the bond or the stock?

   (4) Exactly how large would the expected profit (or the expected rate of return) have to be on the stock investment to make *you* invest in the stock, given the 7.5 percent return on the bond?

   (5) How might your decision be affected if, rather than buying one stock for $0.5 million, you could construct a portfolio consisting of 100 stocks with $5,000 invested in each? Each of these stocks has the same return characteristics as the one stock — that is, a 50-50 chance of being worth either zero or $11,500 at year-end. Would the correlation between returns on these stocks matter?

4-2
Security Market Line

The McAlhany Investment Fund has total capital of $500 million invested in five stocks:

Stock	Investment	Stock's Beta Coefficient
A	$160 million	0.5
B	120 million	2.0
C	80 million	4.0
D	80 million	1.0
E	60 million	3.0

The beta coefficient for a fund like McAlhany Investment can be found as a weighted average of the fund's investments. The current risk-free rate is 8 percent, whereas market returns have the following estimated probability distribution for the next period:

Probability	Market Return
0.1	10%
0.2	12
0.4	13
0.2	16
0.1	17

a. What is the estimated equation for the Security Market Line (SML)? (Hint: First determine the expected market return.)

b. Compute the fund's required rate of return for the next period.

c. Suppose John McAlhany, the president, receives a proposal for a new stock. The investment needed to take a position in the stock is $50 million, it will have an expected return of 18 percent, and its estimated beta coefficient is 2.0. Should the new stock be purchased? At what expected rate of return should McAlhany be indifferent to purchasing the stock?

4-3   Stocks A and B have the following historical returns:

Realized rates of return

Year	Stock A's Returns, k_A	Stock B's Returns, k_B
1988	(18.00%)	(14.50%)
1989	33.00	21.80
1990	15.00	30.50
1991	(0.50)	(7.60)
1992	27.00	26.30

a. Calculate the average rate of return for each stock during the period 1988 through 1992.
b. Assume that someone held a portfolio consisting of 50 percent of Stock A and 50 percent of Stock B. What would have been the realized rate of return on the portfolio in each year from 1988 through 1992? What would have been the average return on the portfolio during this period?
c. Calculate the standard deviation of returns for each stock and for the portfolio.
d. Calculate the coefficient of variation for each stock and for the portfolio.
e. If you are a risk-averse investor, would you prefer to hold Stock A, Stock B, or the portfolio? Why?

EXAM-TYPE PROBLEMS

The problems included in this section are set up in such a way that they could be used as multiple-choice exam problems.

4-4   The market and Stock J have the following probability distributions:

Expected returns

Probability	k_M	k_j
0.3	15%	20%
0.4	9	5
0.3	18	12

a. Calculate the expected rates of return for the market and Stock J.
b. Calculate the standard deviations for the market and Stock J.
c. Calculate the coefficients of variation for the market and Stock J.

4-5   Stocks X and Y have the following probability distributions of expected future returns:

Expected returns

Probability	X	Y
0.1	(10%)	(35%)
0.2	2	0
0.4	12	20
0.2	20	25
0.1	38	45

a. Calculate the expected rate of return, $\hat{k}$, for Stock Y. ($\hat{k}_X = 12\%$.)
b. Calculate the standard deviation of expected returns for Stock X. (That for Stock Y is 20.35 percent.) Now calculate the coefficient of variation for Stock Y. Is it possible that most investors might regard Stock Y as being *less* risky than Stock X? Explain.

4-6   Suppose $k_{RF} = 8\%$, $k_M = 11\%$, and $k_A = 14\%$.

Required rate of return   a. Calculate Stock A's beta.
b. If Stock A's beta were 1.5, what would be A's new required rate of return?

4-7
Required rate of return

Suppose k_{RF} = 9%, k_M = 14%, and b_i = 1.3.
a. What is k_i, the required rate of return on Stock i?
b. Now suppose k_{RF} (1) increases to 10 percent or (2) decreases to 8 percent. The slope of the SML remains constant. How would this affect k_M and k_i?
c. Now assume k_{RF} remains at 9 percent but k_M (1) increases to 16 percent or (2) falls to 13 percent. The slope of the SML does not remain constant. How would these changes affect k_i?

4-8
Portfolio beta

Suppose you hold a diversified portfolio consisting of a $7,500 investment in each of 20 different common stocks. The portfolio beta is equal to 1.12. Now, suppose you have decided to sell one of the stocks in your portfolio with a beta equal to 1.0 for $7,500 and to use these proceeds to buy another stock for your portfolio. Assume the new stock's beta is equal to 1.75. Calculate your portfolio's new beta.

4-9
Portfolio required return

Suppose you are the money manager of a $4 million investment fund. The fund consists of 4 stocks with the following investments and betas:

Stock	Investment	Beta
A	$ 400,000	1.50
B	600,000	(0.50)
C	1,000,000	1.25
D	2,000,000	0.75

If the market required rate of return is 14 percent and the risk-free rate is 6 percent, what is the fund's required rate of return?

4-10
Required rate of return

Stock R has a beta of 1.5, Stock S has a beta of 0.75, the expected rate of return on an average stock is 15 percent, and the risk-free rate of return is 9 percent. By how much does the required return on the riskier stock exceed the required return on the less risky stock?

INTEGRATIVE PROBLEM

4-11
Risk and return

Assume that you recently graduated with a major in finance, and you just landed a job in the trust department of a large regional bank. Your first assignment is to invest $100,000 from an estate for which the bank is trustee. Because the estate is expected to be distributed to the heirs in about one year, you have been instructed to plan for a one-year holding period. Further, your boss has restricted you to the following investment alternatives, shown with their probabilities and associated outcomes. (Disregard for now the items at the bottom of the data; you will fill in the blanks later.)

State of the Economy	Probability	T-Bills	High Tech	Collections	U.S. Rubber	Market Portfolio	2-Stock Portfolio
				Returns on Alternative Investments			
				Estimated Rate of Return			
Recession	0.1	8.0%	(22.0%)	28.0%	10.0%	(13.0%)	
Below average	0.2	8.0	(2.0)	14.7	(10.0)	1.0	
Average	0.4	8.0	20.0	0.0	7.0	15.0	
Above average	0.2	8.0	35.0	(10.0)	45.0	29.0	
Boom	0.1	8.0	50.0	(20.0)	30.0	43.0	____
$\hat{k}$							
σ							
CV							
b							

The bank's economic forecasting staff has developed probability estimates for the state of the economy, and the trust department has a sophisticated computer program which was used to estimate the rate of return on each alternative under each state of the economy. High Tech Inc. is an electronics firm; Collections Inc. collects past-due debts; and U.S. Rubber manufactures tires and various other rubber and plastics products. The bank also maintains an "index fund" which owns a market-weighted fraction of all publicly traded stocks; you can invest in that fund and thus obtain average stock market results. Given the situation as described, answer the following questions.

a. (1) Why is the T-bill's return independent of the state of the economy? Do T-bills promise a completely risk-free return? (2) Why are High Tech's returns expected to move with the economy whereas Collections' are expected to move counter to the economy?

b. Calculate the expected rate of return on each alternative and fill in the row for $\hat{k}$ in the table above.

c. You should recognize that basing a decision solely on expected returns is only appropriate for risk-neutral individuals. Since the beneficiaries of the trust, like virtually everyone, are risk averse, the riskiness of each alternative is an important aspect of the decision. One possible measure of risk is the standard deviation of returns.
   (1) Calculate this value for each alternative, and fill in the row for σ in the table above. (2) What type of risk is measured by the standard deviation? (3) Draw a graph which shows *roughly* the shape of the probability distributions for High Tech, U.S. Rubber, and T-bills.

d. Suppose you suddenly remembered that the coefficient of variation (CV) is generally regarded as being a better measure of total risk than the standard deviation when the alternatives being considered have widely differing expected returns. Calculate the CVs for the different securities, and fill in the row for CV in the table above. Does the CV produce the same risk rankings as the standard deviation?

e. Suppose you created a two-stock portfolio by investing $50,000 in High Tech and $50,000 in Collections. (1) Calculate the expected return ($\hat{k}_p$), the standard deviation (σ_p), and the coefficient of variation (CV_p) for this portfolio and fill in the appropriate rows in the table above. (2) How does the riskiness of this 2-stock portfolio compare to the riskiness of the individual stocks if they were held in isolation?

f. Suppose an investor starts with a portfolio consisting of one randomly selected stock. What would happen (1) to the riskiness and (2) to the expected return of the portfolio as more and more randomly selected stocks were added to the portfolio? What is the implication for investors? Draw two graphs to illustrate your answer.

g. (1) Should portfolio effects impact the way investors think about the riskiness of individual stocks? (2) If you chose to hold a one-stock portfolio and consequently were exposed to more risk than diversified investors, could you expect to be compensated for all of your risk; that is, could you earn a risk premium on that part of your risk that you could have eliminated by diversifying?

h. The expected rates of return and the beta coefficients of the alternatives as supplied by the bank's computer program are as follows:

Security	Return ($\hat{k}$)	Risk (Beta)
High Tech	17.4%	1.29
Market	15.0	1.00
U.S. Rubber	13.8	0.68
T-bills	8.0	0.00
Collections	1.7	(0.86)

(1) What is a beta coefficient, and how are betas used in risk analysis? (2) Do the expected returns appear to be related to each alternative's market risk? (3) Is it pos-

sible to choose among the alternatives on the basis of the information developed thus far? Use the data given at the start of the problem to construct a graph which shows how the T-bill's, High Tech's, and Collections' beta coefficients are calculated. Then discuss what betas measure and how they are used in risk analysis.

i. (1) Write out the Security Market Line (SML) equation, use it to calculate the required rate of return on each alternative, and then graph the relationship between the expected and required rates of return. (2) How do the expected rates of return compare with the required rates of return? (3) Does the fact that Collections has a negative beta make any sense? What is the implication of the negative beta? (4) What would be the market risk and the required return of a 50-50 portfolio of High Tech and Collections? Of High Tech and U.S. Rubber?

j. (1) Suppose investors raised their inflation expectations by 3 percentage points over current estimates as reflected in the 8 percent T-bill rate. What effect would higher inflation have on the SML and on the returns required on high- and low-risk securities? (2) Suppose instead that investors' risk aversion increased enough to cause the market risk premium to increase by 3 percentage points. (Inflation remains constant.) What effect would this have on the SML and on returns of high- and low-risk securities?

COMPUTER-RELATED PROBLEM

Work the problem in this section only if you are using the computer problem diskette.

4-12
Realized rates of return

Using the computerized model in the File C4, rework Problem 4-3, assuming that a third stock, Stock C, is available for inclusion in the portfolio. Stock C has the following historical returns:

Year	Stock C's Returns, k_C
1988	32.00%
1989	(11.75)
1990	10.75
1991	32.25
1992	(6.75)

a. Calculate (or read from the computer screen) the average return, standard deviation, and coefficient of variation for Stock C.

b. Assume that the portfolio now consists of 33.33 percent of Stock A, 33.33 percent of Stock B, and 33.33 percent of Stock C. How does this affect the portfolio return, standard deviation, and coefficient of variation versus when 50 percent was invested in A and in B?

c. Make some other changes in the portfolio, making sure that the percentages sum to 100 percent. For example, enter 25 percent for Stock A, 25 percent for Stock B, and 50 percent for Stock C. (Note that the program will not allow you to enter a zero for the percentage in Stock C.) Notice that $\hat{k}_p$ remains constant and that σ_p changes. Why do these results occur?

d. In Problem 4-3, the standard deviation of the portfolio decreased only slightly, because Stocks A and B were highly positively correlated with one another. In this problem, the addition of Stock C causes the standard deviation of the portfolio to decline dramatically, even though $\sigma_C = \sigma_A = \sigma_B$. What does this indicate about the correlation between Stock C and Stocks A and B?

e. Would you prefer to hold the portfolio described in Problem 4-3 consisting only of Stocks A and B or a portfolio that also included Stock C? If others react similarly, how might this affect the stocks' prices and rates of return?

Appendix 4A

Calculating Beta Coefficients

The CAPM is an *ex ante* model, which means that all of the variables represent before-the-fact, *expected* values. In particular, the beta coefficient used in the SML equation should reflect the expected volatility of a given stock's return versus the return on the market during some *future* period. However, people generally calculate betas using data from some *past* period and then assume that the stock's relative volatility will be the same in the future as it was in the past.

To illustrate how betas are calculated, consider Figure 4A-1. The data at the bottom of the figure show the historical realized returns for Stock J and for the market over the last five years. The data points have been plotted on the scatter diagram, and a regression line has been drawn. If all the data points had fallen on a straight line, as they did in Figure 4-9 in Chapter 4, it would be easy to draw an accurate line. If they do not, as in Figure 4A-1, then you must fit the line either "by eye" as an approximation or with a calculator.

Recall what the term *regression line,* or *regression equation,* means: The equation $Y = a + bX + e$ is the standard form of a simple linear regression. It states that the dependent variable, Y, is equal to a constant, a, plus b times X, where b is the slope coefficient and X is the independent variable, plus an error term, e. Thus, the rate of return on the stock during a given time period (Y) depends on what happens to the general stock market, which is measured by $X = \bar{k}_M$.

Once the data have been plotted and the regression line has been drawn on graph paper, we can estimate its intercept and slope, the a and b values in $Y = a + bX$. The intercept, a, is simply the point where the line cuts the vertical axis. The slope coefficient, b, can be estimated by the "rise over run" method. This involves calculating the amount by which $\bar{k}_J$ increases for a given increase in $\bar{k}_M$. For example, we observe in Figure 4A-1 that $\bar{k}_J$ increases from -8.9 to $+7.1$ percent (the rise) when $\bar{k}_M$ increases from 0 to 10.0 percent (the run). Thus b, the beta coefficient, can be measured as follows:

$$b = \text{Beta} = \frac{\text{Rise}}{\text{Run}} = \frac{\Delta Y}{\Delta X} = \frac{7.1 - (-8.9)}{10.0 - 0.0} = \frac{16.0}{10.0} = 1.6.$$

Note that rise over run is a ratio, and it would be the same if measured using any two arbitrarily selected points on the line.

The regression line equation enables us to predict a rate of return for Stock J, given a value of $\bar{k}_M$. For example, if $\bar{k}_M = 15\%$, we would predict $\bar{k}_J = -8.9\% + 1.6(15\%) = 15.1\%$. However, the actual return would probably differ from the predicted return. This deviation is the error term, e_J, for the year, and it varies randomly from year to year depending on company-specific factors. Note, though, that the higher the correlation coefficient, the closer the points lie to the regression line, and the smaller the errors.

In actual practice, monthly rather than annual returns are generally used for $\bar{k}_J$ and $\bar{k}_M$, and five years of data are often employed; thus, there would be $5 \times 12 = 60$ data points on the scatter diagram. Also, in practice one would use the *least squares method* for finding the regression coefficients a and b; this procedure minimizes the squared values of the error terms. It is discussed in statistics courses.

The least squares value of beta can be obtained quite easily with a financial calculator. The procedures that follow explain how to find the values of beta and the slope using either a Texas Instruments, a Hewlett-Packard, or a Sharp financial calculator.

Figure 4A-1 ▪ Calculating Beta Coefficients

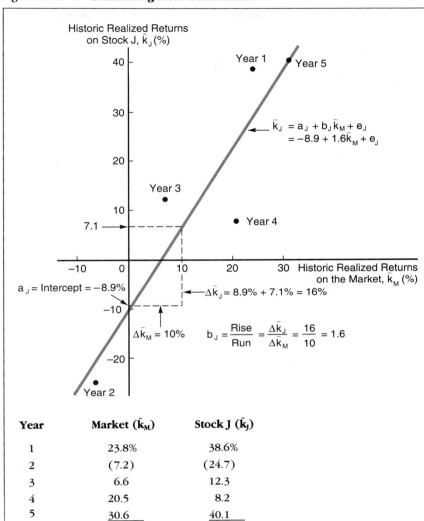

Year	Market ($\bar{k}_M$)	Stock J ($\bar{k}_J$)
1	23.8%	38.6%
2	(7.2)	(24.7)
3	6.6	12.3
4	20.5	8.2
5	30.6	40.1
Average $\bar{k}$	14.9%	14.9%
$\sigma_{\bar{k}}$	15.1%	26.5%

Texas Instruments BA, BA-II, or MBA Calculator

1. Press **2nd** **Mode** until "STAT" shows in the display.

2. Enter the first X value ($\bar{k}_M$ = 23.8 in our example), press **x⇄y**, and then enter the first Y value ($\bar{k}_J$ = 38.6) and press **Σ+** .

3. Repeat Step 2 until all values have been entered.

4. Press **2nd** **b/a** to find the value of Y at X = 0, which is the value of the Y intercept (a), −8.9219, and then press **x≶y** to display the value of the slope (beta), 1.6031.

5. You could also press **2nd** **Corr** to obtain the correlation coefficient, r, which is 0.9134. Putting it all together, you should have this regression line:

$$\bar{k}_J = -8.92 + 1.60\bar{k}_M.$$
$$r = 0.9134.$$

Hewlett-Packard 10B[1]

1. Press **Clear all** to clear your memory registers.

2. Enter the first X value ($\bar{k}_M$ = 23.8 in our example), press **INPUT** , and then enter the first Y value ($\bar{k}_J$ = 38.6) and press **Σ+** . Be *sure* to enter the X variable first.

3. Repeat Step 2 until all values have been entered.

4. To display the vertical axis intercept, press 0 **ŷ,m** . Then −8.9219 should appear.

5. To display the beta coefficient, b, press **SWAP** . Then 1.6031 should appear.

6. To obtain the correlation coefficient, press **x̂,r** and then **SWAP** to get r = 0.9134.

   Putting it all together, you should have this regression line:

$$\bar{k}_J = -8.92 + 1.60\bar{k}_M.$$
$$r = 0.9134.$$

Sharp EL-733

1. Press **2nd F** **Mode** until "STAT" shows in the lower right corner of the display.

2. Press **2nd F** **CA** to clear all memory registers.

3. Enter the first X value ($\bar{k}_M$ = 23.8 in our example) and press **(x,y)** . (This is the RM key; do not press the second F key at all.) Then enter the first Y value ($\bar{k}_J$ = 38.6) and press **DATA** . (This is the M+ key; again do not press the second F key.)

4. Repeat Step 3 until all values have been entered.

5. Press **2nd F** **a** to find the value of Y at X = 0, which is the value of the Y intercept (a), −8.9219, and then press **2nd F** **b** to display the value of the slope (beta), 1.6031.

---

[1]The Hewlett-Packard 17B calculator is even easier to use. If you have one, see Chapter 9 of the *Owner's Manual*.

6. You can also press 2nd F r to obtain the correlation coefficient, r, which is 0.9134.

Putting it all together, you should have this regression line:

$$\bar{k}_J = -8.92 + 1.60\bar{k}_M.$$

$$r = 0.9134.$$

Problems

4A-1

Beta coefficients and rates of return

You are given the following set of data:

Year	Historical Rates of Return ($\bar{k}$) Stock Y($\bar{k}_Y$)	NYSE ($\bar{k}_M$)
1	3.0%	4.0%
2	18.2	14.3
3	9.1	19.0
4	(6.0)	(14.7)
5	(15.3)	(26.5)
6	33.1	37.2
7	6.1	23.8
8	3.2	(7.2)
9	14.8	6.6
10	24.1	20.5
11	18.0	30.6
Mean	9.8%	9.8%
$\sigma_{\bar{k}}$	13.8	19.6

a. Construct a scatter diagram graph (*on graph paper*) showing the relationship between returns on Stock Y and the market as in Figure 4A-1; then draw a freehand approximation of the regression line. What is the approximate value of the beta coefficient? (If you have a calculator with statistical functions, use it to calculate beta.)

b. Give a verbal interpretation of what the regression line and the beta coefficient show about Stock Y's volatility and relative riskiness as compared with other stocks.

c. Suppose the scatter of points had been more spread out but the regression line was exactly where your present graph shows it. How would this affect (1) the firm's risk if the stock were held in a one-asset portfolio and (2) the actual risk premium on the stock if the CAPM held exactly? How would the degree of scatter (or the correlation coefficient) affect your confidence that the calculated beta will hold true in the years ahead?

d. Suppose the regression line had been downward sloping and the beta coefficient had been negative. What would this imply about (1) Stock Y's relative riskiness and (2) its probable risk premium?

e. Construct an illustrative probability distribution graph of returns (see Figure 4-7) for portfolios consisting of (1) only Stock Y, (2) 1 percent each of 100 stocks with beta coefficients similar to that of Stock Y, and (3) all stocks (that is, the distribution of returns on the market). Use as the expected rate of return the arithmetic mean as given previously for both Stock Y and the market and assume that the distributions are normal. Are the expected returns "reasonable" — that is, is it reasonable that $\hat{k}_Y = \hat{k}_M = 9.8\%$?

f. Now suppose that in the next year, Year 12, the market return was 27 percent, but Firm Y increased its use of debt, which raised its perceived risk to investors. Do you think that the return on Stock Y in Year 12 could be approximated by this historical characteristic line?

$$\hat{k}_Y = 3.8\% + 0.62(\hat{k}_M) = 3.8\% + 0.62(27\%) = 20.5\%.$$

g. Now suppose $\bar{k}_Y$ in Year 12, after the debt ratio was increased, had actually been 0 percent. What would the new beta be, based on the most recent 11 years of data (that is, Years 2 through 12)? Does this beta seem reasonable — that is, is the change in beta consistent with the other facts given in the problem?

4A-2 You are given the following historical data on market returns, $\bar{k}_M$, and the returns on
Security Market Line Stocks A and B, $\bar{k}_A$ and $\bar{k}_B$:

Year	$\bar{k}_M$	$\bar{k}_A$	$\bar{k}_B$
1	29.00%	29.00%	20.00%
2	15.20	15.20	13.10
3	(10.00)	(10.00)	0.50
4	3.30	3.30	7.15
5	23.00	23.00	17.00
6	31.70	31.70	21.35

k_{RF}, the risk-free rate, is 9 percent. Your probability distribution for k_M for next year is as follows:

Probability	k_M
0.1	(14%)
0.2	0
0.4	15
0.2	25
0.1	44

a. Determine graphically the beta coefficients for Stocks A and B.
b. Graph the Security Market Line and give its equation.
c. Calculate the required rates of return on Stocks A and B.
d. Suppose a new stock, C, with $\hat{k}_C = 18$ percent and $b_C = 2.0$ becomes available. Is this stock in equilibrium; that is, does the required rate of return on Stock C equal its expected return? Explain. If the stock is not in equilibrium, explain how equilibrium will be restored.

Time Value of Money[1]

A M A N A G E R I A L   P E R S P E C T I V E

The cover story in a recent issue of Fortune *was entitled, "Will You Be Able to Retire?" Although you may laugh when we say the article should be of interest to you, the fact is it should be. The article began with some well-known facts: (1) The savings rate in the United States is the lowest of any major industrial nation. (2) The ratio of workers to retirees, which was 17 to 1 in 1950 and is currently down to 3.3 to 1, will decline to less than 2 to 1 after the Year 2000. (3) Because of points 1 and 2, the Social Security system is in serious trouble. The article then went on to present some figures on how much money the "Baby Boom" generation (people born in the post–World War II period from 1946 through 1968) will need when they retire, given projected trends in inflation. Next, it presented statistics on the amount of money members of that generation are saving, and the rates of return savers are getting on their investments. Finally, the article concluded that even relatively affluent Baby Boomers (those with current incomes of about $85,000) will have trouble maintaining a reasonable standard of living when they retire, and that the children of the Boomers (many of you) will probably end up having to support their parents.*

What does the retirement plight of the Baby Boomers (and their children) have to do with time value of money? Actually, a great deal. The techniques and procedures covered in this chapter are exactly the ones Fortune *used to forecast the Boomers' retirement needs, their probable wealth at retirement, and the resulting shortfall. If you study this chapter carefully, perhaps you can avoid the trap into which many people seem to be falling.*

---

[1]In previous editions, this chapter was written on the assumption that students would not have financial calculators. Today, though, these calculators are relatively inexpensive, and students who cannot use them run the risk of being deemed obsolete and hence uncompetitive before they even graduate. Therefore, the chapter has been rewritten to include a discussion of financial calculator solutions along with the regular calculator and tabular solutions. Those sections which require the use of financial calculators are identified, and instructors may choose to permit students to skip them.

In Chapter 1 we saw that the primary goal of managerial finance is to maximize the value of the firm's stock. We also saw that stock values depend in part on the timing of the cash flows investors expect to receive from an investment — a dollar expected soon is worth more than a dollar expected in the distant future. Therefore, it is essential that financial managers have a clear understanding of the time value of money and its impact on the value of the firm. These concepts are discussed in this chapter, where we show how the timing of cash flows affects asset values and rates of return.

The principles of time value analysis as developed here have many applications, ranging from setting up schedules for paying off loans to decisions about whether to acquire new equipment. *In fact, of all the techniques used in finance, none is more important than the concept of time value of money, or discounted cash flow (DCF) analysis.* Since this concept is used throughout the remainder of the book, it is vital that you understand time value before you move on to other topics.

TIME LINES

time line

An important tool used in time value of money analysis; it is a graphical representation which is used to show the timing of cash flows.

One of the most important tools in time value of money analysis is the **time line,** which is used to help us visualize what is happening in a particular problem and then to help us set up the problem for solution. To illustrate the time line concept, consider the following diagram:

```
Time:  0        1        2        3        4        5
       |--------|--------|--------|--------|--------|
```

Time 0 is today; Time 1 is one period from today, or the end of Period 1; Time 2 is two periods from today, or the end of Period 2; and so on. Thus, the values on top of the tick marks represent end-of-period values. Often the periods are years, but other time intervals such as semiannual periods, quarters, months, or even days are also used. If each period on the time line represents a year, the interval from the tick mark corresponding to 0 to the tick mark corresponding to 1 would be Year 1, the interval from the tick mark corresponding to 1 to the tick mark corresponding to 2 would be Year 2, and so on. Note that each tick mark corresponds to the end of one period as well as the beginning of the next period. In other words, the tick mark at Time 1 represents the *end* of Year 1; it also represents the *beginning* of Year 2 because Year 1 has just passed.

Cash flows are placed directly below the tick marks, and interest rates are shown directly above the time line. Unknown cash flows, which you are trying to find in the analysis, are indicated by question marks. Now consider the following time line:

outflow

A deposit, a cost, or an amount paid.

inflow

A receipt.

Here the interest rate for each of the three periods is 5 percent; a single amount (or lump sum) cash **outflow** is made at Time 0; and the Time 3 value is an unknown **inflow.** Since the initial $100 is an outflow (an investment), it has a minus sign. Since the Period 3 amount is an inflow, it does not have a minus sign. Note that no cash flows occur at Times 1 and 2. Note also that we do not show dollar signs on time lines; this reduces clutter.

Now consider the following situation, where a $100 cash outflow is made today, and we will receive an unknown amount at the end of Time 2:

$$
\begin{array}{c c c c c}
0 & 5\% & 1 & 10\% & 2 \\
\vdash & & \vdash & & \dashv \\
-100 & & & & ?
\end{array}
$$

Here the interest rate is 5 percent during the first period, but it rises to 10 percent during the second period. If the interest rate is constant in all periods, we show it only in the first period, but if it changes, we show all the relevant rates on the time line.

Time lines are essential when you are first learning time value of money concepts, but even experts use time lines to analyze complex problems. We will be using time lines throughout the book, and you should get into the habit of using them when you work problems.

 Self-Test Question

Draw a 3-year time line which illustrates the following situation: (1) An outflow of $10,000 occurs at Time 0.   (2) Inflows of $5,000 occur at the end of Years 1, 2, and 3.   (3) The interest rate during the three years is 10 percent.

FUTURE VALUE

compounding
The arithmetic process of determining the final value of a cash flow or series of cash flows when compound interest is applied.

A dollar in hand today is worth more than a dollar to be received in the future because, if you had it now, you could invest it, earn interest, and end up with more than one dollar in the future. The process of going from today's values, or present values (PV), to future values (FV) is called **compounding**. To illustrate, suppose you deposited $100 in a bank account that paid 5 percent interest each year. How much would you have at the end of one year? To begin, we define the following terms:

PV = present value, or beginning amount, in your account. Here PV = $100.

i = interest rate the bank pays on the account per year. The interest earned is based on the balance at the beginning of each year, and we assume that it is paid at the end of the year. Here i = 5%, or, expressed as a decimal, i = 0.05. Throughout this chapter, we designate the interest rate as i (or I) because that symbol is used on most financial calculators. Note, though, that in later chapters we use the symbol k to denote interest rates because k is used more often in the financial literature.

INT = dollars of interest you earn during the year = Beginning amount $\times$ i. Here INT = $100(0.05) = $5.

FV_n = future value, or ending amount, of your account at the end of n years. Whereas PV is the value now, or the *present value*, FV_n is the value n years into the *future*, after the interest earned has been added to the account.

n = number of periods involved in the analysis. Here n = 1.

In our example, n = 1, so FV_n can be calculated as follows:

$$
\begin{aligned}
FV_n = FV_1 &= PV + INT \\
&= PV + PV(i) \\
&= PV(1 + i).
\end{aligned}
$$

$$= \$100(1 + 0.05) = \$100(1.05) = \$105.$$

future value (FV)

The amount to which a cash flow or series of cash flows will grow over a given period of time when compounded at a given interest rate.

Thus, the **future value (FV)** at the end of one year, FV_1, equals the present value multiplied by 1.0 plus the interest rate, so you will have $105 after one year.

What would you end up with if you left your $100 in the account for five years? Here is a time line set up to show the amount at the end of each year:

	0	5%	1	2	3	4	5
Initial deposit: −100			FV_1 = ?	FV_2 = ?	FV_3 = ?	FV_4 = ?	FV_5 = ?
Interest earned:			5	5.25	5.51	5.79	6.08
Amount at the end of each period:			105	110.25	115.76	121.55	**127.63**

Note the following points: (1) You start by depositing $100 in the account—this is shown as an outflow at t = 0. (2) You earn $100(0.05) = $5 of interest during the first year, so the amount at the end of Year 1 (or t = 1) is $100 + $5 = $105. (3) You start the second year with $105, earn $5.25 on the now larger amount, and end the second year with $110.25. Your interest during Year 2, $5.25, is higher than the first year's interest, $5, because you earned $5(0.05) = $0.25 interest on the first year's interest. (4) This process continues, and because the beginning balance is higher in each succeeding year, the annual interest earned increases. (5) The total interest earned, $27.63, is reflected in the final balance at t = 5, $127.63.

Note that the value at the end of Year 2, $110.25, is equal to

$$
\begin{aligned}
FV_2 &= FV_1(1 + i) \\
&= PV(1 + i)(1 + i) \\
&= PV(1 + i)^2 \\
&= \$100(1.05)^2 = \$110.25.
\end{aligned}
$$

Continuing, the balance at the end of Year 3 is

$$
\begin{aligned}
FV_3 &= FV_2(1 + i) \\
&= PV(1 + i)^3 \\
&= \$100(1.05)^3 = \$115.76,
\end{aligned}
$$

and

$$FV_5 = \$100(1.05)^5 = \$127.63.$$

In general, the future value of an initial sum at the end of n years can be found by applying Equation 5-1:

$$FV_n = PV(1 + i)^n. \tag{5-1}$$

Equation 5-1 and most other time value of money problems can be solved in three ways: numerically with a regular calculator, with interest tables, or with a financial calculator.

Numerical Solution

One can use a regular calculator and either (1) multiply $(1 + i)$ by itself $n - 1$ times or (2) use the exponential function to raise $(1 + i)$ to the nth power. With most calculators, you would enter $1 + i = 1.05$ and multiply it by itself four times, or else enter 1.05, then press the y^x (exponential) function key, and then enter 5. In either case, your answer would be 1.2763 (if you set your calculator to display four decimal places), which you would multiply by $100 to get the final answer, $127.6282, which would be rounded to $127.63.

In certain time value of money problems, it is extremely difficult to arrive at a solution using a regular calculator. We will tell you this when we have such a problem, and in these cases we will not show a numerical solution. Also, at times we show the numerical solution just below the time line, as a part of the diagram, rather than in a separate section.

Interest Tables (Tabular Solution)

Future Value Interest Factor for i and n (FVIF$_{i,n}$)
The future value of $1 left on deposit for n periods at a rate of i percent per period.

The **Future Value Interest Factor for i and n (FVIF$_{i,n}$)** is defined as $(1 + i)^n$, and these factors can be found by using a regular calculator as discussed above. Table 5-1 is illustrative, while Table A-3 in Appendix A at the back of the book contains FVIF$_{i,n}$ values for a wide range of i and n values.

Since $(1 + i)^n = $ FVIF$_{i,n}$, Equation 5-1 can be rewritten as follows:

$$FV_n = PV(FVIF_{i,n}). \tag{5-1a}$$

To illustrate, the FVIF for our 5-year, 5 percent interest problem can be found in Table 5-1 by looking down the first column to Period 5, and then looking across that row to the 5 percent column, where we see that FVIF$_{5\%,5} = 1.2763$. Then, the value of $100 after 5 years is found as follows:

$$
\begin{aligned}
FV_n &= PV(FVIF_{i,n}) \\
&= \$100(1.2763) = \$127.63.
\end{aligned}
$$

Financial Calculator Solution

Equation 5-1 and a number of other equations have been programmed directly into financial calculators, and such a calculator can be used to find future values. Note that calculators have five keys which correspond to the five most commonly used time value of money variables:

Table 5-1   ▪   **Future Value Interest Factors: $FVIF_{i,n} = (1 + i)^n$**

Period (n)	4%	5%	6%
1	1.0400	1.0500	1.0600
2	1.0816	1.1025	1.1236
3	1.1249	1.1576	1.1910
4	1.1699	1.2155	1.2625
5	1.2167	<u>1.2763</u>	1.3382
6	1.2653	1.3401	1.4185

Here

N = the number of periods; some calculators use n rather than N.

I = interest rate per period; again, some calculators use i rather than I.

PV = present value.

PMT = payment. This key is used only if the cash flows involve a series of equal, or constant, payments (an annuity). If there are no periodic payments in the particular problem, then PMT = 0.

FV = future value.

On some financial calculators, these keys are actually buttons on the face of the calculator, while on others they are shown on a screen after going into the time value of money (TVM) menu.

In this chapter, we will deal with equations which involve only four of the variables at any one time—three of the variables will be known, and the calculator will then solve for the fourth (unknown) variable. In the next chapter, when we deal with bonds, we will use all five variables in the bond valuation equation.[2]

To find the future value of $100 after 5 years at 5 percent interest using a financial calculator, note again that we are dealing with Equation 5-1:

$$FV_n = PV(1 + i)^n. \tag{5-1}$$

The equation has four variables, FV_n, PV, i, and n. If we know any three, we can solve for the fourth. In our example, we can enter PV = 100, I = 5, PMT = 0, and N = 5. Then, when we press the FV key, we will get the answer, FV = 127.63 (rounded to two decimal places).

Many financial calculators require that all cash flows be designated as either inflows or outflows, and then outflows must be entered as negative numbers. In our illustration, you deposit, or put in, the initial amount (which is an outflow to you) and you take out, or receive, the ending amount (which is an inflow to you). If your calculator requires that you follow this sign convention, the PV would be entered as − 100. (If you entered 100, then the FV would appear as

---

[2]The equation programmed into the calculators actually has five variables, one for each key. In this chapter, the value of one of the variables is always zero. It is a good idea to get into the habit of inputting a zero for the unused variable (whose value is automatically set equal to zero when you clear the calculator's memory); if you forget to clear your calculator, this procedure will help you avoid trouble.

−127.63.) Also, on some calculators you are required to press a "Compute" key before pressing the FV key.

Sometimes the convention of changing signs can be confusing. For example, if you have $100 in the bank now and want to find out how much you will have after 5 years if your account pays 5 percent interest, the calculator will give you a negative answer, in this case −127.63, because the calculator assumes you are going to withdraw the funds. This sign convention should cause you no problem if you think about what you are doing.

We should also note that financial calculators permit you to specify the number of decimal places that are displayed. Twelve significant digits are actually used in the calculations, but we generally use two places for answers when working with dollars or percentages and four places when working with decimals. The nature of the problem dictates how many decimal places should be displayed.

Technology has progressed to the point where it is far more efficient to solve most time value of money problems with a financial calculator. However, you must understand the concepts behind the calculations and know how to set up time lines in order to work complex problems. This is true for stock and bond valuation, capital budgeting, lease analysis, and many other important types of problems.

Problem Format

To help you understand the various types of time value problems, we will generally use a standard format in the book. First, we state the problem in words. Next, we diagram the problem on a time line. Then, beneath the time line, we show the equation that must be solved. Finally, we present three alternative procedures for solving the equation to obtain the answer: (1) use a regular calculator to obtain a numerical solution, (2) use the tables, or (3) use a financial calculator. Generally, the financial calculator solution is the most efficient.

To illustrate the format, we use the 5-year, 5 percent example:

Time Line:

```
0    5%    1         2         3         4         5
|----------|---------|---------|---------|---------|
-100                                          FV = ?
```

Equation:

$$FV_n = PV(1 + i)^n = \$100(1.05)^5.$$

1. Numerical Solution:

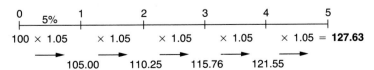

```
0    5%    1         2         3         4         5
|----------|---------|---------|---------|---------|
100 × 1.05   × 1.05    × 1.05    × 1.05    × 1.05 = 127.63

            105.00    110.25    115.76    121.55
```

Using a regular calculator, raise 1.05 to the 5th power and multiply by $100 to get $FV_5 = \$127.63$.

2. Tabular Solution:

Look up FVIF$_{5\%,5}$ in Table 5-1 or Table A-3 at the end of the book and then multiply by $100:

$$FV_5 = \$100(FVIF_{5\%,5}) = \$100(1.2763) = \$127.63.$$

3. Financial Calculator Solution:

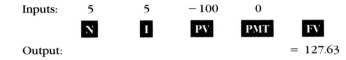

Inputs: 5   5   −100   0

N   I   PV   PMT   FV

Output: = 127.63

Note that the calculator diagram tells you to input N = 5, PV = −100, I = 5, and PMT = 0, and then to press the FV key to get the answer, 127.63. Also, note that in this particular problem, the PMT key does not really come into play, as no constant series of payments is involved.[3] Finally, you should recognize that small rounding differences will often occur among the various solution methods because tables use fewer significant digits (4) than do calculators (12) and also because rounding sometimes is done at intermediate steps in long problems.

Graphic View of the Compounding Process: Growth

Figure 5-1 shows how $1 (or any other sum) grows over time at various interest rates. The data used to plot the curves could be obtained from Table A-3, or it could be generated with a calculator. The higher the rate of interest, the faster the rate of growth. The interest rate is, in fact, a growth rate: If a sum is deposited and earns 5 percent interest, then the funds on deposit will grow at a rate of 5 percent per period. Note also that time value concepts can be applied to anything that is growing—sales, population, earnings per share, or whatever.

Self-Test Questions

Explain what is meant by the following statement: "A dollar in hand today is worth more than a dollar to be received next year."

What is compounding? What is "interest on interest"?

Explain the following equation: $FV_1 = PV + INT$.

Set up a time line that shows the following situation: (1) Your initial deposit is $100.   (2) The account pays 5 percent interest annually.   (3) You want to know how much money you will have at the end of 3 years.

What equation could you use to solve the preceding problem?

What are the five TVM (time value of money) input keys on a financial calculator?

---

[3]We input PMT = 0, but if you cleared the calculator before you started, that would already have been done.

Figure 5-1 ▪ **Relationships among Future Value, Growth, Interest Rates, and Time**

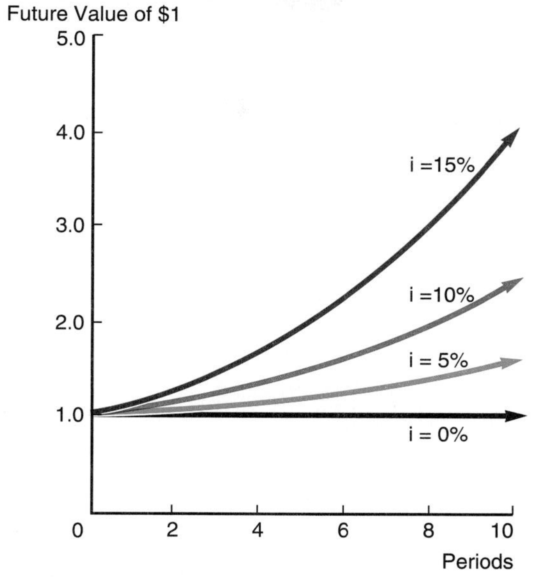

PRESENT VALUE

opportunity cost rate

The rate of return on the best available alternative investment of equal risk.

Suppose you have some extra cash, and you have a chance to buy a low-risk security which will pay $127.63 at the end of 5 years. Your local bank is currently offering 5 percent interest on 5-year certificates of deposit, and you regard the security as being as safe as a CD. The 5 percent rate is defined as being your **opportunity cost rate,** or the rate of return you could earn on alternative investments of similar risk. How much should you be willing to pay for the security?

present value (PV)

The value today of a future cash flow or series of cash flows.

From the future value example presented in the previous section, we saw that an initial amount of $100 invested at 5 percent per year would be worth $127.63 at the end of 5 years. As we will see in a moment, you should be indifferent to the choice between $100 today and $127.63 at the end of 5 years, and the $100 is defined as the **present value,** or **PV,** of $127.63 due in 5 years when the opportunity cost rate is 5 percent. If the price of the security is anything less than $100, you should definitely buy it because it would cost you exactly $100 to produce the $127.63 in 5 years if you earned a 5 percent return. Therefore, if you could find another investment with the same risk that would produce the same future amount ($127.63) but it cost less than $100 (say $95.00), then you could earn a return higher than 5 percent by purchasing that investment. Similarly, if the price of the security is greater than $100, you should not buy it because it would cost you only $100 to produce the same future amount at the given rate of return. If the price is exactly $100, then you could either buy it or turn it down, for $100 is the security's fair value.

In general, *the present value of a cash flow due n years in the future is the amount which, if it were on hand today, would grow to equal the future amount.* Since $100 would grow to $127.63 in 5 years at a 5 percent interest rate, $100 is the present value of $127.63 due 5 years in the future when the opportunity cost rate is 5 percent.

discounting

The process of finding the present value of a cash flow or a series of cash flows; the reverse of compounding.

Finding present values is called **discounting,** and it is simply the reverse of compounding — if you know the PV, you can compound to find the FV, while if you know the FV, you can discount to find the PV. When discounting, you would follow these steps:

Time Line:

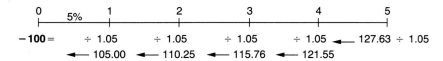

$$PV = ?$$ $$127.63$$

Equation:

To develop the discounting equation, we begin with Equation 5-1,

$$FV_n = PV(1 + i)^n = PV(FVIF_{i,n}), \tag{5-1}$$

and then solve it for PV in several equivalent forms:

$$PV = \frac{FV_n}{(1 + i)^n} = FV_n\left(\frac{1}{1 + i}\right)^n = FV_n(PVIF_{i,n}). \tag{5-2}$$

The last form of Equation 5-2 recognizes that the interest factor $PVIF_{i,n}$ is equal to the term in parentheses in the second section of the equation.

1. Numerical Solution:

```
      0       5%    1          2          3          4          5
      ├─────────────┼──────────┼──────────┼──────────┼──────────┤
  -100 =        ÷ 1.05     ÷ 1.05     ÷ 1.05     ÷ 1.05  ◄── 127.63 ÷ 1.05
              ◄── 105.00  ◄── 110.25  ◄── 115.76  ◄── 121.55
```

Divide $127.63 by 1.05 five times, or by $(1.05)^5$.

2. Tabular Solution:

Present Value Interest Factor for i and n (PVIF_{i,n})

The present value of $1 due n periods in the future discounted at i percent per period.

The term in parentheses in Equation 5-2 is called the **Present Value Interest Factor for i and n (PVIF_{i,n}),** and Table A-1 in Appendix A contains present value interest factors for selected values of i and n. The value of $PVIF_{i,n}$ for i = 5% and n = 5 is 0.7835, so the present value of $127.63 to be received after 5 years when the opportunity cost rate is 5 percent equals $100:

$$PV = \$127.63(PVIF_{5\%,5}) = \$127.63(0.7835) = \$100.$$

Figure 5-2 ▪ **Relationships among Present Value, Interest Rates, and Time**

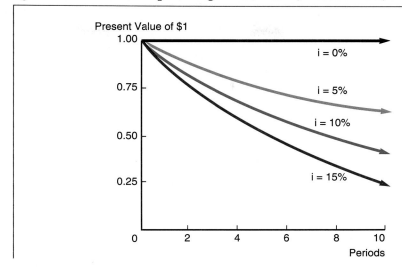

3. Financial Calculator Solution:

 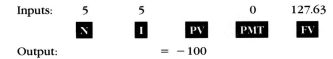

Inputs: 5   5   0   127.63

          [N]   [I]   [PV]   [PMT]   [FV]

Output: = −100

Enter N = 5, I = 5, PMT = 0, and FV = 127.63, and then press PV to get PV = −100.

Graphic View of the Discounting Process

Figure 5-2 shows how the present value of $1 (or any other sum) to be received in the future diminishes as the years to receipt increases. Again, the data used to plot the curves could be obtained either with a calculator or from Table A-1, and the graph shows (1) that the present value of a sum to be received at some future date decreases and approaches zero as the payment date is extended further into the future and (2) that the rate of decrease is greater the higher the interest (discount) rate. At relatively high interest rates, funds due in the future are worth very little today, and even at a relatively low discount rate, the present value of a sum due in the very distant future is quite small. For example, at a 20 percent discount rate, $1 million due in 100 years is worth only 1 cent today. (However, 1 cent would grow to $1 million in 100 years at 20 percent.)

Self-Test Questions

What is meant by the term "opportunity cost rate"?

What is discounting? How is it related to compounding?

How does the present value of an amount to be received in the future change as the time is extended and as the interest rate increases?

SOLVING FOR TIME AND INTEREST RATES

At this point, you should realize that the compounding and discounting processes are reciprocals of one another and that we have been dealing with one equation in two different forms:

FV Form:

$$FV_n = PV(1 + i)^n = PV(FVIF_{i,n}).$$ (5-1)

PV Form:

$$PV = \frac{FV_n}{(1 + i)^n} = FV_n\left(\frac{1}{1 + i}\right)^n = FV_n(PVIF_{i,n}).$$ (5-2)

There are four variables in these equations—PV, FV, i, and n—and if you know the values of any three, you (or your financial calculator) can find the value of the fourth. Thus far, we have always given you the interest rate (i) and the number of years (n) plus either the PV or the FV. In many situations, though, you will need to solve for either i or n, as we discuss below.

Solving for i

Suppose you can buy a security at a price of $78.35 which will pay you $100 after 5 years. Here we know PV, FV, and n, but we do not know i, the interest rate you will earn on your investment. Problems such as this one are solved as follows:

Time Line:

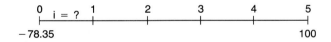

Equation:

$$FV_n = PV(1 + i)^n$$ (5-1)

$100 = \$78.35(1 + i)^5$. Solve for i.

 1. Numerical Solution:

Go through a trial-and-error process in which you insert different values of i into Equation 5-1 until you find a value which "works" in the sense that the right-hand side of the equation equals $100. The solution value is i = 0.05, or 5 percent. The trial-and-error procedure is extremely tedious and inefficient for most time value problems, so no one in the "real world" uses it.

 2. Tabular Solution:

$$FV_n = PV(1 + i)^n = PV(FVIF_{i,n})$$

$$\$100 = \$78.35(FVIF_{i,5})$$

$$FVIF_{i,5} = \$100/\$78.35 = 1.2763.$$

Find the value of the FVIF as shown above, and then look across the Period 5 row in Table A-3 until you find FVIF = 1.2763. This value is in the 5% column, so the interest rate at which $78.35 grows to $100 over 5 years is 5 percent.[4] This procedure can be used only if the interest rate is in the table; therefore, it will not work for fractional interest rates or where n is not a whole number. Approximation procedures can be used, but they are laborious and inexact.

3. Financial Calculator Solution:

Enter N = 5, PV = −78.35, PMT = 0, and FV = 100, and then press I to get I = 5. This procedure can be used for any interest rate or any value of n, including fractional values.

Solving for n

Suppose you know that the security will provide a return of 5 percent per year, that it will cost $78.35, and that you will receive $100 at maturity, but you do not know when the security matures. Thus, you know PV, FV, and i, but you do not know n, the number of periods. Here is the situation:

Time Line:

```
0    5%    1         2        n−1        n = ?
├─────────┼─────────┼── . . . ──┼──────────┤
−78.35                                  100
```

Equation:

$$FV_n = PV(1 + i)^n \tag{5-1}$$

$100 = \$78.35(1.05)^n$. Solve for n.

1. Numerical Solution:

Again, you could go through a trial-and-error process wherein you substituted different values for n into the equation. You would find (eventually) that n = 5 "works," so 5 is the number of years it takes for $78.35 to grow to $100 if the interest rate is 5 percent.

---

[4]The solution could also be set up in present value format:

$$PV = FV_n(PVIF_{i,n})$$

$$\$78.35 = \$100(PVIF_{i,5})$$

$$PVIF_{i,5} = \$78.35/\$100 = 0.7835.$$

This value corresponds to i = 5 percent in Table A-1.

2. Tabular Solution:

$$FV_n = PV(1 + i)^n = PV(FVIF_{i,n})$$

$$\$100 = \$78.35(FVIF_{5\%,n})$$

$$FVIF_{5\%,n} = \$100/\$78.35 = 1.2763.$$

Now look down the 5% column in Table A-3 until you find FVIF = 1.2763. This value is in Row 5, which indicates that it takes 5 years for $78.35 to grow to $100 at a 5 percent interest rate.[5]

3. Financial Calculator Solution:

Inputs: 5   −78.35   0   100

                    N   I   PV   PMT   FV

Output: = 5.0

Enter I = 5, PV = −78.35, PMT = 0, and FV = 100, and then press N to get N = 5.

Self-Test Questions

Assuming that you are given PV, FV, and the interest rate, i, write out an equation that can be used to determine the time period, n.

Assuming that you are given PV, FV, and the time period, n, write out an equation that can be used to determine the interest rate, i.

Explain how financial calculators can be used to solve for i and n.

FUTURE VALUE OF AN ANNUITY

annuity

A series of payments of an equal amount at fixed intervals for a specified number of periods.

ordinary (deferred) annuity

An annuity whose payments occur at the end of each period.

annuity due

An annuity whose payments occur at the beginning of each period.

An **annuity** is a series of equal payments made at fixed intervals for a specified number of periods. For example, $100 at the end of each of the next three years is a 3-year annuity. The payments are given the symbol PMT, and they can occur at either the beginning or the end of each period. If the payments occur at the *end* of each period, as they typically do, the annuity is called an **ordinary**, or **deferred, annuity.** If payments are made at the *beginning* of each period, the annuity is an **annuity due.** Since ordinary annuities are more common in finance, when the term "annuity" is used in this book, you should assume that the payments occur at the end of each period unless otherwise noted.

Ordinary Annuities

An ordinary, or deferred, annuity consists of a series of equal payments made at the *end* of each period. If you deposit $100 at the end of each year for 3 years in a savings account that pays 5 percent interest per year, how much will you

---

[5]The problem could also be solved as follows:

$$PV = FV_n(PVIF_{i,n})$$

$$\$78.35 = \$100(PVIF_{5\%,n})$$

$$PVIF_{5\%,n} = \$78.35/\$100 = 0.7835.$$

This value corresponds to n = 5 years in Table A-1.

FVA$_n$

The future value of an annuity over n periods.

have at the end of 3 years? To answer this question, we must find the future value of the annuity, **FVA$_n$**. Each payment is compounded out to the end of Period n, and the sum of the compounded payments is the future value of the annuity, FVA$_n$.

Time Line:

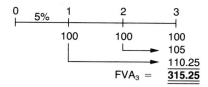

Here we show the regular time line as the top portion of the diagram, but we also show how each cash flow is processed to produce the value FVA$_n$ in the lower portion of the diagram.

Equation:

$$FVA_n = PMT(1 + i)^0 + PMT(1 + i)^1 + PMT(1 + i)^2 + \ldots + PMT(1 + i)^{n-1}$$

$$= PMT \sum_{t=1}^{n} (1 + i)^{n-t}.$$

$$(5\text{-}3)$$

Notice that the first line of Equation 5-3 presents the annuity payments in reverse order of payment, and the superscript in each term indicates the number of periods of interest each payment receives. In other words, because the first annuity payment was made at the end of Period 1, interest would be earned in Period 2 through Period n only; thus, compounding would be for n − 1 periods rather than n periods, compounding for the second annuity payment would be for Period 3 through Period n, or n − 2 periods, and so on. The last annuity payment is made at the same time the computation is made, so there is no time for interest to be earned; thus, the superscript 0 represents the fact that no interest is earned. Simplifying the first line produces the last line of Equation 5-3.

Future Value Interest Factor for an Annuity (FVIFA$_{i,n}$)

The future value interest factor for an annuity of n periods compounded at i percent.

1. Numerical Solution:

The lower section of the time line shows the numerical solution. The future value of each cash flow is found, and those FVs are summed to find the FV of the annuity. This is a tedious process for long annuities.

2. Tabular Solution:

The summation term in Equation 5-3 is called the **Future Value Interest Factor for an Annuity (FVIFA$_{i,n}$):**[6]

---

[6]The third term in Equation 5-3a is found by applying the algebra of geometric progressions. This equation is useful in situations where the required values of i and n are not in the tables and no financial calculator is available.

$$FVIFA_{i,n} = \sum_{t=1}^{n} (1 + i)^{n-t} = \frac{(1 + i)^n - 1}{i}. \qquad (5\text{-}3a)$$

FVIFAs have been calculated for various combinations of i and n; Table A-4 in Appendix A contains a set of FVIFA factors. To find the answer to the 3-year, $100 annuity problem, first refer to Table A-4 and look down the 5% column to the third period; the FVIFA is 3.1525. Thus, the future value of the $100 annuity is $315.25:

$$FVA_n = PMT(FVIFA_{i,n})$$
$$FVA_3 = \$100(FVIFA_{5\%,3}) = \$100(3.1525) = \$315.25.$$

3. Financial Calculator Solution:

Note that in annuity problems, the PMT key is used in conjunction with the N and I keys, plus either the PV or the FV key, depending on whether you are trying to find the PV or the FV of the annuity. In our example, you want the FV, so press the FV key to get the answer, $315.25. Since there is no initial payment, we input PV = 0.

Annuities Due

Had the three $100 payments in the previous example been made at the *beginning* of each year, the annuity would have been an *annuity due*. In the time line, each payment would be shifted to the left one year; therefore, each payment would be compounded for one extra year.

1. Time Line and Numerical Solution:

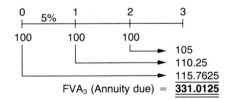

Again, the regular time line is shown at the top of the diagram, and the values as calculated with a regular calculator are shown in the right column.

2. Tabular Solution:

In an annuity due, each payment is compounded for one additional period, so the future value of the entire annuity is equal to the future value of an ordinary annuity compounded for one additional period. Here is the tabular solution:

$$\text{FVA}_n \text{ (Annuity due)} = \text{PMT(FVIFA}_{i,n})(1 + i) \qquad \text{(5-3b)}$$

$$= \$100(3.1525)(1.05) = \$331.0125.$$

The payments occur earlier, so more interest is earned. Therefore, the future value of the annuity due is larger, \$331.01 versus \$315.25 for the ordinary annuity.

3. Financial Calculator Solution:

Most financial calculators have a switch, or key, marked "DUE" or "BEG" that permits you to switch from end-of-period payments (ordinary annuity) to beginning-of-period payments (annuity due). When the beginning mode is activated, the display will normally show the word "BEGIN." Thus, to deal with annuities due, switch your calculator to "BEGIN" and proceed as before:

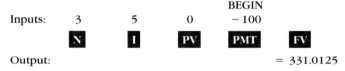

```
                                         BEGIN
Inputs:      3        5        0        −100

             N        I        PV       PMT       FV

Output:                                          = 331.0125
```

Enter N = 3, I = 5, PV = 0, PMT = −100, and then press FV to get the answer, \$331.01. *Since most problems specify end-of-period cash flows, you should always switch your calculator back to "END" mode after you work an annuity due problem.*

Self-Test Questions

What is the difference between an ordinary annuity and an annuity due?

How do you modify the equation for determining the value of an ordinary annuity in order to determine the value of an annuity due?

Which annuity has the greater *future* value: an ordinary annuity or an annuity due? Why?

Explain how financial calculators can be used to solve future value of annuity problems.

PRESENT VALUE OF AN ANNUITY

Suppose you were offered the following alternatives: (1) a 3-year annuity with payments of \$100 at the end of each year or (2) a lump sum payment today. You have no need for the money during the next three years, so if you accept the annuity, you would simply deposit the payments in a savings account that pays 5 percent interest per year. Similarly, the lump sum payment would be deposited into the same account. How large must the lump sum payment today be to make it equivalent to the annuity? Here is the setup:

Time Line:

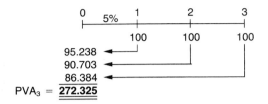

$$\text{PVA}_3 = \underline{\mathbf{272.325}}$$

The regular time line is shown at the top of the diagram, and the numerical solution values are shown in the left column. The PV of the annuity, **PVA$_n$**, is $272.325.

PVA$_n$

The present value of an annuity of n periods.

Equation:

The general equation used to find the PV of an ordinary annuity is shown below:[7]

$$\text{PVA}_n = \text{PMT}\left(\frac{1}{1+i}\right)^1 + \text{PMT}\left(\frac{1}{1+i}\right)^2 + \ldots + \text{PMT}\left(\frac{1}{1+i}\right)^n$$

$$= \text{PMT}\sum_{t=1}^{n}\left(\frac{1}{1+i}\right)^t. \tag{5-4}$$

1. Numerical Solution:

The present value of each cash flow is found and then summed to find the PV of the annuity. This procedure is shown in the lower section of the time line diagram, where we see that the PV of the annuity is $272.325.

2. Tabular Solution:

The summation term in Equation 5-4 is called the **Present Value Interest Factor for an Annuity (PVIFA$_{i,n}$),** and values for the term at different values of i and n are shown in Table A-2 at the back of the book. Thus,

$$\text{PVA}_n = \text{PMT}(\text{PVIFA}_{i,n}). \tag{5-4a}$$

Present Value Interest Factor for an Annuity (PVIFA$_{i,n}$)

The present value interest factor for an annuity of n periods discounted at i percent.

[7]The summation term is called the PVIFA, and, using the geometric progression solution process, its value is found to be

$$\sum_{t=1}^{n}\left(\frac{1}{1+i}\right)^t = \frac{1 - \dfrac{1}{(1+i)^n}}{i} = \frac{1}{i} - \frac{1}{i(1+i)^n}.$$

This form of the equation is useful for dealing with annuities when the values for i and n are not in the tables and no financial calculator is available.

To find the answer to the 3-year, $100 annuity problem, simply refer to Table A-2 and look down the 5% column to the third period. The PVIFA is 2.7232, so the present value of the $100 annuity is $272.32:

$$PVA_n = PMT(PVIFA_{i,n})$$

$$PVA_3 = \$100(PVIFA_{5\%,3}) = \$100(2.7232) = \$272.32.$$

3. Financial Calculator Solution:

Inputs: 3   5   −100   0

| N | I | PV | PMT | FV |

Output: = 272.32

Enter N = 3, I = 5, PMT = −100, and FV = 0, and then press the PV key to find the PV, $272.32.

One especially important application of the annuity concept relates to loans with constant payments, such as mortgages and auto loans. With such loans, called *amortized loans,* the amount borrowed is the present value of an ordinary annuity, and the payments constitute the annuity stream. We will examine constant payment loans in more depth in a later section of this chapter.

Annuities Due

Had the three $100 payments in our earlier example been made at the beginning of each year, the annuity would have been an *annuity due.* Each payment would be shifted to the left one year, so each payment would be discounted for one less year. Here is the time line setup:

1. Time Line and Numerical Solution:

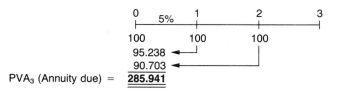

PVA₃ (Annuity due) = **285.941**

Again, we find the PV of each cash flow and then sum these PVs to find the PV of the annuity due. This procedure is illustrated in the lower section of the time line diagram. Since the cash flows occur sooner, the PV of the annuity due exceeds that of the ordinary annuity, $285.94 versus $272.32.

2. Tabular Solution:

In an annuity due, each payment is discounted for one less period. Since its payments come in faster, an annuity due is more valuable than an ordinary annuity, and this higher value is found by multiplying the PV of an ordinary annuity by $(1 + i)$:

$$PVA_n \text{ (Annuity due)} = PMT(PVIFA_{i,n})(1 + i) \qquad (5\text{-}4b)$$

$$= \$100(2.7232)(1.05) = \$285.94.$$

3. Financial Calculator Solution:

			BEGIN	
Inputs:	3	5	− 100	0
	N	**I**	**PV**	**PMT**	**FV**
Output:			= 285.94	

Switch to the beginning-of-period mode, and then enter N = 3, I = 5, PMT = − 100, and FV = 0, and then press PV to get the answer, $285.94. *Again, since most problems deal with end-of-period cash flows, don't forget to switch your calculator back to the "END" mode.*

 Self-Test Questions

Which annuity has the greater present value: an ordinary annuity or an annuity due? Why?

Explain how financial calculators can be used to find present values of annuities.

PERPETUITIES

perpetuity
A stream of equal payments expected to continue forever.

Most annuities call for payments to be made over some finite period of time—for example, $100 per year for three years. However, some annuities go on indefinitely, or perpetually, and these annuities are called **perpetuities.** The present value of a perpetuity is found by applying Equation 5-5.[8]

$$PV \text{ (Perpetuity)} = \frac{\text{Payment}}{\text{Interest rate}} = \frac{PMT}{i}. \qquad (5\text{-}5)$$

consol
A perpetual bond issued by the British government to consolidate past debts; in general, any perpetual bond.

Perpetuities can be illustrated by some British securities issued after the Napoleonic Wars. In 1815, the British government sold a huge bond issue and used the proceeds to pay off many smaller issues that had been floated in prior years to pay for the wars. Since the purpose of the bonds was to consolidate past debts, the bonds were called **consols.** Suppose each consol promised to pay $100 per year in perpetuity. (Actually, interest was stated in pounds.) What would each bond be worth if the opportunity cost rate, or discount rate, was 5 percent? The answer is $2,000:

$$PV \text{ (Perpetuity)} = \frac{\$100}{0.05} = \$2,000 \text{ if } i = 5\%.$$

Suppose the interest rate rose to 10 percent; what would happen to the consol's value? The value would drop to $1,000:

$$PV \text{ (Perpetuity)} = \frac{\$100}{0.10} = \$1,000 \text{ at } i = 10\%.$$

---

[8]The derivation of Equation 5-5 is given in Appendix 4A of Eugene F. Brigham and Louis C. Gapenski, *Intermediate Financial Management,* 4th ed. (Forth Worth, Tex.: Dryden Press, 1993).

We see that the value of a perpetuity changes dramatically when interest rates change. Perpetuities are discussed further in Chapter 6, where procedures for finding the value of various types of securities are discussed.

Self-Test Questions

What happens to the value of a perpetuity when interest rates increase?

What happens when interest rates decrease? Why do these changes occur?

UNEVEN CASH FLOW STREAMS

uneven cash flow stream
A series of cash flows in which the amount varies from one period to the next.

payment (PMT)
This term designates constant cash flows.

cash flow (CF)
This term designates uneven cash flows.

The definition of an annuity includes the words *constant amount* — in other words, annuities involve payments that are equal in every period. Although many financial decisions do involve constant payments, some important decisions involve uneven, or nonconstant, cash flows; for example, common stocks typically pay an increasing stream of dividends over time, and fixed asset investments such as new equipment normally do not generate constant cash flows. Consequently, it is necessary to extend our time value discussion to include **uneven cash flow streams.**

Throughout the book, we will follow convention and reserve the term **payment (PMT)** for annuity situations where the cash flows are constant, and we will use the term **cash flow (CF)** to denote uneven cash flows. Financial calculators are set up to follow this convention, so if you are using one and dealing with uneven cash flows, you will need to use the cash flow register.

Present Value of an Uneven Cash Flow Stream

The PV of an uneven cash flow stream is found as the sum of the PVs of the individual cash flows of the stream. For example, suppose we must find the PV of the following cash flow stream, discounted at 6 percent:

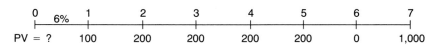

The PV will be found by applying this general present value equation:

$$PV = CF_1\left(\frac{1}{1+i}\right)^1 + CF_2\left(\frac{1}{1+i}\right)^2 + \ldots + CF_n\left(\frac{1}{1+i}\right)^n$$

$$= \sum_{t=1}^{n} CF_t\left(\frac{1}{1+i}\right)^t = \sum_{t=1}^{n} CF_t(PVIF_{i,t}). \tag{5-6}$$

We could find the PV of each individual cash flow using the numerical, tabular, or financial calculator methods, and then sum these values to find the present value of the stream. Here is what the process would look like:

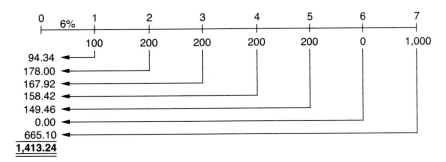

All we did was to apply Equation 5-6, show the individual PVs in the left column of the diagram, and then sum these individual PVs to find the PV of the entire stream.

The present value of a cash flow stream can always be found by summing the present values of the individual cash flows as shown above. However, cash flow regularities within the stream may allow the use of shortcuts. For example, notice that cash flows 2 through 5 represent an annuity. We can use that fact to solve the problem in a slightly different manner:

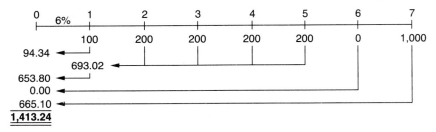

The Year 2−5 cash flows represent an ordinary annuity, so we find its PV at Year 1 (one period before the first payment). This PV ($693.02) must then be discounted back one more period to get its Year 0 value.

Problems involving uneven cash flows can be solved in one step with most financial calculators. First, you input the individual cash flows, in chronological order, into the cash flow register. Cash flows are usually designated CF_0, CF_1, CF_2, CF_3, and so on. Next, you enter the interest rate. At this point, you have substituted in all the known values of Equation 5-6, so you only need to press the NPV key to find the present value of the stream. The calculator has been programmed to find the PV of each cash flow and then to sum these values to find the PV of the entire stream. To input the cash flows for this problem, enter 0 (because $CF_0 = 0$), 100, 200, 200, 200, 200, 0, 1000 in that order into the cash flow register, enter I = 6, and then press NPV to obtain the answer, $1,413.19, which differs slightly from the long-form solution because of rounding errors.

Two points should be noted. First, when dealing with the cash flow register, the calculator uses the term "NPV" rather than "PV." The N stands for "net," so NPV is the abbreviation for "Net Present Value," which is simply the net present value of a series of positive and negative cash flows. Our example has no negative cash flows, but if it did, we would simply input them with negative signs.

The second point to note is that annuities can be entered into the cash f[...] register more efficiently by using the N_j key. (On some calculators, you [...] prompted to enter the number of times the cash flow occurs, and on still ot[...] calculators the procedures for inputting data, as we discuss next, may be diff[...] ent. You should consult your calculator manual to determine the approp[...] ate steps for your specific calculator.) In this illustration, you would ent[...] $CF_0 = 0$, $CF_1 = 100$, $CF_2 = 200$, $N_j = 4$ (which tells the calculator that th[...] 200 occurs 4 times), $CF_6 = 0$, and $CF_7 = 1000$. Then enter I = 6 and pres[...] the NPV key, and 1,413.19 will appear in the display. Also, note that amounts entered into the cash flow register remain in the register until they are cleared. Thus, if you had previously worked a problem with eight cash flows and then moved to a problem with only four cash flows, the calculator would assume that the cash flows from the first problem belonged to the second problem. Therefore, you must be sure to clear the cash flow register before starting a new problem.

Future Value of an Uneven Cash Flow Stream

terminal value

The future value of an uneven cash flow stream.

The future value of an uneven cash flow stream (sometimes called the **terminal value**) is found by compounding each payment to the end of the stream and then summing the future values:

$$FV_n = CF_1(1 + i)^{n-1} + CF_2(1 + i)^{n-2} + \ldots + CF_n(1 + i)^{n-t}$$

$$= \sum_{t=1}^{n} CF_t(1 + i)^{n-t} = \sum_{t=1}^{n} CF_t(FVIF_{i,t}). \tag{5-7}$$

The future value of our illustrative uneven cash flow stream is \$2,124.92:

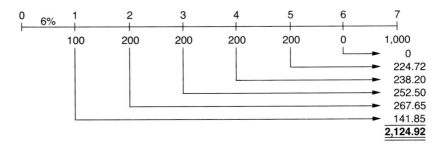

Some financial calculators have a net future value (NFV) key which, after the cash flows and interest rate have been entered into the calculator, can be used to obtain the future value of an uneven cash flow stream. In any event, it is easy enough to compound the individual cash flows to the terminal year and then to sum them to find the FV of the stream. Also, we are generally more interested in the present value of an asset's cash flow stream than in the future value because the present value represents today's value, which we can compare to the price of the asset.

Solving for i with Uneven Cash Flow Streams

It is relatively easy to solve for i numerically or with the tables when the cash flows are lump sums or annuities. However, it is *extremely difficult* to solve for i if the cash flows are uneven, as you will have to go through many tedious trial-and-error calculations. With a financial calculator, though, it is easy to find the value of i. Simply input the CF values into the cash flow register and then press the IRR key. IRR stands for "internal rate of return," which is the return on an investment. We will defer further discussion of this calculation for now, but we will take it up later in our discussion of capital budgeting methods in Chapter 14.

Self-Test Questions

Give two examples of financial decisions that would typically involve uneven flows of cash.

What is meant by the term "terminal value"?

annual compounding
The arithmetic process of determining the final value of a cash flow or series of cash flows when interest is added once a year.

semiannual compounding
The arithmetic process of determining the final value of a cash flow or series of cash flows when interest is added twice a year.

SEMIANNUAL AND OTHER COMPOUNDING PERIODS

In all of our examples thus far, we have assumed that interest is compounded once a year, or annually. This is called **annual compounding.** Suppose, however, that you put $100 into a bank which states that it pays a 6 percent annual interest rate but that interest is added each six months. This is called **semiannual compounding.** How much would you accumulate at the end of one year, two years, or some other period under semiannual compounding?

To illustrate semiannual compounding, assume that $100 is placed into an account at an interest rate of 6 percent and left there for 3 years. First, consider again what happens under annual compounding:

 1. Time Line, Equation, and Numerical Solution:

$$
\begin{array}{ccccc}
0 & \!\!6\% & 1 & 2 & 3 \\
\vdash\!\!\!\!\!-\!\!\!\!\!\!-\!\!\!\!\!\!\!\!-\! & & & \\
-100 & & & & FV = ?
\end{array}
$$

$$FV_n = PV(1 + i)^n = \$100(1.06)^3$$
$$= \$119.10.$$

 2. Tabular Solution:

$$FV_3 = \$100(FVIF_{6\%,3}) = \$100(1.1910) = \$119.10.$$

 3. Financial Calculator Solution:

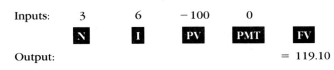

Inputs:	3	6	−100	0	
	N	I	PV	PMT	FV
Output:					= 119.10

Now consider what happens under semiannual compounding. Here we have n = 2 × 3 = 6 semiannual periods, and you will earn i = 6%/2 = 3% every six months. Note that on all types of contracts, interest is always quoted as an annual rate, and if compounding occurs more frequently than once a year, that fact is stated, along with the rate. In our example, the quoted rate is "6 percent, compounded semiannually." Here is how we find the FV after 3 years at 6 percent with semiannual compounding:

Time Line:

1. Equation and Numerical Solution:

$$FV_n = PV(1 + i)^n = \$100(1.03)^6$$
$$= \$100(1.1941) = \$119.41.$$

Here i = rate per period = annual rate/compounding periods per year = 6%/2 = 3%, and n = the total number of periods = years × periods per year = 3 × 2 = 6.

2. Tabular Solution:

$$FV_6 = \$100(FVIF_{3\%, 6}) = \$100(1.1941) = \$119.41.$$

Look up FVIF for 3%, 6 periods in Table A-3 and complete the arithmetic.

3. Financial Calculator Solution:

Enter N = years × periods per year = 3 × 2 = 6, I = annual rate/periods per year = 6/2 = 3, PV = −100, and PMT = 0, and then press FV to find the answer, $119.41 versus $119.10 under annual compounding. The FV is larger under semiannual compounding because interest on interest is being earned more frequently.

Throughout the world economy, different compounding periods are used for different types of investments. For example, bank accounts generally pay interest daily; most bonds pay interest semiannually; and stocks generally pay dividends quarterly.[9] If we are to properly compare securities with different compounding periods, we need to put them on a common basis. This requires

---

[9]Some banks and savings and loans even pay interest compounded *continuously*. Continuous compounding is discussed in Appendix 5A.

nominal (quoted) interest rate

The contracted, or quoted, interest rate.

effective annual rate (EAR)

The annual rate of interest actually being earned, as opposed to the quoted rate.

us to distinguish between **nominal,** or **quoted, interest rates** and **effective annual rates.**[10]

The nominal, or quoted, interest rate in our example is 6 percent. *The effective annual rate (EAR) is defined as that rate which would produce the same ending (future) value if annual compounding had been used.* In our example, the effective annual rate is the rate which would produce an FV of $119.41 at the end of Year 3.

We can determine the effective annual rate, given the nominal rate and the number of compounding periods per year, by solving this equation:

$$\text{Effective annual rate} = \text{EAR} = \left(1 + \frac{i_{\text{Nom}}}{m}\right)^{m} - 1.0. \qquad (5\text{-}8)$$

Here i_{Nom} is the nominal, or quoted, interest rate, and m is the number of compounding periods per year. For example, to find the effective annual rate if the nominal rate is 6 percent and semiannual compounding is used, we have[11]

$$\text{Effective annual rate} = \text{EAR} = \left(1 + \frac{0.06}{2}\right)^{2} - 1.0$$

$$= (1.03)^{2} - 1.0$$

$$= 1.0609 - 1.0 = 0.0609 = 6.09\%.$$

Semiannual compounding (or any nonannual compounding) can be handled in two ways: (1) State everything on a periodic basis rather than on an annual basis. For example, use n = 6 periods rather than n = 3 years, and use i = 3% per period rather than i = 6% per year. (2) Alternatively, find the effective annual rate by applying Equation 5-8, and then use this rate as an annual rate over the given number of years. In our example, use i = 6.09% and n = 3 years. Here are the time lines for the two alternative procedures:

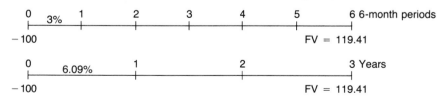

We see that both procedures produce the same result, $119.41. Of course, once you start dealing with noninteger interest rates such as 6.09 percent, the use of a calculator is essential.

---

[10]The term *nominal rate* as it is used here has a different meaning than the way it was used in Chapter 3. There, nominal interest rates referred to stated market rates as opposed to real (zero inflation) rates. In this chapter, the term *nominal rate* means the stated, or quoted, annual rate as opposed to the effective annual rate. In both cases, though, *nominal* means *stated,* or *quoted,* as opposed to some adjusted rate.

[11]Most financial calculators are programmed to find the EAR or, given the EAR, to find the nominal rate. This is called "interest rate conversion," and you simply enter the nominal rate and the number of compounding periods per year and then press the EFF% key to find the EAR.

The points made about semiannual compounding can be generalized as follows. When compounding occurs more frequently than once a year, we can use a modified version of Equation 5-1 to find the future value of any lump sum:

$$\text{Annual compounding: } FV_n = PV(1 + i)^n. \tag{5-1}$$

$$\text{More frequent compounding: } FV_n = PV\left(1 + \frac{i_{Nom}}{m}\right)^{mn}. \tag{5-9}$$

Here i_{Nom} is the nominal, or quoted, rate, m is the number of times compounding occurs per year, and n is the number of years. For example, when banks pay daily interest, the value of m is set at 365 and Equation 5-9 is applied.[12]

Annual Percentage Rate (APR)

The periodic rate × the number of periods per year.

To illustrate further the effects of compounding more frequently than annually, consider the interest rate charged on credit cards. Many banks charge 1.5 percent per month, and, in their advertising, they state that the **Annual Percentage Rate (APR)** is 18.0 percent. However, the true rate is the effective annual rate of 19.6 percent:[13]

$$\text{Effective annual rate} = EAR = \left(1 + \frac{0.18}{12}\right)^{12} - 1$$
$$= (1.015)^{12} - 1.0$$
$$= 0.196 = 19.6\%.$$

Semiannual and other compounding periods can also be used for discounting, and for both lump sums and annuities. First, consider the case where we want to find the PV of an ordinary annuity of $100 per year for 3 years when the interest rate is 8 percent, compounded annually:

Time Line:

```
        0   8%   1        2        3
        ├────────┼────────┼────────┤
PV = ?      − 100    − 100    − 100
```

1. Numerical Solution:

Find the PV of each cash flow and sum them. The PV of the annuity is $257.71.

---

[12]To illustrate, the future value of $1 invested at 10 percent for 1 year under daily compounding is $1.1052:

$$FV_n = \$1\left(1 + \frac{0.10}{365}\right)^{365(1)} = \$1(1.105156) = \$1.1052.$$

[13]The *annual percentage rate (APR)* is the rate often used in bank loan advertisements since it meets the minimum requirements contained in "truth in lending" laws. Typically, the APR is defined as (Periodic rate)(Number of periods in one year). For example, the APR on a credit card with interest charges of 1.5 percent per month is 1.5%(12) = 18.0%. The APR understates the effective annual rate, so banks tend to use the APR when advertising what they charge on loans, but they use the effective annual rate when advertising rates on savings accounts and certificates of deposit because they want to make their deposit rates look high. Their marketing people took finance!

2. Tabular Solution:

$$PVA_n = PMT(PVIFA_{i,n})$$
$$= \$100(PVIFA_{8\%,3}) = \$100(2.5771) = \$257.71.$$

3. Financial Calculator Solution:

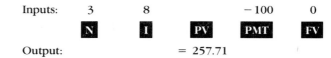

Inputs: 3   8   −100   0

            N   I   PV   PMT   FV

Output: = 257.71

Now let's change the situation. For example, suppose the annuity calls for payments of $50 each 6 months rather than for $100 per year, and the rate is 8 percent, compounded semiannually. Here is the time line:

Time Line:

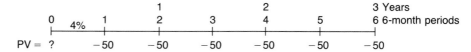

```
                    1              2          3 Years
    0    4%    1    2      3       4     5    6 6-month periods
    ├──────────┼─────┼──────┼───────┼─────┼──────┤
PV = ?      −50   −50    −50     −50   −50    −50
```

1. Numerical Solution:

Find the PV of each cash flow by discounting at 4 percent. Treat each tick mark on the time line as a period, so there would be 6 periods. The PV of the annuity is $262.11 versus $257.71 under annual compounding.

2. Tabular Solution:

$$PVA_n = PMT(PVIFA_{i,n})$$
$$= \$50(PVIFA_{4\%,6}) = \$50(5.2421) = \$262.11.$$

3. Financial Calculator Solution:

Inputs: 6   4   −50   0

            N   I   PV   PMT   FV

Output: = 262.11

The semiannual payments come in sooner, so the $50 semiannual annuity is more valuable than the $100 annual annuity.

Self-Test Questions

What changes must you make in your calculations to determine the future value of an amount that is being compounded at 8 percent semiannually versus one being compounded annually at 8 percent?

Why is semiannual compounding better than annual compounding from a saver's standpoint?

What are meant by the terms "annual percentage rate," "effective annual rate," and "nominal interest rate"?

How does the term "nominal rate" used in this chapter differ from the term as it was used in Chapter 3?

FRACTIONAL TIME PERIODS

In all of the examples used thus far in the chapter, we have assumed that payments occur at either the beginning or the end of periods but not at some date *within* a period. However, we often encounter situations that require compounding or discounting over fractional periods. For example, suppose you deposited $100 in a bank that pays 10 percent interest, compounded annually. If you leave your money in the bank for 9 months, or 0.75 of the year, how much would you have in your account? Problems such as this can be handled easily, but the tables generally cannot be used.

Time Line and Equation:

$$FV_n = PV(1 + i)^n.$$

1. Numerical Solution:

$$FV_n = \$100(1.10)^{0.75} = \$100(1.0741) = \$107.41.$$

2. Financial Calculator Solution:[14]

Inputs:	0.75	10	−100	0	
	N	**I**	**PV**	**PMT**	**FV**
Output:					= 107.41

Present values, annuities, and problems where you must find interest rates or numbers of periods can all be handled with ease. Note, though, that financial calculators are essential for many fractional year problems—the tables are useless.

 Self-Test Question

Why are the tables useless for fractional time periods?

AMORTIZED LOANS

One of the most important applications of compound interest involves loans that are paid off in installments over time. Included are automobile loans, home mortgage loans, student loans, and most business debt other than very short-term loans and long-term bonds. If a loan is to be repaid in equal periodic amounts (monthly, quarterly, or annually), it is said to be an **amortized loan.**[15]

amortized loan

A loan that is repaid in equal payments over its life.

---

[14]Some older calculators will produce an answer of FV = 107.50. This result occurs because these calculators solve for fractional time periods using a straight-line interpolation procedure.

[15]The word *amortized* comes from the Latin *mors,* meaning "death," so an amortized loan is one that is "killed off" over time.

To illustrate, suppose a firm borrows $1,000, and the loan is to be repaid in 3 equal payments at the end of each of the next 3 years. The lender is to receive 6 percent interest on the loan balance that is outstanding at the beginning of each year. The first task is to determine the amount the firm must repay each year, or the annual payment. To find this amount, recognize that the $1,000 represents the present value of an annuity of PMT dollars per year for 3 years, discounted at 6 percent:

Time Line and Equation:

$$
\begin{array}{ccccc}
0 & \underline{\quad 6\% \quad} & 1 & 2 & 3 \\
\vdash & & \vdash & \vdash & \vdash \\
-1,000 & & \text{PMT} & \text{PMT} & \text{PMT}
\end{array}
$$

$$PV = \frac{PMT}{(1 + i)^1} + \frac{PMT}{(1 + i)^2} + \frac{PMT}{(1 + i)^3} = \sum_{t=1}^{n} \frac{PMT}{(1 + i)^t}$$

$$\$1,000 = \sum_{t=1}^{n} \frac{PMT}{(1.06)^t}.$$

Here we know everything except PMT, so we can solve the equation for PMT.

1. Numerical Solution:

You could follow the trial-and-error procedure, inserting values for PMT in the equation until you found a value that "worked" and caused the right side of the equation to equal $1,000. This would be a tedious process, but you would eventually find PMT = $374.11.

2. Tabular Solution:

Substitute in known values and look up PVIFA for 6%, 3 periods in Table A-2:

$$PVA_n = PMT(PVIFA_{i,n})$$
$$\$1,000 = PMT(PVIFA_{6\%,3}) = PMT(2.6730)$$
$$PMT = \$1,000/2.6730 = \$374.11.$$

3. Financial Calculator Solution:

Inputs:	3	6	−1000		0
	N	I	PV	PMT	FV
Output:				= 374.11	

amortization schedule
A schedule showing precisely how a loan will be repaid. It gives the required payment on each payment date and a breakdown of the payment, showing how much is interest and how much is repayment of principal.

Enter N = 3, I = 6, PV = −1000, and FV = 0, and then press the PMT key to find PMT = $374.11.

Therefore, the firm must pay the lender $374.11 at the end of each of the next 3 years, and the percentage cost to the borrower, which is also the rate of return to the lender, will be 6 percent.

Each payment consists partly of interest and partly of repayment of principal. This breakdown is given in the **amortization schedule** shown in Table 5-2. The interest component is largest in the first year, and it declines as the outstanding balance of the loan decreases. For tax purposes, a business bor-

Table 5-2 ▪ Loan Amortization Schedule, 6 Percent Interest Rate

Year	Beginning Amount (1)	Payment (2)	Interest[a] (3)	Repayment of Principal[b] (2) − (3) = (4)	Remaining Balance (1) − (4) = (5)
1	$1,000.00	$ 374.11	$ 60.00	$ 314.11	$685.89
2	685.89	374.11	41.15	332.96	352.93
3	352.93	374.11	21.18	352.93	0.00
		$1,122.33	$122.33	$1,000.00	

[a]Interest is calculated by multiplying the loan balance at the beginning of the year by the interest rate. Therefore, interest in Year 1 is $1,000(0.06) = $60; in Year 2 it is $685.89(0.06) = $41.15; and in Year 3 it is $352.93(0.06) = $21.18.

[b]Repayment of principal is equal to the payment of $374.11 minus the interest charge for each year.

rower reports the interest component shown in Column 3 as a deductible cost each year, while the lender reports this same amount as taxable income.

Financial calculators are programmed to calculate amortization tables—you simply enter the input data, and then press one key to get each entry in Table 5-2. If you have a financial calculator, it is worthwhile to read the appropriate section of the manual and learn how to use its amortization feature.

 Self-Test Questions

To construct an amortization schedule, how do you determine the amount of the periodic payments?

How do you determine the amount of each payment that goes to interest and to principal?

COMPARISON OF DIFFERENT TYPES OF INTEREST RATES

Up to this point, we have discussed three different types of interest rates. If you will be working with relatively difficult time value problems, then it is useful to compare the three types and to know when each should be used, as we discuss below.

1. **Nominal, or quoted, rate.** This is the rate that is quoted by borrowers and lenders. Practitioners in the stock, bond, mortgage, commercial loan, consumer loan, banking, and other markets express all financial contracts in terms of nominal rates. So, if you talk with a banker, broker, mortgage lender, auto finance company, or student loan officer about rates, the nominal rate is the one he or she will normally quote you. However, to be meaningful, the nominal rate quotation must also include the number of compounding periods per year. For example, a bank might offer 8.5 percent, compounded quarterly, on CDs, or a mutual fund might offer 8 percent, compounded monthly, on its money market account.

Nominal rates can be compared with one another, *but only if the instruments being compared use the same number of compounding periods per year.* Thus, to compare an 8.5 percent, annual payment CD with an 8 percent, daily payment money market fund, we would need to put both instruments on an *effective annual rate (EAR)* basis as discussed later in this section.

Note also that the nominal rate is never shown on a time line, and it is never used as an input in a financial calculator unless compounding occurs only once a year (in which case i_{Nom} = periodic rate = EAR). If more frequent compounding occurs, you must use either the periodic rate or the effective annual rate as discussed below.[16]

2. **Periodic rate, i_{PER}.** This is the rate charged by a lender or paid by a borrower each period. It can be a rate per year, per 6-month period, per quarter, per month, per day, or per any other time interval (usually one year or less). For example, a bank might charge 1 percent per month on its credit card loans, or a finance company might charge 3 percent per quarter on consumer loans. We find the periodic rate as follows:

$$\text{Periodic rate, } i_{PER} = i_{Nom}/m, \qquad (5\text{-}10)$$

which implies that

$$i_{Nom} = (\text{Periodic rate})(m) = \text{APR}. \qquad (5\text{-}11)$$

Here i_{Nom} is the nominal annual rate and m is the number of compounding periods per year. APR, which is the annual percentage rate, represents the periodic rate stated on an annual basis without considering interest compounding; it is i_{Nom}. *The APR is never used in actual calculations; it is simply reported to borrowers.* To illustrate, consider a finance company loan at 3 percent per quarter:

$$\text{Nominal annual rate} = i_{Nom} = (\text{Periodic rate})(m) = (3\%)(4) = 12\%,$$

and

$$\text{Periodic rate} = i_{Nom}/m = 12\%/4 = 3\% \text{ per quarter.}$$

If there is one payment per year, or if interest is added only once a year, then m = 1 and the periodic rate is equal to the nominal rate. *But, in all cases where interest is added or payments are made more frequently than annually, the periodic rate is less than the nominal rate.*

The periodic rate is used for calculations in problems where these two conditions hold: (1) payments occur on a regular basis more frequently

---

[16]Some calculators have a switch which permits you to specify the number of payments per year. We find it less confusing to set this switch to 1 and then leave it there. We prefer to work with "periods" when more than one payment occurs each year because this maintains a consistency between number of periods and the periodic interest rate.

than once a year, and (2) a payment is made on each compounding (or discounting) date. Thus, if you were dealing with an auto loan which required monthly payments, with a semiannual payment bond, or with an education loan which called for quarterly payments, then on your time line and in your calculations you would use the Periodic rate = i_{Nom}/m. The periodic rate would not be used to find the PV of an annuity calling for annual payments but where discounting occurred quarterly, because in that case the payments and discounting periods per year do not coincide.

Note that in each of the above examples the interest compounding period is the same as the payment period. *The periodic rate can be used directly in calculations, but only if the number of payments per year is consistent with the number of interest compounding periods.*

To illustrate use of the periodic rate, suppose you make eight quarterly payments of $100 into an account which pays 12 percent, compounded quarterly. How much would you have after two years?

Time Line and Equation:

$$FVA_n = \sum_{t=1}^{n} PMT(1 + i)^{n-t} = \sum_{t=1}^{8} \$100(1.03)^{8-t}.$$

 1. Numerical Solution:

Compound each $100 payment at 12/4 = 3 percent for the appropriate number of periods, and then sum these individual FVs to find the FV of the payment stream, $889.23.

 2. Tabular Solution:

Look up FVIFA for 3%, 8 periods, in Table A-4, and complete the arithmetic:

$$FVA_n = PMT(FVIFA_{i,n})$$
$$= \$100(FVIFA_{3\%,8}) = \$100(8.8923) = \$889.23.$$

3. Financial Calculator Solution:

Inputs:	8	3	0	-100	
	N	**I**	**PV**	**PMT**	**FV**
Output:					= 889.23

Input N = 2 × 4 = 8, I = 12/4 = 3, PV = 0, and PMT = -100, and then press the FV key to get FV = $889.23.

3. Effective annual rate (EAR).   This is the rate with which, under annual compounding (m = 1), we would obtain the same result as if we had used a given periodic rate with m compounding periods per year. The EAR is found as follows:

$$\text{EAR} = \left(1 + \frac{i_{\text{Nom}}}{m}\right)^m - 1.0. \tag{5-8}$$

In the EAR equation, i_{Nom}/m is the periodic rate and m is the number of periods per year. For example, suppose you could borrow using either a credit card which charges 1 percent per month or a bank loan with a 12 percent quoted nominal interest rate that is compounded quarterly. Which should you choose? To answer this question, the cost rate of each alternative must be expressed as an EAR:

$$\text{Credit card loan: EAR} = (1 + 0.01)^{12} - 1.0 = (1.01)^{12} - 1.0$$
$$= 1.126825 - 1.0 = 0.126825 = 12.6825\%.$$
$$\text{Bank loan: EAR} = (1 + 0.03)^4 - 1.0 = (1.03)^4 - 1.0$$
$$= 1.125509 - 1.0 = 0.125509 = 12.5509\%.$$

Thus, the credit card loan is slightly more costly than the bank loan. This result should have been intuitive to you—both loans have the same 12 percent nominal rate, yet you would have to make monthly payments on the credit card versus quarterly payments under the bank loan.

Self-Test Questions

Define the nominal (or quoted) rate, the periodic rate, and the effective annual rate.

How are the nominal rate, the periodic rate, and the effective annual rate related? Can you think of a situation where all three of these rates will be the same?

SUMMARY

Financial decisions often involve situations in which someone pays money at one point in time and receives money at some later time. Dollars that are paid or received at two different points in time are different, and this difference is recognized and accounted for by *time value of money (TVM) analysis.* We summarize below the types of TVM analysis and the key concepts covered in this chapter, using the data shown in Figure 5-3 to illustrate the various points. Refer to the figure constantly, and try to find in it an example of the points covered as you go through this summary.

▪ **Compounding** is the process of determining the **future value (FV)** of a cash flow or a series of cash flows. The compounded amount, or future value, is equal to the beginning amount plus the interest earned.

▪ Future value: $FV_n = PV(1 + i)^n = PV(FVIF_{i,n})$.
(single payment)

Example: $961.50 compounded for 1 year at 4 percent:

$$FV_1 = \$961.50(1.04)^1 = \$1,000.$$

Figure 5-3 ▪ Illustration for Chapter Summary (i = 4%)

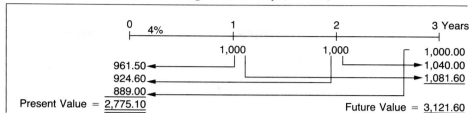

▪ **Discounting** is the process of finding the **present value (PV)** of a future cash flow or a series of cash flows; discounting is the reciprocal of compounding.

▪ Present value: (single payment)
$$PV = \frac{FV_n}{(1 + i)^n} = FV_n \left(\frac{1}{1 + i} \right)^n = FV_n(PVIF_{i,n}).$$

Example: $1,000 discounted back for 2 years at 4 percent:

$$PV = \frac{\$1,000}{(1.04)^2} = \$1,000 \left(\frac{1}{1.04} \right)^2 = \$1,000(0.9246) = \$924.60.$$

▪ An **annuity** is defined as a series of equal periodic payments (PMT) for a specified number of periods.

▪ Future value: (annuity)
$$FVA_n = PMT(1+i)^0 + PMT(1+i)^1 + PMT(1+i)^2 + \ldots + PMT(1+i)^{n-1}$$

$$= PMT \sum_{t=1}^{n} (1 + i)^{n-t}$$

$$= PMT \left[\frac{(1 + i)^n - 1}{i} \right] = PMT(FVIFA_{i,n}).$$

Example: FVA of 3 payments of $1,000 when i = 4%:

$$FVA_3 = \$1,000(3.1216) = \$3,121.60.$$

▪ Present value: (annuity)
$$PVA_n = \frac{PMT}{(1 + i)^1} + \frac{PMT}{(1 + i)^2} + \ldots + \frac{PMT}{(1 + i)^n}$$

$$= PMT \sum_{t=1}^{n} \left[\frac{1}{1+i} \right]^t = PMT \left[\frac{1 - \frac{1}{(1+i)^n}}{i} \right] = PMT(PVIFA_{i,n}).$$

Example: PVA of 3 payments of $1,000 when i = 4%:

$$PVA_3 = \$1,000(2.7751) = \$2,775.10.$$

▪ An annuity whose payments occur at the *end* of each period is called an **ordinary annuity.** The formulas above are for ordinary annuities.

▪ If each payment occurs at the beginning of the period rather than at the end, then we have an **annuity due.** In Figure 5-3, the payments would be shown at Years 0, 1, and 2 rather than at Years 1, 2, and 3. The PV of each payment would be larger, because each payment would be discounted back one year less, and hence the PV of the annuity would also be larger.

Similarly, the FV of the annuity due would also be larger because each payment would be compounded for an extra year. The following formulas can be used to convert the PV and FV of an ordinary annuity to an annuity due:

$$\text{PVA(annuity due)} = \text{PVA of an ordinary annuity} \times (1 + i).$$

Example: PVA of 3 beginning-of-year payments of $1,000 when i = 4%:
PVA (annuity due) = $1,000(2.7751)(1.04) = $2,886.10.

$$\text{FVA(annuity due)} = \text{FVA of an ordinary annuity} \times (1 + i).$$

Example: FVA of 3 beginning-of-year payments of $1,000 when
i = 4%:
FVA (annuity due) = $1,000(3.1216)(1.04) = $3,246.46.

▪ If the time line in Figure 5-3 were extended out forever so that the $1,000 payments went on forever, we would have a **perpetuity** whose value could be found as follows:

$$\text{Value of perpetuity} = \frac{\text{PMT}}{i} = \frac{\$1,000}{0.04} = \$25,000.$$

▪ If the cash flows in Figure 5-3 were unequal, we could not use the annuity formulas. To find the PV or FV of an uneven series, find the PV or FV of each individual cash flow and then sum them. However, if some of the cash flows constitute an annuity, then the annuity formula can be used to calculate the present value of that part of the cash flow stream.

▪ **Financial calculators** have built-in programs which perform all of the operations discussed in this chapter. It would be useful for you to buy such a calculator and to learn how to use it. Even if you do, though, it is essential that you understand the logical processes involved.

▪ TVM calculations generally involve equations which have four variables, so if you know three of the values, you (or your calculator) can solve for the fourth.

▪ If you know the cash flows and the PV (or FV) of a cash flow stream, you can **determine the interest rate.** For example, in the Figure 5-3 illustration, if you were given the information that a loan called for 3 payments of $1,000 each, and that the loan had a value today of PV = $2,775.10, then you could find the interest rate that caused the sum of the PVs of the payments to equal $2,775.10. Since we are dealing with an annuity, we could proceed as follows:

a. Recognize that $\text{PVA}_n = \$2,775.10 = \$1,000(\text{PVIFA}_{i,3})$.
b. Solve for $\text{PVIFA}_{i,3}$:

$$\text{PVIFA}_{i,3} = \$2,775.10/\$1,000 = 2.7751.$$

c. Look up 2.7751 in Table A-2, on the third row. It is in the 4% column, so the interest rate must be 4 percent. If the factor did not appear in the table, this would indicate that the interest rate was not a whole number. In this case, you could not use this procedure to find the exact rate. In practice, though, this is not a problem, because most people use financial calculators to find interest rates.

▌ Thus far in the summary we have assumed that payments are made, and interest is earned, at the end of each year, or annually. However, many contracts call for more frequent payments; for example, mortgage and auto loans call for monthly payments, and most bonds pay interest semi-annually. Similarly, most banks compute interest daily. When compounding occurs more frequently than once a year, this fact must be recognized. We can use the Figure 5-3 example to illustrate the procedures. First, the following formula is used to find an **effective annual rate (EAR)**:

$$\text{Effective annual rate} = \text{EAR} = \left(1 + \frac{i_{\text{Nom}}}{m}\right)^m - 1.0.$$

For semiannual compounding, the effective annual rate is 4.04 percent:

$$\left(1 + \frac{0.04}{2}\right)^2 - 1.0 = (1.02)^2 - 1.0 = 1.0404 - 1.0 = 0.0404 = 4.04\%.$$

This rate could then be used (with a calculator but not with the tables) to find the PV or FV of each payment in Figure 5-3.

If the $1,000 per-year payments were actually payable as $500 each 6 months, you would simply redraw Figure 5-3 to show 6 payments of $500 each, but you would also need to use a **periodic interest rate** of 4%/2 = 2% for determining the PV or FV of the payments.

▌ The general equation for finding the future value for any number of compounding periods per year is:

$$\text{FV}_n = \text{PV}\left(1 + \frac{i_{\text{Nom}}}{m}\right)^{mn},$$

where

i_{Nom} = quoted interest rate.
$\quad m$ = number of compounding periods per year.
$\quad n$ = number of years.

▌ An **amortized loan** is one that is paid off in equal payments over a specified period. An **amortization schedule** shows how much of each payment constitutes interest, how much is used to reduce the principal, and the remaining balance of the loan at each point in time.

The concepts covered in this chapter will be used throughout the remainder of the book. For example, in Chapter 6 we will apply present value concepts to the process of valuing stocks and bonds, and we will see that the market prices of securities are established by determining the present values of the cash flows they are expected to provide. In later chapters, the same basic concepts are applied to corporate decisions involving both expenditures on capital assets and determining the types of capital that should be used to pay for assets.

Questions

5-1 What is an *opportunity cost rate*? How is this rate used in time value analysis, and where is it shown on a time line? Is the opportunity rate a single number which is used in all situations?

5-2 An *annuity* is defined as a series of payments of a fixed amount for a specific number of periods. Thus, $100 a year for 10 years is an annuity, but $100 in Year 1, $200 in Year 2, and $400 in Years 3 through 10 does *not* constitute an annuity. However, the second series *contains* an annuity. Is this statement true or false?

5-3 If a firm's earnings per share grew from $1 to $2 over a 10-year period, the *total growth* would be 100 percent, but the *annual growth rate* would be *less than* 10 percent. True or false? Explain.

5-4 Would you rather have a savings account that pays 5 percent interest compounded semiannually or one that pays 5 percent interest compounded daily? Explain.

5-5 To find the present value of an uneven series of cash flows, you must find the PVs of the individual cash flows and then sum them. Annuity procedures can never be of use, even if some of the cash flows constitute an annuity (for example, $100 each for Years 3, 4, 5, and 6), because the entire series is not an annuity. Is this statement true or false? Explain.

5-6 The present value of a perpetuity is equal to the payment on the annuity, PMT, divided by the interest rate, i: $PV = PMT/i$. What is the *sum,* or future value, of a perpetuity of PMT dollars per year? (Hint: The answer is infinity, but explain why.)

Self-Test Problems *(Solutions Appear in Appendix B)*

ST-1
Key terms

Define each of the following terms:
a. PV; i; INT; FV_n; n; PVA_n; FVA_n; PMT; m; i_{Nom}
b. $FVIF_{i,n}$; $PVIF_{i,n}$; $FVIFA_{i,n}$; $PVIFA_{i,n}$
c. Opportunity cost rate
d. Annuity; lump sum payment; cash flow; uneven cash flow stream
e. Ordinary (deferred) annuity; annuity due
f. Perpetuity; consol
g. Outflow; inflow; time line
h. Compounding; discounting
i. Annual, semiannual, quarterly, monthly, and daily compounding
j. Effective annual rate (EAR); nominal (quoted) interest rate; APR; periodic rate
k. Amortization schedule; principal component versus interest component of a payment; amortized loan
l. Terminal value

ST-2
Future value

Assume that it is now January 1, 1993. On January 1, 1994, you will deposit $1,000 into a savings account that pays 8 percent.
a. If the bank compounds interest annually, how much will you have in your account on January 1, 1997?
b. What would your January 1, 1997, balance be if the bank used quarterly compounding rather than annual compounding?
c. Suppose you deposited the $1,000 in 4 payments of $250 each on January 1 of 1994, 1995, 1996, and 1997. How much would you have in your account on January 1, 1997, based on 8 percent annual compounding?
d. Suppose you deposited 4 equal payments in your account on January 1 of 1994, 1995, 1996, and 1997. Assuming an 8 percent interest rate, how large would each of your payments have to be for you to obtain the same ending balance as you calculated in Part a?

ST-3
Time value
of money

Assume that it is now January 1, 1993, and you will need $1,000 on January 1, 1997. Your bank compounds interest at an 8 percent annual rate.
a. How much must you deposit on January 1, 1994, to have a balance of $1,000 on January 1, 1997?

b. If you want to make equal payments on each January 1 from 1994 through 1997 to accumulate the $1,000, how large must each of the 4 payments be?

c. If your father were to offer either to make the payments calculated in Part b ($221.92) or to give you a lump sum of $750 on January 1, 1994, which would you choose?

d. If you have only $750 on January 1, 1994, what interest rate, compounded annually, would you have to earn to have the necessary $1,000 on January 1, 1997?

e. Suppose you can deposit only $186.29 each January 1 from 1994 through 1997, but you still need $1,000 on January 1, 1997. What interest rate, with annual compounding, must you seek out to achieve your goal?

f. To help you reach your $1,000 goal, your father offers to give you $400 on January 1, 1994. You will get a part-time job and make 6 additional payments of equal amounts each 6 months thereafter. If all of this money is deposited in a bank which pays 8 percent, compounded semiannually, how large must each of the 6 payments be?

g. What is the effective annual rate being paid by the bank in Part f?

h. *Reinvestment rate risk* was defined in Chapter 3 as being the risk that maturing securities (and coupon payments on bonds) will have to be reinvested at a lower rate of interest than they were previously earning. Is there a reinvestment rate risk involved in the preceding analysis? If so, how might this risk be eliminated?

ST-4
Effective annual rates

Bank A pays 8 percent interest, compounded quarterly, on its money market account. The managers of Bank B want its money market account to equal Bank A's effective annual rate, but interest is to be compounded on a monthly basis. What nominal, or quoted, rate must Bank B set?

Problems

5-1
Present and future values
for different periods

Find the following values, *using the equations,* and then work the problems using a financial calculator or the tables to check your answers. Disregard rounding errors. (Hint: If you are using a financial calculator, you can enter the known values and then press the appropriate key to find the unknown variable. Then, without clearing the TVM register, you can "override" the variable which changes by simply entering a new value for it and then pressing the key for the unknown variable to obtain the second answer. This procedure can be used in Parts b and d, and in many other situations, to see how changes in input variables affect the output variable.)

a. An initial $500 compounded for 1 year at 6 percent.

b. An initial $500 compounded for 2 years at 6 percent.

c. The present value of $500 due in 1 year at a discount rate of 6 percent.

d. The present value of $500 due in 2 years at a discount rate of 6 percent.

5-2
Present and future values for
different interest rates

Use the tables or a financial calculator to find the following values. See the hint for Problem 5-1.

a. An initial $500 compounded for 10 years at 6 percent.

b. An initial $500 compounded for 10 years at 12 percent.

c. The present value of $500 due in 10 years at a 6 percent discount rate.

d. The present value of $1,552.90 due in 10 years at a 12 percent discount rate and at a 6 percent rate. Give a verbal definition of the term *present value,* and illustrate it using a time line with data from this problem. As a part of your answer, explain why present values are dependent upon interest rates.

5-3
Time for a lump
sum to double

To the closest year, how long will it take $200 to double if it is deposited and earns the following rates? [Notes: (1) See the hint for Problem 5-1. (2) This problem cannot be solved exactly with some financial calculators. For example, if you enter PV = −200, FV = 400, and I = 7 in an HP-12C, and then press the N key, you will get 11 years for Part a. The correct answer is 10.2448 years, which rounds to 10, but the calculator rounds up. However, the HP-10B and HP-17B give the correct answer. You should look up FVIF = 400/200 = 2 in the tables for Parts a, b, and c, but figure out Part d.]

a. 7 percent.
b. 10 percent.
c. 18 percent.
d. 100 percent.

5-4

Future value of an annuity

Find the *future value* of the following annuities. The first payment in these annuities is made at the *end* of Year 1; that is, they are *ordinary annuities*. (Note: See the hint to Problem 5-1. Also, note that you can leave values in the TVM register, switch to "BEG," press FV, and find the FV of the annuity due.)

a. $400 per year for 10 years at 10 percent.
b. $200 per year for 5 years at 5 percent.
c. $400 per year for 5 years at 0 percent.
d. Now rework Parts a, b, and c assuming that payments are made at the *beginning* of each year; that is, they are *annuities due*.

5-5

Present value of an annuity

Find the *present value* of the following *ordinary annuities* (see note to Problem 5-4.):

a. $400 per year for 10 years at 10 percent.
b. $200 per year for 5 years at 5 percent.
c. $400 per year for 5 years at 0 percent.
d. Now rework Parts a, b, and c assuming that payments are made at the *beginning* of each year; that is, they are *annuities due*.

5-6

Uneven cash flow stream

a. Find the present values of the following cash flow streams. The appropriate interest rate is 8 percent. (Hint: It is fairly easy to work this problem dealing with the individual cash flows. However, if you have a financial calculator, read the section of the manual which describes how to enter cash flows such as the ones in this problem. This will take a little time, but the investment will pay huge dividends throughout the course. Note, if you do work with the cash flow register, that you must enter $CF_0 = 0$.)

Year	Cash Stream A	Cash Stream B
1	$100	$300
2	400	400
3	400	400
4	400	400
5	300	100

b. What is the value of each cash flow stream at a 0 percent interest rate?

5-7

Effective rate of interest

Find the interest rates, or rates of return, on each of the following:

a. You *borrow* $700 and promise to pay back $749 at the end of 1 year.
b. You *lend* $700 and receive a promise to be paid $749 at the end of 1 year.
c. You borrow $85,000 and promise to pay back $201,229 at the end of 10 years.
d. You borrow $9,000 and promise to make payments of $2,684.80 per year for 5 years.

5-8

Future value for various compounding periods

Find the amount to which $500 will grow under each of the following conditions:

a. 12 percent compounded annually for 5 years.
b. 12 percent compounded semiannually for 5 years.
c. 12 percent compounded quarterly for 5 years.
d. 12 percent compounded monthly for 5 years.

5-9

Present value for various compounding periods

Find the present value of $500 due in the future under each of the following conditions:

a. 12 percent nominal rate, semiannual compounding, discounted back 5 years.
b. 12 percent nominal rate, quarterly compounding, discounted back 5 years.
c. 12 percent nominal rate, monthly compounding, discounted back 1 year.

5-10

Future value of an annuity for various compounding periods

Find the future values of the following ordinary annuities:

a. FV of $400 each 6 months for 5 years at a nominal rate of 12 percent, compounded semiannually.
b. FV of $200 each 3 months for 5 years at a nominal rate of 12 percent, compounded quarterly.
c. The annuities described in Parts a and b have the same amount of money paid into them during the 5-year period and both earn interest at the same nominal rate, yet the annuity in Part b earns $101.60 more than the one in Part a over the 5 years. Why does this occur?

5-11

Effective versus nominal interest rates

The First City Bank pays 7 percent interest, compounded annually, on time deposits. The Second City Bank pays 6 percent interest, compounded quarterly.

a. Based on effective interest rates, in which bank would you prefer to deposit your money?
b. Could your choice of banks be influenced by the fact that you might want to withdraw your funds during the year as opposed to at the end of the year? In answering this question, assume that funds must be left on deposit during the entire compounding period in order for you to receive any interest.

5-12

Amortization schedule

a. Set up an amortization schedule for a $25,000 loan to be repaid in equal installments at the end of each of the next 5 years. The interest rate is 10 percent.
b. How large must each annual payment be if the loan is for $50,000? Assume that the interest rate remains at 10 percent and that the loan is paid off over 5 years.
c. How large must each payment be if the loan is for $50,000, the interest rate is 10 percent, and the loan is paid off in equal installments at the end of each of the next 10 years? This loan is for the same amount as the loan in Part b, but the payments are spread out over twice as many periods. Why are these payments not half as large as the payments on the loan in Part b?

5-13

Effective rates of return

Assume that AT&T's pension fund managers are considering two alternative securities as investments: (1) Security Z (for zero intermediate year cash flows), which costs $422.41 today, pays nothing during its 10-year life, and then pays $1,000 after 10 years or (2) Security B, which has a cost today of $1,000 and which pays $80 at the end of each of the next 9 years and then $1,080 at the end of Year 10.

a. What is the rate of return on each security?
b. Assume that the interest rate AT&T's pension fund managers can earn on the fund's money falls to 6 percent immediately after the securities are purchased and is expected to remain at that level for the next 10 years. What would the price of each security change to, what would the fund's profit be on each security, and what would be the percentage profit (profit divided by cost) for each security?
c. Assuming that the cash flows for each security had to be reinvested at the new 6 percent market interest rate, (1) what would be the value attributable to each security at the end of 10 years and (2) what "actual, after-the-fact" rate of return would the fund have earned on each security? (Hint: The "actual" rate of return is found as the interest rate which causes the PV of the compounded Year 10 amount to equal the original cost of the security.)
d. Now assume all the facts as given in Parts b and c except assume that the interest rate *rose* to 12 percent rather than fell to 6 percent. What would happen to the profit figures as developed in Part b and to the "actual" rates of return as determined in Part c? Explain your results.

5-14
Required annuity payments

A father is planning a savings program to put his daughter through college. His daughter is now 13 years old. She plans to enroll at the university in 5 years, and it should take her 4 years to complete her education. Currently, the cost per year (for everything —food, clothing, tuition, books, transportation, and so forth) is $12,500, but a 5 percent inflation rate in these costs is forecasted. The daughter recently received $7,500 from her grandfather's estate; this money, which is invested in a bank account paying 8 percent interest compounded annually, will be used to help meet the costs of the daughter's education. The rest of the costs will be met by money the father will deposit in the savings account. He will make 6 equal deposits to the account in each year from now until his daughter starts college. These deposits will begin today and will also earn 8 percent interest.

a. What will be the present value of the cost of four years of education at the time the daughter becomes 18? [Hint: Calculate the future value of the cost (at 5%) for each year of her education, then discount three of these costs back (at 8%) to the year in which she turns 18, then sum the four costs.]

b. What will be the value of the $7,500 which the daughter received from her grandfather's estate when she starts college at age 18? (Hint: Compound for 5 years at 8%.)

c. If the father is planning to make the first of 6 deposits today, how large must each deposit be for him to be able to put his daughter through college?

EXAM-TYPE PROBLEMS

The problems in this section are set up in such a way that they could be used as multiple-choice exam problems.

5-15
Present value comparison

Which amount is worth more at 14 percent: $1,000 in hand today or $2,000 due in 6 years?

5-16
Growth rates

Martell Corporation's 1992 sales were $12 million. Sales were $6 million 5 years earlier (in 1987).

a. To the nearest percentage point, at what rate have sales been growing?

b. Suppose someone calculated the sales growth for Martell Corporation in Part a as follows: "Sales doubled in 5 years. This represents a growth of 100 percent in 5 years, so, dividing 100 percent by 5, we find the growth rate to be 20 percent per year." Explain what is wrong with this calculation.

5-17
Expected rate of return

Oregon-Pacific invests $4 million to clear a tract of land and to set out some young pine trees. The trees will mature in 10 years, at which time Oregon-Pacific plans to sell the forest at an expected price of $8 million. What is Oregon-Pacific's expected rate of return?

5-18
Effective rate of interest

Your broker offers to sell you a note for $13,250 that will pay $2,345.05 per year for 10 years. If you buy the note, what rate of interest (to the closest percent) will you be earning?

5-19
Effective rate of interest

A mortgage company offers to lend you $85,000; the loan calls for payments of $8,273.59 per year for 30 years. What interest rate is the mortgage company charging you?

5-20
Required lump sum payment

To complete your last year in business school and then go through law school, you will need $10,000 per year for 4 years, starting next year (that is, you will need to withdraw the first $10,000 one year from today). Your rich uncle offers to put you through school, and he will deposit in a bank paying 7 percent interest a sum of money that is sufficient to provide the four payments of $10,000 each. His deposit will be made today.

a. How large must the deposit be?

b. How much will be in the account immediately after you make the first withdrawal? After the last withdrawal?

5-21

Repaying a loan

While Steve Bouchard was a student at the University of Florida, he borrowed $12,000 in student loans at an annual interest rate of 9 percent. If Steve repays $1,500 per year, how long, to the nearest year, will it take him to repay the loan?

5-22

Reaching a financial goal

You need to accumulate $10,000. To do so, you plan to make deposits of $1,250 per year, with the first payment being made a year from today, in a bank account which pays 12 percent annual interest. Your last deposit will be less than $1,250 if less is needed to round out to $10,000. How many years will it take you to reach your $10,000 goal, and how large will the last deposit be?

5-23

Present value of a perpetuity

What is the present value of a perpetuity of $100 per year if the appropriate discount rate is 7 percent? If interest rates in general were to double and the appropriate discount rate rose to 14 percent, what would happen to the present value of the perpetuity?

5-24

Financial calculator needed; PV and effective annual rate

Assume that you inherited some money. A friend of yours is working as an unpaid intern at a local brokerage firm, and her boss is selling some securities which call for four payments, $50 at the end of each of the next 3 years, plus a payment of $1,050 at the end of Year 4. Your friend says she can get you some of these securities at a cost of $900 each. Your money is now invested in a bank that pays an 8 percent nominal (quoted) interest rate but with quarterly compounding. You regard the securities as being just as safe, and as liquid, as your bank deposit, so your required effective annual rate of return on the securities is the same as that on your bank deposit. You must calculate the value of the securities to decide whether they are a good investment. What is their present value to you?

5-25

Loan amortization

Assume that your aunt sold her house on December 31 and that she took a mortgage in the amount of $10,000 as part of the payment. The mortgage has a quoted (or nominal) interest rate of 10%, but it calls for payments every 6 months, beginning on June 30, and the mortgage is to be amortized over 10 years. Now, one year later, your aunt must file a Form 1099 with the IRS and with the person who bought the house, informing them of the interest that was included in the two payments made during the year. (This interest will be income to your aunt and a deduction to the buyer of the house.) To the closest dollar, what is the total amount of interest that was paid during the first year?

5-26

Loan amortization

Your company is planning to borrow $1,000,000 on a 5-year, 15%, annual payment, fully amortized term loan. What fraction of the payment made at the end of the second year will represent repayment of principal?

5-27

Nonannual compounding

a. It is now January 1, 1993. You plan to make 5 deposits of $100 each, one every 6 months, with the first payment being made *today*. If the bank pays a nominal interest rate of 12 percent but uses semiannual compounding, how much will be in your account after 10 years?

b. You must make a payment of $1,432.02 ten years from today. To prepare for this payment, you will make 5 equal deposits, beginning today and for the next 4 quarters, in a bank that pays a nominal interest rate of 12 percent, quarterly compounding. How large must each of the 5 payments be?

5-28

Nominal rate of return

Sue Sharpe, manager of Oaks Mall Jewelry, wants to sell on credit, giving customers 3 months in which to pay. However, Sue will have to borrow from her bank to carry the accounts payable. The bank will charge a nominal 15 percent, but with monthly compounding. Sue wants to quote a nominal rate to her customers (all of whom are expected to pay on time) which will exactly cover her financing costs. What nominal annual rate should she quote to her credit customers?

5-29

Financial calculator needed;
Required annuity payments

Assume that your father is now 50 years old, that he plans to retire in 10 years, and that he expects to live for 25 years after he retires, that is, until he is 85. He wants a fixed retirement income that has the same purchasing power at the time he retires as $40,000 has today (he realizes that the real value of his retirement income will decline year by year after he retires). His retirement income will begin the day he retires, 10 years from today, and he will then get 24 additional annual payments. Inflation is expected to be 5 percent per year from today forward; he currently has $100,000 saved up; and he expects to earn a return on his savings of 8 percent per year, annual compounding. To the nearest dollar, how much must he save during each of the next 10 years (with deposits being made at the end of each year) to meet his retirement goal?

INTEGRATIVE PROBLEM

5-30

Time value of
money analysis

Assume that you are nearing graduation and that you have applied for a job with a local bank. As part of the bank's evaluation process, you have been asked to take an examination which covers several financial analysis techniques. The first section of the test addresses time value of money analysis. See how you would do by answering the following questions.

a. Draw time lines for (a) a $100 lump sum cash flow at the end of Year 2, (b) an ordinary annuity of $100 per year for 3 years, and (c) an uneven cash flow stream of − $50, $100, $75, and $50 at the end of Years 0 through 3.

b. (1) What is the future value of an initial $100 after 3 years if it is invested in an account paying 10 percent annual interest?
    (2) What is the present value of $100 to be received in 3 years if the appropriate interest rate is 10 percent?

c. We sometimes need to find how long it will take a sum of money (or anything else) to grow to some specified amount. For example, if a company's sales are growing at a rate of 20 percent per year, how long will it take sales to double?

d. What is the difference between an ordinary annuity and an annuity due? What type of annuity is shown below? How would you change it to the other type of annuity?

e. (1) What is the future value of a 3-year ordinary annuity of $100 if the appropriate interest rate is 10 percent?
    (2) What is the present value of the annuity?
    (3) What would the future and present values be if the annuity were an annuity due?

f. What is the present value of the following uneven cash flow stream? The appropriate interest rate is 10 percent, compounded annually.

g. What annual interest rate will cause $100 to grow to $125.97 in 3 years?

h. (1) Will the future value be larger or smaller if we compound an initial amount more often than annually, for example, every 6 months, or *semiannually,* holding the stated interest rate constant? Why?

    (2) Define (a) the stated, or quoted, or nominal, rate, (b) the periodic rate, and (c) the effective annual rate (EAR).

    (3) What is the effective annual rate for a nominal rate of 10 percent, compounded semiannually? Compounded quarterly? Compounded daily?

    (4) What is the future value of $100 after 3 years under 10 percent semiannual compounding? Quarterly compounding?

i. Will the effective annual rate ever be equal to the nominal (quoted) rate?

j. (1) What is the value at the end of Year 3 of the following cash flow stream if the quoted interest rate is 10 percent, compounded semiannually?

    (2) What is the PV of the same stream?

    (3) Is the stream an annuity?

    (4) An important rule is that you should *never* show a nominal rate on a time line or use it in calculations unless what condition holds? (Hint: Think of annual compounding, when $i_{Nom} = EAR = i_{PER}$.) What would be wrong with your answer to questions j (1) and j (2) if you used the nominal rate 10% rather than the periodic rate $i_{Nom}/2 = 10\%/2 = 5\%$?

k. (1) Construct an amortization schedule for a $1,000, 10 percent annual rate loan with 3 equal installments.

    (2) What is the annual interest expense for the borrower, and the annual interest income for the lender, during Year 2?

(Parts l through o require a financial calculator.)

l. Suppose on January 1, 1993, you deposit $100 in an account that pays a nominal, or quoted, interest rate of 11.33463 percent, with interest added (compounded) daily. How much will you have in your account on October 1, or after 9 months?

m. Now suppose you leave your money in the bank for 21 months. Thus, on January 1, 1993, you deposit $100 in an account that pays a 12 percent effective annual interest rate. How much will be in your account on October 1, 1994?

n. Suppose someone offered to sell you a note calling for the payment of $1,000 15 months from today. They offer to sell it to you for $850. You have $850 in a bank time deposit which pays a 6.76649 percent nominal rate with daily compounding, which is a 7 percent effective annual interest rate, and you plan to leave the money in the bank unless you buy the note. The note is not risky—you are sure it will be paid on schedule. Should you buy the note? Check the decision in three ways: (1) by comparing your future value if you buy the note versus leaving your money in the bank, (2) by comparing the PV of the note with your current bank account, and (3) by comparing the EAR on the note versus that of the bank account.

o. Suppose the note discussed in Part n had a cost of $850, but called for 5 quarterly payments of $190 each, with the first payment due in 3 months rather than $1,000 at the end of 15 months. Would it be a good investment for you?

Work the problem in this section only if you are using the computer problem diskette.

5-31

Amortization schedule

Use the computerized model in the File C5 to solve this problem.

a. Set up an amortization schedule for a $30,000 loan to be repaid in equal install-ments at the end of each of the next 20 years at an interest rate of 10 percent. What is the annual payment?

b. Set up an amortization schedule for a $60,000 loan to be repaid in 20 equal annual installments at an interest rate of 10 percent. What is the annual payment?

c. Set up an amortization schedule for a $60,000 loan to be repaid in 20 equal annual installments at an interest rate of 20 percent. What is the annual payment?

Appendix 5A

Continuous Compounding and Discounting

In Chapter 5, we dealt only with situations where interest is added at discrete intervals—annually, semiannually, monthly, and so forth. In some instances, though, it is possible to have instantaneous, or *continuous,* growth. In this appendix, we discuss present value and future value calculations when the interest rate is compounded continuously.

Continuous Compounding

continuous compounding

A situation in which inter-est is added continuously rather than at discrete points in time.

The relationship between discrete and **continuous compounding** is illustrated in Fig-ure 5A-1. Panel a shows the annual compounding case, where interest is added once a year; Panel b shows the situation when compounding occurs twice a year; and Panel c shows interest being earned continuously. As the graphs show, the more frequent the compounding period, the larger the final compounded amount because interest is earned on interest more often.

Equation 5-9 in the chapter can be applied to any number of compounding periods per year:

$$\text{More frequent compounding: } FV_n = PV \left(1 + \frac{i_{Nom}}{m} \right)^{mn}. \tag{5-9}$$

To illustrate, let PV = $100, i = 10%, and n = 5. At various compounding periods per year, we obtain the following future values at the end of 5 years:

$$\text{Annual: } FV_5 = \$100 \left(1 + \frac{0.10}{1} \right)^{1(5)} = \$100(1.10)^5 = \$161.05.$$

$$\text{Semiannual: } FV_5 = \$100 \left(1 + \frac{0.10}{2} \right)^{2(5)} = \$100(1.05)^{10} = \$162.89.$$

$$\text{Monthly: } FV_5 = \$100 \left(1 + \frac{0.10}{12} \right)^{12(5)} = \$100(1.0083)^{60} = \$164.53.$$

$$\text{Daily: } FV_5 = \$100 \left(1 + \frac{0.10}{365} \right)^{365(5)} = \$164.86.$$

Figure 5A-1 ▪ **Annual, Semiannual, and Continuous Compounding: Future Value with i = 25%**

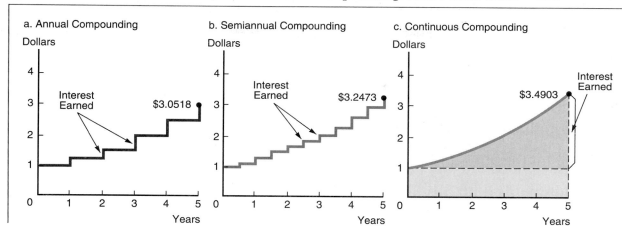

We could keep going, compounding every hour, every minute, every second, and so on. At the limit, we could compound every instant, or *continuously*. The equation for continuous compounding is

$$FV_n = PV(e^{in}). \tag{5A-1}$$

Here e is the value 2.7183... .[1] If $100 is invested for 5 years at 10 percent compounded continuously, then FV_5 is calculated as follows:

$$\text{Continuous: } FV_5 = \$100[e^{0.10(5)}] = \$100(2.7183...)^{0.5}$$
$$= \$164.872.$$

Continuous Discounting

Equation 5A-1 can be transformed into Equation 5A-2 and used to determine present values under continuous discounting:

$$PV = \frac{FV_n}{e^{in}} = FV_n(e^{-in}). \tag{5A-2}$$

Thus, if $1,649 is due in 10 years, and if the appropriate *continuous* discount rate, i, is 5 percent, then the present value of this future payment is

$$PV = \frac{\$1,649}{(2.7183...)^{0.5}} = \frac{\$1,649}{1.649} = \$1,000.$$

---

[1]Calculators with exponential functions can be used to evaluate Equation 5A-1.

Bond and Stock Valuation

A M A N A G E R I A L   P E R S P E C T I V E

A major battle in 1992 concerned the issue of whether banks, savings and loans, insurance companies, and credit unions should "mark to market" their security holdings. Richard Breeden, Chairman of the Securities and Exchange Commission (SEC), argued that they should. He noted that one reason for the S&L debacle was that those institutions were reporting bonds and other securities at cost on their financial statements even though the securities' market values had fallen drastically since they were acquired. As a result, when liabilities were subtracted from the overvalued assets, a positive net worth was shown, whereas in reality the institutions were insolvent because their liabilities exceeded the true value of their assets. This situation prevented federal regulators from closing institutions down; they stayed in business and continued to incur losses for which taxpayers will be paying over the next 30 to 40 years.

The financial institutions and their accountants are lobbying against the mark-to-market policy—they want to continue to report securities on the basis of historical costs. Their primary argument is that banks, insurance companies, and the like generally hold securities until they mature, at which time they are paid off at face value. Thus, if a security's market value declines below its cost, this is just a paper loss that will not be realized, and it should be ignored for accounting purposes. The bankers also argue that in view of the volatility of our financial markets, a requirement to mark to market could easily make fundamentally sound institutions appear to be insolvent, and this would have a serious adverse effect on our financial system. Finally, the bankers argue that it is often hard to determine the value of a security, hence an element of arbitrariness as opposed to objectivity would be injected if the mark-to-market rule were imposed.

As you read this chapter, think about how the concepts we cover could be applied if the mark-to-market rule were imposed. Would financial statements developed under such a rule be more useful than statements developed under the historical cost rule? All things considered, do you think the rule should be imposed?

In Chapter 1 we noted that the goal of managerial finance is to maximize the value of firms. Then, in Chapter 4, we saw how investors determine the rates of return they require on securities, and in Chapter 5 we examined time value of money analysis. These TVM concepts are used by managers and investors to establish the worth of any asset whose value is derived from future cash flows; such assets include real estate, factories, machinery, oil wells, coal mines, farmland, stocks, and bonds. Now, in this chapter, we use time value of money techniques to explain how investors establish the values of stocks and bonds. The material covered in the chapter is obviously important to investors, and it is equally important to financial managers. *Indeed, since all important corporate decisions should be analyzed in terms of how they will affect the price of the firm's stock, it is essential that managers know how stock prices are determined.*

BOND VALUATION

Corporations raise capital in two primary forms—debt and common equity. Our first task in this chapter is to examine the valuation process for bonds, the principal type of long-term debt.

bond
A long-term debt instrument.

A **bond** is a long-term promissory note issued by a business or governmental unit. For example, on January 2, 1993, Allied Food Products borrowed $50 million by selling 50,000 individual bonds for $1,000 each. Allied received the $50 million, and it promised to pay the bondholders annual interest and to repay the $50 million on a specified date. The lenders were willing to give Allied $50 million, so the value of the bond issue was $50 million. But how did the investors decide that the issue was worth $50 million? As a first step in explaining how the values of this and other bonds are determined, we need to define some terms:

par value
The nominal or face value of a stock or bond.

1. **Par value.** The **par value** is the stated face value of the bond; it is usually set at $1,000, although multiples of $1,000 (for example, $5,000) are often used. The par value generally represents the amount of money the firm borrows and promises to repay at some future date.

coupon payment
The specified number of dollars of interest paid each period, generally each six months, on a bond.

coupon interest rate
The stated annual rate of interest on a bond.

2. **Coupon interest rate.** The bond requires the issuer to pay a specified number of dollars of interest each year (or, more typically, each six months). When this **coupon payment,** as it is called, is divided by the par value, the result is the **coupon interest rate.** For example, Allied's bonds have a $1,000 par value, and they pay $150 in interest each year.

The bond's coupon interest is $150, so its coupon interest rate is $150/$1,000 = 15 percent. The $150 is the yearly "rent" on the $1,000 loan. This payment, which is fixed at the time the bond is issued, remains in force, by contract, during the life of the bond. Incidentally, some time ago, most bonds literally had a number of small (½- by 2-inch) dated coupons attached to them, and on the interest payment date, the owner would clip off the coupon for that date and either cash it at his or her bank or mail it to the company's paying agent, who then mailed back a check for the interest. A 30-year, semiannual bond would start with 60 coupons, whereas a 5-year annual payment bond would start with only 5 coupons. Today most bonds are *registered*—no physical coupons are involved, and interest checks are mailed automatically to the registered owners of the bonds. Even so, people continue to use the terms *coupon* and *coupon interest rate* when discussing registered bonds.

maturity date

A specified date on which the par value of a bond must be repaid.

original maturity

The number of years to maturity at the time a bond is issued.

call provision

A provision in a bond contract that gives the issuer the right to pay off the bonds under specified terms prior to the stated maturity date.

3. **Maturity date.** Bonds generally have a specified **maturity date** on which the par value must be repaid. Allied's bonds, which were issued on January 2, 1993, will mature on January 1, 2008; thus, they had a 15-year maturity at the time they were issued. Most bonds have **original maturities** (the maturity at the time the bond is issued) of from 10 to 40 years, but any maturity is legally permissible. Of course, the effective maturity of a bond declines each year after it has been issued. Thus, Allied's bonds had a 15-year original maturity, but in 1994 they will have a 14-year maturity, and so on.

4. **Call provisions.** Most bonds have a provision whereby the issuer may pay them off prior to maturity. This feature is known as a **call provision,** and it is discussed in detail in Chapter 20. If a bond is callable, and if interest rates in the economy decline, then the company can sell a new issue of low-interest-rate bonds and use the proceeds to retire the old, high-interest-rate issue, just as a homeowner can refinance a home mortgage.

5. **New issues versus outstanding bonds.** As we shall see, a bond's market price is determined primarily by its coupon interest payments—the higher the coupon, other things held constant, the higher the market price of the bond. At the time a bond is issued, the coupon is generally set at a level that will cause the market price of the bond to equal its par value. If a lower coupon were set, investors simply would not be willing to pay $1,000 for the bond, while if a higher coupon were set, investors would clamor for the bond and bid its price up over $1,000. Investment bankers can judge quite precisely the coupon rate that will cause a bond to sell at its $1,000 par value.

A bond that has just been issued is known as a *new issue.* (*The Wall Street Journal* classifies a bond as a new issue for about one month after it has first been issued.) Once the bond has been on the market for a while, it is classified as an *outstanding bond,* also called a *seasoned issue.* Newly issued bonds generally sell very close to par, but the prices of outstanding bonds vary widely from par. Coupon interest payments are constant, so when economic conditions change, a bond with a $150 coupon that sold at par when it was issued will sell for more or less than $1,000 thereafter.

The Basic Bond Valuation Model[1]

The value of any financial asset — a stock, a bond, a lease, and even a physical asset such as an apartment building or a piece of machinery — is based on the present value of the cash flows the asset is expected to produce. In the case of a bond, the cash flows consist of interest payments during the life of the bond plus a return of the principal amount borrowed, generally the par value, when the bond matures. In a time line format, here is the situation:

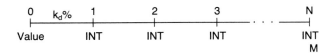

Here

k_d = the appropriate interest rate on the bond = 15%. We used the term "i" or "I" to designate the interest rate in Chapter 5 because those terms are used on financial calculators, but "k," with the subscript "d" to designate the rate on a debt security is normally used in finance.[2]

N = the number of years before the bond matures = 15. Note that N declines each year after the bond has been issued, so a bond that had a maturity of 15 years when it was issued (original maturity = 15) will have N = 14 after one year, N = 13 after two years, and so on. Note also that at this point we assume that the bond pays interest once a year, or annually, so N is measured in years. Later on, we will deal with semiannual payment bonds, which pay interest each six months.[3]

INT = dollars of interest paid each year = Coupon rate × Par value = 0.15($1,000) = $150. In calculator terminology, INT = PMT = 150. If the bond had been a semiannual payment bond, the payment would have been $75 each six months.

M = the par value of the bond = $1,000. This amount must be paid off at maturity.

We can now redraw the time line to show the numerical values for all variables except the bond's value:

---

[1]In finance, the term *model* refers to an equation or set of equations designed to show how one or more variables affect some other variable. Thus, a bond valuation model shows the mathematical relationship between a bond's price and the set of variables that determine the price.

[2]The appropriate interest rate on debt securities was discussed in Chapter 3. The bond's riskiness, liquidity, and years to maturity, as well as supply and demand conditions in the capital markets, all influence the interest rate on bonds.

[3]We should note that some bonds issued in recent years either pay no interest during their lives (*zero coupon bonds*) or else pay very low coupon rates. Such bonds are sold at a discount below par, and hence they are called *original issue discount bonds*. The "interest" earned on a zero coupon bond comes at the end when the company pays off at par ($1,000) a bond which was purchased for, say, $321.97. The discount of $1,000 − $321.97 = $678.03 substitutes for interest. Original issue discount bonds are discussed at length in Chapter 20.

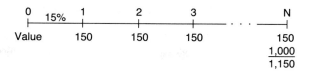

Now the following general equation can be solved to find the value of any bond:

$$
\begin{aligned}
\text{Bond value} = V_B &= \frac{INT}{(1 + k_d)^1} + \frac{INT}{(1 + k_d)^2} + \cdots + \frac{INT}{(1 + k_d)^N} + \frac{M}{(1 + k_d)^N} \\
&= \sum_{t=1}^{N} \frac{INT}{(1 + k_d)^t} + \frac{M}{(1 + k_d)^N}.
\end{aligned} \tag{6-1}
$$

Equation 6-1 can also be rewritten for use with the tables:

$$
V_B = INT(PVIFA_{k_d,N}) + M(PVIF_{k_d,N}). \tag{6-2}
$$

Inserting values for our particular bond, we have

$$
\begin{aligned}
V_B &= \sum_{t=1}^{15} \frac{\$150}{(1.15)^t} + \frac{\$1,000}{(1.15)^{15}} \\
&= \$150(PVIFA_{15\%,15}) + \$1,000(PVIF_{15\%,15}).
\end{aligned}
$$

Notice that the cash flows consist of an annuity of N years plus a lump sum payment at the end of Year N, and this fact is reflected in Equations 6-1 and 6-2. Further, Equation 6-1 can be solved by the three procedures discussed in Chapter 5: (1) numerically, (2) using the tables, and (3) with a financial calculator.

Numerical Solution:

Simply discount each cash flow back to the present and sum these PVs to find the value of the bond; see Figure 6-1 for an example. This procedure is not very efficient, especially if the bond has many years to maturity.

Tabular Solution:

Simply look up the appropriate PVIFA and PVIF values in Tables A-1 and A-2 at the end of the book, insert them into the equation, and complete the arithmetic:

$$
\begin{aligned}
V_B &= \$150(5.8474) + \$1,000(0.1229) \\
&= \$877.11 + \$122.90 \approx \$1,000.
\end{aligned}
$$

There is a one cent rounding error, which results from the fact that the tables only go to four decimal places.

Figure 6-1   ▪   Time Line for Allied Food Products' Bonds, 15% Interest Rate

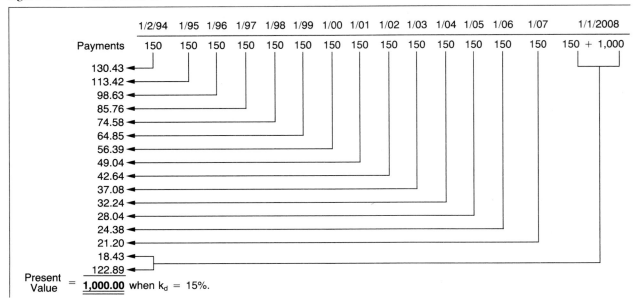

Financial Calculator Solution:

In Chapter 5 we worked problems where only four of the five time value of money (TVM) keys were used, but all five keys are used with bond problems. Here is the setup:

Inputs:	15	15		150	1000
	N	**I**	**PV**	**PMT**	**FV**
Output:			−1,000		

Simply input N = 15, I = k = 15, INT = PMT = 150, M = FV = 1000, and then press the PV key to find the value of the bond, $1,000. Since the PV is an outflow to the investor, it is shown with a negative sign.

Changes in Bond Values over Time

If k_d remained constant at 15 percent, what would the value of the bond be 1 year after it was issued? We can find this value using Equation 6-2 and the tables, but now the term to maturity is only 14 years—that is, N = 14. We see that V_B remains constant at $1,000:

$$V_B = \$150(5.7245) + \$1,000(0.1413)$$
$$= \$999.98 \approx \$1,000.$$

With a financial calculator, just override N = 15 with N = 14, press the PV key, and you will get the same answer. The value of the bond will remain at

$1,000 as long as the appropriate interest rate for it remains constant at 15 percent.[4]

Now suppose interest rates in the economy fell after the Allied bonds were issued, and, as a result, k_d *fell below the coupon rate*, decreasing from 15 to 10 percent. Both the coupon interest payments and the maturity value remain constant, but now 10 percent values for PVIF and PVIFA would have to be used in Equation 6-2. The value of the bond at the end of the first year would be $1,368.31:

$$V_B = \$150(\text{PVIFA}_{10\%,14}) + \$1,000(\text{PVIF}_{10\%,14})$$
$$= \$150(7.3667) + \$1,000(0.2633)$$
$$= \$1,105.01 + \$263.30$$
$$= \$1,368.31.$$

Thus, if k_d fell and went *below* the coupon rate, the bond would sell above par, or at a *premium*. With a financial calculator, just change $k_d = I$ from 15 to 10, and then press the PV key to get the answer, $1,368.33.

The arithmetic of the bond value increase should be clear, but what is the logic behind it? The fact that k_d has fallen to 10 percent means that if you had $1,000 to invest, you could buy new bonds like Allied's (every day some 10 to 12 companies sell new bonds), except that these new bonds would pay $100 of interest each year rather than $150. Naturally, you would prefer $150 to $100, so you would be willing to pay more than $1,000 for Allied's bonds to obtain its higher coupons. All investors would recognize these facts, and, as a result, the Allied bonds would be bid up in price to $1,368.31, at which point they would provide the same rate of return to a potential investor as the new bonds — 10 percent.

Assuming that interest rates remain constant at 10 percent for the next 14 years, what would happen to the value of an Allied bond? It would fall gradually from $1,368.31 at present to $1,000 at maturity, when Allied will redeem each bond for $1,000. This point can be illustrated by calculating the value of the bond 1 year later, when it has 13 years remaining to maturity. With a financial calculator, merely input the values for N, I, PMT, and FV, now using N = 13, and press the PV key to find the value of the bond, $1,355.17. Using the tables, we have

$$V_B = \$150(\text{PVIFA}_{10\%,13}) + \$1,000(\text{PVIF}_{10\%,13})$$
$$= \$150(7.1034) + \$1,000(0.2897) = \$1,355.21 \text{ (rounding error)}.$$

---

[4]The bond prices quoted by brokers are calculated as described. However, if you bought a bond between interest payment dates, you would have to pay the basic price plus accrued interest. Thus, if you purchased an Allied bond 6 months after it was issued, your broker would send you an invoice stating that you must pay $1,000 as the basic price of the bond plus $75 interest, representing one-half the annual interest of $150. The seller of the bond would receive $1,075. If you bought the bond the day before its interest payment date, you would pay $1,000 + (364/365)($150) = $1,149.59. Of course, you would receive an interest payment of $150 at the end of the next day. See Self-Test Problem 3 for a detailed discussion of bond quotations between interest payment dates.

Throughout the chapter we assume that the bond is being evaluated immediately after an interest payment date. The more expensive financial calculators have a built-in calendar which permits the calculation of exact values between interest payment dates.

Thus, the value of the bond will have fallen from $1,368.31 to $1,355.21, or by $13.10. If you were to calculate the value of the bond at other future dates, the price would continue to fall as the maturity date approached.

Notice that if you purchased the bond at a price of $1,368.31 and then sold it 1 year later with k_d still at 10 percent, you would have a capital loss of $13.10, or a total return of $150.00 − $13.10 = $136.90. Your percentage rate of return would consist of an *interest yield* (also called a *current yield*) plus a *capital gains yield,* calculated as follows:

$$\text{Interest, or current, yield} = \$150/\$1,368.31 = 0.1096 = 10.96\%$$
$$\text{Capital gains yield} = -\$13.10/\$1,368.31 = -0.0096 = \underline{-0.96\%}$$
$$\text{Total rate of return, or yield} = \$136.90/\$1,368.31 = 0.1001 \approx \underline{10.00\%}$$

Had interest rates risen from 15 to 20 percent during the first year after issue rather than fallen, the value of the bond would have declined to $769.49:

$$
\begin{aligned}
V_B &= \$150(\text{PVIFA}_{20\%,14}) + \$1,000(\text{PVIF}_{20\%,14}) \\
&= \$150(4.6106) + \$1,000(0.0779) \\
&= \$691.59 + \$77.90 \\
&= \$769.49.
\end{aligned}
$$

In this case, the bond would sell at a *discount* of $230.51 below its par value:

$$
\begin{aligned}
\text{Discount} = \text{Price} - \text{Par value} &= \$769.49 - \$1,000.00 \\
&= -\$230.51.
\end{aligned}
$$

The total expected future yield on the bond would again consist of a current yield and a capital gains yield, but now the capital gains yield would be *positive.* The total yield would be 20 percent. To see this, calculate the price of the bond with 13 years left to maturity, assuming that interest rates remain at 20 percent. With a calculator, enter N = 13, I = 20, PMT = 150, and FV = 1000, and then press PV to obtain the bond's value, $773.37. Using the tables, proceed as follows:

$$
\begin{aligned}
V_B &= \$150(\text{PVIFA}_{20\%,13}) + \$1,000(\text{PVIF}_{20\%,13}) \\
&= \$150(4.5327) + \$1,000(0.0935) \\
&= \$679.91 + \$93.50 \\
&= \$773.41.
\end{aligned}
$$

Notice that the capital gain for the year is the difference between the bond's value in Year 13 and the bond's value in Year 14, or $773.41 − $769.49 = $3.92. The interest yield, capital gains yield, and total yield are calculated as follows:

$$\text{Interest, or current, yield} = \$150/\$769.49 = 0.1949 = 19.49\%$$
$$\text{Capital gains yield} = \$3.92/\$769.49 = 0.0051 = \underline{0.51\%}$$
$$\text{Total rate of return, or yield} = \$153.92/\$769.49 = 0.2000 = \underline{20.00\%}$$

The discount or premium on a bond may also be calculated as the PV of the difference in interest payments, discounted at the new interest rate:

$$
\begin{array}{c}
\text{Discount} \\
\text{or premium}
\end{array} =
\left[
\begin{array}{c}
\text{Interest payment} \\
\text{on the old bond}
\end{array}
-
\begin{array}{c}
\text{Interest payment} \\
\text{on the new bond}
\end{array}
\right]
(\text{PVIFA}_{k_d,N}).
$$

Figure 6-2 ▪ **Time Path of the Value of a 15% Coupon, $1,000 Par Value Bond When Interest Rates Are 10%, 15%, and 20%**

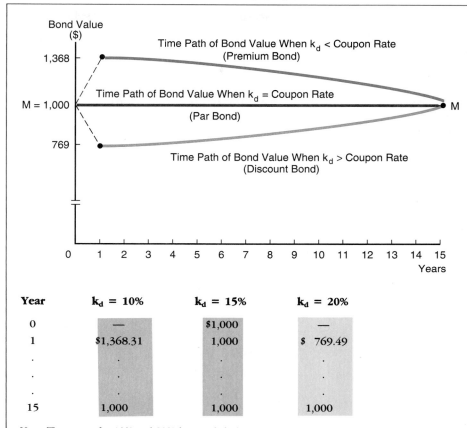

Year	$k_d = 10\%$	$k_d = 15\%$	$k_d = 20\%$
0	—	$1,000	—
1	$1,368.31	1,000	$ 769.49
.	.	.	.
.	.	.	.
.	.	.	.
15	1,000	1,000	1,000

Note: The curves for 10% and 20% have a slight bow.

Here N = years to maturity on the old bond and k_d = current rate of interest on a new bond. For example, if interest rates had risen to 20 percent 1 year after the Allied bonds were issued, the discount on them would have been calculated as follows:

$$\text{Discount} = (\$150 - \$200)(4.6106) = -\$230.53.$$

(The minus sign indicates discount.) This value agrees, except for rounding, with the −$230.51 value calculated previously. From these calculations, we see that the discount is equal to the present value of the interest payments you would sacrifice if you were to buy a low-coupon old bond rather than a high-coupon new bond. The longer the bond has left to maturity, the greater the sacrifice, hence the greater the discount.

Figure 6-2 graphs the value of the bond over time, assuming that interest rates in the economy (1) remain constant at 15 percent, (2) fall to 10 percent and then remain constant at that level, or (3) rise to 20 percent and remain constant at that level. Of course, if interest rates do *not* remain constant, then the price of the bond will fluctuate. However, regardless of what future interest rates do, the bond's price will approach $1,000 as it nears the maturity date (barring bankruptcy, in which case the bond's value might drop to zero).

Figure 6-2 illustrates the following key points:

1. Whenever the going rate of interest, k_d, is equal to the coupon rate, a bond will sell at its par value. Normally, the coupon rate is set equal to the going interest rate when a bond is issued, so it sells at par initially.

2. Interest rates do change over time, but the coupon rate remains fixed after the bond has been issued. Whenever the going rate of interest is *greater than* the coupon rate, a bond's price will fall *below* its par value. Such a bond is called a **discount bond.**

3. Whenever the going rate of interest is *less than* the coupon rate, a bond's price will rise *above* its par value. Such a bond is called a **premium bond.**

4. Thus, an *increase* in interest rates will cause the price of an outstanding bond to *fall,* whereas a *decrease* in rates will cause it to *rise.*

5. The market value of a bond will always approach its par value as its maturity date approaches, provided the firm does not go bankrupt.

These points are very important, for they show that bondholders may suffer capital losses or make capital gains, depending on whether interest rates rise or fall after the bond was purchased. And, as we saw in Chapter 3, interest rates do indeed change over time.

discount bond

A bond that sells below its par value; occurs whenever the going rate of interest *rises above* the coupon rate.

premium bond

A bond that sells above its par value; occurs whenever the going rate of interest *falls below* the coupon rate.

Finding the Interest Rate on a Bond: Yield to Maturity

Suppose you were offered a 14-year, 15 percent coupon, $1,000 par value bond at a price of $1,368.31. What rate of interest would you earn on your investment if you bought the bond and held it to maturity? This rate is called the bond's **yield to maturity (YTM),** and it is the interest rate discussed by bond traders when they talk about rates of return. To find the yield to maturity, you could solve Equation 6-1 or 6-2 for k_d:

yield to maturity (YTM)

The rate of return earned on a bond if it is held to maturity.

$$V_B = \$1,368.31 = \frac{\$150}{(1 + k_d)^1} + \ldots + \frac{\$150}{(1 + k_d)^{14}} + \frac{\$1,000}{(1 + k_d)^{14}}$$

$$= \$150(PVIFA_{k_d,14}) + \$1,000(PVIF_{k_d,14}).$$

If you have a financial calculator, you would simply enter N = 14, PMT = 150, FV = 1000, and PV = 1368.31 ($-$1368.31 on some calculators), and then press the I key. The calculator will blink for several seconds, and then the answer, 10 percent, will appear.[5]

If you do not have a financial calculator, you can substitute values for PVIFA and PVIF until you find a pair that "works" and forces this equality:

$$\$1,368.31 = \$150(PVIFA_{k_d,14}) + \$1,000(PVIF_{k_d,14}).$$

---

[5]If you are using a Sharp calculator, make sure that it is *not* in BGN mode, and press the compute key before pressing the I button.

What would be a good interest rate to use as a starting point? First, you know that the bond is selling at a premium over its par value ($1,368.31 versus $1,000), so the bond's yield to maturity must be *below* its 15 percent coupon rate. Therefore, you might try a rate of 12 percent. Substituting interest factors for 12 percent, you obtain

$$\$150(6.6282) + \$1,000(0.2046) = \$1,198.83 \neq \$1,368.31.$$

The calculated bond value, $1,198.83, is *below* the actual market price, so the YTM is *not* 12 percent. To raise the calculated value, you must *lower* the interest rate used in the process, because lower interest rates mean higher bond prices. Inserting interest factors for 10 percent, you obtain

$$
\begin{aligned}
V_B &= \$150(7.3667) + \$1,000(0.2633) \\
&= \$1,105.01 + \$263.30 \\
&= \$1,368.31.
\end{aligned}
$$

This calculated value is equal to the market price of the bond, so 10 percent is the bond's yield to maturity: $k_d = YTM = 10.0\%$.[6]

The yield to maturity is identical to the total rate of return discussed in the preceding section. The YTM for a bond that sells at par consists entirely of an interest yield, but if the bond sells at a price other than its par value, the YTM consists of the interest yield plus a positive or negative capital gains yield. Note also that a bond's yield to maturity changes whenever interest rates in the economy change, and this is almost daily. One who purchases a bond and holds it until it matures will receive the YTM that existed on the purchase date, but the bond's calculated YTM will change frequently between the purchase date and the maturity date.

Yield to Call

If you purchased a bond that was callable and the company called it, you would not have the option of holding it until it matured, so the yield to maturity would not be earned. For example, if Allied's 15 percent coupon bonds were callable, and if interest rates fell from 15 percent to 10 percent, then the company could call in the 15 percent bonds, replace them with 10 percent bonds, and save $150 − $100 = $50 interest per bond per year. This would be beneficial to the company, but not to its bondholders.

yield to call (YTC)
The rate of return earned on a bond if it is called before its maturity date.

If current interest rates are well below an outstanding bond's coupon rate, then a callable bond is likely to be called, and investors should estimate the expected rate of return on the bond as the **yield to call (YTC)** rather than as the yield to maturity. To calculate the YTC, solve this equation for k_d:

$$\text{Price of bond} = \sum_{t=1}^{N} \frac{INT}{(1 + k_d)^t} + \frac{\text{Call price}}{(1 + k_d)^N}. \tag{6-3}$$

---

[6]A few years ago, bond traders all had specialized tables called *bond tables* that gave yields on bonds of different maturities selling at different premiums and discounts. Because calculators are so much more efficient (and accurate), bond tables are rarely used any more.

Here N is the number of years until the company can call the bond; call price is the price the company must pay in order to call the bond (it is often set equal to the par value plus one year's interest); and k_d is the YTC.

To illustrate the yield-to-call calculation, suppose Allied's bonds had a provision that the company, if it wanted to, could call the bonds 10 years after the issue date at a price of $1,150. Suppose further that interest rates had fallen, such that one year after issuance k_d was 10 percent and the price of the bonds was $1,368.31. Here is the setup for finding the bond's YTC with a financial calculator:

9.78

The YTC is 9.78 percent — this is the return you would earn if you bought the bond at a price of $1,368.31 and it was called 9 years from today. (The bond could not be called for 10 years after issuance, and 1 year has gone by, so there are 9 years left until the first call date.)

Do you think Allied *will* call the bonds when they become callable? Allied's action would depend on what the going interest rate is when the bonds become callable. If the going rate remains at $k_d = 10\%$, then Allied could save $15\% - 10\% = 5\%$, or $50 per bond per year, by calling them and replacing the 15 percent bonds with a new 10 percent issue. There would be costs to the company to refund the issue, but the interest savings would probably be worth the cost, so Allied would probably refund the bonds. Therefore, there is a good chance that you would actually end up earning YTC = 9.78% rather than YTM = 10% if you bought the bonds under the indicated conditions.

The analysis used to decide whether or not to call a bond is covered in detail in Chapter 20 and Appendix 20B. In the balance of this chapter, we assume that bonds are not callable unless otherwise noted, but some of the end-of-chapter problems deal with yield to call.

Bond Values with Semiannual Compounding

Although some bonds pay interest annually, most actually pay interest semiannually. To evaluate semiannual payment bonds, we must modify the valuation models (Equations 6-1 and 6-2) as follows:

1. Divide the annual coupon interest payment by 2 to determine the amount of interest paid each 6 months.

2. Multiply the years to maturity, N, by 2 to determine the number of semiannual periods.

3. Divide the annual interest rate, k_d, by 2 to determine the periodic (semiannual) interest rate.

By making these changes, we obtain the following equations for finding the value of a bond that pays interest semiannually:

$$V_B = \sum_{t=1}^{2N} \frac{INT/2}{(1 + k_d/2)^t} + \frac{M}{(1 + k_d/2)^{2N}} \qquad (6\text{-}1a)$$

$$= \frac{INT}{2} (PVIFA_{k_d/2,2N}) + M(PVIF_{k_d/2,2N}). \qquad (6\text{-}2a)$$

To illustrate, assume now that Allied Food Products' bonds pay $75 interest each 6 months rather than $150 at the end of each year. Thus, each interest payment is only half as large, but there are twice as many of them. When the going (nominal) rate of interest is 10 percent with semiannual compounding, the value of this 15-year bond is found as follows:[7]

$$V_B = \$75(PVIFA_{5\%,30}) + \$1,000(PVIF_{5\%,30})$$
$$= \$75(15.3725) + \$1,000(0.2314)$$
$$= \$1,152.94 + \$231.40$$
$$= \$1,384.34.$$

With a financial calculator, enter N = 30, k = I = 5, PMT = 75, FV = 1000, and then press the PV key to obtain the bond's value, $1,384.31. The value with semiannual interest payments is slightly larger than $1,380.32, the value when interest is paid annually. This higher value occurs because interest payments are received somewhat faster under semiannual compounding.

Students sometimes want to discount the maturity value at 10 percent over 15 years rather than at 5 percent over 30 six-month periods. This is incorrect. Logically, all cash flows in a given contract must be discounted at the same periodic rate, the 5 percent semiannual rate in this instance. For consistency, bond traders *must* use the same discount rate for all cash flows, including the cash flow at maturity, and they do.

Interest Rate Risk on a Bond

As we saw in Chapter 3, interest rates go up and down over time. Further, changes in interest rates affect the holders of outstanding bonds in two ways: (1) An increase in interest rates leads to a decline in the values of outstanding bonds. Since interest rates can rise, bondholders face the risk of losses in the values of their portfolios. This risk is called **interest rate price risk.** (2) Many bondholders (including such institutional bondholders as pension funds and life insurance companies) buy bonds to build funds for some future use. These bondholders reinvest the cash flows (interest payments plus repayment of principal when the bonds mature or are called). If interest rates decline, the bondholders will earn a lower rate of return on reinvested cash flows, and this will reduce the future value of their portfolios relative to the values they would have

interest rate price risk
The risk of declines in bond prices to which investors are exposed due to changing interest rates.

---

[7]We are also assuming a change in the effective annual interest rate, from 10 percent to

$$EAR = (1.05)^2 - 1 = 1.1025 - 1.0 = 0.1025 = 10.25\%.$$

Most bonds pay interest semiannually, and the rates quoted are on a semiannual basis. Therefore, effective annual rates for most bonds are somewhat higher than the quoted rates.

interest rate reinvestment rate risk

The risk that income from a bond portfolio will decline due to having to reinvest cash flows at a lower rate.

had if interest rates had not fallen. This is called **interest rate reinvestment rate risk.**

We see, then, that any given change in interest rates has two separate effects on bondholders — it changes the current values of their portfolios (price risk), and it also changes the rates of return at which the cash flows from their portfolios can be reinvested (reinvestment rate risk). Note that these two risks tend to offset one another. For example, an increase in interest rates will lower the current value of a bond portfolio, but since the future cash flows produced by the portfolio will then be reinvested at a higher rate of return, the future value of the portfolio will be increased. In this section we will look at just how these two effects operate to affect bondholders' positions.[8]

Suppose you bought some 15 percent Allied bonds at a price of $1,000, and interest rates subsequently rose to 20 percent. As we saw before, the price of the bonds would fall to $769.49, so you would have a loss of $230.51 per bond.[9] Interest rates can and do rise, and rising rates cause a loss of value for bondholders. Thus, people or firms who invest in bonds are exposed to risk from changing interest rates, which is called interest rate price risk.

One's exposure to interest rate price risk is higher on bonds with long maturities than on those maturing in the near future. This point can be demonstrated by showing how the value of a 1-year bond with a 15 percent coupon fluctuates with changes in k_d and then comparing these changes with those on a 14-year bond as calculated previously. The 1-year bond's values at different interest rates are shown below:

Value at $k_d = 10\%$:

$$V_B = \$150(\text{PVIFA}_{10\%,1}) + \$1,000(\text{PVIF}_{10\%,1})$$
$$= \$150(0.9091) + \$1,000(0.9091)$$
$$= \$136.37 + \$909.10$$
$$= \$1,045.47.$$

Value at $k_d = 15\%$:

$$V_B = \$150(0.8696) + \$1,000(0.8696)$$
$$= \$130.44 + \$869.60$$
$$= \$1,000.04 \approx \$1,000.$$

Value at $k_d = 20\%$:

$$V_B = \$150(0.8333) + \$1,000(0.8333)$$
$$= \$125.00 + \$833.30$$
$$= \$958.30.$$

---

[8]Actually, we will stop far short of a full examination of the effects of interest rate changes on bondholders' positions, as such an examination would go well beyond the scope of the text. We can note, though, that a concept called "duration" has been developed to help fixed income investors deal with changing interest rates, and, with a properly structured portfolio (one that has the proper duration), most of the risks of changing interest rates can be eliminated because price risk and reinvestment rate risk can be made to exactly offset one another.

[9]You would have an *accounting* (and tax) loss only if you sold the bond; if you held it to maturity, you would not have such a loss. However, even if you did not sell, you would still have suffered a *real economic loss in an opportunity cost sense* because you would have lost the opportunity to invest at 20 percent and would be stuck with a 15 percent bond in a 20 percent market. Thus, in an economic sense "paper losses" are just as bad as realized accounting losses.

Figure 6-3 ▪ Value of Long- and Short-Term 15% Annual Coupon Rate Bonds at Different Market Interest Rates

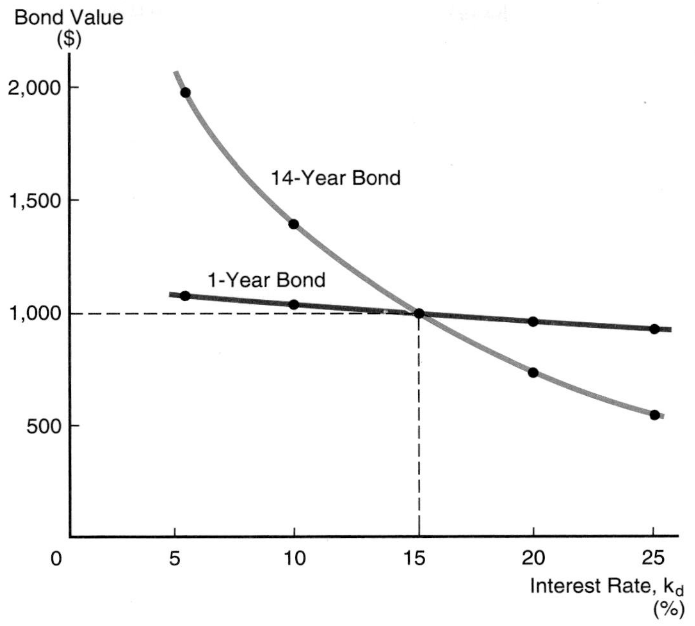

Current Market Interest Rate, k_d	Value of	
	1-Year Bond	14-Year Bond
5%	$1,095.24	$1,989.86
10	1,045.45	1,368.33
15	1,000.00	1,000.00
20	958.33	769.47
25	920.00	617.59

Note: Bond values were calculated using a financial calculator.

You could obtain the first value with a financial calculator by entering N = 1, I = 10, PMT = 150, and FV = 1000, and then pressing PV to get $1,045.45. With everything still in your calculator, enter I = 15 to override the old I = 10, and press PV to find the bond's value at k_d = I = 15; it is $1,000. Then enter I = 20 and press the PV key to find the last bond value, $958.33.

The values of the 1-year and 14-year bonds at several current market interest rates are summarized and plotted in Figure 6-3. Notice how much more sensitive the price of the long-term bond is to changes in interest rates. At a 15 percent interest rate, both the long- and the short-term bonds are valued at $1,000. When rates rise to 20 percent, the long-term bond falls to $769.47, but the short-term bond falls only to $958.33.

For bonds with similar coupons, this differential sensitivity to changes in interest rates always holds true—the longer the maturity of the bond, the greater its price changes in response to a given change in interest rates. Thus, even if the risk of default on two bonds is exactly the same, the one with the longer maturity is typically exposed to more price risk from a rise in interest rates.[10]

The logical explanation for this difference in interest rate price risk is simple. Suppose you bought a 14-year bond that yielded 15 percent, or $150 a year. Now suppose interest rates on comparable-risk bonds rose to 20 percent. You would be stuck with only $150 of interest for the next 14 years. On the other hand, had you bought a 1-year bond, you would have had a low return for only 1 year. At the end of the year, you would get your $1,000 back, and you could then reinvest it and receive 20 percent, or $200 per year, for the next 13 years. Thus, interest rate price risk reflects the length of time one is committed to a given investment.

Although a 1-year bond has less interest rate price risk than a 14-year bond, the 1-year bond exposes the buyer to more interest rate reinvestment rate risk. Suppose you bought a 1-year bond that yielded 15 percent, and then interest rates on comparable-risk bonds fell to 10 percent. After 1 year, when you got your $1,000 back, you would have to invest it at only 10 percent, so you would lose $150 − $100 = $50 in annual interest. Had you bought the 14-year bond, you would have continued to receive $150 in annual interest payments even if rates fell. If you reinvested those coupon payments, you would have to accept a lower rate of return, but you would still be much better off than if you had been holding the 1-year bond.

Bond Prices in Recent Years

We know from Chapter 3 that interest rates fluctuate, and we have just seen that the prices of outstanding bonds rise and fall inversely with changes in interest rates. Figure 6-4 shows what has happened to the price of a typical bond, Alabama Power's 8½ percent, 30-year bond which matures in 2001. When this bond was issued in 1971 it was worth $1,000, but at the 1981 interest rate peak, it sold for only $530. However, the ensuing drop in interest rates caused the price of the bond to rise, and by 1987 it was back over par, selling at a slight premium. In 1988, interest rates rose again, and the bond's price fell back below par, but by 1992 interest rates were again low, so the bond was selling at a premium once again. The graph also shows that if interest rates remain at the 1992 level, the price of the bond will gradually fall, and it will sell for $1,000 (plus accrued interest) just before it matures in 2001.

Bond Markets

Corporate bonds are traded primarily in the over-the-counter market. Most bonds are owned by and traded among the large financial institutions (for example, life insurance companies, mutual funds, and pension funds, all of which deal in very large blocks of securities), and it is relatively easy for the over-the-

---

[10]If a 10-year bond were plotted in Figure 6-3, its curve would lie between those of the 14-year bond and the 1-year bond. The curve of a 1-month bond would be almost horizontal, indicating that its price would change very little in response to an interest rate change, but a perpetuity would have a very steep slope.

Figure 6-4   ▪   **Alabama Power 8½%, 30-Year Bond: Market Value as Interest Rates Change**

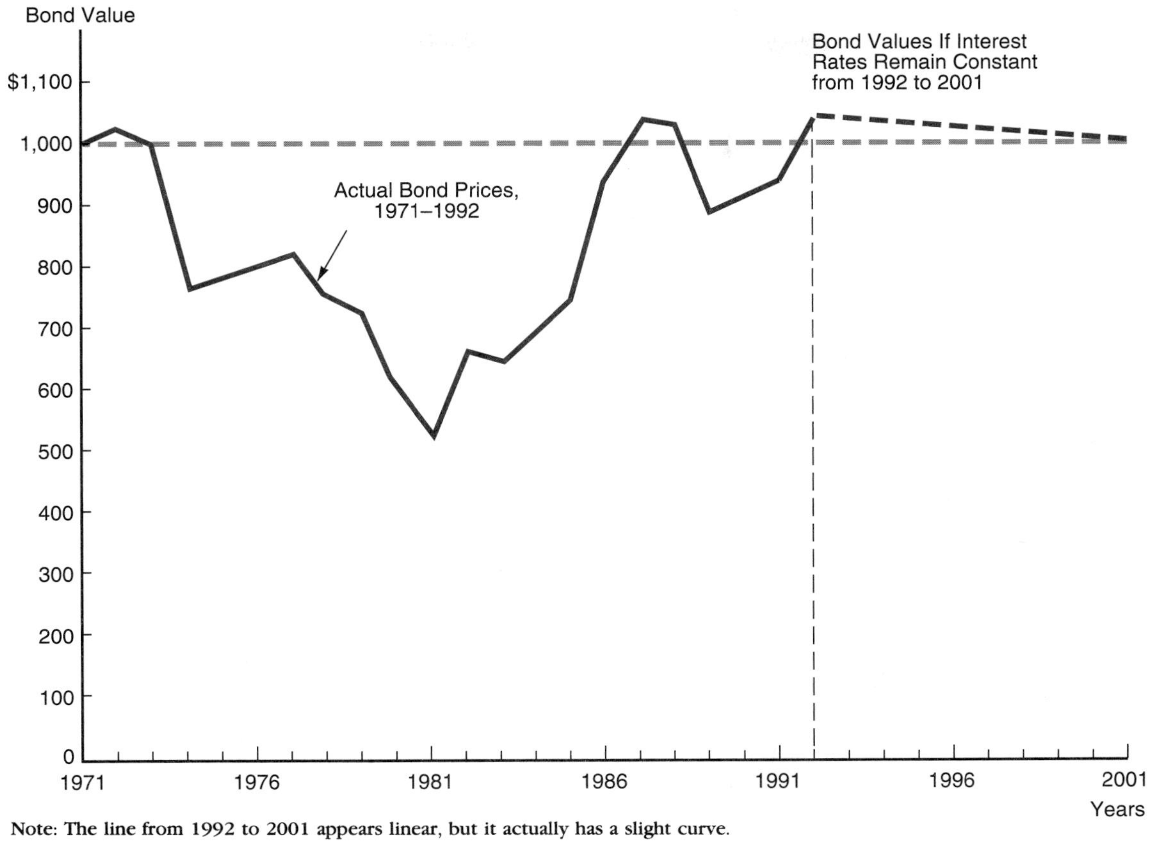

Note: The line from 1992 to 2001 appears linear, but it actually has a slight curve.

counter bond dealers to arrange the transfer of large blocks of bonds among the relatively few holders of the bonds. It would be much more difficult to conduct similar operations in the stock market among the literally millions of large and small stockholders, so a higher percentage of stock trades occur on the exchanges.

Information on bond trades in the over-the-counter market is not published, but a representative group of bonds is listed and traded on the bond division of the NYSE. Figure 6-5 gives a section of the bond market page of *The Wall Street Journal* for trading on January 17, 1992. A total of 609 issues were traded on that date, but we show only the bonds of Alabama Power. Note that Alabama Power had 6 different bonds that were traded on January 17; the company actually had more than 20 bond issues outstanding, but some of them did not trade on that date.

The Alabama Power and other bonds can have various denominations, but for convenience we generally think of each bond as having a par value of $1,000—this is how much per bond the company borrowed and how much it must someday repay. However, since other denominations are possible, for trad-

Figure 6-5 ▪ **NYSE Bond Market Transactions, January 17, 1992**

		Corporation Bonds Volume, $49,510,000			
Bonds	**Cur Yld**	**Vol**	**Close**		**Net Chg.**
AlaP 9s2000	8.8	3	102⅛	−	⅝
AlaP 8½s01	8.3	32	102⅞	−	⅛
AlaP 7¾s02	7.8	5	99¼	−	¾
AlaP 10⅞05	10.1	4	107⅜	+	1⅜
AlaP 9⅝08	9.2	21	104¼	+	⅝
AlaP10s18	9.5	20	105	−	1

Source: *The Wall Street Journal,* January 20, 1992.

current yield

The annual interest payment on a bond divided by its current market value.

ing and reporting purposes bonds are quoted as percentages of par. Looking at the second bond listed, which is the one we plotted in Figure 6-4, we see that there is an 8½ just after the company's name; this indicates that the bond is of the series which pays 8½ percent interest, or 0.0850($1,000) = $85.00 of interest per year. The 8½ percent is the bond's *coupon rate.* The 01 which comes next indicates that this bond matures and must be repaid in the year 2001; it is not shown in the figure, but this bond was issued in 1971, so it had a 30-year original maturity. The 8.3 in the second column is the bond's **current yield,** which is defined as the annual interest payment divided by the closing price of the bond: Current yield = $85/$1,028.75 = 8.26%, rounded to 8.3 percent. The 32 in the third column indicates that 32 of these bonds were traded on January 17, 1992. Since the price shown in the fourth column is expressed as a percentage of par, the bond closed at 102.875 percent, which translates to $1,028.75, down ⅛ of 1 percent, or $1.25 from the previous day's close.

Coupon rates are generally set at levels which reflect the "going rate of interest" on the day a bond is issued. If the rates were set lower, investors simply would not buy the bonds at the $1,000 par value, so the company could not borrow the money it needed. Thus, bonds generally sell at their par values on the day they are issued, but bond prices fluctuate thereafter as interest rates change.

As you can see from Figure 6-5, Alabama Power's 8½ percent bonds maturing in 2001 were recently selling for $1,028.75, while its 7¾ percent bonds maturing in 2002 were selling for $992.50. The difference in coupon rates reflects the fact that the going rate of interest in 1971, when the 8½'s were sold, was higher than in 1972, when the 7¾'s were sold. The current (January 1992) interest rate is between 7¾ and 8½ percent, so the 7¾'s now sell at a discount while the 8½'s sell at a premium.

All of the bonds traded on a given day are listed in the newspaper (and hence in Figure 6-5) in alphabetical order by company and in the order of the dates on which they were originally issued, beginning with the earliest bond issued. Thus, the coupon rates shown in Figure 6-5 decline and then rise as we move down the list, reflecting the facts that interest rates have generally risen in recent years and that Alabama Power has not had to raise much new debt capital since interest rates declined.

? *Self-Test Questions*

In what two primary forms do corporations raise capital?

What is meant by the terms "new issue" and "seasoned issue"?

Explain, verbally, the following equation:

$$V_B = \sum_{t=1}^{N} \frac{INT}{(1 + k_d)^t} + \frac{M}{(1 + k_d)^N}.$$

Explain what happens to the price of a bond if (1) interest rates rise above the bond's coupon rate or (2) interest rates fall below the bond's coupon rate.

Write out a formula that can be used to calculate the discount or premium on a bond, and explain it.

Differentiate between interest rate price risk and reinvestment rate risk.

How does the calculation of a bond's price differ between a bond that is likely to be called and one that is not?

How is the bond valuation formula shown above changed to deal with bonds that have semiannual coupons rather than annual coupons?

PREFERRED STOCK VALUATION

Preferred stock is a *hybrid*—it is similar to bonds in some respects and to common stock in other respects. Preferred dividends are similar to interest payments on bonds in that they are fixed in amount and generally must be paid before common stock dividends can be paid. However, like common dividends, preferred dividends can be omitted without bankrupting the firm, and many preferred issues have no specific maturity date.

Most preferred stocks entitle their owners to regular, fixed dividend payments. If the payments last forever, the issue is a perpetuity whose value V_{ps}, is found as follows:

$$V_{ps} = \frac{D_{ps}}{k_{ps}}. \qquad (6\text{-}4)$$

V_{ps} is the value of the preferred stock, D_{ps} is the preferred dividend, and k_{ps} is the required rate of return. Allied Food Products has preferred stock outstanding which pays a dividend of $10 per year. If the required rate of return on this preferred stock is 10 percent, its value is $100, found by solving Equation 6-4 as follows:

$$V_{ps} = \frac{\$10.00}{0.10} = \$100.00.$$

If we know the current price of a preferred stock and its dividend, we can solve
for the current rate being earned, as follows:

$$k_{ps} = \frac{D_{ps}}{V_{ps}}. \qquad\qquad (6\text{-}4a)$$

Self-Test Question

In what way is preferred stock similar to bonds, and in what respect is it similar to common stock?

COMMON STOCK VALUATION

Common stock represents an ownership interest in a corporation, but to the
typical investor, a share of common stock is simply a piece of paper characterized by two features:

1. It entitles its owner to dividends, but only if the company has earnings out
   of which dividends can be paid and only if management chooses to pay
   dividends rather than to retain and reinvest all the earnings. Whereas a
   bond contains a *promise* to pay interest, common stock provides no such
   promise to pay dividends—if you own a stock, you may *expect* a dividend,
   but your expectations may not in fact be met. To illustrate, Long Island
   Lighting Company (LILCO) had paid dividends on its common stock for
   more than 50 years, and people expected these dividends to continue.
   However, when the company encountered severe problems a few years
   ago, it stopped paying dividends. Note, though, that LILCO continued to
   pay interest on its bonds; if it had not, then it would have been declared
   bankrupt, and the bondholders could have taken over the company.

2. Stock can be sold at some future date, hopefully at a price greater than the
   purchase price. If the stock is actually sold at a price above its purchase
   price, the investor will receive a *capital gain.* Generally, at the time people buy common stocks, they do expect to receive capital gains; otherwise, they would not buy the stocks. However, after the fact, one can end
   up with capital losses rather than capital gains. LILCO's stock price
   dropped from $17.50 to $3.75 in one year, so the *expected* capital gains
   on that stock turned out to be *actual* capital losses.

Definitions of Terms Used in the
Stock Valuation Models

Common stocks provide an expected future cash flow stream, and a stock's
value is found in the same manner as the values of other financial assets—
namely, as the present value of the expected future cash flow stream. The expected cash flows consist of two elements: (1) the dividends expected in each
year and (2) the price investors expect to receive when they sell the stock. The

expected final stock price includes the return of the original investment plus a capital gain.

We saw in Chapter 1 that managers seek to maximize the values of their firms' stocks. A manager's actions affect both the stream of income to investors and the riskiness of that stream. Therefore, the manager needs to know how alternative actions are likely to affect stock prices, so at this point we develop some models to help show how the value of a share of stock is determined. We begin by defining the following terms:

D_t = dividend the stockholder *expects* to receive at the end of Year t. D_0 is the most recent dividend, which has already been paid; D_1 is the first dividend expected, and it will be paid at the end of this year; D_2 is the dividend expected at the end of 2 years; and so forth. D_1 represents the first cash flow a new purchaser of the stock will receive. Note that D_0, the dividend which has just been paid, is known with certainty. However, all future dividends are expected values, so the estimate of D_t may differ among investors.[11]

market price, P_0

The price at which a stock sells in the market.

intrinsic value, $\hat{P}_0$

The value of an asset that in the mind of a particular investor is justified by the facts; $\hat{P}_0$ may be different from the asset's current market price, its book value, or both.

P_0 = actual **market price** of the stock today.

$\hat{P}_t$ = expected price of the stock at the end of each Year t (pronounced "P hat t"). $\hat{P}_0$ is the **intrinsic,** or *theoretical,* **value** of the stock today as seen by the particular investor doing the analysis; $\hat{P}_1$ is the price expected at the end of 1 year; and so on. Note that $\hat{P}_0$ is the intrinsic value of the stock today based on a particular investor's estimate of the stock's expected dividend stream and the riskiness of that stream. Hence, whereas P_0 is fixed and is identical for all investors, $\hat{P}_0$ could differ among investors depending on how optimistic they are regarding the company. The caret, or "hat," is used to indicate that $\hat{P}_t$ is an estimated value. $\hat{P}_0$, the individual investor's estimate of the intrinsic value today, could be above or below P_0, the current stock price, but an investor would buy the stock only if his or her estimate of $\hat{P}_0$ were equal to or greater than P_0.

Since there are many investors in the market, there can be many values for $\hat{P}_0$. However, we can think of a group of "average," or "marginal," investors whose actions actually determine the market price. For these marginal investors, P_0 must equal $\hat{P}_0$; otherwise, a disequilibrium would exist, and buying and selling in the market would change P_0 until $P_0 = \hat{P}_0$ for a marginal investor.

growth rate, g

The expected rate of growth in dividends per share.

g = expected **growth rate** in dividends as predicted by a marginal investor. (If we assume that dividends are expected to grow at a constant rate, g is also equal to the expected rate of growth in the stock's price.) Different investors may use different g's to evaluate

---

[11]Stocks generally pay dividends quarterly, so theoretically we should evaluate them on a quarterly basis. However, in stock valuation, most analysts work on an annual basis because the data generally are not precise enough to warrant refinement to a quarterly model. For additional information on the quarterly model, see Charles M. Linke and J. Kenton Zumwalt, "Estimation Biases in Discounted Cash Flow Analysis of Equity Capital Cost in Rate Regulation," *Financial Management,* Autumn 1984, 15–21.

a firm's stock, but the market price, P_0, is set on the basis of the g estimated by marginal investors.

required rate of return, k_s

The minimum rate of return on a common stock that a stockholder considers acceptable.

k_s = minimum acceptable, or **required, rate of return** on the stock, considering both its riskiness and the returns available on other investments. Again, this term generally relates to marginal investors. The determinants of k_s were discussed in detail in Chapter 4.

expected rate of return, $\hat{k}_s$

The rate of return on a common stock that an individual stockholder expects to receive.

$\hat{k}_s$ = **expected rate of return** which an investor who buys the stock actually expects to receive. $\hat{k}_s$ (pronounced "k hat s") could be above or below k_s, but one would buy the stock only if $\hat{k}_s$ were equal to or greater than k_s.

actual (realized) rate of return, $\bar{k}_s$

The rate of return on a common stock actually received by stockholders. $\bar{k}_s$ may be greater than or less than $\hat{k}_s$ and/or k_s.

$\bar{k}_s$ = **actual,** or **realized,** *after the fact* **rate of return,** pronounced "k bar s." You may *expect* to obtain a return of $\hat{k}_s$ = 15 percent if you buy Exxon stock today, but if the market goes down, you may end up next year with an actual realized return that is much lower, perhaps even negative.

dividend yield

The expected dividend divided by the current price of a share of stock.

D_1/P_0 = expected **dividend yield** on the stock during the coming year. If the stock is expected to pay a dividend of $1 during the next 12 months, and if its current price is $10, then the expected dividend yield is $1/$10 = 0.10 = 10%.

capital gains yield

The capital gain during a given year divided by the beginning price.

$\dfrac{\hat{P}_1 - P_0}{P_0}$ = expected **capital gains yield** on the stock during the coming year. If the stock sells for $10 today, and if it is expected to rise to $10.50 at the end of 1 year, then the expected capital gain is $\hat{P}_1 - P_0$ = $10.50 − $10.00 = $0.50, and the expected capital gains yield is $0.50/$10 = 0.05 = 5%.

expected total return

The sum of the expected dividend yield and the expected capital gains yield on a share of stock.

Expected total return = $\hat{k}_s$ = expected dividend yield (D_1/P_0) plus expected capital gains yield $[(\hat{P}_1 - P_0)/P_0]$. In our example, the **expected total return** = $\hat{k}_s$ = 10% + 5% = 15%.

Expected Dividends as the Basis for Stock Values

In our discussion of bonds, we found the value of a bond as the present value of interest payments over the life of the bond plus the present value of the bond's maturity (or par) value:

$$V_B = \frac{INT}{(1 + k_d)^1} + \frac{INT}{(1 + k_d)^2} + \cdots + \frac{INT}{(1 + k_d)^N} + \frac{M}{(1 + k_d)^N}.$$

Stock prices are likewise determined as the present value of a stream of cash flows, and the basic stock valuation equation is similar to the bond valuation equation. What are the cash flows that corporations provide to their stockholders? First, think of yourself as an investor who buys a stock with the intention of holding it (in your family) forever. In this case, all that you (and your heirs) will receive is a stream of dividends, and the value of the stock today is calculated as the present value of an infinite stream of dividends:

$$\text{Value of stock} = \hat{P}_0 = \text{PV of expected future dividends}$$

$$= \frac{D_1}{(1 + k_s)^1} + \frac{D_2}{(1 + k_s)^2} + \ldots + \frac{D_\infty}{(1 + k_s)^\infty}$$

$$= \sum_{t=1}^{\infty} \frac{D_t}{(1 + k_s)^t}. \tag{6-5}$$

What about the more typical case, where you expect to hold the stock for a finite period and then sell it—what will be the value of $\hat{P}_0$ in this case? Unless the company is likely to be liquidated and thus to disappear, *the value of the stock is again determined by Equation 6-5.* To see this, recognize that for any individual investor, the expected cash flows consist of expected dividends plus the expected sale price of the stock. However, the sale price the current investor receives will depend on the dividends some future investor expects. Therefore, for all present and future investors in total, expected cash flows must be based on expected future dividends. To put it another way, unless a firm is liquidated or sold to another concern, the cash flows it provides to its stockholders will consist only of a stream of dividends; therefore, the value of a share of its stock must be established as the present value of that expected dividend stream.

The general validity of Equation 6-5 can also be confirmed by asking the following question: Suppose I buy a stock and expect to hold it for 1 year. I will receive dividends during the year plus the value $\hat{P}_1$ when I sell out at the end of the year. But what will determine the value of $\hat{P}_1$? The answer is that it will be determined as the present value of the dividends during Year 2 plus the stock price at the end of that year, which in turn will be determined as the present value of another set of future dividends and an even more distant stock price. This process can be continued ad infinitum, and the ultimate result is Equation 6-5.[12]

Equation 6-5 is a generalized stock valuation model in the sense that the time pattern of D_t can be anything: D_t can be rising, falling, or constant, or it can even be fluctuating randomly, and Equation 6-5 will still hold. Often, however, the projected stream of dividends follows a systematic pattern, in which case we can develop a simplified (that is, easier to evaluate) version of the stock valuation model expressed in Equation 6-5. In the following sections we consider the cases of zero growth, constant growth, and nonconstant growth.

---

[12]We should note that investors periodically lose sight of the long-run nature of stocks as investments and forget that in order to sell a stock at a profit, one must find a buyer who will pay the higher price. If you analyzed a stock's value in accordance with Equation 6-5, concluded that the stock's market price exceeded a reasonable value, and then bought the stock anyway, then you would be following the "bigger fool" theory of investment—you think that you may be a fool to buy the stock at its excessive price, but you also think that when you get ready to sell it, you can find someone who is an even bigger fool. The bigger fool theory was widely followed in the summer of 1987, just before the stock market lost over one-third of its value in the October 1987 crash.

Stock Values with Zero Growth

zero growth stock
A common stock whose future dividends are not expected to grow at all; that is, $g = 0$.

Suppose dividends are not expected to grow at all but to remain constant. Here we have a **zero growth stock,** for which the dividends expected in future years are equal to some constant amount—that is, $D_1 = D_2 = D_3$ and so on. Therefore, we can drop the subscripts on D and rewrite Equation 6-5 as follows:

$$\hat{P}_0 = \frac{D}{(1 + k_s)^1} + \frac{D}{(1 + k_s)^2} + \ldots + \frac{D}{(1 + k_s)^\infty}. \qquad (6\text{-}5a)$$

As we noted in Chapter 5 in connection with the British consol bond and also in our discussion of preferred stocks, a security that is expected to pay a constant amount each year forever is called a perpetuity. *Therefore, a zero growth stock is a perpetuity.*

Although a zero growth stock is expected to provide a constant stream of dividends into the indefinite future, each dividend has a smaller present value than the preceding one, and as N gets very large, the present value of the future dividends approaches zero. To illustrate, suppose $D = \$1.15$ and $k_s = 13.4\%$. We can rewrite Equation 6-5a as follows:

$$\hat{P}_0 = \frac{\$1.15}{(1.134)^1} + \frac{\$1.15}{(1.134)^2} + \frac{\$1.15}{(1.134)^3} + \ldots + \frac{\$1.15}{(1.134)^{50}} + \ldots + \frac{\$1.15}{(1.134)^{100}} + \ldots$$

$$= \$1.01 + \$0.89 + \$0.79 + \ldots + \$0.002 + \ldots + \$0.000004 + \ldots$$

We can also show the perpetuity in graph form, as in Figure 6-6. The horizontal line shows the constant dividend stream, $D_t = \$1.15$. The descending step function curve shows the present value of each future dividend. If we extended the analysis on out to infinity and then summed the present values of all the future dividends, the sum would be equal to the value of the stock.

As we saw in Chapter 5, the value of any perpetuity is simply the payment divided by the discount rate, so the value of a zero growth stock reduces to this formula:

$$\hat{P}_0 = \frac{D}{k_s}. \qquad (6\text{-}6)$$

Therefore, the value of our illustrative stock is $8.58:

$$\hat{P}_0 = \frac{\$1.15}{0.134} = \$8.58.$$

If you extended Figure 6-6 on out forever and then added up the present value of each individual dividend, you would end up with the intrinsic value of the stock, $8.58.[13] The actual market value of the stock, P_0, could be greater than,

---

[13]If you think that having a stock pay dividends forever is unrealistic, then think of it as lasting only for 50 years. Here you would have an annuity of $1.15 per year for 50 years. The PV of a 50-year annuity would be $1.15(7.4488) = $8.57, which would differ by only a penny from that of the perpetuity. Thus, the dividends from Years 51 to infinity contribute almost nothing to the value of the stock.

Figure 6-6 ▪ Present Values of Dividends of a Zero Growth Stock (Perpetuity)

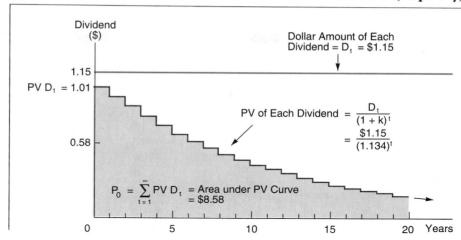

less than, or equal to $8.58, depending on other investors' perceptions of the dividend pattern and riskiness of the stock.

We could transpose the $\hat{P}_0$ and the k_s in Equation 6-6 and solve for k_s to produce Equation 6-7:

$$\hat{k}_s = \frac{D}{P_0}. \qquad (6\text{-}7)$$

We could then look up the price of the stock and the latest dividend, P_0 and D, in the newspaper, and the value D/P_0 would be the rate of return we could expect to earn if we bought the stock. Since we are dealing with an *expected rate of return,* we put a "hat" on the k value. Thus, if we bought the stock at a price of $8.58 and expected to receive a constant dividend of $1.15, our expected rate of return would be

$$\hat{k}_s = \frac{\$1.15}{\$8.58} = 0.134 = 13.4\%.$$

Normal, or Constant, Growth

normal (constant) growth

Growth which is expected to continue into the foreseeable future at about the same rate as that of the economy as a whole; g = a constant.

Although the zero growth model is applicable to a few companies, the earnings and dividends of most companies are expected to increase each year. Expected growth rates vary from company to company, but dividend growth in general is expected to continue in the foreseeable future at about the same rate as that of the nominal gross national product (real GNP plus inflation). On this basis, one may expect the dividend of an average, or "normal," company to grow at a rate of 6 to 8 percent a year. Thus, if a **normal,** or **constant, growth** company's last dividend, which has already been paid, was D_0, its dividend in any future Year t may be forecasted as $D_t = D_0(1 + g)^t$, where g is the constant expected rate of growth. For example, if Allied Food Products just paid a dividend of $1.15 (that is, $D_0 = \$1.15$), and if investors expect an 8 percent growth rate, then the estimated dividend 1 year hence would be $D_1 = \$1.15(1.08) = \$1.24$; D_2 would be $\$1.34$; and the estimated dividend 5 years hence would be

$$D_t = D_0(1 + g)^t = \$1.15(1.08)^5 = \$1.69.$$

Using this method for estimating future dividends, we can determine the current stock value, $\hat{P}_0$, using Equation 6-5 as set forth previously — in other words, we can find the expected future cash flow stream (the dividends), then calculate the present value of each dividend payment, and finally sum these present values to find the value of the stock. Thus, the intrinsic value of the stock is equal to the present value of its expected future dividends.

If g is constant, Equation 6-5 may be rewritten as follows:[14]

$$\hat{P}_0 = \frac{D_0(1 + g)^1}{(1 + k_s)^1} + \frac{D_0(1 + g)^2}{(1 + k_s)^2} + \cdots + \frac{D_0(1 + g)^\infty}{(1 + k_s)^\infty}$$

$$= \frac{D_0(1 + g)}{k_s - g} = \frac{D_1}{k_s - g}. \tag{6-8}$$

Inserting values into the last version of Equation 6-8, we find the value of our illustrative stock to be $23.00:

$$\hat{P}_0 = \frac{\$1.15(1.08)}{0.134 - 0.08} = \frac{\$1.242}{0.054} = \$23.00.$$

constant growth model
Also called the Gordon Model, it is used to find the value of a constant growth stock.

The **constant growth model** as set forth in the last term of Equation 6-8 is often called the Gordon Model, after Myron J. Gordon, who did much to develop and popularize it.

Note that Equation 6-8 is sufficiently general to encompass the zero growth case described earlier: If growth is zero, this is simply a special case of constant growth, and Equation 6-8 is equal to Equation 6-6. Note also that a necessary condition for the derivation of the simplified form of Equation 6-8 is that k_s be greater than g. If the equation is used in situations where k_s is not greater than g, the results will be meaningless.

The concept underlying the valuation process for a constant growth stock is graphed in Figure 6-7. Dividends are growing at the rate g = 8%, but because $k_s > g$, the present value of each future dividend is declining. For example, the dividend in Year 1 is $D_1 = D_0(1 + g)^1 = \$1.15(1.08) = \$1.242$. However, the present value of this dividend, discounted at 13.4 percent, is $PV(D_1) = \$1.242/(1.134)^1 = \$1.095$. The dividend expected in Year 2 grows to $\$1.242(1.08) = \$1.341$, but the present value of this dividend falls to $1.04. Continuing, $D_3 = \$1.449$ and $PV(D_3) = \$0.993$, and so on. Thus, the expected dividends are growing, but the present value of each successive dividend is

---

[14]The last term in Equation 6-8 is derived in Appendix 4A of Eugene F. Brigham and Louis C. Gapenski, *Intermediate Financial Management*, 4th ed. (Fort Worth, Tex.: Dryden Press, 1993). In essence, the full-blown version of Equation 6-8 is the sum of a geometric progression, and the last term is the solution value of the progression.

Figure 6-7   ∎   **Present Values of Dividends of a Constant Growth Stock:**
$D_0 = \$1.15, g = 8\%, k_s = 13.4\%$

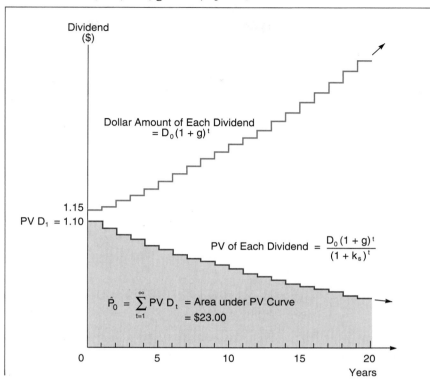

declining, because the dividend growth rate (8%) is less than the rate used for discounting the dividends to the present (13.4%).

If we summed the present values of each future dividend, this summation would be the value of the stock, $\hat{P}_0$. When g is a constant, this summation is equal to $D_1/(k_s - g)$, as shown in Equation 6-8. Therefore, if we extended the lower step function curve in Figure 6-7 on out to infinity and added up the present values of each future dividend, the summation would be identical to the value given by Equation 6-8, $23.00.

Growth in dividends occurs primarily as a result of growth in *earnings per share (EPS)*. Earnings growth, in turn, results from a number of factors, including (1) inflation, (2) the amount of earnings the company retains and reinvests, and (3) the rate of return the company earns on its equity (ROE). Regarding inflation, if output (in units) is stable and if both sales prices and input costs rise at the inflation rate, then EPS will also grow at the inflation rate. EPS will also grow as a result of the reinvestment, or plowback, of earnings. If the firm's earnings are not all paid out as dividends (that is, if some fraction of earnings is retained), the dollars of investment behind each share will rise over time, which should lead to growth in earnings and dividends.

Expected Rate of Return on a Constant Growth Stock

We can solve Equation 6-8 for k_s, again using the hat to denote that we are dealing with an expected rate of return:[15]

$$
\begin{array}{ccccc}
\text{Expected rate} & = & \text{Expected} & + & \text{Expected growth} \\
\text{of return} & & \text{dividend} & & \text{rate, or capital} \\
& & \text{yield} & & \text{gains yield} \\
\hat{k}_s & = & \dfrac{D_1}{P_0} & + & g.
\end{array}
\qquad (6\text{-}9)
$$

Thus, if you buy a stock for a price $P_0 = \$23$, and if you expect the stock to pay a dividend $D_1 = \$1.242$ one year from now and to grow at a constant rate $g = 8\%$ in the future, then your expected rate of return will be 13.4 percent:

$$
\hat{k}_s = \frac{\$1.242}{\$23} + 8\% = 5.4\% + 8\% = 13.4\%.
$$

In this form, we see that $\hat{k}_s$ is the *expected total return* and that it consists of an *expected dividend yield,* $D_1/P_0 = 5.4\%$, plus an *expected growth rate or capital gains yield,* $g = 8\%$.

Suppose this analysis had been conducted on January 1, 1993, so $P_0 = \$23$ is the January 1, 1993, stock price and $D_1 = \$1.242$ is the dividend expected at the end of 1993. What is the expected stock price at the end of 1993 (or the beginning of 1994)? We would again apply Equation 6-8, but this time we would use the 1994 dividend, $D_2 = D_1(1 + g) = \$1.242(1.08) = \$1.3414$:

$$
\hat{P}_{1/1/1994} = \frac{D_{1994}}{k_s - g} = \frac{\$1.3414}{0.134 - 0.08} = \$24.84.
$$

Now notice that $\$24.84$ is 8 percent greater than P_0, the $23 price on January 1, 1993:

$$
\$23(1.08) = \$24.84.
$$

Thus, we would expect to make a capital gain of $\$24.84 - \$23 = \$1.84$ during the year, and a capital gains yield of 8 percent:

$$
\text{Capital gains yield}_{1993} = \frac{\text{Capital gain}}{\text{Beginning price}} = \frac{\$1.84}{\$23} = 0.08 = 8\%.
$$

We could extend the analysis on out, and in each future year the expected capital gains yield would always equal g, the expected dividend growth rate.

---

[15]The k_s value of Equation 6-8 is a *required* rate of return, but when we transform to obtain Equation 6-9, we are finding an *expected* rate of return. Obviously, the transformation requires that $k_s = \hat{k}_s$. This equality holds if the stock market is in equilibrium, a condition that will be discussed later in the chapter.

Continuing, the dividend yield in 1994 could be estimated as follows:

$$\text{Dividend yield}_{1994} = \frac{D_{1994}}{\hat{P}_{1/1/94}} = \frac{\$1.3414}{\$24.84} = 0.054 = 5.4\%.$$

The dividend yield for 1995 could also be calculated, and again it would be 5.4 percent. Thus, *for a constant growth stock,* the following conditions must hold:

1. The dividend is expected to grow forever at a constant rate, g.

2. The stock price is expected to grow at this same rate.

3. The expected dividend yield is a constant.

4. The expected capital gains yield is also a constant, and it is equal to g.

5. The expected total rate of return, $\hat{k}_s$, is equal to the expected dividend yield plus the expected growth rate: $\hat{k}_s$ = dividend yield + g.

The term *expected* should be clarified—it means expected in a probabilistic sense, as the statistically expected outcome. Thus, if we say the growth rate is expected to remain constant at 8 percent, we mean that the best prediction for the growth rate in any future year is 8 percent, not that we literally expect the growth rate to be exactly equal to 8 percent in each future year. In this sense, the constant growth assumption is a reasonable one for many large, mature companies.

Supernormal, or Nonconstant, Growth

supernormal (nonconstant) growth

The part of the life cycle of a firm in which its growth is much faster than that of the economy as a whole.

Firms typically go through *life cycles.* During the early part of their lives, their growth is much faster than that of the economy as a whole; then they match the economy's growth; and finally their growth is slower than that of the economy.[16] Automobile manufacturers in the 1920s and computer software firms such as Microsoft in the 1990s are examples of firms in the early part of the cycle; these firms are called **supernormal,** or **nonconstant, growth** firms. Figure 6-8 illustrates nonconstant growth and also compares it with normal growth, zero growth, and negative growth.[17]

In the figure, the dividends of the supernormal growth firm are expected to grow at a 30 percent rate for 3 years, after which the growth rate is expected

---

[16]The concept of life cycles could be broadened to *product cycle,* which would include both small, start-up companies and large companies like IBM, which periodically introduce new products that give sales and earnings a boost. We should also mention *business cycles,* which alternately depress and boost sales and profits. The growth rate just after a major new product has been introduced, or just after a firm emerges from the depths of a recession, is likely to be much higher than the "expected long-run average growth rate," which is the proper number for a DCF analysis.

[17]A negative growth rate indicates a declining company. A mining company whose profits are falling because of a declining ore body is an example. Someone buying such a company would expect its earnings, and consequently its dividends and stock price, to decline each year, and this would lead to capital losses rather than capital gains. Obviously, a declining company's stock price will be relatively low, and its dividend yield must be high enough to offset the expected capital loss and still produce a competitive total return. Students sometimes argue that they would not be willing to buy a stock whose price was expected to decline. However, if the annual dividends are large enough to *more than offset* the falling stock price, the stock still could provide a good return.

Figure 6-8   ▪   Illustrative Dividend Growth Rates

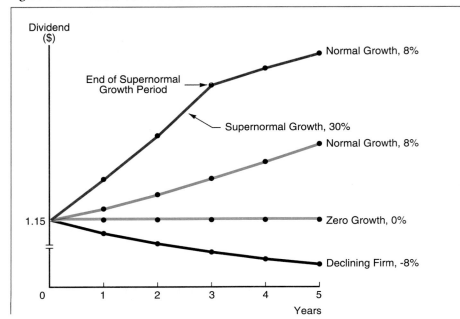

to fall to 8 percent, the assumed average for the economy. The value of this firm, like any other, is the present value of its expected future dividends as determined by Equation 6-5. In the case in which D_t is growing at a constant rate, we simplified Equation 6-5 to $\hat{P}_0 = D_1/(k_s - g)$. In the supernormal case, however, the expected growth rate is not a constant—it declines at the end of the period of supernormal growth. To find the value of such a stock, or of any nonconstant growth stock when the growth rate will eventually stabilize, we proceed in three steps:

1. Find the PV of the dividends during the period of nonconstant growth.

2. Find the price of the stock at the end of the nonconstant growth period, at which point it has become a constant growth stock, and discount this price back to the present.

3. Add these two components to find the intrinsic value of the stock, $\hat{P}_0$.

Figure 6-9 can be used to illustrate the process for valuing nonconstant growth stocks, assuming the following five facts exist:

k_s = stockholders' required rate of return = 13.4%. This rate is used to discount the cash flows.

N = years of supernormal growth = 3.

g_s = rate of growth in both earnings and dividends during the supernormal growth period = 30%. (Note: The growth rate during the supernormal growth period could vary from year to year. Also, there could be several different supernormal growth periods, e.g., 30% for 3 years, then 20% for 3 years, and then a constant 8%.) This rate is shown directly on the time line.

(continued on page 266)

Figure 6-9 ▪ Process for Finding the Value of a Supernormal Growth Stock

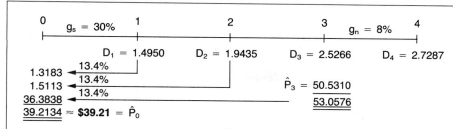

Step 1. Calculate the dividends expected at the end of each year during the supernormal growth period. Calculate the first dividend, $D_1 = D_0(1 + g_s) = \$1.15(1.30) = \$1.4950$. Here g_s is the growth rate during the 3-year supernormal growth period, 30 percent. Show the $1.4950 on the time line as the cash flow for Year 1.

Step 2. Now calculate $D_2 = D_1(1 + g_s) = \$1.4950(1.30) = \$1.9435$, and then $D_3 = D_2(1 + g_s) = \$1.9435(1.30) = \$2.5266$. Show these values on the time line as the cash flows for Years 2 and 3.

Step 3. The price of the stock is the PV of dividends from Year 1 to infinity, so in theory we could project each future dividend, with growth at the normal growth rate, $g_n = 8\%$, used to calculate D_4 and other dividends. However, we know that after D_3 has been paid, which is at Year 3, the stock becomes a constant growth stock, so we can use the constant growth formula to find $\hat{P}_3$, which is the PV of the dividends from Year 4 to infinity as evaluated at Year 3.

First, we determine $D_4 = \$2.5266(1.08) = \$2.7287$ for use in the formula, and then we calculate $\hat{P}_3$ as follows:

$$\hat{P}_3 = \frac{D_4}{k_s - g_n} = \frac{\$2.7287}{0.134 - 0.08} = \$50.5310.$$

Now we show this $50.5310 on the time line as a second cash flow at Year 3. The $50.5310 is a Year 3 cash flow in the sense that the owner of the stock could sell it for $50.5310 at Year 3 and also in the sense that $50.5310 is the present value equivalent of the dividend cash flows from Year 4 to infinity. Note that the *total cash flow* at Year 3 consists of the sum of $D_3 + \hat{P}_3 = \$2.5266 + \$50.5310 = \$53.0576$.

Step 4. Now that the cash flows have been placed on the time line, we can discount each cash flow at the required rate of return, $k_s = 13.4\%$. Since 13.4% is not shown in the tables, it is necessary to discount each flow by dividing by $(1.134)^t$, where $t = 1$ for Year 1, $t = 2$ for Year 2, and $t = 3$ for Year 3. If you do this, you should get the PVs shown to the left below the time line. The sum of the PVs is the value of the supernormal growth stock, $39.21.

If you have a financial calculator, you can find the PV of the cash flows as shown on the time line by using the cash flow (CFLO) register of your calculator. Here you would enter 0 for CF_0 because you get no cash flow at Time 0, $CF_1 = 1.495$, $CF_2 = 1.9435$, and $CF_3 = 2.5266 + 50.531 = 53.0576$. Then enter $I = 13.4$, and press the NPV key to find the value of the stock, $39.21.

g_n = rate of normal, constant growth after the supernormal period = 8%. This rate is also shown on the time line, after Year 3.

D_0 = last dividend the company paid = $1.15.

The valuation process as diagrammed in Figure 6-9 is explained in the steps set forth below the time line. The value of the supernormal growth stock is calculated to be $39.21.

Self-Test Questions

Explain the following statement: "Whereas a bond contains a promise to pay interest, common stock provides an expectation but no promise of dividends."

What are the two elements of a stock's expected returns?

Write out and explain the valuation model for a zero growth stock.

Write out and explain the valuation model for a constant growth stock.

How does one calculate the capital gains yield and the dividend yield of a stock?

Explain how one would find the value of a supernormal growth stock.

STOCK MARKET EQUILIBRIUM

Recall from Chapter 4 that the required return on Stock X, k_X, can be found using the Security Market Line (SML) equation as it was developed in our discussion of the Capital Asset Pricing Model (CAPM):

$$k_X = k_{RF} + (k_M - k_{RF}) b_X.$$

If the risk-free rate of return is 8 percent, if the market risk premium is 4 percent, and if Stock X has a beta of 2, then the marginal investor will require a return of 16 percent on Stock X, calculated as follows:

$$k_X = 8\% + (12\% - 8\%) 2.0$$
$$= 16\%.$$

This 16 percent required return is shown as a point on the SML in Figure 6-10.

The marginal investor will want to buy Stock X if the expected rate of return is more than 16 percent, will want to sell it if the expected rate of return is less than 16 percent, and will be indifferent, hence will hold but not buy or sell, if the expected rate of return is exactly 16 percent. Now suppose the investor's portfolio contains Stock X, and he or she analyzes the stock's prospects and concludes that its earnings, dividends, and price can be expected to grow at a constant rate of 5 percent per year. The last dividend was D_0 = $2.8571, so the next expected dividend is

$$D_1 = \$2.8571(1.05) = \$3.$$

Our marginal investor observes that the present price of the stock, P_0, is $30. Should he or she purchase more of Stock X, sell the present holdings, or maintain the present position?

Figure 6-10   ▪   **Expected and Required Returns on Stock X**

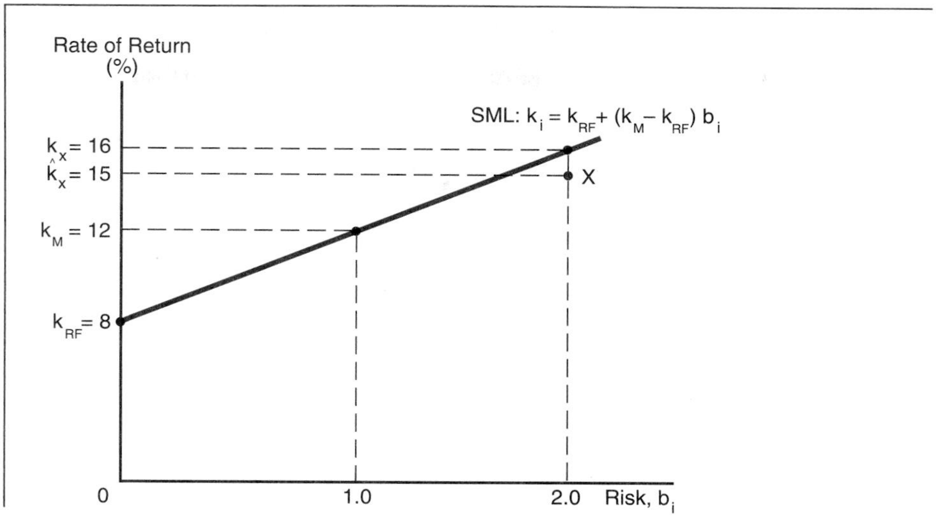

The investor can calculate Stock X's *expected rate of return* as follows:

$$\hat{k}_X = \frac{D_1}{P_0} + g = \frac{\$3}{\$30} + 5\% = 15\%.$$

This value is plotted on Figure 6-10 as Point X, which is below the SML. Because the expected rate of return is less than the required return, this marginal investor would want to sell the stock, as would other holders. However, few people would want to buy at the $30 price, so the present owners would be unable to find buyers unless they cut the price of the stock. Thus, the price would decline, and this decline would continue until the stock's price reached $27.27, at which point the market for this security would be in **equilibrium,** because the expected rate of return, 16 percent, would be equal to the required rate of return:

equilibrium

The condition under which the expected return on a security is just equal to its required return, $\hat{k} = k$, and the price is stable.

$$\hat{k}_X = \frac{\$3}{\$27.27} + 5\% = 11\% + 5\% = 16\% = k_X.$$

Had the stock initially sold for less than $27.27, say at $25, events would have been reversed. Investors would have wanted to buy the stock because its expected rate of return would have exceeded its required rate of return, and buy orders would have driven the stock's price up to $27.27.

To summarize, in equilibrium these two conditions must hold:

1. The expected rate of return as seen by the marginal investor must equal the required rate of return: $\hat{k}_i = k_i$.

2. The actual market price of the stock must equal its intrinsic value as estimated by the marginal investor: $P_0 = \hat{P}_0$.

Of course, some individual investors may believe that $\hat{k}_i > k$ and $\hat{P}_0 > P_0$, and hence they would invest most of their funds in the stock, while other investors may have an opposite view and would sell all of their shares. However, it is the marginal investor who establishes the actual market price, and for this investor,

$\hat{k}_i = k_i$ and $P_0 = \hat{P}_0$. If these conditions do not hold, trading will occur until they do hold.

Changes in Equilibrium Stock Prices

Stock market prices are not constant—they undergo violent changes at times. For example, on October 19, 1987, the Dow Jones average dropped 508 points, and the average stock lost about 23 percent of its value in just one day. Some stocks lost over half of their value that day. To see how such changes can occur, let us assume that Stock X is in equilibrium, selling at a price of $27.27 per share. If all expectations were exactly met, during the next year the price would gradually rise to $28.63, or by 5 percent. However, many different events could occur to cause a change in the equilibrium price of the stock. To illustrate, consider again the set of inputs used to develop Stock X's price of $27.27, along with a new set of assumed input variables:

	Variable Value	
	Original	**New**
Risk-free rate, k_{RF}	8%	7%
Market risk premium, $k_M - k_{RF}$	4%	3%
Stock X's beta coefficient, b_X	2.0	1.0
Stock X's expected growth rate, g_X	5%	6%
D_0	$2.8571	$2.8571
Price of Stock X	$27.27	?

Now give yourself a test: How would the change in each variable, by itself, affect the price, and what is your guess as to the new stock price?

Every change, taken alone, would lead to an increase in the price. The first three variables influence k_X, which declines from 16 to 10 percent:

$$\text{Original } k_X = 8\% + 4\%(2.0) = 16\%.$$

$$\text{New } k_X = 7\% + 3\%(1.0) = 10\%.$$

Using these values, together with the new g value, we find that $\hat{P}_0$ rises from $27.27 to $75.71.[18]

$$\text{Original } \hat{P}_0 = \frac{\$2.8571(1.05)}{0.16 - 0.05} = \frac{\$3}{0.11} = \$27.27.$$

$$\text{New } \hat{P}_0 = \frac{\$2.8571(1.06)}{0.10 - 0.06} = \frac{\$3.0285}{0.04} = \$75.71.$$

At the new price, the expected and required rates of return will be equal:[19]

---

[18]A price change of this magnitude is by no means rare. The prices of *many* stocks double or halve during a year. For example, during 1990 Cabletron increased in value by 204 percent; on the other hand, Monarch Capital fell from $18\frac{3}{4}$ to $\frac{9}{16}$th, a 97 percent loss.

[19]It should be obvious by now that *actual realized* rates of return are not necessarily equal to expected and required returns. Thus, an investor might have *expected* to receive a return of 15 percent if he or she had bought Cabletron or Monarch Capital stock in 1990, but, after the fact, the realized return on Cabletron was far above 15 percent, whereas that on Monarch Capital was far below.

$$\hat{k}_X = \frac{\$3.0285}{\$75.71} + 6\% = 10\% = k_X.$$

Evidence suggests that stocks, especially those of large NYSE companies, adjust rapidly to disequilibrium situations. Consequently, equilibrium ordinarily exists for any given stock, and, in general, required and expected returns are equal. Stock prices certainly change, sometimes violently and rapidly, but this simply reflects changing conditions and expectations. There are, of course, times when a stock continues to react for several months to a favorable or unfavorable development, but this does not signify a long adjustment period; rather, it simply illustrates that as more new pieces of information about the situation become available, the market adjusts to them. The ability of the market to adjust to new information is discussed in the next section.

The Efficient Markets Hypothesis

Efficient Markets Hypothesis (EMH)

The hypothesis that securities are typically in equilibrium—that they are fairly priced in the sense that the price reflects all publicly available information on each security.

A body of theory called the **Efficient Markets Hypothesis (EMH)** holds (1) that stocks are always in equilibrium and (2) that it is impossible for an investor to consistently "beat the market." Essentially, those who believe in the EMH note that there are 100,000 or so full-time, highly trained, professional analysts and traders operating in the market, while there are fewer than 3,000 major stocks. Therefore, if each analyst followed 30 stocks (which is about right, as analysts tend to specialize in the stocks in a specific industry), there would be 1,000 analysts following each stock. Further, these analysts work for organizations such as Citibank, Merrill Lynch, Prudential Insurance, and the like, which have billions of dollars available with which to take advantage of bargains. As a result of SEC disclosure requirements and electronic information networks, as new information about a stock becomes available, these 1,000 analysts all receive and evaluate it at approximately the same time. Therefore, the price of the stock adjusts almost immediately to reflect any new developments.

Financial theorists generally define three forms, or levels, of market efficiency:

1. The *weak-form* of the EMH states that all information contained in past price movements is fully reflected in current market prices. Therefore, information about recent trends in stock prices is of no use in selecting stocks—the fact that a stock has risen for the past three days, for example, gives us no useful clues as to what it will do today or tomorrow. People who believe that weak-form efficiency exists also believe that "tape watchers" and "chartists" are wasting their time.[20]

2. The *semistrong-form* of the EMH states that current market prices reflect all *publicly available* information. If this is true, no abnormal returns can be earned by analyzing stocks.[21] Thus, if semistrong-form efficiency exists,

---

[20]Tape watchers are people who watch the NYSE tape, while chartists plot past patterns of stock price movements. Both are called "technicians," and both believe that they can see if something is happening to the stock that will cause its price to move up or down in the near future.

[21]An abnormal return is one that exceeds the return justified by the riskiness of the investment; that is, a return that plots above the SML in a graph like Figure 6-10.

it does no good to pore over annual reports or other published data because market prices will have adjusted to any good or bad news contained in such reports as soon as they came out. However, insiders (say, the presidents of companies), even under semistrong-form efficiency, can still make abnormal returns on their own companies' stocks.

3. The *strong-form* of the EMH states that current market prices reflect all pertinent information, whether publicly available or privately held. If this form holds, even insiders would find it impossible to earn abnormal returns in the stock market.[22]

Many empirical studies have been conducted to test for the three forms of market efficiency. Most of these studies suggest that the stock market is indeed highly efficient in the weak form and reasonably efficient in the semistrong form, at least for the larger and more widely followed stocks. However, the strong-form EMH does not hold, so abnormal profits can be made by those who possess inside information.

What bearing does the EMH have on financial decisions? Since stock prices do seem to reflect public information, most stocks appear to be fairly valued. This does not mean that new developments could not cause a stock's price to soar or to plummet, but it does mean that stocks, in general, are neither overvalued nor undervalued — they are fairly priced and in equilibrium. However, there are certainly cases in which corporate insiders have information not known to outsiders.

If the EMH is correct, it is a waste of time for most of us to analyze stocks by looking for those that are undervalued. If stock prices already reflect all publicly available information and hence are fairly priced, one can "beat the market" only by luck, and it is difficult, if not impossible, for anyone to consistently outperform the market averages. Empirical tests have shown that the EMH is, in its weak and semi-strong forms, valid. However, people such as corporate officers who have inside information can do better than the averages, and individuals and organizations that are especially good at digging out information on small, new companies also seem to do consistently well. Also, some investors may be able to analyze and react more quickly than others to releases of new information, and these investors may have an advantage over others. However, the buy-sell actions of those investors quickly bring market prices into equilibrium. Therefore, it is generally safe to assume that $\hat{k} = k$, that $\hat{P}_0 = P_0$, and that stocks plot on the SML.[23]

---

[22]Several cases of illegal insider trading have made the news headlines recently. These cases involved employees of several major investment banking houses and even an employee of the SEC. In the most famous case, Ivan Boesky admitted to making $50 million by purchasing the stock of firms he knew were about to merge. He went to jail, and he had to pay a large fine, but he helped disprove the strong-form EMH.

[23]Market efficiency also has important implications for managerial decisions, especially those pertaining to common stock issues, stock repurchases, and tender offers. Stocks appear to be fairly valued, so decisions based on a stock's being undervalued or overvalued must be approached with caution. However, managers do have better information about their own companies than outsiders, and this information can legally be used to the companies' (but not the managers') advantage.

Actual Stock Prices and Returns

Our discussion thus far has focused on *expected* stock prices and *expected* rates of return. Anyone who has ever invested in the stock market knows that there can be, and there generally are, large differences between *expected* and *realized* prices and returns.

We can use Commonwealth Edison, the Chicago utility, to illustrate this point. In early 1990, Edison's stock price was about $38 per share. Its 1989 dividend, D_0, had been $3.00, but analysts expected the company to grow at a rate of about 4 percent in the future. Thus, an average investor who bought Edison at a price of $38 would have expected to earn a return of about 12.2 percent:

$$\hat{k}_s = \begin{array}{c} \text{Expected dividend} \\ \text{yield} \end{array} + \begin{array}{c} \text{Expected growth rate, which is also} \\ \text{the expected capital gains yield} \end{array}$$

$$= \frac{D_0(1 + g)}{P_0} + g$$

$$= \frac{\$3.12}{\$38} + 4\%$$

$$= 8.2\% + 4.0\% = 12.2\%.$$

In fact, things did not work out as expected. The economy in 1990 was weaker than had been predicted, so Edison's earnings did not grow as fast as expected, and its dividend remained at $3.00. So, rather than growing, Edison's stock price declined, and it closed on December 31, 1990, at $34.75, down $3.25 for the year. Thus, on a beginning-of-the-year investment of $38, the actual return on Edison for 1990 was -0.7 percent:

$$\bar{k}_s = \text{Actual dividend yield} + \text{Actual capital gains yield}$$

$$= \frac{\$3.00}{\$38} + \frac{-\$3.25}{\$38}$$

$$= 7.9\% - 8.6\% = -0.7\%.$$

Most other stocks performed similarly to Edison's, or worse, in 1990.

Figure 6-11 shows how the price of an average share of stock has varied in recent years, and Figure 6-12 shows how total realized returns have varied. The market trend has been strongly up, but it has gone up in some years and down in others, and the stocks of individual companies have likewise gone up and down. We know from theory that expected returns as estimated by a marginal investor are always positive, but in some years, as Figure 6-12 shows, negative returns have been realized. Of course, even in bad years some individual companies do well, so the "name of the game" in security analysis is to pick the winners. Financial managers attempt to take actions which will put their companies into the winners' column, but they don't always succeed. In subsequent chapters, we will examine the actions that managers can take to increase the odds of their firms doing relatively well in the marketplace.

Stock Market Reporting

Figure 6-13, taken from a daily newspaper, is a section of the stock market page for stocks listed on the NYSE. For each stock, the NYSE report provides specific data on the trading that took place the prior day. Similar information is available

Figure 6-11   ▪   **S&P 500 Index, 1967–1991**

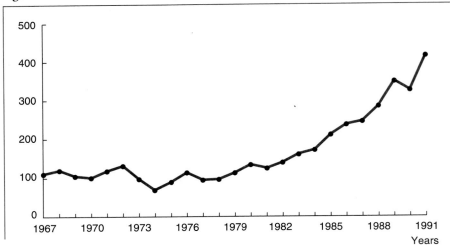

Figure 6-12   ▪   **S&P 500 Index, Total Returns:**
                    Dividend Yield + Capital Gain or Loss, 1967–1991

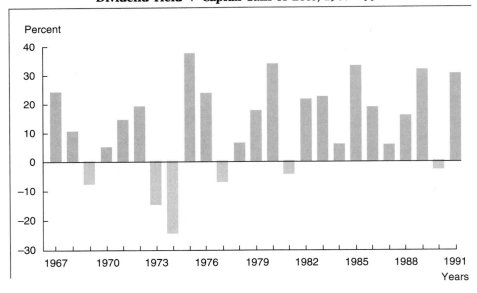

for stocks listed on the other exchanges as well as for stocks traded over-the-counter.

Stocks are listed alphabetically, from AAR Industries to Zweig; the data in Figure 6-13 were taken from the top of the listing. We will examine the data for Abbott Laboratories, AbbotLab, shown about halfway down the table. The two columns on the left show the highest and lowest prices at which the stocks have sold during the past year; Abbott Labs has traded in the range from $69½ to $39¼ during the preceding 52 weeks. The figure just to the right of the company's abbreviated name is the dividend; Abbott Labs had a current indi-

Figure 6-13 ▮ Stock Market Transactions, January 17, 1992

Quotations as of 5 p.m. Eastern Time
Friday, January 17, 1992

	52 Weeks Hi	52 Weeks Lo	Stock	Sym	Div	Yld %	PE	Vol 100s	Hi	Lo	Close	Net Chg
			-A-A-A-									
	16⅞	9¼	AAR	AIR	.48	3.6	18	1440	13¾	13½	13½	...
	11⅝	10⅜	ACM Gvt Fd	ACG	1.26	11.1	...	732	11½	11⅜	11⅜	...
	10⅜	8¾	ACM OppFd	AOF	1.01e	10.2	...	167	10	9⅞	9⅞	− ⅛
	11⅛	9⅜	ACM SecFd	GSF	1.26	11.5	...	1497	11	10⅞	11	...
	9½	8¼	ACM SpctmFd	SI	1.01	10.8	...	783	9⅜	9¼	9⅜	+ ¼
n	9⅛	7⅝	ACM MgdIncFd	AMF	1.01	11.2	...	145	9⅛	9	9	...
	12⅞	11½	ACM MgdMultFd	MMF	1.35	10.7	...	260	12¾	12⅝	12⅝	...
	21½	5	ADT adr	ADTA	.32e	3.9	3	253	8⅜	7¾	8¼	+ ⅜
n	**9½**	**5**	**ADT**	**ADT**		...	...	**7104**	**8½**	**8**	**8⅜**	+ ½
	32⅞	18½	AFLAC	AFL	.40	1.3	17	1513	30	29½	29⅞	+ ¼
	26	14⅜	AL Labs A	BMD	.16	.7	25	361	23⅜	22⅞	22⅞	− ¼
	1⅞	**¾**	**AM Int**	**AM**		...	...	**280**	1⅛	1	1	− ⅛
	12	4⅛	AM Int pf		1.50j	...	...	21	5½	5¼	5⅜	+ ¼
x	11¾	9⅛	AMEV Sec	AMV	1.05	9.2	...	x83	11⅜	11¼	11⅜	...
	75½	44¼	AMR	AMR		...	...	7236	74⅜	72	72½	−2
	44¼	33½	ARCO Chm	RCM	2.50	6.3	21	128	40	39¾	40	+ ⅛
	2⅝	**1**	**ARX**	**ARX**		...	...	**77**	**1¾**	**1⅝**	**1¾**	+ ⅛
	56	41½	ASA	ASA	3.00	5.9	...	1691	51⅝	51	51⅛	− ½
	6½	2½	ATT Cap yen wt			...	...	89	5½	5⅛	5½	+ ¼
	69½	39¼	AbbotLab	ABT	1.00	1.6	25	8623	63½	61	62⅝	+ ⅜
	14⅝	9⅞	Abitibi g	ABY	.50	...	...	86	13⅛	12⅞	13⅛	+ ⅜
	6	3⅜	AcmeElec	ACE		...	...	3	5⅛	5	5	...
	8¾	4¾	AcmeCleve	AMT	.40	4.8	...	187	8⅜	8⅛	8⅜	...
	40	24⅝	Acuson	ACN		...	22	1752	32⅝	31¾	32	− ⅜
	20¼	14¼	AdamsExp	ADX	1.63e	8.6	...	159	19¼	19	19	− ⅛
	9⅛	3⅞	AdobeRes	ADB		...	...	257	5⅛	4¾	5	...
	20⅛	12⅞	AdobeRes pfB			...	...	44	14½	14⅛	14½	+ ⅜
	18	10¾	AdobeRes pfA			...	...	19	12⅝	12⅛	12⅝	+ ⅜
	20½	4⅝	AdvMicro	AMD		...	12	26376	19	17⅜	18⅝	+ ⅞
	46½	19¼	AdvMicro pf		3.00	6.7	...	771	45¼	43¼	44⅞	+ ⅞
	7	2¼	Advest	ADV		...	...	89	6⅝	6½	6½	− ⅛
	49⅛	31⅞	AetnaLife	AET	2.76	6.2	9	1549	44⅝	44⅛	44⅝	+ ¼
	10⅝	6⅝	AffilPub	AFP	.24	2.4	91	822	10⅛	9¾	10	− ⅛
n▲	23¾	21½	AgriMinl	AMC		...	...	1439	24	23⅜	23⅜	+ ⅛
	20⅞	12	Ahmanson	AHM	.88	5.2	10	3642	17	16½	16⅞	+ ¼
	26¼	24	Ahmanson pf		2.40	9.3	...	242	25⅞	25¾	25¾	...
	20	2⅞	Aileen	AEE		...	16	112	19	18½	18½	− ⅜
	80¾	53	AirProduct	APD	1.56	2.0	18	845	80½	79¼	80	...
	30	**16⅝**	**AirbornFrght**	**ABF**	**.30**	1.1	**20**	**4433**	**27**	**25⅝**	**27**	+1⅝
	24½	12½	Airgas	ARG		...	26	122	24⅜	24	24¼	+ ½
	15½	**8⅛**	**Airlease**	FLY	**1.68**	**16.2**	**6**	**141**	**10⅜**	**10**	**10⅜**	+ ½
	26⅜	22	AlaPwr pf		2.06e	7.8	...	17	26¼	26⅛	26¼	+ ⅛
	11	9⅜	AlaPwr pf		.87	8.0	...	29	10⅞	10½	10⅞	+ ¼
	102	88¾	AlaPwr pf		8.16	8.0	...	z3200	101½	101¼	101½	− ½
▲	103	87½	AlaPwr pf		8.28	7.9	...	z4760	105	103	105	+3

Source: *The Wall Street Journal,* January 20, 1992.

cated annual dividend rate of $1.00 per share and a dividend yield (which is the dividend divided by the closing stock price) of 1.6 percent. Next comes the ratio of the stock's price to its annual earnings (the P/E ratio), followed by the volume of trading for the day: 862,300 shares of Abbott Labs stock were traded on January 17, 1992. Following the volume come the high and low prices for the day, and then the closing price. On January 17, Abbott Labs traded as high as $63½ and as low as $61, while the last trade was at $62⅝. The last column gives the change from the closing price on the previous day. Abbott Labs was up ⅜, or $0.375, so the previous close must have been $62.625 − $0.375 = $62.25.

There are several other points to note in Figure 6-13. First, the "pf" following the stock name of the second AM Int listing tells us that this one is a preferred stock rather than a common stock. Second, a "▲" preceding the columns containing a stock's 52-week high and low prices indicates that the price hit a new 52-week high, whereas a "▼" preceding the columns containing a stock's 52-week high and low prices indicates a new 52-week low. The last Alabama Power preferred stock issue shown hit a new high on January 17, 1992. Third, an "x" preceding the columns containing the 52-week high and low prices and also preceding the stock's sales volume indicates that the stock went ex-dividend that day; this means that someone who buys the stock will not receive the next dividend. AMEV is an example of a company that is trading ex-dividend on January 17, 1992. We discuss ex-dividend effects in detail in Chapter 18. Fourth, a "z" preceding a stock's sales volume indicates sales in full, not shown in hundreds. The last two Alabama preferred stock issues shown indicate sales in full. Fifth, an "s" preceding the 52-week high and low prices indicates that the stock was split within the past 52 weeks; we will discuss stock splits in Chapter 18. None of the stocks presented in Figure 6-13 reported a split during the past 52-week period. An "n" preceding the 52-week high and low prices indicates that the stock is newly issued within the past 52 weeks. There were three stocks that were newly issued within the past 52 weeks; ADT was one of those stocks. Next, issues that appear in boldface had a 5 percent or more change in price from their previous closing price. Airborne Freight is an example of a company that had a price change greater than 5 percent from the previous day's closing price. Finally, an "e" following the dividend column indicates that a dividend was declared or paid in the preceding 12 months, but there is no regular dividend rate. Adams Express is an example of a company which has no regular dividend rate but declared or paid a dividend in the previous 12-month period. Dividend policy is discussed in Chapter 18.

We have discussed only a few of the more common footnotes that appear in the NYSE and AMEX exchange listings. For additional footnotes and their explanations, see the explanatory notes in *The Wall Street Journal* on the first page of the section where these listings are published.

Self-Test Questions

When a stock is in equilibrium, what two conditions must hold?

What is the major conclusion of the Efficient Markets Hypothesis (EMH)?

What is the difference between the three forms of the EMH: (1) weak-form, (2) semistrong-form, and (3) strong-form?

If a stock is *not* in equilibrium, explain how financial markets adjust to bring it into equilibrium.

SMALL BUSINESS   Valuation of Small Firms

In this chapter we presented several equations for valuing a firm's common stock. These equations had one common element: they all assumed that the firm is currently paying a dividend. However, many small firms, even highly profitable ones whose stock is traded in the market, have never paid a dividend. How does one value the stock of such firms? If a firm is expected to begin paying dividends in the future, we can modify the equations presented in the chapter and use them to determine the value of the stock.

A new business often expects to have very low sales during its first few years of operation as it develops its product. Then, if the product catches on, sales will grow rapidly for several years. For example, Compaq Computer Company had only three employees when it was incorporated in 1982. Its first year was devoted to product development, and 1982 sales were zero. In 1983, however, Compaq began marketing its personal computer, and its sales hit $111 million, a record first-year volume for any new firm, and by 1986 Compaq was included in Fortune's 500 largest U.S. industrial firms. Obviously, Compaq has been more successful than most new businesses, but it is common for small firms to have growth rates of 100 percent, 500 percent, or even 1,000 percent during their first few years of operation.

Sales growth brings with it the need for additional assets—Compaq could not have increased its sales as it did without also increasing its assets, and asset growth requires an increase in liability and/or equity accounts. Small firms can generally obtain some bank credit, but they must maintain a reasonable balance between debt and equity. Thus, additional bank borrowings require increases in equity, and getting the equity capital needed to support growth can be difficult for small firms. They have limited access to the capital markets, and, even when they can sell common stock, the owners of small firms are reluctant to do so for fear of losing voting control. Therefore, the best source of equity for most small businesses is retained earnings, and for this reason most small firms pay no dividends during their rapid growth years. Eventually, though, successful small firms do pay dividends, and those dividends generally grow rapidly at first but slow down to a sustainable constant rate once the firm reaches maturity.

If a small firm currently pays no dividend but is expected to pay dividends in the future, the value of its stock can be found as follows:

1.   Estimate when dividends will be paid, the amount of the first dividend, the growth rate during the supernormal growth period, the length of the supernormal period, the long-run (constant) growth rate, and the rate of return required by investors.

2.   Use the constant growth model to determine the price of the stock after the firm reaches a stable growth situation.

3.   Set out on a time line the cash flows (dividends during the supernormal growth period and the stock price once the constant growth state is reached) and then find the present value of these cash flows. That present value represents the value of the stock today.

To illustrate this process, consider the situation for WonderLure Inc., a company that was set up in 1992 to produce and market a new high-tech fishing lure. WonderLure's sales are currently growing at a rate of 200 percent per year. The company expects to experience a high but declining rate of growth in sales and earnings during the next 10 years, after which analysts estimate that it will grow at a steady 10 percent per year. The firm's management has announced that it will pay no dividends for 5 years, but, if earnings materialize as forecasted, it will pay a dividend of $0.20 per share at the end of Year 6, $0.30 in Year 7, $0.40 in Year 8, $0.45 in Year 9, and $0.50 in Year 10. After Year 10, current plans are to increase the dividend by 10 percent per year.

WonderLure's investment bankers estimate that investors require a 15 percent return on similar stocks. Therefore, we find the value of a share of WonderLure's stock as follows:

$$P_0 = \frac{\$0}{(1.15)^1} + \ldots + \frac{\$0}{(1.15)^5}$$

$$+ \frac{\$0.20}{(1.15)^6} + \frac{\$0.30}{(1.15)^7}$$

$$+ \frac{\$0.40}{(1.15)^8} + \frac{\$0.45}{(1.15)^9} + \frac{\$0.50}{(1.15)^{10}}$$

$$+ \left(\frac{\$0.50(1.10)}{0.15 - 0.10}\right)\left(\frac{1}{(1.15)^{10}}\right)$$

$$= \$3.30.$$

The last term finds the expected price of the stock in Year 10 and then finds the present value of that price. Thus, we see that the valuation concepts discussed in the chapter can be applied to small firms which currently pay no dividends, provided an estimate of future dividends can be made.

SUMMARY

Corporate decisions should be analyzed in terms of how alternative courses of action are likely to affect the value of a firm. However, it is necessary to know how bond and stock prices are established before attempting to measure how a given decision will affect a specific firm's value. Accordingly, this chapter showed how bond and stock values are determined as well as how investors go about estimating the rates of return they expect to earn. The key concepts covered in the chapter are summarized below.

- A **bond** is a long-term promissory note issued by a business or governmental unit. The firm receives the selling price of the bond in exchange for promising to make interest payments and to repay the principal on a specified future date.

- The **value of a bond** is found as the present value of an **annuity** (the interest payments) plus the present value of a lump sum (the **principal**). The bond is evaluated at the appropriate periodic interest rate over the number of periods for which interest payments are made.

- The equation used to find the value of an annual coupon bond is:

$$V_B = \sum_{t=1}^{N} \frac{INT}{(1 + k_d)^t} + \frac{M}{(1 + k_d)^N}$$
$$= INT(PVIFA_{k_d,N}) + M(PVIF_{k_d,N}).$$

An adjustment to the formula must be made if the bond pays interest **semiannually**: divide INT and k_d by 2, and multiply N by 2.

- The return earned on a bond held to maturity is defined as the bond's **yield to maturity (YTM).** If the bond can be redeemed before maturity, it is **callable**, and the return investors will receive if it is called is defined as the **yield to call (YTC).** The YTC is found as the present value of the interest payments received while the bond is outstanding plus the present value of the call price (the par value plus a call premium).

- The longer the maturity of a bond, the more its price will change in response to a given change in interest rates; this is called **interest rate price risk.** Bonds with short maturities, however, expose the investor to high **interest rate reinvestment rate risk,** which is the risk that income will decline because cash flows received from bonds will have to be reinvested at lower interest rates.

- Most preferred stocks are **perpetuities,** and the value of a share of perpetual preferred stock is found as the dividend divided by the required rate of return:

$$V_{ps} = \frac{D_{ps}}{k_{ps}}.$$

- The **value of a share of stock** is calculated as the **present value of the stream of dividends** it is expected to provide in the future.

- The equation used to find the **value of a constant,** or **normal, growth stock** is: $\hat{P}_0 = D_1/(k_s - g)$.

▪ The **expected total rate of return** from a stock consists of an **expected dividend yield** plus an **expected capital gains yield.** For a constant growth firm, both the expected dividend yield and the expected capital gains yield are constant.

▪ The equation for $\hat{k}_s$, **the expected rate of return on a constant growth stock,** can be expressed as follows: $\hat{k}_s = D_1/P_0 + g$.

▪ A **zero growth stock** is one whose future dividends are not expected to grow at all, while a **supernormal growth stock** is one whose earnings and dividends are expected to grow much faster than the economy as a whole over some specified time period.

▪ To find the **present value of a supernormal growth stock,** (1) find the dividends expected during the supernormal growth period, (2) find the price of the stock at the end of the supernormal growth period, (3) discount the dividends and the projected price back to the present, and (4) sum these PVs to find the current value of the stock, $\hat{P}_0$.

▪ The **Efficient Markets Hypothesis (EMH)** holds (1) that stocks are always in equilibrium and (2) that it is impossible for an investor to consistently "beat the market." Therefore, according to the EMH, stocks are always fairly valued ($\hat{P}_0 = P_0$), the required return on a stock is equal to its expected return ($k = \hat{k}$), and all stocks' expected returns plot on the SML.

▪ Finally, in this chapter we saw that differences can and do exist between expected and actual returns in the stock and bond markets—only for short-term, risk-free assets are expected and actual (or realized) returns equal.

Questions

6-1 Two investors are evaluating IBM's stock for possible purchase. They agree on the expected value of D_1 and also on the expected future dividend growth rate. Further, they agree on the riskiness of the stock. However, one investor normally holds stocks for 2 years, while the other normally holds stocks for 10 years. On the basis of the type of analysis done in this chapter, they should both be willing to pay the same price for IBM's stock. True or false? Explain.

6-2 A bond that pays interest forever and has no maturity date is a perpetual bond. In what respect is a perpetual bond similar to a no-growth common stock, and to a share of preferred stock?

6-3 Is it true that the following equation can be used to find the value of an N-year bond that pays interest once a year?

$$V_B = \sum_{t=1}^{N} \frac{\text{Annual interest}}{(1 + k_d)^t} + \frac{\text{Par value}}{(1 + k_d)^N}.$$

6-4 "The values of outstanding bonds change whenever the going rate of interest changes. In general, short-term interest rates are more volatile than long-term interest rates. Therefore, short-term bond prices are more sensitive to interest rate changes than are long-term bond prices." Is this statement true or false? Explain.

6-5 The rate of return you would get if you bought a bond and held it to its maturity date is called the bond's yield to maturity. If interest rates in the economy rise after a bond has been issued, what will happen to the bond's price and to its YTM? Does the length of time to maturity affect the extent to which a given change in interest rates will affect the bond's price?

6-6   If you buy a *callable* bond and interest rates decline, will the value of your bond rise by as much as it would have risen if the bond had not been callable? Explain.

6-7   If you bought a share of common stock, you would typically expect to receive dividends plus capital gains. Would you expect the distribution between dividend yield and capital gains to be influenced by the firm's decision to pay more dividends rather than to retain and reinvest more of its earnings?

6-8   Is it true that the following expression can be used to find the value of a constant growth stock?

$$\hat{P}_0 = \frac{D_0}{k_s + g}.$$

Self-Test Problems   (Solutions Appear in Appendix B)

ST-1
Key terms

Define each of the following terms:
a.   Bond
b.   Par value; maturity date; call provision
c.   Coupon payment; coupon interest rate
d.   Premium bond; discount bond
e.   Current yield (on a bond); yield to maturity (YTM); yield to call (YTC)
f.   Interest rate price risk; interest rate reinvestment rate risk
g.   Intrinsic value ($\hat{P}_0$); market price (P_0)
h.   Required rate of return, k_s; expected rate of return, $\hat{k}_s$; actual, or realized, rate of return, $\bar{k}_s$
i.   Capital gains yield; dividend yield; expected total return
j.   Zero growth stock
k.   Normal, or constant, growth; supernormal, or nonconstant, growth
l.   Equilibrium
m.   Efficient Markets Hypothesis (EMH); three forms of EMH

ST-2
Stock growth rates
and valuation

You are considering buying the stocks of two companies that operate in the same industry; they have very similar characteristics except for their dividend payout policies. Both companies are expected to earn $6 per share this year. However, Company D (for "dividend") is expected to pay out all of its earnings as dividends, while Company G (for "growth") is expected to pay out only one-third of its earnings, or $2 per share. D's stock price is $40. G and D are equally risky. Which of the following is most likely to be true?
a.   Company G will have a faster growth rate than Company D. Therefore, G's stock price should be greater than $40.
b.   Although G's growth rate should exceed D's, D's current dividend exceeds that of G, and this should cause D's price to exceed G's.
c.   An investor in Stock D will get his or her money back faster because D pays out more of its earnings as dividends. Thus, in a sense, D is like a short-term bond, and G is like a long-term bond. Therefore, if economic shifts cause k_d and k_s to increase and if the expected streams of dividends from D and G remain constant, Stocks D and G will both decline, but D's price should decline further.
d.   D's expected and required rate of return is $\hat{k}_s = k_s = 15\%$. G's expected return will be higher because of its higher expected growth rate.
e.   On the basis of the available information, the best estimate of G's growth rate is 10 percent.

ST-3

Bond valuation

The Pennington Corporation issued a new series of bonds on January 1, 1970. The bonds were sold at par ($1,000), have a 12 percent coupon, and mature in 30 years, on December 31, 1999. Coupon payments are made semiannually (on June 30 and December 31).

a. What was the YTM of Pennington's bonds on January 1, 1970?

b. What was the price of the bond on January 1, 1975, 5 years later, assuming that the level of interest rates had fallen to 10 percent?

c. Find the current yield and capital gains yield on the bond on January 1, 1975, given the price as determined in Part b.

d. On July 1, 1993, Pennington's bonds sold for $916.42. What was the YTM at that date?

e. What were the current yield and capital gains yield on July 1, 1993?

f. Now assume that you purchased an outstanding Pennington bond on March 1, 1993, when the going rate of interest was 15.5 percent. How large a check must you have written to complete the transaction? This is a hard question! (Hint: $PVIFA_{7.75\%,13}$ = 8.0136 and $PVIF_{7.75\%,13}$ = 0.3789.)

ST-4

Constant growth
stock valuation

Ewald Company's current stock price is $36, and its last dividend was $2.40. In view of Ewald's strong financial position and its consequent low risk, its required rate of return is only 12 percent. If dividends are expected to grow at a constant rate, g, in the future, and if k_s is expected to remain at 12 percent, what is Ewald's expected stock price 5 years from now?

ST-5

Supernormal growth
stock valuation

Snyder Computer Chips Inc. is experiencing a period of rapid growth. Earnings and dividends are expected to grow at a rate of 15 percent during the next 2 years, at 13 percent in the third year, and at a constant rate of 6 percent thereafter. Snyder's last dividend was $1.15, and the required rate of return on the stock is 12 percent.

a. Calculate the value of the stock today.

b. Calculate $\hat{P}_1$ and $\hat{P}_2$.

c. Calculate the dividend yield and capital gains yield for Years 1, 2, and 3.

Problems

6-1

Bond valuation

Suppose Ford Motor Company sold an issue of bonds with a 10-year maturity, a $1,000 par value, a 10 percent coupon rate, and semiannual interest payments.

a. Two years after the bonds were issued, the going rate of interest on bonds such as these fell to 6 percent. At what price would the bonds sell?

b. Suppose that, 2 years after the initial offering, the going interest rate had risen to 12 percent. At what price would the bonds sell?

c. Suppose that the conditions in Part a existed—that is, interest rates fell to 6 percent 2 years after the issue date. Suppose further that the interest rate remained at 6 percent for the next 8 years. What would happen to the price of the Ford Motor Company bonds over time?

6-2

Perpetual bond valuation

The bonds of the Lange Corporation are perpetuities with a 10 percent coupon. Bonds of this type currently yield 8 percent, and their par value is $1,000.

a. What is the price of the Lange bonds?

b. Suppose interest rate levels rise to the point where such bonds now yield 12 percent. What would be the price of the Lange bonds?

c. At what price would the Lange bonds sell if the yield on these bonds were 10 percent?

d. How would your answers to Parts a, b, and c change if the bonds were not perpetuities but had a maturity of 20 years?

6-3

Constant growth
stock valuation

Your broker offers to sell you some shares of Wingler & Co. common stock that paid a dividend of $2 *yesterday.* You expect the dividend to grow at the rate of 5 percent per year for the next 3 years, and if you buy the stock you plan to hold it for 3 years and then sell it.

a. Find the expected dividend for each of the next 3 years; that is, calculate D_1, D_2, and D_3. Note that $D_0 = \$2$.

b. Given that the appropriate discount rate is 12 percent and that the first of these dividend payments will occur 1 year from now, find the present value of the dividend stream; that is, calculate the PV of D_1, D_2, and D_3, and then sum these PVs.

c. You expect the price of the stock 3 years from now to be $34.73; that is, you expect $\hat{P}_3$ to equal $34.73. Discounted at a 12 percent rate, what is the present value of this expected future stock price? In other words, calculate the PV of $34.73.

d. If you plan to buy the stock, hold it for 3 years, and then sell it for $34.73, what is the most you should pay for it?

e. Use Equation 6-8 to calculate the present value of this stock. Assume that $g = 5\%$, and it is constant.

f. Is the value of this stock dependent upon how long you plan to hold it? In other words, if your planned holding period were 2 years or 5 years rather than 3 years, would this affect the value of the stock today, $\hat{P}_0$?

6-4

Return on common stock

You buy a share of Damanpour Corporation stock for $21.40. You expect it to pay dividends of $1.07, $1.1449, and $1.2250 in Years 1, 2, and 3, respectively, and you expect to sell it at a price of $26.22 at the end of 3 years.

a. Calculate the growth rate in dividends.

b. Calculate the expected dividend yield.

c. Assuming that the calculated growth rate is expected to continue, you can add the dividend yield to the expected growth rate to get the expected total rate of return. What is this stock's expected total rate of return?

6-5

Constant growth
stock valuation

Investors require a 15 percent rate of return on Goulet Company's stock ($k_s = 15\%$).

a. What will be Goulet's stock value if the previous dividend was $D_0 = \$2$ and if investors expect dividends to grow at a constant compound annual rate of (1) -5 percent, (2) 0 percent, (3) 5 percent, and (4) 10 percent?

b. Using data from Part a, what is the Gordon (constant growth) model value for Goulet's stock if the required rate of return is 15 percent and the expected growth rate is (1) 15 percent or (2) 20 percent? Are these reasonable results? Explain.

c. Is it reasonable to expect that a constant growth stock would have $g > k_s$?

6-6

Stock and bond reporting

Look up the prices of Southwestern Bell's stock and bonds in *The Wall Street Journal* (or some other newspaper which provides this information).

a. What was the stock's price range during the last year?

b. What is Southwestern Bell's current dividend? What is its dividend yield?

c. What change occurred in Southwestern Bell's stock price the day the newspaper was published?

d. If Southwestern Bell were to sell a new issue of $1,000 par value long-term bonds, approximately what coupon interest rate would it have to set on the bonds if it wanted to bring them out at par? (Note: Southwestern Bell bonds trade on the AMEX.)

e. If you had $10,000 and wanted to invest it in Southwestern Bell, what return would you expect to get if you bought the bonds and what return if you bought Southwestern Bell's stock? (Hint: Think about capital gains when you answer the latter part of this question.)

6-7

Discount bond valuation

Assume that in February 1966 the Los Angeles Airport authority issued a series of 3.4 percent, 30-year bonds. Interest rates rose substantially in the years following the issue, and as they did, the price of the bonds declined. In February 1979, 13 years later, the price of the bonds had dropped from $1,000 to $650. In answering the following questions, assume that the bond requires annual interest payments.

a. Each bond originally sold at its $1,000 par value. What was the yield to maturity of these bonds when they were issued?

b. Calculate the yield to maturity in February 1979.

c. Assume that interest rates stabilized at the 1979 level and stayed there for the remainder of the life of the bonds. What would have been the bonds' price in February 1992, when they had 4 years remaining to maturity?

d. What will the price of the bonds be the day before they mature in 1996? (Disregard the last interest payment.)

e. In 1979 the Los Angeles Airport bonds were classified as "discount bonds." What happens to the price of a discount bond as it approaches maturity? Is there a "built-in capital gain" on such bonds?

f. The coupon interest payment divided by the market price of a bond is called the bond's *current yield*. Assuming the conditions in Part c, what would have been the current yield of a Los Angeles Airport bond (1) in February 1979 and (2) in February 1992? What would have been its capital gains yields and total yields (total yield equals yield to maturity) on those same two dates?

6-8

Supernormal growth stock valuation

It is now January 1, 1993. Swink Electric Inc. has just developed a solar panel capable of generating 200 percent more electricity than any solar panel currently on the market. As a result, Swink is expected to experience a 15 percent annual growth rate for the next 5 years. By the end of 5 years, other firms will have developed comparable technology, and Swink's growth rate will slow to 5 percent per year indefinitely. Stockholders require a return of 12 percent on Swink's stock. The most recent annual dividend (D_0), which was paid yesterday, was $1.75 per share.

a. Calculate Swink's expected dividends for 1993, 1994, 1995, 1996, and 1997.

b. Calculate the value of the stock today, $\hat{P}_0$. Proceed by finding the present value of the dividends expected at the end of 1993, 1994, 1995, 1996, and 1997 plus the present value of the stock price which should exist at the end of 1997. The year-end 1997 stock price can be found by using the constant growth equation. Notice that to find the December 31, 1997, price, you use the dividend expected in 1998, which is 5 percent greater than the 1997 dividend.

c. Calculate the expected dividend yield, D_1/P_0, the capital gains yield expected in 1993, and the expected total return (dividend yield plus capital gains yield) for 1993. (Assume that $\hat{P}_0 = P_0$, and recognize that the capital gains yield is equal to the total return minus the dividend yield.) Also calculate these same three yields for 1997.

d. How might an investor's tax situation affect his or her decision to purchase stocks of companies in the early stages of their lives, when they are growing rapidly, versus stocks of older, more mature firms? When does Swink's stock become "mature" in this example?

e. Suppose your boss tells you she believes that Swink's annual growth rate will be only 12 percent during the next 5 years and that the firm's normal growth rate will be only 4 percent. Without doing any calculations, what general effect would these growth-rate changes have on the price of Swink's stock?

f. Suppose your boss also tells you that she regards Swink as being quite risky and that she believes the required rate of return should be 14 percent, not 12 percent. Again without doing any calculations, how would the higher required rate of return affect the price of the stock, its capital gains yield, and its dividend yield?

6-9

Supernormal growth stock valuation

Tanner Technologies Corporation (TTC) has been growing at a rate of 20 percent per year in recent years. This same growth rate is expected to last for another 2 years.

a. If $D_0 = \$1.60$, $k = 10\%$, and $g_n = 6\%$, what is TTC's stock worth today? What are its expected dividend yield and capital gains yield at this time?

b. Now assume that TTC's period of supernormal growth is to last another 5 years rather than 2 years. How would this affect its price, dividend yield, and capital gains yield? Answer in words only.

c. What will be TTC's dividend yield and capital gains yield once its period of supernormal growth ends? (Hint: These values will be the same regardless of whether you examine the case of 2 or 5 years of supernormal growth; the calculations are very easy.)

d. Of what interest to investors is the changing relationship between dividend yield and capital gains yield over time?

6-10

Yield to call

It is now January 1, 1993, and you are considering the purchase of an outstanding Puckett Corporation bond that was issued on January 1, 1991. The Puckett bond has a 9.5 percent annual coupon and a 30-year original maturity (it matures on December 31, 2020). There is a 5-year call protection (until December 31, 1995), after which time the bond can be called at 109 (that is, at 109 percent of par, or $1,090). Interest rates have declined since the bond was issued, and the bond is now selling at 116.575 percent of par, or $1,165.75. You want to determine both the yield to maturity and the yield to call for this bond. (Note: The yield to call considers the effect of a call provision on the bond's probable yield. In the calculation, we assume that the bond will be outstanding until the call date, at which time it will be called. Thus, the investor will have received interest payments for the call-protected period and then will receive the call price—in this case, $1,090—on the call date.)

a. What is the yield to maturity in 1993 for the Puckett bond? What is its yield to call?

b. If you bought this bond, which return do you think you would actually earn? Explain your reasoning.

c. Suppose the bond had sold at a discount. Would the yield to maturity or the yield to call have been more relevant?

6-11

Equilibrium stock price

The risk-free rate of return, k_{RF}, is 11 percent; the required rate of return on the market, k_M, is 14 percent; and Altman Company's stock has a beta coefficient of 1.5.

a. If the dividend expected during the coming year, D_1, is $2.25, and if g = a constant 5%, at what price should Altman's stock sell?

b. Now suppose the Federal Reserve Board increases the money supply, causing the risk-free rate to drop to 9 percent and k_M to fall to 12 percent. What would this do to the price of the stock?

c. In addition to the change in Part b, suppose investors' risk aversion declines; this fact, combined with the decline in k_{RF}, causes k_M to fall to 11 percent. At what price would Altman's stock sell?

d. Now suppose Altman has a change in management. The new group institutes policies that increase the expected constant growth rate to 6 percent. Also, the new management stabilizes sales and profits and thus causes the beta coefficient to decline from 1.5 to 1.3. Assume tht k_{RF} and k_M are equal to the values in Part c. After all these changes, what is Altman's new equilibrium price? (Note: D_1 goes to $2.27.)

6-12

Beta coefficients

Suppose Sartoris Chemical Company's management conducts a study and concludes that if Sartoris expanded its consumer products division (which is less risky than its primary business, industrial chemicals), the firm's beta would decline from 1.2 to 0.9. However, consumer products have a somewhat lower profit margin, and this would cause Sartoris's constant growth rate in earnings and dividends to fall from 7 to 5 percent.

a. Should management make the change? Assume the following: $k_M = 12\%$; $k_{RF} = 9\%$; $D_0 = \$2$.

b. Assume all the facts as given above except the change in the beta coefficient. How low would the beta have to fall to cause the expansion to be a good one? (Hint: Set $\hat{P}_0$ under the new policy equal to $\hat{P}_0$ under the old one, and find the new beta that will produce this equality.)

EXAM-TYPE PROBLEMS

The problems included in this section are set up in such a way that they could be used as multiple-choice exam problems.

6-13
Bond valuation

The Desreumaux Company has two bond issues outstanding. Both bonds pay $100 annual interest plus $1,000 at maturity. Bond L has a maturity of 15 years and Bond S a maturity of 1 year.

a. What will be the value of each of these bonds when the going rate of interest is (1) 5 percent, (2) 8 percent, and (3) 12 percent? Assume that there is only one more interest payment to be made on Bond S.

b. Why does the longer-term (15-year) bond fluctuate more when interest rates change than does the shorter-term bond (1-year)?

6-14
Yield to maturity

The Severn Company's bonds have 4 years remaining to maturity. Interest is paid annually; the bonds have a $1,000 par value; and the coupon interest rate is 9 percent.

a. What is the yield to maturity at a current market price of (1) $829 or (2) $1,104?

b. Would you pay $829 for one of these bonds if you thought that the appropriate rate of interest was 12 percent — that is, if $k_d = 12\%$? Explain your answer.

6-15
Perpetual bond rate of return

What will be the rate of return on a perpetual bond with a $1,000 par value, an 8 percent coupon rate, and a current market price of (a) $600, (b) $800, (c) $1,000, and (d) $1,400? Assume interest is paid annually.

6-16
Declining growth stock valuation

McCue Mining Company's ore reserves are being depleted, so its sales are falling. Also, its pit is getting deeper each year, so its costs are rising. As a result, the company's earnings and dividends are declining at the constant rate of 5 percent per year. If $D_0 = \$5$ and $k_s = 15\%$, what is the value of McCue Mining's stock?

6-17
Rates of return and equilibrium

The beta coefficient for Stock C is $b_c = 0.4$, whereas that for Stock D is $b_D = -0.5$. (Stock D's beta is negative, indicating that its rate of return rises whenever returns on most other stocks fall. There are very few negative beta stocks, although collection agency stocks are sometimes cited as an example.)

a. If the risk-free rate is 9 percent and the expected rate of return on an average stock is 13 percent, what are the required rates of return on Stocks C and D?

b. For Stock C, suppose the current price, P_0, is $25; the next expected dividend, D_1, is $1.50; and the stock's expected constant growth rate is 4 percent. Is the stock in equilibrium? Explain, and describe what will happen if the stock is not in equilibrium.

6-18
Supernormal growth stock valuation

Assume that the average firm in your company's industry is expected to grow at a constant rate of 6 percent, and its dividend yield is 7 percent. Your company is about as risky as the average firm in the industry, but it has just successfully completed some R&D work which leads you to expect that its earnings and dividends will grow at a rate of 50 percent [$D_1 = D_0(1 + g) = D_0(1.50)$] this year and 25 percent the following year, after which growth should match the 6 percent industry average rate. The last dividend paid (D_0) was $1. What is the value per share of your firm's stock?

6-19
Financial calculator needed; Effective annual rate

Assume that as investment manager of Florida Electric Company's pension plan (which is exempt from income taxes), you must choose between IBM bonds and AT&T preferred stock. The bonds have a $1,000 par value, they mature in 20 years, they pay $40 each 6 months, they are callable at IBM's option at a price of $1,080 after 5 years (ten 6-month periods), and they sell at a price of $897.40 per bond. The preferred stock is a perpetuity; it pays a dividend of $2 each quarter, and it sells for $95 per share. What is the *most likely* effective annual rate of return (EAR) on the *higher* yielding security?

6-20
Nominal interest rate

Tapley Corporation's 14 percent coupon rate, semiannual payment, $1,000 par value bonds which mature in 30 years are callable at a price of $1,050 5 years from now. The bonds sell at a price of $1,353.54, and the yield curve is flat. Assuming that interest rates in the economy are expected to remain at their current level, what is the best estimate of Tapley's nominal interest rate on new bonds?

6-21
Supernormal growth
stock valuation

Microtech Corporation is expanding rapidly, and it currently needs to retain all of its earnings, hence it does not pay any dividends. However, investors expect Microtech to begin paying dividends, with the first dividend of $1.00 coming 3 years from today. The dividend should grow rapidly—at a rate of 50 percent per year—during Years 4 and 5. After Year 5, the company should grow at a constant rate of 8 percent per year. If the required return on the stock is 15 percent, what is the value of the stock today?

INTEGRATIVE PROBLEM

6-22
Bond/stock valuation

Robert Balik and Carol Kiefer are senior vice presidents of the Mutual of Chicago Insurance Company. They are co-directors of the company's pension fund management division, with Balik having responsibility for fixed income securities (primarily bonds) and Kiefer being responsible for equity investments. A major new client, the California League of Cities, has requested that Mutual of Chicago present an investment seminar to the mayors of the represented cities, and Balik and Kiefer, who will make the actual presentation, have asked you to help them by answering the following questions.

Section I: Bond valuation

a. What are the key features of a bond?
b. How is the value of any asset whose value is based on expected future cash flows determined?
c. How is the value of a bond determined? What is the value of a 1-year, $1,000 par value bond with a 10 percent annual coupon if its required rate of return is 10 percent? What is the value of a similar 10-year bond?
d. (1) What would be the value of the bond described in Part c if, just after it had been issued, the expected inflation rate rose by 3 percentage points, causing investors to require a 13 percent return? Would we now have a discount or a premium bond? (Hint: $PVIF_{13\%,1} = 0.8850$; $PVIF_{13\%,10} = 0.2946$; $PVIFA_{13\%,10} = 5.4262$.)
   (2) What would happen to the bond's value if inflation fell, and k_d declined to 7 percent? Would we now have a premium or a discount bond?
   (3) What would happen to the value of the 10-year bond over time if the required rate of return remained at 13 percent or remained at 7 percent?
e. (1) What is the yield to maturity on a 10-year, 9 percent annual coupon, $1,000 par value bond that sells for $887.00? That sells for $1,134.20? What does the fact that a bond sells at a discount or at a premium tell you about the relationship between k_d and the bond's coupon rate?
   (2) What is the current yield, the capital gains yield, and the total return in each case?
f. What is interest rate price risk? Which bond in Part c has more interest rate price risk, the 1-year bond or the 10-year bond?
g. What is interest rate reinvestment rate risk? Which bond in Part c has more interest rate reinvestment rate risk, assuming a 10-year investment horizon?
h. Redo Parts c and d, assuming the bonds have semiannual rather than annual coupons. (Hint: $PVIF_{6.5\%,2} = 0.8817$; $PVIFA_{6.5\%,2} = 1.8206$; $PVIF_{6.5\%,20} = 0.2838$; $PVIFA_{6.5\%,20} = 11.0185$; $PVIF_{3.5\%,2} = 0.9335$; $PVIFA_{3.5\%,2} = 1.8997$; $PVIF_{3.5\%,20} = 0.5026$; $PVIFA_{3.5\%,20} = 14.2124$.)

   i. Suppose you could buy, for $1,000, either a 10 percent, 10-year, annual payment bond or a 10 percent, 10-year, semiannual payment bond. They are equally risky. Which would you prefer? If $1,000 is the proper price for the semiannual bond, what is the proper price for the annual payment bond?

   j. What is the value of a perpetual bond with an annual coupon of $100 if its required rate of return is 10 percent? 13 percent? 7 percent? Assess the following statement: "Because perpetual bonds match an infinite investment horizon, they have little interest rate price risk."

   k. Suppose a 10-year, 10 percent, semiannual coupon bond with a par value of $1,000 is currently selling for $1,135.90, producing a yield to maturity of 8 percent. However, the bond can be called after 5 years for a price of $1,050.

     (1) What is the bond's yield to call (YTC)? (2) If you bought this bond, do you think you would be more likely to earn the YTM or the YTC?

Section II: Stock valuation

To illustrate the common stock valuation process, Balik and Kiefer have asked you to analyze the Bon Temps Company, an employment agency that supplies word processor operators and computer programmers to businesses with temporarily heavy workloads. You are to answer the following questions.

   a. (1) Write out a formula that can be used to value any stock, regardless of its dividend pattern.

     (2) What is a constant growth stock? How are constant growth stocks valued?

     (3) What happens if the constant $g > k_s$? Will many stocks have $g > k_s$?

   b. Assume that Bon Temps has a beta coefficient of 1.2, that the risk-free rate (the yield on T-bonds) is 10 percent, and that the required rate of return on the market is 15 percent. What is the required rate of return on the firm's stock?

   c. Assume that Bon Temps is a constant growth company whose last dividend (D_0, which was paid yesterday) was $2.00 and whose dividend is expected to grow indefinitely at a 6 percent rate.

     (1) What is the firm's expected dividend stream over the next 3 years?

     (2) What is the firm's current stock price?

     (3) What is the stock's expected value one year from now?

     (4) What are the expected dividend yield, the capital gains yield, and the total return during the first year?

   d. Now assume that the stock is currently selling at $21.20. What is the expected rate of return on the stock?

   e. What would the stock price be if its dividends were expected to have zero growth?

   f. Now assume that Bon Temps is expected to experience supernormal growth of 30 percent for the next 3 years, then to return to its long-run constant growth rate of 6 percent. What is the stock's value under these conditions? What is its expected dividend yield and capital gains yield in Year 1? In Year 4?

   g. Suppose Bon Temps is expected to experience zero growth during the first 3 years and then to resume its steady-state growth of 6 percent in the fourth year. What is the stock's value now? What is its expected dividend yield and its capital gains yield in Year 1? In Year 4?

   h. Finally, assume that Bon Temps's earnings and dividends are expected to decline by a constant 6 percent per year, that is, $g = -6\%$. Why would anyone be willing to buy such a stock, and at what price should it sell? What would be the dividend yield and capital gains yield in each year?

   i. What does market equilibrium mean?

   j. If equilibrium does not exist, how will it be established?

   k. What is the Efficient Markets Hypothesis, and what are its three forms?

COMPUTER-RELATED PROBLEM

Work the problem in this section only if you are using the computer problem diskette.

6-23

Supernormal growth stock valuation

Use the model on the computer problem diskette in the File C6 to solve this problem.

a. Refer back to Problem 6-8. Rework Part e, using the computerized model to determine what Swink's expected dividends and stock price would be under the conditions given.

b. Suppose your boss tells you that she regards Swink as being quite risky and that she believes the required rate of return should be higher than the 12 percent originally specified. Rework the problem under the conditions given in Part e, except change the required rate of return to (1) 13 percent, (2) 15 percent, and (3) 20 percent to determine the effects of the higher required rates of return on Swink's stock price.

Financial Forecasting, Planning, and Control

Chapter 7   Financial Forecasting

Chapter 8   Financial Planning and Control

Financial Forecasting

Economic forecasts play a critical role in managerial finance. Economists forecast the general level of economic activity, and then firms' own forecasters estimate demand, both in total and by type of product, for their companies. People are hired, products are designed, plants are built, and inventories are stocked to be ready for the forecasted level of demand. If the forecasts are correct, then the firm will have the right number and mix of people, plants, and equipment. However, if there are serious errors, the firm will be in trouble.

Steven Schnaars, a marketing professor at Baruch College in New York, recently conducted a survey to determine just how accurate forecasters have been at predicting the effects of technological and social developments on actual economic conditions in various industries. He found that approximately 80 percent of the "mega-forecasts" were way off the mark —some predictions never materialized, while others did, but decades later than had been predicted. For example, the fax machine was invented over 100 years ago, and in the late 1940s, forecasters predicted that in a few years faxes would replace regular mail and other delivery systems. However, fax technology did not take off until nearly 40 years later, when the breakup of AT&T and the development of fiber-optic transmission systems brought the cost of long-distance telecommunications down to the point where large-scale fax usage was economically feasible.

Note, though, that technological developments sometimes occur rapidly, creating problems for those who do not anticipate them and opportunities for those who do. The personal computer is a good example. IBM, DEC, and the other major computer companies assumed that computing in the future would be done on mainframes, and they dismissed PCs when Apple introduced them in the late 1970s. Eventually, IBM did bring out its own PC, but even then, the company failed to foresee that the power of PCs would increase so rapidly and they could be networked so efficiently that networked PCs would rapidly erode the market for mainframes. Microsoft, under Chairman Bill Gates, correctly anticipated the situation and led the charge of the PC revolution. As a result, IBM's stock now sells at about half of its earlier high, and Gates has become the richest man in the United States while still in his mid-30s.

The moral of these stories is twofold: First, Schnaars's observation that most changes in the economy come in small increments is undoubtedly true. Therefore, forecasts based on the assumption of huge changes in the short run are likely to be off base, while forecasts based on the assumption of slow but sure progress are likely to be on the mark. Second, we can be certain that major changes will occur, probably when we least expect them; thus, we must be ready to deal with changing conditions. The watchword is "flexibility"—financial managers should make their basic forecasts on the assumption of small, incremental technological changes but also be prepared to deal with larger changes when they occur. Keep this in mind as you read this chapter.

Source: "Where Forecasters Go Wrong," *Across the Board,* December 1989.

Thus far we have focused primarily on analysis of financial statements, the financial environment, risk and return, the time value of money, and valuation techniques. Now we turn to the process of financial planning and control.

Well-run companies generally base their operating plans on a set of forecasted financial statements. The planning process begins with a sales forecast for the next five or so years. Then the assets required to meet the sales targets are determined, and a decision is made concerning how to finance the required assets. At that point, income statements and balance sheets can be projected, and earnings and dividends per share, as well as the key ratios, can be forecasted.

Once the "base case" forecasted statements and ratios have been prepared, top managers will ask questions such as these: Are the forecasted results as good as we can realistically expect, and, if not, how might we change our operating plans to produce better earnings and a higher stock price? How sure are we that we will be able to achieve the projected results? For example, if our base case forecast assumes a reasonably strong economy, but a recession occurs, would we be better off under an alternative operating plan? In the balance of this chapter and the next one, we explore in some depth the financial planning process.

sales forecast

A forecast of a firm's unit and dollar sales for some future period; generally based on recent sales trends plus forecasts of the economic prospects for the nation, region, industry, and so forth.

SALES FORECASTS

The **sales forecast** generally starts with a review of sales during the past five to ten years, expressed in a graph such as that in Figure 7-1. The first part of the graph shows five years of historical sales for Allied Food Products, the diversified

Figure 7-1 ▪ **Allied Food Products: 1993 Sales Projection (Millions of Dollars)**

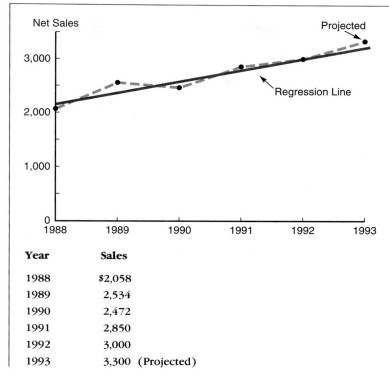

Year	Sales	
1988	$2,058	
1989	2,534	
1990	2,472	
1991	2,850	
1992	3,000	
1993	3,300	(Projected)

food processor and distributor that we first analyzed back in Chapter 2. The graph could have contained 10 years of sales data, but Allied typically focuses on sales figures for the latest 5 years because the firm's studies have shown that future growth is more closely related to the recent than to the distant past.

Allied had its ups and downs during the period from 1988 to 1992. In 1990, poor weather in California's fruit-producing regions resulted in low production, which caused 1990 sales to fall below the 1989 level. Then, a bumper crop in 1991 pushed sales up by 15 percent, an unusually high growth rate for a mature food processor. Based on a regression analysis, Allied's forecasters determined that the average annual growth rate in sales over the past 5 years was 9.1 percent. On the basis of this historical sales trend, on new product and market introductions, and on Allied's forecast for the economy, the firm's planning committee projects a 10 percent sales growth rate during 1993, to sales of $3,300 million. Here are some of the factors that Allied considered in developing its sales forecast:

1. Allied Food Products is divided into three divisions: canned foods, frozen foods, and packaged foods, such as dried fruits. Sales growth is seldom the same for each of the divisions, so to begin the forecasting process, divisional projections are made on the basis of historical growth, and then the divisional forecasts are combined to produce a "first approximation" corporate sales forecast.

2. Next, the level of economic activity in each of the company's marketing areas is forecasted—for example, how strong will the economies be in each of Allied's six domestic and two foreign distribution territories, and what population changes are forecasted in each area?

3. Allied's planning committee also looks at the firm's probable market share in each distribution territory. Consideration is given to such factors as the firm's production and distribution capacity, its competitors' capacities, new product introductions that are planned by Allied or its competitors, and potential changes in shelf-space allocations, which are vital for food sales. Pricing strategies are also considered—for example, does the company have plans to raise prices to boost margins or to lower prices to increase market share and take advantage of economies of scale in purchasing and processing raw foods? Obviously, such factors could greatly affect future sales. In addition, Allied's export sales are affected by exchange rates, governmental policies, and the like.

4. Allied's planners must also consider the effects of inflation on the firm's prices. Over the next five years, the inflation rate is expected to average 4 to 5 percent, and Allied plans to increase prices, on average, by a like amount. In addition, the firm expects to expand its market share in certain products, resulting in a 4 percent growth rate in unit sales. The combination of unit sales growth and increases in sales prices has resulted in historical revenue growth rates in the 8 to 10 percent range, and this same situation is expected in the future.

5. Advertising campaigns, promotional discounts, credit terms, and the like also affect sales, so probable developments in these areas are factored in.

6. Forecasts are made for each division both in total and on an individual product basis. The individual product sales forecasts are summed, and this sum is compared with the overall divisional forecasts. Differences are reconciled, and the end result is a sales forecast for the company as a whole but with breakdowns by the three divisions and by individual products.

If the sales forecast is off, the consequences can be serious. First, if the market expands *more* than Allied has geared up for, the company will not be able to meet demand. Its customers will end up buying competitors' products, and Allied will lose market share, which will be hard to regain. On the other hand, if its projections are overly optimistic, Allied could end up with too much plant, equipment, and inventory. This would mean low turnover ratios, high costs for depreciation and storage, and, possibly, write-offs of spoiled inventory. All of this would result in a low rate of return on equity, which in turn would depress the company's stock price. If Allied had financed an unnecessary expansion with debt, its problems would, of course, be compounded. Thus, an accurate sales forecast is critical to the well-being of the firm.[1]

---

[1] A sales forecast is actually the *expected value of a probability distribution* with many possible levels of sales. Because any sales forecast is subject to a greater or lesser degree of uncertainty, for financial planning we are often just as interested in the degree of uncertainty inherent in the sales forecast (σ sales) as we are in the expected value of sales.

Self-Test Questions

How do past trends affect a sales forecast?

List some factors that should be considered when developing a sales forecast.

Briefly explain why an accurate sales forecast is critical to profitability.

THE PROJECTED BALANCE SHEET METHOD

Any forecast of financial requirements involves (1) determining how much money the firm will need during a given period, (2) determining how much money the firm will generate internally during the same period, and (3) subtracting the funds generated from the funds required to determine the external financial requirements. Two methods are used to estimate external requirements: the *projected, or pro forma, balance sheet method* and the *formula method.* We discuss the balance sheet method in this section and illustrate it with data on Allied Food Products. The formula method is discussed in a later section.

The projected balance sheet method is straightforward—one simply projects the asset requirements for the coming period, then projects the liabilities and equity that will be generated under normal operations, and subtracts the projected liabilities/capital from the required assets to estimate the **additional funds needed (AFN).** The steps in the procedure are explained below.

additional funds needed (AFN)

Funds that a firm must raise externally through borrowing or by selling new common or preferred stock.

projected balance sheet method

A method of forecasting financial requirements based on forecasted financial statements.

Step 1. Forecast the 1993 Income Statement

The **projected balance sheet method** begins with a forecast of sales. Next, the income statement for the coming year is forecasted in order to obtain an estimate of the amount of retained earnings the company will generate during the year. This requires assumptions about the operating cost ratio, the tax rate, interest charges, and the dividend payout ratio. In the simplest case, the assumption is made that costs will increase at the same rate as sales; in more complicated situations, cost changes will be forecasted separately. Still, the objective of this part of the analysis is to determine how much income the company will earn and then retain for reinvestment in the business during the forecasted year.

Table 7-1 shows Allied's actual 1992 and forecasted 1993 income statements. To begin, we assume that sales and costs grow by 10 percent in 1993 over the 1992 levels. Therefore, we show the factor $(1 + g) = 1.10$ in the first three rows of Column 2, and in the same rows of Column 3 we show the forecasted 1993 sales, operating costs, and depreciation. EBIT is found by subtraction, while the interest charges in Column 3 are simply carried over from Column 1. Note, though, that interest charges will change once we know how much additional debt will be required.

Earnings before taxes (EBT) are then calculated, as is net income before preferred dividends. Preferred dividends are carried over from the 1992 column, and they will remain constant unless Allied decides to issue additional preferred stock in 1993. Net income available to common is calculated, and then the 1993 initial dividends are forecasted as follows: The 1992 dividend per

Table 7-1 ▪ **Allied Food Products: Actual 1992 and Projected 1993 Income Statements (Millions of Dollars)**

	Actual 1992 (1)	Forecast Basis (2)	1993 Forecast			
			First Pass (3)	Feedback (4)	Second Pass (5)	Final (6)
1. Sales	$3,000	× 1.10[a]	$3,300		$3,300	$3,300
2. Costs except depreciation	2,616	× 1.10	2,878		2,878	2,878
3. Depreciation	100	× 1.10	110		110	110
4. Total operating costs	$2,716		$2,988		$2,988	$2,988
5. EBIT	$ 284		$ 312		$ 312	$ 312
6. Less interest	88		88[b]	+5	93	93
7. Earnings before taxes (EBT)	$ 196		$ 224		$ 219	$ 219
8. Taxes (40%)	78		89	−1	88	88
9. NI before preferred dividends	$ 118		$ 135		$ 131	$ 131
10. Dividends to preferred	4		4[b]		4	4
11. NI available to common	$ 114		$ 131		$ 127	$ 127
12. Dividends to common	$ 58		$ 63[c]	+3	$ 66	$ 66
13. Addition to retained earnings	$ 56		$ 68	−7	$ 61	$ 61

[a] × 1.10 indicates "times 1 + g"; used for items which grow proportionally with sales.

[b] Indicates a 1992 figure carried over for first pass forecast.

[c] Indicates a projected figure. See text for explanation.

share is $1.15, and this dividend will be increased by about 8 percent, to $1.25. Since there are 50 million shares outstanding, the initially projected dividends are $1.25(50,000,000) = $62.5 million, rounded to $63 million. (Again, like interest, this figure will be increased later in the analysis, if additional shares are sold.)

As the last part of the first pass forecasted income statement, the $63 million projected dividends are subtracted from the $131 million projected net income to common shareholders to determine the first pass projection of funds available from retained earnings, $131 − $63 = $68 million. *Note, though, that this $68 million forecast for retained earnings will turn out to be too high because it understates the actual amount of interest and common stock dividends for 1993. Allied will have to borrow as well as sell additional shares of common stock to finance its asset requirements, and these actions will change the forecasted income statement.* Those modifications will be made after we know how much additional financing will be required.

Step 2. Forecast the 1993 Balance Sheet

If Allied's sales are to increase, then its assets must also grow. Since the company was operating at full capacity in 1992, each asset account must increase if the higher sales level is to be attained: More cash will be needed for transactions, higher sales will lead to higher receivables, additional inventory will have to be stocked, and new plant and equipment must be added.

spontaneously generated funds

Funds that are obtained automatically from routine business transactions.

Further, if Allied's assets are to increase, its liabilities and equity must also increase — the additional assets must be financed in some manner. **Spontaneously generated funds** will be provided by accounts payable and accruals. For example, as sales increase, so will Allied's purchases of raw materials, and these larger purchases will spontaneously lead to higher levels of accounts payable. Similarly, a higher level of operations will require more labor, while higher sales will result in higher taxable income. Therefore, both accrued wages and accrued taxes will increase. In general, these spontaneous liability accounts will increase at the same rate as sales.

Retained earnings will also increase, but not at the same rate as sales: The new level of retained earnings will be the old level plus the addition to retained earnings, and the new retained earnings must be calculated by working down through the projected income statement as we did in Step 1. Also, notes payable, long-term bonds, preferred stock, and common stock will not rise spontaneously with sales — rather, the projected levels of these accounts will depend on financing decisions that will be made later.

In summary, (1) higher sales must be supported by higher asset levels, (2) some of the asset increases can be financed by spontaneous increases in accounts payable and accruals and by retained earnings, and (3) any shortfall must be financed from external sources, either by borrowing or by selling new common stock.

Table 7-2 contains Allied's 1992 actual and its projected 1993 balance sheets. The mechanics of the balance sheet forecast are similar to those used to develop the forecasted income statement. First, those balance sheet accounts that are expected to increase directly with sales are multiplied by 1.10 to obtain the initial 1993 forecasts. Thus, 1993 cash is projected to be $10(1.10) = $11 million, accounts receivable are projected to be $375(1.10) ≈ $412 million, and so on. In our example, all assets increase with sales, so once the individual assets have been forecasted, they can be summed to complete the asset side of the forecasted balance sheet. For example, the total current assets forecasted for 1993 are $11 + $412 + $677 = $1,100 million.

Next, the spontaneously increasing liabilities (accounts payable and accruals) are forecasted and shown in Column 3. Then those liability accounts whose values reflect conscious management decisions — notes payable, long-term bonds, preferred stock, and common stock — are initially forecasted to remain at their 1992 levels. Thus, 1993 notes payable are initially set at $110 million, the long-term bond account is forecasted at $754 million, and so on. The 1993 value for the retained earnings (RE) account is obtained by adding the projected addition to retained earnings as developed in the 1993 income statement (see Table 7-1) to the 1992 ending balance:

$$1993 \text{ RE} = 1992 \text{ RE} + 1993 \text{ forecasted addition to RE}$$
$$= \$766 + \$68 = \$834 \text{ million.}$$

Table 7-2 ▪ **Allied Food Products: Actual 1992 and Projected 1993 Balance Sheets (Millions of Dollars)**

	Actual 1992 (1)	Forecast Basis (2)	1993 Forecast			
			First Pass (3)	AFN[a] (4)	Second Pass (5)	Final (6)
Cash	$ 10	× 1.10[b]	$ 11		u	u
Accounts receivable	375	× 1.10	412		n	n
Inventories	615	× 1.10	677		c	c
Total current assets	$1,000		$1,100		h	h
Net plant and equipment	1,000	× 1.10	1,100		a	a
					n	n
					g	g
					e	e
					d	d
Total assets	$2,000		$2,200		$2,200	$2,200
Accounts payable	$ 60	× 1.10	$ 66		$ 66	$ 66
Notes payable	110		110	+ 28	138	140
Accruals	140	× 1.10	154		154	154
Total current liabilities	$ 310		$ 330		$ 358	$ 360
Long-term bonds	754		754	+ 28	782	784
Total debt	$1,064		$1,084		$1,140	$1,144
Preferred stock	40		40		40	40
Common stock	130		130	+ 56	186	189
Retained earnings	766		834		827	827
Total common equity	$ 896		$ 964		$1,013	$1,016
Total liabilities and equity	$2,000		$2,088	+112	$2,193	$2,200
Additional funds needed (AFN)			$ 112		$ 7	$ 0

[a]AFN stands for "Additional Funds Needed." This figure is determined at the bottom of Column 3, and Column 4 shows how the required $112 of AFN will be raised.

[b]× 1.10 indicates "times $1 + g$"; used for items which grow proportionally with sales.

The forecast of total assets as shown in Column 3 (first pass forecast) in Table 7-2 is $2,200 million, which indicates that Allied must add $200 million of new assets in 1993 to support the higher sales level. However, the forecasted liability and equity accounts as shown in the lower portion of Column 3 total to only $2,088 million. Since the balance sheet must balance, Allied must raise an additional $2,200 − $2,088 = $112 million, which we designate as *Additional Funds Needed (AFN)*. The AFN will be raised by borrowing from the bank as notes payable, by issuing long-term bonds, by selling new common stock, or by some combination of these actions.

Step 3. Raising the Additional Funds Needed

Allied's financial manager will base the financing decision on several factors, including the effect of short-term borrowing on its current ratio, conditions in the debt and equity markets, and restrictions imposed by existing debt agreements. Allied's financial manager, after considering all of the relevant factors, decided on the following additional funds financing mix to raise the needed $112 million:

	Amount of New Capital		
Type of Capital	**Percent**	**Dollars (Millions)**	**Interest Rate**
Notes payable	25%	$ 28	8%
Long-term bonds	25	28	10
Common stock	50	56	—
	100%	$112	

These amounts, which are shown in Column 4 of Table 7-2, are added to the initially forecasted account totals as shown in Column 3 to generate the second pass balance sheet. Thus, in Column 5, the notes payable account increases to $110 + $28 = $138 million, long-term bonds rise to $754 + $28 = $782 million, and common stock increases to $130 + $56 = $186 million.

If there were no changes in any other income statement item or balance sheet account, the forecast would be complete—the initial shortfall was $112 million, and Allied would raise that amount as shown above. However, when Allied takes on new debt, its interest expenses will rise, and the additional shares of common stock will cause the total dividend payments to increase. These changes will affect the amount of retained earnings, as shown in the next section.

Step 4. Financing Feedbacks

financing feedbacks

The effects on the income statement and balance sheet of actions taken to finance increases in assets.

One complexity that arises in financial forecasting relates to **financing feedbacks.** The external funds raised to pay for new assets create additional expenses which must be reflected in the income statement, and that lowers the initially forecasted addition to retained earnings. To handle the financing feedback process, we first forecast the additional interest expense and any additional dividends that will be paid as a result of the external financings. New short-term debt costs 8 percent, so the $28 million of new notes payable will increase Allied's projected 1993 interest expense by 0.08($28) = $2.24 million. Similarly, the new long-term bonds will add 0.10($28) = $2.80 million in interest expense, so the total increase in interest expense will be $5.04 million. When these feedbacks are considered, interest expense as shown in the projected 1993 second pass income statement in Column 5 of Table 7-1 increases to $88 + $5 = $93 million. The higher interest charges will, of course, also affect the remainder of the income statement.

The financing plan also calls for $56 million of new common stock to be sold. Allied's stock price was $23 per share at the end of 1992, and if we assume that new shares would be sold at this price, then $56/$23 = 2.4 million shares of new stock will have to be sold. Further, Allied's 1993 dividend payment is projected to be $1.25 per share, so the 2.4 million shares of new stock will require 2.4($1.25) = $3 million of additional dividend payments. Thus, dividends to common stockholders as shown in the second pass income statement increase to $63 + $3 = $66 million.

The net effect of the financing feedbacks on the income statement is to reduce the addition to retained earnings by $7 million, from $68 million to $61 million. This reduction in the addition to retained earnings reduces the balance sheet forecast of retained earnings by a like amount, so in Table 7-2 the second pass 1993 balance sheet projection for retained earnings becomes $766 + $61 = $827 million, or $7 million less than in the initial forecast. Thus, a shortfall of $7 million will still exist as a direct result of financing feedback effects— the additional interest and dividend payments reduce the projected retained earnings account by $7 million from the initial forecast, so an additional shortfall exists. This amount is shown at the bottom of Column 5 in Table 7-2.

How would the second pass shortfall be financed? In Allied's case, 25 percent of the $7 million would be obtained as short-term debt, 25 percent as long-term bonds, and 50 percent as new common stock.

We could create a third pass balance sheet by using this financing mix to add another $7 million to the liabilities and equity side. Would the third pass balance? No, because the additional $7 million in capital would require another increase in interest and dividend payments, and this would affect the third pass income statement. There would still be a shortfall, although it would be much smaller than the $7 million shortfall on the second pass. We could then construct a fourth pass forecasted income statement and balance sheet, fifth pass statements, and so on. In each iteration, the additional financing needed would become smaller and smaller, and after about five iterations, the AFN would become so small that we could consider the forecast to be completed. We do not show the additional iterations, but the final results are shown in Column 6 of Tables 7-1 and 7-2.[2]

Analysis of the Forecast

The 1993 forecast as developed above is only the first part of Allied's total forecasting process. Next, the projected statements must be analyzed to determine whether the forecast meets the firm's financial targets as laid down in the 5-year financial plan. If the statements do not meet the targets, then elements of the forecast must be changed.

Table 7-3 shows Allied's 1992 ratios as they were reported back in Table 2-6 of Chapter 2, plus the projected 1993 ratios and the latest industry average ratios. (The table also shows some "Revised" data which we will discuss later.) As we noted back in Chapter 2, the firm's financial condition at the close of 1992 was weak, with many ratios being well below the industry averages. The preliminary final forecast for 1993 (after financing feedbacks are considered), which assumes that Allied's past practices will continue into the future, also shows a relatively weak financial condition—naturally, this condition will persist unless management takes some actions to improve things.

---

[2]It is rather tedious to make financial forecasts by hand. Fortunately, it is easy to make a model using *Lotus 1-2-3* or some other spreadsheet program which can be used to do the iterations and arrive at the final forecast.

Table 7-3   ▪   **Projected AFN and Key Ratios**

	1992	Final Preliminary[a] 1993	Industry Average	Revised[a] 1993
Initial AFN		$112		($64)
Current ratio	3.2	3.1	4.2	3.6
Inventory turnover	4.9	4.9	9.0	6.0
Days sales outstanding	45.0	45.0	36.0	42.5
Total assets turnover	1.5	1.5	1.8	1.6
Debt ratio[b]	55.2%	53.8%	40.0%	51.6%
Profit margin	3.8%	3.8%	5.0%	4.8%
Return on assets	5.7%	5.8%	9.0%	7.7%
Return on equity	12.7%	12.5%	15.0%	15.9%

[a]The calculated ratios are after all financing feedback effects.
[b]Includes preferred stock.

Allied's management actually plans to take three steps to improve its financial condition: (1) Management plans to lay off some workers and close certain operations. These steps should lower operating costs (excluding depreciation) from the current 87.2 percent of sales to 86 percent. (2) By screening credit customers more closely and by being more aggressive in collecting past due accounts, the days sales outstanding on receivables can be reduced from 45 to 42.5 days. (3) Finally, management thinks that the inventory turnover ratio can be raised from 4.9 to 6 times through the use of tighter inventory controls.[3]

These proposed operational changes were then used to create a revised set of forecasted statements for 1993. We do not show the new financial statements, but their impact on the key ratios is shown in Table 7-3 in the Revised 1993 column. Here are the highlights:

1. By decreasing operating costs from 87.2 to 86 percent of sales, Allied's forecasted cost figures on Rows 2 and 3 of Table 7-2 were changed. These changes worked on through the statement, and as a result the profit margin improved from 3.8 to 4.8 percent, which is closer to the industry average.

2. The increase in the profit margin resulted in an increase in projected retained earnings. Further, by tightening inventory controls and reducing the days sales outstanding, Allied projected a reduction in the forecasted levels of inventories and receivables. Taken together, these actions resulted in a *negative* AFN of $64 million, which means that Allied would actually generate $64 million more from internal operations than it needs to spend on new assets. Thus, its cash requirements would change from a positive $112 million to a negative $64 million. This $64 million of surplus funds could be used to reduce short-term debt, which would lead to a decrease in the forecasted debt ratio from 53.8 to 51.6 percent. The debt ratio

---

[3]We will discuss receivables and inventory management in detail in Chapters 11 and 12.

would still be well above the industry average, but this would be a step in the right direction.

3. The indicated changes would also affect Allied's current ratio, which would improve from 3.1 to 3.6.

4. These actions also resulted in a forecasted improvement in the rate of return on assets from 5.8 to 7.7 percent, and they gave a boost to the return on equity from 12.5 to 15.9 percent, which even exceeds the industry average.

Although Allied's managers believe that the revised forecast is achievable, they cannot be sure of this. Accordingly, they also want to know how variations in sales would affect the forecast. Therefore, a *Lotus 1-2-3* model was run using alternative sales growth rates, and the results were analyzed to see how the firm's financial condition would change under alternative growth scenarios. To illustrate, if the sales growth rate forecast increased from 10 to 20 percent, the additional funding requirement would change dramatically, from a $64 million surplus to an $83 million shortfall.

The *Lotus 1-2-3* model was also used to evaluate dividend policy. If Allied decided to reduce its dividend growth rate, then additional funds would be generated, and these funds could be invested in plant, equipment, and inventories, used to reduce debt, or, possibly, used to repurchase stock.

The model was also used to evaluate financing alternatives. For example, Allied could use the forecasted $64 million of surplus funds to retire long-term bonds rather than to reduce short-term debt. Under this financing alternative, the current ratio would drop from 3.6 to 2.9, but the total debt ratio would still decline, and the interest coverage ratio would also improve.

Forecasting is an iterative process, both in the way the financial statements are generated and in the way the financial plan is developed. For planning purposes, the financial staff develops a preliminary forecast based on a continuation of past policies and trends. This provides the executives with a starting point, or "straw man" forecast. Next, the model is modified to see what effects alternative operating plans would have on the firm's earnings and financial condition. This results in a revised forecast. In addition, alternative operating plans are examined under different sales growth rate scenarios, and the model is used to evaluate both dividend policy and capital structure decisions. Dividend policy and capital structure will be discussed in later chapters.

The model can also be used to analyze alternative working capital policies —that is, to determine the effects of changes in cash management, credit policy, inventory policy, and the use of different types of short-term credit. We will examine Allied's working capital policy within the model framework in Chapters 9 through 13, but in the remainder of this chapter we consider some other aspects of the financial forecasting process.

Self-Test Questions

What is the AFN, and how is the projected balance sheet method used to estimate it?

What is a financing feedback, and how do financing feedbacks affect the estimate of AFN?

THE FORMULA METHOD FOR FORECASTING AFN

Although most firms' forecasts of capital requirements are made by constructing pro forma income statements and balance sheets as described above, the following formula also is sometimes used to forecast financial requirements:

$$\begin{array}{ccccc} \text{Additional} & & \text{Required} & \text{Spontaneous} & \text{Increase in} \\ \text{funds} & = & \text{increase} - & \text{increase in} - & \text{retained} \\ \text{needed} & & \text{in assets} & \text{liabilities} & \text{earnings} \\ \text{AFN} & = & (A^*/S)\Delta S - & (L^*/S)\Delta S & - MS_1(1 - d). \end{array} \qquad (7\text{-}1)$$

Here

AFN = additional funds needed.

A^*/S = assets that must increase if sales are to increase expressed as a percentage of sales, or the required dollar increase in assets per \$1 increase in sales. $A^*/S = \$2,000/\$3,000 = 0.6667$ for Allied. Thus, for every \$1 increase in sales, assets must increase by about 67 cents. Note that A designates total assets and A^* designates those assets that must increase if sales are to increase. When the firm is operating at full capacity, as is the case here, $A^* = A$. Often, though, A^* and A are not equal, and the equation must be modified or the financial statement forecasting method must be used.

L^*/S = liabilities that increase spontaneously with sales as a percentage of sales or spontaneously generated financing per \$1 increase in sales. $L^*/S = (\$60 + \$140)/\$3,000 = 0.0667$ for Allied. Thus, every \$1 increase in sales generates about 7 cents of spontaneous financing. Again, L^* represents liabilities that increase spontaneously, and L^* is normally less than total liabilities (L).

S_1 = total sales projected for next year. Note that S_0 designates last year's sales. $S_1 = \$3,300$ million for Allied.

ΔS = change in sales $= S_1 - S_0 = \$3,300$ million $- \$3,000$ million $= \$300$ million for Allied.

M = profit margin or rate of profit per \$1 of sales. $M = \$114/\$3,000 = 0.0380$ for Allied.

dividend payout ratio
The percentage of earnings paid out in dividends.

d = percentage of earnings paid out in common dividends, or the **dividend payout ratio**; $d = \$58/\$114 = 0.5088$ for Allied.

Inserting values for Allied into Equation 7-1, we find the additional funds needed to be \$118 million:

$$\begin{aligned} \text{AFN} &= 0.667(\Delta S) - 0.067(\Delta S) - 0.038(S_1)(1 - 0.509) \\ &= 0.667(\$300 \text{ million}) - 0.067(\$300 \text{ million}) - 0.038(\$3,300 \text{ million})(0.491) \\ &= \$200 \text{ million} - \$20 \text{ million} - \$62 \text{ million} \\ &= \$118 \text{ million}. \end{aligned}$$

To increase sales by $300 million, the formula suggests that Allied must increase assets by $200 million. The $200 million of new assets must be financed in some manner. Of the total, $20 million will come from a spontaneous increase in liabilities, while another $62 million will be obtained from retained earnings. The remaining $118 million must be raised from external sources. This value is only an approximation, and it is somewhat different from the AFN figure we developed in Table 7-2.

Inherent in the formula are the assumptions (1) that each asset item must increase in direct proportion to sales increases, (2) that designated liability accounts also grow at the same rate as sales, and (3) that the profit margin is constant. Obviously, these assumptions do not always hold, so the formula does not always produce reliable results. Therefore, the formula is used primarily to get a rough-and-ready forecast of financial requirements and as a supplement to the projected balance sheet method.

Relationship between Growth and Financial Requirements

The faster Allied's growth rate in sales, the greater its need for additional financing; we can use Equation 7-1, which is plotted in Figure 7-2, to demonstrate this relationship. The lower section shows Allied's additional financial requirements at various growth rates, and these data are plotted in the graph. The figure illustrates the following four important points:

1. **Financial planning.** At low growth rates Allied needs no external financing, and it even generates surplus cash. However, if the company grows faster than 3.21 percent, it must raise capital from outside sources.[4] Further, the faster the growth rate, the greater the capital requirements. If management foresees difficulties in raising the required capital, then management should reconsider the feasibility of the expansion plans.

2. **Effect of dividend policy on financing needs.** Dividend policy as reflected in the payout ratio (d in Equation 7-1) also affects external capital requirements—the higher the payout ratio, the smaller the addition to retained earnings, hence the greater the requirements for external capital. Therefore, if Allied foresees difficulties in raising capital, it might want to consider a reduction in the dividend payout ratio. This would lower (or shift to the right) the line in Figure 7-2, indicating smaller external capital requirements at all growth rates. However, before changing its dividend policy, management should consider the effects of such a decision on stock prices. These effects are considered in Chapter 18.

Notice that the line in Figure 7-2 does *not* pass through the origin; thus, at low growth rates (below 3.21 percent), surplus funds will be produced, because new retained earnings plus spontaneous funds will exceed the required asset increases. Only if the dividend payout ratio were 100

---

[4]We found the 3.21 percent growth rate by setting AFN equal to zero, substituting gS_0 for ΔS and $S_0 + g(S_0)$ for S_1 in the AFN equation, and then solving the equation $0 = 0.667(g)(S_0) - 0.067(g)(S_0) - 0.038(S_0 + gS_0)(1 - 0.509)$ for g. The g that solved this equation was about 0.0321, or 3.21 percent.

Figure 7-2 ▪ **Allied Food Products: Relationship between Growth in Sales and Financial Requirements, Assuming S_0 = \$3,000 (Millions of Dollars)**

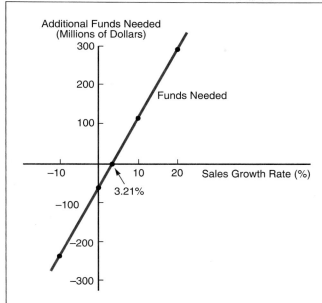

Growth Rate in Sales (1)	Increase (Decrease) in Sales, ΔS (2)	Forecasted Sales, S_1 (3)	Additional Funds Needed (4)
20%	\$600	\$3,600	\$293
10	300	3,300	118
3.21	96	3,096	0
0	0	3,000	(56)
(10)	(300)	2,700	(230)

Explanation of Columns:

Column 1: Assumed growth rate in sales, g.

Column 2: Increase (decrease) in sales, $\Delta S = g(S_0) = g(\$3,000)$.

Column 3: Forecasted sales, $S_1 = S_0 + g(S_0) = S_0(1 + g) = \$3,000(1 + g)$.

Column 4: Additional funds needed $= 0.667(\Delta S) - 0.067(\Delta S) - 0.019(S_1)$.

percent, meaning that the firm did not retain any of its earnings, would the "funds needed" line pass through the origin.

capital intensity ratio

The amount of assets required per dollar of sales (A^*/S).

3. **Capital intensity.** The amount of assets required per dollar of sales, A^*/S in Equation 7-1, is often called the **capital intensity ratio.** This ratio has a major effect on capital requirements per unit of sales growth. If the capital intensity ratio is low, sales can grow rapidly without much outside capital. However, if the firm is capital intensive, even a small growth in output will require a great deal of new outside capital.

4. **Profit margin.** The profit margin, M, is also an important determinant of the funds-required equation—the higher the margin, the lower the funds requirements, other things held constant. In terms of the graph, an in-

crease in the profit margin would cause the line to shift down, and its slope would also become less steep. Because of the relationship between profit margins and additional capital requirements, some very rapidly growing firms do not need much external capital. For example, for many years Xerox grew at a rapid rate with very little borrowing or stock sales. However, as the company lost patent protection and as competition intensified in the copier industry, Xerox's profit margin declined, its needs for external capital rose, and it began to borrow from banks and other sources. IBM has had a similar experience.

 Self-Test Questions

Under certain conditions a simple formula can be used to forecast AFN. Give the formula and briefly explain it.

How do the following factors affect external capital requirements?
a. Dividend policy.
b. Capital intensity.
c. Profit margin.

FORECASTING FINANCIAL REQUIREMENTS WHEN THE BALANCE SHEET RATIOS ARE SUBJECT TO CHANGE

Both the AFN formula and the projected balance sheet method as we used it assume that the balance sheet ratios of assets and liabilities to sales (A*/S and L*/S) remain constant over time, which in turn requires the assumption that each "spontaneous" asset and liability item increases at the same rate as sales. In graph form, this implies the type of relationship shown in Panel a of Figure 7-3, a relationship that is (1) linear and (2) passes through the origin. Under those conditions, if the company's sales increase from $200 million to $400 million, inventory must increase at the same rate, or proportionately, from $100 million to $200 million.

The assumption of constant ratios and identical growth rates is appropriate at times, but there are times when it is incorrect. Three such conditions are described in the following sections.

Economies of Scale

There are economies of scale in the use of many kinds of assets, and when economies occur, the ratios are likely to change over time as the size of the firm increases. For example, firms often need to maintain base stocks of different inventory items even if current sales levels are quite low. As sales expand, inventories grow less rapidly than sales, so the ratio of inventory to sales declines. This situation is depicted in Panel b of Figure 7-3. Here we see that the inventory/sales ratio is 1.5, or 150 percent, when sales are $200 million, but the ratio declines to 1.0 when sales climb to $400 million.

The relationship used to illustrate economies of scale is linear, but nonlinear relationships often exist. Indeed, as we shall see in Chapter 12, if the firm uses

Figure 7-3 ▪ **Three Possible Ratio Relationships (Millions of Dollars)**

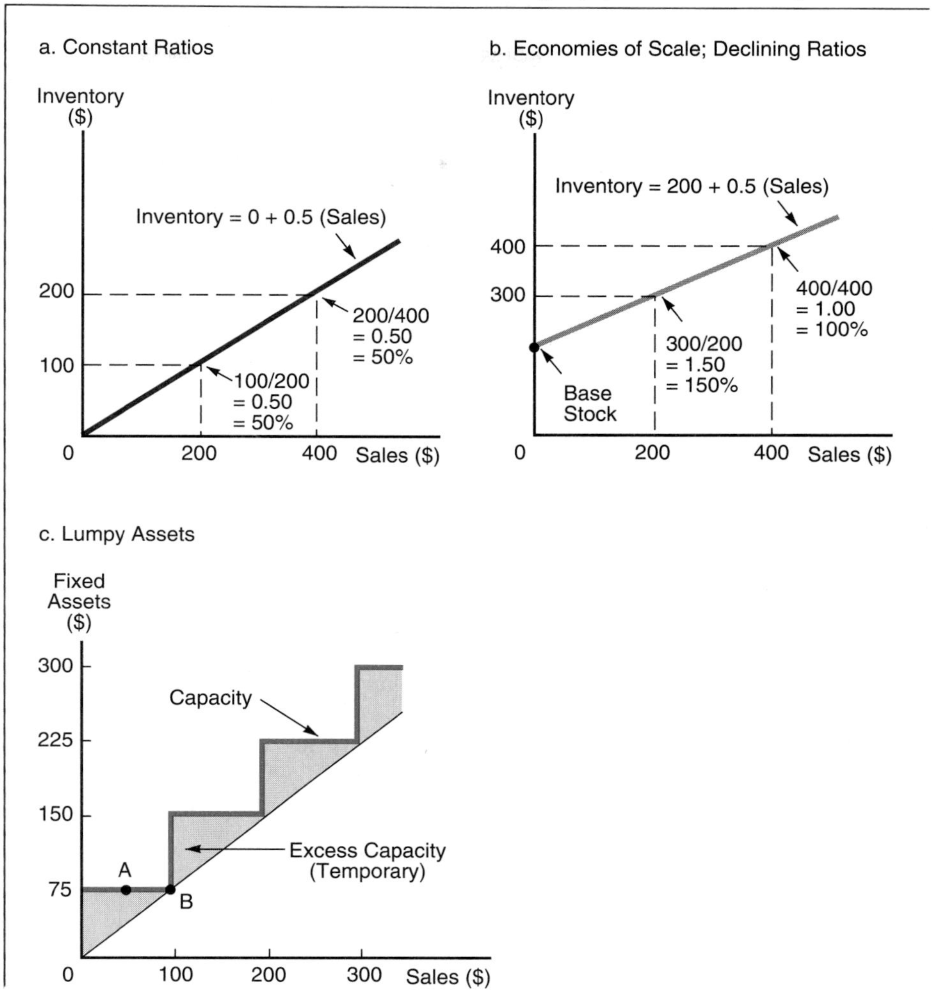

a. Constant Ratios
Inventory ($)
Inventory = 0 + 0.5 (Sales)
200
100
200/400
= 0.50
= 50%
100/200
= 0.50
= 50%
0
200
400
Sales ($)
b. Economies of Scale; Declining Ratios
Inventory ($)
Inventory = 200 + 0.5 (Sales)
400
300
400/400
= 1.00
= 100%
300/200
= 1.50
= 150%
Base Stock
0
200
400
Sales ($)
c. Lumpy Assets
Fixed Assets ($)
300
225
150
75
Capacity
Excess Capacity (Temporary)
A
B
0
100
200
300
Sales ($)

the most popular model for establishing inventory levels, the EOQ model, its inventories will rise with the square root of sales. In this case, the graph in Figure 7-3b would show a curved line whose slope decreases at higher sales levels.

Lumpy Assets

lumpy assets
Assets that cannot be acquired in small increments but must be obtained in large, discrete amounts.

In many industries, technological considerations dictate that if a firm is to be competitive, it must add fixed assets in large, discrete units; such assets are often referred to as **lumpy assets**. In the paper industry, for example, there are strong economies of scale in basic paper mill equipment, so when a paper company expands capacity, it must do so in large, lumpy increments. This type of situation is depicted in Panel c of Figure 7-3. Here we assume that the minimum economically efficient plant has a cost of $75 million and that such a plant can produce enough output to attain a sales level of $100 million. If the firm is to be competitive, it simply must have at least $75 million of fixed assets.

Lumpy assets have a major effect on the fixed assets/sales ratio at different sales levels and, consequently, on financial requirements. At Point A in Figure 7-3c, which represents a sales level of $50 million, the fixed assets are $75 million, so the ratio FA/S = $75/$50 = 1.5. Sales can expand by $50 million, out to $100 million, with no additions to fixed assets. At that point, represented by Point B, the ratio FA/S = $75/$100 = 0.75. However, if the firm is operating at capacity (sales of $100 million), even a small increase in sales would require a doubling of plant capacity, so a small projected sales increase would bring with it a very large financial requirement.[5]

Excess Assets due to Forecasting Errors

Panels a, b, and c of Figure 7-3 all focus on target, or projected, relationships between sales and assets. Actual sales, however, are often different from projected sales, and the actual asset/sales ratio for a given period may thus be quite different from the planned ratio. To illustrate, the firm depicted in Panel b of Figure 7-3 might, when its sales are at $200 million and its inventories at $300 million, project a sales expansion to $400 million and then increase its inventories to $400 million in anticipation of the sales expansion. However, suppose an unforeseen economic downturn were to hold sales to only $300 million. Actual inventories would then be $400 million, but inventories of only $350 million would be needed to support actual sales of $300 million. Thus, inventories would be $50 million larger than needed. In this situation, if the firm were making its forecast for the following year, it would need to recognize that sales could expand by $100 million with no increase whatever in inventories but that any sales expansion beyond $100 million would require additional financing to build inventories.

 Self-Test Question

Describe three conditions under which the assumption that each "spontaneous" asset and liability item increases at the same rate as sales is *not* correct.

---

[5]Several other points should be noted about Panel c of Figure 7-3. First, if the firm is operating at a sales level of $100 million or less, any expansion that calls for a sales increase above $100 million will require a *doubling* of the firm's fixed assets. A much smaller percentage increase would be involved if the firm were large enough to be operating a number of plants. Second, firms generally go to multiple shifts and take other actions to minimize the need for new fixed asset capacity as they approach Point B. However, these efforts can go only so far, and eventually a fixed asset expansion will be required. Third, firms often make arrangements to share excess capacity with other firms in their industry. For example, consider the situation in the electric utility industry, which is very much like that depicted in Panel c. Electric companies often build jointly owned plants, or else they "take turns" building plants, and then they buy power from or sell power to other utilities to avoid building new plants that may be underutilized.

Figure 7-4   ▪   Allied Food Products: Linear Regression Models (Millions of Dollars)

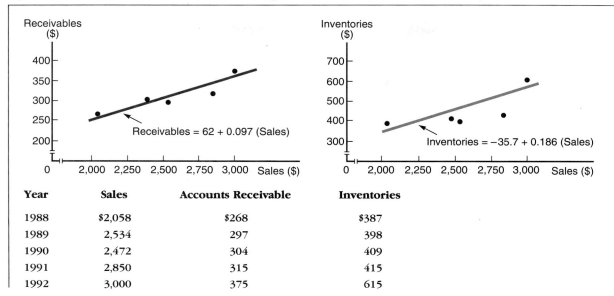

Year	Sales	Accounts Receivable	Inventories
1988	$2,058	$268	$387
1989	2,534	297	398
1990	2,472	304	409
1991	2,850	315	415
1992	3,000	375	615

OTHER FORECASTING TECHNIQUES

If any of the conditions noted above apply (economies of scale, excess capacity, or lumpy assets), the A*/S ratio will not be a constant, and the constant growth forecasting method should not be used. Rather, other techniques must be used to forecast asset levels and additional financing requirements. Two of these methods—linear regression and excess capacity adjustments—are discussed in the following sections.

Simple Linear Regression

If we assume that the relationship between a certain type of asset and sales is linear, then we can use simple linear regression techniques to estimate the requirements for that type of asset for any given sales increase. For example, Allied's levels of sales, receivables, and inventories during the last 5 years are shown in the lower section of Figure 7-4, and each current asset item is plotted in the upper section as a scatter diagram versus sales. Estimated regression equations determined using a financial calculator are also shown with each graph. For example, the estimated relationship between inventories and sales (in millions of dollars) is

$$\text{Inventories} = -\$35.7 + 0.186(\text{Sales}).$$

The plotted points are not very close to the regression line, which indicates a low degree of correlation. In fact, the correlation coefficient between inventories and sales is 0.71, indicating that there is only a moderate linear relationship between these two variables. Still, management regards the regression relationship as providing a reasonable basis for forecasting target inventory levels.

We can use the estimated relationship between inventories and sales to forecast 1993 inventory levels. Since 1993 sales are projected at $3,300 million, 1993 inventories should be $578 million:

$$\text{Inventories} = -\$35.7 + 0.186(\$3,300) = \$578 \text{ million.}$$

This is $99 million less than the preliminary forecast based on the projected balance sheet method. The difference occurs because the projected balance sheet method assumed that the ratio of inventories to sales would remain constant, when in fact it will probably decline, because the regression line in Figure 7-4 does not pass through the origin. Note also that although our graphs show linear relationships, we could have easily used a nonlinear regression model had such a relationship been indicated.

After analyzing the regression results, Allied's managers directed that a new forecast of AFN be developed in which a lower days sales outstanding and a higher inventory turnover ratio are assumed. Management recognized that the 1992 levels of these accounts were above the industry averages, hence that the preliminary results projected for 1993 were below the optimal levels. When simple linear regression was used to forecast the receivables and inventories accounts, the 1993 levels reflect both the average relationships of these accounts to sales over the 5-year period and the trend in the variables' values. The projected balance sheet method assumed that the nonoptimal 1992 levels would remain constant in 1993 and beyond. The new preliminary 1993 forecast for Allied, based on the Figure 7-4 linear regression relationships for receivables and inventories, projected a 1993 funds surplus of $17 million.

Excess Capacity Adjustments

Consider again the Allied Food Products example set forth in Tables 7-1 and 7-2. Now assume that excess capacity exists in fixed assets. Specifically, assume that fixed assets in 1992 were being utilized to only 96 percent of capacity. If fixed assets had been used to full capacity, 1992 sales could have been as high as $3,125 million:

$$\text{Full capacity sales} = \frac{\text{Actual sales}}{\substack{\text{Percentage of capacity} \\ \text{at which fixed assets} \\ \text{were operated}}} = \frac{\$3,000 \text{ million}}{0.96} = \$3,125 \text{ million.} \qquad (7\text{-}2)$$

This suggests that Allied's Fixed assets/Sales ratio should be 32 percent:

$$\text{Target fixed assets/Sales ratio} = \frac{\text{Actual fixed assets}}{\text{Full capacity sales}} \qquad (7\text{-}3)$$

$$= \frac{\$1,000}{\$3,125} = 0.32 = 32\%.$$

Therefore, if sales are to increase to $3,300 million, then fixed assets would have to increase to $1,056 million:

$$\begin{array}{|l}
\text{Required level} \\
\text{of fixed assets}
\end{array} = \text{Target fixed assets/Sales ratio (Projected sales)}\quad (7\text{-}4)$$

$$= 0.32(\$3,300) = \$1,056\ \text{million.}$$

We had previously forecasted that Allied would need to increase fixed assets at the same rate as sales, or by 10 percent, which meant an increase from $1,000 million to $1,100 million, or by $100 million. Now we see that the actual required increase is only from $1,000 million to $1,056 million, or by $56 million. Thus, the capacity-adjusted forecast is $100 million − $56 million = $44 million less than the earlier forecast. Therefore, the projected AFN would decline from an estimated $112 million (before financing feedback effects) to $112 million − $44 million = $68 million.

Note also that, when excess capacity exists, sales growth up to the capacity sales as determined above can occur with no increase whatever in fixed assets and that sales beyond that growth will require fixed asset additions as calculated in our example. The same situation could occur with respect to inventories, and the required additions would be determined in exactly the same manner as for fixed assets. Theoretically, the same situation could occur with other types of assets, but as a practical matter, excess capacity normally exists primarily with respect to fixed assets and inventories.

Self-Test Question

Identify two methods which can be used to forecast asset levels when the assets-to-sales ratio is not constant.

COMPUTERIZED FINANCIAL PLANNING MODELS

Although the types of financial forecasting described in this chapter can be done with a hand calculator, virtually all corporate forecasts are made using computerized forecasting models. Most computerized financial forecasting models are based on a spreadsheet program such as *Lotus 1-2-3*. Spreadsheet models have two major advantages over pencil and paper calculations. First, it is much faster to construct a spreadsheet model than to make a "by hand" forecast if the forecast period extends beyond two or three years. Second, and more important, a spreadsheet model can almost instantaneously recompute the projected financial statements and ratios when one of the input variables is changed, thus making it feasible for managers to determine the effects of changes in variables such as sales.

We developed forecasts for Allied using a 5-year financial planning model based on *Lotus 1-2-3*. The model begins with 5 years of historical data, which are used to establish basic relationships. Other input data include forecasted sales growth rates, the financing mix to apply to any additional funds needed, the cost rates on incremental debt financing, and the tax rate. The model calculates projected financial statements for 5 years, including financing feedback effects, along with some key financial ratios. We used *Lotus*'s linear regression capability to develop Allied's historical sales growth rate and the historical relationships between accounts receivable, inventories, and sales. Thus, it was quite easy to examine the effects of alternative assumptions on Allied's forecasts.[6]

 ### Self-Test Question

Why are computerized planning models playing an increasingly important role in corporate management?

SUMMARY

This chapter described in broad outline how firms project their financial statements and determine their capital requirements. The key concepts covered are listed below.

- Management establishes a **target balance sheet** on the basis of ratio analysis.
- **Financial forecasting** generally begins with a forecast of the firm's sales, in terms of both units and dollars, for some future period.
- **The projected,** or **pro forma, balance sheet method** and the **formula method** are used to forecast financial requirements.
- A firm can determine the amount of **additional funds needed (AFN)** by estimating the amount of new assets necessary to support the forecasted level of sales and then subtracting from that amount the spontaneous funds that will be generated from operations. The firm can then plan to raise the AFN through bank borrowing, by issuing securities, or both.
- The **higher a firm's sales growth rate,** the **greater** will be its need for additional financing. Similarly, the **larger a firm's dividend payout ratio,** the **greater** its need for additional funds.

---

[6]It is becoming increasingly easy for companies to develop planning models as a result of the dramatic improvements that have been made in computer hardware and software in recent years. *Lotus 1-2-3* is the most widely used system, although many companies also employ more complex and elaborate modeling systems. Increasingly, a knowledge of *Lotus 1-2-3* or some similar spreadsheet program is becoming a requirement for getting even an entry-level job in many corporations. Indeed, surveys indicate that the probability of a business student getting an attractive job offer increases dramatically if he or she has a working knowledge of *Lotus 1-2-3*. In addition, starting salaries are materially higher for those students who have such a knowledge.

Note also that we have concentrated on long-run, or strategic, financial planning. Within the framework of the long-run strategic plan, firms also develop short-run financial plans. For example, in Table 7-2 we saw that Allied Food Products expects to need $112 million by the end of 1993, and that it plans to raise this capital by using short-term debt, long-term debt, and common stock. However, we do not know when during the year the funds will be needed or when Allied will obtain each of its different types of capital. To address these issues, the firm must develop a short-run financial plan, the centerpiece of which is the *cash budget*, which is a projection of cash inflows and outflows on a daily, weekly, or monthly basis during the coming year (or other budget period). We will discuss cash budgeting in Chapter 8, where we continue our discussion of financial planning and control.

▪ Adjustments must be made if **economies of scale** exist in the use of assets, if **excess capacity** exists, or if assets must be added in **lumpy increments.**

▪ **Linear regression** and **specific item forecasting techniques** can be used to forecast asset requirements in situations in which assets cannot be expected to grow at the same rate as sales.

The type of forecasting described in this chapter is important for several reasons. First, if the projected operating results are unsatisfactory, management can "go back to the drawing board," reformulate its plans, and develop more reasonable targets for the coming year. Second, it is possible that the funds required to meet the sales forecast simply cannot be obtained; if so, it is obviously better to know this in advance and to scale back the projected level of operations than to suddenly run out of cash and have operations grind to a halt. And third, even if the required funds can be raised, it is desirable to plan for their acquisition well in advance.

Questions

7-1   Certain liability and net worth items generally increase spontaneously with increases in sales. Put a check ($\sqrt{}$) by those items that typically increase spontaneously:

Accounts payable   _____
Notes payable to banks   _____
Accrued wages   _____
Accrued taxes   _____
Mortgage bonds   _____
Common stock   _____
Retained earnings   _____

7-2   The following equation can, under certain assumptions, be used to forecast financial requirements:

$$AFN = (A^*/S)(\Delta S) - (L^*/S)(\Delta S) - MS_1(1 - d).$$

Under what conditions does the equation give satisfactory predictions, and when should it not be used?

7-3   Assume that an average firm in the office supply business has a 6 percent after-tax profit margin, a 40 percent debt/assets ratio, a total assets turnover of 2 times, and a dividend payout ratio of 40 percent. Is it true that if such a firm is to have *any* sales growth ($g > 0$), it will be forced either to borrow or to sell common stock (that is, it will need some nonspontaneous, external capital even if g is very small)?

7-4   Is it true that computerized corporate planning models were a fad during the 1980s but, because of a need for flexibility in corporate planning, they have been dropped by most firms?

7-5   Suppose a firm makes the following policy changes. If the change means that external, nonspontaneous financial requirements (AFN) will increase, indicate this by a (+); indicate a decrease by a (−); and indicate indeterminate or no effect by a (0). Think in terms of the immediate, short-run effect on funds requirements.

a. The dividend payout ratio is increased.   _____
b. The firm contracts to buy, rather than make, certain components used in its products.   _____
c. The firm decides to pay all suppliers on delivery, rather than after a 30-day delay, to take advantage of discounts for rapid payment.   _____

d. The firm begins to sell on credit (previously all sales had been on a cash basis).   _____

e. The firm's profit margin is eroded by increased competition; sales are steady.   _____

f. Advertising expenditures are stepped up.   _____

g. A decision is made to substitute long-term mortgage bonds for short-term bank loans.   _____

h. The firm begins to pay employees on a weekly basis (previously it had paid at the end of each month).   _____

Self-Test Problems   *(Solutions Appear in Appendix B)*

ST-1
Key terms

Define each of the following terms:

a. Sales forecast
b. Projected balance sheet method
c. Spontaneously generated funds
d. Dividend payout ratio
e. Pro forma financial statement
f. Additional funds needed (AFN); AFN formula
g. Capital intensity ratio
h. Lumpy assets
i. Financing feedback

ST-2
Maximum growth rate

Weatherford Industries Inc. has the following ratios: $A^*/S = 1.6$; $L^*/S = 0.4$; profit margin $= 0.10$; and dividend payout ratio $= 0.45$, or 45 percent. Sales last year were $100 million. Assuming that these ratios will remain constant, use the AFN formula to determine the maximum growth rate Weatherford can achieve without having to employ nonspontaneous external funds.

ST-3
Additional funds needed

Suppose Weatherford's financial consultants report (1) that the inventory turnover ratio is sales/inventory = 3 times versus an industry average of 4 times, and (2) that Weatherford could reduce inventories and thus raise its turnover to 4 without affecting sales, the profit margin, or the other asset turnover ratios. Under these conditions, use the AFN formula to determine the amount of additional funds Weatherford would require during each of the next 2 years if sales grew at a rate of 20 percent per year.

ST-4
Proportional growth

Using the projected balance sheet method, construct Allied Food Products' third pass income statement and balance sheet. What is the AFN for this iteration?

Problems

7-1
Pro forma statements and ratios

Magee Computers makes bulk purchases of small computers, stocks them in conveniently located warehouses, and ships them to its chain of retail stores. Magee's balance sheet as of December 31, 1992, is shown here (millions of dollars):

Cash	$ 3.5	Accounts payable	$ 9.0
Receivables	26.0	Notes payable	18.0
Inventories	58.0	Accruals	8.5
Total current assets	$ 87.5	Total current liabilities	$ 35.5
Net fixed assets	35.0	Mortgage loan	6.0
		Common stock	15.0
		Retained earnings	66.0
Total assets	$122.5	Total liabilities and equity	$122.5

Sales for 1992 were $350 million, while net income for the year was $10.5 million. Magee paid dividends of $4.2 million to common stockholders. The firm is operating at full capacity. Assume that all ratios remain constant.

a. If sales are projected to increase by $70 million, or 20 percent, during 1993, use the AFN equation to determine Magee's projected external capital requirements.

b. Construct Magee's pro forma balance sheet for December 31, 1993. Assume that all external capital requirements are met by bank loans and are reflected in notes payable. Do not consider any financing feedback effects.

c. Now calculate the following ratios, based on your projected December 31, 1993, balance sheet. Magee's 1992 ratios and industry average ratios are shown here for comparison:

	Magee Computers		Industry Average
	12/31/93	**12/31/92**	**12/31/92**
Current ratio	_____	2.5×	3×
Debt/total assets	_____	33.9%	30%
Rate of return on equity	_____	13%	12%

d. Now assume that Magee grows by the same $70 million but that the growth is spread over 5 years—that is, that sales grow by $14 million each year. Do not consider any financing feedback effects.

   (1) Calculate total additional financial requirements over the 5-year period. (Hint: Use 1992 ratios, $\Delta S = \$70$, but *total* sales for the 5-year period.)

   (2) Construct a pro forma balance sheet as of December 31, 1997, using notes payable as the balancing item.

   (3) Calculate the current ratio, total debt/total assets ratio, and rate of return on equity as of December 31, 1997. [Hint: Be sure to use *total sales*, which amount to $1,960 million, to calculate retained earnings but 1997 profits to calculate the rate of return on equity—that is, return on equity = (1997 profits)/(12/31/97 equity).]

e. Do the plans outlined in Parts b and/or d seem feasible to you? That is, do you think Magee could borrow the required capital, and would the company be raising the odds on its bankruptcy to an excessive level in the event of some temporary misfortune?

7-2

Additional funds needed

Trivoli Textile's 1992 financial statements are shown below.

Trivoli Textile:
Balance Sheet as of December 31, 1992
(Thousands of Dollars)

Cash	$ 1,080	Accounts payable	$ 4,320
Receivables	6,480	Accruals	2,880
Inventories	9,000	Notes payable	2,100
Total current assets	$16,560	Total current liabilities	$ 9,300
Net fixed assets	12,600	Mortgage bonds	3,500
		Common stock	3,500
		Retained earnings	12,860
Total assets	$29,160	Total liabilities and equity	$29,160

Trivoli Textile:
Income Statement for December 31, 1992
(Thousands of Dollars)

Sales	$36,000
Operating costs	32,440
Earnings before interest and taxes	$ 3,560
Interest	560
Earnings before taxes	$ 3,000
Taxes (40%)	1,200
Net Income	$ 1,800
Dividends (45%)	$810
Addition to retained earnings	$990

a. Suppose 1993 sales are projected to increase by 15 percent over 1992 sales. Determine the additional funds needed. Assume that the company was operating at full capacity in 1992, that it cannot sell off any of its fixed assets, and that any required financing will be borrowed as notes payable. Also, assume that assets, spontaneous liabilities, and operating costs are expected to increase by the same percentage as sales. Use the projected balance sheet method to develop a pro forma balance sheet and income statement for December 31, 1993. (Do not incorporate any financing feedback effects. Use the pro forma income statement to determine the addition to retained earnings.)

b. Use the financial statements developed in Part a to incorporate the financing feedback as a result of the addition to notes payable. (That is, do the next financial statement iteration.) For the purpose of this part, assume that the notes payable interest rate is 10 percent. What is the AFN for this iteration?

7-3

Excess capacity

Van Auken Lumber's 1992 financial statements are shown below.

Van Auken Lumber:
Balance Sheet as of December 31, 1992
(Thousands of Dollars)

Cash	$ 1,800	Accounts payable	$ 7,200
Receivables	10,800	Notes payable	3,472
Inventories	12,600	Accruals	2,520
Total current assets	$25,200	Total current liabilities	$13,192
		Mortgage bonds	5,000
		Common stock	2,000
Net fixed assets	21,600	Retained earnings	26,608
Total assets	$46,800	Total liabilities and equity	$46,800

Van Auken Lumber:
Income Statement for December 31, 1992
(Thousands of Dollars)

Sales	$36,000
Operating costs	30,783
Earnings before interest and taxes	$ 5,217
Interest	1,017
Earnings before taxes	$ 4,200
Taxes (40%)	1,680
Net Income	$ 2,520
Dividends (60%)	$1,512
Addition to retained earnings	$1,008

a. Assume that the company was operating at full capacity in 1992 with regard to all items *except* fixed assets; fixed assets in 1992 were being utilized to only 75 percent of capacity. By what percentage could 1993 sales increase over 1992 sales without the need for an increase in fixed assets?

b. Now suppose 1993 sales increase by 25 percent over 1992 sales. How much additional external capital will be required? Assume that Van Auken cannot sell any fixed assets. (Hint: Use the projected balance sheet method to develop a pro forma balance sheet and income statement as in Tables 7-1 and 7-2.) Assume that any required financing is borrowed as notes payable. Do not include any financing feedbacks, and use a pro forma income statement to determine the addition to retained earnings. (Another hint: Notes payable = $6,021.)

c. Use the financial statements developed in Part b to incorporate the financing feedback which results from the addition to notes payable. (That is, do the next financial statement iteration.) For purposes of this part, assume that the notes payable interest rate is 12 percent. What is the AFN for this iteration?

d. Suppose the industry average DSO and inventory turnover ratio are 90 days and 3.33, respectively, and that Van Auken Lumber matches these figures in 1993 and then uses the funds released to reduce equity. (It pays a special dividend out of retained earnings.) What would this do to the rate of return on year-end 1993 equity? Use the second pass balance sheet and income statement as developed in Part c, and assume that the additional AFN amount calculated in that iteration is added to notes payable. (Hint: Notes payable is now $6,094.)

7-4

Additional funds needed

Patrick Technologies Inc.'s 1992 financial statements are shown below.

Patrick Technologies Inc.:
Balance Sheet as of December 31, 1992

Cash	$ 180,000	Accounts payable	$ 360,000
Receivables	360,000	Notes payable	156,000
Inventories	720,000	Accruals	180,000
Total current assets	$1,260,000	Total current liabilities	$ 696,000
Fixed assets	1,440,000	Common stock	1,800,000
		Retained earnings	204,000
Total assets	$2,700,000	Total liabilities and equity	$2,700,000

Patrick Technologies Inc.:
Income Statement for December 31, 1992

Sales	$3,600,000
Operating costs	3,279,720
EBIT	$ 320,280
Interest	20,280
EBT	$ 300,000
Taxes (40%)	120,000
Net Income	$ 180,000

Per share data:

Common stock price	$24.00
Earnings per share (EPS)	$1.80
Dividends per share (DPS)	$1.08

a. Suppose that in 1993 sales increase by 10 percent over 1992 sales and that 1993 DPS will increase to $1.12. Construct the pro forma financial statements using the projected balance sheet method. How much additional capital will be required? Assume the firm operated at full capacity in 1992. Do not include any financing feedbacks.

b. Now assume that 50 percent of the additional capital required will be financed by selling common stock and the remainder by borrowing as notes payable. Assume that the interest rate on notes payable is 13 percent. Do the next iteration of financial statements incorporating financing feedbacks. What is the AFN for this iteration?

c. If the profit margin were to remain at 5 percent and the dividend payout rate were to remain at 60 percent, at what growth rate in sales would the additional financing requirements be exactly zero? (Hint: Set AFN equal to zero and solve for g.)

7-5
External financing
requirements

The 1992 balance sheet and income statement for the Woods Company are shown below.

Woods Company: Balance Sheet as of
December 31, 1992 (Thousands of Dollars)

Cash	$ 80	Accounts payable	$ 160
Accounts receivable	240	Accruals	40
Inventories	720	Notes payable	252
Total current assets	$1,040	Total current liabilities	$ 452
Fixed assets	3,200	Long-term debt	1,244
		Total debt	$1,696
		Common stock	1,605
		Retained earnings	939
Total assets	$4,240	Total liabilities and equity	$4,240

**Woods Company: Income Statement for
December 31, 1992 (Thousands of Dollars)**

Sales	$8,000
Operating costs	7,450
EBIT	$ 550
Interest	150
EBT	$ 400
Taxes (40%)	160
Net income	$ 240
Per share data	
Common stock price	$16.96
Earnings per share (EPS)	$1.60
Dividends per share (DPS)	$1.04

a. The firm operated at full capacity in 1992. It expects sales to increase by 20 percent during 1993 and expects 1993 dividends per share to increase to $1.10. Use the projected balance sheet method to determine how much outside financing is required, developing the firm's pro forma balance sheet and income statement, and use AFN as the balancing item.

b. If the firm must maintain a current ratio of 2.3 and a debt ratio of 40 percent, how much financing, after the first pass, will be obtained using notes payable, long-term debt, and common stock?

c. Make the second pass financial statements incorporating financing feedbacks, using the ratios in Part b. Assume that the interest rate on debt averages 10 percent.

EXAM-TYPE PROBLEMS

The problems in this section are set up in such a way that they could be used as multiple-choice exam problems.

Long-term
financing needed

At year-end 1992, total assets for Shome Inc. were $1.2 million and accounts payable were $375,000. Sales, which in 1992 were $2.5 million, are expected to increase by 25 percent in 1993. Total assets and accounts payable are proportional to sales and that relationship will be maintained. Shome typically uses no current liabilities other than accounts payable. Common stock amounted to $425,000 in 1992, and retained earnings were $295,000. Shome plans to sell new common stock in the amount of $75,000. The firm's profit margin on sales is 6 percent; 40 percent of earnings will be paid out as dividends.

a. What was Shome's total debt in 1992?

b. How much new, long-term debt financing will be needed in 1993? (Hint: AFN − New stock = New long-term debt.) Do not consider any financing feedback effects.

7-7

Additional funds needed

The McGill Company's sales are forecasted to increase from $1,000 in 1992 to $2,000 in 1993. Here is the December 31, 1992, balance sheet:

Cash	$ 100	Accounts payable	$ 50
Accounts receivable	200	Notes payable	150
Inventories	200	Accruals	50
Net fixed assets	500	Long-term debt	400
		Common stock	100
		Retained earnings	250
Total assets	$1,000	Total liabilities and equity	$1,000

McGill's fixed assets were used to only 50 percent of capacity during 1992, but its current assets were at their proper levels. All assets except fixed assets increase at the same rate as sales, and fixed assets would also increase at the same rate if the current excess capacity did not exist. McGill's after-tax profit margin is forecasted to be 5 percent, and its payout ratio will be 60 percent. What is McGill's additional funds needed (AFN) for the coming year? Ignore financing feedback effects.

INTEGRATIVE PROBLEM

7-8

Financial forecasting

Sue Wilson, the new financial manager of Northwest Chemicals (NWC), an Oregon producer of specialized chemicals for use in fruit orchards, must prepare a financial forecast for 1993. NWC's 1992 sales were $2 billion, and the marketing department is forecasting a 25 percent increase for 1993. Sue thinks the company was operating at full capacity in 1992, but she is not sure about this. The 1992 financial statements, plus some other data, are given in Table IP7-1.

Assume that you were recently hired as Sue's assistant, and your first major task is to help her develop the forecast. She asked you to begin by answering the following set of questions.

a. Assume (1) that NWC was operating at full capacity in 1992 with respect to all assets, (2) that all assets must grow proportionally with sales, (3) that accounts payable and accruals will also grow in proportion to sales, and (4) that the 1992 profit margin and dividend payout will be maintained. Under these conditions, what will the company's financial requirements be for the coming year? Use the AFN equation to answer this question.

b. Now estimate the 1993 financial requirements using the projected financial statement approach, making an initial forecast plus one additional "pass" to determine the effects of "financing feedbacks." Assume (1) that each type of asset, as well as payables, accruals, and fixed and variable costs, grow at the same rate as sales; (2) that the payout ratio is held constant at 30 percent; (3) that external funds needed are financed 50 percent by notes payable and 50 percent by long-term debt (no new common stock will be issued); and (4) that all debt carries an interest rate of 8 percent.

c. Why do the two methods produce somewhat different AFN forecasts? Which method provides the more accurate forecast?

d. Calculate NWC's forecasted ratios, and compare them with the company's 1992 ratios and with the industry averages. How does NWC compare with the average firm in its industry, and is the company expected to improve during the coming year?

e. Suppose you now learn that NWC's 1992 receivables and inventories were in line with required levels, given the firm's credit and inventory policies, but that excess capacity existed with regard to fixed assets. Specifically, fixed assets were operated at only 75 percent of capacity.

Table IP7-1   ▮   **Financial Statements and Other Data on NWC**
(Millions of Dollars)

A. 1992 Balance Sheet

Cash and securities	$ 20	Accounts payable and accruals	$ 100	
Accounts receivable	240	Notes payable	100	
Inventories	240	Total current liabilities	$ 200	
Total current assets	$ 500	Long-term debt	100	
Net fixed assets	500	Common stock	500	
		Retained earnings	200	
Total assets	$ 1,000	Total liabilities and equity	$1,000	

B. 1992 Income Statement

Sales	$2,000.00
Less: Variable costs	1,200.00
Fixed costs	700.00
Earnings before interest and taxes	$ 100.00
Interest	16.00
Earnings before taxes	$ 84.00
Taxes (40%)	33.60
Net income	$ 50.40
Dividends (30%)	15.12
Addition to retained earnings	$ 35.28

C. Key Ratios

	NWC	Industry	Comment
Basic earning power	10.00%	20.00%	
Profit margin	2.52	4.00	
Return on equity	7.20	15.60	
Days sales outstanding (360 days)	43.20 days	32.00 days	
Inventory turnover	8.33×	11.00×	
Fixed assets turnover	4.00	5.00	
Total assets turnover	2.00	2.50	
Debt/assets	30.00%	36.00%	
Times interest earned	6.25×	9.40×	
Current ratio	2.50	3.00	
Payout ratio	30.00%	30.00%	

(1) What level of sales could have existed in 1992 with the available fixed assets? What would the fixed assets/sales ratio have been if NWC had been operating at full capacity?

(2) How would the existence of excess capacity in fixed assets affect the additional funds needed during 1993?

f. Without actually working out the numbers, how would you expect the ratios to change in the situation where excess capacity in fixed assets exists? Explain your reasoning.

g. Based on comparisons between NWC's days sales outstanding (DSO) and inventory turnover ratios with the industry average figures, does it appear that NWC is operating efficiently with respect to its inventories and accounts receivable? If the company were able to bring these ratios into line with the industry averages, what effect would this have on its AFN and its financial ratios? (Note: Inventories and receivables will be discussed in detail in later chapters.)

h. The relationship between sales and the various types of assets is important in financial forecasting. The balance sheet approach, under the assumption that each asset item grows at the same rate as sales, leads to an AFN forecast that is reasonably close to the forecast using the AFN equation. Explain how each of the following factors would affect the accuracy of financial forecasts based on the AFN equation: (1) excess capacity, (2) base stocks of assets, such as shoes in a shoe store, (3) economies of scale in the use of assets, and (4) lumpy assets.

i. (1) How could regression analysis be used to detect the presence of the situations described above and then to improve the financial forecasts? Plot a graph of the following data, which is for a typical well-managed company in NWC's industry, to illustrate your answer.

Year	Sales	Inventories
1990	$1,280	$118
1991	1,600	138
1992	2,000	162
1993E	2,500	192

(2) On the same graph that plots the above data, draw a line which shows how the regression line must appear to justify the use of the AFN formula and the projected balance sheet forecasting procedure. As a part of your answer, show the growth rate in inventories that results from a 10 percent increase in sales from a sales level of (a) $200 and (b) $2,000 based on both the actual regression line and a *hypothetical* regression line which is linear and which goes through the origin.

j. How would changes in these items affect the AFN? (1) The dividend payout ratio, (2) the profit margin, (3) the capital intensity ratio, and (4) NWC begins buying from its suppliers on terms which permit it to pay after 60 days rather than after 30 days. (Consider each item separately and hold all other things constant.)

COMPUTER-RELATED PROBLEM

Work the problem in this section only if you are using the computer problem diskette.

7-9   Use the model in File C7 to solve this problem. Stendardi Industries' 1992 financial
Forecasting   statements are shown on the next page.

Stendardi Industries:
Balance Sheet as of December 31, 1992
(Millions of Dollars)

Cash	$ 4.0	Accounts payable	$ 8.0
Receivables	12.0	Notes payable	5.0
Inventories	16.0	Total current liabilities	$13.0
Total current assets	$32.0	Long-term debt	12.0
Net fixed assets	40.0	Common stock	20.0
		Retained earnings	27.0
Total assets	$72.0	Total liabilities and equity	$72.0

Stendardi Industries:
Income Statement for December 31, 1992
(Millions of Dollars)

Sales	$80.0
Operating costs	71.3
EBIT	$ 8.7
Interest	2.0
EBT	$ 6.7
Taxes (40%)	2.7
Net income	$ 4.0
Dividends (40%)	$1.60
Addition to retained earnings	$2.40

Assume that the firm has no excess capacity in fixed assets, that the average interest rate for debt is 12 percent, and that the projected annual sales growth rate for the next 5 years is 15 percent.

a. Stendardi plans to finance its additional funds needed with 50 percent short-term debt and 50 percent long-term debt. Using the projected balance sheet method, prepare the pro forma financial statements for 1993 through 1997, and then determine (1) additional funds needed, (2) the current ratio, (3) the debt ratio, and (4) the return on equity.

b. Sales growth could be 5 percentage points above or below the projected 15 percent. Determine the effect of such variances on AFN and the key ratios.

c. Perform an analysis to determine the sensitivity of AFN and the key ratios for 1997 to changes in the dividend payout ratio as specified in the following, assuming sales grow at a constant 15 percent. What happens to AFN if the dividend payout ratio (1) is raised from 40 to 70 percent or (2) is lowered from 40 to 20 percent?

Financial Planning and Control

Business is becoming increasingly competitive, and corporate profitability is increasingly dependent upon operating efficiency. This situation is desirable from a social standpoint, for consumers are getting higher quality goods at lower prices, but intense competition does make life tough on corporate managers. No longer can firms afford to sit back and assume that the strategies that got them where they are will work in the future.

These points are clearly illustrated with events that are currently happening within three different firms in different industries: Sears, Federal Express, and UAL Corp. (the parent company of United Airlines).

Sears operates in an extremely competitive environment—retailing—which has seen a number of recent bankruptcies. Since August 1990, Sears has eliminated a total of 40,500 jobs, including 600 salaried positions in its regional management structure, in cost-cutting moves designed to increase operating efficiency. Sears also plans pay cuts for salespeople in its U.S. stores. To date, these cost-reduction programs have reduced Sears's selling, general, and administrative expenses from $0.30 per dollar of revenue in 1990 to $0.29 per dollar of revenue in 1991. However, Wal-Mart's expenses per revenue dollar are about half of Sears's, and Wal-Mart recently unseated Sears as the nation's largest retailer.

Federal Express, an overnight door-to-door deliverer of packages, is planning restructurings and "business arrangements" with third parties to cut costs and improve profitability. Fed Ex faces increasing competition from faxes, computer-to-computer transmissions, and new entrants to its market such as Airborne Express. The source of Federal Express's problem is fixed costs—they need to be reduced. The "business arrangement" that the company is considering is sharing space on its airplanes. One of Federal Express's competitors, DHL Worldwide Express, has already done this. DHL recently signed an agreement with the Emery Worldwide unit of Consolidated Freightways Inc. which allows Emery to share space on DHL's jet flights between New York and Brussels. If Federal Express were to follow DHL's lead, it would be a first for the company, which has long had a philosophy of independence.

Because of uncertain times in the airline industry, UAL Corp. has reduced its projected capital expenditures during the next three years by $3.6 billion. With this action, UAL hopes to improve its balance sheet and to avoid the kinds of problems which led to the bankruptcies of Eastern, Pan American, Braniff, and other airlines in recent years. UAL is not alone in its actions—other carriers, including USAIR and American Airlines, have taken similar actions. The airlines hope that these actions (which will leave them with less seats to fill) will improve future profits.

All of these companies—Sears, Federal Express, and United Airlines—are attempting to lower their fixed costs and reduce their breakeven points so that they can stem losses during bad times and boost profits when times are good. Keep these examples in mind as you read this chapter.

Sources: "Sears to Slash 600 Salary Posts, Salespeople Pay," *The Wall Street Journal*, February 13, 1992; "Federal Express Mulls Options to Stem Losses," *The Wall Street Journal*, February 12, 1992; and "UAL to Trim Capital Outlays by $3.6 Billion," *The Wall Street Journal*, February 11, 1992.

financial planning
The projection of sales, income, and assets based on alternative production and marketing strategies, as well as the determination of the resources needed to achieve these projections.

financial control
The phase in which financial plans are implemented; control deals with the feedback and adjustment process required to ensure adherence to plans and modification of plans because of unforeseen changes.

In the last chapter we focused on financial forecasting, emphasizing how growth in sales requires additional investment in assets, which in turn generally requires the firm to raise new external capital. We now go on to consider the planning and control systems used by financial managers. First, we look at the relationship between sales volume and profitability under different sets of operating conditions. These relationships are used by managers when forecasting the firm's level of operations, financing needs, and profitability. Next, since one of the financial manager's key jobs in the planning process is forecasting the firm's needs for funds, or cash budgeting, we consider this important topic. Finally, we examine the control phase of the planning and control process, because a good control system is essential both to ensure that plans are properly executed and to facilitate timely modifications to plans if the assumptions upon which the initial plans were based turn out to be incorrect.

FINANCIAL PLANNING AND CONTROL PROCESSES

Financial planning involves making projections of sales, income, and assets based on alternative production and marketing strategies and then deciding how to meet the forecasted financial requirements. In the financial planning process, managers should also evaluate plans and identify changes in operations that would improve results. **Financial control** moves on to the implementation

Figure 8-1   ▪   **Overview of the Financial Planning and Control Process**

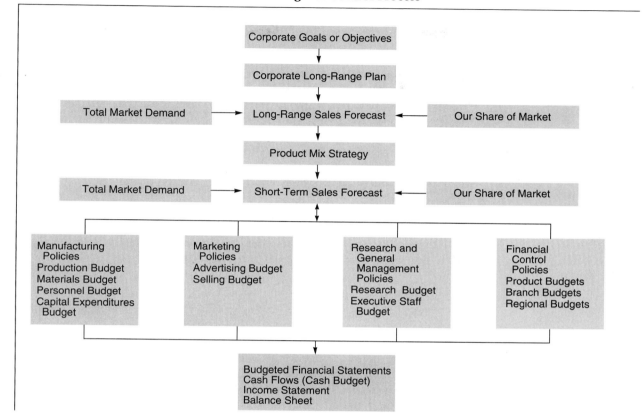

phase, dealing with the feedback and adjustment process that is required (1) to ensure that plans are followed and (2) to modify existing plans in response to changes in the operating environment. The process begins with the specification of the corporate goals, after which management lays out a series of forecasts and budgets for every significant area of the firm's activities, as shown in Figure 8-1.

Financial forecasting analysis begins with projections of sales revenues and production costs. In standard business terminology, a **budget** is a plan which sets forth the projected expenditures for a certain activity and explains where the required funds will come from. Thus, the *production budget* presents a detailed analysis of the required investments in materials, labor, and plant necessary to support the forecasted sales level. Each of the major elements of the production budget is likely to have a sub-budget of its own; thus, there will be a materials budget, a personnel budget, and a facilities budget. The marketing staff will also develop selling and advertising budgets. Typically, these budgets will be set up on a monthly basis, and as time goes by, actual figures will be compared with projected figures, differences will be explained or corrected, and projected figures for the remainder of the year will be adjusted if it appears that the original projections were unrealistic.

budget

Projected financial data which are compared with actual performance.

During the planning process, the projected levels of each of the different operating budgets will be combined, and from this set of data the firm's cash flows will be set forth in its *cash budget*. If a projected increase in sales leads to a projected cash shortage, management can make arrangements to obtain the required funds in the least-cost manner.

After all the cost and revenue elements have been forecasted, the firm's *pro forma*, or projected, income statement and balance sheet can be developed. These pro forma statements are later compared with the actual statements; such comparisons can help the firm pinpoint reasons for deviations, correct operating problems, and adjust projections for the remainder of the budget period to reflect actual operating conditions. Through its financial planning and control processes, management seeks to avoid cash squeezes and to improve the profitability of the individual divisions and thus the entire company.

? *Self-Test Question*

Briefly explain the relationship between the operating budget, the cash budget, and the pro forma income statement and balance sheet.

BREAKEVEN ANALYSIS

breakeven analysis

An analytical technique for studying the relationship between fixed costs, variable costs, sales volume, and profits.

The relationship between sales volume and profitability is explored in cost-volume-profit planning, or breakeven analysis. **Breakeven analysis** is a method of determining the point at which sales will just cover costs—that is, the point at which the firm will break even—but it also shows the magnitude of the firm's profits or losses if sales exceed or fall below that point. Breakeven analysis is important in the planning process because the cost-volume-profit relationship can be greatly influenced by the proportion of the firm's investment in assets which are fixed, and changes in the ratio of fixed to variable assets are determined when financial plans are set. A sufficient volume of sales must be anticipated and achieved if fixed and variable costs are to be covered, or else the firm will incur losses. In other words, if a firm is to avoid accounting losses, its sales must cover all costs—those that vary directly with production and those that do not change as production levels change. Costs that fall into each of these categories are listed in Table 8-1.

Note that interest charges are not listed in Table 8-1. Interest is a *financial cost* as opposed to an *operating cost*. Thus, breakeven analysis, as we develop it in this chapter, shows the breakeven point *before* interest charges. The reason for this emphasis is that, at this point, we are concerned with the firm's *operating plan* rather than its *financing plan*. We will expand the analysis to include financial charges in Chapter 17, when we take up the issue of debt versus equity financing.

Breakeven Chart

The essentials of breakeven analysis are depicted in Figure 8-2, the basic breakeven chart. Here units produced and sold are shown on the horizontal axis, and revenues and costs are measured on the vertical axis. We assume that the number of units sold is equal to the number of units produced. Fixed operating costs

Table 8-1   ▪   **Fixed and Variable Operating Costs**

Fixed Operating Costs[a]	Direct (Variable) Operating Costs
Depreciation on plant and equipment	Factory labor
Rentals	Materials
Salaries of research staff	Sales commissions
Salaries of executive staff	
General office expenses	

[a]Some of these costs—for example, salaries and office expenses—can be variable to some degree; hence, they are often called *semivariable* costs. However, firms are reluctant to reduce these expenditures in response to temporary fluctuations in sales, and they are often constrained from doing so by labor agreements and other contractual arrangements. Hence, de facto, fixed costs are generally greater than one might think.

Figure 8-2   ▪   **Breakeven Chart**

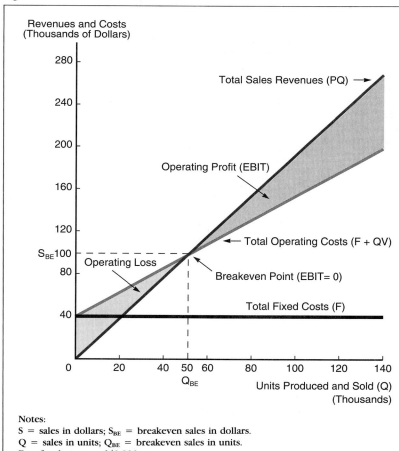

Notes:
S = sales in dollars; S_{BE} = breakeven sales in dollars.
Q = sales in units; Q_{BE} = breakeven sales in units.
F = fixed costs = $40,000.
V = variable costs per unit = $1.20.
P = price per unit = $2.00.

of $40,000 are represented by a horizontal line; they are the same (fixed) regardless of the number of units produced. Variable costs are assumed to be $1.20 a unit, so (1) total variable costs are found by multiplying $1.20 by the number of units sold, and (2) the total cost line rises at a rate of 1.2 dollars per one-unit increase in units produced and sold. Therefore, the total operating costs function, which is equal to fixed costs plus total variable costs, is shown on the graph as a straight line with a Y intercept of $40,000 and a slope of $1.20.

Each unit produced is assumed to be sold at a price of $2. Therefore, a second straight line, with a Y intercept of zero and a slope of $2, is used to depict total sales revenues. The slope of the total revenues line is steeper than that of the total operating costs line because the firm is gaining $2 of revenue for every $1.20 it pays out for labor and materials as each new unit is produced and sold. At the point where the total revenues line cuts the total operating costs line, the firm's total revenues are just equal to its total operating costs, and at that volume the firm breaks even. Before the breakeven volume is reached, the firm suffers operating losses, but after that point, it earns larger and larger operating profits as sales increase.

Breakeven Sales Volume

Figure 8-2 shows that the breakeven sales volume is 50,000 units; at that volume, sales revenues and total operating costs are both $100,000. We could calculate the breakeven point algebraically, rather than graphically. From the data given, the firm's total sales revenues are

$$S = PQ \qquad (8\text{-}1)$$

$$= \$2Q,$$

where S is total sales in dollars, P is the sales price per unit, and Q is the volume in units. The total operating cost equation is

$$TC = F + VQ \qquad (8\text{-}2)$$

$$= \$40,000 + \$1.20Q,$$

where F is total fixed operating costs and V is the variable operating cost per unit.

breakeven point (Q$_{BE}$)
The volume of sales at which total operating costs equal total revenues, and operating income (EBIT) equals zero.

At the **breakeven point, Q$_{BE}$**, total sales revenues and total operating costs are equal. Therefore, the sales and cost functions are equal to one another, and, solving, we find the breakeven volume to be 50,000 units:

$$\$2Q_{BE} = \$40,000 + \$1.20Q_{BE}$$
$$Q_{BE} = 50,000 \text{ units.}$$

As a generalization, we can use this formula to find the breakeven volume in units, Q_{BE}:[1]

$$Q_{BE} = \frac{F}{P - V}. \qquad (8\text{-}3)$$

Thus, with our example,

$$Q_{BE} = \frac{\$40,000}{\$2.00 - \$1.20} = \frac{\$40,000}{\$0.80} = 50,000 \text{ units.}$$

If we know both the breakeven volume in units and the sales price, then we can find the breakeven volume in dollars, S_{BE}:

$$S_{BE} = PQ_{BE}. \qquad (8\text{-}3a)$$

Thus,

$$S_{BE} = \$2(50,000) = \$100,000.$$

Thus, the breakeven point in either units or in dollar sales can be calculated by use of Equations 8-3 and 8-3a.

Breakeven analysis based on dollar sales rather than on units of output is useful in determining the breakeven volume for a firm which sells many products at varying prices. This analysis requires only that total sales, total fixed costs, and total variable costs at the given sales level be known. The breakeven volume then is calculated as

$$S_{BE} = \frac{FC}{1 - \dfrac{VC}{Sales}}. \qquad (8\text{-}4)$$

When a project is being planned, it is relatively easy to estimate the fixed and variable costs associated with that project. These costs can be estimated by identifying and summing the major components of fixed expenses, such as rent, depreciation, and general and administrative expenses, and using this sum as total fixed costs. Total variable costs can then be calculated as total costs minus total fixed costs. Once a firm is operational, however, it is much more difficult

---

[1]Equation 8-3 is derived as follows. At breakeven, total sales revenues are equal to total operating costs.

$$TR = TC.$$

TR is equal to PQ, while TC is equal to fixed costs (F) plus total variable costs (VQ), so

$$PQ = F + VQ.$$

Solving for $Q = Q_{BE}$, we obtain

$$Q_{BE} = \frac{F}{P - V}. \qquad (8\text{-}3)$$

to separate the firm's fixed and variable costs in order to calculate the firm's breakeven sales level.

Breakeven analysis can shed light on three important types of business decisions: (1) When one is making new product decisions, breakeven analysis can help determine how large the sales of a new product must be for the firm to achieve profitability. (2) Breakeven analysis can be used to study the effects of a general expansion in the level of the firm's operations; an expansion would cause the levels of both fixed and variable costs to rise, but it would also increase expected sales. (3) When the firm is considering modernization and automation projects, where the fixed investment in equipment is increased in order to lower variable costs, particularly the cost of labor, breakeven analysis can help management analyze the consequences of these projects.

Limitations of Breakeven Analysis

When one attempts to apply breakeven analysis in practice, a number of issues immediately arise. Here are some examples:

1. The total revenue function as graphed in Figure 8-2 is based on the assumption that the price per unit is constant at $2 regardless of the volume of sales and production. Is that realistic? For example, if demand were low, might the company not lower the sales price in an effort to boost sales? Conversely, if demand were high, might that not be a good time to boost the price and widen profit margins?

2. Is it realistic to expect variable cost per unit to be constant at all output levels? For example, at very low outputs, the cost per unit might be high because the labor force would not be producing enough units to learn how to produce them efficiently and because the firm would not be able to take advantage of quantity discounts in purchasing parts and materials. Similarly, at high volumes, the firm might have to employ labor on an overtime basis (at double-time wages) or to utilize its least efficient equipment, both of which would lead to high unit costs. These considerations suggest that the cost curve would probably be nonlinear, rising at a declining rate over a range where economies of scale exist, then rising at a constant rate, and finally rising at an increasing rate, indicating that diseconomies of scale had set in. If the cost curve is nonlinear, a situation might exist where the firm has a loss at low sales levels, earns a profit over some range of sales volumes, and then has a loss at very high sales volumes.

3. The firm might also want to consider changing its level of fixed costs. Higher fixed costs are not good, other things held constant, but they are generally associated with a more automated production process, which reduces variable costs per unit. Breakeven analysis as set forth in Figure 8-2 must be modified to deal with such changes.

These limitations make the use of a single breakeven chart as set forth in Figure 8-2 impractical—such a chart provides useful information, but the fact that it cannot deal with changes in the price of the product, with changing variable cost rates, and with changes in fixed cost levels suggests the need for a more flexible type of analysis. Today, such analysis is provided by computer simulation. Functions such as those expressed in Equations 8-1, 8-2, and 8-3 (or more complicated versions of them) are put into a *Lotus 1-2-3* or similar model, and then variables such as sales price (P), the variable cost rate (V), and the level of fixed costs (F) may be changed. The model can instantaneously produce new versions of Figure 8-2, or a whole set of such graphs, to show what the breakeven point would be under different production setups and price-cost situations. This point is discussed in the following section.

? *Self-Test Questions*

Is interest paid considered in a breakeven analysis? Why or why not?

Give the equations used to calculate the breakeven point in units and in dollar sales.

Why might you want to use breakeven analysis based on dollar sales rather than on units of output? (Hint: Think of a multiproduct firm.)

Give some examples of business decisions for which breakeven analysis might be useful.

Identify some limitations to the use of a single breakeven chart.

OPERATING LEVERAGE

operating leverage

The extent to which fixed costs are used in a firm's operations.

If a high percentage of a firm's total costs are fixed, the firm is said to have a high degree of **operating leverage.** In physics, leverage implies the use of a lever to raise a heavy object with a small amount of force. In politics, people who have leverage can accomplish a great deal with their smallest word or action. *In business terminology, a high degree of operating leverage, other things held constant, means that a relatively small change in sales will result in a large change in operating income.*

The concept of operating leverage is illustrated in Figure 8-3, where we compare three firms—A, B, and C—which use differing degrees of operating leverage. Firm A uses the least amount of operating leverage, so it has a relatively small amount of fixed charges; it does not have much automated equipment, so its depreciation cost, maintenance expense, and property taxes are low. Note, however, that A's variable cost line has a relatively steep slope, indicating that its variable costs per unit are higher than those of the other firms, which use more leverage.

Firm B is considered to have a normal amount of operating leverage, hence normal fixed costs. It uses automated equipment (with which an operator can turn out a few or many units at the same labor cost) to about the same extent as the average firm in the industry. Firm B breaks even at a higher level of operations (50,000 units) than does Firm A. At a production level of 40,000 units, B loses $8,000 but A breaks even.

Firm C uses operating leverage to a greater extent than either Firm A or Firm B. It is highly automated, using expensive, high-speed machines that require very little labor per unit produced. With such an operation, Firm C has high fixed costs, but its variable costs rise slowly. Because of the high overhead resulting from depreciation and maintenance expenses associated with the expensive machinery, Firm C's breakeven point is higher than that for either Firm

Figure 8-3 ▪ Operating Leverage

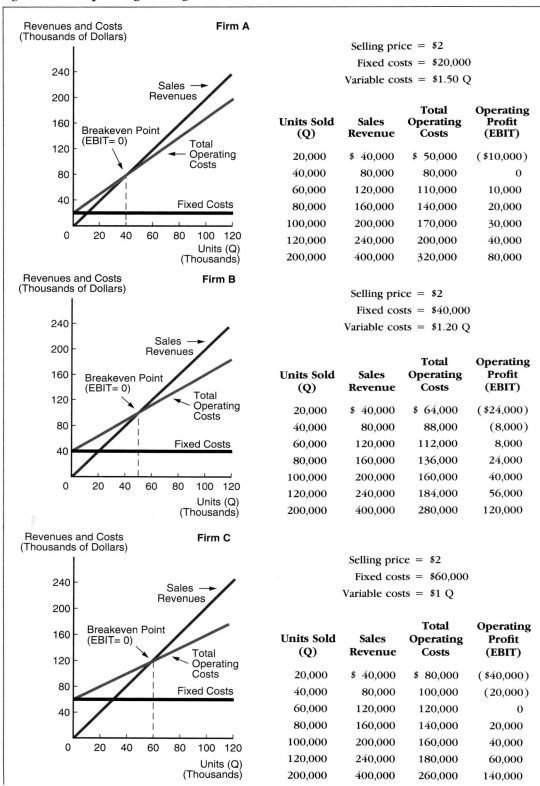

Firm A

Selling price = $2
Fixed costs = $20,000
Variable costs = $1.50 Q

Units Sold (Q)	Sales Revenue	Total Operating Costs	Operating Profit (EBIT)
20,000	$ 40,000	$ 50,000	($10,000)
40,000	80,000	80,000	0
60,000	120,000	110,000	10,000
80,000	160,000	140,000	20,000
100,000	200,000	170,000	30,000
120,000	240,000	200,000	40,000
200,000	400,000	320,000	80,000

Firm B

Selling price = $2
Fixed costs = $40,000
Variable costs = $1.20 Q

Units Sold (Q)	Sales Revenue	Total Operating Costs	Operating Profit (EBIT)
20,000	$ 40,000	$ 64,000	($24,000)
40,000	80,000	88,000	(8,000)
60,000	120,000	112,000	8,000
80,000	160,000	136,000	24,000
100,000	200,000	160,000	40,000
120,000	240,000	184,000	56,000
200,000	400,000	280,000	120,000

Firm C

Selling price = $2
Fixed costs = $60,000
Variable costs = $1 Q

Units Sold (Q)	Sales Revenue	Total Operating Costs	Operating Profit (EBIT)
20,000	$ 40,000	$ 80,000	($40,000)
40,000	80,000	100,000	(20,000)
60,000	120,000	120,000	0
80,000	160,000	140,000	20,000
100,000	200,000	160,000	40,000
120,000	240,000	180,000	60,000
200,000	400,000	260,000	140,000

A or Firm B. Once Firm C reaches its breakeven point, however, its profits rise faster than do those of the other firms.

Each firm's use of operating leverage can have a great impact on its average cost per unit. When only 40,000 units are sold, the average cost per unit of production for each firm (calculated by dividing total costs by the 40,000 units sold) is highest for Firm C and lowest for Firm A. The reverse holds true when output rises to 200,000 units.

	Average Cost Per Unit	
	40,000 Units	**200,000 Units**
Firm A	$2.00	$1.60
Firm B	2.20	1.40
Firm C	2.50	1.30

These results have important implications. At a high volume of operations, say 200,000 units per period, Firm C has a substantial cost savings over the other two firms, particularly over Firm A. Firm C could cut the price of its product to $1.50 per unit and still have a profit margin in excess of 13 percent ($0.20/ $1.50); at that same price level, Firm A would be losing 10 cents on each unit produced.

The competitive advantage of high-volume, low-unit-cost operations may be made clear by an actual example. IBM introduced its personal computer (the PC) in the early 1980s. Less than 10 years later, volume was up to 9 million units per year. Because of the low costs associated with higher volumes, IBM had been able to cut PC prices by 70 percent, in spite of continued general inflation. Those price cuts put great pressure on IBM's low-volume, high-cost competitors, driving some of them out of business and further increasing IBM's market position, sales volume, and total profits. This example demonstrates the extreme importance of the relationship between market position, volume, costs, and profits, and the need to take this relationship into account in strategic planning. High-cost, low-volume producers have a hard time surviving against low-cost, high-volume competitors.

Degree of Operating Leverage

degree of operating leverage (DOL)

The percentage change in EBIT resulting from a given percentage change in sales.

Operating leverage can be defined more precisely in terms of the way a given change in volume affects earnings before interest and taxes (EBIT). To measure the effect of a change in volume on profitability, we calculate the **degree of operating leverage (DOL)**, defined as the percentage change in EBIT (or operating income) associated with a given percentage change in sales:

$$\text{DOL} = \frac{\text{Percentage change in EBIT}}{\text{Percentage change in sales}} = \frac{\dfrac{\Delta \text{EBIT}}{\text{EBIT}}}{\dfrac{\Delta Q}{Q}}. \qquad (8\text{-}5)$$

In effect, the DOL is an index number which measures the effect of a change in sales on operating income or EBIT. For Firm B in Figure 8-3, the degree of operating leverage (DOL_B) for a change in units of output from 100,000 to 120,000 is 2.0:

$$DOL_B = \frac{\frac{\$56,000 - \$40,000}{\$40,000}}{\frac{120,000 - 100,000}{100,000}} = \frac{\frac{\$16,000}{\$40,000}}{\frac{20,000}{100,000}}$$

$$= \frac{40\%}{20\%} = 2.0.$$

The degree of operating leverage can also be calculated as follows:[2]

$$DOL_Q = \text{Degree of operating leverage at Point Q}$$
$$= \frac{Q(P - V)}{Q(P - V) - F}, \tag{8-6}$$

or, based on dollar sales rather than units,

$$DOL_S = \frac{S - VC}{S - VC - F}. \tag{8-6a}$$

Here Q is the initial units of output, P is the average sales price per unit of output, V is the variable cost per unit, F is fixed operating costs, S is initial sales in dollars, and VC is total variable costs. Equation 8-6 is normally used to analyze a single product, such as IBM's PC, whereas Equation 8-6a is used to evaluate an entire firm with many types of products and, hence, for which "quantity in units" and "sales price" are not meaningful.

---

[2]Equation 8-6 is developed from Equation 8-5 as follows. The change in units of output is defined as ΔQ. Since both price and fixed costs are constant, the change in EBIT is $\Delta Q(P - V)$, where P is the price per unit and V is the variable cost per unit. The initial EBIT is $Q(P - V) - F$, so the percentage change in EBIT is

$$\% \Delta EBIT = \frac{\Delta Q(P - V)}{Q(P - V) - F}.$$

The percentage change in output is $\Delta Q/Q$, so the ratio of the percentage change in EBIT to the percentage change in output is

$$DOL = \frac{\frac{\Delta Q(P - V)}{Q(P - V) - F}}{\frac{\Delta Q}{Q}} = \left(\frac{\Delta Q(P - V)}{Q(P - V) - F}\right)\left(\frac{Q}{\Delta Q}\right)$$

$$= \frac{Q(P - V)}{Q(P - V) - F}. \tag{8-6}$$

For Firm B, we can calculate the degree of operating leverage at 100,000 units, using either Equation 8-6 or 8-6a, as 2.0:

$$\text{DOL}_B = \frac{100,000\,(\$2.00 - \$1.20)}{100,000\,(\$2.00 - \$1.20) - \$40,000} \tag{8-6}$$

$$= \frac{\$200,000 - \$120,000}{\$200,000 - \$120,000 - \$40,000}$$

$$= \frac{\$80,000}{\$40,000}$$

$$= 2.0,$$

or

$$\text{DOL}_B = \frac{\$200,000 - \$120,000}{\$200,000 - \$120,000 - \$40,000} \tag{8-6a}$$

$$= \frac{\$80,000}{\$40,000}$$

$$= 2.0,$$

with both equations producing the same value found using Equation 8-5.

The DOL of 2.0 indicates that an X percent increase in sales will produce a 2X percent increase in EBIT or operating income. For example, if units sold increase by, say, 20 percent, from 100,000 to 120,000 units, operating profits will increase by $2.0 \times 20\% = 40\%$. This can be confirmed by reference to Firm B's tabular data in Figure 8-3 and noting that $(1 + 40\%) \times \$40,000 = 1.40 \times \$40,000 = \$56,000$.

It should also be noted that the degree of operating leverage for a given firm is specific to the initial sales level. In our example, we calculated DOL_B for Firm B at a sales level of 100,000 units. Had we examined DOL_B at sales of 60,000 units, DOL_B would have been 6.0:

$$\text{DOL}_B = \frac{\$120,000 - \$72,000}{\$120,000 - \$72,000 - \$40,000}$$

$$= 6.0.$$

Thus, from a base of 60,000 units, a 33.3 percent increase in sales, from 60,000 to 80,000 units, would have led to a $6 \times 33.3\% = 200\%$ increase in operating profits, or from $8,000 to $8,000 + 2.0(\$8,000) = \$24,000$.

In general, if a firm is operating at close to its breakeven level, the degree of operating leverage will be high, but DOL declines the higher the base level of sales is above breakeven sales. Looking back at Firm B's tabular data in Figure 8-3, we see that the company's breakeven point is at sales of 50,000 units or $100,000. At that level, DOL_B is infinite:

$$\text{DOL}_B = \frac{\$100,000 - \$60,000}{\$100,000 - \$60,000 - \$40,000}$$

$$= \frac{\$40,000}{0} = \text{undefined but} \approx \text{infinity.}$$

When evaluated at higher and higher sales levels, DOL_B progressively declines.

Using Equation 8-6, the degree of operating leverage at 100,000 units is 1.67 for Firm A and 2.5 for Firm C. Thus, for a 10 percent change in sales, Firm

A, the company with the least operating leverage, will experience a profit gain of only 16.7 percent, while Firm C, the one with the most leverage, will enjoy a 25 percent profit gain. Clearly, the profits of Firm C, which has higher fixed costs and a higher degree of operating leverage, are more sensitive to changes in sales volume than are those of Firm A, with its lower fixed costs and lower DOL. *Thus, the higher the degree of operating leverage, the more profits will fluctuate, in both an upward and a downward direction, in response to changes in sales volume.*

A firm's degree of operating leverage has a number of important implications. First, Firm C's high degree of operating leverage suggests that it could make gains from increasing its sales volume even if it had to lower its price to do so. Suppose Firm C could increase its quantity sold from 100,000 units to 120,000 units by cutting the price per unit from $2 to $1.90. Its EBIT would then rise from $40,000 to $48,000:

$$EBIT = PQ - VQ - F \qquad (8\text{-}7)$$

$$= \$1.90(120,000) - \$1(120,000) - \$60,000$$
$$= \$228,000 - \$120,000 - \$60,000$$
$$= \$48,000.$$

Thus, Firm C could increase its earnings from operations from $40,000 at a volume of 100,000 units to $48,000 at a volume of 120,000 units by lowering its price from $2.00 to $1.90. This demonstrates that a firm with a high degree of operating leverage and consequently low variable costs per unit, like IBM, will be inclined to follow an aggressive price policy, particularly if its competitors have higher costs and thus cannot respond to price cuts.

At the same time, though, Firm C's high degree of operating leverage also indicates that the company would be subject to large swings in profits if its volume fluctuates. Thus, if Firm C's industry is one whose sales are greatly affected by changes in the overall level of economic activity (as, for example, such durable goods industries as machine tools, steel, and autos are), then its profits would be subject to wide fluctuations. Hence, although Firm C's profit potential is increased by its greater use of operating leverage, the riskiness of its earnings stream is also increased.

 Self-Test Questions

What does the term "high degree of operating leverage" imply, and what are some implications of having a high degree of operating leverage?

Give the general equation used to calculate the degree of operating leverage.

What is the association between the concepts of breakeven and operating leverage?

CASH BREAKEVEN ANALYSIS

cash breakeven point (Q$_{CBE}$)
The breakeven point when noncash items are subtracted from fixed costs.

Because some of the firm's fixed costs are noncash outlays, it is often useful for management to know what the **cash breakeven point** is. The cash breakeven chart for Firm B is shown in Figure 8-4, which was constructed on the assump-

Figure 8-4   ▪   **Cash Breakeven Analysis for Firm B**

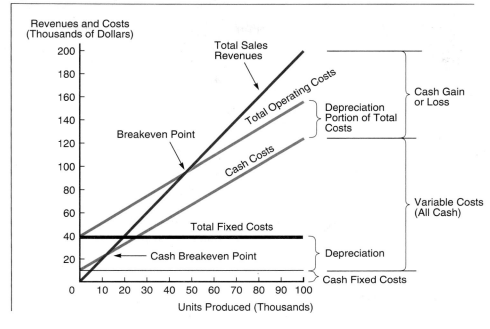

tion that $30,000 of the fixed costs from the previous illustration are depreciation charges and, therefore, are noncash outlays. Fixed cash outlays, then, are only $10,000, resulting in a cash breakeven point of 12,500 units rather than the previous 50,000 units operating income breakeven point.

An equation for the cash breakeven point can be derived from the equation for the operating income breakeven point. The only change required is to reduce fixed costs by the amount of noncash outlays:

$$Q_{CBE} = \frac{F - \text{Noncash outlays}}{P - V}. \tag{8-8}$$

For Firm B,

$$Q_{CBE} = \frac{\$40,000 - \$30,000}{\$0.80}$$

$$= 12,500 \text{ units.}$$

If noncash outlays are a large percentage of total fixed costs, the cash breakeven point will be much lower than the operating income breakeven point.

Cash breakeven analysis does not fully represent cash flows; for this a cash budget is required. However, cash breakeven analysis is useful in providing a general picture of the flow of funds from operations. A firm may incur a level of fixed costs that will result in losses during business downswings but in large profits during upswings. If cash outlays are small, then even during periods of loss the firm may still be able to operate above the cash breakeven point. If the risk of insolvency (in the sense of being unable to meet cash obligations) is small, a firm may be willing to increase its use of operating leverage in the hopes of earning higher profits. A firm with a high cash breakeven point, however, could not risk using a high degree of operating leverage without seriously exposing the firm to the possibility of bankruptcy.

⁇ *Self-Test Questions*

Differentiate between the equations used to calculate the operating income breakeven point and the cash breakeven point.

Why would a firm want to calculate its cash breakeven point?

THE CASH BUDGET

cash budget

A schedule showing cash flows (receipts, disbursements, and cash balances) for a firm over a specified period.

The firm estimates its needs for cash as a part of its general budgeting, or forecasting, process. First, it forecasts both fixed asset and inventory requirements, along with the times when payments must be made. This information is combined with projections about the delay in collecting accounts receivable, tax payment dates, dividend and interest payment dates, and so on. All of this information is summarized in the **cash budget,** which shows the firm's projected cash inflows and outflows over some specified period. Generally, firms use a monthly cash budget forecasted over the next year plus a more detailed daily or weekly cash budget for the coming month. The monthly cash budgets are used for planning purposes and the daily or weekly budgets for actual cash control.

The cash budget provides much more detailed information concerning a firm's future cash flows than do the forecasted financial statements. Back in Chapter 7, we developed Allied Food Products' 1993 forecasted financial statements. Allied's projected 1993 sales were $3,300 million, resulting in a net cash flow from operations of $162 million. When all expenditures and financing flows are considered, Allied's cash account is projected to increase by $1 million in 1993. Does this mean that Allied will not have to worry about cash shortages during 1993? To answer this question, we must construct Allied's cash budget for 1993.

To simplify the example, we will only consider Allied's cash budget for the last half of 1993. Further, we will not list every cash flow that is expected to occur but rather focus on the operating flows. Allied's sales peak is in September, shortly after the majority of its raw food inputs have been harvested. All sales are made on terms that allow a 2 percent cash discount for payments made within 10 days, and, if the discount is not taken, the full amount is due in 40 days. However, like most companies, Allied finds that some of its customers delay payment up to 90 days. Experience has shown that payment on 20 percent of Allied's dollar sales is made during the month in which the sale is made—these are the discount sales. On 70 percent of sales, payment is made during the month immediately following the month of sale, and payment is made on 10 percent of sales in the second month following the month of sale.

The costs to Allied of foodstuffs, spices, preservatives, and packaging materials average 70 percent of the sales prices of the finished products. These purchases are generally made one month before the firm expects to sell the finished products, but Allied's purchase terms with its suppliers allow it to delay payments for 30 days. Accordingly, if July sales are forecasted at $300 million, then purchases during June will amount to $210 million, and this amount will actually be paid in July.

target cash balance

The desired cash balance that a firm plans to maintain in order to conduct business.

Such other cash expenditures as wages and rent are also built into the cash budget, and Allied must make estimated tax payments of $30 million on September 15 and $20 million on December 15, while a $100 million payment for a new plant must be made in October. Assuming that Allied's **target cash balance** is $10 million and that it projects $15 million to be on hand on July 1, 1993, what will the firm's monthly cash surpluses or shortfalls be for the period from July to December?[3]

The monthly cash flows are shown in Table 8-2. Section I of the table provides a worksheet for calculating both collections on sales and payments on purchases. Line 1 gives the sales forecast for the period from May through December. (May and June sales are necessary to determine collections for July and August.) Next, Lines 2 through 5 show cash collections. Line 2 shows that 20 percent of the sales during any given month are collected during that month. Customers who pay in the first month, however, typically take the discount, so the cash collected in the month of sale is reduced by 2 percent; for example, collections during July for the $300 million of sales in that month will be 20 percent times sales less the 2 percent discount $= (0.2)(0.98)(\$300) \approx \$59$ million. Line 3 shows the collections on the previous month's sales, or 70 percent of sales in the preceding month; for example, in July, 70 percent of the $250 million June sales, or $175 million, will be collected. Line 4 gives collections from sales two months earlier, or 10 percent of sales in that month; for example, the July collections for May sales are $(0.10)(\$200) = \$20$ million. The collections during each month are summed and shown on Line 5; thus, the July collections represent 20 percent of July sales (minus the discount) plus 70 percent of June sales plus 10 percent of May sales, or $254 million in total.

Next, payments for purchases of raw materials are shown. July sales are forecasted at $300 million, so Allied will purchase $210 million of materials in June (Line 6) and pay for these purchases in July (Line 7). Similarly, Allied will purchase $280 million of materials in July to meet August's forecasted sales of $400 million.

With Section I completed, Section II can be constructed. Cash from collections is shown on Line 8. Lines 9 through 14 list payments made during each month, and these payments are summed on Line 15. The difference between cash receipts and cash payments (Line 8 minus Line 15) is the net cash gain or loss during the month; for July there is a net cash loss of $11 million, as shown on Line 16.

In Section III, we first determine Allied's cash balance at the start of each month, assuming no borrowing is done; this is shown on Line 17. We assume that Allied will have $15 million on hand on July 1. The beginning cash balance (Line 17) is then added to the net cash gain or loss during the month (Line 16) to obtain the cumulative cash that would be on hand if no financing were done

---

[3]Setting the target cash balance is an important part of cash management. We will discuss this topic later, in Chapter 10.

Table 8-2 ▪ **Allied Food Products: Cash Budget (Millions of Dollars)**

	May	Jun	Jul	Aug	Sep	Oct	Nov	Dec
I. Collections and Purchases Worksheet								
(1) Sales (gross)[a]	$200	$250	$300	$400	$500	$350	$250	$200
Collections:								
(2) During month of sale: (0.2)(0.98)(month's sales)			59	78	98	69	49	39
(3) During first month after sale: 0.7 (previous month's sales)			175	210	280	350	245	175
(4) During second month after sale: 0.1 (sales 2 months ago)			20	25	30	40	50	35
(5) Total collections (2 + 3 + 4)			$254	$313	$408	$459	$344	$249
Purchases:								
(6) 0.7 (next month's sales)		$210	$280	$350	$245	$175	$140	
(7) Payments (1-month lag)			$210	$280	$350	$245	$175	$140
II. Cash Gain or Loss for Month								
(8) Collections (from Section I)			$254	$313	$408	$459	$344	$249
(9) Payments for purchases (from Section I)			$210	$280	$350	$245	$175	$140
(10) Wages and salaries			30	40	50	40	30	30
(11) Rent			15	15	15	15	15	15
(12) Other expenses			10	15	20	15	10	10
(13) Taxes					30			20
(14) Payment for plant construction						100		
(15) Total payments			$265	$350	$465	$415	$230	$215
(16) Net cash gain (loss) during month (Line 8 − Line 15)			($ 11)	($ 37)	($ 57)	$ 44	$114	$ 34
III. Cash Surplus or Loan Requirement								
(17) Cash at start of month if no borrowing is done[b]			$ 15	$ 4	($ 33)	($ 90)	($ 46)	$ 68
(18) Cumulative cash (cash at start, + gain or − loss = Line 16 + Line 17)			$ 4	($ 33)	($ 90)	($ 46)	$ 68	$102
(19) Target cash balance			10	10	10	10	10	10
(20) Cumulative surplus cash or loans outstanding to maintain $10 target cash balance: (Line 18 − Line 19)[c]			($ 6)	($ 43)	($100)	($ 56)	$ 58	$ 92

[a]Although the budget period is July through December, sales and purchases data for May and June are needed to determine collections and payments during July and August.

[b]The amount shown on Line 17 for July, the $15 balance (in millions), is assumed to be on hand initially. The values shown for each of the following months on Line 17 are equal to the cumulative cash as shown on Line 18 for the preceding month; for example, the $4 shown on Line 17 for August is taken from Line 18 in the July column.

[c]When the target cash balance of $10 (Line 19) is deducted from the cumulative cash balance (Line 18), a resulting negative figure on Line 20 represents a required loan, whereas a positive figure represents surplus cash. Loans are required from July through October, and surpluses are expected during November and December. Note also that firms can borrow or pay off loans on a daily basis, so the $6 borrowed during July would be done on a daily basis, as needed, and during October the $100 loan that existed at the beginning of the month would be reduced daily to the $56 ending balance, which in turn would be completely paid off during November.

(Line 18); at the end of July, Allied forecasts a cumulative cash balance of $4 million in the absence of borrowing.

The target cash balance, $10 million, is then subtracted from the cumulative cash balance to determine the firm's borrowing requirements, shown in parentheses, or its surplus cash. Because Allied expects to have cumulative cash, as shown on Line 18, of only $4 million in July, it will have to borrow $6 million to bring the cash account up to the target balance of $10 million. Assuming that this amount is indeed borrowed, loans outstanding will total $6 million at the end of July. (We assume that Allied did not have any loans outstanding on July 1 because its beginning cash balance exceeded the target balance.) The cash surplus or required loan balance is given on Line 20; a positive value indicates a cash surplus, whereas a negative value indicates a loan requirement. Note that the surplus cash or loan requirement shown on Line 20 is a *cumulative amount*. Thus, Allied must borrow $6 million in July; it has a cash shortfall during August of $37 million as reported on Line 16, so its total loan requirement at the end of August is $6 + $37 = $43 million, as reported on Line 20. Allied's arrangement with the bank permits it to increase its outstanding loans on a daily basis, up to a prearranged maximum, just as you could increase the amount you owe on a credit card. Allied will use any surplus funds it generates to pay off its loans, and because the loan can be paid down at any time, on a daily basis, the firm will never have both a cash surplus and an outstanding loan balance.

This same procedure is used in the following months. Sales will peak in September, accompanied by increased payments for purchases, wages, and other items. Receipts from sales will also go up, but the firm will still be left with a $57 million net cash outflow during the month. The total loan requirement at the end of September will hit a peak of $100 million, the cumulative cash plus the target cash balance. This amount is also equal to the $43 million needed at the end of August plus the $57 million cash deficit for September.

Sales, purchases, and payments for past purchases will fall sharply in October, but collections will be the highest of any month because they will reflect the high September sales. As a result, Allied will enjoy a healthy $44 million net cash gain during October. This net gain can be used to pay off borrowings, so loans outstanding will decline by $44 million, to $56 million.

Allied will have an even larger cash surplus in November, which will permit it to pay off all of its loans. In fact, the company is expected to have $58 million in surplus cash by the month's end, and another cash surplus in December will swell the excess cash to $92 million. With such a large amount of unneeded funds, Allied's treasurer will certainly want to invest in interest-bearing securities or to put the funds to use in some other way. Various types of investments into which Allied might put its excess funds are discussed in Chapter 10.

Before concluding our discussion of the cash budget, we should make some additional points:

1. For simplicity, our illustrative budget for Allied omitted many important cash flows that are anticipated for 1993, such as dividends, proceeds from stock and bond sales, and additional fixed asset additions. Some of these are projected to occur in the first half of the year, but those that are projected for the July–December period could easily be added to the exam-

ple. The final cash budget should contain all projected cash inflows and outflows.

2. Our cash budget example does not reflect interest on loans or income from investing surplus cash. This refinement could easily be added.

3. If cash inflows and outflows are not uniform during the month, we could seriously understate the firm's peak financing requirements. The data in Table 8-2 show the situation expected on the last day of each month, but on any given day during the month it could be quite different. For example, if all payments had to be made on the fifth of each month, but collections came in uniformly throughout the month, the firm would need to borrow much larger amounts than those shown in Table 8-2. In this case, we would have to prepare a cash budget identifying requirements on a daily basis.

4. Since depreciation is a noncash charge, it does not appear on the cash budget other than through its effect on taxable income, hence on taxes paid.

5. Since the cash budget represents a forecast, all the values in the table are *expected* values. If actual sales, purchases, and so on are different from the forecasted levels, then the projected cash deficits and surpluses will also be incorrect. Thus, Allied might end up needing to borrow larger amounts than are indicated on Line 20, so it should arrange a line of credit in excess of that amount. For example, if Allied's monthly sales are only 80 percent of their forecasted levels, the firm's maximum cumulative borrowing requirement will turn out to be $126 million, a 26 percent increase from the expected cash budget.

6. Computerized spreadsheet programs such as *Lotus 1-2-3* are particularly well suited for constructing and analyzing cash budgets, especially with respect to the sensitivity of cash flows to changes in sales levels, collection periods, and the like. We could change any assumption, say the projected monthly sales or the time that customers pay, and the cash budget would automatically and instantly be recalculated. This would show us exactly how the firm's borrowing requirements would change if various other things changed. Also, with a computer model, it is easy to add features like interest paid on loans, interest earned on marketable securities, and so on. We have written such a model for the computer-related problem at the end of the chapter.

7. Finally, we should note that the target cash balance probably will be adjusted over time, rising and falling with seasonal patterns and with long-term changes in the scale of the firm's operations. Thus, Allied will probably plan to maintain larger cash balances during August and September than at other times, and, as the company grows, so will its required cash balance. Also, the firm might even set the target cash balance at zero — this could be done if it carried a portfolio of marketable securities which could be sold to replenish the cash account or if it had an arrangement with its bank that permitted it to borrow any funds needed on a daily basis. In that event, the cash budget would simply stop with Line 18, and the amounts on that line would represent projected loans outstanding or surplus cash. Note, though, that most firms would find it difficult to operate with a zero-balance bank account, just as you would, and the costs of such an operation would in most instances offset the costs associated with maintaining a positive cash balance. Therefore, most firms do set a positive target cash balance. Factors that influence the target cash balance are discussed in Chapter 10.

?   *Self-Test Questions*

What is the purpose of a cash budget?

What are the three major sections of a cash budget?

Suppose a firm's cash flows do not occur uniformly throughout the month. What impact might this have on the accuracy of the forecasted borrowing requirements?

How is uncertainty handled in a cash budget?

Is depreciation reflected in a cash budget? Explain.

CONTROL IN MULTIDIVISIONAL COMPANIES

The concepts, techniques, and procedures described thus far in the chapter must be extended when applied to large national and multinational firms. Such corporations have plants and sales offices all across the nation and even around the world. To permit faster decisions and to increase operating efficiency, large firms are generally set up on a decentralized basis. For example, General Electric has established separate divisions for heavy appliances, light appliances, power transformers, fossil fuel generating equipment, nuclear generating equipment, and so on. Each division is defined as a *profit center*, and each has its own plant, equipment, and working capital, as well as a share of such general corporate assets as research labs and headquarters buildings. Further, each division is expected to earn an appropriate return on its operating assets. Corporate headquarters, through its central staff, typically uses a form of the *Du Pont* system to control the various divisions. The Du Pont system was introduced in Chapter 2, and here we expand our discussion to show how this system can be used in controlling the firm.

Du Pont System of Financial Analysis

As we noted in Chapter 2, the Du Pont system facilitates an integrated analysis of the turnover ratios and the profit margin on sales, and it shows how the various ratios interact to determine the rate of return on assets.

return on assets (ROA) control

The use of the Du Pont system of analysis for divisional control in multidivisional firms.

When the Du Pont system is used for divisional control, the process is often called **return on assets (ROA) control**, where return is measured by operating income, or earnings before interest and taxes (EBIT). Target levels for ROA are established, and actual ROAs are compared with target levels to see just how well each division is operating. If problems arise, corporate headquarters will investigate and take corrective action, including firing the managers of poorly performing divisions. Superior performers are rewarded with bonuses and stock options. However, for meaningful comparisons, a corporation that uses ROA control must take into account certain differences among divisions and adjust for them. For example, some divisions might have older fixed assets which were acquired at pre-inflation prices, and much of their equipment might have been depreciated down to a low book value yet still be serviceable. This division might well have a higher rate of return than another division with newer assets even though both divisions are equally well-managed. If management believes the differences in asset book values are great enough to warrant an adjustment, earnings figures may be calculated on the basis of replacement cost depreciation, and asset values may be increased to a current cost basis to put the divisions on a comparable basis.[4]

If a particular division's ROA falls below a target figure, the centralized corporate staff will help the division's own financial staff trace back through the Du Pont system to determine the cause of its substandard performance. Each division manager is judged by his or her division's ROA and rewarded or penalized accordingly. Division managers are thus motivated to keep their ROAs up to the target level.

In addition to its use in managerial control, ROA can be used to allocate funds to the various divisions. The firm as a whole has financial resources—cash flows from retained earnings, from depreciation, and from external financing. The available capital can be allocated on the basis of the divisional ROAs, with those divisions having the highest ROAs receiving more funds than those with lower ROAs. However, capital budgeting analysis as discussed in Chapter 14 is better for allocating capital than is the use of divisional ROAs.

Pitfalls in the Use of ROA Control

Increasingly, managers are being compensated on some type of performance-based system: They receive a relatively low base salary, but they then receive bonuses or stock options which depend on how well their divisions meet certain stated objectives. One of the most important of those objectives is, generally, their divisions' ROAs. This is quite logical, because the firm's ROA has a major effect on the value of its stock, and the firm's ROA obviously depends on the ROAs of its different divisions.

However, any such control-by-incentive system runs the risk that executives will devise methods for "beating the system," so safeguards are required. Also, since the divisional managers are rewarded on the basis of their ROA performance, maintaining morale makes it essential that managers feel that their divisional ROA targets are reasonable and that earned ROAs do indeed provide an accurate measure of relative performance. But ROA depends on a number of factors in addition to managerial competence, and these factors must be considered when judging performance on an ROA standard. Some of the key factors are listed below.

1. **Depreciation.** ROA is very sensitive to depreciation policy. A division which is currently writing off assets at a relatively rapid rate will have high

---

[4]Replacement cost depreciation is depreciation calculated by dividing the cost that would have to be incurred to replace an asset by the life of the asset. This type of depreciation is not used for taxes or for stockholder reporting, but it is occasionally used for internal management purposes. Depreciation is discussed in Appendix 15A.

current depreciation expenses, a relatively low profit, and hence a lower ROA than a division using a slower depreciation method. Depreciation will be discussed in Appendix 15A.

2. **Book value of assets.** If an older division is using assets that were acquired before the period of rapid inflation in the late 1970s and early 1980s and if these assets have been largely written off, then both its current depreciation charges and its asset base will be low. This will make its ROA high in relation to rapidly growing divisions with newer assets.

transfer price

The price at which goods are transferred between divisions within a firm.

3. **Transfer pricing.** In most corporations, some divisions make sales to other divisions. At General Motors, for example, the Fisher Body Division sells to the Chevrolet Division. In such cases, the price at which goods are transferred between divisions, called the **transfer price**, has a fundamental effect on divisional profits. If the transfer price of auto bodies is set relatively high, then Fisher Body's ROA will be relatively high and Chevrolet's will be relatively low.

4. **Time periods.** Many projects have long gestation periods, during which expenditures must be made for research and development, for plant construction, for market development, and so on. Such expenditures add to the asset base without a commensurate increase in profits for several years. During this period, a division's ROA can be seriously reduced, and without proper adjustments, its managers might be improperly penalized. This, in turn, would lead division managers to seek short-term, fast payback projects. Given the frequency of personnel transfers in larger corporations, it is easy to see how the timing problem, if it is not recognized and taken into account, would make managers resist taking on the long-term projects even when such investments are in the best interests of the firm.

5. **Industry conditions.** If one division is operating in an industry where conditions are favorable and rates of return are high while another is in an industry that is suffering from excessive competition, this factor may cause the favored division to look good and the unfavored one to look bad, quite apart from any differences in the abilities of their managers. For example, Boeing's defense electronics division could hardly have been expected to perform as well as its commercial aircraft division in 1992, when the entire defense industry was suffering severe problems but aircraft sales were soaring. Therefore, external conditions must be taken into account when appraising ROA performance.

Because of these factors, a division's ROA must be supplemented with other criteria when evaluating performance. For example, its growth rate in sales, its profit margins, and its ROA should be compared with other firms in its own industry, as well as with its sister divisions. As with most other tools, ROA control can be helpful if used properly, but it can also be destructive if misused.

? *Self-Test Question*

Identify and explain some key factors that must be considered when judging performance on an ROA standard.

SUMMARY

In this chapter we considered several planning and control systems used by financial managers. The key concepts covered are listed below.

- **Financial planning** involves making projections of sales, income, and assets based on alternative production and marketing strategies and then deciding how to meet the forecasted financial requirements.

- **Financial control** deals with the feedback and adjustment process that is required (1) to ensure that plans are followed or (2) to modify existing plans in response to changes in the operating environment.

- **Breakeven analysis** is a method of determining the point at which sales will just cover costs, and it shows the magnitude of the firm's operating profits or losses if sales exceed or fall below that point.

- The **breakeven point** is the sales volume at which total operating costs equal total revenues and operating income (EBIT) equals zero. The equation used to calculate the breakeven point is

$$Q_{BE} = \frac{F}{P - V}.$$

- **Operating leverage** is a measure of the extent to which fixed costs are used in a firm's operations. A firm with a high percentage of fixed costs is said to have a high *degree of operating leverage.*

- The **degree of operating leverage (DOL)** shows how a change in sales will affect operating income. Whereas *breakeven analysis* emphasizes the volume of sales the firm needs to be profitable, the *degree of operating leverage* measures how sensitive the firm's profits are to changes in the volume of sales. The equation used to calculate the DOL is

$$DOL = \frac{Q(P - V)}{Q(P - V) - F}.$$

- A **cash breakeven point** can be calculated; it is the breakeven point when noncash items are subtracted from fixed costs. The equation is

$$Q_{CBE} = \frac{F - \text{Noncash outlays}}{P - V}.$$

- The *budgeting process* provides a detailed plan of how funds will be spent. A **budget** is a plan stated in terms of specific expenditures for specific purposes, and it is used for both planning and control.

- A **cash budget** is a schedule showing projected cash inflows and outflows over a specified period. The cash budget is used to determine when the firm will have cash surpluses and shortfalls, and it thus can help management plan to invest surpluses or to finance shortfalls.

- **Return on assets (ROA) control** refers to the use of the Du Pont system for divisional control.

Although the entire budget system is vital to corporate management, the cash budget is especially important to the financial manager. The cash budget is, in fact, the single most important tool for making short-run financial forecasts.

If used properly, it can pinpoint the amount of funds that will be needed, when they will be needed, and when cash flows will be available to retire any loans the company has taken out.

As a firm becomes larger, it becomes necessary to decentralize operations. However, decentralized operations still require some degree of centralized control, and the principal tool used for such control is the ROA method. There are potential pitfalls with ROA control, but if it is used properly, then overall operations can be improved.

Questions

8-1   What benefits can be derived from breakeven analysis? What are some problems with breakeven analysis?

8-2   Explain how profits or losses will be magnified for a firm with high operating leverage as opposed to a firm with lower operating leverage.

8-3   What data are necessary to construct a breakeven chart?

8-4   What would be the effect of each of the following on a firm's breakeven point?
a. An increase in the sales price with no change in unit costs.
b. A reduction in variable labor costs; other things are held constant.

8-5   Why is a cash budget important even when there is plenty of cash in the bank?

8-6   What is the difference between the projected balance sheet method used for forecasting financial requirements and the cash budget? How might they be used together?

8-7   Assume that a firm is developing its long-run financial plan. What period should this plan cover—one month, six months, one year, three years, five years, or some other period? Justify your answer.

8-8   Would a detailed budget be more important to a large, multidivisional firm or to a small, single-product, owner-managed firm? Why?

8-9   Assume that your uncle is a major stockholder in a multidivisional firm that uses a naive ROA criterion for evaluating divisional managers and that bases managers' salaries in large part on this evaluation. You can have the job of division manager in any division you choose. If you are a salary maximizer, what divisional characteristics would you seek? If, because of your good performance, you become president of the firm, what changes would you make?

Self-Test Problems   (Solutions Appear in Appendix B)

ST-1
Key terms

Define each of the following terms:
a. Financial planning; financial control
b. Breakeven analysis; breakeven point, Q_{BE}; cash breakeven point, Q_{CBE}
c. Operating leverage; degree of operating leverage (DOL)
d. Budget; cash budget; target cash balance
e. ROA control
f. Transfer price

ST-2
Operating leverage and breakeven analysis

Olinde Electronics Inc. produces stereo components which sell for P = $100. Olinde's fixed costs are $200,000; 5,000 components are produced and sold each year; EBIT is currently $50,000; and Olinde's assets (all equity financed) are $500,000. Olinde estimates that it can change its production process, adding $400,000 to investment and $50,000 to fixed operating costs. This change will (1) reduce variable costs per unit by $10 and (2) increase output by 2,000 units, but (3) the sales price on all units will have to be lowered to $95 to permit sales of the additional output. Olinde has tax loss carry-forwards that cause its tax rate to be zero. Olinde uses no debt, and its average cost of capital is 10 percent.

a. Should Olinde make the change?

b. Would Olinde's degree of operating leverage increase or decrease if it made the change? What about its breakeven point?

c. Suppose Olinde were unable to raise additional equity financing and had to borrow the $400,000 to make the investment at an interest rate of 10 percent. Use the Du Pont equation to find the expected ROA of the investment. Should Olinde make the change if debt financing must be used?

Problems

8-1
Breakeven analysis

The Weaver Watch Company manufactures a line of ladies' watches which is sold through discount houses. Each watch is sold for $25; the fixed costs are $140,000 for 30,000 watches or less; variable costs are $15 per watch.

a. What is the firm's gain or loss at sales of 8,000 watches? Of 18,000 watches?

b. What is the breakeven point? Illustrate by means of a chart.

c. What is Weaver's degree of operating leverage at sales of 8,000 units? Of 18,000 units? (Hint: Use Equation 8-6 to solve this problem.)

d. What happens to the breakeven point if the selling price rises to $31? What is the significance of the change to the financial manager?

e. What happens to the breakeven point if the selling price rises to $31 but variable costs rise to $23 a unit?

8-2
Breakeven analysis

The following relationships exist for Dellva Industries, a manufacturer of electronic components. Each unit of output is sold for $45; the fixed costs are $175,000, of which $110,000 are annual depreciation charges; variable costs are $20 per unit.

a. What is the firm's gain or loss at sales of 5,000 units? Of 12,000 units?

b. What is the operating income breakeven point?

c. What is the cash breakeven point?

d. Assume Dellva is operating at a level of 4,000 units. Are creditors likely to seek the liquidation of the company if it is slow in paying its bills?

8-3
Cash budgeting

Patricia Smith recently leased space in the Southside Mall and opened a new business, Smith's Coin Shop. Business has been good, but Smith has frequently run out of cash. This has necessitated late payment on certain orders, which in turn is beginning to cause a problem with suppliers. Smith plans to borrow from the bank to have cash ready as needed, but first she needs a forecast of just how much she must borrow. Accordingly, she has asked you to prepare a cash budget for the critical period around Christmas, when needs will be especially high.

Sales are made on a cash basis only. Smith's purchases must be paid for during the following month. Smith pays herself a salary of $4,800 per month, and the rent is $2,000 per month. In addition, she must make a tax payment of $12,000 in December. The current cash on hand (on December 1) is $400, but Smith has agreed to maintain an average bank balance of $6,000—this is her target cash balance. (Disregard till cash, which is insignificant because Smith keeps only a small amount on hand in order to lessen the chances of robbery.)

The estimated sales and purchases for December, January, and February are shown below. Purchases during November amounted to $140,000.

	Sales	Purchases
December	$160,000	$40,000
January	40,000	40,000
February	60,000	40,000

a. Prepare a cash budget for December, January, and February.
b. Now suppose Smith were to start selling on a credit basis on December 1, giving customers 30 days to pay. All customers accept these terms, and all other facts in the problem are unchanged. What would the company's loan requirements be at the end of December in this case? (Hint: The calculations required to answer this question are minimal.)

8-4

Cash budgeting

Carol Moerdyk, owner of Carol's Fashion Designs Inc., is planning to request a line of credit from her bank. She has estimated the following sales forecasts for the firm for parts of 1993 and 1994:

May 1993	$180,000
June	180,000
July	360,000
August	540,000
September	720,000
October	360,000
November	360,000
December	90,000
January 1994	180,000

Collection estimates obtained from the credit and collection department are as follows: collections within the month of sale, 10 percent; collections the month following the sale, 75 percent; collections the second month following the sale, 15 percent. Payments for labor and raw materials are typically made during the month following the one in which these costs have been incurred. Total labor and raw materials costs are estimated for each month as follows:

May 1993	$ 90,000
June	90,000
July	126,000
August	882,000
September	306,000
October	234,000
November	162,000
December	90,000

General and administrative salaries will amount to approximately $27,000 a month; lease payments under long-term lease contracts will be $9,000 a month; depreciation charges will be $36,000 a month; miscellaneous expenses will be $2,700 a month; income tax payments of $63,000 will be due in both September and December; and a progress payment of $180,000 on a new design studio must be paid in October. Cash on hand on July 1 will amount to $132,000, and a minimum cash balance of $90,000 will be maintained throughout the cash budget period.
a. Prepare a monthly cash budget for the last six months of 1993.
b. Prepare an estimate of the required financing (or excess funds)—that is, the amount of money Carol will need to borrow (or will have available to invest)—for each month during that period.
c. Assume that receipts from sales come in uniformly during the month (that is, cash receipts come in at the rate of ⅟₃₀ each day), but all outflows are paid on the fifth of the month. Will this have an effect on the cash budget—in other words, would the

cash budget you have prepared be valid under these assumptions? If not, what can be done to make a valid estimate of peak financing requirements? No calculations are required, although calculations can be used to illustrate the effects.

d. Carol produces on a seasonal basis, just ahead of sales. Without making any calculations, discuss how the company's current ratio and debt ratio would vary during the year assuming all financial requirements were met by short-term bank loans. Could changes in these ratios affect the firm's ability to obtain bank credit?

8-5
Return on assets control

G. Pogue & Co., is a diversified multinational corporation that produces a wide variety of goods and services, including rubber, soaps, tobacco products, toys, plastics, pollution control equipment, canned food, sugar, motion pictures, and computer software. The corporation's major divisions were brought together in the early 1970s under a decentralized form of management; each division was evaluated in terms of its profitability, efficiency, and return on investments. This decentralized organization was used for approximately 20 years, during which Pogue experienced a high average growth rate in total assets, earnings, and stock prices.

Toward the end of 1991, however, those trends were reversed. The organization was faced with declining earnings, unstable stock prices, and a generally uncertain future. This situation persisted into 1992, but during that year a new president, Herbert Quigley, was appointed by the board of directors. Quigley, who had served for a time on the financial staff of E. I. Du Pont, used the Du Pont system to evaluate the various divisions. All showed definite weaknesses.

Quigley reported to the board that a principal reason for the poor overall performance was a lack of control by central management over each division's activities. He was particularly disturbed by the consistently poor results of the corporation's budgeting procedures. Under those procedures, each division manager drew up a projected budget for the next quarter, along with estimated sales, revenues, and profit; funds were then allocated to the divisions, basically in proportion to their budget requests. However, actual budgets seldom matched the projections and wide discrepancies occurred; this, of course, resulted in a highly inefficient use of capital.

In an attempt to correct the situation, Quigley asked the firm's chief financial officer to draw up a plan to improve the budgeting, planning, and control processes. When the plan was submitted, its basic provisions included the following:

1. To improve the quality of the divisional budgets, the division managers should be informed that the continuance of wide variation between their projected and actual budgets would result in dismissal.

2. A system should be instituted under which funds would be allocated to divisions on the basis of their average return on assets (ROA) during the last four quarters. Since funds were short, divisions with high ROAs would get most of the available money.

3. About half of each division manager's present compensation should be received as salary; the rest should be in the form of a bonus related to the division's average ROA for the quarter.

4. Each division should submit to the central office for approval all capital expenditure requests, production schedules, and price changes. Thus, the company would be recentralized.
   a. (1) Is it reasonable to expect the new procedures to improve the accuracy of budget forecasts?
      (2) Should all divisions be expected to maintain the same degree of accuracy?
      (3) In what other ways might the budgets be made?
   b. (1) What problems would be associated with the use of the ROA criterion in allocating funds among the divisions?

(2) What effect would the period used in computing ROA (that is, one quarter, four quarters, two years, and so on) have on the effectiveness of this method?

(3) What problems might occur in evaluating the ROA in the crude rubber and auto tires divisions? What problems would occur between the sugar products and pollution control equipment divisions?

c. What problems would be associated with rewarding each manager on the basis of the division's ROA?

EXAM-TYPE PROBLEMS

The problems included in this section are set up in such a way that they could be used as multiple-choice exam problems.

8-6
Operating leverage

The Niendorf Corporation produces tea kettles, which it sells for $15 each. Fixed costs are $700,000 for up to 400,000 units of output. Variable costs are $10 per kettle.
a. What is the firm's gain or loss at sales of 125,000 units? Of 175,000 units?
b. What is the breakeven point? Illustrate by means of a chart.
c. What is Niendorf's degree of operating leverage at sales of 125,000 units? Of 150,000 units? Of 175,000 units? (Hint: You may use either Equation 8-6 or 8-6a to solve this problem.)

8-7
Degree of operating leverage

a. Given the following graphs, calculate the total fixed costs, variable costs per unit, and sales price for Firm A. Firm B's fixed costs are $120,000, its variable costs per unit are $4, and its sales price is $8 per unit.
b. Which firm has the higher degree of operating leverage? Explain.
c. At what *sales level,* in units, do both firms earn the same profit?

Breakeven Charts for Problem 8-7

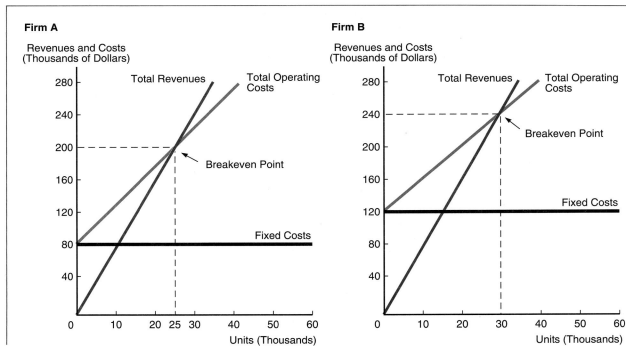

INTEGRATIVE PROBLEM

8-8
Cash budget and
breakeven analysis

Betty Rose, financial manager of Golf World Inc. (GWI), a Washington, D.C.-based chain of golf supply stores, was asked by Kitty Barton, the president, to consider the company's cash and marketable securities position. Currently, GWI has $300,000 of cash and no marketable securities, and Barton wonders if the company needs that much cash, given that cash earns no return.

GWI's business is highly seasonal. Here is a forecast of sales for the last two months of 1992 and the first eight months of 1993, in thousands:

November 1992	$ 500	April	$5,800
December	500	May	3,300
January 1993	200	June	1,000
February	200	July	800
March	3,200	August	1,000

GWI's credit terms allow customers to take a 2 percent discount if they pay within 10 days of the purchase date; otherwise, the full invoice amount is due within 30 days. In the past, 40 percent of the customers have taken the discount and thus paid in the month of the sale, 50 percent have paid the following month, and 10 percent have paid during the second month after the sale. These percentages are expected to continue. Also, GWI purchases goods for resale two months prior to when they should be sold and pays for them the month after receipt, and purchases amount to 75 percent of sales. Thus, the $3,200,000 of goods to be sold in March will be purchased in January at a cost of $3,200,000 (0.75) = $2,400,000, and this amount will be paid in February.

Wages, administrative, and selling expenses are projected at $140,000 per month, and depreciation expenses at $42,500 per month. Quarterly income tax payments of $125,000 must be made in March and June, and $250,000 will be needed in April to pay for the spring advertising campaign. Betty Rose estimates that there will be $300,000 of cash in the bank on January 1.

Part I. Cash budget

As Rose's assistant, you have been asked to answer the following questions.
a. What is financial planning? What is financial control, and what is its relationship to financial planning?
b. What is a budget, and where does it fit into the financial planning process?
c. Prepare a cash budget for the first six months of 1993. Assume that $300,000 of cash will be on hand on January 1 and that Rose wants to begin each subsequent month with $200,000 of cash on hand. What is the maximum cash surplus GWI will enjoy during the period studied? The maximum cash shortfall?
d. (1) Should depreciation expense be explicitly included in the cash budget? Why or why not?
  (2) Suppose the outflows all occur on the 5th day of each month, but the inflows all occur on the 25th day. This situation occurs because of the credit terms used by GWI and its suppliers. How would this affect March's cash budget? What could be done to incorporate such nonuniform flows into the cash budget?
  (3) GWI's only receipts are collections. What are some other types of inflows that could occur? List both fairly regular cash inflows and also some cash inflows that could be forecasted, but which would have to be planned for (negotiated with someone).
  (4) Rose plans to "sweep" any excess cash balances into marketable securities. Further, GWI would have to pay interest on its short-term borrowings. Explain how

these flows could be incorporated into the cash budget. Be specific — say exactly where lines would be added to the budget, exactly what the entries on those lines would be, and how the effects would be carried through the remainder of the statement.

e. We have assumed that all sales are collected and thus that GWI has no bad debts. Is this realistic? If not, how would bad debts be dealt with in a cash budgeting sense? For purposes of this question, assume that 3 percent of sales end up as bad debts. (Hint: Bad debts will affect collections but not purchases.)

f. The cash budget is a *forecast,* so many of the flows are expected values rather than amounts known with certainty. If actual sales, hence collections and production, were different from the forecasted levels, then the forecasted surpluses and deficits would also be incorrect. In words, how would you expect the funds needed or surplus cash position to be affected if sales were to rise or fall 15 percent above or below the levels originally forecasted? How would the company's ability to react in a timely manner to falling sales affect the outcome? How could scenario analysis be used to help forecast the net cash inflows and required beginning-of-month cash balances? Assume zero bad debt losses.

Part II. Breakeven analysis

Kitty Barton has recently come up with the idea that GWI should expand its product lines to include golfing shoes. Kitty has asked Betty Rose to perform a breakeven analysis as a first step in determining whether the company should proceed with the idea. The fixed costs attributed to the golf shoes would be $250,000 (of which $25,000 includes noncash outlays), the average variable cost per unit has been calculated as $35 per unit, and the average price per unit is $50 per unit. As Rose's assistant, you have been asked to answer the following questions.

a. What is breakeven analysis?

b. What is the breakeven point in units and in dollars for the golf shoes?

c. What is meant by the term "cash breakeven point"? Find the cash breakeven point in units and in dollars for the golf shoes.

d. Draw the breakeven chart for the golf shoes.

e. Draw the cash breakeven chart for the golf shoes.

f. As a final task, Rose has asked you to do some analysis on the firm's degree of operating leverage. The firm's total dollar sales for the current year are expected to be $17,500,000, total variable costs are estimated at $11,000,000, and total fixed costs are expected to total $5,000,000.
  (1) What is operating leverage?
  (2) Calculate the firm's degree of operating leverage at the expected sales level using Equation 8-6a.
  (3) What would be GWI's percentage increase in operating profits if sales were expected to increase by 10 percent during the coming year?

COMPUTER-RELATED PROBLEM

Work the problem in this section only if you are using the computer problem diskette.

8-9

Cash budget

Use the model in File C8 to solve this problem.

a. Refer back to Problem 8-4. Suppose that by offering a 2 percent cash discount for paying within the month of sale, the credit manager of Carol's Fashion Designs Inc. has revised the collection percentages to 50 percent, 35 percent, and 15 percent, respectively. How will this affect the loan requirements?

b. Return the payment percentages to their base case values: 10 percent, 75 percent, and 15 percent, respectively, and the discount to zero percent. Now suppose sales fall to only 70 percent of the forecasted level. Production is maintained, so cash out-flows are unchanged. How does this affect Carol's financial requirements?

c. Return sales to the forecasted level (100%), and suppose collections slow down to 3 percent, 10 percent, and 87 percent for the three months, respectively. How does this affect financial requirements? If Carol went to a cash-only sales policy, how would that affect requirements, other things held constant?

Working Capital Management

Chapter 9   Working Capital Policy

Chapter 10   Cash and Marketable Securities Management

Chapter 11   Credit Management

Chapter 12   Inventory Management

Chapter 13   Short-Term Financing

Working Capital Policy

Typically, firms operate to maintain a specified balance between current assets and current liabilities and between sales and each category of current assets. So long as the target balance is maintained, current liabilities can be paid on time, suppliers will continue shipping goods and replenishing inventories, and inventories will be sufficient to meet the sales demand. However, if the financial situation gets out of balance, problems arise and multiply, and a company can quickly go into a downward spiral that leads to bankruptcy.

R. H. Macy & Company, one of the oldest and largest U.S. department store chains, is a case in point. In 1986 Macy's management arranged for the company to "go private" in a leveraged buyout (LBO). The company issued a huge amount of debt, used the proceeds to buy up all the publicly held stock, and left the management group as the owners and the company with a great deal of high-interest debt and relatively little common equity. Management expected sales to grow by 9 percent per year, and they anticipated being able to pay down the debt out of operating cash flows.

Things were going along reasonably well, but then, in 1988, Macy's management entered into a bidding war with Canadian Robert Campeau for Federated Department Stores. In the end, Campeau owned most of Federated (which later went bankrupt), but Macy did acquire two big California retailers, Bullock's and I. Magnin, as well as $1.1 billion of new debt.

Macy's forecast of 9 percent sales growth turned out to be wildly optimistic; 1991 growth was minus 7 percent. As a result, inventories built up, cash flows declined, and Macy began paying its debts late. As the pressure mounted, prices were slashed and inventories were sold off to raise cash, but losses increased, and debts kept piling up. Finally, in early 1992, Macy's management concluded that the company could not continue in business without a complete overhaul. Suppliers looked at those huge current liabilities supported by inadequate cash and other current assets, and many refused to continue shipping the merchandise Macy had to have to stay in business. At that point, the company filed for bankruptcy.

It is not clear what will happen to the Macy organization. We do know, though, that the top managers have been replaced, that thousands of employees have lost their jobs, that the company's creditors can expect to receive less than 50 cents of every dollar that they are owed, and that the stockholders (primarily the managers) will probably be wiped out. You should keep the Macy story in mind as you read this chapter.

Sources: "Cash Pinch Leads Macy to Delay Paying Bills and Plan Other Steps," *The Wall Street Journal*, January 13, 1992; and "Macy Files for Chapter 11, Listing Assets of $4.95 Billion, Liabilities of $5.32 Billion," *The Wall Street Journal*, January 28, 1992.

About 60 percent of a financial manager's time is devoted to working capital management, and many finance students' first assignment on the job will involve working capital. For these reasons, working capital policy and management is an essential topic of study. Chapter 9 provides an overview of working capital policy. Then, Chapter 10 focuses on cash and marketable securities, Chapter 11 covers accounts receivable, Chapter 12 focuses on inventory management, and Chapter 13 covers short-term financing.

WORKING CAPITAL TERMINOLOGY

It is useful to begin the discussion of working capital policy by reviewing some basic definitions and concepts:

working capital
A firm's investment in short-term assets — cash, marketable securities, inventory, and accounts receivable.

net working capital
Current assets minus current liabilities.

1. **Working capital,** sometimes called *gross working capital,* simply refers to current assets.

2. **Net working capital** is defined as current assets minus current liabilities.

3. The *current ratio,* which was discussed in Chapter 2, is calculated by dividing current assets by current liabilities, and it is intended to measure a firm's liquidity. However, a high current ratio does not insure that a firm will have the cash required to meet its needs. If inventories cannot be sold, or if receivables cannot be collected in a timely manner, then the apparent safety reflected in a high current ratio could be illusory.

4. The *quick ratio,* or *acid test,* also attempts to measure liquidity, and it is found by subtracting inventories from current assets and then dividing by current liabilities. The quick ratio removes inventories from current assets because they are the least liquid of current assets, so it is an "acid test" of a company's ability to meet its current obligations.

5. The best and most comprehensive picture of a firm's liquidity position is obtained by examining its *cash budget.* This statement, which forecasts cash inflows and outflows, focuses on what really counts, the firm's ability to generate sufficient cash inflows to meet its required cash outflows. Cash budgeting was discussed in detail in Chapter 8.

6. Working capital policy refers to the firm's basic policies regarding (1) target levels for each category of current assets and (2) how current assets will be financed.

7. *Working capital management* involves the administration, within policy guidelines, of current assets and current liabilities.

working capital policy
Basic policy decisions regarding (1) target levels for each category of current assets and (2) how current assets will be financed.

The term *working capital* originated with the old Yankee peddler, who would load up his wagon with goods and then go off on his route to peddle his wares. The merchandise was called working capital because it was what he actually sold, or "turned over," to produce his profits. The wagon and horse were his fixed assets. He generally owned the horse and wagon, so they were financed with "equity" capital, but he borrowed the funds to buy the merchandise. These borrowings were called *working capital loans,* and they had to be repaid after each trip to demonstrate to the bank that the credit was sound. If the peddler was able to repay the loan, then the bank would make another loan, and banks that followed this procedure were said to be employing sound banking practices.

We must distinguish between those current liabilities which are specifically used to finance current assets and those current liabilities which represent (1) current maturities of long-term debt; (2) financing associated with a construction program which will, after the project is completed, be funded with the proceeds of a long-term security issue; or (3) the use of short-term debt to finance fixed assets.

Table 9-1 contains three balance sheets for Allied Food Products. According to the definitions given, Allied's December 31, 1992, working capital was $1,000 million, and its net working capital was $1,000 − $310 = $690 million. Also, Allied's year-end 1992 current ratio was 3.23 and its quick ratio was 1.24.

Note that the total current liabilities of $310 million at the end of 1992 includes the current portion of long-term debt, which was $20 million. This account is unaffected by changes in working capital policy since it is a function of past long-term debt financing decisions. Thus, even though we define long-term debt coming due in the next accounting period as a current liability, it is not a working capital decision variable. Similarly, if Allied were building a new canning factory and initially financed the construction with a short-term loan which would be replaced later with mortgage bonds, the construction loan would not be considered part of working capital management. Although such accounts are not part of Allied's working capital decision process, they cannot be ignored, and they must be taken into account when Allied's managers construct the cash budget and assess the firm's liquidity.

Self-Test Questions

Why is the quick ratio also called an acid test?

Where did the term "working capital" originate?

Table 9-1 ■ **Allied Food Products:**
Historical and Projected Balance Sheets
(Millions of Dollars)

	12/31/92 (Historical)	9/30/93 (Projected)	12/31/93 (Projected)
Cash	$ 10	$ 15	$ 11
Accounts receivable	375	562	412
Inventories	615	922	677
Total current assets	$1,000	$1,499	$1,100
Net plant and equipment	1,000	1,075	1,100
Total assets	$2,000	$2,574	$2,200
Accounts payable	$ 60	$ 90	$ 66
Notes payable	110	451	140
Accruals	140	210	154
Total current liabilities	$ 310	$ 751	$ 360
Long-term bonds	754	784	784
Total debt	$1,064	$1,535	$1,144
Preferred stock	$ 40	$ 40	$ 40
Common stock	130	189	189
Retained earnings	766	810	827
Total common equity	$ 896	$ 999	$1,016
Total liabilities and equity	$2,000	$2,574	$2,200
Current ratio	3.23	2.00	3.06
Quick ratio	1.24	0.77	1.18

THE REQUIREMENT FOR EXTERNAL WORKING CAPITAL FINANCING

Food processing is a seasonal business. Most of Allied's output consists of non-citrus fruits and vegetables, and the harvest season for these crops generally runs from May through September. Thus, at the end of September Allied's inventories are significantly higher than they are at the end of the calendar year. Allied offers significant sales incentives to wholesalers during August and September in an effort to move inventories out of its warehouses and into those of its customers; otherwise, inventories would be even higher than shown in Table 9-1. Because of this sales surge, Allied's receivables are also much higher at the end of September than at the end of December.

    Consider what will happen to Allied's current assets and current liabilities from December 31, 1992, to September 30, 1993. Current assets increase from $1,000 million to $1,499 million, or by $499 million. Since increases on the asset side of the balance sheet must be financed by identical increases on the liabilities and equity side, the firm must raise $499 million to meet its increase in working capital over the period. However, the higher volume of purchases, plus labor expenditures associated with increased production, will cause accounts payable and accruals to increase spontaneously from $60 + $140 =

$200 million to $90 + $210 = $300 million, or by $100 million. This leaves a projected $499 − $100 = $399 million current asset financing requirement, which Allied will finance primarily by a $341 million increase in notes payable. Therefore, for September 30, 1993, notes payable are projected to rise to $451 million. Note that Allied's current ratio falls from 3.23 to 2.00, and its quick ratio declines from 1.24 to 0.77, from December to September because most of the funds invested in current assets come from current liabilities.

The fluctuations in Allied's working capital position shown in Table 9-1 result from seasonal variations. Similar fluctuations in working capital requirements, and hence in financing needs, also occur during business cycles—working capital needs typically decline during recessions but increase during booms. For food companies, seasonal fluctuations are much greater than business cycle fluctuations, but for other companies—for example, appliance manufacturers—cyclical fluctuations are larger. In the following sections we look in more detail at the requirement for working capital financing, and we examine some alternative working capital policies.

Self-Test Question

Describe how both seasonal and cyclical sales fluctuations influence current asset levels and financing requirements.

THE CASH CONVERSION CYCLE

As we noted above, the concept of working capital management originated with the old Yankee peddler, who would borrow to buy inventory, sell the inventory to pay off the bank loan, and then repeat the cycle. That general concept has been applied to more complex businesses, and it is useful when analyzing the effectiveness of a firm's working capital management process.

We can illustrate the process with data from Real Time Computer Corporation (RTC), which in early 1992 introduced a new super-minicomputer that can perform 15 million instructions per second and that will sell for $250,000. The effects of this new product on RTC's working capital position were analyzed in terms of the following five steps:

1. RTC will order and then receive the materials it needs to produce the 100 computers that are expected to be sold. Because RTC and most other firms purchase materials on credit, this transaction will create an account payable. However, the purchase will have no immediate cash flow effect.

2. Labor will be used to convert the materials into finished computers. However, wages will not be fully paid at the time the work is done, so accrued wages will build up.

3. The finished computers will be sold, but on credit, so sales will create receivables, not immediate cash inflows.

4. At some point during the cycle, RTC must pay off its accounts payable and accrued wages. Because these payments will be made before RTC has collected cash from its receivables, a net cash outflow will occur, and this outflow must be financed.

5. The cycle will be completed when RTC's receivables have been collected. At that time, the company will be in a position to pay off the credit that was used to finance production, and it can then repeat the cycle.

cash conversion cycle
The length of time from the payment for the purchase of raw materials to the collection of accounts receivable generated by the sale of the final product.

The **cash conversion cycle** model, which focuses on the length of time between when the company makes payments and when it receives cash inflows, formalizes the steps outlined above.[1] The following terms are used in the model:

1. *Inventory conversion period,* which is the average length of time required to convert materials into finished goods and then to sell those goods. Note that the inventory conversion period is calculated by dividing inventory by sales per day. For example, if average inventories are $2 million and sales are $10 million, then the inventory conversion period is 72 days:

$$\text{Inventory conversion period} = \frac{\text{Inventory}}{\text{Sales per day}}$$

$$= \frac{\$2,000,000}{\$10,000,000/360}$$
$$= 72 \text{ days.}$$

Thus, it takes an average of 72 days to convert materials into finished goods and then to sell those goods.

2. *Receivables collection period,* which is the average length of time required to convert the firm's receivables into cash, that is, to collect cash following a sale. The receivables collection period is also called the days sales outstanding (DSO), and it is calculated by dividing accounts receivable by the average credit sales per day. If receivables are $666,667 and sales are $10 million, the receivables collection period is

$$\text{Receivables collection period} = \text{DSO} = \frac{\text{Receivables}}{\text{Sales/360}}$$

$$= \frac{\$666,667}{\$10 \text{ million}/360} = 24 \text{ days.}$$

Thus, it takes 24 days after a sale to convert the receivables into cash.

3. *Payables deferral period,* which is the average length of time between the purchase of materials and labor and the payment of cash for them. For example, if the firm on average has 30 days to pay for labor and materials, if its cost of goods sold are $8 million per year, and if its accounts payable average $666,667, then its payables deferral period can be calculated as follows:

[1]See Verlyn D. Richards and Eugene J. Laughlin, "A Cash Conversion Cycle Approach to Liquidity Analysis," *Financial Management,* Spring 1980, 32–38.

$$\text{Payables deferral period} = \text{Payables/Credit purchases per day}$$
$$= \text{Payables/(Cost of goods sold/360)}$$

$$= \$666,667/(\$8,000,000/360)$$
$$= 30 \text{ days.}$$

4. *Cash conversion cycle,* which nets out the three periods just defined and which therefore equals the length of time between the firm's actual cash expenditures to pay for productive resources (materials and labor) and its own cash receipts from the sale of products (that is, the length of time between paying for labor and materials and collecting on receivables). The cash conversion cycle thus equals the average length of time a dollar is tied up in current assets.

We can now use these definitions to analyze the cash conversion cycle. First, the concept is diagrammed in Figure 9-1. Each component is given a number, and the cash conversion cycle can be expressed by this equation:

$$
\begin{array}{ccccccc}
(1) & + & (2) & - & (3) & = & (4) \\
\text{Inventory} & & \text{Receivables} & & \text{Payables} & & \text{Cash} \\
\text{conversion} & + & \text{collection} & - & \text{deferral} & = & \text{conversion.} \\
\text{period} & & \text{period} & & \text{period} & & \text{cycle}
\end{array}
$$

To illustrate, suppose it takes Real Time an average of 72 days to convert raw materials to make computers and then sell them and another 24 days to collect on receivables. However, 30 days normally elapse between receipt of raw materials and payment for them. In this case, the cash conversion cycle would be 66 days:

$$72 \text{ days} + 24 \text{ days} - 30 \text{ days} = 66 \text{ days.}$$

To look at it another way,

$$
\begin{array}{ccc}
\text{Receipts delay} & - \text{ Payment delay} = \text{Net delay} \\
(72 \text{ days} + 24 \text{ days}) - & 30 \text{ days} & = \ \ 66 \text{ days.}
\end{array}
$$

Given these data, RTC knows when it starts producing a computer that it will have to finance the manufacturing costs for a 66-day period. The firm's goal should be to shorten its cash conversion cycle as much as possible without hurting operations. This would improve profits because the longer the cash conversion cycle, the greater the need for external financing, and such financing has a cost.

The cash conversion cycle can be shortened (1) by reducing the inventory conversion period by processing and selling goods more quickly, (2) by reducing the receivables collection period by speeding up collections, or (3) by lengthening the payables deferral period by slowing down its own payments. To the extent that these actions can be taken *without increasing costs or depressing sales,* they should be carried out.

Figure 9-1 ▪ The Cash Conversion Cycle Model

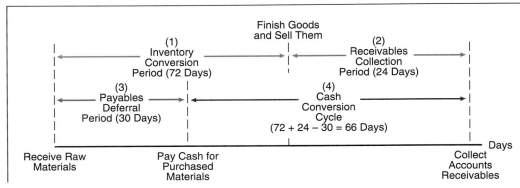

We can illustrate the benefits of shortening the cash conversion cycle by looking again at Real Time Computer Corporation. Suppose RTC must spend $200,000 on materials and labor to produce one computer, and it can turn out three computers per day. Thus, it must invest $600,000 for each day's production. This investment must be financed for 66 days—the length of the cash conversion cycle—so the company's working capital financing needs will be 66 × $600,000 = $39.6 million. If RTC could reduce the cash conversion cycle to 56 days, say by deferring payment of its accounts payable an additional 10 days, or by speeding up either the production process or the collection of its receivables, it could reduce its working capital financing requirements by $6 million. We see, then, that actions which affect the inventory conversion period, the receivables collection period, and the payables deferral period all affect the cash conversion cycle, hence they influence the firm's need for current assets and current asset financing. You should keep the cash conversion cycle concept in mind as you go through the remainder of this chapter and the other chapters on working capital management.

？ *Self-Test Questions*

What steps are involved in estimating the cash conversion cycle?

What do the following terms mean?
a. Inventory conversion period.
b. Receivables collection period.
c. Payables deferral period.

What is the cash conversion cycle model? How can it be used to improve current asset management?

WORKING CAPITAL INVESTMENT AND FINANCING POLICIES

Working capital policy involves two basic questions: (1) What is the appropriate level for current assets, both in total and by specific accounts, and (2) how should current assets be financed?

Alternative Current Asset Investment Policies

relaxed current asset investment policy

A policy under which relatively large amounts of cash, marketable securities, and inventories are carried and under which sales are stimulated by a liberal credit policy, resulting in a high level of receivables.

restricted current asset investment policy

A policy under which holdings of cash, securities, inventories, and receivables are minimized.

moderate current asset investment policy

A policy that is between the relaxed and restricted policies.

Figure 9-2 shows three alternative policies regarding the total amount of current assets carried. Essentially, these policies differ in that different amounts of current assets are carried to support any given level of sales. The line with the steepest slope represents a **relaxed current asset investment** (or "fat cat") **policy,** where relatively large amounts of cash, marketable securities, and inventories are carried and where sales are stimulated by the use of a credit policy that provides liberal financing to customers and a corresponding high level of receivables. Conversely, with the **restricted current asset investment** (or "lean-and-mean") **policy,** the holdings of cash, securities, inventories, and receivables are minimized. The **moderate current asset investment policy** is between the two extremes.

Under conditions of certainty—when sales, costs, lead times, payment periods, and so on, are known for sure—all firms would hold only minimal levels of current assets. Any larger amounts would increase the need for external funding without a corresponding increase in profits, while any smaller holdings would involve late payments to labor and suppliers and lost sales due to inventory shortages and an overly restrictive credit policy.

However, the picture changes when uncertainty is introduced. Here the firm requires some minimum amount of cash and inventories based on expected payments, expected sales, expected order lead times, and so on, plus additional amounts, or *safety stocks,* which enable it to deal with departures from the expected values. Similarly, accounts receivable levels are determined by credit terms, and the tougher the credit terms, the lower the receivables for any given level of sales. With a restricted current asset investment policy, the firm would hold minimal levels of safety stocks for cash and inventories, and it would have a tight credit policy even though this meant running the risk of losing sales. A restricted, lean-and-mean current asset investment policy generally provides the highest expected return on investment, but it entails the greatest risk, while the reverse is true under a relaxed policy. The moderate policy falls in between the two extremes in terms of expected risk and return.

In terms of the cash conversion cycle, a restricted investment policy would tend to reduce the inventory conversion and receivables collection periods, hence result in a relatively short cash conversion cycle. Conversely, a relaxed policy would create higher levels of inventories and receivables, longer inventory conversion and receivables collection periods, and a relatively long cash conversion cycle. A moderate policy would produce a cash conversion cycle which falls between the two extremes.

Alternative Current Asset Financing Policies

permanent current assets

Current assets that are still on hand at the trough of a firm's cycles.

Most businesses experience seasonal and/or cyclical fluctuations. For example, construction firms have peaks in the spring and summer, retailers peak around Christmas, and the manufacturers who supply both construction companies and retailers follow similar patterns. Similarly, virtually all businesses must build up current assets when the economy is strong, but they then sell off inventories and have net reductions of receivables when the economy slacks off. Still, current assets rarely drop to zero, and this realization has led to the development of the idea of **permanent current assets.** Applying this idea to Allied Food

Figure 9-2 ▪ Alternative Current Asset Investment Policies
(Millions of Dollars)

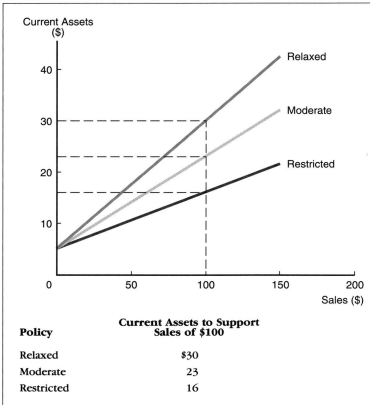

Policy	Current Assets to Support Sales of $100
Relaxed	$30
Moderate	23
Restricted	16

Note: The sales/current assets relationship is shown here as being linear, but the relationship is often curvilinear.

temporary current assets

Current assets that fluctuate with seasonal or cyclical variations in a firm's business.

maturity matching, or "self-liquidating," approach

A financing policy that matches asset and liability maturities. This is a moderate policy.

Products, Table 9-1 (presented earlier) suggests that, at this stage in its life, Allied's total assets are growing at a 10 percent rate, from $2,000 million to $2,200 million, but seasonal fluctuations push total assets up to $2,574 million during the firm's peak season. Thus, at the end of September, Allied's total assets of $2,574 million consist of about $2,150 million of permanent assets (9/12ths of the increase from $2,000 to $2,200 million) and $2,574 − $2,150 = $424 million of seasonal, or **temporary, current assets.** Allied's temporary current assets fluctuate from zero during the slow season in March to $424 million during the peak season in September. The manner in which the permanent and temporary current assets are financed is called the firm's *current asset financing policy.*

Maturity Matching, or "Self-Liquidating," Approach. The **maturity matching,** or **"self-liquidating," approach** calls for matching asset and liability maturities as shown in Panel a of Figure 9-3. This strategy minimizes the risk that the firm will be unable to pay off its maturing obligations. To illustrate, suppose Allied borrows on a 1-year basis and uses the funds obtained to build

Figure 9-3 ▪ Alternative Current Asset Financing Policies

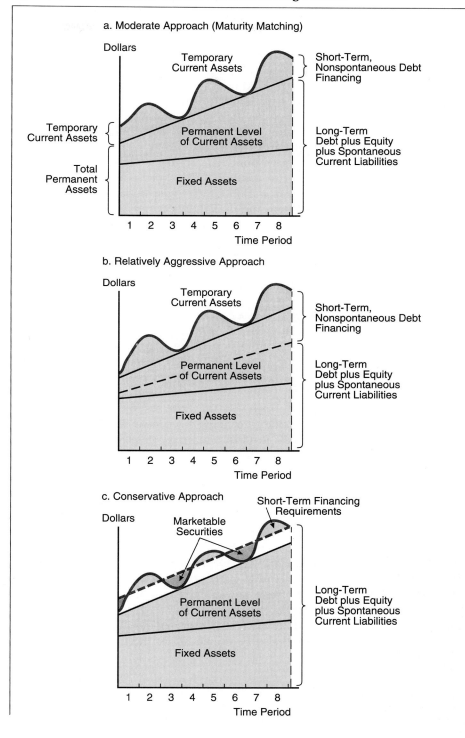

and equip a plant. Cash flows from the plant (profits plus depreciation) would not be sufficient to pay off the loan at the end of only one year, so the loan would have to be renewed. If for some reason the lender refused to renew the loan, then Allied would have problems. Had the plant been financed with long-term debt, however, the required loan payments would have been better matched with cash flows from profits and depreciation, and the problem of renewal would not have arisen.

At the limit, a firm could attempt to match exactly the maturity structure of its assets and liabilities. Inventory expected to be sold in 30 days could be financed with a 30-day bank loan; a machine expected to last for 5 years could be financed by a 5-year loan; a 20-year building could be financed by a 20-year mortgage bond; and so forth. Actually, of course, two factors prevent this exact maturity matching: (1) there is uncertainty about the lives of assets, and (2) some common equity must be used, and common equity has no maturity. To illustrate the uncertainty factor, Allied might finance inventories with a 30-day loan, expecting to sell the inventories and to use the cash generated to retire the loan. But if sales were slow, the cash would not be forthcoming, and the use of short-term credit could end up causing a problem. Still, if Allied makes an attempt to match asset and liability maturities, we would define this as a moderate current asset financing policy.

Aggressive Approach. Panel b of Figure 9-3 illustrates the situation for a relatively aggressive firm which finances all of its fixed assets with long-term capital but part of its permanent current assets with short-term, nonspontaneous credit. A look back at Table 9-1 will show that Allied actually follows this strategy. Allied has $1,075 million in permanent current assets projected for September 1993, so its temporary current assets must be $1,499 − $1,075 = $424 million.[2] However, the firm has $451 million in notes payable as well as some temporary financing from peak levels of accounts payable and accruals. Thus, Allied's level of temporary financing exceeds its level of temporary current assets, so some part of its permanent assets are financed with temporary capital.

Returning to Figure 9-3, note that we used the term "relatively" in the title for Panel b, because there can be different *degrees* of aggressiveness. For example, the dashed line in Panel b could have been drawn *below* the line designating fixed assets, indicating that all of the permanent current assets and part of the fixed assets were financed with short-term credit; this would be a highly aggressive, extremely nonconservative position, and the firm would be very much subject to dangers from rising interest rates as well as to loan renewal problems. However, short-term debt is often cheaper than long-term debt, and some firms are willing to sacrifice safety for the chance of higher profits.

Conservative Approach. As shown in Panel c of Figure 9-3, the dashed line could also be drawn *above* the line designating permanent current assets, indi-

---

[2]We estimated in an earlier section that as of September, Allied Food Products had $2,150 million of permanent assets, and of that amount, $1,075 million is fixed assets. Therefore, permanent current assets = $2,150 million − $1,075 million = $1,075 million.

cating that permanent capital is being used to finance all permanent asset requirements and also to meet some or all of the seasonal demands. In the situation depicted in our graph, the firm uses a small amount of short-term, nonspontaneous credit to meet its peak requirements, but it also meets a part of its seasonal needs by "storing liquidity" in the form of marketable securities during the off-season. The humps above the dashed line represent short-term financing; the troughs below the dashed line represent short-term security holdings. Panel c represents a very safe, conservative current asset financing policy.

Self-Test Questions

What two key issues does working capital policy involve?

What is meant by the term "current asset financing policy"?

What are three alternative current asset financing policies? Is one best?

What is meant by the term "permanent current assets"?

ADVANTAGES AND DISADVANTAGES OF SHORT-TERM FINANCING

The three possible financing policies described above were distinguished by the relative amounts of short-term debt used under each policy. The aggressive policy called for the greatest use of short-term debt, while the conservative policy called for the least. Maturity matching fell in between. Although using short-term credit is generally riskier than using long-term credit, short-term credit does have some significant advantages. The pros and cons of short-term financing are considered in this section.

Speed

A short-term loan can be obtained much faster than long-term credit. Lenders will insist on a more thorough financial examination before extending long-term credit, and the loan agreement will have to be spelled out in considerable detail because a lot can happen during the life of a 10- or 20-year loan. Therefore, if funds are needed in a hurry, the firm should look to the short-term markets.

Flexibility

If its needs for funds are seasonal or cyclical, a firm may not want to commit itself to long-term debt for three reasons: (1) Flotation costs are generally high when raising long-term debt but trivial for short-term credit. (2) Although long-term debt can be repaid early, provided the loan agreement includes a prepayment provision, prepayment penalties can be expensive. Accordingly, if a firm thinks its need for funds will diminish in the near future, it should choose short-term debt for the flexibility it provides. (3) Long-term loan agreements always contain provisions, or covenants, which constrain the firm's future actions. Short-term credit agreements are generally much less onerous in this regard.

Cost of Long-Term versus Short-Term Debt

The yield curve is normally upward sloping, indicating that interest rates are generally lower on short-term than on long-term debt. Thus, under normal conditions, interest costs at the time the funds are obtained will be lower if the firm borrows on a short-term rather than on a long-term basis.

Risk of Long-Term versus Short-Term Debt

Even though short-term debt is often less expensive than long-term debt, short-term credit subjects the firm to more risk than does long-term financing. This occurs for two reasons: (1) If a firm borrows on a long-term basis, its interest costs will be relatively stable over time, but if it uses short-term credit, its interest expense will fluctuate widely, at times going quite high. For example, the rate banks charge large corporations for short-term debt more than tripled over a two-year period in the 1980s, rising from 6.25 to 21 percent. Many firms that had borrowed heavily on a short-term basis simply could not meet their rising interest costs, and as a result bankruptcies hit record levels during that period. (2) If a firm borrows heavily on a short-term basis, it may find itself unable to repay this debt, and it may be in such a weak financial position that the lender will not extend the loan; this too could force the firm into bankruptcy. Braniff Airlines, which failed during a credit crunch in the 1980s, is an example.

Another good example of the riskiness of short-term debt is provided by Transamerica Corporation, a major financial services company. Transamerica's chairman, Mr. Beckett, described how his company was moving to reduce its dependency on short-term loans whose costs vary with short-term interest rates. According to Mr. Beckett, Transamerica had reduced its variable-rate (short-term) loans by about $450 million over a two-year period. "We aren't going to go through the enormous increase in debt expense again that had such a serious impact on earnings," he said. The company's earnings fell sharply because money rates rose to record highs. "We were almost entirely in variable-rate debt," he said, but currently "about 65 percent is fixed rate and 35 percent variable. We've come a long way, and we'll keep plugging away at it." Transamerica's earnings were badly depressed by the increase in short-term rates, but other companies were even less fortunate—they simply could not pay the rising interest charges, and this forced them into bankruptcy.

 ### Self-Test Questions

Which of the three alternative current asset financing policies uses the most short-term debt?

What are some advantages of short-term debt over long-term debt as a source of capital?

What are some disadvantages of short-term debt?

SMALL BUSINESS | Growth and Working Capital Needs

Working capital is the requirement that entrepreneurs most often underestimate when seeking funds to finance a new business. The entrepreneur generally plans for research and development and for the plant and equipment required for production. Working capital, however, frequently comes as a surprise to the entrepreneur, who probably expects to develop a product the market will immediately accept and for which the market will pay a substantial premium. This premium will, he or she assumes, lead to high profit margins, which will then "finance" all of the firm's other needs. As naive as this point of view may seem, it nevertheless is common among less experienced founders of new businesses.

Ned was one of the founders of a new microcomputer software company that began seeking venture capital to support its products in early 1992. When speaking with a venture capitalist, who was concerned about the low level of funding being sought, Ned explained that the company's products had such a high profit margin that the company would be essentially self-financing.

Ned's company made and sold a computer software package. The package was shipped in the form of three diskettes and a set of manuals. The total cost of those materials was about $20, and the package sold for $500. With such a high profit margin, Ned claimed, there would be no need for financing once the marketing was under way. In fact, he said, there would be plenty of cash to pay for new product development.

Joanna, the venture capitalist, was somewhat disconcerted by Ned's reasoning. She pointed out some of the errors in Ned's "analysis": The $500 was only a suggested retail price; discounters would probably sell the package for closer to $275. This $275, in turn, was at the *end* of a marketing chain that included distributors and dealers; Ned's firm would only receive $80 to $90 per package. This $80 to $90 would initially be added to accounts receivable — not received as cash — and probably not collected, on average, for about 60 days. Meanwhile, Ned would have to write checks to pay for overhead, for high R&D expenses, for a marketing staff, and for advertising space. Instead of $480 per package of cash flowing *in,* the firm would be, on balance, paying cash *out* for the first few years of its life.

Rapid growth consumes cash; it does not generate cash. Rapid growth may generate profits, but profits do not pay the bills — cash does. Consider what a firm must do to sustain a high growth rate. If it is a manufacturer, the components of its assets include raw materials inventory, work-in-process inventory, finished goods inventory, and accounts receivable, as well as fixed assets. With the exception of fixed assets, these items are all components of gross working capital. When the firm produces a product, it makes an investment in each of these working capital items before any cash is received from collection of receivables, assuming all sales are credit sales.

Consider a small firm that finances its activities solely through the funds it generates. Recall the financial analysis presented earlier in this chapter. Suppose the firm has an average of 120 days of sales in inventory and an average of 60 days of sales in receivables. If the firm pays cash for all of its materials and labor, it has a cash conversion cycle of 180 days; that is, between the payment for goods at the beginning of the cycle and the receipt of cash at the end, 180 days pass. Thus, the company "turns over" its cash only twice per year.

If the company earns, say, 3 percent on its sales dollar (as measured by the net profit margin), it has about 3 percent more money available after a cycle than before it. With two cycles per year, about 6 percent more is available for investment at the end of the year than at the beginning. Thus, annual growth of approximately 6 percent can be supported.

If the company is growing at a rate of 20 percent per year, but it can generate only 6 percent internally, it must either obtain funds externally or face enormous pressures.

How can the company improve its ability to fund growth internally? Generally, the firm can grow at a rate equal to the product of its net profit margin times the number of cash conversion cycles per year.[3] Thus, it can support more rapid growth either by raising the profit margin or by shortening the cash conversion cycle (increasing the number of cycles per year).

To raise the profit margin, the company must raise prices, cut costs, or both. Raising prices may reduce growth (because customers will be less eager to

---

[3]Several factors may mitigate the accuracy of this approximation. First, this example ignores the fact that some expenses, such as depreciation, are not cash expenses. Furthermore, no spontaneous sources of financing, discussed in Chapter 7, have been considered. Finally, the example assumes a zero dividend payout ratio, which may not fit every situation.

buy at higher prices), but it may also help bring growth and financial resources more into balance.

Shortening the cash conversion cycle requires reducing inventory, collecting receivables more efficiently, or paying suppliers more slowly. Consider the effects of these changes. Reducing inventory by 25 percent (to 90 days) and cutting receivables to 30 days (normal credit terms), reduces the cycle to 120 days. In addition, if suppliers are willing to wait 30 days for payment, then the time cash is outstanding can be further shortened to 90 days. Cash turnover changes to four times per year from two, and internally fundable growth becomes 12 percent rather than 6 percent. Improving the cash conversion cycle and thus increasing the rate at which the firm can

support growth internally reduces the firm's needs for outside funds to a more manageable level.

For the small business with serious constraints on obtaining outside funds, these discretionary policies can help bring the firm's rate of growth into balance with its ability to finance that growth. Furthermore, such control on the part of management may impress bankers and others who have funds, and this may help the firm get the outside financing it would have preferred to have had all along.[4]

[4]Limits on growth and the concept of "sustainable growth" are explored in Chapter 6 of Robert C. Higgins, *Analysis for Financial Management,* 2nd Edition (Homewood, Ill.: Irwin, 1989).

SUMMARY

This chapter examined working capital policy and alternative ways of financing current assets. The key concepts covered are listed below.

- **Working capital** refers to current assets, and **net working capital** is defined as current assets minus current liabilities. **Working capital policy** refers to decisions relating to the level of current assets and the way they are financed.

- The **inventory conversion period** is the average length of time required to convert raw materials into finished goods and then to sell them.

- The **receivables collection period** is the average length of time required to convert the firm's receivables into cash, and it is equal to the days sales outstanding.

- The **payables deferral period** is the average length of time between the purchase of raw materials and labor and paying for them.

- The **cash conversion cycle** is the length of time between paying for purchases and receiving cash from the sale of finished goods. The cash conversion cycle can be calculated as follows:

$$\begin{array}{ccccc} \text{Inventory} & & \text{Receivables} & & \text{Payables} & & \text{Cash} \\ \text{conversion} & + & \text{collection} & - & \text{deferral} & = & \text{conversion.} \\ \text{period} & & \text{period} & & \text{period} & & \text{cycle} \end{array}$$

- Under a **relaxed current asset investment policy,** a firm holds relatively large amounts of each type of current asset. Under a **restricted current asset investment policy,** the firm holds minimal amounts of these items.

- **Permanent current assets** are those current assets that the firm holds even during slack times, whereas **temporary current assets** are the additional current assets that are needed during seasonal or cyclical peaks. The methods used to finance permanent and temporary current assets constitute the firm's **current asset financing policy.**

▪ A **moderate** approach to current asset financing involves matching, to the extent possible, the maturities of assets and liabilities, so that temporary current assets are financed with short-term nonspontaneous debt and permanent current assets and fixed assets are financed with long-term debt or equity plus spontaneous debt. Under an **aggressive** approach, some permanent current assets and perhaps even some fixed assets are financed with short-term debt. A **conservative** approach would be to use long-term capital to finance all permanent assets and some of the temporary current assets.

▪ The advantages of short-term credit are (1) the **speed** with which short-term loans can be arranged, (2) increased **flexibility,** and (3) the fact that short-term **interest rates** are generally **lower** than long-term rates. The principal disadvantage of short-term credit is the **extra risk** that the borrower must bear because (1) the lender can demand payment on short notice and (2) the cost of the loan will increase if interest rates rise.

Questions

9-1   How does the seasonal nature of a firm's sales influence its decision regarding the amount of short-term credit to use in its financial structure?

9-2   Assuming the firm's sales volume remained constant, would you expect it to have a higher cash balance during a tight-money period or during an easy-money period? Why?

9-3   What are the advantages of matching the maturities of assets and liabilities? What are the disadvantages?

9-4   From the standpoint of the borrower, is long-term or short-term credit riskier? Explain. Would it ever make sense to borrow on a short-term basis if short-term rates were above long-term rates?

9-5   If long-term credit exposes a borrower to less risk, why would people or firms ever borrow on a short-term basis?

Self-Test Problems   (Solutions Appear in Appendix B)

ST-1   Define each of the following terms:
Key terms   a. Working capital; net working capital; working capital policy
   b. Permanent current assets; temporary current assets
   c. Cash conversion cycle; inventory conversion period; receivables collection period; payables deferral period
   d. Relaxed current asset investment policy; restricted current asset investment policy; moderate current asset investment policy
   e. Moderate current asset financing policy; aggressive current asset financing policy; conservative current asset financing policy
   f. Maturity matching, or "self-liquidating," approach

ST-2
Current asset financing

Vanderheiden Press Inc. and the Herrenhouse Publishing Company had the following balance sheets as of December 31, 1992 (thousands of dollars):

	Vanderheiden Press	Herrenhouse Publishing
Current assets	$100,000	$ 80,000
Fixed assets (net)	100,000	120,000
Total assets	$200,000	$200,000
Current liabilities	$ 20,000	$ 80,000
Long-term debt	80,000	20,000
Common stock	50,000	50,000
Retained earnings	50,000	50,000
Total liabilities and equity	$200,000	$200,000

Earnings before interest and taxes (EBIT) for both firms are $30 million, and the federal-plus-state tax rate is 40 percent.

a. What is the return on equity for each firm if the interest rate on current liabilities is 10 percent and the rate on long-term debt is 13 percent?

b. Assume that the short-term rate rises to 20 percent. While the rate on new long-term debt rises to 16 percent, the rate on existing long-term debt remains unchanged. What would be the return on equity for Vanderheiden Press and Herrenhouse Publishing under these conditions?

c. Which company is in a riskier position? Why?

ST-3
Working capital policy

The Calgary Company is attempting to establish a current assets policy. Fixed assets are $600,000, and the firm plans to maintain a 50 percent debt-to-assets ratio. The interest rate is 10 percent on all debt. Three alternative current asset policies are under consideration: 40, 50, and 60 percent of projected sales. The company expects to earn 15 percent before interest and taxes on sales of $3 million. Calgary's federal-plus-state tax rate is 40 percent. What is the expected return on equity under each alternative?

Problems

9-1
Cash conversion cycle

Look back in the chapter to Table 9-1, which showed the balance sheets for Allied Food Products on three different dates. Allied's sales fluctuate during the year due to the seasonal nature of its business; however, we can calculate its sales on an average day as total sales divided by 360, recognizing that daily sales will be much higher than this value during its peak selling season and much lower during its slack time. Allied's sales for 1993 totaled $3,300 million, so an average day's sales were $9.167 million. Assume that the balance sheet on December 31, 1992 is also the same balance sheet that existed on January 1, 1993.

a. Calculate Allied's inventory conversion period as of January 1 and September 30. (Hint: The inventory conversion period is equal to the number of average days' sales held in inventory, and it is calculated as inventory divided by an average day's sales.)

b. Calculate Allied's receivables collection period as of January 1 and September 30.

c. Assume Allied's purchases are 50 percent of sales and all purchases are made on credit. Using this information, calculate the payables deferral period as of January 1 and September 30 as accounts payable divided by average daily purchases.

d. Using the values calculated in Parts a through c, calculate the length of Allied's cash conversion cycle on the two balance sheet dates.

e. In Part d, you should have found that the cash conversion cycle was longer on September 30 than on January 1. Why did these results occur?

f. Can you think of any reason why the cash conversion cycle of a firm with seasonal sales might be different during the slack selling season than during the peak selling season?

9-2
Working capital investment

Verbrugge Corporation is a leading U.S. producer of automobile batteries. Verbrugge turns out 1,500 batteries a day at a cost of $6 per battery for materials and labor. It takes the firm 22 days to convert raw materials into a battery. Verbrugge allows its customers 40 days in which to pay for the batteries, and the firm generally pays its suppliers in 30 days.

a. What is the length of Verbrugge's cash conversion cycle?
b. At a steady state in which Verbrugge produces 1,500 batteries a day, what amount of working capital must it finance?
c. By what amount could Verbrugge reduce its working capital financing needs if it was able to stretch its payables deferral period to 35 days?
d. Verbrugge's management is trying to analyze the effect of a proposed new production process on the working capital investment. The new production process would allow Verbrugge to decrease its inventory conversion period to 20 days and to increase its daily production to 1,800 batteries. However, the new process would cause the cost of materials and labor to increase to $7. Assuming the change does not affect the receivables collection period (40 days) or the payables deferral period (30 days), what will be the length of the cash conversion cycle and the working capital financing requirement if the new production process is implemented?

9-3
Working capital policy

The Hawley Corporation is attempting to determine the optimal level of current assets for the coming year. Management expects sales to increase to approximately $2 million as a result of an asset expansion presently being undertaken. Fixed assets total $1 million, and the firm wishes to maintain a 60 percent debt ratio. Hawley's interest cost is currently 8 percent on both short-term and longer-term debt (which the firm uses in its permanent structure). Three alternatives regarding the projected current asset level are available to the firm: (1) a tight policy requiring current assets of only 45 percent of projected sales, (2) a moderate policy of 50 percent of sales in current assets, and (3) a relaxed policy requiring current assets of 60 percent of sales. The firm expects to generate earnings before interest and taxes (EBIT) at a rate of 12 percent on total sales.

a. What is the expected return on equity under each current asset level? (Assume a 40 percent federal-plus-state tax rate.)
b. In this problem we have assumed that the level of expected sales is independent of current asset policy. Is this a valid assumption?
c. How would the overall riskiness of the firm vary under each policy?

EXAM-TYPE PROBLEMS

The problems included in this section are set up in such a way that they could be used as multiple-choice exam problems.

9-4
Cash conversion cycle

The Prestopino Corporation has an inventory conversion period of 75 days, a receivables collection period of 38 days, and a payables deferral period of 30 days.

a. What is the length of the firm's cash conversion cycle?
b. If Prestopino's annual sales are $3,375,000 and all sales are on credit, what is the firm's investment in accounts receivable?
c. How many times per year does Prestopino turn over its inventory?

9-5
Working capital cash flow cycle

The Broske Corporation is trying to determine the effect of its inventory turnover ratio and days sales outstanding (DSO) on its cash flow cycle. Broske's 1992 sales (all on credit) were $150,000, and it earned a net profit of 6 percent, or $9,000. It turned over its inventory 6 times during the year, and its DSO was 36 days. The firm had fixed assets totaling $40,000. Broske's payables deferral period is 40 days.

a. Calculate Broske's cash conversion cycle.

b. Assuming Broske holds negligible amounts of cash and marketable securities, calculate its total assets turnover and ROA.

c. Suppose Broske's managers believe that the inventory turnover can be raised to 8 times. What would Broske's cash conversion cycle, total assets turnover, and ROA have been if the inventory turnover had been 8 for 1992?

INTEGRATIVE PROBLEM

9-6

Working capital policy and financing

Daniel Barnes, financial manager of New York Fuels (NYF), a heating oil distributor, is concerned about the company's working capital policy, and he is considering three alternative policies: (1) a "restrictive" ("lean and mean" or "tight") policy, which calls for reducing receivables by $100,000 and inventories by $200,000; (2) a "relaxed" ("loose" or "fat cat") policy, which calls for increasing receivables by $100,000 and inventories by $200,000; and (3) a "moderate" policy, which would mean leaving receivables and inventories at their current levels. NYF's 1992 financial statements and key ratios, plus some industry average data, are given in Table IP9-1.

The cost of long-term debt is 12 percent versus only 8 percent for short-term notes payable. Variable costs as a percentage of sales (74 percent) would not be affected by the firm's working capital policy, but fixed costs would be affected due to the storage, handling, and insurance costs associated with inventory. Here are the assumed fixed costs under the three policies:

Policy	Fixed Costs
Restrictive	$ 950,000
Moderate	1,000,000
Relaxed	1,100,000

Sales would also be affected by the policy chosen: Carrying larger inventories and using easier credit terms would stimulate sales, so sales would be highest under the relaxed policy and lowest under the restrictive policy. Also, these effects would vary depending on the strength of the economy. Here are the relationships Barnes assumes would have held in 1992:

State of the Economy	Sales (Millions of Dollars)		
	Restrictive	Moderate	Relaxed
Weak	$4.3	$4.5	$5.0
Average	4.7	5.0	5.5
Strong	5.3	5.5	6.0

Barnes considers the 1992 economy to be average.

You have been asked to answer the following questions to help determine NYF's optimal working capital policy.

a. How does NYF's current working capital policy as reflected in its financial statements compare with an average firm's policy? Do the differences suggest that NYF's policy is better or worse than that of the average firm in its industry?

b. Based on the 1992 ratios and financial statements, what were the company's inventory conversion period, its receivables collection period, and, assuming a 29-day

Table IP9-1 ▪ **Financial Statements and Other Data on NYF (Thousands of Dollars)**

A. 1992 Balance Sheet

Cash and securities	$ 100	Accounts payable and accruals	$ 300
Accounts receivable	600	Notes payable (8%)	500
Inventories	1,000	Total current liabilities	$ 800
Total current assets	$1,700	Long-term debt (12%)	600
Net fixed assets	800	Common equity	1,100
Total assets	$2,500	Total liabilities and equity	$2,500

B. 1992 Income Statement

Sales	$5,000.00
Less: Variable costs	3,700.00
Fixed costs	$1,000.00
EBIT	$ 300.00
Interest	112.00
Earnings before taxes (EBT)	$ 188.00
Taxes (40%)	75.20
Net income	$ 112.80
Dividends (30% payout)	$ 33.84
Addition to retained earnings	$ 78.96

C. Key Ratios

	NYF	Industry
Basic earning power	12.00%	15.8%
Profit margin	2.3%	3.0%
Return on equity	10.3%	15.0%
Days sales outstanding (360 days)	43.2	30.0
Accounts receivable turnover	8.3×	12.0×
Inventory turnover	5.0	7.5
Fixed assets turnover	6.3	6.0
Total assets turnover	2.0	2.5
Debt/assets	56.0%	50.0%
Times interest earned	2.7×	4.8×
Current ratio	2.1	2.3
Quick ratio	0.9	1.3

payables deferral period, its cash conversion cycle? How could the cash conversion cycle concept be used to help improve the firm's working capital management?

c. Barnes has asked you to recast the 1992 financial statements, and calculate some key ratios, assuming an average economy and a restrictive (tight) working capital policy, and to check some calculations he has made. Construct these statements, and then calculate the new current ratio and ROE. Assume that common stock is used to make the balance sheet balance, but do not get into financing feedbacks. (Hint: You need to change sales, fixed costs, receivables, inventories, and common equity, plus items affected by those changes, and then calculate new ratios.)

Table IP9-2 ▪ **ROEs under the Alternative Policies**

	Working Capital Policy		
State of the Economy	**Tight**	**Moderate**	**Easy**
Weak	4.2%	3.2%	3.8%
Average	12.0	10.3	9.3
Strong	23.7	17.3	14.9
Average	13.3%	10.3%	9.3%

d. Barnes himself has actually analyzed the situation for each of the policies under each economic scenario; the ROEs he has calculated are shown in Table IP9-2. What are the implications of these data for the working capital policy decision?

e. The working capital policy discussion thus far has focused entirely on current assets, and not at all on the current asset financing policy. How would you bring financing policy into the analysis?

COMPUTER-RELATED PROBLEM

Work the problem in this secion only if you are using the computer problem diskette.

9-7

Working capital financing

Three companies—Aggressive, Moderate, and Conservative—have different working capital management policies as implied by their names. For example, Aggressive employs only minimal current assets, and it finances almost entirely with current liabilities plus equity. This restricted approach has a dual effect. It keeps total assets low, which tends to increase return on assets; but because of stock-outs and credit rejections, total sales are reduced, and because inventory is ordered more frequently and in smaller quantities, variable costs are increased. Condensed balance sheets for the three companies follow:

	Aggressive	Moderate	Conservative
Current assets	$225,000	$300,000	$450,000
Fixed assets	300,000	300,000	300,000
Total assets	$525,000	$600,000	$750,000
Current liabilities (cost = 12%)	$300,000	$150,000	$ 75,000
Long-term debt (cost = 10%)	0	150,000	300,000
Total debt	$300,000	$300,000	$375,000
Equity	225,000	300,000	375,000
Total liabilities and equity	$525,000	$600,000	$750,000
Current ratio	0.75:1	2:1	6:1

The cost of goods sold functions for the three firms are as follows:

Cost of goods sold = Fixed costs + Variable costs.
Aggressive: Cost of goods sold = $300,000 + 0.70(Sales).
Moderate: Cost of goods sold = $405,000 + 0.65(Sales).
Conservative: Cost of goods sold = $577,500 + 0.60(Sales).

Because of the working capital differences, sales for the three firms under different economic conditions are expected to vary as follows:

	Aggressive	**Moderate**	**Conservative**
Strong economy	$1,800,000	$1,875,000	$1,950,000
Average economy	1,350,000	1,500,000	1,725,000
Weak economy	1,050,000	1,200,000	1,575,000

a. Construct income statements for each company for strong, average, and weak economies using the following format:

> Sales
> Less cost of goods sold
> Earnings before interest and taxes (EBIT)
> Less interest expense
> Earnings before taxes (EBT)
> Less taxes (at 40%)
> Net income (NI)

b. Compare the basic earning power (EBIT/assets) and return on equity for the companies. Which company is best in a strong economy? In an average economy? In a weak economy?

c. Suppose that, with sales at the average-economy level, short-term interest rates rose to 20 percent. How would this affect the three firms?

d. Suppose that because of production slowdowns caused by inventory shortages, the aggressive company's variable cost ratio rose to 80 percent. What would happen to its ROE? Assume a short-term interest rate of 12 percent.

e. What considerations for the management of working capital are indicated by this problem?

Cash and Marketable Securities Management

Cash is the oil that lubricates the wheels of business. Without adequate oil, machines grind to a halt, and a business with inadequate cash will do likewise. However, carrying cash is expensive—since cash is a non-earning asset, a firm that holds cash beyond its minimum requirements is lowering its potential earnings.

Cash management is a very professional, highly refined activity. The following excerpt from a United California Bank (UCB) advertisement illustrates what is involved:

> *Using any lockbox will accelerate cash flow. But a UCB Lock Box System does it with maximum efficiency. One difference is our unique city-wide zip code system for California lockbox customers. It speeds the receipt of your lockbox mail by several hours.*
>
> *Another difference: We work around the clock, seven days a week. So you can be sure your funds will be deposited, regardless of absenteeism or seasonal work loads.*
>
> *A third difference: We're the only West Coast bank using helicopters to speed collections of checks, thus reducing float.*
>
> *Also, using our computerized optimization models, we can determine how many lockboxes you should use, where they should be located, and how much money you'll save with them.*
>
> *Finally—you need not keep idle cash balances to guard against a failure to receive expected payments or to be ready for unexpected outflows. We can arrange a line of credit for you, let you know by 11 A.M. how much (if any) you need to borrow to cover the checks that have cleared, and have the money in your account by 4 P.M. Or, if your account has net inflows on a given day, we will use these funds to reduce your loan balance or to purchase securities, as you direct. With this service, you'll never have funds sitting idle.*
>
> *The cost is surprisingly low. Call us, and let us show you how UCB can make your cash work harder.*

> *For some companies, these ideas make good sense. However, firms sometimes go too far with their cash management systems. For example, the general practice in the securities brokerage business (until Merrill Lynch lost a major suit and agreed to stop doing it) was to write checks to customers located east of the Mississippi on a West Coast bank and checks to customers located west of the river on an East Coast bank. This slowed down payments on checks, deprived customers of the use of their money, and gave the brokerage firms the use of billions of dollars of their customers' money for extended periods of time. According to the SEC, this practice, although it increased brokerage firms' profits by millions of dollars each year, was "inconsistent with a broker-dealer's obligation to deal fairly with its customers."*
>
> *As you read this chapter, consider just how important the various cash management techniques discussed in this chapter really are. The lessons to be learned from this chapter apply to the cash holdings of individuals and nonprofit organizations, including government agencies. Maybe you will be able to take some of the ideas discussed in this chapter and improve the handling of your own cash balances.*

Approximately 1.5 percent of the average industrial firm's assets are held in the form of cash, which is defined as demand deposits plus currency. In addition, sizable holdings of near-cash short-term marketable securities such as U.S. Treasury bills (T-bills), bank certificates of deposit (CDs), money market funds, and floating rate preferred stock are often reported on corporations' financial statements. Moreover, cash and marketable securities balances vary widely both across industries and between firms within a given industry. In this chapter, we analyze the factors that determine how much cash and marketable securities firms hold, and we describe the most commonly held types of marketable securities.

CASH MANAGEMENT

Cash is often called a "nonearning asset." It is needed to pay for labor and raw materials, to buy fixed assets, to pay taxes, to service debt, to pay dividends, and so on. However, cash itself (and also commercial checking accounts) earns no interest. Thus, the goal of the cash manager is to minimize the amount of cash the firm must hold for use in conducting its normal business activities, yet, at the same time, to have sufficient cash (1) to take trade discounts, (2) to maintain its credit rating, and (3) to meet unexpected cash needs. We begin our analysis with a discussion of the reasons for holding cash.

Rationale for Holding Cash

Firms hold cash for two primary reasons:

transactions balance

A cash balance associated with payments and collections; the balance necessary for day-to-day operations.

1. **Transactions.** Cash balances are necessary in business operations. Payments must be made in cash, and receipts are deposited in the cash account. Cash balances associated with routine payments and collections are known as **transactions balances.**

2. **Compensation to banks for providing loans and services.** A bank makes money by lending out funds that have been deposited with it, so the larger its deposits, the better the bank's profit position. In addition, if a bank is providing services to a customer, it may require the customer to leave a minimum balance on deposit to help offset the costs of providing the services. This type of balance, defined as a **compensating balance,** is discussed in detail later in this chapter.

compensating balance

A checking account balance that a firm must maintain with a bank to compensate the bank for services rendered or for granting a loan.

Two other reasons for holding cash have been noted in the finance and economics literature: for *precaution* and for *speculation.* Cash inflows and outflows are somewhat unpredictable, with the degree of predictability varying among firms and industries. Therefore, firms need to hold some cash in reserve for random, unforeseen fluctuations in inflows and outflows. These "safety stocks" are called **precautionary balances,** and the less predictable the firm's cash flows, the larger such balances should be. However, if the firm has easy access to borrowed funds—that is, if it can borrow on short notice—its need for precautionary balances is reduced. Also, as we note later in this chapter, firms that would otherwise need large precautionary balances tend to hold highly liquid marketable securities rather than cash per se; marketable securities serve many of the purposes of cash, but they provide greater interest income than bank deposits.

precautionary balance

A cash balance held in reserve for random, unforeseen fluctuations in cash inflows and outflows.

Some cash balances may be held to enable the firm to take advantage of bargain purchases that might arise; these funds are called **speculative balances.** However, as with precautionary balances, firms today are more likely to rely on reserve borrowing capacity and/or marketable securities portfolios than on cash per se for speculative purposes.

speculative balance

A cash balance that is held to enable the firm to take advantage of any bargain purchases that might arise.

Although the cash accounts of most firms can be thought of as consisting of transactions, compensating, precautionary, and speculative balances, we cannot calculate the amount needed for each purpose, sum them, and produce a total desired cash balance, because the same money often serves more than one purpose. For instance, precautionary and speculative balances can also be used to satisfy compensating balance requirements. Firms do, however, consider all four factors when establishing their target cash positions.

Advantages of Holding Adequate Cash and Near-Cash Assets

In addition to the four motives just discussed, sound working capital management requires that an ample supply of cash be maintained for several specific reasons:

discount

A price reduction that suppliers offer customers for early payment of bills.

1. It is essential that the firm have sufficient cash and near-cash assets to take **discounts.** Suppliers frequently offer customers discounts for early pay-

ment of bills. As we will see in Chapter 13, the cost of not taking discounts is very high, so firms should have enough cash and near-cash assets to permit payment of bills in time to take discounts.

2. Adequate holdings of cash and near-cash assets can help the firm maintain its credit rating by keeping its current and acid test ratios in line with those of other firms in its industry. A strong credit rating enables the firm both to purchase goods from suppliers on favorable terms and to maintain an ample line of credit with its bank.

3. Cash and near-cash assets are useful for taking advantage of favorable business opportunities, such as special offers from suppliers or the chance to acquire another firm.

4. The firm should have sufficient cash and near-cash assets to meet such emergencies as strikes, fires, or competitors' marketing campaigns and to weather seasonal and cyclical downturns.

Self-Test Questions

Why is cash management important?

What are the two primary motives for holding cash?

What are the two secondary motives for holding cash as noted in the finance and economics literature?

CASH MANAGEMENT TECHNIQUES

Cash management has changed significantly over the last 20 years as a result of two factors. First, interest rates have, for much of that time, been trending up, which has increased the opportunity cost of holding cash and encouraged financial managers to search for more efficient ways of managing the firm's cash. Second, new technologies, particularly computerized electronic funds transfer mechanisms, have made improved cash management possible.

Most cash management activities are performed jointly by the firm and its primary bank, but the financial manager is responsible for the effectiveness of the cash management program. Effective cash management encompasses proper management of both the cash inflows and the cash outflows of a firm. More specifically, managing cash inflows and cash outflows entails (1) synchronizing cash flows, (2) using float, (3) accelerating collections, (4) getting available funds to where they are needed, and (5) controlling disbursements. Most business is conducted by large firms, many of which operate regionally, nationally, or even worldwide. They collect cash from many sources and make payments from a number of different cities. For example, companies like IBM, General Motors, and Hewlett-Packard have manufacturing plants all around the world, even more sales offices, and bank accounts in virtually every city where they do business. Their collection points are typically spread out, following sales patterns. Some disbursements are made from local offices, but most disbursements are made in the areas where manufacturing occurs or else from the home office (dividend and interest payments, taxes, debt repayments, and the like). Thus, a major corporation might have hundreds or even thousands of bank accounts, and since there is no reason to think that inflows and outflows will balance in each account, a system must be in place to transfer funds from where they currently are to where they are needed, to arrange loans to cover net corporate shortfalls, and to invest net corporate surpluses without delay. We discuss the most commonly used techniques for accomplishing these tasks in the following sections.

Cash Flow Synchronization

If you as an individual were to receive income once a year, you would probably put it in the bank, draw down your account periodically, and have an average balance during the year equal to about half your annual income. If you received income monthly instead of once a year, you would operate similarly, but now your average balance would be much smaller. If you could arrange to receive income daily and to pay rent, tuition, and other charges on a daily basis, and if you were quite confident of your forecasted inflows and outflows, then you could hold a very small average cash balance.

synchronized cash flows
A situation in which inflows coincide with outflows, thereby permitting a firm to hold low transactions balances.

Exactly the same situation holds for business firms—by improving their forecasts and by arranging things so that cash receipts coincide with required cash outflows, firms can reduce their transactions balances to a minimum. Recognizing this point, utility companies, oil companies, credit card companies, and so on arrange to bill customers, and to pay their own bills, on regular "billing cycles" throughout the month. This improves the **synchronization of cash flows,** which in turn enables a firm to reduce its cash balances, decrease its bank loans, lower interest expenses, and boost profits.

Check-Clearing Process

check clearing
The process of converting a check that has been written and mailed into cash in the payee's account.

When a customer writes and mails a check, this does *not* mean that the funds are immediately available to the receiving firm. Most of us have been told by someone that "the check is in the mail," and we have also deposited a check in our account and then been told that we cannot write our own checks against this deposit until the **check-clearing** process has been completed. Our bank must first make sure that the check we deposited is good and then receive funds itself from the customer's bank before it will give us cash.

As shown on the left side of Figure 10-1, quite a bit of time may be required for a firm to process incoming checks and obtain the use of the money. A check must first be delivered through the mail and then be cleared through the banking system before the money can be put to use. Checks received from customers in distant cities are especially subject to delays because of mail time and also because more parties are involved. For example, assume that we receive a check and deposit it in our bank. Our bank must send the check to the bank on which it was drawn. Only when this latter bank transfers funds to our bank are the funds available for us to use. Checks are generally cleared through the Federal Reserve System or through a clearinghouse set up by the banks in a particular city. Of course, if the check is deposited in the same bank on which it was drawn, that bank merely transfers funds by bookkeeping entries from one of its depositors to another. The length of time required for checks to clear is thus a function of the distance between the payer's and the payee's banks. In the case of private clearinghouses, it can range from one to three days. The maximum

Figure 10-1   ▪   **Diagram of the Check-Clearing Process**

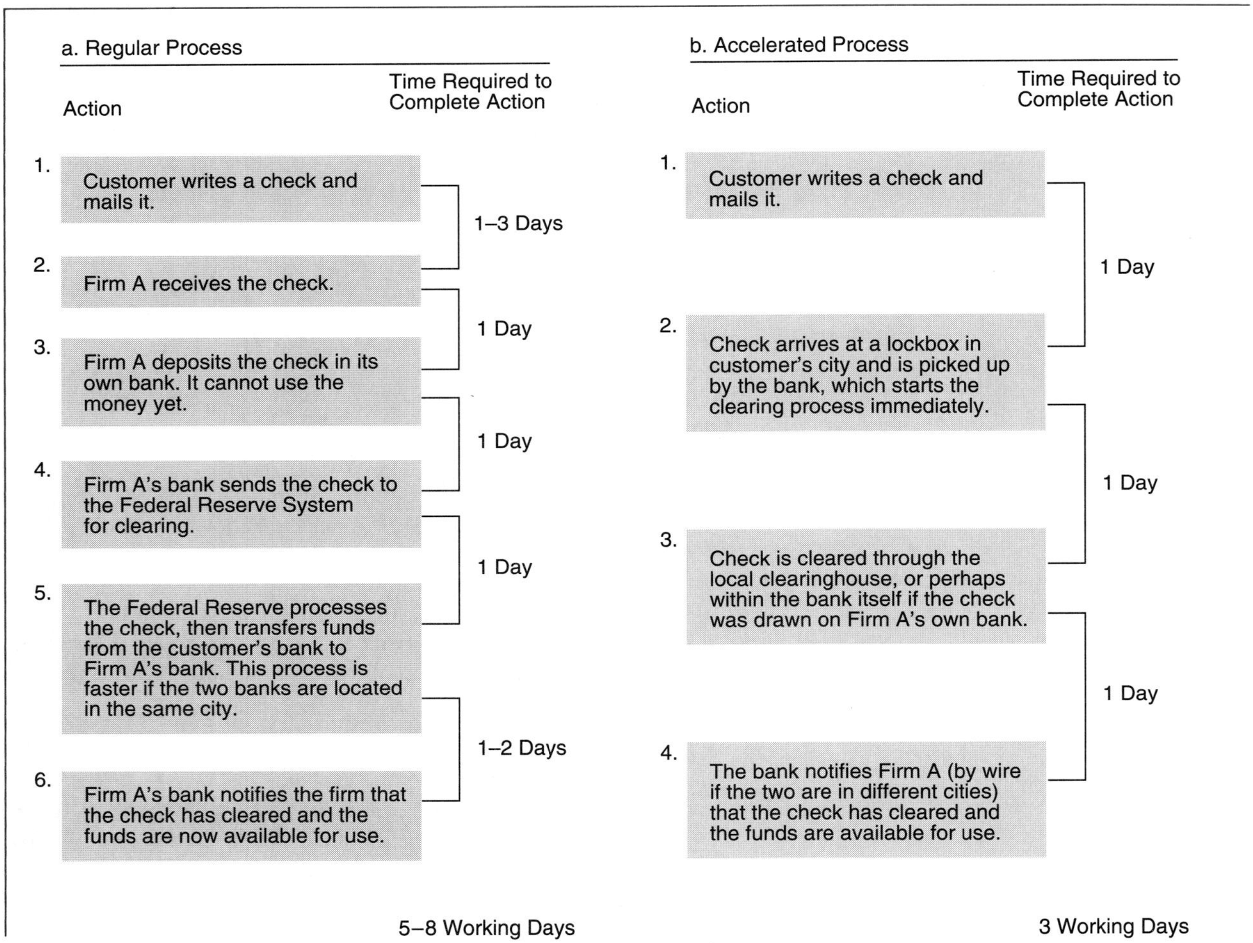

a. Regular Process

| Action | Time Required to Complete Action |

1. Customer writes a check and mails it.

1–3 Days

2. Firm A receives the check.

1 Day

3. Firm A deposits the check in its own bank. It cannot use the money yet.

1 Day

4. Firm A's bank sends the check to the Federal Reserve System for clearing.

1 Day

5. The Federal Reserve processes the check, then transfers funds from the customer's bank to Firm A's bank. This process is faster if the two banks are located in the same city.

1–2 Days

6. Firm A's bank notifies the firm that the check has cleared and the funds are now available for use.

5–8 Working Days

b. Accelerated Process

| Action | Time Required to Complete Action |

1. Customer writes a check and mails it.

1 Day

2. Check arrives at a lockbox in customer's city and is picked up by the bank, which starts the clearing process immediately.

1 Day

3. Check is cleared through the local clearinghouse, or perhaps within the bank itself if the check was drawn on Firm A's own bank.

1 Day

4. The bank notifies Firm A (by wire if the two are in different cities) that the check has cleared and the funds are available for use.

3 Working Days

time required for checks to clear through the Federal Reserve System is two days, but mail delays can slow down things on each end of the Fed's involvement in the process.

Using Float

disbursement float

The value of the checks which we have written but which are still being processed and thus have not been deducted from our account balance by the bank.

Float is defined as the difference between the balance shown in a firm's (or individual's) checkbook and the balance on the bank's records. Suppose a firm writes, on the average, checks in the amount of $5,000 each day, and it takes six days for these checks to clear and to be deducted from the firm's bank account. This will cause the firm's own checkbook to show a balance $30,000 smaller than the balance on the bank's records; this difference is called **disbursement float**. Now suppose the firm also receives checks in the amount of $5,000 daily, but it loses four days while they are being deposited and cleared.

collections float

The amount of checks that we have received but which have not yet been credited to our account.

net float

The difference between our checkbook balance and the balance shown on the bank's books.

This will result in $20,000 of **collections float.** In total, the firm's **net float**— the difference between $30,000 positive disbursement float and the $20,000 negative collections float—will be $10,000.

If the firm's own collection and clearing process is more efficient than that of the recipients of its checks—which is generally true of larger, more efficient firms—then the firm could actually show a *negative* balance on its own books but have a *positive* balance on the records of its bank. Some firms indicate that they *never* have positive book cash balances. One large manufacturer of construction equipment stated that while its account, according to its bank's records, shows an average cash balance of about $20 million, its *book* cash balance is *minus* $20 million—it has $40 million of net float. Obviously the firm must be able to forecast its disbursements and collections accurately in order to make such heavy use of float.

E. F. Hutton provides an example of pushing cash management too far. Hutton, a leading brokerage firm at the time, did business with banks all across the country, and it had to keep compensating balances in these banks. The sizes of the required compensating balances were known, and any excess funds in these banks were sent electronically, on a daily basis, to concentration banks, where they were immediately invested in interest-bearing securities. However, rather than waiting to see what the end-of-day balances actually were, Hutton began estimating inflows and outflows, and it transferred out for investment the *estimated* end-of-day excess. But then Hutton got greedy and began *kiting* checks. Hutton deliberately overestimated its deposits and underestimated clearings of its own checks, thereby deliberately overstating the estimated end-of-day balances. As a result, Hutton was chronically overdrawn at its local banks, and it was in effect earning interest on funds which really belonged to those local banks. It is entirely proper to forecast what your bank will have recorded as your balance and then to make decisions based on the estimate, even if that balance is different from the balance your own books show. However, it is illegal to forecast an overdrawn situation but then to tell the bank that you expect to have a positive balance.[1]

Delays that cause float arise because it takes time for checks (1) to travel through the mail (mail float), (2) to be processed by the receiving firm (processing float), and (3) to clear through the banking system (clearing, or availability, float). Basically, the size of a firm's net float is a function of its ability to speed up collections on checks received and to slow down collections on checks written. Efficient firms go to great lengths to speed up the processing of

---

[1]A question raised during the Hutton investigation was this: "Why didn't the banks recognize that Hutton was systematically overdrawing its account and call the company to task?" The answer is that some banks, with tight controls, did exactly that—they refused to let Hutton get away with the practice. Other banks were lax. Still other banks apparently let Hutton get away with being chronically overdrawn out of fear of losing its business: Hutton used its economic muscle to force the banks to let it get away with an illegal act. In many people's opinion, the banks were as much at fault as Hutton. Still, in business dealings, honesty is presumed, and Hutton was dishonest in its dealings with the banks. This dishonesty severely damaged Hutton's reputation, cost the company profits totaling hundreds of millions of dollars, cost its top managers their jobs, and contributed to the ultimate demise of the company.

incoming checks, thus putting the funds to work faster, and they try to stretch their own payments out as long as possible.

Acceleration of Receipts

Financial managers have been searching for ways to collect receivables faster since credit transactions began. Although cash collection is the financial manager's responsibility, the speed with which checks are cleared is dependent on the banking system. Several techniques are now used both to speed collections and to get funds where they are needed. Included are lockbox plans, pre-authorized debits, and concentration banking.

lockbox plan
A procedure used to speed up collections and reduce float through the use of post office boxes in payers' local areas.

Lockboxes. A **lockbox plan** is one of the oldest cash management tools. In a lockbox system, incoming checks are sent to post office boxes rather than to corporate headquarters. For example, a firm headquartered in New York City might have its West Coast customers send their payments to a box in San Francisco, its customers in the Southwest send their checks to Dallas, and so on, rather than having all checks sent to New York City. Several times a day a local bank will collect the contents of the lockbox and deposit the checks into the company's local account. The bank would then provide the firm with a daily record of the receipts collected, usually via an electronic data transmission system in a format that permits on-line updating of the firm's receivables accounts.

A lockbox system reduces the time required for a firm to receive incoming checks, to deposit them, and to get them cleared through the banking system so that the funds are available for use. As shown on the right side of Figure 10-1, this time reduction occurs because mail time and check collection time are both reduced if the lockbox is located in the geographic area where the customer is located. Lockbox services can often increase the availability of funds by two to five days over the "regular" system.

Pre-Authorized Debits. A *pre-authorized debit* allows funds to be automatically transferred from a customer's account to the firm's account on specified dates. These transactions are also called "checkless" or "paperless" transactions since they are accomplished without using traditional paper checks. However, a record of payment does appear on both parties' bank statements. Pre-authorized debiting accelerates the transfer of funds because mail and check-clearing time are totally eliminated. Although pre-authorized debits are efficient, and they appear to be the trend of the future, the pace of acceptance by payers has been much slower than originally predicted. Of course, a payer who agrees to a pre-authorized debit system loses the disbursement float that is inherent in the paper-based system.

Concentration Banking. Lockbox systems and pre-authorized debits, although efficient in speeding up collections, result in the firm's cash being spread around among many banks. The primary purpose of *concentration banking* is to mobilize funds from decentralized receiving locations, whether they be lockboxes or decentralized company locations, into one or more central cash pools. The cash manager then uses these pools for short-term investing or reallocation among the firm's banks.

concentration bank

Larger bank to which the firm channels funds from the local depository banks which operate its lock-boxes.

depository transfer check (DTC)

A check that is restricted to use in making deposits to a particular account at a particular bank.

electronic depository transfer

The electronic transfer of funds via a telecommunications network that makes funds collected at one bank immediately available from another bank.

In a typical concentration system, the firm's collection banks record deposits received each day. Then, based on disbursement needs, the corporate cash manager transfers the funds from these collection points to a **concentration bank.** Concentration accounts allow firms to take maximum advantage of economies of scale in cash management and investment.

One of the keys to concentration banking is the ability to quickly transfer funds from collecting banks to concentration banks. One commonly used transfer tool is the **depository transfer check (DTC).** Here's how it works: Collection (lockbox) banks report the amounts on hand daily to the firm's concentration bank. The concentration bank, based on preset cash balance targets for the collection accounts, automatically writes DTCs that transfer funds to the concentration bank.

A relatively new development in funds transfer is the **electronic depository transfer,** sometimes called an *ACH-DTC.* The ACH stands for automated clearinghouse, which is an electronic communications network that provides a means of sending data from one bank to another. Instead of using paper checks, magnetic tape files are processed by the ACH, and all entries for a particular bank are placed on a single file which is sent to that bank. Previously banks sent and received their data on tapes, but today most have direct computer links to the ACH. There are actually 32 regional ACH associations, but all of the ACH facilities, except for the New York ACH, are operated by the Federal Reserve System. All ACHs guarantee one-day clearing regardless of the location of the bank on which the check was written. The ACH network sorts all transactions daily, the entries are then forwarded for processing the following day, and the processing accomplishes the actual transfer.

In addition to the automated clearinghouses, the Federal Reserve wire system can be used for cash concentration or other cash transfers. This system is used to move large sums that occur on a sporadic basis, such as would occur if a firm borrowed $10 million in the commercial paper market.

Disbursement Control

Efficient cash management requires that both inflows and outflows be effectively managed. Accelerating collections represents one side of cash management, and controlling funds outflows is the flip side.

Payables Centralization.   No single action controls cash outflows more effectively than the centralized processing of payables. This permits the financial manager to evaluate the payments coming due for the entire firm and to schedule the availability of funds to meet these needs on a companywide basis. Centralizing disbursements also permits more efficient monitoring of payables and float balances. Of course, there are also disadvantages to a centralized disbursement system—regional offices may not be able to make prompt payment for services rendered, which can create ill will and raise the company's operating costs. More than one firm has saved a few pennies by using a cheaper check-disbursing system but lost far more as a result of higher operating costs caused by ill will.

Zero-Balance Accounts.   *Zero-balance accounts (ZBAs)* are special disbursement accounts having a zero-dollar balance on which checks are written. Typically, a firm establishes several ZBAs in the concentration bank and funds them from a master account. As checks are presented to a ZBA for payment, funds are automatically transferred from the master account. If the master account goes negative, it is replenished by borrowing from the bank against a line of credit, by borrowing in the commercial paper market, or by selling some T-bills from the marketable securities portfolio. Zero-balance accounts simplify the control of disbursements and cash balances, hence reduce the amount of idle (non-interest-bearing) cash.

Controlled Disbursement Accounts.   Whereas zero-balance accounts are typically established at concentration banks, *controlled disbursement accounts* can be set up at any bank. In fact, controlled disbursement accounts were initially used only in relatively remote banks, hence this technique was originally called *remote disbursement.* The basic technique is simple: Controlled disbursement accounts are not funded until the day's checks are presented against the account. The key to controlled disbursement is the ability of the bank having the account to report the total daily amount of checks received for clearance by 11 A.M., New York time. This early notification gives financial managers sufficient time (1) to wire funds to the controlled disbursement account to cover the checks presented for payment or (2) to invest excess cash at midday, when money market trading is at a peak.

Cash Management in the Multidivisional Firm

The concepts, techniques, and procedures described thus far in the chapter must be extended when applied to large, national firms. Such corporations have plants and sales offices all across the nation (or around the world), and they deal with banks in all of their operating territories. These companies must maintain compensating balances in each of their banks, and they must be sure that no bank account becomes overdrawn. (After E. F. Hutton's problems, this has become especially important.) Cash inflows and outflows are subject to random fluctuations, so in the absence of close control and coordination, there would be a tendency for some accounts to have shortages while others had excess balances.

An example of such a firm is General Motors, which has extended the electronic transfer system for use in paying its suppliers. GM's electronic system utilizes eight banks across the nation, and it not only speeds up the payment process but also decreases uncertainty about the timing of the payment. This system benefits both GM and its suppliers because it reduces the required level of each firms' transactions and precautionary cash balances. GM's suppliers especially like the electronic system because overdue bills from GM have been reduced considerably, and suppliers take this into account when they bid for GM's business.

Self-Test Questions

What is float? How do firms use float to increase cash management efficiency?

What are some methods firms can use to accelerate receipts?

What are some techniques for controlling disbursements?

INDUSTRY PRACTICE	Where to Stash the Cash?

A high level of corporate cash has been a worldwide phenomenon, fueled by a long economic expansion and relatively high interest rates that have existed in recent years. Large companies with huge stockpiles of cash can handle it in a variety of ways. Some are fairly conservative and keep it mostly untouched, while others apply a more aggressive approach. Four companies' cash management styles are presented here to illustrate some of the possibilities.

Chrysler Corporation believes in active, inventive management of its $2.5 billion in "usable" cash, according to David Chrisco, manager for corporate cash and banking administration. This total does not include "balance sheet cash" such as floats on receipts and disbursements, or cash belonging to wholly owned foreign subsidiaries. Four full-time staff members assist Chrisco, and this structure is different from the arrangement in some companies where, he says, cash management is treated "as more or less a custodial type of function, . . . as some kind of part-time job for some employee."

None of the Chrysler cash goes into bonds — Treasury or otherwise — because of the interest rate price risk associated with their longer maturities. However, Chrisco does work with the company's tax department on strategies for tax-advantaged securities like municipal bonds and preferred stock. He also has explored an area that most large companies avoid — loan participations, in which commercial banks pass along short-term loans to third parties. In another program, Chrysler is experimenting with the idea of outside management for the cash involved with a dividend reinvestment plan.

While Chrysler's $2.5 billion in excess cash seems like a large amount, Chrisco says it is needed as a cushion to protect the firm against unforeseen events. "If you get a wildcat strike and the plants get shut down, it doesn't take very long for the cash supply to run out the door very quickly."

At General Motors the philosophy is simple and conservative — liquidity and protection of principal. Averaging $4.5 billion, the company's cash is stashed in five types of investments — U.S. Treasury bills and notes; Ginnie Mae, Fannie Mae, and Federal Home Loan Mortgage Corporation securities; certificates of deposit and other items from domestic and foreign

Source: "A Portfolio of Cash Management Strategies," *Institutional Investor,* February 1989.

banks; municipal obligations; and commercial paper. Loan participations are not used because "It takes an awful lot of manpower to review individual transactions," says Ned Case, director of corporate financing and investments.

Large amounts of available cash protect GM against such possibilities as a recession in the car business, strikes at suppliers' companies, and lawsuits, and these funds facilitate major acquisitions. The last large purchases for the company — Electronic Data Systems and Hughes Aircraft — each required more than $1 billion in cash. Case says, "We can't afford to risk principal. It's not our money to play with. If it's a choice between making a few more basis points and being comfortable with having bought a high-quality, liquid asset, we will always choose high quality and liquidity."

GM's philosophy corresponds with that of Lloyd Mistele, treasury manager of Toyota Motor Sales U.S.A., whose cash fund of between $1 and $2 billion grew by $500 million in a recent three-year period. Profitability, while desirable, is last among his priorities, after safety, liquidity, and timely availability for known expenditures. Mistele defines "cash" as a portfolio of securities, usually with maturities of a year or less. His staff needs a detailed knowledge of federal and state tax laws to manage the tax-advantaged investments in which the company stows some of its cash — included are such things as money market preferred, auction-rate preferred, municipal bonds, and tax-exempt commercial paper. Toyota U.S.A.'s taxable investments consist primarily of very short-term domestic securities and Eurodollar time deposits. Mistele and his staff are also conservative about transferring their funds. They review interest rates and investment guidelines regularly, but they only shift their cash a few times a year.

Not surprisingly, Mistele's policies are in line with those of his company's parent, Toyota Motor Corporation, which invests most of its 2 trillion yen cash stockpile ($13,080,000,000) in short-term bank deposits, commercial paper, or government securities. In keeping with its risk-averse approach, Toyota won't touch loan participations, stocks, or corporate bonds.

When talking about big hoards of cash, the deepest pockets in the world may belong to the German electronics firm, Siemens, jokingly known to fellow countrymen as "the bank that runs an electronics workshop on the side." Its 24 billion deutsche mark cache ($14,565,840,000) was barely affected by the $2.7 billion withdrawal for two acquisitions in 1989.

Aside from about 5 billion deutsche marks used to cover one month's costs, Siemens' money is invested in short-term time deposits, in fixed-rate bonds and notes with maturities averaging more than three years, and in an equity portfolio. The firm's money-market investments director Reinhard Warkocz's investments of choice are German federal government bonds, U.S. Treasury or government agency paper, and blue-chip German bank and insurance stocks ("safe as bonds"). Even with all that cash, Warkocz is not averse to borrowing. "In countries where we see a currency risk," he says, "we hesitate to invest our stable deutsche marks in accounts receivable and inventories, so we borrow."

The company monitors its performance by comparing it with those of outside cash managers in London and New York. Warkocz says, "From time to time, we learn from other people. But I am very proud that during the 15 years I have been at this job, we have achieved the same or even better performance than [outsiders]. It confirms that we should continue managing our own cash."

COMPENSATING BANKS FOR SERVICES

In addition to lending firms money, banks provide a great many services — they clear checks, operate lockbox plans, supply credit information, and the like. Because these services cost the bank money, the bank must be compensated for rendering them.

Compensating Balances

Banks earn most of their income by lending money at interest, and most of the funds they lend are obtained in the form of deposits. If a firm maintains a deposit account with an average balance of $100,000, and if the bank can lend these funds at a net return of $8,000, then the account is, in a sense, worth $8,000 to the bank. Thus, it is to the bank's advantage to provide services worth up to $8,000 to attract and hold the account.

Banks first determine the costs of the services rendered to their larger customers, and then they estimate the average account balances necessary to provide enough income to compensate for these costs. Firms can make direct fee payments for these services, but they often find it more convenient to maintain compensating balances rather than to pay monthly cash service charges to the bank.[2]

Compensating balances are also required by some banks under loan agreements. During periods when the supply of credit is restricted and interest rates are high, banks frequently require that borrowers maintain accounts which average a specified percentage of the loan amount as a condition for granting a loan; 10 percent is a typical figure. If the required balance is larger than the firm would otherwise maintain, the effective cost of the loan is increased; the excess balance presumably "compensates" the bank for making a loan at a rate below what it could earn on the funds if they were invested elsewhere.[3]

---

[2]Compensating balance arrangements apply to individuals as well as to business firms. Thus, you might get "free" checking services if you maintain a minimum balance of $500 but be charged 25 cents per check if your balance falls below that amount during the month.

[3]The effect of compensating balances on interest rates will be discussed in Chapter 13.

Compensating balances can be established (1) as an *absolute minimum* — say, $100,000 — below which the actual balance must never fall or (2) as a *minimum average balance* — perhaps $100,000 — over some period, generally a month. The absolute minimum is a much more restrictive requirement, because the total amount of cash held during the month must exceed $100,000 by the amount of the firm's transactions balances. The $100,000 in this case is "dead money" from the firm's standpoint. With a minimum average balance, however, the account could fall to zero on one day provided it was $200,000 on some other day, with the average working out to $100,000. Thus, the $100,000 in this case would be available for transactions.

Statistics on compensating balance requirements are not available, but average balances are typical and absolute minimums rare for business accounts. Discussions with bankers, however, indicate that absolute balance requirements are less rare during times of extremely tight money.

Overdraft Systems

overdraft system

A system whereby depositors may write checks in excess of their balances, with the banks automatically extending loans to cover the shortages.

One of the services provided by banks is an **overdraft system.** In such a system, a depositor firm writes checks in excess of its actual balance, and its bank automatically extends loans to cover the shortage. The maximum amount of such loans must, of course, be established beforehand. Although statistics are not available on the usage of overdrafts in the United States, a number of firms have worked out informal, and in some cases formal, overdraft arrangements. Also, both banks and credit card companies regularly establish cash reserve systems for individuals. In general, the use of overdrafts has been increasing in recent years, and, if this trend continues, it will lead to a reduction of cash balances.

? Self-Test Questions

What are compensating balances, and why are they used?

Differentiate between an absolute minimum and a minimum average compensating balance.

What are overdraft systems, and how do they work?

MATCHING THE COSTS AND BENEFITS OF CASH MANAGEMENT

Although a number of techniques have been discussed to reduce cash balance requirements, implementing these procedures is not a costless operation. How far should a firm go in making its cash operations more efficient? As a general rule, the firm should incur these expenses as long as the marginal returns exceed the marginal costs.

For example, suppose that by establishing a lockbox system a firm can reduce its investment in cash by $1 million without increasing the risk of running short of cash. Further, suppose the firm borrows at a cost of 12 percent. The lockbox system will release $1 million, which can be used to reduce bank loans and thus save $120,000 per year. If the costs of setting up and operating the lockbox system are less than $120,000, the move is a good one, but if the costs exceed $120,000, the improvement in efficiency is not worth the cost. It is clear that larger firms, with larger cash balances, can better afford to hire the personnel necessary to maintain tight control over their cash positions. Cash management is one element of business operations in which economies of scale are present.

Very clearly, the value of careful cash management depends upon the costs of funds invested in cash, which in turn depend upon the current rate of interest. In recent years, with interest rates at relatively high levels, firms have been devoting a great deal of care to cash management.[4] As we write this in early 1992, the country is in the midst of a recession, and even though interest rates are lower, the importance of cash management has become even more critical due to the need to boost profits.

Self-Test Question

How far should a firm go in its cash management effort; that is, how much should be spent on cash management?

MARKETABLE SECURITIES

marketable securities
Securities that can be sold on short notice without loss of principal or original investment.

Realistically, the management of cash and marketable securities cannot be separated — management of one implies management of the other. In the first part of the chapter, we focused on cash management. Now we turn to **marketable securities.**

Rationale for Holding Marketable Securities

Marketable securities typically provide much lower yields than operating assets; for example, IBM holds a multibillion-dollar portfolio of marketable securities that yields about 6 percent, while its operating assets provide a return of about 14 percent. Why would a company such as IBM have such large holdings of low-yielding assets? There are two basic reasons for these holdings: (1) They serve as a substitute for cash balances, and (2) they are used as a temporary investment. These points are considered next.

Marketable Securities as a Substitute for Cash.   Some firms hold portfolios of marketable securities in lieu of larger cash balances, liquidating part of the portfolio to increase the cash account when cash outflows exceed inflows. In such situations, the marketable securities could be used as a substitute for transactions balances, for precautionary balances, for speculative balances, or for all three. In most cases, the securities are held primarily for precautionary purposes — most firms prefer to rely on bank credit to make temporary trans-

---

[4]Banks have also placed considerable emphasis on developing and marketing cash management services. Because of scale economies, banks can generally provide these services to smaller companies at lower costs than the companies could achieve by operating in-house cash management systems.

actions or to meet speculative needs, but they may still hold some liquid assets to guard against a possible shortage of bank credit.

A few years ago, IBM had substantially more marketable securities than it does today. Those large liquid balances had been built up primarily as a reserve for possible damage payments resulting from pending antitrust suits. When it became clear that IBM would win most of the suits, its liquidity needs declined, and the company spent some of the funds on other assets, including repurchases of its own stock. This is a good example of a firm's building up its precautionary balances to handle possible emergencies.

Marketable Securities Held as a Temporary Investment.   Temporary investments in marketable securities generally occur in one of the following two situations:

1. **To finance seasonal or cyclical operations.** If the firm has a conservative financing policy as we defined it back in Panel c of Figure 9-3, then its long-term capital will exceed its permanent assets, and marketable securities will be held when inventories and receivables are low. On the other hand, with a highly aggressive policy it will never carry any securities, and it will borrow heavily to meet peak needs. With a moderate policy, where maturities are matched, permanent assets will be matched with long-term financing, most seasonal increases in inventories and receivables will be met by short-term loans, but the firm will also carry marketable securities at certain times.

2. **To meet known financial requirements.** Marketable securities are frequently built up immediately preceding quarterly corporate tax payment dates. Further, if a major plant construction program is planned for the near future, if an acquisition is planned, or if a bond issue is about to mature, a firm may build up its marketable securities portfolio to provide the required funds. For example, Commonwealth Edison, the electric utility serving Chicago, has a permanent, ongoing construction program, generating a continuous need for new capital. Since there are substantial fixed costs involved in stock or bond flotations, these securities are issued infrequently and in large amounts.

    During the 1970s, Edison followed the practice of selling bonds and stock *before* the capital was needed, investing the proceeds in marketable securities, and then liquidating the securities to finance plant construction. Plan A in Figure 10-2 illustrates this procedure. However, during the 1980s, Edison encountered financial stress. It was forced to use up its liquid assets and to switch to its present policy of financing plant construction with short-term bank loans and then selling long-term securities to retire the bank loans when they had built up to some target level. This policy is illustrated by Plan B of Figure 10-2.

Plan A is the more conservative, less risky one. First, the company is minimizing its liquidity problems because it has no short-term debt hanging over its head. Second, it is sure of having the funds available to meet construction payments as they come due. On the other hand, firms generally have to pay higher interest rates when they borrow than the return they receive on marketable securities, so following the less risky strategy has a cost.

Figure 10-2   ▪   **Alternative Methods of Financing a Continuous Construction Program**

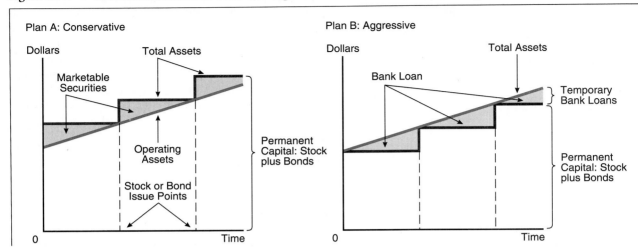

Factors Influencing the Choice of Marketable Securities

A wide variety of securities, differing in terms of default risk, interest rate price risk, liquidity risk, and expected rate of return, are available to firms that choose to hold marketable securities. In this section we first consider the different types of risk, then we look at the extent to which each type of risk is found in different securities, and, finally, we look at some specific instruments which are suitable investments for temporary excess cash.

default risk

The risk that a borrower will not pay the interest or principal on a loan.

Default Risk.   The risk that a borrower will be unable to make interest payments, or to repay the principal amount on schedule, is known as **default risk.** If the issuer is the U.S. Treasury, default risk is negligible, so Treasury securities are regarded as being default-free. (Treasury securities are not completely free of risk, since U.S. government bonds are subject to risk caused by interest rate fluctuations, and they are also subject to loss of purchasing power due to inflation.) Recall that in Chapter 3 we developed this equation for determining the nominal interest rate:

$$k_{Nom} = k^* + IP + DRP + LP + MRP.$$

Here k^* is the real risk-free rate, IP is a premium for expected inflation, DRP is the default risk premium, LP is the liquidity (or marketability) risk premium, and MRP is the maturity (or interest rate) risk premium. Also, remember from Chapter 3 that the risk-free rate, k_{RF}, is equal to $k^* + IP$. As we learned in Chapter 3, a U.S. Treasury bill comes closest to the risk-free rate, while a U.S. Treasury bond has no default or liquidity risk premiums, but it is exposed to interest rate price risk, so a maturity risk premium is included in its nominal interest rate. Corporate securities, as well as bonds issued by state and local governments, are subject to some degree of default risk, so these securities' returns include a default risk premium. Several organizations (for example, Moody's Investment Service and Standard & Poor's Corporation) rate bonds.

They classify them on a scale that ranges from very high quality to highly speculative, with a definite chance of going into default. Ratings change from time to time as the issuer's situation changes.

Event Risk.   The probability that some event (such as a recapitalization or a leveraged buyout) will occur and suddenly increase a firm's default risk is called **event risk.** Bonds issued by industrial and service companies generally have more event risk than bonds issued by regulated companies such as banks or electric utilities. Also, long-term securities are affected more by unfavorable events than are short-term securities. Treasury securities do not carry any event risk, barring national disaster.

event risk
The risk that an event will occur that suddenly increases a firm's default risk.

Interest Rate Price Risk.   We saw in Chapter 6 that bond prices vary with changes in interest rates. Also, the prices of long-term bonds are much more sensitive to changes in interest rates than are prices of short-term securities — long-term bonds have more **interest rate price risk.** Thus, if Allied's treasurer purchased at par $1 million of 25-year U.S. government bonds paying 9 percent interest, and if interest rates then rose to 14.5 percent, the market value of the bonds would fall from $1 million to just below $635,000 — a loss of almost 40 percent. (This actually happened from 1980 to 1982.) If 90-day Treasury bills had been held, however, the loss would have been negligible. Thus, the Treasury bill would have a zero maturity risk premium, but the long-term Treasury bond would have a positive maturity risk premium included in its nominal interest rate.

interest rate price risk
The risk of declines in bond prices to which investors are exposed due to rising interest rates.

Inflation Risk.   Another type of risk is **inflation risk,** or the risk that inflation will reduce the purchasing power of a given sum of money. Inflation risk, which is important both to firms and to individual investors during times of rising prices, is lower on assets whose returns tend to rise with inflation than on assets whose returns are fixed. Thus, real estate and common stocks are generally better hedges against inflation than are bonds and other fixed-income securities. As you should recall from our discussion in Chapter 3, a security's interest rate reflects the average rate of inflation expected over the security's life. Therefore, a 90-day Treasury bill would include the average rate of inflation expected over the 90-day period, while a 30-year Treasury bond would include the average rate of inflation expected over a 30-year period. Thus, if a high rate of inflation is expected in the future, that expectation is built into interest rates. Accordingly, the real risk of inflation to bondholders is the possibility that actual inflation will exceed the expected level.

inflation risk
The risk that inflation will reduce the purchasing power of a given sum of money.

Marketability Risk.   An asset that can be sold on short notice for close to its quoted market price is considered to be highly marketable. If Allied purchased $1 million of infrequently traded bonds of a relatively obscure company like Bigham Pork Products, it would probably have to accept a price reduction in order to sell the bonds on short notice. On the other hand, if Allied invested in U.S. Treasury bonds, or in bonds issued by AT&T, General Motors, or Exxon, it would be able to dispose of them almost instantaneously at close to the quoted market price. These latter bonds are therefore said to have very little **marketability risk.** If we go back to the nominal interest rate equation discussed

marketability risk
The risk that securities cannot be sold easily at close to the quoted market price.

earlier, the required return for any bond includes a premium for inflation, default, maturity, and liquidity risk. Marketability risk would be closely associated with liquidity risk. Therefore, the bonds of Bigham Pork Products would have a greater liquidity premium than the bonds of AT&T, General Motors, and Exxon.

Of course, long-term bonds are exposed to significantly more interest rate price risk than are short-term instruments. There are many types of safe, highly liquid short-term securities in which a company can invest temporary excess cash. These instruments will be discussed shortly.

Returns on Securities (Yields). As we know from earlier chapters, the higher a security's risk, the higher its required return. Thus corporate treasurers, like other investors, must make a tradeoff between risk and return when choosing marketable securities. Because these securities are generally held either for a specific known need or for use in emergencies, the firm might be financially embarrassed should the portfolio decline in value. Also, most corporations do not have investment departments specializing in appraising securities and determining the probability of their going into default. Accordingly, the marketable securities portfolio is generally composed of highly liquid short-term securities issued either by the U.S. government or by the very strongest corporations. Given the purpose of the portfolio, treasurers should not sacrifice safety for higher rates of return.

Types of Marketable Securities

Table 10-1 lists the major types of securities available for investment, with yields as of June 10, 1977, February 10, 1982, and February 11, 1992. Depending on how long they will be held, the financial manager decides upon a suitable set of securities, and a suitable maturity pattern, to hold as **near-cash reserves.**

It should be noted that larger corporations, with large amounts of surplus cash, tend to own directly Treasury bills, commercial paper, and CDs, as well as Euromarket securities. Smaller firms, on the other hand, are more likely to invest through a money market or preferred stock mutual fund because the small firm's volume of investment simply does not warrant the hiring of specialists who can manage the portfolio and make sure that the securities held mature (or can be sold) at the same time cash is required. Firms can use a mutual fund and then literally write checks on the fund to meet cash needs as they arise. Interest rates on money funds are somewhat lower than rates on direct investments of equivalent risk because of management fees, but for smaller companies the net returns may well be higher on money funds.

near-cash reserves
Reserves that can be quickly and easily converted to cash.

? Self-Test Questions

Why do firms hold marketable securities?

What criteria are applied when selecting securities for a firm's liquid asset portfolio?

What are some securities commonly held as marketable securities?

Table 10-1 ▪ **Securities Available for Investment of Surplus Cash**

Security	Typical Maturity at Time of Issue	Approximate Yields		
		6/10/77	2/10/82	2/11/92
Suitable to Hold as Near-Cash Reserves				
U.S. Treasury bills[a]	91 days to 1 year	4.8%	15.1%	3.8%
Commercial paper[a]	Up to 270 days	5.5	15.3	4.0
Negotiable certificates of deposit (CDs) of U.S. banks	Up to 1 year	6.0	15.5	3.6
Money market mutual funds	Instant liquidity	5.1	14.0	4.0
Floating rate and market auction preferred stock[b]	Instant liquidity	N.A.	N.A.	3.4
Eurodollar time deposits	Up to 1 year	6.1	16.2	4.0
Not Suitable to Hold as Near-Cash Reserves				
U.S. Treasury notes	3 to 10 years	6.8	14.8	7.2
U.S. Treasury bonds	Up to 30 years	7.6	14.6	7.8
Corporate bonds (AAA)[c]	Up to 40 years	8.2	16.0	8.4
State and local government bonds (AAA)[c,d]	Up to 30 years	5.7	12.8	6.6
Preferred stocks (AAA)[c,d]	30 years to perpetual	7.5	14.0	7.6
Common stocks of other corporations	Unlimited	Variable	Variable	Variable
Common stock of the firm in question	Unlimited	Variable	Variable	Variable

[a]Treasury bills and commercial paper are sold at a discount but are paid off at par upon maturity, so their returns are quoted on a *discount basis rate*. To obtain an interest rate which can be compared to quoted yields on coupon bonds—called a *yield basis rate*—we use the following formula:

$$\text{Yield basis rate} \atop \text{(Effective annual rate)} = \frac{365(\text{Discount basis rate})}{360 - (\text{Discount basis rate})(\text{Days to maturity})}.$$

To illustrate, if we assume a 3-month (91-day) maturity, the T-bills' 3.8 percent discount basis rate on February 11, 1992, translates into a yield basis rate (or effective annual rate) of 3.89 percent:

$$\text{Yield basis rate} = \frac{365(0.038)}{360 - 0.038(91)}$$

$$= 0.0389 = 3.89\%.$$

See Robert C. Radcliffe, *Investment Concepts, Analysis, and Strategy* (Glenview, Ill.: Scott, Foresman, 1990), for a further discussion.

[b]Floating rate and market auction preferred stocks are recent innovations in near-cash securities. They are held by corporations (often through money funds designed for this purpose) because of the 70 percent dividend tax exclusion.

[c]Rates shown for corporate and state/local government bonds, and for preferred stock, are for longer maturities rated AAA. Lower-rated securities have higher yields. The slope of the yield curve determines whether shorter- or longer-term securities of a given rating would have higher yields.

[d]Rates are lower on state/municipal government bonds because the interest they pay is exempt from federal income taxes, and the rate on preferred stocks is low because 70 percent of the dividends paid on them is exempt from federal taxes for corporate owners, who own most preferred stocks.

Figure 10-3   ∎   **Cash Balances under the Baumol Model's Assumptions**

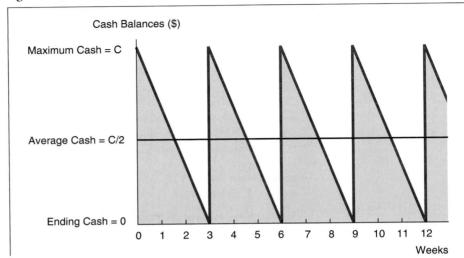

THE BAUMOL MODEL FOR BALANCING CASH AND MARKETABLE SECURITIES

In Chapter 8, when we discussed Allied's cash budget, we took as a given the $10 million target cash balance. In this chapter, we have discussed how lockboxes, synchronizing inflows and outflows, and float can reduce the required cash balance. Now we consider a formal model which can be used for establishing the target cash balance.

William Baumol first noted that cash balances are in many respects similar to inventories, and that the EOQ inventory model, which will be developed in Chapter 12, can be used to establish a target cash balance.[5] Baumol's model assumes that the firm uses cash at a steady, predictable rate—say, $1 million per week—and that the firm's cash inflows from operations also occur at a steady, predictable rate—say, $900,000 per week. Therefore, the firm's net cash outflows, or net need for cash, also occur at a steady rate—in this case, $100,000 per week.[6] Under these steady-state assumptions, the firm's cash position will resemble the situation shown in Figure 10-3.

If our illustrative firm started at Time 0 with a cash balance of C = $300,000, and if its outflows exceeded its inflows by $100,000 per week, then its cash balance would drop to zero at the end of Week 3, and its average cash

---

[5]William J. Baumol, "The Transactions Demand for Cash: An Inventory Theoretic Approach," *Quarterly Journal of Economics,* November 1952, 545–556.

[6]Our hypothetical firm is experiencing a $100,000 weekly cash shortfall, but this does not necessarily imply that it is headed for bankruptcy. The firm could, for example, be highly profitable and be enjoying high earnings but be expanding so rapidly that it is experiencing chronic cash shortages that must be made up by borrowing or by selling common stock. Or the firm could be in the construction business and therefore receive major cash inflows at wide intervals but have net cash outflows of $100,000 per week between major inflows.

Figure 10-4 ▪ **Determination of the Target Cash Balance**

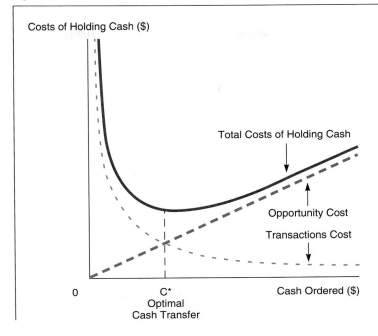

balance would be C/2 = \$300,000/2 = \$150,000. Therefore, at the end of Week 3 the firm would have to replenish its cash balance, either by selling marketable securities, if it had any, or by borrowing.

If C were set at a higher level, say, \$600,000, then the cash supply would last longer (6 weeks), and the firm would have to sell securities (or borrow) less frequently, but its average cash balance would rise from \$150,000 to \$300,000. Brokerage or some other type of transactions cost must be incurred to sell securities (or to borrow), so holding larger cash balances will lower the transactions costs associated with obtaining cash. On the other hand, cash provides no income, so the larger the average cash balance, the higher the opportunity cost, which is the return that could have been earned on securities or other assets held in lieu of cash. Thus, we have the situation that is graphed in Figure 10-4. The optimal cash balance is found by using the following variables and equations:

C = amount of cash raised by selling marketable securities or by borrowing. $C/2$ = average cash balance.

C^* = optimal amount of cash to be raised by selling marketable securities or by borrowing. $C^*/2$ = optimal average cash balance.

F = fixed costs of making a securities trade or of obtaining a loan.

T = total amount of net new cash needed for transactions during the entire period (usually a year).

k = opportunity cost of holding cash, set equal to the rate of return forgone on marketable securities or the cost of borrowing to hold cash.

The total costs of cash balances consist of holding (or opportunity) costs plus transactions costs:[7]

$$\begin{aligned} \text{Total} \atop \text{costs} &= \qquad \text{Holding costs} \qquad + \qquad \text{Transactions costs} \\ &= \left(\begin{matrix}\text{Average cash} \\ \text{balance}\end{matrix}\right)\left(\begin{matrix}\text{Opportunity} \\ \text{cost}\end{matrix}\right) + \left(\begin{matrix}\text{Number of} \\ \text{transactions}\end{matrix}\right)\left(\begin{matrix}\text{Cost per} \\ \text{transaction}\end{matrix}\right) \\ &= \frac{C}{2}(k) + \frac{T}{C}(F). \end{aligned} \qquad (10\text{-}1)$$

The minimum total costs are achieved when C is set equal to C*, the optimal cash transfer. C* is found as follows:[8]

$$C^* = \sqrt{\frac{2(F)(T)}{k}}. \qquad (10\text{-}2)$$

Baumol model

An economic model that determines the optimal cash balance by using economic ordering quantity (EOQ) concepts.

Equation 10-2 is the **Baumol model** for determining optimal cash balances. To illustrate its use, suppose F = \$150; T = 52 weeks × \$100,000/week = \$5,200,000; and k = 15% = 0.15. Then

$$C^* = \sqrt{\frac{2(\$150)(\$5,200,000)}{0.15}} = \$101,980.$$

Therefore, the firm should sell securities in the amount of \$101,980 when its cash balance approaches zero, thus building its cash balance back up to \$101,980. If we divide T by C*, we have the number of transactions per year: \$5,200,000/\$101,980 = 50.99 ≈ 51, or about once a week. The firm's average cash balance is \$101,980/2 = \$50,990 ≈ \$51,000.

Notice that the optimal cash balance increases less than proportionately with increases in the amount of cash needed for transactions. For example, if the firm's size and consequently its net new cash needs doubled from \$5,200,000 to \$10,400,000 per year, average cash balances would increase by only 41 percent, from \$51,000 to \$72,000. This suggests that there are economies of scale in holding cash balances, and this in turn gives larger firms an edge over smaller ones.[9]

Of course, the firm would probably want to hold a safety stock of cash designed to reduce the probability of a cash shortage to some specified level.

---

[7]Total costs can be expressed on either a before-tax or an after-tax basis. Both methods lead to the same conclusions regarding target cash balances and comparative costs. For simplicity, we present the model here on a before-tax basis.

[8]Equation 10-1 is differentiated with respect to C. The derivative is set equal to zero, and we then solve for C = C* to derive Equation 10-2. This model, applied to inventories and called the EOQ model, is discussed further in Chapter 12.

[9]This edge may, of course, be more than offset by other factors—after all, cash management is only one aspect of running a business.

However, if the firm is able to sell securities or to borrow on short notice — and most larger firms can do so in a matter of just a couple of hours simply by making a telephone call — the safety stock of cash can be quite low.

The Baumol model is obviously simplistic in many respects. Most important, it assumes relatively stable, predictable cash inflows and outflows, and it does not take into account any seasonal or cyclical trends. Other models have been developed to deal both with uncertainty in the cash flows and with trends. Any of these models, including the Baumol model, can provide a useful starting point for establishing a target cash balance, but all of them have limitations and must be applied with judgment.

Self-Test Questions

What is the purpose of the Baumol model?

Write out the equation for the model and then list its key assumptions.

SUMMARY

In this chapter, we discussed cash and marketable securities. First, we examined some cash management techniques, and then we discussed marketable securities. Finally, we discussed the Baumol model for setting the target cash balance. The key concepts covered are listed below.

- The **primary goal of cash management** is to reduce the amount of cash held to the minimum necessary to conduct business.

- The **transactions balance** is the cash necessary to conduct day-to-day business, whereas the **precautionary balance** is a cash reserve held to meet random, unforeseen needs. A **compensating balance** is a minimum checking account balance that a bank requires as compensation either for services provided or as part of a loan agreement. Firms also hold **speculative balances,** which allow them to take advantage of bargain purchases. Note, though, that borrowing capacity and marketable security holdings reduce the need for both precautionary and speculative balances.

- **Effective cash management** encompasses the proper management of cash inflows and outflows, which entails (1) synchronizing cash flows, (2) using float, (3) accelerating collections, (4) determining where and when funds will be needed and insuring that they are available at the right place at the right time, and (5) controlling disbursements.

- **Disbursement float** is the amount of funds associated with checks written by our firm that are still in process and hence have not yet been deducted by the bank from our account.

- **Collections float** is the amount of funds associated with checks written to our firm that have not been cleared and hence are not yet available for our use.

- **Net float** is the difference between disbursement float and collections float, and it also is equal to the difference between the balance in our firm's checkbook and the balance on the bank's records. The larger the net float, the smaller the cash balances we must maintain, so net float is good.

▪ Two techniques that can be used to speed up collections are (1) **lock-boxes** and (2) **pre-authorized debits.** Also, a **concentration banking system** consolidates cash into a centralized pool that can be managed more efficiently than a large number of individual accounts.

▪ Three techniques for controlling disbursements are (1) **payables centralization,** (2) **zero-balance accounts,** and (3) **controlled disbursement accounts.**

▪ The implementation of a sophisticated cash management system is costly, so all cash management actions must be evaluated to insure that **benefits exceed costs.**

▪ Firms can reduce their cash balances by holding **marketable securities,** which can be easily sold on short notice at close to their quoted market values. Marketable securities serve both as a substitute for cash and as a temporary investment for funds that will be needed in the near future. Safety is the primary consideration when selecting marketable securities.

▪ The **Baumol model** is used to help determine the optimal cash balance. This model balances the opportunity cost of holding cash against the transactions costs associated with replenishing the cash account by selling off marketable securities or by borrowing.

$$\text{Optimal cash transfer} = C^* = \sqrt{\frac{2(F)(T)}{k}}.$$

Questions

10-1 What are the two principal reasons for holding cash? Can a firm estimate its target cash balance by summing the cash held to satisfy each of the two?

10-2 Explain how each of the following factors would probably affect a firm's target cash balance if all other factors were held constant.
  a. The firm institutes a new billing procedure which better synchronizes its cash inflows and outflows.
  b. The firm develops a new sales forecasting technique which improves its forecasts.
  c. The firm reduces its portfolio of U.S. Treasury bills.
  d. The firm arranges to use an overdraft system for its checking account.
  e. The firm borrows a large amount of money from its bank and also begins to write far more checks than it did in the past.
  f. Interest rates on Treasury bills rise from 5 percent to 10 percent.

10-3 Why would a lockbox plan make more sense for a firm that makes sales all over the United States than for a firm with the same volume of business but concentrated in its home city?

10-4 Would a corporate treasurer be more tempted to invest the firm's liquidity portfolio in long-term as opposed to short-term securities when the yield curve was upward sloping or downward sloping?

10-5 What does the term "liquidity" mean? Which would be more important to a firm that held a portfolio of marketable securities as precautionary balances against the possibility of losing a major lawsuit—liquidity or rate of return? Explain.

10-6 Firm A's management is very conservative whereas Firm B's is more aggressive. Is it true that, other things the same, Firm B would probably have larger holdings of marketable securities? Explain.

10-7 Is it true that interest rate price risk refers to the risk that a firm will be unable to pay the interest on its bonds? Explain.

10-8 When selecting securities for portfolio investments, corporate treasurers must make a tradeoff between risk and returns. Is it true that most treasurers are willing to assume a fairly high exposure to risk to gain higher expected returns?

Self-Test Problems   *(Solutions Appear in Appendix B)*

ST-1
Key terms

Define each of the following terms:

a. Transactions balance; compensating balance; precautionary balance; speculative balance
b. Trade discounts
c. Synchronized cash flows
d. Check clearing; net float; disbursement float; collections float
e. Lockbox plan; pre-authorized debit
f. Depository transfer check (DTC); electronic depository transfer; concentration bank
g. Overdraft system; zero-balance accounts; controlled disbursement accounts
h. Marketable securities; near-cash reserves
i. Default risk; interest rate price risk; inflation (purchasing power) risk; marketability risk; event risk
j. Baumol model

ST-2
Float

The Upton Company is setting up a new checking account with Howe National Bank. Upton plans to issue checks in the amount of $1 million each day and to deduct them from its own records at the close of business on the day they are written. On average, the bank will receive and clear the checks at 5 P.M. the third day after they are written; for example, a check written on Monday will be cleared on Thursday afternoon. The firm's agreement with the bank requires it to maintain a $500,000 average compensating balance; this is $250,000 greater than the cash balance the firm would otherwise have on deposit. It makes a $500,000 deposit at the time it opens the account.

a. Assuming that the firm makes deposits at 4 P.M. each day (and the bank includes them in that day's transactions), how much must it deposit daily in order to maintain a sufficient balance once it reaches a steady state? (To do this, set up a table which shows the daily balance recorded on the company's books and the daily balance at the bank until a steady state is reached.) Indicate the required deposit on Day 1, Day 2, Day 3, if any, and each day thereafter, assuming that the company will write checks for $1 million on Day 1 and each day thereafter.
b. How many days of float does Upton have?
c. What ending daily balance should the firm try to maintain (1) on the bank's records and (2) on its own records?

ST-3
Comparison of transfer methods

Kroncke Inc. has grown from a small Boston firm with customers concentrated in New England to a large, national firm serving customers throughout the United States. It has, however, kept its central billing system in Boston. On average, 5 days elapse from the time customers mail payments until Kroncke is able to receive, process, and deposit them. To shorten the collection period, Kroncke is considering the installation of a lockbox system consisting of 30 local depository banks, or lockbox operators, and 8 regional concentration banks. The fixed costs of operating the system are estimated to be $14,000 per month. Under this system, customers' checks would be received by the lockbox operator 1 day after they are mailed, and daily collections should average $30,000 at each location. The collections would be transferred daily to the regional concentration banks. One transfer mechanism involves having the local depository banks use "mail depository transfer checks," or DTCs, to move the funds to the concentration banks; the alternative would be to use electronic (wire) transfers. A DTC would cost only 75 cents, but it would take 2 days before funds were in the concentration bank and thus available to Kroncke. Therefore, float time under the DTC system would be 1 day for mail plus 2 days for transfers, or 3 days total, down from 5 days. A wire transfer would cost $11, but funds would be available immediately, so float time would be only 1 day. If Kroncke's opportunity cost is 11 percent, should it initiate the lockbox system? If so, which transfer method should be used? (Assume that there are 52 × 5 = 260 working days in a year.)

Problems

10-1
Net float

The Garvin Company is setting up a new checking account with Barngrover National Bank. Garvin plans to issue checks in the amount of $1.6 million each day and to deduct them from its own records at the close of business on the day they are written. On average, the bank will receive and clear (that is, deduct from the firm's bank balance) the checks at 5 P.M. the fourth day after they are written; for example, a check written on Monday will be cleared on Friday afternoon. The firm's agreement with the bank requires it to maintain a $1.2 million average compensating balance; this is $400,000 greater than the cash balance the firm would otherwise have on deposit. It makes a $1.2 million deposit at the time it opens the account.

a. Assuming that the firm makes deposits at 4 P.M. each day (and the bank includes them in that day's transactions), how much must it deposit daily in order to maintain a sufficient balance once it reaches a steady state? (To do this, set up a table which shows the daily balance recorded on the company's books and the daily balance at the bank until a steady state is reached.) Indicate the required deposit on Day 1, Day 2, Day 3, Day 4, if any, and each day thereafter, assuming that the company will write checks for $1.6 million on Day 1 and each day thereafter.

b. How many days of float does Garvin carry?

c. What ending daily balance should the firm try to maintain (1) on the bank's records and (2) on its own records?

d. Explain how net float can help increase the value of the firm's common stock.

10-2
Lockbox system

Durst Corporation began operations 5 years ago as a small firm serving customers in the Denver area. However, its reputation and market area grew quickly, so that today Durst has customers throughout the entire United States. Despite its broad customer base, Durst has maintained its headquarters in Denver and keeps its central billing system there. Durst's management is considering an alternative collection procedure to reduce its mail time and processing float. On average, it takes 5 days from the time customers mail payments until Durst is able to receive, process, and deposit them. Durst would like to set up a lockbox collection system, which it estimates would reduce the time lag from customer mailing to deposit by 3 days—bringing it down to 2 days. Durst receives an average of $1,400,000 in payments per day.

a. How many days of collection float now exist (Durst's customers' disbursement float) and what would it be under the lockbox system? What reduction in cash balances could Durst achieve by initiating the lockbox system?

b. If Durst has an opportunity cost of 10 percent, how much is the lockbox system worth on an annual basis?

c. What is the maximum monthly charge Durst should pay for the lockbox system?

10-3

Comparison of
transfer mechanisms

The San Francisco field office of the Metallux Corporation has sold a quantity of silver ingots for $22,500. Metallux wants to transfer this amount to its concentration bank in New York as economically as possible. Two means of transfer are being considered:

(1) A mail depository transfer check (DTC), which costs $0.75 and takes three days.

(2) A wire transfer, which costs $8.00 and for which funds are immediately available in New York.

a. Metallux earns 12 percent annual interest on funds in its concentration bank. Which transfer method should Metallux use to minimize the total cost of the transfer?

b. At what dollar transfer amount would Metallux be indifferent to the two transfer procedures? (Hint: Set the cost of the two methods equal.)

c. What other factors might influence the decision?

EXAM-TYPE PROBLEMS

The problems included in this section are set up in such a way that they could be used as multiple-choice exam problems.

10-4

Optimal cash transfer

Bildersee Industries projects that cash outlays of $4.5 million will occur uniformly throughout the year. Bildersee plans to meet its cash requirements by periodically selling marketable securities from its portfolio. The firm's marketable securities are invested to earn 12 percent, and the cost per transaction of converting securities to cash is $27.

a. Use the Baumol model to determine the optimal transaction size for transfers from marketable securities to cash.

b. What will be Bildersee's average cash balance?

c. How many transfers per year will be required?

d. What will be Bildersee's total annual cost of maintaining cash balances? What would the total cost be if the company maintained an average cash balance of $50,000 or of $0 (it deposits funds daily to meet cash requirements)?

10-5

Lockbox system

Koehl and Daughters Inc. operates a mail-order firm doing business on the West Coast. Koehl receives an average of $325,000 in payments per day. On average it takes 4 days from the time customers mail checks until Koehl receives and processes them. Koehl is considering the use of a lockbox system to reduce collection and processing float. The system will cost $6,500 per month and will consist of 10 local depository banks and a concentration bank located in San Francisco. Under this system, customers' checks should be received at the lockbox locations 1 day after they are mailed, and daily totals will be transferred to San Francisco using wire transfers costing $9.75 each. Assume that Koehl has an opportunity cost of 10 percent and that there are $52 \times 5 = 260$ working days, hence 260 transfers from each lockbox location, in a year.

a. What is the total annual cost of operating the lockbox system?

b. What is the annual benefit of the lockbox system to Koehl?

c. Should Koehl initiate the system?

INTEGRATIVE PROBLEM

10-6

Cash and marketable
securities management

Ray Smith, a retired librarian, recently opened a sportsman's shop called Ray's Camping & Fishing Gear, Unlimited. Ray decided at age 62 that he wasn't quite ready to stay at home, living the life of leisure. It had always been his dream to open an outdoor sportsman's shop, so his friends convinced him to go ahead. Because Ray's educational background was in literature and not in business, he hired you, a finance expert, to help him with the store's cash management. Ray is very eager to learn, so he asked you to develop a set of questions to help him understand cash management. Now answer the following questions:

a. What is the goal of cash management?

b. For what two primary reasons do firms hold cash?

c. What is meant by the terms "precautionary" and "speculative" balances?

d. What are some specific advantages for a firm holding adequate cash balances?

e. How can a firm synchronize its cash flows, and what good would this do?

f. You have been going through the store's checkbook and bank balances. In the process, you discovered that Ray, on average, writes checks in the amount of $500 each day and that it takes about 5 days for these checks to clear. Also, the firm receives checks in the amount of $500 daily, but loses 4 days while they are being deposited and cleared. What is the firm's disbursement float, collections float, and net float?

g. How can a firm speed up collections and slow down disbursements?

h. Identify two funds transfer "tools" and explain how they work. Would they be appropriate for Ray's business?

i. Define compensating balances, overdraft systems, zero balance accounts, and controlled disbursement accounts, and explain how each is used.

j. Why would a firm hold marketable securities?

k. What factors should a firm consider in building its marketable securities portfolio? What are some securities which should and which should not be held?

l. What is the Baumol model, and what are its major assumptions? How might the firm use the Baumol model? Assume that Ray's opportunity cost of holding cash is 9.5 percent, the fixed cost of obtaining a loan is $75, and the total amount of cash needed for transactions during the year is $200,000. What is the optimal cash balance, and what is the total cost associated with the average cash balance? If Ray tries to use the Baumol model to determine his cash balances, what could go wrong? Should Ray hold a "safety stock" of cash?

COMPUTER-RELATED PROBLEM

Work the problem in this section only if you are using the computer problem diskette.

10-7

Lockbox system

Use the model in File C10 to work this problem.

a. Refer back to Problem 10-5. Would the lockbox system be beneficial if Koehl could operate it with only 8 lockbox locations while achieving the same reduction in float?

b. Suppose that interest rates rise so that Koehl can now earn 11 percent on its invested funds. What will be the benefit (or loss) of operating the lockbox system with 8 lockbox locations?

Credit Management

Most security analysts were forecasting Xerox's sales and earnings to fall during a recent recession. But it did not happen—earnings rose 10 percent on a 23 percent sales gain. The secret, analysts learned, was that Xerox had instituted a major change in its credit policy—it had built up a pool of cash which it then loaned to its customers at bargain rates in order to increase sales of its products. Profits on the added sales more than offset the cost to Xerox of the low-rate loans, boosting the company's net income at a time when its competitors' profits were falling.

Xerox liberalized its credit policy and gained, but other companies, faced with different conditions, have increased their profits by tightening or even eliminating credit. For example, Atlantic Richfield Company (Arco) recently eliminated the use of credit cards at all of its service stations. Its management believed (1) that customers were very sensitive to gasoline prices; (2) that the cost of extending credit to customers amounted to about 4 cents per gallon; (3) that if it eliminated credit sales it could cut gas prices at the pump by 3 cents a gallon, which would boost profit per gallon by 1 cent and at the same time double its number of customers; and (4) that consequently it would enjoy a substantial increase in net profits. The plan worked beautifully, and it contributed to Arco's overall success.

Our goal in this chapter is to examine the factors that companies like Xerox and Arco consider when they establish credit policies.

Since the typical firm has about 25 percent of its assets in receivables, its effectiveness in managing receivables is important to its profitability and risk—and thus to its stock price. Techniques for managing receivables are covered in this chapter.

RECEIVABLES MANAGEMENT

account receivable

A balance due from a customer.

Firms would, in general, rather sell for cash than on credit, but competitive pressures force most firms to offer credit. Thus, goods are shipped, inventories are reduced, and an **account receivable** is created.[1] Eventually, the customer will pay the account, at which time (1) the firm will receive cash, and (2) its receivables will decline. Carrying receivables has both direct and indirect costs, but it also has an important benefit—granting credit will increase sales.

Receivables management begins with the decision of whether or not to grant credit. In this section, we discuss the manner in which a firm's receivables build up, and we also present several alternative means of monitoring receivables. A monitoring system is important because without it, receivables will build up to excessive levels, cash flows will decline, and bad debts will offset the profits on sales. Corrective action is often needed, and the only way to know whether the situation is getting out of hand is to set up and then follow a good receivables control system.

The Accumulation of Receivables

The total amount of accounts receivable outstanding at any given time is determined by two factors: (1) the volume of credit sales and (2) the average length of time between sales and collections. For example, suppose the Boston Lumber Company (BLC), a wholesale distributor of lumber products, opens a warehouse on January 1 and, starting the first day, makes sales of $1,000 each day. For simplicity, we assume that all sales are on credit, and customers are given 10 days in which to pay. At the end of the first day, accounts receivable will be $1,000; they will rise to $2,000 by the end of the second day; and by January 10, they will have risen to 10($1,000) = $10,000. On January 11, another $1,000 will be added to receivables, but payments for sales made on January 1 will reduce receivables by $1,000, so total accounts receivable will remain constant at $10,000. In general, once the firm's operations have stabilized, this situation will exist:

$$\begin{array}{ccc} \text{Accounts} \\ \text{receivable} \end{array} = \begin{array}{c} \text{Credit sales} \\ \text{per day} \end{array} \times \begin{array}{c} \text{Length of} \\ \text{collection period} \end{array} \qquad \text{(11-1)}$$

$$= \quad \$1,000 \quad \times \quad 10 \text{ days} \quad = \$10,000.$$

If either credit sales or the collection period changes, such changes will be reflected in accounts receivable.

Notice that the $10,000 investment in receivables must be financed. To illustrate, suppose that when the warehouse opened on January 1, BLC's share-

---

[1]Whenever goods are sold on credit, two accounts are created—an asset item entitled *accounts receivable* appears on the books of the selling firm, and a liability item called *accounts payable* appears on the books of the purchaser. At this point we are analyzing the transaction from the viewpoint of the seller, so we are concentrating on the variables under its control, in this case, the receivables. We will examine the transaction from the viewpoint of the purchaser in Chapter 13, where we will discuss accounts payable as a source of funds and will consider their cost relative to the cost of funds obtained from other sources.

holders had put up $800 as common stock and used this money to buy the goods sold the first day. The $800 worth of inventory will be sold for $1,000; thus, BLC's gross profit on the $800 investment is $200, or 25 percent. In this situation, the initial balance sheet would be as follows:[2]

Inventories	$800	Common equity	$800
Total assets	$800	Total liabilities and equity	$800

At the end of the day, the balance sheet would look like this:

Accounts receivable	$1,000	Common equity	$ 800
Inventories	0	Retained earnings	200
Total assets	$1,000	Total liabilities and equity	$1,000

In order to remain in business, BLC must replenish inventories. To do so requires that $800 of goods be purchased, and this requires $800 in cash. Assuming that BLC borrows the $800 from the bank, the balance sheet at the start of the second day will be as follows:

Accounts receivable	$1,000	Notes payable to bank	$ 800
Inventories	800	Common equity	800
		Retained earnings	200
Total assets	$1,800	Total liabilities and equity	$1,800

At the end of the second day, the inventories will have been converted to receivables, and the firm will have to borrow another $800 to restock for the third day.

This process will continue, provided the bank is willing to lend the necessary funds, until the beginning of the eleventh day, when the balance sheet reads as follows:

Accounts receivable	$10,000	Notes payable to bank	$ 8,000
Inventories	800	Common equity	800
		Retained earnings	2,000
Total assets	$10,800	Total liabilities and equity	$10,800

From this point on, $1,000 of receivables will be collected every day, and $800 of these funds can be used to purchase new inventories.

This example should make it clear (1) that accounts receivable depend jointly on the level of credit sales and the collection period, (2) that any increase in receivables must be financed in some manner, but (3) that the entire amount of receivables does not have to be financed because the profit portion

---

[2]Note that the firm would need other assets such as cash, fixed assets, and a permanent stock of inventory. Also, overhead costs and taxes would have to be deducted, so retained earnings would be less than the figures shown here. We abstract from these details here so that we may focus on receivables.

($200 of each $1,000 of sales) does not represent a cash outflow. In our example, we assumed bank financing, but, as we will discuss in Chapter 13, there are many alternative ways to finance current assets.

Monitoring the Receivables Position

The optimal credit policy, hence the optimal level of accounts receivable, depends on the firm's own unique operating conditions. For example, a firm with excess capacity and low variable production costs should extend credit more liberally, and carry a higher level of receivables, than a firm operating at full capacity on a slim profit margin. However, even though optimal credit policies vary among firms, or even for a single firm over time, it is still useful to analyze the effectiveness of the firm's credit policy in an overall, aggregate sense. Investors—both stockholders and bank loan officers—should pay close attention to accounts receivable management, for, as we shall see, one can be misled by reported financial statements and later suffer serious losses on an investment.

When a credit sale is made, the following events occur: (1) Inventories are reduced by the cost of goods sold; (2) accounts receivable are increased by the sales price; and (3) the difference is profit, which is added to retained earnings. If the sale is for cash, the profit is definitely earned, but if the sale is on credit, the profit is not actually earned unless and until the account is collected. Firms have been known to encourage "sales" to very weak customers in order to report high profits. This could boost the firm's stock price, at least until credit losses begin to lower earnings, at which time the stock price will fall. Analyses along the lines suggested in the following sections will detect any such questionable practice as well as any unconscious deterioration in the quality of accounts receivable. Such early detection could help both investors and bankers avoid losses.[3]

days sales outstanding (DSO)

The average length of time required to collect credit sales.

Days Sales Outstanding (DSO).   Suppose Super Sets Inc., a television manufacturer, sells 200,000 television sets a year at a sales price of $198 each. Further, assume that all sales are on credit, with terms which allow customers who pay within 10 days to take a 2 percent discount, and those customers who do not take the discount to pay the full invoice amount within 30 days. These credit terms are often stated as 2/10, net 30. Finally, assume that 70 percent of the customers take discounts and pay on Day 10, while the other 30 percent pay on Day 30.

Super Sets' **days sales outstanding (DSO),** sometimes called the *average collection period (ACP),* is 16 days:

$$DSO = ACP = 0.7(10 \text{ days}) + 0.3(30 \text{ days}) = 16 \text{ days}.$$

---

[3]Accountants are increasingly interested in these matters. Investors have sued several of the major accounting firms for substantial damages when (1) profits were overstated and (2) it could be shown that the auditors should have conducted an analysis along the lines described here and then should have reported the results to stockholders in their audit opinion.

Super Sets' *average daily sales (ADS)*, assuming a 360-day year, is $110,000:

$$ADS = \frac{\text{Annual sales}}{360} = \frac{(\text{Units sold})(\text{Sales price})}{360} \qquad (11\text{-}2)$$

$$= \frac{200,000(\$198)}{360} = \frac{\$39,600,000}{360} = \$110,000.$$

Super Sets' accounts receivable, assuming a constant, uniform rate of sales all during the year, will at any point in time be $1,760,000:

$$\text{Receivables} = (\text{ADS})(\text{DSO}) \qquad (11\text{-}3)$$

$$= (\$110,000)(16) = \$1,760,000.$$

Note also that its DSO is a measure of the average length of time it takes Super Sets' customers to pay off their credit purchases, and the DSO is often compared with an industry average DSO. For example, if all television manufacturers sell on the same credit terms, and if the industry average DSO is 25 days versus Super Sets' 16-day DSO, then Super Sets either has a higher percentage of discount customers or else its credit department is exceptionally good at ensuring prompt payment.

Finally, note that if you know annual sales and the receivables balance, you can calculate DSO as follows:

$$DSO = \frac{\text{Receivables}}{\text{Annual sales}/360} = \frac{\$1,760,000}{\$39,600,000/360} = \frac{\$1,760,000}{\$110,000} = 16 \text{ days.}$$

The DSO can be compared with the firm's own credit terms. For example, suppose Super Sets' DSO had been running at a level of 35 days versus its 2/10, net 30 credit terms. With a 35-day DSO, some customers would obviously be taking more than 30 days to pay their bills. In fact, if many customers were paying within 10 days to take advantage of the discount, the others would, on average, have to be taking much longer than 35 days. One way to check this possibility is to use an aging schedule as described in the next section.

aging schedule

A report showing how long accounts receivable have been outstanding; it gives the percentage of receivables currently past due, and the percentages past due by specified periods.

Aging Schedules.   An **aging schedule** breaks down a firm's receivables by age of account. Table 11-1 contains the December 31, 1992, aging schedules of two television manufacturers, Super Sets and Wonder Vision. Both firms offer the same credit terms, 2/10, net 30, and both show the same total receivables. However, Super Sets' aging schedule indicates that all of its customers pay on time—70 percent pay on Day 10 while 30 percent pay on Day 30. Wonder Vision's schedule, which is more typical, shows that many of its customers are not abiding by its credit terms—some 27 percent of its receivables are more than 30 days past due, even though Wonder Vision's credit terms call for full payment by Day 30.

Aging schedules cannot be constructed from the type of summary data that are reported in financial statements; they must be developed from the firm's

Table 11-1 ▪ **Aging Schedules**

Age of Account (Days)	Super Sets Value of Account	Percentage of Total Value	Wonder Vision Value of Account	Percentage of Total Value
0–10	$1,232,000	70%	$ 825,000	47%
11–30	528,000	30	460,000	26
31–45	0	0	265,000	15
46–60	0	0	179,000	10
Over 60	0	0	31,000	2
Total receivables	$1,760,000	100%	$1,760,000	100%

accounts receivable ledger. However, well-run firms have computerized their accounts receivable records, so it is easy to determine the age of each invoice, to sort electronically by age categories, and thus to generate an aging schedule.

Management should constantly monitor the days sales outstanding and the aging schedule to detect trends, to see how the firm's collection experience compares with its credit terms, and to see how effectively the credit department is operating in comparison with other firms in the industry. If the DSO starts to lengthen, or if the aging schedule begins to show an increasing percentage of past-due accounts, then the firm's credit policy may need to be tightened.

Although a change in the DSO or the aging schedule should be a signal to the firm to investigate its credit policy, a deterioration in either of these measures does not necessarily indicate that the firm's credit policy has weakened. In fact, if a firm experiences sharp seasonal variations, or if it is growing rapidly, then both the aging schedule and the DSO may be distorted. This point can be illustrated using Allied Food Products. Recall from Chapter 9 that Allied's peak selling season is in the summer, so 1993 forecasted receivables are expected to be high, at $562 million, in September just after the peak season ends, and receivables are expected to be low, at $412 million, at the end of December 1993. Allied's average daily sales are expected to be $9.167 million ($3,300 million annually), so its DSO would be $562/$9.167 = 61 days on September 30, but only $412/$9.167 = 45 days on December 31, 1993. This decline in DSO would not indicate that Allied had tightened its credit policy, only that its sales had fallen due to seasonal factors. Similar problems arise with the aging schedule when sales fluctuate widely. Therefore, a change in either the DSO or the aging schedule should be taken as a signal to investigate further, but not necessarily as a sign that the firm's credit policy has weakened. Still, days sales outstanding and the aging schedule are useful tools for reviewing the credit department's performance.[4]

---

[4]See Eugene F. Brigham and Louis C Gapenski, *Intermediate Financial Management,* 4th ed., Chapter 23, for a more complete discussion of the problems with the DSO and aging schedule and how to correct for them.

Use of Computers in Receivables Management

Except possibly in the inventory and payroll areas, nowhere in the typical firm have computers had more of an impact than in accounts receivable management. A well-run business will use a computer system to record sales, to send out bills, to keep track of when payments are made, to alert the credit manager when an account becomes past due, and to insure that actions are taken to collect past due accounts (for example, to prepare form letters requesting payment). Additionally, the payment history of each customer can be summarized and used to help establish credit limits for customers and classes of customers, and the data on each account can be aggregated and used for the firm's accounts receivable monitoring system. Finally, historical data can be stored in the firm's data base and used to develop inputs for studies related to credit policy changes, as we discuss in the next section.

 ### *Self-Test Questions*

Explain how a new firm's receivables balance is built up over time.

Define days sales outstanding (DSO). What can be learned from it? How is it affected by sales fluctuations?

What is an aging schedule? What can be learned from it? How is it affected by sales fluctuations?

INDUSTRY PRACTICE | Trade Credit and Bankruptcy

As we reported in Chapter 9, R. H. Macy & Company, one of the largest U.S. retailers, recently filed for protection from its creditors under Chapter 11 of the Bankruptcy Act. Macy had undergone a leveraged buyout (LBO), which involved the company's borrowing huge sums at high interest rates and using the proceeds to buy up the publicly held stock. Macy's managers thought they could service the debt out of operating cash flows, but they were wrong—sales did not come up to the forecasted levels, so cash flows were insufficient to cover current obligations.

As events unfolded, Macy's suppliers began to worry about the company's ability to pay for the merchandise they were ordering. Those suppliers knew that they would be exposed to losses if Macy defaulted, so many of them reduced shipments or insisted on payment in advance. As a result, Macy's accounts payable declined from a normal level of $800 million to $275 million at the time of the bankruptcy filing.

Sources: "Macy Files for Chapter 11, Listing Assets of $4.95 Billion, Liabilities of $5.32 Billion," *The Wall Street Journal,* January 28, 1992; and "Macy Suppliers May Collect Half or Less of Claims, Bankruptcy Specialists Say," *The Wall Street Journal,* January 29, 1992.

It is anticipated that the holders of the $275 million of trade credit will collect between 35 and 55 cents on the dollar, and then only after about a two-year delay. Those suppliers who simply cannot wait will sell their receivables for perhaps 30 cents on the dollar, and Wall Street firms are now gearing up to buy this paper.

After such losses, why would any company be willing to supply goods to Macy? And if it cannot get merchandise to sell, how can the company hope to stay in business? The answer is bankruptcy. Under our bankruptcy laws, credit extended after the filing receives preferential treatment over prebankruptcy debts. Accordingly, Macy has arranged a $600 million line of debtor-in-possession financing from two New York banks, Chemical and Bankers Trust. This credit can be used to pay for the new merchandise which Macy needs to continue operations. Shep Porter, president of Porter House Ltd, a women's sportswear maker, expressed surprise and disappointment about the losses he will incur on his prefiling receivables, but he went on to say, "In this market, more doors are closing than opening. I intend to ship again as soon as I get the debtor-in-possession number."

CREDIT POLICY

The success or failure of a business depends primarily on the demand for its products — as a rule, the higher its sales, the larger its profits and the higher the value of its stock. Sales, in turn, depend on a number of factors, some exogenous but others under the control of the firm. The major controllable variables which affect demand are sales prices, product quality, advertising, and the firm's **credit policy.** Credit policy, in turn, consists of these four variables:

credit policy

A set of decisions that include a firm's credit period, credit standards, collection procedures, and discounts offered.

1. The *credit period,* which is the length of time buyers are given to pay for their purchases.
2. The *credit standards,* which refer to the minimum financial strength of acceptable credit customers and the amount of credit available to different customers.
3. The firm's *collection policy,* which is measured by its toughness or laxity in following up on slow-paying accounts.
4. Any *discounts* given for early payment, including the discount amount and period.

The credit manager has the responsibility for administering the firm's credit policy. However, because of the pervasive importance of credit, the credit policy itself is normally established by the executive committee, which usually consists of the president plus the vice-presidents in charge of finance, marketing, and production.

 Self-Test Question

What are the four credit policy variables?

SETTING THE CREDIT PERIOD AND STANDARDS

credit terms

A statement of the credit period and any discounts offered — for example, 2/10, net 30.

credit period

The length of time for which credit is granted.

credit standards

Standards that stipulate the minimum financial strength that an applicant must demonstrate in order to be granted credit.

A firm's regular **credit terms,** which include the **credit period** and *discount,* might call for sales on a 2/10, net 30 basis to all "acceptable" customers. Its *credit standards* would be applied to determine which customers are qualified for the regular credit terms and the amount of credit available to each customer.

Credit Standards

Credit standards refer to the strength and creditworthiness a customer must exhibit in order to qualify for credit. If a customer does not qualify for the regular credit terms, it can still purchase from the firm, but under more restrictive terms. For example, a firm's "regular" credit terms might call for payment after 30 days, and these terms might be extended to all qualified customers. The firm's credit standards would be applied to determine which customers qualified for the regular credit terms and how much credit each customer should receive. The major factors considered when setting credit standards relate to the likelihood that a given customer will pay slowly or perhaps even end up as a bad debt loss.

Setting credit standards implicitly requires a measurement of *credit quality,* which is defined in terms of the probability of a customer's default. The probability estimate for a given customer is for the most part a subjective judgment. Nevertheless, credit evaluation is a well-established practice, and a good credit manager can make reasonably accurate judgments of the probability of default by different classes of customers. In this section we discuss some of the methods used by firms to measure credit quality.

Credit-Scoring Systems.   Although most credit decisions are subjective, many firms now use a sophisticated statistical method called *multiple discriminant analysis (MDA)* to assess credit quality. MDA is similar to multiple regression analysis. The dependent variable is, in essence, the probability of default, and the independent variables are factors associated with financial strength and the ability to pay off the debt if credit is granted. MDA models are set up to "score" the quality of credit based on variables considered important for differentiating between potentially good and potentially bad credit customers. For example, if a firm such as Sears is evaluating consumers' credit quality, then the independent variables in the credit scoring system would be such factors as these: (1) Does the credit applicant own his or her own home? (2) How long has the applicant worked on his or her current job? (3) What is the applicant's outstanding debt in relation to his or her annual income? (4) Does the potential customer have a history of paying his or her debts on time?

One major advantage of an MDA credit-scoring system is that a customer's credit quality is expressed in a single numerical value rather than as a subjective assessment of various factors. This is a tremendous advantage for a large firm that must evaluate many customers in many different locations using many different credit employees, for without an automated procedure, the firm would have a hard time applying equal standards to all credit applicants. Therefore, most credit card companies, department stores, oil companies, and the like use credit-scoring systems to determine who gets how much credit, as do the larger building supply chains and manufacturers of electrical products, machinery, and so on.

To illustrate the use of MDA, suppose Hanover Company, a North Carolina furniture manufacturer, has historical information on 500 of its customers, all of whom are retail businesses. Of these 500, assume that 400 have always paid on time, but the other 100 either paid late or, in some cases, went bankrupt and did not pay at all. Further, the firm has historical data on each customer's quick ratio, times-interest-earned ratio, debt ratio, years in existence, and so on. Multiple discriminant analysis relates the experienced record (or historical probability) of late payment or nonpayment with various measures of a firm's financial condition and then assigns weights to each of the critical factors. In effect, MDA produces an equation that looks much like a regression equation, and when data on a customer are plugged into the equation, then a credit score for that customer is produced.

For example, suppose Hanover's multiple discriminant analysis indicates that the critical factors affecting prompt payment are the customer's times-interest-earned ratio (TIE), quick ratio, debt/assets ratio, and number of years in business. Here is the equation produced, which is termed the discriminant function:

Score = 3.5(TIE) + 10.0(Quick ratio) − 25.0(Debt/Assets) + 1.3(Years in business).

Further, assume that a score less than 40 indicates a poor credit risk, 40-50 indicates an average credit risk, and a score above 50 signifies a good credit risk. Now suppose a firm with the following conditions applies for credit:

$$\text{TIE} = 4.2$$
$$\text{Quick ratio} = 3.1$$
$$\text{Debt/assets} = 0.30$$
$$\text{Years in business} = 10$$

This firm's credit score would be $3.5(4.2) + 10.0(3.1) - 25.0(0.30) + 1.3(10) = 51.2$. Therefore, it would be considered a good credit risk, and consequently it would be offered favorable credit terms.

The Five Cs System

No matter what the approach is, methods used to measure credit quality are concerned with evaluating five areas generally considered important to determining a customer's creditworthiness. These five areas, which are referred to with words beginning with the letter C, are called the **five Cs of credit:**

five Cs of credit

The factors used to evaluate credit risk: character, capacity, capital, collateral, and conditions.

1. *Character* refers to the probability that customers will *try* to honor their obligations. This factor is of considerable importance because every credit transaction implies a *promise* to pay: Will debtors make an honest effort to pay their debts, or are they likely to try to get away with something? Experienced credit managers frequently insist that the moral factor is the most important issue in a credit evaluation. Thus, credit reports provide background information on people's and firms' past performances. Often credit analysts will seek this type of information from a firm's bankers, its other suppliers, its customers, and even its competitors.

2. *Capacity* is a subjective judgment of customers' abilities to pay. It is gauged in part by the customers' past records and business methods, and it may be supplemented by physical observation of their plants or stores. Again, credit analysts will obtain judgmental information on this factor from a variety of sources.

3. *Capital* is measured by the general financial condition of a firm as indicated by an analysis of its financial statements. Special emphasis is given to the risk ratios—the debt/assets ratio, the current ratio, and the times-interest-earned ratio.

4. *Collateral* is represented by assets that customers may offer as security in order to obtain credit.

5. *Conditions* refers both to general economic trends and to special developments in certain geographic regions or sectors of the economy that might affect customers' abilities to meet their obligations.

Information on these five factors comes from the firm's previous experience with its customers, and it is supplemented by a well-developed system of external information gatherers. Of course, once the information on the five Cs is developed, the credit manager must still make a final decision on the potential customer's overall credit quality. This decision is normally judgmental in nature, and credit managers must rely on their background knowledge and instincts.

Sources of Credit Information.   Two major sources of credit information are available. The first is a set of *credit associations,* which are local groups that meet frequently and which correspond with one another to exchange information on credit customers. These local groups have also banded together to create Credit Interchange, a system developed by the National Association of Credit Management for assembling and distributing information about debtors' past performances. The interchange reports show the paying records of different debtors, the industries from which they are buying, and the geographic areas in which they are making purchases. The second source of external information is the work of the *credit-reporting agencies,* which collect credit information and sell it for a fee. The best known of these agencies are Dun & Bradstreet (D&B), Equifax, and TRW. These and other agencies provide factual data that can be used in credit analysis, and they also provide ratings similar to those available on corporate bonds.[5]

Managing a credit department requires fast, accurate, up-to-date information, and to help get such information, the National Association of Credit Management (a group with 43,000 member firms) persuaded TRW to develop a computer-based telecommunications network for the collection, storage, retrieval, and distribution of credit information. The TRW system contains credit data on more than 120 million individuals, and it electronically transmits credit reports which are available within seconds to its thousands of subscribers. Dun & Bradstreet has a similar electronic system which covers businesses, plus another service which provides more detailed reports through the U.S. mail.

A typical business credit report would include the following pieces of information:

1. A summary balance sheet and income statement.
2. A number of key ratios, with trend information.
3. Information obtained from the firm's suppliers telling whether it has been paying promptly or slowly and whether it has recently failed to make any payments.
4. A verbal description of the physical condition of the firm's operations.
5. A verbal description of the backgrounds of the firm's owners, including any previous bankruptcies, lawsuits, divorce settlement problems, and the like.
6. A summary rating, ranging from A for the best credit risks down to F for those that are deemed likely to default.

Although a great deal of credit information is available, it must still be processed in a judgmental manner. Computerized information systems can assist in making better credit decisions, but, in the final analysis, most credit decisions are really exercises in informed judgment. Even credit scoring systems require judgment in deciding where to draw the lines, given the set of derived scores.

---

[5]For additional information, see *Credit Management,* a publication of the National Association of Credit Management; and also see Peter Nulty, "An Upstart Takes on Dun & Bradstreet," *Fortune,* April 9, 1979, 98–100.

Self-Test Questions

What is a credit-scoring system?

Identify and briefly explain the five Cs of credit.

What are some sources of credit information?

SETTING THE COLLECTION POLICY

collection policy
The procedures that a firm follows to collect accounts receivable.

Collection policy refers to the procedures the firm follows to collect past-due accounts. For example, a letter may be sent to customers when a bill is 10 days past due; a more severe letter, followed by a telephone call, may be used if payment is not received within 30 days; and the account may be turned over to a collection agency after 90 days.

The collection process can be expensive in terms of both out-of-pocket expenditures and lost goodwill—customers dislike being turned over to a collection agency. However, at least some firmness is needed to prevent an undue lengthening of the collection period and to minimize outright losses. A balance must be struck between the costs and benefits of different collection policies.

Changes in collection policy influence sales, the collection period, and the bad debt loss percentage. The effects of a change in collection policy, along with changes in the other credit policy variables, will be analyzed later in the chapter.

 Self-Test Question

What does the term "collection policy" mean, and how does it affect sales and profitability?

CASH DISCOUNTS

cash discount
A reduction in the price of goods given to encourage early payment.

The last element in the credit policy decision, the use of **cash discounts** for early payment, is analyzed by balancing the costs and benefits of different cash discounts. For example, a firm might decide to change its credit terms from "net 30," which means that customers must pay within 30 days, to "2/10, net 30," which means that it will allow a 2 percent discount if payment is received within 10 days, while the full invoice price must otherwise be paid within 30 days. This change should produce two benefits: (1) It should attract new customers who consider the discount to be a type of price reduction, and (2) the discount should cause a reduction in the days sales outstanding since some established customers will pay more promptly in order to take advantage of the discount. Offsetting these benefits is the dollar cost of the discounts taken. The optimal discount is established at the point where the marginal costs and benefits are exactly offsetting. The methodology for analyzing changes in the discount is developed later in the chapter.

seasonal dating
Terms to induce customers to buy early by not requiring payment until the purchaser's selling season, regardless of when the goods are shipped.

If sales are seasonal, a firm may use **seasonal dating** on discounts. For example, Slimware Inc., a swimsuit manufacturer, sells on terms of 2/10, net 30, May 1 dating. This means that the effective invoice date is May 1, even if the sale was made back in January. The discount may be taken up to May 10; otherwise, the full amount must be paid on May 30. Slimware produces throughout the year, but retail sales of bathing suits are concentrated in the spring and early summer, and by offering seasonal dating, the company induces some of its customers to stock up early, saving Slimware storage costs and also "nailing down sales."

Self-Test Questions

How can cash discounts be used to influence sales volume and the DSO?

What is seasonal dating?

OTHER FACTORS INFLUENCING CREDIT POLICY

In addition to the factors discussed in the previous sections, several other points should be made regarding credit policy.

Profit Potential

Thus far, we have emphasized the costs of granting credit. *However, if it is possible to sell on credit and also to assess a carrying charge on the receivables that are outstanding, then credit sales can actually be more profitable than cash sales.* This is especially true for consumer durables (autos, appliances, clothing, and so on), but it is also true for certain types of industrial equipment. Thus, GM's General Motors Acceptance Corporation (GMAC) unit, which finances automobiles, is highly profitable, as is Sears's credit subsidiary.[6] Some encyclopedia companies are even reported to lose money on cash sales but to more than make up these losses from the carrying charges on their credit sales; obviously, such companies would rather sell on credit than for cash!

The carrying charges on outstanding credit are generally about 18 percent on a nominal interest rate basis: 1.5 percent per month, so $1.5\% \times 12 = 18\%$. This is equivalent to an effective annual rate of $(1.015)^{12} - 1.0 = 19.6\%$. Except in the type of situation that occurred in the early 1980s, when short-term interest rates rose to unprecedented levels, having receivables outstanding that earn over 18 percent is highly profitable.

Legal Considerations

It is illegal, under the Robinson-Patman Act, for a firm to charge prices that discriminate between customers unless these differential prices are cost-justified. The same holds true for credit — it is illegal to offer more favorable credit terms to one customer or class of customers than to another unless the differences are cost-justified.

---

[6]Companies that do a large volume of sales financing typically set up subsidiary companies called *captive finance companies* to do the actual financing. Thus, General Motors, Chrysler, and Ford all have captive finance companies, as do Sears, Montgomery Ward, and General Electric.

Credit Instruments

open account

A credit arrangement whereby an invoice is signed by the buyer upon receipt of goods, after which both the buyer and the seller record the purchase on their books.

promissory note

A document specifying the amount, percentage interest rate, repayment schedule, and other terms and conditions of a loan.

commercial draft

An instrument drawn up by and made out to the seller that must be signed by the buyer before taking possession of goods.

sight draft

An instrument that calls for payment upon acceptance of goods by the buyer.

time draft (trade acceptance)

A draft that is payable on a specified future date.

banker's acceptance

A time draft that has been guaranteed by a bank. It is a promissory note by a business arising out of a business transaction, but a bank, by endorsing it, assumes the obligation of payment at the due date.

conditional sales contract

A method of financing in which the seller retains title to the goods until the buyer has completed payment.

Most credit is offered on **open account,** which means that the only formal evidence of credit is an invoice which accompanies the shipment and which the buyer signs to indicate that goods have been received. Then, the buyer and the seller each record the purchase on their books of account. Under certain circumstances, the selling firm may require the buyer to sign a **promissory note** evidencing the credit obligation. Promissory notes are useful (1) if the order is very large; (2) if the seller anticipates the possibility of having trouble collecting, because a note is a stronger legal claim than a simple signed invoice; or (3) if the buyer wants a longer-than-usual time in which to pay for the order, because in that case interest should be charged, and interest charges can be built into a promissory note.

Another instrument used in trade credit, especially in international trade, is the **commercial draft.** Here the seller draws up a draft—which is a combination check and promissory note—calling for the buyer to pay a specific amount to the seller by a specified date. This draft is then sent to the buyer's bank, along with the shipping invoices necessary to take possession of the goods. The bank forwards the draft to the buyer, who signs it and returns it to the bank. The bank then delivers the shipping documents to its customer, who at this point can claim the goods. If the draft is a **sight draft,** then upon delivery of the shipping documents and acceptance of the draft by the buyer, the bank actually withdraws money from the buyer's account and forwards it to the selling firm. If the draft is a **time draft,** payable on a specific future date, then the bank returns it to the selling firm. In this case, the draft is called a **trade acceptance,** and it amounts to a promissory note that the seller can hold for future payment or use as collateral for a loan. The bank, in such a situation, has served as an intermediary, making sure that the buyer does not receive title to the goods until the note (or draft) has been executed for the benefit of the seller.

A seller who lacks confidence in the ability or willingness of the buyer to pay off a time draft may refuse to ship without a guarantee of payment by the buyer's bank. Presumably, the bank knows its customer, and, for a fee, the bank will guarantee payment of the draft. In this instance, the draft is called a **banker's acceptance.** Such instruments are widely used, especially in foreign trade. They have a low degree of risk if guaranteed by a strong bank, and there is a ready market for acceptances, making it easy for the seller of the goods to sell the instrument to raise immediate cash. (Banker's acceptances are sold at a discount below face value, and then paid off at face value when they mature, so the discount amounts to interest on the acceptance. The effective interest rate on a strong banker's acceptance is a little above the Treasury bill rate of interest.)

Another type of credit instrument is the **conditional sales contract,** under which the seller retains legal ownership of the goods until the buyer has completed payment. Conditional sales contracts are used primarily for such items as machinery, dental equipment, and the like, which are often purchased on an installment basis over a period of two or three years. The significant advantage of a conditional sales contract is that it is easier for the seller to repossess the equipment in the event of default than it would be if title had passed. This feature makes possible some credit sales that otherwise would not be feasible.

Conditional sales contracts generally have a market interest rate built into their payment schedules.

? *Self-Test Questions*

How do profit potential and legal considerations affect a firm's credit policy?

Describe some instruments used to document trade credit transactions, and indicate when each type of instrument is likely to be used.

ANALYZING PROPOSED CHANGES IN CREDIT POLICY

If the firm's credit policy is *eased* by such actions as lengthening the credit period, relaxing credit standards, following a less tough collection policy, or offering cash discounts, then sales should increase: *Easing the credit policy stimulates sales.* Of course, if the credit policy is eased and sales rise, then costs will also rise because more labor, materials, and so on will be required to produce the additional goods. Additionally, receivables outstanding will also increase, which will increase carrying costs, and bad debt and/or discount expenses may also rise. Thus, the key question when deciding on a proposed credit policy change is this: Will sales revenues rise more than costs, including credit-related costs, causing cash flow to increase, or will the increase in sales revenues be more than offset by the higher costs?

Table 11-2 illustrates the general idea behind credit policy analysis. Column 1 shows the projected 1993 income statement for Monroe Manufacturing under the assumption that the firm's current credit policy is maintained throughout the year. Column 2 shows the expected effects of easing the credit policy by extending the credit period, offering larger discounts, relaxing credit standards, and easing collection efforts. Specifically, Monroe is analyzing the effects of changing its credit terms from 1/10, net 30 to 2/10, net 40, relaxing its credit standards, and putting less pressure on slow-paying customers. Column 3 shows the projected 1993 income statement incorporating the expected effects of an easing in credit policy. The generally looser policy is expected to increase sales and lower collection costs, but discounts and several other types of costs would rise. The overall, bottom-line effect is a $7 million increase in projected net income. In the following paragraphs, we explain how the numbers in the table were calculated.

Monroe's annual sales are $400 million. Under its current credit policy, 50 percent (by dollar value) of those customers who pay do so on Day 10 and take the discount, 40 percent pay on Day 30, and 10 percent pay late, on Day 40. Thus, Monroe's days sales outstanding is $(0.5)(10) + (0.4)(30) + (0.1)(40) = 21$ days, and discounts total $(0.01)($400,000,000)(0.5) = $2,000,000$.

The cost of carrying receivables is equal to the average receivables balance times the variable cost ratio times the cost of money used to carry receivables. The firm's variable cost ratio is 70 percent, and its pre-tax cost of capital

Table 11-2 ▪ **Monroe Manufacturing Company: Analysis of Changing Credit Policy (Millions of Dollars)**

	Projected 1993 Net Income under Current Credit Policy (1)	Effect of Credit Policy Change (2)	Projected 1993 Net Income under New Credit Policy (3)
Gross sales	$400	+ $130	$530
Less discounts	2	+ 4	6
Net sales	$398	+ $126	$524
Production costs, including overhead	280	+ 91	371
Profit before credit costs and taxes	$118	+ $ 35	$153
Credit-related costs:			
Cost of carrying receivables	3	+ 2	5
Credit analysis and collection expenses	5	− 3	2
Bad debt losses	10	+ 22	32
Profit before taxes	$100	+ $ 14	$114
Federal-plus-state taxes (50%)	50	+ 7	57
Net income	$ 50	+ $ 7	$ 57

Note: The above statements include only those cash flows which are affected by credit policy.

invested in receivables is 20 percent. Thus, its cost of carrying receivables before a change in credit policy is $3 million:

$$(\text{DSO})\left(\begin{array}{c}\text{Sales} \\ \text{per} \\ \text{day}\end{array}\right)\left(\begin{array}{c}\text{Variable} \\ \text{cost} \\ \text{ratio}\end{array}\right)\left(\begin{array}{c}\text{Cost} \\ \text{of} \\ \text{funds}\end{array}\right) = \text{Cost of carrying receivables} \quad (11\text{-}4)$$

$$(21)(\$400,000,000/360)(0.70)(0.20) = \$3,266,667 \approx \$3 \text{ million.}$$

Only variable costs enter this calculation because this is the only cost element in receivables that must be financed. We are seeking the cost of carrying receivables, and variable costs represent the firm's investment in the cost of goods sold.

Even though Monroe spends $5 million annually to analyze accounts and to collect bad debts, 2.5 percent of sales will never be collected. Bad debt losses therefore amount to $(0.025)(\$400,000,000) = \$10,000,000$.

Monroe's new credit policy would be 2/10, net 40 versus the old policy of 1/10, net 30, so it would call for a larger discount and a longer payment period, as well as a relaxed collection effort and lower credit standards. The company believes that these changes would lead to a $130 million increase in sales, to $530 million per year. Under the new terms, management believes that 60 percent (by dollar value) of the customers who pay would take the 2 percent discount, so discounts would increase to $(0.02)(\$530,000,000)(0.60) = \$6,360,000 \approx \$6$ million. Half of the nondiscount customers would pay on Day 40 and the remainder on Day 50. The new DSO is thus estimated to be 24 days:

$$(0.6)(10) + (0.2)(40) + (0.2)(50) = 24 \text{ days.}$$

Therefore, the cost of carrying receivables would increase to $5 million:

$$(24)(\$530,000,000/360)(0.70)(0.20) = \$4,946,667 \approx \$5 \text{ million.}[7]$$

Also, the company plans to reduce its annual credit analysis and collection expenditures to $2 million. The reduced credit standards and the relaxed collection effort are expected to raise bad debt losses to about 6 percent of sales, or to $(0.06)(\$530,000,000) = \$31,800,000 \approx \$32,000,000$, which is an increase of $22 million from the previous level.

The combined effect of all the changes in credit policy is a projected $7 million annual increase in net income. There might, of course, be corresponding changes on the projected balance sheet—the higher sales might necessitate somewhat more cash, receivables, inventories, and, depending on the capacity situation, more fixed assets. Since these asset increases would have to be financed, certain liabilities and/or equity would have to be increased. Any associated costs would be reflected in the variable cost ratio.

The $7 million expected increase in net income is, of course, an estimate, and the actual effects of the change could be quite different. In the first place, there is uncertainty—perhaps quite a lot—about the projected $130 million increase in sales. Conceivably, if the firm's competitors matched its changes, sales would not rise at all. Similar uncertainties must be attached to the number of customers who would take discounts, to production costs at higher or lower sales levels, to the costs of carrying additional receivables, and to bad debt losses.

The analysis in Table 11-2 provides Monroe's managers with a vehicle for considering the impact of credit policy changes on the firm's income statement and balance sheet variables. However, a great deal of judgment must be applied to the decision because customers' responses to credit policy changes are very difficult to estimate. Nevertheless, this type of numerical analysis can provide a good starting point for credit policy decisions.

Self-Test Questions

Describe the procedure used to evaluate a change in credit policy.

Should credit policy decisions be made more on the basis of numerical analyses or judgmental factors?

---

[7]Since the credit policy change will result in a longer DSO, the firm will have to wait longer to receive its profit on the goods it sells. Therefore, the firm will incur an opportunity cost due to not having the cash from these profits available for investment. The dollar amount of this opportunity cost is equal to the old sales per day times the change in DSO times the contribution margin $(1 - \text{Variable cost ratio})$ times the firm's cost of carrying receivables, or

$$\text{Opportunity cost} = (\text{Old sales}/360)(\Delta DSO)(1 - v)(k)$$
$$= (\$400/360)(3)(0.3)(0.20)$$
$$= \$0.2 \text{ million} = \$200,000.$$

For simplicity, and because it is small, we have ignored this opportunity cost in our analysis. For a more complete discussion of credit policy change analysis, see Eugene F. Brigham and Louis C. Gapenski, *Intermediate Financial Management,* 4th ed., Chapter 23.

SUMMARY

This chapter discussed receivables management. The key concepts covered are listed below.

- When a firm sells goods to a customer on credit, an **account receivable** is created.

- Firms can use an **aging schedule** and the **days sales outstanding (DSO)** to help keep track of their receivables position and to help avoid an increase in bad debts.

- A firm's **credit policy** consists of four elements: (1) credit period, (2) discounts given for early payment, (3) credit standards, and (4) collection policy. The first two, when combined, are called the **credit terms.**

- Two major sources of external credit information are **credit associations,** which are local groups that meet frequently and correspond with one another to exchange information on credit customers, and **credit reporting agencies,** which collect credit information and sell it for a fee.

- Additional factors that influence a firm's overall credit policy are (1) **profit potential** and (2) **legal considerations.**

- The basic objective of the credit manager is to increase profitable sales by extending credit to worthy customers and therefore adding value to the firm.

- If a firm **eases its credit policy,** its sales should increase. Actions which ease the credit policy include lengthening the credit period, relaxing credit standards and collection policy, and offering cash discounts. Each of these actions, however, increases costs. A firm should ease its credit policy only if the costs of doing so will be more than offset by higher sales revenues.

Questions

11-1   Is it true that when one firm sells to another on credit, the seller records the transaction as an account receivable while the buyer records it as an account payable and that, disregarding discounts, the receivable typically exceeds the payable by the amount of profit on the sale?

11-2   What are the four elements of a firm's credit policy? To what extent can firms set their own credit policies as opposed to having to accept policies that are dictated by "the competition"?

11-3   Suppose that a firm makes a purchase and receives the shipment on February 1. The terms of trade as stated on the invoice read "2/10, net 40, May 1 dating." What is the latest date on which payment can be made and the discount still be taken? What is the date on which payment must be made if the discount is not taken?

11-4   a. What is the days sales outstanding (DSO) for a firm whose sales are $2,880,000 per year and whose accounts receivable are $312,000? (Use 360 days per year.)
   b. Is it true that if this firm sells on terms of 3/10, net 40, its customers probably all pay on time?

11-5   Is it true that if a firm calculates its days sales outstanding, it has no need for an aging schedule?

11-6   Firm A had no credit losses last year, but 1 percent of Firm B's accounts receivable proved to be uncollectible and resulted in losses. Should Firm B fire its credit manager and hire A's?

11-7   Indicate by a (+), (−), or (0) whether each of the following events would probably cause accounts receivable (A/R), sales, and profits to increase, decrease, or be affected in an indeterminant manner:

	A/R	Sales	Profits
The firm tightens its credit standards.	_____	_____	_____
The terms of trade are changed from 2/10, net 30 to 3/10, net 30.	_____	_____	_____
The terms are changed from 2/10, net 30 to 3/10, net 40.	_____	_____	_____
The credit manager gets tough with past-due accounts.	_____	_____	_____

Self-Test Problems   (Solutions Appear in Appendix B)

ST-1
Key terms

Define each of the following terms:
a. Account receivable; days sales outstanding (DSO)
b. Aging schedule
c. Credit policy; credit period; credit standards; five Cs of credit; collection policy; credit terms
d. Cash discounts
e. Seasonal dating
f. Open account; promissory note; commercial draft; sight draft; time draft, or trade acceptance; banker's acceptance; conditional sales contract

ST-2
Change in credit policy

The Boca Grande Company expects to have sales of $10 million this year under its current operating policies. Its variable costs as a percentage of sales are 80 percent, and its cost of capital is 16 percent. Currently, Boca Grande's credit policy is net 25 (no discount for early payment). However, its DSO is 30 days, and its bad debt loss percentage is 2 percent. Boca Grande spends $50,000 per year to collect bad debts, and its federal-plus-state tax rate is 40 percent.

The credit manager is considering two alternative proposals for changing Boca Grande's credit policy. Find the expected change in net income, taking into consideration anticipated changes in carrying costs for accounts receivable, the probable bad debt losses, and the discounts likely to be taken, for each proposal. Should a change in credit policy be made?

Proposal 1: Lengthen the credit period by going from net 25 to net 30. Collection expenditures will remain constant. Under this proposal, sales are expected to increase by $1 million annually, and the bad debt loss percentage on *new* sales is expected to rise to 4 percent (the loss percentage on old sales should not change). In addition, the DSO is expected to increase from 30 to 45 days on all sales.

Proposal 2: Shorten the credit period by going from net 25 to net 20. Again, collection expenses will remain constant. The anticipated effects of this change are a decrease in sales of $1 million per year, a decline in the DSO from 30 to 22 days, and a decline in the bad debt loss percentage to 1 percent on all sales.

Problems

11-1
Easing credit terms

Bey Technologies is considering changing its credit terms from 2/15, net 30 to 3/10, net 30 in order to speed collections. At present, 40 percent of Bey's customers take the 2 percent discount. Under the new terms, discount customers are expected to rise to

50 percent. Regardless of the credit terms, half of the customers who do not take the discount are expected to pay on time, whereas the remainder will pay 10 days late. The change does not involve a relaxation of credit standards; therefore, bad debt losses are not expected to rise above their present 2 percent level. However, the more generous cash discount terms are expected to increase sales from $2 million to $2.6 million per year. Bey's variable cost ratio is 75 percent, the interest rate on funds invested in accounts receivable is 9 percent, and the firm's federal-plus-state tax rate is 40 percent.

a. What is the days sales outstanding before and after the change?
b. Calculate the discount costs before and after the change.
c. Calculate the dollar cost of carrying receivables before and after the change.
d. Calculate the bad debt losses before and after the change.
e. What is the incremental profit from the change in credit terms? Should Bey change its credit terms?

11-2
Credit analysis

Flint Distributors makes all sales on a credit basis, selling on terms of 2/10, net 30. Once a year it evaluates the creditworthiness of all its customers. The evaluation procedure ranks customers from 1 to 5, with 1 indicating the "best" customers. Results of the ranking are as follows:

Customer Category	Percentage of Bad Debts	Days Sales Outstanding	Credit Decision	Annual Sales Lost Because of Credit Restrictions
1	None	10	Unlimited credit	None
2	1	12	Unlimited credit	None
3	3	20	Limited credit	$375,000
4	9	60	Limited credit	$190,000
5	16	90	Limited credit	$220,000

The variable cost ratio is 70 percent, and its federal-plus-state tax rate is 40 percent. The cost of capital invested in receivables is 12 percent. What would be the effect on the profitability of extending unlimited credit to each of Categories 3, 4, and 5? (Hint: Determine the effect of changing each policy separately on the income statement. In other words, find the change in sales, change in production costs, change in receivables and cost of carrying receivables, change in bad debt costs, and so forth, down to the change in net profits. Assume that none of the customers in these three categories will take the discount.)

11-3
Relaxing collection efforts

The Pettit Corporation has annual credit sales of $2 million. Current expenses for the collection department are $30,000, bad debt losses are 2 percent, and the days sales outstanding is 30 days. Pettit is considering easing its collection efforts so that collection expenses will be reduced to $22,000 per year. The change is expected to increase bad debt losses to 3 percent and to increase the days sales outstanding to 45 days. In addition, sales are expected to increase to $2.2 million per year.

Should Pettit relax collection efforts if the opportunity cost of funds is 12 percent, the variable cost ratio is 75 percent, and its federal-plus-state tax rate is 40 percent?

EXAM-TYPE PROBLEMS

The problems included in this section are set up in such a way that they could be used as multiple-choice exam problems.

11-4
Receivables investment

Morrissey Industries sells on terms of 3/10, net 30. Total sales for the year are $900,000. Forty percent of the customers pay on the tenth day and take discounts; the other 60 percent pay, on average, 40 days after their purchases.

a. What is the days sales outstanding?

b. What is the average amount of receivables?

c. What would happen to average receivables if Morrissey toughened up on its collection policy with the result that all nondiscount customers paid on the thirtieth day?

11-5

Tightening credit terms

Helen Bowers, the new credit manager of the Muscarella Corporation, was alarmed to find that Muscarella sells on credit terms of net 50 days while industrywide credit terms have recently been lowered to net 30 days. On annual credit sales of $3 million, Muscarella currently averages 60 days' sales in accounts receivable. Bowers estimates that tightening the credit terms to 30 days would reduce annual sales to $2.6 million, but accounts receivable would drop to 35 days of sales, and the savings on investment in them should more than overcome any loss in profit.

Muscarella's variable cost ratio is 70 percent, and its federal-plus-state tax rate is 40 percent. If the interest rate on funds invested in receivables is 11 percent, should the change in credit terms be made?

11-6

Cost of carrying receivables

The McCollough Company has a variable operating cost ratio of 70 percent, its cost of capital is 10 percent, and current sales are $10,000. All of its sales are on credit, and it currently sells on terms of net 30. Its accounts receivable balance is $1,500. Mc-Collough is considering a new credit policy with terms of net 45. Under the new policy, sales will increase to $12,000, and accounts receivable will rise to $2,500. If McCollough changes its credit policy to net 45, by how much will its cost of carrying receivables increase? Assume a 360-day year.

INTEGRATIVE PROBLEM

11-7

Credit policy

Dan Edwards, Financial Vice-President of Shield Chemicals Corporation, recently received a report from the company's marketing department recommending that Shield's credit policy be eased. Specifically, the report recommended that the credit terms be changed from 2/10, net 30 to 3/20, net 45 and that both the credit standards and the collection policy be relaxed. According to the report, such a change would cause sales to increase from $18 million to $22 million.

Currently, 63 percent of Shield's *paying* customers pay on Day 10 and take the discount, 34 percent pay on Day 30, and the remaining 3 percent pay (on average) on Day 60. Only 2 percent of sales currently end up as bad debt losses. If the new credit policy is adopted, Edwards thinks that 70 percent of *paying* customers would take the discount, 11 percent would pay on Day 45, and 19 percent would pay late, on Day 90. However, because of the relaxed credit standards, bad debt losses would rise from 2 percent to 4 percent.

Variable operating costs are currently 75 percent of sales, the cost of funds used to carry receivables is 10 percent, and its federal-plus-state tax rate is 40 percent. None of these factors would change as a result of a credit policy change.

To help decide whether or not to adopt the new policy, Edwards has asked you to answer the following questions.

a. What four variables make up a firm's credit policy? In what direction would each be changed if the credit policy were to be *tightened*? How would each variable tend to affect sales, the level of receivables, and bad debt losses?

b. What are the 5 Cs of credit, which credit policy variables do they affect, and how are they used in credit management?

c. How are the days sales outstanding (DSO) and the average collection period (ACP) related to one another? What would the DSO be if the current credit policy is maintained? If the proposed policy is adopted?

d. What is the dollar amount of bad debt losses under the current and the proposed credit policies?

e. What is the dollar amount of discounts granted under the current and the proposed credit policies?

f. What is the dollar cost of carrying receivables under the current and the proposed credit policies?

g. What is the expected incremental profit associated with the proposed change in credit policy? Based on the analysis thus far, should the change be made?

h. If the proposed changes were made, how sure would Edwards be that the changes would actually produce the expected results? What variables in this analysis are especially uncertain? Can you think of anything that the company might do to get more accurate, less uncertain estimates of the effects of the proposed changes?

i. Suppose the company makes the proposed change, but its competitors react by making changes in their own credit terms, with the net result being that gross sales remain at the $18 million level. What would be the impact on the company's after-tax profits?

j. (1) What does the term "monitoring accounts receivable" mean?

   (2) Why would a firm want to monitor its receivables?

   (3) How might the DSO and the aging schedule be used in this process?

   (4) How would seasonal fluctuations affect the validity of the DSO and the aging schedule for monitoring purposes?

COMPUTER-RELATED PROBLEM

Work the problem in this section only if you are using the computer problem diskette.

11-8

Tightening credit terms

Use the model in File C11 to work this problem.

a. Refer back to Problem 11-5. When Bowers analyzed her proposed credit policy changes, she found that they would reduce Muscarella's profits and, therefore, should not be enacted. Bowers has reevaluated her sales estimates since all other firms in the industry have recently tightened their credit policies. She now estimates that sales would decline to only $2,800,000 if she tightened the credit policy to net 30 days. Would the credit policy change be profitable under these circumstances?

b. On the other hand, Bowers believes that she could tighten the credit policy to net 45 days and pick up some sales from her competitors. She estimates that sales would increase to $3.3 million and that the days sales outstanding would fall to 50 days under this policy. What would be Muscarella's profits if Bowers enacted this change?

c. Bowers also believes that, if she leaves the credit policy as it is, sales will increase to $3.4 million, and the days sales outstanding will remain at 60 days. Should Bowers leave the credit policy alone or tighten it as described in either Part a or Part b? Which credit policy produces the largest profits for Muscarella Corporation?

Inventory Management

A MANAGERIAL PERSPECTIVE

Companies are very much concerned with their inventory policies. The cost of money used to buy and carry inventories is about 15 percent for many firms, and storage, insurance, pilferage, and obsolescence amount to another 10 to 15 percent. Thus, holding $100 of inventory for a year has a cost in the range of $25 to $30. With these high costs, holding excessive inventories can literally ruin a company. On the other hand, inventory shortages can lead to lost sales, to production interruptions, and to customer ill will, so shortages can be just as harmful as excesses.

Many firms today are using computerized inventory control models to match stocks on hand with forecasted sales levels, and they are coordinating closely with suppliers to reduce average inventory levels. For example, Huffy Corporation, the largest U.S. bicycle manufacturer, was able to reduce its peak spring inventory from $69 million to $36 million through a better inventory control process. Huffy is saving millions of dollars in interest and storage costs by keeping a pared-down inventory, with no adverse effect on sales. However, such a policy is not without dangers—if bicycle sales surge, Huffy's inventories might not be sufficient to meet demand, causing the company to lose sales to its rivals, who are continuing to carry higher inventories. Note, though, that if sales fall, Huffy will be in a better position than its rivals, and if consumers begin to demand bicycles of different styles, Huffy will be able to adapt more easily than its competitors, who will be stuck with obsolete bicycles.

Our goal in this chapter is to examine the factors that companies like Huffy consider when they establish their inventory policies.

Inventories are essential for sales, and sales are necessary for profits. Actual inventory control is generally not under the direct control of the financial manager. Rather, in manufacturing companies, production people typically have control over inventories, whereas in retail concerns this control is exercised by merchandising people. However, the financial manager is still vitally concerned with inventory levels, for he or she has responsibility for tracking factors which affect the overall profitability of the firm, and, because inventories generally amount to some 20 to 40 percent of total assets, poor inventory control will hurt the firm's profitability. You know from your study of the Du Pont equation that ineffective inventory management can result in excessive inventories, which in turn can lead to a low rate of return on invested capital.

Inventory management also has an effect on the cash conversion cycle, which was discussed in Chapter 9. Remember that one of the components of the cash conversion cycle is the inventory conversion period, the average length of time required to convert raw materials into finished goods and then to sell these goods. Naturally, the larger the amount of inventories held, the longer the inventory conversion period, hence the longer the cash conversion cycle. In this chapter we discuss in general terms the basics of inventory management.[1]

INVENTORIES

Inventories, which may be classified as (1) *raw materials,* (2) *work-in-process,* and (3) *finished goods,* are an essential part of virtually all business operations. As is the case with accounts receivable, inventory levels depend heavily upon sales. However, whereas receivables build up *after* sales have been made, inventories must be acquired *ahead* of sales. This is a critical difference, and the necessity of forecasting sales before establishing target inventory levels makes inventory management a difficult task. Also, since errors in the establishment of inventory levels quickly lead either to lost sales or to excessive carrying costs, inventory management is as important as it is difficult.

Inventory management techniques are covered in depth in production management courses, but since financial managers have a responsibility both for raising the capital needed to carry inventory and for the overall profitability of the firm, we need to cover the basics of inventory management here. Two examples will make clear the types of issues involved in inventory management and the problems poor inventory control can cause.

Retail Clothing Store

Chicago Discount Clothing Company (CDCC) must order swimsuits for summer sales in January, and it must take delivery by April to be sure of having enough suits to meet the heavy May–June demand. Bathing suits come in many styles, colors, and sizes, and if CDCC stocks incorrectly, either in total or in terms of the style-color-size distribution, then the store will have trouble. It will lose

---

[1]Students often cover the materials presented in this chapter in production management or other courses. In that event, this chapter can be used as a review, or it can be omitted.

potential sales if it stocks too few suits, and it will be forced to lower prices and take losses if it stocks too many or the wrong types.

The effects of inventory changes on the balance sheet are important. For simplicity, assume that CDCC has a $10,000 base stock of inventory which is financed by common stock. Its balance sheet is as follows:

Inventory (base stock)	$10,000	Common stock	$10,000
Total assets	$10,000	Total claims	$10,000

Now it anticipates that it will sell $5,000 worth of swimsuit inventory this summer. Dollar sales will actually be greater than $5,000 since CDCC makes about $200 in profits for every $1,000 of inventory sold. CDCC finances its seasonal inventory with bank loans, so its pre-summer balance sheet would look like this:

Inventory (seasonal)	$ 5,000	Notes payable to bank	$ 5,000
Inventory (base stock)	10,000	Common stock	10,000
Total assets	$15,000	Total claims	$15,000

If everything works out as planned, sales will be made, inventories will be converted to cash, the bank loan will be retired, and the company will earn a profit. The balance sheet, after a successful season, might look like this:

Cash	$ 1,000	Notes payable to bank	$ 0
Inventory (seasonal)	0	Common stock	10,000
Inventory (base stock)	10,000	Retained earnings	1,000
Total assets	$11,000	Total claims	$11,000

The company is now in a highly liquid position and is ready to begin a new season.

But suppose the season had not gone well, and CDCC had only sold $1,000 of its inventory. As fall approached, the balance sheet would look like this:

Cash	$ 200	Notes payable to bank	$ 4,000
Inventory (seasonal)	4,000	Common stock	10,000
Inventory (base stock)	10,000	Retained earnings	200
Total assets	$14,200	Total claims	$14,200

Now suppose the bank insists on repayment of the $4,000 outstanding on the loan, and it wants cash, not swimsuits. But if the swimsuits did not sell well in the summer, how will out-of-style suits sell in the fall? Assume that CDCC is forced to mark the suits down to half their cost (not half the selling price) in order to sell them to raise cash to repay the bank loan. The result will be as follows:

Cash	$ 2,200	Notes payable to bank	$ 4,000
Inventory (base stock)	10,000	Common stock	10,000
		Retained earnings	(1,800)
Total assets	$12,200	Total claims	$12,200

At this point, CDCC is in serious trouble. It does not have the cash to pay off the loan, and the firm's shareholders have lost $1,800 of their equity. If the bank will not extend the loan, and if other sources of cash are not available, CDCC will have to mark down its base stock prices in an effort to stimulate sales, and if this does not work, CDCC could be forced into bankruptcy. Clearly, poor inventory decisions can spell trouble.

Appliance Manufacturer

Now consider a different type of situation, that of Housepro Corporation, a well-established appliance manufacturer whose inventory position, in millions of dollars, follows:

Raw materials	$ 200
Work-in-process	200
Finished goods	600
Total inventory	$1,000

Suppose Housepro anticipates that the economy is about to get much stronger and that the demand for appliances will rise sharply. If it is to share in the expected boom, Housepro will have to increase production. This means it will have to increase inventory, and, since the inventory buildup must precede sales, additional financing will be required—some liability account, perhaps notes payable, would have to be increased in order to support the additional inventory.

Proper inventory management requires close coordination among the sales, purchasing, production, and finance departments. The sales/marketing department is generally the first to spot changes in demand. These changes must be worked into the company's purchasing and manufacturing schedules, and the financial manager must arrange any financing that will be needed to support the inventory buildup. Lack of coordination among departments, poor sales forecasts, or both, can lead to disaster.

INVENTORY MANAGEMENT

Inventory management focuses on four basic questions. (1) How many units should be ordered (or produced) at a given time? (2) At what point should inventory be ordered (or produced)? (3) What inventory items warrant special attention? (4) Can changes in the costs of inventory items be hedged? The remainder of the chapter is devoted to providing answers to these four questions.

INVENTORY COSTS

The goal of inventory management is to provide the inventories required to sustain operations at the lowest possible cost. The first step in inventory management is to identify all the costs involved in purchasing and maintaining inventory. Table 12-1 gives a listing of the typical costs associated with inventory. We have broken down costs into three categories: those associated with carry-

Table 12-1 ▪ **Costs Associated with Inventory**

	Approximate Annual Cost as a Percentage of Inventory Value
I. Carrying Costs	
Cost of capital tied up	12.0%
Storage and handling costs	0.5
Insurance	0.5
Property taxes	1.0
Depreciation and obsolescence	12.0
Total	26.0%
II. Ordering, Shipping, and Receiving Costs	
Cost of placing orders, including production and setup costs	Varies
Shipping and handling costs	2.5%
III. Costs of Running Short	
Loss of sales	Varies
Loss of customer goodwill	Varies
Disruption of production schedules	Varies

Note: These costs vary from firm to firm, from item to item, and also over time. The figures shown are U.S. Department of Commerce estimates for an average manufacturing firm. Where costs vary so widely that no meaningful numbers can be assigned, the term "Varies" is reported.

ing inventory, those associated with ordering and receiving inventory, and those associated with running short of inventory.

Although they may well be the most important element, we shall at this point disregard the third category of costs—the costs of running short. These costs are dealt with by adding safety stocks, as we will discuss later. Similarly, we shall discuss quantity discounts in a later section. The costs that remain for consideration at this stage, then, are carrying costs and ordering, shipping, and receiving costs.

Carrying Costs

carrying costs

The costs associated with carrying inventory, including storage, capital, and depreciation costs; these costs generally increase in proportion to the average amount of inventory held.

Carrying costs generally rise in direct proportion to the average amount of inventory carried. Inventory carried, in turn, depends on the frequency with which orders are placed. To illustrate, if a firm sells S units per year, and if it places equal-sized orders N times per year, then S/N units will be purchased with each order. If the inventory is used evenly over the year, and if no safety stocks are carried, then the average inventory, A, will be

$$\text{Average inventory} = A = \frac{\text{Units per order}}{2} = \frac{S/N}{2}. \qquad (12\text{-}1)$$

For example, if S = 120,000 units a year and N = 4, then the firm will order 30,000 units at a time, and its average inventory will be 15,000 units:

$$A = \frac{120{,}000/4}{2} = \frac{30{,}000}{2} = 15{,}000 \text{ units.}$$

Just after a shipment arrives, the inventory will be 30,000 units; just before the next shipment arrives, it will be zero; and on average, 15,000 units will be carried.

Now assume the firm purchases its inventory at a price P = $2 per unit. The average inventory value is, thus, (P)(A) = $2(15,000) = $30,000. If the firm has a cost of capital of 10 percent, it will incur $3,000 in financing charges to carry the inventory for one year. Further, assume that each year the firm incurs $2,000 of storage costs (space, utilities, security, taxes, and so forth), that its inventory insurance costs are $500, and that it must mark down inventory by $1,000 because of depreciation and obsolescence. The firm's total cost of carrying the $30,000 average inventory is thus $3,000 + $2,000 + $500 + $1,000 = $6,500, and the annual percentage cost of carrying the inventory is $6,500/$30,000 = 0.217 = 21.7%.

Defining the annual percentage carrying cost as C, we can, in general, find the annual total carrying cost, TCC, as the percentage carrying cost, C, times the price per unit, P, times the average inventory in units, A:

$$\text{TCC} = \text{Total carrying cost} = (C)(P)(A). \qquad (12\text{-}2)$$

In our example,

$$\text{TCC} = (0.217)(\$2)(15{,}000) \approx \$6{,}500.$$

Ordering Costs

ordering costs

The costs of placing and receiving an order; these costs are fixed regardless of the average size of inventory.

Although we assume that carrying costs are entirely variable and rise in direct proportion to the average size of inventory, **ordering costs** are usually fixed. For example, the costs of placing and receiving an order—interoffice memos, long-distance telephone calls, setting up a production run, and taking delivery—are essentially fixed regardless of the size of an order, so this part of inventory cost is simply the fixed cost of placing and receiving orders times the number of orders placed per year.[2] We define the fixed costs associated with ordering

---

[2]Note that, in reality, both carrying and ordering costs can have variable and fixed cost elements, at least over certain ranges of average inventory. For example, security and utilities charges are probably fixed in the short run over a wide range of inventory levels. Similarly, labor costs in receiving inventory could be tied to the quantity received, hence could be variable. To simplify matters, we treat all carrying costs as variable and all ordering costs as fixed. However, if these assumptions do not fit the situation at hand, the cost definitions can be changed. For example, one could add another term for shipping costs if there are economies of scale in shipping such that the cost of shipping a unit is smaller if shipments are larger. However, in most situations, shipping costs are not sensitive to order size, so total shipping costs are simply the shipping cost per unit times the units ordered (and sold) during the year. Under this condition, shipping costs are not influenced by inventory policy, and hence may be disregarded for purposes of determining the optimal inventory level and the optimal order size.

inventories as F, and if we place N orders per year, the total ordering cost is given by Equation 12-3:

$$\text{Total ordering cost} = \text{TOC} = (F)(N). \qquad (12\text{-}3)$$

Here TOC = total ordering cost, F = fixed costs per order, and N = number of orders placed per year.

Equation 12-1 can be rewritten as N = S/2A, and then substituted into Equation 12-3:

$$\text{Total ordering cost} = \text{TOC} = F\left(\frac{S}{2A}\right). \qquad (12\text{-}4)$$

To illustrate the use of Equation 12-4, if F = $100, S = 120,000 units, and A = 15,000 units, then TOC, the total annual ordering cost, is $400:

$$\text{TOC} = \$100\left(\frac{120,000}{30,000}\right) = \$100(4) = \$400.$$

Total Inventory Costs

Total carrying cost, TCC, as defined in Equation 12-2, and total ordering cost, TOC, as defined in Equation 12-4, may be combined to find total inventory costs, TIC, as follows:

$$\text{Total inventory costs} = \text{TIC} = \quad \text{TCC} \quad + \quad \text{TOC}$$
$$= (C)(P)(A) + F\left(\frac{S}{2A}\right). \qquad (12\text{-}5)$$

Recognizing that the average inventory carried is A = Q/2, or one-half the size of each order quantity, Q, we may rewrite Equation 12-5 as follows:

$$\text{TIC} = \quad \text{TCC} \quad + \quad \text{TOC}$$
$$= (C)(P)\left(\frac{Q}{2}\right) + (F)\left(\frac{S}{Q}\right). \qquad (12\text{-}6)$$

Here we see that total carrying cost equals average inventory in units, Q/2, multiplied by unit price, P, times the percentage annual carrying cost, C. Total ordering cost equals the number of orders placed per year, S/Q, multiplied by the fixed cost of placing and receiving an order, F. We will use this equation in the next section to develop the optimal inventory ordering quantity.

Self-Test Questions

What are the three categories of inventory costs?

What are some specific inventory carrying costs?

What are some inventory ordering costs?

Explain in words what Equation 12-6 is doing.

THE ECONOMIC ORDERING QUANTITY (EOQ) MODEL

Inventories are obviously necessary, but it is equally obvious that a firm's profitability will suffer if it has too much or too little inventory. How can we determine the optimal inventory level? One commonly used approach is based on the economic ordering quantity (EOQ) model, which is described next.

Derivation of the EOQ Model

Figure 12-1 illustrates the basic premise on which the EOQ model is built, namely, that some costs rise with larger inventories while other costs decline, and there is an optimal order size (and associated average inventory) which minimizes the total costs of inventories. First, as noted earlier, the average investment in inventory depends on how frequently orders are placed and the size of each order—if we order every day, average inventory will be much smaller than if we order once a year. Further, as Figure 12-1 shows, the firm's carrying costs rise with larger orders: Larger orders mean larger average inventory, so warehousing costs, interest on funds tied up in inventory, insurance, and obsolescence costs will all increase. However, ordering costs decline with larger orders of inventories: The cost of placing orders, suppliers' production setup costs, and order handling costs will all decline if we order infrequently and consequently hold larger quantities.

If the carrying and ordering cost curves in Figure 12-1 are summed, the sum represents total inventory costs, TIC. The point where the TIC is minimized represents the **economic ordering quantity (EOQ),** and this, in turn, determines the optimal average inventory level.

The EOQ is found by differentiating Equation 12-6 with respect to ordering quantity, Q, and setting the derivative equal to zero:

economic ordering quantity (EOQ)

The optimal, or least-cost, quantity of inventory that should be ordered.

$$EOQ = \sqrt{\frac{2(F)(S)}{(C)(P)}}. \qquad (12\text{-}7)$$

Here

EOQ = economic ordering quantity, or the optimum quantity to be ordered each time an order is placed.

F = fixed costs of placing and receiving an order.

S = annual sales in units.

Figure 12-1   ▪   **Determination of the Optimal Order Quantity**

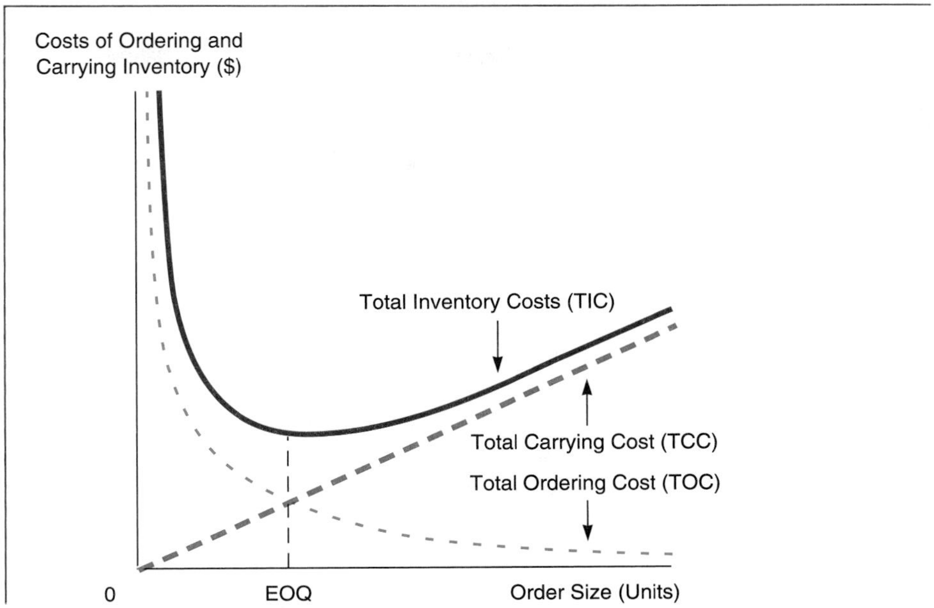

EOQ model

A formula for determining the order quantity that will minimize total inventory costs:

$$EOQ = \sqrt{\frac{2(F)(S)}{(C)(P)}}.$$

C = annual carrying costs expressed as a percentage of average inventory value.

P = purchase price the firm must pay per unit of inventory.

Equation 12-7 is the **EOQ model.**[3] The assumptions of the model, which will be relaxed shortly, include the following: (1) sales can be forecasted perfectly, (2) sales are evenly distributed throughout the year, and (3) orders are received when expected.

EOQ Model Illustration

To illustrate the EOQ model, consider the following data, supplied by Cotton Tops Inc., a distributor of custom-designed T-shirts which supplies concessionaires at Daisy World:

S = annual sales = 26,000 shirts per year.

C = percentage carrying cost = 25 percent of inventory value.

P = purchase price per shirt = $4.92 per shirt. (The shirts sell for $9, but this is irrelevant for our purposes here.)

---

[3]The EOQ model can also be written as

$$EOQ = \sqrt{\frac{2(F)(S)}{C^*}},$$

where C^* is the annual carrying cost per unit expressed in *dollars.*

F = fixed cost per order = $1,000. Cotton Tops designs and distributes the shirts, but the actual production is done by another company. The bulk of this $1,000 cost is the labor cost for setting up the equipment for the production run, which the manufacturer bills separately from the $4.92 cost per shirt.

Substituting these data into Equation 12-7, we find an EOQ of 6,500 units:

$$EOQ = \sqrt{\frac{2(F)(S)}{(C)(P)}} = \sqrt{\frac{(2)(\$1,000)(26,000)}{(0.25)(\$4.92)}}$$
$$= \sqrt{42,276,423} \approx 6,500 \text{ units.}$$

With an EOQ of 6,500 shirts and annual usage of 26,000 shirts, Cotton Tops will place 26,000/6,500 = 4 orders per year. Notice that average inventory holdings depend directly on the EOQ: This relationship is illustrated graphically in Figure 12-2, where we see that average inventory = EOQ/2. Immediately after an order is received, 6,500 shirts are in stock. The usage rate, or sales rate, is 500 shirts per week (26,000/52 weeks), so inventories are drawn down by this amount each week. Thus, the actual number of units held in inventory will vary from 6,500 shirts just after an order is received to zero just before a new order arrives. With a 6,500 beginning balance, a zero ending balance, and a uniform sales rate, inventory will average one-half the EOQ, or 3,250 shirts, during the year. At a cost of $4.92 per shirt, the average investment in inventory will be (3,250)($4.92) ≈ $16,000. If inventories are financed by bank loans, the loan will vary from a high of $32,000 to a low of $0, but the average amount outstanding over the course of a year will be $16,000.

Figure 12-2 ▪ **Inventory Position without Safety Stock**

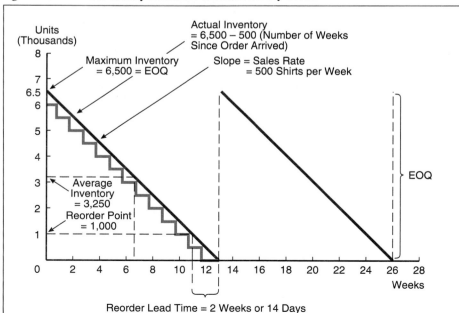

Reorder Lead Time = 2 Weeks or 14 Days

Notice that the EOQ, hence average inventory holdings, rises with the square root of sales. Therefore, a given increase in sales will result in a less-than-proportionate increase in inventory, so the inventory/sales ratio will tend to decline as a firm grows. For example, Cotton Tops' EOQ is 6,500 shirts at an annual sales level of 26,000, and the average inventory is 3,250 shirts, or $16,000. However, if sales were to increase by 100 percent, to 52,000 shirts per year, the EOQ would rise only to 9,195 shirts, or by 41 percent, and the average inventory would rise by this same percentage. This suggests that there are economies of scale in holding inventories.[4]

Finally, look at Cotton Tops' total inventory costs for the year, assuming that the EOQ is ordered each time. Using Equation 12-6, we find total inventory costs of $8,000:

$$
\begin{aligned}
\text{TIC} &= \quad\quad \text{TCC} \quad\quad + \quad\quad \text{TOC} \\[2mm]
&= \quad (C)(P)\left(\frac{Q}{2}\right) \quad + \quad (F)\left(\frac{S}{Q}\right) \\[2mm]
&= \ 0.25(\$4.92)\left(\frac{6{,}500}{2}\right) + (\$1{,}000)\left(\frac{26{,}000}{6{,}500}\right) \\[2mm]
&\approx \quad\quad \$4{,}000 \quad\quad + \quad\quad \$4{,}000 \quad = \$8{,}000.
\end{aligned}
$$

Note these two points: (1) The $8,000 total inventory cost represents the total of carrying costs and ordering costs, but this amount does *not* include the 26,000($4.92) = $127,920 annual purchasing cost of the inventory itself. (2) As we see both in Figure 12-1 and in the numbers just above, at the EOQ, total carrying cost (TCC) equals total ordering cost (TOC). This property is not unique to our Cotton Tops illustration; it always holds.

Setting the Reorder Point

reorder point

The inventory level at which an order should be placed.

If a 2-week lead time is required for production and shipping, what is Cotton Tops' **reorder point,** or the inventory level at which an order should be placed? The firm sells 26,000/52 = 500 shirts per week. Thus, if a 2-week lag occurs between the order and the delivery, Cotton Tops must place the order when there are 1,000 shirts on hand:

> Reorder point = Lead time in weeks × Weekly usage   (12-8)

$$= 2 \times 500 = 1{,}000.$$

At the end of the 2-week production and shipping period, the inventory balance will be down to zero — but just at that time, the order of new shirts will arrive.

---

[4]Note, however, that these scale economies relate to each particular item, not to the entire firm. Thus, a large distributor with $500 million of sales might have a higher inventory/sales ratio than a much smaller distributor if the small firm has only a few high-sales-volume items while the large firm distributes a great many low-volume items.

Goods in Transit

goods in transit
Goods which have been ordered but have not been received.

If a new order must be placed before the previous order is received, a **goods-in-transit** inventory will build up. Goods in transit are goods which have been ordered but have not been received. A goods-in-transit inventory will exist if the normal delivery lead time is longer than the time between orders. This complicates matters somewhat, but the simplest solution to the problem is to deduct goods in transit when calculating the reorder point. In other words, the reorder point is calculated as follows:

$$\text{Reorder} \atop \text{point} = \left({\text{Lead time} \atop \text{in weeks}} \times {\text{Weekly} \atop \text{usage}} \right) - {\text{Goods in} \atop \text{transit}} \qquad (12\text{-}9)$$

Goods in transit is not an issue for Cotton Tops because the firm orders $26{,}000/6{,}500 = 4$ times a year, or once every 13 weeks, and the delivery lead time is 2 weeks. However, suppose that Cotton Tops ordered 1,000 shirts every 2 weeks and the delivery lead time was 3 weeks. Then, whenever an order was placed, another order of 1,000 shirts would be in transit. Therefore, Cotton Tops' reorder point would be

$$\begin{aligned}
\text{Reorder point} &= (3 \times 500) - 1{,}000 \\
&= 1{,}500 - 1{,}000 \\
&= 500.
\end{aligned}$$

Self-Test Questions

What is the purpose of the EOQ model?

What is the relationship between total carrying cost and total ordering cost at the EOQ?

What assumptions are inherent in the EOQ model as presented here?

EOQ MODEL EXTENSIONS

The basic EOQ model was derived under several restrictive assumptions. In this section, we relax some of those assumptions and, in the process, extend the model to make it more useful.

The Concept of Safety Stocks

safety stocks
Additional inventory carried to guard against changes in sales rates or production/shipping delays.

If Cotton Tops knew for certain that both the sales rate and the order lead time would never vary, it could operate exactly as shown in Figure 12-2. However, because sales do change, and because production and shipping delays do occur, the firm must carry additional inventory, or **safety stocks.**

The concept of a safety stock is illustrated in Figure 12-3. First, note that the slope of the sales line measures the expected rate of sales. The company *expects* to sell 500 shirts per week, but let us assume that the maximum likely sales rate is twice this amount, or 1,000 units each week. Further, assume that Cotton Tops sets the safety stock at 1,000 shirts, so it initially orders 7,500 shirts, the EOQ of 6,500 plus the 1,000-unit safety stock. Subsequently, it reor-

Figure 12-3   ▪   **Inventory Position with Safety Stock Included**

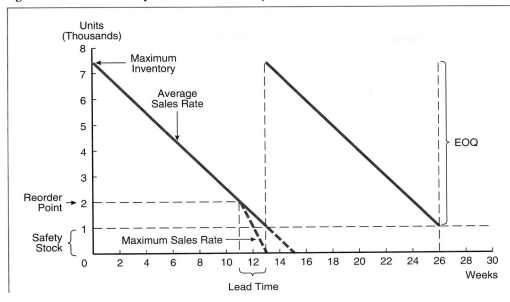

ders the EOQ whenever the inventory level falls to 2,000 shirts, the safety stock of 1,000 shirts plus the 1,000 shirts expected to be used while awaiting delivery of the order.

Notice that the company could, over the 2-week delivery period, sell 1,000 units a week, or double its normal expected sales. This maximum rate of sales is shown by the steeper dashed line in Figure 12-3. The condition that makes possible this higher maximum sales rate is the safety stock of 1,000 shirts.

The safety stock is also useful to guard against delays in receiving orders. The expected delivery time is 2 weeks, but with a 1,000-unit safety stock, the company could maintain sales at the expected rate of 500 units per week for an additional 2 weeks if production or shipping delays held up an order.

However, carrying a safety stock has a cost. The average inventory is now EOQ/2 plus the safety stock, or $6,500/2 + 1,000 = 3,250 + 1,000 = 4,250$ shirts, and the average inventory value is now $(4,250)($4.92) = $20,910$. This increase in average inventory causes an increase in annual inventory carrying costs equal to (Safety stock)(P)(C) = $1,000($4.92)(0.25) = $1,230$.

The optimal safety stock varies from situation to situation, but, in general, it *increases* (1) with the uncertainty of demand forecasts, (2) with the costs (in terms of lost sales and lost goodwill) that result from inventory shortages, and (3) with the probability that delays will occur in receiving shipments. The optimum safety stock *decreases* as the cost of carrying this additional inventory increases.

Quantity Discounts

Now suppose the T-shirt manufacturer offered Cotton Tops a *quantity discount* of 2 percent on large orders. If the quantity discount applied to orders of 5,000 or more, then Cotton Tops would continue to place the EOQ order of 6,500 shirts and take the quantity discount. However, if the quantity discount required orders of 10,000 or more, then Cotton Tops' inventory manager would have to compare the savings in purchase price that would result if its ordering quantity were increased to 10,000 units versus the increase in total inventory costs caused by the departure from the 6,500-unit EOQ.

First, consider the total costs associated with Cotton Tops' EOQ of 6,500 shirts. We found earlier that total inventory costs are $8,000:

$$
\begin{aligned}
\text{TIC} &= \qquad\quad \text{TCC} \qquad\qquad + \qquad \text{TOC} \\[6pt]
&= \qquad (C)(P)\left(\frac{Q}{2}\right) \qquad + \qquad (F)\left(\frac{S}{Q}\right) \\[6pt]
&= \quad 0.25(\$4.92)\left(\frac{6{,}500}{2}\right) \;+\; (\$1{,}000)\left(\frac{26{,}000}{6{,}500}\right) \\[6pt]
&\approx \qquad\quad \$4{,}000 \qquad\quad + \qquad \$4{,}000 \qquad = \$8{,}000.
\end{aligned}
$$

Now, what would the total inventory costs be if Cotton Tops ordered 10,000 shirts instead of 6,500? The answer is $8,625:

$$
\begin{aligned}
\text{TIC} &= \; 0.25(\$4.82)\left(\frac{10{,}000}{2}\right) \;+\; (\$1{,}000)\left(\frac{26{,}000}{10{,}000}\right) \\[6pt]
&= \qquad\quad \$6{,}025 \qquad\quad + \qquad \$2{,}600 \qquad = \$8{,}625.
\end{aligned}
$$

Notice that when the discount is taken, the price, P, is reduced by the amount of the discount; the new price per unit would be 0.98($4.92) = $4.82. Also note that when the ordering quantity is increased, carrying costs increase because the firm is carrying a larger average inventory, but ordering costs decrease since the number of orders per year decreases. If we were to calculate total inventory costs at an ordering quantity of 5,000, we would find that carrying costs would be less than $4,000, and ordering costs would be more than $4,000, but the total inventory costs would be more than $8,000 since they are at a minimum when 6,500 shirts are ordered.[5]

Thus, inventory costs would increase by $8,625 − $8,000 = $625 if Cotton Tops were to increase its order size to 10,000 shirts. *However, this cost increase must be compared with Cotton Tops' savings if it takes the discount.* Taking the discount would save 0.02($4.92) = $0.0984 per shirt. Over the year, Cotton Tops orders 26,000 shirts, so the annual savings is $0.0984(26,000) ≈ $2,558. Here is a summary:

Reduction in purchase price = 0.02($4.92)(26,000) = $2,558
Increase in total inventory cost   =   625
Net savings from taking discounts   = $1,933

Obviously, the company should order 10,000 shirts and take advantage of the quantity discount.

---

[5]At an ordering quantity of 5,000 units, total inventory costs are $8,275:

$$
\begin{aligned}
\text{TIC} &= (0.25)(\$4.92)\left(\frac{5{,}000}{2}\right) \;+\; (\$1{,}000)\left(\frac{26{,}000}{5{,}000}\right) \\[6pt]
&= \$3{,}075 + \$5{,}200 = \$8{,}275.
\end{aligned}
$$

Inflation

Moderate inflation—say 3 percent per year—can largely be ignored for purposes of inventory management, but higher rates of inflation must be explicitly considered. If the rate of inflation in the types of goods the firm stocks tends to be relatively constant, it can be dealt with quite easily—simply deduct the expected annual rate of inflation from the carrying cost percentage, C, in Equation 12-7, and use this modified version of the EOQ model to establish the working stock. The reason for making this deduction is that inflation causes the value of the inventory to rise, thus offsetting somewhat the effects of depreciation and other carrying costs factors. Since C will now be smaller, the calculated EOQ, and the average inventory, will increase. However, the higher the rate of inflation, the higher are interest rates, and this factor will cause C to increase, thus lowering the EOQ and average inventory.

On balance, there is no evidence that inflation either raises or lowers the optimal inventory of firms in the aggregate. Inflation should still be explicitly considered, however, for it will raise the individual firm's optimal holdings if the rate of inflation for its own inventories is above average (and is greater than the effects of inflation on interest rates) and vice versa.

Seasonal Demand

For most firms, it is unrealistic to assume that the demand for an inventory item is uniform throughout the year. What happens when there is seasonal demand, as would hold true for an ice cream company? Here the standard annual EOQ model is obviously not appropriate. However, the model does provide a point of departure for setting inventory parameters, which are then modified to fit the particular seasonal pattern. The procedure here is to divide the year into the seasons in which annualized sales are relatively constant, say the summer, the spring and fall, and the winter. Then, the EOQ model can be applied separately to each period. During the transitions between seasons, inventory would be either run down or else built up with special seasonal orders.

Self-Test Questions

Why are inventory safety stocks required?

How would you decide whether or not to accept a quantity discount offer from a supplier?

What impact does inflation have on the EOQ?

How can the EOQ model be used when a company faces seasonal demand fluctuations?

INVENTORY CONTROL SYSTEMS

The EOQ model, together with safety stock analysis, can be used to establish the proper inventory level, but inventory management also involves the establishment of an *inventory control system*. Inventory control systems run the gamut from very simple to extremely complex, depending on the size of the firm and the nature of its inventories. For example, one simple control proce-

red-line method

An inventory control procedure in which a red line is drawn around the inside of an inventory-stocked bin to indicate the reorder point level.

two-bin method

An inventory control procedure in which an order is placed when one of two inventory-stocked bins is empty.

computerized inventory control system

A system of inventory control in which a computer is used to determine reorder points and to adjust inventory balances.

dure is the **red-line method**—inventory items are stocked in a bin, a red line is drawn around the inside of the bin at the level of the reorder point, and the inventory clerk places an order when the red line shows. The **two-bin method** has inventory items stocked in two bins. When the working bin is empty, an order is placed and inventory is drawn from the second bin. These procedures work well for parts such as bolts in a manufacturing process or for many items in retail businesses.

Computerized Systems

Larger companies employ **computerized inventory control systems.** The computer starts with an inventory count in memory. As withdrawals are made, they are recorded by the computer, and the inventory balance is revised. When the reorder point is reached, the computer automatically places an order, and when the order is received, the recorded balance is increased. Retailers such as Wal-Mart have carried this system quite far—each item has a bar code, and, as an item is checked out, the code is read, a signal is sent to the computer, and the inventory balance is adjusted at the same time the price is fed into the cash register tape. When the balance drops to the reorder point, an order is placed, in Wal-Mart's case directly from its computers to those of its suppliers.

A good inventory control system is dynamic, not static. A company such as IBM or General Motors (GM) stocks hundreds of thousands of different items. The sales (or use) of these various items can rise or fall quite separately from rising or falling overall corporate sales. As the usage rate for an individual item begins to rise or fall, the inventory manager must adjust its balance to avoid running short or ending up with obsolete items. If the change in the usage rate appears to be permanent, then the EOQ should be recomputed, the safety stock level should be reconsidered, and the computer model used in the control process should be reprogrammed.

Just-in-Time Systems

just-in-time system

A system of inventory control in which a manufacturer coordinates production with suppliers so that raw materials or components arrive just as they are needed in the production process.

A relatively new approach to inventory control called the **just-in-time system** has been developed by Japanese firms and is gaining popularity throughout the world. Toyota provides a good example of the just-in-time system. Eight of Toyota's ten factories, along with most of Toyota's suppliers, dot the countryside around Toyota City. Delivery of components is tied to the speed of the assembly line, and parts are generally delivered no more than a few hours before they are used. The just-in-time system reduces the need for Toyota and other manufacturers to carry large inventories, but it requires a great deal of coordination between the manufacturer and its suppliers, both in the timing of deliveries and the quality of the parts.

Not surprisingly, U.S. automobile manufacturers were among the first domestic firms to move toward just-in-time systems. Ford has been restructuring its production system with a goal of increasing its inventory turnover from 20 times a year to 30 or 40 times. Of course, just-in-time systems place considerable pressure on suppliers. GM formerly kept a 10-day supply of seats and other parts made by Lear Siegler; now GM sends in orders at four- to eight-hour intervals and expects immediate shipment. A Lear Siegler spokesman stated, "We can't afford to keep things sitting around either," so Lear Siegler has had to be tougher on its own suppliers.

Just-in-time systems are also being adopted by smaller firms. In fact, some production experts say that small companies are better positioned than large ones to use just-in-time methods because it is easier to redefine job functions and to educate people in small firms. One small-firm example is Fireplace Manufacturers Inc., a manufacturer of prefabricated fireplaces. The company was recently having cash flow problems, and it was carrying $1.1 million in inventories to support annual sales of about $8 million. The company used just-in-time methods to trim its raw material and work-in-process inventories to $750,000, freeing up $350,000 of cash, even as sales doubled.

It has been argued that just-in-time inventory controls do not really increase overall economic efficiency because they merely shift costs of purchases to other firms further up the supply chain. However, this view is probably incorrect—the close coordination required between the parties has led to an overall reduction of inventories throughout the production-distribution system, and hence to a general improvement in economic efficiency. This point is made by companies such as Wal-Mart and Toyota, and it is borne out by economic statistics, which indicate that inventories as a percentage of sales have been declining since the use of just-in-time procedures began.

Out-Sourcing

out-sourcing
The practice of purchasing components rather than making them in-house.

Another important development related to inventories is **out-sourcing,** which is the practice of purchasing components rather than making them in-house. Thus, if GM arranged to buy radiators, axles, and other parts from suppliers rather than making them itself, it would be increasing its use of out-sourcing. Out-sourcing is often combined with just-in-time systems to reduce inventory levels. However, perhaps the major reason for out-sourcing has nothing to do with inventory policy—a bureaucratic, unionized company like GM can often buy parts from a smaller, nonunionized supplier at a lower cost than if it made them itself.

The Relationship between Production Scheduling and Inventory Levels

A final point relating to inventory levels is *the relationship between production scheduling and inventory levels.* A firm like a greeting card manufacturer has highly seasonal sales. Such a firm could produce on a steady, year-round basis, or it could let production rise and fall with sales. If it established a level production schedule, its inventories would rise sharply during periods when sales were low and then would decline during peak sales periods, but the average inventory held would be substantially higher than if production rose and fell with sales.

Our discussions of just-in-time systems, out-sourcing, and production scheduling all point out the necessity of coordinating inventory policy with manufacturing/procurement policies. Companies try to minimize *total production and distribution costs,* and inventory costs are just one part of total costs. Still, they are an important cost, and financial managers should be aware of the determinants of inventory costs and how they can be minimized.

Self-Test Questions

Describe some inventory control systems used in practice.

What are just-in-time systems? What are their advantages?

What is out-sourcing?

Describe the dependency between production scheduling and inventory levels.

MONITORING INVENTORY LEVELS

ABC system

A system used to categorize inventory items to insure that the most important ones are reviewed most often.

The EOQ model can give some insights into the optimal ordering quantity and average inventories for a firm's major items, but usage rates change over time, and a good inventory management system must respond promptly to such changes. One system that is used to monitor inventory EOQs and levels is the **ABC system.** Under this system, the firm analyzes each inventory item on the basis of its cost, frequency of usage, seriousness of a stock-out, reorder lead time, and other criteria. Items that are expensive, are frequently used, have serious consequences if a stock-out occurs, and have long reorder lead times are put into the A category; less important items are placed in the B category; and the least important items are designated as C items. Management reviews the A items' usage rates, stock positions, and delivery times frequently—say, monthly—and adjusts the EOQ and reorder points as necessary. Category B items are reviewed and adjusted less frequently—say, every quarter—and C items are reviewed even less often, perhaps annually. Thus, inventory management resources are focused on where they will do the most good.

Major inventory changes should also be evaluated using the firm's forecasting model and cash budget. For example, increases in inventory, if not accompanied by increases in sales, would tend to decrease profitability and increase the need for additional funding. Further, cash outlays for the additional inventory would increase cash outflows as reported on the firm's cash budget. Efficient inventory management will result in relatively low levels of inventories, in low write-offs of obsolete or deteriorated inventories, and in few work stoppages or lost sales due to inventory shortages. All this, in turn, will contribute to a high total assets turnover, a high profit margin, a high return on equity, and a high stock price.

Self-Test Question

Explain the key features of the ABC system of inventory management.

SUMMARY

This chapter discussed inventory management. The key concepts covered are listed below.

- **Inventory management** involves determining how much inventory to hold, when to place orders, and how many units to order.
- **Inventory** can be grouped into three categories: (1) raw materials, (2) work-in-process, and (3) finished goods.

▪ **Inventory costs** can be divided into three types: carrying costs, ordering costs, and stock-out costs. In general, carrying costs increase as the level of inventory rises, but ordering costs and stock-out costs decline with larger inventory holdings.

▪ **Total carrying cost (TCC)** is equal to the percentage cost of carrying inventory (C) times the purchase price per unit of inventory (P) times the average number of units held (A): TCC = (C)(P)(A).

▪ **Total ordering cost (TOC)** is equal to the fixed cost of placing an order (F) times the number of orders placed per year (N): TOC = (F)(N).

▪ **Total inventory costs (TIC)** are equal to carrying costs plus ordering costs: TIC = TCC + TOC.

▪ The **economic ordering quantity (EOQ) model** is a formula for determining the order quantity that will minimize total inventory costs:

$$EOQ = \sqrt{\frac{2(F)(S)}{(C)(P)}}.$$

Here F is the fixed cost per order, S is annual sales in units, C is the percentage cost of carrying inventory, and P is the purchase price per unit.

▪ The **reorder point** is the inventory level at which new items must be ordered.

▪ **Safety stocks** are held to avoid shortages (1) if demand increases or (2) if shipping delays are encountered. The cost of carrying safety stocks is equal to the percentage cost of carrying inventories times the purchase price per unit times the number of units held as the safety stock. These costs are separate from those used in the EOQ model.

▪ Firms use inventory control systems such as the **red-line method** and the **two-bin method,** as well as **computerized inventory control systems,** to help them keep track of actual inventory levels and to insure that inventory levels are adjusted as sales change. **Just-in-time (JIT) systems** are also used to hold down inventory costs and, simultaneously, to improve the production process. The **ABC system** categorizes inventory items to insure that the most important ones are reviewed most often.

Questions

12-1 If a firm calculates its optimal inventory of widgets to be 1,000 units when the general rate of inflation is 2 percent, is it true that the optimal inventory (in units) will almost certainly rise if the general rate of inflation climbs to 10 percent?

12-2 Indicate by a (+), (−), or (0) whether each of the following events would probably cause average annual inventories (the sum of the inventories held at the end of each month of the year divided by 12) to rise, fall, or be affected in an indeterminant manner:

Our suppliers switch from delivering by train to air freight. ⎯⎯⎯⎯

We change from producing just in time to meet seasonal sales to steady, year-round production. (Sales peak at Christmas.) ⎯⎯⎯⎯

> Competition in the markets in which we sell increases.   _____
>
> The rate of general inflation increases.   _____
>
> Interest rates rise; other things are constant.   _____

12-3   A firm can reduce its investment in inventory by having its suppliers hold raw materials inventories and its customers hold finished goods inventories. Explain actions a firm can take which would result in larger inventories for its suppliers and customers and smaller inventories for itself. What are the limitations of such actions?

12-4   The toy business is subject to large seasonal demand fluctuations. What effect would such fluctuations have on inventory decisions of toy manufacturers and toy retailers?

Self-Test Problems   *(Solutions Appear in Appendix B)*

ST-1
Key terms

a. Carrying costs; ordering costs
b. Economic ordering quantity (EOQ); EOQ model
c. Reorder point; stock-out cost; goods in transit; safety stocks
d. Red-line method; two-bin method; computerized inventory control system
e. Just-in-time system; out-sourcing; ABC system

ST-2
EOQ and total
inventory costs

The Homemade Bread Company buys and then sells (as bread) 2.6 million bushels of wheat annually. The wheat must be purchased in multiples of 2,000 bushels. Ordering costs, which include grain elevator removal charges of $3,500, are $5,000 per order. Annual carrying costs are 2 percent of the purchase price of $5 per bushel. The company maintains a safety stock of 200,000 bushels. The delivery time is 6 weeks.
a. What is the EOQ?
b. At what inventory level should an order be placed to prevent having to draw on the safety stock?
c. What are the total inventory costs, including the costs of carrying the safety stock?
d. The wheat processor agrees to pay the elevator removal charges if Homemade Bread will purchase wheat in quantities of 650,000 bushels. Would it be to Homemade Bread's advantage to order under this alternative?

Problems

12-1
Inventory cost

Computer Supplies Inc. must order floppy diskettes from its supplier in lots of one dozen boxes. Given the following information, complete the table below and determine the economic ordering quantity of floppy diskettes for Computer Supplies Inc.

> Annual demand: 2,600 dozen
> Cost per order placed: $7.00
> Carrying cost: 15%
> Price per dozen: $20

Order Size (dozens)	26	50	100	130	200	2,600
Number of orders	____	____	____	____	____	____
Average inventory	____	____	____	____	____	____
Carrying cost	____	____	____	____	____	____
Order cost	____	____	____	____	____	____
Total cost	____	____	____	____	____	____

12-2
EOQ

Krogh Toys, a large manufacturer of toys and dolls, uses large quantities of flesh-colored cloth in its doll production process. Throughout the year, the firm uses 1,250,000 square yards of this cloth. The fixed costs of placing and receiving an order are $2,000, which includes a $1,500 setup charge at the mill. The price of the cloth is $2.50 per square yard, and the annual cost of carrying this inventory item is 20 percent of the price. Krogh maintains a 12,500 square yard safety stock. The cloth supplier requires a 2-week lead time from order to delivery.

a. What is the EOQ for this cloth?

b. What is the average inventory dollar value, including the safety stock?

c. What is the total cost of ordering and carrying the inventory, including the safety stock? (Assume that the safety stock is on hand at the beginning of the year.)

d. Using a 52-week year, at what inventory unit level should an order be placed? (Again, assume the 12,500 square yard safety stock is on hand.)

12-3
EOQ and total
ordering costs

The following inventory data have been established for the Thompson Company:

(1) Orders must be placed in multiples of 100 units.

(2) Annual sales are 338,000 units.

(3) The purchase price per unit is $6.

(4) Carrying cost is 20 percent of the purchase price of goods.

(5) Fixed order cost is $48.

(6) Desired safety stock is 12,000 units; this amount is on hand initially.

(7) Two weeks are required for delivery.

a. What is the EOQ?

b. How many orders should Thompson place each year?

c. At what inventory level should an order be made? [Hint: Reorder point = Safety stock + (Lead time × Usage rate) − Goods in transit.]

d. Calculate the total cost of ordering and carrying inventories if the order quantity is (1) 4,000 units, (2) 4,800 units, or (3) 6,000 units. (4) What are the total costs if the order quantity is the EOQ?

12-4
Changes in the EOQ

The following relationships for inventory costs have been established for the Dalrymple Corporation:

(1) Annual sales are 560,000 units.

(2) The purchase price per unit is $1.50.

(3) The carrying cost is 15 percent of the purchase price of goods.

(4) The cost per order placed is $35.

(5) Desired safety stock is 10,000 units (on hand initially).

(6) One week is required for delivery.

a. What is the economic ordering quantity? (Round to the hundreds.) What is the total cost of ordering and carrying inventories at the EOQ?

b. What is the optimal number of orders to be placed?

c. At what inventory level should Dalrymple order?

d. If annual unit sales double, what is the percent increase in the EOQ? What is the elasticity of EOQ with respect to sales (percent change in EOQ/percent change in sales)?

e. If the cost per order doubles, what is the elasticity of EOQ with respect to cost per order?

f. If the carrying cost declines by 50 percent, what is the elasticity of EOQ with respect to that change?

g. If the purchase price declines by 50 percent, what is the elasticity of EOQ with respect to that change?

EXAM-TYPE PROBLEM

The problem included in this section is set up in such a way that it could be used as a multiple-choice exam problem.

12-5
Economic ordering quantity

Green Thumb Garden Centers sells 240,000 bags of lawn fertilizer annually. The optimal safety stock (which is on hand initially) is 1,200 bags. Each bag costs Green Thumb $4, inventory carrying costs are 20 percent, and the cost of placing an order with its supplier is $25.
a. What is the economic ordering quantity?
b. What is the maximum inventory of fertilizer?
c. What will Green Thumb's average inventory be?
d. How often must the company order?

INTEGRATIVE PROBLEM

12-6
EOQ model

Dan Edwards, Financial Vice President of Shield Chemicals Corporation, was requested by the company's president to take a look at the company's inventory position. The president thinks that inventories may be too high as a result of the production manager's tendency to make large production runs. Edwards has decided to examine the situation for one key product, 100-pound drums of general purpose insecticide. Each drum costs $320 to produce, but there is a $10,000 setup cost for each production run. Annual sales of the product are 25,000 drums, and the annual carrying cost is 20 percent of inventory value. The company has been producing 5,000 drums per run and making another production run when the stock on hand falls to 2,000 drums. Sales are uniform throughout the year.
a. Edwards believes that the EOQ model should be used to help determine the optimal inventory situation for this product. What is the EOQ formula, and what are the key assumptions underlying this model?
b. What is the formula for total inventory costs?
c. What is the EOQ for the 100-pound drum of insecticide? What will the total inventory costs be for this product if the EOQ is produced?
d. What is Shield's added cost if it produces 2,000 drums per run rather than the EOQ quantity? What if it produces 3,500 drums per production run?
e. Suppose it takes 2 weeks for Shield to set up production, make and test the insecticide, and package it before the product is ready for sale. Assuming certainty in production time and usage, at what inventory level should Shield begin production? (Assume a 52-week year, and assume that Shield produces the EOQ amount.)
f. Of course, there is uncertainty in Shield's usage rate, as well as in the length of the production process, so the company must carry a safety stock to avoid running out of the 100-pound drums of insecticide and having to lose sales. If a 500-drum safety stock is carried, what effect would this have on total inventory costs? At what inventory level will the firm have to make another production run? What protection does the safety stock provide if usage increases or if production is delayed?
g. Now suppose that if Shield produced quantities of 3,500 or more drums per run, its $320 per drum production cost could be reduced by 1 percent. Should the company do this? Why or why not?
h. For most of Shield's products, inventory usage is not uniform throughout the year but, rather, follows some seasonal pattern. Could the EOQ model be used in this situation? If so, how?
i. How would these factors affect the use of the EOQ model?
   (1) "Just-in-time" (JIT) procedures.
   (2) The use of air freight for deliveries.

(3) Computerized inventory control systems.

(4) Flexible plant designs which reduce setup costs and make small production runs more feasible.

COMPUTER-RELATED PROBLEM

Work the problem in this section only if you are using the computer problem diskette.

12-7

EOQ and total inventory costs

Use the model in File C12 to work this problem.

a. Refer back to Problem 12-2. Suppose the mill offers to lower the fixed cost to $750 if Krogh will increase its order size from 100,000 (as found in Part a of Problem 12-2) to 183,500 square yards. Would it be to Krogh's advantage to order under this alternative?

b. Now suppose the mill offers to lower the fixed cost to $1,250 if Krogh will order 140,000 yards at a time. Should Krogh accept this alternative?

Short-Term Financing

A MANAGERIAL PERSPECTIVE

In early 1992 Fortune *reported that the United States was in the midst of the worst credit crunch since World War II. Business loans on the books of U.S. banks were down 8 percent from the prior year, and in certain states the decline was even worse—for example, New Hampshire was down 43 percent, and Connecticut, Washington, D.C., and Massachusetts had declines of 20 percent or more.*

Some of the decline could be explained by the decrease in loan demand which normally accompanies recessions, because businesses need less money to finance expansion. However, the major reason for the credit contraction is that so many banks themselves were in trouble—124 banks failed in 1991, and twice that number are expected to fail in 1992. As a result, bank regulators were stressing soundness in loan portfolios to the point that bankers thought the best way of avoiding trouble was to avoid risk. Banks, which were laying off staff to reduce expenses and rebuilding capital to comply with tightened international standards, were just not willing to take risks by making loans that required them to add still more reserves.

Ben Bernanke of Princeton University and Cara Lown of the Federal Reserve Bank of New York argued that the decline in lending was caused by a sharp drop in overall demand for credit, but they did note that a shortage of bank capital had limited banks' ability to make loans. Frank Cahouet, chief executive of Mellon Bank, added that a big part of the decline came from a bank-induced "invisible credit crunch": Borrowers were not asking for loans because they knew they would be turned down, and they were not using their credit lines because they knew that their bankers would object. In other words, bankers were sending signals to be cautious, and, as a result, would-be borrowers were cutting back on capital spending, were not hiring, and were deferring expansion plans.

How do tighter bank lending standards affect the economy? First, the effects are not distributed evenly. The strongest companies have no problems getting credit, but smaller companies at the lower end of the acceptable credit range are severely restricted and are examined extremely carefully. Given the importance of a bank's financial condition today, it is even possible for two borrowers in the same town, in similar financial situations, to face drastically different loan prospects depending on the condition of their banks. Finally, no businesses are harder hit by the credit crunch than are real-estate developers—commercial real-estate loans declined by almost 18 percent during 1991, more than twice the drop in any other category.

While companies were asking banks to give them a break, banks were asking the same thing of regulators, and Treasury Secretary Nicholas Brady was leaning on the regulators to relax and let the money flow. Alan Greenspan and the Federal Reserve were doing their part, cutting the discount rate to its lowest level in 27 years. Under normal circumstances, lower interest rates would eventually make even marginal businesses creditworthy. However, we were in the midst of a vicious cycle: Bad loans were making bankers reluctant to lend, and that, in turn, was slowing down the recovery, which was turning once-attractive borrowers into shaky credit risks.

As you read this chapter, think about what happens to companies which use different sources of short-term financing under different economic conditions. As you will soon find out, costs and availability can vary widely, both over time and from alternative sources.

Source: "Victims of the Credit Crunch," *Fortune*, January 27, 1992.

In Chapter 9 we discussed the decisions the financial manager must make concerning alternative current asset financing policies. We also showed how debt maturities can affect both risk and expected returns: while short-term debt is generally riskier than long-term debt, it is also generally less expensive, and it can be obtained faster and under more flexible terms. The primary purpose of this chapter is to examine the different types of short-term credit that are available to the financial manager. We also examine the types of issues the financial manager must consider when selecting among the various types of short-term credit.

SOURCES OF SHORT-TERM FINANCING

Statements about the flexibility, cost, and riskiness of short-term versus long-term debt depend, to a large extent, on the type of short-term credit that is actually used. *Short-term credit* is defined as any liability originally scheduled for payment within one year. There are numerous sources of short-term funds, and in the following sections we describe four major types: (1) accruals, (2) accounts payable (trade credit), (3) bank loans, and (4) commercial paper. In addition, we discuss the cost of bank loans and the factors that influence a firm's choice of a bank.

ACCRUALS

accruals
Continually recurring short-term liabilities, especially accrued wages and accrued taxes.

Firms generally pay employees on a weekly, biweekly, or monthly basis, so the balance sheet will typically show some accrued wages. Similarly, the firm's own estimated income taxes, the social security and income taxes withheld from employee payrolls, and the sales taxes collected are generally paid on a weekly, monthly, or quarterly basis, so the balance sheet will typically show some accrued taxes along with accrued wages.

   Accruals increase automatically, or spontaneously, as a firm's operations expand. Further, this type of debt is "free" in the sense that no explicit interest is paid on funds raised through accruals. However, a firm cannot ordinarily control its accruals: The timing of wage payments is set by economic forces and industry custom, while tax payment dates are established by law. Thus, firms use all the accruals they can, but they have little control over the levels of these accounts.

 Self-Test Questions

What types of short-term credits are classified as accruals?

What is the cost of accruals?

How much control do financial managers have over the dollar amount of accruals?

ACCOUNTS PAYABLE (TRADE CREDIT)

trade credit
Interfirm debt arising from credit sales and recorded as an account receivable by the seller and as an account payable by the buyer.

Firms generally make purchases from other firms on credit, recording the debt as an *account payable*. Accounts payable, or **trade credit,** is the largest single category of short-term debt, representing about 40 percent of the current liabilities of the average nonfinancial corporation. The percentage is somewhat larger for smaller firms: Because small companies often do not qualify for financing from other sources, they rely especially heavily on trade credit.[1]

---

[1]In a credit sale, the seller records the transaction as a receivable; the buyer, as a payable. We examined accounts receivable as an asset investment in Chapter 11. Our focus in this chapter is on accounts payable, a liability item. We might also note that if a firm's accounts payable exceed its receivables, it is said to be *receiving net trade credit,* whereas if its receivables exceed its payables, it is *extending net trade credit.* Smaller firms frequently receive net credit; larger firms generally extend it.

Trade credit is a spontaneous source of financing in the sense that it arises from ordinary business transactions. For example, suppose a firm makes average purchases of $2,000 a day on terms of net 30, meaning that it must pay for goods 30 days after the invoice date. On average, it will owe 30 times $2,000, or $60,000, to its suppliers. If its sales, and consequently its purchases, were to double, then its accounts payable would also double, to $120,000. So, simply by growing, the firm would have spontaneously generated an additional $60,000 of financing. Similarly, if the terms under which it bought were extended from 30 to 40 days, its accounts payable would expand from $60,000 to $80,000. Thus, lengthening the credit period, as well as expanding sales and purchases, generates additional financing.

The Cost of Trade Credit

Firms that sell on credit have a *credit policy* that includes certain *terms of credit*. For example, Microchip Electronics sells on terms of 2/10, net 30, meaning that a 2 percent discount is given if payment is made within 10 days of the invoice date, with the full invoice amount being due and payable within 30 days if the discount is not taken.

Note that the true price of Microchip's products is the net price, or 0.98 (list price), because any customer can purchase an item at a 2 percent "discount" as long as the customer pays within 10 days. Consider Personal Computer Company (PCC), which buys its memory chips from Microchip. One commonly used memory chip is listed at $100, so the true cost to PCC is $98. Now if PCC wants an additional 20 days of credit beyond the 10-day discount period, it must incur a finance charge of $2 per chip for that credit. Thus, the $100 list price can be thought of as follows:

$$\text{List price} = \$98 \text{ true price} + \$2 \text{ finance charge.}$$

The question that PCC must ask before it takes the additional 20 days of credit from Microchip is whether the firm could obtain similar credit under better terms from some other lender, say a bank. In other words, could 20 days of credit be obtained for less than $2 per item?

PCC buys an average of $11,760,000 of memory chips from Microchip each year at the net or true price, which amounts to $11,760,000/360 = $32,666.67 per day. For simplicity, assume that Microchip is PCC's only supplier. If PCC declines the additional trade credit offered by Microchip—that is, if it pays on the 10th day and takes the discount—its payables will average 10($32,666.67) = $326,667. Thus, PCC will be receiving $326,667 of credit from its only supplier, Microchip Electronics.

Now suppose PCC decides to take the additional 20 days credit and thus must pay the finance charge. Since PCC will now pay on the 30th day, its accounts payable will increase to 30($32,666.67) = $980,000.[2] Microchip will

---

[2]A question arises here: Should accounts payable reflect gross purchases or purchases net of discounts? Although generally accepted accounting principles permit either treatment on the grounds that the difference is not material, most accountants prefer to record payables net of discounts, or at "true" prices, and then to report the higher payments that result from not taking discounts as an additional expense, called "discounts lost." *Thus, we show accounts payable net of discounts even if the company does not expect to take the discount.*

now be supplying PCC with an additional $653,333 of credit, which it could use to build up its cash account, to pay off debt, to expand inventories, or even to extend more credit to its own customers and hence to increase its own accounts receivable.

The additional credit offered by Microchip has a cost—PCC must pay the finance charge by foregoing the 2 percent discount on its purchases from Microchip. Since PCC buys $11,760,000 of chips at the true price of 0.98 (list price), the added finance charge increases the total cost to PCC to $11,760,000/0.98 = $12 million, so the annual financing cost is $12,000,000 − $11,760,000 = $240,000. Dividing the $240,000 financing cost by the $653,333 in average annual additional credit, we find the implicit cost of the additional trade credit to be 36.7 percent:

$$\text{Approximate percentage cost} = \frac{\$240,000}{\$653,333} = 36.7\%.$$

Assuming that PCC can borrow from its bank (or from other sources) at an interest rate less than 36.7 percent, it should not obtain credit in the form of accounts payable by foregoing discounts.

The following equation can be used to calculate the approximate percentage cost, on an annual basis, of not taking discounts:

$$\text{Approximate percentage cost} = \frac{\text{Discount percent}}{100 - \text{Discount percent}} \times \frac{360}{\text{Days credit is outstanding} - \text{Discount period}}. \quad \text{(13-1)}$$

The numerator of the first term, Discount percent, is the cost per dollar of credit, while the denominator in this term, 100 − Discount percent, represents the funds made available by not taking the discount. Thus, the first term is the periodic cost of the trade credit. The denominator of the second term is the number of days of extra credit obtained by not taking the discount, so the entire second term shows how many times each year the cost is incurred. To illustrate the equation, the approximate cost of not taking a discount when the terms are 2/10, net 30, is calculated as follows:

$$\text{Approximate percentage cost} = \frac{2}{98} \times \frac{360}{20} = 2.04\% \times 18 = 36.7\%.$$

The approximation formula does not take account of compounding, and in effective annual interest terms, the cost of trade credit is seen to be much higher. The discount amounts to interest, and with terms of 2/10, net 30, the firm gains use of the funds for 30 − 10 = 20 days, so there are 360/20 = 18 "interest periods" per year. Remember that the first term in Equation 13-1, (Discount percent)/(100 − Discount percent) = 0.02/0.98 = 0.0204, is the periodic interest rate. This rate is paid 18 times each year, so the effective annual cost rate of trade credit is

$$\text{Effective annual rate} = (1.0204)^{18} - 1.0 = 1.439 - 1.0 = 43.9\%.$$

Thus, the 36.7 percent approximate cost calculated with Equation 13-1 understates the true cost of trade credit.

Notice, however, that the cost of trade credit can be reduced by paying late. Thus, if PCC could get away with paying in 60 days rather than in the specified 30, then the effective credit period would become $60 - 10 = 50$ days, the number of times the discount would be lost would fall to $360/50 = 7.2$, and the approximate cost would drop from 36.7 percent to $2.04\% \times 7.2 = 14.7\%$. The effective annual rate would drop from 43.9 to 15.7 percent:

$$\text{Effective annual rate} = (1.0204)^{7.2} - 1.0 = 1.157 - 1.0 = 15.7\%.$$

stretching accounts payable

The practice of deliberately paying accounts payable late.

In periods of excess capacity, firms may be able to get away with late payments, but they will also suffer a variety of problems associated with **stretching accounts payable** and being branded a "slow payer." These problems are discussed later in the chapter.

The cost of the additional trade credit that is incurred by not taking discounts can be worked out for other purchase terms. Some illustrative costs are shown below:

| | Cost of Additional Credit If the Cash Discount Is Not Taken | |
Credit Terms	Approximate Cost	Effective Cost
1/10, net 20	36%	44%
1/10, net 30	18	20
2/10, net 20	73	107
3/15, net 45	37	44

As these figures show, the cost of not taking discounts can be substantial. Incidentally, throughout the chapter, we assume that payments are made either on the *last day* for taking discounts or on the *last day* of the credit period, unless otherwise noted. It would be foolish to pay, say, on the fifth day or on the twentieth day if the credit terms were 2/10, net 30.

Effects of Trade Credit on the Financial Statements

A firm's policy with regard to taking or not taking discounts can have a significant effect on its financial statements. To illustrate, let us assume that PCC is just beginning its operations. On the first day, it makes net purchases of $32,666.67. This amount is recorded on its balance sheet under accounts payable.[3] The second day it buys another $32,666.67. The first day's purchases are not yet paid for, so at the end of the second day, accounts payable total $65,333.34. Accounts payable increase by another $32,666.67 on the third day, for a total of $98,000, and after 10 days, accounts payable are up to $326,667.

If PCC takes discounts, then on the 11th day it will have to pay for the $32,666.67 of purchases made on the first day, which will reduce accounts payable. However, it will buy another $32,666.67, which will increase payables.

---

[3]Inventories also increase by $32,666.67, but we are not now concerned with inventories. Again note that both inventories and receivables are recorded net of discounts regardless of whether discounts are taken.

Table 13-1 ▪ **PCC's Financial Statements with Different Trade Credit Policies**

	Take Discounts; Borrow from Bank (1)	Do Not Take Discounts; Use Maximum Trade Credit (2)	Difference (1) − (2)
I. Balance Sheets			
Cash	$ 500,000	$ 500,000	$ 0
Receivables	1,000,000	1,000,000	0
Inventories	2,000,000	2,000,000	0
Fixed assets	2,980,000	2,980,000	0
Total assets	$ 6,480,000	$ 6,480,000	$ 0
Accounts payable	$ 326,667	$ 980,000	$ − 653,333
Notes payable (10%)	653,333	0	+ 653,333
Accruals	500,000	500,000	0
Common equity	5,000,000	5,000,000	0
Total claims	$ 6,480,000	$ 6,480,000	$ 0
II. Income Statements			
Sales	$15,000,000	$15,000,000	$ 0
Less: Purchases	11,760,000	11,760,000	0
Labor	2,000,000	2,000,000	0
Interest	65,333	0	+ 65,333
Discounts lost	0	240,000	− 240,000
Earnings before taxes (EBT)	$ 1,174,667	$ 1,000,000	$ + 174,667
Taxes (40%)	469,867	400,000	+ 69,867
Net income	$ 704,800	$ 600,000	$ + 104,800

Thus, after the 10th day of operations, PCC's balance sheet will level off, showing a balance of $326,667 in accounts payable, assuming that the company pays on the 10th day in order to take discounts.

Now suppose PCC decides not to take discounts. In this case, on the 11th day it will add another $32,666.67 to payables, but it will not pay for the purchases made on the 1st day. Thus, the balance sheet figure for accounts payable will rise to 11($32,666.67) = $359,333.37. This buildup will continue through the 30th day, at which point payables will total 30($32,666.67) = $980,000. On the 31st day, PCC will buy another $32,666.67 of goods, which will increase accounts payable, but it will also pay for the purchases made the 1st day, which will reduce payables. Thus, the balance sheet item accounts payable will stabilize at $980,000 after 30 days, assuming PCC does not take discounts.

The upper section of Table 13-1 shows PCC's balance sheet, after it reaches a steady state, under the two trade credit policies. Total assets are unchanged by this policy decision, and we also assume that the accruals and common equity accounts are unchanged. The differences show up in accounts payable and notes payable; when PCC elects to take discounts and thus gives up some of the trade credit it otherwise could have obtained, it will have to raise $653,333 from some other source. It could have sold more common stock, or it could have used long-term bonds, but it chose to use bank credit, which has a 10 percent cost and is reflected in the notes payable account.

The lower section of Table 13-1 shows PCC's income statement under the two policies. If the company does not take discounts, then its interest expense will be zero, but it will have a $240,000 expense for discounts lost. On the other hand, if it does take discounts, it will incur an interest expense of $65,333, but it will avoid the cost of discounts lost. Since discounts lost exceed the interest expense, the take-discounts policy results in a higher net income and, thus, in a higher stock price.

Components of Trade Credit: Free versus Costly

free trade credit
Credit received during the discount period.

costly trade credit
Credit taken in excess of free trade credit, whose cost is equal to the discount lost.

On the basis of the preceding discussion, trade credit can be divided into two components: (1) **free trade credit,** which involves credit received during the discount period and which for PCC amounts to 10 days' net purchases, or $326,667, and (2) **costly trade credit,** which involves credit in excess of the free trade credit and whose cost is an implicit one based on the foregone discounts.[4] PCC could obtain $653,333, or 20 days' net purchases, of nonfree trade credit at a cost of approximately 37 percent. *Financial managers should always use the free component, but they should use the costly component only after analyzing the cost of this capital to make sure that it is less than the cost of funds which could be obtained from other sources.* Under the terms of trade found in most industries, the costly component will involve a relatively high percentage cost, so stronger firms will avoid using it.

We noted earlier that firms sometimes can and do deviate from the stated credit terms, thus altering the percentage cost figures cited earlier. For example, a California manufacturing firm that buys on terms of 2/10, net 30, makes a practice of paying in 15 days (rather than 10), but it still takes discounts. Its treasurer simply waits until 15 days after receipt of the goods to pay, and then writes a check for the invoiced amount less the 2 percent discount. The company's suppliers want its business, so they tolerate this practice. Similarly, a Wisconsin firm that also buys on terms of 2/10, net 30, does not take discounts, but it pays in 60 rather than in 30 days, thus "stretching" its trade credit. As we saw earlier, both practices reduce the cost of trade credit. Neither of these firms is "loved" by its suppliers, and neither could continue these practices in times when suppliers were operating at full capacity and had order backlogs, but these practices can and do reduce the costs of trade credit during times when suppliers have excess capacity.

 Self-Test Questions

What is trade credit?

What is the difference between free trade credit and costly trade credit?

---

[4]There is some question as to whether any credit is really "free," because the supplier will have a cost of carrying receivables which must be passed on to the customer in the form of higher prices. Still, if suppliers sell on standard terms such as 2/10, net 30, and if the base price cannot be negotiated downward for early payment, then for all intents and purposes the 10 days of trade credit is indeed "free."

What is the formula for finding the approximate cost of trade credit? What is the formula for the effective annual cost rate of trade credit?

How does the cost of costly trade credit generally compare with the cost of short-term bank loans?

SHORT-TERM BANK LOANS

Commercial banks, whose loans generally appear on firms' balance sheets as notes payable, are second in importance to trade credit as a source of short-term financing.[5] The banks' influence is actually greater than it appears from the dollar amounts they lend because banks provide *nonspontaneous* funds. As a firm's financing needs increase, it requests additional funds from its bank. If the request is denied, the firm may be forced to abandon attractive growth opportunities. The key features of bank loans are discussed in the following paragraphs.

Maturity

Although banks do make longer-term loans, *the bulk of their lending is on a short-term basis*—about two-thirds of all bank loans mature in a year or less. Bank loans to businesses are frequently written as 90-day notes, so the loan must be repaid or renewed at the end of 90 days. Of course, if a borrower's financial position has deteriorated, the bank may well refuse to renew the loan. This can mean serious trouble for the borrower.

Promissory Note

promissory note

A document specifying the terms and conditions of a loan, including the amount, interest rate, and repayment schedule.

When a bank loan is approved, the agreement is executed by signing a **promissory note.** The note specifies (1) the amount borrowed; (2) the percentage interest rate; (3) the repayment schedule, which can call for either a lump sum or a series of installments; (4) any collateral that might have to be put up as security for the loan; and (5) any other terms and conditions to which the bank and the borrower may have agreed. When the note is signed, the bank credits the borrower's checking account with the amount of the loan, so on the borrower's balance sheet both cash and notes payable increase.

Compensating Balances

compensating balance (CB)

A minimum checking account balance that a firm must maintain with a commercial bank, generally equal to 10 to 20 percent of the amount of loans outstanding.

Banks sometimes require borrowers to maintain an average demand deposit (checking account) balance equal to from 10 to 20 percent of the face amount of the loan. This is called a **compensating balance (CB),** and such balances raise the effective interest rate on the loans. For example, if a firm needs $80,000 to pay off outstanding obligations, but if it must maintain a 20 percent compensating balance, then it must borrow $100,000 to obtain a usable

---

[5]Although commercial banks remain the primary source of short-term loans, other sources are available. For example, in 1991 GE Capital Corporation (GECC) had several billion dollars in commercial loans outstanding. Firms such as GECC, which was initially established to finance consumers' purchases of GE's durable goods, often find business loans to be more profitable than consumer loans.

$80,000. If the stated interest rate is 8 percent, the effective cost is actually 10 percent: $8,000 interest divided by $80,000 of usable funds equals 10 percent.[6]

Line of Credit

line of credit

An arrangement in which a bank agrees to lend up to a specified maximum amount of funds during a designated period.

A **line of credit** is an agreement between a bank and a borrower indicating the maximum credit the bank will extend to the borrower. For example, on December 31 a bank loan officer might indicate to a financial manager that the bank regards the firm as being "good" for up to $80,000 during the forthcoming year. If on January 10 the financial manager signs a promissory note for $15,000 for 90 days, this would be called "taking down" $15,000 of the total line of credit. This amount would be credited to the firm's checking account at the bank, and before repayment of the $15,000, the firm could borrow additional amounts up to a total of $80,000 outstanding at any one time.

Revolving Credit Agreement

revolving credit agreement

A formal, committed line of credit extended by a bank or other lending institution.

A **revolving credit agreement** is a formal line of credit often used by large firms. To illustrate, in 1992 Texas Petroleum Company negotiated a revolving credit agreement for $100 million with a group of banks. The banks were formally committed for 4 years to lend the firm up to $100 million if the funds were needed. Texas Petroleum, in turn, paid an annual commitment fee of one-quarter of 1 percent on the unused balance of the commitment to compensate the banks for making the commitment. Thus, if Texas Petroleum did not take down any of the $100 million commitment during a year, it would still be required to pay a $250,000 annual fee, normally in monthly installments of $20,833.33. If it borrowed $50 million on the first day of the agreement, the unused portion of the line of credit would fall to $50 million, and the annual fee would fall to $125,000. Of course, interest would also have to be paid on the money Texas Petroleum actually borrowed. As a general rule, the rate of interest on "revolvers" is pegged to the prime rate, so the cost of the loan varies over time as interest rates change.[7] Texas Petroleum's rate was set at prime plus 0.5 percentage points.

---

[6]Note, however, that the compensating balance may be set as a minimum monthly *average,* and if the firm would maintain this average anyway, the compensating balance requirement would not raise the effective interest rate. Also, note that these *loan* compensating balances are added to any compensating balances that the firm's bank may require for *services performed,* such as clearing checks.

[7]Each bank sets its own prime rate, but, because of competitive forces, most banks' prime rates are identical. Further, most banks follow the rate set by the large New York City banks, and they, in turn, generally follow the rate set by Citibank, the largest bank in the United States. Citibank formerly set the prime rate each week at 1¼ to 1½ percentage points above the average rate on certificates of deposit (CDs) during the three weeks immediately preceding. CD rates represent the "price" of money in the open market, and they rise and fall with the supply and demand of money, so CD rates are "market-clearing" rates. By tying the prime rate to CD rates, the banking system insured that the prime rate would also clear the market.

Except for the cut in the prime rate from 7.5 percent to 6.5 percent in late December 1991, which was the immediate result of the Federal Reserve Board's actions to lower the discount and federal funds rates in order to spur the economy, in recent years the prime rate has been held relatively constant even during periods when open market rates fluctuated. Also, in recent years

Note that a revolving credit agreement is very similar to a regular line of credit. However, there is an important distinguishing feature: The bank has a *legal obligation* to honor a revolving credit agreement, and it receives a commitment fee. Neither the legal obligation nor the fee exists under the typical line of credit.

? Self-Test Question

Explain how a firm that expects to need funds during the coming year might make sure the needed funds will be available.

THE COST OF BANK LOANS

prime rate
A published rate of interest charged by commercial banks to large, strong corporations.

The cost of bank loans varies for different types of borrowers at any given point in time, and for all borrowers over time. Interest rates are higher for riskier borrowers, and rates are also higher on smaller loans because of the fixed costs involved in making and servicing loans. If a firm can qualify as a "prime credit" because of its size and financial strength, it can borrow at the **prime rate,** which has traditionally been the lowest rate banks charge. Rates on other loans are generally scaled up from the prime rate.

Bank rates vary widely over time depending on economic conditions and Federal Reserve policy. When the economy is weak, then (1) loan demand is usually slack, (2) inflation is low, and (3) the Fed also makes plenty of money available to the system. As a result, rates on all types of loans are relatively low. Conversely, when the economy is booming, loan demand is typically strong, and the Fed restricts the money supply; the result is high interest rates. As an indication of the kinds of fluctuations that can occur, the prime rate during 1980 rose from 11 percent to 21 percent in just four months. Interest rates on other bank loans also vary, generally moving with the prime rate.

Interest rates on bank loans are calculated in three ways: (1) *simple interest,* (2) *discount interest,* and (3) *add-on interest.* These three methods are explained in the following sections.

Regular, or Simple, Interest

simple interest
Interest that is charged on the basis of the amount borrowed; it is paid when the loan ends rather than when it begins.

In a **simple interest** loan, the borrower receives the face value of the loan and repays the principal and interest at maturity. For example, in a simple interest loan of $10,000 at 12 percent for one year, the borrower receives the $10,000 upon approval of the loan and pays back the $10,000 principal plus $10,000(0.12) = $1,200 in interest at maturity (one year later). The 12 per-

---

many banks have been lending to the very strongest companies at rates below the prime rate. As we discuss later in this chapter, larger firms have ready access to the commercial paper market, and if banks want to do business with these larger companies, they must match or at least come close to the commercial paper rate. As competition in financial markets increases, as it has been doing because of the deregulation of banks and other financial institutions, "administered" rates such as the prime rate are giving way to flexible, negotiated rates based on market conditions.

cent is the quoted, or nominal, rate. On this 1-year loan, the effective annual rate is also 12 percent:

$$\text{Effective annual rate}_{\text{Simple}} = \frac{\text{Interest}}{\text{Amount received}} \qquad (13\text{-}2)$$

$$= \frac{\$1,200}{\$10,000} = 12\%.$$

Here is the time line set up:

```
0      i = ?      1
├──────────────┤
10,000        − 10,000
              − 1,200
              − 11,200
```

To solve with a financial calculator, enter PV = 10000, FV = − 11200, and N = 1, and then press I to obtain 12.0.

On a simple interest loan of one year or more, the nominal rate equals the effective rate. However, if the loan had a term of less than one year, say 90 days, then the effective annual rate would be calculated as follows:

$$\text{Effective annual rate}_{\text{Simple}} = \left(1 + \frac{k_{\text{Nom}}}{m}\right)^m - 1.0 \qquad (13\text{-}3)$$

$$= (1 + 0.12/4)^4 - 1.0 = 12.55\%.$$

Here k_{Nom} is the nominal, or quoted, rate and m is the number of loan periods per year, or 360/90 = 4. The bank gets the interest sooner than under a 1-year loan, hence the effective rate is higher.

Note that the interest payment on a \$10,000 90-day loan is \$10,000(0.12)(90/360) = \$300, so the time line looks like this:

```
0      i = ?                              1
├──────┼───────────┼───────────┼─────────┤
10,000      − 10,000
            − 300
            − 10,300
```

To solve with a financial calculator, enter PV = 10000, FV = − 10300, and N = 1, and then press I to obtain 3.0. But this is a quarterly rate, so the effective annual rate = $(1.03)^4 - 1.0 = 12.55\%$.

An alternative way to calculate the effective rate is to enter PV = 10000, FV = − 10300, and N = 0.25, and then press I to obtain 12.55%.

Discount Interest

discount interest
Interest that is calculated on the face amount of a loan but is paid in advance.

In a **discount interest** loan, the bank deducts the interest in advance (*discounts* the loan). Thus, the borrower receives less than the face value of the loan. On a 1-year, \$10,000 loan with a 12 percent (nominal) rate, discount basis, the interest is $10,000(0.12) = $1,200$, so the borrower obtains the use of only $10,000 - $1,200 = $8,800$. The effective annual rate is 13.64 percent versus 12 percent on a 1-year simple interest loan:[8]

$$\text{Effective annual rate}_{\text{Discount}} = \frac{\text{Interest}}{\text{Amount received}} = \frac{\text{Interest}}{\text{Face value} - \text{Interest}} \quad (13\text{-}4)$$

$$= \frac{\$1,200}{\$10,000 - \$1,200} = 13.64\%.$$

An alternative procedure for finding the effective annual rate on a discount interest loan is

$$\text{Effective annual rate}_{\text{Discount}} = \frac{\text{Nominal rate }(\%)}{1.0 - \text{Nominal rate (fraction)}} \quad (13\text{-}4a)$$

$$= \frac{12\%}{1.0 - 0.12} = \frac{12\%}{0.88} = 13.64\%.$$

Here's how the loan looks on a time line:

```
0        i = ?      1
├────────────────┤
8,800          -10,000
```

With a financial calculator, enter PV = 8800, FV = -10000, and N = 1, and then press I to obtain 13.64.

If the discount loan is for a period of less than one year, its effective annual rate is found as follows:

$$\text{Effective annual rate}_{\text{Discount}} = \left(1.0 + \frac{\text{Interest}}{\text{Face value} - \text{Interest}}\right)^m - 1.0. \quad (13\text{-}4b)$$

---

[8]Note that the firm actually receives less than the face amount of the loan:

$$\text{Funds received} = \text{Face amount of loan }(1.0 - \text{Nominal interest rate}).$$

We can solve for the face amount as follows:

$$\text{Face amount of loan} = \frac{\text{Funds received}}{1.0 - \text{Nominal rate (fraction)}}.$$

Therefore, if the borrowing firm actually requires $10,000 of cash, it must borrow $11,363.64:

$$\text{Face value} = \frac{\$10,000}{1.0 - 0.12} = \frac{\$10,000}{0.88} = \$11,363.64.$$

Now, the borrower will receive $11,363.64 - 0.12($11,363.64) = $10,000$. Increasing the face value of the loan does not change the effective rate of 13.64 percent on the $10,000 of usable funds.

For example, if we borrow $10,000 face value at a nominal rate of 12 percent, discount interest, for 3 months, then m = 12/3 = 4, and the interest payment is (0.12/4)($10,000) = $300, so

$$\text{Effective annual rate}_{\text{Discount}} = \left(1.0 + \frac{\$300}{\$10,000 - \$300}\right)^4 - 1.0$$

$$= 0.1296 = 12.96\%.$$

Thus, discount interest imposes less of a penalty on shorter-term than on longer-term loans.

Here's the time line situation:

```
0    i = ?                                      1
├──────────┼──────────┼──────────┼──────────┤
9,700    -10,000
```

With a financial calculator, enter PV = 9700, FV = −10000, and N = 1, and then press I to obtain 3.0928. Then, the effective annual rate is $(1.030928)^4 - 1.0 = 12.96\%$.

An alternative way to calculate the effective rate is to enter PV = 9700, FV = −10000, and N = 0.25, and then press I to obtain 12.96%.

Installment Loans: Add-On Interest

add-on interest

Interest that is calculated and added to funds received to determine the face amount of an installment loan.

Lenders typically charge **add-on interest** on automobile and other types of installment loans. The term "add-on" means that the interest is calculated and then added to the amount received to obtain the loan's face value. To illustrate, suppose you borrow $10,000 on an add-on basis at a nominal rate of 12 percent to buy a car, with the loan to be repaid in 12 monthly installments. At a 12 percent add-on rate, you will pay a total interest charge of $10,000(0.12) = $1,200. However, since the loan is paid off in monthly installments, you have the use of the full $10,000 for only the first month, and the outstanding balance declines until, during the last month, only 1/12 of the original loan will still be outstanding. Thus, you are paying $1,200 for the use of only about half the loan's face amount, as the average outstanding balance of the loan is only about $5,000. Therefore, we can approximate the effective rate as follows:

$$\text{Approximate effective annual rate}_{\text{Add-on}} = \frac{\text{Interest}}{(\text{Amount received})/2} \quad \text{(13-5)}$$

$$= \frac{\$1,200}{\$10,000/2} = 24.0\%.$$

To determine the precise effective rate of an add-on loan, we proceed as follows:

1. The total amount to be repaid is $10,000 of principal, plus $1,200 of interest, or $11,200.

2. The monthly payment is $11,200/12 = $933.33.

3. The bank is, in effect, buying a 12-period annuity of $933.33 for $10,000, so $10,000 is the present value of the annuity. Here is the time line:

```
   0        1        2          11       12
   |        |        |          |        |
 -10,000  933.33  933.33 . . . 933.33  933.33
```

4. With a financial calculator, enter PV = −10000, PMT = 933.33, N = 12, and then press I to obtain 1.7880. However, this is a monthly rate.

5. The effective annual rate is found as follows:[9]

$$\text{Effective annual rate}_{\text{Add-on}} = (1 + k_d)^{12} - 1.0$$
$$= (1.01788)^{12} - 1.0$$
$$= 1.2370 - 1.0 = 23.7\%.$$

Simple Interest with Compensating Balances

Compensating balances tend to raise the effective rate on a loan. To illustrate, suppose a firm needs $10,000 to pay for some equipment that it recently purchased. A bank offers to lend the company money for one year at a 12 percent simple rate, but the company must maintain a *compensating balance (CB)* equal to 20 percent of the loan amount. If the firm did not take the loan, it would keep no deposits with the bank. What is the effective annual rate on the loan?

First, note that if the firm requires $10,000, it must, assuming it does not currently have cash balances that can be used as all or part of the compensating balance, borrow $12,500:

$$\text{Face value} = \frac{\text{Funds required}}{1.0 - \text{CB (fraction)}} \qquad (13\text{-}6)$$

$$= \frac{\$10,000}{1.0 - 0.20} = \$12,500.$$

The interest paid at the end of the year will be $12,500(0.12) = $1,500, but the firm will only get the use of $10,000. Therefore, the effective annual rate is 15 percent:

$$\text{Effective annual rate}_{\text{Simple/CB}} = \frac{\text{Interest}}{\text{Amount received}} \qquad (13\text{-}7)$$

$$= \frac{\$1,500}{\$10,000} = 15\%.$$

---

[9]Note that if an installment loan is paid off ahead of schedule, additional complications arise. For a discussion of this point, see Dick Bonker, "The Rule of 78," *Journal of Finance,* June 1976, 877–888.

An alternative formula is

$$\text{Effective annual rate}_{\text{Simple/CB}} = \frac{\text{Nominal rate (\%)}}{1.0 - \text{CB (fraction)}} \quad \text{(13-7a)}$$

$$= \frac{12\%}{1.0 - 0.2} = 15\%.$$

Here's the time line solution:

```
         0        i = ?        1
         ├─────────────────────┤
Face value      12,500    -12,500  Principal repayment
Less CB         -2,500      2,500  CB returned
Amount received 10,000     -1,500  Interest payment
                          -11,500  Amount repaid
```

With a financial calculator, enter PV = 10000, FV = −11500, and N = 1, and then press I to obtain 15.0.

Note that if a firm normally carries cash balances with the bank, then those balances can be used to meet all or part of the compensating balance requirement, and this will reduce the effective cost of the loan. In this case, the calculations required to determine the effective annual rate are a bit more complicated, and we must go through the following three-step process:

1. $\begin{pmatrix} \text{Additional funds} \\ \text{needed to meet} \\ \text{compensating balance} \\ \text{requirement} \end{pmatrix} = \begin{pmatrix} \text{Compensating} \\ \text{balance} \\ \text{percentage} \times \text{Loan} \end{pmatrix} - \begin{pmatrix} \text{Cash available} \\ \text{for compensating} \\ \text{balance} \end{pmatrix}.$

2. $\text{Loan} = \begin{pmatrix} \text{Funds} \\ \text{needed} \end{pmatrix} + \begin{pmatrix} \text{Required additional funds} \\ \text{for compensating balance} \end{pmatrix}$

   $= \begin{pmatrix} \text{Funds} \\ \text{needed} \end{pmatrix} + \begin{pmatrix} \text{Compensating} \\ \text{balance percentage} \times \text{Loan} \end{pmatrix} - \begin{pmatrix} \text{Available} \\ \text{cash} \end{pmatrix}.$

3. $\text{Effective annual rate} = \dfrac{\text{Interest rate(Loan)}}{\text{Funds needed}}.$

To illustrate, if our firm normally carried a working balance of $1,000, then the effective annual cost of a $10,000 loan requiring a 20 percent compensating balance would be found as follows:

Step 1. $\begin{matrix} \text{Additional funds to meet} \\ \text{compensating balance} \end{matrix} = 0.2(\text{Loan} - \$1,000).$

Step 2. $\text{Loan} = \$10,000 + 0.2(\text{Loan}) - \$1,000$

$0.8(\text{Loan}) = \$9,000$

$\text{Loan} = \$11,250.$

Step 3. $\text{Effective interest rate} = \dfrac{\text{Nominal rate(Loan)}}{\text{Funds needed}}$

$= \dfrac{0.12(\$11,250)}{\$10,000} = 13.5\%.$

Thus, the firm will borrow $11,250, use $10,000 of this amount to meet its obligations, leave $1,250 on deposit as part of the compensating balance requirement, meet the remainder of the compensating balance requirement with the currently available $1,000, and pay an effective interest rate of 13.5 percent for the $10,000 net usable funds it received.

We can confirm the interest cost with a financial calculator. Note that when the loan matures at year end, the firm must pay the $11,250 loan amount plus interest of 0.12($11,250) = $1,350, or $12,600 in total, but it can use the $11,250 − $10,000 = $1,250 borrowed compensating balance, so its net repayment will be $12,600 − $1,250 = $11,350. Therefore, we can enter N = 1, PV = 10000, FV = −11350 and then press I to find the effective rate, 13.5%.

In our experience, most firms that require significant bank loans do not have much in the way of cash balances available for compensating balances. Therefore, in most situations Equation 13-7a can be used to find the cost of a bank loan with compensating balance requirements. However, if cash balances are available, it is easy enough to go through the three-step process described.

Discount Interest with Compensating Balances

The analysis can be extended to the case where compensating balances are required and the loan is on a discount basis. In this situation, if a firm needs $10,000 for one year and a 20 percent compensating balance (CB) is required on a 12 percent discount loan, it must borrow $14,705.88:

$$\text{Face value} = \frac{\text{Funds required}}{1.0 - \text{Nominal rate (fraction)} - \text{CB (fraction)}} \quad \text{(13-8)}$$

$$= \frac{\$10,000}{1.0 - 0.12 - 0.2} = \$10,000/0.68 = \$14,705.88.$$

The firm would record this $14,705.88 as a note payable offset by these asset accounts (note that a small rounding error occurs):

To cash account	$10,000.00
Prepaid interest (12% of $14,705.88)	1,764.71
Compensating balance (20% of $14,705.88)	2,941.18
	$14,705.89

Now the effective annual rate is 17.65 percent:

$$\text{Effective annual rate}_{\text{Discount/CB}} = \frac{\text{Nominal rate (\%)}}{1.0 - \text{Nominal rate (fraction)} - \text{CB (fraction)}} \quad \text{(13-9)}$$

$$= \frac{12\%}{1.0 - 0.12 - 0.2} = 12\%/0.68 = 17.65\%.$$

On a time line, the situation looks like this:

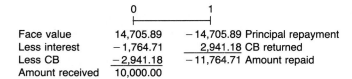

	0	1
Face value	14,705.89	−14,705.89 Principal repayment
Less interest	−1,764.71	2,941.18 CB returned
Less CB	−2,941.18	−11,764.71 Amount repaid
Amount received	10,000.00	

With a financial calculator, enter PV = 10000, FV = −11764.71, and N = 1, and then press I to obtain 17.65.

In our example, compensating balances and discount interest combined to push the effective rate of interest up from 12 to 17.65 percent. Note, however, that in this analysis we assumed that the compensating balance requirement forced the firm to increase its bank deposits. If the company normally carried cash balances which could be used to supply all or part of the compensating balances, we would have to adjust the calculations along the lines discussed in the preceding section, and the effective annual rate would have been less than 17.65 percent. Also, if the firm earns interest on its bank deposits, including the compensating balance, then the effective annual rate would be further decreased.

Self-Test Questions

What are some different ways that banks can calculate interest on loans?

What is a compensating balance? What effect does a compensating balance requirement have on the effective interest rate on a loan?

CHOOSING A BANK

Individuals whose only contact with their bank is through the use of its checking services generally choose a bank for the convenience of its location and the competitive cost of its services. However, a business that borrows from banks must look at other criteria, and a potential borrower seeking banking relations should recognize that important differences exist among banks. Some of these differences are considered next.

Willingness to Assume Risks

Banks have different basic policies toward risk. Some banks are inclined to follow relatively conservative lending practices, while others engage in what are properly termed "creative banking practices." These policies reflect partly the personalities of officers of the bank and partly the characteristics of the bank's deposit liabilities. Thus, a bank with fluctuating deposit liabilities in a static community will tend to be a conservative lender, while a bank whose deposits are growing with little interruption may follow more liberal credit policies. Similarly, a large bank with broad diversification over geographic regions or across industries can obtain the benefit of combining and averaging risks. Thus, marginal credit risks that might be unacceptable to a small bank or specialized bank can be pooled by a large branch banking system to reduce the overall risk of a group of marginal accounts.

Advice and Counsel

Some bank loan officers are active in providing counsel and in stimulating development loans to firms in their early and formative years. Certain banks have specialized departments which make loans to firms expected to grow and thus to become more important customers. The personnel of these departments can provide valuable counseling to customers: The bankers' experience with other firms in growth situations may enable them to spot, and then to warn their customers about, developing problems.

Loyalty to Customers

Banks differ in the extent to which they will support the activities of borrowers in bad times. This characteristic is referred to as the degree of *loyalty* of the bank. Some banks may put great pressure on a business to liquidate its loans when the firm's outlook becomes clouded, whereas others will stand by the firm and work diligently to help it get back on its feet. An especially dramatic illustration of this point was Bank of America's bailout of Memorex Corporation. The bank could have forced Memorex into bankruptcy, but instead it loaned the company additional capital and helped it survive a bad period. Memorex's stock price subsequently rose on the New York Stock Exchange from $1.50 to $68, so Bank of America's help was indeed beneficial.

Specialization

Banks differ greatly in their degrees of loan specialization. Larger banks have separate departments that specialize in different kinds of loans—for example, real estate loans, farm loans, and commercial loans. Within these broad categories, there may be a specialization by line of business, such as steel, machinery, cattle, or textiles. The strengths of banks are also likely to reflect the nature of the business and the economic environment in which they operate. For example, some California banks have become specialists in lending to electronics companies, while many Midwestern banks are agricultural specialists. A sound firm can obtain more creative cooperation and more active support by going to a bank that has experience and familiarity with its particular type of business. Therefore, a bank that is excellent for one firm may be unsatisfactory for another.

Maximum Loan Size

The size of a bank can be an important factor. Since the maximum loan a bank can make to any one customer is limited to 15 percent of the bank's capital accounts (capital stock plus retained earnings), it is generally not appropriate for large firms to develop borrowing relationships with small banks.

Merchant Banking

The term "merchant bank" was originally applied to banks which not only loaned depositors' money but also provided customers with equity capital and financial advice. Prior to 1933, U.S. commercial banks performed all types of merchant banking functions. However, about one-third of the U.S. banks failed during the Great Depression, in part because of these activities, so in 1933 the Glass-Steagall Act was passed in an effort to reduce banks' exposure to risk. In recent years, commercial banks have been attempting to get back into merchant banking, in part because their foreign competitors offer such services, and U.S. banks need to be able to compete with their foreign counterparts for multinational corporations' business. Currently, the larger banks, often through holding companies, are being permitted to get back into merchant banking, at least to a limited extent. This trend will probably continue, and, if it does, corporations will need to consider a bank's ability to provide a full range of commercial and merchant banking services when choosing a bank.

Other Services

Banks can also provide cash management services (see Chapter 10), assist with electronic funds transfers, help firms obtain foreign exchange, and the like, and the availability of such services should be taken into account when selecting a bank. Also, if the firm is a small business whose manager owns most of its stock, the bank's willingness and ability to provide trust and estate services should also be considered.

Self-Test Question

What are some of the factors that should be considered when choosing a bank?

COMMERCIAL PAPER

commercial paper
Unsecured, short-term promissory notes of large firms, usually issued in denominations of $100,000 or more and having an interest rate somewhat below the prime rate.

Commercial paper is a type of unsecured promissory note issued by large, strong firms, and it is sold primarily to other business firms, to insurance companies, to pension funds, to money market mutual funds, and to banks. Although the amount of commercial paper outstanding is smaller than bank loans outstanding, this form of financing has grown rapidly in recent years. In early 1992, there was approximately $540 billion of commercial paper outstanding, versus about $615 billion of regular business loans.

Maturity and Cost

Maturities of commercial paper generally vary from one to nine months, with an average of about five months.[10] The rate on commercial paper fluctuates with supply and demand conditions — it is determined in the marketplace, varying daily as conditions change. Recently, commercial paper rates have ranged from 1½ to 2½ percentage points below the stated prime rate and about ½ of a percentage point above the T-bill rate. For example, on February 18, 1992, the average rate on 3-month commercial paper was 4.1 percent, the stated prime rate was 6.5 percent, and the 3-month T-bill rate was about 3.8 percent.

---

[10]The maximum maturity without SEC registration is 270 days. Also, commercial paper can only be sold to "sophisticated" investors; otherwise, SEC registration would be required even for maturities of 270 days or less.

Use of Commercial Paper

The use of commercial paper is restricted to a comparatively small number of concerns that are exceptionally good credit risks. Dealers prefer to handle the paper of firms whose net worth is $100 million or more and whose annual borrowing exceeds $10 million. One potential problem with commercial paper is that a debtor who is in temporary financial difficulty may receive little help because commercial paper dealings are generally less personal than are bank relationships. Thus, banks are generally more able and willing to help a good customer weather a temporary storm than is a commercial paper dealer. On the other hand, using commercial paper permits a corporation to tap a wide range of credit sources, including financial institutions outside its own area and industrial corporations across the country, and this can reduce interest costs.

Self-Test Questions

What is commercial paper?

What types of companies can use commercial paper to meet their short-term financing needs?

How does the cost of commercial paper compare to the cost of short-term bank loans? To the cost of Treasury bills?

USE OF SECURITY IN SHORT-TERM FINANCING

secured loan
A loan backed by collateral, often inventories or receivables.

Thus far we have not addressed the question of whether or not loans should be secured. Commercial paper is never secured, but all other types of loans can be secured if this is deemed necessary or desirable. Given a choice, it is ordinarily better to borrow on an unsecured basis since the bookkeeping costs of **secured loans** are often high. However, weak firms may find that they can borrow only if they put up some type of security to protect the lender, or that by using security they can borrow at a much lower rate.

Several different kinds of collateral can be employed, including marketable stocks or bonds, land or buildings, equipment, inventory, and accounts receivable. Marketable securities make excellent collateral, but few firms that need loans also hold portfolios of stocks and bonds. Similarly, real property (land and buildings) and equipment are good forms of collateral, but they are generally used as security for long-term loans rather than for working capital loans. Therefore, most secured short-term business borrowing involves the use of accounts receivable and inventories as collateral.

To understand the use of security, consider the case of a Chicago hardware dealer who wanted to modernize and expand his store. He requested a $200,000 bank loan. After examining his business's financial statements, the bank indicated that it would lend him a maximum of $100,000 and that the interest rate would be 12 percent, discount interest, for an effective rate of 13.6 percent. The owner had a substantial personal portfolio of stocks, and he offered to put up $300,000 of high-quality stocks to support the $200,000 loan. The bank then granted the full $200,000 loan, and at a rate of only 10 percent, simple interest. The store owner might also have used his inventories or receivables as security for the loan, but processing costs would have been high.[11]

In the past, state laws varied greatly with regard to the use of security in financing. Today, however, all states except Louisiana operate under the **Uniform Commercial Code,** which standardized and simplified the procedures for establishing loan security. The heart of the Uniform Commercial Code is the *Security Agreement,* a standardized document on which the specific pledged assets are listed. The assets can be items of equipment, accounts receivable, or inventories. Procedures under the Uniform Commercial Code for using accounts receivable and inventories as security for short-term credit are described in the following sections.

Uniform Commercial Code

A system of standards that simplifies and standardizes procedures for establishing loan security.

Accounts Receivable Financing

Accounts receivable financing involves either the pledging of receivables or the selling of receivables (called factoring). The **pledging of accounts receivable** is characterized by the fact that the lender not only has a claim against the receivables but also has **recourse** to the borrower: If the person or firm that bought the goods does not pay, the selling firm must take the loss. Therefore, the risk of default on the pledged accounts receivable remains with the borrower. The buyer of the goods is not ordinarily notified about the pledging of the receivables, and the financial institution that lends on the security of accounts receivable is generally either a commercial bank or one of the large industrial finance companies.

pledging receivables

Putting accounts receivable up as security for a loan.

recourse

The lender can seek payment from the selling firm if an account receivable is uncollectable.

factoring

Outright sale of accounts receivable.

Factoring, or *selling accounts receivable,* involves the purchase of accounts receivable by the lender, generally without recourse to the borrower, which means that if the purchaser of the goods does not pay for them, the lender rather than the seller of the goods takes the loss. Under factoring, the buyer of the goods is typically notified of the transfer and is asked to make payment directly to the financial institution. Since the factoring firm assumes the risk of default on bad accounts, it must make the credit check. Accordingly, factors provide not only money but also a credit department for the borrower. Incidentally, the same financial institutions that make loans against pledged receivables also serve as factors. Thus, depending on the circumstances and the wishes of the borrower, a financial institution will provide either form of receivables financing.

Procedure for Pledging Accounts Receivable.   The financing of accounts receivable is initiated by a legally binding agreement between the seller of the goods and the financing institution. The agreement sets forth in detail the pro-

---

[11]The term "asset-based financing" is often used as a synonym for "secured financing." In recent years accounts receivable have been used as security for long-term bonds, and this permits corporations to borrow from lenders such as pension funds rather than being restricted to banks and other traditional short-term lenders.

cedures to be followed and the legal obligations of both parties. Once the work-ing relationship has been established, the seller periodically takes a batch of invoices to the financing institution. The lender reviews the invoices and makes credit appraisals of the buyers. Invoices of companies that do not meet the lender's credit standards are not accepted for pledging.

The financial institution seeks to protect itself at every phase of the opera-tion. First, selection of sound invoices is one way the lender safeguards itself. Second, if the buyer of the goods does not pay the invoice, the lender still has recourse against the seller. Third, additional protection is afforded the lender because the loan will generally be less than 100 percent of the pledged receiv-ables; for example, the lender may advance the selling firm only 75 percent of the amount of the pledged invoices.

Procedure for Factoring Accounts Receivable.   The procedures used in fac-toring are somewhat different from those for pledging. Again, an agreement be-tween the seller and the factor specifies legal obligations and procedural arrangements. When the seller receives an order from a buyer, a credit approval slip is written and immediately sent to the factoring company for a credit check. If the factor approves the credit, shipment is made and the invoice is stamped to notify the buyer to make payment directly to the factoring company. If the factor does not approve the sale, the seller generally refuses to fill the order; if the sale is made anyway, the factor will not buy the account.

The factor normally performs three functions: (1) credit checking, (2) lend-ing, and (3) risk bearing. However, the seller can select various combinations of these functions by changing provisions in the factoring agreement. For ex-ample, a small- or medium-sized firm may have the factor perform the risk-bearing function and thus avoid having to establish a credit department. The factor's service is often less costly than a credit department that would have excess capacity for the firm's credit volume. At the same time, if the selling firm uses someone who is not really qualified for the job to perform credit checking, then that person's lack of education, training, and experience could result in excessive losses.

The seller may have the factor perform the credit-checking and risk-taking functions without performing the lending function. The following procedure illustrates the handling of a $10,000 order under this arrangement. The factor checks and approves the invoices. The goods are shipped on terms of net 30. Payment is made to the factor, who remits to the seller. If the buyer defaults, however, the $10,000 must still be remitted to the seller, and if the $10,000 is never paid, the factor sustains a $10,000 loss. Note that in this situation, the factor does not remit funds to the seller until either they are received from the buyer of the goods or the credit period has expired. Thus, the factor does not supply any credit.

Now consider the more typical situation in which the factor performs the lending, risk-bearing, and credit-checking functions. The goods are shipped, and even though payment is not due for 30 days, the factor immediately makes funds available to the seller. Suppose $10,000 worth of goods are shipped. Fur-ther, assume that the factoring commission for credit checking and risk bearing is 2.5 percent of the invoice price, or $250, and that the interest expense is computed at a 9 percent annual rate on the invoice balance, or $75.[12] The selling firm's accounting entry is as follows:

Cash	$9,175	
Interest expense	75	
Factoring commission	250	
Reserve due from factor on collection of account	500	
Accounts receivable		$10,000

The $500 due from the factor upon collection of the account is a reserve established by the factor to cover disputes between the seller and buyers over damaged goods, goods returned by the buyers to the seller, and the failure to make an outright sale of goods. The reserve is paid to the selling firm when the factor collects on the account.

Factoring is normally a continuous process instead of the single cycle just described. The firm that sells the goods receives an order; it transmits this order to the factor for approval; upon approval, the firm ships the goods; the factor advances the invoice amount minus withholdings to the seller; the buyer pays the factor when payment is due; and the factor periodically remits any excess in the reserve to the seller of the goods. Once a routine has been established, a continuous circular flow of goods and funds takes place between the seller, the buyers of the goods, and the factor. Thus, once the factoring agreement is in force, funds from this source are *spontaneous* in the sense that an increase in sales will automatically generate additional credit.

Cost of Receivables Financing. Both accounts receivable pledging and factoring are convenient and advantageous, but they can be costly. The credit-checking and risk-bearing fee is 1 to 3 percent of the amount of invoices accepted by the factor, and it may be even more if the buyers are poor credit risks. The cost of money is reflected in the interest rate (usually 2 to 3 percentage points over the prime rate) charged on the unpaid balance of the funds advanced by the factor.

Evaluation of Receivables Financing. It cannot be said categorically that accounts receivable financing is either a good or a bad way to raise funds. Among the advantages is, first, the flexibility of this source of financing: As the firm's sales expand, more financing is needed, but a larger volume of invoices, and hence a larger amount of receivables financing, is generated automatically. Second, receivables can be used as security for loans that would otherwise not be granted. Third, factoring can provide the services of a credit department that might otherwise be available only at a higher cost.

---

[12]Since the interest is only for 1 month, we multiply 1/12 of the quoted rate (9 percent) by the $10,000 invoice price:

$$(1/12)(0.09)(\$10,000) = \$75.$$

The effective rate of interest is really above 9 percent because (1) the term is for less than 1 year and (2) a discounting procedure is used and the borrower does not get the full $10,000. In many instances, however, the factoring contract calls for interest to be calculated on the invoice price minus the factoring commission and the reserve account.

Accounts receivable financing also has disadvantages. First, when invoices are numerous and relatively small in dollar amount, the administrative costs involved may be excessive. Second, since receivables represent the firm's most liquid noncash assets, some trade creditors may refuse to sell on credit to a firm that factors or pledges its receivables on the grounds that this practice weakens the position of other creditors.

Future Use of Receivables Financing.   We may make a prediction at this point: In the future, accounts receivable financing will increase in relative importance. Computer technology is rapidly advancing toward the point where credit records of individuals and firms can be kept on disks and magnetic tapes. For example, one device used by retailers consists of a box which, when an individual's magnetic credit card is inserted, gives a signal that the credit is "good" and that a bank is willing to "buy" the receivable created as soon as the store completes the sale. The cost of handling invoices will be greatly reduced over present-day costs because the new systems will be so highly automated. This will make it possible to use accounts receivable financing for very small sales, and it will reduce the cost of all receivables financing. The net result will be a marked expansion of accounts receivable financing. In fact, when consumers use credit cards such as MasterCard or Visa, the seller is in effect factoring receivables. The seller receives the amount of the purchase, minus a percentage fee, the next working day. The buyer receives 30 days' (or so) credit, at which time he or she remits payment directly to the credit card company or sponsoring bank.

Inventory Financing

A substantial amount of credit is secured by business inventories. If a firm is a relatively good credit risk, the mere existence of the inventory may be a sufficient basis for receiving an unsecured loan. However, if the firm is a relatively poor risk, the lending institution may insist upon security in the form of a *lien* against the inventory. Methods for using inventories as security are discussed in this section.

Blanket Liens.   The *inventory blanket lien* gives the lending institution a lien against all of the borrower's inventories. However, the borrower is free to sell inventories, and thus the value of the collateral can be reduced below the level that existed when the loan was granted.

Trust Receipts.   Because of the inherent weakness of the blanket lien, another procedure for inventory financing has been developed — the *trust receipt,* which is an instrument acknowledging that the goods are held in trust for the lender. Under this method, the borrowing firm, as a condition for receiving funds from the lender, signs and delivers a trust receipt for the goods. The goods can be stored in a public warehouse or held on the premises of the borrower. The trust receipt states that the goods are held in trust for the lender or are segregated on the borrower's premises on the lender's behalf and that any proceeds from the sale of the goods must be transmitted to the lender at the end of each day. Automobile dealer financing is one of the best examples of trust receipt financing.

One defect of trust receipt financing is the requirement that a trust receipt be issued for specific goods. For example, if the security is autos in a dealer's inventory, the trust receipts must indicate the cars by registration number. In order to validate its trust receipts, the lending institution must send someone to the borrower's premises periodically to see that the auto numbers are correctly listed, because auto dealers who are in financial difficulty have been known to sell cars backing trust receipts and then use the funds obtained for other operations rather than to repay the bank. Problems are compounded if the borrower has a number of different locations, especially if they are separated geographically from the lender. To offset these inconveniences, *warehousing* has come into wide use as a method of securing loans with inventory.

Warehouse Receipts.   Warehouse receipt financing is another way to use inventory as security. A *public warehouse* is an independent third-party operation engaged in the business of storing goods. Items which must age, such as tobacco and liquor, are often financed and stored in public warehouses. Sometimes a public warehouse is not practical because of the bulkiness of goods and the expense of transporting them to and from the borrower's premises. In such cases, a *field warehouse* may be established on the borrower's grounds. To provide inventory supervision, the lending institution employs a third party in the arrangement, the field warehousing company, which acts as its agent.

Field warehousing can be illustrated by a simple example. Suppose a firm which has iron stacked in an open yard on its premises needs a loan. A field warehousing concern can place a temporary fence around the iron, erecting a sign stating, "This is a field warehouse supervised by the Smith Field Warehousing Corporation," and then assign an employee to supervise and control the fenced-in inventory.

This example illustrates the three essential elements for the establishment of a field warehouse: (1) public notification, (2) physical control of the inventory, and (3) supervision by a custodian of the field warehousing concern. When the field warehousing operation is relatively small, the third condition is sometimes violated by hiring an employee of the borrower to supervise the inventory. This practice is viewed as undesirable by most lenders, because there is no control over the collateral by a person independent of the borrowing firm.[13]

The field warehouse financing operation is best described by an actual case. A California tomato cannery was interested in financing its operations by bank borrowing. It had sufficient funds to finance 15 to 20 percent of its operations during the canning season. These funds were adequate to purchase and process an initial batch of tomatoes. As the cans were put into boxes and rolled into the storerooms, the cannery needed additional funds for both raw materials and

---

[13]This absence of independent control was the main cause of a breakdown that resulted in more than $200 million of losses on loans to the Allied Crude Vegetable Oil Company by Bank of America and other banks. American Express Field Warehousing Company was handling the operation, but it hired men from Allied's own staff as custodians. Their dishonesty was not discovered because of another breakdown—the fact that the American Express touring inspector did not actually take a physical inventory of the warehouses. As a consequence, the swindle was not discovered until losses running into the hundreds of millions of dollars had been suffered.

labor. Because of the cannery's poor credit rating, the bank decided that a field warehousing operation was necessary to secure its loans.

The field warehouse was established, and the custodian notified the bank of the description, by number, of the boxes of canned tomatoes in storage and under warehouse control. With this inventory as collateral, the lending institution established for the cannery a deposit on which it could draw. From this point on, the bank financed the operations. The cannery needed only enough cash to initiate the cycle. The farmers brought in more tomatoes; the cannery processed them; the cans were boxed; the boxes were put into the field warehouse; field warehouse receipts were drawn up and sent to the bank; the bank established further deposits for the cannery on the basis of the additional collateral; and the cannery could draw on the deposits to continue the cycle.

Of course, the cannery's ultimate objective was to sell the canned tomatoes. As it received purchase orders, it transmitted them to the bank, and the bank directed the custodian to release the inventories. It was agreed that as remittances were received by the cannery, they would be turned over to the bank. These remittances thus paid off the loans.

Note that a seasonal pattern existed. At the beginning of the tomato harvesting and canning season, the cannery's cash needs and loan requirements began to rise, and they reached a peak just as the season ended. It was expected that well before the new canning season began, the cannery would have sold a sufficient volume to pay off the loan. If the cannery had experienced a bad year, the bank might have carried the loan over for another year to enable the company to work off its inventory.

Acceptable Products.   In addition to canned foods, which account for about 17 percent of all field warehouse loans, many other types of products provide a basis for field warehouse financing. Some of these are miscellaneous groceries, which represent about 13 percent; lumber products, about 10 percent; and coal and coke, about 6 percent. These products are relatively nonperishable and are sold in well-developed, organized markets. Nonperishability protects the lender if it should have to take over the security. For this reason, a bank would not make a field warehousing loan on perishables such as fresh fish, but frozen fish, which can be stored for a long time, can be field warehoused.

Cost of Financing.   The fixed costs of a field warehousing arrangement are relatively high; such financing is therefore not suitable for a very small firm. If a field warehousing company sets up a field warehouse, it will typically set a minimum charge of about $25,000 per year, plus about 1 to 2 percent of the amount of credit extended to the borrower. Furthermore, the financing institution will charge an interest rate of two to three percentage points over the prime rate. An efficient field warehousing operation requires a minimum inventory of at least $1 million.

Evaluation of Inventory Financing.   The use of inventory financing, especially field warehouse financing, as a source of funds has many advantages. First, the amount of funds available is flexible because the financing is tied to the growth of inventories, which in turn is related directly to financing needs. Second, the field warehousing arrangement increases the acceptability of inventories as loan collateral; some inventories simply would not be accepted by a bank as security without such an arrangement. Third, the necessity for inventory control and safekeeping as well as the use of specialists in warehousing often results in improved warehouse practices, which in turn save handling costs, insurance charges, theft losses, and so on. Thus, field warehousing companies often save money for firms in spite of the costs of financing that we have discussed. The major disadvantages of field warehousing include the paperwork, physical separation requirements, and, for small firms, the fixed-cost element.

Self-Test Questions

What is a secured loan?

What two types of current assets are pledged as security for short-term loans?

Differentiate between pledging accounts receivable and factoring accounts receivable.

Identify the services a factor normally provides.

List the advantages and disadvantages of accounts receivable financing.

Describe three methods of inventory financing.

What are some advantages and disadvantages of inventory financing?

SMALL BUSINESS   Receivables Financing by a Small Firm

To stimulate growth, small firms often find that they must offer customers credit. If rapid sales growth does result, then accounts receivable will grow equally or perhaps even faster. This, in turn, brings with it a need for additional financing. Larger firms, with established earning power, generally have no trouble raising growth capital, but a small firm with no track record may face a real problem.

Accounts receivable are highly liquid; hence, they are attractive to lenders as collateral. The small firm can either pledge its receivables or factor them to help bring in growth capital.

In the case of pledged receivables, the firm needing capital merely uses its receivables as collateral for the loan. To illustrate, Ray Johnson and Rod Lease decided to acquire an old, slow-growth firm, Main Street Builders' Supply, and to revitalize it using modern management techniques. Main Street sells directly to builders, and, to increase sales, Johnson and Lease decided to offer better credit terms than those of their competitors. Specifically, they began offering terms of 2/10, net 60, versus the old terms of net 30.

Because many builders are themselves undercapitalized, many of Main Street's customers elected to delay payment. As Main Street began to grow, its cash reserves were depleted, which made it difficult to finance its own inventory requirements. To solve this problem, Main Street is considering pledging its receivables as security for a bank loan. The bank would review Main Street's major receivable accounts and select those accounts which it regards as acceptable for collateral purposes. The bank would then lend Main Street 70 percent of the face value of the acceptable accounts. Projections have indicated that this would relieve Main Street's financial pressures.

Pledging receivables is especially sensible for the small firm that has customers with better credit histories than the firm itself, as this allows the firm to take advantage of the strength of its customer base. However, the firm must ultimately bear the risk of nonpayment, and it gets only part of the funds due from its customers.

Main Street's other alternative is factoring, which involves the sale of receivables to a third party, called the "factor." This arrangement would be without recourse, meaning that the factor must bear any credit risk inherent in the receivable. Thus, it would be up to the factor to check the customers' creditworthiness and to collect the receivables.

A small firm employing a factor therefore gets more than just credit. If Main Street uses factoring, the factor would take over Main Street's credit analysis and collection functions almost entirely. The factor would decide which customers merit credit, and if a customer does not pay, the factor must absorb the loss. Of course, if Main Street goes ahead and sells to a customer that the factor finds unacceptable, then Main Street would have to bear the credit risk itself.

If Main Street decides to use a factor, it would not need a credit department either for checking credit or for collecting receivables. But factors are in business to make money, so it stands to reason that Main Street would have to pay for the factor's services. Main Street's problem, then, is to decide whether the comparatively high cost of the factor is warranted in view of the full set of services that it would receive, including short-term capital, credit analysis, and collection services.

There are good reasons why many small firms find that factors are indeed an economical alternative. The small firm has its own special expertise—in Main Street's case, buying and selling building materials—while factors have their own expertise—credit services. Economies of scale exist, so the factor's services may be a bargain when compared to the costs of maintaining a credit department and being exposed to credit risks.

The fees charged by factors normally include interest paid on funds advanced, a fee for evaluating customers' credit, and an additional charge to reflect the credit risk of the customers. Also, the factor does not generally advance the full amount of the receivable, holding back an allowance for possible returns due to disputes between the buyer and seller. For example, suppose Main Street agrees to deliver $25,000 in building supplies to Reliable Homes on terms of net 60, and Main Street has worked out an arrangement with Factor Inc., a wholly owned subsidiary of the ma-

jor local bank holding company. Factor accepts the account and charges Main Street interest at the rate of 11½ percent, 5 points over prime, resulting in an interest charge of $1/6 \times 11.5\% \times \$25,000 = \$479.17$ on the $25,000 invoice amount. Factor charges an additional 2 percent, or $500, as a credit fee. Finally, Factor advances only $21,520.83 rather than $24,020.83, holding a 10 percent (or $2,500) allowance in the event that Reliable disputes the order or finds something wrong with the materials.

At the end of the 60 days, Reliable pays $24,000 directly to Factor after deducting $1,000 for defective sinks which it returned to Main Street. At that point, Factor pays Main Street the remainder of the $2,500 allowance, or $1,500, due the firm on the net $24,000 sale of materials to Reliable Homes.

Therefore, Main Street will incur a cost of $479.17 + $500 = $979.17 for the use of $21,521 for 60 days. This translates into an effective annual rate of 30.6 percent. However, one must bear in mind that Factor bore the cost of credit verification as well as the risk of nonpayment or delayed payment by Reliable. In deciding on the use of a factor, Main Street must consider not only the financial cost of other forms of financing, such as that offered by the bank, but also the cost of the credit services provided by the factor.

For small firms with limited managerial resources and limited experience in monitoring and collecting credit accounts, factors may be more than worth the cost. The small firm's comparative advantage is its ability to deliver a product; the factor's advantage is its ability to provide financial and credit services. Therefore, it may be best to have the firm do what it does best and to have the factor provide financing and credit services.

SUMMARY

This chapter examined (1) the different types of short-term credit available to firms, (2) the decisions financial managers make when selecting among types of short-term credit, and (3) decisions regarding the use of security to obtain credit. The key concepts covered are listed below.

▪ **Short-term credit** is defined as any liability originally scheduled for payment within one year. The four major sources of short-term credit are (1) accruals, (2) accounts payable, (3) bank loans, and (4) commercial paper.

▪ **Accruals,** which are continually recurring short-term liabilities, represent free, spontaneous credit.

▪ **Accounts payable,** or **trade credit,** is the largest category of short-term debt. This credit arises spontaneously as a result of purchases on credit. Firms should use all the **free trade credit** they can obtain, but they should use **costly trade credit** only if it is less expensive than other forms of short-term debt. Suppliers often offer discounts to customers who pay within a stated discount period. The following equation may be used to calculate the approximate percentage cost, on an annual basis, of not taking discounts:

$$\begin{array}{c}\text{Approximate}\\\text{percentage}\\\text{cost}\end{array} = \frac{\text{Discount percent}}{100 - \begin{array}{c}\text{Discount}\\\text{percent}\end{array}} \times \frac{360}{\begin{array}{c}\text{Days credit}\\\text{is outstanding}\end{array} - \begin{array}{c}\text{Discount}\\\text{period}\end{array}}.$$

▪ **Bank loans** are an important source of short-term credit. Interest on bank loans may be quoted as **simple interest, discount interest,** or **add-on interest.** The effective rate on a discount or add-on loan always exceeds the quoted nominal rate.

▪ When a bank loan is approved, a **promissory note** is signed. It specifies: (1) the amount borrowed, (2) the percentage interest rate, (3) the repayment schedule, (4) the collateral, and (5) any other conditions to which the parties have agreed.

▪ Banks sometimes require borrowers to maintain **compensating balances,** which are deposit requirements set at between 10 and 20 percent of the loan amount. Compensating balances raise the effective rate of interest on bank loans.

▪ A **line of credit** is an understanding between the bank and the borrower indicating the maximum amount of credit the bank will extend to the borrower.

▪ A **revolving credit agreement** is a formal line of credit which involves a **commitment fee.**

▪ **Commercial paper** is unsecured short-term debt issued by a large, financially strong corporation. Although the cost of commercial paper is lower than the cost of bank loans, commercial paper's maturity is limited to 270 days, and it can be used only by large firms with exceptionally strong credit ratings.

▪ Sometimes a borrower will find it necessary to borrow on a **secured basis,** in which case the borrower pledges assets such as real estate, securities, equipment, inventories, or accounts receivable as collateral for the loan.

▪ Accounts receivable financing involves either **pledging** or **factoring receivables.** Under a pledging arrangement the lender not only gets a claim against the receivables but also has recourse to the borrower. Factoring involves the purchase of accounts receivable by the lender, generally without recourse to the borrower.

▪ There are three primary methods of inventory financing: (1) An **inventory blanket lien** gives the lender a lien against all of the borrower's inventories. (2) A **trust receipt** is an instrument that acknowledges that goods are held in trust for the lender. (3) **Warehouse receipt financing** is an arrangement under which the lender employs a third party to exercise control over the borrower's inventory and to act as the lender's agent.

▪ **Pledging receivables** is especially sensible for a small firm which has customers with better credit histories than the firm itself, as this allows the firm to take advantage of the strength of its customer base.

▪ For small firms with limited managerial resources and limited experience in monitoring and collecting credit accounts, **factoring** may be more than worth the cost. The small firm's comparative advantage is its ability to deliver a product; the factor's advantage is its ability to provide financial and credit services.

Questions

13-1   "Firms can control their accruals within fairly wide limits; depending on the cost of accruals, financing from this source will be increased or decreased." Discuss.

13-2   Is it true that both trade credit and accruals represent a spontaneous source of capital for financing growth? Explain.

13-3   Is it true that most firms are able to obtain some free trade credit and that additional trade credit is often available, but at a cost? Explain.

13-4   The availability of bank credit is often more important to a small firm than to a large one. Why?

13-5   What kinds of firms use commercial paper? Could Mama and Papa Gus's Corner Grocery borrow using this form of credit?

13-6   Given that commercial paper interest rates are generally lower than bank loan rates to a given borrower, why might firms which are capable of selling commercial paper also use bank credit?

13-7   Suppose a firm can obtain funds by borrowing at the prime rate or by selling commercial paper.
   a. If the prime rate is 6½ percent, what is a reasonable estimate for the cost of commercial paper?
   b. If a substantial cost differential exists, why might a firm like this one actually borrow some of its funds in each market?

Self-Test Problems   *(Solutions Appear in Appendix B)*

ST-1   Define each of the following terms:
Key terms
   a. Accruals
   b. Trade credit; stretching accounts payable; free trade credit; costly trade credit
   c. Promissory note; line of credit; revolving credit agreement
   d. Prime rate
   e. Simple interest; discount interest; add-on interest
   f. Compensating balance (CB)
   g. Commercial paper
   h. Secured loan
   i. Uniform Commercial Code
   j. Pledging receivables; factoring
   k. Recourse
   l. Inventory blanket lien; trust receipt; warehouse receipt financing; field warehouse

ST-2
Receivables financing

The Naylor Corporation is considering two methods of raising working capital: (1) a commercial bank loan secured by accounts receivable and (2) factoring accounts receivable. Naylor's bank has agreed to lend the firm 75 percent of its average monthly accounts receivable balance of $250,000 at an annual interest rate of 9 percent. The bank loan is in the form of a series of 30-day loans. The loan would be discounted, and a 20 percent compensating balance would also be required.

A factor has agreed to purchase Naylor's accounts receivable and to advance 85 percent of the balance to the firm. The 15 percent of receivables not loaned to the firm under the factoring arrangement is held in a reserve account. The factor would charge a 3.5 percent factoring commission and annual interest of 9 percent on the invoice price, less both the factoring commission and the reserve account. The monthly interest payment would be deducted from the advance. If Naylor chooses the factoring arrangement, it can eliminate its credit department and reduce operating expenses by $4,000 per month. In addition, bad debt losses of 2 percent of the monthly receivables will be avoided.

a. What is the annual cost associated with each financing arrangement?

b. Discuss some considerations other than cost that may influence management's decision between factoring and a commercial bank loan.

Problems

13-1
Cash discounts

Suppose a firm makes purchases of $3.6 million per year under terms of 2/10, net 30 and takes discounts.

a. What is the average amount of accounts payable net of discounts? (Assume that the $3.6 million of purchases is net of discounts—that is, gross purchases are $3,673,469, discounts are $73,469, and net purchases are $3.6 million. Also, use 360 days in a year.)

b. Is there a cost of the trade credit the firm uses?

c. If the firm did not take discounts but it did pay on the due date, what would be its average payables and the approximate and effective annual costs of this nonfree trade credit? Assume the firm records accounts payable net of discounts.

d. What would its approximate and effective annual costs of not taking discounts be if it could stretch its payments to 40 days?

13-2
Trade credit versus bank credit

Gallinger Corporation projects an increase in sales from $1.5 million to $2 million, but it needs an additional $300,000 of current assets to support this expansion. The money can be obtained from the bank at an interest rate of 13 percent, discount interest; no compensating balance is required. Alternatively, Gallinger can finance the expansion by no longer taking discounts, thus increasing accounts payable. Gallinger purchases under terms of 2/10, net 30, but it can delay payment for an additional 35 days—paying in 65 days and thus becoming 35 days past due—without a penalty because of its suppliers' current excess capacity problems.

a. Based strictly on effective annual interest rate comparisons, how should Gallinger finance its expansion?

b. What additional qualitative factors should Gallinger consider before reaching a decision?

13-3
Bank financing

The O'Brien Corporation had sales of $3.5 million last year, and it earned a 5 percent return, after taxes, on sales. Recently the company has fallen behind in its accounts payable. Although its terms of purchase are net 30 days, its accounts payable represent 60 days' purchases. The company's treasurer is seeking to increase bank borrowings in order to become current in meeting its trade obligations (that is, to have 30 days' payables outstanding). The company's balance sheet is as follows (thousands of dollars):

Cash	$ 100	Accounts payable	$ 600
Accounts receivable	300	Bank loans	700
Inventories	1,400	Accruals	200
Current assets	$1,800	Current liabilities	$1,500
Land and buildings	600	Mortgage on real estate	700
Equipment	600	Common stock, $0.10 par	300
		Retained earnings	500
Total assets	$3,000	Total liabilities and equity	$3,000

a. How much bank financing is needed to eliminate the past-due accounts payable?

b. Would you as a bank loan officer make the loan? Why?

13-4
Cost of bank loans

Gifts Galore Inc. borrowed $1.5 million from National City Bank. The loan was made at a simple annual interest rate of 9 percent a year for three months. A 20 percent compensating balance requirement raised the effective interest rate.

a. The approximate interest rate on the loan was 11.25 percent. What is the true effective rate?

b. What would be the effective cost of the loan if the note required discount interest?

c. What would be the approximate annual interest rate on the loan if National City Bank required Gifts Galore to repay the loan and interest in three equal monthly installments?

13-5
Short-term financing analysis

Bankston Feed and Supply Company buys on terms of 1/10, net 30, but it has not been taking discounts and has actually been paying in 60 rather than 30 days. Bankston's balance sheet follows (thousands of dollars):

Cash	$ 50	Accounts payable[a]	$ 500
Accounts receivable	450	Notes payable	50
Inventories	750	Accruals	50
Current assets	$1,250	Current liabilities	$ 600
		Long-term debt	150
Fixed assets	750	Common equity	1,250
Total assets	$2,000	Total liabilities and equity	$2,000

[a]Stated net of discounts.

Now Bankston's suppliers are threatening to stop shipments unless the company begins making prompt payments (that is, paying in 30 days or less). The firm can borrow on a 1-year note (call this a current liability) from its bank at a rate of 15 percent, discount interest, with a 20 percent compensating balance required. (Bankston's $50,000 of cash is needed for transactions; it cannot be used as part of the compensating balance.)

a. Determine what action Bankston should take by calculating (1) the cost of nonfree trade credit and (2) the cost of the bank loan.

b. Assume that Bankston forgoes discounts and then borrows the amount needed to become current on its payables from the bank. How large will the bank loan be?

c. Based on your conclusion in Part b, construct a pro forma balance sheet. (Hint: Remember that the interest for a discount loan is paid "up front"; therefore, you will need to include an account entitled "prepaid interest" under current assets.)

13-6

Alternative financing
arrangements

Suntime Boats Limited estimates that because of the seasonal nature of its business, it will require an additional $2 million of cash for the month of July. Suntime Boats has the following four options available for raising the needed funds:

(1) Establish a one-year line of credit for $2 million with a commercial bank. The commitment fee will be 0.5 percent per year on the unused portion, and the interest charge on the used funds will be 11 percent per annum. Assume that the funds are needed only in July and that there are 30 days in July and 360 days in the year.

(2) Forgo the trade discount of 2/10, net 40 on $2 million of purchases during July.

(3) Issue $2 million of 30-day commercial paper at a 9.5 percent per annum interest rate. The total transactions fee, including the cost of a backup credit line, on using commercial paper is 0.5 percent of the amount of the issue.

(4) Issue $2 million of 60-day commercial paper at a 9 percent per annum interest rate, plus a transactions fee of 0.5 percent. Since the funds are required for only 30 days, the excess funds ($2 million) can be invested in 9.4 percent per annum marketable securities for the month of August. The total transactions cost of purchasing and selling the marketable securities is 0.4 percent of the amount of the issue.

a. What is the dollar cost of each financing arrangement?

b. Is the source with the lowest expected cost necessarily the one to select? Why or why not?

13-7

Receivables financing

Fogler's Funtime Company manufactures plastic toys. It buys raw materials, manufactures the toys in the spring and summer, and ships them to department stores and toy stores by late summer or early fall. Funtime factors its receivables; if it did not, its October 1992 balance sheet would appear as follows (thousands of dollars):

Cash	$ 40	Accounts payable	$1,200
Receivables	1,200	Notes payable	800
Inventories	800	Accruals	80
Current assets	$2,040	Current liabilities	$2,080
		Mortgages	200
		Common stock	400
Fixed assets	800	Retained earnings	160
Total assets	$2,840	Total liabilities and equity	$2,840

Funtime provides extended credit to its customers, so its receivables are not due for payment until January 31, 1993. Also, Funtime would have been overdue on some $800,000 of its accounts payable if the preceding situation had actually existed.

Funtime has an agreement with a finance company to factor the receivables for the period October 31 through January 31 of each selling season. The factoring company charges a flat commission of 2 percent of the invoice price, plus 6 percent per year interest on the outstanding balance; it deducts a reserve of 8 percent for returned and damaged materials. Interest and commissions are paid in advance. Note, however, that interest is not recognized as an expense until the end of the 90-day period. No interest is charged on the reserved funds or on the commission.

a. Show Funtime's balance sheet on October 31, 1992, including the purchase of all the receivables by the factoring company and the use of the funds to pay accounts payable. Ignore tax effects, and assume all proceeds from receivables factored are applied to accounts payable.

b. If the $1.2 million is the average level of outstanding receivables, and if they turn over four times a year (hence the commission is paid four times a year), what are the total dollar costs of receivables financing (factoring) and the effective annual interest rate?

13-8

Factoring arrangement

Cooley Industries needs an additional $500,000, which it plans to obtain through a factoring arrangement. The factor would purchase Cooley's accounts receivable and advance the invoice amount, minus a 2 percent commission, on the invoices purchased each month. Cooley sells on terms of net 30 days. In addition, the factor charges a 12 percent annual interest rate on the total invoice amount, to be deducted in advance.

a. What amount of accounts receivable must be factored to net $500,000?
b. If Cooley can reduce credit expenses by $3,500 per month and avoid bad debt losses of 2.5 percent on the factored amount, what is the total dollar cost of the factoring arrangement?
c. What would be the total cost of the factoring arrangement if Cooley's funds needed rose to $750,000? Would the factoring arrangement be profitable under these circumstances?

13-9

Field warehousing arrangement

Because of crop failures last year, the San Joaquin Packing Company has no funds available to finance its canning operations during the next six months. It estimates that it will require $1,200,000 from inventory financing during the period. One alternative is to establish a six-month, $1,500,000 line of credit with terms of 9 percent annual interest on the used portion, a 1 percent commitment fee on the unused portion, and a $300,000 compensating balance at all times. The other alternative is to use field warehouse financing. The costs of the field warehouse arrangement in this case would be a flat fee of $2,000, plus 8 percent annual interest on all outstanding credit, plus 1 percent of the maximum amount of credit extended.

Expected inventory levels to be financed are as follows:

Month	Amount
July 1993	$ 250,000
August	1,000,000
September	1,200,000
October	950,000
November	600,000
December	0

a. Calculate the cost of funds from using the line of credit. Be sure to include interest charges and commitment fees. Note that each month's borrowings will be $300,000 greater than the inventory level to be financed because of the compensating balance requirement.
b. Calculate the total cost of the field warehousing operation.
c. Compare the cost of the field warehousing arrangement to the cost of the line of credit. Which alternative should San Joaquin choose?

EXAM-TYPE PROBLEMS

The problems included in this section are set up in such a way that they could be used as multiple-choice exam problems.

13-10

Cost of trade credit

Calculate the approximate cost of nonfree trade credit under each of the following terms. Assume payment is made either on the due date or on the discount date.

a. 1/15, net 20.
b. 2/10, net 60.
c. 3/10, net 45.
d. 2/10, net 45.
e. 2/15, net 40.

13-11
Cost of credit

a. If a firm buys under terms of 3/15, net 45, but actually pays on the 20th day and *still takes the discount*, what is the approximate cost of its nonfree trade credit?

b. Does it receive more or less credit than it would if it paid within 15 days?

13-12
Cost of bank loans

Susan Visscher, owner of Visscher's Hardware, is negotiating with First Merchant's Bank for a $50,000, 1-year loan. First Merchant's has offered Visscher the following alternatives. Calculate the effective interest rate for each alternative. Which alternative has the lowest effective interest rate?

a. A 12 percent annual rate on a simple interest loan with no compensating balance required and interest due at the end of the year.

b. A 9 percent annual rate on a simple interest loan with a 20 percent compensating balance required and interest again due at the end of the year.

c. An 8.75 percent annual rate on a discounted loan with a 15 percent compensating balance.

d. Interest is figured as 8 percent of the $50,000 amount, *payable at the end of the year,* but the $50,000 is repayable in monthly installments during the year.

13-13
Cost of trade credit

Howe Industries sells on terms of 2/10, net 40. Gross sales last year were $4.5 million, and accounts receivable averaged $437,500. Half of Howe's customers paid on the tenth day and took discounts. What is the cost of trade credit to Howe's nondiscount customers? (Hint: Calculate sales/day based on a 360-day year; then get average receivables of discount customers; then find the DSO for the nondiscount customers.)

13-14
Effective cost of short-term credit

Boles Corporation needs to raise $500,000 for one year to supply working capital to a new store. Boles buys from its suppliers on terms of 3/10, net 90, and it currently pays on the 10th day and takes discounts, but it could forego discounts, pay on the 90th day, and get the needed $500,000 in the form of costly trade credit. Alternatively, Boles could borrow from its bank on a 12 percent discount interest rate basis. What is the effective annual interest rate of the lower cost source?

13-15
Effective cost of short-term credit

The Meyer Company must arrange financing for its working capital requirements for the coming year. Meyer can (a) borrow from its bank on a simple interest basis (interest payable at the end of the loan) for one year at a 12 percent nominal rate; (b) borrow on a 3-month, but renewable, loan at an 11.5 percent nominal rate; (c) borrow on an installment loan basis at a 6.0 percent add-on rate with 12 end-of-month payments; or (d) obtain the needed funds by no longer taking discounts and thus increasing its accounts payable. Meyer buys on terms of 1/15, net 60. What is the effective annual cost (*not* the approximate cost) of the *least expensive* type of credit, assuming 360 days per year?

INTEGRATIVE PROBLEM

13-16
Short-term financing

C. Charles Smith was recently hired as president of Dellvoe Office Equipment Inc., a small manufacturer of metal office equipment. As his assistant, you have been asked to review the company's short-term financing policies and to prepare a report for Smith and the board of directors. To help you get started, Smith has prepared some questions which, when answered, will give him a better idea of the company's short-term financing policies.

a. What is short-term credit, and what are the four major sources of this credit?

b. Is there a cost to accruals, and do firms have much control over them?

c. What is trade credit?

d. Like most small companies, Dellvoe has two primary sources of short-term debt: trade credit and bank loans. One supplier, which supplies Dellvoe with $50,000 of materials a year, offers Dellvoe terms of 2/10, net 50.

(1) What are Dellvoe's net daily purchases from this supplier?

(2) What is the average level of Dellvoe's accounts payable to this supplier if the discount is taken? What is the average level if the discount is not taken? What are the amounts of free credit and costly credit under both discount policies?

(3) What is the approximate cost of the costly trade credit? What is its effective annual cost?

e. In discussing a possible loan with the firm's banker, Smith has found that the bank is willing to lend Dellvoe up to $800,000 for 1 year at a 9 percent nominal, or quoted, rate. However, he forgot to ask what the specific terms would be.

(1) Assume the firm will borrow $800,000. What would be the effective interest rate if the loan were based on simple interest? If the loan had been an 8 percent simple interest loan for 6 months rather than for a year, would that have affected the effective annual rate?

(2) What would be the effective rate if the loan were a discount interest loan? What would be the face amount of a loan large enough to net the firm $800,000 of usable funds?

(3) Assume now that the terms call for an installment (or add-on) loan with equal monthly payments. The add-on loan is for a period of one year. What would be Dellvoe's monthly payment? What would be the approximate cost of the loan? What would be the effective annual rate?

(4) Now assume that the bank charges simple interest, but it requires the firm to maintain a 20 percent compensating balance. How much must Dellvoe borrow to obtain its needed $800,000 and to meet the compensating balance requirement? What is the effective annual rate on the loan?

(5) Now assume that the bank charges discount interest of 9 percent and also requires a compensating balance of 20 percent. How much must Dellvoe borrow, and what is the effective annual rate under these terms?

(6) Now assume all the conditions in Part 4, that is, a 20 percent compensating balance and a 9 percent simple interest loan, but assume also that Dellvoe has $100,000 of cash balances which it normally holds for transactions purposes and which can be used as part of the required compensating balance. How does this affect (a) the size of the required loan and (b) the effective cost of the loan?

f. Dellvoe is considering using secured short-term financing. What is a secured loan? What two types of current assets can be used to secure loans?

g. What are the differences between pledging receivables and factoring receivables? Is one type generally considered better?

h. What are the differences among the three forms of inventory financing? Is one type generally considered best?

i. Dellvoe had expected a really strong market for office equipment for the year just ended, and in anticipation of strong sales, the firm increased its inventory purchases. However, sales for the last quarter of the year did not meet its expectations, and now Dellvoe finds itself short on cash. The firm expects that its cash shortage will be temporary, only lasting 3 months. (The inventory has been paid for and cannot be returned to suppliers. The office equipment market is one where designs change nearly every two years, and Dellvoe's inventory reflects the new design changes, so its inventory is not obsolete.) Dellvoe has decided to use inventory financing to meet its short-term cash needs. It estimates that it will require $800,000 for inventory financing during this three-month period. Dellvoe has negotiated with the bank for a three-month, $1,000,000 line of credit with terms of 10 percent annual interest on the used portion, a 1 percent commitment fee on the unused portion, and a $125,000 compensating balance at all times.

Expected inventory levels to be financed are as follows:

Month	Amount
January 1993	$800,000
February	500,000
March	300,000

Calculate the cost of funds from this source, including interest charges and commitment fees. (Hint: Each month's borrowings will be $125,000 greater than the inventory level to be financed because of the compensating balance requirement.)

COMPUTER-RELATED PROBLEM

Work the problem in this section only if you are using the computer problem diskette.

13-17
Factoring receivables

Use the model in File C13 to work this problem. Refer back to Problem 13-8.
a. Would it be to Cooley's advantage to offer to pay the factor a commission of 2.5 percent if it would lower the interest rate to 10.5 percent annually?
b. Assume a commission of 2 percent and an interest rate of 12 percent. What would be the total cost of the factoring arrangement if Cooley's funds needed rose to $650,000? Would the factoring arrangement be profitable under these circumstances?

Strategic Long-Term Investment Decisions: Capital Budgeting

Chapter 14   Capital Budgeting Techniques

Chapter 15   Project Cash Flows and Risk

Appendix 15A   Depreciation

Capital Budgeting Techniques

A MANAGERIAL PERSPECTIVE

Imagine an American car dealership with Hondas, Toyotas, and Acuras displayed side by side in the showroom, along with a new domestic model designed expressly to compete with them. That's one of the marketing strategies under discussion at General Motors, where $3 billion has gone into the creation of a new compact car—the Saturn. After five years in planning, production began in the summer of 1990 on the Saturn, which comes as a two-door coupe or a four-door sedan. Originally scheduled at a 500,000-car-a-year rate, the first-year production goal was lowered to only 120,000 cars. One analyst says that number means "The car will be a marketing success but a financial flop." GM does plan to double production before the first year is over, but there are no immediate plans to do more than that. Saturn's vice president for finance admits that 500,000 cars are needed for the project to be viable, but he also says that expanding the plant is not an option at this time.

After being burned by a six-year, $40 billion capital spending spree in the early 1980s that did not pay off, GM is trying to correct its errors, and it is using the Saturn project as a prototype. Under their previously faulty strategy, GM managers invested most of their funds in fancy technology, robots, and lasers. When the company subsequently lost rather than gained market share to Japanese automakers, Chief Financial Officer F. Alan Smith quipped ruefully that with the amount of money GM spent, it could have simply bought Nissan and Toyota instead. In their capital budgeting planning, Smith and his colleagues had failed to take into account the environment in which they operated. While they were improving their production capacity with all the new equipment, their foreign competitors were doing even more. As a result, between 1985 and 1990, U.S. companies' share of the passenger-car market shrank 11 percentage points, to 33 percent, while the Japanese companies' share climbed 7 points, to 26 percent.

Saturn is GM's hope for turning things around. The Saturn team has been set free to create a whole new company. A Ford executive observed, "They've had an opportunity to look at the entire manufacturing process with no holds barred. They may learn a lot about making cars that will have a profound effect on the way GM makes cars in the future."

The Saturn team has set a formidable goal—to sell 80 percent of its cars to drivers who otherwise would not have bought a GM product. According to one study, more than 40 percent of car shoppers will not even consider GM. In order to compete with Japanese companies, the team designed its new car to "feel" like a Honda. When the Saturn project first got under way, the company bought 70 imported cars of various makes and told the planners and engineers to drive them. They adopted the feel, as well as the look, of Japanese cars, especially in dashboard design. By enlarging the original subcompact car and by increasing its selling price from a planned $6,000 to between $10,000 and $12,000, Saturn also matched the increased size and higher costs of its chief rivals, the Honda Civic and the Toyota Corolla. Furthermore, the dealers who test-drove pre-production Saturns found them superior to Honda and Toyota in terms of handling and smoothness of ride.

Although the product itself is an imitation, the division that makes it is an original that the other GM divisions may eventually imitate. In December 1987, GM's directors approved a capital outlay of $1.9 billion for a new factory, for equipment, and for tooling. After its painful lessons of the past, however, the technology is not the expensive, superautomated, computerized, robot-in-the-dark equipment that was initially visualized. Instead, it is designed to make human workers more efficient.

Former GM Chairman Roger Smith created Saturn as an independent subsidiary after a team of GM managers and union laborers studied and formulated the project. Smith's goal, inspired by the earlier capital-spending debacle, was to stress good management more than expensive equipment. In keeping with that, it is the innovative relationships between people that make the Saturn team unique, particularly in the ponderous bureaucracy of GM.

GM's Saturn project was a massive capital budgeting venture, but the principles set forth in this chapter offer insights into how its managers should consider all projects, large and small.

Sources: "GM Is Tougher Than You Think," *Fortune,* November 10, 1986; "Here Comes GM's Saturn," *Business Week,* April 9, 1990.

In previous chapters we have seen how investors value corporate securities and how investors determine required rates of return, and we have also seen how managers make working capital decisions, including decisions to increase current assets. Now we turn to investment decisions involving fixed assets, or *capital budgeting.* Here the term *capital* refers to fixed assets used in production, while a *budget* is a plan which details projected inflows and outflows during some future period. Thus, the *capital budget* is an outline of planned expenditures on fixed assets, and **capital budgeting** is the whole process of analyzing projects and deciding whether they should be included in the capital budget.

capital budgeting
The process of planning expenditures on assets whose cash flows are expected to extend beyond one year.

Our treatment of capital budgeting is divided into two chapters. First, this chapter gives an overview and explains the basic techniques used in capital budgeting analysis. Then, in Chapter 15, we go on to consider how cash flows are estimated and how risk is brought into the analysis.

IMPORTANCE OF CAPITAL BUDGETING

A number of factors combine to make capital budgeting decisions perhaps the most important ones financial managers must make. First, since the results of capital budgeting decisions continue for many years, the decision maker loses some of his or her flexibility. For example, the purchase of an asset with an economic life of 10 years "locks in" the firm for a 10-year period. Further, because asset expansion is fundamentally related to expected future sales, a decision to buy a fixed asset that is expected to last 10 years involves an implicit 10-year sales forecast.

An error in the forecast of asset requirements can have serious consequences. If the firm invests too much in assets, it will incur unnecessarily heavy expenses. However, if it does not spend enough on fixed assets, two problems may arise. First, its equipment may not be efficient enough to enable it to produce competitively. Second, if it has inadequate capacity, it may lose a portion of its market share to rival firms, and regaining lost customers requires heavy selling expenses and price reductions, both of which are costly.

Timing is also important in capital budgeting — capital assets must be ready to come "on line" when they are needed. Edward Ford, executive vice president of Western Design, a decorative tile company, gave the authors an illustration of the importance of capital budgeting. His firm tried to operate near capacity most of the time. During a four-year period, Western experienced intermittent spurts in the demand for its products, which forced it to turn away orders. After these sharp increases in demand, Western would add capacity by renting an additional building, then purchasing and installing the appropriate equipment. It would take six to eight months to get the additional capacity ready, but frequently by that time demand had dried up — other firms had already expanded their operations and had taken an increased share of the market. If Western had properly forecasted demand and planned its capacity requirements a year or so in advance, it would have been able to maintain or perhaps even increase its market share.

Effective capital budgeting can improve both the timing of asset acquisitions and the quality of assets purchased. A firm which forecasts its needs for capital assets in advance will have an opportunity to purchase and install the assets before they are needed. Unfortunately, many firms do not order capital goods until they approach full capacity or are forced to replace worn-out equipment. If sales increase because of an increase in general market demand, all firms in the industry will tend to order capital goods at about the same time. This results in backlogs, long waiting times for machinery, a deterioration in the quality of the capital goods, and an increase in their prices. If a firm foresees its needs and purchases capital assets early, it can avoid these problems. Note, though, that if a firm forecasts an increase in demand and then expands to meet the anticipated demand, but sales then do not increase, it will be saddled with excess capacity and high costs. This can lead to losses or even bankruptcy. Thus, an accurate sales forecast is critical.

Finally, capital budgeting is also important because asset expansion typically involves substantial expenditures, and before a firm can spend a large amount of money, it must have the funds available—large amounts of money are not available automatically. Therefore, a firm contemplating a major capital expenditure program should arrange its financing several years in advance to be sure the funds required are available.

 Self-Test Questions

Why are capital budgeting decisions so important to the success of a firm?

Why is the sales forecast a key element in a capital budgeting decision?

GENERATING IDEAS FOR CAPITAL PROJECTS

The same general concepts that we developed for security analysis are involved in capital budgeting. However, whereas a set of stocks and bonds exists in the securities market, and investors select from this set, *capital budgeting projects are created by the firm.* For example, a sales representative may report that customers are asking for a particular product that the company does not now produce. The sales manager then discusses the idea with the marketing research group to determine the size of the market for the proposed product. If it appears likely that a significant market does exist, cost accountants and engineers will be asked to estimate production costs. If it appears that the product can be produced and sold at a sufficient profit, the project will be undertaken.

A firm's growth, and even its ability to remain competitive and to survive, depends upon a constant flow of ideas for new products, ways to make existing products better, and ways to produce output at a lower cost. Accordingly, a well-managed firm will go to great lengths to develop good capital budgeting proposals. For example, the executive vice president of one very successful corporation indicated that his company takes the following steps to generate projects:

strategic business plan
A long-run plan which outlines in broad terms the firm's basic strategy for the next 5 to 10 years.

Our R&D department is constantly searching for new products and also for ways to improve existing products. In addition, our executive committee, which consists of senior executives in marketing, production, and finance, identifies the products and markets in which our company will compete, and the committee sets long-run targets for each division. These targets, which are spelled out in the corporation's **strategic business plan,** provide a general guide to the operating executives who must meet them. These executives then seek new products, set expansion plans for existing products, and look for ways to reduce production and distribution costs. Since bonuses and promotions are based in large part on each unit's ability to meet or exceed its targets, these economic incentives encourage our operating executives to seek out profitable investment opportunities.

While our senior executives are judged and rewarded on the basis of how well their units perform, people further down the line are given bonuses for specific suggestions, including ideas that lead to profitable investments. Additionally, a percentage of our corporate profit is set aside for distribution to nonexecutive employees, and we have an Employees' Stock Ownership Plan (ESOP) to provide further incentives. Our objective is to encourage employees at all levels to keep on the lookout for good ideas, including those that lead to capital investments.

If a firm has capable and imaginative executives and employees, and if its incentive system is working properly, many ideas for capital investment will be advanced. Because some capital investment ideas will be good and others will not, procedures must be established for evaluating the worth of such projects to the firm. Our topic in the remainder of this chapter is the evaluation of the worth (acceptability) of capital projects.

 Self-Test Question

How does a firm get ideas for capital projects?

PROJECT CLASSIFICATIONS

Analyzing capital expenditure proposals is not a costless operation — benefits can be gained, but analysis does have a cost. For certain types of projects, a relatively detailed analysis may be warranted; for others, simpler procedures should be used. Accordingly, firms generally classify projects into the following categories, and they analyze projects in each category somewhat differently:

1. **Replacement: maintenance of business.** One category consists of expenditures to replace worn-out or damaged equipment used in the production of profitable products. These replacement projects are necessary if the operation is to continue, so the only issues here are (a) should we continue to produce these products or services, and (b) should we continue to use our existing production processes? The answers are usually "yes," so maintenance decisions are normally made without going through an elaborate decision process.

2. **Replacement: cost reduction.** This category includes expenditures to replace serviceable but obsolete equipment. The purpose here is to lower the costs of labor, materials, or other inputs such as electricity. These decisions are discretionary, and a more detailed analysis is generally required to support them.

3. **Expansion of existing products or markets.** Expenditures to increase output of existing products, or to expand outlets or distribution facilities in markets now being served, are included here. These decisions are more complex because they require an explicit forecast of growth in demand.

Mistakes are more likely, so a still more detailed analysis is required, and the final decision is made at a higher level within the firm.

4. **Expansion into new products or markets.** These are expenditures necessary to produce a new product or to expand into a geographic area not currently being served. These projects involve strategic decisions that could change the fundamental nature of the business, and they normally require the expenditure of large sums of money over long periods. Invariably, a very detailed analysis is required, and the final decision is generally made at the very top—by the board of directors as a part of the firm's strategic plan.

5. **Safety and/or environmental projects.** Expenditures necessary to comply with government orders, labor agreements, or insurance policy terms fall into this category. These expenditures are often called *mandatory investments,* or *nonrevenue-producing projects.* How they are handled depends on their size, with small ones being treated much like the Category 1 projects described above.

6. **Other.** This catch-all includes office buildings, parking lots, executive aircraft, and so on. How they are handled varies among companies.

In general, relatively simple calculations, and only a few supporting documents, are required for replacement decisions, especially maintenance-type investments in profitable plants. More detailed analysis is required for cost-reduction replacements, for expansion of existing product lines, and especially for investments in new products or areas. Also, within each category projects are broken down by their dollar costs: Larger investments require both more detailed analysis and approval at a higher level within the firm. Thus, although a plant manager may be authorized to approve maintenance expenditures up to $10,000 on the basis of a relatively unsophisticated analysis, the full board of directors may have to approve decisions which involve either amounts over $1 million or expansions into new products or markets. Statistical data are generally lacking for new product decisions, so here judgments, as opposed to detailed cost data, are especially important.

Self-Test Question

Identify and briefly explain how capital project classification categories are used.

SIMILARITIES BETWEEN CAPITAL BUDGETING AND SECURITY VALUATION

Conceptually, capital budgeting involves exactly the same six steps that are used in security analysis:

1. First, the cost of the project must be determined. This is similar to finding the price that must be paid for a stock or bond.

2. Next, management estimates the expected cash flows from the project, including the salvage value of the asset at the end of its expected life. This is

similar to estimating the future dividend or interest payment stream on a stock or bond, along with the stock's expected sales price or the bond's maturity value.

3. Third, the riskiness of the projected cash flows must be estimated. For this assessment, management needs information about the probability distributions of the cash flows.

4. Then, given the project's riskiness, management determines the appropriate cost of capital at which to discount cash flows.

5. Next, the expected cash inflows are put on a present value basis to obtain an estimate of the asset's value to the firm. This is equivalent to finding the present value of a stock's expected future dividends.

6. Finally, the present value of the expected cash inflows is compared with the required outlay, or cost; if the PV of the cash flows exceeds the cost, the project should be accepted. Otherwise, it should be rejected. Alternatively, the expected rate of return on the project can be calculated, and if this rate of return exceeds the project's cost of capital, the project should be accepted.

If an individual investor identifies and invests in a stock or bond whose market price is less than its true value, the value of the investor's portfolio will increase. Similarly, if a firm identifies (or creates) an investment opportunity with a present value greater than its cost, the value of the firm will increase. Thus, there is a very direct link between capital budgeting and stock values: The more effective the firm's capital budgeting procedures, the higher the price of its stock.

Self-Test Questions

List the six steps in the capital budgeting process, and compare them with the steps in security valuation.

Explain how capital budgeting is related to the wealth-maximization goal that should be pursued by the financial manager of a firm.

CAPITAL BUDGETING EVALUATION TECHNIQUES

Five primary methods are used to evaluate projects and to decide whether or not they should be accepted for inclusion in the capital budget: (1) payback, (2) discounted payback, (3) net present value (NPV), (4) internal rate of return (IRR), and (5) modified internal rate of return (MIRR). We will explain how each evaluation criterion is calculated, and then we will determine how well each performs in terms of identifying those projects which will maximize the firm's stock price.

We use the tabular and time line cash flow data shown in Figure 14-1 for Projects S and L to illustrate all the methods, and throughout this chapter we assume that the projects are equally risky. Note that the cash flows, CF_t, are expected values and that they have been adjusted to reflect taxes, depreciation, and salvage values. Further, since many projects require an investment in both fixed assets and working capital, the investment outlays shown as CF_0 include

Figure 14-1   ▪   **Net Cash Flows for Projects S and L**

Year (t)	Expected After-Tax Net Cash Flows, CF_t	
	Project S	**Project L**
0^a	($1,000)	($1,000)
1	500	100
2	400	300
3	300	400
4	100	600

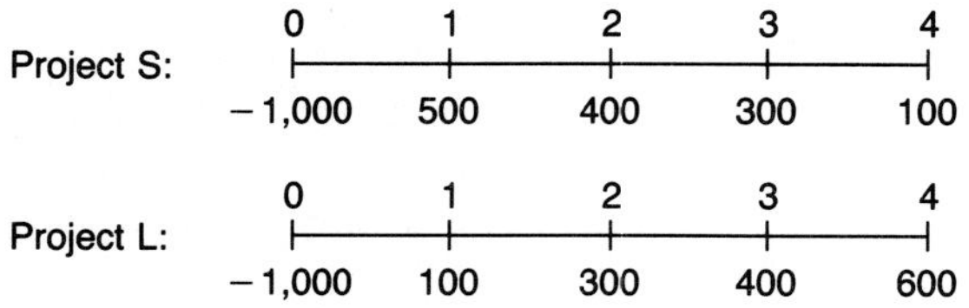

Project S:

```
     0      1      2      3      4
     ├──────┼──────┼──────┼──────┤
  -1,000   500    400    300    100
```

Project L:

```
     0      1      2      3      4
     ├──────┼──────┼──────┼──────┤
  -1,000   100    300    400    600
```

^{a}CF_0 represents the net investment outlay, or initial cost.

any necessary changes in net working capital.[1] Finally, we assume that all cash flows occur at the end of the designated year. Incidentally, the S stands for *short* and the L for *long:* Project S is a short-term project in the sense that its cash inflows tend to come in sooner than L's.

Payback Period

payback period
The length of time required for the net revenues of an investment to recover the cost of the investment.

The **payback period,** defined as the expected number of years required to recover the original investment, was the first formal method used to evaluate capital budgeting projects. The process is a simple one—sum the future cash flows for each year until the initial cost of the capital project is at least covered. The total amount of time, including the fraction of a year if appropriate, that it takes to recapture the original amount invested is the payback period. The payback calculation process for both Project S and Project L is diagrammed in Figure 14-2. Using your calculator, the payback for Project S can be calculated as described below.

1. Enter $CF_0 = -1000$ in your calculator. (You do not need to use the cash flow register—just have your display show -1000.)

2. Now add $CF_1 = 500$ to get the cumulative cash flow at the end of Year 1. This is -500.

---

[1]Perhaps the most difficult part of the capital budgeting process is the estimation of the relevant cash flows. For simplicity, the net cash flows are treated as a given in this chapter, which allows us to focus on our main area of concern, the capital budgeting evaluation techniques. However, in Chapter 15 we will discuss cash flow estimation in detail. Also, remember that *working capital* is defined as the firm's current assets and that *net working capital* is current assets minus current liabilities.

Figure 14-2 ▪ Projects S and L: Payback Period

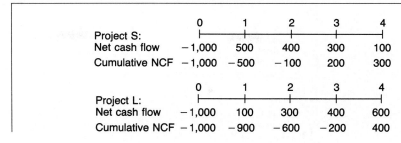

3. Next, add $CF_2 = 400$ to get the cumulative cash flow at the end of Year 2. This is -100.

4. Now add $CF_3 = 300$ to get the cumulative cash flow at the end of Year 3. This is $+200$.

5. You see that by the end of Year 3 the cumulative inflows have more than recovered the initial outflow. Thus, the payback occurred during the third year. If the $300 of inflows come in evenly during Year 3, then the exact payback can be found as follows:

$$Payback_s = \text{Year before full recovery} + \frac{\text{Unrecovered cost at start of year}}{\text{Cash flow during year}}$$

$$= 2 + \frac{100}{300} = 2.33 \text{ years.}$$

Applying the same procedure to Project L, we find $Payback_L = 3.33$ years.

The lower the payback the better. Therefore, if the firm required a payback of three years or less, Project S would be accepted, but Project L would be rejected. If the projects were **mutually exclusive,** S would be ranked over L because S has the shorter payback. *Mutually exclusive* means that if one project is taken on, the other must be rejected. For example, the installation of a conveyor-belt system in a warehouse and the purchase of a fleet of forklift trucks for the same warehouse would be mutually exclusive projects—accepting one implies rejection of the other. **Independent projects** are projects whose cash flows are not affected by one another, which means the acceptance of one project does not affect the acceptance of the other project.

mutually exclusive projects

A set of projects where only one can be accepted.

independent projects

Projects whose cash flows are not affected by the acceptance or nonacceptance of other projects.

discounted payback period

The length of time required for *discounted* cash flows to recover the cost of the investment.

Discounted Payback Period

Some firms use a variant of the regular payback, the **discounted payback period,** which is similar to the regular payback period except that the expected cash flows are discounted by the project's cost of capital. Thus, the discounted payback period is defined as the number of years required to recover the investment from *discounted* net cash flows. Figure 14-3 contains the discounted net cash flows for Projects S and L, assuming both projects have a cost of capital of 10 percent. To construct Figure 14-3, each cash inflow is divided by $(1 + k)^t = (1.10)^t$, where t is the year in which the cash flow occurs, and k is the project's cost of capital. After 3 years, Project S will have generated $1,011 in discounted cash inflows. Since the cost is $1,000, the discounted payback is

Figure 14-3 ▪ Projects S and L: Discounted Payback Period

	0	1	2	3	4
Project S:					
Net cash flow	−1,000	500	400	300	100
Discounted NCF	−1,000	455	331	225	68
Cumulative discounted NCF	−1,000	−545	−214	11	79
	0	1	2	3	4
Project L:					
Net cash flow	−1,000	100	300	400	600
Discounted NCF	−1,000	91	248	301	410
Cumulative discounted NCF	−1,000	−909	−661	−360	50

just under 3 years, or, to be precise, 2 + ($214/$225) = 2.95 years. Project L's discounted payback is 3.88 years:

$$\text{Discounted payback}_S = 2.0 + \$214/\$225 = 2.95 \text{ years.}$$

$$\text{Discounted payback}_L = 3.0 + \$360/\$410 = 3.88 \text{ years.}$$

For Projects S and L, the rankings are the same regardless of which payback method is used; that is, Project S is preferred to Project L, and Project S would still be selected if the firm were to require a discounted payback of three years or less. Often, however, the regular and the discounted paybacks produce conflicting rankings.

Note that the payback is a type of "breakeven" calculation in the sense that if cash flows come in at the expected rate until the payback year, then the project will break even. However, the regular payback does not take account of the cost of capital—no cost for the debt or equity used to undertake the project is reflected in the cash flows or the calculation. The discounted payback does take account of capital costs—it shows the breakeven year after covering debt and equity costs. Still, as we shall see, both payback methods have some serious deficiencies, and other procedures are less likely to lead to errors in project selection. Therefore, we will not dwell on the finer points of payback analysis.[2]

Although both payback methods have serious faults as project ranking criteria, they do provide information on how long funds will be tied up in a project. Thus, the shorter the payback period, other things held constant, the greater is the project's *liquidity*. Also, since cash flows expected in the distant future are generally regarded as being riskier than near-term cash flows, the payback is often used as one indicator of a project's *riskiness*. Unfortunately, neither payback method considers the cash flows beyond the payback period, and sometimes these cash flows are substantial.

---

[2]Another capital budgeting technique that was once used widely is the *accounting rate of return (ARR)*, which examines a project's contribution to the firm's net income. Although some companies still calculate an ARR, it really has no redeeming features, so we will not discuss it in this text. See Eugene F. Brigham and Louis C. Gapenski, *Intermediate Financial Management,* 4th Edition, Chapter 7. Yet another technique which we omit here is the *profitability index,* or *benefit/cost ratio.* Brigham and Gapenski also discuss this criterion and show that it is inferior to several other methods.

net present value (NPV) method

A method of evaluating capital investment proposals by finding the present value of future net cash flows, discounted at the firm's cost of capital or required rate of return.

discounted cash flow (DCF) techniques

Methods of evaluating investment proposals that employ time value of money concepts; two of these are the *net present value* and *internal rate of return* methods.

Net Present Value (NPV)

As the flaws in the payback and other early methods were recognized, people began to search for ways to improve the effectiveness of project evaluations. One such method is the **net present value (NPV) method,** which relies on **discounted cash flow (DCF) techniques.** To implement this approach, we proceed as follows:

1. Find the present value of each cash flow, including both inflows and outflows, discounted at the project's cost of capital.

2. Sum these discounted cash flows; this sum is defined as the project's NPV.

3. If the NPV is positive, the project should be accepted, while if the NPV is negative, it should be rejected. If two projects are mutually exclusive, the one with the higher NPV should be chosen, provided the NPV is positive.

The NPV can be expressed as follows:

$$NPV = CF_0 + \frac{CF_1}{(1 + k)^1} + \frac{CF_2}{(1 + k)^2} + \ldots + \frac{CF_n}{(1 + k)^n}$$

$$= \sum_{t=0}^{n} \frac{CF_t}{(1 + k)^t}. \qquad (14\text{-}1)$$

Here CF_t is the expected net cash flow at Period t, and k is the project's cost of capital. Cash outflows (expenditures on the project, such as the cost of buying equipment or building factories) are treated as *negative* cash flows. For our Projects S and L, only CF_0 is negative, but for many large projects such as the Alaska Pipeline, an electric generating plant, or General Motors's Saturn project, outflows occur for several years before operations begin and cash flows turn positive.

At a 10 percent cost of capital, Project S's NPV is $78.82:

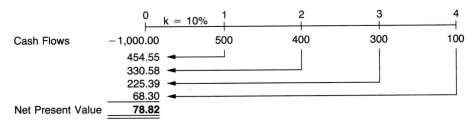

By a similar process, we find $NPV_L = \$49.18$. On this basis, both projects should be accepted if they are independent, but S should be the one chosen if they are mutually exclusive.

It is not hard to calculate the NPV as was done in the time line by using Equation 14-1 and a regular calculator, along with the interest rate tables. However, the most efficient way to find the NPV is with a financial calculator. Different calculators are set up somewhat differently, but they all have a section of memory called the "cash flow register" which is used for uneven cash flows such as those in Projects S and L (as opposed to equal annuity cash flows). A solution process for Equation 14-1 is literally programmed into financial calculators, and all you have to do is enter the cash flows (being sure to observe the signs), along with the value of k = I. At that point you have (in your calculator) this equation:

$$NPV_s = -1,000 + \frac{500}{(1.10)^1} + \frac{400}{(1.10)^2} + \frac{300}{(1.10)^3} + \frac{100}{(1.10)^4}.$$

Notice that the equation has one unknown, NPV. Now all you need to do is to ask the calculator to solve the equation for you, which you do by pressing the NPV key (and, on some calculators, the "compute" key). The answer, 78.82, will appear on the screen.[3]

Rationale for the NPV Method

The rationale for the NPV method is straightforward. An NPV of zero signifies that the project's cash flows are just sufficient to repay the invested capital and to provide the required rate of return on that capital. If a project has a positive NPV, then it is generating more cash than is needed to service its debt and to provide the required return to shareholders, and this excess cash accrues solely to the firm's stockholders. Therefore, if a firm takes on a project with a positive NPV, the position of the stockholders is improved. In our example, sharehold-

---

[3]The steps for two popular calculators, the HP 10B and the HP 17B, are shown below. If you have another type of financial calculator, see its manual.

HP 10B:

1. Clear the memory.
2. Enter CF_0 as follows: 1000 $\boxed{+/-}$ $\boxed{CF_j}$.
3. Enter CF_1 as follows: 500 $\boxed{CF_j}$.
4. Repeat the process to enter the other cash flows. Note that CF 0, CF 1, and so forth flash on the screen as you press the $\boxed{CF_j}$ key. If you hold the key down, CF 0 and so forth will remain on the screen until you release it.
5. Once the CFs have been entered, enter k = I = 10%: 10 $\boxed{I/YR}$.
6. Now that all of the inputs have been entered, you can press ▮ $\boxed{NPV}$ to get the answer, NPV = $78.82.
7. If a cash flow is repeated for several years, you can avoid having to enter the CFs for each year. For example, if the $500 cash flow for Year 1 had also been the CF for Years 2 through 10, making 10 of these $500 cash flows, then after entering 500 $\boxed{CF_j}$ the first time, you could enter 10 ▮ $\boxed{N_j}$. This would automatically enter 10 CFs of 500.

HP 17B:

1. Go to the cash flow (CFLO) menu, clear if FLOW(0) = ? does not appear on the screen.
2. Enter CF_0 as follows: 1000 $\boxed{+/-}$ $\boxed{INPUT}$.
3. Enter CF_1 as follows: 500 $\boxed{INPUT}$.
4. Now the calculator will ask you if the 500 is for Period 1 only or if it is also used for several following periods. Since it is only used for Period 1, press $\boxed{INPUT}$ to answer "1." Alternatively, you could press $\boxed{EXIT}$ and then $\boxed{\#T?}$ to turn off the prompt for the remainder of the problem. For some problems you will want to use the repeat feature.
5. Enter the remaining CFs, being sure to turn off the prompt or else to specify "1" for each entry.
6. Once the CFs have all been entered, press $\boxed{EXIT}$ and then $\boxed{CALC}$.
7. Now enter k = I = 10% as follows: 10 $\boxed{I\%}$.
8. Now press $\boxed{NPV}$ to get the answer, NPV = $78.82.

internal rate of return (IRR) method

A method of evaluating investment proposals using the rate of return on an asset investment, calculated by finding the discount rate that equates the present value of future cash inflows to the investment's cost.

IRR

The discount rate which forces the PV of a project's inflows to equal the PV of its costs. IRR is similar to the YTM on a bond.

ers' wealth would increase by $78.82 if the firm takes on Project S but by only $49.18 if it takes on Project L. Viewed in this manner, it is easy to see why S is preferred to L, and it is also easy to see the logic of the NPV approach.[4]

Internal Rate of Return (IRR)

In Chapter 6, we presented procedures for finding the yield to maturity, or rate of return, on a bond—if you invest in the bond and hold it to maturity, you can expect to earn the YTM on the money you invested. Exactly the same concepts are employed in capital budgeting when the **internal rate of return (IRR) method** is used. The **IRR** is defined as that discount rate which equates the present value of a project's expected cash inflows to the present value of its expected costs:

$$PV(\text{Inflows}) = PV(\text{Investment costs}),$$

or, equivalently,

$$CF_0 + \frac{CF_1}{(1 + IRR)^1} + \frac{CF_2}{(1 + IRR)^2} + \ldots + \frac{CF_n}{(1 + IRR)^n} = 0$$

$$\sum_{t=0}^{n} \frac{CF_t}{(1 + IRR)^t} = 0. \quad (14\text{-}2)$$

For our Project S, here is the time line setup:

	0 IRR	1	2	3	4
Cash Flows	−1,000	500	400	300	100
Sum of PVs for CF₁₋₄	1,000				
Net Present Value	0				

$$-1{,}000 + \frac{500}{(1 + IRR)^1} + \frac{400}{(1 + IRR)^2} + \frac{300}{(1 + IRR)^3} + \frac{100}{(1 + IRR)^4} = 0.$$

---

[4]This description of the process is somewhat oversimplified. Both analysts and investors anticipate that firms will identify and accept positive NPV projects, and current stock prices reflect these expectations. Thus, stock prices react to announcements of new capital projects only to the extent that such projects were not already expected. In this sense, we may think of a firm's value as consisting of two parts: (1) the value of its existing assets and (2) the value of its "growth opportunities," or projects with positive NPVs. AT&T is a good example of this: The company has the world's largest long-distance network plus telephone manufacturing facilities, both of which provide current earnings and cash flows, and it has Bell Labs, which has the *potential* for coming up with new products in the computer/telecommunications area that could be extremely profitable. Security analysts (and investors) thus analyze AT&T as a company with a set of cash-producing assets plus a set of growth opportunities that will materialize if and only if the company can come up with a number of positive NPV projects through its capital budgeting process.

Although it is easy to find the NPV without a financial calculator, this is *not* true of the IRR. If the cash flows are constant from year to year, then we have an annuity, and we can use annuity factors as discussed in Chapter 5 to find the IRR. However, if the cash flows are not constant, as is generally the case in capital budgeting, then it is difficult to find the IRR without a financial calculator. Without a calculator, you basically have to solve Equation 14-2 by trial and error — try some discount rate (or corresponding PVIF factors), and see if the equation solves to zero, and if it does not, try a different discount rate until you find one that forces the equation to equal zero. The discount rate that causes the equation to equal zero is defined as the IRR. For a realistic project with a fairly long life, the trial and error approach is a tedious, time-consuming task.

Fortunately, it is easy to find IRRs with a financial calculator. You follow almost identical procedures to those used to find the NPV. First, you enter the cash flows as shown on the preceding time line into the calculator's cash flow register. In effect, you have entered the cash flows into the equation shown below the time line. Note that we now have one unknown, IRR, or the discount rate which forces the equation to equal zero. The calculator has been programmed to solve for the IRR, and you activate this program by pressing the key labeled "IRR." Then the calculator solves for IRR and displays it on the screen. Here are the IRRs for Projects S and L as found with a financial calculator:[5]

$$IRR_S = 14.5\%$$
$$IRR_L = 11.8\%.$$

hurdle rate

The discount rate (cost of capital) which the IRR must exceed if a project is to be accepted.

If both projects have a 10 percent cost of capital, or **hurdle rate,** then the internal rate of return rule indicates that if the projects are independent, both should be accepted — they are both expected to earn more than the cost of the capital needed to finance them. If they are mutually exclusive, S ranks higher and should be accepted, while L should be rejected. If the cost of capital is above 14.5 percent, both projects should be rejected.

Notice that the internal rate of return formula, Equation 14-2, is simply the NPV formula, Equation 14-1, solved for the particular discount rate that forces the NPV to equal zero. Thus, the same basic equation is used for both methods, but in the NPV method the discount rate, k, is specified and the NPV is found, whereas in the IRR method the NPV is specified to equal zero, and the interest rate that forces this equality (the IRR) is determined.

Mathematically, the NPV and IRR methods will always lead to the same accept/reject decisions for independent projects: If a project's NPV is positive, its IRR will exceed k, while if NPV is negative, k will exceed the IRR. However, NPV and IRR can give conflicting rankings for mutually exclusive projects. This point will be discussed in more detail shortly.

---

[5]To find the IRR with an HP 10B or HP 17B, repeat the steps given in footnote 3. Then, with an HP 10B, press ▇ IRR/YR , and after a pause 14.49, Project S's IRR, will appear. With the HP 17B, simply press IRR% to get the IRR. With both calculators, you would always want to get both the NPV and the IRR after entering the input data, before clearing the cash flow register.

Rationale for the IRR Method

Why is the particular discount rate that equates a project's cost with the present value of its receipts so special? Because the IRR on a project is its expected rate of return, and if the internal rate of return exceeds the cost of the funds used to finance the project, a surplus remains after paying for the capital, and this surplus accrues to the firm's stockholders. Therefore, taking on a project whose IRR exceeds its cost of capital increases shareholders' wealth. On the other hand, if the internal rate of return is less than the cost of capital, then taking on the project imposes a cost on current stockholders. It is this "breakeven" characteristic that makes the IRR useful in evaluating capital projects.

Self-Test Questions

What four methods for evaluating capital budgeting proposals were discussed in this section?

Describe each method, and give the rationale for its use.

What two methods always lead to the same accept/reject decision for independent projects?

What two pieces of information does the payback provide that are not provided by the other methods?

COMPARISON OF THE NPV AND IRR METHODS

In many respects the NPV method is better than IRR, so it is tempting to explain NPV only, to state that it should be used to select projects, and to go on to the next topic. However, the IRR method is familiar to many corporate executives, it is widely entrenched in industry, and it does have some virtues. Therefore, it is important that finance students understand the IRR method and be prepared to explain why, at times, a project with a lower IRR may be preferable to one with a higher IRR.

NPV Profiles

net present value profile

A curve showing the relationship between a project's NPV and the cost of capital.

A graph which relates a project's NPV to the discount rate used to calculate the NPV is defined as the project's **net present value profile;** profiles for Projects L and S are shown in Figure 14-4. To construct the profiles, we first note that at a zero discount rate, the NPV is simply the total of the undiscounted cash flows of the project; thus, at a zero discount rate $NPV_S = \$300$, and $NPV_L = \$400$. These values are plotted as the vertical axis intercepts in Figure 14-4. Next, we calculate the projects' NPVs at three discount rates, say 5, 10, and 15 percent, and plot these values. The four points plotted on our graph for each project are shown at the bottom of the figure.[6]

---

[6]To calculate the points with a financial calculator, enter the cash flows into the cash flow register, enter k = I = 0, and press the NPV key to find the NPV at a zero cost of capital. Then enter k = I = 5 to override the zero, and press NPV to get the NPV at 5 percent. Repeat these steps for 10 and 15 percent.

Figure 14-4 ▪ **Net Present Value Profiles: NPVs of Projects S and L at Different Costs of Capital**

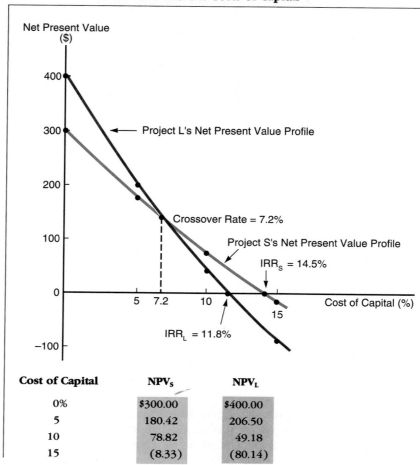

Cost of Capital	NPV$_S$	NPV$_L$
0%	$300.00	$400.00
5	180.42	206.50
10	78.82	49.18
15	(8.33)	(80.14)

Recall that the IRR is defined as the discount rate at which a project's NPV equals zero. Therefore, *the point where its net present value profile crosses the horizontal axis indicates a project's internal rate of return*. Since we calculated IRR$_S$ and IRR$_L$ in an earlier section, we have two other points which we can use in plotting the projects' NPV profiles.

When we connect the data points, we have the net present value profiles.[7] NPV profiles can be very useful in project analysis, and we will use them often in the remainder of the chapter.

----

[7]Notice that the NPV profiles are curved—they are *not* straight lines. Also, the NPVs approach the t = 0 cash flow (the cost of the project) as the discount rate increases without limit. The reason is that, at an infinitely high discount rate, the PV of the inflows would be zero, so NPV at (k = ∞) is CF$_0$, which in our example is − $1,000. We should also note that under certain conditions the NPV profiles can cross the horizontal axis several times or never cross it. This point is discussed later in the chapter.

NPV Rankings Depend on the Cost of Capital

crossover rate

The discount rate at which the NPV profiles of two projects cross and, thus, at which the projects' NPVs are equal.

We saw in Figure 14-4 that the NPV profiles of both Project L and Project S decline as the discount rate increases. But notice in the figure that Project L has the higher NPV at low discount rates, while NPV_S exceeds NPV_L if the discount rate is greater than the 7.2 percent **crossover rate.** Notice also that Project L's NPV is "more sensitive" to changes in the discount rate than is NPV_S; that is, Project L's net present value profile has the steeper slope, indicating that a given change in k has a larger effect on NPV_L than on NPV_S.

To see why L has the greater sensitivity, recall first that the cash flows from S are received faster than those from L—in a payback sense, S is a short-term project, while L is a long-term project. Next, recall the equation for the NPV:

$$NPV = \frac{CF_0}{(1 + k)^0} + \frac{CF_1}{(1 + k)^1} + \ldots + \frac{CF_n}{(1 + k)^n}.$$

The impact of an increase in the discount rate is much greater on distant than on near-term cash flows. To illustrate, consider the following:

$$\text{PV of \$100 after 1 year @ k = 5\%}: \frac{\$100}{(1.05)^1} = \$95.24.$$

$$\text{PV of \$100 after 1 year @ k = 10\%}: \frac{\$100}{(1.10)^1} = \$90.91.$$

$$\text{Percentage decline} = \frac{\$95.24 - \$90.91}{\$95.24} = 4.5\%.$$

$$\text{PV of \$100 after 20 years @ k = 5\%}: \frac{\$100}{(1.05)^{20}} = \$37.69.$$

$$\text{PV of \$100 after 20 years @ k = 10\%}: \frac{\$100}{(1.10)^{20}} = \$14.86.$$

$$\text{Percentage decline} = \frac{\$37.69 - \$14.86}{\$37.69} = 60.6\%.$$

Thus, a 5 percentage point increase in the discount rate causes only a 4.5 percent decline in the PV of a Year 1 cash flow, but the same 5 percentage point increase in the discount rate causes the PV of a Year 20 cash flow to fall by over 60 percent. Thus, if a project has most of its cash flows coming in the early years, its NPV will not be lowered very much if the cost of capital increases, but a project whose cash flows come later will be severely penalized by high capital costs. Accordingly, Project L, which has its largest cash flows in the later years, is hurt badly when the cost of capital is high, while Project S, which has relatively rapid cash flows, is affected less by high capital costs.

Independent Projects

If two projects are *independent,* then the NPV and IRR criteria always lead to the same accept/reject decision: if NPV says accept, IRR also says accept. To see why this is so, look back at Figure 14-4, focus on Project L's profile, and notice (1) that the IRR criterion for acceptance is that the cost of capital is less than (or to the left of) the IRR and (2) that whenever the cost of capital is less than the IRR, its NPV is positive. Thus, at any cost of capital less than 11.8 percent, Project L will be acceptable by both the NPV and the IRR criteria, while both methods reject the project if the cost of capital is greater than 11.8 percent. Project S—and all other independent projects under consideration—could be analyzed similarly, and it will always turn out that if the IRR method says accept, then so will the NPV method.

Mutually Exclusive Projects

Now assume that Projects S and L are *mutually exclusive* rather than independent. That is, we can choose either Project S or Project L, or we can reject both, but we cannot accept both projects. Notice in Figure 14-4 that as long as the cost of capital is *greater than* the crossover rate of 7.2 percent, NPV_S is larger than NPV_L, and IRR_S also exceeds IRR_L. Therefore, if k is *greater* than the crossover rate of 7.2 percent, the two methods lead to the selection of the same project. However, if the cost of capital is *less than* the crossover rate, the NPV method ranks Project L higher, but the IRR method says that Project S is better. *Thus, a conflict exists if the cost of capital is less than the crossover rate:* NPV says choose mutually exclusive L, while IRR says take S. Which answer is correct? Logic suggests that the NPV method is better since it selects the project that adds the most to shareholder wealth.[8]

There are two basic conditions which can cause NPV profiles to cross and thus which can lead to conflicts between NPV and IRR: (1) when *project size (or scale) differences* exist, meaning that the cost of one project is larger than that of the other, or (2) when *timing differences* exist, meaning that the timing of cash flows from the two projects differs such that most of the cash flows from one project come in the early years and most of the cash flows from the other project come in the later years, as occurred with Projects L and S.[9]

When either size or timing differences occur, the firm will have different amounts of funds to invest in the various years, depending on which of the two mutually exclusive projects it chooses. For example, if one project costs more than the other, then the firm will have more money at t = 0 to invest elsewhere if it selects the smaller project. Similarly, for projects of equal size, the one with the larger early cash inflows provides more funds for reinvestment in the early years. Given this situation, the rate of return at which differential cash flows can be invested is an important consideration.

The critical issue in resolving conflicts between mutually exclusive projects is this: How useful is it to generate cash flows earlier rather than later? The value of early cash flows depends on the rate at which we can reinvest these cash flows. *The NPV method implicitly assumes that the rate at which cash flows can be reinvested is the cost of capital, whereas the IRR method implies*

---

[8]The crossover rate is easy to calculate. Simply go back to Figure 14-1, where we set forth the two projects' cash flows, and calculate the difference in those cash flows in each year. The differences are $CF_S - CF_L$ = $0, + $400, + $100, − $100, and − $500, respectively. Enter these values into the cash flow register of a financial calculator, press the IRR key, and the crossover rate, $7.17 \approx 7.2$, appears. Be sure to enter $CF_0 = 0$.

[9]Of course, it is possible for mutually exclusive projects to differ with respect to both scale and timing. Also, if mutually exclusive projects have different lives (as opposed to different cash flow patterns over a common life), this introduces further complications, and for meaningful comparisons, some mutually exclusive projects must be evaluated over a common life. This point will be discussed in detail in Chapter 15.

that the firm has the opportunity to reinvest at the IRR. These assumptions are inherent in the mathematics of the discounting process. The cash flows may actually be withdrawn as dividends by the stockholders and spent on beer and pizza, but the NPV method still assumes that cash flows can be reinvested at the cost of capital, while the IRR method assumes reinvestment at the project's IRR.

Which is the better assumption—that cash flows can be reinvested at the cost of capital or that they can be reinvested at the project's IRR? It can be demonstrated that the best assumption is that projects' cash flows are reinvested at the cost of capital.[10] Therefore, we conclude that *the best **reinvestment rate assumption** is the cost of capital, which is implicit in the NPV method.* This, in turn, leads us to prefer the NPV method, at least for firms willing and able to obtain capital at a cost reasonably close to their current cost of capital.

We should reiterate that, when projects are *independent,* the NPV and IRR methods both make exactly the same accept/reject decision. However, *when evaluating mutually exclusive projects, especially those that differ in scale and/or timing, the NPV method should be used.*

Multiple IRRs

There is one other situation in which the IRR approach may not be usable—this is when nonnormal projects are involved. A project is *normal* if it has one or more cash outflows (costs) followed by a series of cash inflows. If, however, a project has a large cash outflow either sometime during or at the end of its life, then it is a *nonnormal* project. Nonnormal projects can present unique difficulties when evaluated by the IRR method, including the problem of **multiple IRRs.**

When one solves Equation 14-2 to find the IRR for a nonnormal project,

$$\sum_{t=0}^{n} \frac{CF_t}{(1 + IRR)^t} = 0, \qquad \textbf{(14-2)}$$

it is possible to obtain more than one value of IRR, which means that multiple IRRs occur. Notice that Equation 14-2 is a polynomial of degree n, so it has n different roots, or solutions. All except one of the roots are imaginary numbers when investments are normal (one or more cash outflows followed by cash inflows), so in the normal case, only one value of IRR appears. However, the possibility of multiple real roots, hence multiple IRRs, arises when the project is nonnormal (negative net cash flows occur during some year after the project has been placed in operation). Each time there is an interruption in the direction of the cash flows associated with the implementation of the project, there will be an IRR solution. For example, the normal cash flow pattern only has one net cash outflow at the beginning of the project's life, so the direction of the cash flows changes (is interrupted) once from negative (outflow) to positive (inflow), and there is only one IRR solution. A project that requires two net cash outflows in nonconsecutive years after the project is in operation will have three IRR solutions because the cash flow pattern has three direction changes, or interruptions, one after the initial cost is paid and two others caused by the net cash outflows required later in the life of the project.

reinvestment rate assumption

The assumption that cash flows from a project can be reinvested (1) at the cost of capital, if using the NPV method, or (2) at the internal rate of return, if using the IRR method.

multiple IRRs

The situation where a project has two or more IRRs.

---

[10]Again, see Eugene F. Brigham and Louis C. Gapenski, *Intermediate Financial Management,* 4th ed., Chapter 7, for a demonstration of this point.

To illustrate this problem, suppose a firm is considering the expenditure of $1.6 million to develop a strip mine (Project M). The mine will produce a cash flow of $10 million at the end of Year 1. Then, at the end of Year 2, $10 million must be expended to restore the land to its original condition. Therefore, the project's expected net cash flows are as follows (in millions of dollars):

Expected Net Cash Flows

Year 0	End of Year 1	End of Year 2
− $1.6	+ $10	− $10

These values can be substituted into Equation 14-2 to derive the IRR for the investment:

$$\text{NPV} = \frac{-\$1.6 \text{ million}}{(1 + \text{IRR})^0} + \frac{\$10 \text{ million}}{(1 + \text{IRR})^1} + \frac{-\$10 \text{ million}}{(1 + \text{IRR})^2} = 0.$$

When solved, we find that NPV = 0 when IRR = 25% and also when IRR = 400%.[11] Therefore, the IRR of the investment is both 25 and 400 percent. This relationship is depicted graphically in Figure 14-5.[12] Note that no dilemma would arise if the NPV method were used; we would simply use Equation 14-1, find the NPV, and use this to evaluate the project. If Project M's cost of capital is 10 percent, then its NPV is − $0.77 million, and the project should be rejected. If k were between 25 and 400 percent, the NPV would be positive.

The authors encountered another example of multiple internal rates of return when a major California bank *borrowed* funds from an insurance company and then used these funds (plus an initial investment of its own) to buy a number of jet engines, which it then leased to a major airline. The bank expected to receive positive net cash flows (lease payments plus tax savings minus interest on the insurance company loan) for a number of years, then several large negative cash flows as it repaid the insurance company loan, and, finally, a large inflow from the sale of the engines when the lease expired.

The bank discovered two IRRs and wondered which was correct. It could not ignore the IRR and use the NPV method since the lease was already on the

---

[11]If you attempted to find the IRR of Project M with many financial calculators, you would get an error message. However, you could still find Project M's IRRs by first calculating NPVs using several different values for k and then plotting the NPV profile. The intersections with the X-axis give a rough idea of the IRR values, and you could then use trial and error to find the exact values of k which force NPV = 0.

Note, too, that some calculators, including the HP 10B and 17B, can find the IRR. Rather than giving you an error message, they tell you to enter a guess. If you enter as your guess a cost of capital less than the one at which the NPV in Figure 14-5 is maximized (about 100%), the lower IRR, 25%, is displayed. If you guess a higher rate, the upper IRR is given.

[12]Does Figure 14-5 suggest that the firm should try to *raise* its cost of capital to about 100 percent in order to maximize the NPV of the project? Certainly not. The firm should seek to *minimize* its cost of capital; this will cause the price of its stock to be maximized. Actions taken to raise the cost of capital might make this particular project look good, but those actions would be terribly harmful to the firm's more numerous normal projects. Only if the firm's cost of capital is high, in spite of efforts to keep it down, will the illustrative project have a positive NPV.

Figure 14-5 ▪ **NPV Profile for Project M**

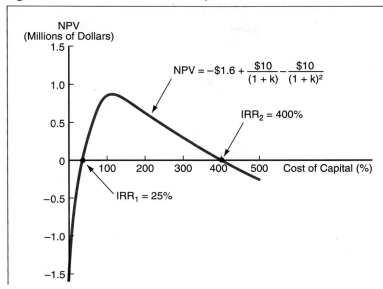

$$NPV = -\$1.6 + \frac{\$10}{(1+k)} - \frac{\$10}{(1+k)^2}$$

$IRR_2 = 400\%$

$IRR_1 = 25\%$

books, and the bank's senior loan committee, as well as Federal Reserve bank examiners, wanted to know the return on the lease. The bank asked the authors for help, and our recommended solution called for calculating and then using the "modified internal rate of return," as discussed in the next section.

The examples just presented illustrate one problem, multiple IRRs, that can arise when the IRR criterion is used with a project that has nonnormal cash flows. Use of the IRR method on nonnormal cash flow projects could produce other problems such as no IRR or an IRR which leads to an incorrect accept/ reject decision. In all such cases, the NPV criterion could be easily applied, and the NPV leads to conceptually correct capital budgeting decisions.

Self-Test Questions

Describe how NPV profiles are constructed.

What is the crossover rate, and how does it affect the choice between mutually exclusive projects?

What are the two basic conditions that can lead to conflicts between the NPV and IRR methods?

What is the underlying cause of conflicts between the NPV and IRR methods?

If a conflict exists, should the capital budgeting decision be made on the basis of the NPV or the IRR ranking? Why?

Explain the difference between normal and nonnormal projects.

What is the "multiple IRR problem," and what condition is necessary for its occurrence?

MODIFIED INTERNAL RATE OF RETURN (MIRR)

modified IRR (MIRR)
The discount rate at which the present value of a project's cost is equal to the present value of its terminal value, where the terminal value is found as the sum of the future values of the cash inflows, compounded at the firm's cost of capital.

In spite of a strong academic preference for NPV, surveys indicate that business executives prefer IRR over NPV by a margin of 3 to 1. Apparently, managers find it intuitively more appealing to analyze investments in terms of percentage rates of return than dollars of NPV. Given this fact, can we devise a percentage evaluator that is better than the regular IRR? The answer is yes—we can modify the IRR and make it a better indicator of relative profitability, hence better for use in capital budgeting. The new measure is called the **modified IRR,** or **MIRR,** and it is defined as follows:

$$\text{PV costs} = \text{PV terminal value}$$

$$\sum_{t=0}^{n} \frac{\text{COF}_t}{(1+k)^t} = \frac{\sum_{t=0}^{n} \text{CIF}_t (1+k)^{n-t}}{(1+\text{MIRR})^n}$$

$$\text{PV costs} = \frac{\text{TV}}{(1+\text{MIRR})^n}. \tag{14-2a}$$

Here COF refers to cash outflows (negative numbers), or the cost of the project, and CIF refers to cash inflows (all positive numbers). The left term is simply the PV of the investment outlays when discounted at the cost of capital, and the numerator of the right term is the future value of the inflows, assuming that the cash inflows are reinvested at the cost of capital. The future value of the cash inflows is also called the *terminal value,* or *TV.* The discount rate that forces the PV of the TV to equal the PV of the costs is defined as the MIRR.[13]

If the investment costs are all incurred at t = 0, and if the first operating inflow occurs at t = 1, as is true for our illustrative Projects S and L which we first presented in Figure 14-1, then this equation may be used:

$$\text{Cost} = \frac{\text{TV}}{(1+\text{MIRR})^n} = \frac{\sum_{t=1}^{n} \text{CIF}_t (1+k)^{n-t}}{(1+\text{MIRR})^n}. \tag{14-2b}$$

We can illustrate the calculation with Project S:

[13]There are several alternative definitions for the MIRR. The differences relate primarily to whether negative cash flows which occur after positive cash flows begin should be compounded and treated as part of the TV or discounted and treated as a cost. Our definition (which treats all negative cash flows as investments and thus discounts them) is generally the most appropriate procedure. For a complete discussion, see William R. McDaniel, Daniel E. McCarty, and Kenneth A. Jessell, "Discounted Cash Flow with Explicit Reinvestment Rates: Tutorial and Extension," *The Financial Review,* August 1988, 369–385.

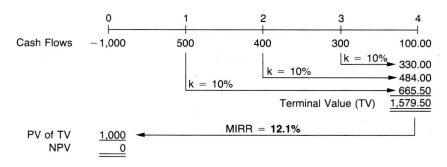

Using the cash flows as set out on the time line, first find the terminal value by compounding each cash inflow at the 10 percent cost of capital. Then, enter PV = −1000, FV = 1579.5, and N = 4, and press the I key to find $MIRR_S$ = 12.1%. Similarly, we find $MIRR_L$ = 11.3%.

The modified IRR has a significant advantage over the regular IRR. MIRR assumes that cash flows are reinvested at the cost of capital, while the regular IRR assumes that cash flows are reinvested at the project's own IRR. Since reinvestment at the cost of capital is generally more correct, the modified IRR is a better indicator of a project's true profitability. MIRR also solves the multiple IRR problem. To illustrate, with k = 10%, Project M (the strip mine project) has MIRR = 5.6% versus the 10 percent cost of capital, so it should be rejected. This is consistent with the decision based on the NPV method because at k = 10%, NPV = − $0.77 million.

Is MIRR as good as NPV for choosing between mutually exclusive projects? If two projects are of equal size and have the same life, then NPV and MIRR will always lead to the same project selection decision. Thus, for any projects like our Projects S and L, if NPV_S > NPV_L, then $MIRR_S$ > $MIRR_L$, and the kinds of conflicts we encountered between NPV and the regular IRR will not occur. Also, if the projects are of equal size, but differ in lives, the MIRR will always lead to the same decision as the NPV if the MIRRs are both calculated using as the terminal year the life of the longer project. (Just fill in zeros for the shorter project's missing cash flows.) However, if the projects differ in size, then conflicts can still occur. For example, if we were choosing between a large project and a small mutually exclusive one, then we might find NPV_L > NPV_S, but $MIRR_S$ > $MIRR_L$.

Our conclusion is that the modified IRR is superior to the regular IRR as an indicator of a project's "true" rate of return, or "expected long-term rate of return," but the NPV method is still better for choosing among competing projects that differ in size because it provides a better indicator of the extent to which each project will increase the value of the firm.

Self-Test Questions

Briefly describe how the modified IRR (MIRR) is calculated.

What is the primary difference between the MIRR and the regular IRR?

What advantages does the MIRR have over the regular IRR?

What condition can cause the MIRR and NPV methods to produce conflicting rankings?

CONCLUSIONS ON THE CAPITAL BUDGETING DECISION METHODS

We have discussed five capital budgeting decision methods in this chapter. In this discussion, we compared the methods against one another to highlight their relative strengths and weaknesses, and in the process we probably created the impression that "sophisticated" firms should use only one method in the decision process, NPV. However, virtually all capital budgeting decisions are analyzed by computer, so it is easy to calculate and list all the decision measures: payback, discounted payback, NPV, IRR, and modified IRR (MIRR). In making the accept/reject decision, most large, sophisticated firms such as IBM, GE, and General Motors calculate and consider all five measures because each provides decision makers with a somewhat different piece of relevant information.

Payback and discounted payback provide an indication of both the *risk* and the *liquidity* of a project—a long payback means (1) that the investment dollars will be locked up for many years, hence the project is relatively illiquid, and (2) that the project's cash flows must be forecast far out into the future, hence the project is probably quite risky. A good analogy for this is the bond valuation process. An investor should never compare the yields to maturity on two bonds without considering their terms to maturity because a bond's riskiness is significantly influenced by its maturity.

NPV is important because it gives a direct measure of the dollar benefit (on a present value basis) to the firm's shareholders, so we regard NPV as the best single measure of *profitability*. IRR also measures profitability, but here it is expressed as a percentage rate of return, which many decision makers, especially nonfinancial managers, seem to prefer. Further, IRR contains information concerning a project's "safety margin" which is not inherent in NPV. To illustrate, consider the following two projects: Project S (for small) costs $10,000 at t = 0 and is expected to return $16,500 at the end of 1 year, while Project L (for large) costs $100,000 and has an expected payoff of $115,500 after 1 year. At a 10 percent cost of capital, both projects have an NPV of $5,000, so by the NPV rule we should be indifferent between the two. However, Project S actually provides a much larger margin for error. Even if its realized cash inflow were almost 40 percent below the $16,500 forecast, the firm would still recover its $10,000 investment. On the other hand, if Project L's inflows fell by only 14 percent from the forecasted $115,500, the firm would not recover its investment. Further, if no inflows were generated at all, the firm would lose only $10,000 with Project S but $100,000 if it took on Project L.

The NPV contains no information about either the "safety margin" inherent in a project's cash flow forecasts or the amount of capital at risk, but the IRR does provide "safety margin" information—Project S's IRR is a whopping 65.0 percent, while Project L's IRR is only 15.5 percent. As a result, the realized return could fall substantially for Project S, and it would still make money. Note, though, that the modified IRR has all the virtues of the IRR, but it also incorporates the correct reinvestment rate assumption, and it avoids the multiple rate of return problem.

In summary, the different methods provide different types of information to decision makers. Since it is easy to calculate them, all should be considered in the decision process. For any specific decision, more weight might be given to one method than another, but it would be foolish to ignore the information provided by any of the methods.

Self-Test Questions

Describe the advantages and disadvantages of the five capital budgeting methods.

Should capital budgeting decisions be made solely on the basis of a project's NPV?

THE POST-AUDIT

post-audit

A comparison of the actual and expected results for a given capital project.

An important aspect of the capital budgeting process is the **post-audit,** which involves (1) comparing actual results with those predicted by the project's sponsors and (2) explaining why any differences occurred. For example, many firms require that the operating divisions send a monthly report for the first six months after a project goes into operation, and a quarterly report thereafter, until the project's results are up to expectations. From then on, reports on the project are handled like those of other operations.

The post-audit has two main purposes:

1. **Improve forecasts.** When decision makers are forced to compare their projections to actual outcomes, there is a tendency for estimates to improve. Conscious or unconscious biases are observed and eliminated; new forecasting methods are sought as the need for them becomes apparent; and people simply tend to do everything better, including forecasting, if they know that their actions are being monitored.

2. **Improve operations.** Businesses are run by people, and people can perform at higher or lower levels of efficiency. When a divisional team has made a forecast about an investment, its members are, in a sense, putting their reputations on the line. If costs are above predicted levels, sales below expectations, and so on, executives in production, marketing, and other areas will strive to improve operations and to bring results into line with forecasts. In a discussion related to this point, an IBM executive made this statement: "You academicians worry only about making good decisions. In business, we also worry about making decisions good."

The post-audit is not a simple process—a number of factors can cause complications. First, we must recognize that each element of the cash flow forecast is subject to uncertainty, so a percentage of all projects undertaken by any reasonably venturesome firm will necessarily go awry. This fact must be considered when appraising the performances of the operating executives who submit capital expenditure requests. Second, projects sometimes fail to meet expectations for reasons beyond the control of the operating executives and for reasons that no one could realistically be expected to anticipate. For example, the 1990–1992 recession adversely affected many projects. Third, it is often difficult to separate the operating results of one investment from those of a larger system. Although some projects stand alone and permit ready identification of costs and revenues, the actual cost savings that result from a new computer system, for example, may be very hard to measure. Fourth, it is often hard to hand out blame or praise because the executives who were actually responsible for a given decision may have moved on by the time the results of a long-term investment are known.

Because of these difficulties, some firms tend to play down the importance of the post-audit. However, observations of both businesses and governmental units suggest that the best-run and most successful organizations are the ones that put the greatest emphasis on post-audits. Accordingly, we regard the post-audit as being one of the most important elements in a good capital budgeting system.

 Self-Test Questions

What is done in the post-audit?

Identify several purposes of the post-audit.

What are some factors which can cause complications in the post-audit?

SMALL BUSINESS   Capital Budgeting in the Small Firm

The allocation of capital in small firms is as important as it is in large ones. In fact, given their lack of access to the capital markets, it is often more important in the small firm because the funds necessary to correct mistakes may not be available. Also, large firms with capital budgets of $100 million or more allocate capital to numerous projects, so a mistake on one project can be offset by successes with others.

In spite of the importance of capital expenditures to small business, studies of the way capital budgeting decisions are made generally suggest that many small firms use "back-of-the-envelope" analysis, or perhaps no analysis at all. For example, when L. R. Runyon studied 214 firms with net worths of from $500,000 to $1,000,000, he found that almost 70 percent relied upon either payback or some other questionable criteria; only 14 percent used a discounted cash flow analysis; and about 9 percent indicated that they used no formal analysis at all.[14] Studies of larger firms, on the other hand, generally find that most analyze capital budgeting decisions using discounted cash flow techniques.

We are left with a puzzle. Capital budgeting is clearly important to small firms, yet these firms tend not to use the tools that have been developed to im-

prove capital budgeting decisions. Why does this situation exist? One argument is that managers of small firms are simply not well trained; they are unsophisticated. This argument suggests that the managers would make greater use of sophisticated techniques if they understood them better.

Another argument relates to the fact that management talent is a scarce resource in small firms. That is, even if the managers were exceptionally sophisticated, the demands on their time may be such that they simply cannot take the time to use elaborate techniques to analyze proposed projects. In other words, small business managers may be capable of doing careful discounted cash flow analysis, but it would be irrational for them to take the time required for such an analysis.

A third argument relates to the cost of analyzing capital projects. To some extent, these costs are fixed; the costs may be larger for bigger projects, but not by much. To the extent that the costs of analysis are indeed fixed, it may not be economical to incur them if the project itself is relatively small. This argument suggests that small firms with small projects may actually be making the sensible decision when they rely upon management's "gut feeling."

Note also that a major part of the capital budgeting process in large firms involves having lower level analysts marshal facts needed by higher-level decision

[14]L. R. Runyon, "Capital Expenditure Decision Making in Small Firms," *Journal of Business Research*, September 1983, 389–397.

makers. This step may not be necessary in the small firm.

Thus, a cursory examination of a small firm's decision process might suggest that capital budgeting decisions are based on snap judgment, but if that judgment is exercised by someone with a total knowledge of the firm and its markets, it could represent a better decision than one based on an elaborate analysis by a lower-level analyst in a large firm.

Also, as Runyon reported in his study, small firms tend to be cash oriented. They are concerned with basic survival, so they tend to look at expenditures from the standpoint of near-term effects on cash. This cash and survival orientation leads to a focus on a relatively short time horizon, and this, in turn, may lead to an emphasis on the payback method. The limitations of payback are well known, but in spite of those limitations, the technique is popular in small business, as it gives the firm a "feel" for when the cash committed to an investment will be recovered and thus be available to repay loans or for new opportunities. Therefore, small firms that are cash oriented and have limited managerial resources may find the payback method an appealing compromise between the need for extensive analysis on the one hand and the high costs of analysis on the other.

Small firms also face greater uncertainty in the cash flows they might generate beyond the immediate future. Large firms such as IBM have "staying power" —they can make an investment and then ride out business downturns or situations of excess capacity in an industry. Such periods are called "shakeouts," and it is the smaller firms that are generally shaken out. Therefore, most small business managers are uncomfortable making forecasts beyond a few years. Since discounted cash flow techniques require explicit estimates of cash flows through the life of the project, small business managers may not take seriously an analysis that hinges on "guesstimate" numbers which, if wrong, could lead to bankruptcy.

The Value of the Firm and Capital Budgeting.
The single most appealing argument for the use of net present value in capital expenditure decisions is that NPV gives an explicit measure of the effect of the investment on the value of the firm: if NPV is positive, the investment will increase the value of the firm and make its owners wealthier. In small firms, however,

the stock is often not traded in public markets, so its value cannot be observed. Also, for reasons of control many small business owners and managers may not want to broaden ownership by going public.

It is difficult to argue for value-based techniques when the value of the firm itself is unobservable. Furthermore, in a closely held firm the objectives of the individual owner-manager may extend beyond the firm's monetary value. For example, the owner-manager may value his or her firm's reputation for quality and service and therefore may make an investment that would be rejected on purely economic grounds. In addition, the owner-manager may not hold a well-diversified investment portfolio but may instead have all of his or her eggs in this one basket. In that case, the manager would logically be sensitive to the total risk of the firm, not just to its systematic or undiversifiable component. Thus, one project might be viewed as desirable because of its contribution to risk reduction in the firm as a whole, whereas another project with a low beta but high unsystematic risk might be unacceptable, even though in a CAPM framework it would be judged superior.

Another problem faced by a firm that is not publicly traded is that its cost of equity capital is not easily determined—the P_0 term in the cost of equity equation $k = D_1/P_0 + g$ is not observable, nor is its beta. Since a cost of capital estimate is required to use either the NPV or the IRR method, a small firm in an industry of small firms may simply have no good basis for estimating its cost of capital.

Conclusions.   Small firms make less extensive use of DCF techniques than larger firms. This may be a rational decision resulting from a conscious or subconscious conclusion that the costs of sophisticated analyses outweigh their benefits; it may reflect nonmonetary goals of small businesses' owner-managers; or it may reflect difficulties in estimating the cost of capital, which is required for DCF analyses but not for payback. However, nonuse of DCF methods may also reflect a weakness in many small business organizations. We simply do not know. We do know that small businesses must do all they can to compete effectively with big business, and to the extent that a small business fails to use DCF methods because its manager is unsophisticated or uninformed, it may be putting itself at a serious competitive disadvantage.

SUMMARY

This chapter discussed the capital budgeting process, and the key concepts covered are listed below.

- **Capital budgeting** is the process of analyzing potential fixed asset investments. Capital budgeting decisions are probably the most important ones financial managers must make.

- The **payback period** is defined as the expected number of years required to recover a project's cost. The regular payback method ignores cash flows beyond the payback period, and it does not consider the time value of money. The payback does, however, provide an indication of a project's risk and liquidity because it shows how long the invested capital will be "at risk."

- The **discounted payback method** is similar to the regular payback method except that it discounts cash flows at the project's cost of capital. Like the regular payback, it ignores cash flows beyond the discounted payback period.

- The **net present value (NPV) method** discounts all cash flows at the project's cost of capital and then sums those cash flows. The project is accepted if this sum, called the NPV, is positive.

- The **internal rate of return (IRR)** is defined as the discount rate which forces a project's NPV to equal zero. The project is accepted if the IRR is greater than the project's cost of capital.

- The NPV and IRR methods make the same accept/reject decisions for **independent projects,** but if projects are **mutually exclusive,** then ranking conflicts can arise. If conflicts arise, the NPV method should generally be used. The NPV and IRR methods are both superior to the payback, but NPV is generally the single best measure of a project's profitability.

- The NPV method assumes that cash flows can be reinvested at the firm's cost of capital, while the IRR method assumes reinvestment at the project's IRR. Because **reinvestment at the cost of capital is generally a better (closer to the truth) assumption,** the NPV is superior to the IRR.

- The **modified IRR (MIRR) method** corrects some of the problems with the regular IRR. MIRR involves finding the terminal value (TV) of the cash inflows, compounded at the firm's cost of capital, and then determining the rate (MIRR) which forces the present value of the TV to equal the present value of the outflows.

- Sophisticated managers consider all five of the project evaluation measures because the different measures provide different types of information.

- The **post-audit** is a key element of capital budgeting. By comparing actual results with predicted results, and then determining why differences occurred, decision makers can improve both their operations and their forecasts of projects' outcomes.

- Small firms tend to use the payback method rather than a "sophisticated" method. This may be a rational decision because (1) the **cost** of a DCF analysis **may outweigh the benefits** for the project being considered,

(2) **the firm's cost of capital cannot be estimated accurately**, or
(3) the small business owner may be considering **nonmonetary goals.**

Although this chapter has presented the basic elements of the capital budgeting process, there are many other aspects of this crucial topic. Some of the more important ones are discussed in the following chapter.

Questions

14-1   How is a project classification scheme (for example, replacement, expansion into new markets, and so forth) used in the capital budgeting process?

14-2   Explain why the NPV of a relatively long-term project, defined as one for which a high percentage of its cash flows are expected in the distant future, is more sensitive to changes in the cost of capital than is the NPV of a short-term project.

14-3   Explain why, if two mutually exclusive projects are being compared, the short-term project might have the higher ranking under the NPV criterion if the cost of capital is high, but the long-term project might be deemed better if the cost of capital is low. Would changes in the cost of capital ever cause a change in the IRR ranking of two such projects?

14-4   In what sense is a reinvestment rate assumption embodied in the NPV, IRR, and MIRR methods? What is the assumed reinvestment rate of each method?

14-5   "If a firm has no mutually exclusive projects, only independent ones, and it also has both a constant cost of capital and normal projects in the sense that each project has one or more outflows followed by a stream of inflows, then the NPV and IRR methods will always lead to identical capital budgeting decisions." Discuss this statement. What does it imply about using the IRR method in lieu of the NPV method? If each of the assumptions made in the question were changed (one by one), how would these changes affect your answer?

14-6   Are there conditions under which a firm might be better off if it were to choose a machine with a rapid payback rather than one with a larger NPV?

14-7   A firm has $100 million available for capital expenditures. It is considering investing in one of two projects; each has a cost of $100 million. Project A has an IRR of 20 percent and an NPV of $9 million. It will be terminated at the end of one year at a profit of $20 million, resulting in an immediate increase in earnings per share (EPS). Project B, which cannot be postponed, has an IRR of 30 percent and an NPV of $50 million. However, the firm's short-run EPS will be reduced if it accepts Project B because no revenues will be generated for several years.
a.   Should the short-run effects on EPS influence the choice between the two projects?
b.   How might situations like the one described here influence a firm's decision to use payback as a part of the capital budgeting process?

Self-Test Problems   *(Solutions Appear in Appendix B)*

ST-1   Define each of the following terms:
Key terms   a.   The capital budget; capital budgeting; strategic business plan
b.   Regular payback period; discounted payback period
c.   Independent projects; mutually exclusive projects
d.   DCF techniques; net present value (NPV) method
e.   Internal rate of return (IRR) method; IRR
f.   Modified internal rate of return (MIRR) method
g.   NPV profile; crossover rate

    h. Nonnormal projects; multiple IRRs
    i. Hurdle rate
    j. Reinvestment rate assumption
    k. Post-audit

ST-2

Project analysis

You are a financial analyst for Damon Electronics Company. The director of capital budgeting has asked you to analyze two proposed capital investments, Projects X and Y. Each project has a cost of $10,000, and the cost of capital for each project is 12 percent. The projects' expected net cash flows are as follows:

	Expected Net Cash Flows	
Year	Project X	Project Y
0	($10,000)	($10,000)
1	6,500	3,500
2	3,000	3,500
3	3,000	3,500
4	1,000	3,500

    a. Calculate each project's payback period, net present value (NPV), internal rate of return (IRR), and modified internal rate of return (MIRR).
    b. Which project or projects should be accepted if they are independent?
    c. Which project should be accepted if they are mutually exclusive?
    d. How might a change in the cost of capital produce a conflict between the NPV and IRR rankings of these two projects? Would this conflict exist if k were 5%? (Hint: Plot the NPV profiles.)
    e. Why does the conflict exist?

Problems

14-1

Payback, NPV, IRR, and
MIRR calculations

Project K has a cost of $52,125, and its expected net cash inflows are $12,000 per year for 8 years.
    a. What is the project's payback period (to the closest year)?
    b. The cost of capital is 12 percent. What is the project's NPV?
    c. What is the project's IRR? (Hint: Recognize that the project is an annuity.)
    d. What is the project's discounted payback period, assuming a 12 percent cost of capital?
    e. Calculate the project's MIRR assuming a 12 percent cost of capital.

14-2

NPV and IRR analysis

Petry Products Company is considering two mutually exclusive investments. The projects' expected net cash flows are as follows:

	Expected Net Cash Flows	
Year	Project A	Project B
0	($300)	($405)
1	(387)	134
2	(193)	134
3	(100)	134
4	600	134
5	600	134
6	850	134
7	(180)	0

a. Construct NPV profiles for Projects A and B.

b. What is each project's IRR?

c. If you were told that each project's cost of capital was 12 percent, which project should be selected? If the cost of capital was 18 percent, what would the proper choice be?

d. What is each project's MIRR at a cost of capital of 12 percent? At k = 18%? (Hint: Consider Period 7 as the end of Project B's life.)

e. Looking at the NPV profiles constructed in Part a, what is the approximate crossover rate, and what is its significance?

14-3
Timing differences

The Southwestern Oil Exploration Company is considering two mutually exclusive plans for extracting oil on property for which it has mineral rights. Both plans call for the expenditure of $12,000,000 to drill development wells. Under Plan A, all the oil will be extracted in one year, producing a cash flow at t = 1 of $14,400,000. Under Plan B, cash flows will be $2,100,000 per year for 20 years.

a. Construct NPV profiles for Plans A and B, identify each project's IRR, and indicate the approximate crossover rate of return.

b. Suppose a company has a cost of capital of 12 percent, and it can get unlimited capital at that cost. Is it logical to assume that it would take on all available independent projects (of average risk) with returns greater than 12 percent? Further, if all available projects with returns greater than 12 percent have been taken on, would this mean that cash flows from past investments would have an opportunity cost of only 12 percent, because all the firm could do with these cash flows would be to replace money that has a cost of 12 percent? Finally, does this imply that the cost of capital is the correct rate to assume for the reinvestment of a project's cash flows?

14-4
Scale differences

The Chaplinsky Publishing Company is considering two mutually exclusive expansion plans. Plan A calls for the expenditure of $40 million on a large-scale, integrated plant which will provide an expected cash flow stream of $6.4 million per year for 20 years. Plan B calls for the expenditure of $12 million to build a somewhat less efficient, more labor-intensive plant which has an expected cash flow stream of $2.72 million per year for 20 years. Chaplinsky's cost of capital is 10 percent.

a. Calculate each project's NPV and IRR.

b. Graph the NPV profiles for Plan A and Plan B. From the NPV profiles constructed, approximate the crossover rate.

c. Give a logical explanation, based on reinvestment rates and opportunity costs, as to why the NPV method is better than the IRR method when the firm's cost of capital is constant at some value such as 10 percent.

14-5
Multiple rates of return

The Upton Uranium Company is deciding whether or not it should open a strip mine, the net cost of which is $2 million. Net cash inflows are expected to be $13 million, all coming at the end of Year 1. The land must be returned to its natural state at a cost of $12 million, payable at the end of Year 2.

a. Plot the project's NPV profile. (Hint: Calculate NPV at k = 0, 10, 80, and 450%, and possibly at other k values.)

b. Should the project be accepted if k = 10%? If k = 20%? Explain your reasoning.

c. Can you think of some other capital budgeting situations in which negative cash flows during or at the other end of the project's life might lead to multiple IRRs?

d. What is the project's MIRR at k = 10%? At k = 20%? Does the MIRR method lead to the same accept/reject decision as the NPV method?

EXAM-TYPE PROBLEMS

The problems included in this section are set up in such a way that they could be used as multiple-choice exam problems.

14-6

NPVs, IRRs, and MIRRs for independent projects

Olsen Engineering is considering including two pieces of equipment, a truck and an overhead pulley system, in this year's capital budget. The projects are independent. The cash outlay for the truck is $17,100 and that for the pulley system is $22,430. The firm's cost of capital is 14 percent. After-tax cash flows, including depreciation, are as follows:

Year	Truck	Pulley
1	$5,100	$7,500
2	5,100	7,500
3	5,100	7,500
4	5,100	7,500
5	5,100	7,500

Calculate the IRR, the NPV, and the MIRR for each project, and indicate the correct accept/reject decision for each.

14-7

NPVs and IRRs for mutually exclusive projects

Horrigan Industries must choose between a gas-powered and an electric-powered forklift truck for moving materials in its factory. Since both forklifts perform the same function, the firm will choose only one. (They are mutually exclusive investments.) The electric-powered truck will cost more, but it will be less expensive to operate; it will cost $22,000, whereas the gas-powered truck will cost $17,500. The cost of capital that applies to both investments is 12 percent. The life for both types of truck is estimated to be 6 years, during which time the net cash flows for the electric-powered truck will be $6,290 per year and those for the gas-powered truck will be $5,000 per year. Annual net cash flows include depreciation expenses. Calculate the NPV and IRR for each type of truck, and decide which to recommend.

14-8

Capital budgeting methods

Project S costs $15,000 and is expected to produce benefits (cash flows) of $4,500 per year for 5 years. Project L costs $37,500 and is expected to produce cash flows of $11,100 per year for 5 years. Calculate the two projects' NPVs, IRRs, and MIRRs, assuming a cost of capital of 14 percent. Which project would be selected, assuming they are mutually exclusive, using each evaluation technique? Which should actually be selected?

14-9

Present value of costs

The Cordell Coffee Company is evaluating the within-plant distribution system for its new roasting, grinding, and packing plant. The two alternatives are (1) a conveyor system with a high initial cost but low annual operating costs and (2) several forklift trucks, which cost less but have considerably higher operating costs. The decision to construct the plant has already been made, and the choice here will have no effect on the overall revenues of the project. The cost of capital for the plant is 9 percent, and the projects' expected net costs are listed below:

	Expected Net Cash Flows	
Year	Conveyor	Forklift
0	($300,000)	($120,000)
1	(66,000)	(96,000)
2	(66,000)	(96,000)
3	(66,000)	(96,000)
4	(66,000)	(96,000)
5	(66,000)	(96,000)

a. What is the IRR of each alternative?

b. What is the present value of costs of each alternative? Which method should be chosen?

14-10

MIRR and NPV

Your company is considering two mutually exclusive projects, X and Y, whose costs and cash flows are shown below:

Year	X	Y
0	($1,000)	($1,000)
1	100	1,000
2	300	100
3	400	50
4	700	50

The projects are equally risky, and their cost of capital is 12 percent. You must make a recommendation, and you must base it on the modified IRR. What is the MIRR of the better project?

14-11

NPV and IRR

A company is analyzing two mutually exclusive projects, S and L, whose cash flows are shown below:

Years	0	1	2	3	4
S	−1,000	900	250	10	10
L	−1,000	0	250	400	800

The company's cost of capital is 10 percent, and it can get an unlimited amount of capital at that cost. What is the *regular IRR* (not MIRR) of the *better* project? (Hint: Note that the better project may or may not be the one with the higher IRR.)

14-12

MIRR

Project X has a cost of $1,000 at t = 0, and it is expected to produce a uniform cash flow stream for 10 years, i.e., the CFs are the same in Years 1 through 10, and it has a regular IRR of 12 percent. The cost of capital for the project is 10 percent. What is the project's modified IRR (MIRR)?

INTEGRATIVE PROBLEM

14-13

Basics of capital budgeting

Your boss, the chief financial officer (CFO) for Allied Food Products, has just handed you the estimated cash flows for two proposed projects. Project L involves adding a new item to the firm's frozen foods line; it would take some time to build up the market for this product, so the cash inflows would increase over time. Project S involves an add-on to an existing line, and its cash flows would decrease over time. Both projects have 3-year lives because Allied is planning to introduce an entirely new frozen foods line at that time.

Here are the net cash flow estimates (in thousands of dollars):

	Expected Net Cash Flows	
Year	Project L	Project S
0	($100)	($100)
1	10	70
2	60	50
3	80	20

Depreciation, salvage values, net working capital requirements, and tax effects are all included in these cash flows.

The CFO also made subjective risk assessments of each project, and he concluded that the projects both have risk characteristics which are similar to the firm's average project. Allied's cost of capital is 10 percent. You must now determine whether one or both of the projects should be accepted.

a. What is capital budgeting? Are there any similarities between a firm's capital budgeting decisions and an individual's investment decisions?

b. What is the difference between independent and mutually exclusive projects? Between normal and nonnormal projects?

c. (1) What is the payback period? Find the paybacks for Projects L and S.

   (2) What is the rationale for the payback? According to the payback criterion, which project or projects should be accepted if the firm's maximum acceptable payback is 2 years, and Projects L and S are independent? Mutually exclusive?

   (3) What is the difference between the regular payback and the discounted payback?

   (4) What are the main disadvantages of the regular payback? Is the payback method of any real usefulness in capital budgeting decisions?

d. (1) Define the term net present value (NPV). What is each project's NPV?

   (2) What is the rationale behind the NPV method? According to NPV, which project or projects should be accepted if they are independent? Mutually exclusive?

   (3) Would the NPVs change if the cost of capital changed?

e. (1) Define the term internal rate of return (IRR). What is each project's IRR?

   (2) How is the IRR on a project related to the YTM on a bond?

   (3) What is the logic behind the IRR method? According to IRR, which projects should be accepted if they are independent? Mutually exclusive?

   (4) Would the projects' IRRs change if the cost of capital changed?

f. (1) Draw the NPV profiles for Projects L and S. At what discount rate do the profiles cross?

   (2) Look at the NPV profile graph without referring to the actual NPVs and IRRs. Which project or projects should be accepted if they are independent? Mutually exclusive? Explain. Do your answers apply for any discount rate less than 23.6 percent?

g. (1) What is the underlying cause of ranking conflicts between NPV and IRR?

   (2) What is the "reinvestment rate assumption," and how does it affect the NPV versus IRR conflict?

   (3) Which method is the best? Why?

h. (1) Define the term modified IRR (MIRR). Find the MIRR for Projects L and S.

   (2) What are the MIRR's advantages and disadvantages vis-à-vis the regular IRR? What are the MIRR's advantages and disadvantages vis-à-vis the NPV?

i. As a separate project (Project P), the firm is considering sponsoring a pavilion at the upcoming World's Fair. The pavilion would cost $800,000, and it is expected to result in $5 million of incremental cash inflows during its one year of operation. However, it would then take another year, and $5 million of costs, to demolish the site and return it to its original condition. Thus, Project P's expected net cash flows look like this (in millions of dollars):

Year	Cash Flows
0	($0.8)
1	5
2	(5)

The project is estimated to be of average risk, so its cost of capital is 10 percent.

(1) What is Project P's NPV? What is its IRR? Its MIRR?

(2) Draw Project P's NPV profile. Does Project P have normal or nonnormal cash flows? Should this project be accepted?

COMPUTER-RELATED PROBLEM

Work the problem in this section only if you are using the computer problem diskette.

14-14

NPV and IRR analysis

Use the model in File C14 to solve this problem. West Coast Chemical Company (WCCC) is considering two mutually exclusive investments. The projects' expected net cash flows are as follows:

| Year | Expected Net Cash Flows | |
	Project A	Project B
0	($46,800)	($63,600)
1	(21,600)	20,400
2	43,200	20,400
3	43,200	20,400
4	43,200	20,400
5	(28,800)	20,400

a. Construct NPV profiles for Projects A and B.

b. Calculate each project's IRR and MIRR. Assume the cost of capital is 13 percent.

c. If the cost of capital for each project is 13 percent, which project should West Coast select? If the cost of capital were 9 percent, what would be the proper choice? If the cost of capital were 15 percent, what would be the proper choice?

d. At what rate do the NPV profiles of the two projects cross?

e. Project A has a large negative outflow in Year 5 associated with ending the project. WCCC's management is confident of Project A's cash flows in Years 0 to 4 but is uncertain about what its Year 5 cash flow will be. (There is no uncertainty about Project B's cash flows.) Under a worst case scenario, Project A's Year 5 cash flow will be − $36,000, whereas under a best case scenario, the cash flow will be − $24,000. Redo Parts a, b, and d for each scenario, assuming a 13 percent cost of capital. Press the F10 function key on the computer keyboard to see the new NPV profiles. If the cost of capital for each project is 13 percent, which project should be selected under each scenario?

Project Cash Flows and Risk[*]

When RJR Nabisco canceled its smokeless cigarette project, **The Wall Street Journal** *called it "one of the most stunning new product disasters in recent history." RJR had spent over $300 million on the product and had test marketed it for five months. The company had even built a new plant and was all set to produce smokeless cigarettes in huge quantities.*

The new cigarette had two fatal flaws—it had to be lit with a special lighter and even then it was hard to light, and many, if not most, smokers didn't like the taste. These problems were well known early on, yet RJR still pumped money into the project.

What led RJR's top managers to downplay the flaws and to spend $300 million on a bad product? According to industry observers, many people inside the company were aware of the seriousness of the situation, but they were afraid to voice their concerns for fear of offending the top managers. The top managers, meantime, were so infatuated with their "new toy" that they assumed consumers would embrace the smokeless cigarette in spite of its obvious flaws. Interestingly, most of the top managers smoked, but none smoked the new smokeless cigarette!

RJR was not a well-run company, even though it was entrenched in highly profitable markets and was generating billions of dollars of cash each year. The smokeless cigarette project didn't kill the company, but it did contribute to the downfall of the management team that backed the project. Had RJR's top managers followed the procedures set forth in this chapter, perhaps they would still be in control of the company.

---

[*]Parts of this chapter are relatively technical, and all or parts of it can be omitted without loss of continuity if time pressures do not permit full coverage.

The basic principles of capital budgeting were covered in Chapter 14. Now we examine some additional issues, including (1) cash flow estimation, (2) replacement decisions, (3) mutually exclusive projects with unequal lives, (4) the effects of inflation on capital budgeting analysis, and (5) incorporating risk into the capital budgeting decision.

CASH FLOW ESTIMATION

cash flow

The actual net cash, as opposed to accounting net income, that flows into (or out of) a firm during some specified period.

The most important, but also the most difficult, step in the analysis of a capital project is estimating its **cash flows**—the investment outlays and the annual net cash inflows after the project goes into operation. Many variables are involved in cash flow estimation, and many individuals and departments participate in the process. For example, the forecasts of unit sales and sales prices are normally made by the marketing group based on their knowledge of advertising effects, the state of the economy, competitors' reactions, and trends in consumers' tastes. Similarly, the capital outlays associated with a new product are generally obtained from the engineering and product development staffs, while operating costs are estimated by cost accountants, production experts, personnel specialists, purchasing agents, and so forth.

Because it is difficult to make accurate forecasts of the costs and revenues associated with a large, complex project, forecast errors can be quite large. For example, when several major oil companies decided to build the Alaska Pipeline, the original cost estimates were in the neighborhood of $700 million, but the final cost was closer to $7 billion. Similar (or even worse) miscalculations are common in forecasts of product design costs, such as the costs to develop a new personal computer. Further, as difficult as plant and equipment costs are to estimate, sales revenues and operating costs over the life of the project are generally even more uncertain. For example, several years ago Federal Express developed an electronic delivery service system (ZapMail). It used the correct capital budgeting technique, NPV, but it incorrectly estimated the project's cash flows: Projected revenues were too high, and projected costs were too low, and virtually no one was willing to pay the price required to cover the project's costs. As a result, cash flows failed to meet the forecasted levels, and Federal Express ended up losing about $200 million on the venture. This example demonstrates a basic truth—if cash flow estimates are not reasonably accurate, any analytical technique, no matter how sophisticated, can lead to poor decisions and hence to operating losses and lower stock prices. Because of its financial strength, Federal Express was able to absorb losses on the project with no problem, but the ZapMail venture could have forced a weaker firm into bankruptcy.

The financial staff's role in the forecasting process includes (1) coordinating the efforts of the other departments, such as engineering and marketing, (2) ensuring that everyone involved with the forecast uses a consistent set of economic assumptions, and (3) making sure that no biases are inherent in the forecasts. This last point is extremely important, because division managers often become emotionally involved with pet projects or develop empire-building complexes, both of which can lead to cash flow forecasting biases which make bad projects look good—on paper. The RJR smokeless cigarette project discussed above is an example of this problem.

It is almost impossible to overstate the difficulties one can encounter in cash flow forecasts. It is also difficult to overstate the importance of these forecasts. Still, observing the principles discussed in the next several sections will help to minimize forecasting errors.

Self-Test Questions

What is the most important step in the analysis of a capital project?

What is the financial staff's role in the capital projects forecasting process?

IDENTIFYING THE RELEVANT CASH FLOWS

relevant cash flows

The specific cash flows that should be considered in a capital budgeting decision.

One important element in cash flow estimation is the identification of **relevant cash flows,** which are defined as the specific set of cash flows that should be considered in the decision at hand. Errors are often made here, but two cardinal rules can help financial analysts avoid mistakes: (1) Capital budgeting decisions must be based on *cash flows,* not accounting income, and (2) only *incremental cash flows* are relevant to the accept/reject decision. These two rules are discussed in detail in the following sections.

Cash Flow versus Accounting Income

In capital budgeting analysis, *annual cash flows, not accounting profits,* are used. Cash flows and accounting profits can be very different. To illustrate, consider Table 15-1, which shows how accounting profits and cash flows are related to one another. We assume that Allied Food Products is planning to start a new division at the end of 1993; that sales and all costs except depreciation represent actual cash flows and are projected to be constant over time; and that the division will use accelerated depreciation, which will cause its reported depreciation charges to decline over time.[1]

The top section of the table shows the situation in the first year of operations, 1994. Accounting profits are $12 million, but the division's net cash flow —money which is available to Allied—is $42 million. The $12 million profit is the return *on the invested capital,* while the $30 million of depreciation is a return *of part of the invested capital,* so the $42 million cash flow consists of both a return *on* and a return *of* part of the invested capital.

The bottom part of the table shows the situation projected for 1999. Here reported profits have doubled (because of the decline in depreciation), but net cash flow is down sharply. Accounting profits are important for some purposes, but for purposes of setting a value on a project using DCF techniques, cash flows

---

[1]Depreciation procedures are discussed in detail in accounting courses, but we do provide a summary and review in Appendix 15A at the end of this chapter. The tables provided in Appendix 15A are used to calculate depreciation charges used in the chapter examples. In some instances, we simplify the depreciation assumptions in order to reduce the arithmetic. Since Congress changes depreciation procedures fairly frequently, it is always necessary to consult the latest tax regulations before developing actual capital budgeting cash flows.

Table 15-1 ▪ Accounting Profit versus Net Cash Flow (Thousands of Dollars)

I. *1994 Situation*	Accounting Profits	Cash Flows
Sales	$100,000	$100,000
Costs except depreciation	50,000	50,000
Depreciation	30,000	—
Operating income	$ 20,000	$ 50,000
Federal-plus-state taxes (40%)	8,000	8,000
Net income or net cash flow	$ 12,000	$ 42,000

Net cash flow = Net income plus depreciation = $12,000 + $30,000 = $42,000.

II. *1999 Situation*		
Sales	$100,000	$100,000
Costs except depreciation	50,000	50,000
Depreciation	10,000	—
Operating income	$ 40,000	$ 50,000
Federal-plus-state taxes (40%)	16,000	16,000
Net income or net cash flow	$ 24,000	$ 34,000

Net cash flow = Net income plus depreciation = $24,000 + $10,000 = $34,000.

are what is relevant. Therefore, in capital budgeting, we are interested in net cash flows, defined as

$$
\begin{aligned}
\text{Net cash flow} &= \text{Net income} &&+ \text{Depreciation} \\
&= \text{Return } on \text{ capital} &&+ \text{Return } of \text{ capital,}
\end{aligned} \qquad \text{(15-1)}
$$

not in accounting profits per se.[2]

Incremental Cash Flows

In evaluating a capital project, we are concerned only with those cash flows that result directly from the decision to accept the project. These cash flows, called **incremental cash flows,** represent the changes in the firm's total cash flows that occur as a direct result of accepting the project. Four special problems in determining incremental cash flows are discussed next.

incremental cash flow
The net cash flow attributable to an investment project.

---

[2]Actually, net cash flow should be adjusted to reflect all noncash charges, not just depreciation. However, for most projects, depreciation is by far the largest noncash charge. Also, notice that Table 15-1 ignores interest charges, which would be present if the firm used debt. Most firms do use debt and hence finance part of their capital budgets with debt. Therefore, the question has been raised as to whether or not interest charges should be reflected in capital budgeting cash flow analysis. The consensus is that interest charges should *not* be dealt with explicitly in capital budgeting—rather, the effects of debt financing are reflected in the cost of capital which is used to discount the cash flows. If interest were subtracted, and cash flows were then discounted, we would be double counting the cost of debt.

sunk cost

A cash outlay that has already been incurred and which cannot be recovered regardless of whether the project is accepted or rejected.

Sunk Costs.   Sunk costs are not incremental costs, and they should not be included in the analysis. A **sunk cost** is an outlay that has already been committed or that has already occurred and hence is not affected by the accept/reject decision under consideration. To illustrate, in 1992 Northeast BankCorp was considering the establishment of a branch office in a newly developed section of Boston. To help with its evaluation, Northeast had, back in 1991, hired a consulting firm to perform a site analysis; the cost was $100,000, and this amount was expensed for tax purposes in 1991. Is this 1991 expenditure a relevant cost with respect to the 1992 capital budgeting decision? The answer is no—the $100,000 is a sunk cost, and Northeast cannot recover it regardless of whether or not the new branch is built. It often turns out that a particular project has a negative NPV when all the associated costs, including sunk costs, are considered. However, on an incremental basis the project may be a good one because the incremental cash flows are large enough to produce a positive NPV on the incremental investment.

opportunity cost

The return on the best *alternative* use of an asset; the highest return that will *not* be earned if funds are invested in a particular project.

Opportunity Costs.   The second potential problem relates to **opportunity costs,** defined here as the cash flows that could be generated from assets the firm already owns provided they are not used for the project in question. To illustrate, Northeast BankCorp already owns a piece of land that is suitable for the branch location. When evaluating the prospective branch, should the cost of the land be disregarded because no additional cash outlay would be required? The answer is no, because there is an opportunity cost inherent in the use of the property. In this case, the land could be sold to yield $150,000 after taxes. Use of the site for the branch would require forgoing this inflow, so the $150,000 must be charged as an opportunity cost against the project. Note that the proper land cost in this example is the $150,000 market-determined value, irrespective of whether Northeast originally paid $50,000 or $500,000 for the property. (What Northeast paid would, of course, have an effect on taxes and hence on the after-tax opportunity cost.)

externalities

Effects of a project on cash flows in other parts of the firm.

Effects on Other Parts of the Firm: Externalities.   The third potential problem involves the effects of a project on other parts of the firm; economists call these effects **externalities.** For example, some of Northeast's customers who would use the new branch are already banking with Northeast's downtown office. The loans and deposits, and hence profits, generated by these customers would not be new to the bank; rather, they would represent a transfer from the main office to the branch. Thus, the net revenues produced by these customers should not be treated as incremental income in the capital budgeting decision. On the other hand, having a suburban branch would help the bank attract new business to its downtown office, because some people like to be able to bank both close to home and close to work. In this case, the additional revenues that would actually flow to the downtown office should be attributed to the branch. Although they are often difficult to quantify, externalities such as these should be considered.

Shipping and Installation Costs.   When a firm acquires fixed assets, it often must incur substantial costs for shipping and installing the equipment. These charges are added to the invoice price of the equipment when the cost of the project is being determined. Also, the full cost of the equipment, including shipping and installation costs, is used as the depreciable basis when depreciation charges are being calculated. Thus, if Northeast BankCorp bought a computer with an invoice price of $100,000, and paid another $10,000 for shipping and installation, then the full cost of the computer, and its depreciable basis, would be $110,000.

 Self-Test Questions

Briefly explain the difference between accounting income and net cash flow. Which should be used in capital budgeting? Why?

Explain what these terms mean, and assess their relevance in capital budgeting: incremental cash flow, sunk cost, opportunity cost, externality, and shipping plus installation costs.

Explain why incremental analysis is important in capital budgeting.

CHANGES IN NET WORKING CAPITAL

change in net working capital
The increased current assets resulting from a new project, minus the simultaneous increase in accounts payable and accruals.

Normally, additional inventories are required to support a new operation, and expanded sales also lead to additional accounts receivable. Both of these asset increases must be financed. However, accounts payable and accruals will increase spontaneously as a result of the expansion, and this will reduce the net cash needed to finance inventories and receivables. The difference between the required increase in current assets and the spontaneous increase in current liabilities is the **change in net working capital.** If this change is positive, as it generally is for expansion projects, this indicates that additional financing, over and above the cost of the fixed assets, is needed to fund the increase in current assets.

As the project approaches termination, inventories will be sold off and not replaced, and receivables will also be converted to cash. As these changes occur, the firm will receive an end-of-project cash flow that is equal to the net working capital requirement that occurred when the project was begun.

 Self-Test Questions

How is an increase in net working capital dealt with in capital budgeting?

Explain how the company gets back the dollars it invests in working capital.

CAPITAL BUDGETING PROJECT EVALUATION

Up to this point, we have discussed several important aspects of cash flow analysis. Now we illustrate cash flow estimation for expansion projects and for replacement projects.

Expansion Projects

expansion project
A project that is intended to increase sales.

An **expansion project** is defined as one that calls for the firm to invest in new facilities to increase sales. We illustrate expansion project analysis with a project that is being considered by Brandt-Quigley Corporation (BQC), an Atlanta-based technology company. BQC's research and development department has been applying its expertise in microprocessor technology to develop a small computer specifically designed to control home appliances. Once programmed, the computer will automatically control the heating and air-conditioning systems, security system, hot water heater, and even small appliances such as a coffee maker. By increasing a home's energy efficiency, the computer can save enough on costs to pay for itself within a few years. Developments have now reached the stage at which a decision must be made about whether or not to go forward with full-scale production.

BQC's marketing department plans to target sales of the appliance computer toward the owners of larger homes; the computer is cost effective only in homes with 2,000 or more square feet of heated/air-conditioned space. The marketing vice president believes that annual sales would be 20,000 units if the units were priced at $2,000 each, so annual sales are estimated at $40 million. The engineering department has reported that the firm would need additional manufacturing capability, and BQC currently has an option to purchase an existing building, at a cost of $12 million, which would meet this need. The building would be bought and paid for in one payment, on December 31, 1993, and for depreciation purposes it would fall into the MACRS 31.5-year class. (MACRS classes are discussed in Appendix 15A.)

The necessary equipment would be purchased and installed late in 1993, and it would also be paid for on December 31, 1993. The equipment would fall into the MACRS 5-year class, and it would cost $8 million, including transportation and installation.

The project also would require an initial investment of $6 million in net working capital. The initial working capital investment would also be made on December 31, 1993. The project's estimated economic life is 4 years. At the end of that time, the building is expected to have a market value of $7.5 million and a book value of $10.74 million, whereas the equipment would have a market value of $2 million and a book value of $1.36 million. The production department has estimated that variable manufacturing costs would total 60 percent of sales and that fixed overhead costs, excluding depreciation, would be $5 million a year. Depreciation expenses would vary from year to year in accordance with the MACRS rates.

BQC's federal-plus-state tax rate is 40 percent; its cost of capital is 12 percent; and, for capital budgeting purposes, the company's policy is to assume that operating cash flows occur at the end of each year. Because the plant would begin operations on January 1, 1994, the first operating cash flows would occur on December 31, 1994.

As one of the company's financial analysts, you have been assigned the task of supervising the capital budgeting analysis. For now, you may assume that the project has the same amount of risk as the firm's average project, and you may use the corporate required rate of return, 12 percent, for this project. Later in this chapter, we will examine additional information about the riskiness of the project, but at this point assume that the project is of average risk.

Analysis of the Cash Flows. The first step in the analysis is to summarize the investment outlays required for the project; this is done in the 1993 column of Table 15-2. For BQC's computer project, the cash outlays consist of the pur-

Table 15-2 ∎ **BQC Expansion Project Net Cash Flows, 1993–1997 (Thousands of Dollars)**

	1993	1994	1995	1996	1997
Building	($12,000)				
Equipment	(8,000)				
Increase in NWC[a]	(6,000)				
Sales revenues		$40,000	$40,000	$40,000	$40,000
Variable costs (60% of sales)		24,000	24,000	24,000	24,000
Fixed costs		5,000	5,000	5,000	5,000
Depreciation (building)[b]		180	360	360	360
Depreciation (equipment)[b]		1,600	2,560	1,520	960
Earnings before taxes (EBT)		$ 9,220	$ 8,080	$ 9,120	$ 9,680
Taxes (40%)		3,688	3,232	3,648	3,872
Net income		$ 5,532	$ 4,848	$ 5,472	$ 5,808
Add back depreciation		1,780	2,920	1,880	1,320
Cash flow from operations		$ 7,312	$ 7,768	$ 7,352	$ 7,128
Return of NWC					6,000
Net salvage value (see Table 15-3)					10,540
Net cash flow	($26,000)	$ 7,312	$ 7,768	$ 7,352	$23,668
Net present value (12%)	$ 6,996				

[a]NWC = net working capital. These funds will be recovered at the end of the project's operating life, 1997, as inventories are sold off and not replaced and as receivables are collected.

[b]MACRS depreciation expenses were calculated using the following rates:

Year	1	2	3	4
Depreciation rates (building)	1.5%	3.0%	3.0%	3.0%
Depreciation rates (equipment)	20.0%	32.0%	19.0%	12.0%

These percentages were multiplied by the depreciable basis ($12,000 for the building and $8,000 for the equipment, in thousands) to determine the depreciation expense for each year. Thus, depreciation on the building for 1994 is 0.015($12,000) = $180, while that on the equipment is 0.2($8,000) = $1,600. The allowances have been rounded for ease of computation. See Appendix 15A for a review of MACRS.

chase price of the building, the price of the needed equipment, and the required investment in net working capital (NWC).

Having estimated the capital requirements, we must now estimate the cash flows that will occur once production begins; these are set forth in the 1994 through 1997 columns of Table 15-2. The operating cash flow estimates are based on information provided by BQC's various departments. The depreciation amounts were obtained by multiplying the depreciable basis by the MACRS recovery allowance rates as set forth in Note b to Table 15-2.

The $6 million investment in net working capital will be recovered in 1997. Also, an estimate of the cash flows from the salvage values is required, and Table 15-3 summarizes this analysis. The building has an estimated salvage value which is less than its book value—it will be sold at a loss for tax purposes. This loss will reduce taxable income and thus will generate a tax savings. In effect, the company has been depreciating the building too slowly, and it will write off the loss against its ordinary income, saving taxes that it would otherwise have to pay. The equipment, on the other hand, will be sold for more than its book value, and the company will have to pay taxes on the $640,000 profit. In both

Table 15-3 ▪ **Net Salvage Values, 1997**

	Building	**Equipment**
Initial cost	$12,000,000	$8,000,000
1997 salvage (market) value	7,500,000	2,000,000
1997 book value[a]	10,740,000	1,360,000
Gain (loss) on sale[b]	($ 3,240,000)	$ 640,000
Taxes (40%)	(1,296,000)	256,000
Net salvage value[c]	$ 8,796,000	$1,744,000

Total cash flow from salvage value = $8,796,000 + $1,744,000 = $10,540,000.

[a]The book values equal depreciable basis (initial cost in this case) minus accumulated MACRS depreciation. For the building, accumulated depreciation equals $1,260,000, so book value equals $12,000,000 − $1,260,000 = $10,740,000; for the equipment, accumulated depreciation equals $6,640,000, so book value equals $8,000,000 − $6,640,000 = $1,360,000.

[b]Building: $7,500,000 market value − $10,740,000 book value = − $3,240,000. This represents a shortfall in depreciation taken versus "true" depreciation, and it is treated as an operating expense for 1997.

Equipment: $2,000,000 market value − $1,360,000 book value = $640,000. Here the depreciation charge exceeds the "true" depreciation, and the difference is called "depreciation recapture." It is taxed as ordinary income in 1997.

[c]Net salvage value equals salvage (market) value minus taxes. For the building, the loss results in a tax credit, so net salvage value = $7,500,000 − (− $1,296,000) = $8,796,000.

cases, the book value is calculated as the initial cost minus the accumulated depreciation. The total cash flow from salvage is merely the sum of the net salvage values of the building and equipment components.

Making the Decision.   To summarize the data and get them ready for evaluation, it is useful to combine all of the net cash flows on a time line like the one shown in Figure 15-1, using data taken from Table 15-2. (Actually, the "net cash flow" line in Table 15-2 could be treated as a time line.) Figure 15-1 also shows the payback period, IRR, MIRR, and NPV (at the 12 percent cost of capital). The project appears to be acceptable using the NPV, IRR, and MIRR methods, and it also would be acceptable if BQC required a payback period of four years. Note, however, that the analysis thus far has been based on the assumption that the project has the same degree of risk as the company's average project. If the project were judged to be riskier than an average project, it would be necessary to increase the cost of capital, which in turn might cause the NPV to become negative and the IRR and the MIRR to fall below k. Later in this chapter, we will extend the evaluation of this project to include a risk analysis.

Replacement Analysis

replacement analysis

An analysis involving the decision of whether or not to replace an existing asset that is still productive with a new one.

Brandt-Quigley's appliance control computer project was used to show how an expansion project is analyzed. All companies, including this one, also make replacement decisions, and the analysis relating to replacements is somewhat different from that for expansion because the cash flows from the old asset must be considered. **Replacement analysis** is illustrated with another BQC example, this time from the company's research and development (R&D) division.

Figure 15-1 ▪ **Time Line of Consolidated Net Cash Flows, 1993–1997 (In Thousands)**

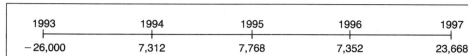

1993	1994	1995	1996	1997
−26,000	7,312	7,768	7,352	23,668

Payback period: 3.15 years.
IRR: 21.9% versus a 12% cost of capital.
MIRR: 18.9% versus a 12% cost of capital.
NPV: $6,995,624.

A lathe for trimming molded plastics was purchased 10 years ago at a cost of $7,500. The machine had an expected life of 15 years at the time it was purchased, and management originally estimated, and still believes, that the salvage value will be zero at the end of the 15-year life. The machine is being depreciated on a straight line basis; therefore, its annual depreciation charge is $500, and its present book value is $2,500.

The R&D manager reports that a new special-purpose machine can be purchased for $12,000 (including freight and installation), and, over its 5-year life, it will reduce labor and raw materials usage sufficiently to cut operating costs from $7,000 to $4,000. This reduction in costs will cause before-tax profits to rise by $7,000 − $4,000 = $3,000 per year.

It is estimated that the new machine can be sold for $2,000 at the end of 5 years; this is its estimated salvage value. The old machine's actual current market value is $1,000, which is below its $2,500 book value. If the new machine is acquired, the old lathe will be sold to another company rather than exchanged for the new machine. The company's federal-plus-state tax rate is 40 percent, and the replacement project is of slightly below-average risk. Net working capital requirements will also increase by $1,000 at the time of replacement. By an IRS ruling, the new machine falls into the 3-year MACRS class, and, since the cash flows are relatively certain, the project's cost of capital is only 11.5 percent. Should the replacement be made?

Table 15-4 shows the worksheet format the company uses to analyze replacement projects. Each line is numbered, and a line-by-line description of the table follows.

Line 1.   The top section of the table, Lines 1 through 5, sets forth the cash flows which occur at (approximately) t = 0, the time the investment is made. Line 1 shows the purchase price of the new machine, including installation and freight charges. Since it is an outflow, it is negative.

Line 2.   Here we show the price received from the sale of the old equipment.

Line 3.   Since the old equipment would be sold at less than book value, the sale would create a loss which would reduce the firm's taxable income and hence its next quarterly income tax payment. The tax saving is equal to (Loss)(T) = ($1,500)(0.40) = $600, where T is the marginal corporate tax rate. The Tax Code defines this loss as an operating loss because it reflects the fact that inadequate depreciation was taken on the old asset. If there had been

Table 15-4 ▪ **Replacement Analysis Worksheet**

Year:	0	1	2	3	4	5
I. Investment Outlay						
1. Cost of new equipment	($12,000)					
2. Market value of old equipment	1,000					
3. Tax savings on sale of old equipment	600					
4. Increase in net working capital	(1,000)					
5. Total net investment	($11,400)					
II. Operating Inflows over the Project's Life						
6. After-tax decrease in costs		$1,800	$1,800	$1,800	$1,800	$1,800
7. Depreciation on new machine		$3,960	$5,400	$1,800	$ 840	$ 0
8. Depreciation on old machine		500	500	500	500	500
9. Change in depreciation (7 − 8)		$3,460	$4,900	$1,300	$ 340	($ 500)
10. Tax savings from depreciation (0.4 × 9)		1,384	1,960	520	136	(200)
11. Net operating cash flows (6 + 10)		$3,184	$3,760	$2,320	$1,936	$1,600
III. Terminal Year Cash Flows						
12. Estimated salvage value of new machine						$2,000
13. Tax on salvage value						(800)
14. Return of net working capital						1,000
15. Total termination cash flows						$2,200
IV. Net Cash Flows						
16. Total net cash flows	($11,400)	$3,184	$3,760	$2,320	$1,936	$3,800
V. Results						

Payback period: 4.1 years.

IRR: 10.1% versus an 11.5% cost of capital.

MIRR: 10.7% versus an 11.5% cost of capital.

NPV: − $388.77.

a profit on the sale (that is, if the sale price had exceeded book value), Line 3 would have shown taxes *paid,* a cash outflow. In the actual case, the equipment would be sold at a loss, so no taxes would be paid, and the company would realize a tax savings of $600.[3]

Line 4.   The investment in additional net working capital (new current asset requirements minus increases in accounts payable and accruals) is shown here. This investment will be recovered at the end of the project's life (see Line 14). No taxes are involved.

---

[3]If the old asset were being exchanged for the new asset, rather than being sold to a third party, the tax consequences would be different. In an exchange of similar assets, no gain or loss is recognized. If the market value of the old asset is greater than its book value, the depreciable basis of the new asset is decreased by the excess amount. Conversely, if the market value of the old asset is less than its book value, the depreciable basis is increased by the shortfall.

Line 5.   Here we show the total net cash outflow at the time the replacement is made. The company writes a check for $12,000 to pay for the machine, and another $1,000 is invested in net working capital. However, these outlays are partially offset by proceeds from the sale of the old equipment and reduced taxes.

Line 6.   Section II of the table shows the *incremental operating cash flows,* or benefits, that are expected if the replacement is made. The first of these benefits is the reduction in operating costs shown on Line 6. Cash flows increase because operating costs are reduced by $3,000, but reduced costs also mean higher taxable income, hence higher income taxes:

Reduction in costs $= \Delta$ cost $=$	$3,000
Associated increase in taxes $= T(\Delta$ cost$) = 0.4(\$3,000) =$	1,200
Increase in net after-tax cash flows due to cost reduction $= \Delta$ NCF $=$	$1,800
Note also that Δ NCF $= (\Delta$ cost$)(1 - T) = (\$3,000)(0.6) =$	$1,800

Had the replacement resulted in an increase in sales in addition to the reduction in costs (that is, if the new machine had been both larger and more efficient), then this amount would also be reported on Line 6 (or a separate line could be added). Also, note that the $3,000 cost savings is constant over Years 1 through 5; had the annual savings been expected to change over time, this fact would have to be built into the analysis.

Line 7.   The depreciable basis of the new machine, $12,000, is multiplied by the appropriate MACRS recovery allowance for 3-year class property (see Table 15A-2) to obtain the depreciation figures shown on Line 7. Note that if you summed across Line 7, the total would be $12,000, the depreciable basis.

Line 8.   Line 8 shows the $500 straight line depreciation on the old machine.

Line 9.   The depreciation expense on the old machine as shown on Line 8 can no longer be taken if the replacement is made, but the new machine's depreciation will be available. Therefore, the $500 depreciation on the old machine is subtracted from that on the new machine to show the net change in annual depreciation. The change is positive in Years 1 through 4 but negative in Year 5. The Year 5 negative net change in annual depreciation signifies that the purchase of the replacement machine results in a *decrease* in depreciation expense during that year.

Line 10.   The net change in depreciation results in a tax reduction which is equal to the change in depreciation multiplied by the tax rate: Depreciation tax savings $= T($Change in depreciation$) = 0.40(\$3,460) = \$1,384$ for Year 1. Note that the relevant cash flow is the tax savings on the *net change* in depreciation, not just the depreciation on the new equipment. Capital budgeting decisions are based on *incremental* cash flows, and since BQC will lose $500 of depreciation if it replaces the old machine, that fact must be taken into account.

Line 11.   Here we show the net operating cash flows over the project's 5-year life. These flows are found by adding the after-tax cost decrease to the depreciation tax savings, or Line 6 + Line 10.

Line 12. Part III shows the cash flows associated with the termination of the project. To begin, Line 12 shows the estimated salvage value of the new machine at the end of its 5-year life, $2,000.[4]

Line 13. Since the book value of the new machine at the end of Year 5 is zero, the company will have to pay taxes of $2,000(0.4) = $800.

Line 14. An investment of $1,000 in net working capital was shown as an outflow at t = 0. This investment, like the new machine's salvage value, will be recovered when the project is terminated at the end of Year 5. Accounts receivable will be collected, inventories will be drawn down and not replaced, and the result will be an inflow of $1,000 at t = 5.

Line 15. Here we show the total cash flows resulting from terminating the project.

Line 16. Part IV shows, on Line 16, the total net cash flows in a form suitable for capital budgeting evaluation. In effect, Line 16 is a "time line."

Part V of the table, "Results," shows the replacement project's payback, IRR, MIRR, and NPV. Because of the nature of the project, it is less risky than the firm's average project, so a cost of capital of only 11.5 percent is appropriate. However, even at this cost of capital, the NPV is negative, the project is not acceptable, and hence the old lathe should not be replaced.

Self-Test Question

Explain and differentiate between the capital budgeting analyses required for expansion and for replacement projects.

COMPARING PROJECTS WITH UNEQUAL LIVES

Note that a replacement decision involves comparing two mutually exclusive projects: retaining the old asset versus buying a new one. To simplify matters, in our replacement example we assumed that the new machine had a life equal to the remaining life of the old machine. If, however, we were choosing between two mutually exclusive alternatives with significantly different lives, an adjustment would be necessary. We now discuss two procedures—(1) the replacement chain (common life) method and (2) the equivalent annual annuity method—to illustrate the problem and to show how to deal with it.

Suppose BQC is planning to modernize its production facilities, and as a part of the process, it is considering either a conveyor system (Project C) or some forklift trucks (Project F) for moving materials from the parts department to the main assembly line. Figure 15-2 shows both the expected net cash flows and the NPVs for these two mutually exclusive alternatives. We see that Project

---

[4]In this analysis, the salvage value of the old machine is zero. However, if the old machine was expected to have a positive salvage value at the end of 5 years, replacing the old machine now would eliminate this cash flow. Thus, the after-tax salvage value of the old machine would represent an opportunity cost to the firm, and it would be included as a Year 5 cash outflow in the terminal cash flow section of the worksheet.

Figure 15-2 ▪ Expected Net Cash Flows for Projects C and F

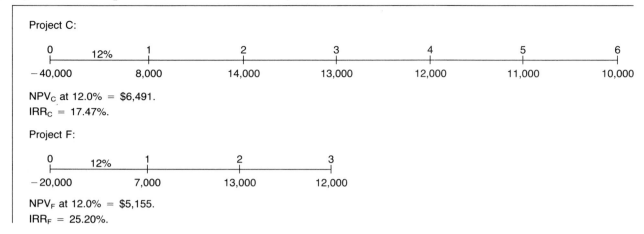

Project C:

0	1	2	3	4	5	6
−40,000	8,000	14,000	13,000	12,000	11,000	10,000

12%

NPV_C at 12.0% = \$6,491.
IRR_C = 17.47%.

Project F:

0	1	2	3
−20,000	7,000	13,000	12,000

12%

NPV_F at 12.0% = \$5,155.
IRR_F = 25.20%.

C, when discounted at a 12 percent cost of capital, has the higher NPV and thus appears to be the better project, in spite of the fact that F has the higher IRR.

Replacement Chain (Common Life) Approach

Although the analysis in Figure 15-2 suggests that Project C should be selected, this analysis is incomplete, and the decision to choose Project C is actually incorrect. If we choose Project F, we will have the opportunity to make a similar investment in 3 years, and if cost and revenue conditions continue at the Figure 15-2 levels, this second investment will also be profitable. However, if we choose Project C, we will not have this second investment opportunity. Therefore, to make a proper comparison of Projects C and F, we could apply the **replacement chain (common life) approach**; that is, we could find the NPV of Project F over a 6-year period and then compare this extended NPV with the NPV of Project C over the same 6 years.

replacement chain (common life) approach

A method of comparing projects of unequal lives which assumes that each project can be replicated as many times as necessary to reach a common life span; the NPVs over this life span are then compared, and the project with the higher common life NPV is chosen.

The NPV for Project C as calculated in Figure 15-2 is already over the 6-year common life. For Project F, however, we must expand the analysis to include the replacement of F in Year 3, resulting in the following 6-year time line:[5]

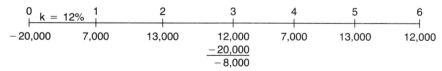

0	1	2	3	4	5	6
−20,000	7,000	13,000	12,000	7,000	13,000	12,000
			−20,000			
			−8,000			

k = 12%

Extended life NPV = \$8,824.

---

[5]We could also set up Project F's extended time line as follows:

1. The Stage 1 NPV is \$5,155.

2. The Stage 2 NPV is also \$5,155, but this value will not accrue until Year 3, so its value today, discounted at 12 percent, is \$3,669.

3. The extended life NPV is thus \$5,155 + \$3,669 = \$8,824.

Here we make the assumption that Project F's cost and annual cash inflows will not change if the project is repeated in 3 years, and that BQC's cost of capital will remain at 12 percent. Project F's extended NPV is $8,824. This is the value which should be compared with Project C's NPV, $6,491. Since Project F's "true" NPV is greater than that of Project C, Project F should be selected.

Equivalent Annual Annuity Approach

Although the preceding example illustrates why an extended analysis is necessary if we are comparing mutually exclusive projects with different lives, the arithmetic is generally more complex in practice. For example, one project might have a 6-year life versus a 10-year life for the other. This would require a replacement chain analysis over 30 years, the lowest common denominator of the two lives. In such a situation, it is often simpler to use a second procedure, the **equivalent annual annuity (EAA) method**, which involves three steps:

equivalent annual annuity (EAA) method

A method which calculates the annual payments a project would provide if it were an annuity. When comparing projects of unequal lives, the one with the higher equivalent annual annuity should be chosen.

1. Find each project's NPV over its initial life. In Figure 15-2, we found $NPV_C = \$6,491$ and $NPV_F = \$5,155$.

2. Find the constant annuity cash flow (the equivalent annual annuity [EAA]) that has the same present value as each project's NPV. For Project F, here is the time line:

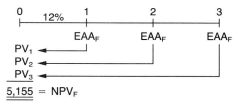

To find the value of EAA_F, with a financial calculator, enter -5155 as the PV, k = I = 12, and N = 3, and solve for PMT. The answer is $2,146. This cash flow stream, when discounted back 3 years at 12 percent, has a present value equal to Project F's original NPV, $5,155. The payment figure we found, $2,146, is called the project's "equivalent annual annuity (EAA)." The EAA for Project C was found similarly to be $1,579. Thus, Project C has an NPV which is equivalent to an annuity of $1,579 per year, while Project F's NPV is equivalent to an annuity of $2,146.

3. Assuming that continuous replacements can and will be made each time a project's life ends, these EAAs will continue on out to infinity; that is, they will constitute perpetuities. Recognizing that the value of a perpetuity is $V = PMT/k$, we can find the net present values of the infinite EAAs of Projects C and F as follows:

$$\text{Infinite horizon } NPV_C = \$1,579/0.12 = \$13,158.$$

$$\text{Infinite horizon } NPV_F = \$2,146/0.12 = \$17,883.$$

In effect, the EAA method assumes that each project will, if taken on, be replaced each time it wears out and will provide cash flows equivalent to the calculated annuity value. The PV of this infinite annuity is then the infinite horizon NPV for the project. Since the infinite horizon NPV of F exceeds that of C, Project F should be accepted. Therefore, the EAA method leads to the same decision rule as the replacement chain method—accept Project F.

The EAA method is often easier to apply than the replacement chain method, but the replacement chain method is easier to explain to decision makers. Still, the two methods always lead to the same decision if consistent assumptions are used. Also, note that Step 3 of the EAA method is not really necessary—we could have stopped after Step 2 because the project with the higher EAA will always have the higher NPV over any common life if the same required rate of return is used for the projects.

When should we worry about unequal life analysis? As a general rule, the unequal life issue (1) does not arise for independent projects, but (2) can arise if mutually exclusive projects with significantly different lives are being evaluated. However, even for mutually exclusive projects, it is not always appropriate to extend the analysis to a common life. This should only be done if there is a high probability that the projects will actually be replicated beyond their initial lives.

We should note several potentially serious weaknesses inherent in this type of unequal life analysis: (1) If inflation is expected, then replacement equipment will have a higher price, and both sales prices and operating costs will probably change. Thus, the static conditions built into the analysis would be invalid. (2) Replacements that occur down the road would probably employ new technology, which in turn might change the cash flows. This factor is not built into either replacement chain analysis or the EAA approach. (3) It is difficult enough to estimate the lives of most projects, so estimating the lives of a series of projects is often just a speculation. (4) If reasonably strong competition is present, the profitability of projects will be eroded over time, and that would reduce the need to extend the analysis beyond the projects' initial lives.

In view of these problems, no experienced financial analyst would be too concerned about comparing mutually exclusive projects with lives of, say, 8 years and 10 years. Given all the uncertainties in the estimation process, such projects would, for all practical purposes, be assumed to have the same life. Still, it is important to recognize that a problem does exist if mutually exclusive projects have substantially different lives. When we encounter such problems in practice, we build expected inflation and/or possible efficiency gains directly into the cash flow estimates, and then use the replacement chain approach (but not the equivalent annual annuity method). The cash flow estimation is more complicated, but the concepts involved are exactly the same as in our example.

Self-Test Questions

Why is it not always necessary to adjust project cash flow analyses for unequal lives?

Briefly describe the replacement chain (common life) approach.

Briefly describe the equivalent annual annuity (EAA) approach.

DEALING WITH INFLATION

Inflation is a fact of life, and it should be explicitly recognized in capital budgeting decisions. Some important points follow:

1. Recall from Chapter 3 that inflationary expectations are built into interest rates and money costs: $k_i = k^* + IP + LP + MRP + DRP$, with IP being the inflation factor. This factor is reflected in the required rate of return which is used to find NPVs and as the hurdle rate if the IRR or MIRR method is used. Therefore, inflation is reflected in the cost of capital part of a capital budgeting analysis.

2. The NPV method involves finding the PV of each future CF, discounted at the cost of capital, as follows:

$$NPV = \sum_{t=0}^{n} \frac{CF_t}{(1 + k)^t}.$$

Note that k includes a premium for expected inflation, so the higher the expected inflation rate, the larger the value of k, and, other things held constant, the smaller will be the NPV.

3. If inflation is expected, but this expectation is not built into the forecasted cash flows as shown in Table 15-2, then the calculated NPV will be incorrect — it will be downward biased. To see this, recognize that sales prices over the life of the project are built into the sales revenues shown in Table 15-2, the cash flow projections for BQC's expansion project. If sales prices do not reflect expected inflation, this bias will be present — the denominator of the NPV equation will be increased because expected inflation is automatically built into the cost of capital by participants in the capital market, but the cash flows in the numerator will not be increased, so the NPV will be biased downward.

It is easy enough to avoid the inflation bias — simply build inflationary expectations into the cash flows used in the analysis. In other words, when making a table such as Table 15-2, simply reflect expected inflation in the revenue and cost figures, hence in the annual net cash flow forecasts. Then the NPV will be unbiased.

? *Self-Test Questions*

How can inflation cause a downward bias in a project's estimated NPV?

What is the best way of handling inflation in a capital budgeting analysis, and how does this procedure eliminate the potential bias?

stand-alone risk
The risk an asset would have if it were a firm's only asset; it is measured by the variability of the asset's expected returns.

INTRODUCTION TO PROJECT RISK ANALYSIS

Three separate and distinct types of project risk can be identified: (1) the project's own **stand-alone risk,** or its risk disregarding the facts that it is but one asset within the firm's portfolio of assets and that the firm in question is but one

corporate (within-firm) risk
Risk not considering the effects of stockholders' diversification; it is measured by a project's effect on the firm's earnings variability.

beta (market) risk
That part of a project's risk that cannot be eliminated by diversification; it is measured by the project's beta coefficient.

stock in most investors' stock portfolios; (2) **corporate, or within-firm, risk,** which is the effect a project has on the company's risk without considering the effects of the stockholders' own personal diversification; and (3) **beta, or market, risk,** which is project risk assessed from the standpoint of an equity investor who holds a highly diversified portfolio. As we shall see, a particular project may have high stand-alone risk, yet taking it on may not have much effect on either the firm's risk or that of its owners because of portfolio effects.

A project's stand-alone risk is measured by the variability of the project's expected returns; its corporate risk is measured by the project's impact on the firm's earnings variability; and its beta risk is measured by the project's effect on the firm's beta coefficient. Taking on a project with a high degree of either stand-alone or corporate risk will not necessarily affect the firm's beta to any great extent. However, if the project has highly uncertain returns, and if those returns are highly correlated with returns on the firm's other assets and also with most other assets in the economy, the project will have a high degree of all types of risk. For example, suppose General Motors decides to undertake a major expansion to build solar-powered autos. GM is not sure how its technology will work on a mass production basis, so there are great risks in the venture — its stand-alone risk is high. Management also estimates that the project will have a higher probability of success if the economy is strong, for then people will have more money to spend on the new autos. This means that the project will tend to do well if GM's other divisions also do well and to do badly if other divisions do badly. This being the case, the project will also have high corporate risk. Finally, since GM's profits are highly correlated with those of most other firms, the project's beta coefficient will also be high. Thus, this project will be risky under all three definitions of risk.

Beta risk is important because of its direct effect on a firm's stock price: Beta affects k, and k affects the stock price. Corporate risk is also important for three primary reasons:

1. Undiversified stockholders, including the owners of small businesses, are more concerned about corporate risk than about beta risk.

2. Empirical studies of the determinants of required rates of return (k) generally find that both beta and corporate risk affect stock prices. This suggests that investors, even those who are well diversified, consider factors other than beta risk when they establish required returns.

3. The firm's stability is important to its managers, workers, customers, suppliers, and creditors, as well as to the community in which it operates. Firms that are in serious danger of bankruptcy, or even of suffering low profits and reduced output, have difficulty attracting and retaining good managers and workers. Also, both suppliers and customers are reluctant to depend on weak firms, and such firms have difficulty borrowing money at reasonable interest rates. These factors tend to reduce risky firms' profitability and hence the prices of their stocks, and, thus, they also make corporate risk significant.

For these three reasons, corporate risk is important even if a firm's stockholders are well diversified.

? *Self-Test Questions*

What are the three types of project risk?

How is a project's stand-alone risk measured?

How is corporate risk measured?

How is beta risk measured?

List three reasons why corporate risk is important.

TECHNIQUES FOR MEASURING STAND-ALONE RISK

What about a project's stand-alone risk — is it of any importance to anyone? In theory, this type of risk should be of little or no concern. However, it is of great importance, for the following reasons:

1. It is easier to estimate a project's stand-alone risk than its corporate risk, and it is far easier to measure stand-alone risk than beta risk.

2. In the vast majority of cases, all three types of risk are highly correlated — if the general economy does well, so will the firm, and if the firm does well, so will most of its projects. Thus, stand-alone risk is generally a good proxy for hard-to-measure corporate and beta risk.

3. Because of Points 1 and 2, if management wants a reasonably accurate assessment of a project's riskiness, it ought to spend considerable effort on ascertaining the riskiness of the project's own cash flows — that is, its stand-alone risk.

The starting point for analyzing a project's stand-alone risk involves determining the uncertainty inherent in the project's cash flows. This analysis can be handled in a number of ways, ranging from informal judgments to complex economic and statistical analyses involving large-scale computer models. To illustrate what is involved, we shall refer to Brandt-Quigley Corporation's appliance control computer project that we discussed earlier. Many of the individual cash flows that were shown in Table 15-2 are subject to uncertainty. For example, sales for each year were projected at 20,000 units to be sold at a net price of $2,000 per unit, or $40 million in total. Actual unit sales would almost certainly be somewhat higher or lower than 20,000, however, and the sales price would probably turn out to be different from the projected $2,000 per unit. *In effect, the sales quantity and the sales price estimates are really expected values taken from probability distributions, as are many of the other values that were shown in Table 15-2.* The distributions could be relatively "tight," reflecting small standard deviations and low risk, or they could be "flat," denoting a great deal of uncertainty about the final value of the variable in question and hence a high degree of stand-alone risk.

The nature of the individual cash flow distributions, and their correlations with one another, determine the nature of the NPV distribution and, thus, the project's stand-alone risk. We next discuss three techniques for assessing a project's stand-alone risk: (1) sensitivity analysis, (2) scenario analysis, and (3) Monte Carlo simulation.

Sensitivity Analysis

sensitivity analysis
A risk analysis technique in which key variables are changed and the resulting changes in the NPV and the IRR are observed.

Intuitively, we know that many of the variables which determine a project's cash flows are subject to a probability distribution rather than being known with certainty. We also know that if a key input variable, such as units sold, changes, the project's NPV will also change. **Sensitivity analysis** is a technique which indicates exactly how much the NPV will change in response to a given change in an input variable, other things held constant.

Sensitivity analysis begins with a *base case* situation, which is developed using the *expected* values for each input. To illustrate, consider the data given back in Table 15-2, in which projected income statements for Brandt-Quigley's computer project were shown. The values used to develop the table, including unit sales, sales price, fixed costs, and variable costs, are the most likely, or base case, values, and the resulting $6,996,000 NPV shown in Table 15-2 is called the *base case NPV.* Now we ask a series of "what if" questions: "What if unit sales fall 20 percent below the most likely level?" "What if the sales price per unit falls?" "What if variable costs are 65 percent of dollar sales rather than the expected 60 percent?" Sensitivity analysis is designed to provide the decision maker with answers to questions such as these.

In a sensitivity analysis, each variable is changed by several specific percentage points above and below the expected value, holding other things constant; then a new NPV is calculated for each of these values; and, finally, the set of NPVs is plotted against the variable that was changed. Figure 15-3 shows the computer project's sensitivity graphs for three of the key input variables. The

Figure 15-3 ▮ **Sensitivity Analysis (Thousands of Dollars)**

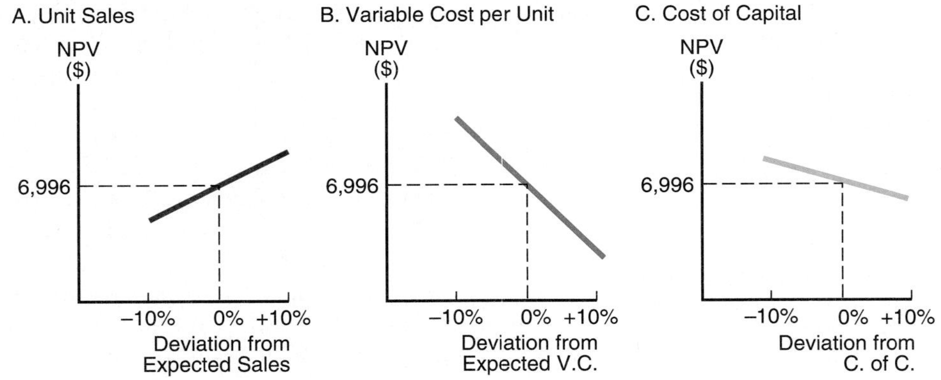

Deviation from Base Level (%)	Net Present Value		
	Units Sold	Variable Cost/Unit	Cost of Capital
−10	$4,080	$11,369	$8,035
0 (base case)	6,996	6,996	6,996
+10	9,911	2,622	6,003

Note: This analysis was performed using *Lotus 1-2-3,* so the values are slightly different than those that would be obtained using interest factor tables because of rounding differences.

table below the graphs gives the NPVs that were used to construct the graphs. The slopes of the lines in the graphs show how sensitive NPV is to changes in each of the inputs: *the steeper the slope, the more sensitive the NPV is to a change in the variable.* In the figure we see that the project's NPV is very sensitive to changes in variable costs, fairly sensitive to changes in unit sales, and not very sensitive to changes in the cost of capital.

If we were comparing two projects, the one with the steeper sensitivity lines would be regarded as riskier because for that project a relatively small error in estimating a variable such as unit sales would produce a large error in the project's expected NPV. Thus, sensitivity analysis can provide useful insights into the riskiness of a project.

Before we move on, two additional points about sensitivity analysis warrant attention. First, spreadsheet computer models, such as *Lotus 1-2-3* models, are ideally suited for performing sensitivity analysis. We used a *Lotus 1-2-3* model to conduct the analyses represented in Figure 15-3; it generated the NPVs and then drew the graphs. Second, we could have plotted all of the sensitivity lines on one graph; this would have facilitated direct comparisons of the sensitivities among different input variables.

Scenario Analysis

scenario analysis

A risk analysis technique in which "bad" and "good" sets of financial circumstances are compared with a most likely, or base case, situation.

worst case scenario

An analysis in which all of the input variables are set at their worst reasonably forecasted values.

best case scenario

An analysis in which all of the input variables are set at their best reasonably forecasted values.

base case

An analysis in which all of the input variables are set at their most likely values.

Although sensitivity analysis is probably the most widely used risk analysis technique, it does have limitations. Consider, for example, a proposed coal mine project whose NPV is highly sensitive to changes in output, in variable costs, and in sales price. However, if a utility company has contracted to buy a fixed amount of coal at an inflation-adjusted price per ton, the mining venture may be quite safe in spite of its steep sensitivity lines. *In general, a project's stand-alone risk depends on both (1) the sensitivity of its NPV to changes in key variables and (2) the range of likely values of these variables as reflected in their probability distributions.* Because sensitivity analysis considers only the first factor, it is incomplete.

Scenario analysis is a risk analysis technique that considers both the sensitivity of NPV to changes in key variables and the likely range of variable values. In a scenario analysis, the financial analyst asks operating managers to pick a "bad" set of circumstances (low unit sales, low sales price, high variable cost per unit, high construction cost, and so on) and a "good" set. The NPVs under the bad and good conditions are then calculated and compared to the expected, or base case, NPV.

As an example, let us return to the appliance control computer project. Assume that Brandt-Quigley's managers are fairly confident of their estimates of all the project's cash flow variables except price and unit sales. Further, they regard a drop in sales below 15,000 units or a rise above 25,000 units as being extremely unlikely. Similarly, they expect the sales price as set in the marketplace to fall within the range of $1,500 to $2,500. Thus, 15,000 units at a price of $1,500 defines the lower bound, or the **worst case scenario,** whereas 25,000 units at a price of $2,500 defines the upper bound, or the **best case scenario.** Remember that the **base case** values are 20,000 units and a price of $2,000.

Table 15-5 ▪ **Scenario Analysis**

Scenario	Sales Volume (Units)	Sales Price	NPV (Thousands of Dollars)	Probability of Outcome (P_i)	NPV × P_i (Thousands of Dollars)
Worst case	15,000	$1,500	($ 5,761)	0.25	($ 1,440)
Most likely case	20,000	2,000	6,996	0.50	3,498
Best case	25,000	2,500	23,397	0.25	5,849
				Expected NPV =	$ 7,907
				σ_{NPV} =	$10,349
				CV_{NPV} =	1.3

To carry out the scenario analysis, we use the worst case variable values to obtain the worst case NPV and the best case variable values to obtain the best case NPV.[6] We actually performed the analysis using a *Lotus* model, and Table 15-5 summarizes the results of this analysis. We see that under the base case (or most likely case) forecast a positive NPV results; the worst case produces a negative NPV; and the best case results in a very large positive NPV.

We can use the results of the scenario analysis to determine the expected NPV, the standard deviation of NPV, and the coefficient of variation. To begin, we need an estimate of the probabilities of occurrence of the three scenarios, the P_i values. Suppose management estimates that there is a 25 percent probability of the worst case scenario occurring, a 50 percent probability of the base case, and a 25 percent probability of the best case. Of course, it is *very difficult* to estimate scenario probabilities accurately.

The scenario probabilities and NPVs constitute a probability distribution of returns just like those we dealt with in Chapter 4, except that the returns are measured in dollars instead of in percentages (rates of return). The expected NPV (in thousands of dollars) is $7,907:[7]

$$\text{Expected NPV} = \sum_{i=1}^{n} P_i(NPV_i)$$
$$= 0.25(-\$5,761) + 0.50(\$6,996) + 0.25(\$23,397)$$
$$= \$7,907.$$

---

[6]We could have included worst and best case values for fixed and variable costs, income tax rates, salvage values, and so on. For illustrative purposes, we limited the changes to only two variables. Also, note that we are treating sales price and quantity as independent variables; that is, a low sales price could occur when unit sales were low, and a high sales price could be coupled with high unit sales, or vice versa. As we discuss in the next section, it is relatively easy to vary these assumptions if the facts of the situation suggest a different set of conditions.

[7]Note that the expected NPV is *not* the same as the base case NPV, $6,996 (in thousands). This is because the two uncertain variables, sales volume and sales price, are multiplied together to obtain dollar sales, and this process causes the NPV distribution to be skewed to the right. A big number times another big number produces a very big number, which in turn causes the average, or expected value, to be increased.

The standard deviation of the NPV is $10,349 (in thousands of dollars):

$$\sigma_{NPV} = \sqrt{\sum_{i=1}^{n} P_i(NPV_i - \text{Expected NPV})^2}$$

$$= \sqrt{\begin{array}{c} 0.25(-\$5,761 - \$7,907)^2 + 0.50(\$6,996 - \$7,907)^2 \\ + \ 0.25(\$23,397 - \$7,907)^2 \end{array}}$$

$$= \$10,349.$$

Finally, the project's coefficient of variation is 1.3:

$$CV_{NPV} = \frac{\sigma_{NPV}}{E(NPV)} = \frac{\$10,349}{\$7,907} = 1.3.$$

Now the project's coefficient of variation can be compared with the coefficient of variation of Brandt-Quigley's "average" project to get an idea of the relative riskiness of the appliance control computer project. Brandt-Quigley's existing projects, on average, have a coefficient of variation of about 1.0, so, on the basis of this stand-alone risk measure, Brandt-Quigley's managers would conclude that the appliance computer project is riskier than the firm's "average" project.

Scenario analysis provides useful information about a project's stand-alone risk. However, it is limited in that it only considers a few discrete outcomes (NPVs) for the project, even though there really are an infinite number of possibilities. In the next section, we describe a more rigorous method of assessing a project's stand-alone risk.

Monte Carlo Simulation

Monte Carlo simulation

A risk analysis technique in which probable future events are simulated on a computer, generating estimated rates of return and risk indexes.

Monte Carlo simulation, so named because this type of analysis grew out of work on the mathematics of casino gambling, ties together sensitivities and input variable probability distributions.[8] However, simulation requires a relatively powerful computer, coupled with an efficient financial planning software package, whereas scenario analysis can be done using a PC with a spreadsheet program or even using a calculator.

The first step in a computer simulation is to specify the probability distribution of each uncertain cash flow variable. Once this has been done, the simulation proceeds as follows:

1. The computer chooses at random a value for each uncertain variable based on the variable's specified probability distribution. For example, a value for unit sales would be chosen and used in the first model run.

2. The value selected for each uncertain variable, along with values for fixed factors such as the tax rate and depreciation charges, are then used in the model to determine the net cash flows for each year, and these cash flows are then used to determine the project's NPV in the first run.

---

[8]The use of simulation analysis in capital budgeting was first reported by David B. Hertz, "Risk Analysis in Capital Investments," *Harvard Business Review,* January–February 1964, 95–106.

3. Steps 1 and 2 are repeated many times, say 500, resulting in 500 NPVs, which make up a probability distribution.

Using this procedure, we performed a simulation analysis on Brandt-Quigley's appliance control computer project. We simplified the illustration by specifying a probability distribution for only one key variable—we assumed that unit sales is best specified by a normal distribution with an expected value of 20,000 units and a standard deviation of 2,000 units. For all of the other variables, we simply used their expected values. The resulting NPV distribution is graphed in Figure 15-4. Note that the standard deviation and the expected NPV are smaller in the simulation than in the scenario analysis. This occurred as a result of the probability distribution of sales we used in the simulation analysis.

The primary advantage of simulation is that it shows us the range of possible outcomes along with their attached probabilities, rather than merely a point estimate of the NPV. From Figure 15-4 we can see that the expected NPV is $7.3 million and that the standard deviation of the NPV is $10.2 million. Thus, the coefficient of variation is $10.2 million/$7.3 million = 1.40. These figures differ slightly from those developed in the scenario analysis because we used different assumptions in the two analyses. Simulation software packages can be used to estimate the probability of NPV > 0, of IRR > k, and so on. This additional information can be quite helpful in assessing the riskiness of a project.

Limitations of Scenario and Simulation Analysis

In spite of its obvious appeal, Monte Carlo simulation has not been widely used in industry. One of the major problems is specifying the correlations among the uncertain cash flow variables. Mechanically, it is easy to incorporate any type of correlation among variables into a simulation analysis; for example, @RISK, the *Lotus* add-in simulation software that we used to create Figure 15-4, permits one to specify both intervariable and intertemporal correlations. However, it is *not* easy to specify what the correlations should be. Indeed, people who have tried to obtain such relationships from the operating managers who must estimate them have eloquently emphasized the difficulties involved. The problem is not insurmountable, as simulation is used in business, but it is important not to underestimate the difficulty of obtaining valid estimates of probability distributions and correlations among the variables.[9]

Another problem with both scenario and simulation analyses is that even when the analysis has been completed, no clear-cut decision rule emerges. We end up with an expected NPV and a distribution about this expected value, and we can use these statistics to judge the project's stand-alone risk. However, the analysis provides no mechanism to indicate whether a project's profitability as measured by its expected NPV is sufficient to compensate for its risk as measured by its σ_{NPV} or CV_{NPV}.

Finally, scenario and simulation analyses ignore the effects of diversification, both among projects within the firm and by investors in their personal invest-

---

[9]For more insight into the difficulties involved in estimating probability distributions and correlations in practice, see K. Larry Hastie, "One Businessman's View of Capital Budgeting," *Financial Management,* Winter 1974, 36–43. Hastie was treasurer of Bendix Corporation.

Figure 15-4   ▪   **NPV Probability Distribution (Millions of Dollars)**

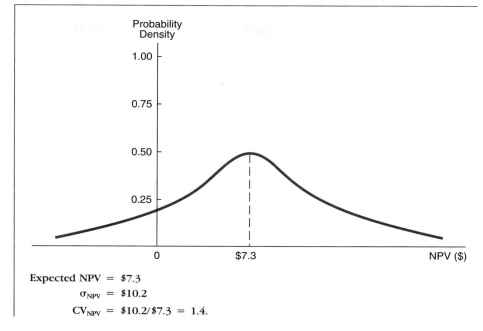

Expected NPV = $7.3

σ_{NPV} = $10.2

CV_{NPV} = $10.2/$7.3 = 1.4.

ment portfolios. Thus, an individual project might have highly uncertain returns when evaluated on a stand-alone basis, but if those returns are not correlated with the returns on the firm's other assets, the project may not be very risky in terms of either corporate or market risk.

? *Self-Test Questions*

List three reasons why, in practice, a project's stand-alone risk is important.

Differentiate between sensitivity and scenario analyses. Why might scenario analysis be preferable to sensitivity analysis?

What is Monte Carlo simulation?

Identify some problems with (1) sensitivity analysis, (2) scenario analysis, and (3) Monte Carlo simulation.

BETA (OR MARKET) RISK

The types of risk analysis discussed thus far in the chapter provide insights into a project's risk and thus help managers make better accept/reject decisions. However, these risk measures do not take account of portfolio risk, and they do not specify whether a project should be accepted or rejected. In this section, we show how the CAPM can be used to help overcome those shortcomings. Of course, the CAPM has shortcomings of its own, but it nevertheless offers useful insights into risk analysis in capital budgeting.

To begin, recall from Chapter 4 that the Security Market Line equation expresses the risk/return relationship as follows:

$$k_s = k_{RF} + (k_M - k_{RF})b_i.$$

As an example, consider the case of Erie Steel Company, an integrated steel producer operating in the Great Lakes region. For simplicity, assume that Erie is all equity financed, so its cost of equity is also its overall cost of capital. Erie's beta $= b = 1.1$; $k_{RF} = 8\%$; and $k_M = 12\%$. Thus, Erie's cost of equity is 12.4 percent:

$$k_s = 8\% + (12\% - 8\%)1.1$$
$$= 8\% + (4\%)1.1$$
$$= 12.4\%.$$

This suggests that investors should be willing to give Erie money to invest in average risk projects if the company expects to earn 12.4 percent or more on this money. Here again, by average risk we mean projects having risk similar to the firm's existing assets. *Therefore, as a first approximation, Erie should invest in capital projects if and only if these projects have an expected return of 12.4 percent or more.*[10] In other words, Erie should use 12.4 percent as its discount rate to determine the NPVs of any average risk project which it is considering.

Suppose, however, that taking on a particular project would cause a change in Erie's beta coefficient and hence change the company's cost of equity. For example, suppose Erie is considering the construction of a fleet of barges to haul iron ore, and barge operations have betas of 1.5 rather than 1.1. Since the firm itself may be regarded as a "portfolio of assets," and since the beta of any portfolio is a weighted average of the betas of its individual assets, taking on the barge project would cause the overall corporate beta to rise to somewhere between the original beta of 1.1 and the barge project's beta of 1.5. The exact value of the new beta would depend on the relative size of the investment in barge operations versus Erie's other assets. If 80 percent of Erie's total funds ended up in basic steel operations with a beta of 1.1 and 20 percent in barge operations with a beta of 1.5, the new corporate beta would be 1.18:

$$\text{New beta} = 0.8(1.1) + 0.2(1.5)$$
$$= 1.18.$$

This increase in Erie's beta coefficient would cause its stock price to decline *unless the increased beta were offset by a higher expected rate of return.* Note that taking on the new project would cause the overall corporate cost of capital to rise from the original 12.4 percent to 12.72 percent:

$$k_s = 8\% + (4\%)1.18$$
$$= 12.72\%.$$

Therefore, to keep the barge investment from lowering the value of the firm, Erie's overall expected rate of return must rise from 12.4 to 12.72 percent.

---

[10]To simplify things somewhat, we assume at this point that the firm uses only equity capital. If debt is used, the cost of capital used must be a weighted average of the costs of debt and equity. This point is discussed at length in Chapter 16.

If investments in basic steel must earn 12.4 percent, how much must the barge investment earn for the new overall rate of return to equal 12.72 percent? We know that if Erie undertakes the barge investment, it will have 80 percent of its assets invested in basic steel projects earning 12.4 percent and 20 percent in barge operations earning "X" percent, and the average required rate of return will be 12.72 percent. Therefore,

$$0.8(12.4\%) + 0.2X = 12.72\%$$
$$0.2X = 2.8\%$$
$$X = 14\%.$$

Since X = 14%, we see that the barge project must have an expected return of 14 percent if the corporation is to earn its new cost of capital.

In summary, if Erie takes on the barge project, its corporate beta will rise from 1.1 to 1.18; its cost of capital will rise from 12.4 to 12.72 percent; and the barge investment will have to earn 14 percent if the company is to earn its new overall cost of capital.

This line of reasoning leads to the conclusion that if the beta coefficient for each project, b_p, could be determined, then a **project cost of capital, k_p,** for each individual project could be found as follows:

project cost of capital, k_p
The risk-adjusted cost of capital for an individual project.

$$k_p = k_{RF} + (k_M - k_{RF})b_p.$$

Thus, for basic steel projects with b = 1.1, Erie should use 12.4 percent as the cost of capital. The barge project, with b = 1.5, should be evaluated at a 14 percent cost of capital:

$$k_{Barge} = 8\% + (4\%)1.5$$
$$= 8\% + 6\%$$
$$= 14\%.$$

On the other hand, a low risk project such as a new steel distribution center with a beta of only 0.5 would have a cost of capital of 10 percent:

$$k_{Center} = 8\% + (4\%)0.5$$
$$= 10\%.$$

Figure 15-5 gives a graphic summary of these concepts as applied to Erie Steel. Note the following points:

1. The SML is a Security Market Line like the one we developed in Chapter 4. It shows how investors are willing to make tradeoffs between risk as measured by beta and expected returns. The higher the beta risk, the higher the rate of return needed to compensate investors for bearing this risk. The SML specifies the nature of this relationship.

2. Erie Steel initially had a beta of 1.1, so its required rate of return on average risk investments was 12.4 percent.

3. High risk investments such as the barge line require higher rates of return, whereas low risk investments such as the distribution center require lower rates of return. If Erie concentrates its new investments in either high or low risk projects as opposed to average risk ones, its corporate beta will either rise or fall from the current value of 1.1. Consequently, Erie's re-

Figure 15-5 ▪ Using the Security Market Line Concept in Capital Budgeting

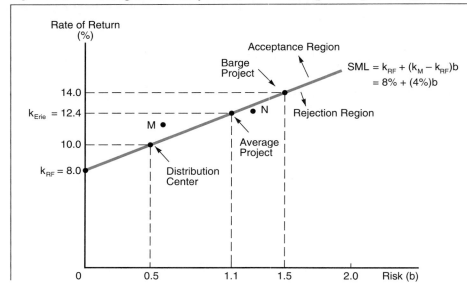

quired rate of return on common stock would change from its current value of 12.4 percent.

4. If the expected rate of return on a given capital project lies *above* the SML, the expected rate of return on the project is more than enough to compensate for its risk, and the project should be accepted. Conversely, if the project's rate of return lies *below* the SML, it should be rejected. Thus, Project M in Figure 15-5 is acceptable, whereas Project N should be rejected. N has a higher expected return than M, but the differential is not enough to offset its much higher risk.

Self-Test Questions

What is meant by the term "average risk project"? How would one find the cost of capital for such a project, for a low risk project, and for a high risk project?

Complete the following sentence: An increase in a company's beta coefficient would cause its stock price to decline unless . . .

Explain why a firm should accept a given capital project if its expected rate of return lies above the SML. What if the expected rate of return lies on the SML? Below the SML?

TECHNIQUES FOR MEASURING BETA RISK

In Chapter 4, we discussed the estimation of betas for stocks, and we indicated that it is difficult to estimate true future betas. The estimation of project betas is even more difficult and more fraught with uncertainty. However, two approaches can be used to estimate individual assets' betas—the pure play method and the accounting beta method.

The Pure Play Method

pure play method

An approach used for estimating the beta of a project in which a firm identifies several companies whose only business is the product in question, determines the beta for each firm, and then averages the betas to find an approximation of its own project's beta.

In the **pure play method,** the company tries to find several single-product companies in the same line of business as the project being evaluated, and it then applies these betas to determine the cost of capital for its own project. For example, suppose Erie could find three existing single-product firms that operate barges, and suppose also that Erie's management believes its barge project would be subject to the same risks as these firms. Erie could then determine the betas of those firms, average them, and use this average beta as a proxy for the barge project's beta.[11]

The pure play approach can only be used for major assets such as whole divisions, and even then it is frequently difficult to implement because it is often impossible to find pure play proxy firms. However, when IBM was considering going into personal computers, it was able to obtain data on Apple Computer and several other essentially pure play personal computer companies. This is often the case when a firm considers a major investment outside its primary field.

The Accounting Beta Method

accounting beta method

A method of estimating a project's beta by running a regression of the company's basic earning power against the average basic earning power for a large sample of firms.

As noted above, it is often impossible to find single-product, publicly traded firms suitable for the pure play approach. If that is the case, we may be able to use the **accounting beta method.** Betas normally are found as described in Appendix 4A—by regressing the returns of a particular company's stock against returns on a stock market index. However, we could run a regression of the company's basic earning power (EBIT/Total assets) over time against the average basic earning power for a large sample of companies, such as those included in the S&P 400. Betas determined in this way (that is, by using accounting data rather than stock market data) are called *accounting betas.*

Accounting betas for projects can be calculated only after the project has been accepted, has been placed in operation, and has begun to generate output and accounting results. However, to the extent that management thinks a given project is similar to other projects the firm has undertaken in the past, other projects' accounting betas can be used as proxies for that of the project in question. In practice, accounting betas are normally calculated for divisions or other large units, not for single assets, and divisional betas are then used for the division's projects.

Self-Test Question

What is the difference between the pure play and the accounting beta methods for estimating individual projects' betas?

---

[11] If the pure play firms employ different capital structures than that of Erie, this fact must be dealt with by adjusting the beta coefficients. See Eugene F. Brigham and Louis C. Gapenski, *Intermediate Financial Management,* 4th ed., Chapter 9, for a discussion of this aspect of the pure play method.

SHOULD FIRMS DIVERSIFY TO REDUCE RISK?

As we learned in Chapter 4, a security may be risky if held in isolation but not very risky if held as part of a well-diversified portfolio. The same is true of capital budgeting; returns on an individual project may be highly uncertain, but if the project is small relative to the total firm, and if its returns are not highly correlated with the firm's other assets, the project may not be very risky in the corporate or the beta sense.

Many firms make a serious effort to diversify; often this is a specific objective of the long-run strategic plan. For example, KeyCorp, a bank holding company with offices in New England, has weathered that region's economic storms because it also owns banks in the Pacific Northwest that have been profitable. Similarly, NCNB, a North Carolina–based banking concern that acquired Atlanta–based C&S/Sovran to become NationsBank, the third largest U.S. bank, stated: "We like having textiles and tobacco in North Carolina, citrus growing and tourism in Florida, cattle ranching and oil in Texas." One objective of moves such as those of KeyCorp and NCNB is to stabilize earnings, reduce corporate risk, and raise the value of the firm's stock.

The wisdom of corporate diversification designed to reduce risk has been questioned — why should a firm diversify when stockholders can easily diversify themselves? In other words, although it may be true that if the returns on NCNB's and C&S/Sovran's stocks are not perfectly positively correlated, then merging the companies will reduce their risks somewhat, would it not be as easy for investors to diversify directly, without the trouble and expense of a merger?

The answer is not simple. Although stockholders could directly obtain some of the risk-reducing benefits through personal diversification, other benefits can be gained only by diversification at the corporate level. For example, a more stable bank might be able to attract a better work force and also obtain funds cheaper than could two less stable banks. Also, there may be spillover effects from mergers. For example, NCNB became expert at cleaning up bad real estate loans after it acquired banks in Texas, and that expertise will help it clean up bad loans at C&S/Sovran. Finally, combining the administrative offices of the two banks, and closing some branches, will result in economies of scale, lower costs, and, thus, higher profits.

? *Self-Test Questions*

Does a merger which lowers a company's risk by stabilizing earnings necessarily benefit stockholders?

Are there any good reasons why a firm might want to engage in mergers even though its stockholders could diversify on their own?

PROJECT RISK CONCLUSIONS

We have discussed the three types of risk normally considered in capital budgeting analysis — stand-alone risk, within-firm (or corporate) risk, and beta (or market) risk — and we have discussed ways of assessing each. However, two important questions remain: (1) Should a firm be concerned with stand-alone and corporate risk in its capital budgeting decisions, and (2) what do we do when the stand-alone or within-firm risk assessments and the beta risk assessment lead to different conclusions?

These questions do not have easy answers. From a theoretical standpoint, well-diversified investors should be concerned only with beta risk, managers should be concerned only with stock price maximization, and these two factors should lead to the conclusion that beta risk ought to be given virtually all the weight in capital budgeting decisions. However, if investors are not well diversified, if the CAPM does not operate exactly as theory says it should, or if measurement problems keep managers from having confidence in the CAPM approach in capital budgeting, it may be appropriate to give stand-alone and corporate risk more weight than financial theorists suggest. Note also that the CAPM ignores bankruptcy costs, even though such costs can be substantial, and that the probability of bankruptcy depends on a firm's corporate risk, not on its beta risk. Therefore, one can easily conclude that even well-diversified investors should want a firm's management to give at least some consideration to a project's corporate risk instead of concentrating entirely on beta risk.

Although it would be desirable to reconcile these problems and to measure project risk on some absolute scale, the best we can do in practice is to determine project risk in a somewhat nebulous, relative sense. For example, we can generally say with a fair degree of confidence that a particular project has more or less stand-alone risk than the firm's average project. Then, assuming that stand-alone and corporate risk are highly correlated (which is typical), the project's stand-alone risk will be a good measure of its corporate risk. Finally, assuming that beta risk and corporate risk are highly correlated (as is true for most companies), a project with more corporate risk than average will also have more beta risk, and vice versa for projects with low corporate risk.[12]

Self-Test Questions

In theory, is it correct for a firm to be concerned with stand-alone and corporate risk in its capital budgeting decisions? Should the firm be concerned with these risks in practice?

If a project's stand-alone, corporate, and beta risk are highly correlated, would this make the task of measuring risk easier or harder? Explain.

INCORPORATING PROJECT RISK AND CAPITAL STRUCTURE INTO CAPITAL BUDGETING

Thus far, we have seen that capital budgeting can affect a firm's beta risk, its corporate risk, or both. We have also seen that it is extremely difficult to quantify either type of risk. In other words, although it may be possible to reach the

---

[12]For example, see M. Chapman Findlay III, Arthur E. Gooding, and Wallace Q. Weaver, Jr., "On the Relevant Risk for Determining Capital Expenditure Hurdle Rates," *Financial Management,* Winter 1976, 9–16.

general conclusion that one project is riskier than another, it is difficult to develop a really good *measure* of project risk. This lack of precision in measuring project risk makes it difficult to incorporate differential risk into capital budgeting decisions.

There are two methods for incorporating project risk into the capital budgeting decision process. One is called the *certainty equivalent* approach, under which the expected cash flows in each year are adjusted to reflect project risk. Here all cash flows that are not known with certainty are scaled down, and the riskier the flows, the lower their certainty equivalent values. However, the certainty equivalent approach is difficult to implement in practice, and hence we will focus on the **risk-adjusted discount rate** approach, under which differential project risk is dealt with by changing the discount rate. Average risk projects are discounted at the firm's average cost of capital, above-average risk projects are discounted at a higher cost of capital, and below-average risk projects are discounted at a rate below the firm's average cost of capital. Unfortunately, because risk cannot be measured precisely, there is no good way of specifying exactly *how much* higher or lower these discount rates should be; given the present state of the art, risk adjustments are necessarily judgmental and somewhat arbitrary.

Capital structure must also be taken into account if a firm finances different assets in different ways. For example, one division might have a lot of real estate which is well suited as collateral for loans, whereas some other division might have most of its capital tied up in special-purpose machinery, which is not good collateral. As a result, the division with the real estate might have a higher *debt capacity* than the division with the machinery, hence an optimal capital structure which contains a higher percentage of debt. In this case, the financial manager might calculate the cost of capital differently for the two divisions.[13]

Although the process is not exact, many companies use a two-step procedure to develop risk-adjusted discount rates for use in capital budgeting. First, *divisional costs of capital* are established for each of the major operating divisions on the basis of each division's estimated average riskiness and its capital structure. Second, within each division, all projects are classified into three categories—high risk, average risk, and low risk. Then, each division uses its basic divisional cost of capital as the discount rate for average risk projects, reduces the divisional cost of capital by one or two percentage points when evaluating low risk projects, and raises the cost of capital by several percentage points for high risk projects. For example, if a division's basic cost of capital is estimated to be 10 percent, a 12 percent discount rate might be used for a high risk project and a 9 percent rate for a low risk project. Average risk projects, which constitute about 80 percent of most capital budgets, would be evaluated at the 10 percent divisional cost of capital. This procedure is far from precise, but it does at least recognize that different divisions have different characteristics and hence different costs of capital, and it also acknowledges differential project riskiness within divisions.

risk-adjusted discount rate

The discount rate that applies to a particular risky stream of income; it is equal to the risk-free rate of interest plus a risk premium appropriate to the level of risk attached to a particular project's income stream.

---

[13]We will say much more about optimal capital structure and debt capacity in Chapters 16 and 17.

Self-Test Questions

How are risk-adjusted discount rates used to incorporate project risk into the capital budget decision process?

Briefly explain the two-step process many companies use to develop risk-adjusted discount rates for use in capital budgeting.

CAPITAL RATIONING

capital rationing
A situation in which a constraint is placed on the total size of the firm's capital investment.

Capital budgeting decisions are typically made on the basis of the techniques presented in Chapter 14 and applied as described in this chapter — independent projects are accepted if their NPVs are positive, and choices among mutually exclusive projects are made by selecting the one with the highest NPV. In this analysis, it is assumed that if in a particular year the firm has an especially large number of good projects, management simply will go into the financial markets and raise whatever funds are required to finance all of the acceptable projects. However, some firms do set limits on the amount of funds they are willing to raise, and, if this is done, the capital budget must also be limited. This situation is known as **capital rationing.**

Elaborate and mathematically sophisticated models have been developed to help firms maximize their values when they are subject to capital rationing. However, a firm which subjects itself to capital rationing is deliberately forgoing profitable projects, and hence it is not truly maximizing its value. This point is well known, so few sophisticated firms ration capital today. Therefore, we shall not discuss it further, but you should know what the term *capital rationing* means.

Self-Test Questions

What is meant by the term "capital rationing"?

Why do few sophisticated firms ration capital today?

SUMMARY

This chapter presented two issues in capital budgeting: cash flow estimation and evaluation and risk analysis in capital budgeting. The key concepts covered are listed below.

- The most important, but also the most difficult, step in analyzing a capital budgeting project is **estimating the incremental after-tax cash flows** the project will produce.

- **Net cash flows** consist of net income plus depreciation. In most situations, net cash flows are estimated by forecasting annual cash flow statements.

- In determining incremental cash flows, **opportunity costs** (the cash flow foregone by using an asset) must be included, but **sunk costs** (cash outlays that have been made and that cannot be recouped) should not be included. Any **externalities** (effects of a project on other parts of the firm) should also be reflected in the analysis.

▪ Capital projects often require an additional investment in **net working capital (NWC).** An increase in NWC must be included in the Year 0 initial cash outlay and then shown as a cash inflow in the project's final year.

▪ **Replacement analysis** is slightly different from that for **expansion projects** because the cash flows from the old asset must be considered in replacement decisions.

▪ If mutually exclusive projects have **unequal lives,** it may be necessary to adjust the analysis to place the projects on an equal life basis. This can be done using either the **replacement chain approach** or the **equivalent annual annuity approach.**

▪ **Inflation effects** must be considered in project analysis. The best procedure is to build inflation directly into the cash flow estimates.

▪ A project's **stand-alone risk** is the risk the project would have if it were the firm's only asset and if the firm's stockholders held only that one stock. Stand-alone risk is measured by the variability of the asset's expected returns, and it is often used as a proxy for both beta and corporate risk because (1) beta and corporate risk are difficult to measure and (2) the three types of risk are usually highly correlated.

▪ **Within-firm,** or **corporate, risk** reflects the effects of a project on the firm's risk, and it is measured by the project's effect on the firm's earnings variability. Stockholder diversification is not taken into account.

▪ **Beta risk** reflects the effects of a project on the risks borne by stockholders, assuming stockholders hold diversified portfolios. In theory, beta risk should be the most relevant type of risk.

▪ **Corporate risk** is important because it influences the firm's ability to use low-cost debt, to maintain smooth operations over time, and to avoid crises that might consume management's energy and disrupt employees, customers, suppliers, and the community.

▪ **Sensitivity analysis** is a technique which shows how much an output variable such as NPV will change in response to a given change in an input variable such as sales, other things held constant.

▪ **Scenario analysis** is a risk analysis technique in which the best and worst case NPVs are compared with the project's expected NPV.

▪ **Monte Carlo simulation** is a risk analysis technique in which a computer is used to simulate probable future events and thus to estimate the profitability distribution and riskiness of a project.

▪ The **pure play method** and the **accounting beta method** can be used to estimate betas for large projects or for divisions.

▪ The **risk-adjusted discount rate** is the rate used to evaluate a particular project. The discount rate is increased for projects which are riskier than the firm's average project but is decreased for less risky projects.

▪ **Capital rationing** occurs when management places a constraint on the size of the firm's capital budget during a particular period.

Both the measurement of risk and its incorporation into capital budgeting involve judgment. It is possible to use a quantitative technique such as simulation as an aid to judgment, but in the final analysis the assessment of risk in capital budgeting is a subjective process.

Questions

15-1   Cash flows rather than accounting profits are listed in Table 15-2. What is the basis for this emphasis on cash flows as opposed to net income?

15-2   Look at Table 15-4 and answer these questions:
   a. Why is the salvage value shown on Line 12 reduced for taxes on Line 13?
   b. Why is depreciation on the old machine deducted on Line 8 to get Line 9?
   c. What would happen if the new machine permitted a *reduction* in net working capital?
   d. Why were the cost savings shown on Line 6 reduced by multiplying the before-tax figure by $(1 - T)$, whereas the change in depreciation figure on Line 9 was multiplied by T?

15-3   Explain why sunk costs should not be included in a capital budgeting analysis, but opportunity costs and externalities should be included.

15-4   Explain how net working capital is recovered at the end of a project's life, and why it is included in a capital budgeting analysis.

15-5   In general, is an explicit recognition of incremental cash flows more important in new project or replacement analysis? Why?

15-6   Why is it true, in general, that a failure to adjust expected cash flows for expected inflation biases the calculated NPV downward?

15-7   Suppose a firm is considering two mutually exclusive projects. One has a life of 6 years and the other a life of 10 years. Would the failure to employ some type of replacement chain analysis bias an NPV analysis against one of the projects? Explain.

15-8   Define (a) simulation analysis, (b) scenario analysis, and (c) sensitivity analysis. If AT&T were considering two investments, one calling for the expenditure of $200 million to develop a satellite communications system and the other involving the expenditure of $12,000 for a new truck, on which one would the company be more likely to use simulation analysis?

15-9   Distinguish between beta (or market) risk, within-firm (or corporate) risk, and stand-alone risk for a project being considered for inclusion in the capital budget. Which type of risk do you believe should be given the greatest weight in capital budgeting decisions? Explain.

15-10   Suppose Reading Engine Company, which has a high beta as well as a great deal of corporate risk, merged with Simplicity Patterns Inc. Simplicity's sales rise during recessions, when people are more likely to make their own clothes, and, consequently, its beta is negative but its corporate risk is relatively high. What would the merger do to the costs of capital in the consolidated company's locomotive engine division and in its patterns division?

15-11   Suppose a firm estimates its cost of capital for the coming year to be 10 percent. What are reasonable costs of capital for evaluating average risk projects, high risk projects, and low risk projects?

Self-Test Problems   *(Solutions Appear in Appendix B)*

ST-1
Key terms

Define each of the following terms:
a. Cash flow; accounting income; relevant cash flow
b. Incremental cash flow; sunk cost; opportunity cost; externalities
c. Change in net working capital; expansion project
d. Salvage value
e. Replacement analysis
f. Replacement chain (common life) approach
g. Equivalent annual annuity (EAA) method
h. Stand-alone risk; within-firm risk; market risk
i. Corporate risk
j. Sensitivity analysis
k. Scenario analysis
l. Monte Carlo simulation analysis
m. Coefficient of variation versus standard deviation
n. Project beta versus corporate beta
o. Pure play method of estimating divisional betas; accounting beta method
p. Corporate diversification versus stockholder diversification
q. Risk-adjusted discount rate; project cost of capital
r. Capital rationing

ST-2
New project analysis

You have been asked by the president of Ellis Construction Company, headquartered in Toledo, to evaluate the proposed acquisition of a new earthmover. The mover's basic price is $50,000, and it will cost another $10,000 to modify it for special use by Ellis Construction. Assume that the mover falls into the MACRS 3-year class. (See Table 15A-2 for MACRS recovery allowance percentages.) It will be sold after 3 years for $20,000, and it will require an increase in net working capital (spare parts inventory) of $2,000. The earthmover purchase will have no effect on revenues, but it is expected to save Ellis $20,000 per year in before-tax operating costs, mainly labor. Ellis's federal-plus-state tax rate is 40 percent.
a. What is the company's net investment if it acquires the earthmover? (That is, what are the Year 0 cash flows?)
b. What are the operating cash flows in Years 1, 2, and 3?
c. What are the additional (nonoperating) cash flows in Year 3?
d. If the project's cost of capital is 10 percent, should the earthmover be purchased?

ST-3
Replacement analysis

The Dauten Toy Corporation currently uses an injection molding machine that was purchased 2 years ago. This machine is being depreciated on a straight line basis toward a $500 salvage value, and it has 6 years of remaining life. Its current book value is $2,600, and it can be sold for $3,000 at this time. Thus, the annual depreciation expense is ($2,600 − $500)/6 = $350 per year.

Dauten is offered a replacement machine which has a cost of $8,000, an estimated useful life of 6 years, and an estimated salvage value of $800. This machine falls into the MACRS 5-year class. (See Table 15A-2 for MACRS recovery allowance percentages.) The replacement machine would permit an output expansion, so sales would rise by $1,000 per year; even so, the new machine's much greater efficiency would still cause operating expenses to decline by $1,500 per year. The new machine would require that inventories be increased by $2,000, but accounts payable would simultaneously increase by $500.

Dauten's federal-plus-state tax rate is 40 percent, and its cost of capital is 15 percent. Should it replace the old machine?

ST-4
Corporate risk analysis

The staff of Heymann Manufacturing has estimated the following net cash flows and probabilities for a new manufacturing process:

| | **Net Cash Flows** | | |
Year	P = 0.2	P = 0.6	P = 0.2
0	($100,000)	($100,000)	($100,000)
1	20,000	30,000	40,000
2	20,000	30,000	40,000
3	20,000	30,000	40,000
4	20,000	30,000	40,000
5	20,000	30,000	40,000
5*	0	20,000	30,000

Line 0 gives the cost of the process, Lines 1 through 5 give operating cash flows, and Line 5* contains the estimated salvage values. Heymann's cost of capital for an average risk project is 10 percent.

a. Assume that the project has average risk. Find the project's expected NPV. (Hint: Use expected values for the net cash flow in each year.)

b. Find the best case and worst case NPVs. What is the probability of occurrence of the worst case if the cash flows are perfectly dependent (perfectly positively correlated) over time? If they are independent over time?

c. Assume that all the cash flows are perfectly positively correlated, that is, there are only three possible cash flow streams over time: (1) the worst case, (2) the most likely, or base, case, and (3) the best case, with probabilities of 0.2, 0.6, and 0.2, respectively. These cases are represented by each of the columns in the table. Find the expected NPV, its standard deviation, and its coefficient of variation.

d. The coefficient of variation of Heymann's average project is in the range 0.8 to 1.0. If the coefficient of variation of a project being evaluated is greater than 1.0, 2 percentage points are added to the firm's cost of capital. Similarly, if the coefficient of variation is less than 0.8, 1 percentage point is deducted from the cost of capital. What is the project's cost of capital? Should Heymann accept or reject the project?

Problems

15-1
New project analysis

You have been asked by the president of your company to evaluate the proposed acquisition of a spectrometer for the firm's R&D department. The equipment's base price is $140,000, and it would cost another $30,000 to modify it for special use by your firm. The spectrometer, which falls into the MACRS 3-year class, would be sold after 3 years for $60,000. (See Table 15A-2 for MACRS recovery allowance percentages.) Use of the equipment would require an increase in net working capital (spare parts inventory) of $8,000. The spectrometer would have no effect on revenues, but it is expected to save the firm $50,000 per year in before-tax operating costs, mainly labor. The firm's federal-plus-state tax rate is 40 percent.

a. What is the net cost of the spectrometer? (That is, what is the Year 0 net cash flow?)
b. What are the net operating cash flows in Years 1, 2, and 3?
c. What is the additional (nonoperating) cash flow in Year 3?
d. If the project's cost of capital is 12 percent, should the spectrometer be purchased?

15-2
New project analysis

The Ewert Company is evaluating the proposed acquisition of a new milling machine. The machine's base price is $108,000, and it would cost another $12,500 to modify it for special use by the firm. The machine falls into the MACRS 3-year class, and it would be sold after 3 years for $65,000. (See Table 15A-2 for MACRS recovery allowance percentages.) The machine would require an increase in net working capital (inventory) of $5,500. The milling machine would have no effect on revenues, but it is expected to save the firm $44,000 per year in before-tax operating costs, mainly labor. Ewert's tax rate is 34 percent.

a.   What is the net cost of the machine for capital budgeting purposes? (That is, what is the Year 0 net cash flow?)

b.   What are the net operating cash flows in Years 1, 2, and 3?

c.   What is the additional (nonoperating) cash flow in Year 3?

d.   If the project's cost of capital is 12 percent, should the machine be purchased?

15-3

Replacement analysis

The Tysseland Equipment Company purchased a machine 5 years ago at a cost of $100,000. The machine had an expected life of 10 years at the time of purchase and an expected salvage value of $10,000 at the end of the 10 years. It is being depreciated by the straight line method toward a salvage value of $10,000, or by $9,000 per year.

A new machine can be purchased for $150,000, including installation costs. During its 5-year life, it will reduce cash operating expenses by $50,000 per year. Sales are not expected to change. At the end of its useful life, the machine is estimated to be worthless. MACRS depreciation will be used, and the machine will be depreciated over its 3-year class life rather than its 5-year economic life. (See Table 15A-2 for MACRS recovery allowance percentages.)

The old machine can be sold today for $65,000. The firm's tax rate is 34 percent. The appropriate discount rate is 16 percent.

a.   If the new machine is purchased, what is the amount of the initial cash flow at Year 0?

b.   What incremental operating cash flows will occur at the end of Years 1 through 5 as a result of replacing the old machine?

c.   What incremental nonoperating cash flow will occur at the end of Year 5 if the new machine is purchased?

d.   What is the NPV of this project? Should Tysseland replace the old machine?

15-4

Replacement analysis

The Boyd Bottling Company is contemplating the replacement of one of its bottling machines with a newer and more efficient one. The old machine has a book value of $600,000 and a remaining useful life of 5 years. The firm does not expect to realize any return from scrapping the old machine in 5 years, but it can sell it now to another firm in the industry for $265,000. The old machine is being depreciated toward a zero salvage value, or by $120,000 per year, using the straight line method.

The new machine has a purchase price of $1,175,000, an estimated useful life and MACRS class life of 5 years, and an estimated salvage value of $145,000. (See Table 15A-2 for MACRS recovery allowance percentages.) It is expected to economize on electric power usage, labor, and repair costs, as well as to reduce the number of defective bottles. In total, an annual savings of $255,000 will be realized if the new machine is installed. The company's tax rate is 34 percent and it has a 12 percent cost of capital.

a.   What is the initial cash outlay required for the new machine?

b.   Calculate the annual depreciation allowances for both machines, and compute the change in the annual depreciation expense if the replacement is made.

c.   What are the operating cash flows in Years 1 through 5?

d.   What is the cash flow from the salvage value in Year 5?

e.   Should the firm purchase the new machine? Support your answer.

f.   In general, how would each of the following factors affect the investment decision, and how should each be treated?

(1) The expected life of the existing machine decreases.

(2) The cost of capital is not constant but is increasing as Boyd adds more projects into its capital budget for the year.

15-5

Risky cash flows

The Singleton Company must decide between two mutually exclusive investment projects. Each project costs $6,750 and has an expected life of 3 years. Annual net cash flows from each project begin 1 year after the initial investment is made and have the following probability distributions:

Project A		Project B	
Probability	**Net Cash Flows**	**Probability**	**Net Cash Flows**
0.2	$6,000	0.2	$ 0
0.6	6,750	0.6	6,750
0.2	7,500	0.2	18,000

Singleton has decided to evaluate the riskier project at a 12 percent rate and the less risky project at a 10 percent rate.

a. What is the expected value of the annual net cash flows from each project? What is the coefficient of variation (CV_{NPV})? (Hint: Use Equation 4-3 from Chapter 4 to calculate the standard deviation of Project A. $\sigma_B = \$5,798$ and $CV_B = 0.76$.)

b. What is the risk-adjusted NPV of each project?

c. If it were known that Project B was negatively correlated with other cash flows of the firm whereas Project A was positively correlated, how would this knowledge affect the decision? If Project B's cash flows were negatively correlated with gross national product (GNP), would that influence your assessment of its risk?

15-6

CAPM approach to
risk adjustments

Goodtread Rubber Company has two divisions: the tire division, which manufactures tires for new autos, and the recap division, which manufactures recapping materials that are sold to independent tire recapping shops throughout the United States. Since auto manufacturing fluctuates with the general economy, the tire division's earnings contribution to Goodtread's stock price is highly correlated with returns on most other stocks. If the tire division were operated as a separate company, its beta coefficient would be about 1.50. The sales and profits of the recap division, on the other hand, tend to be countercyclical because recap sales boom when people cannot afford to buy new tires. The recap division's beta is estimated to be 0.5. Approximately 75 percent of Goodtread's corporate assets are invested in the tire division and 25 percent are invested in the recap division.

Currently, the rate of interest on Treasury securities is 9 percent, and the expected rate of return on an average share of stock is 13 percent. Goodtread uses only common equity capital, so it has no debt outstanding.

a. What is the required rate of return on Goodtread's stock?

b. What discount rate should be used to evaluate capital budgeting projects? Explain your answer fully, and, in the process, illustrate your answer with a project which costs $160,000, has a 10-year life, and provides expected after-tax net cash flows of $30,000 per year.

15-7

Scenario analysis

Your firm, Agrico Products, is considering the purchase of a tractor which will have a net cost of $36,000, will increase pretax operating cash flows before taking account of depreciation effects by $12,000 per year, and will be depreciated on a straight line basis to zero over 5 years at the rate of $7,200 per year, beginning the first year. (Annual cash flows will be $12,000, before taxes, plus the tax savings that result from $7,200 of depreciation.) The board of directors is having a heated debate about whether the tractor will actually last 5 years. Specifically, Joan Lamm insists that she knows of some tractors that have lasted only 4 years. Alan Grunewald agrees with Lamm, but he argues that most tractors do give 5 years of service. Judy Maese says she has known some to last for as long as 8 years.

Given this discussion, the board asks you to prepare a scenario analysis to ascertain the importance of the uncertainty about the tractor's life. Assume a 40 percent federal-plus-state tax rate, a zero salvage value, and a cost of capital of 10 percent. (Hint: Here straight line depreciation is based on the MACRS class life of the tractor and is not affected by the actual life. Also, ignore the half-year convention for this problem.)

EXAM-TYPE PROBLEMS

The problems included in this section are set up in such a way that they could be used as multiple-choice exam problems.

15-8
Replacement analysis

The Gehr Company is considering the purchase of a new machine tool to replace an obsolete one. The machine being used for the operation has both a tax book value and a market value of zero; it is in good working order, however, and will last physically for at least another 10 years. The proposed replacement machine will perform the operation so much more efficiently that Gehr engineers estimate it will produce after-tax cash flows (labor savings and depreciation) of $9,000 per year. The new machine will cost $40,000 delivered and installed, and its economic life is estimated to be 10 years. It has zero salvage value. The firm's cost of capital is 10 percent, and its tax rate is 34 percent. Should Gehr buy the new machine?

15-9
Replacement analysis

Galveston Shipyards is considering the replacement of an 8-year-old riveting machine with a new one that will increase earnings before depreciation from $27,000 to $54,000 per year. The new machine will cost $82,500, and it will have an estimated life of 8 years and no salvage value. The new machine will be depreciated over its 5-year MACRS recovery period. (See Table 15A-2 for MACRS recovery allowance percentages.) The firm's federal-plus-state tax rate is 40 percent, and the firm's cost of capital is 12 percent. The old machine has been fully depreciated and has no salvage value. Should the old riveting machine be replaced by the new one?

15-10
Unequal lives

Keenan Clothes Inc. is considering the replacement of its old, fully depreciated knitting machine. Two new models are available: Machine 190-3, which has a cost of $190,000, a 3-year expected life, and after-tax cash flows (labor savings and depreciation) of $87,000 per year; and Machine 360-6, which has a cost of $360,000, a 6-year life, and after-tax cash flows of $98,300 per year. Knitting machine prices are not expected to rise because inflation will be offset by cheaper components (microprocessors) used in the machines. Assume that Keenan's cost of capital is 14 percent.
a. Should the firm replace its old knitting machine, and, if so, which new machine should it use?
b. Suppose the firm's basic patents will expire in 9 years, and the company expects to go out of business at that time. Assume further that the firm depreciates its assets using the straight line method, that its federal-plus-state tax rate is 40 percent, and that the used machines can be sold at their book values. Under these circumstances, should the company replace the old machine? Explain.

15-11
Risk adjustment

The risk-free rate of return is 9 percent, and the market risk premium is 5 percent. The beta of the project under analysis is 1.4, with expected net cash flows estimated to be $1,500 per year for 5 years. The required investment outlay on the project is $4,500.
a. What is the required risk-adjusted return on the project?
b. Should the project be accepted?

15-12
Divisional required rates of return

Pappas Computer Corporation, a producer of office equipment, currently has assets of $15 million and a beta of 1.4. The risk-free rate is 8 percent and the market risk premium is 5 percent. Pappas would like to expand into the risky home computer market. If the expansion is undertaken, Pappas would create a new division with $3.75 million in assets. The new division would have a beta of 1.8.
a. What is Pappas's current required rate of return?

b. If the expansion is undertaken, what would be the firm's new beta? What is the new overall required rate of return, and what rate of return must the home computer division produce to leave the new overall required rate of return unchanged?

15-13

Unequal lives

Zappe Airlines is considering two alternative planes. Plane A has an expected life of 5 years, will cost $100, and will produce net cash flows of $30 per year. Plane B has a life of 10 years, will cost $132, and will produce net cash flows of $25 per year. Zappe plans to serve the route for 10 years. Inflation in operating costs, airplane costs, and fares is expected to be zero, and the company's cost of capital is 12 percent. By how much would the value of the company increase if it accepted the better project (plane)? Assume all costs and cash flows are in millions of dollars.

INTEGRATIVE PROBLEMS

15-14

Capital budgeting and cash flow estimation

Allied Food Products is evaluating a new product, fresh lemon juice. Assume that you were recently hired as assistant to the director of capital budgeting, and you must evaluate the new project.

The lemon juice would be produced in an unused building adjacent to Allied's Fort Myers plant; Allied owns the building, which is fully depreciated. The required equipment would cost $200,000, plus an additional $40,000 for shipping and installation. In addition, inventories would rise by $25,000, while accounts payable would go up by $5,000. All of these costs would be incurred at t = 0. By a special ruling, the machinery could be depreciated under the MACRS system as 3-year property.

The project is expected to operate for 4 years, at which time it will be terminated. The cash inflows are assumed to begin one year after the project is undertaken, or at t = 1, and to continue out to t = 4. At the end of the project's life (t = 4), the equipment is expected to have a salvage value of $25,000.

Unit sales are expected to total 100,000 cans per year, and the expected sales price is $2.00 per can. Cash operating costs for the project (total operating costs less depreciation) are expected to total 60 percent of dollar sales. Allied's federal-plus-state tax rate is 40 percent, and its required rate of return is 10 percent. Tentatively, the lemon juice project is assumed to be of equal risk to Allied's other assets.

You have been asked to evaluate the project and to make a recommendation as to whether it should be accepted or rejected. To guide you in your analysis, your boss gave you the following set of questions.

a. Draw a time line which shows when the net cash inflows and outflows will occur, and explain how the time line can be used to help structure the analysis.

b. Allied has a standard form which is used in the capital budgeting process; see Table IP15-1. Part of the table has been completed, but you must replace the blanks with the missing numbers. Complete the table in the following steps:

(1) Complete the unit sales, sales price, total revenues, and operating costs excluding depreciation lines.

(2) Complete the depreciation line.

(3) Now complete the table down to net income and then down to net operating cash flows.

(4) Now fill in the blanks under Year 0 and Year 4 for the initial cost and the termination cash flows, and complete the "time line (net cash flow)" line. Discuss working capital. What would have happened if the machinery were sold for less than its book value?

c. (1) Allied uses debt in its capital structure, so some of the money used to finance the project will be debt. Given this fact, should the projected cash flows be revised to show projected interest charges? Explain.

Table IP15-1   ▪   **Allied's Lemon Juice Project (Total Cost in Thousands)**

End of Year:	0	1	2	3	4
Unit sales (thousands)			100		
Price/unit		$2.00	$2.00		
Total revenues					$200.0
Operating costs excluding depreciation			$120.0		
Depreciation				36.0	16.8
Total costs		$199.2	$228.0		
Earnings before taxes (EBT)				$44.0	
Taxes		0.3			25.3
Net income				$26.4	
Depreciation		79.2		36.0	
Net operating cash flow	$0.0	$ 79.7			$ 54.7
Equipment cost					
Installation					
Increase in inventory					
Increase in accounts payable					
Salvage value					
Tax on salvage value					
Return of net working capital					
Time line (net cash flow):	($260.0)				$ 89.7
Cumulative cash flow for payback:	(260.0)	(180.3)			63.0
Compounded inflows for MIRR:		106.1			89.7
Terminal value of inflows:					

$$\text{NPV} =$$
$$\text{IRR} =$$
$$\text{MIRR} =$$
$$\text{Payback} =$$

(2) Suppose you learned that Allied had spent $50,000 to renovate the building last year, expensing these costs. Should this cost be reflected in the analysis? Explain.

(3) Now suppose you learned that Allied could lease its building to another party and earn $25,000 per year. Should that fact be reflected in the analysis? If so, how?

(4) Now assume that the lemon juice project would take away profitable sales from Allied's fresh orange juice business. Should that fact be reflected in your analysis? If so, how?

d. Disregard all the assumptions made in Part c, and assume there was no alternative use for the building over the next 4 years. Now calculate the project's NPV, IRR, MIRR, and regular payback. Do these indicators suggest that the project should be accepted?

e. If this project had been a replacement rather than an expansion project, how would the analysis have changed? Think about the changes that would have to occur in the cash flow table, but no calculations are required.

f. Assume that inflation is expected to average 5 percent over the next 4 years; that this expectation is reflected in the required rate of return; and that inflation will increase variable costs and revenues by the same percentage, 5 percent. Does it appear that inflation has been dealt with properly in the analysis? If not, what should be done, and how would the required adjustment affect the decision? You can modify the numbers in the table to quantify your results.

g. In an unrelated analysis, you have also been asked to choose between the following two mutually exclusive projects:

	Expected Net Cash Flows	
Year	Project S	Project L
0	($100,000)	($100,000)
1	60,000	33,500
2	60,000	33,500
3	—	33,500
4	—	33,500

The projects provide a necessary service, so whichever one is selected is expected to be repeated into the foreseeable future. Both projects are of average risk.

(1) What is each project's initial NPV without replication?

(2) Now construct a time line, and then apply the replacement chain approach to determine the projects' extended NPVs. Which project should be chosen?

(3) Repeat the analysis using the equivalent annual annuity approach.

(4) Now assume that the cost to replicate Project S in Year 2 will increase to $105,000 because of inflationary pressures. How should the analysis be handled now, and which project should be chosen?

15-15
Risk analysis

Problem 15-14 contained the details of a new-project capital budgeting evaluation being conducted by Allied Food Products. Although inflation was considered in the initial analysis, the riskiness of the project was not considered. The expected cash flows considering inflation as they were estimated in Problem 15-14 (in thousands of dollars) are given in the table on the next page. Allied's required rate of return is 10 percent. You have been asked to answer the following questions.

a. (1) What are the three levels, or types, of project risk that are normally considered?

(2) Which type is the most relevant?

(3) Which type is the easiest to measure?

(4) Are the three types of risk generally highly correlated?

b. (1) What is sensitivity analysis?

(2) Discuss how one would perform a sensitivity analysis on the unit sales, salvage value, and cost of capital for the project. Assume that each of these variables deviates from its base case, or expected, value by plus and minus 10, 20, and 30 percent. Explain how you would calculate the NPV, IRR, MIRR, and the payback for each case. Include a sensitivity diagram, and discuss the results.

(3) What is the primary weakness of sensitivity analysis? What are its primary advantages?

c. Assume that you are confident about the estimates of all the variables that affect the project's cash flows except unit sales. If product acceptance is poor, sales would be only 75,000 units a year, while a strong consumer response would produce sales of

			Year		
	0	1	2	3	4
Investment in:					
Fixed assets	($240)				
Net working capital	(20)				
Unit sales (Thousands)		100	100	100	100
Sales price (dollars)		$2.100	$2.205	$2.315	$2.431
Total revenues		$210.0	$220.5	$231.5	$243.1
Cash operating costs (60%)		126.0	132.3	138.9	145.9
Depreciation		79.2	108.0	36.0	16.8
Earnings before taxes (EBT)		$ 4.8	($ 19.8)	$ 56.6	$ 80.4
Taxes (40%)		1.9	(7.9)	22.6	32.1
Net income		$ 2.9	($ 11.9)	$ 34.0	$ 48.3
Plus depreciation		79.2	108.0	36.0	16.8
Net operating cash flow		$ 82.1	$ 96.1	$ 70.0	$ 65.1
Salvage value					25.0
Tax on SV (40%)					(10.0)
Recovery of NWC					20.0
Net cash flow	($260)	$ 82.1	$ 96.1	$ 70.0	$100.1
Cumulative cash flow for payback:	(260.0)	(177.9)	(81.8)	(11.8)	88.2
Compounded inflows for MIRR:		109.2	116.3	77.0	100.1
Terminal value of inflows:					402.6

NPV at 10% cost of capital = $15.0

IRR   = 12.6%

MIRR   = 11.6%

125,000 units. In either case, cash costs would still amount to 60 percent of revenues. You believe that there is a 25 percent chance of poor acceptance, a 25 percent chance of excellent acceptance, and a 50 percent chance of average acceptance (the base case).

(1) What is the worst case NPV? The best case NPV?

(2) Use the worst, most likely (or base), and best case NPVs and probabilities of occurrence to find the project's expected NPV, standard deviation (σ_{NPV}), and coefficient of variation (CV_{NPV}).

d. (1) Assume that Allied's average project has a coefficient of variation (CV_{NPV}) in the range of 1.25 to 1.75. Would the lemon juice project be classified as high risk, average risk, or low risk? What type of risk is being measured here?

(2) Based on common sense, how highly correlated do you think the project would be to the firm's other assets? (Give a correlation coefficient, or range of coefficients, based on your judgment.)

(3) How would this correlation coefficient and the previously calculated σ combine to affect the project's contribution to corporate, or within-firm, risk? Explain.

e. (1) Based on your judgment, what do you think the project's correlation coefficient would be with respect to the general economy and thus with returns on "the market"?

(2) How would correlation with the economy affect the project's market risk?

f. (1) Allied typically adds or subtracts 3 percentage points to the overall cost of capital to adjust for risk. Should the lemon juice project be accepted?

(2) What subjective risk factors should be considered before the final decision is made?

g. Define scenario analysis and simulation analysis, and discuss their principal advantages and disadvantages. (Note that you have already done scenario analysis in Part c.)

h. (1) Assume that the risk-free rate is 10 percent, the market risk premium is 6 percent, and the new project's beta is 1.2. What is the project's required rate of return on equity based on the CAPM?

(2) How does the project's market risk compare with the firm's overall market risk?

(3) How does the project's stand-alone risk compare with that of the firm's average project?

(4) Briefly describe two methods that you could conceivably have used to estimate the project's beta. How feasible do you think those procedures would actually be in this case?

(5) What are the advantages and disadvantages of focusing on a project's market risk?

i. As a completely different project, Allied is also evaluating two different systems for disposing of wastes associated with another product, fresh grapefruit juice. Plan W requires more workers but less capital, while Plan C requires more capital but fewer workers. Both systems have 3-year lives. Since the production line choice has no impact on revenues, you will base your decision on the relative costs of the two systems as set forth next:

	Expected Net Costs	
Year	Plan W	Plan C
0	($500)	($1,000)
1	(500)	(300)
2	(500)	(300)
3	(500)	(300)

(1) Assume initially that the two systems are both of average risk. Which one should be chosen?

(2) Now assume that the worker-intensive plan (W) is judged to be riskier than average because future wage rates are very difficult to forecast. Under this condition, which system should be chosen? Base your answer on the lowest reasonable PV of future costs.

(3) What are the two plans' IRRs?

COMPUTER-RELATED PROBLEM

Work the problem in this section only if you are using the computer problem diskette.

15-16

Expansion project

Use the computerized model in the File C15 to work this problem.

Golden State Bakers Inc. (GSB) has an opportunity to invest in a new dough machine. GSB needs more productive capacity, so the new machine will not replace an existing machine. The new machine costs $260,000 and will require modifications costing $15,000. It has an expected useful life of 10 years, will be depreciated using the

MACRS method over its 5-year class life, and has an expected salvage value of $12,500 at the end of Year 10. (See Table 15A-2 for MACRS recovery allowance percentages.) The machine will require a $22,500 investment in net working capital. It is expected to generate additional sales revenues of $125,000 per year, but its use also will increase annual cash operating expenses by $55,000. GSB's cost of capital is 10 percent, and its federal-plus-state tax rate is 40 percent. The machine's book value at the end of Year 10 will be zero, so GSB will have to pay taxes on the $12,500 salvage value.

a. What is the NPV of this expansion project? Should GSB purchase the new machine?
b. Should GSB purchase the new machine if it is expected to be used for only 5 years and then sold for $31,250? (Note that the model is set up to handle a 5-year life; you need only enter the new life and salvage value.)
c. Would the machine be profitable if revenues increased by only $105,000 per year? Assume a 10-year project life and a salvage value of $12,500.
d. Suppose that revenues rose by $125,000 but that expenses rose by $65,000. Would the machine be acceptable under these conditions? Assume a 10-year project life and a salvage value of $12,500.

Appendix 15A

Depreciation

Suppose a firm buys a milling machine for $100,000 and uses it for 5 years, after which it is scrapped. The cost of the goods produced by the machine must include a charge for the machine, and this charge is called *depreciation*. In the following sections we review some of the depreciation concepts covered in your accounting course.

Companies often calculate depreciation one way when figuring taxes and another way when reporting income to investors: many use the *straight line* method for stockholder reporting (or "book" purposes), but they use the fastest rate permitted by law for tax purposes. Under the straight line method used for stockholder reporting, one normally takes the cost of the asset, subtracts its estimated salvage value, and divides the net amount by the asset's useful economic life. For an asset with a 5-year life, which costs $100,000 and has a $12,500 salvage value, the annual straight line depreciation charge is ($100,000 − $12,500)/5 = $17,500. Note, however, as we discuss later in this appendix, that salvage value is *not* considered for tax depreciation purposes.

For tax purposes, Congress changes the permissible tax depreciation methods from time to time. Prior to 1954, the straight line method was required for tax purposes, but in 1954 *accelerated* methods (double declining balance and sum-of-years'-digits) were permitted. Then, in 1981, the old accelerated methods were replaced by a simpler procedure known as the Accelerated Cost Recovery System (ACRS). The ACRS system was changed again in 1986 as a part of the Tax Reform Act, and it is now known as the *Modified Accelerated Cost Recovery System (MACRS)*.

Tax Depreciation Life

For tax purposes, the cost of an asset is expensed over its depreciable life. Historically, an asset's depreciable life was determined by its estimated useful economic life; it was intended that an asset would be fully depreciated at approximately the same time that it reached the end of its useful economic life. However, MACRS totally abandoned that practice and set simple guidelines which created several classes of assets, each with a

Table 15A-1   ▪   **Major Classes and Asset Lives for MACRS**

Class	Type of Property
3-year	Certain special manufacturing tools.
5-year	Automobiles, light-duty trucks, computers, and certain special manufacturing equipment.
7-year	Most industrial equipment, office furniture, and fixtures.
10-year	Certain longer-lived types of equipment.
27.5-year	Residential rental real property such as apartment buildings.
31.5-year	All nonresidential real property, including commercial and industrial buildings.

more-or-less arbitrarily prescribed life called a *recovery period* or *class life.* The MACRS class life bears only a rough relationship to the expected useful economic life.

A major effect of the MACRS system has been to shorten the depreciable lives of assets, thus giving businesses larger tax deductions and thereby increasing their cash flows available for reinvestment. Table 15A-1 describes the types of property that fit into the different class life groups, and Table 15A-2 sets forth the MACRS recovery allowances (depreciation rates) for selected classes of investment property.

Consider Table 15A-1 first. The first column gives the MACRS class life, while the second column describes the types of assets which fall into each category. Property in the 27.5- and 31.5-year categories (real estate) must be depreciated by the straight line method, but 3-, 5-, 7-, and 10-year property (personal property) can be depreciated either by the accelerated method using the rates shown in Table 15A-2 or by an alternate straight line method.[1]

As we saw earlier in the chapter, higher depreciation expenses result in lower taxes, hence higher cash flows. Therefore, since a firm has the choice of using the alternate straight line rates or the accelerated rates shown in Table 15A-2, most elect to use the accelerated rates. The yearly recovery allowance, or depreciation expense, is determined by multiplying each asset's *depreciable basis* by the applicable recovery percentage shown in Table 15A-2. Calculations are discussed in the following sections.

Half-Year Convention.   Under MACRS, the assumption is generally made that property is placed in service in the middle of the first year. Thus, for 3-year class life property, the recovery period begins in the middle of the year the asset is placed in service and ends 3 years later. The effect of the *half-year convention* is to extend the recovery period out one more year, so 3-year class life property is depreciated over 4 calendar years, 5-year property is depreciated over 6 calendar years, and so on. This convention is incorporated into Table 15A-2's recovery allowance percentages.[2]

---

[1] As a benefit to very small companies, the Tax Code also permits companies to *expense,* which is equivalent to depreciating over one year, up to $10,000 of equipment. Thus, if a small company bought one asset worth up to $10,000, it could write the asset off in the year it was acquired. This is called "Section 179 expensing." We shall disregard this provision throughout the book.

[2] The half-year convention also applies if the straight line alternative is used, with half of one year's depreciation taken in the first year, a full year's depreciation taken in each of the remaining years of the asset's class life, and the remaining half-year's depreciation taken in the year following the end of the class life. You should recognize that virtually all companies have computerized depreciation systems. Each asset's depreciation pattern is programmed into the system at the time of its acquisition, and the computer aggregates the depreciation allowances for all assets when the accountants close the books and prepare the financial statements and tax returns.

Table 15A-2 ▪ **Recovery Allowance Percentages for Personal Property**

Ownership Year	Class of Investment			
	3-Year	**5-Year**	**7-Year**	**10-Year**
1	33%	20%	14%	10%
2	45	32	25	18
3	15	19	17	14
4	7	12	13	12
5		11	9	9
6		6	9	7
7			9	7
8			4	7
9				7
10				6
11				3
	100%	100%	100%	100%

Notes:

a. We developed these recovery allowance percentages based on the 200 percent declining balance method prescribed by MACRS, with a switch to straight line depreciation at some point in the asset's life. For example, consider the 5-year recovery allowance percentages. The straight line percentage would be 20 percent per year, so the 200 percent declining balance multiplier is $2.0(20\%) = 40\% = 0.4$. However, because the half-year convention applies, the MACRS percentage for Year 1 is 20 percent. For Year 2, there is 80 percent of the depreciable basis remaining to be depreciated, so the recovery allowance percentage is $0.40(80\%) = 32\%$. In Year 3, $20\% + 32\% = 52\%$ of the depreciation has been taken, leaving 48%, so the percentage is $0.4(48\%) \approx 19\%$. In Year 4, the percentage is $0.4(29\%) \approx 12\%$. After 4 years, straight line depreciation exceeds the declining balance depreciation, so a switch is made to straight line (this is permitted under the law). However, the half-year convention must also be applied at the end of the class life, and the remaining 17 percent of depreciation must be taken (amortized) over 1.5 years. Thus, the percentage in Year 5 is $17\%/1.5 \approx 11\%$, and in Year 6, $17\% - 11\% = 6\%$. Although the tax tables carry the allowance percentages out to two decimal places, we have rounded to the nearest whole number for ease of illustration.

b. Residential rental property (apartments) is depreciated over a 27.5-year life, whereas commercial and industrial structures are depreciated over 31.5 years. In both cases, straight line depreciation must be used. The depreciation allowance for the first year is based, pro rata, on the month the asset was placed in service, with the remainder of the first year's depreciation being taken in the 28th or 32nd year.

Depreciable Basis.   The *depreciable basis* is a critical element of MACRS because each year's allowance (depreciation expense) depends jointly on the asset's depreciable basis and its MACRS class life. The depreciable basis under MACRS is equal to the purchase price of the asset plus any shipping and installation costs. The basis is *not* adjusted for *salvage value* (which is the estimated market value of the asset at the end of its useful life) regardless of whether accelerated or the alternate straight line method is used.

Sale of a Depreciable Asset.   If a depreciable asset is sold, the sale price (actual salvage value) minus the then-existing undepreciated book value is added to operating income and taxed at the firm's tax rate. For example, suppose a firm buys a 5-year class life asset for $100,000 and sells it at the end of the fourth year for $25,000. The asset's book value is equal to $100,000(0.11 + 0.06) = $100,000(0.17) = $17,000$. Therefore, $25,000 - $17,000 = $8,000 is added to the firm's operating income and is taxed.

Depreciation Illustration.   Assume that Allied Food Products buys a $150,000 machine which falls into the MACRS 5-year class life and places it into service on March 15, 1993. Allied must pay an additional $30,000 for delivery and installation. Salvage value is not considered, so the machine's depreciable basis is $180,000. (Delivery and installation charges are included in the depreciable basis rather than expensed in the year incurred.) Each year's recovery allowance (tax depreciation expense) is determined by multiplying the depreciable basis by the applicable recovery allowance percentage. Thus, the depreciation expense for 1993 is 0.20($180,000) = $36,000, and for 1994 it is 0.32($180,000) = $57,600. Similarly, the depreciation expense is $34,200 for 1995, $21,600 for 1996, $19,800 for 1997, and $10,800 for 1998. The total depreciation expense over the 6-year recovery period is $180,000, which is equal to the depreciable basis of the machine.

As noted above, most firms use straight line depreciation for stockholder reporting purposes but MACRS for tax purposes. *For these firms, for capital budgeting, MACRS should be used.* The reason is that, in capital budgeting, we are concerned with cash flows, not reported income. Since MACRS depreciation is used for taxes, this type of depreciation must be used to determine the taxes that will be assessed against a particular project. Only if the depreciation method used for tax purposes is also used for capital budgeting will the analysis produce accurate cash flow estimates.

Problem

15A-1
Depreciation effects

Christina Manning, great granddaughter of the founder of Manning Tile Products and current president of the company, believes in simple, conservative accounting. In keeping with her philosophy, she has decreed that the company shall use alternative straight line depreciation, based on the MACRS class lives, for all newly acquired assets. Your boss, the financial vice president and the only nonfamily officer, has asked you to develop an exhibit which shows how much this policy costs the company in terms of market value. Ms. Manning is interested in increasing the value of the firm's stock because she fears a family stockholder revolt which might remove her from office. For your exhibit, assume that the company spends $100 million each year on new capital projects, that the projects have on average a 10-year class life, that the company has a 9 percent cost of debt, and that its tax rate is 34 percent. (Hint: Show how much the NPV of projects in an average year would increase if Manning used the standard MACRS recovery allowances.)

P A R T

VI

The Cost of Capital, Leverage, and Dividend Policy

Chapter 16   The Cost of Capital

Chapter 17   Capital Structure and Leverage

Chapter 18   Dividend Policy

The Cost of Capital

*During the decade of the 1980s, the United States was generally prosper-
ous, and things seemed to be going well. However, even in the best of
those years, some observers argued that problems loomed. The United
States was running a massive foreign trade deficit—we were buying more
from abroad than we were selling overseas, and we were covering this
shortfall by borrowing from the Japanese, Germans, British, and the others who were selling goods to us. In effect, we were paying for our imports by selling foreigners massive amounts of the stocks and bonds of
companies such as GE and General Motors, whole companies such as Columbia Records and MCA, and real estate such as Rockefeller Center in
New York and the IBM building in Atlanta.*

*At the same time, U.S. companies were setting up manufacturing
plants overseas to take advantage of cheaper and more flexible labor, less
restrictive environmental controls, and expanding markets. We were losing jobs, especially in manufacturing, and becoming more and more of a
"service economy." Increasingly, we were becoming a nation of lawyers,
accountants, stockbrokers, advertising executives, retail clerks, hamburger
flippers, and the like, and less and less a nation of engineers, production
workers, and others who produce goods as opposed to services. Even
worse, we were paying for foreign-produced goods by borrowing from and
selling assets to non-U.S. producers. Knowledgeable people are concerned
about how long that trend can continue.*

*Obviously, as a nation we are not saving a very high percentage of
our income, so we have been unable to invest as much as we might have
(and as our competitors have) in research and development, in education, in new capital equipment, and in infrastructure such as modern
roads and highways. Our low savings rate has also led to a shortage of
capital, and to a high cost of capital, in comparison with our global competitors. This high capital cost has had a feed-back effect on the capital*

investment situation—if the cost of capital is high, investment will be low, low investment will hurt our competitive position, and the economy can spiral downward.

Things continue to look bad in 1992 as we struggle through a recession brought on by the excesses of the 1980s, but all is not gloom and doom. During the 1980s, too many people forgot the fundamentals of finance and investments. But the recession is forcing us to relearn these fundamentals. If you understand the topics covered here, you can help us avoid the mistakes of the past and get and keep the United States moving forward.

The most important use of the cost of capital is in capital budgeting, but it is also used for other purposes. For example, the cost of capital is a key factor in lease-versus-purchase decisions, in bond refunding decisions, and in decisions relating to the use of debt versus equity capital. The cost of capital is also important in the regulation of electric, gas, and telephone companies. These utilities are natural monopolies in the sense that one firm can supply service at a lower cost than could two or more firms. Since it has a monopoly, your electric or telephone company could, if it were unregulated, exploit you. Therefore, regulators (1) determine the cost of the capital investors have provided to utilities and (2) then set electric, gas, and telephone rates which permit the companies to just earn their costs of capital.

Our first topic in this chapter is the logic of the weighted average cost of capital. Next, we consider the costs of the major types of capital, after which we see how the costs of the individual components of the capital structure are brought together to form a weighted average cost of capital.

It should be noted that the cost of capital models and formulas used in this chapter are the same ones we developed in Chapter 6, where we were concerned with the rates of return investors require on different securities. Those same models and formulas are used to estimate the firm's cost of capital. Indeed, the rate of return on a security to an investor is the same as the cost of capital to a firm, so exactly the same models are used by investors and by corporate treasurers.

THE LOGIC OF THE WEIGHTED AVERAGE COST OF CAPITAL

It is possible to finance a firm entirely with equity funds. In that case, the cost of capital used to analyze capital budgeting decisions should be the company's required return on equity. However, most firms raise a substantial portion of their capital as long-term debt, and many also use preferred stock. For these firms, their cost of capital must reflect the average cost of the various sources of long-term funds used, not just the firms' costs of equity.

Assume that Allied Food Products has a 10 percent cost of debt and a 13.4 percent cost of equity. Further, assume that Allied has made the decision to finance next year's projects by selling debt. The argument is sometimes made that the cost of capital for these projects is 10 percent because only debt will be used to finance them. However, this position is incorrect. If Allied finances a particular set of projects with debt, the firm will be using up some of its potential for obtaining new debt in the future. As expansion occurs in subsequent years, Allied will at some point find it necessary to raise additional equity to prevent the debt ratio from becoming too large.

To illustrate, suppose Allied borrows heavily at 10 percent during 1993, using up its debt capacity in the process, to finance projects yielding 11.5 percent. In 1994 it has new projects available that yield 13 percent, well above the return on 1993 projects, but it cannot accept them because they would have to be financed with 13.4 percent equity money. *To avoid this problem, Allied should be viewed as an ongoing concern, and the cost of capital used in capital budgeting should be calculated as a weighted average, or composite, of the various types of funds it generally uses, regardless of the specific financing used to fund a particular project.*

? Self-Test Question

Why should the cost of capital used in capital budgeting be calculated as a weighted average of the various types of funds the firm generally uses, regardless of the specific financing used to fund a particular project?

BASIC DEFINITIONS

capital component

One of the types of capital used by firms to raise money.

The items on the right-hand side of a firm's balance sheet — various types of debt, preferred stock, and common equity — are its **capital components.** Any increase in total assets must be financed by an increase in one or more of these capital components.

Capital is a necessary factor of production, and, like any other factor, it has a cost. The cost of each component is called the *component cost* of that particular type of capital; for example, if Allied can borrow money at 10 percent, its component cost of debt is 10 percent.[1] Throughout this chapter we concentrate on debt, preferred stock, retained earnings, and new issues of common stock, which are the four major capital structure components; their component costs are identified by the following symbols:

k_d = interest rate on the firm's new debt = before-tax component cost of debt. For Allied, $k_d = 10\%$.

$k_d(1 - T)$ = after-tax component cost of debt, where T is the firm's marginal tax rate. $k_d(1 - T)$ is the debt cost used to calculate the weighted average cost of capital. For Allied, $T = 40\%$, so $k_d(1 - T) = 10\%(1 - 0.4) = 10\%(0.6) = 6.0\%$.

k_p = component cost of preferred stock. For Allied, $k_p = 10.3\%$.

---

[1]We will see shortly that there is both a before-tax and an after-tax cost of debt; for now it is sufficient to know that 10 percent is the before-tax component cost of debt.

k_s = component cost of retained earnings (or internal equity). It is identical to the k_s developed in Chapters 4 and 6 and defined there as the required rate of return on common stock. It is quite difficult to estimate k_s, but, as we shall see shortly, for Allied, $k_s \approx 13.4\%$.

k_e = component cost of external equity obtained by issuing new common stock as opposed to retaining earnings. As we shall see, it is necessary to distinguish between equity raised by retained earnings and that raised by selling new stock. This is why we distinguish between internal and external equity, k_s and k_e. Further, k_e is always greater than k_s. For Allied, $k_e \approx 14\%$.

WACC = the weighted average cost of capital. If Allied raises new capital to finance asset expansion, and if it is to keep its capital structure in balance (that is, if it is to keep the same percentage of debt, preferred stock, and common equity funds), then it must raise part of its new funds as debt, part as preferred stock, and part as common equity (with equity coming either from retained earnings or from the issuance of new common stock).[2] We will calculate WACC for Allied Food Products shortly.

These definitions and concepts are explained in detail in the remainder of the chapter, where we develop a marginal cost of capital (MCC) schedule that can be used in capital budgeting. Later, in Chapter 17, we will extend the analysis to determine the mix of types of capital that will minimize the firm's cost of capital and thereby maximize its value.

Self-Test Question

Identify the firm's four major capital structure components, and give their respective component cost symbols.

COST OF DEBT, $k_d(1 - T)$

after-tax cost of debt, $k_d(1 - T)$
The relevant cost of new debt, taking into account the tax deductibility of interest; used to calculate the WACC.

The **after-tax cost of debt, $k_d(1 - T)$,** is used to calculate the weighted average cost of capital, and it is the interest rate on debt, k_d, less the tax savings that result because interest is deductible. This is the same as k_d multiplied by $(1 - T)$, where T is the firm's marginal tax rate:[3]

---

[2]Firms try to keep their debt, preferred stock, and common equity in optimal proportions; we will learn how they establish these proportions in Chapter 17. However, firms do not try to maintain any proportional relationship between the common stock and retained earnings accounts as shown on the balance sheet—for capital structure purposes, common equity is common equity, whether it comes from selling new common stock or from retaining earnings.

[3]The federal tax rate for most corporations is 34 percent. However, most corporations are also subject to state income taxes, so the marginal tax rate on most corporate income is about 40 percent. For illustrative purposes, we assume that the effective federal-plus-state tax rate on marginal income is 40 percent. Also, note that the cost of debt is considered in isolation. The effect of debt on the cost of equity, as well as on future increments of debt, is ignored when the weighted cost of a combination of debt and equity is derived in this chapter, but it will be treated in Chapter 17, "Capital Structure and Leverage."

> After-tax component cost of debt = Interest rate − Tax savings
>
> $$= k_d - k_dT$$
>
> $$= k_d(1 - T). \qquad (16\text{-}1)$$

In effect, the government pays part of the cost of debt because interest is deductible. Therefore, if Allied can borrow at an interest rate of 10 percent, and if it has a marginal federal-plus-state tax rate of 40 percent, then its after-tax cost of debt is 6 percent:

$$k_d(1 - T) = 10\%(1.0 - 0.4)$$
$$= 10\%(0.6)$$
$$= 6.0\%.$$

The reason for using the after-tax cost of debt is as follows. The value of the firm's stock, which we want to maximize, depends on *after-tax* cash flows. Because interest is a deductible expense, it produces tax savings which reduce the net cost of debt, making the after-tax cost of debt less than the before-tax cost. We are concerned with after-tax cash flows, and since cash flows and rates of return should be on a comparable basis, we adjust the interest rate downward to take account of the preferential tax treatment of debt.[4]

Note that the cost of debt is the interest rate on *new* debt, not that on already outstanding debt; in other words, we are interested in the *marginal* cost of debt. Our primary concern with the cost of capital is to use it for capital budgeting decisions — for example, a decision about whether or not to obtain the capital needed to acquire a new machine tool. The rate at which the firm has borrowed in the past is a sunk cost, and it is irrelevant for cost of capital purposes.

Self-Test Questions

Why is the after-tax cost of debt rather than the before-tax cost used to calculate the weighted average cost of capital?

Is the relevant cost of debt the interest rate on already *outstanding* debt or that on *new* debt? Why?

---

[4]The tax rate is *zero* for a firm with losses. Therefore, for a company that does not pay taxes, the cost of debt is not reduced; that is, in Equation 16-1 the tax rate equals zero, so the after-tax cost of debt is equal to the interest rate.

It should also be noted that we have ignored flotation costs (the costs incurred for new issuances) on debt because the vast majority of debt (over 99 percent) is privately placed and hence has no flotation cost. However, if bonds are publicly placed and do involve flotation costs, the solution value of k_d in this formula is used as the after-tax cost of debt:

$$M(1 - F) = \sum_{t=1}^{N} \frac{INT(1 - T)}{(1 + k_d)^t} + \frac{M}{(1 + k_d)^N}.$$

Here F is the percentage amount of the bond flotation cost, N is the number of periods to maturity, INT is the dollars of interest per period, T is the corporate tax rate, M is the maturity value of the bond, and k_d is the after-tax cost of debt adjusted to reflect flotation costs. If we assume that the bond in the example calls for annual payments, that it has a 20-year maturity, and that F = 2%, then the flotation-adjusted, after-tax cost of debt is 6.18 percent versus 6 percent before the flotation adjustment.

COST OF PREFERRED STOCK, k_p

The component **cost of preferred stock, k_p,** used to calculate the weighted average cost of capital is the preferred dividend, D_p, divided by the net issuing price, P_n, or the price the firm receives after deducting flotation costs:

$$\text{Component cost of preferred stock} = k_p = \frac{D_p}{P_n}. \qquad (16\text{-}2)$$

cost of preferred stock, k_p

The rate of return investors require on the firm's preferred stock. k_p is calculated as the preferred dividend, D_p, divided by the net issuing price, P_n.

For example, Allied has preferred stock that pays a \$10 dividend per share and sells for \$100 per share in the market. If it issues new shares of preferred, it will incur an underwriting (or flotation) cost of 2.5 percent, or \$2.50 per share, so it will net \$97.50 per share. Therefore, Allied's cost of preferred stock is 10.3 percent:

$$k_p = \$10/\$97.50 = 10.3\%.$$

No tax adjustments are made when calculating k_p because preferred dividends, unlike interest expense on debt, are *not* deductible, and hence there are no tax savings associated with the use of preferred stock.

 Self-Test Questions

Does the component cost of preferred stock include or exclude flotation costs? Explain.

Is a tax adjustment made to the cost of preferred stock? Why or why not?

COST OF RETAINED EARNINGS, k_s

cost of retained earnings, k_s

The rate of return required by stockholders on a firm's common stock.

The costs of debt and preferred stock are based on the returns investors require on these securities. Similarly, the **cost of retained earnings, k_s,** is the rate of return stockholders require on equity capital the firm obtains by retaining earnings.[5]

The reason we must assign a cost of capital to retained earnings involves the *opportunity cost principle.* The firm's after-tax earnings literally belong to its stockholders. Bondholders are compensated by interest payments, and preferred stockholders by preferred dividends, but the earnings remaining after interest and preferred dividends belong to the common stockholders, and these earnings serve to compensate stockholders for the use of their capital. Management may either pay out the earnings in the form of dividends or retain earnings and reinvest them in the business. If management decides to retain earnings,

[5]The term *retained earnings* can be interpreted to mean either the balance sheet item "retained earnings," consisting of all the earnings retained in the business throughout its history, or the income statement item "additions to retained earnings." The income statement item is used in this chapter; for our purpose, *retained earnings* refers to that part of current earnings not paid out in dividends and hence available for reinvestment in the business this year.

there is an opportunity cost involved—stockholders could have received the earnings as dividends and invested this money in other stocks, in bonds, in real estate, or in anything else. Thus, the firm should earn on its retained earnings at least as much as its stockholders themselves could earn on alternative investments of comparable risk.

What rate of return can stockholders expect to earn on equivalent-risk investments? First, recall from Chapter 6 that stocks are normally in equilibrium, with the expected and required rates of return being equal: $\hat{k}_s = k_s$. Therefore, we can assume that Allied's stockholders expect to earn a return of k_s on their money. *If the firm cannot invest retained earnings and earn at least k_s, it should pay these funds to its stockholders and let them invest directly in other assets that do provide this return.*[6]

Whereas debt and preferred stocks are contractual obligations that have easily determined costs, it is not at all easy to measure k_s. However, we can employ the principles developed in Chapters 4 and 6 to produce reasonably good cost of equity estimates. To begin, we know that if a stock is in equilibrium (which is the typical situation), then its required rate of return, k_s, is also equal to its expected rate of return, $\hat{k}_s$. Further, its *required* return is equal to a risk-free rate, k_{RF}, plus a risk premium, RP, whereas the *expected* return on a constant growth stock is equal to the stock's dividend yield, D_1/P_0, plus its expected growth rate, g:

$$\text{Required rate of return} = \text{Expected rate of return}$$
$$k_s = k_{RF} + RP \qquad = \qquad D_1/P_0 + g = \hat{k}_s. \qquad (16\text{-}3)$$

Since the two must be equal, we can estimate k_s either as $k_s = k_{RF} + RP$ or as $k_s = D_1/P_0 + g$. Actually, three methods are commonly used for finding the cost of retained earnings: (1) the CAPM approach, (2) the bond-yield-plus-risk-premium approach, and (3) the discounted cash flow (DCF) approach. These three approaches are discussed in the following sections.

The CAPM Approach

To use the Capital Asset Pricing Model (CAPM) as developed in Chapter 4, we proceed as follows:

Step 1.   Estimate the risk-free rate, k_{RF}, generally taken to be either the U.S. Treasury bond rate or the short-term (30-day) Treasury bill rate.

Step 2.   Estimate the stock's beta coefficient, b_i, and use this as an index of the stock's risk. The i signifies the *i*th company's beta.

Step 3.   Estimate the expected rate of return on the market, or on an "average" stock, k_M.

---

[6]Dividends and capital gains are taxed differently, with long-term gains being taxed at a lower rate than dividends for many stockholders. That makes it beneficial for companies to retain earnings rather than to pay them out as dividends, and that, in turn, results in a relatively low cost of capital for retained earnings. This point is discussed in detail in Chapter 18.

Step 4. Substitute the preceding values into the CAPM equation to estimate the required rate of return on the stock in question:

$$k_s = k_{RF} + (k_M - k_{RF})b_i. \tag{16-4}$$

Equation 16-4 shows that the CAPM estimate of k_s begins with the risk-free rate, k_{RF}, to which is added a risk premium set equal to the risk premium on an average stock, $k_M - k_{RF}$, scaled up or down to reflect the particular stock's risk as measured by its beta coefficient.

To illustrate the CAPM approach, assume that $k_{RF} = 8\%$, $k_M = 13\%$, and $b_i = 0.7$ for a given stock. This stock's k_s is calculated as follows:

$$\begin{aligned} k_s &= 8\% + (13\% - 8\%)(0.7) \\ &= 8\% + (5\%)(0.7) \\ &= 8\% + 3.5\% \\ &= 11.5\%. \end{aligned}$$

Had b_i been 1.8, indicating that the stock was riskier than average, its k_s would have been

$$\begin{aligned} k_s &= 8\% + (5\%)(1.8) \\ &= 8\% + 9\% \\ &= 17\%. \end{aligned}$$

For an average stock,

$$k_s = k_M = 8\% + (5\%)(1.0) = 13\%.$$

It should be noted that although the CAPM approach appears to yield accurate, precise estimates of k_s, there are actually several problems with it. First, as we saw in Chapter 4, if a firm's stockholders are not well diversified, they may be concerned with *total risk* rather than with market risk only; in that case the firm's true investment risk will not be measured by its beta, and the CAPM procedure will understate the correct value of k_s. Further, even if the CAPM method is valid, it is hard to obtain correct estimates of the inputs required to make it operational: (1) there is controversy about whether to use long-term or short-term Treasury yields for k_{RF}; (2) it is hard to estimate the beta that investors expect the company to have in the future; and (3) it is especially difficult to estimate the market risk premium.

Bond-Yield-plus-Risk-Premium Approach

Although it is essentially an ad hoc, subjective procedure, analysts often estimate a firm's cost of common equity by adding a risk premium of three to five percentage points to the interest rate on the firm's own long-term debt. It is logical to think that firms with risky, low-rated, and consequently high-interest-rate debt will also have risky, high-cost equity, and the procedure of basing the cost of equity on a readily observable debt cost utilizes this precept. For example, if an extremely strong firm such as IBM has bonds that yield 9 percent, its cost of equity might be estimated as follows:

$$k_s = \text{Bond yield} + \text{Risk premium} = 9\% + 4\% = 13\%.$$

The debt of a riskier company such as Chrysler might carry a yield of 12 percent, making its estimated cost of equity 16 percent:

$$k_s = 12\% + 4\% = 16\%.$$

Because the 4 percent risk premium is a judgmental estimate, the estimated value of k_s is also judgmental. Empirical work in recent years suggests that the risk premium over a firm's own bond yield has generally ranged from 3 to 5 percentage points, so this method is not likely to produce a precise cost of equity—about all it can do is get us "into the right ballpark."

Dividend-Yield-plus-Growth-Rate, or Discounted Cash Flow (DCF), Approach

In Chapter 6 we learned that both the price and the expected rate of return on a share of common stock depend, ultimately, on the dividends expected on the stock:

$$P_0 = \frac{D_1}{(1 + k_s)^1} + \frac{D_2}{(1 + k_s)^2} + \cdots \cdot$$
$$= \sum_{t=1}^{\infty} \frac{D_t}{(1 + k_s)^t}. \qquad (16\text{-}5)$$

Here P_0 is the current price of the stock; D_t is the dividend expected to be paid at the end of Year t; and k_s is the required rate of return. If dividends are expected to grow at a constant rate, then, as we saw in Chapter 6, Equation 16-5 reduces to this important formula:

$$P_0 = \frac{D_1}{k_s - g}. \qquad (16\text{-}6)$$

We can solve for k_s to obtain the required rate of return on common equity, which for the marginal investor is also equal to the expected rate of return:

$$k_s = \hat{k}_s = \frac{D_1}{P_0} + \text{Expected g.} \qquad (16\text{-}7)$$

Thus, investors expect to receive a dividend yield, D_1/P_0, plus a capital gain, g, for a total expected return of $\hat{k}_s$, and in equilibrium this expected return is also equal to the required return, k_s. This method of estimating the cost of equity is called the *discounted cash flow, or DCF, method.* Henceforth, we will assume that equilibrium exists, and we will use the terms k_s and $\hat{k}_s$ interchangeably.

It is relatively easy to determine the dividend yield, but it is difficult to establish the proper growth rate. If past growth rates in earnings and dividends have been relatively stable, and if investors appear to be projecting a continuation of past trends, then g may be based on the firm's historical growth rate.

However, if the company's past growth has been abnormally high or low, either because of its own unique situation or because of general economic fluctuations, then investors will not project the past growth rate into the future. In this case, g must be estimated in some other manner.

Security analysts regularly make earnings and dividend growth forecasts, looking at such factors as projected sales, profit margins, and competitive factors. For example, *Value Line,* which is available in most libraries, provides growth rate forecasts for 1,700 companies, and Merrill Lynch, Salomon Brothers, and other organizations make similar forecasts. Therefore, someone making a cost of capital estimate can obtain several analysts' forecasts, average them, use the average as a proxy for the growth expectations of investors in general, and then combine this g with the current dividend yield to estimate $\hat{k}_s$ as follows:

$$\hat{k}_s = \frac{D_1}{P_0} + \text{Growth rate as projected by security analysts.}$$

Again, note that this estimate of $\hat{k}_s$ is based on the assumption that g is expected to remain constant in the future.[7]

To illustrate the DCF approach, suppose Allied's stock sells for $23; its next expected dividend is $1.24; and its expected growth rate is 8 percent. Allied's expected and required rate of return, and hence its cost of retained earnings, is 13.4 percent:

$$\hat{k}_s = k_s = \frac{\$1.24}{\$23} + 8.0\%$$
$$= 5.4\% + 8.0\%$$
$$= 13.4\%.$$

This 13.4 percent is the minimum rate of return that management must expect to earn to justify retaining earnings and plowing them back into the business rather than paying them out to stockholders as dividends.

People experienced in estimating equity capital costs recognize that both careful analysis and sound judgment are required. It would be nice to pretend that judgment is unnecessary and to specify an easy, precise way of determining the exact cost of equity capital. Unfortunately, this is not possible—finance is in large part a matter of judgment, and we simply must face that fact.

Self-Test Questions

Why must a cost be assigned to retained earnings?

What are the three approaches for estimating the cost of retained earnings?

---

[7]Analysts' growth rate forecasts are usually for five years into the future, and the rates provided represent the average growth rate over that five-year horizon. Studies have shown that analysts' forecasts represent the best source of growth rate data for DCF cost of capital estimates. See Robert Harris, "Using Analysts' Growth Rate Forecasts to Estimate Shareholder Required Rates of Return," *Financial Management,* Spring 1986.

Another method for estimating g involves first forecasting the firm's average future dividend payout ratio and its complement, the *retention rate,* and then multiplying the retention rate by the company's average future projected rate of return on equity (ROE):

$$g = (\text{Retention rate})(\text{ROE}) = (1.0 - \text{Payout rate})(\text{ROE}).$$

Security analysts often use this procedure when they estimate growth rates.

Identify some problems with the CAPM approach.

What is the reasoning behind the bond-yield-plus-risk-premium approach?

Which of the components of the constant growth DCF formula, the dividend yield or the growth rate, is more difficult to estimate? Why?

COST OF NEWLY ISSUED COMMON STOCK, OR EXTERNAL EQUITY, k_e

cost of new common equity, k_e

The cost of external equity; based on the cost of retained earnings, but increased for flotation costs.

The **cost of new common equity, k_e**, or external equity capital, is higher than the cost of retained earnings, k_s, because of flotation costs involved in selling new common stock. What rate of return must be earned on funds raised by selling stock in order to make issuing new stock worthwhile? To put it another way, what is the cost of new common stock?

In general, the answer is found by applying the following formula:[8]

$$k_e = \frac{D_1}{P_0(1 - F)} + g. \qquad (16\text{-}8)$$

flotation cost, F

The percentage cost of issuing new common stock.

Here **F** is the percentage **flotation cost** incurred in selling the new stock issue, so $P_0(1 - F)$ is the net price per share received by the company.

Assuming that Allied has a flotation cost of 10 percent, its cost of new outside equity is computed as follows:

$$k_e = \frac{\$1.24}{\$23(1 - 0.10)} + 8.0\%$$

$$= \frac{\$1.24}{\$20.70} + 8.0\%$$

$$= 6.0\% + 8.0\% = 14.0\%.$$

---

[8]Equation 16-8 is derived as follows:

Step 1. The old stockholders expect the firm to pay a stream of dividends, D_t, which will be derived from existing assets with a per-share value of P_0. New investors will likewise expect to receive the same stream of dividends, but the funds available to invest in assets will be less than P_0 because of flotation costs. For new investors to receive their expected dividend stream *without impairing the D_t stream of the old investors*, the new funds obtained from the sale of stock must be invested at a return high enough to provide a dividend stream whose present value is equal to the price the firm will receive:

$$P_0(1 - F) = P_n = \sum_{t=1}^{\infty} \frac{D_t}{(1 + k_e)^t}. \qquad (16\text{-}9)$$

Here D_t is the dividend stream to new (and old) stockholders, and k_e is the cost of new outside equity.

Step 2. When growth is constant, Equation 16-9 reduces to

$$P_n = P_0(1 - F) = \frac{D_1}{k_e - g}. \qquad (16\text{-}9a)$$

Step 3. Equation 16-9a can be rearranged to produce Equation 16-8:

$$k_e = \frac{D_1}{P_0(1 - F)} + g.$$

Investors require a return of k_s = 13.4% on the stock. However, because of flotation costs the company must earn *more* than 13.4 percent on funds obtained by selling stock if it is to provide a 13.4 percent return. Specifically, if the firm earns 14 percent on funds obtained from new stock, then earnings per share will not fall below previously expected earnings, the firm's expected dividend can be maintained, and, as a result, the price per share will not decline. If the firm earns less than 14 percent, then earnings, dividends, and growth will fall below expectations, causing the price of the stock to decline. If it earns more than 14 percent, the price of the stock will rise.[9]

The reason for the flotation adjustment can perhaps be made clear by a simple example. Suppose Weaver Realty Company has $100,000 of assets and no debt, it earns a 15 percent return (or $15,000) on its assets, and it pays all earnings out as dividends, so its growth rate is zero. The company has 1,000 shares of stock outstanding, so EPS = DPS = $15, and P_0 = $100. Weaver's cost of equity is thus k_s = $15/$100 + 0 = 15%. Now suppose Weaver can get a return of 15 percent on new assets. Should it sell new stock to acquire new assets? If it sold 1,000 new shares of stock to the public for $100 per share, but it incurred a 10 percent flotation cost on the issue, it would net $100 − 0.10($100) = $90 per share, or $90,000 in total. It would then invest this $90,000 and earn 15 percent, or $13,500. Its new total earnings would be $15,000 from the old assets plus $13,500 from the new, or $28,500 in total, but it would now have 2,000 shares of stock outstanding. Therefore, its EPS and DPS would decline from $15 to $14.25:

$$\text{New EPS and DPS} = \frac{\$28,500}{2,000} = \$14.25.$$

Because its EPS and DPS would fall, the price of the stock also would fall from P_0 = $100 to P_1 = $14.25/0.15 = $95.00. This result occurs because investors have put up $100 per share, but the company has received and invested only $90 per share. Thus, we see that the $90 must earn more than 15 percent to provide investors with a 15 percent return on the $100 they put up.

Now suppose Weaver earned a return of k_e based on Equation 16-8 on the $90,000 of new assets:

$$k_e = \frac{D_1}{P_0(1 - F)} + g$$

$$= \frac{\$15}{\$100(0.90)} + 0 = 16.667\%.$$

---

[9]On occasion it is useful to use another equation to calculate the cost of external equity:

$$k_e = \frac{\text{Dividend yield}}{(1 - F)} + g = \frac{D_1/P_0}{(1 - F)} + g. \qquad \text{(16-8a)}$$

Equation 16-8a is derived algebraically from Equation 16-8, and it is useful when information on dividend yields, but not on dollar dividends and stock prices, is available.

Here is the new situation:

$$\begin{aligned}
\text{New total earnings} &= \$15,000 + \$90,000(0.16667) \\
&= \$15,000 + \$15,000 \\
&= \$30,000. \\
\text{New EPS and DPS} &= \$30,000/2,000 = \$15. \\
\text{New price} &= \$15/0.15 = \$100 = \text{Original price.}
\end{aligned}$$

Thus, if the return on the new assets is equal to k_e as calculated by Equation 16-8, then EPS, DPS, and the stock price will all remain constant. If the return on the new assets exceeds k_e, then EPS, DPS, and P_0 will rise. This confirms the fact that because of flotation costs, the cost of external equity exceeds the cost of equity raised internally from retained earnings.

Self-Test Questions

Why is the cost of external equity capital higher than the cost of retained earnings?

How can the DCF model be changed to account for flotation costs?

WEIGHTED AVERAGE, OR COMPOSITE, COST OF CAPITAL, WACC

target (optimal) capital structure

The percentages of debt, preferred stock, and common equity that will maximize the price of the firm's stock.

weighted average cost of capital (WACC)

A weighted average of the component costs of debt, preferred stock, and common equity.

As we shall see in Chapter 17, each firm has an optimal capital structure, defined as that mix of debt, preferred stock, and common equity that causes its stock price to be maximized. Therefore, a rational, value-maximizing firm will establish a **target (optimal) capital structure** and then raise new capital in a manner that will keep the actual capital structure on target over time. In this chapter we assume that the firm has identified its optimal capital structure, that it uses this optimum as the target, and that it finances so as to remain constantly on target. How the target is established will be examined in Chapter 17.

The target proportions of debt, preferred stock, and common equity, along with the component costs of capital, are used to calculate the firm's **weighted average cost of capital (WACC).** To illustrate, suppose Allied Food Products has a target capital structure calling for 45 percent debt, 2 percent preferred stock, and 53 percent common equity (retained earnings plus common stock). Its before-tax cost of debt, k_d, is 10 percent; its after-tax cost of debt $= k_d(1 - T) = 10\%(0.6) = 6.0\%$; its cost of preferred stock, k_p, is 10.3 percent; its cost of common equity from retained earnings, k_s, is 13.4 percent; its marginal tax rate is 40 percent, and all of its new equity will come from retained earnings. Now we can calculate Allied's weighted average cost of capital (WACC) as follows:

$$\text{WACC} = w_d k_d(1 - T) + w_p k_p + w_s k_s \qquad (16\text{-}10)$$

$$\begin{aligned}
&= 0.45(10\%)(0.6) + 0.02(10.3\%) + 0.53(13.4\%) \\
&= 10.0\%.
\end{aligned}$$

Here w_d, w_p, and w_s are the weights used for debt, preferred stock, and common equity, respectively.

Every dollar of new capital that Allied obtains consists of 45 cents of debt with an after-tax cost of 6 percent, 2 cents of preferred stock with a cost of 10.3 percent, and 53 cents of common equity (all from additions to retained earnings) with a cost of 13.4 percent. The average cost of each whole dollar, WACC, is 10 percent.

The weights could be based either on the accounting values shown on the firm's balance sheet (book values) or on the market values of the different securities. Theoretically, the weights should be based on market values, but if a firm's book value weights are reasonably close to its market value weights, book value weights can be used as a proxy for market value weights. This point is discussed further in Chapter 17, but in the remainder of this chapter we shall assume that the firm's market values are reasonably close to its book values, and we will use book value capital structure weights.

Self-Test Question

How does one calculate the weighted average cost of capital? Write out the equation.

THE MARGINAL COST OF CAPITAL, MCC

The *marginal cost* of any item is the cost of another unit of that item; for example, the marginal cost of labor is the cost of adding one additional worker. The marginal cost of labor may be $25 per person if 10 workers are added but $35 per person if the firm tries to hire 100 new workers because it will be harder to find that many people willing and able to do the work. The same concept applies to capital. As the firm tries to attract more new dollars, the cost of each dollar will at some point rise. *Thus, the **marginal cost of capital (MCC)** is defined as the cost of the last dollar of new capital that the firm raises, and the marginal cost rises as more and more capital is raised during a given period.*

marginal cost of capital (MCC)

The cost of obtaining another dollar of new capital; the weighted average cost of the last dollar of new capital raised.

We can use Allied Food Products to illustrate the marginal cost of capital concept. The company's target capital structure and other data follow:

Long-term debt	$ 754,000,000	45%
Preferred stock	40,000,000	2
Common equity	896,000,000	53
Total capital	$1,690,000,000	100%

$k_d = 10\%$.

$k_p = 10.3\%$.

$T = 40\%$.

$P_0 = \$23$.

$g = 8\%$, and growth is expected to remain constant.

$D_0 = \$1.15 =$ dividends per share in the *last* period. D_0 has already been paid, so someone who purchased this stock today would *not* receive D_0 — rather, he or she would receive D_1, the *next* dividend.

$D_1 = D_0(1 + g) = \$1.15(1.08) = \$1.24.$

$k_s = D_1/P_0 + g = (\$1.24/\$23) + 0.08 = 0.054 + 0.08 = 0.134 = 13.4\%.$

On the basis of these data, the weighted average cost of capital (WACC) is 10 percent:

$$\text{WACC} = \begin{pmatrix} \text{Fraction} \\ \text{of} \\ \text{debt} \end{pmatrix} \begin{pmatrix} \text{Interest} \\ \text{rate} \end{pmatrix}(1 - T) + \begin{pmatrix} \text{Fraction} \\ \text{of} \\ \text{preferred} \\ \text{stock} \end{pmatrix} \begin{pmatrix} \text{Cost} \\ \text{of} \\ \text{preferred} \\ \text{stock} \end{pmatrix} + \begin{pmatrix} \text{Fraction of} \\ \text{common} \\ \text{equity} \end{pmatrix} \begin{pmatrix} \text{Cost} \\ \text{of} \\ \text{equity} \end{pmatrix}$$

$$= \quad (0.45)(10\%)(0.6) \quad + \quad (0.02)(10.3\%) \quad + \quad (0.53)(13.4\%)$$

$$= \quad\quad 2.7\% \quad\quad\quad + \quad\quad 0.2\% \quad\quad + \quad\quad 7.1\%$$

$$= \quad\quad 10.0\%.$$

Note that only long-term debt is included in the capital structure. Allied uses its cost of capital in the capital budgeting process, which involves long-term assets, and it finances those assets with long-term capital. Thus, current liabilities do not enter the calculation. We will discuss this point in more detail in Chapter 17.[10]

As long as Allied keeps its capital structure on target, and as long as its debt has an after-tax cost of 6 percent, its preferred stock a cost of 10.3 percent, and its common equity a cost of 13.4 percent, then its weighted average cost of capital will be WACC = 10%. Each dollar the firm raises will consist of some long-term debt, some preferred stock, and some common equity, and the cost of the whole dollar will be 10 percent.

A graph which shows how the WACC changes as more and more new capital is raised during a given year is called the **marginal cost of capital schedule.** The graph shown in Figure 16-1 is Allied's MCC schedule. Here the dots represent dollars raised, and because each dollar of new capital has a cost of 10 percent, the marginal cost of capital (MCC) for Allied is constant at 10 percent under the assumptions we have used thus far.[11]

marginal cost of capital (MCC) schedule

A graph that relates the firm's weighted average cost of each dollar of capital to the total amount of new capital raised.

Breaks in the MCC Schedule

Could Allied raise an unlimited amount of new capital at the 10 percent cost? The answer is no. As a practical matter, as a company raises larger and larger sums during a given time period, the costs of debt, preferred stock, and common equity begin to rise, and as this occurs, the weighted average cost of each new dollar also rises. Thus, just as corporations cannot hire unlimited numbers of workers at a constant wage, they cannot raise unlimited amounts of capital at a constant cost. At some point, the cost of each new dollar will increase.

---

[10]Also see Eugene F. Brigham and Louis C. Gapenski, *Intermediate Financial Management,* 4th ed., Chapter 6.

[11]Allied's MCC schedule in Figure 16-1 would be different (higher) if the company used any capital structure other than 45 percent debt, 2 percent preferred, and 53 percent equity. This point will be developed in Chapter 17. However, as a general rule, a different MCC schedule exists for every possible capital structure, and the optimal structure is the one that produces the lowest MCC schedule.

Figure 16-1   ▪   **Marginal Cost of Capital (MCC) Schedule
for Allied Food Products**

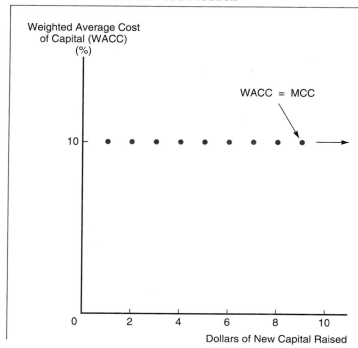

Where will this point occur for Allied? As a first step to determining the point at which the MCC begins to rise, recognize that although the company's balance sheet shows total long-term capital of $1,690,000,000, all of this capital was raised in the past, and it has been invested in assets which are being used in operations. New (or marginal) capital will presumably be raised so as to maintain the 45/2/53 debt/preferred/common relationship. Therefore, if Allied wants to raise $1,000,000 in new capital, it should obtain $450,000 of debt, $20,000 of preferred stock, and $530,000 of common equity. The new common equity could come from two sources: (1) retained earnings, defined as that part of this year's profits which management decides to retain in the business rather than use for dividends (but not earnings retained in the past, for these have already been invested in plant, equipment, inventories, and so on); or (2) proceeds from the sale of new common stock.

The debt will have an interest rate of 10 percent, or an after-tax cost of 6 percent, and the preferred stock will have a cost of 10.3 percent. *The cost of common equity will be $k_s = 13.4\%$ as long as the equity is obtained as retained earnings, but it will jump to $k_e = 14\%$ once the company uses up all of its retained earnings and is thus forced to sell new common stock.*

Consider first the case in which all the new equity comes from retained earnings. Allied's stock now sells for $23 per share; its last dividend (D_0) was $1.15; its expected growth rate is 8 percent; and its next expected dividend is $1.24. Thus, we estimate the expected and required rate of return on its common equity, k_s, to be 13.4 percent:

Table 16-1 ▪ **Allied's WACC Using New Retained Earnings
and New Common Stock**

I. WACC when Equity Is from New Retained Earnings

	Weight ×	Component Cost =	Product
Debt	0.45	6.0%	2.7%
Preferred stock	0.02	10.3	0.2
Common equity (Retained earnings)	0.53	13.4	7.1
	1.00	WACC$_1$ =	10.0%

II. WACC when Equity Is from Sale of New Common Stock

	Weight ×	Component Cost =	Product
Debt	0.45	6.0%	2.7%
Preferred stock	0.02	10.3	0.2
Common equity (New common stock)	0.53	14.0	7.4
	1.00	WACC$_2$ =	10.3%

$$k_s = \frac{D_1}{P_0} + g = \frac{\$1.24}{\$23} + 8\% = 5.4\% + 8\% = 13.4\%.$$

Now suppose the company expands so rapidly that its retained earnings for the year are not sufficient to meet its needs for new equity, forcing it to sell new common stock. Since the flotation cost on new stock is F = 10 percent, Allied's cost of equity after it exhausts its retained earnings will jump from 13.4 to 14 percent:

$$k_e' = \frac{D_1}{P_0(1 - F)} + g = \frac{\$1.24}{\$23(0.9)} + 8\% = \frac{\$1.24}{\$20.70} + 8\% = 14.0\%.$$

The company will net $20.70 per share when it sells new stock, and it must earn 14 percent on this $20.70 in order to provide investors with a 13.4 per-cent return on the $23 they actually put up.

Allied's weighted average cost of capital, when it uses new retained earnings (earnings retained this year, not in the past) and also when it uses new common stock, is shown in Table 16-1. We see that the weighted average cost of each dollar is 10 percent as long as retained earnings are used, but the WACC jumps to 10.3 percent as soon as the firm exhausts its retained earnings and is forced to sell new common stock.

How much new capital can Allied raise before it exhausts its retained earnings and is forced to sell new common stock; that is, where will an increase in the MCC schedule occur? We find this point as follows:[12]

1. Assume that the company expects to have total earnings of $137.8 million in 1993, and it has a target payout ratio of 45 percent, so it plans to pay

---

[12]The numbers in this set of calculations are rounded. It really makes little sense to carry estimates out to very many decimal places—this is "spurious accuracy."

out 45 percent of its earnings as dividends. Thus, the retained earnings for the year are projected to be $137.8(1.0 - 0.45) = $75.8 million.

2. We know that Allied expects to have $75.8 million of retained earnings for the year. We also know that if the company is to remain at its optimal capital structure, it must raise each dollar as 45 cents of debt, 2 cents of preferred stock, and 53 cents of common equity. Therefore, each 53 cents of retained earnings will support $1 of capital, and the $75.8 million of retained earnings will not be exhausted, hence the WACC will not rise, until $75.8 million of retained earnings, plus some additional amount of debt and preferred stock, have been used up.

3. We now want to know how much *total new capital*—debt, preferred stock, and retained earnings—can be raised before the $75.8 million of retained earnings is exhausted and Allied is forced to sell new common stock. In effect, we are seeking some amount of capital, X, which is called a **break point (BP)** and which represents the total financing that can be raised before Allied is forced to sell new common stock.

break point (BP)

The dollar value of new capital that can be raised before an increase in the firm's weighted average cost of capital occurs.

4. We know that 53 percent, or 0.53, of X, the total capital raised, will be retained earnings, whereas 47 percent will be debt plus preferred stock. We also know that retained earnings will amount to $75.8 million. Therefore,

$$\text{Retained earnings} = 0.53X = \$75,800,000.$$

5. Solving for X, which is the *retained earnings break point,* we obtain $BP_{RE} = \$143$ million:

$$X = BP_{RE} = \frac{\text{Retained earnings}}{\text{Equity fraction}} = \frac{\$75,800,000}{0.53} = \$143,018,868 \approx 143 \text{ million.}$$

6. Thus, Allied can raise a total of $143 million, consisting of 0.53($143 million) = $75.8 million of retained earnings plus 0.02($143 million) = $2.9 million of preferred stock and 0.45($143 million) = $64.3 million of new debt supported by these new retained earnings, without altering its capital structure (dollars in millions):

New debt supported by retained earnings	$64.3	45%
Preferred stock supported by retained earnings	2.9	2
Retained earnings	75.8	53
Total capital supported by retained earnings, or break point for retained earnings	$143.0	100%

7. The value of X, or $BP_{RE} = \$143$ million, is defined as the *retained earnings break point,* and it is the amount of total capital at which a break, or jump, occurs in the MCC schedule.

Figure 16-2 graphs Allied's marginal cost of capital schedule with the retained earnings break point. Each dollar has a weighted average cost of 10 percent until the company has raised a total of $143 million. This $143 million will consist of $64.3 million of new debt with an after-tax cost of 6 percent, $2.9 million of preferred stock with a cost of 10.3 percent, and $75.8 million of

Figure 16-2 ▪ Marginal Cost of Capital Schedule for Allied Food Products Using Both Retained Earnings and New Common Stock

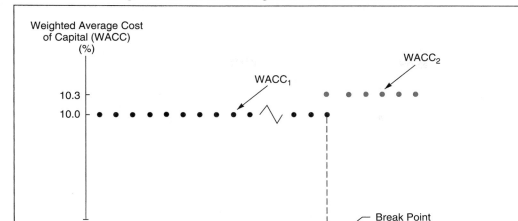

retained earnings with a cost of 13.4 percent. However, if Allied raises one dollar over $143 million, each new dollar will contain 53 cents of equity *obtained by selling new common equity at a cost of 14 percent;* therefore, WACC jumps from 10 percent to 10.3 percent, as calculated in Table 16-1.

Note that we really don't think the MCC jumps by precisely 0.3 percent when we raise $1 over $143 million. Thus, Figure 16-2 should be regarded as an approximation rather than as a precise representation of reality. We will return to this point later in the chapter.

Other Breaks in the MCC Schedule

There is a jump, or break, in Allied's MCC schedule at $143 million of new capital. Could there be other breaks in the schedule? Yes, there could. For example, suppose Allied could obtain only $90 million of debt at a 10 percent interest rate, with additional debt costing 12 percent. This would result in a second break point in the MCC schedule, at the point where the $90 million of 10 percent debt is exhausted. At what amount of *total financing* would the 10 percent debt be used up? We know that this total financing will amount to $90 million of debt plus some amount of preferred stock and common equity. If we let BP_{Debt} represent the total financing at this second break point, then we know that 45 percent, or 0.45, of BP_{Debt} will be debt, so

$$0.45(BP_{Debt}) = \$90,000,000,$$

and, solving for BP_{Debt}, we obtain

$$BP_{Debt} = \frac{\text{Amount of 10\% debt}}{\text{Debt fraction}} = \frac{\$90,000,000}{0.45} = \$200,000,000.$$

Figure 16-3   ▪   **Marginal Cost of Capital Schedule for Allied Food Products Using Retained Earnings, New Common Stock, and Higher-Cost Debt**

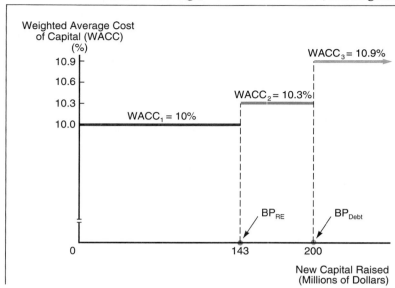

Thus, there will be another break in the MCC schedule after Allied has raised a total of $200 million, and this second break results from an increase in the cost of debt.

As we have seen, from $0 to $143 million of new capital the WACC is 10 percent, whereas just beyond $143 million the WACC rises to 10.3 percent. Then, at $200 million of new capital, the WACC rises again, to 10.9 percent, as a result of the increase in k_d from 10 percent to 12 percent:

WACC above $200 Million

Component	Weight		Component Cost		Product
Debt	0.45	×	7.2%[a]	=	3.24%
Preferred stock	0.02	×	10.3	=	0.21
Common equity	0.53	×	14.0	=	7.42
				$WACC_3$ =	10.87% ≈ 10.9%

[a]12%(1 − T) = 12%(0.6) = 7.2%, up from 10%(0.6) = 6%.

In other words, the next dollar beyond $200 million will consist of 45 cents of 12 percent debt (7.2 percent after taxes), 2 cents of 10.3 percent preferred stock, and 53 cents of new common stock at a cost of 14 percent (retained earnings were used up much earlier), and this marginal dollar will have a cost of $WACC_3$ = 10.9%.

The effect of this second WACC increase is shown in Figure 16-3. Now there are two break points, one caused by using up all the retained earnings and the other by using up all the 10 percent debt. With the two breaks, there are three different WACCs: $WACC_1$ = 10% for the first $143 million of new capital; $WACC_2 = 10.3\%$ in the interval between \$143 million and \$200 million; and $WACC_3 = 10.9\%$ for all new capital beyond \$200 million.[13]

There could, of course, be still more break points; they would occur if the interest rate continued to rise, if the cost of preferred stock rose, or if the cost of common stock rose.[14] *In general, a break point will occur whenever the cost of one of the capital components rises, and the break point can be determined by the following equation:*

$$\frac{\text{Break}}{\text{point}} = \frac{\text{Total amount of lower-cost capital of a given type}}{\text{Fraction of this type of capital in the capital structure}}. \qquad (16\text{-}11)$$

We see, then, that numerous break points can occur. At the limit, we can even think of an MCC schedule with so many break points that it rises almost continuously beyond some given level of new financing. Such an MCC schedule is shown in Figure 16-4.

The easiest sequence for calculating MCC schedules is as follows:

1. Use Equation 16-11 to determine each point at which a break occurs. A break will occur any time the cost of one of the capital components rises. (It is possible, however, that two capital components could both increase at the same point.) After determining the exact break points, make a list of them.

2. Determine the cost of capital for each component in the intervals between breaks.

3. Calculate the weighted averages of these component costs to obtain the WACCs in each interval, as we did in Table 16-1. The WACC is constant within each interval, but it rises at each break point.

Notice that if there are n separate breaks, there will be n + 1 different WACCs. For example, in Figure 16-3 we see two breaks and three different WACCs.

---

[13]When we use the term *weighted average cost of capital,* we are referring to the WACC, which is the cost of \$1 raised partly as debt, partly as preferred, and partly as equity. We could also calculate the average cost of all the capital the firm raised during a given year. For example, if Allied raised \$300 million, the first \$143 million would have a cost of 10 percent, the next \$57 million a cost of 10.3 percent, and the last \$100 million a cost of 10.9 percent. The entire \$300 million would have an average cost of

$$(143/300)(10\%) + (57/300)(10.3\%) + (100/300)(10.9\%) = 10.4\%.$$

In general, this particular cost of capital should not be used for financial decisions — it usually has no relevance in finance. The only exception to this rule occurs when the firm is considering a very large asset which must be accepted in total or else rejected, and the capital required for it includes capital with different WACCs. For example, if Allied were considering one \$300 million project, that project should be evaluated with a 10.4 percent cost.

[14]The first break point is not necessarily the point at which retained earnings are used up; it is possible for low-cost debt to be exhausted *before* retained earnings have been used up. For example, if Allied had available only \$50 million of 10 percent debt, BP_{Debt} would occur at \$111.1 million:

$$BP_{Debt} = \frac{\$50,000,000}{0.45} = \$111.1 \text{ million.}$$

This is well before the break point for retained earnings, which occurs at \$143 million.

Figure 16-4 ▪ Smooth, or Continuous, Marginal Cost of Capital Schedule

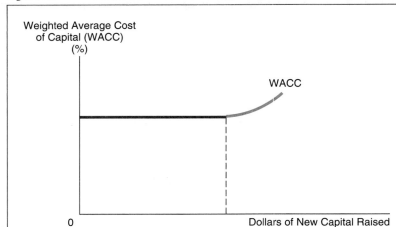

Before closing this section, we should note again that a different MCC schedule would result if a different capital structure were used. As we will show in Chapter 17, the optimal capital structure produces the lowest MCC schedule.

Self-Test Questions

What are break points, and why do they occur in MCC schedules?

Write out and explain the equation for determining break points.

How does one calculate a firm's MCC schedule?

If there are n breaks in the MCC schedule, how many different WACCs are there? Why?

COMBINING THE MCC AND INVESTMENT OPPORTUNITY SCHEDULES

Now that we have calculated the MCC schedule, we can use it to develop a discount rate for use in the capital budgeting process; *that is, we can use the MCC schedule to find the cost of capital for determining projects' net present values (NPVs) as discussed in Chapter 14.*

To understand how the MCC schedule is used in capital budgeting, assume that Allied Food Products has three financial executives: a financial vice-president (VP), a treasurer, and a director of capital budgeting (DCB). The financial VP asks the treasurer to develop the firm's MCC schedule, and the treasurer produces the schedule shown earlier in Figure 16-3. At the same time, the financial VP asks the DCB to draw up a list of all projects that are potentially acceptable. The list shows each project's cost, projected annual net cash inflows, life, and IRR. These data are presented at the bottom of Figure 16-5. For example, Project A has a cost of $80 million, it is expected to produce inflows of $15.10 million per year for 8 years, and, therefore, it has an IRR of 10.2 percent. Simi-

Figure 16-5 ▪ **Combining the MCC and IOS Schedules to Determine the Optimal Capital Budget**

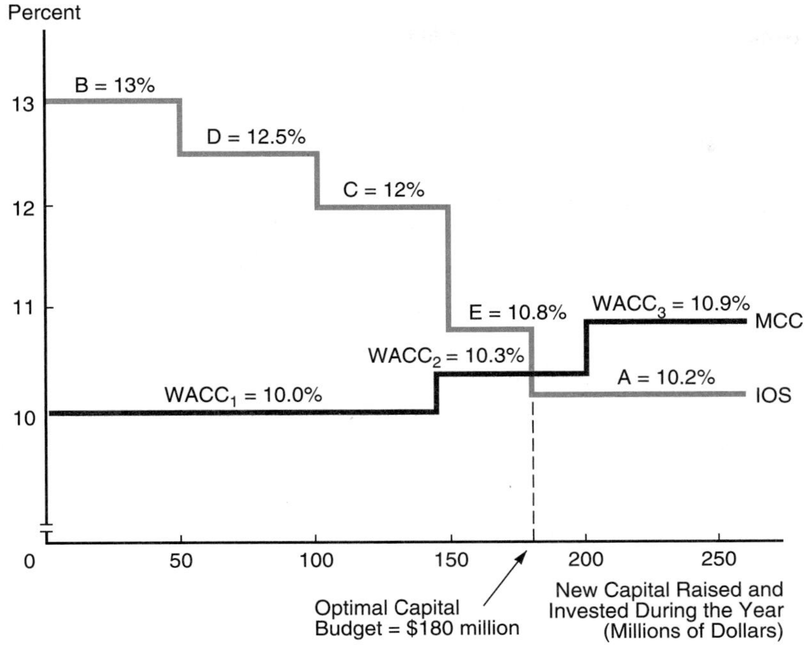

Project	Cost (in Millions)	Annual Inflows (in Millions)	Project Life (Years)	IRR, or Discount Rate, at which NPV = 0
A	$80	$15.10	8	10.2%
B	50	11.31	7	13.0
C	50	13.87	5	12.0
D	50	9.03	10	12.5
E	30	12.23	3	10.8

larly, Project B has a cost of $50 million, it is expected to produce inflows of $11.31 million per year for 7 years, and thus it has an IRR of 13 percent. (NPVs and MIRRs cannot be shown yet because we do not yet know the marginal cost of capital.) For simplicity, we assume now that all projects are independent as opposed to mutually exclusive, that they are equally risky, and that their risks are all equal to those of the firm's average existing assets.

The DCB then plots the IRR data shown at the bottom of Figure 16-5 as the **investment opportunity schedule (IOS)** shown in the graph. The IOS schedule shows, in rank order, how much money Allied could invest at different rates of return. Figure 16-5 also shows Allied's MCC schedule as it was developed by the treasurer and plotted in Figure 16-3. Now consider Project B: its IRR is 13 percent, and it can be financed with capital that costs only 10 percent; consequently, it should be accepted. Recall from Chapter 14 that if a project's IRR exceeds its cost of capital, its NPV will also be positive; therefore, Project B must also be acceptable by the NPV criterion. Projects D, C, and E can be ana-

investment opportunity schedule (IOS)

A graph of the firm's investment opportunities ranked in order of the projects' rates of return.

lyzed similarly; they are all acceptable because IRR > MCC and hence NPV > 0. Project A, on the other hand, should be rejected because its IRR < MCC and therefore its NPV < 0.

Notice that if the cost of capital had started at a point above 13 percent, none of the available projects would have had positive NPVs; hence, none of them would be accepted. In that case, Allied simply would not expand. However, in the actual situation, where the MCC starts at 10 percent and then rises, Allied would accept the four projects (B, D, C, and E) which have rates of return in excess of the cost of the capital that would be used to finance them, ending up with a capital budget of $180 million.

People sometimes ask this question: "If we took Project A first, it would be acceptable because its 10.2 percent return would exceed the 10 percent cost of money used to finance it. Why couldn't we do this?" The answer is that we are seeking, in effect, to maximize the *excess of returns over costs,* or the area that is above the WACC but below the IOS. We accomplish this by graphing (and accepting) the most profitable projects first.

Another question that sometimes arises is this: "What would happen if the MCC cut through one of the projects? For example, suppose the second break point in the MCC schedule had occurred at $170 million rather than at $200 million, causing the MCC schedule to cut through Project E. Should we then accept Project E?" If Project E could be accepted in part, we would take on only part of it. Otherwise, the answer would be determined by (1) finding the average cost of the funds needed to finance Project E (some of the money would cost 10.3 percent and some 10.9 percent) and (2) comparing the average cost of this money with the 10.8 percent return on the project. We should accept Project E if its return exceeds the average cost of the $30 million needed to finance it.

The preceding analysis as summarized in Figure 16-5 reveals a very important point: *The cost of capital used in the capital budgeting process as discussed in Chapters 14 and 15 is actually determined at the intersection of the IOS and MCC schedules. If the cost of capital at the intersection ($WACC_2 = 10.3\%$ in Figure 16-5) is used, then the firm will make correct accept/reject decisions, and its level of financing and investment will be optimal. If it uses any other rate, its capital budget will not be optimal.*

If Allied had fewer good investment opportunities, its IOS schedule would be shifted to the left, causing the intersection to occur at a lower level on the MCC curve. Conversely, if the firm had more and better investment opportunities, the IOS would be shifted to the right, and the intersection would occur at a higher WACC. In either event, the WACC at the intersection could change. *Thus, we see that the cost of capital used in capital budgeting is influenced both by the shape of the MCC curve and by the set of available projects.*

We have, of course, abstracted from differential project riskiness in this chapter; for simplicity, we have assumed that all projects are equally risky. As we learned in Chapter 15, the cost of capital used to evaluate riskier projects should be adjusted upward, whereas a lower rate should be used for projects with below-average risk. The intersection WACC as determined in Figure 16-5 should be used to find the NPVs of new projects that are about as risky as the firm's existing assets, but this corporate cost of capital should be adjusted up or down to find NPVs for projects with higher or lower risk than the average project. This point was discussed in Chapter 15, in connection with the Brandt-Quigley Corporation appliance control computer example.

? *Self-Test Questions*

Differentiate between the MCC and IOS schedules.

How is the corporate cost of capital, which is used to evaluate average risk projects to determine their NPVs, found?

As a general rule, should a firm's cost of capital as determined in this chapter be used to evaluate all of its capital budgeting projects? Explain.

SOME PROBLEM AREAS IN COST OF CAPITAL

A number of difficult issues relating to the cost of capital either have not been mentioned or were glossed over in this chapter. These topics are covered in advanced finance courses, but they deserve some mention now to alert you to potential dangers as well as to provide you with a preview of some of the matters dealt with in advanced courses.

1. **Depreciation-generated funds.** The largest single source of capital for many firms is depreciation, yet we have not discussed the cost of funds from this source. In brief, depreciation cash flows can either be reinvested or returned to investors (stockholders *and* creditors). The cost of depreciation-generated funds is approximately equal to the weighted average cost of capital in the interval in which capital comes from retained earnings and low-cost debt. See Eugene F. Brigham and Louis C. Gapenski, *Intermediate Financial Management,* 4th ed., Chapter 6, for a discussion.

2. **Privately owned firms.** Our discussion of the cost of equity was related to publicly owned corporations, and we have concentrated on the rate of return required by public stockholders. However, there is a serious question about how one should measure the cost of equity for a firm whose stock is not traded. Tax issues also become especially important in these cases. As a general rule, the same principles of cost of capital estimation apply to both privately held and publicly owned firms, but the problems of obtaining input data are somewhat different for the two cases.

3. **Small businesses.** Small businesses are generally privately owned, making it difficult to estimate their cost of equity, and some of them also obtain debt from government sources, such as the Small Business Administration. The Small Business section of this chapter discusses this issue.

4. **Measurement problems.** One cannot overemphasize the practical difficulties encountered when one actually attempts to estimate the cost of equity. It is very difficult to obtain good input data for the CAPM, for g in the formula $k_s = D_1/P_0 + g$, and for the risk premium in the formula $k_s = $ Bond yield $+$ Risk premium. As a result, we can never be sure just how accurate our estimated cost of capital is.

5. **Costs of capital for projects of differing riskiness.** As we saw in Chapter 15, it is difficult to assign proper risk-adjusted discount rates to capital budgeting projects of differing degrees of riskiness.

6. **Capital structure weights.** In this chapter we have simply taken as given the target capital structure and used it to obtain the weights used to calculate the WACC. As we shall see in Chapter 17, establishing the target capital structure is a major task in itself.

7. **Dynamic considerations.** Capital budgeting and cost of capital estimates are a part of the *planning process*—they deal with ex ante, or estimated, data rather than ex post, or historical, data. Hence, we can be wrong about the location of the IOS and the MCC. For example, we can underestimate the MCC and then accept projects which, with 20-20 hindsight, we should have rejected. In a dynamic, changing world this is a real problem. For example, interest rates and money costs could be low at the time plans are being laid and contracts to build plants are being let, but six or eight months later, when we actually raise the money, capital costs could have risen substantially. Thus, a project that formerly looked good could turn out to be a bad one because we improperly forecasted the MCC schedule.

Although this listing of problems may appear formidable, the state of the art in cost of capital estimation is really not in bad shape. The procedures outlined in this chapter can be used to obtain cost of capital estimates that are sufficiently accurate for practical purposes, and the problems listed here merely indicate the desirability of refinements. The refinements are not unimportant, but the problems we have identified do not invalidate the usefulness of the procedures outlined in the chapter.

Self-Test Question

Identify some problem areas in cost of capital analysis. Do these problems invalidate the cost of capital procedures discussed in the chapter? Explain.

SMALL BUSINESS   The Cost of Equity Capital for Small Firms

The three equity cost estimating techniques discussed in this chapter (DCF, Bond-Yield-plus-Risk-Premium, and CAPM) have serious limitations when applied to small firms. Consider first the constant growth model, $k_s = D_1/P_0 + g$. Imagine a small, rapidly growing firm, such as Bio-Technology General (BTG), which does not now and will not in the foreseeable future pay dividends. For firms like this, the constant growth model is simply not applicable. In fact, it is difficult to imagine any dividend model that would be of practical benefit for such a firm because of the difficulty of estimating dividends and growth rates.

The second method, which calls for adding a risk premium of 3 to 5 percent to the firm's cost of debt, can be used for some small firms, but problems arise if the firm does not have a bond issue outstanding. BTG, for example, has no such debt issue outstanding, so we would have trouble using the bond-yield-plus-risk-premium approach for BTG.

The third approach, the CAPM, is often not usable, because if the firm's stock is not publicly traded, then we cannot calculate that firm's beta. For the privately owned firm, we might use the "pure play" CAPM technique, which involves finding a firm in the same line of business with publicly held stock, estimating that firm's beta, and then using this second firm's beta as a replacement for that of the small business in question.

To illustrate the pure play approach, again consider BTG. The firm is not publicly traded, so we cannot estimate its beta. However, data are available on more established firms, such as Genentech and Genetic Industries, so we could use their betas as representative of the biological and genetic engineering industry. Of course, these firms' betas would have to be subjectively modified to reflect their larger sizes and more established positions, as well as to take account of the differences in the nature of their products and their capital structures as compared to those of BTG. Still, as long as there are public companies in similar lines of business available for comparison, the estimates of their betas can be used to help estimate the cost of capital of a firm whose equity is not publicly traded. Note also that a "liquidity premium" as discussed in Chapter 3 would have to be added to reflect the illiquidity of the small, nonpublic firm's stock.

Flotation Costs for Small Issues.   When external equity capital is raised, flotation costs increase the cost of equity capital beyond what it would be for internal funds. These external flotation costs are especially significant for smaller firms, and they can substantially affect capital budgeting decisions involving external equity funds. To illustrate this point, consider a firm that is expected to pay constant dividends forever, hence its growth rate is zero. In this case, if F is the percentage flotation cost, then the cost of equity capital is $k_e = D_1/[P_0(1 - F)]$. The higher the flotation cost, the higher the cost of external equity.

How big is F? According to the latest Securities and Exchange Commission data, the average flotation cost of large common stock offerings (more than $50 million) is only about 4 percent. For a firm that is expected to provide a 15 percent dividend yield (that is, $D_1/P_0 = 15\%$), the cost of equity is $15\%/(1 - 0.04)$, or 15.6 percent. However, the SEC's data on small stock offerings (less than $1 million) show that flotation costs for such issues average about 21 percent. Thus, the cost of equity capital in the preceding ex-ample would be $15\%/(1 - 0.21)$, or about 19 percent. When we compare this to the 15.6 percent for large firms, it is clear that a small firm would have to earn considerably more on the same project than a large firm. Small firms are therefore at a substantial disadvantage because of the effects of flotation costs.

The Small-Firm Effect.   A number of researchers have observed that portfolios of small-firm stocks have earned consistently higher average returns than those of large-firm stocks; this is called the "small-firm effect." On the surface, it would seem to be advantageous to the small firm to provide average returns in the stock market that are higher than those of large firms. In reality, this is bad news for the small firm—what the small-firm effect means is that the capital market demands higher returns on stocks of small firms than on otherwise similar stocks of large firms. Therefore, the basic cost of equity capital is higher for small firms. This compounds the high flotation cost problem noted above.

It may be argued that stocks of small firms are riskier than those of large ones and that this accounts for the differences in returns. It is true that academic research usually finds that betas are higher for small firms than for large ones. However, the larger returns for small firms remain larger even after adjusting for the effects of their higher risks as reflected in their beta coefficients.

The small-firm effect is an anomaly in the sense that it is not consistent with the CAPM theory. Still, higher returns reflect a higher cost of capital, so we must conclude that small firms do have higher capital costs than otherwise similar large firms. The manager of a small firm should take this factor into account when estimating his or her firm's cost of equity capital. In general, the cost of equity capital appears to be about four percentage points higher for small firms (those with market values of less than $20 million) than for large, New York Stock Exchange firms with similar risk characteristics.

SUMMARY

This chapter showed how the MCC schedule is developed for use in the capital budgeting process. The key concepts covered are listed below.

- The cost of capital to be used in capital budgeting decisions is the **weighted average** of the various types of capital the firm uses, typically debt, preferred stock, and common equity.

▪ The **component cost of debt** is the **after-tax** cost of new debt. It is found by multiplying the cost of new debt by $(1 - T)$, where T is the firm's marginal tax rate: $k_d(1 - T)$.

▪ The **component cost of preferred stock** is calculated as the preferred dividend divided by the net issuing price, where the net issuing price is the price the firm receives after deducting flotation costs: $k_p = D_p/P_n$.

▪ The **cost of common equity** is the cost of retained earnings as long as the firm has retained earnings, but the cost of equity becomes the cost of new common stock once the firm has exhausted its retained earnings.

▪ The **cost of retained earnings** is the rate of return required by stockholders on the firm's common stock, and it can be estimated using one of three methods: (1) the **CAPM approach**, (2) the **bond-yield-plus-risk-premium approach**, and (3) the **dividend-yield-plus-growth-rate, or DCF, approach.**

▪ To use the **CAPM approach**, one (1) estimates the firm's beta, (2) multiplies this beta by the market risk premium to determine the firm's risk premium, and (3) adds the firm's risk premium to the risk-free rate to obtain the firm's cost of retained earnings: $k_s = k_{RF} + (k_M - k_{RF})b_i$.

▪ The **bond-yield-plus-risk-premium approach** calls for adding a risk premium of from 3 to 5 percentage points to the firm's interest rate on long-term debt: $k_s = $ Bond yield $ + $ RP.

▪ To use the **dividend-yield-plus-growth-rate approach,** which is also called the **DCF approach,** one adds the firm's expected growth rate to its expected dividend yield: $k_s = D_1/P_0 + g$.

▪ The **cost of new common equity** is higher than the cost of retained earnings because the firm must incur **flotation expenses** to sell stock. To find the cost of new common equity, the stock price is first reduced by the flotation expense, then the dividend yield is calculated on the basis of the price the firm will actually receive, and finally the expected growth rate is added to this **adjusted dividend yield:** $k_e = D_1/[P_0(1 - F)] + g$.

▪ Each firm has an **optimal capital structure**, defined as that mix of debt, preferred stock, and common equity which minimizes its **weighted average cost of capital (WACC):**

$$WACC = w_d k_d (1 - T) + w_p k_p + w_e (k_s \text{ or } k_e).$$

▪ The **marginal cost of capital (MCC)** is defined as the cost of the last dollar of new capital that the firm raises. The MCC increases as the firm raises more and more capital during a given period. A graph of the MCC plotted against dollars raised is the **MCC schedule.**

▪ A **break point** will occur in the MCC schedule each time the cost of one of the capital components increases.

▪ The **investment opportunity schedule (IOS)** is a graph of the firm's investment opportunities, ranked in order of their rates of return.

▪ The MCC schedule is combined with the IOS schedule, and the intersection defines the **corporate cost of capital,** which is used to evaluate average-risk capital budgeting projects.

▮ The three equity cost estimation techniques discussed in this chapter have **serious limitations when applied to small firms,** thus increasing the need for the small-business manager to use judgment.

▮ Stock offerings of less than $1 million have an average flotation cost of 21 percent, while the average flotation cost on large common stock offerings is about 4 percent. As a result, a small firm would have to earn considerably more on the same project than a large firm. Also, the capital market demands higher returns on stocks of small firms than on otherwise similar stocks of large firms—this is called the **small-firm effect.**

The concepts developed in this chapter are extended in Chapter 17, where we consider the effect of the capital structure on the cost of capital.

Questions

16-1   In what sense does the marginal cost of capital schedule represent a series of average costs?

16-2   How would each of the following affect a firm's cost of debt, $k_d(1 - T)$; its cost of equity, k_s; and its weighted average cost of capital, WACC? Indicate by a plus (+), a minus (−), or a zero (0) if the factor would raise, lower, or have an indeterminate effect on the item in question. Assume other things are held constant. Be prepared to justify your answer, but recognize that several of the parts probably have no single correct answer; these questions are designed to stimulate thought and discussion.

	Effect on		
	$k_d(1 - T)$	k_s	WACC
a. The corporate tax rate is lowered.	_____	_____	_____
b. The Federal Reserve tightens credit.	_____	_____	_____
c. The firm uses more debt; that is, it increases its debt/assets ratio.	_____	_____	_____
d. The dividend payout ratio is increased.	_____	_____	_____
e. The firm doubles the amount of capital it raises during the year.	_____	_____	_____
f. The firm expands into a risky new area.	_____	_____	_____
g. The firm merges with another firm whose earnings are countercyclical both to those of the first firm and to the stock market.	_____	_____	_____
h. The stock market falls drastically, and the firm's stock falls along with the rest.	_____	_____	_____
i. Investors become more risk averse.	_____	_____	_____
j. The firm is an electric utility with a large investment in nuclear plants. Several states propose a ban on nuclear power generation.	_____	_____	_____

16-3   Suppose a firm estimates its MCC and IOS schedules for the coming year and finds that they intersect at the point 10%, $10 million. What cost of capital should be used to evaluate average projects, high-risk projects, and low-risk projects?

Self-Test Problems *(Solutions Appear in Appendix B)*

ST-1
Key terms

Define each of the following terms:

a. After-tax cost of debt, $k_d(1 - T)$; capital component cost
b. Cost of preferred stock, k_p
c. Cost of retained earnings, k_s
d. Cost of new common equity, k_e
e. Flotation cost, F
f. Target capital structure; capital structure components
g. Weighted average cost of capital, WACC
h. Marginal cost of capital, MCC
i. Marginal cost of capital schedule; break point, BP
j. Investment opportunity schedule, IOS

ST-2
Optimal capital budget

Lancaster Engineering Inc. (LEI) has the following capital structure, which it considers to be optimal:

Debt	25%
Preferred stock	15
Common equity	60
	100%

LEI's expected net income this year is $34,285.72; its established dividend payout ratio is 30 percent; its federal-plus-state tax rate is 40 percent; and investors expect earnings and dividends to grow at a constant rate of 9 percent in the future. LEI paid a dividend of $3.60 per share last year, and its stock currently sells at a price of $60 per share.

LEI can obtain new capital in the following ways:

▮ *Common:* New common stock has a flotation cost of 10 percent for up to $12,000 of new stock and 20 percent for all common over $12,000.

▮ *Preferred:* New preferred stock with a dividend of $11 can be sold to the public at a price of $100 per share. However, flotation costs of $5 per share will be incurred for up to $7,500 of preferred, and flotation costs will rise to $10 per share, or 10 percent, on all preferred over $7,500.

▮ *Debt:* Up to $5,000 of debt can be sold at an interest rate of 12 percent; debt in the range of $5,001 to $10,000 must carry an interest rate of 14 percent; and all debt over $10,000 will have an interest rate of 16 percent.

LEI has the following independent investment opportunities:

Project	Cost at t = 0	Annual Net Cash Flow	Project Life	IRR
A	$10,000	$2,191.20	7 years	12.0%
B	10,000	3,154.42	5	17.4
C	10,000	2,170.18	8	14.2
D	20,000	3,789.48	10	13.7
E	20,000	5,427.84	6	

a. Find the break points in the MCC schedule.
b. Determine the cost of each capital structure component.

c. Calculate the weighted average cost of capital in the interval between each break in the MCC schedule.

d. Calculate the IRR for Project E.

e. Construct a graph showing the MCC and IOS schedules.

f. Which projects should LEI accept?

Problems

16-1
Cost of retained earnings

The earnings, dividends, and stock price of Talukdar Technologies Inc. are expected to grow at 7 percent per year in the future. Talukdar's common stock sells for $23 per share, its last dividend was $2.00, and the company will pay a dividend of $2.14 at the end of the current year.

a. Using the discounted cash flow approach, what is its cost of retained earnings?

b. If the firm's beta is 1.6, the risk-free rate is 9 percent, and the average return on the market is 13 percent, what will be the firm's cost of equity using the CAPM approach?

c. If the firm's bonds earn a return of 12 percent, what will k_s be using the bond-yield-plus-risk-premium approach? (Hint: Use the midpoint of the risk premium range discussed in the text.)

d. Based on the results of Parts a through c, what would you estimate Talukdar's cost of retained earnings to be?

16-2
Cost of retained earnings

The Shrieves Company's EPS was $6.50 in 1992 and $4.42 in 1987. The company pays out 40 percent of its earnings as dividends, and the stock sells for $36.

a. Calculate the past growth rate in earnings. (Hint: This is a 5-year growth period.)

b. Calculate the *next* expected dividend per share, D_1. [$D_0 = 0.4($6.50) = $2.60.$] Assume that the past growth rate will continue.

c. What is the cost of retained earnings, k_s, for the Shrieves Company?

16-3
Break point calculations

The Simmons Company expects earnings of $30 million next year. Its dividend payout ratio is 40 percent, and its debt/assets ratio is 60 percent. Simmons uses no preferred stock.

a. What amount of retained earnings does Simmons expect next year?

b. At what amount of financing will there be a break point in the MCC schedule?

c. If Simmons can borrow $12 million at an interest rate of 11 percent, another $12 million at a rate of 12 percent, and any additional debt at a rate of 13 percent, at what points will rising debt costs cause breaks in the MCC schedule?

16-4
Calculation of g and EPS

Rowell Products' stock is currently selling for $60 a share. The firm is expected to earn $5.40 per share this year and to pay a year-end dividend of $3.60.

a. If investors require a 9 percent return, what rate of growth must be expected for Rowell?

b. If Rowell reinvests retained earnings in projects whose average return is equal to the stock's expected rate of return, what will be next year's EPS? [Hint: g = b(ROE), where b = fraction of earnings retained.]

16-5
Weighted average cost of capital

On January 1, 1993, the total assets of the Dexter Company were $270 million. The firm's present capital structure, which follows, is considered to be optimal. Assume that there is no short-term debt.

Long-term debt	$135,000,000
Common equity	135,000,000
Total liabilities and equity	$270,000,000

New bonds will have a 10 percent coupon rate and will be sold at par. Common stock, currently selling at $60 a share, can be sold to net the company $54 a share. Stockholders' required rate of return is estimated to be 12 percent, consisting of a dividend yield of 4 percent and an expected growth rate of 8 percent. (The next expected dividend is $2.40, so $2.40/$60 = 4%.) Retained earnings are estimated to be $13.5 million. The federal-plus-state tax rate is 40 percent. Assuming that all asset expansion (gross expenditures for fixed assets plus related working capital) is included in the capital budget, the dollar amount of the capital budget, ignoring depreciation, is $135 million.

a. To maintain the present capital structure, how much of the capital budget must Dexter finance by equity?
b. How much of the new equity funds needed will be generated internally? Externally?
c. Calculate the cost of each of the equity components.
d. At what level of capital expenditure will there be a break in Dexter's MCC schedule?
e. Calculate the WACC (1) below and (2) above the break in the MCC schedule.
f. Plot the MCC schedule. Also, draw in an IOS schedule that is consistent with both the MCC schedule and the projected capital budget. (Any IOS schedule that is consistent will do.)

16-6

Weighted average
cost of capital

The following tabulation gives earnings per share figures for the Brueggeman Company during the preceding 10 years. The firm's common stock, 7.8 million shares outstanding, is now (1/1/93) selling for $65 per share, and the expected dividend at the end of the current year (1993) is 55 percent of the 1992 EPS. Because investors expect past trends to continue, g may be based on the earnings growth rate. (Note that nine years of growth are reflected in the data.)

Year	EPS	Year	EPS
1983	$3.90	1988	$5.73
1984	4.21	1989	6.19
1985	4.55	1990	6.68
1986	4.91	1991	7.22
1987	5.31	1992	7.80

The current interest rate on new debt is 9 percent. The firm's federal-plus-state tax rate is 40 percent. Its capital structure, considered to be optimal, is as follows:

Debt	$104,000,000
Common equity	156,000,000
Total liabilities and equity	$260,000,000

a. Calculate Brueggeman's after-tax cost of new debt and of common equity, assuming that new equity comes only from retained earnings. Calculate the cost of equity as $k_s = D_1/P_0 + g$.
b. Find Brueggeman's weighted average cost of capital, again assuming that no new common stock is sold and that all debt costs 9 percent.
c. How much can be spent on capital investments before external equity must be sold? (Assume that retained earnings available for 1993 are 45 percent of 1992 earnings. Obtain 1992 earnings by multiplying 1992 EPS by the shares outstanding.)
d. What is Brueggeman's weighted average cost of capital (cost of funds raised in excess of the amount calculated in Part c) if new common stock can be sold to the public at $65 a share to net the firm $58.50 a share? The cost of debt is constant.

16-7
Optimal capital budget

Ezzell Enterprises has the following capital structure, which it considers to be optimal under present and forecasted conditions:

Debt (long-term only)	45%
Common equity	55
Total liabilities and equity	100%

For the coming year, management expects after-tax earnings of $2.5 million. Ezzell's past dividend policy of paying out 60 percent of earnings will continue. Present commitments from its banker will allow Ezzell to borrow according to the following schedule:

Loan Amount	Interest Rate
$0 to $500,000	9% on this increment of debt
$500,001 to $900,000	11% on this increment of debt
$900,001 and above	13% on this increment of debt

The company's federal-plus-state tax rate is 40 percent; the current market price of its stock is $22 per share; its *last* dividend was $2.20 per share; and the expected growth rate is 5 percent. External equity (new common) can be sold at a flotation cost of 10 percent.
Ezzell has the following investment opportunities for the next year:

Project	Cost	Annual Cash Flows	Project Life	IRR
1	$675,000	$155,401	8 years	
2	900,000	268,484	5	15.0%
3	375,000	161,524	3	
4	562,500	185,194	4	12.0
5	750,000	127,351	10	11.0

Management asks you to help determine which projects (if any) should be undertaken. You proceed with this analysis by answering the following questions (or performing the tasks) as posed in a logical sequence:
a. How many breaks are there in the MCC schedule? At what dollar amounts do the breaks occur, and what causes them?
b. What is the weighted average cost of capital in each of the intervals between the breaks?
c. What are the IRR values for Projects 1 and 3?
d. Graph the IOS and MCC schedules.
e. Which projects should Ezzell's management accept?
f. What assumptions about project risk are implicit in this problem? If you learned that Projects 1, 2, and 3 were of above-average risk, yet Ezzell chose the projects which you indicated in Part e, how would this affect the situation?
g. The problem stated that Ezzell pays out 60 percent of its earnings as dividends. How would the analysis change if the payout ratio were changed to zero, to 100 percent, or somewhere in between? (No calculations are necessary.)

EXAM-TYPE PROBLEMS

The problems included in this section are set up in such a way that they could be used as mutliple-choice exam problems.

16-8
After-tax cost of debt

Calculate the after-tax cost of debt under each of the following conditions:
a. Interest rate, 13 percent; tax rate, 0 percent.
b. Interest rate, 13 percent; tax rate, 20 percent.
c. Interest rate, 13 percent; tax rate, 34 percent.

16-9
After-tax cost of debt

The McDaniel Company's financing plans for next year include the sale of long-term bonds with a 10 percent coupon. The company believes it can sell the bonds at a price that will provide a yield to maturity of 12 percent. If the federal-plus-state tax rate is 34 percent, what is McDaniel's after-tax cost of debt?

16-10
Cost of preferred stock

Maness Industries plans to issue some $100 par preferred stock with an 11 percent dividend. The stock is selling on the market for $97.00, and Maness must pay flotation costs of 5 percent of the market price. What is the cost of the preferred stock for Maness?

16-11
Cost of new common stock

The Choi Company's next expected dividend, D_1, is $3.18; its growth rate is 6 percent; and the stock now sells for $36. New stock can be sold to net the firm $32.40 per share.
a. What is Choi's percentage flotation cost, F?
b. What is Choi's cost of new common stock, k_e?

16-12
Weighted average cost of capital

The Gupta Company's cost of equity is 16 percent. Its before-tax cost of debt is 13 percent, and its federal-plus-state tax rate is 40 percent. The stock sells at book value. Using the following balance sheet, calculate Gupta's after-tax weighted average cost of capital:

Assets		**Liabilities and Equity**	
Cash	$ 120	Long-term debt	$1,152
Accounts receivable	240	Equity	1,728
Inventories	360		
Plant and equipment, net	2,160		
Total assets	$2,880	Total liabilities and equity	$2,880

16-13
Optimal capital budget

The Mason Corporation's present capital structure, which is also its target capital structure, calls for 50 percent debt and 50 percent common equity. The firm has only one potential project, an expansion program with a 10.2 percent IRR and a cost of $20 million but which is completely divisible; that is, Mason can invest any amount up to $20 million. The firm expects to retain $3 million of earnings next year. It can raise up to $5 million in new debt at a before-tax cost of 8 percent, and all debt after the first $5 million will have a cost of 10 percent. The cost of retained earnings is 12 percent, and the firm can sell any amount of new common stock desired at a constant cost of new equity of 15 percent. The firm's federal-plus-state tax rate is 40 percent. What is the firm's optimal capital budget?

16-14
Optimal capital budget

The management of Ferri Phosphate Industries (FPI) is planning next year's capital budget. FPI projects its net income at $7,500, and its payout ratio is 40 percent. The company's earnings and dividends are growing at a constant rate of 5 percent; the last dividend, D_0, was $0.90; and the current stock price is $8.59. FPI's new debt will cost 14 percent. If FPI issues new common stock, flotation costs will be 20 percent. FPI is at its optimal capital structure, which is 40 percent debt and 60 percent equity, and the firm's federal-plus-state tax rate is 40 percent. FPI has the following independent, indivisible, and equally risky investment opportunities:

Project	Cost	IRR
A	$15,000	17%
B	20,000	14
C	15,000	16
D	12,000	15

What is FPI's optimal capital budget?

16-15
Risk-adjusted optimal capital budget

Refer to Problem 16-14. Management now decides to incorporate project risk differentials into the analysis. The new policy is to add 2 percentage points to the cost of capital of those projects significantly riskier than average and to subtract 2 percentage points from the cost of capital of those which are substantially less risky than average. Management judges Project A to be of high risk, Projects C and D to be of average risk, and Project B to be of low risk. No projects are divisible. What is the optimal capital budget after adjustment for project risk?

16-16
Weighted average cost of capital

Florida Electric Company (FEC) uses only debt and equity. It can borrow unlimited amounts at an interest rate of 10% as long as it finances at its target capital structure, which calls for 45 percent debt and 55 percent common equity. Its last dividend was $2; its expected constant growth rate is 4 percent; its stock sells at a price of $25; and new stock would net the company $20 per share after flotation costs. FEC's federal-plus-state tax rate is 40 percent, and it expects to have $100 million of retained earnings this year. Two projects are available: Project A has a cost of $200 million and a rate of return of 13 percent, while Project B has a cost of $125 million and a rate of return of 10 percent. All of the company's potential projects are equally risky.
a. What is FEC's cost of equity from newly issued stock?
b. What is FEC's marginal cost of capital; i.e., what WACC cost rate should it use to evaluate capital budgeting projects (these two projects plus any others that might arise during the year, provided the cost of capital schedule remains as it is currently)?

16-17
After-tax cost of debt

A company's 6 percent coupon rate, semiannual payment, $1,000 par value bond which matures in 30 years sells at a price of $515.16. The company's federal-plus-state tax rate is 40 percent. What is the firm's component cost of debt for purposes of calculating the WACC? (Hint: Base your answer on the nominal rate, not the EAR.)

16-18
Marginal cost of equity

Chicago Paints Corporation has a target capital structure of 40 percent debt and 60 percent common equity. The company expects to have $600 of after-tax income during the coming year, and it plans to retain 40 percent of its earnings. The current stock price is $P_0 = \$30$, the last dividend was $D_0 = \$2.00$, and the dividend is expected to grow at a constant rate of 7 percent. New stock can be sold at a flotation cost of $F = 25$ percent. What will Chicago Paints's marginal cost of *equity* capital (not the WACC) be if it raises a total of $500 of new capital?

INTEGRATIVE PROBLEM

16-19
Cost of capital

Assume that you were recently hired as assistant to Jerry Lehman, financial VP of Coleman Technologies. Your first task is to estimate Coleman's cost of capital. Lehman has provided you with the following data, which he believes may be relevant to your task:
(1)   The firm's federal-plus-state tax rate is 40 percent.

(2)   The current price of Coleman's 12% coupon, semiannual payment, noncallable bonds with 15 years remaining to maturity is $1,153.72. Coleman does not use short-term interest-bearing debt on a permanent basis. New bonds would be privately placed with no flotation cost.

(3)   The current price of the firm's 10 percent, $100 par value, quarterly dividend, perpetual preferred stock is $113.10. Coleman would incur flotation costs of $2.00 per share on a new issue.

(4)   Coleman's common stock is currently selling at $50 per share. Its last dividend (D_0) was $4.19, and dividends are expected to grow at a constant rate of 5 percent in the foreseeable future. Coleman's beta is 1.2; the yield on T-bonds is 7 percent; and the market risk premium is estimated to be 6 percent. For the bond-yield-plus-risk-premium approach, the firm uses a 4 percentage point risk premium.

(5)   Up to $300,000 of new common stock can be sold at a flotation cost of 15 percent. Above $300,000, the flotation cost would rise to 25 percent.

(6)   Coleman's target capital structure is 30 percent long-term debt, 10 percent preferred stock, and 60 percent common equity.

(7)   The firm is forecasting retained earnings of $300,000 for the coming year.

To structure the task somewhat, Lehman has asked you to answer the following questions.

a. (1) What sources of capital should be included when you estimate Coleman's weighted average cost of capital (WACC)?
  (2) Should the component costs be figured on a before-tax or an after-tax basis?
  (3) Should the costs be historical (embedded) costs or new (marginal) costs?
b. What is the market interest rate on Coleman's debt and its component cost of debt?
c. (1) What is the firm's cost of preferred stock?
  (2) Coleman's preferred stock is riskier to investors than its debt, yet the yield to investors is lower than the yield to maturity on the debt. Does this suggest that you have made a mistake? (Hint: Think about taxes.)
d. (1) Why is there a cost associated with retained earnings?
  (2) What is Coleman's estimated cost of retained earnings using the CAPM approach?
  (3) Why is the T-bond rate a better estimate of the risk-free rate for cost of capital purposes than the T-bill rate?
e. What is the estimated cost of retained earnings using the discounted cash flow (DCF) approach?
f. What is the bond-yield-plus-risk-premium estimate for Coleman's cost of retained earnings?
g. What is your final estimate for k_s?
h. What is Coleman's cost for up to $300,000 of newly issued common stock, k_{e1}? What happens to the cost of equity if Coleman sells more than $300,000 of new common stock?
i. Explain in words why new common stock has a higher percentage cost than retained earnings.
j. (1) What is Coleman's overall, or weighted average, cost of capital (WACC) when retained earnings are used as the equity component?
  (2) What is the WACC after retained earnings have been exhausted and Coleman uses up to $300,000 of new common stock with a 15 percent flotation cost?
  (3) What is the WACC if more than $300,000 of new common equity is sold?
k. (1) At what amount of new investment would Coleman be forced to issue new common stock? To put it another way, what is the largest capital budget the company could support without issuing new common stock? Assume that the 30/10/60 target capital structure will be maintained.

(2) At what amount of new investment would Coleman be forced to issue new common stock with a 25 percent flotation cost?

(3) What is a marginal cost of capital (MCC) schedule? Construct a graph which shows Coleman's MCC schedule.

l.   Coleman's Director of Capital Budgeting has identified the following potential projects:

Project	Cost	Life	Cash Flow	IRR
A	$700,000	5 years	$218,795	17.0%
B	500,000	5	152,705	16.0
B′	500,000	20	79,881	15.0
C	800,000	5	219,185	11.5

Projects B and B′ are mutually exclusive, whereas the remainder are independent. All of the projects are equally risky.

(1) Plot the IOS schedule on the same graph that contains your MCC schedule. What is the firm's marginal cost of capital for capital budgeting purposes?

(2) What is the dollar size, and the included projects, in Coleman's optimal capital budget? Explain your answer fully.

(3) Would Coleman's MCC schedule remain constant at 12.8 percent beyond $2 million regardless of the amount of capital required?

(4) If WACC$_3$ had been 18.5 percent rather than 12.8 percent, but the second WACC break point had still occurred at $1,000,000, how would that have affected the analysis?

m. Suppose you learned that Coleman could raise only $200,000 of new debt at a 10 percent interest rate and that new debt beyond $200,000 would have a yield to investors of 12 percent. Trace back through your work and explain how this new fact would change the situation.

COMPUTER-RELATED PROBLEM

Work the problem in this section only if you are using the computer problem diskette.

16-20 Use the model in the File C16 to work this problem.

Marginal cost of capital

a. Refer back to Problem 16-7. Now assume that the debt ratio is increased to 65 percent, causing all interest rates to rise by 1 percentage point, to 10 percent, 12 percent, and 14 percent, and causing g to increase from 5 to 6 percent. What happens to the MCC schedule and the capital budget?

b. Assume the facts as in Part a, but suppose Ezzell's federal-plus-state tax rate falls (1) to 20 percent or (2) to 0 percent. How would this affect the MCC schedule and the capital budget?

c. Ezzell's management would now like to know what the optimal capital budget would be if earnings were as high as $3.25 million or as low as $1 million. Assume a 40 percent federal-plus-state tax rate.

d. Would it be reasonable to use the model to analyze the effects of a change in the payout ratio without changing other variables?

Capital Structure and Leverage

The debt ratio of the average U.S. company rose from about 47 percent in 1972 to almost 60 percent in early 1991. When questioned about this trend, a number of respected business and academic leaders debated whether or not corporations are using too much debt. For example, Henry Kaufman, a well-known Wall Street economist whose nickname is "Dr. Gloom," argued that debt levels have risen so high that an otherwise minor economic setback could turn into a major recession. However, John Paulus, Morgan Stanley's chief economist, countered that debt is the cheapest source of capital and that if U.S. firms are to compete effectively in global markets, they should use even more debt. Still others question the basic data—for example, Robert Taggart, a finance professor at Boston University, argued that the accounting data cited above tell us nothing and that market value debt ratios are the only comparisons that make sense. (With most stocks selling at about twice their book values, market value debt ratios are far lower than book value ratios.)

It should also be noted that, while the median rating of companies followed by Standard & Poor's (a leading bond-rating agency) was A in 1981, the median had dropped to the "junk" level, BB, by early 1991. However, in 1981 most smaller, riskier companies were simply unable to obtain capital in the public bond markets, hence they did not have rated debt in 1981, while today the junk bond market has made capital available to creative and venturesome young companies.

However, corporations are beginning to deleverage, substituting new equity for debt. In 1991, for the first time in eight years, the balance sheets of nonfinancial corporations ended the year with lower debt ratios than when the year began. Some of the corporations which led the LBO binge of the 1980s, including Warnaco, Kaiser Aluminum, Duracell International, and RJR Nabisco, sold stock to the public to reduce their debt loads, and, in November 1991, Colgate-Palmolive lowered its debt-to-

> *equity ratio from 50–50 to 30–70. "Equity and balance sheet quality are in fashion," states Brian Heidtke, treasurer of Colgate-Palmolive.*
>
> *The effects of deleveraging are substantial. As new equity is issued and debt is retired, interest costs are reduced, operating restrictions are relaxed, and credit rating agencies view the deleveraging as a favorable sign. In addition, retiring debt frees up cash which companies can spend on capital expenditures and the like. After you read this chapter, you should be in a better position to help a firm decide how much debt is optimal.*
>
> Sources: "A Decade of Debt Is Now Giving Way to the Age of Equity," *The Wall Street Journal,* December 16, 1991, and other related articles.

In Chapter 16, when we calculated the weighted average cost of capital for use in capital budgeting, we took the capital structure weights, or the mix of securities the firm uses to finance its assets, as a given. However, if the weights are changed, the calculated cost of capital, and thus the set of acceptable projects, also will change. Further, changing the capital structure will affect the riskiness inherent in the firm's common stock, and this will affect k_s and P_0. Therefore, the choice of a capital structure is an important decision.

THE TARGET CAPITAL STRUCTURE

target capital structure
The mix of debt, preferred stock, and common equity with which the firm plans to finance its investments.

As we shall see, the firm first analyzes a number of factors, and then it establishes a **target capital structure.** This target may change over time as conditions vary, but at any given moment the firm's management has a specific capital structure in mind, and individual financing decisions should be consistent with this target. If the actual debt ratio is below the target level, expansion capital will probably be raised by issuing debt, whereas if the debt ratio is currently above the target, stock will probably be sold.

Capital structure policy involves a tradeoff between risk and return:

- Using more debt raises the riskiness of the firm's earnings stream.
- However, a higher debt ratio generally leads to a higher expected rate of return.

The higher risk associated with greater debt tends to lower the stock's price, but the higher expected rate of return raises it. *Therefore, the optimal capital structure is the one that strikes a balance between risk and return so as to maximize the price of the stock.*

Four primary factors influence capital structure decisions.

1. The first is the firm's *business risk,* or the riskiness that would be inherent in the firm's operations if it used no debt. The greater the firm's business risk, the lower its optimal debt ratio.

2. The second key factor is the firm's *tax position.* As we shall see, a major reason for using debt is that interest is deductible, which lowers the effective cost of debt. However, if much of a firm's income is already sheltered from taxes by accelerated depreciation or tax loss carry-forwards, its tax rate will be low, and in this case debt will not be as advantageous as it would be to a firm with a higher effective tax rate.

3. The third important consideration is *financial flexibility,* or the ability to raise capital on reasonable terms under adverse conditions. Corporate treasurers know that a steady supply of capital is necessary for stable operations, which in turn are vital for long-run success. They also know that when money is tight in the economy, or when a firm is experiencing operating difficulties, suppliers of capital prefer to advance funds to companies with strong balance sheets. Therefore, both the potential future need for funds and the consequences of a funds shortage have a major influence on the target capital structure—the greater the probable future need for capital, and the worse the consequences of a capital shortage, the stronger the balance sheet should be.

4. The fourth debt-determining factor has to do with *managerial conservatism or aggressiveness.* Some managers are more aggressive than others, hence some firms are more inclined to use debt in an effort to boost profits. This factor does not affect the optimal, or value-maximizing, capital structure, but it does influence the target capital structures that firms actually establish.

These four points largely determine the target capital structure, but, of course, operating conditions can cause the actual capital structure to vary from the target at any given time. For example, Illinois Power has a target debt ratio of about 45 percent, but large losses associated with a nuclear plant forced it to write down its common equity, and that raised the debt ratio above the target level. Subsequently, the company eliminated its dividends and took other steps to get its equity back up to the target level.

Self-Test Questions

What are the four factors that affect the target capital structure?

In what sense does capital structure policy involve a tradeoff between risk and return?

BUSINESS AND FINANCIAL RISK

In Chapter 4, when we examined risk from the viewpoint of the individual investor, we distinguished between *market risk,* which is measured by the firm's beta coefficient, and *total risk,* which includes both beta risk and a type of risk which can be eliminated by diversification. Then, in Chapter 15, we examined risk from the viewpoint of the corporation, and we considered how capital budgeting decisions affect the riskiness of the firm. There again we distinguished between beta risk (the effect of a project on the firm's beta) and corporate risk (the effect of the project on the firm's total risk).

Now we introduce two new dimensions of risk:

1. *Business risk,* which is the riskiness of the firm's operations if it uses no debt.
2. *Financial risk,* which is the additional risk placed on the common stockholders as a result of the firm's decision to use debt.

Conceptually, the firm has a certain amount of risk inherent in its operations; this is its business risk. When it uses debt, it partitions this risk and concentrates most of it on one class of investors—the common stockholders.[1]

Business Risk

business risk

The risk associated with projections of a firm's future returns on assets, or returns on equity (ROE) if the firm uses no debt.

Business risk is defined as the uncertainty inherent in projections of future returns on assets (ROA), or of returns on equity (ROE) if the firm uses no debt, and it is the single most important determinant of capital structure. Consider Bigbee Electronics Company, a firm that currently uses 100 percent equity. Figure 17-1 gives some clues about Bigbee's business risk. The top graph shows the trend in ROE (and ROA) from 1982 through 1992; this graph gives both security analysts and Bigbee's management an idea of the degree to which ROE has varied in the past and might vary in the future. The bottom graph shows the beginning-of-year, subjectively estimated probability distribution of Bigbee's ROE for 1992 based on the trend line in the top section of Figure 17-1. The estimate was made at the beginning of 1992, and the expected value of 12 percent was read from the trend line. As the graphs indicate, actual ROE in 1992 (8%) fell below the expected value (12%).

Bigbee's past fluctuations in ROE were caused by many factors—booms and recessions in the national economy, successful new products introduced both by Bigbee and by its competitors, labor strikes, a fire in Bigbee's major plant, and so on. Similar events will doubtless occur in the future, and when they do, ROE will rise or fall. Further, there is always the possibility that a long-term disaster might strike, permanently depressing the company's earning power. For example, a competitor could introduce a new product that would permanently lower Bigbee's earnings.[2] This element of uncertainty about Bigbee's future ROE is the company's *basic business risk.*

---

[1]Using preferred stock also adds to financial risk. To simplify matters somewhat, in this chapter we shall consider only debt and common equity. Also, if a firm uses an especially large amount of debt in a leveraged buyout (LBO), then its debt will be classified as "junk bonds," and the bondholders will also be exposed to financial risk. Some junk bonds practically amount to equity.

[2]Two examples of "safe" industries that turned out to be risky are the railroads just before automobiles, airplanes, and trucks took away most of their business and the telegraph business just before telephones came on the scene. Also, numerous individual companies have been hurt, if not destroyed, by antitrust actions, fraud, or just plain bad management.

Figure 17-1 ▪ **Bigbee Electronics Company: Trend in ROE, 1982–1992, and Subjective Probability Distribution of ROE, 1992**

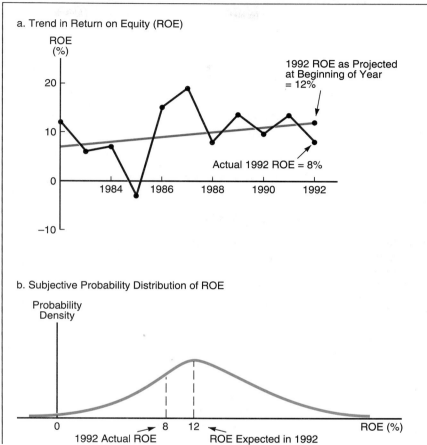

Business risk varies from one industry to another and also among firms in a given industry. Further, business risk can change over time. For example, the electric utilities were regarded for years as having little business risk, but a combination of events in the 1970s and 1980s altered their situation, producing sharp declines in ROE for some companies, and greatly increasing the industry's business risk. Today, food processors and grocery retailers are frequently cited as examples of industries with low business risk, whereas cyclical manufacturing industries, such as steel, are regarded as having especially high business risk. Smaller companies, especially single-product firms, also have a relatively high degree of business risk.[3]

_____

[3]We have avoided any discussion of market versus company-specific risk in this section. We note now (1) that any action which increases business risk will generally increase a firm's beta coefficient but (2) that a part of business risk as we define it will generally be company-specific and hence subject to elimination through diversification by the firm's stockholders.

Business risk depends on a number of factors, the more important of which are the following:

1. **Demand (unit sales) variability.** The more stable the unit sales of a firm's products, other things held constant, the lower its business risk.

2. **Sales price variability.** Firms whose products are sold in highly volatile markets are exposed to more business risk than similar firms whose output prices are relatively stable.

3. **Input price variability.** Firms whose input prices are highly uncertain are exposed to a high degree of business risk.

4. **Ability to adjust output prices for changes in input prices.** Some firms have little difficulty in raising their own output prices when input costs rise, and the greater the ability to adjust output prices, the lower the degree of business risk. This factor is especially important during periods of high inflation.

5. **The extent to which costs are fixed: operating leverage.** If a high percentage of a firm's costs are fixed and hence do not decline when demand falls off, this increases the company's business risk. This factor is called *operating leverage,* and it was discussed at length in Chapter 8.

Each of these factors is determined partly by the firm's industry characteristics, but each is also controllable to some extent by management. For example, most firms can, through their marketing policies, take actions to stabilize both unit sales and sales prices; however, this stabilization may require either large expenditures on advertising or price concessions to induce customers to commit to purchasing fixed quantities at fixed prices in the future. Similarly, firms like Bigbee Electronics can reduce the volatility of future input costs by negotiating long-term labor and materials supply contracts, but they may have to agree to pay prices somewhat above the current market price to obtain these contracts.[4]

Financial Risk

financial leverage
The extent to which fixed-income securities (debt and preferred stock) are used in a firm's capital structure.

financial risk
The portion of stockholders' risk, over and above basic business risk, resulting from the use of financial leverage.

Financial leverage refers to the use of fixed-income securities—debt and preferred stock—and **financial risk** is the additional risk placed on the common stockholders as a result of using financial leverage. Conceptually, the firm has a certain amount of risk inherent in its operations; this is its business risk, which is defined as the uncertainty inherent in projections of future ROA. By using debt and preferred stock (financial leverage), the firm concentrates its business risk on the common stockholders. To illustrate, suppose 10 people decide to form a corporation to manufacture running shoes. There is a certain amount of business risk in the operation. If the firm is capitalized only with common equity, and if each person buys 10 percent of the stock, then each investor will bear an equal share of the business risk. However, suppose the firm is capitalized

---

[4]For example, in 1992 utilities could buy coal in the spot market for about $30 per ton, but under a 5-year contract, the cost was about $50 per ton. Clearly, the price for reducing uncertainty was high!

INDUSTRY PRACTICE | Too Much Debt Hurts Company with Sound Basic Operations

Prime Computer reported a half billion dollar loss during 1991. Its net worth dropped to a negative $725.8 million, and it will be in default on loan agreements if it cannot arrange new financing by the end of 1993. In spite of its financial problems, Prime's president and CEO, John J. Shields, insists that his company is "a pretty good operating company." He states that the bad numbers reflect burdensome debt ($1.26 billion worth), large write-offs, and noncash interest payments. To make matters worse, Prime's industry is struggling—the computer industry is suffering from price cutting, weak markets in the United States and abroad, rapid product cycles, and cautious customers.

Prime is an example of what can happen to a company that takes on huge amounts of debt in an industry where fixed assets cannot be sold, where engineering costs are substantial, and where consumer confidence is important. Because of its problems, Prime has reduced its work force, shifted one of its key subsidiaries from hardware to software, and won two years of breathing room by renegotiating its debt agreements. One analyst states that the company is doing all the right things, but financially it is a house of cards. If Prime goes under, it will not be because of its operating strategy or its technology, but because of its poor financial policies.

Although the numbers do not seem to indicate it, Prime did have a positive cash flow in 1991. The company would have been profitable if it had not had write-offs and huge interest payments. Prime's president insists that the cure for Prime is equity. The board has not made the decision to raise equity yet, but refinancing is a top priority.

An industry analyst at Moody's Investors Service stated that Prime is operating in a difficult industry environment complicated by the recession. "You want customers to commit to you, but with the kind of earnings stream Prime has, it's hard." If the company goes bankrupt, its customers will have a tough time getting spare parts and service. Although Moody's Investors Service rates Prime's bonds Caa, one notch above default, some sophisticated junk bond investors think Prime can emerge as a viable company. Its debt is currently trading at around 50 cents on the dollar, an improvement from 10 cents on the dollar two years ago. One junk bond holder indicated that if the company could demonstrate a few good quarters in the CAD/CAM design systems, the capital markets would be receptive to an equity offering, which would help the debt ratio tremendously.

For the present, on the basis of its current operating assumptions and business outlook, Prime will be able to avoid default. However, the company will have to arrange alternative financing sources to meet its long-term debt service requirements during the coming year. The only solution to Prime's problems appears to be recapitalization—add equity and reduce debt.

Source: "Prime Computer's Forte Is Technology, Not Finance," *The Wall Street Journal*, April 1, 1992.

with 50 percent debt and 50 percent equity, with 5 of the investors putting up their capital as debt and the other 5 putting up their money as equity. In this case, the investors who put up the equity will have to bear essentially all of the business risk, so their common stock will be twice as risky as it would have been had the firm been financed only with equity. *Thus, the use of debt concentrates the firm's business risk on its stockholders.*

In the next section, we will explain how financial leverage affects a firm's expected earnings per share, the riskiness of those earnings, and, consequently, the price of the firm's stock. As you will see, the value of a firm that has no debt first rises as it substitutes debt for equity, then hits a peak, and finally declines as the use of debt becomes excessive. The objective of our analysis is to determine the capital structure at which value is maximized; this point is then used as the *target capital structure.*[5]

? *Self-Test Questions*

What is the difference between business risk and financial risk?

Identify and briefly explain some of the more important factors which affect business risk.

Which of the factors identified in the previous question can management control?

Why does business risk vary from one industry to another?

What creates financial risk?

DETERMINING THE OPTIMAL CAPITAL STRUCTURE

We can illustrate the effects of financial leverage using the data shown in Table 17-1 for an illustrative company which we shall call Firm B. As shown in the top section of the table, the company has no debt. Should it continue the policy of using no debt, or should it start using financial leverage? If it does decide to substitute debt for equity, how far should it go? As in all such decisions, *the correct answer is that it should choose the capital structure that will maximize the price of its stock.*

EBIT/EPS Analysis of the Effects of Financial Leverage

Changes in the use of debt will cause changes in earnings per share (EPS) and, consequently, in the stock price. To understand the relationship between financial leverage and EPS, first consider Table 17-2, which shows how Firm B's cost of debt would vary if it used different percentages of debt in its capital structure. Naturally, the higher the percentage of debt, the riskier the debt, hence the higher the interest rate lenders will charge.

---

[5]In this chapter we examine capital structures on a *book value* (or *balance sheet) basis.* An alternative approach is to calculate the market values of debt, preferred stock, and common equity and then to reconstruct the balance sheet on a *market value basis.* Although the market value approach is more consistent with financial theory, bond rating agencies and most financial executives focus their attention on book values. Moreover, the conversion from book to market values is a complicated process, and since market value capital structures change with stock market fluctuations, they are thought by many to be too unstable to serve as operationally useful targets. Finally, exactly the same insights are gained from the book value and market value analyses. For all these reasons, a market value analysis of capital structure is better suited for advanced finance courses.

Table 17-1 ▪ **Data on Firm B**

I. Balance Sheet on 12/31/92

Current assets	$100,000	Debt	$ 0
Net fixed assets	100,000	Common equity (10,000 shares)	200,000
Total assets	$200,000	Total liabilities and equity	$200,000

II. Income Statement for 1992

Sales			$200,000
Fixed operating costs		$ 40,000	
Variable operating costs		120,000	160,000
Earnings before interest and taxes (EBIT)			$ 40,000
Interest			0
Taxable income			$ 40,000
Taxes (40%)			16,000
Net income			$ 24,000

III. Other Data

1. Earnings per share = EPS = $24,000/10,000 shares = $2.40.
2. Dividends per share = DPS = $24,000/10,000 shares = $2.40. (Thus, Firm B pays out all of its earnings as dividends.)
3. Book value per share = $200,000/10,000 shares = $20.
4. Market price per share = P_0 = $20. (Thus, the stock sells at its book value, so M/B = 1.0.)
5. Price/earnings ratio = P/E = $20/$2.40 = 8.33 times.

Table 17-2 ▪ **Interest Rates for Firm B with Different Debt/Assets Ratios**

Amount Borrowed[a]	Debt/Assets Ratio	Interest Rate, k_d, on All Debt
$ 20,000	10%	8.0%
40,000	20	8.3
60,000	30	9.0
80,000	40	10.0
100,000	50	12.0
120,000	60	15.0

[a]We assume that the firm must borrow in increments of $20,000. We also assume that Firm B is unable to borrow more than $120,000, or 60 percent of assets, because of restrictions in its corporate charter.

Now consider Table 17-3, which shows how expected EPS varies with changes in financial leverage. Section I of the table begins with a probability distribution of sales; we assume for simplicity that sales can take on only three values, $100,000, $200,000, or $300,000. In the remainder of Section I we calculate EBIT at each of the three sales levels. Note that in Section I we assume that both sales and operating costs are independent of financial leverage. There-

Table 17-3 ▪ Firm B: EPS with Different Amounts of Financial Leverage (Thousands of Dollars, except Per-Share Figures)

I. Calculation of EBIT

Probability of indicated sales	0.2	0.6	0.2
Sales	$100.0	$200.0	$300.0
Fixed costs	40.0	40.0	40.0
Variable costs (60% of sales)	60.0	120.0	180.0
Total costs (except interest)	$100.0	$160.0	$220.0
Earnings before interest and taxes (EBIT)	$ 0.0	$ 40.0	$ 80.0

II. Situation if Debt/Assets (D/A) = 0%

EBIT (from Section I)	$ 0.0	$ 40.0	$ 80.0
Less interest	0.0	0.0	0.0
Earnings before taxes (EBT)	$ 0.0	$ 40.0	$ 80.0
Taxes (40%)	0.0	(16.0)	(32.0)
Net income	$ 0.0	$ 24.0	$ 48.0
Earnings per share (EPS) on 10,000 shares[a]	$ 0.0	$ 2.40	$ 4.80
Expected EPS		$ 2.40	
Standard deviation of EPS		$ 1.52	
Coefficient of variation		0.63	

III. Situation if Debt/Assets (D/A) = 50%

EBIT (from Section I)	$ 0.0	$ 40.0	$ 80.0
Less interest (0.12 × $100,000)	12.0	12.0	12.0
Earnings before taxes (EBT)	($ 12.0)	$ 28.0	$ 68.0
Taxes (40%; tax credit on losses)	4.8	(11.2)	(27.2)
Net income	($ 7.2)	$ 16.8	$ 40.8
Earnings per share (EPS) on 5,000 shares[a]	($ 1.44)	$ 3.36	$ 8.16
Expected EPS		$ 3.36	
Standard deviation of EPS		$ 3.04	
Coefficient of variation		0.90	

[a]The EPS figures can also be obtained using the following formula, in which the numerator amounts to an income statement at a given sales level laid out horizontally:

$$\text{EPS} = \frac{(\text{Sales} - \text{Fixed costs} - \text{Variable costs} - \text{Interest})(1 - \text{Tax rate})}{\text{Shares outstanding}} = \frac{(\text{EBIT} - I)(1 - T)}{\text{Shares outstanding}}.$$

For example, with zero debt and Sales = $200,000, EPS is $2.40:

$$\text{EPS}_{D/A=0} = \frac{(\$200,000 - \$40,000 - \$120,000 - 0)(0.6)}{10,000} = \$2.40.$$

With 50 percent debt and Sales = $200,000, EPS is $3.36:

$$\text{EPS}_{D/A=0.5} = \frac{(\$200,000 - \$40,000 - \$120,000 - \$12,000)(0.6)}{5,000} = \$3.36.$$

The sales level at which EPS will be equal under the two financing policies, or the indifference level of sales, S_I, can be found by setting $\text{EPS}_{D/A=0}$ equal to $\text{EPS}_{D/A=0.5}$ and solving for S_I:

$$\text{EPS}_{D/A=0} = \frac{(S_I - \$40,000 - 0.6S_I - 0)(0.6)}{10,000} = \frac{(S_I - \$40,000 - 0.6S_I - \$12,000)(0.6)}{5,000} = \text{EPS}_{D/A=0.5}.$$

$$S_I = \$160,000.$$

By substituting this value of sales into either equation, we can find EPS_I, the earnings per share at this indifference point. In our example, $\text{EPS}_I = \$1.44$.

fore, the three EBIT figures ($0, $40,000, and $80,000) will always remain the same, no matter how much debt Firm B uses.[6]

Section II of Table 17-3, the zero-debt case, calculates Firm B's earnings per share at each sales level under the assumption that the company continues to use no debt. Net income is divided by the 10,000 shares outstanding to obtain EPS. If sales are as low as $100,000, EPS will be zero, but it will rise to $4.80 at a sales level of $300,000. The EPS at each sales level is then multiplied by the probability of that sales level to calculate the expected EPS, which is $2.40 if Firm B uses no debt. We also calculate the standard deviation of EPS and the coefficient of variation as indicators of the firm's risk at a zero debt ratio: $\sigma_{EPS} = 1.52, and $CV_{EPS} = 0.63$.[7]

Section III of the table shows the financial results that could be expected if Firm B were financed with a debt/assets ratio of 50 percent. In this situation, $100,000 of the $200,000 total capital would be debt. The interest rate on the debt, 12 percent, is taken from Table 17-2. With $100,000 of 12 percent debt outstanding, the company's interest expense in Table 17-3 would be $12,000 per year. This is a fixed cost—it is the same regardless of the level of sales—and it is deducted from the EBIT values as calculated in the top section. Next, taxes are taken out to calculate net income. EPS is then calculated as net income divided by shares outstanding. With debt = 0, there would be 10,000 shares outstanding. However, if half of the equity were replaced by debt (debt = $100,000), there would be only 5,000 shares outstanding, and we must use this fact to determine the EPS figures that would result at each of the three possible sales levels.[8] With a debt/assets ratio of 50 percent, the EPS figure would be

---

[6]In the real world, capital structure *does* at times affect EBIT. First, if debt levels are excessive, the firm will probably not be able to finance at all if its earnings are low at a time when interest rates are high. This could lead to stop-start construction and R&D programs, as well as to the necessity of passing up good investment opportunities. Second, a weak financial condition (i.e., too much debt) could cause a firm to lose sales. For example, prior to the time that its huge debt forced Eastern Airlines into bankruptcy, many people refused to buy Eastern tickets because they were afraid the company would go bankrupt and leave them holding unusable tickets. Third, financially strong companies are able to bargain hard with unions as well as with their suppliers, whereas weaker ones may have to give in simply because they do not have the financial resources to carry on the fight. Finally, a company with so much debt that bankruptcy is a serious threat will have difficulty attracting and retaining managers and employees, or it will have to pay premium salaries. People value job security, and financially weak companies simply cannot provide such protection. For all these reasons, it is not totally correct to say that a firm's financial policy has no effect on its operating income.

Note also that EBIT is dependent on operating leverage. If we were analyzing a firm with either more or less operating leverage, the top section of Table 17-3 would be quite different: fixed and variable costs would be different, and the range of EBIT over the various sales levels would be narrower if the company used a lower degree of operating leverage but wider if it used more operating leverage.

[7]See Chapter 4 for a review of procedures for calculating standard deviations and coefficients of variation. Recall that the advantage of the coefficient of variation is that it permits better comparisons when the expected values of EPS vary, as they do here for the two capital structures.

[8]We assume in this example that the firm could change its capital structure by repurchasing common stock at its book value of $100,000/5,000 shares = $20 per share. However, the firm may actually have to pay a higher price to repurchase its stock on the open market. If Firm B had to pay $22 per share, then it could repurchase only $100,000/$22 = 4,545 shares, and in this case, expected EPS would be only $16,800/(10,000 − 4,545) = $16,800/5,455 = $3.08 rather than $3.36.

Figure 17-2 ▪ **Firm B: Probability Distributions of EPS with Different Amounts of Financial Leverage**

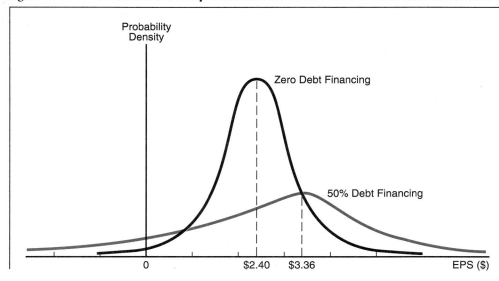

— $1.44 if sales were as low as $100,000; it would rise to $3.36 if sales were $200,000; and it would soar to $8.16 if sales were as high as $300,000.

The EPS distributions under the two financial structures are graphed in Figure 17-2, where we use continuous distributions rather than the discrete distributions contained in Table 17-3. Although expected EPS would be much higher if financial leverage were employed, the graph makes it clear that the risk of low or even negative EPS would also be higher if debt were used.

Another view of the relationships among expected EPS, risk, and financial leverage is presented in Figure 17-3. The tabular data in the lower section were calculated in the manner set forth in Table 17-3, and the graphs plot these data. Here we see that expected EPS rises until the firm is financed with 50 percent debt. Interest charges rise, but this effect is more than offset by the declining number of shares outstanding as debt is substituted for equity. However, EPS peaks at a debt ratio of 50 percent. Beyond this amount, interest rates rise so rapidly that EPS is depressed in spite of the falling number of shares outstanding.

The right panel of Figure 17-3 shows that risk, as measured by the coefficient of variation of EPS, rises continuously, and at an increasing rate, as debt is substituted for equity.

We see, then, that using leverage has both good and bad effects: higher leverage increases expected earnings per share (in this example, until the D/A ratio equals 50 percent), but it also increases the firm's risk. Clearly, the debt ratio should not exceed 50 percent, but where, in the range of 0 to 50 percent, should it be set? This issue is discussed in the following sections.

EPS indifference point
The level of sales at which EPS will be the same whether the firm uses debt or common stock financing.

EPS Indifference Analysis

Another way of considering the data on Firm B's two financing methods is shown in Figure 17-4, which depicts the **EPS indifference point**—that is, the point at which EPS is the same regardless of whether the firm uses debt or

Figure 17-3 ▪ Firm B: Relationships among Expected EPS, Risk, and Financial Leverage

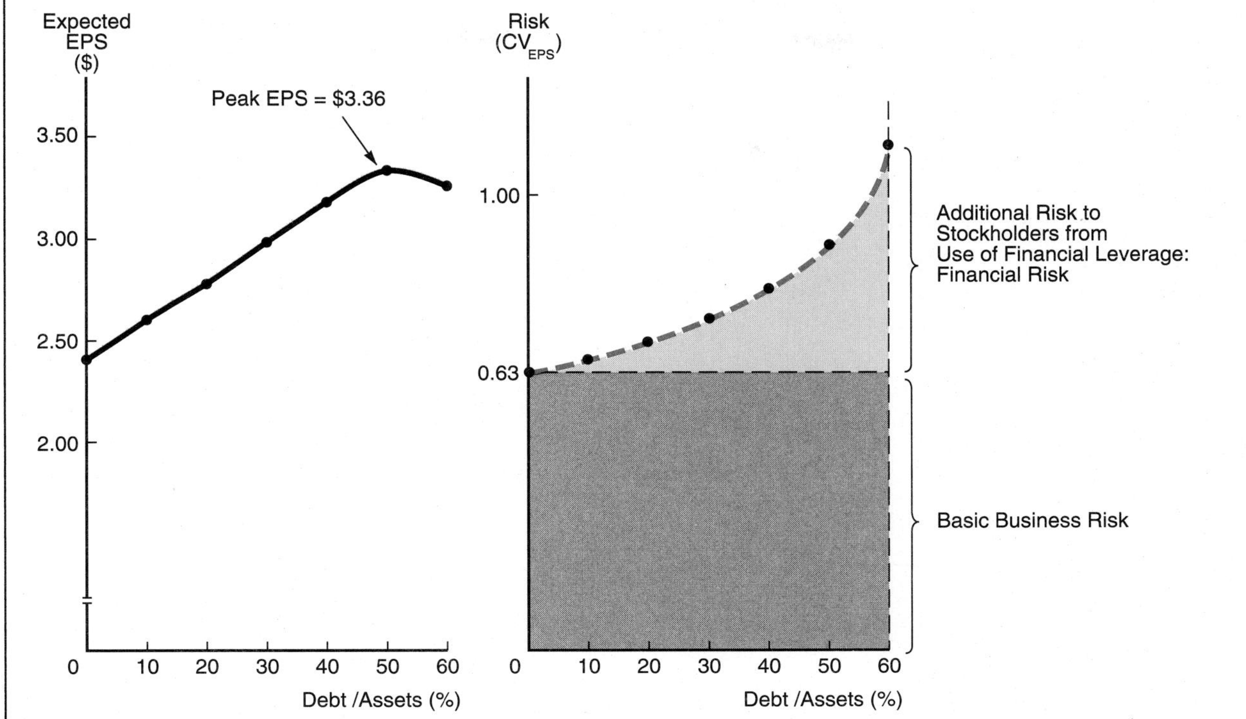

Debt/Assets Ratio	Expected EPS	Standard Deviation of EPS	Coefficient of Variation
0%[a]	$2.40[a]	$1.52[a]	0.63[a]
10	2.56	1.69	0.66
20	2.75	1.90	0.69
30	2.97	2.17	0.73
40	3.20	2.53	0.79
50[a]	3.36[a]	3.04[a]	0.90[a]
60	3.30	3.79	1.15

[a]Values for D/A = 0 and D/A = 50 percent are taken from Table 17-3. Values at other D/A ratios were calculated similarly.

common stock. At a low level of sales, EPS is much higher if stock rather than debt is used. However, the debt line has a steeper slope, showing that earnings per share will go up faster with increases in sales if debt is used. The two lines cross at sales of $160,000. Below that level, EPS would be higher if the firm used more common stock; above it, debt financing would produce higher earnings per share.

If we were certain that sales would never again fall below $160,000, bonds would be the preferred method of financing the asset increase. But we cannot know this for certain. In fact, investors know that in a number of previous years,

Figure 17-4 ▪ **Earnings per Share for Stock and Debt Financing**

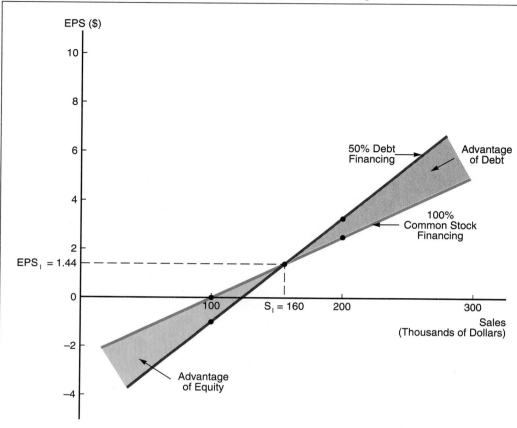

1. These values of the indifference level of sales, S_I and EPS_I, are the same as those obtained algebraically in Table 17-3. These relationships would be somewhat different if we did not assume that stock can be repurchased at book value.

2. We can also develop an equation to find the sales level at which EPS is the same under different degrees of financial leverage:

$$EPS_1 = \frac{S_{BE} - F - V - I_1}{Shares_1} = \frac{S_{BE} - F - V - I_2}{Shares_2} = EPS_2.$$

Here, EPS_1 and EPS_2 are the EPSs at two debt levels; S_{BE} is the sales breakeven (or indifference) level at which $EPS_1 = EPS_2$; I_1 and I_2 are interest charges at the two debt levels; $Shares_1$ and $Shares_2$ are shares outstanding at the two debt levels; F is the fixed costs; and V = variable costs = Sales × v, where v is the variable cost percentage. Solving for S_{BE}, we obtain this expression:

$$S_{BE} = \left[\frac{(Shares_2)(I_1) - (Shares_1)(I_2)}{Shares_2 - Shares_1} + F \right]\left(\frac{1}{1 - v}\right).$$

In our example,

$$S_{BE} = \left[\frac{(5,000)(0) - (10,000)(\$12,000)}{-5,000} + \$40,000 \right]\left(\frac{1}{0.4}\right)$$

$$= \$160,000.$$

Table 17-4   ■   **Stock Price and Cost of Capital Estimates for Firm B with Different Debt/Assets Ratios**

Debt/ Assets (1)	k_d (2)	Expected EPS (and DPS)[a] (3)	Estimated Beta (4)	$k_s = [k_{RF} + (k_M - k_{RF})b]$[b] (5)	Estimated Price[c] (6)	Resulting P/E Ratio (7)	Weighted Average Cost of Capital, WACC[d] (8)
0%	—	$2.40	1.50	12.0%	$20.00	8.33	12.00%
10	8.0%	2.56	1.55	12.2	20.98	8.20	11.46
20	8.3	2.75	1.65	12.6	21.83	7.94	11.08
30	9.0	2.97	1.80	13.2	22.50	7.58	10.86
40	**10.0**	**3.20**	**2.00**	**14.0**	**22.86**	**7.14**	**10.80**
50	12.0	3.36	2.30	15.2	22.11	6.58	11.20
60	15.0	3.30	2.70	16.8	19.64	5.95	12.12

[a]Firm B pays all of its earnings out as dividends, so EPS = DPS.

[b]We assume that k_{RF} = 6% and k_M = 10%. Therefore, at debt/assets equal to zero, k_s = 6% + (10% − 6%)1.5 = 6% + 6% = 12%. Other values of k_s are calculated similarly.

[c]Since all earnings are paid out as dividends, no retained earnings will be plowed back into the business, and growth in EPS and DPS will be zero. Hence, the zero growth stock price model developed in Chapter 6 can be used to estimate the price of Firm B's stock. For example, at debt/assets = 0,

$$P_0 = \frac{DPS}{k_s} = \frac{\$2.40}{0.12} = \$20.$$

Other prices were calculated similarly.

[d]Column 8 is found by use of the weighted average cost of capital (WACC) equation developed in Chapter 16:

$$WACC = w_d k_d (1 - T) + w_s k_s$$
$$= (D/A)(k_d)(1 - T) + (1 - D/A)k_s.$$

For example, at D/A = 40%,

$$WACC = 0.4(10\%)(0.6) + 0.6(14.0\%) = 10.80\%.$$

sales have fallen below this critical level, and if any of several detrimental events should occur in the future, sales would again fall below $160,000. On the other hand, if sales continue to expand, higher earnings per share would result from the use of bonds, and this is an advantage that no investor would want to forgo.

The Effect of Capital Structure on Stock Prices and the Cost of Capital

As we saw in Figure 17-3, Firm B's expected EPS is maximized at a debt/assets ratio of 50 percent. Does this mean that Firm B's optimal capital structure calls for 50 percent debt? The answer is a resounding no—*the optimal capital structure is the one that maximizes the price of the firm's stock, and this always calls for a debt ratio which is lower than the one that maximizes expected EPS.*

This statement is demonstrated in Table 17-4, which develops Firm B's estimated stock price and weighted average cost of capital at different debt/assets ratios. The debt cost and EPS data in Columns 2 and 3 were taken from Table 17-2 and Figure 17-3. The beta coefficients shown in Column 4 were estimated.

Figure 17-5 ▪ **Firm B's Required Rate of Return on Equity at Different Debt Levels**

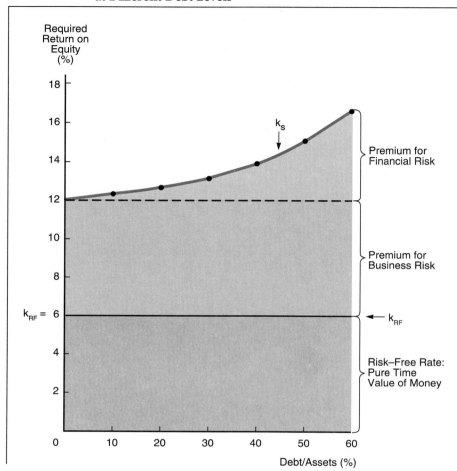

Recall from Chapter 4 that a stock's beta measures its relative volatility as compared with that of an average stock. It has been demonstrated both theoretically and empirically that a firm's beta increases with its degree of financial leverage. The exact nature of this relationship for a given firm is difficult to estimate, but the values given in Column 4 do show the approximate nature of the relationship for Firm B.

Assuming that the risk-free rate of return, k_{RF}, is 6 percent and that the required return on an average stock, k_M, is 10 percent, we can use the CAPM equation to develop estimates of the required rates of return, k_s, for Firm B as shown in Column 5. Here we see that k_s is 12 percent if no financial leverage is used, but k_s rises to 16.8 percent if the company finances with 60 percent debt, the maximum permitted by its charter.

Figure 17-5 graphs Firm B's required rate of return on equity at different debt levels. The figure also shows the composition of Firm B's required return: the risk-free rate of 6 percent and the premiums for both business and financial risk, which were discussed earlier in this chapter. As you can see from the graph, the business risk premium does not depend on the debt level—it remains constant at 6 percent at all debt levels. However, the financial risk premium varies depending on the debt level—the higher the debt level, the greater the premium for financial risk.

The zero growth stock valuation model developed in Chapter 6 is used in Table 17-4, along with the Column 3 values of DPS and the Column 5 values of k_s, to develop the estimated stock prices shown in Column 6. Here we see that the expected stock price first rises with financial leverage, hits a peak of $22.86 at a debt/assets ratio of 40 percent, and then begins to decline. *Thus, Firm B's optimal capital structure calls for 40 percent debt.*

The price/earnings ratios shown in Column 7 were calculated by dividing the price in Column 6 by the expected earnings given in Column 3. We use the pattern of P/E ratios as a check on the "reasonableness" of the other data. Other things held constant, P/E ratios should decline as the riskiness of a firm increases, and that pattern does exist in our illustrative case. Also, at the time Firm B's data were being analyzed, the P/Es shown here were generally consistent with those of zero growth companies with varying amounts of financial leverage. Thus, the data in Column 7 reinforce our confidence in the reasonableness of the estimated prices shown in Column 6.

Finally, Column 8 shows Firm B's weighted average cost of capital, WACC, calculated as described in Chapter 16, at the different capital structures. If the company uses zero debt, its capital is all equity, so WACC = k_s = 12%. As the firm begins to use lower-cost debt, its weighted average cost of capital declines. However, as the debt ratio increases, the costs of both debt and equity rise, and the increasing costs of the two components begin to offset the fact that larger amounts of the lower-cost component are being used. At 40 percent debt, WACC hits a minimum, and it rises after that as the debt ratio is increased.

The EPS, cost of capital, and stock price data shown in Table 17-4 are plotted in Figure 17-6. As the graph shows, the debt/assets ratio that maximizes Firm B's expected EPS is 50 percent. However, the expected stock price is maximized, and the cost of capital is minimized, at a 40 percent debt ratio. *Thus, the optimal capital structure calls for 40 percent debt and 60 percent equity.* Management should set its target capital structure at these ratios, and if the existing ratios are off target, it should move toward the target when new security offerings are made.

Self-Test Questions

Explain the following statement: "Using leverage has both good and bad effects."

What does the EPS indifference point show? What occurs at sales below this point? What occurs at sales above this point?

Is the optimal capital structure the one that maximizes expected EPS? Explain.

Explain the following statement: "At the optimal capital structure, a firm has minimized its cost of capital." Do stockholders want the firm to minimize its cost of capital?

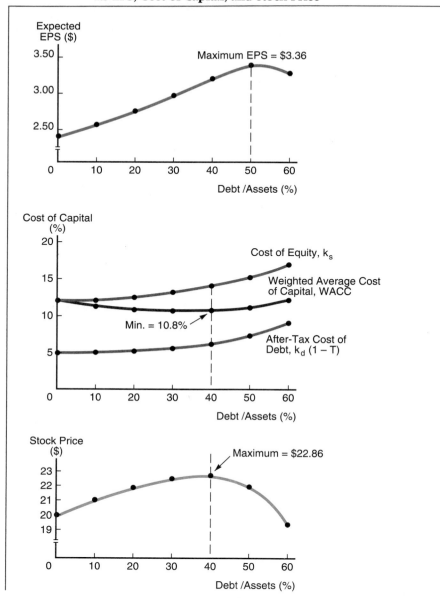

Figure 17-6 ∎ **Relationship between Firm B's Capital Structure and Its EPS, Cost of Capital, and Stock Price**

DEGREE OF LEVERAGE[9]

In our discussion of operating leverage back in Chapter 8, we made no mention of financial leverage, and when we discussed financial leverage in earlier sections of this chapter, operating leverage was assumed to be given. Actually, the two types of leverage are interrelated. For example, if Firm B *reduced* its oper-

---

[9]This section is relatively technical. It can be omitted without loss of continuity if time pressures require omission.

ating leverage, this would probably lead to an *increase* in its optimal use of financial leverage. On the other hand, if it decided to *increase* its operating leverage, its optimal capital structure would probably call for *less* debt.

The theory of finance has not been developed to the point where we can actually specify simultaneously the optimal levels of operating and financial leverage. However, we can see how operating and financial leverage interact through an analysis of the *degree of leverage concept.*

degree of operating leverage (DOL)

The percentage change in EBIT resulting from a given percentage change in sales.

Degree of Operating Leverage (DOL)

The **degree of operating leverage (DOL)** is defined as the percentage change in operating income (or EBIT) associated with a given percentage change in sales:

$$DOL = \frac{\text{Percentage change in EBIT}}{\text{Percentage change in sales}} = \frac{\dfrac{\Delta EBIT}{EBIT}}{\dfrac{\Delta Q}{Q}}. \qquad (17\text{-}1)$$

In effect, the DOL is an index number which measures the effect of a change in sales on operating income, or EBIT.

DOL can also be calculated by using Equation 17-2, which is derived from Equation 17-1:[10]

$$DOL_Q = \text{Degree of operating leverage at Point Q}$$
$$= \frac{Q(P - V)}{Q(P - V) - F}, \qquad (17\text{-}2)$$

or, based on dollar sales rather than units,

$$DOL_S = \frac{S - VC}{S - VC - F}. \qquad (17\text{-}2a)$$

---

[10]Equation 17-2 is developed from 17-1 as follows. The change in units of output is defined as ΔQ. In equation form, $EBIT = Q(P - V) - F$, where Q is units sold, P is the price per unit, V is the variable cost per unit, and F is the total fixed cost. Since both price and fixed costs are constant, the change in EBIT is $\Delta EBIT = \Delta Q(P - V)$. The initial EBIT is $Q(P - V) - F$, so the percentage change in EBIT is

$$\% \Delta EBIT = \frac{\Delta Q(P - V)}{Q(P - V) - F}.$$

The percentage change in output is $\Delta Q/Q$, so the ratio of the percentage change in EBIT to the percentage change in output is

$$DOL = \frac{\dfrac{\Delta Q(P - V)}{Q(P - V) - F}}{\dfrac{\Delta Q}{Q}} = \left(\frac{\Delta Q(P - V)}{Q(P - V) - F} \right) \left(\frac{Q}{\Delta Q} \right) = \frac{Q(P - V)}{Q(P - V) - F}. \qquad (17\text{-}2)$$

Here Q is the initial units of output, P is the average sales price per unit of output, V is the variable cost per unit, F is fixed operating costs, S is initial sales in dollars, and VC is total variable costs. Equation 17-2 is normally used to analyze a single product, such as IBM's PC, whereas Equation 17-2a is used to evaluate an entire firm with many types of products and, hence, for which "quantity in units" and "sales price" are not meaningful.

Applying Equation 17-2a to data for Firm B at a sales level of $200,000 as shown back in Table 17-3, we find its degree of operating leverage to be 2.0:

$$DOL_{\$200,000} = \frac{\$200,000 - \$120,000}{\$200,000 - \$120,000 - \$40,000}$$

$$= \frac{\$80,000}{\$40,000} = 2.0.$$

Thus, an X percent increase in sales will produce a 2X percent increase in EBIT. For example, a 50 percent increase in sales, starting from sales of $200,000, will result in a 50%(2.0)= 100% increase in EBIT. This situation is confirmed by examining Section I of Table 17-3, where we see that a 50 percent increase in sales, from $200,000 to $300,000, causes EBIT to double. Note, however, that if sales decrease by 50 percent, then EBIT will decrease by 100 percent; according to Table 17-3, EBIT decreases to $0 if sales decrease to $100,000.

Note also that the DOL is specific to the initial sales level; thus, if we evaluated it from a sales base of $300,000, there would be a different DOL:

$$DOL_{\$300,000} = \frac{\$300,000 - \$180,000}{\$300,000 - \$180,000 - \$40,000}$$

$$= \frac{\$120,000}{\$80,000} = 1.5.$$

In general, if a firm is operating at close to its breakeven level, the degree of operating leverage will be high, but DOL declines the higher the base level of sales is above breakeven sales. Looking back at the top section of Table 17-3, we see that the company's breakeven point (before consideration of financial leverage) is at sales of $100,000. At that level, DOL is infinite:

$$DOL_{\$100,000} = \frac{\$100,000 - \$60,000}{\$100,000 - \$60,000 - \$40,000}$$

$$= \frac{\$40,000}{0} = \text{undefined but} \approx \text{infinity.}$$

When evaluated at higher and higher sales levels, DOL progressively declines.

Degree of Financial Leverage (DFL)

Operating leverage affects earnings before interest and taxes (EBIT), whereas financial leverage affects earnings after interest and taxes, or the earnings available to common stockholders. In terms of Table 17-3, operating leverage affects the top section, whereas financial leverage affects the lower sections. Thus, if Firm B decided to use more operating leverage, its fixed costs would be higher than $40,000, its variable cost ratio would be lower than 60 percent of sales, and its EBIT would be more sensitive to changes in sales. *Financial leverage*

degree of financial leverage (DFL)

The percentage change in earnings available to common stockholders associated with a given percentage change in earnings before interest and taxes.

takes over where operating leverage leaves off, further magnifying the effects on earnings per share of changes in the level of sales. For this reason, operating leverage is sometimes referred to as *first-stage leverage* and financial leverage as *second-stage leverage.*

The **degree of financial leverage (DFL)** is defined as the percentage change in earnings per share that results from a given percentage change in earnings before interest and taxes (EBIT), and it is calculated as follows:[11]

$$DFL = \frac{\%\,\Delta EPS}{\%\,\Delta EBIT}$$

$$= \frac{EBIT}{EBIT - I}. \qquad (17\text{-}3)$$

For Firm B at sales of \$200,000 and an EBIT of \$40,000, the degree of financial leverage with a 50 percent debt ratio is

$$DFL_{S = \$200,000,\ D = 50\%} = \frac{\$40,000}{\$40,000 - \$12,000}$$

$$= 1.43.$$

Therefore, a 100 percent increase in EBIT would result in a 100(1.43) = 143 percent increase in earnings per share. This may be confirmed by referring to the lower section of Table 17-3, where we see that a 100 percent increase in EBIT, from \$40,000 to \$80,000, produces a 143 percent increase in EPS:

$$\%\,\Delta EPS = \frac{\Delta EPS}{EPS_0} = \frac{\$8.16 - \$3.36}{\$3.36} = \frac{\$4.80}{\$3.36} = 1.43 = 143\%.$$

---

[11]Equation 17-3 is developed as follows:

1. Recall that EBIT = Q(P − V) − F.

2. Earnings per share are found as EPS = [(EBIT − I)(1 − T)]/N, where I is interest paid, T is the corporate tax rate, and N is the number of shares outstanding.

3. I is a constant, so $\Delta I = 0$; hence, ΔEPS, the change in EPS, is

$$\Delta EPS = \frac{(\Delta EBIT - \Delta I)(1 - T)}{N} = \frac{\Delta EBIT(1 - T)}{N}.$$

4. The percentage change in EPS is the change in EPS divided by the original EPS:

$$\frac{\dfrac{\Delta EBIT(1 - T)}{N}}{\dfrac{(EBIT - I)(1 - T)}{N}} = \left[\frac{\Delta EBIT(1 - T)}{N}\right]\left[\frac{N}{(EBIT - I)(1 - T)}\right] = \frac{\Delta EBIT}{EBIT - I}.$$

5. The degree of financial leverage is the percentage change in EPS over the percentage change in EBIT:

$$DFL = \frac{\dfrac{\Delta EBIT}{EBIT - I}}{\dfrac{\Delta EBIT}{EBIT}} = \left(\frac{\Delta EBIT}{EBIT - I}\right)\left(\frac{EBIT}{\Delta EBIT}\right) = \frac{EBIT}{EBIT - I}. \qquad (17\text{-}3)$$

6. This equation must be modified if the firm has preferred stock outstanding.

If no debt were used, the degree of financial leverage would by definition be 1.0, so a 100 percent increase in EBIT would produce exactly a 100 percent increase in EPS. This can be confirmed from the data in Section II of Table 17-3.

Combining Operating and Financial Leverage (DTL)

We have seen (1) that the greater the degree of operating leverage (or fixed operating costs), the more sensitive EBIT will be to changes in sales, and (2) that the greater the degree of financial leverage (fixed financial costs), the more sensitive EPS will be to changes in EBIT. Therefore, if a firm uses a considerable amount of both operating and financial leverage, then even small changes in sales will lead to wide fluctuations in EPS.

Equation 17-2 for the degree of operating leverage can be combined with Equation 17-3 for the degree of financial leverage to produce the equation for the **degree of total leverage (DTL),** which shows how a given change in sales will affect earnings per share. Here are three equivalent equations for DTL:[12]

degree of total leverage (DTL)

The percentage change in EPS brought about by a given percentage change in sales; DTL shows the effects of both operating leverage and financial leverage.

$$DTL = (DOL)(DFL). \tag{17-4}$$

$$DTL = \frac{Q(P - V)}{Q(P - V) - F - I}. \tag{17-4a}$$

$$DTL = \frac{S - VC}{S - VC - F - I}. \tag{17-4b}$$

For Firm B at sales of \$200,000, we can substitute data from Table 17-3 into Equation 17-4b to find the degree of total leverage if the debt ratio is 50 percent:

$$DTL_{\$200,000,\ 50\%} = \frac{\$200,000 - \$120,000}{\$200,000 - \$120,000 - \$40,000 - \$12,000}$$

$$= \frac{\$80,000}{\$28,000} = 2.86.$$

----

[12]Equation 17-4 is simply a definition, while Equations 17-4a and 17-4b are developed as follows:

1. Recognize that $EBIT = Q(P - V) - F$, and then rewrite Equation 17-3 as follows:

$$DFL = \frac{EBIT}{EBIT - I} = \frac{Q(P - V) - F}{Q(P - V) - F - I} = \frac{S - VC - F}{S - VC - F - I}. \tag{17-3a}$$

2. The degree of total leverage is equal to the degree of operating leverage times the degree of financial leverage, or Equation 17-2 times Equation 17-3a:

$$DTL = (DOL)(DFL) \tag{17-4}$$

$$= (\text{Equation 17-2})(\text{Equation 17-3a})$$

$$= \left[\frac{Q(P - V)}{Q(P - V) - F} \right] \left[\frac{Q(P - V) - F}{Q(P - V) - F - I} \right]$$

$$= \frac{Q(P - V)}{Q(P - V) - F - I} \tag{17-4a}$$

$$= \frac{S - VC}{S - VC - F - I}. \tag{17-4b}$$

Equivalently, using Equation 17-4, we get the same result:

$$DTL_{\$200,000,\ 50\%} = (2.00)(1.43) = 2.86.$$

We can also use the degree of total leverage (DTL) to find the new earnings per share (EPS_1) for any given percentage increase in sales (%Δ Sales), proceeding as follows:

$$
\begin{aligned}
EPS_1 &= EPS_0 + EPS_0[(DTL)(\%\,\Delta Sales)] \\
&= EPS_0[1.0 + (DTL)(\%\,\Delta Sales)]. \qquad (17\text{-}5)
\end{aligned}
$$

For example, a 50 percent (or 0.5) increase in sales, from \$200,000 to \$300,000, would cause EPS_0 (\$3.36 as shown in Section III of Table 17-3) to increase to \$8.16:

$$
\begin{aligned}
EPS_1 &= \$3.36[1.0 + (2.86)(0.5)] \\
&= \$3.36(2.43) \\
&= \$8.16.
\end{aligned}
$$

This figure agrees with the one for EPS shown in Table 17-3.

The degree of leverage concept is useful primarily for the insights it provides regarding the joint effects of operating and financial leverage on earnings per share. The concept can be used to show the management of a business, for example, that a decision to automate a plant and to finance the new equipment with debt would result in a situation wherein a 10 percent decline in sales would produce a 50 percent decline in earnings, whereas with a different operating and financial leverage package, a 10 percent sales decline would cause earnings to decline by only 20 percent. Having the alternatives stated in this manner gives decision makers a better idea of the ramifications of alternative actions.[13]

 Self-Test Questions

Give the formula for calculating the degree of operating leverage (DOL), and explain what DOL is.

Why is the DOL different at various sales levels?

What is the value of the DOL at the company's breakeven point?

---

[13]The degree of leverage concept is also useful for investors. If firms in an industry are classified as to their degrees of total leverage, an investor who is optimistic about prospects for the industry might favor those firms with high leverage, and vice versa if industry sales are expected to decline. However, it is very difficult to separate fixed from variable costs. Accounting statements simply do not make this breakdown, so the analyst must make the separation in a necessarily judgmental manner. Note that costs are really fixed, variable, and "semivariable," for if times get tough enough, firms will sell off depreciable assets and thus reduce depreciation charges (a fixed cost), lay off "permanent" employees, reduce salaries of the remaining personnel, and so on. For this reason, the degree of leverage concept is generally more useful in explaining the general nature of the relationship than in developing precise numbers, and any numbers developed should be thought of as approximations rather than as exact specifications.

Give the formula for calculating the degree of financial leverage (DFL), and explain what this calculation means.

Give the formula for calculating the degree of total leverage (DTL), and explain what DTL is.

Why is the degree of leverage concept useful?

LIQUIDITY AND CASH FLOW ANALYSIS

There are some practical difficulties with the types of analyses described thus far in the chapter, including the following:

1. It is virtually impossible to determine exactly how either P/E ratios or equity capitalization rates (k_s values) are affected by different degrees of financial leverage. The best we can do is make educated guesses about these relationships. Therefore, management rarely, if ever, has sufficient confidence in the type of analysis set forth in Table 17-3 and Figure 17-6 to use it as the sole determinant of the target capital structure.

2. The managers may be more or less conservative than the average stockholder, and hence management may set a somewhat different target capital structure than the one that would maximize the stock price. The managers of a publicly owned firm would never admit this, for unless they owned voting control, they would quickly be removed from office. However, in view of the uncertainties about what constitutes the value-maximizing capital structure, management could always say that the target capital structure employed is, in its judgment, the value-maximizing structure, and it would be difficult to prove otherwise. Still, if management is far off target, especially on the low side, then chances are very high that some other firm or management group will take over the company, increase its leverage, and thereby raise its value. This point is discussed in more detail later in the chapter.

3. Managers of large firms, especially those which provide vital services such as electricity or telephones, have a responsibility to provide *continuous* service; therefore, they must refrain from using leverage to the point where the firms' long-run viability is endangered. Long-run viability may conflict with short-run stock price maximization and capital cost minimization.[14]

For all of these reasons, managers are concerned about the effects of financial leverage on the risk of bankruptcy, and an analysis of this factor is therefore an

---

[14]Recognizing this fact, most public service commissions require utilities to obtain the commission's approval before issuing long-term securities, and Congress has empowered the SEC to supervise the capital structures of public utility holding companies. However, in addition to concern over the firms' safety, which suggests low debt ratios, both managers and regulators recognize a need to keep all costs as low as possible, including the cost of capital. Since a firm's capital structure affects its cost of capital, regulatory commissions and utility managers try to select capital structures that will minimize the cost of capital, subject to the constraint that the firm's financial flexibility not be endangered.

Figure 17-7   ▪   **Firm B: Probability Distributions of Times-Interest-Earned Ratios with Different Capital Structures**

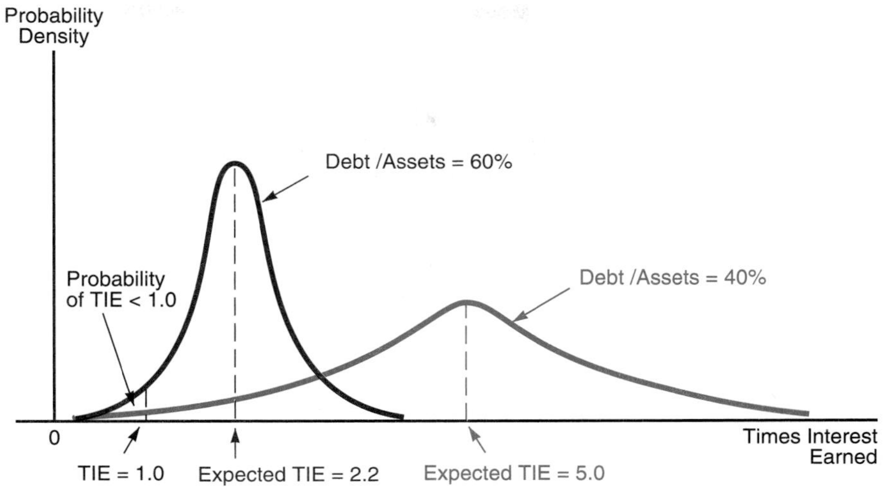

Debt/Assets	Expected TIE[a]
0%	Undefined
10	25.0
20	12.0
30	7.4
40	5.0
50	3.3
60	2.2

[a]TIE = EBIT/Interest. For example, when debt/assets = 50%, TIE = $40,000/$12,000 = 3.3. Data are from Tables 17-2 and 17-3.

times-interest-earned (TIE) ratio

A ratio that measures the firm's ability to meet its annual interest obligations, calculated by dividing earnings before interest and taxes by interest charges.

important input in all capital structure decisions. Accordingly, managements give considerable weight to financial strength indicators such as the **times-interest-earned (TIE) ratio.** The lower this ratio, the higher the probability that a firm will default on its debt and be forced into bankruptcy.

The tabular material in the lower section of Figure 17-7 shows Firm B's expected TIE ratio at several different debt/assets ratios. If the debt/assets ratio were only 10 percent, the expected TIE would be a high 25 times, but the interest coverage ratio would decline rapidly if the debt ratio were increased. Note, however, that these coverages are expected values at different debt ratios; the actual TIE for any debt ratio will be higher if sales exceed the expected $200,000 level, but lower if sales fall below $200,000.

The variability of the TIE ratio is highlighted in the graph in Figure 17-7, which shows the probability distributions of the TIEs at debt/assets ratios of 40 percent and 60 percent. The expected TIE is much higher if only 40 percent debt is used. The relationship between actual companies' TIEs and debt ratios will be examined later, in Table 17-5. Even more important is the fact that with less debt, there is a much lower probability of a TIE of less than 1.0, the level at which the firm is not earning enough to meet its required interest payment and thus is seriously exposed to the threat of bankruptcy.[15]

Self-Test Question

Why do managers give considerable weight to the TIE ratio when they make capital structure decisions? Why not just use the capital structure that maximizes the stock price?

CAPITAL STRUCTURE THEORY

Capital structure theory has been developed along two main lines: (1) tax benefit/bankruptcy cost *tradeoff theory* and (2) *signaling theory.* These two theories are discussed in this section.

Tradeoff Theory

Modern capital structure theory began in 1958, when Professors Franco Modigliani and Merton Miller (hereafter MM) published what has been called the most influential finance article ever written.[16] MM proved, under a very restrictive set of assumptions, that because of the tax deductibility of interest on debt, a firm's value rises continuously as it uses more debt, and hence its value will be maximized by financing almost entirely with debt. MM's assumptions included the following:

1. There are no brokerage costs.
2. There are no personal taxes.
3. Investors can borrow at the same rate as corporations.
4. Investors have the same information as management about the firm's future investment opportunities.
5. All the firm's debt is riskless, regardless of how much debt it uses.
6. EBIT is not affected by the use of debt.

Since several of these assumptions were obviously unrealistic, MM's position was only the beginning of capital structure research.

Subsequent researchers, and MM themselves, extended the basic theory by relaxing the assumptions. Other researchers attempted to test the various theo-

---

[15]Note that cash flows, which include depreciation, can be sufficient to cover required interest payments even though the TIE is less than 1.0. Thus, at least for a while, a firm may be able to avoid bankruptcy even though its operating income is less than its interest charges. However, most debt contracts stipulate that firms must maintain the TIE ratio above some minimum level, say, 2.0 or 2.5, or else they cannot borrow any additional funds, which can severely constrain operations. Such potential constraints, as much as the threat of actual bankruptcy, limit the use of debt.

[16]Franco Modigliani and Merton H. Miller, "The Cost of Capital, Corporation Finance, and the Theory of Investment," *American Economic Review,* June 1958. Modigliani and Miller both won Nobel Prizes for their work.

Figure 17-8 ▪ Effect of Leverage on the Value of Firm B's Stock

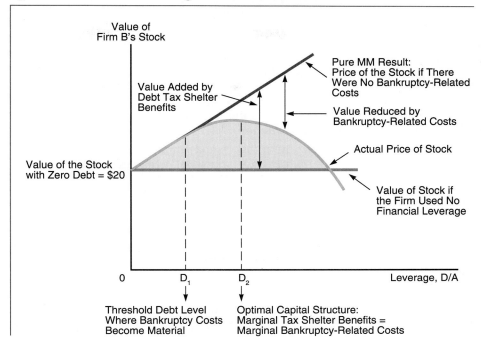

retical models with empirical data to see exactly how stock prices and capital costs are affected by capital structure. Both the theoretical and the empirical results have added to our understanding of capital structure, but none of these studies has produced results that can be used to precisely identify a firm's optimal capital structure. A summary of the theoretical and empirical research to date is expressed graphically in Figure 17-8. Here are the key points in the figure:

1. The fact that interest is a deductible expense makes debt less expensive than common or preferred stock. In effect, the government pays part of the cost of debt capital, or, to put it another way, debt provides *tax shelter benefits*. As a result, using debt causes more of the firm's operating income (EBIT) to flow through to investors, so the more debt a company uses, the higher its value, and the higher the price of its stock. Under the assumptions of the original Modigliani-Miller paper, their analysis led to the conclusion that the firm's stock price will be maximized if it uses virtually 100 percent debt, and the line labeled "Pure MM Result" in Figure 17-8 expressed their relationship between stock prices and debt.

2. The MM assumptions do not hold in the real world. First, interest rates rise as the debt ratio rises. Second, EBIT declines at extreme levels of leverage. Third, expected tax rates fall at high debt levels, and this also reduces the expected value of the debt tax shelter. And, fourth, the probability of bankruptcy, which brings with it lawyers' fees and other costs, increases as the debt ratio rises.

3. There is some threshold level of debt, labeled D_1 in Figure 17-8, below which the effects noted in Point 2 are immaterial. Beyond D_1, however, the bankruptcy-related costs become increasingly important, and they reduce the tax benefits of debt at an increasing rate. In the range from D_1 to D_2, bankruptcy-related costs reduce but do not completely offset the tax benefits of debt, so the firm's stock price rises (but at a decreasing rate) as the debt ratio increases. However, beyond D_2 bankruptcy-related costs exceed the tax benefits, so from this point on increasing the debt ratio lowers the value of the stock. Therefore, D_2 is the optimal capital structure.

4. Both theory and empirical evidence support the preceding discussion. However, statistical problems prevent researchers from identifying Points D_1 and D_2.

5. While theoretical and empirical work supports the general shape of the curves in Figures 17-6 and 17-8, these graphs must be taken as approximations, not as precisely defined functions. The numbers in Figure 17-6 are shown out to two decimal places, but that is merely for illustrative purposes — the numbers are not nearly that accurate in view of the fact that the data on which the graph is based are judgmental estimates.

6. Another disturbing aspect of capital structure theory as expressed in Figure 17-8 is the fact that many large, successful firms, such as Apple and Microsoft, use far less debt than the theory suggests. This point led to the development of signaling theory, which is discussed below.

Signaling Theory

symmetric information
The situation in which investors and managers have identical information about the firm's prospects.

asymmetric information
The situation in which managers have different (better) information about their firm's prospects than do investors.

MM assumed that investors have the same information about a firm's prospects as its managers — this is called **symmetric information.** However, we know that in fact managers often have better information about their firms than outside investors. This is called **asymmetric information,** and it has an important effect on the optimal capital structure. To see why, consider two situations, one in which the company's managers know that its prospects are extremely favorable (Firm F) and one in which the managers know that the future looks very unfavorable (Firm U).

Suppose, for example, that Firm F's R&D labs have just discovered a non-patentable cure for the common cold. Firm F's managers want to keep the new product a secret for as long as possible to delay competitors' entry into the market. New plants and distribution facilities must be built to exploit the new product, so capital must be raised. How should Firm F's managment raise the needed capital? If the firm sells stock, then, when profits from the new product start flowing in, the price of the stock will rise sharply, and the purchasers of the new stock will have made a bonanza. The current stockholders (including the managers) will also do well, but not as well as they would have done if the company had not sold stock before the price increased, because then they would not have had to share the benefits of the new product with the new stockholders. *Therefore, one would expect a firm with very favorable prospects to try to avoid selling stock and, rather, to raise any required new cap-*

ital by other means, including using debt beyond the normal target capital structure.[17]

Now let's consider Firm U. Suppose its managers have information that new orders are off sharply because a competitor has installed new technology which has improved its products' quality. Firm U must upgrade its own facilities, at a high cost, just to maintain its recent sales level. As a result, its return on investment will fall (but not by as much as if it took no action, which would lead to a 100 percent loss through bankruptcy). How should Firm U raise the needed capital? Here the situation is just the reverse of that facing Firm F, which did not want to sell stock so as to avoid having to share the benefits of future developments. *A firm with unfavorable prospects would want to sell stock, which would mean bringing in new investors to share the losses!*[18]

The conclusions from all this are that firms with extremely bright prospects prefer not to finance through new stock offerings, whereas firms with poor prospects do like to finance with outside equity. How would you, as an investor, react to this conclusion? You ought to say, "If I see that a company plans to issue new stock, this should worry me, because I know that management would not want to issue stock if future prospects looked good, but it would want to issue stock if things looked bad. Therefore, I should lower my estimate of the firm's value, other things held constant, if I read an announcement of a new stock offering." Of course, the negative reaction would be stronger if the stock sale was by a large, established company such as GM or IBM, which surely has many financing options, than if it was by a small company such as GeneSplicer. For GeneSplicer, a stock sale might mean truly extraordinary investment opportunities that were so large that they just could not be financed without a stock sale.

If you gave the above answer, your views are completely consistent with those of sophisticated portfolio managers of institutions such as Morgan Guaranty Trust, Prudential Insurance, and so forth. *So, in a nutshell, the announcement of a stock offering by a mature firm that seems to have financing alternatives is taken as a* **signal** *that the firm's prospects as seen by its management are not bright.* This, in turn, suggests that when a mature firm announces a new stock offering, the price of its stock should decline. Empirical studies have shown that this situation does indeed exist.[19]

What are the implications of all this for capital structure decisions? The answer is that firms should, in normal times, maintain a **reserve borrowing capacity** which can be used in the event that some especially good investment opportunities come along. *This means that firms should, in normal times, use less debt than would be suggested by the tax benefit/bankruptcy cost tradeoff expressed in Figure 17-8.*

signal

An action taken by a firm's management which provides clues to investors about how management views the firm's prospects.

reserve borrowing capacity

The ability to borrow money at a reasonable cost when good investment opportunities arise; firms often use less debt than specified by the MM optimal capital structure to insure that they can obtain debt capital later if they need to.

---

[17]It would be illegal for Firm F's managers to purchase more shares on the basis of their inside knowledge of the new product. They could be sent to jail if they did.

[18]Of course, Firm U would have to make certain disclosures when it offered new shares to the public, but it might be able to meet the legal requirements without fully disclosing management's worst fears.

[19]Paul Asquith and David W. Mullins, Jr., "The Impact of Initiating Dividend Payments on Shareholders' Wealth," *Journal of Business,* January 1983, 77–96.

Signaling/asymmetric information concepts also have implications for the marginal cost of capital (MCC) curve as discussed in Chapter 16. There we saw that the weighted average cost of capital (WACC) jumped when retained earnings were exhausted and the firm was forced to sell new common stock to raise equity. The jump in the WACC, or the break in the MCC schedule, was attributed only to flotation costs. However, if the announcement of a stock sale causes a decline in the price of the stock, then k as measured by $k = D_1/P_0 + g$ will rise because of the decline in P_0. This factor reinforces the effects of flotation costs, and perhaps it is an even more important explanation for the jump in the MCC schedule at the point at which new stock must be issued. For example, assume that $P_0 = \$10$, $D_1 = \$1$, $g = 5\%$, and $F = 10\%$. Therefore, $k_s = 10\% + 5\% = 15\%$, and k_e, the cost of external equity, is 16.1 percent:

$$k_e = \frac{D_1}{P_0(1 - F)} + g = \frac{\$1}{\$10(1.0 - 0.10)} + 5\% = 16.1\%.$$

Suppose, however, that the announcement of a stock sale causes the market price of the stock to fall from $P_0 = \$10$ to $P_0 = \$8$. This will produce an increase in the costs of both retained earnings (k_s) and external equity:

$$k_s = \frac{D_1}{P_0} + g = \frac{\$1}{\$8} + 5\% = 17.5\%.$$

$$k_e = \frac{D_1}{P_0(1 - F)} + g = \frac{\$1}{\$8(0.9)} + 5\% = 18.9\%.$$

This would, of course, have further implications for capital budgeting. Specifically, it would make it even more difficult for a marginal project to show a positive NPV if the project required the firm to sell stock to raise capital.

If you find this discussion of capital structure theory somewhat confusing, or at least imprecise, you are not alone. In truth, no one knows how to identify precisely the optimal capital structure for a firm or how to measure precisely the effect of the firm's capital structure on either its value or its cost of capital. In real life, capital structure decisions must be made more on the basis of judgment than numerical analysis. Still, an understanding of the theoretical issues as presented here is essential to making sound judgments on capital structure issues.[20]

? Self-Test Questions

What does it mean when one hears, "The MM capital structure theory involves a tradeoff between the tax benefits of debt and costs associated with actual or potential bankruptcy"?

Explain how "asymmetric information" and "signals" affect capital structure decisions.

---

[20]We can report firsthand the usefulness of financial theory in the actual establishment of corporate capital structures. In recent years we served as consultants to several of the regional telephone companies established as a result of the breakup of AT&T, as well as to several large electric utilities. On the basis of finance theory and computer models which simulated results under a range of conditions, the companies were able to specify "optimal capital structure ranges" with at least a reasonable degree of confidence. Without finance theory, setting a target capital structure would have amounted to little more than throwing darts.

What is meant by *reserve borrowing capacity,* and why is it important for firms?

CAPITAL STRUCTURE AND MERGERS

One of the most dramatic developments in the financial world during the 1980s was the high level of merger activity, especially hostile takeovers, and leveraged buyouts. The target firm's stock was considered to be undervalued by the acquiring firm, so the acquirer was willing to pay a premium of 50 to 100 percent to gain control. For example, General Electric offered $66.50 per share for RCA (which owned the NBC television network, among other things) versus RCA's preannouncement price of $45 per share, and Kohlberg Kravis paid $106 for RJR Nabisco's stock versus RJR's preannouncement price of $55. Mergers are discussed at length in Chapter 22, but it is useful to mention several points now: (1) very often the acquiring firm issues debt and uses it to buy the target firm's stock; (2) the new debt effectively changes the enterprise's capital structure; and (3) the value enhancement resulting from the use of debt is sufficient to cover the premium offered for the stock and still leave a profit for the acquiring company.

An understanding of the type of analysis described in this chapter has led to the creation of companies whose major function is to acquire other companies through debt-financed takeovers. The managers of these acquiring companies have made huge personal fortunes, and shrewd individual investors, including a few finance professors, have selected stock portfolios heavily weighted with prime acquisition targets and have done well in the market.

Of course, the managements of firms with low leverage ratios who do not want to be taken over can be expected to react by attempting to find their optimal debt levels and then issuing debt and repurchasing stock, thus bringing their firms' actual debt ratios up to the levels that maximize the prices of their stocks, which will make these companies less attractive acquisition targets. This is called *restructuring,* and a great deal of it has been going on lately. CBS, for example, did this when it was fighting off an acquisition attempt by Ted Turner, and Phillips Petroleum did likewise to fend off T. Boone Pickens.

Self-Test Questions

Why does capital structure sometimes cause one firm to take over another?

What is meant by the term "restructuring"?

CHECKLIST FOR CAPITAL STRUCTURE DECISIONS

In addition to the types of analysis discussed above, firms generally consider the following factors, which can have an important, though difficult to measure, bearing on the optimal capital structure:

1. **Sales stability.** A firm whose sales are relatively stable can safely take on more debt and incur higher fixed charges than a company with unstable

sales. Utility companies, because of their stable demand, have historically been able to use more financial leverage than industrial firms.

2. **Asset structure.** Firms whose assets are suitable as security for loans tend to use debt rather heavily. General purpose assets which can be used by many businesses make good collateral, whereas special-purpose assets do not. Thus, real estate companies are usually highly leveraged, whereas companies involved in technological research employ less debt.

3. **Operating leverage.** Other things the same, a firm with less operating leverage is better able to employ financial leverage because, as we saw, the interaction of operating and financial leverage determines the overall effect of a decline in sales on operating income and net cash flows.

4. **Growth rate.** Other things the same, faster-growing firms must rely more heavily on external capital (see Chapter 7). Further, the flotation costs involved in selling common stock exceed those incurred when selling debt. Thus, rapidly growing firms tend to use somewhat more debt than slower-growing companies.

5. **Profitability.** One often observes that firms with very high rates of return on investment use relatively little debt. Although there is no theoretical justification for this fact, one practical explanation is that very profitable firms such as Apple, Microsoft, and Coca-Cola simply do not need to do much debt financing. Their high rates of return enable them to do most of their financing with retained earnings.

6. **Taxes.** Interest is a deductible expense, and deductions are most valuable to firms with high tax rates. Hence, the higher a firm's corporate tax rate, the greater the advantage of debt.

7. **Control.** The effect that issuing debt versus stock might have on a management's control position may influence its capital structure. If management currently has voting control (over 50 percent of the stock) but is not in a position to buy any more stock, it may choose debt for new financings. On the other hand, the management group may decide to use equity rather than debt if the firm's financial situation is so weak that the use of debt might subject the firm to serious risk of default because, if the firm goes into default, the managers will almost surely lose their jobs. However, if too little debt is used, management runs the risk of a takeover. Thus, control considerations could lead to the use of *either* debt or equity because the type of capital that best protects management will vary from situation to situation. In any event, if management is at all insecure, it will definitely take account of the effects of capital structure on control.

8. **Management attitudes.** Since no one can prove that one capital structure will lead to higher stock prices than another, management can exercise its own judgment about the proper capital structure. Some managements tend to be more conservative than others and thus use less debt than the average firm in their industry, whereas other managements use more debt in the quest for higher profits.

9. **Lender and rating agency attitudes.** Regardless of managers' own analyses of the proper leverage factors for their firms, there is no question that lenders' and rating agencies' attitudes frequently influence financial struc-

ture decisions (see Chapter 20). In the majority of cases, the corporation discusses its capital structure with lenders and rating agencies and gives much weight to their advice. For example, one large utility was recently told by Moody and Standard & Poor that its bonds would be downgraded if it issued more bonds. This influenced its decision to finance its expansion with common equity.

10. **Market conditions.** Conditions in the stock and bond markets undergo both long- and short-run changes that can have an important bearing on a firm's optimal capital structure. For example, during the credit crunch in the winter of 1991, the junk bond market dried up, and there was simply no market at any "reasonable" interest rate for new long-term bonds rated below triple B. Therefore, low-rated companies in need of capital were forced to go to the stock market or to the short-term debt market, regardless of their target capital structures. When conditions eased, however, these companies sold stock to bring their capital structures back to their target levels.

11. **The firm's internal condition.** A firm's own internal condition can also have a bearing on its target capital structure. For example, suppose a firm has just successfully completed an R&D program, and it projects higher earnings in the immediate future. However, the new earnings are not yet anticipated by investors and hence are not reflected in the price of the stock. This company would not want to issue stock — it would prefer to finance with debt until the higher earnings materialize and are reflected in the stock price. Then it could sell an issue of common stock, retire the debt, and return to its target capital structure.

12. **Financial flexibility.** An astute corporate treasurer made this statement to the authors:

> Our company can earn a lot more money from good capital budgeting and operating decisions than from good financing decisions. Indeed, we are not sure exactly how financing decisions affect our stock price, but we know for sure that having to turn down a promising venture because funds are not available will reduce our long-run profitability. For this reason, my primary goal as treasurer is to always be in a position to raise the capital needed to support operations.
>
> We also know that when times are good, we can raise capital with either stocks or bonds, but when times are bad, suppliers of capital are much more willing to make funds available if we give them a secured position, and this means bonds. Further, when we sell a new issue of stock, this sends a negative "signal" to investors, so stock sales by a mature company such as ours are not generally desirable.

Putting these thoughts together gives rise to the goal of *maintaining financial flexibility,* which, from an operational viewpoint, means *maintaining adequate reserve borrowing capacity.* Determining an "adequate" reserve borrowing capacity is judgmental, but it clearly depends on the factors mentioned previously in the chapter, including the firm's forecasted need for funds, predicted capital market conditions, management's confidence in its forecasts, and the consequences of a capital shortage.

? *Self-Test Questions*

How does sales stability affect capital structure?

How does asset structure affect capital structure?

How do taxes affect capital structure?

How do lender and rating agency attitudes affect capital structure?

How does the firm's internal condition affect capital structure?

What is "financial flexibility," and is it increased or decreased by a high debt ratio?

VARIATIONS IN CAPITAL STRUCTURES AMONG FIRMS

As might be expected, wide variations in the use of financial leverage occur both across industries and among the individual firms in each industry. Table 17-5 illustrates differences for selected industries; the ranking is in descending order of common equity ratios, as shown in Column 1.[21]

The steel and drug companies do not use much debt (their common equity ratios are high); the uncertainties inherent in industries that are cyclical, oriented toward research, or subject to huge product liability suits render the heavy use of debt unwise. Retailers and utility companies, on the other hand, use debt relatively heavily, but for different reasons. Retailers use short-term debt to finance inventories and long-term debt secured by mortgages on their stores. The utilities have traditionally used large amounts of debt, particularly long-term debt — their fixed assets make good security for mortgage bonds, and their relatively stable sales make it safe for them to carry more debt than would be true for firms with more business risk.

Particular attention should be given to the times-interest-earned (TIE) ratio because it gives a measure of how safe the debt is and how vulnerable the company is to financial distress. TIE ratios depend on three factors: (1) the percentage of debt, (2) the interest rate on the debt, and (3) the company's profitability. Generally, the least leveraged industries, such as the drug industry, have the highest coverage ratios, whereas the utility industry, which finances heavily with debt, has a low average coverage ratio.

Wide variations in capital structures also exist among firms within given industries — for example, although the average common equity ratio in 1990 for the drug industry was 69.1 percent, Biopharmaceutics Inc.'s equity ratio was less than 40 percent, but Bristol-Myers' ratio was close to 90 percent. Thus, factors unique to individual firms, including managerial attitudes, play an important role in setting target capital structures.

---

[21]Information on capital structures and financial strength is available from a multitude of sources. We used the *Compustat* data tapes to develop Table 17-5, but published sources include *The Value Line Investment Survey, Robert Morris Association Annual Studies,* and *Dun & Bradstreet Key Business Ratios.*

Table 17-5 ▪ **Capital Structure Percentages, 1990: Four Industries Ranked by Common Equity Ratios**

Industry	Common Equity (1)	Preferred Stock (2)	Total Debt (3)	Long-Term Debt (4)	Short-Term Debt (5)	Times-Interest-Earned Ratio (6)	Return on Equity (7)
Steel	72.4%	0.0%	27.6%	23.7%	3.9%	5.0×	6.0%
Drugs	69.1	0.9	30.0	15.6	14.4	10.2	27.4
Retailing	44.9	1.5	53.6	35.3	18.3	2.6	12.0
Utilities	43.4	5.6	51.0	47.0	4.0	2.4	8.3
Composite (average of all industries, not just those listed above)	40.5%	1.7%	57.8%	35.4%	22.4%	1.9×	10.7%

Note: These ratios are based on accounting (or book) values. Stated on a market-value basis, the equity percentages would rise because most stocks sell at prices that are much higher than their book values.

Source: *Compustat* Industrial Data Tape, 1991.

 Self-Test Question

Why do wide variations in the use of financial leverage occur both across industries and among the individual firms in each industry?

SUMMARY

In this chapter we examined the effects of financial leverage on stock prices, earnings per share, and the cost of capital. The key concepts covered are summarized below.

▪ A firm's **optimal capital structure** is that mix of debt and equity which maximizes the price of the firm's stock. At any point in time, the firm's management has a specific **target capital structure** in mind, presumably the optimal one, although this target may change over time.

▪ Several factors influence a firm's capital structure decisions. These factors include the firm's (1) **business risk,** (2) **tax position,** (3) need for **financial flexibility,** and (4) **managerial conservatism or aggressiveness.**

▪ **Business risk** is the uncertainty associated with projections of a firm's future returns on equity. A firm will tend to have low business risk if the demand for its products is stable, if the prices of its inputs and products remain relatively constant, if it can adjust its prices freely if its costs increase, and if a high percentage of its costs are variable and hence decrease as its output and sales decrease. Other things the same, the lower a firm's business risk, the higher its optimal debt ratio.

▪ **Financial leverage** is the extent to which fixed-income securities (debt and preferred stock) are used in a firm's capital structure. **Financial risk** is the added risk to stockholders which results from financial leverage.

- The **EPS indifference point** is the level of sales at which EPS will be the same whether the firm uses debt or common stock financing. Equity financing will be better if the firm's sales end up below the EPS indifference point, whereas debt financing will be better at higher sales levels.

- The **degree of operating leverage (DOL)** shows how changes in sales affect operating income, whereas the **degree of financial leverage (DFL)** shows how changes in operating income affect earnings per share. The **degree of total leverage (DTL)** shows the percentage change in EPS resulting from a given percentage change in sales: $DTL = DOL \times DFL$.

- **Modigliani and Miller** developed a **tradeoff theory of capital structure,** where debt is useful because interest is **tax deductible,** but debt brings with it costs associated with actual or potential bankruptcy. Under MM's theory the optimal capital structure strikes a balance between the tax benefits of debt and the costs associated with bankruptcy.

- An alternative (or, really, complementary) theory of capital structure relates to the **signals** given to investors by a firm's decision to use debt or stock to raise new capital. The use of stock is a negative signal, while using debt is a positive or at least a neutral signal. Therefore, companies try to maintain a **reserve borrowing capacity,** and this means using less debt in "normal" times than the MM tradeoff theory would suggest.

Although it is theoretically possible to determine the optimal capital structure, as a practical matter we cannot estimate this structure with precision. Accordingly, financial executives generally treat the optimal capital structure as a range—for example, 40 to 50 percent debt—rather than as a precise point, such as 45 percent. The concepts discussed in this chapter help managers understand the factors they should consider when they set the target capital structure ranges for their firms.

Questions

17-1 "One type of leverage affects both EBIT and EPS. The other type affects only EPS." Explain what this statement means.

17-2 Explain why the following statement is true: "Other things the same, firms with relatively stable sales are able to carry relatively high debt ratios."

17-3 Why do public utilities pursue a different financial policy than retail firms?

17-4 Why is EBIT generally considered to be independent of financial leverage? Why might EBIT actually be influenced by financial leverage at high debt levels?

17-5 If a firm went from zero debt to successively higher levels of debt, why would you expect its stock price to first rise, then hit a peak, and then begin to decline?

17-6 Why is the debt level that maximizes a firm's expected EPS generally higher than the one that maximizes its stock price?

17-7 When the Bell System was broken up, the old AT&T was split into a new AT&T plus seven regional telephone companies. The specific reason for forcing the breakup was to increase the degree of competition in the telephone industry. AT&T had a monopoly on local service, long distance, and the manufacture of all the equipment used by telephone companies, and the breakup was expected to open most of these markets to competition. In the court order that set the terms of the breakup, the capital structures of the surviving companies were specified, and much attention was given to the increased competition telephone companies could expect in the future. Do you think the optimal capital structure after the breakup should be the same as the pre-breakup optimal capital structure? Explain your position.

17-8 Assume that you are advising the management of a firm that is about to double its assets to serve its rapidly growing market. It must choose between a highly automated production process and a less automated one, and it must also choose a capital structure for financing the expansion. Should the asset investment and financing decisions be jointly determined, or should each decision be made separately? How would these decisions affect one another? How could the degree of leverage concept be used to help management analyze the situation?

17-9 Your firm's R&D department has been working on a new process which, if it works, can produce oil from coal at a cost of about $5 per barrel versus a current market price of $20 per barrel. The company needs $10 million of external funds at this time to complete the research. The results of the research will be known in about a year, and there is about a 50-50 chance of success. If the research is successful, your company will need to raise a substantial amount of new money to put the idea into production. Your economists forecast that although the economy will be depressed next year, interest rates will be high because of international monetary problems. You must recommend how the currently needed $10 million should be raised—as debt or as equity. How would the potential impact of your project influence your decision?

Self-Test Problems (*Solutions Appear in Appendix B*)

ST-1
Key terms

Define each of the following terms:

a. Target capital structure; optimal capital structure; target range
b. Business risk; financial risk; total risk
c. Financial leverage
d. EPS indifference point
e. Degree of operating leverage (DOL)
f. Degree of financial leverage (DFL)
g. Degree of total leverage (DTL)
h. Times-interest-earned (TIE) ratio
i. Symmetric information; asymmetric information
j. Tradeoff theory; signaling theory
k. Reserve borrowing capacity

ST-2
Financial leverage

Gentry Motors Inc., a producer of turbine generators, is in this situation: EBIT = $4 million; tax rate = T = 35%; debt outstanding = D = $2 million; k_d = 10%; k_s = 15%; shares of stock outstanding = N_0 = 600,000; and book value per share = $10. Since Gentry's product market is stable and the company expects no growth, all earnings are paid out as dividends. The debt consists of perpetual bonds.

a. What are Gentry's earnings per share (EPS) and its price per share (P_0)?
b. What is Gentry's weighted average cost of capital (WACC)?
c. Gentry can increase its debt by $8 million, to a total of $10 million, using the new debt to buy back and retire some of its shares at the current price. Its interest rate on debt will be 12 percent (it will have to call and refund the old debt), and its cost of equity will rise from 15 percent to 17 percent. EBIT will remain constant. Should Gentry change its capital structure?
d. If Gentry did not have to refund the $2 million of old debt, how would this affect things? Assume that the new and the still outstanding debt are equally risky, with k_d = 12%, but that the coupon rate on the old debt is 10 percent.

e. What is Gentry's TIE coverage ratio under the original situation and under the conditions in Part c of this question?

Problems

17-1

Risk analysis

a. Given the following information, calculate the expected value for Firm C's EPS.
$E(EPS_A) = \$5.10$, and $\sigma_A = \$3.61$; $E(EPS_B) = \$4.20$, and $\sigma_B = \$2.96$; and
$\sigma_C = \$4.11$.

	Probability				
	0.1	**0.2**	**0.4**	**0.2**	**0.1**
Firm A: EPS_A	($1.50)	$1.80	$5.10	$8.40	$11.70
Firm B: EPS_B	(1.20)	1.50	4.20	6.90	9.60
Firm C: EPS_C	(2.40)	1.35	5.10	8.85	12.60

b. Discuss the relative riskiness of the three firms' (A, B, and C) earnings.

17-2

Operating leverage effects

Merville Corporation will begin operations next year to produce a single product at a price of $12 per unit. Merville has a choice of two methods of production: Method A, with variable costs of $6.75 per unit and fixed operating costs of $675,000; and Method B, with variable costs of $8.25 per unit and fixed operating costs of $401,250. To support operations under either production method, the firm requires $2,250,000 in assets, and it has established a debt ratio of 40 percent. The cost of debt is $k_d = 10$ percent. The tax rate is irrelevant for the problem, and fixed *operating* costs do not include interest.

a. The sales forecast for the coming year is 200,000 units. Under which method would EBIT be more adversely affected if sales did not reach the expected levels? (Hint: Compare DOLs under the two production methods.)

b. Given the firm's present debt, which method would produce the greater percentage increase in earnings per share for a given increase in EBIT? (Hint: Compare DFLs under the two methods.)

c. Calculate DTL under each method, and then evaluate the firm's total risk under each method.

d. Is there some debt ratio under Method A which would produce the same DTL_A as the DTL_B that you calculated in Part c? (Hint: Let $DTL_A = DTL_B = 2.90$ as calculated in Part c, solve for I, and then determine the amount of debt that is consistent with this level of I. Conceivably, debt could be *negative*, which implies holding liquid assets rather than borrowing.)

17-3

Degree of leverage

Wei Communications Corporation (WCC) supplies headphones to airlines for use with movie and stereo programs. The headphones sell for $288 per set, and this year's sales are expected to be 45,000 units. Variable production costs for the expected sales under present production methods are estimated at $10,200,000, and fixed production (operating) costs at present are $1,560,000. WCC has $4,800,000 of debt outstanding at an interest rate of 8 percent. There are 240,000 shares of common stock outstanding, and there is no preferred stock. The dividend payout ratio is 70 percent, and WCC is in the 40 percent federal-plus-state tax bracket.

The company is considering investing $7,200,000 in new equipment. Sales would not increase, but variable costs per unit would decline by 20 percent. Also, fixed operating costs would increase from $1,560,000 to $1,800,000. WCC could raise the required capital by borrowing $7,200,000 at 10 percent or by selling 240,000 additional shares at $30 per share.

a. What would be WCC's EPS (1) under the old production process, (2) under the new process if it uses debt, and (3) under the new process if it uses common stock?

b. Calculate DOL, DFL, and DTL under the existing setup and under the new setup with each type of financing. Assume that the expected sales level is 45,000 units, or $12,960,000.

c. At what unit sales level would WCC have the same EPS, assuming it undertakes the investment and finances it with debt or with stock? (Hint: V = variable cost per unit = $8,160,000/45,000, and EPS = $[(PQ - VQ - F - I)(1 - T)]/N$. Set $EPS_{Stock} = EPS_{Debt}$ and solve for Q.)

d. At what unit sales level would EPS = 0 under the three production/financing setups — that is, under the old plan, the new plan with debt financing, and the new plan with stock financing? (Hint: Note that $V_{Old} = $10,200,000/45,000$, and use the hints for Part c, setting the EPS equation equal to zero.)

e. On the basis of the analysis in Parts a through d, which plan is the riskiest, which has the highest expected EPS, and which would you recommend? Assume here that there is a fairly high probability of sales falling as low as 25,000 units, and determine EPS_{Debt} and EPS_{Stock} at that sales level to help assess the riskiness of the two financing plans.

17-4
Financing alternatives

The Strasburg Company plans to raise a net amount of $270 million to finance new equipment and working capital in early 1993. Two alternatives are being considered: Common stock may be sold to net $60 per share, or bonds yielding 12 percent may be issued. The balance sheet and income statement of the Strasburg Company prior to financing are as follows:

The Strasburg Company:
Balance Sheet as of December 31, 1992
(Millions of Dollars)

Current assets	$ 900.00	Accounts payable	$ 172.50
Net fixed assets	450.00	Notes payable to bank	255.00
		Other current liabilities	225.00
		Total current liabilities	$ 652.50
		Long-term debt (10%)	300.00
		Common stock, $3 par	60.00
		Retained earnings	337.50
Total assets	$1,350.00	Total liabilities and equity	$1,350.00

The Strasburg Company:
Income Statement for Year Ended
December 31, 1992
(Millions of Dollars)

Sales	$2,475.00
Operating costs	2,227.50
Earnings before interest and taxes (10%)	$ 247.50
Interest on short-term debt	15.00
Interest on long-term debt	30.00
Earnings before taxes	$ 202.50
Federal-plus-state taxes (40%)	81.00
Net income	$ 121.50

The probability distribution for annual sales is as follows:

Probability	Annual Sales (Millions of Dollars)
0.30	$2,250
0.40	2,700
0.30	3,150

Assuming that EBIT is equal to 10 percent of sales, calculate earnings per share under both the debt financing and the stock financing alternatives at each possible level of sales. Then calculate expected earnings per share and σ_{EPS} under both debt and stock financing. Also, calculate the debt ratio and the times-interest-earned (TIE) ratio at the expected sales level under each alternative. The old debt will remain outstanding. Which financing method do you recommend?

EXAM-TYPE PROBLEMS

The problems included in this section are set up in such a way that they could be used as multiple-choice exam problems.

17-5
Financial leverage effects

The firms HL and LL are identical except for their leverage ratios and interest rates on debt. Each has $20 million in assets, earned $4 million before interest and taxes in 1992, and has a 40 percent federal-plus-state tax rate. Firm HL, however, has a leverage ratio (D/TA) of 50 percent and pays 12 percent interest on its debt, whereas LL has a 30 percent leverage ratio and pays only 10 percent interest on debt.
a. Calculate the rate of return on equity (net income/equity) for each firm.
b. Observing that HL has a higher return on equity, LL's treasurer decides to raise the leverage ratio from 30 to 60 percent, which will increase LL's interest rate on all debt to 15 percent. Calculate the new rate of return on equity for LL.

17-6
Financial leverage effects

The Damon Company wishes to calculate next year's return on equity under different leverage ratios. Damon's total assets are $14 million, and its federal-plus-state tax rate is 40 percent. The company is able to estimate next year's earnings before interest and taxes for three possible states of the world: $4.2 million with a 0.2 probability, $2.8 million with a 0.5 probability, and $700,000 with a 0.3 probability. Calculate Damon's expected return on equity, standard deviation, and coefficient of variation for each of the following leverage ratios, and evaluate the results:

Leverage (Debt/Total Assets)	Interest Rate
0%	—
10	9%
50	11
60	14

INTEGRATIVE PROBLEM

17-7

Optimal capital structure

Assume that you have just been hired as business manager of Campus Deli and Sub Shop (CDSS), which is located adjacent to the campus. Sales were $1,350,000 last year; variable costs were 60 percent of sales; and fixed costs were $40,000. Therefore, EBIT totaled $500,000. Because the University's enrollment is capped, EBIT is expected to be constant over time. Since no expansion capital is required, CDSS pays out all earnings as dividends. The management group owns about 50 percent of the stock, which is traded in the over-the-counter market.

CDSS currently has no debt—it is an all equity firm—and its 100,000 shares outstanding sell at a price of $20 per share. The firm's federal-plus-state tax rate is 40 percent. On the basis of statements made in your finance text, you believe that CDSS's shareholders would be better off if some debt financing were used. When you suggested this to your new boss, she encouraged you to pursue the idea, but to provide support for the suggestion.

You then obtained from a local investment banker the following estimates of the costs of debt and equity at different debt levels (in thousands of dollars):

Amount Borrowed	k_d	k_s
$ 0	—	15.0%
250	10.0%	15.5
500	11.0	16.5
750	13.0	18.0
1,000	16.0	20.0

If the firm were recapitalized, debt would be issued, and the borrowed funds would be used to repurchase stock. Stockholders, in turn, would use funds provided by the repurchase to buy equities in other fast food companies similar to CDSS. You plan to complete your report by asking and then answering the following questions.

a. (1) What is business risk? What factors influence a firm's business risk?
   (2) What is operating leverage, and how does it affect a firm's business risk?
b. (1) What is meant by the terms financial leverage and financial risk?
   (2) How does financial risk differ from business risk?
c. Now, to develop an example which can be presented to CDSS's management as an illustration, consider two hypothetical firms, Firm U, with zero debt financing, and Firm L, with $10,000 of 12 percent debt. Both firms have $20,000 in total assets and a 40 percent federal-plus-state tax rate, and they face the following EBIT probability distribution for next year:

Probability	EBIT
0.25	$2,000
0.50	3,000
0.25	4,000

(1) Complete the following partial income statements and the set of ratios for Firm L.

	Firm U			Firm L		
Assets	$20,000	$20,000	$20,000	$20,000	$20,000	$20,000
Equity	$20,000	$20,000	$20,000	$10,000	$10,000	$10,000
Probability	0.25	0.50	0.25	0.25	0.50	0.25
Sales	$ 6,000	$ 9,000	$12,000	$ 6,000	$ 9,000	$12,000
Operating costs	4,000	6,000	8,000	4,000	6,000	8,000
Earnings before interest and taxes	$ 2,000	$ 3,000	$ 4,000	$ 2,000	$ 3,000	$ 4,000
Interest (12%)	0	0	0	1,200		1,200
Earnings before taxes	$ 2,000	$ 3,000	$ 4,000	$ 800	$	$ 2,800
Taxes (40%)	800	1,200	1,600	320		1,120
Net income	$ 1,200	$ 1,800	$ 2,400	$ 480	$	$ 1,680
Basic earning power (BEP = EBIT/Assets)	10.0%	15.0%	20.0%	10.0%	%	20.0%
ROE	6.0%	9.0%	12.0%	4.8%	%	16.8%
TIE	∞	∞	∞	1.7×	×	3.3×
Expected basic earning power		15.0%			%	
Expected ROE		9.0%			10.8%	
Expected TIE		∞			2.5×	
σ_{BEP}		3.5%			%	
σ_{ROE}		2.1%			4.2%	
σ_{TIE}		0			0.6×	

(2) What does this example illustrate concerning the impact of financial leverage on expected rate of return and risk?

d. With the above points in mind, now consider the optimal capital structure for CDSS.

(1) To begin, define the term optimal capital structure.

(2) Describe briefly, without using numbers, the sequence of events that would occur if CDSS decided to recapitalize and to increase its use of debt.

(3) Assume that shares could be repurchased at the current market price of $20 per share. Calculate CDSS's expected EPS and TIE at debt levels of $0, $250,000, $500,000, $750,000, and $1,000,000. How many shares would remain after recapitalization under each scenario?

(4) What would be the new stock price if CDSS recapitalizes with $250,000 of debt? $500,000? $750,000? $1,000,000? Recall that the payout ratio is 100 percent, so g = 0.

(5) Considering only the levels of debt discussed, what is CDSS's optimal capital structure?

(6) Is EPS maximized at the debt level which maximizes share price? Why?

(7) What is the WACC at the optimal capital structure?

e. Suppose you discovered that CDSS had more business risk than you originally estimated. Describe how this would affect the analysis. What if the firm had less business risk than originally estimated?

f. What is meant by the terms degree of operating leverage (DOL), degree of financial leverage (DFL), and degree of total leverage (DTL)? If fixed costs total $40,000 and the company uses $500,000 of debt, what are CDSS's degrees of each type of leverage? Of what practical use is the degree of leverage concept?

g. What are some factors a manager should consider when establishing his or her firm's target capital structure?

h. Put labels on the following graph, and then discuss the graph as you might use it to explain to your boss why CDSS might want to use some debt.

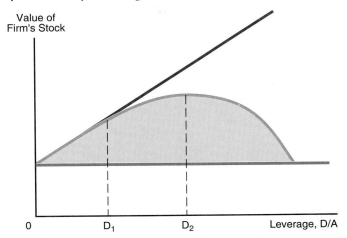

i. How does the existence of asymmetric information and signaling affect capital structure?

COMPUTER-RELATED PROBLEM

Work the problem in this section only if you are using the computer problem diskette.

17-8   Use the model in File C17 to work this problem.

Effects of financial leverage   a. Rework Problem 17-4, assuming that the old long-term debt will not remain outstanding but, rather, that it must be refinanced at the new long-term interest rate of 12 percent. What effect does this have on the decision to refinance?

b. What would be the effect on the refinancing decision if the rate on long-term debt fell to 5 percent or rose to 20 percent, assuming that all long-term debt must be refinanced?

c. Which financing method would be recommended if the stock price (1) rose to $105 or (2) fell to $30? (Assume that all debt will have an interest rate of 12 percent.)

d. With $P_0 = \$60$ and $k_d = 12\%$, change the sales probability distribution to the following:

| | Alternative 1 | | Alternative 2 |
Sales	Probability	Sales	Probability
$2,250	0	$ 0	0.3
2,700	1.0	2,700	0.4
3,150	0	7,500	0.3

What are the implications of these changes?

Dividend Policy

A   M A N A G E R I A L   P E R S P E C T I V E

For 174 straight quarters, since it went public in 1946, Tucson Electric Power Company of Arizona had paid a dividend on its common stock. Then, in January 1990, the directors voted to omit the dividend. That decision followed months of upsetting announcements both from and about the utility company. In February 1989, Chief Financial Officer Joe Coykendall sold his 9,000 shares of stock for $48.25 per share. Then, Moody's downgraded the debt to below investment grade, blaming a trend toward harsh utilities regulation in Arizona. On June 20, 1989, Tucson Electric's vice president, Joseph B. Wilcox, sold 14,916 shares for about $34 each. On June 28, Coykendall resigned, and Einar Greve, chairman, president, and CEO, announced that he had sold two-thirds of his stock, 24,047 shares, at an average price of $32.29 each. The next day, J. Luther Davis, one of the utility's directors, announced that he had sold 5,203 shares at $32.00 each. Each of the sellers claimed personal reasons for divesting. Greve said he needed cash to pay off some loans, to pay taxes, and to offset some gains and losses, and Wilcox said he sold for similar reasons and "absolutely not" because of concerns about the future of the utility. To make matters worse, the resignation and stock sales coincided with the filing of a $40 million lawsuit by an Arizona savings bank against a Tucson Electric subsidiary.

In early July, Greve sold the remainder of his holdings, and then he resigned under pressure from the board of directors, who told him his stock transactions had caused them to lose faith in him. After that meeting, the board warned stockholders that their dividends might have to be reduced, or even eliminated, because of a regulatory decision allowing Tucson Electric to recover only about $3.1 million of the approximately $70 million it had spent for fuel and purchased power. Its most recent dividend payment had been 97.5 cents per common share on June 26, 1989.

The board then elected John P. Schaefer as chairman and Thomas C. Weir as president and CEO. Schaefer, who had chaired an ad hoc committee of the board to investigate the insider stock sales, said he had met with Greve to review the committee's conclusions about the former CEO's sales. "Our findings were that, at a minimum, he exercised what we would call extremely poor judgment, and because of that, the board of directors lost confidence in his ability to lead."

Tucson Electric's directors then warned shareholders that their dividends might be cut or eliminated, and they tried the less difficult option first: In the third quarter of 1989, they reduced the dividend from 97.5 cents to 40 cents per share. This was not enough, though, and in early 1990, President/CEO Weir was forced to make this announcement: "Our negative cash flow mandates that the dividend be eliminated at this time. We will continue to monitor this closely, but there is little probability that a dividend can be paid for several years." He cited "excess generating capacity that will not be fully needed to serve our retail load for several years" as the primary problem. Growth in electricity needs had turned out to be slower than forecasted, and attempts to sell the excess capacity had failed because most other southwestern utility companies were experiencing the same problem.

Tucson's problems were aggravated because it had diversified into some nonutility businesses about which it knew little—real estate ventures and savings and loan institutions. The $40 million lawsuit filed by MeraBank Federal Savings Bank sought recovery of a loan from one of the utility's subsidiaries, Sierrita Resources, Inc., which had invested in a Phoenix land development. Finally, the utility company was under investigation by the Securities and Exchange Commission for possible insider trading by the officers and directors who sold their stock.

As a result of all this, Tucson Electric has suffered severe losses. As we write this in the spring of 1992, the company is restructuring, and the stock is selling for $6.75, down from a high of $65 before the trouble started.

Sources: *The Wall Street Journal,* "Inside Track," July 12, 1989; Frederick Rose, "Tucson Electric's Chief, Greve, Quits Amid Stock Study," July 18, 1989; Frederick Rose, "Tucson Electric Preferred-Stock Auction Fails," October 2, 1989; Earl C. Gottschalk, Jr., "Tucson Electric Omits Dividend on Its Common," January 24, 1990.

Dividend policy involves the decision to pay out earnings or to retain them for reinvestment in the firm. The basic stock price model, $P_0 = D_1/(k_s - g)$, shows that if the firm adopts a policy of paying out more cash dividends, D_1 will rise, which will tend to increase the price of the stock. However, if cash dividends are increased, then less money will be available for reinvestment, the expected future growth rate will be lowered, and this will depress the price of the stock. Thus, changing the dividend has two opposing effects. *The* **optimal dividend policy** *for a firm strikes that balance between current dividends and future growth which maximizes the price of the stock.*

In this chapter, we first examine factors which affect the optimal dividend policy, after which we discuss stock repurchases as an alternative to cash dividends.

optimal dividend policy

The dividend policy that strikes a balance between current dividends and future growth and maximizes the firm's stock price.

DIVIDEND POLICY THEORIES

A number of factors influence dividend policy, including the investment opportunities available to the firm, alternative sources of capital, and stockholders' preferences for current versus future income. The major goal of this chapter is to show how these factors interact to determine a firm's optimal dividend policy. We begin by examining three theories of dividend policy: (1) the dividend irrelevance theory, (2) the "bird-in-the-hand" theory, and (3) the tax preference theory.

Dividend Irrelevance Theory

It has been argued that dividend policy has no effect on either the price of a firm's stock or its cost of capital—that is, that dividend policy is *irrelevant*. The principal proponents of the **dividend irrelevance theory** are Merton Miller and Franco Modigliani (MM).[1] They argued that the value of the firm is determined only by its basic earning power and its business risk; in other words, MM argued that the value of the firm depends only on the income produced by its assets, not on how this income is split between dividends and retained earnings (and hence growth).

MM based their proposition on theoretical grounds. However, as in all theoretical work, they had to make some assumptions in order to develop a manageable theory. Specifically, they assumed (1) that there are no personal or corporate income taxes, (2) that there are no stock flotation or transactions costs, (3) that financial leverage has no effect on the cost of capital, (4) that investors and managers have the same information about the firm's future prospects, (5) that the distribution of income between dividends and retained earnings has no effect on the firm's cost of equity (k_s), and (6) that a firm's capital budgeting policy is independent of its dividend policy. Obviously these assumptions do not hold in the real world. Firms and investors do pay income taxes; firms do incur flotation costs; managers often know more about the firm's future prospects than outside investors know; investors do incur transactions costs;

dividend irrelevance theory

The theory that a firm's dividend policy has no effect on either its value or its cost of capital.

---

[1]Merton H. Miller and Franco Modigliani, "Dividend Policy, Growth, and the Valuation of Shares," *Journal of Business,* October 1961, 411–433.

and both taxes and transactions costs may cause k_s to be affected by dividend policy. MM argued (correctly) that all economic theories are based on simplifying assumptions and that the validity of a theory must be judged on empirical tests, not on the realism of its assumptions. We will discuss empirical tests of the MM dividend theory shortly.

Bird-in-the-Hand Theory

The fifth assumption in MM's dividend irrelevance theory is that dividend policy does not affect investors' required rate of return on equity, k_s. This particular assumption has been hotly debated in academic circles. For example, Myron Gordon and John Lintner argued that k_s decreases as the dividend payout is increased because investors are less certain of receiving the capital gains which should result from retained earnings than they are of receiving dividend payments.[2] Gordon and Lintner said, in effect, that investors value a dollar of expected dividends more highly than a dollar of expected capital gains because the dividend yield component, D_1/P_0, is less risky than the g component in the total expected return equation, $\hat{k}_s = D_1/P_0 + g$.

bird-in-the-hand theory
MM's name for the theory that a firm's value will be maximized by a high dividend payout ratio.

MM disagreed. They argued that k_s is independent of dividend policy, which implies that investors are indifferent between D_1/P_0 and g and, hence, between dividends and capital gains. They called the Gordon-Lintner argument the **bird-in-the-hand** fallacy because, in MM's view, most investors plan to reinvest their dividends in the stock of the same or similar firms, and, in any event, the riskiness of the firm's cash flows to investors in the long run is determined only by the riskiness of its operating cash flows and not by its dividend payout policy.

Tax Preference Theory

There are three tax-related reasons for thinking that investors might prefer a low dividend payout to a high payout: (1) Recall from Chapter 3 that capital gains are taxed at a maximum rate of 28 percent, whereas dividend income is taxed at effective rates which go up to almost 35 percent. Therefore, wealthy investors (who own most of the stock and receive most of the dividends paid) might prefer to have companies retain and plow earnings back into the business. Then, earnings growth would presumably lead to stock price increases, and lower-taxed capital gains would be substituted for higher-taxed dividends. (2) Taxes are not paid on gains until the stock is sold. Due to time value effects, a dollar of taxes paid in the future has a lower effective cost than a dollar paid today. (3) If a stock is held by someone until he or she dies, no capital gains tax is due at all—the beneficiaries who receive the stock can use the stock's value on the death day as their cost basis and thus escape the capital gains tax.

Because of these tax advantages, investors may prefer to have companies retain most of their earnings. If so, investors would be willing to pay more for low payout companies than for otherwise similar high payout companies.

---

[2]Myron J. Gordon, "Optimal Investment and Financing Policy," *Journal of Finance,* May 1963, 264–272, and John Lintner, "Dividends, Earnings, Leverage, Stock Prices, and the Supply of Capital to Corporations," *Review of Economics and Statistics,* August 1962, 243–269.

Illustration of Dividend Policy Theories

Figure 18-1 can be used to explain the three dividend policy theories: (1) Miller and Modigliani's dividend irrelevance theory, (2) Gordon and Lintner's bird-in-the-hand theory, and (3) the tax preference theory. To illustrate the three theories, consider the case of Hardin Electronics, which has, from its inception, plowed all of its earnings back into the business, and consequently, has never paid a dividend. Hardin's management is now considering a change in policy, and it wants to adopt the policy that will maximize its stock price.

Consider first the data presented below the graph. Columns 1 and 2 show three alternative dividend policies: (1) Retain all earnings and pay out zero, which is the present policy, (2) pay out 50 percent of earnings, and (3) pay out 100 percent of earnings. In the example, we assume that the company will have a 15 percent ROE regardless of which payout policy it follows, so with a book value per share of $30, EPS will be 0.15($30) = $4.50 under all payout policies.[3] Given an EPS of $4.50, dividends per share are shown in Column 3 under each payout policy.

Under the assumption of a constant ROE, the growth rate shown in Column 4 will be g = (% Retained)(ROE), and it will vary from 15 percent at a zero payout to zero at a 100 percent payout. If Hardin pays out 50 percent of its earnings, then its dividend growth rate will be 7.5 percent.

Columns 5, 6, and 7 show how the situation would look if MM's irrelevance theory were correct. Under this theory, neither the stock price nor the cost of equity would be affected by the payout policy—the stock price would remain constant at $30, and k_s would be stable at 15 percent. Note that k_s is found as the sum of the growth rate in Column 4 plus the dividend yield in Column 6.

Columns 8, 9, and 10 show how the situation would look if the bird-in-the-hand theory were true. Under this theory, investors prefer dividends, and the more dividends the company pays out, the higher its stock price and the lower its cost of equity. In this example, the bird-in-the-hand argument indicates that adopting a 100 percent payout policy would cause the stock price to rise from $30 to $40, and the cost of equity would decline from 15 percent to 11.25 percent.

Finally, Columns 11, 12, and 13 show the situation that would exist if the tax preference theory were correct. Under this theory, investors want companies to retain earnings and thus provide returns in the form of lightly taxed capital gains rather than heavily taxed dividends. If the tax preference theory were correct, then an increase in the dividend payout ratio would cause the stock price to decline and the cost of equity to rise.

The data in the table can be plotted to produce the two graphs shown in Figure 18-1. The top panel shows how the stock price reacts to dividend policy

---

[3]When the three theories were developed, it was assumed that a company's investment opportunities would be held constant and that if the company increased its dividends, its capital budget could be funded by selling common stock. Conversely, if a high payout company lowered its payout to the point where earnings exceeded good investment opportunities, it was assumed that the company would repurchase shares. Transactions costs were assumed to be zero. We maintain those assumptions in our example.

Figure 18-1 ▪ **The Miller-Modigliani, Bird-in-Hand, and Tax Preference Dividend Hypotheses**

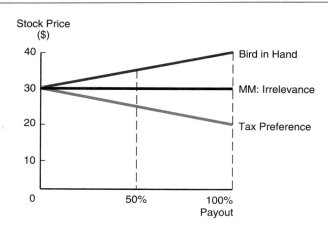

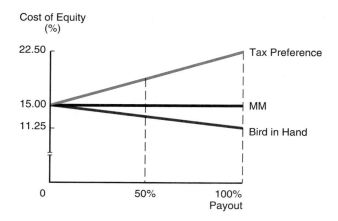

| | | | | | | Possible Situations | | | | | | |
| | | | | | MM | | | Bird-in-Hand | | | Tax Preference | |
Percent Payout (1)	Percent Retained (2)	DPS (3)	g (4)	P_0 (5)	D/P_0 (6)	k_s (7)	P_0 (8)	D/P_0 (9)	k_s (10)	P_0 (11)	D/P_0 (12)	k_s (13)
0%	100%	$0.00	15.0%	$30	0.0%	15.0%	$30	0.00%	15.00%	$30	0.0%	15.0%
50	50	2.25	7.5	30	7.5	15.0	35	6.43	13.93	25	9.0	16.5
100	0	4.50	0.0	30	15.0	15.0	40	11.25	11.25	20	22.5	22.5

Notes:

1. Book value = Initial market value = $30 per share.

2. ROE = 15%.

3. EPS = $30(0.15) = $4.50.

4. g = (% retained)(ROE).

5. k_s = Dividend yield + Growth rate.

under each of the theories, and the bottom panel shows how the cost of equity is affected. Thus, the three theories lead to very different conclusions, and we cannot at this point say which theory is most correct. Before reaching any conclusions, we must examine the available empirical evidence.

Self-Test Questions

Differentiate between the dividend irrelevance theory, the bird-in-the-hand theory, and the tax preference theory. Use a graph such as Figure 18-1 to illustrate your answer.

List the assumptions of Modigliani and Miller concerning the dividend irrelevance theory.

How did the bird-in-the-hand theory get its name?

In what sense does MM's theory represent a middle ground position between the other two theories?

TESTS OF THE DIVIDEND THEORIES

In the preceding section, we presented three dividend theories:

1. MM argued that dividend policy is irrelevant; that is, it does not affect a firm's value or its cost of capital. Thus, according to MM, there is no optimal dividend policy — one dividend policy is as good as any other.

2. Gordon and Lintner disagreed with MM, arguing that dividends are less risky than capital gains, so a firm should set a high dividend payout ratio and offer a high dividend yield in order to maximize its stock price. MM called this the bird-in-the-hand fallacy.

3. A third position is that investors prefer retained earnings to dividends because of the capital gains tax preference situation. This theory suggests that companies should hold dividend payments to low levels if they want to maximize stock prices.

These three theories offer contradictory advice to corporate managers; which, if any, should we believe? The most logical way to proceed is to test the theories empirically. Such tests have been conducted, but the results have been unclear. Indeed, the empirical tests suggest that any of the theories could be correct, or that they could all be incorrect. There are two reasons for this situation: (1) For a valid statistical test, things other than dividend policy must be held constant; that is, the sample companies must differ only in their dividend policies, and (2) we must be able to measure with a high degree of accuracy the costs of equity for the sample firms. Neither of these two conditions actually holds: We cannot find a set of publicly owned firms that differ only in their dividend policies, and we cannot obtain precise estimates of the cost of equity. Therefore, we cannot determine what effect dividend policy has on the cost of equity. Hence, direct tests have been unable to resolve the dividend policy controversy.

Academic researchers have also studied the dividend policy issue from a CAPM perspective. These studies hypothesize that required returns are a function of both market risk, as measured by beta, and dividend yield. As with the direct tests, the results of the CAPM studies have been mixed, and they also suffer from empirical problems. The major problem is that the researchers generally used historical earned rates of return as a proxy for required returns, and with such a poor proxy, the tests were almost bound to have mixed results. Thus, the CAPM-based empirical tests, like the direct tests, have not led to definitive conclusions about which dividend theory is most correct. As a result, the issue is still unresolved; researchers at this time simply cannot tell corporate decision makers how dividend policy affects stock prices and capital costs.

 Self-Test Question

What have been the results of empirical tests of the dividend theories?

OTHER DIVIDEND POLICY ISSUES

Before discussing dividend policy in practice, we must examine two other theoretical issues that could affect our views toward dividend policy: (1) the *information content,* or *signaling, hypothesis* and (2) the *clientele effect.*

Information Content, or Signaling, Hypothesis

If investors expect a company's dividend to increase by 5 percent per year, and if the dividend is in fact increased by 5 percent, then the stock price generally will not change significantly on the day the dividend increase is announced. In Wall Street parlance, such a dividend increase would be "discounted," or anticipated, by the market. However, if investors expect a 5 percent increase, but the company actually increases the dividend by 25 percent—say from $2 to $2.50—this would generally be accompanied by an increase in the price of the stock. Conversely, a less-than-expected dividend increase, or a reduction, would generally result in a price decline.

information content (signaling) hypothesis
The theory that investors regard dividend changes as signals of management's earnings forecasts.

The fact that large dividend increases generally cause stock price increases suggests to some that investors in the aggregate prefer dividends to capital gains. However, MM argued differently. They noted the well-established facts that corporations are always reluctant to cut dividends and, consequently, that managers do not raise dividends unless they anticipate higher, or at least stable, earnings in the future. Therefore, according to MM, this means that a larger-than-expected dividend increase is taken by investors as a "signal" that the firm's management forecasts improved future earnings, whereas a dividend reduction signals a forecast of poor earnings. Thus, MM claimed that investors' reactions to changes in dividend payments do not show that investors prefer dividends to retained earnings; rather, the stock price changes simply indicate that important information is contained in dividend announcements. This theory is referred to as the **information content,** or **signaling, hypothesis.**

Clientele Effect

clientele effect

The tendency of a firm to attract the type of investor who likes its dividend policy.

MM also suggested that a **clientele effect** might exist, and, if so, this might help explain why stock prices change after announced changes in dividend policy. Their argument went like this: A firm sets a particular dividend payout policy, which then attracts a "clientele" consisting of those investors who like this particular dividend policy. For example, some stockholders, such as university endowment funds and retired individuals, prefer current income to future capital gains, so they want the firm to pay out a higher percentage of its earnings. Other stockholders have no need for current investment income—they would simply reinvest any dividend income received, after first paying income taxes on it, so they favor a low payout ratio.

If the firm retained and reinvested earnings rather than paying dividends, those stockholders who need current income would be disadvantaged. They presumably could realize some capital gains, but they would have to go to the trouble and expense of selling some of their shares to obtain cash. Since brokerage costs are quite high on small transactions, selling a few shares to obtain periodic income would be expensive and inefficient. Also, some institutional investors (or trustees for individuals) are precluded from selling stock and then "spending capital." On the other hand, if the firm paid out most of its income, other stockholders who did not need current cash income would be forced to receive such income, pay taxes on it, and then go to the trouble and expense of reinvesting what's left of their dividends after taxes. MM concluded from all this that those investors who desired current investment income would purchase shares in high-dividend-payout firms, whereas those who did not need current cash income would invest in low-payout firms.

This suggests that each firm should establish the specific policy that its management deems most appropriate and then let stockholders who do not like this policy sell their shares to other investors who do. However, investor switching is costly because of (1) brokerage costs, (2) the likelihood that selling stockholders will have to pay taxes on their capital gains, and (3) a possible shortage of investors who like the firm's newly stated dividend policy. This means that firms should not change dividend policies frequently because such changes will result in net losses due to brokerage costs and capital gains taxes. However, if there is a really good business reason for the change, and if there are enough investors in the economy who favor the new policy, then demand for the stock could more than offset the costs associated with a given change and thus lead to an increase in the price of the stock.

Several studies have investigated the importance of the clientele effect.[4] However, like most other issues in the dividend arena, the implications of the clientele effect are still up in the air.

Self-Test Question

Define (1) information content and (2) the clientele effect, and explain how they affect dividend policy.

---

[4]For example, see R. Richardson Pettit, "Taxes, Transactions Costs, and the Clientele Effect of Dividends," *Journal of Financial Economics,* December 1977, 419–436.

INDUSTRY PRACTICE The Tax Bite on Dividends

When considering stocks to buy, investors often look for high dividend yields. However, high yields will increase tax payments, which effectively lowers investment returns. How big are these tax payments? According to the IRS, three million taxpayers earning between $75,000 and $100,000 a year paid approximately $1.5 billion in taxes on $7.4 billion in dividends in 1989. This works out to an average of $500 for each taxpayer.

To see how much taxes reduced stocks' payoffs, a recent study done by *Fortune* looked at the 100 largest corporations and calculated the average annual total return (capital gains or losses, plus dividends) for the period from 1981 through 1991. The pre-tax total return calculation assumed that shareholders reinvested their dividends. The after-tax total return also assumed that dividends were reinvested, but only after they had been taxed at the marginal tax rate for an individual earning $100,000 annually. The results of the study showed that an investor who had bought $100 of stock in each of the 100 largest corporations 10 years ago would have seen the $10,000 investment increase to $61,473 before taxes. However, when taxes were considered, that same $10,000 would have only grown to $53,255 by the end of 1991. The difference of $8,218 went to the IRS.

The *Fortune* study calculated the "tax efficiency" of each stock by dividing the annual average after-tax return by the average annual pre-tax return. A stock which has a large disparity between pre-tax and after-tax returns is considered less tax efficient than one in which pre-tax and after-tax returns are close. The stocks that scored highest on tax efficiency were those that provided most or all of their returns in the form of capital gains.

If an individual investor cannot decide between two stocks, tax efficiency could be the deciding factor. For example, consider Xerox and Hewlett-Packard (HP). During the last 10 years, Xerox's average total pre-tax return averaged 12 percent, while HP's pre-tax return averaged 11.9 percent. But if one considers after-tax returns, HP's return was considerably higher than Xerox's, 11.6 percent versus 9.5 percent. The reason for the difference was that HP paid out a total of $2.69 a share in dividends over the 10-year period, while Xerox paid more than that in each year— $3.00 a share annually during that same 10-year period. PepsiCo is another tax efficient company—it raised its dividend by only 166 percent from 1982 to 1991, while its net profit was increasing by 391 percent. The company's return on this investment has averaged 21.6 percent annually.

The easiest way for investors to achieve tax efficiency is to select companies that pay little or no dividends. But individuals should not select just any low-dividend stock—they should look for a company that will earn more on what it retains than investors could earn if they received the earnings as dividends. In short, if the company's ROE is several percentage points higher than what you could earn on alternative investments, then you are better off letting management retain and reinvest its earnings.

Some companies, such as Archer-Daniels-Midland, prefer to pay stock dividends rather than cash dividends. Stock dividends are not taxed until the shares are sold. However, some academics argue that these paper payouts have no value and only serve to cut the pie into more slices without enhancing stockholders' wealth. Others argue that stockholders get a psychological boost from the stock dividend, and they have a choice whether to cash it immediately or to hold on to it (waiting to pay the taxes until the stock is sold). In addition, many managements believe stock dividends help maintain the firm's stock price within a favorable trading range.

Notwithstanding tax effects, many individual investors still hold investments in high-dividend yielding stocks. Two-thirds of GM stock, and more than half of IBM's, is owned by individuals. Some of these investors hold their stock in tax-exempt accounts, but most do not. Why would investors want dividends even though they realize that a part of them will be paid to the IRS in taxes? Logical or not, investors want dividends for a number of reasons. One of the biggest reasons is that they need cash income to meet living expenses. But many investors in high-yielding stocks are taking their dividends, incurring the tax, and plowing the money back into the company through dividend reinvestment programs. These investors are incurring taxes on income that they clearly do not need, and this is leading many corporations to re-examine their dividend policies.

Source: "How to Find Stocks That Will Beat the Tax Man," *Fortune,* April 20, 1992.

DIVIDEND POLICY IN PRACTICE

We noted earlier that there are three conflicting theories as to what dividend policy firms *should* follow: (1) Miller and Modigliani's theory that dividend policy is irrelevant, (2) the bird-in-the-hand theory which states that dividends are less risky than capital gains and hence that k_s rises as dividend payments are reduced, and (3) the tax preference theory which states that investors prefer retained earnings to dividends. We also saw that dividend payments send signals to investors—an unexpectedly large dividend increase conveys management optimism, whereas a cut conveys pessimism—and that companies' dividend policies attract clienteles of stockholders who are seeking a dividend policy similar to the one the company is following. All of this provides insights that aid corporate decision makers. However, no one has been able to develop a formula that can be used to tell management how a given dividend policy will affect a firm's stock price.

Even though no dividend policy formula exists, managements must still establish dividend policies. This section discusses several alternative policies that are used in practice.

Residual Dividend Policy

residual dividend policy

A policy in which the dividend paid is set equal to the actual earnings minus the amount of retained earnings necessary to finance the firm's optimal capital budget.

In practice, dividend policy is very much influenced by investment opportunities and by the availability of funds with which to finance new investments. This fact has led to the development of a **residual dividend policy,** which states that a firm should follow these steps when deciding on its payout ratio: (1) determine the optimal capital budget as in Chapter 16, (2) determine the amount of capital needed to finance that budget, (3) use retained earnings to supply the equity component to the extent possible, and (4) pay dividends only if more earnings are available than are needed to support the optimal capital budget. The word *residual* means "left over," and the residual policy implies that dividends should be paid only out of "leftover" earnings.

The basis of the residual policy is the fact that *investors prefer to have the firm retain and reinvest earnings rather than pay them out in dividends if the rate of return the firm can earn on reinvested earnings exceeds the rate investors, on average, can themselves obtain on other investments of comparable risk.* For example, if the corporation can reinvest retained earnings at a 14 percent rate of return, whereas the best rate the average stockholder can obtain if the earnings are passed on in the form of dividends is 12 percent, then stockholders will prefer to have the firm retain the profits.

To continue, we saw in Chapter 16 that the cost of retained earnings is an *opportunity cost* which reflects rates of return available to equity investors. If a firm's stockholders can buy other stocks of equal risk and obtain a 12 percent dividend-plus-capital-gains yield, then 12 percent is the firm's cost of retained earnings. The cost of new outside equity raised by selling common stock will be higher than 12 percent because of the costs of floating the issue.

Most firms have a target capital structure that calls for at least some debt, so new financing is done partly with debt and partly with equity. As long as the firm finances with the optimal mix of debt and equity, and as long as it uses only internally generated equity (retained earnings), its marginal cost of each

Figure 18-2   ▪   Texas and Western Transport Company: Marginal Cost of Capital

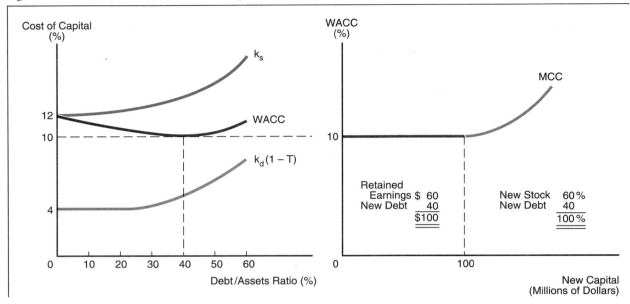

new dollar of capital will be minimized. Internally generated equity is available for financing a certain amount of new investment, but beyond that amount the firm must turn to more expensive new common stock. At the point where new stock must be sold, the cost of equity, and consequently the marginal cost of capital, rises.

These concepts, which were developed in Chapter 16, are illustrated in Figure 18-2 with data from the Texas and Western (T&W) Transport Company. T&W has a marginal cost of capital of 10 percent. However, this cost rate assumes that all new equity comes from retained earnings. Therefore, MCC = 10% as long as retained earnings are available, but MCC begins to rise at the point where new stock must be sold.

T&W has $60 million of net income and a 40 percent optimal debt ratio. Provided it does not pay cash dividends, T&W can make net investments (investments in addition to asset replacements financed from depreciation) of $100 million, consisting of $60 million from retained earnings plus $40 million of new debt supported by the retained earnings, at a 10 percent marginal cost of capital. Therefore, its MCC is constant at 10 percent up to $100 million of capital, beyond which it rises as the firm begins to use more expensive new common stock.

Of course, if T&W does not retain all of its earnings, then its MCC will begin to rise before $100 million. For example, if T&W retains only $30 million, its MCC will begin to rise at $50 million: $30 million of retained earnings + $20 million of debt = $50 million.

Now suppose T&W's director of capital budgeting constructs investment opportunity schedules under three economic scenarios and plots them on a graph. The investment opportunity schedules for three different states of the economy—good (IOS_G), normal (IOS_N), and bad (IOS_B)—are shown in

Figure 18-3   ∎   **Texas and Western Transport Company:**
Investment Opportunity Schedules

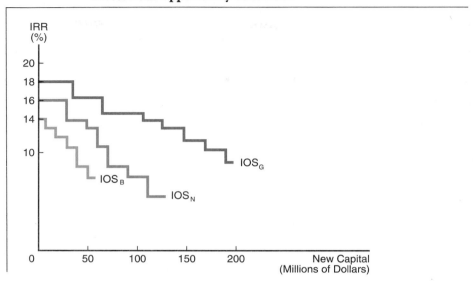

Figure 18-4   ∎   **Texas and Western Transport Company:**
Interrelationships between Cost of Capital, Investment
Opportunities, and New Investment

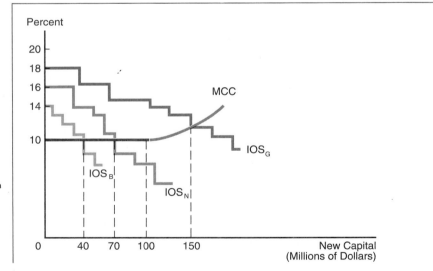

Figure 18-3. T&W can invest the most money, and earn the highest rates of
return, when the investment opportunities as given by IOS_G exist.

In Figure 18-4, we combine these investment opportunity schedules with
the cost of capital schedule that would exist if the company retained all of its
earnings. The point where the relevant IOS curve cuts the MCC curve defines
the proper level of new investment. When investment opportunities are rela-

tively bad (IOS_B), the optimal level of investment is $40 million; when opportunities are normal (IOS_N), $70 million should be invested; and when opportunities are relatively good (IOS_G), T&W should make new investments in the amount of $150 million.[5]

Consider the situation in which IOS_G is the appropriate schedule. T&W should raise and invest $150 million. It has $60 million in earnings and a 40 percent target debt ratio. Thus, if it retained all of its earnings, it could finance $100 million, consisting of $60 million of retained earnings plus $40 million of new debt, at an average cost of 10 percent. The remaining $50 million would include external equity and thus would have a higher cost. If T&W paid out part of its earnings in dividends, it would have to begin to use more costly new common stock earlier than need be, so its MCC curve would rise earlier than it otherwise would. This suggests that under the conditions of IOS_G, T&W should retain all of its earnings. According to the residual policy, T&W's payout ratio should in this case be zero.

Under the conditions of IOS_N, however, T&W should invest only $70 million. How should this investment be financed? First, notice that if T&W retained all of its earnings, $60 million, it would need to sell only $10 million of new debt. However, if T&W retained $60 million and sold only $10 million of new debt, it would move away from its target capital structure. To stay on target, T&W must finance 60 percent of the required $70 million with equity—retained earnings—and 40 percent with debt. This means that it would retain only $42 million and sell $28 million of new debt. Since T&W would retain only $42 million of its $60 million total earnings, it would have to distribute the residual, $18 million, to its stockholders. Thus, its optimal payout ratio would be $18/$60 = 30% if IOS_N prevailed.

Under the conditions of IOS_B, T&W should invest only $40 million. Because it has $60 million in earnings, it could finance the entire $40 million out of retained earnings and still have $20 million available for dividends. Should this be done? Under our assumptions this would not be a good decision because it would force T&W away from its optimal capital structure. To stay at the 40 percent target debt/assets ratio, T&W must retain $24 million of earnings and sell $16 million of debt. When the $24 million of retained earnings is subtracted from the $60 million total earnings, T&W would be left with a residual of $36 million, the amount that should be paid out in dividends. Thus, under IOS_B, the payout ratio as prescribed by the residual policy would be $36/$60 = 60 percent.

Since both the IOS schedule and the earnings level vary from year to year, strict adherence to the residual dividend policy would result in dividend variability—one year the firm might declare zero dividends because investment opportunities were good, but the next year it might pay a large dividend because investment opportunities were poor. Similarly, fluctuating earnings would

---

[5]Figure 18-4 shows one MCC schedule and three IOS schedules for three possible sets of investment opportunities. Actually, both the MCC and the IOS schedules would normally change from year to year as interest rates and stock prices change. Figure 18-4 is designed to illustrate a point, not to duplicate reality. In reality there would be one MCC and one IOS schedule for each year, but those schedules would change from year to year.

also lead to variable dividends even if investment opportunities were stable over time. Thus, following the residual dividend policy would be optimal only if investors were not bothered by fluctuating dividends. However, if investors prefer stable, dependable dividends, k_s would be higher, and the stock price lower, if the firm followed the residual theory in a strict sense rather than attempting to stabilize its dividends over time. *Therefore, firms use the residual policy to help set their long-run target payout ratios, not as a guide to the payout in any one year.*

Constant, or Steadily Increasing, Dividends

In the past, many firms set a specific annual dollar dividend per share and then maintained it, increasing the annual dividend only if it seemed clear that future earnings would be sufficient to allow the new dividend to be maintained. A corollary of that policy was this rule: *Never reduce the annual dividend.*

More recently, inflation plus reinvested earnings have tended to push earnings up, so many firms that would otherwise have followed the stable dividend payment policy have switched over to what is called the "stable growth rate" policy. Here the firm sets a target growth rate for dividends (for example, 6 percent per year, which is a little above the long-run average inflation rate) and strives to increase dividends by this amount each year. Obviously, earnings must be growing at a reasonably steady rate for this policy to be feasible, but where it can be followed, such a policy provides investors with a stable real income.

A fairly typical dividend policy, that of Eastman Kodak, is illustrated in Figure 18-5. Kodak's payout ratio ranged from 41.1 percent to 52.5 percent from 1975 to 1982, and it averaged close to 50 percent during those 8 years. Although the payout ratio fluctuated somewhat, earnings were relatively stable during those years, and dividends clearly tracked earnings. After 1980, Kodak's earnings were much less stable. Global competition intensified, Kodak lost a major suit to Polaroid, and booms and recessions alternated to lead to earnings variability. Management stopped increasing the dividend when earnings fell, but did not cut the dividend, even when earnings failed to cover the dividend. Thus, in 1985 and 1986, the payout ratio averaged more than 100 percent. Maintaining the dividend was Kodak's way of signaling to stockholders that management was confident that the earnings decline was only temporary and that earnings would soon resume their upward trend. This was, indeed, the case. Kodak's earnings increased by almost 300 percent from 1986 to 1990, moving the 1990 dividend payout ratio to about 50 percent, which is about where Kodak likes to keep it. In 1991, Kodak's earnings dropped due to a sluggish economy, but Kodak maintained its dividend at the 1990 level.

The dashed lines beyond 1991 in Figure 18-5 represent the forecasts of a major investment advisory service, *Value Line,* whose analysts believe that Kodak's earnings will grow at a rate of about 10 percent per year and that, over the long term, Kodak will increase dividends as earnings grow. During the forecast period, 1992–1996, *Value Line* projects that Kodak will pay out close to 50 percent of earnings.

There are two good reasons for paying a stable, predictable dividend rather than following the residual dividend policy. First, given the existence of the

Figure 18-5   ▪   **Eastman Kodak: Earnings and Dividends, 1975–1996**

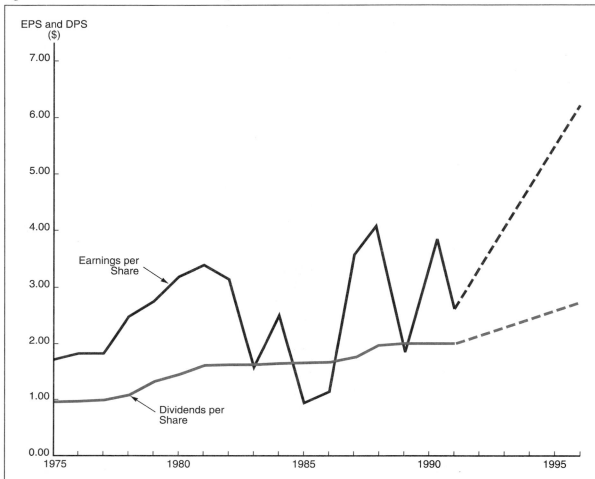

Source: *Value Line,* December 20, 1991. Projected values are shown beyond 1991.

information content, or signaling, idea, a fluctuating payment policy would lead to greater uncertainty, hence to a higher k_s and a lower stock price, than would exist under a stable policy. Second, many stockholders use dividends for current consumption, and they would be put to trouble and expense if they had to sell part of their shares to obtain cash if the company cut the dividend; this is in addition to the anxiety a dividend cut would cause them. Further, it is possible for most firms to avoid these problems. Even though the optimal dividend as prescribed by the residual policy might vary somewhat from year to year, actions such as delaying some investment projects, departing from the target capital structure during a particular year, or even issuing new common stock make it possible for a company to avoid the problems associated with unstable dividends.

Constant Payout Ratio

It would be possible for a firm to pay out a constant percentage of earnings, but since earnings will surely fluctuate, this policy would mean that the dollar amount of dividends would vary. For example, if it had paid out a constant percentage of earnings, Eastman Kodak would have had to cut its dividend in several different years, and this undoubtedly would have caused its stock price to fall sharply. (Kodak's stock price was relatively stable during the 1980s, in spite of earnings fluctuations. Had it cut the dividend to keep the payout ratio constant, the stock price would have "fallen out of bed" several times because investors would have taken the dividend reduction as a signal that management thought the earnings drops were permanent.)

Note, though, that Kodak's long-run target payout ratio has been relatively constant; except for the depressed periods in the 1980s and in 1991, it has fluctuated narrowly about 50 percent. Kodak, like most companies, conducts an analysis similar to the residual analysis set forth earlier in the chapter and then establishes a target payout ratio based on the most likely set of conditions. The target is not hit in every year, but over time the average payout has been close to the target level. Of course, the target would change if fundamental changes in the company's business were to occur.

Low Regular Dividend plus Extras

A policy of paying a low regular dividend plus a year-end extra in good years is a compromise between a stable dividend (or stable growth rate) and a constant payout rate. Such a policy gives the firm flexibility, yet investors can count on receiving at least a minimum dividend. Therefore, if a firm's earnings and cash flows are quite volatile, this policy may well be its best choice. The directors can set a relatively low regular dividend—low enough so that it can be maintained even in low-profit years or in years when a considerable amount of retained earnings is needed—and then supplement it with an **extra dividend** in years when excess funds are available. Ford, General Motors, and other auto companies, whose earnings fluctuate widely from year to year, formerly followed such a policy, but in recent years they have joined the crowd and now follow our first choice, a stable dividend policy.

extra dividend
A supplemental dividend paid in years when excess funds are available.

Payment Procedures

Dividends are normally paid quarterly, and, if conditions permit, the dividend is increased once each year. For example, Kodak paid $0.50 per quarter in 1991, or at an annual rate of $2.00. In common financial parlance, we say that in 1991 Kodak's *regular quarterly dividend* was $0.50, and its *annual dividend* was $2.00. In late 1991, Kodak's board of directors met, reviewed projections for 1992, and decided to keep the 1992 dividend at $2.00. The directors announced the $2 rate, so stockholders could count on receiving it unless the company experienced unanticipated operating problems.

The actual payment procedure is as follows:

declaration date
The date on which a firm's directors issue a statement declaring a dividend.

1. **Declaration date.** On the **declaration date**—say, on November 13—the directors meet and declare the regular dividend, issuing a statement similar to the following: "On November 13, 1992, the directors of the XYZ

Company met and declared the regular quarterly dividend of 50 cents per share, payable to holders of record on December 11, payment to be made on January 4, 1993." For accounting purposes, the declared dividend becomes an actual liability on the declaration date, and if a balance sheet were constructed, the amount ($0.50) $\times$ (Number of shares outstanding) would appear as a current liability, and retained earnings would be reduced by a like amount.

holder-of-record date

If the company lists the stockholder as an owner on this date, then the stockholder receives the dividend.

2. **Holder-of-record date.** At the close of business on the **holder-of-record date**, December 11, the company closes its stock transfer books and makes up a list of shareholders as of that date. If XYZ Company is notified of the sale and transfer of some stock before 5 P.M. on December 11, then the new owner receives the dividend. However, if notification is received on or after December 12, the previous owner of the stock gets the dividend check.

3. **Ex-dividend date.** Suppose Jean Buyer buys 100 shares of stock from John Seller on December 7. Will the company be notified of the transfer in time to list Buyer as the new owner and thus pay the dividend to her? To avoid conflict, the securities industry has set up a convention of declaring that the right to the dividend remains with the stock until four business days prior to the holder-of-record date; on the fourth day before that date, the right to the dividend no longer goes with the shares. The date when the right to the dividend leaves the stock is called the **ex-dividend date.** In this case, the ex-dividend date is four days prior to December 11, or December 7:

ex-dividend date

The date on which the right to the current dividend no longer accompanies a stock; it is usually four working days prior to the holder-of-record date.

	December 6 Buyer receives the dividend
Ex-dividend date:	December 7 Seller receives the dividend
	December 8
	December 9
	December 10
Holder-of-record date:	December 11

Therefore, if Buyer is to receive the dividend, she must buy the stock on or before December 6. If she buys it on December 7 or later, Seller will receive the dividend because he will be the official holder of record.

The XYZ dividend amounts to $0.50, so the ex-dividend date is important. Barring fluctuations in the stock market, one would normally expect the price of a stock to drop by approximately the amount of the dividend on the ex-dividend date. Thus, if XYZ closed at $30½ on December 6, it would probably open at about $30 on December 7.[6]

payment date

The date on which a firm actually mails dividend checks.

dividend reinvestment plan (DRP)

A plan that enables a stockholder to automatically reinvest dividends received back into the stock of the paying firm.

4. **Payment date.** The company actually mails the checks to the holders of record on January 4, the **payment date**.

Dividend Reinvestment Plans

In recent years most larger companies have instituted **dividend reinvestment plans (DRPs),** whereby stockholders can automatically reinvest dividends received in the stock of the paying corporation.[7] There are two types of DRPs: (1) plans which involve only "old" stock that is already outstanding and (2) plans which involve newly issued stock. In either case, the stockholder must pay income taxes on the amount of the dividends even though stock rather than cash is received.

Under the "old-stock" type of plan, the stockholder chooses between receiving dividend checks or having the company use the dividends to buy more stock in the corporation. If the stockholder elects reinvestment, a bank, acting as trustee, takes the total funds available for reinvestment, purchases the corporation's stock on the open market, and allocates the shares purchased to the participating stockholders' accounts on a pro rata basis. The transactions costs of buying shares (brokerage costs) are low because of volume purchases, so these plans benefit small stockholders who do not need cash dividends for current consumption.

The "new-stock" type of DRP provides for dividends to be invested in newly issued stock; hence, these plans raise new capital for the firm. AT&T, Florida

---

[6]December 6, 1992, is a Sunday. Therefore, the buyer would actually have to purchase the stock on Friday, December 4, to receive the dividend. Also, tax effects cause the price decline on average to be less than the full amount of the dividend. Suppose you were an investor in the 40 percent federal-plus-state tax bracket. If you bought XYZ's stock on December 6, you would receive the dividend, but you would almost immediately pay 40 percent of it out in taxes. Thus, you would want to wait until December 7 to buy the stock if you thought you could get it for $0.50 less per share. Your reaction, and those of others, would influence stock prices around dividend payment dates. Here is what would happen:

1. Other things held constant, a stock's price should rise during the quarter, with the daily price increase (for XYZ) equal to $0.50/90 = $0.005556. Therefore, if the price started at $30 just after its last ex-dividend date, it would rise to $30.50 on December 6.

2. In the absence of taxes, the stock's price would fall to $30 on December 7 and then start up as the next dividend accrual period began. Thus, over time, if everything else were held constant, the stock's price would follow a sawtooth pattern if it were plotted on a graph.

3. Because of taxes, the stock's price would neither rise by the full amount of the dividend nor fall by the full dividend amount when it goes ex-dividend.

4. The amount of the rise and subsequent fall would depend on the average investor's marginal tax rate.

See Edwin J. Elton and Martin J. Gruber, "Marginal Stockholder Tax Rates and the Clientele Effect," *Review of Economics and Statistics,* February 1970, 68–74, for an interesting discussion of all this.

[7]See Richard H. Pettway and R. Phil Malone, "Automatic Dividend Reinvestment Plans," *Financial Management,* Winter 1973, 11–18, for an excellent discussion of this topic.

Power & Light, Union Carbide, and many other companies have had such plans in effect in recent years, using them to raise substantial amounts of new equity capital. No fees are charged to stockholders, and many companies offer stock at a discount of 5 percent below the actual market price. The companies absorb these costs as a tradeoff against the flotation costs that would have been incurred had they sold stock through investment bankers rather than through the dividend reinvestment plans.[8]

Self-Test Questions

Explain the logic of the residual dividend policy, the steps a firm would take to implement it, and why it is more likely to be used to establish a long-run payout target than to set the actual year-by-year payout ratio.

Describe the constant, or steadily increasing, dividend policy, and give two reasons why a firm might follow such a policy.

Explain what a low-regular-dividend-plus-extras policy is and why a firm might follow such a policy.

Differentiate between the two types of dividend reinvestment plans.

Describe the constant payout ratio dividend policy. Why is this policy probably not as popular as a constant, or steadily increasing, dividend policy?

Why is the ex-dividend date important to investors?

SUMMARY OF FACTORS INFLUENCING DIVIDEND POLICY

Thus far in the chapter we have described the major theories that deal with the effects of dividend policy on the value of a firm, and we have discussed alternative payment policies. Firms choose a particular policy based on managements' beliefs concerning which dividend theory is most correct, plus a host of other factors as described below. All of the factors firms take into account may be grouped into four broad categories: (1) constraints on dividend payments, (2) investment opportunities, (3) availability and cost of alternative sources of capital, and (4) effects of dividend policy on k_s. Each of these categories has several subparts, which we discuss in the following paragraphs.

---

[8]One interesting aspect of DRPs is that they are forcing corporations to reexamine their basic dividend policies. A high participation rate in a DRP suggests that stockholders might be better off if the firm simply reduced cash dividends, as this would save stockholders some personal income taxes. Quite a few firms are surveying their stockholders to learn more about their preferences and to find out how they would react to a change in dividend policy. A more rational approach to basic dividend policy decisions may emerge from this research.

Also, it should be noted that companies either use or stop using new-stock DRPs depending on their need for equity capital. Florida Power & Light recently stopped offering a new-stock DRP with a 5 percent discount because its need for equity capital declined once it had completed a nuclear-powered generating plant.

Constraints

1. **Bond indentures.** Debt contracts often limit dividend payments to earnings generated after the loan was granted. Also, contracts often stipulate that no dividends can be paid unless the current ratio, times-interest-earned ratio, and other safety ratios exceed stated minimums.

2. **Impairment of capital rule.** Dividend payments cannot exceed the balance sheet item "retained earnings." This legal restriction, known as the *impairment of capital rule,* is designed to protect creditors. Without the rule, a company that was in trouble might distribute most of its assets to stockholders and leave its debtholders out in the cold. (*Liquidating dividends* can be paid out of capital, but they must be indicated as such, and they must not reduce capital below the limits stated in debt contracts.)

3. **Availability of cash.** Cash dividends can be paid only with cash. Thus, a shortage of cash in the bank can restrict dividend payments. However, the ability to borrow can offset this factor.

4. **Penalty tax on improperly accumulated earnings.** To prevent wealthy individuals from using corporations to avoid personal taxes, the Tax Code provides for a special surtax on improperly accumulated income. Thus, if the IRS can demonstrate that a firm's dividend payout ratio is being deliberately held down to help its stockholders avoid personal taxes, the firm is subject to heavy penalties. This factor is generally relevant only to privately owned firms.

Investment Opportunities

1. **Location of the IOS schedule.** If a firm's "typical" IOS schedule as shown earlier in Figure 18-4 is far to the right, this will tend to produce a low target payout ratio, and vice versa if the IOS is far to the left.

2. **Possibility of accelerating or delaying projects.** The ability to accelerate or to postpone projects will permit a firm to adhere more closely to its target dividend policy.

Alternative Sources of Capital

1. **Cost of selling new stock.** If a firm needs to finance a given level of investment, it can obtain equity by retaining earnings or by selling new common stock. If flotation costs (including any negative signaling effects of a stock offering) are high, k_e will be well above k_s, making it better to set a low payout ratio and to finance through retention rather than through sale of new common stock. On the other hand, a high dividend payout ratio is more feasible for a firm whose flotation costs are low. Flotation costs differ among firms — for example, the flotation percentage is generally higher for small firms, so they tend to set low payout ratios.

2. **Ability to substitute debt for equity.** A firm can finance a given level of investment with either debt or equity. As noted above, low stock flotation costs permit a more flexible dividend policy because equity can be raised either by retaining earnings or by selling new stock. A similar situation

holds for debt policy: if the firm can adjust its debt ratio without raising costs sharply, it can maintain a constant dollar dividend, even if earnings fluctuate, by using a variable debt ratio. The shape of the average cost of capital curve (in the left-hand panel of Figure 18-2 shown earlier) determines the practical extent to which the debt ratio can be varied. If the average cost of capital curve is relatively flat over a wide range, then a higher payout ratio is more feasible than it would be if the curve had a V shape.

3. **Control.** If management is concerned about maintaining control, it may be reluctant to sell new stock, hence the company may retain more earnings than it otherwise would. However, if stockholders want higher dividends and a proxy fight looms, then the dividend will be increased.

Effects of Dividend Policy on k_s

The effects of dividend policy on k_s may be considered in terms of four factors: (1) stockholders' desire for current versus future income, (2) perceived riskiness of dividends versus capital gains, (3) the tax advantage of capital gains over dividends, and (4) the information content of dividends (signaling). Since we discussed each of these factors in detail earlier, we need only note here that the importance of each factor in terms of its effect on k_s varies from firm to firm depending on the makeup of its current and possible future stockholders.

It should be apparent from our discussion thus far that dividend policy decisions are truly exercises in informed judgment, not decisions that can be quantified precisely. Even so, to make rational dividend decisions, financial managers must take account of all the points discussed in the preceding sections.

Self-Test Questions

Identify the four broad categories of factors which affect dividend policy.

What constraints affect dividend policy?

How do investment opportunities affect dividend policy?

How does the availability and cost of outside capital affect dividend policy?

STOCK DIVIDENDS AND STOCK SPLITS

Stock dividends and stock splits are related to the firm's cash dividend policy. The rationale for stock dividends and splits can best be explained through an example. We will use Porter Electronic Controls Inc., a $700 million electronic components manufacturer, for this purpose. Since its inception, Porter's markets have been expanding, and the company has enjoyed growth in sales and earnings. Some of its earnings have been paid out in dividends, but some are also retained each year, causing earnings per share and market price per share to grow. The company began its life with only a few thousand shares outstanding, and, after some years of growth, each of Porter's shares had a very high EPS and DPS. When a "normal" P/E ratio was applied, the derived market price was so high that few people could afford to buy a "round lot" of 100 shares. This limited the demand for the stock and thus kept the total market value of the firm below what it would have been if more shares, at a lower price, had been outstanding. To correct this situation, Porter "split its stock," as described in the next section.

Stock Splits

Although there is little empirical evidence to support the contention, there is nevertheless a widespread belief in financial circles that an *optimal price range* exists for stocks. "Optimal" means that if the price is within this range, the price/earnings ratio, hence the value of the firm, will be maximized. Many observers, including Porter's management, believe that the best range for most stocks is from $20 to $80 per share. Accordingly, if the price of Porter's stock rose to $80, management would probably declare a two-for-one **stock split,** thus doubling the number of shares outstanding, halving the earnings and dividends per share, and thereby lowering the price of the stock. Each stockholder would have more shares, but each share would be worth less. If the post-split price were $40, Porter's stockholders would be exactly as well off as they were before the split. However, if the price of the stock were to stabilize above $40, stockholders would be better off. Stock splits can be of any size—for example, the stock could be split two-for-one, three-for-one, one-and-a-half-for-one, or in any other way.[9]

Stock Dividends

Stock dividends are similar to stock splits in that they "divide the pie into smaller slices" without affecting the fundamental position of the current stockholders. On a 5 percent stock dividend, the holder of 100 shares would receive an additional 5 shares (without cost); on a 20 percent stock dividend, the same holder would receive 20 new shares; and so on. Again, the total number of shares is increased, so earnings, dividends, and price per share all decline. If a firm wants to reduce the price of its stock, should it use a stock split or a stock dividend? Stock splits are generally used after a sharp price run-up to produce a large price reduction. Stock dividends are typically used on a regular annual basis to keep the stock price more or less constrained. For example, if a firm's earnings and dividends were growing at about 10 percent per year, its stock price would tend to go up at about that same rate, and it would soon be outside the desired trading range. A 10 percent annual stock dividend would maintain the stock price within the optimal trading range.

Balance Sheet Effects

Although the economic effects of stock splits and stock dividends are virtually identical, accountants treat them somewhat differently. On a two-for-one split,

stock split

An action taken by a firm to increase the number of shares outstanding, such as doubling the number of shares outstanding by giving each stockholder two new shares for each one formerly held.

stock dividend

A dividend paid in the form of additional shares of stock rather than in cash.

[9]*Reverse splits,* which reduce the shares outstanding, can even be used. For example, a company whose stock sells for $5 might employ a one-for-five reverse split, exchanging 1 new share for 5 old ones and raising the value of the shares to about $25, which is within the optimal range. LTV Corporation did this after several years of losses had driven its stock price down below the optimal range.

Table 18-1 ▪ **Porter Electronic Controls Inc.: Stockholders' Equity Accounts, Pro Forma, December 31, 1993**

Before a Stock Split or Stock Dividend

Common stock (6 million shares authorized, 5 million outstanding, $1 par)	$ 5,000,000
Additional paid-in capital	10,000,000
Retained earnings	155,000,000
Total common stockholders' equity	$170,000,000
Book value per share	$34.00

After a Two-for-One Stock Split

Common stock (12 million shares authorized, 10 million outstanding, $0.50 par)	$ 5,000,000
Additional paid-in capital	10,000,000
Retained earnings	155,000,000
Total common stockholders' equity	$170,000,000
Book value per share	$17.00

After a 20 Percent Stock Dividend

Common stock (6 million shares authorized, 6 million outstanding, $1 par)[a]	$ 6,000,000
Additional paid-in capital[b]	89,000,000
Retained earnings[b]	75,000,000
Total common stockholders' equity	$170,000,000
Book value per share	$28.33

[a]Shares outstanding are increased by 20 percent, from 5 million to 6 million.

[b]A transfer equal to the market value of the new shares is made from the retained earnings account to the additional paid-in capital and common stock accounts:

$$\text{Transfer} = (5,000,000 \text{ shares})(0.2)(\$80) = \$80,000,000.$$

Of this $80 million, ($1 par)(1,000,000 shares) = $1,000,000 goes to common stock and $79 million to paid-in capital.

the shares outstanding are doubled, and the stock's par value is halved. This treatment is shown in the middle section of Table 18-1 for Porter Electronic Controls, using a pro forma 1993 balance sheet.

The bottom section of Table 18-1 shows the effect of a 20 percent stock dividend. With a stock dividend, the par value is not reduced, but an accounting entry is made transferring capital from the retained earnings account to the common stock and paid-in capital accounts. The transfer from retained earnings is calculated as follows:

$$\begin{matrix} \text{Dollars} \\ \text{transferred from} \\ \text{retained earnings} \end{matrix} = \begin{pmatrix} \text{Number} \\ \text{of shares} \\ \text{outstanding} \end{pmatrix} \begin{pmatrix} \text{Percentage} \\ \text{of the} \\ \text{stock dividend} \end{pmatrix} \begin{pmatrix} \text{Market} \\ \text{price of} \\ \text{the stock} \end{pmatrix}. \quad \textbf{(18-1)}$$

Porter has 5 million shares outstanding, and they sell for $80 each, so a 20 percent stock dividend would require the transfer of $80 million:

$$\text{Dollars transferred} = (5,000,000)(0.2)(\$80) = \$80,000,000.$$

As shown in the table, $1 million of this $80 million is added to the common stock account and $79 million to the additional paid-in capital account. The retained earnings account is reduced from $155 million to $75 million.[10]

Price Effects

Several empirical studies have examined the effects of stock splits and stock dividends on stock prices.[11] These studies suggest that investors see stock splits and stock dividends for what they are—simply additional pieces of paper. If stock dividends and splits are accompanied by higher earnings and cash dividends, then investors will bid up the price of the stock. However, if stock dividends are not accompanied by increases in earnings and cash dividends, the dilution of earnings and dividends per share causes the price of the stock to drop by the same percentage as the stock dividend. Thus, the fundamental determinants of price are the underlying earnings and cash dividends per share, and stock splits and stock dividends merely cut the pie into thinner slices.

Self-Test Questions

What is the rationale for a stock split?

Differentiate between the accounting treatments for stock splits and stock dividends.

What is the effect of stock splits and dividends on stock prices?

STOCK REPURCHASES

A recent *Fortune* article entitled "Beating the Market by Buying Back Stock" discussed the fact that during a one-year period, more than 600 major corporations repurchased significant amounts of their own stock. It also gave illustrations of some specific companies' repurchase programs and their effects on stock prices. The article's conclusion was that "buybacks have made a mint for shareholders who stay with the companies carrying them out." This section

---

[10]Note that Porter could not pay a stock dividend that exceeded 38.75 percent; a stock dividend of that percentage would exhaust the retained earnings. Thus, a firm's ability to declare stock dividends is constrained by the amount of its retained earnings. Of course, if Porter had wanted to pay a 50 percent stock dividend, it could have just switched to a 1.5-for-one stock split and accomplished the same thing.

[11]See C. A. Barker, "Evaluation of Stock Dividends," *Harvard Business Review,* July–August 1958, 99–114. Barker's study has been replicated several times in recent years, and his results are still valid—they have withstood the test of time. Another excellent study, using an entirely different methodology, reached similar conclusions; see Eugene F. Fama, Lawrence Fisher, Michael C. Jensen, and Richard Roll, "The Adjustment of Stock Prices to New Information," *International Economic Review,* February 1969, 1–21.

stock repurchase

A transaction in which a firm buys back shares of its own stock, thereby decreasing shares outstanding, increasing EPS, and, often, increasing the price of the stock.

explains what a **stock repurchase** is, how a repurchase is carried out, and how the financial manager should analyze a possible repurchase program.

There are two principal types of repurchases: (1) situations in which the firm has cash available for distribution to its stockholders, and it distributes this cash by repurchasing shares rather than by paying cash dividends; and (2) situations in which the firm concludes that its capital structure is too heavily weighted with equity, and then it sells debt and uses the proceeds to buy back its stock.

Stock that has been repurchased by a firm is called *treasury stock*. If some of the outstanding stock is repurchased, fewer shares will remain outstanding. Assuming that the repurchase does not adversely affect the firm's future earnings, the earnings per share on the remaining shares will increase, resulting in a higher market price per share. As a result, capital gains will have been substituted for dividends.

The Effects of Stock Repurchases

Many companies have been repurchasing their stock in recent years. Until the 1980s, most repurchases amounted to a few million dollars, but in 1985 Phillips Petroleum announced plans for the largest repurchase on record—81 million of its shares with a market value of $4.1 billion. Other large repurchases have been made by Texaco, IBM, CBS, Coca Cola, Teledyne, Atlantic Richfield, Goodyear, and Xerox. Indeed, since 1985 more shares have been repurchased than issued.

The effects of a repurchase can be illustrated with data on American Development Corporation (ADC). The company expects to earn $4.4 million in 1993, and 50 percent of this amount, or $2.2 million, has been allocated for distribution to common shareholders. There are 1.1 million shares outstanding, and the market price is $20 a share. ADC believes that it can either use the $2.2 million to repurchase 100,000 of its shares through a tender offer for $22 a share or else pay a cash dividend of $2 a share.[12]

The effect of the repurchase on the EPS and market price per share of the remaining stock can be analyzed in the following way:

1.   Current EPS $= \dfrac{\text{Total earnings}}{\text{Number of shares}} = \dfrac{\$4.4 \text{ million}}{1.1 \text{ million}} = \$4$ per share.

---

[12]Stock repurchases are generally made in one of three ways: (1) A publicly owned firm can simply buy its own stock through a broker on the open market. (2) It can make a *tender offer,* under which it permits stockholders to send in (that is, "tender") their shares to the firm in exchange for a specified price per share. When a firm makes a tender offer, it generally indicates that it will buy up to a specified number of shares within a particular time period (usually about two weeks); if more shares are tendered than the company wishes to purchase, purchases are made on a pro rata basis. (3) The firm can purchase a block of shares from one large holder on a negotiated basis. If a negotiated purchase is employed, care must be taken to insure that this one stockholder does not receive preferential treatment over other stockholders or that any preference given can be justified by "sound business reasons." Texaco's management was sued by stockholders who were unhappy over the company's repurchase of about $600 million of stock from the Bass Brothers' interests at a substantial premium over the market price. The suit charged that Texaco's management, afraid the Bass Brothers would attempt a takeover, used the buyback to get them off its back. Such payments have been dubbed "greenmail."

2. P/E ratio $= \dfrac{\$20}{\$4} = 5\times$.

3. EPS after repurchase of 100,000 shares $= \dfrac{\$4.4 \text{ million}}{1 \text{ million}}$

$= \$4.40$ per share.

4. Expected market price after repurchase $= (\text{P/E})(\text{EPS}) = (5)(\$4.40)$

$= \$22$ per share.

It should be noted from this example that investors would receive before-tax benefits of $2 per share in any case, either in the form of a $2 cash dividend or a $2 increase in the stock price. This result would occur because we assumed, first, that shares could be repurchased at exactly $22 a share and, second, that the P/E ratio would remain constant. If shares could be bought for less than $22, the operation would be even better for *remaining* stockholders, but the reverse would hold if ADC had to pay more than $22 a share. Furthermore, the P/E ratio might change as a result of the repurchase operation, rising if investors viewed it favorably and falling if they viewed it unfavorably. Some factors that might affect P/E ratios are considered next.

Advantages of Repurchases

The advantages of repurchases are as follows:

1. Repurchase announcements are viewed as positive signals by investors because the repurchase is often motivated by management's belief that the firm's shares are undervalued.

2. The stockholders have a choice when the firm repurchases stock—to sell or not to sell. However, stockholders must accept a dividend payment and pay the tax. Thus, those stockholders who need cash can sell back some of their shares, while those who do not want additional cash can simply retain their stock. From a tax standpoint, in a repurchase both types of stockholders get what they want.

3. A third advantage is that a repurchase can remove a large block of stock that is overhanging the market and keeping the price per share down.

4. Dividends are "sticky" in the short run because managements are reluctant to raise the dividend if the increase cannot be maintained in the future—managements dislike cutting cash dividends. Hence, if the excess cash flow is thought to be only temporary, management may prefer to make the distribution in the form of a share repurchase rather than to declare an increased cash dividend that cannot be maintained.

5. Repurchases can be used to produce large-scale changes in capital structures. For example, Consolidated Edison recently decided to repurchase $400 million of its common stock in order to increase its debt ratio. The repurchase was necessary because even if the company financed its capital budget only with debt, it would still have taken years to get the debt ratio up to the target level. Con Ed used repurchases to produce an instantaneous change in its capital structure.

Disadvantages of Repurchases

Disadvantages of repurchases include the following:

1. Stockholders may not be indifferent between dividends and capital gains, and the price of the stock might benefit more from cash dividends than from repurchases. Cash dividends are generally dependable, but repurchases are not. Further, if a firm announced a regular, dependable repurchase program, the improper accumulation tax would become more of a threat.

2. The *selling* stockholders may not be fully aware of all the implications of a repurchase, or they may not have all pertinent information about the corporation's present and future activities. However, firms generally announce repurchase programs before embarking on them to avoid potential stockholder suits.

3. The corporation may pay too high a price for the repurchased stock, to the disadvantage of remaining stockholders. If its shares are inactively traded, and if the firm seeks to acquire a relatively large amount of the stock, then the price may be bid above its equilibrium level and then fall after the firm ceases its repurchase operations.

Conclusions on Stock Repurchases

When all the pros and cons on stock repurchases have been totaled, where do we stand? Our conclusions may be summarized as follows:

1. Because of uncertainties about their tax treatment, repurchases on a regular, systematic, dependable basis are probably not a good idea.

2. However, repurchases do offer investors an opportunity to save taxes, and, for this reason, they should be given careful consideration.

3. Repurchases can be especially valuable to a firm that wants to make a large shift in its capital structure within a short period of time.

On balance, companies probably ought to be doing more repurchasing and distributing less cash as dividends than they are. However, increases in the size and frequency of repurchases in recent years suggest that companies are rapidly reaching this same conclusion.

Self-Test Questions

Explain how repurchases can (1) help stockholders hold down taxes and (2) help firms change their capital structures.

What is treasury stock?

What are the three ways a firm can make repurchases?

What are the key advantages and disadvantages of stock repurchases?

SMALL BUSINESS   Dividend Policy for Small Businesses

The dividend policy decision involves determining the amount of earnings to distribute to stockholders. While most large, mature firms pay out a portion of earnings each year, many small, rapidly growing firms pay no dividends whatsoever. As the small firm grows, so does its need for financing. However, small businesses have limited access to the capital markets, so they must rely on internal financing (retained earnings) to a greater extent than larger firms. Over time, though, as the firm and its products mature, its growth will slow, its financing requirements will lessen, and at some point it will begin to pay dividends.

Apple Computer can be used to illustrate this process. Apple was founded in 1977, and its first year sales were $660,000. In 1978, sales increased by 550 percent, to $3.6 million, and the company earned a profit of $660,000. Growth continued at a rapid pace in the following years. Initially, all of the stock was owned by the founders and a few venture capitalists. These investors wanted to insure the company's success, and they also were more interested in capital gains than in taxable dividends, so the firm did not pay any dividends. Indeed, from 1978 to 1987, all earnings were plowed back and used to support growth, which averaged about 50 percent annually. We should also point out that Apple has never issued debt; it has chosen instead to support its growth by retaining earnings and by occasionally issuing additional shares of common stock. Apple had 118 million shares of stock outstanding in late 1991, up from 33 million in 1978.

By 1988, new competitors had entered the market, and Apple's growth was slowing down. *Value Line*'s analysts estimated that Apple's revenues would grow at an annual rate of 26 percent during the period 1988 to 1993. While a growth rate of 26 percent per year is well above average, it is far below Apple's earlier growth rate of 50 percent. On the basis of these growth forecasts, Apple's board of directors met early in 1987 and declared an annual dividend of $0.24 per share. The stock price reacted favorably, so the annual dividend was raised in 1988 to $0.32, and on up to $0.48 by 1992.

This story illustrates three points. First, small, rapidly growing firms generally need to retain all their earnings, and also to obtain additional capital from outside sources, to support growth. Growth requires cash, and even highly profitable companies like Apple have difficulty generating enough cash from earnings to support rapid growth. Second, as the firm matures, its growth will slow down, and its need for funds will diminish. Thus, when Apple's growth began to slow down, it no longer needed to retain all of its earnings, so it began to pay a small dividend. Third, as we saw earlier in the chapter, the sale of stock by a mature firm is often interpreted by investors to mean that management expects bad times ahead. However, this is not the case when the issuer is a young, rapidly growing firm: the market recognizes that new, profitable firms often grow so fast that they simply must issue common stock and that such issues indicate that the firm's managers anticipate extraordinarily good investment opportunities.

SUMMARY

Dividend policy involves the decision to pay out earnings versus retaining them for reinvestment in the firm, and dividend policy decisions can have either favorable or unfavorable effects on the price of a firm's stock. The key concepts covered are listed below.

- The **optimal dividend policy** is that policy which strikes the exact balance between current dividends and future growth that maximizes the price of the firm's stock.

- Miller and Modigliani developed the **dividend irrelevance theory,** which holds that a firm's dividend policy has no effect either on the value of its stock or on its cost of capital.

▌ The **bird-in-the-hand theory,** advocated by Gordon and Lintner, holds that the value of the firm will be maximized by a high dividend payout ratio because investors regard actual dividends as being less risky than potential capital gains.

▌ The **tax preference theory** states that, because capital gains are subject to less onerous taxes than dividends, investors prefer to have companies retain earnings rather than pay them out as dividends.

▌ Because **empirical tests** of the three theories **have been inconclusive,** academicians simply cannot tell corporate managers how a change in dividend policy will affect stock prices and capital costs. Thus, actually determining the optimal dividend policy is a matter of judgment.

▌ Dividend policy should reflect the existence of the **information content of dividends (signaling)** and the **clientele effect.** The information content, or signaling, hypothesis states that investors regard dividend changes as a signal of management's forecast of future earnings. The clientele effect suggests that a firm will attract investors who like the firm's dividend policy.

▌ In practice, most firms try to follow a policy of paying a **constant, or steadily increasing, dividend.** This policy provides investors with a stable, dependable income, and it also gives investors information about management's expectations for earnings growth through signaling effects.

▌ Other dividend policies used include: (1) the **residual dividend policy,** in which dividends are paid out of earnings left over after the capital budget has been financed; (2) the **constant payout ratio policy,** in which a constant percentage of earnings is targeted to be paid out; and (3) the **low-regular-dividend-plus-extras policy,** in which the firm pays a constant, low dividend which can be maintained even in bad years and then pays an extra dividend in good years.

▌ A **dividend reinvestment plan (DRP)** allows stockholders to have the company automatically use their dividends to purchase additional shares of the firm's stock. DRPs are popular with investors who do not need current income because the plans allow stockholders to acquire additional shares without incurring normal brokerage fees.

▌ Other factors, such as **legal constraints, investment opportunities, availability and cost of funds from other sources,** and **taxes,** are considered by managers when they establish dividend policies.

▌ A **stock split** is an action taken by a firm to increase the number of shares outstanding. Normally, splits reduce the price per share in proportion to the increase in shares because splits merely "divide the pie into smaller slices." A **stock dividend** is a dividend paid in additional shares of stock rather than in cash. Both stock dividends and splits are used to keep stock prices within an "optimal" range.

▌ Under a **stock repurchase plan,** a firm buys back some of its outstanding stock, thereby decreasing the number of shares, which in turn should increase both EPS and the stock price. Repurchases are useful for making major changes in a firm's capital structure, as well as for allowing stock-holders to delay paying taxes on their share of the firm's profits.

▌ Small, rapidly growing firms generally need to **retain all their earnings,** and to obtain additional capital from outside sources, to support growth. As the firm matures, its growth will slow down, and its need for funds will diminish. The market recognizes that new, profitable firms often grow so fast that they simply must issue common stock and that such issues indicate that the **firm's managers anticipate extraordinarily good investment opportunities.**

Questions

18-1 As an investor, would you rather invest in a firm that has a policy of maintaining (a) a constant payout ratio, (b) a constant or steadily increasing dollar dividend per share, (c) a target dividend growth rate, or (d) a constant regular quarterly dividend plus a year-end extra when earnings are sufficiently high or corporate investment needs sufficiently low? Explain your answer, stating how these policies would affect your k_s. Discuss also how your answer might change if you were a student, a 50-year-old professional with peak earnings, or a retiree.

18-2 How would each of the following changes tend to affect aggregate (that is, the average for all corporations) payout ratios, other things held constant? Explain your answers.
a. An increase in the personal income tax rate.
b. A liberalization of depreciation for federal income tax purposes — that is, faster tax write-offs.
c. A rise in interest rates.
d. An increase in corporate profits.
e. A decline in investment opportunities.
f. Permission for corporations to deduct dividends for tax purposes as they now do interest charges.
g. A change in the Tax Code so that both realized and unrealized capital gains in any year were taxed at the same rate as dividends.

18-3 Discuss the pros and cons of having the directors formally announce what a firm's dividend policy will be in the future.

18-4 Most firms would like to have their stock selling at a high P/E ratio, and they would also like to have extensive public ownership (many different shareholders). Explain how stock dividends or stock splits may help achieve these goals.

18-5 What is the difference between a stock dividend and a stock split? As a stockholder, would you prefer to see your company declare a 100 percent stock dividend or a two-for-one split? Assume that either action is feasible.

18-6 "The cost of retained earnings is less than the cost of new outside equity capital. Consequently, it is totally irrational for a firm to sell a new issue of stock and to pay dividends during the same year." Discuss this statement.

18-7 Would it ever be rational for a firm to borrow money in order to pay dividends? Explain.

18-8 "Executive salaries have been shown to be more closely correlated to the size of the firm than to its profitability. If a firm's board of directors is controlled by management instead of by outside directors, this might result in the firm's retaining more earnings than can be justified from the stockholders' point of view." Discuss the statement, being sure (a) to use Figure 18-4 in your answer and (b) to explain the implied relationship between dividend policy and stock prices.

18-9   Modigliani and Miller (MM) on the one hand and Gordon and Lintner (GL) on the other have expressed strong views regarding the effect of dividend policy on a firm's cost of capital and value.

a. In essence, what are the MM and GL views regarding the effect of dividend policy on the cost of capital and stock prices?

b. How does the tax preference theory differ from the views of MM and GL?

c. According to the text, which of the theories, if any, has received statistical confirmation from empirical tests?

d. How could MM use the *information content,* or *signaling, hypothesis* to counter their opponents' arguments? If you were debating MM, how would you counter them?

e. How could MM use the *clientele effect* concept to counter their opponents' arguments? If you were debating MM, how would you counter them?

18-10   More NYSE companies had stock dividends and stock splits during 1983 and 1984 than ever before. What events in these years could have made stock splits and stock dividends so popular? Explain the rationale that a financial vice-president might give his or her board of directors to support a stock split/dividend recommendation.

18-11   One position expressed in the financial literature is that firms set their dividends as a residual after using income to support new investment.

a. Explain what a residual dividend policy implies, illustrating your answer with a graph showing how different conditions could lead to different dividend payout ratios.

b. Could the residual dividend policy be consistent with (1) a constant growth-rate policy, (2) a constant payout ratio policy, and/or (3) a low-regular-dividend-plus-extras policy? Answer in terms of both short-run, year-to-year consistency and longer-run consistency.

c. Think back to Chapter 17, where we considered the relationship between capital structure and the cost of capital. If the WACC-versus-debt-ratio plot was shaped like a sharp V, would this have a different implication for the importance of setting dividends according to the residual policy than if the plot was shaped like a shallow bowl (or a flattened U)?

d. Assume that Companies A and B both have IOS schedules that intersect their MCC schedules at a point which, under the residual policy, calls for a 30 percent payout. In both cases, a 30 percent payout would require a cut in the annual dividend from $3 to $1.50. One company cuts its dividend, whereas the other does not. One company has a relatively steep IOS curve, whereas the other has a relatively flat one. Explain which company probably has the steeper curve.

Self-Test Problems   *(Solutions Appear in Appendix B)*

ST-1
Key terms

Define each of the following terms:

a. Optimal dividend policy

b. Dividend irrelevance theory; bird-in-the-hand theory; tax preference theory

c. Information content, or signaling, hypothesis; clientele effect

d. Residual dividend policy

e. Extra dividend

f. Declaration date; holder-of-record date; ex-dividend date; payment date

g. Dividend reinvestment plan (DRP)

h. Stock split; stock dividend

i. Stock repurchase

ST-2
Alternative dividend policies

Components Manufacturing Corporation (CMC) has an all-common-equity capital structure. It has 200,000 shares of $2 par value common stock outstanding. When CMC's founder, who was also its research director and most successful inventor, retired unexpectedly to the South Pacific in late 1992, CMC was left suddenly and permanently with materially lower growth expectations and relatively few attractive new investment opportunities. Unfortunately, there was no way to replace the founder's contributions to the firm. Previously, CMC found it necessary to plow back most of its earnings to finance growth, which averaged 12 percent per year. Future growth at a 5 percent rate is considered realistic, but that level would call for an increase in the dividend payout. Further, it now appears that new investment projects with at least the 14 percent rate of return required by CMC's stockholders ($k_s = 14\%$) would amount to only $800,000 for 1993 in comparison to a projected $2,000,000 of net income. If the existing 20 percent dividend payout were continued, retained earnings would be $1.6 million in 1993, but, as noted, investments which yield the 14 percent cost of capital would amount to only $800,000.

The one encouraging thing is that the high earnings from existing assets are expected to continue, and net income of $2 million is still expected for 1993. Given the dramatically changed circumstances, CMC's management is reviewing the firm's dividend policy.

a. Assuming that the acceptable 1993 investment projects would be financed entirely by earnings retained during the year, calculate DPS in 1993, assuming that CMC uses the residual payment policy.

b. What payout ratio does your answer to Part a imply for 1993?

c. If a 60 percent payout ratio is maintained for the foreseeable future, what is your estimate of the present market price of the common stock? How does this compare with the market price that should have prevailed under the assumptions existing just before the news about the founder's retirement? If the two values of P_0 are different, comment on why.

d. What would happen to the price of the stock if the old 20 percent payout were continued? Assume that if this payout is maintained, the average rate of return on the retained earnings will fall to 7.5 percent and the new growth rate will be

$$g = (1.0 - \text{Payout ratio})(\text{ROE})$$
$$= (1.0 - 0.2)(7.5\%)$$
$$= (0.8)(7.5\%) = 6.0\%.$$

Problems

18-1

Stock dividend

The McLaughlin Corporation declared a 6 percent stock dividend plus a cash dividend of $0.90 per share. The cash dividend was paid on both the old shares and the new shares received from the stock dividend. Construct a pro forma balance sheet showing the effect of these actions; use one new balance sheet that incorporates both actions. The stock was selling for $37.50 per share, and a condensed version of McLaughlin's balance sheet as of December 31, 1992, before the dividends, follows (millions of dollars):

Cash	$ 112.5	Debt	$1,500
Other assets	2,887.5	Common stock (90 million shares authorized, 75 million shares outstanding, $1 par)	75
		Paid-in capital	300
		Retained earnings	1,125
Total assets	$3,000.0	Total liabilities and equity	$3,000

18-2

Alternative dividend policies

In 1992 the Sirmans Company paid dividends totaling $3,600,000 on net income of $10.8 million. 1992 was a normal year, and for the past 10 years, earnings have grown at a constant rate of 10 percent. However, in 1993, earnings are expected to jump to $14.4 million, and the firm expects to have profitable investment opportunities of $8.4 million. It is predicted that Sirmans will not be able to maintain the 1993 level of earnings growth—the high 1993 earnings level is attributable to an exceptionally profitable new product line introduced that year—and the company will return to its previous 10 percent growth rate. Sirmans's target debt ratio is 40 percent.

a. Calculate Sirmans's total dividends for 1993 if it follows each of the following policies:
   (1) Its 1993 dividend payment is set to force dividends to grow at the long-run growth rate in earnings.
   (2) It continues the 1992 dividend payout ratio.
   (3) It uses a pure residual dividend policy (40 percent of the $8.4 million investment is financed with debt).
   (4) It employs a regular-dividend-plus-extras policy, with the regular dividend being based on the long-run growth rate and the extra dividend being set according to the residual policy.

b. Which of the preceding policies would you recommend? Restrict your choices to the ones listed, but justify your answer.

c. Assume that investors expect Sirmans to pay total dividends of $9,000,000 in 1993 and to have the dividend grow at 10 percent after 1993. The total market value of the stock is $180 million. What is the company's cost of equity?

d. What is Sirmans's long-run average return on equity? [Hint: g = (Retention rate)(ROE) = (1.0 − Payout rate)(ROE).]

e. Does a 1993 dividend of $9,000,000 seem reasonable in view of your answers to Parts c and d? If not, should the dividend be higher or lower?

18-3

Dividend policy and capital structure

Ybor City Tobacco Company has for many years enjoyed a moderate but stable growth in sales and earnings. However, cigar consumption and consequently Ybor's sales have been falling recently, primarily because of an increasing awareness of the dangers of smoking to health. Anticipating further declines in tobacco sales for the future, Ybor's management hopes eventually to move almost entirely out of the tobacco business and into a newly developed, diversified product line in growth-oriented industries. The company is especially interested in the prospects for pollution-control devices because its research department has already done much work on the problems of filtering smoke. Right now the company estimates that an investment of $15 million is necessary to purchase new facilities and to begin operations on these products, but the investment could be earning a return of about 18 percent within a short time. The only other available investment opportunity totals $6 million and is expected to return about 10.4 percent.

The company is expected to pay a $3.00 dividend on its 3 million outstanding shares, the same as its dividend last year. The directors might, however, change the dividend if there are good reasons for doing so. Total earnings after taxes for the year are expected to be $14.25 million; the common stock is currently selling for $56.25; the firm's target debt ratio (debt/assets ratio) is 45 percent; and its federal-plus-state tax rate is 40 percent. The costs of various forms of financing are as follows:

New bonds, $k_d = 11\%$. This is a before-tax rate.

New common stock sold at $56.25 per share will net $51.25.

Required rate of return on retained earnings, $k_s = 14\%$.

a. Calculate Ybor's expected payout ratio, the break point at which MCC rises, and its marginal cost of capital above and below the point of exhaustion of retained earnings at the current payout. (Hint: k_s is given, and D_1/P_0 can be found. Then, knowing k_s and D_1/P_0, g can be determined.)

b. How large should Ybor's capital budget be for the year?

c. What is an appropriate dividend policy for Ybor? How should the capital budget be financed?

d. How might risk factors influence Ybor's cost of capital, capital structure, and dividend policy?

e. What assumptions, if any, do your answers to the preceding parts make about investors' preferences for dividends versus capital gains (in other words, what are investors' preferences regarding the D_1/P_0 and g components of k_s)?

EXAM-TYPE PROBLEMS

The problems included in this section are set up in such a way that they could be used as multiple-choice exam problems.

18-4

External equity financing

Northern California Heating and Cooling Inc. has a six-month backlog of orders for its patented solar heating system. To meet this demand, management plans to expand production capacity by 40 percent with a $10 million investment in plant and machinery. The firm wants to maintain a 40 percent debt-to-total-assets ratio in its capital structure; it also wants to maintain its past dividend policy of distributing 45 percent of last year's net income. In 1992, net income was $5 million. How much external equity must Northern California seek at the beginning of 1993 to expand capacity as desired?

18-5

Dividend payout

The Garlington Corporation expects next year's net income to be $15 million. The firm's debt ratio is currently 40 percent. Garlington has $12 million of profitable investment opportunities, and it wishes to maintain its existing debt ratio. According to the residual dividend policy, how large should Garlington's dividend payout ratio be next year?

18-6

Stock split

After a five-for-one stock split, the Swensen Company paid a dividend of $0.75 per new share, which represents a 9 percent increase over last year's pre-split dividend. What was last year's dividend per share?

18-7

Dividend payout

The Scanlon Company's optimal capital structure calls for 50 percent debt and 50 percent common equity. The interest rate on its debt is a constant 10 percent; its cost of common equity from retained earnings is 14 percent; the cost of equity from new stock is 16 percent; and its federal-plus-state tax rate is 40 percent. Scanlon has the following investment opportunities:

Project A: Cost = $5 million; IRR = 20%.

Project B: Cost = $5 million; IRR = 12%.

Project C: Cost = $5 million; IRR = 9%.

Scanlon expects to have net income of $7,287,500. If Scanlon bases its dividends on the residual policy, what will its payout ratio be?

INTEGRATIVE PROBLEM

18-8

Dividend policy

Information Systems Inc. (ISI), which develops software for the health care industry, was founded 5 years ago by Donald Brown and Margaret Clark, who are still its only stockholders. ISI has now reached the stage where outside equity capital is necessary if the firm is to achieve its growth targets yet still maintain its target capital structure of 60 percent equity and 40 percent debt. Therefore, Brown and Clark have decided to take the company public. Until now, Brown and Clark have paid themselves reasonable salaries but routinely reinvested all after-tax earnings in the firm, so dividend policy has not been an issue. However, before talking with potential outside investors, they must decide on a dividend policy.

Assume that you were recently hired by Arthur Adamson & Company (AA), a national consulting firm, which has been asked to help ISI prepare for its public offering. Martha Millon, the senior AA consultant in your group, has asked you to make a presentation to Brown and Clark in which you review the theory of dividend policy and discuss the following questions.

a. (1) What is meant by the term "dividend policy"?
   (2) The terms "irrelevance," "bird-in-the-hand," and "tax preference" have been used to describe three major theories regarding the way dividend policy affects a firm's value. Explain what these terms mean, and briefly describe each theory.
   (3) What do the three theories indicate regarding the actions management should take with respect to dividend policy?
   (4) Explain the relationships between dividend policy and (1) stock price and (2) the cost of equity under each dividend policy theory by constructing two graphs, such as those shown in Figure 18-1. Dividend policy should be placed on the X axis.
   (5) What results have empirical studies of the dividend theories produced? How does all this affect what we can tell managers about dividend policy?

b. Discuss (1) the information content, or signaling, hypothesis, (2) the clientele effect, and (3) their effects on dividend policy.

c. (1) Assume that ISI has an $800,000 capital budget planned for the coming year. You have determined that its present capital structure (60 percent equity and 40 percent debt) is optimal, and its net income is forecasted at $600,000. Use the residual dividend policy approach to determine ISI's total dollar dividend and payout ratio. In the process, explain what the residual dividend policy is, and use a graph to illustrate your answer. Then, explain what would happen if net income were forecasted at $400,000, or at $800,000.
   (2) In general terms, how would a change in investment opportunities affect the payout ratio under the residual payment policy?
   (3) What are the advantages and disadvantages of the residual policy? (Hint: Don't neglect signaling and clientele effects.)

d. What are some other commonly used dividend payment policies? What are their advantages and disadvantages? Which policy is most widely used in practice?

e. What is a dividend reinvestment plan (DRP), and how do they work?

f. Describe the series of steps that most firms take in setting dividend policy in practice.

g. What are stock repurchases? Discuss the advantages and disadvantages of a firm's repurchasing its own shares.

h. What are stock dividends and stock splits? What are the advantages and disadvantages of stock dividends and splits? When should a stock dividend as opposed to a stock split be used?

COMPUTER-RELATED PROBLEM

Work the problem in this section only if you are using the computer problem diskette.

18-9
Dividend policy and
capital structure

Use the model in the File C18 to work this problem.

Refer back to Problem 18-3. Assume that Ybor's management is considering a change in the firm's capital structure to include more debt; thus, management would like to analyze the effects of an increase in the debt ratio to 60 percent. The treasurer believes that such a move would cause lenders to increase the required rate of return on new bonds to 12 percent and that k_s would rise to 14.5 percent.

a. How would this change affect the optimal capital budget?

b. If k_s rose to 16 percent, would the low-return project be acceptable?

c. Would the project selection be affected if the dividend was reduced to $1.88 from $3.00, still assuming $k_s = 16$ percent?

P A R T

VII

Strategic Long-Term Financing Decisions

Chapter 19   Common Stock and the
             Investment Banking Process

Chapter 20   Long-Term Debt

              Appendix 20A   Bankruptcy and Reorganization

              Appendix 20B   Refunding Operations

Chapter 21   Hybrid Financing: Preferred Stock,
             Leasing, and Option Securities

Chapter 22   Mergers, Divestitures, Holding
             Companies, and LBOs

Chapter 23   Multinational Managerial Finance

Common Stock and the Investment Banking Process

During the third quarter of 1991, insider buying in initial public offerings (IPOs) exceeded selling, reversing the previous trend. Insiders had been using IPOs as an opportunity to sell their personal holdings of stock in a company but not to add to their investment.

According to filings received by the Securities and Exchange Commission (SEC) during the third quarter of 1991, six of the ten companies with the largest number of insiders buying shares were new public companies. A large number of IPOs occurred during the first nine months of 1991 — 220 companies went public and raised $9.3 billion, compared with 152 companies which raised $4.3 billion during the same period of 1990. Company executives stated that institutional investors wanted to see management risk its own money on the deals; insider buying is viewed positively by outsiders because it sends a signal which helps distinguish one new company from another. IPOs in which insiders purchased stock and in which new investors profited included Duracell International and Fisher-Price.

One IPO that did not go well was that of Monro Muffler Brake, a chain of automotive shops based in Rochester, New York. Prior to the IPO, the company had grown rapidly by opening new stores, and it was helped by the increasing number of older cars still on the road. The firm went public in July 1991, selling 28 percent of the company for $16 a share. Two months later, Monro announced that the muffler business had slowed down, and less than three months after the IPO, the stock's price had declined by 23 percent, down to $12.25. Monro is not the first company to deliver bad news after going public; however, what really hurt the IPO investors was that 75 percent of the money raised went into the pockets of 30 inside investors, not into Monro's coffers.

Monro's controlling shareholder and biggest seller of stock in the IPO, Peter J. Solomon, was a former vice-chairman of Shearson Lehman Brothers, the IPO underwriter's parent company. Mr. Solomon still receives a $250,000 retainer from Shearson Lehman, and his private firm receives $160,000 a year to provide Monro with financial advice. Mr. Solomon defends the IPO, stating (1) that demand for the offering was strong, (2) that many other retail-related IPOs have stumbled, some of them by more than Monro, (3) that the underwriters did an enormous amount of research on Monro's books, and (4) that the IPO satisfied a fiduciary responsibility to Massachusetts Mutual Life Insurance, a co-investor. Mr. Solomon insists that he did not get any special treatment from Shearson Lehman but used them for the IPO because he knew them.

What did Mr. Solomon get out of the deal? He sold 340,000 shares of stock for $5.4 million, or about 20 times the amount of money he originally invested in the company. He retains 746,000 shares, or approximately 13 percent, of the common stock. However, due to a special class of preferred stock, he and his brother retain absolute voting control.

What about investors who bought shares through the IPO? At their best, IPOs offer investors a chance to share in the growth of a new publicly held company. If the company needs capital badly enough, investors may get in at a bargain price. But in this case, Monro did not need the public; only its selling shareholders did. No one has stated that Lehman or Mr. Solomon set out to cheat the public. But Monro's IPO serves as a lesson to investors on what things to watch out for in an IPO: Big insider selling, little new money raised by the company, close ties between issuer and underwriter, and a special controlling stock. If you read this chapter and learn the concepts presented here, you can avoid the pitfalls made by Monro's IPO investors.

Sources: "Insiders Gobble IPOs to Reassure Investors," *The Wall Street Journal,* September 25, 1991; and "Tale of How 30 Monro Muffler Inside Investors Made a Killing, Public Buyers of IPO Face Loss," *The Wall Street Journal,* October 14, 1991.

When we discussed capital structure decisions in Chapter 17, we did not spend much time on the specific characteristics of common stock, preferred stock, or debt, nor did we discuss the process through which these securities are issued. However, these "details" are actually quite important. Therefore, in this and the following two chapters we will examine the characteristics of common and preferred stocks, and of the many different types of debt, and we will discuss how firms actually raise long-term capital. The focus in this chapter is on common stock.

BALANCE SHEET ACCOUNTS
AND DEFINITIONS

common equity

The sum of the firm's common stock, paid-in capital, and retained earnings, which equals the common stockholders' total investment in the firm.

par value

The nominal or face value of a stock or bond.

retained earnings

The balance sheet account which indicates the total amount of earnings the firm has not paid out as dividends throughout its history; these earnings have been reinvested in the firm.

additional paid-in capital

Funds received in excess of par value when a firm sells new stock.

book value per share

The accounting value of a share of common stock; equal to the common equity (common stock plus paid-in capital plus retained earnings) divided by the number of shares outstanding.

An understanding of legal and accounting terminology is vital to both investors and financial managers if they are to avoid misinterpretations and possibly costly mistakes. Therefore, we begin our analysis of common stock with a discussion of accounting and legal issues. Consider first Table 19-1, which shows the **common equity** section of Allied Food Products' balance sheet. Allied's owners— its stockholders—have authorized management to issue a total of 60 million shares, and management has thus far actually issued (or sold) 50 million shares. Each share has a **par value** of $1; this is the minimum amount for which new shares can be issued.[1]

Allied is an old company—it was established back in 1873. Its initial equity capital consisted of 5,000 shares sold at the $1 par value, so on its first balance sheet the total stockholders' equity was $5,000. The initial paid-in capital and retained earnings accounts showed zero balances. Over the years Allied retained some of its earnings, and the firm issued new stock to raise capital from time to time. During 1992 Allied earned $113.5 million, paid $57.5 million in dividends, and retained $56 million. The $56 million was added to the $710 million accumulated **retained earnings** shown on the year-end 1991 balance sheet to produce the $766 million retained earnings at year-end 1992. Thus, since its inception in 1873, Allied has retained, or plowed back, a total of $766 million. This is money that belongs to the stockholders and that they could have received in the form of dividends. Instead, the stockholders chose to let management reinvest the $766 million in the business.

Now consider the $80 million **additional paid-in capital.** This account shows the difference between the stock's par value and what new stockholders paid when they bought newly issued shares. As we noted, Allied Food Products was formed in 1873 with 5,000 shares issued at the $1 par value; thus, the first balance sheet showed a zero balance for additional paid-in capital. By 1888 the company had demonstrated its profitability, and it was earning 50 cents per share. Further, it had built up the retained earnings account to a total of $10,000, so the total stockholders' equity was $5,000 of par value plus $10,000 of retained earnings = $15,000, and the **book value per share** was $15,000/ 5,000 shares = $3. Allied had also borrowed heavily, and, in spite of its retained earnings, the company's debt ratio had risen to an unacceptable level, precluding further use of debt without an infusion of equity.

The company had profitable investment opportunities, so to take advantage of them, management decided to issue another 2,000 shares of stock. The market price at the time was $4 per share, which was eight times the 50 cents earnings per share (the price/earnings ratio was $8 \times$). This $4 market value per

---

[1]A stock's par value is an arbitrary figure that originally indicated the minimum amount of money stockholders had put up. Today, firms are not required to establish a par value for their stock. Thus, Allied Food Products could have elected to use "no-par" stock, in which case the common stock and additional paid-in capital accounts would have been consolidated under one account called *common stock*, which would show a 1992 balance of $130 million. For simplicity, in Chapter 2 we did not show the detailed breakdown of Allied's common equity accounts. For purposes of the present discussion it is necessary to show the detail as given in Table 19-1.

Table 19-1 ▪ **Allied Food Products: Common Stockholders' Equity Accounts as of December 31 (Millions of Dollars)**

	1992	1991
Common stock (60 million shares authorized, 50 million shares outstanding, $1 par)	$ 50	$ 50
Additional paid-in capital	80	80
Retained earnings	766	710
Total common stockholders' equity (or common net worth)	$896	$840

$$\text{Book value per share} = \frac{\text{Total common stockholders' equity}}{\text{Shares outstanding}} = \frac{\$896}{50} = \$17.92.$$

Table 19-2 ▪ **Effects of Stock Sale on Allied Food Products' Common Equity Accounts in 1888**

Before Sale of Stock

Common stock (5,000 shares outstanding, $1 par)	$ 5,000
Additional paid-in capital	0
Retained earnings	10,000
Total stockholders' equity	$15,000
Book value per share = $15,000/5,000 =	$ 3.00

After Sale of Additional 2,000 Shares

Common stock (7,000 shares outstanding, $1 par)	$ 7,000
Additional paid-in capital ($4 − $1) × 2,000 shares	6,000
Retained earnings	10,000
Total stockholders' equity	$23,000
Book value per share = $23,000/7,000 =	$ 3.29

share was well in excess of the $1 par value and also higher than the $3 book value per share, demonstrating that par value, book value, and market value are not necessarily equal. Had the company lost money since its inception, it would have had negative retained earnings, the book value would have been below par, and the market price may well have been below book. After the 2,000 new shares had been sold to investors back in 1888 at the market price of $4 per share, Allied's partial balance sheet changed as shown in Table 19-2. Each share brought in $4, of which $1 represented the par value and $3 represented the excess of the sale price above par. Since 2,000 shares were involved, a total of $2,000 was added to common stock, and $6,000 was entered in additional paid-in capital. Also, book value per share rose from $3 to $3.29; whenever stock is sold at a price above book, the book value increases, and vice versa if stock is sold below book value. Similar transactions have taken place through the years to produce the current situation, as shown on Allied's latest balance sheet in Table 19-1.[2]

 Self-Test Questions

How is book value per share calculated, and is it generally equal to the par and market values?

What differences would there be in the stockholders' equity accounts of a firm that has par value stock and one that has no-par stock?

LEGAL RIGHTS AND PRIVILEGES OF COMMON STOCKHOLDERS

The common stockholders are the *owners* of a corporation, and as such they have certain rights and privileges. The most important of these rights are discussed in this section.

Control of the Firm

The stockholders have the right to elect the firm's directors, who in turn elect the officers who manage the business. In a small firm, the major stockholder typically assumes the positions of president and chairperson of the board of directors. In a large, publicly owned firm, the managers typically have some stock, but their personal holdings are insufficient to provide voting control. Thus, the managements of most publicly owned firms can be removed by the stockholders if they decide a management team is not effective.

Various state and federal laws stipulate how stockholder control is to be exercised. First, corporations must hold an election of directors periodically, usually once a year, with the vote taken at the annual meeting. Frequently, one-third of the directors are elected each year for a three-year term. Each share of stock has one vote; thus, the owner of 1,000 shares has 1,000 votes. Stockholders can appear at the annual meeting and vote in person, but typically they transfer their right to vote to a second party by means of an instrument known as a **proxy.** Management always solicits stockholders' proxies and usually gets them. However, if earnings are poor and stockholders are dissatisfied, an outside group may solicit the proxies in an effort to overthrow management and take control of the business. This is known as a **proxy fight.**

The question of control has become a central issue in finance in recent years. The frequency of proxy fights has increased, as have attempts by one corporation to take over another by purchasing a majority of the outstanding

proxy

A document giving one person the authority to act for another, typically the power to vote shares of common stock.

proxy fight

An attempt by a person or group of people to gain control of a firm by getting its stockholders to grant that person or group the authority to vote their shares in order to vote a new management into office.

---

[2]Stock dividends, stock splits, and stock repurchases (the reverse of stock issues) also affect the capital accounts. These topics were discussed in Chapter 18.

takeover

An action whereby a person or group succeeds in ousting a firm's management and taking control of the company.

stock. This latter action, which is called a **takeover,** will be discussed in detail in Chapter 22. Some well-known examples of recent takeover battles include KKR's acquisition of RJR Nabisco, Chevron's acquisition of Gulf Oil, and AT&T's takeover of NCR.

Managers who do not have majority control (more than 50 percent of their firms' stock) are very much concerned about proxy fights and takeovers, and many of them are attempting to get stockholder approval for changes in their corporate charters that would make takeovers more difficult. For example, a number of companies have gotten their stockholders to agree (1) to elect only one-third of the directors each year (rather than electing all directors each year), (2) to require 75 percent of the stockholders (rather than 50 percent) to approve a merger, and (3) to vote in a "poison pill" provision which would allow the stockholders of a firm that is taken over by another firm to buy shares in the second firm at a reduced price. The third provision makes the acquisition unattractive and, thus, wards off hostile takeover attempts. Managements seeking such changes generally cite a fear that the firm will be picked up at a bargain price, but it often appears that managers' concerns about their own positions might be an even more important consideration.

The Preemptive Right

preemptive right

A provision in the corporate charter or bylaws that gives common stockholders the right to purchase on a pro rata basis new issues of common stock (or convertible securities).

Common stockholders often have the right, called the **preemptive right,** to purchase any additional shares sold by the firm. In some states the preemptive right is automatically included in every corporate charter; in others it is necessary to insert it specifically into the charter.

The purpose of the preemptive right is twofold. First, it protects the power of control of current stockholders. If it were not for this safeguard, the management of a corporation under criticism from stockholders could prevent stockholders from removing it from office by issuing a large number of additional shares and purchasing these shares itself. Management could thereby secure control of the corporation and frustrate the will of the current stockholders.

The second, and by far the most important, reason for the preemptive right is that it protects stockholders against a dilution of value. For example, suppose 1,000 shares of common stock, each with a price of $100, were outstanding, making the total market value of the firm $100,000. If an additional 1,000 shares were sold at $50 a share, or for $50,000, this would raise the total market value of the firm to $150,000. When the total market value is divided by the new total shares outstanding, a value of $75 a share is obtained. The old stockholders thus lose $25 per share, and the new stockholders have an instant profit of $25 per share. Thus, selling common stock at a price below the market value would dilute its price and would transfer wealth from the present stockholders to those who were allowed to purchase the new shares. The preemptive right prevents such occurrences.

Self-Test Questions

Identify some actions that companies have taken to make takeovers more difficult.

What are the two primary reasons for the existence of the preemptive right?

TYPES OF COMMON STOCK

classified stock

Common stock that is given a special designation, such as Class A, Class B, and so forth, to meet special needs of the company.

Although most firms have only one type of common stock, in some instances **classified stock** is used to meet the special needs of the company. Generally, when special classifications of stock are used, one type is designated *Class A,* another *Class B,* and so on. Small, new companies seeking to obtain funds from outside sources frequently use different types of common stock. For example, when Genetic Concepts went public recently, its Class A stock was sold to the public and paid a dividend, but this stock had no voting rights for five years. Its Class B stock, which was retained by the organizers of the company, had full voting rights for five years, but the legal terms stated that dividends could not be paid on the Class B stock until the company had established its earning power by building up retained earnings to a designated level. The use of classified stock thus enabled the public to take a position in a conservatively financed growth company without sacrificing income, while the founders retained absolute control during the crucial early stages of the firm's development. At the same time, outside investors were protected against excessive withdrawals of funds by the original owners. As is often the case in such situations, the Class B stock was called **founders' shares.**

founders' shares

Stock owned by the firm's founders that has sole voting rights but restricted dividends for a specified number of years.

Note that "Class A," "Class B," and so on, have no standard meanings. Most firms have no classified shares, but a firm that does could designate its Class B shares as founders' shares and its Class A shares as those sold to the public, while another could reverse these designations. Still other firms could use stock classifications for entirely different purposes. For example, when General Motors acquired Hughes Aircraft for $5 billion, it paid in part with a new Class H common, GMH, which had limited voting rights and whose dividends were tied to Hughes's performance as a GM subsidiary. The reasons for the new stock were reported to be (1) that GM wanted to limit voting privileges on the new classified stock because of management's concern about a possible takeover and (2) that Hughes employees wanted to be rewarded more directly on Hughes's own performance than would have been possible through regular GM stock.

GM's deal posed a problem for the NYSE, which had a rule against listing any company's common stock if the company had any nonvoting common stock outstanding. GM made it clear that it was willing to delist if the NYSE did not change its rules. The NYSE concluded that such arrangements as GM had made were logical and were likely to be made by other companies in the future, so it changed its rules to accommodate GM.

? *Self-Test Question*

What are some reasons why a company might use classified stock?

EVALUATION OF COMMON STOCK AS A SOURCE OF FUNDS

Thus far the chapter has covered the main characteristics of common stock. Now we will appraise stock financing both from the viewpoint of the corporation and from a social perspective.

From the Corporation's Viewpoint

Advantages.   Common stock offers several advantages to the corporation:

1. Common stock does not obligate the firm to make payments to stockholders: Only if the company generates earnings and has no pressing internal needs for them will it pay dividends. Had it used debt, it would have incurred a legal obligation to pay interest, regardless of its operating condition and cash flows.

2. Common stock carries no fixed maturity date—it never has to be "repaid" as would a debt issue.

3. Since common stock cushions creditors against losses, the sale of common stock increases the creditworthiness of the firm. This, in turn, raises its bond rating, lowers its cost of debt, and increases its future ability to use debt.

4. If a company's prospects look bright, then common stock can often be sold on better terms than debt. Stock appeals to certain groups of investors because (a) it typically carries a higher expected total return (dividends plus capital gains) than does preferred stock or debt, and (b) since stock represents the ownership of the firm, it provides the investor with a better hedge against unanticipated inflation because common dividends tend to rise during inflationary periods.[3]

5. When a company is having operating problems, it often needs new funds to overcome its problems. However, investors are reluctant to supply capital to a troubled company, and if they do they generally require some type of security. From a practical standpoint, this often means that a firm which is experiencing problems can only obtain new capital by issuing debt, which is safer from the investor's standpoint. Because corporate treasurers are well aware of this, they often opt to finance with common stock during good times in order to maintain a **reserve borrowing capacity.** Indeed, surveys have indicated that maintenance of an adequate reserve of borrowing capacity is the most important consideration in many financing decisions.

Disadvantages.   Disadvantages associated with issuing common stock include the following:

1. The sale of common stock gives some voting rights, and perhaps even control, to new stockholders. For this reason, additional equity financing is often avoided by managers who are concerned about maintaining control. The use of founders' shares, and shares such as those GM issued to acquire Hughes Aircraft, can mitigate this problem.

2. Common stock gives new owners the right to share in the income of the firm; if profits soar, then new stockholders will share in this bonanza,

reserve borrowing capacity

Unused debt capacity that permits borrowing if a firm needs capital in troubled times.

---

[3]For common stock in general, the rate of increase in dividends has slightly exceeded the rate of inflation since 1970.

whereas if debt had been used, new investors would have received only a fixed return, no matter how profitable the company had been.[4]

3. As we shall see, the costs of underwriting and distributing common stock are usually higher than those for preferred stock or debt. Flotation costs for common stock are characteristically higher because (a) the costs of investigating an equity security investment are higher than those for a comparable debt security, and (b) stocks are riskier than debt, meaning that investors must diversify their equity holdings, so a given dollar amount of new stock must be sold to a larger number of purchasers than the same amount of debt.

4. As we saw in Chapter 17, if the firm has more equity than is called for in its optimal capital structure, the average cost of capital will be higher than necessary. Therefore, a firm would not want to sell stock if the sale caused its equity ratio to exceed the optimal level.

5. Under current tax laws, common stock dividends are not deductible as an expense for tax purposes, but bond interest is deductible. As we saw in Chapter 16, taxes raise the relative cost of equity as compared with debt.

From a Social Viewpoint

From a social viewpoint, common stock is a desirable form of financing because it makes businesses less vulnerable to the consequences of declines in sales and earnings. Common stock financing involves no fixed charge payments which might force a faltering firm into bankruptcy. From the standpoint of the economy as a whole, if too many firms used too much debt, business fluctuations would be amplified, and minor recessions could turn into major ones. Recently, when many leveraged mergers and buyouts were occurring and were raising the aggregate debt ratio (the average debt ratio of all firms), the Federal Reserve and other authorities voiced concern over the situation, and congressional leaders debated the wisdom of social controls over corporations' use of debt. Like most important issues, this one is debatable, and the debate centers around who can better determine "appropriate" capital structures—corporate managers or government officials.[5]

Self-Test Questions

What are the major advantages of common stock financing? The major disadvantages?

From a social viewpoint, why is common stock a desirable form of financing?

---

[4]This point has given rise to an important theory: "If a firm sells a large issue of bonds, this is a *signal* that management expects the company to earn high profits on investments financed by the new capital and that it does not wish to share these profits with new stockholders. On the other hand, if the firm issues stock, this is a signal that its prospects are not so bright." This issue was discussed earlier in Chapters 17 and 18.

[5]When business executives hear someone say, "I'm from Washington and I'm here to help you," they generally cringe, and often with good reason. On the other hand, a stable national economy does require sound businesses, and too much debt can lead to corporate instability.

THE MARKET FOR COMMON STOCK

closely held corporation

A corporation that is owned by a few individuals who are typically associated with the firm's management.

publicly owned corporation

A corporation that is owned by a relatively large number of individuals who are not actively involved in its management.

over-the-counter (OTC) market

The network of dealers that provides for trading in unlisted securities.

organized security exchange

A formal organization, having a tangible physical location, that facilitates trading in designated ("listed") securities. The two major U.S. security exchanges are the New York Stock Exchange (NYSE) and the American Stock Exchange (AMEX).

secondary market

The market in which "used" stocks are traded after they have been issued by corporations.

primary market

The market in which firms issue new securities to raise corporate capital.

Some companies are so small that their common stocks are not actively traded; they are owned by only a few people, usually the companies' managers. Such firms are said to be *privately owned,* or **closely held, corporations,** and their stock is called *closely held stock.* In contrast, the stocks of most larger companies are owned by a large number of investors, most of whom are not active in management. Such companies are said to be **publicly owned corporations,** and their stock is called *publicly held stock.*

As we saw in Chapter 3, the stocks of smaller publicly owned firms are not listed on an exchange; they trade in the **over-the-counter (OTC) market,** and the companies and their stocks are said to be *unlisted.* However, larger publicly owned companies generally apply for listing on an **organized security exchange,** and they and their stocks are said to be *listed.* As a general rule, companies are first listed on a regional exchange, such as the Pacific Coast or Midwest Exchange. Then, as they grow, they move up to the American Stock Exchange (AMEX). Finally, if they grow large enough, they are listed on the "Big Board," the New York Stock Exchange (NYSE). About 7,000 stocks are traded in the OTC market, but in terms of market value of both outstanding shares and daily transactions, the NYSE is most important, having about 60 percent of the business.

Institutional investors such as pension trusts, insurance companies, and mutual funds own about 35 percent of all common stocks. These institutions buy and sell relatively actively, however, so they account for about 75 percent of all transactions. Thus, the institutional investors have a heavy influence on the prices of individual stocks.

Types of Stock Market Transactions

We can classify stock market transactions into three distinct types:

1. **Trading in the outstanding shares of established, publicly owned companies: the secondary market.** Allied Food Products has 50 million shares of stock outstanding. If the owner of 100 shares sells his or her stock, the trade is said to have occurred in the **secondary market.** Thus, the market for outstanding shares, or *used shares,* is the secondary market. The company receives no new money when sales occur in this market.

2. **Additional shares sold by established, publicly owned companies: the primary market.** If Allied decides to sell (or issue) an additional 1 million shares to raise new equity capital, this transaction is said to occur in the **primary market.**[6]

3. **New public offerings by privately held firms: the primary market.** Recently the Coors Brewing Company, which was owned by the Coors

---

[6]Recall that Allied has 60 million shares authorized but only 50 million outstanding; thus, it has 10 million authorized but unissued shares. If it had no authorized but unissued shares, management could increase the authorized shares by obtaining stockholders' approval, which would generally be granted without any arguments.

going public

The act of selling stock to the public at large by a closely held corporation or its principal stockholders.

initial public offering (IPO) market

The market consisting of stocks of companies that have just gone public.

family at the time, decided to sell some stock to raise capital needed for a major expansion program.[7] This type of transaction is called **going public** —whenever stock in a closely held corporation is offered to the public for the first time, the company is said to be going public. The market for stock that has recently gone public is often called the **initial public offering (IPO) market.**

Firms can go public without raising any additional capital. For example, the Ford Motor Company was once owned exclusively by the Ford family. When Henry Ford died, he left a substantial part of his stock to the Ford Foundation. When the Foundation later sold some of this stock to the general public, the Ford Motor Company went public, even though the company raised no capital in the transaction.

The Decision to Go Public

As noted in Chapter 1, most businesses begin life as proprietorships or partnerships, and the more successful ones, as they grow, find it desirable at some point to convert into corporations. Initially, these new corporations' stocks are owned by the firms' officers, key employees, and a few investors who are not actively involved in management. If growth continues, however, the companies may decide at some point to go public. The advantages and disadvantages of public ownership are discussed next.

Advantages of Going Public

1. **Facilitates stockholder diversification.** As a company grows and becomes more valuable, its founders often have most of their wealth tied up in the company. By selling some of their stock in a public offering, the founders can diversify their holdings and thereby reduce somewhat the riskiness of their personal portfolios.

2. **Increases liquidity.** The stock of a closely held firm is illiquid: no ready market exists for it. If one of the holders wants to sell some shares to raise cash, it is hard to find potential buyers, and even if a buyer is located, there is no established price at which to complete the transaction. These problems do not exist with publicly held firms.

3. **Makes it easier to raise new corporate cash.** If a privately held company wants to raise cash by a sale of new stock, it must either go to its existing owners, who may neither have any money nor want to put any more eggs into this particular basket, or it must shop around for wealthy investors who are willing to make an investment in the company. However, it is usually difficult to get outsiders to put money into a closely held company, because if the managers have voting control (over 50 percent)

---

[7]The stock Coors offered to the public was designated Class B, and it was nonvoting. The Coors family retained the founders' shares, called Class A stock, which carried full voting privileges. The company was large enough to obtain an NYSE listing, but at that time the Exchange had a requirement that listed common stocks must have full voting rights, which precluded Coors from obtaining an NYSE listing. Now that GM has forced the Exchange to change its rules, Coors might be able to list its stock.

of the stock, then they can run roughshod over outsiders. The insiders can pay or not pay dividends, pay themselves exorbitant salaries, have private deals with the company, and so on. For example, the president might buy a warehouse and lease it to the company at a high rental, get the use of a Rolls Royce, and enjoy "all-the-frills" travel to conventions. The insiders can even keep the outsiders from knowing the company's actual earnings or its real worth. There are not many positions more vulnerable than that of an outside stockholder in a closely held company, and for this reason it is hard for closely held companies to raise new equity capital. Going public, which brings with it disclosure requirements and regulation by the Securities and Exchange Commission (SEC), greatly reduces these problems and thus makes people more willing to invest in the company.

4. **Establishes a value for the firm.** For a number of reasons, it is often useful to establish a firm's value in the marketplace. For one thing, when the owner of a privately owned business dies, state and federal inheritance tax appraisers must set a value on the company for estate tax purposes. Often, these appraisers set too high a value, which creates all sorts of problems. A company that is publicly owned, however, has its value established with little room for argument. Similarly, if a company wants to give incentive stock options to key employees, it is useful to know the exact value of these options. In addition, employees much prefer to own stock, or options on stock, that is publicly traded, because public trading increases liquidity.

Disadvantages of Going Public

1. **Cost of reporting.** A publicly owned company must file quarterly and annual reports with the SEC, with various state officials, or with both. These reports can be costly, especially for very small firms.

2. **Disclosure.** Management may not like the idea of reporting operating data, because such data will then be available to competitors. Similarly, the owners of the company may not want people to know their net worth. Because publicly owned companies must disclose the number of shares owned by officers, directors, and major stockholders, it is easy enough for anyone to multiply shares held by price per share to estimate the net worth of an insider.

3. **Self-dealings.** The owners-managers of closely held companies have many opportunities for various types of questionable but legal self-dealings, including the payment of high salaries, nepotism, personal transactions with the business (such as leasing arrangements), excellent retirement programs, and not-truly-necessary fringe benefits. Such self-dealings are much harder to arrange if a company is publicly owned — they must be disclosed, and the managers are also subject to stockholder suits.

4. **Inactive market/low price.** If a firm is very small, and if its shares are not traded with much frequency, then its stock will not really be liquid, and the market price may not be representative of the stock's true value. Security analysts and stockbrokers simply will not follow the stock because

there will not be sufficient trading activity to generate enough sales commissions to cover the analysts' or brokers' costs of keeping up with it.

5. **Control.** Because of the dramatic increase in tender offers and proxy fights in the 1980s, the managers of publicly owned firms who do not have at least 50 percent of the stock must be concerned about maintaining control. Further, there is pressure on such managers to produce annual earnings gains, even when it would be in the shareholders' best long-term interests to adopt a strategy that might penalize short-run earnings but lead to higher earnings in future years. These factors have led a number of public companies to "go private" in leveraged buyout (LBO) deals in which the managers and some related investors borrow the money to buy out the public stockholders. The RJR Nabisco deal, the largest LBO on record at about $25 billion, is an example.

Conclusions on Going Public

It should be obvious from this discussion that there are no hard and fast rules about whether a company should go public, or when it should do so. This is an individual decision that should be made on the basis of the company's and its stockholders' own unique circumstances.

If a company does decide to go public, either by the sale of newly issued stock to raise new capital for the corporation or by the sale of stock by the current owners, setting the price at which shares will be offered to the public is a key issue. The company and its current owners want to set the price as high as possible—the higher the offering price, the smaller the fraction of the company the current owners will have to give up to obtain any specified amount of money. On the other hand, potential buyers will want to buy the stock at as low a price as possible. We will return to the establishment of the offering price later in the chapter, after we have described some other aspects of common stock financing.

The Decision to List the Stock

The decision to go public, as discussed previously, is a truly significant milestone in a company's life; it marks a major transition in the relationship between the firm and its owners. The decision to *list,* on the other hand, is not a major event. The company will have to file a few new reports with an exchange, it will have to abide by the rules of the exchange, and the stock's price will be quoted in the newspaper under a stock exchange rather than in the over-the-counter section. These are not very important differences.

In order to have its stock listed, a company must apply to an exchange, pay a relatively small fee, and meet the exchange's minimum requirements. These requirements relate to the size of the company's net income as well as to the number of shares outstanding and in the hands of outsiders (as opposed to the number held by insiders, who generally do not trade their stock very actively). The company also must agree to disclose certain information to the exchange; this information is designed to help the exchange track trading patterns and thus try to prevent manipulation of the stock's price.[8] The size qualifications increase as one moves from the regional exchanges to the AMEX and on to the NYSE.

Assuming that a company qualifies, many people believe that listing is beneficial both to it and to its stockholders. Listed companies receive a certain amount of free advertising and publicity, and their status as a listed company enhances their prestige and reputation. This may have a beneficial effect on the sales of the firm's products, and it is probably advantageous in terms of lowering the required rate of return on its common stock. Investors respond favorably to increased information, increased liquidity, and confidence that the quoted price is not being manipulated. By providing investors with these benefits in the form of listing their companies' stock, financial managers may lower their firms' costs of capital and increase the value of their stocks.

Regulation of Securities Markets

Securities and Exchange Commission (SEC)

The U.S. government agency that regulates the issuance and trading of stocks and bonds.

registration statement

A statement of facts filed with the SEC about a company which plans to issue securities.

prospectus

A document describing a new security issue and the issuing company.

red herring prospectus

A preliminary prospectus distributed to potential buyers of a new security issue prior to approval of the registration statement by the SEC.

Sales of new securities, as well as operations in the secondary markets, are regulated by the **Securities and Exchange Commission (SEC)** and, to a lesser extent, by each of the 50 states. The following are the primary elements of SEC regulation.

1. The SEC has jurisdiction over all interstate offerings of new securities to the public in amounts of $1.5 million or more.

2. Newly issued securities must be registered with the SEC at least 20 days before they are publicly offered. The **registration statement** provides financial, legal, and technical information about the company. A **prospectus** summarizes this information for use in selling the securities. SEC lawyers and accountants analyze both the registration statement and the prospectus; if the information is inadequate or misleading, the SEC will delay or stop the public offering.

3. After the registration has become effective, new securities may be offered, but any sales solicitation must be accompanied by the prospectus. Preliminary, or **red herring, prospectuses** may be distributed to potential buyers during the 20-day waiting period, but no sales may be finalized during this time. The red herring prospectus contains all the key information that will appear in the final prospectus except the price.

4. If the registration statement or prospectus contains misrepresentations or omissions of material facts, any purchaser who suffers a loss may sue for damages. Severe penalties may be imposed on the issuer or its officers, di-

---

[8]It is illegal for anyone to attempt to manipulate the price of a stock. Prior to the creation of the SEC in the 1930s, syndicates would buy and sell stock back and forth at rigged prices for the purpose of deceiving the public into thinking that a particular stock was worth more or less than its true value. The exchanges, with the encouragement and support of the SEC, utilize sophisticated computer programs to help spot any irregularities that suggest manipulation. They can identify the exact day and time of each trade, and the broker who executed it, and they can require the broker to disclose the name of the person for whom the trade was made. Such a system can obviously help identify manipulators. This same system also helps to identify illegal insider trading, as discussed in the next section.

rectors, accountants, engineers, appraisers, underwriters, and all others who participated in the preparation of the registration statement or prospectus.

5. The SEC also regulates all national securities exchanges, and companies whose securities are listed on an exchange must file annual reports similar to the registration statement with both the SEC and the exchange.

insiders

Officers, directors, major stockholders, or others who may have inside information on a company's operations.

6. The SEC has control over stock trades by corporate **insiders.** Officers, directors, and major stockholders must file monthly reports of changes in their holdings of the corporation's stock. Any short-term profits from such transactions must be handed over to the corporation.

7. The SEC has the power to prohibit manipulation by such devices as pools (aggregations of funds used to affect prices artificially) or wash sales (sales between members of the same group to record artificial transaction prices).

8. The SEC has control over the form of the proxy and the way the company uses it to solicit votes.

margin requirements

The percentage of a security's purchase price that must be deposited by investors.

margin call

Call from a broker asking for more money to support a stock purchase loan.

Control over the flow of credit into securities transactions is exercised by the Board of Governors of the Federal Reserve System. The Fed exercises this control through **margin requirements,** which represent the percentage of the purchase price that must be deposited (invested) by investors—the percentage that can be borrowed is equal to 100 percent less the margin requirement set by the Fed. If a great deal of margin borrowing has been going on, a decline in stock prices can result in inadequate loan coverages, which would force stock brokers to issue **margin calls,** which in turn would require investors either to put up more money or to have their margined stock sold to pay off their loans. Such forced sales would further depress the stock market and could set off a downward spiral. The margin requirement is currently 50 percent.

States also have some control over the issuance of new securities within their boundaries. This control is usually exercised by a "corporation commissioner" or someone with a similar title. State laws relating to securities sales are called **blue sky laws,** because they were put into effect to keep unscrupulous promoters from selling securities that offered the "blue sky" but which actually had little or no asset backing.

blue sky laws

State laws that prevent the sale of securities having little or no asset backing.

The securities industry itself realizes the importance of stable markets, sound brokerage firms, and no perception of stock manipulation. Therefore, the various exchanges work closely with the SEC to police transactions on the exchanges and to maintain the integrity and credibility of the system. Similarly, the **National Association of Securities Dealers (NASD)** cooperates with the SEC to police trading in the OTC market. These industry groups also cooperate with regulatory authorities to set net worth and other standards for securities firms, to develop insurance programs to protect the customers of brokerage houses, and the like.

National Association of Securities Dealers (NASD)

An organization of securities dealers that works with the SEC to regulate operations in the over-the-counter market.

In general, government regulation of securities trading, as well as industry self-regulation, is designed to insure that investors receive information that is as accurate as possible, that no one artificially manipulates the market price of a given stock, and that corporate insiders do not take advantage of their position to profit in their companies' stocks at the expense of other stockholders. Nei-

INDUSTRY PRACTICE   SCOR Aids Small Firms in Going Public

SCOR, an acronym for Small Company Offering Registration, is a legal procedure which can help small businesses obtain funds in the stock market. SCOR, also known as ULOR (Uniform Limited Offering Registration), was created in the late 1980s by securities attorneys and government regulators and makes it easier and cheaper for small companies to sell stock.

With a SCOR, a company can raise a maximum of $1 million from each offering, and each share must be sold for at least $5.00 per share. Therefore, a maximum of 200,000 shares may be offered at one time. These rules were devised to make the stock less attractive to stock scam artists, who find it more difficult to manipulate a $5 stock than a 5¢ stock. SCOR permits multiple-state stock offerings with minimal notification to the SEC, and there is a standardized disclosure form.

Nobody knows the total number of companies nationwide that have used a SCOR, but they are gaining acceptance. The Pacific Stock Exchange has even asked the SEC to permit it to list smaller companies that go public though SCOR, as more and more companies are using SCOR. Thus far, 21 states have adopted the process—double the number of states that had adopted it only two years earlier. One drawback of SCOR is the absence of an active aftermarket to help maintain prices for SCOR securities, but a Pacific Exchange listing might help relieve that problem.

To understand its usefulness, consider the situation at Spokane Pres-To-Log, a company that for 40 years had converted waste wood to logs. The company had been acquired by an investment group three years earlier, and it needed capital to expand. Banks were not interested (the company needed equity, not debt) and venture capitalists wanted too big a stake in the company. Therefore, Pres-To-Log is using a $1 million SCOR offering in three states—Washington, Idaho, and Montana—to obtain the capital it needs to expand. If Pres-To-Log sells all 200,000 shares at $5 a share, or $1 million total, the offering will cost $130,000—half of what it would have cost in a traditional offering. Most of Pres-To-Log's SCOR costs will come from using a broker to market its new shares.

The SCOR process could be a tremendous benefit to small companies, especially in these times of tight credit and economic doldrums. Small businesses need to tap into the equity markets, and the time is ripe. Stock prices are high, and with interest rates cyclically low, investors are turning to the stock market to obtain higher returns. SEC Chairman Richard Breeden has said that his top priority for 1992 is to provide small firms with greater access to the capital markets. Proponents of the SCOR procedure believe it will eventually be a major element in United States capital formation.

Source: "SCOR Funding Provides Short Form for Going Public," *The Wall Street Journal*, January 21, 1992.

---

ther the SEC, the state regulators, nor the industry itself can prevent investors from making foolish decisions or from having bad luck, but regulators can and do help investors obtain the best data possible for making sound investment decisions.

 ## Self-Test Questions

Differentiate between a closely held corporation and a publicly owned corporation.

Differentiate between a listed stock and an unlisted stock.

Differentiate between the primary and secondary markets.

What are the major advantages and disadvantages of going public?

Which is more important, the decision to list or the decision to go public? Why?

Differentiate between a registration statement, a prospectus, and a red herring prospectus.

What is the primary purpose of regulating securities trading, whether it is imposed by law or self-imposed?

THE INVESTMENT BANKING PROCESS

The role of investment bankers was discussed in general terms in Chapter 3, where we learned (1) that investment banking is quite different from commercial banking, (2) that the major investment banking houses are often divisions of large financial service corporations engaged in a wide range of activities, and (3) that investment bankers help firms issue new securities in the primary markets and also operate as brokers in the secondary markets. Sears is one of the largest financial services corporations; in addition to its insurance and credit card operations, it owns a large brokerage house and a major investment banking house. Similarly, Merrill Lynch has a brokerage department which operates thousands of offices, as well as an investment banking department which helps companies issue securities, take over other companies, and the like. Of course, Merrill Lynch's and Sears's brokers also sell securities that have been issued through their investment banking departments. In this section we describe how securities are issued, and we explain the role of investment bankers in this process.

Raising Capital: Stage I Decisions

The firm itself makes some preliminary decisions on its own, including the following:

1. **Dollars to be raised.** How much new capital do we need?

2. **Type of securities used.** Should stock, bonds, or a combination be used? Further, if stock is to be issued, should it be offered to existing stockholders or sold directly to the general public? (See Chapters 20 and 21 for a detailed discussion of different types of securities.)

3. **Competitive bid versus negotiated deal.** Should the company simply offer a block of its securities for sale to the highest bidder, or should it sit down with an investment banker and negotiate a deal? These two procedures are called *competitive bids* and *negotiated deals.* Only about 100 of the largest firms on the NYSE, whose securities are already well-known to the investment banking community, are in a position to use the competitive bid process. The investment banks would have to do a large amount of investigative work in order to bid on an issue unless they were already quite familiar with the firm, and the costs involved would be too high to make it worthwhile unless the investment bank was sure of getting the deal. Therefore, the vast majority of offerings of stock or bonds are made on a negotiated basis.

4. **Selection of an investment banker.** Assuming the issue is to be negotiated, which investment banker should the firm use? Older firms that have

Table 19-3 ▪ **Top Ten Global Investment Bankers, 1991**

1. Merrill Lynch	6. Kidder Peabody
2. Goldman Sachs	7. Salomon Brothers
3. First Boston	8. Bear Sterns
4. Lehman Brothers	9. Nomura Securities
5. Morgan Stanley	10. Daiwa Securities

Note: Rankings are based on the dollar volume of underwritings by global firms managed during 1991.

Source: *The Wall Street Journal,* January 2, 1992.

"been to market" before will have already established a relationship with an investment banker, although it is easy enough to change bankers if the firm is dissatisfied. However, a firm that is just going public will have to choose an investment bank, and different investment banking houses are better suited for different companies. The older, larger "establishment houses" like Morgan Stanley deal mainly with large companies like AT&T, IBM, and Exxon. Other bankers handle more speculative issues. There are some houses that specialize in new issues and others that are not well suited to handle new issues because their brokerage clients are relatively conservative. (Because the investment banking firms sell the issues largely to their own regular investment customers, the nature of these customers has a major effect on the house's ability to do a good job for a corporate security issuer.) Table 19-3 lists in ranked order the top ten global investment bankers in 1991, as measured by the dollar amount of securities underwritten.

Raising Capital: Stage II Decisions

Stage II decisions, which are made jointly by the firm and its selected investment banker, include the following:

1. **Reevaluating the initial decisions.** The firm and its investment banker will reevaluate the initial decisions about the size of the issue and the type of securities to use. For example, the firm may have initially decided to raise $50 million by selling common stock, but the investment banker may convince management that it would be better off, in view of current market conditions, to limit the stock issue to $25 million and to raise the other $25 million as debt.

2. **Best efforts or underwritten issues.** The firm and its investment banker must decide whether the investment banker will work on a best efforts basis or underwrite the issue. In a **best efforts arrangement,** the investment banker does not guarantee that the securities will be sold or that the company will get the cash it needs. In an **underwritten arrangement,** the company does get a guarantee, so the investment banker bears significant risks in such an offering. For example, the very day IBM signed an underwritten agreement to sell $1 billion of bonds in 1979, interest rates rose sharply, and bond prices fell. IBM's investment bankers lost somewhere between $10 million and $20 million. Had the offering been on a

best efforts arrangement
Agreement for the sale of securities in which the investment bank handling the transaction gives no guarantee that the securities will be sold.

underwritten arrangement
Agreement for the sale of securities in which the investment bank guarantees the sale of the securities, thus agreeing to bear any risks involved in the transaction.

best efforts basis, IBM would have been the loser. This well-known instance of risk-bearing by investment bankers is described in more detail later in the chapter.

3. **Issuance costs.** The investment banker's fee must be negotiated, and the firm also must estimate the other expenses it will incur in connection with the issue—lawyers' fees, accountants' costs, printing and engraving, and so on. Usually, the investment banker will buy the issue from the company at a discount below the price at which the securities are to be offered to the public, and this spread covers the banker's costs and provides a profit.

flotation costs

The costs of issuing new stocks or bonds.

Table 19-4 gives an indication of the **flotation costs** associated with public issues of bonds, preferred stock, and common stock. As the table shows, costs as a percentage of the proceeds are higher for stocks than for bonds, and costs are also higher for small issues than for large issues. The relationship between size of issue and flotation costs is primarily due to the existence of fixed costs: certain costs must be incurred regardless of the size of the issue, so the percentage flotation cost is quite high for small issues.

When relatively small companies go public to raise new capital, the investment bankers frequently take part of their compensation in the form of options to buy stock in the firm. For example, when Data Technologies went public with a $10 million issue in 1992 by selling 1 million shares at a price of $10 per share, its investment bankers bought the stock from the company at a price of $9.75, so the direct underwriting fee was only $1,000,000($10.00 − $9.75) = $250,000$, or 2.5 percent. However, the investment bankers also received a 5-year option to buy 200,000 shares at a price of $10, so if the stock goes up to $15, which the investment bankers expect it to do, they will make a $1 million profit on top of the $250,000 underwriting fee.

4. **Setting the offering price.** If the company is already publicly owned, the **offering price** will be based on the existing market price of the stock or the yield on the bonds. For common stock, the most typical arrangement calls for the investment banker to buy the securities at a prescribed number of points below the closing price on the last day of registration. For example, on July 1, 1992, the stock of Allied Food Products had a current price of $23.00, and it had traded between $20 and $25 a share during the previous three months. Allied and its underwriter agreed that the investment banker would buy 10 million new shares at $1 below the closing price on the last day of registration, which was expected to be in early October. The stock actually closed at $20.50 on the day the SEC released the issue, so the company received $19.50 a share. The shares were then sold to the public at a price of $20.50. As is typical, Allied's agreement had an escape clause that provided for the contract to be voided if the price of the stock had fallen below a predetermined figure. In the illustrative case, this "upset" price was set at $18.50 a share. Thus, if the closing price of the shares on the last day of registration had been $18, Allied would have had the option of withdrawing from the agreement.

offering price

The price at which common stock is sold to the public.

Investment bankers have an easier job if an issue is priced relatively low, but the issuer of the securities naturally wants as high a price as possible. There-

Table 19-4 ▪ **Costs of Flotation for Underwritten, Nonrights Offerings (Expressed as a Percentage of Gross Proceeds)**

Size of Issue (Millions of Dollars)	Bonds			Preferred Stock			Common Stock		
	Underwriting Commission	Other Expenses	Total Costs	Underwriting Commission	Other Expenses	Total Costs	Underwriting Commission	Other Expenses	Total Costs
Under 1.0	10.0%	4.0%	14.0%	—	—	—	13.0%	9.0%	22.0%
1.0–1.9	8.0	3.0	11.0	—	—	—	11.0	5.9	16.9
2.0–4.9	4.0	2.2	6.2	—	—	—	8.6	3.8	12.4
5.0–9.9	2.4	0.8	3.2	1.9%	0.7%	2.6%	6.3	1.9	8.2
10.0–19.9	1.2	0.7	1.9	1.4	0.4	1.8	5.1	0.9	6.0
20.0–49.9	1.0	0.4	1.4	1.4	0.3	1.7	4.1	0.5	4.6
50.0 and over	0.9	0.2	1.1	1.4	0.2	1.6	3.3	0.2	3.5

Notes:

1. Small issues of preferred are rare, so no data on preferred issues below $5 million are given.

2. Flotation costs tend to rise somewhat when interest rates are cyclically high, because when money is in relatively tight supply, the investment bankers will have a more difficult time placing issues with permanent investors. Thus, the figures shown in the table represent averages, and actual flotation costs vary somewhat over time.

Sources: Securities and Exchange Commission, *Cost of Flotation of Registered Equity Issues* (Washington, D.C.: U.S. Government Printing Office, December 1974); Richard H. Pettway, "A Note on the Flotation Costs of New Equity Capital Issues of Electric Companies," *Public Utilities Fortnightly,* March 18, 1982; Robert Hansen, "Evaluating the Costs of a New Equity Issue," *Midland Corporate Finance Journal,* Spring 1986; and informal surveys of common stock, preferred stock, and bond issues conducted by the authors.

fore, an inherent conflict of interest on price exists between the investment banker and the issuer. However, if the issuer is financially sophisticated and makes comparisons with similar security issues, the investment banker will be forced to price close to the market.

As we discussed in Chapters 17 and 18, the announcement of a new stock offering by a mature firm is generally taken as a negative signal. If the firm's prospects were very good, management would not want to issue new stock and thus share the rosy future with new stockholders. Because the announcement of a new stock offering is generally taken as bad news, the price will probably fall when the announcement is made; therefore, the offering price will probably have to be set at a price well below the preoffering market price. Consider Figure 19-1, in which d_0 is the estimated market demand curve for Allied's stock and S_0 is the number of shares currently outstanding. Initially, there are 50 million shares outstanding, and the initial equilibrium price of the stock is $23.00. As we saw in Chapter 6, the equilibrium price of a constant-growth stock is found in accordance with the following equation:

$$P_0 = \hat{P}_0 = \frac{D_1}{k_s - g}$$

$$= \frac{\$1.242}{0.134 - 0.08}$$

$$= \$23.00.$$

Figure 19-1   ▪   **Estimated Demand Curves for Allied Food Products' Common Stock**

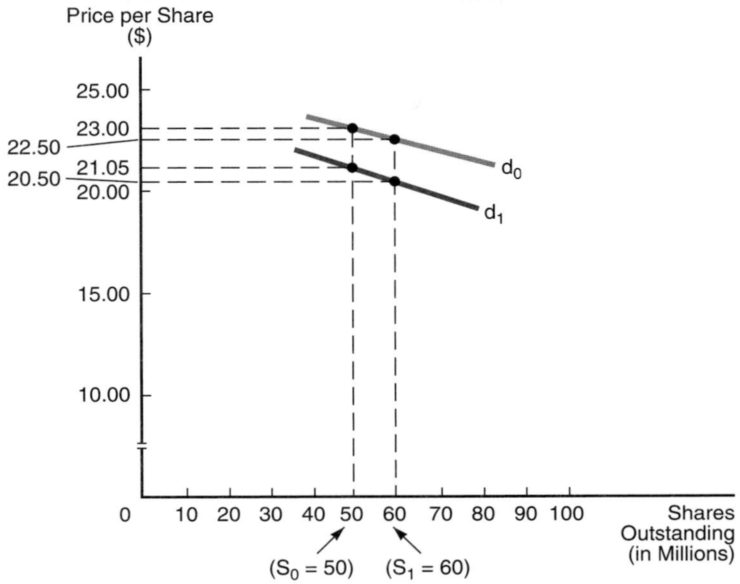

The values shown for D_1, k_s, and g are *estimates made by the marginal stockholder.* Some stockholders doubtlessly regard Allied as being less risky than others and hence assign it a lower value for k_s. Similarly, some stockholders have a higher estimate of the company's growth rate than others, so they will use g > 8 percent when calculating the stock's intrinsic value. Thus, there are some investors who think Allied's stock is worth more than $23.00 and others who think it is worth less, but the **marginal investor** thinks the stock is worth $23.00. Accordingly, this is its current price.

When Allied announces that it plans to sell another 10 million shares, this is taken as a negative signal, so k_s rises from 13.4 to 13.7 percent and the expected g declines from 8 to 7.8 percent. Consequently, the demand curve shifts from d_0 to d_1, and the price falls. The new equilibrium price, if 50 million shares were outstanding, would be $21.05:

marginal investor

A representative investor whose actions reflect the beliefs of those people who are currently trading a stock. It is the marginal investor who determines a stock's price.

$$P_1 = \frac{\$1.242}{0.137 - 0.078} = \$21.05.$$

However, if Allied is to sell another 10 million shares of stock, it will have to either attract some investors who are not willing to own the stock at the $21.05 price or else induce present stockholders to buy additional shares. There are two ways this can be accomplished: (1) by reducing the price of the stock or (2) by "promoting" the company and thus shifting the demand curve to the right.[9] If the demand curve does not shift at all from d_1, we see from Figure 19-1 that the only way the 10 million additional shares can be sold will be by setting the offering price at $20.50 per share. However, if the investment bankers can promote the stock sufficiently to shift the demand curve back to d_0, the offering price can be set at $22.50, which is close to the pre-announcement equilibrium price.[10]

The extent to which the demand curve can be shifted depends primarily on two factors: (1) what investors think the company can do with the money brought in by the stock sale and (2) how effectively the brokers promote the issue. If investors can be convinced that the new money will be invested in highly profitable projects that will substantially raise earnings and the earnings growth rate, then the demand curve may be shifted back to or even to the right of the original curve, d_0, so the stock price might even go above the initial price of $23.00. Even if investors do not radically change their expectations about the company's fundamental factors, the fact that thousands of stockbrokers telephone their clients with suggestions that they consider purchasing Allied's stock might shift the demand curve. The extent to which this promotional campaign succeeds in shifting the demand curve depends, of course, on the effectiveness of the investment banking firm. Therefore, Allied's financial manager's perceptions about the effectiveness of different investment bankers will be an important factor in its choice of an underwriter.

One final point should be made: *If pressure from the new shares drives down the price of the stock, all shares outstanding, not just the new shares, will be affected.* Thus, if Allied's stock fell from $23.00 to $20.50 as a result of the financing, and if the price remained at that new level, the company would incur a loss of $2.50 on each of the 50 million shares previously outstanding, or a total market value loss of $125 million. In a sense, that loss would be a *flotation cost* because it would be a cost associated with the new issue. However, if the company's prospects really were poorer than investors had thought, then most of the price decline would have occurred sooner or later anyway. On the other hand, if the company's prospects are not really all that bad (if the signal was incorrect), then over time Allied's demand curve would move back to d_0, or even to the right of d_0, and in that case the company would not suffer a permanent loss of $125 million.

---

[9]It should be noted that investors can buy newly issued stock without paying normal brokerage commissions, and brokers are careful to point this out to potential purchasers. Thus, if an investor were to buy Allied's stock at $23.00 in the regular market, the commission would be about 1 percent, or 23 cents per share. If the stock were purchased in an underwriting, this commission would be avoided.

For years many academicians argued that the demand curve for a firm's stock is either horizontal or has only a slight downward slope and that signaling effects are minimal. Most corporate treasurers, on the other hand, think that both effects exist for mature companies, and recent empirical studies have confirmed the treasurers' position. One such study is Andrei Shleifer, "Do Demand Curves for Stocks Slope Down?" *Journal of Finance,* July 1986, 579–590.

[10]The supply curve is a vertical line, first at 50 million shares and then, after the new issue, at 60 million.

If the company is going public for the first time, it will have no established price (or demand curve), so the investment bankers will have to estimate the *equilibrium price* at which the stock will sell after issue. Both the "Small Business" section and Problem 19-2 at the end of this chapter illustrate in some detail the process involved. If the offering price is set below the true equilibrium price, the stock will rise sharply after issue, and the company and its original stockholders will have given away too many shares to raise the required capital. If the offering price is set above the true equilibrium price, either the issue will fail or, if the bankers succeed in selling the stock, their investment clients will be unhappy when the stock subsequently falls to its equilibrium level. Therefore, it is important that the equilibrium price be approximated as closely as possible.

Selling Procedures

Once the company and its investment bankers have decided how much money to raise, the type of securities to issue, and the basis for pricing the issue, they will prepare and file a registration statement and prospectus with the SEC, as described earlier in the chapter. It generally takes about 20 days for the issue to be approved by the SEC. The final price of the stock (or the interest rate on a bond issue) is set at the close of business the day the issue clears the SEC, and the securities are then offered to the public the following day.

Investors are not required to pay for the stock until ten days after they place their buy orders, but the investment bankers must pay the issuing firm within four days of the time the offering officially begins. Typically, the investment bankers sell the stock within a day or two after the offering begins, but on occasion they miscalculate, set the offering price too high, and are unable to move the issue. Similarly, the market might decline during the offering period, which again would force the investment bankers to reduce the price of the stock. In either instance, on an underwritten offering the firm would still receive the price that was agreed upon, and the investment bankers would have to absorb any losses that were incurred.

underwriting syndicate

A syndicate of investment firms formed to spread the risk associated with the purchase and distribution of a new issue of securities.

lead, or **managing, underwriter**

The member of an underwriting syndicate that actually manages a new security offering.

selling group

A group of brokerage firms formed for the purpose of distributing a new issue of securities.

Because they are exposed to large potential losses, investment bankers typically do not handle the purchase and distribution of an issue singlehandedly unless it is a very small one. If the amount of money involved is large and the risk of price fluctuations substantial, investment bankers form an **underwriting syndicate** in an effort to minimize the amount of risk each one carries. The investment banking house which sets up the deal is called the **lead,** or **managing, underwriter.**

In addition to the underwriting syndicate, on larger offerings still more investment bankers are included in a **selling group,** which handles the distribution of securities to individual investors. The selling group includes all members of the underwriting syndicate plus additional dealers who take relatively small participations (or shares of the total issue) from the syndicate members. Thus, the underwriters act as *wholesalers,* whereas members of the selling group act as *retailers.* The number of houses in a selling group depends partly on the size of the issue; for example, the one set up when Communications Satellite Corporation (Comsat) went public consisted of 385 members.

Shelf Registrations

The selling procedures described previously, including the 20-day minimum waiting period between registration with the SEC and sale of the issue, apply to most security sales. However, large, well-known public companies which issue securities frequently may file a *master registration statement* with the SEC and then update it with a *short-form statement* just prior to each individual offering. In such a case, a company could decide at 10 A.M. to sell registered securities and have the sale completed before noon. This procedure is known as **shelf registration** because in effect the company puts its new securities "on the shelf" and then sells them to investors when it thinks the market is right.

shelf registration

A procedure under which a large, well-established firm can sell new securities on very short notice.

Maintenance of the Secondary Market

In the case of a large, established firm like Allied Food Products, the investment banking firm's job is finished once it has disposed of the stock and turned the net proceeds over to the company. However, in the case of a company going public for the first time, the investment banker is under an obligation to maintain a market for the shares after the issue has been completed. Such stocks are typically traded in the over-the-counter market, and the lead underwriter generally agrees to "make a market" in the stock and to keep it reasonably liquid. The company wants a good market to exist for its stock, as do its stockholders. Therefore, if the investment banking house wants to do business with the company in the future, to keep its own brokerage customers happy, and to have future referral business, it will hold an inventory of the shares and help to maintain an active secondary market in the stock.

? Self-Test Questions

What is the sequence of events when a firm decides to issue new securities?

What type of firm would use a shelf registration? Explain.

What is an underwriting syndicate, and why is it important in the investment banking process?

IBM'S INITIAL DEBT OFFERING

IBM's first public debt offering provides an interesting case study of investment banking.[11] The offering, at the time the largest in U.S. corporate history, consisted of $500 million in 7-year notes and $500 million in 25-year debentures (unsecured long-term debt) for a total of $1 billion. IBM's customary investment banker had been Morgan Stanley & Co. However, for this offering IBM requested separate underwriting proposals from Morgan Stanley and from Salomon Brothers, another major investment banking house; these proposals were presented in September 1979. IBM's financial staff was of the opinion that two

---

[11]This summary is based on contemporary accounts in the financial press and in the article by Walter Guzzardi, Jr., "The Bomb IBM Dropped on Wall Street," *Fortune,* November 19, 1979, 52–56.

managers would provide better execution of the sale and would back it up with a larger amount of capital. John H. Gutfreund, Salomon Brothers' managing partner, is quoted as stating, "A major corporation is best served by two sets of eyes and ears." Robert H. B. Baldwin, president of Morgan Stanley, is said to have responded, "You need only one brain surgeon." Morgan Stanley dropped out, refusing to participate if it could not be sole manager, and Salomon Brothers and Merrill Lynch became co-managers, with an underwriting group totaling 227 members.

During the month of September, the prime rate was increased five times, reaching a level of 13.5 percent on September 28. A "pricing meeting" took place on Wednesday, October 3, 1979. At the time, yields were rising rapidly in the money markets. It was agreed that IBM's 7-year notes would be priced to yield 7 basis points more than Treasury notes and that the 25-year debentures would be priced to yield 12 basis points more than Treasury bonds.[12] This meant that IBM would have to pay 9.62 percent for the 7-year notes and 9.41 percent for the 25-year debentures. The underwriting spread, or commission, was set at $\frac{5}{8}$ of 1 percent, or $6.25, per note and $\frac{7}{8}$ of 1 percent, or $8.75, per debenture. Since there were $500,000,000/$1,000 = 500,000 notes and an equal number of debentures, the total underwriting fees were ($6.25)(500,000) + ($8.75)(500,000) = $7,500,000.

Only hours after the meeting in which the securities' yields and prices were fixed, and the contracts signed, the market yield for Treasury bonds moved up by 5 basis points. The IBM offering began the next day, Thursday, October 4. On that same day, the Treasury auctioned $2.5 billion of 4-year notes yielding 9.79 percent, which was well above the 9.62 percent on the IBM 7-year notes. Naturally, the IBM securities did not sell at all well.

On Saturday, October 6, the Federal Reserve System announced an increase in its discount rate from 11 percent to 12 percent in an effort to combat the high rate of inflation that was developing. At the same time, a number of other credit-tightening policies, which Wall Street experts called "draconian" in their severity, were implemented. As a result of the Fed's weekend actions, on Tuesday, October 9, the New York banks announced a full percentage point increase in the prime rate, to 14.5 percent. The next morning, the underwriting syndicate was disbanded, and the prices of both the notes and the debentures fell by about $50 each, with yields rising to 10.65 percent on the notes and to 10.09 percent on the debentures.

When the syndicate was disbanded, it was estimated that only $650 million of the $1 billion issue had been sold, earning syndicate members less than $5 million in underwriting fees. The remaining $350 million portion of the issue was sold after prices had fallen, and the investment bankers took an estimated loss of between $10 and $20 million. To put it mildly, the underwriters "took a bath."

A controversy arose over whether the IBM issue was priced "too tight." During the entire month preceding the offering, the prime rate and the discount rate had both been increasing, and the financial markets were hectic, if not

---

[12]One basis point is equal to one-hundredth of 1 percent. Therefore, IBM's notes were priced to yield 0.07 percent more than Treasury notes of the same maturity.

chaotic. Undoubtedly, the severe measures taken by the Federal Reserve System on Saturday, October 6, 1979, were being anticipated. Whether the underwriters should have given themselves more of a cushion to avoid the subsequent price decline is a matter of judgment. Differences in judgment are natural, and differences are what make markets.

The IBM offering illustrates a number of basic characteristics of investment banking. First, the risks are real. Second, competition among investment bankers for deals is vigorous and tough. Third, an offering by a well-managed, financially strong firm which is taking on debt in moderate quantity in relation to its total assets will be rated high and priced close to Treasury issues. Fourth, turbulence in the financial markets during the period immediately preceding an offering makes the task of the underwriters extremely difficult, and both a willingness to take risks and good judgment are required when making decisions in an extremely volatile financial environment. In sum, the episode illustrates the high drama, the considerable financial sophistication, and the continued great challenges that exist in the field of financial decision making.[13]

Self-Test Question

Identify some basic characteristics of investment banking as illustrated through the IBM offering.

EMERGING TRENDS

The Depository Institutions Deregulation and Monetary Control Act of 1980 had the desirable effect of increasing competition among financial institutions, which benefitted both savers and borrowers, and it also slowed the decline of U.S. banks in the world markets. However, the act had several serious shortcomings, and at the time this text is being written (spring 1992), Congress and the Bush administration are nearing agreement on some important changes in the law. Here is a summary:

1. In the 1980 act, Congress was right to deregulate institutions and free them to make loans and investments in markets beyond their traditional ones. However, Congress was misguided in permitting the S&Ls to invest insured deposits in risky ventures. This encouraged S&L managers to make wildly speculative loans which, if they worked out, would make the S&L owners rich but, if they did not, would leave the federal insurance program with huge losses. The situation was a bit like inviting someone to

---

[13]To close out the story, at least some of the underwriters had hedged their IBM positions in the futures market, so they were protected against rising interest rates. Salomon Brothers, the lead underwriter, was at the time aggressively (and successfully) seeking to expand its operations, and that required taking some chances. Salomon's overall strategy has certainly worked well, even if this one issue did not, for in 1991 Salomon was one of the top ten global investment bankers.

play poker with your money, where the player gets to keep the winnings but you have to absorb the losses. The S&L bailout, for which taxpayers will be paying for many years, is a direct result of this aspect of the 1980 act. Therefore, one feature of the legislation will be to correct this problem. Financial institutions will be allowed to compete in a wide spectrum of markets, but new restrictions will be imposed on the use of capital raised as insured deposits.

2. Currently banks are not allowed to branch beyond state lines except under highly restricted conditions. This limits the size and scope of U.S. banks vis-à-vis their global competitors, and it also impedes the free flow of capital within the United States. The new legislation will probably give banks and other financial institutions nationwide branching powers, which will lead to much larger, national banks.

3. Because of abuses, commercial and investment banking were separated by Congress in the 1930s, so U.S. banks have been prohibited from underwriting securities and participating in equity market activities. Banks in Japan and Europe have far greater powers, and this has helped them surpass U.S. banks in size and profitability. U.S. banks will probably be given permission to engage in underwriting activities, but these new powers will only be given to the strongest, best capitalized banks, and banks will not be able to use insured deposits to fund these activities.

4. Since expanded lending and other powers will be granted only to the strongest banks, this will encourage the banking system to raise additional equity capital.

5. The most controversial aspect of the legislation under discussion is a Bush administration proposal that would permit industrial companies to own banks and insurance companies, and vice versa. Many in Congress are opposed to this proposal on the grounds that it might lead to another costly bailout, but proponents argue that Japanese and European financial institutions are affiliated with industrial companies and that if U.S. institutions are to compete effectively in world markets, then they need the same powers.

It is unclear how the final legislation will shape up, but it is likely that U.S. banks will gain new powers to engage in security underwritings and that branching powers will be extended. However, only the strongest banks will be given these expanded powers. The result is likely to be a system of larger, stronger, and more diversified banks, yet more competition will probably exist in our financial markets.

Self-Test Question

What are some important new developments that are taking place in the financial markets?

SMALL BUSINESS   Why Go Public for Less Than You're Worth?

For many entrepreneurs, making an initial public offering (IPO) of their company's equity is a dream come true. After their years of sacrifice and hard work, the company is finally a success. The value of that sacrifice is realized by going public. Many observers are amazed that the successful entrepreneur appears willing to sell equity in his or her firm for too little money—IPOs are "underpriced" on average.

Stocks are underpriced if they begin trading in the public markets at a price that is higher than the offering price. An example would be a stock that was sold in an IPO for $12.00 which begins trading immediately after the IPO for $15.00 per share. Some stocks have traded for as much as twice their IPO prices in the public market.

This underpricing is a puzzle. The company going public, and any current shareholders of the privately owned firm who are selling as part of the public offering, receive, on average, the IPO price minus a commission or "discount" of roughly 8 percent. Thus, shareholders selling for $12.00 per share in an IPO would typically receive about $11.00 per share. If the share price increases to $15.00 after the IPO, then the former shareholders (and the company) have received $4.00 per share less than their shares were worth. Even if the shareholders do not sell any of their own shares in the IPO, but instead sell only the company's shares, they are still hurt by underpricing because their ownership in the firm is diluted more than it would have been had the shares been fully priced.

Underpricing is especially severe during periods known as "hot issue periods" in the market. During such periods, the *average* issue sold in an IPO has increased in price by 25 percent to 50 percent immediately after issuance. In general, the definition of a hot issue period is one in which issue values increase sharply after the IPO in the public market.

The large returns of IPOs in the public market are not caused by the companies' performance after the IPOs. They do not mean that the firms showed high earnings growth after the IPOs—the higher returns generally occur on the *first trading day*. This simply means that the IPO securities were sold at a price below their value.

Why would issuers in IPOs (i.e., selling companies) willingly sell their stocks for less than their true value? There are a number of theories to explain underpricing, which are being tested by scholars, but there is no widespread consensus on the reasons for underpricing. Some possible explanations are described next.

One theory holds that issues are underpriced because the issuing companies' owners do not know everything that their underwriters know. The assumption is that there is an "information asymmetry" between issuers and underwriters, and that without this asymmetry, issues would be fully priced. This theory may explain some occurrences of underpricing, such as isolated instances in which an unethical underwriter (who presumably would not last long in the business) knowingly misinforms the issuer. However, some underwriters themselves have gone public, acting as their own underwriters, and they have also had substantial first-day returns.

A popular theory among academicians is that underpricing occurs to keep uninformed investors in the market. According to this theory, there are some well-informed investors who regularly watch the IPO market. They see new issues, and they can tell which ones are mispriced. They, therefore, buy only the underpriced issues and avoid all others. However, such informed investors do not have enough capital to buy all of the shares of any offering.

An uninformed investor may place an offer to buy some shares in every offering. This uninformed investor will get to buy a lot of stock in the overpriced or correctly priced offerings, but will obtain only a small portion of the offerings in which the informed investors are active. Unless the set of all offerings is underpriced on average, then uninformed investors would consistently lose money, they would leave the market, and the market would break down. Thus, this theory argues, the IPO market must experience general underpricing to function. Early empirical evidence is consistent with this theory. In particular, it shows that offerings about which there is great uncertainty will tend to be more underpriced, and that is observed in practice.

The most popular theory with underwriters and venture capitalists is what might be called the "good taste in the mouth" theory. According to this theory, if the company underprices its issue in an IPO, investors will be more receptive to future "seasoned" issues from the same firm. Note, too, that most IPOs involve only 10 to 20 percent of the stock, so the original owners still have 80 to 90 percent of the shares.

All of these theories have a similar implication: An IPO with less uncertainty concerning its value will tend to be more fully priced. This suggests some ways that firms can prepare themselves for public offerings at higher prices. For example, offerings through more prestigious underwriters are, on average, less underpriced than offerings through less reputable underwriters. Issuers that use reputable, visible accountants for their audits are also less underpriced than those with less reputable accountants, and firms that received venture capital investment from more reputable capitalists are less underpriced. In fact, even the successful application for a bank loan that is revealed in the offering prospectus is associated with less underpricing. Firms with a longer financial history and which have achieved a higher level of sales also appear to be able to obtain a better price for their shares.

The phenomenon of underpricing IPO shares remains a puzzle to finance academicians. We think we have some of the answers, but the questions are not yet settled. Meanwhile, an issuer should be aware that most IPOs are underpriced by a meaningful amount and that this underpricing is almost certainly related to the risk and uncertainty of the business. This is important information to consider when deciding when the firm should make its initial public offering.

SUMMARY

This chapter is more descriptive than analytical, but a knowledge of the issues discussed here is essential to an understanding of finance. The key concepts covered are listed below.

- **Stockholders' equity** consists of the firm's common stock, paid-in capital (funds received in excess of the par value), and retained earnings (earnings not paid out as dividends).

- **Book value per share** is equal to stockholders' equity divided by the number of shares of stock outstanding. A stock's book value is often different from its par value and its market value.

- A **proxy** is a document which gives one person the power to act for another person, typically the power to vote shares of common stock. A proxy fight occurs when an outside group solicits stockholders' proxies in order to vote a new management team into office.

- Stockholders often have the right to purchase any additional shares sold by the firm. This right, called the **preemptive right,** protects the control of the present stockholders and prevents dilution of the value of their stock.

- The major **advantages of common stock financing** are as follows: (1) there is no obligation to make fixed payments, (2) common stock never matures, (3) the use of common stock increases the creditworthiness of the firm, (4) stock can often be sold on better terms than debt, and (5) using stock helps the firm maintain its reserve borrowing capacity.

- The major **disadvantages of common stock financings** are (1) they extend voting privileges to new stockholders, (2) new stockholders share in the firm's profits, (3) the costs of stock financings are high, (4) using stock can raise the firm's cost of capital, and (5) dividends paid on common stock are not tax deductible.

- A **closely held corporation** is one that is owned by a few individuals who are typically associated with the firm's management.

▪ A **publicly owned corporation** is one that is owned by a relatively large number of individuals who are not actively involved in its management.

▪ **Going public** facilitates stockholder diversification, increases liquidity of the firm's stock, makes it easier for the firm to raise capital, and establishes a value for the firm. However, reporting costs are high, operating data must be disclosed, management self-dealings are harder to arrange, the price may sink to a low level if the stock is not traded actively, and public ownership may make it harder for management to maintain control of the firm.

▪ Security markets are regulated by the **Securities and Exchange Commission (SEC).**

▪ An **investment banker** assists in the issuing of securities by helping the firm determine the size of the issue and the type of securities to be used, by establishing the selling price, by selling the issue, and, in some cases, by maintaining an after-market for the stock.

▪ A *small firm's stock* sold in an **initial public offering (IPO)** often rises in price immediately after issue, with the largest price increases being associated with issues where uncertainties are greatest.

Questions

19-1 Examine Table 19-1. Suppose Allied Food Products sold 2 million shares, with the company netting $25 per share. Construct a statement of the equity accounts to reflect this sale.

19-2 Is it true that the flatter, or more nearly horizontal, the demand curve for a particular firm's stock, and the less important investors regard the signaling effect of the offering, the more important the role of investment bankers when the company sells a new issue of stock?

19-3 The SEC attempts to protect investors who are purchasing newly issued securities by requiring issuers to provide relevant financial information to prospective investors. However, the SEC does not provide an opinion about the real value of the securities; hence, an investor might pay too much for some stock and consequently lose heavily. Do you think the SEC should, as a part of every new stock or bond offering, render an opinion to investors on the proper value of the securities being offered? Explain.

19-4 How do you think each of the following items would affect a company's ability to attract new capital and the flotation costs involved in doing so?
a. A decision to list a company's stock; the stock now trades in the over-the-counter market.
b. A decision of a privately held company to go public.
c. The increasing importance of institutions in the stock and bond markets.
d. The trend toward financial conglomerates as opposed to stand-alone investment banking houses.
e. Elimination of the preemptive right.
f. The introduction of shelf registrations.

19-5 Before entering a formal agreement, investment bankers carefully investigate the companies whose securities they underwrite; this is especially true of the issues of firms going public for the first time. Since the bankers do not themselves plan to hold the securities but intend to sell them to others as soon as possible, why are they so concerned about making careful investigations?

19-6   It is frequently stated that the primary purpose of the preemptive right is to allow individuals to maintain their proportionate share of the ownership and control of a corporation.

   a. How important do you suppose this consideration is for the average stockholder of a firm whose shares are traded on the New York or American Stock Exchanges?

   b. Is the preemptive right likely to be of more importance to stockholders of publicly owned or closely held firms? Explain.

19-7   a. Is a firm likely to get a wider distribution of shares if it sells new stock through a preemptive rights offering to existing stockholders or directly to underwriters?

   b. Why would management be interested in getting a wider distribution of its shares?

Self-Test Problem

ST-1

Key terms

Define each of the following terms:

   a. Common equity; paid-in capital; retained earnings
   b. Par value; book value per share; market value per share
   c. Proxy; proxy fight; takeover
   d. Preemptive right
   e. Classified stock; founders' shares
   f. Reserve borrowing capacity
   g. Closely held corporation; publicly owned corporation
   h. Over-the-counter (OTC) market; organized security exchange
   i. Primary market; secondary market
   j. Going public; new issue market; initial public offering (IPO)
   k. Securities and Exchange Commission (SEC); registration statement; shelf registration; blue sky laws; margin requirements; margin call; insiders
   l. Prospectus; red herring prospectus
   m. National Association of Securities Dealers (NASD)
   n. Best efforts arrangement; underwritten arrangement
   o. Spread; flotation costs; offering price
   p. Marginal investor
   q. Underwriting syndicate; lead, or managing, underwriter; selling group

Problems

19-1

Profit (loss) on new stock issue

Security Brokers Inc. specializes in underwriting new issues by small firms. On a recent offering of Barenbaum Inc., the terms were as follows:

Price to public	$7.50 per share
Number of shares	3 million
Proceeds to Barenbaum	$21,000,000

The out-of-pocket expenses incurred by Security Brokers in the design and distribution of the issue were $450,000. What profit or loss would Security Brokers incur if the issue were sold to the public at an average price of

   a. $7.50 per share?
   b. $9.00 per share?
   c. $6.00 per share?

19-2

Setting the price of a new stock issue

U-Fix-It, a small home improvement building supplier, has been successful and has enjoyed a good growth trend. Now U-Fix-It is planning to go public with an issue of common stock, and it faces the problem of setting an appropriate price on the stock. The company's management and its investment bankers believe that the proper procedure is to select several similar firms with publicly traded common stock and to make relevant comparisons.

Several home improvement building suppliers are reasonably similar to U-Fix-It with respect to product mix, size, asset composition, and debt/equity proportions. Of these companies, Home Headquarters and Lows are most similar. When analyzing the following data, assume that 1987 and 1992 were reasonably normal years for all three companies; that is, these years were neither especially good nor especially bad in terms of sales, earnings, and dividends. At the time of the analysis, k_{RF} was 10 percent and k_M was 15 percent. Home Headquarters is listed on the AMEX and Lows on the NYSE, while U-Fix-It will be traded in the OTC market.

	Home Headquarters	Lows	U-Fix-It (Totals)
Earnings per share			
1992	$ 3.60	$ 6.00	$ 960,000
1987	2.40	4.40	652,800
Price per share			
1992	$28.80	$52.00	—
Dividends per share			
1992	$ 1.80	$ 3.00	$ 480,000
1987	1.20	2.20	336,000
Book value per share, 1992	$24.00	$44.00	$7,200,000
Market/book ratio, 1992	120%	118%	—
Total assets, 1992	$22.4 million	$ 65.6 million	$16.0 million
Total debt, 1992	$ 9.6 million	$ 24.0 million	$ 8.8 million
Sales, 1992	$32.8 million	$112.0 million	$29.6 million

a. Assume that U-Fix-It has 100 shares of stock outstanding. Use this information to calculate earnings per share (EPS), dividends per share (DPS), and book value per share for U-Fix-It. (Hint: U-Fix-It's 1992 EPS = $9,600.)

b. Calculate earnings and dividend growth rates for the three companies. (Hint: U-Fix-It's EPS g is 8%.)

c. On the basis of your answer to Part a, do you think U-Fix-It's stock would sell at a price in the same "ballpark" as that of Home Headquarters and Lows—that is, in the range of $25 to $100 per share?

d. Assuming that U-Fix-It's management can split the stock so that the 100 shares could be changed to 1,000 shares, 100,000 shares, or any other number, would such an action make sense in this case? Why?

e. Now assume that U-Fix-It did split its stock and has 400,000 shares. Calculate new values for EPS, DPS, and book value per share. (Hint: U-Fix-It's new 1992 EPS is $2.40.)

f. Return on equity (ROE) can be measured as EPS/book value per share or as total earnings/total equity. Calculate ROEs for the three companies for 1992. (Hint: U-Fix-It's 1992 ROE = 13.3%.)

g. Calculate dividend payout ratios for the three companies. (Hint: U-Fix-It's 1992 payout ratio is 50%.)

h. Calculate debt/total assets ratios for the three companies. (Hint: U-Fix-It's 1992 debt ratio is 55%.)

i. Calculate the P/E ratios for Home Headquarters and Lows based on 1992 data. Are these P/E ratios reasonable in view of relative growth, payout, and ROE data? If not, what other factors might explain them? (Hint: Home Headquarters' P/E $= 8 \times$.)

j. Now determine a range of values for U-Fix-It's stock price, with 400,000 shares outstanding, by applying Home Headquarters' and Lows's P/E ratios, price/dividends ratios, and price/book value ratios to your data for U-Fix-It. For example, one possible price for U-Fix-It's stock is (P/E Home Headquarters)(EPS U-Fix-It) $= 8(\$2.40) =$ \$19.20 per share. Similar calculations would produce a range of prices based on both Home Headquarters' and Lows's data. (Hint: Our range was \$19.20 to \$21.60.)

k. Using the equation $k_s = D_1/P_0 + g$, find approximate k_s values for Home Headquarters and Lows. Then use these values in the constant growth stock price model to find a price for U-Fix-It's stock. (Hint: We averaged the EPS and DPS g's for U-Fix-It.)

l. At what price do you think U-Fix-It's shares should be offered to the public? You will want to select a price that will be low enough to induce investors to buy the stock but not so low that it will rise too sharply immediately after it is issued. Think about relative growth rates, ROEs, dividend yields, and total returns ($k_s = D_1/P_0 + g$).

EXAM-TYPE PROBLEMS

The problems included in this section are set up in such a way that they could be used as multiple-choice exam problems.

19-3
Book value per share

Atlantic Coast Resources Company had the following balance sheet at the end of 1992:

Atlantic Coast Resources Company: Balance Sheet December 31, 1992

		Accounts payable	$ 64,400
		Notes payable	71,400
		Long-term debt	151,200
		Common stock (30,000 shares authorized, 20,000 shares outstanding)	364,000
		Retained earnings	336,000
Total assets	$987,000	Total liabilities and equity	$987,000

a. What is the book value per share of Atlantic's common stock?

b. Suppose the firm sold the remaining authorized shares and netted \$32.55 per share from the sale. What would be the new book value per share?

19-4
Underwriting and flotation expenses

The Taussig Company, whose stock price is now \$30, needs to raise \$15 million in common stock. Underwriters have informed Taussig's management that it must price the new issue to the public at \$27.53 per share because of a downward-sloping demand curve. The underwriters' compensation will be 7 percent of the issue price, so Taussig will net \$25.60 per share. Taussig will also incur expenses in the amount of \$360,000.

How many shares must Taussig sell to net \$15 million after underwriting and flotation expenses?

INTEGRATIVE PROBLEM

19-5
Investment banking process

Gonzales Food Stores, a family-owned grocery store chain headquartered in El Paso, is considering a major expansion. The proposed expansion would require Gonzales to raise \$10 million in additional capital. Because Gonzales currently has a debt ratio of 50 percent, and because the family members already have all their funds tied up in the business, the owners cannot supply any additional equity, so the company will have to sell stock to the public. However, the family wants to insure that they retain control of the company. This would be Gonzales's first stock sale, and the owners are not sure just what would be involved. Therefore, they have asked you to research the process and to help them decide exactly how to raise the needed capital. In doing so, you should answer the following questions.

a. What are the advantages to Gonzales of financing with stock rather than bonds? What are the disadvantages of using stock?

b. Is the stock of Gonzales Food Stores currently publicly held or privately owned? Would this situation change if the stock sale were made?

c. What is classified stock? Would there be any advantage to Gonzales of designating the stock currently outstanding as "founders' shares"? What type of common stock should Gonzales sell to the public to allow the family to retain control of the business?

d. What does the term "going public" mean? What would be the advantages to the Gonzales family of having the firm go public? What would be the disadvantages?

e. What does the term "listed stock" mean? Do you think that Gonzales's stock would be listed shortly after the company goes public? If not, where would the stock trade?

f. Suppose the firm has decided to issue $10 million of Class B nonvoting stock. Now Gonzales must select an investment banker. Do you think it should select a banker on the basis of a competitive bid or do a negotiated deal? Explain.

g. Without doing any calculations, give a brief description of the procedures by which Gonzales and its investment banker will determine the price at which the stock will be offered to the public.

h. What is a prospectus? What is a red herring prospectus? Why does the SEC require all firms to file registration statements and distribute prospectuses to potential stockholders before selling stock? What steps does the SEC take to insure that the information in the prospectus presents a fair and accurate portrayal of the issuing firm's financial position?

i. If Gonzales goes public and sells shares which the public buys at a price of $10 per share, what will be the approximate percentage cost, including both underwriting costs and other costs? Assume the company sells 1.5 million shares. Would the cost be higher or lower if the company were already publicly owned?

j. Would you recommend that Gonzales have the issue underwritten or sold on a best efforts basis? Why? What would be the difference in costs between the two procedures?

k. If some of the Gonzales family members wanted to sell some of their own shares in order to diversify at the same time the company was selling new shares to raise expansion capital, would this be feasible?

l. Would it be a good idea to use a rights offering for the issue? Why or why not?

Long-Term Debt

At a recent junk bond conference held in Greenwich, Connecticut, Sumner Redstone, CEO of National Amusements (which owns Viacom, a firm that operates Nickelodeon and MTV, among other things), told the attendees of the conference that this was the last junk bond conference he would be attending. He stated that if they did see him at the next conference, Viacom would have a new chief financial officer. The message was clear: Viacom had amassed close to $3 billion of debt, and it was now time to reduce that debt. The jargon for reducing debt is to "deleverage."

A study by Indepth Data, an investment research firm based in Oklahoma City, found that in 1986, during the height of the takeover and leveraged buyout frenzy, only $2.2 billion of debt was taken off corporate books through exchange offers, tender offers, and redemptions. As of early 1991, however, debt reductions totaled $11.2 billion, including $3.4 billion which disappeared through bankruptcy settlements.

There are good reasons for this deleveraging trend. Credit is the lifeblood of any business, especially companies that are growing. But credit is harder to come by for low-rated companies these days because of bankers' reluctance to add to their risk exposure by making additional loans to companies which already have high debt levels. Federal bank regulators have been pressuring commercial banks and savings and loans to stop lending to companies whose bonds are rated below investment grade (BBB) because these firms' balance sheets showed high debt-to-equity ratios. Because of the leveraging that occurred in the 1980s, only 400 corporations' bonds remained in the investment-grade category, and the HLT (highly leveraged transaction) list of the bank regulators now blackballs most U.S. companies. Nearly 95 percent of corporations with annual sales of more than $35 million are in the "junk bond brigade." As a result, net new bank loans to nonfinancial companies decreased from $33.1 billion in 1989 to just $2 billion in 1990. Many corporations' executives argue *that the HLT definitions ignore cash flow—earnings before interest, taxes, depreciation, and amortization. They argue that arbitrary balance sheet ratios have replaced sound credit analysis and that these rules have aggravated the credit shortage that many firms now face.*

Deleveraging strategies can take many forms. Declining interest rates have enabled financial managers to restructure their balance sheets by replacing high-cost debt with low-cost debt. Stock issuances are also very popular; however, dividend payments are not tax deductible, while interest payments on debt obligations are tax deductible. In addition, companies have tried to raise money to reduce their debt by selling assets, but these efforts have been met with varying degrees of success. The most common strategy for deleveraging is to use a combination of actions: Issue new equity, retire old high-interest debt for new low-cost debt, and sell assets if possible. The lower a firm's debt-to-equity ratio, the easier it is for the firm to refinance its bank debt, to borrow in the commercial paper markets, and maybe even to get an upgrade on its debt from the bond-rating agencies. Clearly, deleveraging has many advantages for firms that pushed the use of debt too far.

Consider Viacom's deleveraging strategy. Between 1987 and 1990, Viacom sold assets and paid off $600 million in costly bank debt. Then, it extended maturities on some notes from 1991 to 1998, issued $200 million in senior subordinated debentures at a comfortable rate of 10.25 percent, and retired its old 15.5 percent bonds. Because of its lighter debt burden, Viacom has been able to continue to invest in its fastest-growing businesses. In fact, in August 1991, Viacom gave up 2.2 million shares of common equity to acquire MTV Europe from Robert Maxwell's sinking empire.

As long as (1) banks have to adhere to HLT regulations, (2) stock prices keep increasing, and (3) interest rates remain low or continue to decline, highly leveraged companies will continue to find ways to beef up the equity on their balance sheets and to rid themselves of high-rate debt. However, these actions may not be entirely good for the economy. The attack on leverage due to the pressure from bank regulators may be slowing down our economic recovery. The hundreds of billions of dollars raised recently in stock and bond offerings have been used primarily to pay down old debt rather than to invest in new projects which could create jobs and stimulate economic growth. (As corporate debt has been paid down, the funds have been used mainly to purchase Treasury securities sold to finance the huge U.S. fiscal deficit.)

However, deleveraging can only go so far. The equity that disappeared from firms' balance sheets in the 1980s may never be replaced. Between

1980 and 1990, $640 billion of equity was converted into debt. To restore equity to the level that existed in 1980, companies would have to keep issuing new stock at the 1991 record pace for the next 17 years. It appears that many companies will be saddled with their costly old liabilities for a long time. As you read this chapter, consider both the positive and negative effects that debt may have on our economy.

Source: "The Big Drive to Reduce Debt," *Fortune,* February 10, 1992.

Different groups of investors prefer different types of securities, and investors' tastes change over time. Thus, astute financial managers offer a variety of securities, and they package their new security offerings at each point in time to appeal to the greatest possible number of potential investors. In this chapter, we consider the various types of long-term debt available to financial managers.

funded debt

Long-term debt; "funding" means replacing short-term debt with securities of longer maturity.

Long-term debt is often called **funded debt.** When a firm "funds" its short-term debt, this means that it replaces short-term debt with securities of longer maturity. Funding does not imply that the firm places money with a trustee or other repository; it is simply part of the jargon of finance, and it means that the firm replaces short-term debt with permanent capital. Pacific Gas & Electric Company (PG&E) provides a good example of funding. PG&E has a continuous construction program, and it typically uses short-term debt to finance construction expenditures. However, once short-term debt has built up to about $100 million, the company sells a stock or bond issue, uses the proceeds to pay off (or fund) its bank loans, and starts the cycle again. There is a fixed cost involved in selling stocks or bonds which makes it quite expensive to issue small amounts of these securities. Therefore, the process used by PG&E and other companies is quite logical.

TRADITIONAL DEBT INSTRUMENTS

There are many types of long-term debt instruments: term loans, bonds, secured and unsecured notes, marketable and nonmarketable debt, and so on. In this section, we discuss briefly the traditional long-term debt instruments, after which we examine some important features of debt contracts. Finally, we consider some recent innovations in long-term debt financing.

term loan

A loan, generally obtained from a bank or insurance company, with a maturity period greater than one year.

Term Loans

A **term loan** is a contract under which a borrower agrees to make a series of interest and principal payments on specific dates to the lender. Term loans are usually negotiated directly between the borrowing firm and a financial institution—generally a bank, an insurance company, or a pension fund. Although term loans' maturities vary from 2 to 30 years, most are for periods in the 3-year to 15-year range.[1]

Term loans have three major advantages over public offerings — *speed, flexibility,* and *low issuance costs.* Because they are negotiated directly between the lender and the borrower, formal documentation is minimized. The key provisions of a term loan can be worked out much more quickly than those for a public issue, and it is not necessary for the loan to go through the Securities and Exchange Commission registration process. A further advantage of term loans has to do with future flexibility. If a bond issue is held by many different bondholders, it is virtually impossible to obtain permission to alter the terms of the agreement, even though new economic conditions may make such changes desirable. With a term loan, the borrower can generally sit down with the lender and work out mutually agreeable modifications to the contract.

The interest rate on a term loan can either be fixed for the life of the loan or be variable. If a fixed rate is used, it will generally be set close to the rate on bonds of equivalent maturity and risk. If the rate is variable, it will usually be set at a certain number of percentage points over either the prime rate, the commercial paper rate, the T-bill rate, the T-bond rate, or the London Inter-Bank Offered Rate (LIBOR), which is the rate of interest offered by the largest and strongest London banks on deposits of other large banks of the highest credit standing. Then, when the index rate goes up or down, so does the rate charged on the outstanding balance of the term loan. Rates may be adjusted annually, semiannually, quarterly, monthly, or on some other basis, depending on what the contract specifies. In 1992, about 60 percent of the dollar amount of all term loans made by banks had floating rates, up from virtually zero in 1970. Banks obtain most of the funds they themselves lend by selling certificates of deposit, and because the CD rate rises when other market rates rise, banks need to increase the rate they charge in order to cover their own interest costs. With the increased volatility of interest rates in recent years, banks and other lenders have become increasingly reluctant to make long-term, fixed-rate loans.

Bonds

bond

A long-term debt instrument.

A **bond** is a long-term contract under which a borrower agrees to make payments of interest and principal on specific dates to the holder of the bond. Although bonds have traditionally been issued with maturities of between 20 and 30 years, in recent years shorter maturities, such as 7 to 10 years, have been used to an increasing extent. Bonds are similar to term loans, but a bond issue is generally advertised, offered to the public, and actually sold to many different investors. Indeed, thousands of individual and institutional investors may purchase bonds when a firm sells a bond issue, whereas there is generally

---

[1]Most term loans are *amortized,* which means they are paid off in equal installments over the life of the loan. Amortization protects the lender against the possibility that the borrower will not make adequate provisions for the loan's retirement during the life of the loan. See Chapter 5 for a review of amortization. Also, if the interest and principal payments required under a term loan agreement are not met on schedule, the borrowing firm is said to have *defaulted,* and it can then be forced into bankruptcy. Bankruptcy is covered briefly later in this chapter, and Appendix 20A presents a detailed discussion of bankruptcy.

only one lender in the case of a term loan.[2] With bonds the interest rate is generally fixed, although in recent years there has been an increase in the use of various types of floating rate bonds. There are also a number of different types of bonds, the more important of which are discussed below.

mortgage bond

A bond backed by fixed assets. *First mortgage bonds are senior in priority to claims of second mortgage bonds.*

Mortgage Bonds.   Under a **mortgage bond,** the corporation pledges certain assets as security for the bond. To illustrate, in 1992 Billingham Corporation needed $10 million to build a major regional distribution center. Bonds in the amount of $4 million, secured by a mortgage on the property, were issued. (The remaining $6 million was financed with equity capital.) If Billingham defaults on the bonds, the bondholders can foreclose on the property and sell it to satisfy their claims.

If Billingham chooses to, it can issue *second mortgage bonds* secured by the same $10 million plant. In the event of liquidation, the holders of these second mortgage bonds would have a claim against the property, but only after the first mortgage bondholders had been paid off in full. Thus, second mortgages are sometimes called *junior mortgages,* because they are junior in priority to the claims of *senior mortgages,* or *first mortgage bonds.*

indenture

A formal agreement between the issuer of a bond and the bondholders.

All mortgage bonds are written subject to an **indenture**, which is a legal document that spells out in detail the rights of both the bondholders and the corporation. The indentures of most major corporations were written 20, 30, 40, or more years ago. These indentures are generally "open ended," meaning that new bonds may be issued from time to time under the existing indenture. However, the amount of new bonds that can be issued is virtually always limited to a specified percentage of the firm's total "bondable property," which generally includes all plant and equipment.

For example, Savannah Electric Company can issue first mortgage bonds totaling up to 60 percent of its fixed assets. If its fixed assets totaled $1 billion, and if it had $500 million of first mortgage bonds outstanding, it could, by the property test, issue another $100 million of bonds (60% of $1 billion = $600 million).

At times, Savannah Electric has been unable to issue any new first mortgage bonds because of another indenture provision: its times-interest-earned (TIE) ratio was below 2.5, the minimum coverage that it must maintain in order to sell new bonds. Thus, although Savannah Electric passed the property test, it failed the coverage test, so it could not issue first mortgage bonds, and it had to finance with junior securities. Since first mortgage bonds carry lower rates of interest than junior long-term debt, this restriction was a costly one.

Savannah Electric's neighbor, Georgia Power Company, has more flexibility under its indenture — its interest coverage requirement is only 2.0. In hearings before the Georgia Public Service Commission, it was suggested that Savannah Electric should change its indenture coverage to 2.0 so that it could issue more first mortgage bonds. However, this was simply not possible — the holders

---

[2]However, for very large term loans, 20 or more financial institutions may form a syndicate to grant the credit. Also, it should be noted that a bond issue can be sold to one lender (or to just a few); in this case, the issue is said to be "privately placed." Companies that place bonds privately do so for the same reasons that they use term loans — speed, flexibility, and low issuance costs.

of the outstanding bonds would have to approve the change, and it is inconceivable that they would vote for a change that would seriously weaken their position.

debenture

A long-term bond that is not secured by a mortgage on specific property.

Debentures. A **debenture** is an unsecured bond, and as such it provides no lien against specific property as security for the obligation. Debenture holders are, therefore, general creditors whose claims are protected by property not otherwise pledged. In practice, the use of debentures depends both on the nature of the firm's assets and on its general credit strength. An extremely strong company, such as IBM, will tend to use debentures; it simply does not need to put up property as security for its debt. Debentures are also issued by companies in industries in which it would not be practical to provide security through a mortgage on fixed assets. Examples of such industries are the large mail-order houses and commercial banks, which characteristically hold most of their assets in the form of inventory or loans, neither of which is satisfactory security for a mortgage bond.

subordinated debenture

A bond having a claim on assets only after the senior debt has been paid off in the event of liquidation.

Subordinated Debentures. The term *subordinate* means "below," or "inferior to," and, in the event of bankruptcy, subordinated debt has claims on assets only after senior debt has been paid off. **Subordinated debentures** may be subordinated either to designated notes payable (usually bank loans) or to all other debt. In the event of liquidation or reorganization, holders of subordinated debentures cannot be paid until all senior debt, as named in the debentures' indenture, has been paid. Precisely how subordination works, and how it strengthens the position of senior debtholders, is explained in detail in Appendix 20A.

convertible bond

A bond that is exchangeable, at the option of the holder, for common stock of the issuing firm.

warrant

A long-term option to buy a stated number of shares of common stock at a specified price.

income bond

A bond that pays interest to the holder only if the interest is earned.

putable bond

A bond that can be redeemed at the bondholder's option.

Other Types of Bonds. Several other types of bonds are used sufficiently often to warrant mention. First, **convertible bonds** are securities that are convertible into shares of common stock, at a fixed price, at the option of the bondholder. Convertibles have a lower coupon rate than nonconvertible debt, but they offer investors a chance for capital gains in exchange for the lower coupon rate. Bonds issued with **warrants** are similar to convertibles. Warrants are options which permit the holder to buy stock for a stated price, thereby providing a capital gain if the price of the stock rises. Bonds that are issued with warrants, like convertibles, carry lower coupon rates than straight bonds, and both types of bonds are discussed in detail in Chapter 21. **Income bonds** pay interest only when the interest is earned. Thus, these securities cannot bankrupt a company, but from an investor's standpoint they are riskier than "regular" bonds. **Putable bonds** may be turned in and exchanged for cash at the *holder's* option; generally, the put option can be exercised only if the issuer takes some specified action, such as being acquired by a weaker company or increasing its outstanding debt by a large amount.[3]

---

[3]Putable bonds have not been used to a large extent, but the recent spate of leveraged buyouts (LBOs) will probably increase their use in the coming years. A good example of why putable bonds are needed is the situation that arose with RJR Nabisco. RJR's management announced that it planned to undertake an LBO in which it would issue billions of new debt and use the proceeds to buy all the publicly held stock. The company's debt ratio would thus be changed, instantly, from

indexed (purchasing power) bond

A bond that has interest payments based on an inflation index so as to protect the holder from inflation.

Another type of bond that has been discussed in the United States but is not yet used here to any extent is the **indexed, or purchasing power, bond,** which is popular in Brazil, Israel, and a few other countries plagued by high rates of inflation. The interest rate paid on these bonds is based on an inflation index such as the consumer price index, so the interest paid rises automatically when the inflation rate rises, thus protecting the bondholders against inflation. The British government has issued an indexed bond whose interest rate is set equal to the British inflation rate plus 3 percent. Thus, these bonds provide a "real return" of 3 percent. Also, Mexico has used bonds whose interest rate is pegged to the price of oil to finance the development of its huge petroleum reserves; since oil prices and inflation are correlated, these bonds offer some protection to investors against inflation.

? *Self-Test Questions*

What are the three major advantages that term loans have over public offerings?

Differentiate between term loans and bonds.

Differentiate between mortgage bonds and debentures.

Define convertible bonds, bonds with warrants, income bonds, putable bonds, and indexed bonds.

Why do bonds with warrants and convertible bonds have lower coupons than bonds that do not have these features?

SPECIFIC DEBT CONTRACT FEATURES

A firm's managers are concerned with both the effective cost of debt and any restrictions in debt contracts which might limit the firm's future actions. In this section, we discuss features which could affect either the cost of the firm's debt or the firm's future flexibility.

Bond Indentures

In Chapter 1 we discussed *agency problems,* which relate to conflicts of interest among corporate stakeholders—stockholders, bondholders, and managers. Bondholders have a legitimate fear that once they lend money to a company and are "locked in" for up to 30 years, the company will take some action that is designed to benefit stockholders but that harms bondholders. For example, RJR Nabisco, when it was highly rated, sold 30-year bonds with a low coupon rate, and investors bought those bonds in spite of the low yield because of their low risk. Then, after the bonds had been sold, the company announced plans to issue a great deal more debt, increasing the expected rate of return to stockholders but also increasing the riskiness of the bonds. RJR's bonds fell 20 per-

---

about 40 percent to about 95 percent. The currently outstanding bonds were rated A+, but as soon as the announcement was made, investors knew that they would soon become junk bonds, and their price fell by about 20 percent in two days. That event virtually paralyzed the bond market, and it will lead to wider use of putable bonds in the future.

cent the week the announcement was made. Safeway Stores and a number of other companies have done the same thing, and their bondholders also lost heavily as the market yield on the bonds rose and drove the prices of the bonds down.

Investors attempt to reduce agency problems by use of legal restrictions designed to insure, insofar as possible, that the company does nothing to cause the quality of its bonds to deteriorate after they have been issued. The indenture is the legal document which spells out the rights of the bondholders and the corporation. A **trustee,** usually a bank, is assigned to represent the bondholders and to make sure that the terms of the indenture are carried out. The indenture may be several hundred pages in length, and it will include **restrictive covenants** that cover such points as the conditions under which the issuer can pay off the bonds prior to maturity, the level at which the issuer's times-interest-earned ratio must be maintained if the company is to sell additional bonds, and restrictions against the payment of dividends when earnings do not meet certain specifications.

The trustee is responsible both for making sure the covenants are not violated and for taking appropriate action if they are. What constitutes "appropriate action" varies with the circumstances. It might be that to insist on immediate compliance would result in bankruptcy, which in turn might lead to large losses on the bonds. In such a case, the trustee might decide that the bondholders would be better served by giving the company a chance to work out its problems rather than by forcing it into bankruptcy.

The Securities and Exchange Commission approves indentures for publicly traded bonds and makes sure that all indenture provisions are met before allowing a company to sell new securities to the public. The indentures of many larger corporations were written back in the 1930s or 1940s, and many issues of new bonds, all covered by the same indenture, have been sold down through the years. The interest rates on the bonds, and perhaps also the maturities, will change from issue to issue, but bondholders' protection as spelled out in the indenture will be the same for all bonds of a given type.[4]

trustee

An official who ensures that the bondholders' interests are protected and that the terms of the indenture are carried out.

restrictive covenant

A provision in a debt contract that constrains the actions of the borrower.

Call Provisions

call provision

A provision in a bond contract that gives the issuer the right to redeem the bonds under specified terms prior to the normal maturity date.

Most bonds contain a **call provision,** which gives the issuing corporation the right to call the bonds for redemption. The call provision generally states that the company must pay the bondholders an amount greater than the par value for the bonds when they are called. The additional sum, which is termed a *call premium,* is typically set equal to one year's interest if the bonds are called during the first year, and the premium declines at a constant rate of INT/N each year thereafter, where INT = annual interest and N = original maturity in years. For example, the call premium on a $1,000 par value, 10-year, 10 percent bond would generally be $100 if it were called during the first year, $90 during the second year (calculated by reducing the $100, or 10 percent, premium by one-tenth), and so on. However, bonds are often not callable until several years (generally 5 to 10) after they were issued.

---

[4]A firm will have different indentures for each major type of bonds it issues, including its first mortgage bonds, its debentures, its convertibles, and so on.

Suppose a company sold bonds or preferred stock when interest rates were relatively high. Provided the issue is callable, the company could sell a new issue of low-yielding securities if and when interest rates drop. It could then use the proceeds to retire the high-rate issue and thus reduce its interest or preferred dividend expenses. This process is called a *refunding operation,* and it is discussed briefly at the end of this chapter and in greater detail in Appendix 20B.

The call privilege is valuable to the firm but potentially detrimental to the investor, especially if the bonds were issued in a period when interest rates were cyclically high. Accordingly, the interest rate on a new issue of callable bonds will exceed that on a new issue of noncallable bonds. For example, on May 2, 1992, Pacific Timber Company sold a bond issue yielding 8.875 percent; these bonds were callable immediately. On the same day, Northwest Milling Company sold an issue of similar risk and maturity which yielded 8.5 percent; its bonds were noncallable for 10 years. (This is known as a *deferred call,* and the bonds are said to have *call protection.*) Investors were apparently willing to accept a 0.375 percent lower interest rate on Northwest's bonds for the assurance that the rate of interest would be earned for at least 10 years. Pacific, on the other hand, had to incur a 0.375 percent higher annual interest rate to obtain the option of calling the bonds in the event of a subsequent decline in interest rates.

Sinking Funds

sinking fund

A required annual payment designed to amortize a bond or preferred stock issue.

A **sinking fund** is a provision that facilitates the orderly retirement of a bond issue (or an issue of preferred stock). Typically, the sinking fund provision requires the firm to retire a portion of the bond issue each year. On rare occasions the firm may be required to deposit money with a trustee, which invests the funds and then uses the accumulated sum to retire the bonds when they mature. Usually, though, the sinking fund is used to buy back a certain percentage of the issue each year. A failure to meet the sinking fund requirement causes the bond issue to be thrown into default, which may force the company into bankruptcy. Obviously, a sinking fund can constitute a dangerous cash drain on the firm.

In most cases, the firm is given the right to handle the sinking fund in either of two ways:

1. The company can call in for redemption (at par value) a certain percentage of the bonds each year; for example, it might be able to call 2 percent of the total original amount of the issue at a price of $1,000 per bond. The bonds are numbered serially, and those called for redemption are determined by a lottery administered by the trustee.

2. The company may buy the required amount of bonds on the open market.

The firm will choose the least-cost method. If interest rates have risen, causing bond prices to fall, it will buy bonds in the open market at a discount; if interest rates have fallen, it will call the bonds. Note that a call for sinking fund purposes is quite different from a refunding call as discussed above. A sinking fund call requires no call premium, but only a small percentage of the issue is normally callable in any one year.

Although sinking funds are designed to protect bondholders by insuring that an issue is retired in an orderly fashion, it must be recognized that sinking funds will at times work to the detriment of bondholders. For example, suppose the bond carries a 12 percent interest rate and yields on similar bonds have fallen to 8.5 percent. A sinking fund call at par would require an investor to give up $120 of interest and then to reinvest in a bond that pays only $85 per year. This obviously disadvantages those bondholders whose bonds are called. On balance, however, bonds that provide for a sinking fund are regarded as being safer than those without such a provision, so at the time they are issued sinking fund bonds have lower coupon rates than otherwise similar bonds without sinking funds.

? *Self-Test Questions*

How do trustees and indentures reduce agency problems for bondholders?

What are the two ways a sinking fund can be handled? Which method will be chosen by the firm if interest rates have risen? If interest rates have fallen?

What is the difference between a call for sinking fund purposes and a refunding call?

Are securities that provide for a sinking fund regarded as being riskier than those without this type of provision? Explain.

Why is a call provision so advantageous to a bond issuer? When will the issuer initiate a refunding call? Why?

RECENT INNOVATIONS

Zero (or Very Low) Coupon Bonds

zero coupon bond
A bond that pays no annual interest but is sold at a discount below par, thus providing compensation to investors in the form of capital appreciation.

Some bonds pay no interest but are offered at a substantial discount below their par values and hence provide capital appreciation rather than interest income. These securities are called **zero coupon bonds** *("zeros"),* or *original issue discount bonds (OIDs).* Corporations first used zeros in a major way in 1981. In recent years IBM, Alcoa, J. C. Penney, ITT, Cities Service, GMAC, Martin-Marietta, and many other companies have used them to raise billions of dollars. Municipal governments also sell "zero munis," and investment bankers have in effect created zero coupon Treasury bonds.

To understand how zeros are used and analyzed, consider the zeros that are going to be issued by Vandenberg Corporation, a shopping center developer. Vandenberg is developing a new shopping center in Orange County, California, and it needs $50 million. The company does not anticipate major cash flows from the project for about 5 years. However, Pieter Vandenberg, the president, plans to sell the center once it is fully developed and rented, which should take about 5 years. Therefore, Vandenberg wants to use a financing vehicle that will not require cash outflows for 5 years, and he has decided on a 5-year zero coupon bond, with a maturity value of $1,000.

Vandenberg Corporation is an A-rated company, and A-rated zeros with 5-year maturities yield 9 percent at this time (5-year coupon bonds also yield 9

Table 20-1 ▪ Analysis of a Zero Coupon Bond

Basic Data

Maturity value	$1,000
k_d	9.00%
Maturity	5 years
Corporate tax rate	40.00%
Issue price	$649.93

Analysis

				Years		
	0	1	2	3	4	5
(1) Year-end accrued value	$649.93	$708.42	$772.18	$841.68	$917.43	$1,000.00
(2) Interest deduction		58.49	63.76	69.50	75.75	82.57
(3) Tax savings (40%)		23.40	25.50	27.80	30.30	33.03
(4) Cash flow	+649.93	+23.40	+25.50	+27.80	+30.30	−966.97
After-tax cost of debt	5.40%					

Number of $1,000 zeros the company must issue to raise $50 million = Amount needed/Price per bond
= $50,000,000/$649.93
= 76,931 bonds.

percent). The company is in the 40 percent federal-plus-state tax bracket. Pieter Vandenberg wants to know the firm's after-tax cost of capital if it uses 9 percent, 5-year maturity zeros, and he also wants to know what the bond's cash flows will be. Table 20-1 provides an analysis of the situation, and the following numbered paragraphs explain the table itself.

1. The information in the "Basic Data" section, except the issue price, was given in the preceding paragraph, and the information in the "Analysis" section was calculated using the known data. The maturity value of the bond is always set at $1,000 or some multiple thereof.

2. The issue price is the PV of $1,000, discounted back 5 years at the rate $k_d = 9\%$. Using the tables, we find PV = $1,000(0.6499) = $649.90. Using a financial calculator, we input N = 5, I = 9, and FV = 1000, then press the PV key to find PV = $649.93. Note that $649.93, compounded annually for 5 years at 9 percent, will grow to $1,000 as shown on the time line in Table 20-1.

3. The accrued values as shown on Line 1 in the analysis section represent the compounded value of the bond at the end of each year. The accrued value for Year 0 is the issue price; the accrued value for Year 1 is found as $649.93(1.09) = $708.42; the accrued value at the end of Year 2 is $649.93(1.09)^2 = $772.18; and, in general, the value at the end of any Year n is

O━┳

Accrued value at the end of Year n = Issue price $\times (1 + k_d)^n$.

4. The interest deduction as shown on Line 2 represents the increase in accrued value during the year. Thus, interest in Year 1 = \$708.42 − \$649.93 = \$58.49. In general,

<table>
<tr><td>Interest in Year n = Accrued value$_n$ − Accrued value$_{n-1}$.</td></tr>
</table>

This method of calculating taxable interest is specified in the Tax Code.

5. The company can deduct interest each year, even though the payment is not made in cash. This deduction lowers the taxes that would otherwise be paid, producing the following savings:

<table>
<tr><td>Tax savings = (Interest deduction)(T)</td></tr>
</table>

$$= \$58.49(0.4)$$

$$= \$23.40 \text{ in Year 1.}$$

6. Line 4 represents cash flows on a time line; it shows the cash flow at the end of Years 0 through 5. At Year 0, the company receives the \$649.93 issue price. The company also has positive cash inflows equal to the tax savings during Years 1 through 4. Finally, in Year 5, it must pay the \$1,000 maturity value, but it gets one more interest tax savings for the year. Therefore, the net cash flow in Year 5 is − \$1,000 + \$33.03 = − \$966.97.

7. We can find the IRR of the cash flows shown on Line 4 using the IRR function of a financial calculator by simply inputting the annual cash flows in the cash flow register; the IRR is the after-tax cost of zero coupon debt to the company. Conceptually, here is the situation:

$$\sum_{t=0}^{n} \frac{CF_n}{(1 + k_{d(AT)})^n} = 0.$$

$$\frac{\$649.93}{(1 + k_{d(AT)})^0} + \frac{\$23.40}{(1 + k_{d(AT)})^1} + \frac{\$25.50}{(1 + k_{d(AT)})^2} + \frac{\$27.80}{(1 + k_{d(AT)})^3} + \frac{\$30.30}{(1 + k_{d(AT)})^4} + \frac{-\$966.97}{(1 + k_{d(AT)})^5} = 0.$$

The value $k_{d(AT)}$ = 0.054 = 5.4%, found with a financial calculator, produces the equality, and it is the cost of this debt.

8. Note that $k_d(1 − T)$ = 9%(0.6) = 5.4%. As we saw in Chapter 16, the cost of capital for regular coupon debt is found using the formula $k_d(1 − T)$. Thus, there is symmetrical treatment for tax purposes for zero coupon and regular coupon debt; that is, both types of debt have the same

after-tax cost effects. This was Congress's intent, and it is why the Tax Code specifies the treatment set forth in Table 20-1.[5]

Not all original issue discount bonds (OIDs) have zero coupons. For example, Vandenberg might have sold an issue of 5-year bonds with a 5 percent coupon at a time when other bonds with similar ratings and maturities were yielding 9 percent. Such bonds would have had a value of $844.41:

$$\text{Bond value} = \sum_{t=1}^{5} \frac{\$50}{(1.09)^t} + \frac{\$1,000}{(1.09)^5} = \$844.41.$$

If an investor had purchased these bonds at a price of $844.41, the yield to maturity would have been 9 percent. The discount of $1,000 − $844.41 = $155.59 would have been amortized over the bond's 5-year life, and it would have been handled by both Vandenberg and the bondholders exactly as the discount on the zeros was handled.

Thus, zero coupon bonds are just one type of original issue discount bond. Any nonconvertible bond whose coupon rate is set below the going market rate at the time of its issue will sell at a discount, and it will be classified (for tax and other purposes) as an OID bond.

Shortly after corporations began to issue zeros, investment bankers figured out a way to create zeros from U.S. Treasury bonds, which are issued only in coupon form. In 1982 Salomon Brothers bought $1 billion of 12 percent, 30-year Treasuries. Each bond had 60 coupons worth $60 each, which represented the interest payments due every 6 months. Salomon then in effect clipped the coupons and placed them in 60 piles; the last pile also contained the now "stripped" bond itself, which represented a promise of $1,000 in the year 2012. These 60 piles of U.S. Treasury promises were then placed with the trust department of a bank and used as collateral for "zero coupon U.S. Treasury Trust Certificates," which are, in essence, zero coupon Treasury bonds. A pension fund that expected to need money in 1993 could have bought 11-year certificates backed by the interest the Treasury will pay in 1993. Treasury zeros are, of course, safer than corporate zeros, so they are very popular with pension fund managers.

Corporate (and municipal) zeros are generally callable at the option of the issuer, just like coupon bonds, after some stated call protection period. The call price is set at a premium over the accrued value at the time of the call. Stripped U.S. Treasury bonds (Treasury zeros) generally are not callable because the

---

[5]The purchaser of a zero coupon bond must calculate interest income on the bond in the same manner as the issuer calculates the interest deduction. Thus, in Year 1, a buyer of a bond would report interest income of $58.49 and would pay taxes in the amount of T(Interest income), even though no cash was received. T, of course, would be the bondholder's personal tax rate. Because of the tax situation, most zero coupon bonds are bought by pension funds and other tax-exempt entities. Individuals do, however, buy taxable zeros for their Individual Retirement Accounts (IRAs). Also, state and local governments issue "tax exempt muni zeros," which are purchased by individuals in high tax brackets.

Note too that we have analyzed the bond as if the cash flows accrued annually. Generally, to facilitate comparisons with semiannual payment coupon bonds, the analysis is conducted on a semiannual basis.

Treasury normally sells noncallable bonds. Thus, Treasury zeros are completely protected against reinvestment risk (the risk of having to invest cash flows from a bond at a lower rate because of a decline in interest rates).

Floating Rate Debt

In the early 1980s, inflation pushed interest rates up to unprecedented levels, causing sharp declines in the prices of long-term bonds. Even some supposedly "risk-free" U.S. Treasury bonds lost fully half their value, and a similar situation occurred with corporate bonds, mortgages, and other fixed-rate, long-term securities. As a result, many lenders became reluctant to lend money at fixed rates on a long-term basis, and they would do so only at extraordinarily high rates.

There is normally a *maturity risk premium* embodied in long-term interest rates; this premium is designed to offset the risk of declining bond prices if interest rates rise. Prior to the 1970s, the maturity risk premium on 30-year bonds was about one percentage point, meaning that under normal conditions, a firm might expect to pay about one percentage point more to borrow on a long-term than on a short-term basis. However, in the early 1980s, the maturity risk premium is estimated to have jumped to about three percentage points, which made long-term debt very expensive relative to short-term debt. Lenders were able and willing to lend on a short-term basis, but corporations were correctly reluctant to borrow on a short-term basis to finance long-term assets—such action is extremely dangerous. Therefore, there was a situation in which lenders did not want to lend on a long-term basis, but corporations needed long-term money. The problem was solved by the introduction of long-term, floating rate debt.

floating rate bond

A bond whose interest rate fluctuates with shifts in the general level of interest rates.

A typical **floating rate bond** works as follows. The coupon rate is set for, say, the initial six-month period, after which it is adjusted every six months based on some market rate. Some corporate issues have been tied to the Treasury bond rate, while other issues have been tied to short-term rates. Many additional provisions can be included in floating rate issues; for example, some are convertible to fixed rate debt, whereas others have upper and lower limits ("caps" and "collars") on how high or low the yield can go.

Floating rate debt is advantageous to investors because the interest rate moves up if market rates rise. This causes the market value of the debt to be stabilized, and it also provides lenders such as banks with income which is better geared to their own obligations. (Banks' deposit costs rise with interest rates, so the income on floating rate loans rises just when banks' deposit costs are rising.) Moreover, floating rate debt is advantageous to corporations because by using it, firms can issue debt with a long maturity without committing themselves to paying a historically high rate of interest for the entire life of the loan. Of course, if interest rates were to move even higher after a floating rate note had been signed, the borrower would have been better off issuing conventional, fixed rate debt.

Junk Bonds

Prior to the 1980s, fixed income investors such as pension funds and insurance companies were generally unwilling to buy risky bonds, so it was almost impossible for risky companies to raise capital in the public bond markets. These companies, if they could raise debt capital at all, had to do so in the term loan market, where the loan could be tailored to satisfy the lender. Then, in the late 1970s, Michael Milken of the investment banking firm Drexel Burnham Lambert, relying on historical studies which showed that risky bonds yielded more than enough to compensate for their risk, began to convince certain institutional investors of the merits of purchasing risky debt. Thus was born the **junk bond,** a high-risk, high-yield bond issued to finance a leveraged buyout, a merger, or a troubled company. For example, when Ted Turner attempted to buy CBS, he planned to finance the acquisition by issuing junk bonds to CBS's stockholders in exchange for their shares. Similarly, Public Service of New Hampshire financed construction of its troubled Seabrook nuclear plant with junk bonds, and junk bonds were used in the RJR Nabisco LBO. In junk bond deals, the debt ratio is generally extremely high, so the bondholders must bear as much risk as stockholders normally would. The bonds' yields reflect this fact—a coupon rate of 25 percent per annum was required to sell the Public Service of New Hampshire bonds.

junk bond
A high-risk, high-yield bond used to finance mergers, leveraged buyouts, and troubled companies.

The emergence of junk bonds as an important type of debt is another example of how the investment banking industry adjusts to and facilitates new developments in capital markets. In the 1980s, mergers and takeovers increased dramatically. People like T. Boone Pickens and Ted Turner thought that certain old-line, established companies were run inefficiently and were financed too conservatively, and they wanted to take these companies over and restructure them. Michael Milken and his staff at Drexel Burnham Lambert began an active campaign to persuade certain institutions (often S&Ls) to purchase high-yield bonds. Milken developed expertise in putting together deals that were attractive to the institutions yet apparently feasible in the sense that projected cash flows were sufficient to meet the required interest payments. The fact that interest on the bonds was tax deductible, combined with the much higher debt ratios of the restructured firms, also increased after-tax cash flows and helped make the deals appear feasible.

The development of junk bond financing has done as much as any single factor to reshape the U.S. financial scene. The existence of these securities led directly to the loss of independence of Gulf Oil and hundreds of other companies, and it led to major shake-ups in such companies as CBS, Union Carbide, and USX (formerly U.S. Steel). It also caused Drexel Burnham Lambert to leap from essentially nowhere in the 1970s to become the most profitable investment banking firm during the 1980s.

The phenomenal growth of the junk bond market was impressive, but controversial. In early 1989, Drexel Burnham Lambert was forced into bankruptcy, and "junk bond king" Michael Milken is now in jail. These events badly tarnished the junk bond market, which also came under severe criticism for fueling takeover fires and adding to the cost of the S&L bailout. Additionally, the realization that high leverage can spell trouble—as when Campeau, with $3 billion in junk financing, filed for bankruptcy in early 1990—has slowed the growth in the junk bond market.

Do junk bonds have a future role in corporate finance aside from takeovers and LBOs? In Chapter 17, we discussed the signaling theory of capital structure, which implies that companies should first use retained earnings plus debt supported by retained earnings, then use "reserve borrowing capacity" debt, and only issue new common stock as a last resort, after all the debt capacity has been exhausted. The development of the junk bond market has effectively extended the limits of firms' debt capacities beyond the earlier limits, and in spite of all the publicity surrounding the use of junk bonds in mergers and acquisitions, statistics show that well over half of the junk bond issues in recent years have been used for normal expansion purposes.

The final verdict on junk bonds is not yet in. However, at this point it appears that junk bonds will play a smaller role in corporate financings in the 1990s than they did in the 1980s, but that they will remain an important part of the financial scene.

Self-Test Questions

Explain how the cash flows related to an issue of zero coupon bonds are determined.

What problem was solved by the introduction of long-term floating rate debt, and how is the rate on such bonds actually set?

For what purposes have junk bonds typically been used?

BOND RATINGS

Since the early 1900s, bonds have been assigned quality ratings that reflect their probability of going into default. The two major rating agencies are Moody's Investors Service (Moody's) and Standard & Poor's Corporation (S&P). These agencies' rating designations are shown in Table 20-2.[6] The triple- and double-A bonds are extremely safe. Single-A and triple-B bonds are strong enough to be called **investment grade bonds,** and they are the lowest-rated bonds that many banks and other institutional investors are permitted by law to hold. Double-B and lower bonds are speculative, or junk bonds; they have a significant probability of going into default, and many financial institutions are prohibited from buying them.

investment grade bonds

Bonds rated A or triple-B; many banks and other institutional investors are permitted by law to hold only investment grade or better bonds.

Bond Rating Criteria

Bond ratings are based on both qualitative and quantitative factors, some of which are as follows:

1. Various ratios, including the debt ratio, the times-interest-earned ratio, the fixed charge coverage ratio, and the current ratio.

2. Mortgage provisions: Is the bond secured by a mortgage? If it is, and if the property has a high value in relation to the amount of bonded debt, the bond's rating is enhanced.

3. Subordination provisions: Is the bond subordinated to other debt? If so, it will be rated at least one notch below the rating it would have if it were

---

[6]In the discussion to follow, reference to the S&P code is intended to imply the Moody's code as well. Thus, triple-B bonds mean both BBB and Baa bonds; double-B bonds mean both BB and Ba bonds; and so on.

Table 20-2   ▪   **Moody's and S&P Bond Ratings**

| | High Quality | | Investment Grade | | Junk Bonds | | | |
					Substandard		Speculative	
Moody's	Aaa	Aa	A	Baa	Ba	B	Caa	C
S&P	AAA	AA	A	BBB	BB	B	CCC	D

Note: Both Moody's and S&P use "modifiers" for bonds rated below triple A. S&P uses a plus and minus system; thus, A+ designates the strongest A-rated bonds and A− the weakest. Moody's uses a 1, 2, or 3 designation, with 1 denoting the strongest and 3 the weakest; thus, within the double-A category, Aa1 is the best, Aa2 is average, and Aa3 is the weakest.

not subordinated. Conversely, a bond with other debt subordinated to it will have a somewhat higher rating.

4. Guarantee provisions: Some bonds are guaranteed by other firms. If a weak company's debt is guaranteed by a strong company (usually the weak company's parent), the bond will be given the strong company's rating.

5. Sinking fund: Does the bond have a sinking fund to insure systematic repayment? This feature is a plus factor to the rating agencies.

6. Maturity: Other things the same, a bond with a shorter maturity will be judged less risky than a longer-term bond, and this will be reflected in the ratings.

7. Stability: Are the issuer's sales and earnings stable?

8. Regulation: Is the issuer regulated, and could an adverse regulatory climate cause the company's economic position to decline? Regulation is especially important for utilities, railroads, and telephone companies.

9. Antitrust: Are any antitrust actions pending against the firm that could erode its position?

10. Overseas operations: What percentage of the firm's sales, assets, and profits are from overseas operations, and what is the political climate in the host countries?

11. Environmental factors: Is the firm likely to face heavy expenditures for pollution control equipment?

12. Pension liabilities: Does the firm have unfunded pension liabilities that could pose a future problem?

13. Labor unrest: Are there potential labor problems on the horizon that could weaken the firm's position? As this is written, a number of airlines face this problem, and it has caused their ratings to be lowered.

14. Accounting policies: If a firm uses relatively conservative accounting policies, its reported earnings will be of "higher quality" than if it uses less conservative procedures. Thus, conservative accounting policies are a plus factor in bond ratings.

Representatives of the rating agencies have consistently stated that no precise formula is used to set a firm's rating; all the factors listed, plus others, are taken into account, but not in a mathematically precise manner. Statistical studies have borne out this contention, for researchers who have tried to predict bond ratings on the basis of quantitative data have had only limited success, indicating that the agencies use subjective judgment when establishing a firm's rating.[7]

Importance of Bond Ratings

Bond ratings are important both to firms and to investors. First, because a bond's rating is an indicator of its default risk, the rating has a direct, measurable influence on the bond's interest rate and the firm's cost of debt capital. Second, most bonds are purchased by institutional investors rather than individuals, and many institutions are restricted to investment-grade securities. Thus, if a firm's bonds fall below BBB, it will have a difficult time selling new bonds since many potential purchasers will not be allowed to buy them.

As a result of their higher risk and more restricted market, lower-grade bonds have higher required rates of return, k_d, than high-grade bonds. Figure 20-1 illustrates this point. In each of the years shown on the graph, U.S. government bonds have had the lowest yields, AAAs have been next, and BBB bonds have had the highest yields. The figure also shows that the gaps between yields on the three types of bonds vary over time, indicating that the cost differentials, or risk premiums, fluctuate from year to year. This point is highlighted in Figure 20-2, which gives the yields on the three types of bonds and the risk premiums for AAA and BBB bonds in June 1963 and January 1992.[8] Note first that the risk-free rate, or vertical axis intercept, rose more than 3 percentage points from 1963 to 1992, primarily reflecting the increase in realized and anticipated inflation. Second, the slope of the line also has increased since 1963, indicating an increase in investors' risk aversion. Thus, the penalty for having a low credit rating varies over time. Occasionally, as in 1963, the penalty is quite small, but at other times, as in 1992, it is large. These slope differences reflect investors' risk aversion. In 1992, there was fear of a lingering recession, and at such times there is a "flight to quality," Treasuries are in great demand, and the premium on low-quality over high-quality bonds increases.

Changes in Ratings

Changes in a firm's bond rating affect both its ability to borrow long-term capital and the cost of that capital. Rating agencies review outstanding bonds on a periodic basis, occasionally upgrading or downgrading a bond as a result of its

---

[7]See Ahmed Belkaoui, *Industrial Bonds and the Rating Process* (London: Quorum Books, 1983).

[8]The term *risk premium* ought to reflect only the difference in expected (and required) returns between two securities that results from differences in their risk. However, the differences between *yields to maturity* on different types of bonds consist of (1) a true risk premium; (2) a liquidity premium, which reflects the fact that U.S. Treasury bonds are more readily marketable than most corporate bonds; (3) a call premium, because most Treasury bonds are not callable whereas corporate bonds are; and (4) an expected loss differential, which reflects the probability of loss on the corporate bonds. As an example of the last point, suppose the yield to maturity on a BBB bond was 10 percent versus 7 percent on government bonds, but there was a 5 percent probability of total default loss on the corporate bond. In this case, the expected return on the BBB bond would be $0.95(10\%) + 0.05(0\%) = 9.5\%$, and the risk premium would be 2.5 percent, not the full 3 percentage point difference in "promised" yields to maturity. Because of all these points, the risk premiums given in Figure 20-2 overstate somewhat the true (but unmeasurable) risk premiums.

Figure 20-1   ▪   **Yields on Selected Long-Term Bonds, 1955–1992**

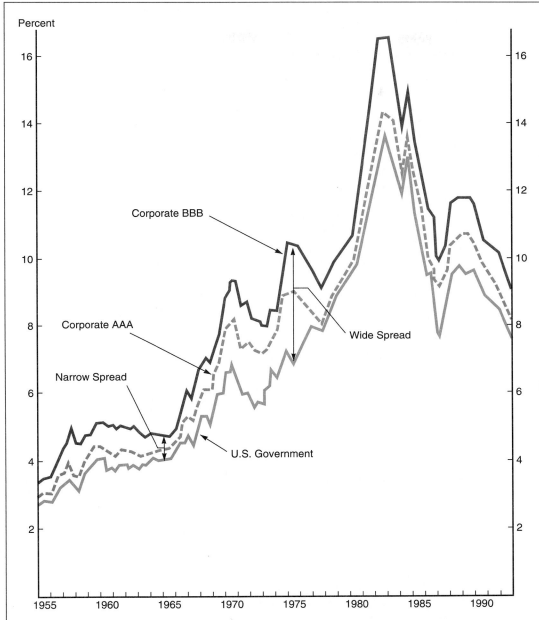

Sources: Federal Reserve Board, *Historical Chart Book,* 1983, and *Federal Reserve Bulletin,* various issues.

issuer's changed circumstances. For example, the April 6, 1992, issue of *Standard & Poor's CreditWeek* reported that Arkla Inc.'s senior debt ratings were lowered from BBB to BB+, reflecting the company's weak financial profile and continuing concerns about the effects of depressed natural gas prices on the company's pipeline and gas production businesses. In the same issue, S&P up-

Figure 20-2 ▪ **Relationship between Bond Ratings and Bond Yields, 1963 and 1992**

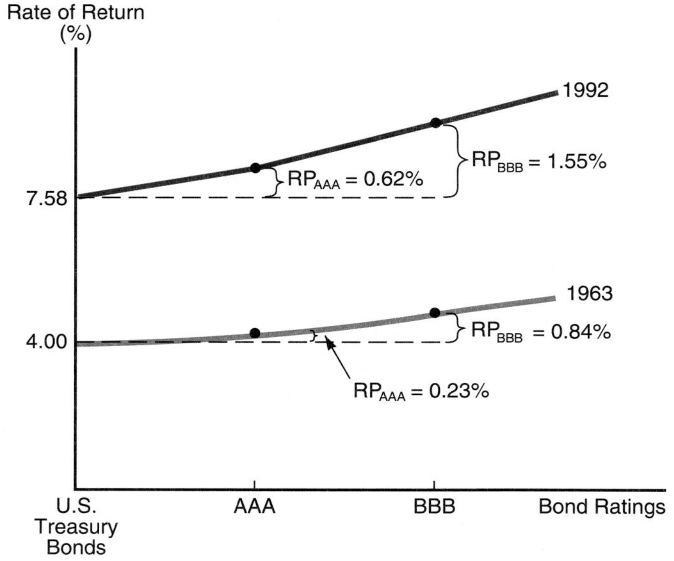

	Long-Term Government Bonds (Default-Free) (1)	AAA Corporate Bonds (2)	BBB Corporate Bonds (3)	Risk Premiums	
				AAA (4) = (2) − (1)	BBB (5) = (3) − (1)
June 1963	4.00%	4.23%	4.84%	0.23%	0.84%
January 1992	7.58	8.20	9.13	0.62	1.55

RP_{AAA} = risk premium on AAA bonds.

RP_{BBB} = risk premium on BBB bonds.

Sources: *Federal Reserve Bulletin,* December 1963, and April 1992.

graded Chicago & North Western Acquisition Corporation's subordinated debt ratings from B− to B+. Chicago & North Western Acquisition is the parent company of CNW Corporation, which owns Chicago & North Western Transportation Company, the eighth largest U.S. rail system. The rating upgrade is a result of the company's improved operational performance and the completion of a public stock offering and debt restructuring. Through the company's recapitalization, it is anticipated that earnings and cash flow will increase by lowering its annual interest expense and eliminating its preferred stock dividends.

? Self-Test Questions

Name the two major rating agencies and some factors that affect bond ratings.

Why are bond ratings important both to firms and to investors?

RATIONALE FOR USING DIFFERENT TYPES OF SECURITIES

Why are there so many different types of long-term securities? At least a partial answer to this question may be seen in Figure 20-3, which depicts the now familiar risk/return tradeoff function drawn to show the risk and the expected after-personal-tax returns for the various securities of Allied Food Products.[9] First, U.S. Treasury bills, which represent the risk-free rate, are shown for reference. The lowest-risk long-term securities offered by Allied are its floating rate notes; these securities are free of interest rate risk, but they are exposed to some risk of default. The first mortgage bonds are somewhat riskier than the notes (because the bonds are exposed to interest rate risk), and they sell at a somewhat higher required and expected after-tax return. The second mortgage bonds are even riskier, so they have a still higher expected return. Subordinated debentures, income bonds, and preferred stocks are all increasingly risky, and their expected returns increase accordingly. The firm's convertible preferred is riskier than its straight preferred, but less risky than its common stock. Allied's warrants, the riskiest security it issues, have the highest required return. (Preferred stock, warrants, and convertibles all will be discussed in Chapter 21.)

Why does Allied issue so many different classes of securities? Why not offer just one type of bond, plus common stock? The answer lies in the fact that different investors have different risk/return tradeoff preferences, so to appeal to the broadest possible market, Allied must offer securities that attract as many different types of investors as possible. Also, different securities are more popular at different points in time, and firms tend to issue whatever is popular at the time they need money. Used wisely, a policy of selling differentiated securities to take advantage of market conditions can lower a firm's overall cost of capital below what it would be if the firm used only one class of debt.

 Self-Test Questions

List the different types of securities in order of highest to lowest risk.

Why do corporations issue so many different classes of securities?

FACTORS INFLUENCING LONG-TERM FINANCING DECISIONS

As we show in this section, many factors influence a firm's long-term financing decisions. The factors' relative importance varies among firms at any point in time and for any given firm over time, but any company planning to raise new long-term capital should consider each of these points.

---

[9]The yields in Figure 20-3 are shown on an after-tax basis to the recipient. If yields were on a before-tax basis, those on preferred stocks would lie below those on bonds because of the tax treatment of preferreds. In essence, 70 percent of preferred dividends are tax exempt to corporations owning preferred shares, so a preferred stock with a 10 percent pre-tax yield will have a higher after-tax return to a corporation in the 34 percent tax bracket than will a bond with a 12 percent yield. This point will be discussed in more detail in Chapter 21.

Figure 20-3 ▪ **Allied Food Products: Risk and Expected Returns on Different Classes of Securities**

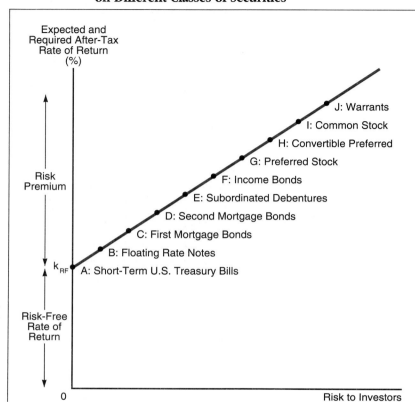

Target Capital Structure

As we discussed in Chapter 17, firms typically establish target capital structures, and one of the most important considerations in any financing decision is how the firm's actual capital structure compares to its target structure. However, few firms finance each year exactly in accordance with their target capital structures, primarily because exact adherence would increase their flotation costs: since smaller issues of new securities have proportionally larger flotation costs, firms tend to use debt one year and stock the next.

For example, Allied Food Products, a processor and distributor of a wide variety of staple foods discussed earlier in the text, needs $15 million of new external capital in each of the next two years. Its target capital structure calls for 45 percent debt, so if Allied were to raise debt each year, it would issue $6.75 million of new bonds each year. The flotation costs, based on data back in Table 19-4 (in Chapter 19), would be 3.2 percent of each $6.75 million issue. To net $6.75 million, Allied would have to sell $6,750,000/0.968 = $6,973,140 each year and thus pay $223,140 in flotation costs on each issue, for a total of $446,280 in flotation costs over the two years. Alternatively, Allied could raise the entire $13.5 million of debt in one year. The flotation cost for a $13.5 million issue would be about 1.9 percent, so the firm would float an issue for

$13,500,000/0.981 = $13,761,468 and pay $261,468 in total flotation costs. By issuing debt only once, Allied could cut its debt flotation costs by more than 40 percent. The same relationship would apply to sales of preferred stock and to new common equity issues.

Making fewer but larger security offerings would cause Allied's capital structure to fluctuate above and below its optimal level rather than stay right on target. However, as we discussed in Chapter 17, small fluctuations about the optimal capital structure have little effect either on a firm's cost of debt and equity or on its overall cost of capital. Also, investors would recognize that its actions were prudent and that the firm would save substantial amounts of flotation costs by financing in this manner. Therefore, even though firms such as Allied do tend to finance over the long haul in accordance with their target capital structures, flotation costs have a definite influence on the specific financing decisions in any given year.

Maturity Matching

Assume that Allied decides to float a single $13.5 million nonconvertible bond issue with a sinking fund. It must next choose a maturity for the issue, taking into consideration the shape of the yield curve, management's own expectations about future interest rates, and the maturity of the assets being financed. In the case at hand, Allied's capital projects during the next two years consist primarily of new, automated food processing machinery for one of its Midwestern plants. This machinery has an expected economic life of 10 years (even though it falls into the MACRS 5-year class life). Should Allied finance the debt portion of the capital raised for this equipment with 5-year, 10-year, 20-year, or 30-year debt, or with debt of some other maturity? *One approach is to match the maturity of the liabilities with the maturity of the assets being financed.*

Note that some of the new capital for the machinery will come from common stock, which is generally considered to be a perpetual security with an infinite maturity. Of course, common stock can always be repurchased on the open market or by a tender offer, so its effective maturity can be reduced significantly, but generally it has no maturity.

Debt maturities, however, are specified at the time of issue. If Allied financed its capital budgets over the next two years with 10-year sinking fund bonds, it would be matching its asset and liability maturities. The cash flows resulting from the new machinery should be sufficient to make the interest and sinking fund payments on the issue, and the bonds would be retired as the machinery wore out. If Allied used 1-year debt, it would have to pay off the loan with cash flows derived from assets other than the machinery in question. If its operations were stable, the company could probably roll over the 1-year debt, but if interest rates rose, then it would have to pay a higher rate. If Allied subsequently experienced difficulties, its lenders might be hesitant to extend the loan, and the company might be unable to obtain new short-term debt at any reasonable rate. At the other extreme, if it used 20-year or 30-year debt, Allied would still have to service the debt long after the assets purchased with the debt had been scrapped and had ceased providing cash flows, and this would worry potential lenders.

For all these reasons, one commonly used financing strategy is to match debt maturities with asset maturities. In recognition of this fact, firms do consider maturity relationships, and this factor has a major influence on the type of debt securities used.

Interest Rate Levels

Financial managers also consider interest rate levels, both absolute and relative, when making financing decisions. For example, long-term interest rates were high by historic standards in 1981 and 1982, so many managers were reluctant to issue long-term debt and thus lock in those high costs for long periods. We already know that one solution to this problem is to use long-term debt with a call provision. Callability permits the company to refund the issue should interest rates drop, but there is a cost, because firms must pay more if they make their debt callable. Alternatively, a firm may finance with short-term debt whenever long-term rates are historically high, and then, assuming that interest rates subsequently fall, sell a long-term issue to replace the short-term debt. Of course, this strategy has its risks. If interest rates climb even higher, the firm will be forced to renew the short-term debt at higher and higher rates, or to replace the short-term debt with a long-term bond which costs more than it would have cost earlier.

Forecasted Interest Rates

At a time when the interest rate on AAA corporate bonds was over 10 percent, which was high by historical standards, Exxon's investment bankers advised the company to tap the Eurodollar bond market for relatively cheap fixed rate financing.[10] At the time, Exxon could have issued its bonds in London at 0.4 percentage points *below* comparable-maturity Treasury bonds. However, one Exxon officer was quoted as cautioning, "I say so what. The absolute level of rates is too high. We would rather wait." The managers of Exxon, as well as those of many other companies, were betting that the next move in interest rates would be down.

This example illustrates that firms do base their financing decisions on expectations about future interest rates. In Exxon's case, the financial staff turned out to be correct. However, the success of such a strategy requires interest rate forecasts to be right more often than they are wrong, and it is very difficult to find someone with a long-term forecasting record better than 50-50.

The Firm's Current and Forecasted Conditions

If a firm's current financial condition is poor, its managers may be reluctant to issue new long-term debt, because (1) a new bond issue would probably trigger a review by the rating agencies, and (2) long-term debt issued when a firm is in poor financial condition costs more and is subject to more severe restrictive covenants than debt issued from a strong position. Thus, a firm that is in a

---

[10]A *Eurodollar bond* is a bond sold outside of the United States but denominated in U.S. dollars.

weakened condition but which is forecasting an improvement would be inclined to delay permanent financing until things improved. Conversely, a firm that is strong now but whose forecasts indicate a potentially bad time just ahead would be motivated to finance long term now rather than to wait. These scenarios imply that the capital markets are inefficient in the sense that investors do not have as much information about the firm's future as does its management. This situation is undoubtedly true at times.

The firm's earnings outlook, and the extent to which forecasted higher earnings per share are reflected in stock prices, also has an effect on the choice of securities. If a successful R&D program has just been concluded, and, consequently, management forecasts higher earnings than do most investors, the firm would not want to issue common stock. It would use debt, and then, after earnings had risen and pushed up the stock price, it would sell common stock to restore the capital structure to its target level.

Restrictions in Existing Debt Contracts

Earlier we discussed the fact that Savannah Electric has at times been restricted from issuing new first mortgage bonds by its indenture coverage requirements. This is just one example of how indenture covenants can influence a firm's financing decisions. Restrictions on the current ratio, the debt ratio, and so on, can also restrict a firm's ability to use different types of financing at a given time.

Availability of Collateral

Generally, secured long-term debt will be less costly than unsecured debt. Thus, firms with large amounts of general-purpose (as opposed to specialized) fixed assets are likely to use a relatively large amount of debt, especially mortgage bonds. Additionally, each year's financing decision will be influenced by the amount of newly acquired assets that are available as security for new bonds.

Self-Test Questions

Do most firms finance each year exactly in accordance with their target capital structures? Why or why not?

Why is the matching of debt maturities with asset maturities a commonly used financing strategy?

If a firm's current financial condition is expected to improve shortly, why might its managers be reluctant to issue new long-term debt?

Which type of firm is more likely to use a relatively large amount of debt, a firm with general-purpose fixed assets or one with specialized fixed assets? Explain.

BANKRUPTCY AND REORGANIZATION

During recessions bankruptcies normally rise, and the recession of 1991–1992 was no exception. The 1991–1992 casualties included Pan Am, Carter Hawley Hale Stores, Continental Airlines, R. H. Macy & Company, Zale Corporation, and

INDUSTRY PRACTICE   Fast-Track Bankruptcies for Small Businesses

Under the existing bankruptcy laws, small and large companies seeking protection from creditors while they reorganize are lumped together under Chapter 11 of the federal bankruptcy code. The complexity of major corporate failures slows down the court process, which results in increasing the reorganization time required for all bankruptcies, even relatively simple small-business failures. Therefore, credit managers are seeking a "fast-track" bankruptcy procedure for small businesses.

The National Association of Credit Management, the largest trade group for credit managers, recently proposed that Congress simplify existing bankruptcy procedures for small companies under a new section called Chapter 10. Under this new proposal, a single trustee, rather than an unwieldy creditors committee, would monitor creditor payments while the company recoups its losses. In addition to this change, a company would have just 90 days to file its reorganization plan, and a hearing on the plan would have to be held within 45 days from the reorganization plan's filing.

The new Chapter 10 is modeled after a three-year-old program run by Judge A. Thomas Small of the federal bankruptcy court in Raleigh, North Carolina. Judge Small's system has decreased the average time from the bankruptcy filing to confirmation of the reorganization plan from the national average of two years to only six months. As Judge Small explains, the proposed Chapter 10 is a good idea; speed is important because it saves money.

The last major revision to the bankruptcy code, which took place in 1978, gave family farmers and consumers their own bankruptcy chapters. However, no separate chapters were created for small businesses. Under the proposed Chapter 10, small-business debtors would get out of court faster, creditors would get their money faster, less money would be spent on court costs, and the IRS would get its money faster. Thus, "fast-track" bankruptcies for small businesses seem to be a good idea for everyone involved.

Source: "Finding a Quick Route through Bankruptcy," *The Wall Street Journal,* September 12, 1991.

McCrory Corporation. Because of its importance, at least a brief discussion of bankruptcy is warranted within the chapter, and a more detailed discussion is presented in Appendix 20A.

When a business becomes *insolvent,* it does not have enough cash to meet scheduled interest and principal payments. A decision must then be made whether to dissolve the firm through *liquidation* or to permit it to *reorganize* and thus stay alive. These issues are addressed in Chapters 7 and 11 of the federal bankruptcy statutes, and the final decision is made by a federal bankruptcy court judge.

The decision to force a firm to liquidate or to permit it to reorganize depends on whether the value of the reorganized firm is likely to be greater than the value of the firm's assets if they were sold off piecemeal. In a reorganization, a committee of unsecured creditors is appointed by the court to negotiate with management on the terms of a potential reorganization. The reorganization plan may call for a *restructuring* of the firm's debt, in which case the interest rate may be reduced, the term to maturity lengthened, or some of the debt may be exchanged for equity. The point of the restructuring is to reduce the financial charges to a level that the firm's cash flows can support. Of course, the common stockholders also have to give up something—they normally see their position eroded as a result of additional shares being given to debtholders in exchange for accepting a reduced amount of debt principal and interest. A trustee may be appointed by the court to oversee the reorganization, or the existing management may be allowed to retain control.

Liquidation occurs if the company is deemed to be too far gone to be saved—if it is worth more dead than alive. If the bankruptcy court orders a liquidation, assets are distributed as specified in Chapter 7 of the Bankruptcy Act. Here is the priority of claims:

1. Secured creditors are entitled to the proceeds of the sale of the specific property that was used to support their loans.

2. The trustee's costs of administering and operating the bankrupt firm are next in line.

3. Expenses incurred after bankruptcy was filed but before a trustee was appointed come next.

4. Wages due workers, up to a limit of $2,000 per worker, follow.

5. Claims for unpaid contributions to employee benefit plans are next. This amount, together with wages, cannot exceed $2,000 per worker.

6. Unsecured claims for customer deposits up to $900 per customer are sixth in line.

7. Federal, state, and local taxes due come next.

8. Unfunded pension plan liabilities are next. (Limitations exist as specified in Appendix 20A.)

9. General unsecured creditors are ninth on the list.

10. Preferred stockholders come next, up to the par value of their stock.

11. Common stockholders are finally paid, if anything is left.

Appendix 20A provides an illustration of how a firm's assets are distributed after it has been liquidated. For now, you should know (1) that the Federal bankruptcy statutes govern both reorganization and liquidation, (2) that bankruptcies occur frequently, and (3) that a priority of the specified claims must be followed when distributing the assets of a liquidated firm.

Self-Test Questions

When a business becomes insolvent, what two alternatives are available?

Differentiate between a *liquidation* and a *reorganization*.

List the priority of claims for the distribution of the assets of a liquidated firm.

REFUNDING OPERATIONS

A great deal of long-term debt was issued at very high interest rates during the late 1970s and early 1980s. Since then, interest rates have fallen, and the call protection periods of many bonds have expired. As a result, corporations and government units are retiring old bonds and replacing them with lower interest rate new bonds.

Bond refunding analysis is similar to capital budgeting analysis, as discussed in Chapters 14 and 15. To simplify things, we assume that the "refunding" corporation has a zero percent tax rate. This avoids some complicated but important tax issues, which are addressed in Appendix 20B.

The refunding decision actually involves two separate questions: (1) Would it be profitable to call an outstanding issue now and to replace it with a new issue? (2) Even if refunding is currently profitable, would it be better to call now or to postpone the refunding to a later date? We consider the first question here, but the second issue is deferred to Appendix 20B.

As noted above, refunding decisions are similar to capital budgeting decisions, and the net present value method is the primary tool. In essence, the costs of undertaking the refunding operation (the investment outlay) are compared to the present value of the interest that will be saved if the high interest rate bond is called and replaced with a new, low interest rate bond. If the net present value of refunding is positive, then the refunding should take place. The costs of the refunding operation consist primarily of the call premium on the old bond issue and the flotation costs associated with selling the new issue. The cash flow benefits consist primarily of the interest expenses that will be saved if the company replaces high-cost debt with low-cost debt. The discount rate used to find the present value of the interest savings is the after-tax cost of new debt — the interest saved is the difference between two relatively certain cash flow streams, so the difference is essentially riskless. Therefore, a low discount rate should be used, and that rate is today's after-tax cost of new debt in the market.

For simplification, we assume that the new bond will have the same maturity as the remaining maturity of the old bond. If this is not the case, then a replacement chain analysis must be used, as is done in capital budgeting analysis when replacement projects have unequal lives.

To illustrate the refunding decision, consider the Strasburg Communications Corporation, which has a $100 million, 13 percent, semiannual coupon bond outstanding with 10 years remaining to maturity. The bond has a call provision which permits the company to retire the issue by calling the bonds in at a 10 percent call premium. Investment bankers have assured Strasburg that it could issue an additional $100 million of new 10-year bonds with a semiannual coupon of 10 percent. Flotation costs on the new refunding issue will amount to $4,000,000. Strasburg has suffered losses in recent years, so its marginal tax rate is zero percent. Predictions are that long-term interest rates are unlikely to fall below 10 percent. Should the company refund the $100 million of 13 percent semiannual coupon bonds?

Strasburg's refunding analysis is presented below. Since the marginal tax rate is zero, its before-tax cash flows are equal to its after-tax cash flows, and its before-tax cost of new debt is equal to its after-tax cost, 10 percent per year or 5 percent per 6-month period. Since the bonds have semiannual coupons, there will be 20 semiannual periods in the analysis, and the discount rate must be halved.

Cost of Refunding at t = 0

Call premium on old bond (0.1 × $100 million)	$10,000,000
Flotation costs on new issue	4,000,000
Total investment outlay	$14,000,000

Semiannual Interest Savings Due to Refunding: t = 1 to 20

Interest on old bond (0.065 × $100 million)	$ 6,500,000
Interest on new bond (0.05 × $100 million)	5,000,000
Net interest savings	$ 1,500,000

Refunding Time Line:

	0	1	2		20
Investment outlay	−14,000,000				
Interest savings	0	1,500,000	1,500,000	· · ·	1,500,000
Net cash flow	−14,000,000	1,500,000	1,500,000	· · ·	1,500,000

NPV at 5% = $4,693,316.

Since the NPV of refunding is positive, Strasburg should refund the old bond issue. The firm's value will be increased by $4,693,316 if it retires the old bonds.

Self-Test Questions

In what respects is bond refunding analysis similar to capital budgeting analysis?

What two questions are involved in the bond refunding decision?

What are the primary costs and the primary benefits in a bond refunding analysis?

Why is the after-tax cost of debt used as the discount rate in a bond refunding analysis?

SUMMARY

This chapter described the characteristics, advantages, and disadvantages of the major types of long-term debt securities. The key concepts covered are listed below.

- **Term loans** and **bonds** are long-term debt contracts under which a borrower agrees to make a series of interest and principal payments on specific dates to the lender. A term loan is generally sold to one lender (or a few), while a bond is typically offered to the public and sold to many different investors.

- There are many different types of bonds. They include **mortgage bonds, debentures, convertibles, bonds with warrants, income bonds, putable bonds,** and **purchasing power (indexed) bonds.** The return required on each type of bond is determined by the bond's riskiness.

- A bond's **indenture** is a legal document that spells out the rights of the bondholders and of the issuing corporation. A **trustee** is assigned to make sure that the terms of the indenture are carried out.

- A **call provision** gives the issuing corporation the right to redeem the bonds prior to maturity under specified terms, usually at a price greater than the maturity value (the difference is a **call premium**). A firm will typically call a bond and refund it if interest rates fall substantially.

▪ A **sinking fund** is a provision which requires the corporation to retire a portion of the bond issue each year. The purpose of the sinking fund is to provide for the orderly retirement of the issue. No call premium is paid to the holders of bonds called for sinking fund purposes.

▪ Some recent innovations in long-term financing include **zero coupon bonds,** which pay no annual interest but which are issued at a discount; **floating rate debt,** whose interest payments fluctuate with changes in the general level of interest rates; and **junk bonds,** which are high-risk, high-yield instruments issued by firms which use a great deal of financial leverage.

▪ Bonds are assigned **ratings** which reflect the probability of their going into default. The higher a bond's rating, the lower its interest rate.

▪ A firm's long-term financing decisions are influenced by its **target capital structure,** the **maturity of its assets,** current and forecasted **interest rate levels,** the firm's current and forecasted **financial condition, restrictions** in its existing debt contracts, and the suitability of its **assets for use as collateral.**

Two related issues are discussed in detail in Appendixes 20A and 20B: bankruptcy and bond refundings. Bankruptcy is an important consideration both to companies that issue debt and to investors, for it has a profound effect on all parties. Refunding, or paying off high interest rate debt with new, lower cost debt, is also an important consideration, especially today (1992), because many firms that issued long-term debt in the early 1980s at rates of 12 percent or more now have an opportunity to refund this debt at a cost of 10 percent or less.

Questions

20-1 What effect would each of the following items have on the interest rate a firm must pay on a new issue of long-term debt? Indicate whether each factor would tend to raise, lower, or have an indeterminate effect on the interest rate, and then explain *why*.

a. The firm uses bonds rather than a term loan.

b. The firm uses nonsubordinated debentures rather than first mortgage bonds.

c. The firm makes its bonds convertible into common stock.

d. If the firm makes its debentures subordinate to its bank debt, what will the effect be
   (1) On the cost of the debentures?
   (2) On the cost of the bank debt?
   (3) On the average cost of total debt?

e. The firm sells income bonds rather than debentures.

f. The firm must raise $100 million, all of which will be used to construct a new plant, and it is debating the sale of first mortgage bonds or debentures. If it decides to issue $50 million of each type, as opposed to $75 million of first mortgage bonds and $25 million of debentures, how will this affect
   (1) The cost of debentures?
   (2) The cost of mortgage bonds?
   (3) The weighted average cost of the $100 million?

g. The firm puts a call provision on its new issue of bonds.

h. The firm uses zero coupon bonds rather than regular coupon bonds.

i. The firm includes a sinking fund on its new issue of bonds.

j. The firm's bonds are downgraded from A to BBB.

k. The firm sells Eurobonds rather than U.S. domestic bonds.

20-2   Rank the following securities from lowest (1) to highest (9) in terms of their riskiness for an investor. All securities (except the Treasury bond) are for a given firm. If you think two or more securities are equally risky, indicate so.

a. Income bond   _____

b. Subordinated debentures—noncallable   _____

c. First mortgage bond—no sinking fund   _____

d. Common stock   _____

e. U.S. Treasury bond   _____

f. First mortgage bond—with sinking fund   _____

g. Subordinated debentures—callable   _____

h. Amortized term loan   _____

i. Nonamortized term loan   _____

20-3   A sinking fund can be set up in one of two ways:

(1) The corporation makes annual payments to the trustee, who invests the proceeds in securities (frequently government bonds) and uses the accumulated total to retire the bond issue at maturity.

(2) The trustee uses the annual payments to retire a portion of the issue each year, either calling a given percentage of the issue by a lottery and paying a specified price per bond or buying bonds on the open market, whichever is cheaper.

Discuss the advantages and disadvantages of each procedure from the viewpoint of both the firm and its bondholders.

20-4   Draw an SML graph. Put dots on the graph to show (approximately) where you think a particular company's (a) common stock and (b) bonds would lie. Now put on dots to represent a riskier company's stock and bonds.

Self-Test Problems   *(Solutions Appear in Appendix B)*

ST-1   Define each of the following terms:

Key terms

a. Funded debt

b. Term loan; bond

c. Mortgage bond

d. Debenture; subordinated debenture

e. Convertible bond; warrant; income bond; putable bond; indexed, or purchasing power, bond

f. Indenture; restrictive covenant

g. Trustee

h. Call provision; sinking fund

i. Zero coupon bond; original issue discount bond (OID)

j. Floating rate bond

k. Junk bond

l. Investment grade bonds

m. Maturity matching

ST-2   The Vancouver Development Company has just sold a $100 million, 10-year, 12 per-

Sinking fund   cent bond issue. A sinking fund will retire the issue over its life. Sinking fund payments are of equal amounts and will be made *semiannually,* and the proceeds will be used to retire bonds as the payments are made. Bonds can be called at par for sinking fund purposes, or the funds paid into the sinking fund can be used to buy bonds in the open market.

a. How large must each semiannual sinking fund payment be?
b. What will happen, under the conditions of the problem thus far, to the company's debt service requirements per year for this issue over time?
c. Now suppose Vancouver Development set up its sinking fund so that *equal annual amounts,* payable at the end of each year, are paid into a sinking fund trust held by a bank, with the proceeds being used to buy government bonds that pay 9 percent interest. The payments, plus accumulated interest, must total $100 million at the end of 10 years, and the proceeds will be used to retire the bonds at that time. How large must the annual sinking fund payment be now?
d. What are the annual cash requirements for covering bond service costs under the trusteeship arrangement described in Part c? (Note: Interest must be paid on Vancouver's outstanding bonds but not on bonds that have been retired.)
e. What would have to happen to interest rates to cause the company to buy bonds on the open market rather than call them under the original sinking fund plan?

Problems

20-1
Amortization schedule

Set up an amortization schedule for a $1 million, 3-year, 9 percent loan.

20-2
Perpetual bond analysis

In 1936 the Canadian government raised $55 million by issuing bonds at a 3 percent annual rate of interest. Unlike most bonds issued today, which have a specific maturity date, these bonds can remain outstanding forever; they are, in fact, perpetuities.

At the time of issue, the Canadian government stated in the bond indenture that cash redemption was possible at face value ($100) on or after September 1966; in other words, the bonds were callable at par after September 1966. Believing that the bonds would in fact be called, many investors purchased these bonds in 1965 with expectations of receiving $100 in 1966 for each perpetual bond they had. In 1965 the bonds sold for $55, but a rush of buyers drove the price to just below the $100 par value by 1966. Prices fell dramatically, however, when the Canadian government announced that these perpetual bonds were indeed perpetual and would not be paid off. A new, 30-year supply of coupons was sent to each bondholder.

The bonds' market price declined to $42 in December 1966. Because of their severe losses, hundreds of Canadian bondholders formed the Perpetual Bond Association to lobby for face value redemption of the bonds, claiming that the government had reneged on an implied promise to redeem the bonds. Government officials in Ottawa insisted that claims for face value payment were nonsense, for the bonds were and always had been clearly identified as perpetuals. One Ottawa official stated, "Our job is to protect the taxpayer. Why should we pay $55 million for less than $25 million worth of bonds?"

The issue is heating up again, as 1996 approaches. Here are some questions relating to the Canadian issue that will test your understanding of bonds in general:

a. Would it make sense for a business firm to issue bonds like the Canadian government bonds described here? Would it matter whether the firm was a proprietorship or a corporation?
b. Suppose the U.S. government today sold $100 million each of these four types of bonds: 5-year bonds, 50-year bonds, "regular" perpetuities, and Canadian-type perpetuities. What do you think the relative order of interest rates would be? In other words, rank the bonds from the one with the lowest to the one with the highest rate of interest. Explain your answer.

c. (1) Suppose that because of pressure by the Perpetual Bond Association, you believe that the Canadian government will redeem this particular perpetual bond issue in 4 years. Which course of action would be more advantageous to you if you owned the bonds: (a) sell your bonds today at $55.99, or (b) wait 4 years and have them redeemed? Assume that similar-risk bonds earn 9 percent today and that interest rates are expected to remain at this level for the next 4 years.

(2) If you had the opportunity to invest your money in bonds of similar risk, at what rate of return would you be indifferent to the choice of selling your perpetuals today or having them redeemed in 4 years — that is, what is the expected yield to maturity on the Canadian bonds?

d. Show mathematically the perpetuities' value if they yield 6.1 percent, pay $3 interest annually, and are considered "regular" perpetuities. Show what would happen to the price of the bonds if the going interest rate fell to 2 percent.

e. Are the Canadian bonds more likely to be valued as "regular" perpetuities if the going rate of interest is above or below 3 percent? Why?

f. Do you think the Canadian government would have taken the same action with regard to retiring the bonds if the interest rate had fallen rather than risen after they were issued?

g. Do you think the Canadian government was fair or unfair in its actions? Give the pros and cons, and justify your reason for thinking that one outweighs the other. Would it matter if the bonds had been sold to "sophisticated" as opposed to "naive" purchasers?

20-3
Zero coupon bond

Filkins Farm Equipment needs to raise $4.5 million for expansion, and its investment bankers have indicated that 5-year zero coupon bonds could be sold at a price of $567.44 for each $1,000 bond. Filkins's federal-plus-state tax rate is 40 percent.

a. How many $1,000 par value zero coupon bonds would Filkins have to sell to raise the needed $4.5 million?

b. What would be the after-tax yield on the zeros (1) to an investor who is tax exempt and (2) to a taxpayer in the 31 percent marginal tax bracket?

c. What would be the after-tax cost of debt to Filkins if it decides to issue the zeros?

EXAM-TYPE PROBLEMS

The problems included in this section are set up in such a way that they could be used as multiple-choice exam problems.

20-4
Loan amortization

Suppose a firm is setting up an amortized term loan. What are the annual payments for a $10 million loan under the following terms:

a. 8 percent, 5 years?
b. 8 percent, 10 years?
c. 14 percent, 5 years?
d. 14 percent, 10 years?

20-5
Yield to call

Six years ago The Parrish Company sold a 20-year bond issue with a 14 percent annual coupon rate and a 9 percent call premium. Today Parrish called the bonds. The bonds originally were sold at their face value of $1,000. Compute the realized rate of return for investors who purchased the bonds when they were issued and who surrender them today in exchange for the call price.

20-6
Zero coupon bonds and EAR

Assume that the city of Tampa sold an issue of $1,000 maturity value, tax-exempt (muni), zero coupon bonds 5 years ago. The bonds had a 25-year maturity when they were issued, and the interest rate built into the issue was a nominal 10 percent, but with semiannual compounding. The bonds are now callable at a premium of 10 percent over the accrued value. What effective annual rate of return would an investor who bought the bonds when they were issued and who still owns them earn if they are called today?

20-7
Bond refunding

The city of Gainesville issued $1,000,000 of 14 percent coupon, 30-year, semiannual payment, tax-exempt muni bonds 10 years ago. The bonds had 10 years of call protection, but now Gainesville can call the bonds if it chooses to do so. The call premium would be 10 percent of the face amount. New 20-year, 12 percent, semiannual payment bonds can be sold at par, but flotation costs on this issue would be 2 percent, or $20,000. What is the net present value of the refunding?

INTEGRATIVE PROBLEM

20-8
Long-term debt financing

Hospital Development Corporation (HDC) needs $10 million to build a regional testing laboratory in Birmingham. Once the lab is completed and fully operational, which should take about 5 years, HDC will sell it to a health maintenance organization (HMO). HDC tentatively plans to raise the $10 million by selling 5-year bonds, and its investment bankers have indicated that either regular or zero coupon bonds can be used. Regular coupon bonds would sell at par and would have annual payment coupons of 12 percent, and zero coupon bonds would also be priced to yield 12 percent annually. Either bond would be callable after 3 years, on the anniversary date of the issue, at a premium of 6 months' interest for the regular bonds or 5 percent over the accrued value on the ca' date for zero coupon bonds. HDC's federal-plus-state tax rate is 40 percent. As assi. t to HDC's treasurer, you have been assigned the task of making a recommendation as ﾐ which type of bonds to issue. As part of your analysis, you have been asked to answer the following questions.

a. What is the difference between a bond and a term loan? What are the advantages of a term loan over a bond?

b. Suppose HDC issues bonds and uses the medical center (land and buildings) as collateral to secure the issue. What type of bond would this be? Suppose that instead of using secured bonds HDC had decided to sell debentures. How would this affect the interest rate that HDC would have to pay on the $10 million of debt?

c. What is a bond indenture? What are some typical provisions the bondholders would require HDC to include in its indenture?

d. HDC's bonds will be callable after 3 years. If the bonds were not callable, would the required interest rate be higher or lower than 12 percent? What would be the effect on the rate if the bonds were callable immediately? What are the advantages to HDC of making the bonds callable?

e. (1) Suppose HDC's indenture included a sinking fund provision which required the company to retire one-fifth of the bonds each year. Would this provision raise or lower the interest rate required on the bonds?
(2) How would the sinking fund operate?
(3) Why might HDC's investors require it to use a sinking fund?
(4) For this particular issue, would it make sense to include a sinking fund?

f. If HDC were to issue zero coupon bonds, what initial price would cause the zeros to have an annual (EAR) return of 12 percent? How many $1,000 par value zeros would HDC have to sell to raise the needed $10 million? How many regular 12 percent coupon bonds would HDC have to sell?

g. Set up a time line which shows the accrued value of the zeros at the end of Years 1 through 5, along with the annual after-tax cash flows from the zeros (1) to an investor in the 28 percent tax bracket and (2) to HDC.

h. What would be the after-tax yield to maturity on each type of bond to an investor in the 28 percent tax bracket? What would be the after-tax cost of debt to HDC?

i. If interest rates were to fall, causing HDC to call the bonds (either the zero or the coupon) at the end of Year 3, what would be the after-tax yield to call on each type of bond to an investor in the 28 percent tax bracket?

j. HDC is an A-rated firm. Suppose HDC's bond rating was (1) lowered to triple-B or (2) raised to double-A. Who would make these changes, and what would the changes mean? What would be the effect of these changes on the interest rate required on HDC's new long-term debt and on the market value of HDC's outstanding debt?

k. What are some of the factors a firm like HDC should consider when deciding whether to issue long-term debt, short-term debt, or equity? Why might long-term debt be HDC's best choice for this project?

l. What is meant by the terms "default," "insolvent," "liquidation," "reorganization," "bankruptcy," "Chapter 11," and "Chapter 7"?

m. Explain briefly the order of asset distribution for a firm that is being liquidated.

n. In what sense is a bond refunding decision similar to a capital budgeting decision? Assume that HDC has a $40 million bond issue outstanding that has a 16 percent semiannual coupon and 15 years remaining to maturity. The bond has a call provision which makes it possible for the company to retire the issue at this time by calling the bonds in at a 12 percent call premium. Investment bankers have assured the company that it could sell new 15-year bonds at a semiannual coupon interest rate of 14 percent. Predictions are that long-term interest rates are unlikely to fall below 14 percent. Flotation costs on a new refunding issue will amount to $2.2 million. Assume for purposes of this part only, that HDC has a marginal tax rate of zero percent. Should the company refund the $40 million of 16 percent semiannual coupon bonds?

Appendix 20A

Bankruptcy and Reorganization

In the event of bankruptcy, debtholders have a prior claim to a firm's income and assets over the claims of both common and preferred stockholders. Further, different classes of debtholders are treated differently in the event of bankruptcy. Since bankruptcy is a fairly common occurrence, and since it affects both the bankrupt firm and its customers, suppliers, and creditors, it is important to know who gets what if a firm fails. These topics are discussed in this appendix.[1]

Federal Bankruptcy Laws

Bankruptcy actually begins when a firm is unable to meet scheduled payments on its debt or when the firm's cash flow projections indicate that it will soon be unable to meet payments. As the bankruptcy proceedings go forward, the following central issues arise:

1. Does the firm's inability to meet scheduled payments result from a temporary cash flow problem, or does it represent a permanent problem caused by asset values having fallen below debt obligations?

This appendix was coauthored by Arthur L. Herrmann of the University of Hartford.

[1]Much of the current work in this area is based on writings by Edward I. Altman. For a summary of his work, and that of others, see Edward I. Altman, "Bankruptcy and Reorganization," in *Handbook of Corporate Finance,* Edward I. Altman, ed. (New York: Wiley, 1986), Chapter 19.

2. If the problem is a temporary one, then an agreement which stretches out payments may be worked out to give the firm time to recover and to satisfy everyone. However, if basic long-run asset values have truly declined, economic losses will have occurred. In this event, who should bear the losses?

3. Is the company "worth more dead than alive"—that is, would the business be more valuable if it were maintained and continued in operation or if it were liquidated and sold off in pieces?

4. Who should control the firm while it is being liquidated or rehabilitated? Should the existing management be left in control, or should a trustee be placed in charge of operations?

These are the primary issues that are addressed in the federal bankruptcy statutes.

Our bankruptcy laws were first enacted in 1898, modified substantially in 1938, changed again in 1978, and further fine-tuned in 1984. The 1978 Act, which provides the basic laws which govern bankruptcy today, was a major revision designed to streamline and expedite proceedings, and it consists of eight odd-numbered chapters, the even-numbered chapters of the earlier Act having been deleted. Chapters 1, 3, and 5 of the 1978 Act contain general provisions applicable to the other chapters; Chapter 7 details the procedures to be followed when liquidating a firm; Chapter 9 deals with financially distressed municipalities; Chapter 11 is the business reorganization chapter; Chapter 13 covers the adjustment of debts for "individuals with regular income"; and Chapter 15 sets up a system of trustees who help administer proceedings under the Act.

Chapters 11 and 7 are the most important ones for managerial finance purposes. When you read in the paper that McCrory Corporation or some other company has "filed for Chapter 11," this means that the company is bankrupt and is trying to reorganize under Chapter 11 of the Act. If a reorganization plan cannot be worked out, then the company will be liquidated as prescribed in Chapter 7 of the Act.

The 1978 Act is quite flexible, and it provides a great deal of scope for informal negotiations between a company and its creditors. Under this Act, a case is opened by the filing of a petition with a federal district bankruptcy court. The petition may be either voluntary or involuntary—that is, it may be filed either by the firm's management or by its creditors. A committee of unsecured creditors is then appointed by the court to negotiate with management for a reorganization, which may include the restructuring of debt and other claims against the firm. (A "restructuring" could involve lengthening the maturity of debt, lowering the interest rate on it, reducing the principal amount owed, exchanging common or preferred stock for debt, or some combination of these actions.) A trustee may be appointed by the court if that is deemed to be in the best interests of the creditors and stockholders; otherwise, the existing management will retain control. If no fair and feasible reorganization can be worked out under Chapter 11, the firm will be liquidated under the procedures spelled out in Chapter 7.

Financial Decisions in Bankruptcy

When a business becomes insolvent, a decision must be made whether to dissolve the firm through *liquidation* or to keep it alive through *reorganization*. To a large extent, this decision depends on a determination of the value of the firm if it is rehabilitated versus the value of its assets if they are sold off individually. The procedure that promises higher returns to the creditors and owners will be adopted. However, the "public interest" will also be considered, and this generally means attempting to salvage the firm, even if the salvaging effort may be costly to bondholders. For example, the bankruptcy court kept Eastern Airlines alive, at the cost of millions of dollars which could have been paid to bondholders, until it was obvious even to the judge that Eastern could not be saved. Note too that if the decision is made to reorganize the firm, the courts and possibly the SEC will be called upon to determine the fairness and the feasibility of the proposed reorganization plan.

Standard of Fairness.   The basic doctrine of *fairness* states that claims must be recognized in the order of their legal and contractual priority. Carrying out this concept of fairness in a reorganization (as opposed to a liquidation) involves the following steps.

1.   Future sales must be estimated.

2.   Operating conditions must be analyzed so that the future earnings and cash flows can be predicted.

3.   A capitalization (or discount) rate to be applied to these future cash flows must be determined.

4.   This capitalization rate must then be applied to the estimated cash flows to obtain a present value figure, which is the indicated value for the reorganized company.

5.   Provisions for the distribution of the restructured firm's securities to its claimants must be made.

Standard of Feasibility.   The primary test of *feasibility* in a reorganization is whether the fixed charges after reorganization can be covered by cash flows. Adequate coverage generally requires an improvement in operating earnings, a reduction of fixed charges, or both. Among the actions that must generally be taken are the following:

1.   Debt maturities are usually lengthened, interest rates may be scaled back, and some debt may be converted into equity.

2.   When the quality of management has been substandard, a new team must be given control of the company.

3.   If inventories have become obsolete or depleted, they must be replaced.

4.   Sometimes the plant and equipment must be modernized before the firm can operate on a competitive basis.

Liquidation Procedures

If a company is too far gone to be reorganized, it must be liquidated. Liquidation should occur if a business is worth more dead than alive, or if the possibility of restoring it to financial health is so remote that the creditors would face a high risk of even greater losses if operations were continued.

Chapter 7 of the Bankruptcy Act is designed to do three things: (1) provide safeguards against the withdrawal of assets by the owners of the bankrupt firm, (2) provide for an equitable distribution of the assets among the creditors, and (3) allow insolvent debtors to discharge all of their obligations and to start over unhampered by a burden of prior debt.

The distribution of assets in a liquidation under Chapter 7 of the Bankruptcy Act is governed by the following priority of claims:

1.   **Secured creditors, who are entitled to the proceeds of the sale of specific property pledged for a lien or a mortgage.** If the proceeds do not fully satisfy the secured creditors' claims, the remaining balance is treated as a general creditor claim. (See Item 9.)

2.   **Trustee's costs to administer and operate the bankrupt firm.**

3. **Expenses incurred after an involuntary case has begun but before a trustee is appointed.**

4. **Wages due workers if earned within three months prior to the filing of the petition of bankruptcy.** The amount of wages is limited to $2,000 per person.

5. **Claims for unpaid contributions to employee benefit plans that were to have been paid within six months prior to filing.** However, these claims, plus wages in Item 4, are not to exceed the $2,000 per employee limit.

6. **Unsecured claims for customer deposits, not to exceed a maximum of $900 per individual.**

7. **Taxes due to federal, state, county, and any other government agency.**

8. **Unfunded pension plan liabilities.** Unfunded pension plan liabilities have a claim above that of the general creditors for an amount up to 30 percent of the common and preferred equity; any remaining unfunded pension claims rank with the general creditors.

9. **General, or unsecured, creditors.** Holders of trade credit, unsecured loans, the unsatisfied portion of secured loans, and debenture bonds are classified as *general creditors.* Holders of subordinated debt also fall into this category, but they must turn over required amounts to the holders of senior debt, as discussed later in this section.

10. **Preferred stockholders, who can receive an amount up to the par value of the issue.**

11. **Common stockholders, who receive any remaining funds.**

To illustrate how this priority system works, consider the balance sheet of Chiefland Inc., shown in Table 20A-1. The assets have a book value of $90 million. The claims are indicated on the right-hand side of the balance sheet. Note that the debentures are subordinate to the notes payable to banks. Chiefland had filed for reorganization under Chapter 11, but since no fair and feasible reorganization could be arranged, the trustee is liquidating the firm under Chapter 7. The firm also has $15 million of unfunded pension liabilities.[2]

The assets as reported in the balance sheet in Table 20A-1 are greatly overstated; they are, in fact, worth about half of the $90 million at which they are carried. The following amounts are realized on liquidation:

---

[2]Under the federal statutes which regulate pension funds, corporations are required to estimate the amount of money needed to provide for the pensions which have been promised to their employees. This determination is made by professional actuaries, taking into account when employees will retire, how long they are likely to live, and the rate of return that can be earned on pension fund assets. If the assets currently in the pension fund are deemed sufficient to make all required payments, the plan is said to be *fully funded.* If assets in the plan are less than the present value of expected future payments, an *unfunded liability* exists. Under federal laws, companies are given up to 30 years to fund any unfunded liabilities. (Note that if a company were fully funded in 1992 but then agreed, in 1993, to double pension benefits, this would immediately create a large unfunded liability, and it would need time to make the adjustment. Otherwise, it would be difficult for companies to agree to increase pension benefits.)

Unfunded pension liabilities, including medical benefits to retirees, represent a time bomb ticking in the bowels of many companies. If a company has a relatively old labor force, and if it has promised them substantial retirement benefits but has not set aside assets in a funded pension fund to cover these benefits, it could experience severe trouble in the future. These unfunded pension benefits could even drive the company into bankruptcy, at which point the pension plan would be subject to the bankruptcy laws.

Table 20A-1 ▪ **Chiefland Inc.: Balance Sheet Just before Liquidation (Thousands of Dollars)**

Current assets	$80,000	Accounts payable	$20,000
Net fixed assets	10,000	Notes payable (to banks)	10,000
		Accrued wages, 1,400 @ $500	700
		U.S. taxes	1,000
		State and local taxes	300
		Current liabilities	$32,000
		First mortgage	6,000
		Second mortgage	1,000
		Subordinated debentures[a]	8,000
		Total long-term debt	$15,000
		Preferred stock	2,000
		Common stock	26,000
		Paid-in capital	4,000
		Retained earnings	11,000
		Total equity	$43,000
Total assets	$90,000	Total liabilities and equity	$90,000

[a]Subordinated to $10 million of notes payable to banks.

Note: Unfunded pension liabilities are $15 million; this is not reported on the balance sheet.

Proceeds from sale of current assets	$41,950,000
Proceeds from sale of fixed assets	5,000,000
Total receipts	$46,950,000

The allocation of available funds is shown in Table 20A-2. The holders of the first mortgage bonds receive the $5 million of net proceeds from the sale of fixed assets. Note that a $1 million unsatisfied claim of the first mortgage holders remains; this claim is added to those of the other general creditors. Next come the fees and expenses of administration, which are typically about 20 percent of gross proceeds; in this example, they are assumed to be $6 million. Next in priority are wages due workers, which total $700,000; taxes due, which amount to $1.3 million; and unfunded pension liabilities of up to 30 percent of the common plus preferred equity, or $12.9 million. Thus far, the total of claims paid from the $46.95 million is $25.90 million, leaving $21.05 million for the general creditors.

The claims of the general creditors total $42.1 million. Since $21.05 million is available, claimants will initially be allocated 50 percent of their claims, as shown in Column 2 of Table 20A-2, before the subordination adjustment. This adjustment requires that the holders of subordinated debentures turn over to the holders of notes payable all amounts received until the notes are satisfied. In this situation, the claim of the notes payable is $10 million, but only $5 million is available; the deficiency is therefore $5 million. After transfer of $4 million from the subordinated debentures, there remains a deficiency of $1 million on the notes. This amount will remain unsatisfied.

Note that 92 percent of the first mortgage, 90 percent of the notes payable, and 93 percent of the unfunded pension fund claims are satisfied, whereas a maximum of 50 percent of unsecured claims will be satisfied. These figures illustrate the usefulness of

Table 20A-2 ▪ **Chiefland Inc.: Order of Priority of Claims**

Distribution of Proceeds on Liquidation

1. Proceeds from sale of assets			$46,950,000
2. First mortgage, paid from sale of fixed assets		$5,000,000	
3. Fees and expenses of administration of bankruptcy		6,000,000	
4. Wages due workers earned within three months prior to filing of bankruptcy petition		700,000	
5. Taxes		1,300,000	
6. Unfunded pension liabilities		12,900,000[a]	25,900,000
7. Available to general creditors			$21,050,000

Distribution to General Creditors

Claims of General Creditors	Claim[b] (1)	Application of 50 Percent[c] (2)	After Subordination Adjustment[d] (3)	Percentage of Original Claims Received[e] (4)
Unsatisfied portion of first mortgage	$ 1,000,000	$ 500,000	$ 500,000	92%
Unsatisfied portion of second mortgage	1,000,000	500,000	500,000	50
Notes payable	10,000,000	5,000,000	9,000,000	90
Accounts payable	20,000,000	10,000,000	10,000,000	50
Subordinated debentures	8,000,000	4,000,000	0	0
Pension plan	2,100,000	1,050,000	1,050,000	93
	$42,100,000	$21,050,000	$21,050,000	

[a]Unfunded pension liabilities are $15,000,000, and common and preferred equity total $43,000,000. Unfunded pension liabilities have a prior claim of up to 30 percent of the equity, or $12,900,000, with the remainder, $2,100,000, being treated as a general creditor claim.

[b]Column 1 is the claim of each class of general creditor. Total claims equal $42.1 million.

[c]From Line 7 in the upper section of the table, we see that $21.05 million is available for general creditors. This sum, divided by the $42.1 million of claims, indicates that general creditors will initially receive 50 percent of their claims; this is shown in Column 2.

[d]The debentures are subordinated to the notes payable, so $4 million is reallocated from debentures to notes payable in Column 3.

[e]Column 4 shows the results of dividing the amount in Column 3 by the original claim amount given in Column 1, except for the first mortgage, for which the $5 million received from the sale of fixed assets is included, and the pension plan, for which the $12.9 million is included.

the subordination provision to the security to which the subordination is made. Because no other funds remain, the claims of the holders of preferred and common stock are completely wiped out. Studies of bankruptcy liquidations indicate that unsecured creditors receive on the average about 15 cents on the dollar, whereas common stockholders generally receive nothing.

Social Issues in Bankruptcy Proceedings

An interesting social issue arose in connection with bankruptcy during the 1980s—the role of bankruptcy in settling labor disputes and product liability suits. Normally, bankruptcy proceedings originate after a company has become so financially weak that it cannot meet its current obligations. However, provisions in the Bankruptcy Act permit a company to file for protection under Chapter 11 if *financial forecasts* indicate that a continuation of business under current conditions will lead to insolvency. These provisions were applied by Frank Lorenzo, the principal stockholder of Continental Airlines, who demonstrated that if Continental continued to operate under its then-current union contract, it would become insolvent in a matter of months. The company then filed a plan of reorganization which included major changes in its union contract. The court found for Continental and allowed the company to abrogate its contract. It then reorganized as a nonunion carrier, and that reorganization turned the company from a money loser into a money maker. (However, in 1990 Continental's financial situation reversed again, partly due to rising fuel prices, and the company once again filed for bankruptcy.) Under pressure from labor, Congress changed the bankruptcy laws after the Continental affair to make it more difficult to use the laws to break union contracts.

The bankruptcy laws have also been used to bring about settlements in major product liability suits, the Manville asbestos case being the first, followed by the Dalkon Shield case. In both instances, the companies were being bombarded by literally thousands of lawsuits, and the very existence of such huge contingent liabilities made continued operations virtually impossible. Further, in both cases, it was relatively easy to prove (1) that if the plaintiffs won, the companies would be unable to pay off the full amounts claimed, (2) that a larger amount of funds would be available if the companies continued to operate than if they were liquidated, (3) that continued operations were possible only if the suits were brought to a conclusion, and (4) that a timely resolution of all the suits was impossible because of the number of suits and the different positions taken by different parties. At any rate, the bankruptcy statutes were used to consolidate all the suits and to reach a settlement under which all the plaintiffs obtained more money than they otherwise would have gotten, and the companies were able to stay in business. The stockholders did not do very well because most of the companies' future cash flows were assigned to the plaintiffs, but, even so, the stockholders probably came out better than they would have if the individual suits had been carried through the jury system to a conclusion.

We have no opinion about the use of the bankruptcy laws to settle social issues such as labor disputes and product liability suits. However, the examples do illustrate how financial projections can be used to demonstrate the effects of different legal decisions. Financial analysis is being used to an increasing extent in various types of legal work, from antitrust cases to suits against stockbrokers by disgruntled customers, and this trend is likely to continue.

Problems

20A-1
Bankruptcy distributions

The Mathys Marble Company has the following balance sheet:

Current assets	$5,040		Accounts payable	$1,080
Fixed assets	2,700		Notes payable (to bank)	540
			Accrued taxes	180
			Accrued wages	180
			Total current liabilities	$1,980
			First mortgage bonds	900
			Second mortgage bonds	900
			Total mortgage bonds	$1,800
			Subordinated debentures	1,080
			Total debt	$4,860
			Preferred stock	360
			Common stock	2,520
Total assets	$7,740		Total liabilities and equity	$7,740

The debentures are subordinated only to the notes payable. Suppose Mathys Marble goes bankrupt and is liquidated, with $1,800 being received from the sale of the fixed assets, which were pledged as security for the first and second mortgage bonds, and $2,880 received from the sale of current assets. The trustee's costs total $480. How much will each class of investors receive?

20A-2
Bankruptcy distributions

Southeast Furniture Inc. has the following balance sheet:

Current assets	$1,875,000	Accounts payable	$ 375,000
Fixed assets	1,875,000	Notes payable	750,000
		Subordinated debentures	750,000
		Total debt	$1,875,000
		Common equity	1,875,000
Total assets	$3,750,000	Total liabilities and equity	$3,750,000

The trustee's costs total $281,250, and Southeast Furniture has no accrued taxes or wages. The debentures are subordinated only to the notes payable. If the firm goes bankrupt, how much will each class of investors receive under each of the following conditions?
a. A total of $2.5 million is received from sale of the assets.
b. A total of $1.875 million is received from sale of the assets.

COMPUTER-RELATED PROBLEM

Work the problem in this section only if you are using the computer problem diskette.

20A-3
Bankruptcy distributions

Use the computerized model in the File C20A to solve this problem.
a. Rework Problem 20A-1, assuming that $960 is received from the sale of fixed assets and $2,040 from the sale of current assets.
b. Rework Problem 20A-1, assuming that $1,680 is received from the sale of fixed assets and $3,720 from the sale of current assets.

Appendix 20B

Refunding Operations

A great deal of long-term debt was sold during the period 1979–1984 at interest rates going up to 18 percent for double-A companies. Because the period of call protection on much of this debt is, or soon will be, ending, many companies are analyzing the pros and cons of bond refundings. Refunding decisions actually involve two separate questions: (1) Is it profitable to call an outstanding issue in the current period and replace it with a new issue; and (2) even if refunding is currently profitable, would the expected value of the firm be increased even more if the refunding were postponed to a later date? We consider both questions in this appendix.

Note that the decision to refund a security is analyzed in much the same way as a capital budgeting expenditure. The costs of refunding (the investment outlays) are (1) the call premium paid for the privilege of calling the old issue, (2) the costs of selling the new issue, (3) the tax savings from writing off the unexpensed flotation costs on the old issue, and (4) the net interest that must be paid while both issues are outstanding (the new issue is often sold one month before the refunding to insure that the funds will be available). The annual cash flows, in a capital budgeting sense, are the interest payments that are saved each year plus the net tax savings which the firm receives for amortizing the flotation expenses. For example, if the interest expense on the old issue is $1,000,000 whereas that on the new issue is $700,000, the $300,000 reduction in interest savings constitutes an annual benefit.

The net present value method is used to analyze the advantages of refunding: the future cash flows are discounted back to the present, and then this discounted value is compared with the cash outlays associated with the refunding. The firm should refund the bond only if the present value of the savings exceeds the cost — that is, if the NPV of the refunding operation is positive.

In the discounting process, the after-tax cost of the new debt, k_d, should be used as the discount rate. The reason is that there is relatively little risk to the savings — cash flows in a refunding are known with relative certainty, which is quite unlike the situation with cash flows in most capital budgeting decisions.

The easiest way to examine the refunding decision is through an example. McCarty Publishing Company has a $60 million bond issue outstanding that has a 15 percent annual coupon interest rate and 20 years remaining to maturity. This issue, which was sold 5 years ago, had flotation costs of $3 million that the firm has been amortizing on a straight line basis over the 25-year original life of the issue. The bond has a call provision which makes it possible for the company to retire the issue at this time by calling the bonds in at a 10 percent call premium. Investment bankers have assured the company that it could sell an additional $60 million to $70 million worth of new 20-year bonds at an interest rate of 12 percent. To insure that the funds required to pay off the old debt will be available, the new bonds will be sold one month before the old issue is called, so for one month, interest will have to be paid on two issues. Current short-term interest rates are 11 percent. Predictions are that long-term interest rates are unlikely to fall below 12 percent.[1] Flotation costs on a new refunding issue will amount to $2,650,000. McCarty's marginal federal-plus-state tax rate is 40 percent. Should the company refund the $60 million of 15 percent bonds?

The following steps outline the decision process; they are summarized in worksheet form in Table 20B-1. The paragraph numbers below correspond with line numbers in the table.

Step 1: Determine the investment outlay required to refund the issue.

1. *Call premium on old issue:*

$$\text{Before tax: } 0.10(\$60,000,000) = \$6,000,000.$$
$$\text{After tax: } \$6,000,000(1 - T) = \$6,000,000(0.6)$$
$$= \$3,600,000.$$

Although McCarty must expend $6 million on the call premium, this is a deductible expense in the year the call is made. Because the company is in the 40 percent tax bracket, it saves $2.4 million in taxes; therefore, the after-tax cost of the call is only $3.6 million. This amount is shown on Line 1 of Table 20B-1.

2. *Flotation costs on new issue:*
   Flotation costs on the new issue will be $2,650,000. This amount cannot be expensed for tax purposes, so it has no immediate tax benefit.

---

[1]The firm's management has estimated that interest rates will probably remain at their present level of 12 percent or else rise; there is only a 25 percent probability that they will fall further.

Table 20B-1 ▪ **Worksheet for the Bond Refunding Decision**

	Amount before Tax	Amount after Tax
Cost of Refunding at t = 0		
1. Call premium on old bond	$ 6,000,000	$ 3,600,000
2. Flotation costs on new issue	2,650,000	2,650,000
3. Immediate tax savings on old flotation cost expense	(2,400,000)	(960,000)
4. Extra interest paid on old issue	750,000	450,000
5. Interest earned on short-term investment	(550,000)	(330,000)
6. Total after-tax investment		$ 5,410,000
Annual Flotation Cost Tax Effects: t = 1 to 20		
7. Annual benefit from new issue flotation costs	$ 132,500	$ 53,000
8. Annual lost benefit from old issue flotation costs	(120,000)	(48,000)
9. Net amortization tax effect	$ 12,500	$ 5,000
Annual Interest Savings Due to Refunding: t = 1 to 20		
10. Interest on old bond	$ 9,000,000	$ 5,400,000
11. Interest on new bond	(7,200,000)	(4,320,000)
12. Net interest savings	$ 1,800,000	$ 1,080,000

Refunding NPV

13. NPV = PV of flotation tax effects + PV of interest savings − Investment

$$= \$5,000(10.4313) + \$1,080,000(10.4313) - \$5,410,000$$

$$= \$52,157 + \$11,265,804 - \$5,410,000$$

$$= \$11,317,961 - \$5,410,000$$

$$= \$5,907,961.$$

Alternatively, using a financial calculator, input N = 20, I = 7.2, PMT = 1085000, and then press PV to find PV = $11,317,974. NPV = $11,317,974 − $5,410,000 = $5,907,974. (Difference due to rounding.)

3. *Flotation costs on old issue:*
   The old issue has an unamortized flotation cost of (20/25)($3,000,000) = $2,400,000 at this time. If the issue is retired, the unamortized flotation cost may be recognized immediately as an expense, thus creating an after-tax savings of $2,400,000(T) = $960,000. Because this is a cash inflow, it is shown as a negative outflow on Line 3.

4 and 5. *Additional interest:*
   One month's "extra" interest on the old issue, after taxes, costs $450,000:

$$\text{(Dollar amount)}(1/12 \text{ of } 15\%)(1 - T) = \text{Interest cost}$$
$$(\$60,000,000)(0.0125)(0.6) = \$450,000.$$

   However, the proceeds from the new issue can be invested in short-term securities for one month. Thus, $60 million invested at a rate of 11 percent will return $330,000 in after-tax interest:

$$(\$60,000,000)(1/12 \text{ of } 11\%)(1 - T) = \text{Interest earned}$$
$$(\$60,000,000)(0.009167)(0.6) = \$330,000.$$

The net after-tax additional interest cost is thus $120,000:

Interest paid on old issue	$450,000
Interest earned on short-term securities	(330,000)
Net additional interest	$120,000

These figures are reflected on Lines 4 and 5 of Table 20B-1.

6. *Total after-tax investment:*
   The total investment outlay required to refund the bond issue, which will be financed by debt, is thus $5,410,000:[2]

Call premium	$3,600,000
Flotation costs, new	2,650,000
Flotation costs, old, tax savings	(960,000)
Net additional interest	120,000
Total investment	$5,410,000

This total is shown on Line 6 of Table 20B-1.

Step 2: Calculate the annual flotation cost tax effects.

7. *Tax savings on flotation costs on the new issue:*
   For tax purposes, flotation costs must be amortized over the life of the new bond, or for 20 years. Therefore, the annual tax deduction is

$$\frac{\$2,650,000}{20} = \$132,500.$$

Because McCarty is in the 40 percent tax bracket, it has a tax savings of $132,500(0.4) = $53,000 a year for 20 years. This is an annuity of $53,000 for 20 years, and it is shown on Line 7.

8. *Tax benefits lost on flotation costs on the old issue:*
   The firm, however, will no longer receive a tax deduction of $120,000 a year for 20 years, so it loses an after-tax benefit of $48,000 a year. This is shown on Line 8.

9. *Net amortization tax effect:*
   The after-tax difference between the amortization tax effects of flotation on the new and old issues is $5,000 a year for 20 years. This is shown on Line 9.

Step 3: Calculate the annual interest savings.

10. *Interest on old bond, after tax:*
    The annual after-tax interest on the old issue is $5.4 million:

$$(\$60,000,000)(0.15)(0.6) = \$5,400,000.$$

This is shown on Line 10 of Table 20B-1.

---

[2]The investment outlay (in this case, $5,410,000) is usually obtained by increasing the amount of the new bond issue. In the example given, the new issue would be $65,410,000. However, the interest on the additional debt *should not* be deducted at Step 3 because the $5,410,000 itself will be deducted at Step 4. If additional interest on the $5,410,000 were deducted at Step 3, interest would, in effect, be deducted twice. The situation here is exactly like that in regular capital budgeting decisions. Even though some debt may be used to finance a project, interest on that debt is not subtracted when developing the annual cash flows. Rather, the annual cash flows are *discounted* at the project's cost of capital.

11. *Interest on new bond, after tax:*
The new issue has an annual after-tax cost of $4,320,000:

$$(\$60,000,000)(0.12)(0.6) = \$4,320,000.$$

This is shown on Line 11.

12. *Net annual interest savings:*
Thus, the net annual interest savings is $1,080,000:

Interest on old bonds, after tax	$ 5,400,000
Interest on new bonds, after tax	(4,320,000)
Annual interest savings	$ 1,080,000

This is shown on Line 12.

Step 4: Determine the NPV of the refunding.

13. *PV of the benefits:*
The PV of the annual after-tax flotation cost benefit of $5,000 a year for 20 years is $52,157, and the PV of the $1,080,000 annual after-tax interest savings for 20 years is $11,265,804:[3]

$$
\begin{aligned}
PV &= \$5,000(PVIFA_{7.2\%,20}) \\
&= \$5,000(10.4313) \\
&= \$52,157. \\
PV &= \$1,080,000(PVIFA_{7.2\%,20}) \\
&= \$1,080,000(10.4313) \\
&= \$11,265,804.
\end{aligned}
$$

These values are used on Line 13 when finding the NPV of the refunding operation:

Amortization tax effects	$ 52,157
Interest savings	11,265,804
Net investment outlay	(5,410,000)
NPV from refunding	$ 5,907,961

Because the net present value of the refunding is positive, it will be profitable to refund the old bond issue.

We can summarize the data shown in Table 20B-1 using a time line (amounts in thousands) as shown below:

Time Period	0	1	2		20
After-tax investment	−5,410				
Flotation cost tax effects		5	5	· · ·	5
Interest savings		1,080	1,080	· · ·	1,080
Net cash flows	−5,410	1,085	1,085	· · ·	1,085

$NPV_{7.2\%} = \$5,908.$

---

[3] The PVIFA for 7.2 percent over 20 years is 10.4313, found with a financial calculator.

Several other points should be made. First, because the cash flows are based on differences between contractual obligations, their risk is the same as that of the underlying obligations. Therefore, the present values of the cash flows should be found by discounting at the firm's least risky rate—its after-tax cost of marginal debt. Second, since the refunding operation is advantageous to the firm, it must be disadvantageous to bondholders; they must give up their 15 percent bonds and reinvest in new ones yielding 12 percent. This points out the danger of the call provision to bondholders, and it also explains why bonds without a call feature command higher prices than callable bonds. Third, although it is not emphasized in the example, we assumed that the firm raises the investment required to undertake the refunding operation (the $5,410,000 shown on Line 6 of Table 20B-1) as debt. This should be feasible, because the refunding operation will improve the interest coverage ratio, even though a larger amount of debt is outstanding.[4] Fourth, we set up our example in such a way that the new issue had the same maturity as the remaining life of the old one. Often, the old bonds have a relatively short time to maturity (say, 5 to 10 years), whereas the new bonds have a much longer maturity (say, 25 to 30 years). In such a situation, the analysis should be set up similarly to a replacement chain analysis in capital budgeting. Fifth, refunding decisions are well suited for analysis with a computer spreadsheet such as *Lotus 1-2-3*. The spreadsheet is simple to set up, and once the model has been constructed, it is easy to vary the assumptions (especially the assumption about the interest rate on the refunding issue) and to see how such changes affect the NPV. See Problem 20B-3 for an example.

One final point should be addressed: Although our analysis shows that the refunding would increase the value of the firm, would refunding *at this time* truly maximize the firm's expected value? If interest rates continue to fall, the company might be better off waiting, for this could increase the NPV of the refunding operation even more. The mechanics of calculating the NPV in a refunding are easy, but the decision of *when* to refund is not simple at all because it requires a forecast of future interest rates. Thus, the final decision on refunding now versus waiting for a possibly more favorable time is a judgmental decision.

Problems

20B-1
Refunding analysis

Susan Long, financial manager of West Coast Transportation (WCT), has been asked by her boss to review WCT's outstanding debt issues for possible bond refunding. Five years ago, WCT issued $40,000,000 of 13 percent, 25-year debt. The issue, with semiannual coupons, is currently callable at a premium of 11 percent, or $110 for each $1,000 par value bond. Flotation costs on this issue were 3 percent, or $1,200,000.

Long believes that WCT could issue 20-year debt today with a coupon rate of 11 percent. The firm has placed many issues in the capital markets during the last 10 years, and its debt flotation costs are currently estimated to be 2 percent of the issue's value. WCT's federal-plus-state tax rate is 34 percent.

Help Long conduct the refunding analysis by answering the following questions:
a. What is the total dollar call premium required to call the old issue? Is it tax deductible? What is the net after-tax cost of the call?

[4]See Ahron R. Ofer and Robert A. Taggart, Jr., "Bond Refunding: A Clarifying Analysis," *Journal of Finance,* March 1977, 21–30, for a discussion of how the method of financing the refunding affects the analysis. Ofer and Taggart prove that if the refunding investment outlay is to be raised as common equity, the before-tax cost of debt is the proper discount rate, whereas if these funds are to be raised as debt, the after-tax cost of debt is the proper discount rate. Since a profitable refunding will virtually always raise the firm's debt-carrying capacity (because total interest charges after the refunding will be lower than before it), it is more logical to use debt than either equity or a combination of debt and equity to finance the operation. Therefore, firms generally do use additional debt to finance refunding operations.

b. What is the dollar flotation cost on the new issue? Is it immediately tax deductible? What is the after-tax flotation cost?

c. What amount of old-issue flotation costs have not been expensed? Can these deferred costs be expensed immediately if the old issue is refunded? What is the value of the tax savings?

d. What is the net after-tax cash outlay required to refund the old issue?

e. What is the semiannual tax savings which arises from amortizing the flotation costs on the new issue? What is the forgone semiannual tax savings on the old-issue flotation costs?

f. What is the semiannual after-tax interest savings that would result from the refunding?

g. Thus far, Long has identified two future cash flows: (1) the net of new-issue flotation cost tax savings and old-issue flotation cost tax savings which are lost if refunding occurs and (2) after-tax interest savings. What is the sum of these two semiannual cash flows? What is the appropriate discount rate to apply to these future cash flows? What is the present value of these cash flows? (Hint: The $PVIFA_{3.63\%,40} = 20.9310$.)

h. What is the NPV of refunding? Should WCT refund now or wait until later?

20B-2
Refunding analysis

Tosar Technologies is considering whether or not to refund a $75 million, 15 percent coupon, 30-year bond issue that was sold 5 years ago. It is amortizing $3 million of flotation costs on the 15 percent bonds over the issue's 30-year life. Tosar's investment bankers have indicated that the company could sell a new 25-year issue at an interest rate of 13 percent in today's market. Neither they nor Tosar's management anticipate that interest rates will fall below 13 percent any time soon, but there is a chance that rates will increase.

A call premium of 15 percent would be required to retire the old bonds, and flotation costs on the new issue would amount to $3 million. Tosar's marginal federal-plus-state tax rate is 40 percent. The new bonds would be issued one month before the old bonds are called, with the proceeds being invested in short-term government securities returning 11 percent annually during the interim period.

a. Perform a complete bond refunding analysis. What is the bond refunding's NPV? (Hint: $PVIFA_{7.8\%,25} = 10.8597$.)

b. What factors would influence Tosar's decision to refund now rather than later?

COMPUTER-RELATED PROBLEM

Work the problem in this section only if you are using the computer problem diskette.

20B-3
Refunding analysis

Use the computerized model in the File C20B to solve this problem.

a. Refer back to Problem 20B-2. Determine the interest rate on new bonds at which Tosar would be indifferent to refunding the bond issue. (Hint: You will need to perform this analysis using different rates of interest on new bonds until you find the one which causes the NPV to be zero.)

b. How would the refunding decision be affected if the corporate tax rate were lowered from 40 percent to 34 percent, assuming the rate on new bonds was 13 percent? At what interest rate on new bonds would Tosar be indifferent to refunding at a 34 percent corporate tax rate?

Hybrid Financing: Preferred Stock, Leasing, and Option Securities

A   M A N A G E R I A L   P E R S P E C T I V E

One of 1991's hottest financial products was preferred stock, but analysts warn that individuals may be ignoring some of preferred's disadvantages. Preferred stock was popular in the 1970s, it gave way to high-yield junk bonds in the 1980s, but it is making a comeback in the 1990s. As of early December 1991, corporations had sold a record $16.5 billion of preferred stock, which was more than four times the total sold in 1990, and four of 1991's six largest stock offerings were preferred stock issues.

Preferred stock is a hybrid which resembles both debt and common stock. Like debt, preferred is a fixed-income obligation, but it does not offer investors the same protection as bonds if the company runs into financial difficulty. Bondholders have a superior position to preferred stock investors, who in turn have a superior position to common stockholders. Preferred stock resembles common equity because it pays a dividend; however, the dividend is usually fixed for the life of the security. Also, preferred stock does not offer the same potential for price increases as common stock.

Why has preferred stock become so popular with investors and the corporations that issued it? For investors, preferred stock offered high yields compared with money-market funds, which dropped sharply during 1991. For corporate issuers worried about credit ratings, selling preferred increases the equity shown on the balance sheet, even though these companies will have to pay hefty dividends.

Among the preferred issuers were Ford Motor Company and General Motors—two cyclical companies caught up in a recession which limited their capacity to borrow to meet their massive capital expenditure pro-

grams. Ford's issue allowed it to sell equity even though its common stock price had declined by more than 50 percent from its 1989 high. Besides the auto companies, banks were heavy preferred issuers: 10 of 1991's 20 largest preferred stock issues were sold by banks, which were trying to bolster their equity capital to meet regulatory requirements. Finally, RJR Nabisco sold $2 billion of preferred stock as part of its plan to regain the investment grade credit rating it lost following a 1988 LBO that saddled the company with large amounts of debt.

The types of preferred stock that were issued in 1991 were as varied as the corporations issuing them. The offerings included (1) straight preferred, which provides a hefty dividend but without any capital appreciation for common stock price gains; (2) convertible preferred, which is convertible into common stock but at a premium over the common stock's price at the time the preferred is issued; and (3) a newly created version, PERCs (preference equity redemption convertible stock), which lets investors share in any price gains on a company's common stock, but only up to pre-established limits.

Some portfolio managers endorse preferred issues for individuals, particularly in a declining interest environment. They note that while preferred stock prices do not appreciate as much as common stock prices in a rising stock market, they do not decline as drastically in a falling market. On the other hand, other experts comment that a company's preferred dividends may be only slightly higher than the company's bond yields, so individuals are not being compensated sufficiently for the risks they are undertaking. Corporate investors have a tax advantage in owning preferred stock because they do not have to pay taxes on 70 percent of their preferred dividend income, while individual investors do not receive this tax break. Therefore, prices on preferred issues are generally set by corporate investors, so individuals are at a price disadvantage in buying preferred issues. In addition, some of the preferred issues, like the PERCs, are difficult to understand, so individuals could be mislead.

At the very least, most experts caution individuals not to put large portions of their investments in any single preferred issue. Instead, they recommend diversifying either by investing in six or more issues, preferably in safer utility preferreds, or through a mutual fund that holds preferreds. Once you have read this chapter and understand the concepts presented, you should be able to make informed decisions regarding preferred stock and the other hybrid securities.

Source: "Preferreds: A Perennial Wallflower Blooms," *The Wall Street Journal*, December 6, 1991.

In the two preceding chapters, we examined the use of common stock and various types of debt. In this chapter, we examine three other types of long-term capital which financial managers can use to lower their firms' costs of capital: *preferred stock,* which is a hybrid security that represents a cross between bonds and common stock; *leasing,* which is used by financial managers as an alternative to borrowing to finance fixed assets; and option securities, particularly *warrants* and *convertibles*, which are attractive to investors because they allow debtholders to acquire common stock at bargain prices and thus to share in the capital gains if a company is especially successful.[1]

PREFERRED STOCK

Preferred stock is a *hybrid*—it is similar to bonds in some respects and to common stock in others. The hybrid nature of preferred stock becomes apparent when we try to classify it in relation to bonds and common stock. Like bonds, preferred stock has a par value. Preferred dividends are also similar to interest payments in that they are fixed in amount and generally must be paid before common stock dividends can be paid. However, if the preferred dividend is not earned, the directors can omit (or "pass") it without throwing the company into bankruptcy. So, although preferred stock has a fixed payment like bonds, a failure to make this payment will not lead to bankruptcy.

Accountants classify preferred stock as equity and report it in the equity portion of the balance sheet under "preferred stock" or "preferred equity." However, financial analysts sometimes treat preferred stock as debt and sometimes treat it as equity, depending on the type of analysis being made. If the analysis is being made by a common stockholder, the key consideration is the fact that the preferred dividend is a fixed charge which reduces earnings on the common, so from the common stockholder's point of view preferred stock is similar to debt. Suppose, however, that the analysis is being made by a bondholder studying the firm's vulnerability to failure in the event of a decline in sales and income. If the firm's income declines, the debtholders have a prior claim to the available income ahead of preferred stockholders, and if the firm fails, debtholders have a prior claim to assets when the firm is liquidated. Thus, to a bondholder, preferred stock is similar to common equity.

From management's perspective, preferred stock lies between debt and common equity. Since failure to pay dividends on preferred stock will not force the firm into bankruptcy, preferred stock is safer to use than debt. At the same time, if the firm is highly successful, the common stockholders will not have to share that success with the preferred stockholders because preferred dividends are fixed. Remember, however, that the preferred stockholders do have a higher priority claim than the common stockholders. We see, then, that preferred stock has some of the characteristics of debt and some of the characteristics of com-

---

[1]Even though all three of the topics covered in this chapter are important, time pressures may preclude detailed coverage of all of them. Accordingly, the chapter is written in a modular form so as to permit instructors to cover one, two, or all three topics.

mon stock, and it is used in situations in which conditions are such that neither debt nor common stock is entirely appropriate.

Major Provisions of Preferred Stock Issues

Preferred stock has a number of features, the most important of which are discussed in the following sections.

Priority to Assets and Earnings.   Preferred stockholders have priority over common stockholders with regard to earnings and assets. Thus, dividends must be paid on preferred stock before they can be paid on the common stock, and, in the event of bankruptcy, the claims of the preferred shareholders must be satisfied before the common stockholders receive anything. To reinforce these features, most preferred stocks have coverage requirements similar to those on bonds. These restrictions limit the amount of preferred stock a company can use, and they also require a minimum level of retained earnings before common dividends can be paid.

Par Value.   Unlike common stock, preferred stock always has a par value (or its equivalent under some other name), and this value is important. First, the par value establishes the amount due the preferred stockholders in the event of liquidation. Second, the preferred dividend is frequently stated as a percentage of the par value. For example, an issue of Duke Power's preferred stock has a par value of $100 and a stated dividend of 7.8 percent of par. The same results would, of course, be produced if this issue of Duke's preferred stock simply called for an annual dividend of $7.80.

cumulative dividends

A protective feature on preferred stock that requires preferred dividends previously not paid to be paid before any common dividends can be paid.

Cumulative Dividends.   Most preferred stock provides for **cumulative dividends;** that is, any preferred dividends not paid in previous periods must be paid before common dividends can be paid. The cumulative feature is a protective device, for if the preferred stock dividends were not cumulative, a firm could avoid paying preferred and common stock dividends for, say, 10 years, plowing back all of its earnings, and then pay a huge common stock dividend but pay only the stipulated annual dividend to the preferred stockholders. Obviously, such an action would effectively void the preferred position the preferred stockholders are supposed to have. The cumulative feature helps prevent such abuses.[2]

Convertibility.   Approximately 40 percent of the preferred stock that has been issued in recent years is convertible into common stock. For example, each share of Enron's $10.50 Class J preferred stock can be converted into 3.413 shares of its common stock at the option of the preferred shareholders. (Convertibility is discussed in detail later in this chapter.)

---

[2]Note, however, that compounding is absent in most cumulative plans — in other words, the unpaid preferred dividends themselves earn no return. Also, many preferred issues have a limited cumulative feature; for example, unpaid preferred dividends might accumulate for only three years.

Other Provisions.   Some other provisions one occasionally encounters in preferred stocks include the following:

1. **Voting rights.** Preferred stockholders are generally given the right to vote for directors if the company has not paid the preferred dividend for a specified period, such as ten quarters. This feature motivates management to make every effort to pay preferred dividends.

2. **Participating.** A rare type of preferred stock is one that participates with the common stock in sharing the firm's earnings. Participating preferred stocks generally work as follows: (a) the stated preferred dividend is paid —for example, $5 a share; (b) the common stock is then entitled to a dividend in an amount up to the preferred dividend; (c) if the common dividend is raised, say to $5.50, the preferred dividend must likewise be raised to $5.50.

3. **Sinking fund.** In the past (before the mid-1970s), few preferred issues had sinking funds. Today, however, most newly issued preferred stocks have sinking funds which call for the purchase and retirement of a given percentage of the preferred stock each year. If the amount is 2 percent, which is used frequently, the preferred issue will have an average life of 25 years and a maximum life of 50 years.

4. **Call provision.** A call provision gives the issuing corporation the right to call in the preferred stock for redemption. As in the case of bonds, call provisions generally state that the company must pay an amount greater than the par value of the preferred stock, the additional sum being termed a **call premium.** For example, Trivoli Corporation's 12 percent, $100 par value preferred stock, issued in 1988, is noncallable for 10 years, but it may be called at a price of $112 after 1998.

5. **Maturity.** Before the mid-1970s, most preferred stock was perpetual—it had no maturity and never needed to be paid off. However, today most new preferred stock has a sinking fund and thus an effective maturity date.

call premium

The amount in excess of par value that a company must pay when it calls a security.

Pros and Cons of Preferred Stock

As noted below, there are both advantages and disadvantages to financing with preferred stock.

Issuer's Viewpoint.   By using preferred stock, a firm can fix its financial costs and thus keep more of the potential future profits for its existing set of common stockholders, yet still avoid the danger of bankruptcy if earnings are too low to meet these fixed charges. Also, by selling preferred rather than common stock, the firm avoids sharing control with new investors.

However, preferred stock does have a major disadvantage from the issuer's standpoint: It has a higher after-tax cost of capital than debt. The major reason for this higher cost is taxes: Preferred dividends are not deductible as a tax expense, whereas interest expense is deductible.[3] This makes the component cost of preferred stock much greater than that of bonds—the after-tax cost of debt is approximately two-thirds of the stated coupon rate for profitable firms, whereas the cost of preferred stock is the full percentage amount of the preferred dividend. Of course, the deductibility differential is most important for issuers that are in relatively high tax brackets. If a company pays little or no taxes because it is unprofitable or because it has a great deal of accelerated depreciation, the deductibility of interest does not make much difference. Thus, the lower a company's tax bracket, the more likely it is to issue preferred stock.

Investor's Viewpoint.   In designing securities, the financial manager must consider the investor's point of view. It is sometimes asserted that preferred stock has so many disadvantages to both the issuer and the investor that it should never be issued. Nevertheless, as we saw at the beginning of this chapter, preferred stock is being issued in substantial amounts. It provides investors with a steadier and more assured income than common stock, and it has a preference over common in the event of liquidation. In addition, 70 percent of the preferred dividends received by corporations are not taxable. For this reason, most preferred stock is owned by corporations.

The principal disadvantage of preferred stock from an investor's standpoint is that although preferred stockholders bear some of the ownership risks, their returns are limited. Other disadvantages are that (1) preferred stockholders have no legally enforceable right to dividends, even if a company earns a profit, and (2) for individual as opposed to corporate investors, after-tax bond yields are generally higher than those on preferred stock, even though the preferred is riskier.

Recent Trends

Because preferred dividends are not tax deductible, many companies have retired their preferred stocks and replaced them with debentures or subordinated debentures. However, as the following examples illustrate, preferred is still

---

[3]One would think that a given firm's preferred stock would carry a higher coupon rate than its bonds because of the preferred's greater risk from the holder's viewpoint. However, 70 percent of preferred dividends received by corporate owners are exempt from income taxes, and this has made preferred stock very attractive to corporate investors. Therefore, most preferred stock is owned by corporations, and in recent years high-grade preferreds, on average, have sold on a lower-yield basis than high-grade bonds. As an example, Alabama Power recently sold a preferred issue yielding 11 percent to investors. On the day the preferred was issued, Alabama Power's bonds yielded 13 percent, or 2 percentage points more than the preferred. The tax treatment accounted for this differential; the *after-tax* yield to a corporate investor was greater on the preferred stock than on the bonds. For a corporate investor in the 40 percent tax bracket,

$$\text{After-tax yield on bonds} = \text{Yield} - \text{Yield(T)}$$
$$= \text{Yield}(1 - T) = 13\%(0.6) = 7.8\%.$$
$$\text{After-tax yield on preferred} = \text{Yield} - \text{Yield}(1 - \text{Exclusion})(T)$$
$$= 11\% - 11\%(0.3)(0.4)$$
$$= 11\%(1 - 0.12) = 11\%(0.88) = 9.68\%.$$

being used to raise long-term capital under a number of different conditions, including situations where neither common stock nor long-term debt can be issued on reasonable terms.

1. Chrysler's issue of preferred stock with warrants several years ago proved a successful means of raising capital in the face of adverse circumstances. Because of its losses, Chrysler's common stock was depressed and very much out of favor. Investors were so worried about the company's ability to survive that they were unwilling to make additional commitments without receiving some sort of senior position. Therefore, common stock was ruled out. Chrysler had already borrowed to the hilt, and it could not obtain any more debt without first building its equity base (and preferred is equity from the bondholders' viewpoint). Various incentives were offered to the brokers who handled the preferred issue, and a relatively high yield was set. As a result, the issue was so successful that its size was raised from $150 to $200 million while the underwriting was under way. Chrysler got the money it needed, and that money helped the company survive.

2. Utility companies often use preferred stock to bolster the equity component of their capital structures. These companies are capital intensive, and they make heavy use of debt financing, but lenders and rating agencies require minimum equity ratios as a condition for maintaining bond ratings. Also, the utilities have made very heavy investments in fixed assets and thus have high depreciation charges, which has held down their effective tax rates and thus has lowered the tax disadvantage of preferred stock in relation to debt.

3. In recent years there has also been a pronounced movement toward convertible preferred, which is often used in connection with mergers. For example, when Belco Petroleum was negotiating its acquisition by Enron, it was pointed out that if the buyout were for cash, Belco's stockholders (one of whom owned 40 percent of the stock and thus could block the merger) would be required to immediately pay huge capital gains taxes. However, under U.S. tax laws, if preferred stock is exchanged for the acquired company's common, this constitutes a tax-free exchange of securities. Thus, Belco's stockholders could obtain a fixed-income security yet postpone the payment of taxes on their capital gains.

   Enron actually offered a choice of straight or convertible preferred to Belco's stockholders. Those stockholders who were interested primarily in income could take the straight preferred, whereas those interested in capital gains could take the convertible preferred.

floating rate preferred stock

Preferred stock whose dividend rate fluctuates with changes in the general level of interest rates.

4. In 1984, Alabama Power introduced a new type of security, **floating rate preferred stock.** Since this stock has a floating rate, its price stays relatively constant, making it suitable for liquid asset portfolios (marketable securities held by corporations to provide funds either for planned expenditures or to meet emergencies). The combination of a floating rate, and hence a stable price, plus the 70 percent tax exemption for corporations, made this preferred quite attractive, and it enabled Alabama Power to obtain capital at a low cost.

Self-Test Questions

Explain the following statement: "Preferred stock is a hybrid."

Identify and briefly explain some of the key features of preferred stock.

What are the advantages and disadvantages of preferred stock from an issuer's viewpoint?

What are the advantages and disadvantages of preferred stock from an investor's viewpoint?

LEASING

Firms generally own fixed assets and report them on their balance sheets, but it is the *use* of buildings and equipment that is important, not their ownership per se. One way of obtaining the use of assets is to buy them, but an alternative is to lease them. Prior to the 1950s, leasing was generally associated with real estate—land and buildings. Today, however, it is possible to lease virtually any kind of fixed asset, and in 1992 about 25 percent of all new capital equipment acquired by businesses was leased.

Types of Leases

Leasing takes three different forms: (1) *sale-and-leaseback* arrangements, (2) *operating leases,* and (3) straight *financial,* or *capital, leases.*

sale and leaseback
An operation whereby a firm sells land, buildings, or equipment and simultaneously leases the property back for a specified period under specific terms.

lessee
The party that uses, rather than the one who owns, the leased property.

lessor
The owner of the leased property.

Sale and Leaseback. Under a **sale and leaseback,** a firm that owns land, buildings, or equipment sells the property and simultaneously executes an agreement to lease the property back for a specified period under specific terms. The purchaser could be an insurance company, a commercial bank, a specialized leasing company, or even an individual investor. The sale-and-leaseback plan is an alternative to taking out a mortgage loan.

The firm which is selling the property, or the **lessee,** immediately receives the purchase price put up by the buyer, or the **lessor.**[4] At the same time, the seller-lessee firm retains the use of the property just as if it had borrowed and mortgaged the property to secure the loan. Note that under a mortgage loan arrangement, the financial institution would normally receive a series of equal payments just sufficient to amortize the loan while providing a specified rate of return to the lender on the outstanding balance. Under a sale-and-leaseback arrangement, the lease payments are set up in exactly the same way; the payments are set so as to return the purchase price to the investor-lessor while providing a specified rate of return on the lessor's outstanding investment.

operating lease
A lease under which the lessor maintains and finances the property; also called a *service lease.*

Operating Leases. **Operating leases,** sometimes called *service leases,* provide for both *financing* and *maintenance.* IBM is one of the pioneers of the operating lease contract, and computers and office copying machines, together with automobiles and trucks, are the primary types of equipment involved. Or-

---

[4]The term *lessee* is pronounced "less-ee," not "lease-ee," and *lessor* is pronounced "less-or."

dinarily, these leases call for the lessor to maintain and service the leased equipment, and the cost of providing maintenance is built into the lease payments.

Another important characteristic of operating leases is the fact that they are frequently *not fully amortized;* in other words, the payments required under the lease contract are not sufficient to recover the full cost of the equipment. However, the lease contract is written for a period considerably shorter than the expected economic life of the leased equipment, and the lessor expects to recover all investment costs through subsequent renewal payments, through subsequent leases to other lessees, or by selling the leased equipment.

A final feature of operating leases is that they frequently contain a *cancellation clause,* which gives the lessee the right to cancel the lease before the expiration of the basic agreement. This is an important consideration for the lessee, for it means that the equipment can be returned if it is rendered obsolete by technological developments or if it is no longer needed because of a decline in the lessee's business.

financial lease
A lease that does not provide for maintenance services, is not cancelable, and is fully amortized over its life; also called a *capital lease.*

Financial, or Capital, Leases. **Financial leases,** sometimes called *capital leases,* are differentiated from operating leases in three respects: (1) they do *not* provide for maintenance services, (2) they are *not* cancelable, and (3) they *are* fully amortized (that is, the lessor receives rental payments which are equal to the full price of the leased equipment plus a return on the investment). In a typical financial lease arrangement, the firm that will use the equipment (the lessee) selects the specific items it requires and negotiates the price and delivery terms with the manufacturer. The user firm then negotiates terms with a leasing company and, once the lease terms are set, arranges to have the lessor buy the equipment from the manufacturer or the distributor. When the equipment is purchased, the user firm simultaneously executes the lease agreement.

Financial leases are similar to sale-and-leaseback arrangements, the major difference being that the leased equipment is new and the lessor buys it from a manufacturer or a distributor instead of from the user-lessee. A sale and leaseback may thus be thought of as a special type of financial lease, and both sale and leasebacks and financial leases are analyzed in the same manner.[5]

Financial Statement Effects

off balance sheet financing
Financing in which the assets and liabilities involved do not appear on the firm's balance sheet.

Lease payments are shown as operating expenses on a firm's income statement, but under certain conditions, neither the leased assets nor the liabilities under the lease contract appear on the firm's balance sheet. For this reason, leasing is often called **off balance sheet financing.** This point is illustrated in Table 21-1 by the balance sheets of two hypothetical firms, B (for Buy) and L (for Lease). Initially, the balance sheets of both firms are identical, and both have

---

[5]For a lease transaction to qualify as a lease for *tax purposes,* and thus for the lessee to be able to deduct the lease payments, the life of the lease must not exceed 80 percent of the expected life of the asset, and the lessee cannot be permitted to buy the asset at a nominal value. These conditions are IRS requirements, and they should not be confused with the FASB requirements discussed later in the chapter concerning the capitalization of leases. It is important to consult lawyers and accountants to ascertain whether or not a prospective lease meets current IRS regulations.

Table 21-1 ▪ **Balance Sheet Effects of Leasing**

	Before Asset Increase			After Asset Increase						
	Firms B and L			**Firm B, Which Borrows and Purchases**				**Firm L, Which Leases**		
Current assets	$ 50	Debt	$ 50	Current assets	$ 50	Debt	$150	Current assets	$ 50	Debt	$ 50
Fixed assets	50	Equity	50	Fixed assets	150	Equity	50	Fixed assets	50	Equity	50
Total	$100		$100	Total	$200		$200	Total	$100		$100
		Debt ratio: 50%				Debt ratio: 75%				Debt ratio: 50%

debt ratios of 50 percent. Each firm then decides to acquire fixed assets which cost $100. Firm B borrows $100 to make the purchase, so both an asset and a liability are recorded on its balance sheet, and its debt ratio is increased to 75 percent. Firm L leases the equipment, so its balance sheet is unchanged. The lease may call for fixed charges as high as or even higher than those on the loan, and the obligations assumed under the lease may be equally or more dangerous from the standpoint of financial safety, but the firm's debt ratio remains at 50 percent.

To correct this problem, the Financial Accounting Standards Board issued **FASB #13,** which requires that for an unqualified audit report, firms that enter into financial (or capital) leases must restate their balance sheets to report leased assets as fixed assets and the present value of future lease payments as a debt. This process is called *capitalizing the lease,* and its net effect is to cause Firms B and L to have similar balance sheets, both of which will resemble the one shown for Firm B after the asset increase.[6]

The logic behind FASB #13 is as follows. If a firm signs a lease contract, its obligation to make lease payments is just as binding as if it had signed a loan agreement. The failure to make lease payments can bankrupt a firm just as surely as can the failure to make principal and interest payments on a loan. Therefore, for all intents and purposes, a financial lease is identical to a loan.[7] This being the case, when a firm signs a lease agreement, it has, in effect, raised its "true" debt ratio and thereby has changed its "true" capital structure. Accordingly, if

---

[6]FASB #13, "Accounting for Leases," November 1976, spells out in detail the conditions under which leases must be capitalized, and the procedures for doing so.

[7]There are, however, certain legal differences between loans and leases. In a bankruptcy liquidation, the lessor is entitled to take possession of the leased asset, and, if the value of the asset is less than the required payments under the lease, the lessor can enter a claim (as a general creditor) for one year's lease payments. In a bankruptcy reorganization, the lessor receives the asset plus three years' lease payments if needed to bring the value of the asset up to the remaining investment in the lease. Under a secured loan arrangement, on the other hand, the lender has a security interest in the asset, meaning that if it is sold, the lender will be given the proceeds, and the full unsatisfied portion of the lender's claim will be treated as a general creditor obligation (see Appendix 20A). It is not possible to state as a general rule whether a supplier of capital is in a stronger position as a secured creditor or as a lessor. Since one position is usually regarded as being about as good as the other at the time the financial arrangements are being made, a lease is about as risky as a secured term loan from both the lessor-lender's and the lessee-borrower's viewpoints.

the firm had previously established a target capital structure, and if there is no reason to think that the optimal capital structure has changed, then using lease financing requires additional equity backing in exactly the same manner as does the use of debt financing.

If a disclosure of the lease in the Table 21-1 example were not made, then investors could be deceived into thinking that Firm L's financial position is stronger than it actually is. Even if the lease were disclosed in a footnote, investors might not fully recognize its impact and might not see that Firms B and L are in essentially the same financial position. If this were the case, Firm L would have increased its true amount of debt through a lease arrangement, but its required return on debt, k_d, its required return on equity, k_s, and consequently its weighted average cost of capital, would have increased less than those of Firm B, which borrowed directly. Thus, investors would be willing to accept a lower return from Firm L because they would view it as being in a stronger financial position than Firm B. These benefits of leasing would accrue to stockholders at the expense of new investors, who were, in effect, being deceived by the fact that the firm's balance sheet did not fully reflect its true liability situation. This is why FASB #13 was issued.

A lease will be classified as a capital lease, and hence be capitalized and shown directly on the balance sheet, if any one of the following conditions exists:

1. Under the terms of the lease, ownership of the property is effectively transferred from the lessor to the lessee.
2. The lessee can purchase the property or renew the lease at less than a fair market price when the lease expires.
3. The lease runs for a period equal to or greater than 75 percent of the asset's life. Thus, if an asset has a 10-year life and if the lease is written for more than 7.5 years, the lease must be capitalized.
4. The present value of the lease payments is equal to or greater than 90 percent of the initial value of the asset.[8]

These rules, together with strong footnote disclosures for operating leases, are sufficient to insure that no one will be fooled by lease financing. Thus, leases are recognized to be essentially the same as debt, and they have the same effects as debt on the firm's required rate of return. Therefore, leasing will not generally permit a firm to use more financial leverage than could be obtained with conventional debt.

Evaluation by the Lessee

Any prospective lease must be evaluated by both the lessee and the lessor. The lessee must determine whether leasing an asset will be less costly than buying it, and the lessor must decide whether or not the lease will provide a reasonable rate of return. Since our focus in this book is primarily on managerial finance

---

[8]The discount rate used to calculate the present value of the lease payments must be the lower of (1) the rate used by the lessor to establish the lease payments or (2) the rate of interest which the lessee would have paid for new debt with a maturity equal to that of the lease.

as opposed to investments, we restrict our analysis to that conducted by the lessee.[9]

In the typical case, the events leading to a lease arrangement follow the sequence described in the following list. We should note that a great deal of theoretical literature exists about the correct way to evaluate lease-versus-purchase decisions, and some very complex decision models have been developed to aid in the analysis. The analysis given here, however, leads to the correct decision in every case we have ever encountered.

1. The firm decides to acquire a particular building or piece of equipment. This decision is based on regular capital budgeting procedures, and it is not an issue in the typical lease analysis. In a lease analysis, we are concerned simply with whether to finance the machine by a lease or by a loan. However, if the effective cost of the lease is substantially lower than that of debt—and this could occur for several reasons, including the situation in which the lessor is able to utilize the depreciation tax shelters but the lessee is not—then the capital budgeting decision would have to be reevaluated, and projects formerly deemed unacceptable might become acceptable.

2. Once the firm has decided to acquire the asset, the next question is how to finance it. Well-run businesses do not have excess cash lying around, so new assets must be financed in some manner.

3. Funds to purchase the asset could be obtained by borrowing, by retaining earnings, or by issuing new stock. Alternatively, the asset could be leased. Because of the FASB #13 capitalization/disclosure provision for leases, we assume that a lease would have the same capital structure effect as a loan.

As indicated earlier, a lease is comparable to a loan in the sense that the firm is required to make a specified series of payments, and a failure to make these payments can result in bankruptcy. Thus, it is most appropriate to compare the cost of lease financing with that of debt financing.[10] The lease-versus-borrow-and-purchase analysis is illustrated with data on the Mitchell Electronics Company. The following conditions are assumed:

1. Mitchell plans to acquire equipment with a 5-year life which has a cost of $10,000,000, delivered and installed.

---

[9]The lessee is typically offered a set of lease terms by the lessor, which is generally a bank, a finance company such as General Electric Capital (the largest U.S. lessor), or some other institutional lender. The lessee can accept or reject the lease, or shop around for a better deal. In this chapter, we take the lease terms as given for purposes of our analysis. See Chapter 17 of Eugene F. Brigham and Louis C. Gapenski, *Intermediate Financial Management,* 4th ed., for a discussion of lease analysis from the lessor's standpoint, including a discussion of how a potential lessee can use such an analysis in bargaining for better terms.

[10]The analysis should compare the cost of leasing to the cost of debt financing *regardless* of how the asset is actually financed. The asset may actually be purchased with available cash if it is not leased, but because leasing is a substitute for debt financing, a comparison between the two is still appropriate.

2. Mitchell can borrow the required $10 million, using a 10 percent loan to be amortized over 5 years. Therefore, the loan will call for payments of $2,637,965.60 per year, calculated as follows:

$$\text{Payment} = \frac{\$10,000,000}{\text{PVIFA}_{10\%,5}}$$

$$= \frac{\$10,000,000}{3.7908} = \$2,637,965.60.$$

With a financial calculator, input N = 5, I = 10, PV = −10000000, and FV = 0, and then press PMT to find the payment, $2,637,974.81. Note the rounding difference; the calculator solution is more accurate.

3. Alternatively, Mitchell can lease the equipment for 5 years at a rental charge of $2,800,000 per year, payable at the end of the year, but the lessor will own it upon the expiration of the lease.[11] (The lease payment schedule is established by the potential lessor, and Mitchell can accept it, reject it, or negotiate.)

4. The equipment will definitely be used for 5 years, at which time its estimated net salvage value will be $715,000. Mitchell plans to continue using the equipment, so (1) if it purchases the equipment, the company will keep it, and (2) if it leases the equipment, the company will exercise an option to buy it at its estimated salvage value, $715,000.

5. The lease contract stipulates that the lessor will maintain the equipment. However, if Mitchell borrows and buys, it will have to bear the cost of maintenance, which will be performed by the equipment manufacturer at a fixed contract rate of $500,000 per year, payable at year-end.

6. The equipment falls in the MACRS 5-year class life, and for this analysis we assume that Mitchell's effective federal-plus-state tax rate is 40 percent. Also, the depreciable basis is the original cost of $10,000,000.

NPV Analysis.   Table 21-2 shows the cash flows that would be incurred each year under the two financing plans. The table is set up to produce a time line of cash flows:

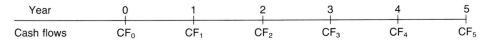

Year	0	1	2	3	4	5
Cash flows	CF_0	CF_1	CF_2	CF_3	CF_4	CF_5

All cash flows occur at the end of the year, and the CF_t values are shown on Lines 5 and 10 of Table 21-2 for buying and leasing respectively.

The top section of the table (Lines 1–6) is devoted to the cost of owning (borrowing and buying). Lines 1–4 show the individual cash flow items. Line 5 summarizes the annual net cash flows that Mitchell will incur if it finances the equipment with a loan. The present values of these cash flows are summed to

---

[11]Lease payments can occur at the beginning of the year or at the end of the year. In this example, we assume end-of-year payments, but we demonstrate beginning-of-year payments in Self-Test Problem ST-2.

Table 21-2 ▪ Mitchell Electronics Company: NPV Lease Analysis (Thousands of Dollars)

	Year					
	0	**1**	**2**	**3**	**4**	**5**
I. Cost of Owning						
1. Net purchase price	($10,000)					
2. Maintenance cost		($ 500)	($ 500)	($ 500)	($ 500)	($ 500)
3. Maintenance tax savings		200	200	200	200	200
4. Depreciation tax savings		800	1,280	760	480	440
5. Net cash flow	($10,000)	$ 500	$ 980	$ 460	$ 180	$ 140
6. PV cost of owning	($ 8,023)					
II. Cost of Leasing						
7. Lease payment		($2,800)	($2,800)	($2,800)	($2,800)	($2,800)
8. Lease payment tax savings		1,120	1,120	1,120	1,120	1,120
9. Purchase option price						(715)
10. Net cash flow	$ 0	($1,680)	($1,680)	($1,680)	($1,680)	($2,395)
11. PV cost of leasing	($ 7,611)					
III. Cost Comparison						

12. Net advantage to leasing = NAL

= PV cost of owning − PV cost of leasing

= $8,023 − $7,611 = $412.

Note: A line-by-line explanation of the table follows.

Explanation of Lines

1. If Mitchell buys the equipment, it will have to spend $10,000,000 on the purchase. Alternatively, we could show all of the financing flows associated with a $10,000,000 loan, net of taxes, but the end result would be the same because the PV of those flows would be exactly $10 million.

2. If the equipment is owned, Mitchell must pay $500,000 at the end of each year for maintenance.

3. The $500,000 maintenance expense is tax deductible, so it will produce a (Tax rate)(Maintenance expense) = 0.4($500,000) = $200,000 tax savings in each year.

4. If Mitchell buys the equipment, it can depreciate the equipment for tax purposes, and thus lower taxable income and taxes. The tax savings in each year is equal to (Tax rate)(Depreciation expense) = 0.4(Depreciation expense). As shown in Appendix 15A, the MACRS rates for 5-year property are 0.20, 0.32, 0.19, 0.12, and 0.11 in Years 1–5, respectively. To illustrate the calculation of the depreciation tax savings, consider Year 2. The depreciation expense is 0.32($10,000,000) = $3,200,000, and the tax savings is 0.4($3,200,000) = $1,280,000.

5. The net cash flows associated with owning are found by summing Lines 1–4.

6. The PV (in thousands) of the Line 5 cash flows, when discounted at 6 percent, is − $8,023.

7. The annual end-of-year lease payment is $2,800,000.

8. Since the lease payment is tax deductible, a tax savings of (Tax rate)(Lease payment) = 0.4($2,800,000) = $1,120,000 results.

9. Because Mitchell plans to continue to use the equipment after the lease expires, it must purchase the equipment for $715,000 at the end of Year 5 if it leases.

10. The net cash flows associated with leasing are found by summing Lines 7–9.

11. The PV (in thousands) of the Line 10 cash flows, when discounted at 6 percent, is − $7,611.

12. The net advantage to leasing is merely the difference between the PV cost of owning (in thousands) and the PV cost of leasing (in thousands) = $8,023 − $7,611 = $412. Since the NAL is positive, leasing is favored over borrowing and buying.

find the *present value of the cost of owning,* which is shown on Line 6 in the Year 0 column. (Note that with a financial calculator, we would input the cash flows as shown on Line 5 into the cash flow register, input the interest rate, I = 6, and then press the NPV key to obtain the PV of owning the equipment.)

Section II of the table calculates the present value cost of leasing. The lease payments are $2,800,000 per year; this rate, which in this example but not in all cases includes maintenance, was established by the prospective lessor and offered to Mitchell Electronics. If Mitchell accepts the lease, the full $2,800,000 will be a deductible expense, so the tax savings is (Tax rate)(Lease payment) = (0.4)($2,800,000) = $1,120,000. These amounts are shown on Lines 7 and 8.

Line 9 in the lease section shows the $715,000 which Mitchell expects to pay in Year 5 to purchase the equipment. We include this amount as a cost of leasing because Mitchell will almost certainly want to continue the operation and thus will be forced to purchase the equipment from the lessor. If we had assumed that the operation would not be continued, then no entry would have appeared on this line. However, in that case, we would have included the $715,000, minus applicable taxes, as a Year 5 inflow in the cost of owning analysis, because if the asset were purchased originally, it would be sold after 5 years. Line 10 shows the net cash flows associated with leasing for each year, and Line 11 shows the PV cost of leasing. (As indicated earlier in the cost of owning analysis, using a financial calculator we would input the cash flows as shown on Line 10 into the cash flow register, input the interest rate, I = 6, and then press the NPV key to obtain the PV cost of leasing the equipment.)

The rate used to discount the cash flows is a critical issue. In Chapter 4, we saw that the riskier a cash flow, the higher the discount rate used to find its present value. This same principle was observed in our discussion of capital budgeting, and it also applies in lease analysis. Just how risky are the cash flows under consideration here? Most of them are relatively certain, at least when compared with the types of cash flow estimates that were developed in capital budgeting. For example, the loan payment schedule is set by contract, as is the lease payment schedule. The depreciation expenses are also established by law and are not subject to change, and the $500,000 annual maintenance cost is fixed by contract as well. The tax savings are somewhat uncertain because tax rates may change, although tax rates do not change very often. The residual value is the least certain of the cash flows, but even here Mitchell's management is fairly confident that it will want to acquire the property and also that the cost of doing so will be close to $715,000.

Since the cash flows under both the lease and the borrow-and-purchase alternatives are all reasonably certain, they should be discounted at a relatively low rate. Most analysts recommend that the company's cost of debt be used, and this rate seems reasonable in our example. Further, since all the cash flows are on an after-tax basis, *the after-tax cost of debt, which is 6 percent, should be used.* Accordingly, in Table 21-2 we used a 6 percent discount rate to obtain the present values of the costs of owning and leasing. The financing method that produces the smaller present value of costs is the one that should be selected. The example shown in Table 21-2 indicates that leasing has a net advantage over buying: the present value of the cost of leasing is $412,000 less than that of buying. Therefore, it is to Mitchell's advantage to lease.

Factors That Affect Leasing Decisions

The basic method of analysis set forth in Table 21-2 is sufficient to handle most situations. However, certain factors warrant additional comments.

residual value

The value of leased property at the end of the lease term.

Estimated Residual Value.   It is important to note that the lessor will own the property upon the expiration of the lease. The estimated end-of-lease value of the property is called the **residual value.** Superficially, it would appear that if residual values are expected to be large, owning would have an advantage over leasing. However, if expected residual values are large—as they may be under inflation for certain types of equipment as well as if real property is involved—then competition among leasing companies will force leasing rates down to the point where potential residual values will be fully recognized in the lease contract rates. Thus, the existence of large residual values on equipment is not likely to bias the decision against leasing.

Increased Credit Availability.   As noted earlier, leasing is sometimes said to have an advantage for firms that are seeking the maximum degree of financial leverage. First, it is sometimes argued that a firm can obtain more money, and for a longer period, under a lease arrangement than under a loan secured by the asset. Second, because some leases do not appear on the balance sheet, lease financing has been said to give the firm a stronger appearance in a *superficial* credit analysis, thus permitting it to use more leverage than it could if it did not lease. There may be some truth to these claims for smaller firms. However, now that larger firms are required to capitalize major leases and to report them on their balance sheets, this point is of questionable validity.

⑦ *Self-Test Questions*

Define each of these terms: (1) sale-and-leaseback arrangements, (2) operating leases, and (3) financial, or capital, leases.

What is off balance sheet financing, what is FASB #13, and how are the two related?

List the sequence of events, for the lessee, leading to a lease arrangement.

Why is it appropriate to compare the cost of lease financing with that of debt financing? Why does the comparison *not* depend on how the asset will actually be financed if it is not leased?

OPTIONS

option

A contract that gives the option holder the right to buy or sell an asset at some predetermined price within a specified period of time.

An **option** is a contract that gives its holder the right to buy (or sell) an asset at some predetermined price within a specified period of time. "Pure options" are instruments that are created by outsiders (generally investment banking firms) rather than by the firm itself; they are bought and sold primarily by investors (or speculators). However, financial managers should understand the nature of options because this will help them structure warrant and convertible financings.

Option Types and Markets

striking (exercise) price

The price that must be paid (buying or selling) for a share of common stock when an option is exercised.

call option

An option to buy, or "call," a share of stock at a certain price within a specified period.

put option

An option to sell a share of stock at a certain price, within a specified period.

There are many types of options and option markets.[12] To understand how options work, suppose you owned 100 shares of IBM stock which on April 16, 1992, sold for $88.625 per share. You could sell to someone else the right to buy your 100 shares at any time during the next 3 months at a price of, say, $95 per share. The $95 is called the **striking, or exercise, price.** Such options exist, and they are traded on a number of stock exchanges, with the Chicago Board Options Exchange (CBOE) being the oldest and largest. This type of option is known as a **call option,** as the purchaser has a "call" on 100 shares of stock. The seller of a call option is known as an *option writer.* An investor who writes a call option against stock held in his or her portfolio is said to be selling *covered options;* options sold without the stock to back them up are called *naked options.*

On April 16, 1992, IBM's 3-month, $95 call options sold on the CBOE for $1.625 each. Thus, for ($1.625)(100) = $162.50, you could buy an option contract that would give you the right to purchase 100 shares of IBM at a price of $95 per share at any time during the next 3 months. If the stock stayed below $95 during that period, you would lose your $162.50, but if the stock's price rose to $105, your $162.50 investment would be worth ($105 − $95)(100) = $1,000. That translates into a very healthy rate of return on your $162.50 investment. Incidentally, if the stock price did go up, you would probably not actually exercise your options and buy the stock; rather, you would sell the options, which would then each have a price of at least $10 versus the $1.625 you had paid, to another option buyer.

You can also buy an option which gives you the right to *sell* a stock at a specified price at some time in the future—this is called a **put option.** For example, suppose you expect IBM's stock price to decline from its current level sometime during the next 3 months. For $118.75 you could buy a 3-month put option giving you the right to sell 100 shares (which you would not necessarily own) at a price of $80 per share ($80 is the put option striking price). If you bought a 100-share put contract for $118.75 and IBM's stock price actually fell to $70, you would make ($80 − $70)(100) = $1,000 minus the $118.75 you paid for the put option, for a net profit (before taxes and commissions) of $881.25.

Options trading is one of the hottest financial activities in the United States today. The leverage involved makes it possible for speculators with just a few dollars to make a fortune almost overnight. Also, investors with sizable portfolios can sell options against their stocks and earn the value of the options (minus brokerage commissions) even if the stocks' prices remain constant. Still, those who have profited most from the development of options trading are security firms, which earn very healthy commissions on such trades.

The corporations on whose stocks options are written, such as IBM, have nothing to do with the options market. They neither raise money in that market nor have any direct transactions in it, and option holders neither receive dividends nor vote for corporate directors (unless they exercise their options to

---

[12]For more information on options, see any standard investments textbook.

purchase the stock, which few actually do). There have been studies by the SEC and others as to whether options trading stabilizes or destabilizes the stock market and whether it helps or hinders corporations seeking to raise new capital. The studies have not been conclusive, but options trading is here to stay, and many regard it as the most exciting game in town.

Formula Value versus Option Price

formula value

The value of an option security, calculated as the stock price minus the striking, or exercise, price.

How is the actual price of an option determined in the market? In this section, we consider some of the basic relationships that can help investors determine the market price of a *call* option. Because a *call* option is the option to *purchase* shares of stock and a *put* option is the option to *sell* shares of stock, the relationships discussed will differ somewhat for puts. To begin, we define an option's **formula value** as follows:

> Formula value = Current price of the stock − Striking price.   **(21-1)**

For example, if a stock sells for $50 and its options have a striking price of $20, then the formula value of the option is $30. As we shall see, options generally sell at a price greater than their formula value.

Now consider Figure 21-1, which presents some data on Space Technology Inc. (STI), a company which recently went public and whose stock has fluctuated widely during its short history. Column 1 in the lower section shows the trading range of the stock; Column 2 shows the striking price of the option; Column 3 shows the formula values for STI's option when the stock sells at different prices; Column 4 gives the actual market prices of the option; and Column 5 shows the premium, or excess of the actual option price over its formula value. These data are plotted in the graph.

In this example, for any stock price below $20, the formula value is negative; above $20, each $1 increase in the price of the stock brings with it a $1 increase in the option's formula value. Note, however, that the actual market price of the option lies above the formula value at all prices of the common stock, but that the premium declines as the price of the stock increases. For example, when the common stock sold for $20 and the option had a zero formula value, its actual price, and the premium, was $9. Then, as the price of the stock rose, the formula value matched the stock increase dollar for dollar, but the market price of the option climbed less rapidly, causing the premium to decline. Thus, the premium was $9 when the stock sold for $20 a share, but it had declined to $1 by the time the stock price reached $73 a share, and beyond that point the premium virtually disappeared.

Why does this pattern exist? Why should the option ever sell for more than its formula value, and why does the premium decline as the price of the stock increases? The answer lies in the speculative appeal of options; they provide an investor with a high degree of leverage when buying securities. To illustrate, suppose STI's stock was selling for $21, and its options sold for exactly their formula value, $1. Now suppose you were thinking of investing in the company. If you bought a share of stock and the price rose to $42, you would make a 100 percent capital gain. However, if you bought the option at its $1 formula value,

Figure 21-1   ▪   **Space Technology Inc.: Option Price and Formula Value**

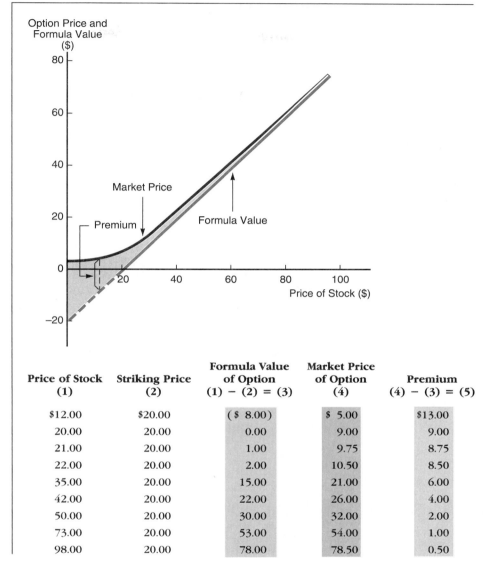

Price of Stock (1)	Striking Price (2)	Formula Value of Option (1) − (2) = (3)	Market Price of Option (4)	Premium (4) − (3) = (5)
$12.00	$20.00	($ 8.00)	$ 5.00	$13.00
20.00	20.00	0.00	9.00	9.00
21.00	20.00	1.00	9.75	8.75
22.00	20.00	2.00	10.50	8.50
35.00	20.00	15.00	21.00	6.00
42.00	20.00	22.00	26.00	4.00
50.00	20.00	30.00	32.00	2.00
73.00	20.00	53.00	54.00	1.00
98.00	20.00	78.00	78.50	0.50

your capital gain would be $21 on a $1 investment, a 2,100 percent gain! At the same time, your total loss potential with the option would be only $1, whereas the potential loss if you purchased the stock would be $21. The huge capital gains potential, combined with the loss limitation, is clearly worth something; the exact amount it is worth to investors is the amount of the premium.

Why does the premium decline as the price of the stock rises? Part of the answer is that both the leverage effect and the loss protection feature decline at high stock prices. For example, if you were thinking of buying the stock when its price was $73 a share, the formula value of the option would be $53. If the stock price doubled to $146, the formula value of STI's option would go from

$53 to $126, an increase of 138 percent versus the 2,100 percent gain when the stock price doubled from $21. Notice also that the potential loss on the option is much greater when the option is selling at a high price. These two factors—the declining leverage effect and the increasing danger of losses—help explain why the premium diminishes as the price of the common stock rises.

In addition to the stock price and the striking price, the value of an option also depends on (1) the option's time to maturity and (2) the variability of the underlying stock's price, as explained below:

1. The longer an option has to run, the greater its value, and the larger its premium. If an option expires at 4 P.M. today, there is not much chance that the stock price will go way up. Therefore, the option will sell at close to its formula value, and its premium will be small. On the other hand, if it has a year to go, the stock price could rise sharply, pulling the option's value up with it.

2. An option on an extremely volatile stock will be worth more than one on a very stable stock. We know that an option on a stock whose price rarely moves will not offer much chance for a large gain. On the other hand, an option on a stock that is highly volatile could provide a large gain, so such an option will be valuable. Note also that because losses on options are limited, large declines in a stock's price do not have a corresponding bad effect on option holders. Therefore, stock price volatility can only enhance the value of an option.[13]

If everything else were held constant, then in a graph like Figure 21-1, the longer an option's life, the higher its market price line would be above the formula value line. Also, the more volatile the price of the underlying stock, the higher the option's market price line would be.

---

[13]To illustrate this point, suppose that for $2 you could buy an option on a stock now selling for $20. The striking price is also $20. Now suppose the stock is highly volatile, and you think it has a 50 percent probability of selling for either $10 or $30 when the option expires in one month. What is the expected value of the option? If the stock sells for $30, the option will be worth $30 − $20 = $10. Since there is a 50-50 chance that the stock will be worth $10 or $30, the expected value of the option is $5:

$$\text{Expected value of option} = 0.5(0) + 0.5(\$10) = \$5.$$

To be exactly correct, we would have to discount the $5 back for one month.

Now suppose the stock was more volatile, with a 50-50 chance of being worth zero or $40. Here the option would be worth

$$\text{Expected value of option} = 0.5(0) + 0.5(\$20) = \$10.$$

This demonstrates that the greater the volatility of the stock, the greater the value of the option. The reason this result occurs is that the large loss on the stock ($20) had no more of an adverse effect on the option holder than the small loss ($10). Thus, option holders benefit greatly if a stock goes way up, but they do not lose too badly if it drops all the way to zero. These concepts have been used to develop formulas for pricing options, with the most widely used formula being the Black-Scholes model, which is discussed in most investments texts.

INDUSTRY PRACTICE | Are the Futures Markets Too
Risky for Pension Funds?

The prevailing wisdom is that the futures markets are too risky for conservative, multibillion-dollar public pension funds, which are among the world's largest investors. However, several of these funds have taken large positions in financial futures in recent years. The managers of these funds assert that pension funds will soon trade futures as actively as they now trade stocks and that funds which do not engage in futures trading will sacrifice potential returns. Virginia's public pension fund recently committed $100 million to trade commodity futures, and in mid-1991, the state of Colorado sold $100 million of Standard & Poor's 500-stock-index futures, betting that the stock market would fall. When the market fell to 360 from 385, the pension fund made a bundle. However, in some states, such as New York, it is against the law to invest public employees' retirement money in futures contracts.

Most pension funds that deal in the futures markets distinguish between commodities, such as soybeans or crude oil, and financial futures, such as those based on stocks, government bonds, and foreign currencies. Pension fund boards of trustees generally resist investments in pork bellies and other commodities even if they permit trading in financial futures.

The state of Wisconsin's pension fund works with interest rate futures contracts to create high-yield "synthetic" bonds. To do this, the fund purchases 10-year government Treasury bonds, which are relatively long-term investments which currently offer higher yields than shorter-term bonds. However, the pension fund does not necessarily want to hold the long-term Treasury bonds to their maturity, so, after it buys the bonds, it sells Treasury-bond futures contracts on the Chicago Board of Trade. By doing this, the pension fund is obliged to sell its Treasury bonds at today's prices on some future date, usually three or six months from now. Through these actions, the fund can turn long-term Treasury bonds into three- or six-month instruments but earn the higher interest yield of a long-term bond in the meantime. As a result, the pension fund does not sacrifice credit quality for a higher return.

If this sounds too good to be true, some experts would agree. First, if interest rates drop and bond prices rise, the Wisconsin fund will not share in this gain because they have presold their long-term bonds. Second, there is at least some danger that interest rates will rise, bond prices will decline, and the buyer of the futures contract will default, leaving the Wisconsin fund with marked-down long-term bonds. Finally, futures market operators do not work for nothing, so funds which engage in futures trading have to pay fees to get into the game.

Other pension funds use futures contracts or similar arrangements with banks, called forward contracts, to eliminate foreign exchange rate risk from their overseas investment earnings. For example, the Pennsylvania State Employees Retirement System has a $200 million portfolio of foreign stocks. Even if the prices of these foreign stocks rise, the gains could be eroded by changes in currency exchange rates. To protect itself from this risk, futures-like forward contracts on foreign currencies are used to lock in the currency exposure of the foreign stocks at today's rates, which eliminates the portfolio's future foreign exchange rate risk. Since 1988, by using this strategy, the Pennsylvania fund has been able to earn a 6.75 percent return on its foreign stock portfolio as compared with a world benchmark return of 4.62 percent.

Source: "State Pension Funds Try Futures Markets," *The Wall Street Journal,* November 5, 1991.

 Self-Test Questions

Differentiate between a call option and a put option.

Do the corporations on whose stocks options are written raise money in the options market? Explain.

How does one calculate the formula value of an option? How is the premium on the option calculated?

Why does the premium on the option decline as the price of the stock increases?

Explain how these factors affect the premium on an option: (1) the time remaining before the option expires and (2) the volatility of the underlying stock.

WARRANTS

warrant

A long-term option to buy a stated number of shares of common stock at a specified price.

A **warrant** is an option issued by a company which gives the holder the right to buy a stated number of shares of the company's stock at a specified price. Generally, warrants are distributed along with debt, and they are used to induce investors to buy a firm's long-term debt at a lower interest rate than would otherwise be required. For example, when Pan-Pacific Airlines (PPA) wanted to sell $50 million of 20-year bonds in 1992, the company's investment bankers informed the financial vice president that straight bonds would be difficult to sell and that an interest rate of 14 percent would be required. However, the bankers suggested as an alternative that investors would be willing to buy bonds with an annual coupon rate as low as 10⅜ percent if the company would offer 30 warrants with each $1,000 bond, each warrant entitling the holder to buy one share of common stock at a price of $22 per share. The stock was selling for $20 per share at the time, and the warrants would expire in 1998 if they had not been exercised previously.

Why would investors be willing to buy Pan-Pacific's bonds at a yield of only 10⅜ percent in a 14 percent market just because warrants were offered as part of the package? The answer is that warrants are long-term *options,* and they have a value for the reasons set forth in the previous section. In the PPA case, this value offset the low interest rate on the bonds and made the entire package of low interest bonds plus warrants attractive to investors.

Initial Market Price of Bond with Warrants

If the PPA bonds had been issued as straight debt, they would have carried a 14 percent interest rate. With warrants attached, however, the bonds were sold to yield 10⅜ percent. Someone buying one of the bonds at its $1,000 initial offering price would thus have been receiving a package consisting of a 10⅜ percent, 20-year bond plus 30 warrants. Since the going interest rate on bonds as risky as those of PPA was 14 percent, we can find the pure-debt value of the bonds, assuming an annual coupon, as follows:

$$PV = \text{Pure-debt value} = \sum_{t=1}^{20} \frac{\$103.75}{(1.14)^t} + \frac{\$1,000}{(1.14)^{20}}$$

$$= \$103.75(\text{PVIFA}_{14\%,20}) + \$1,000(\text{PVIF}_{14\%,20})$$

$$= \$687.15 + \$72.80$$

$$= \$759.95 \approx \$760.$$

Alternatively, using a financial calculator we would input the following data in the TVM register: N = 20, I = 14, PMT = 103.75, and FV = 1000. Then, we would press the PV key to obtain the answer of $759.91, or approximately $760. Thus, a person buying the bonds in the initial underwriting would pay $1,000 and receive in exchange a pure bond worth about $760 plus warrants presumably worth about $1,000 − $760 = $240:

$$\frac{\text{Price paid for}}{\text{bond with warrants}} = \frac{\text{Straight-debt}}{\text{value of bond}} + \frac{\text{Value of}}{\text{warrants}} \qquad (21\text{-}2)$$

$$\$1,000 \quad = \quad \$760 \quad + \quad \$240.$$

Because investors receive 30 warrants with each bond, each warrant has an implied value of $240/30 = $8.

The key issue in setting the terms of a bond-with-warrants offering is finding the value of the warrants. The pure-debt value of the bond can be estimated quite accurately. However, it is much more difficult to estimate the value of the warrants. If their value is overestimated relative to their true market value, it will be difficult to sell the issue at its par value. Conversely, if the warrants' value is underestimated, investors in the issue will receive a windfall profit because they can sell the warrants in the market for more than they implicitly paid for them, and this windfall profit would come out of the pockets of PPA's current stockholders.

Use of Warrants in Financing

Warrants are generally used by small, rapidly growing firms as "sweeteners" to help sell either debt or preferred stock. Such firms are frequently regarded as being highly risky, and their bonds can be sold only if the firms are willing to pay extremely high rates of interest and to accept very restrictive indenture provisions. To avoid this, firms such as Pan-Pacific often offer warrants along with their bonds. However, some strong firms also have used warrants. In one of the largest financings of any type ever undertaken by a business firm, AT&T raised $1.57 billion by selling bonds with warrants. This marked the first use ever of warrants by a large, strong corporation.

Getting warrants along with bonds enables investors to share in a company's growth if that firm does in fact grow and prosper; therefore, investors are willing to accept a lower bond interest rate and less restrictive indenture provisions. A bond with warrants has some characteristics of debt and some of equity. It is a hybrid security that provides the financial manager with an opportunity to expand the firm's mix of securities and to appeal to a broader group of investors, thus lowering the firm's cost of capital.

detachable warrant

A warrant that can be detached from a bond and traded independently of it.

Virtually all warrants today are **detachable warrants,** meaning that after a bond with attached warrants has been sold, the warrants can be detached and traded separately from the bond. Further, when these warrants are exercised, the bonds themselves (with their low coupon rate) will remain outstanding.

Thus, the warrants will bring in additional equity while leaving low interest rate debt on the books.

The warrants' exercise price is generally set at from 10 to 30 percent above the market price of the stock on the date the bond is issued. For example, if the stock sells for $10, the exercise price will probably be set in the $11 to $13 range. If the firm does grow and prosper, and if its stock price rises above the exercise price at which shares may be purchased, warrant holders will turn in their warrants, along with cash equal to the stated exercise price, in exchange for stock. Without some incentive, however, many warrants would never be exercised until just before expiration. Their value in the market would be greater than their formula, or exercise, value, and hence holders would sell warrants rather than exercise them.

There are three conditions which encourage holders to exercise their warrants: (1) Warrant holders will *surely* exercise warrants and buy stock if the warrants are about to expire with the market price of the stock above the exercise price. This means that if a firm wants its warrants exercised soon in order to raise capital, it should set a relatively short expiration date. (2) Warrant holders will tend to exercise *voluntarily* and buy stock if the company raises the dividend on the common stock by a sufficient amount. Since no dividend is paid on the warrant, it provides no current income. However, if the common stock pays a high dividend, it provides an attractive dividend yield. Therefore, the higher the stock's dividend, the greater the opportunity cost of holding the warrant rather than exercising it. Thus, if a firm wants its warrants exercised, it can raise the common stock's dividend. (3) Warrants sometimes have **stepped-up exercise prices,** which prod owners into exercising them. For example, the Shome Scientific Company has warrants outstanding with an exercise price of $25 until December 31, 1994, at which time the exercise price will rise to $30. If the price of the common stock is over $25 just before December 31, 1994, many warrant holders will exercise their options before the stepped-up price takes effect.

Another useful feature of warrants is that they generally bring in funds only if such funds are needed. If the company grows, it will probably need new equity capital. At the same time, this growth will cause the price of the stock to rise and the warrants to be exercised, thereby allowing the firm to obtain additional cash. If the company is not successful and cannot profitably employ additional money, the price of its stock will probably not rise sufficiently to induce exercise of the options.

stepped-up exercise price

An exercise price that is specified to be higher if a warrant is exercised after a designated date.

Self-Test Questions

Explain (showing two formulas, but without doing any calculations) how you would determine the value of warrants attached to bonds.

What three conditions would encourage holders to exercise their warrants?

Do warrants bring in additional funds to the firm when exercised? Explain.

Explain how a firm can use warrants to issue debt with a lower cost than similar debt without warrants.

CONVERTIBLES

convertible security

A security, usually a bond or preferred stock, that is exchangeable at the option of the holder for the common stock of the issuing firm.

Convertible securities are bonds or preferred stocks that can be exchanged for common stock at the option of the holder. Unlike the exercise of warrants, which provides the firm with additional funds, conversion does not bring in additional capital — debt (or preferred stock) is simply replaced by common stock. Of course, this reduction of debt or preferred stock will strengthen the firm's balance sheet and make it easier to raise additional capital, but this is a separate action.

Conversion Ratio and Conversion Price

conversion ratio, CR

The number of shares of common stock that may be obtained by converting a convertible bond or share of convertible preferred stock.

conversion price, P_c

The effective price paid for common stock obtained by converting a convertible security.

One of the most important provisions of a convertible security is the **conversion ratio, CR,** defined as the number of shares of stock the convertible holder receives upon conversion. Related to the conversion ratio is the **conversion price, P_c,** which is the effective price paid for the common stock obtained by converting a convertible security. The relationship between the conversion ratio and the conversion price can be illustrated by the Jackson Electronics Company's convertible debentures, issued at their $1,000 par value in 1992. At any time prior to maturity on July 1, 2012, a debenture holder can exchange a bond for 20 shares of common stock; therefore, CR = 20. The bond has a par value of $1,000, so the holder would be relinquishing this amount upon conversion. Dividing the $1,000 par value by the 20 shares received gives a conversion price of P_c = $50 a share:

$$\text{Conversion price} = P_c = \frac{\text{Par value of bond}}{\text{CR}} \qquad (21\text{-}3)$$

$$= \frac{\$1,000}{20} = \$50.$$

Similarly, if we know the conversion price, we can find CR:

$$\text{CR} = \frac{\text{Par value}}{P_c} \qquad (21\text{-}4)$$

$$= \frac{\$1,000}{\$50} = 20 \text{ shares.}$$

Once CR is set, the value of P_c is established, and vice versa.

Like a warrant's exercise price, the conversion price is characteristically set at from 10 to 30 percent above the prevailing market price of the common stock at the time the convertible issue is sold. Generally, the conversion price and ratio are fixed for the life of the bond, although sometimes a stepped-up conversion price is used. Arden Industries' convertible debentures, for example, are convertible into 12.5 shares until 1995; into 11.76 shares from 1995 until 2000; and into 11.11 shares from 2000 until maturity in 2005. The conversion price thus started at $80, will rise to $85 in 1995, and then will go to $90 in 2000. Arden's convertibles, like most, are callable at the option of the company after a 3-year call protection period.

Another factor that may cause a change in the conversion price and ratio is a standard feature of almost all convertibles—the clause protecting the convertible against dilution from stock splits, stock dividends, and the sale of common stock at prices below the conversion price. The typical provision states that if common stock is sold at a price below the conversion price, the conversion price must be lowered (and the conversion ratio raised) to the price at which the new stock was issued. Also, if the stock is split (or if a stock dividend is declared), the conversion price must be lowered by the percentage of the stock split (or stock dividend). For example, if Jackson Electronics were to have a two-for-one stock split, the conversion ratio would automatically be adjusted from 20 to 40, and the conversion price lowered from $50 to $25. If this protection were not contained in the contract, a company could completely thwart conversion by the use of stock splits. Warrants are similarly protected against such dilution.

The standard protection against dilution from selling new stock at prices below the conversion price can, however, get a company into trouble. For example, Arden Industries' stock was selling for only $64 in 1992 versus the conversion price of $80. Thus, Arden would have had to give its bondholders a tremendous break if it wanted to sell new common stock. Problems like this must be kept in mind by firms considering the use of convertibles or bonds with warrants.[14]

Convertible Bond Analysis

In 1992 Jackson Electronics Company was thinking of issuing 20-year convertible bonds at a price of $1,000 each. Each bond would pay a 10 percent annual coupon interest rate, or $100 per year, and each would be convertible into 20 shares of stock. Thus, the conversion price would be $1,000/20 = $50. If the bonds did not have the conversion feature, investors would require a yield of 12 percent, because $k_d = 12\%$. Knowing k_d, the coupon rate, and the maturity, we can find the pure-debt value of the convertibles at the time of issue, B_0, using the bond valuation model developed back in Chapter 6. The bonds would initially sell at a price of $851:

$$\text{Pure-debt value at time of issue} = B_0 = \sum_{t=1}^{N} \frac{\text{Coupon interest}}{(1 + k_d)^t} + \frac{\text{Maturity value}}{(1 + k_d)^N} \quad \textbf{(21-5)}$$

$$= \sum_{t=1}^{20} \frac{\$100}{(1.12)^t} + \frac{\$1,000}{(1.12)^{20}} = \$851.$$

---

[14]For a more complete discussion of how the terms are set on a convertible offering, see M. Wayne Marr and G. Rodney Thompson, "The Pricing of New Convertible Bond Issues," *Financial Management,* Summer 1984, 31–37.

B_0 is the initial pure debt value of the bond, and B_t is the value each year after issue, as the bond's maturity changes from 20 to 19, then 18, and so forth. As maturity approaches, the pure debt value approaches $1,000.

Jackson's stock is expected to pay a dividend of $2.80 in the coming year; it currently sells at $35 per share, and this price is expected to grow at a constant rate of 8 percent per year. Thus, the stock price expected in each future Year t is $\hat{P}_t = P_0(1 + g)^t = \$35(1.08)^t$. Further, since Jackson's convertibles would allow their holders to convert them into 20 shares of stock, the value a bondholder would expect to receive if he or she converted, defined as C_t, would be

$$\text{Conversion value} = C_t = \text{Initial stock price } (1 + g)^t(\text{CR}) \quad \textbf{(21-6)}$$

$$= \$35(1.08)^t(20).$$

The convertible bonds would not be callable for 10 years, after which they could be called at a price of $1,000. If after 10 years the conversion value exceeded the call price by at least 20 percent, management has indicated that it would call the bonds.

Figure 21-2 shows the expectations of both an average investor and the company:

1. The horizontal line $MM'' = \$1,000$ represents the par (and maturity) value. Also, $1,000 is the price at which the bond would initially be offered to the public.

2. The pure-debt value of the convertible would initially be $851, but it would rise to $1,000 over the 20-year life of the bond. The bond's pure-debt value is shown by the line B_t in Figure 21-2.

conversion value, C_t

The value of common stock obtained by converting a convertible security.

3. The bond's initial **conversion value, C_t,** or the value of the stock the investor would receive if the bond were converted at $t = 0$, is $700: Conversion value $= P_0(\text{CR}) = \$35(20 \text{ shares}) = \$700$. As indicated previously, the stock's price is expected to grow at an 8 percent rate, so $\hat{P}_t = \$35(1.08)^t$. If the price of the stock rises over time, so will the conversion value of the bond. For example, in Year 3 the conversion value should be $C_3 = P_3(\text{CR}) = \$35(1.08)^3(20) = \$882$. The expected conversion value over time is given by the line C_t in Figure 21-2.

4. The actual market price of the bond must always be equal to or greater than the *higher* of its pure-debt value or its conversion value. Therefore, the higher of the bond value or the conversion value curves in Figure 21-2 represents a "floor price" for the bond; this is reperesented by the heavy line B_0XC_t.

5. The market value of a convertible generally will exceed the floor price for the same reasons that an option's or a warrant's price will exceed its formula value. Investors are willing to pay a premium over the pure-debt value (which establishes the initial floor) because of the possibility of earning large capital gains if the stock price shoots up. After Year 3, when the conversion value exceeds the pure-bond value and thus establishes the floor, the market price will still exceed the floor. This is because the con-

Figure 21-2 ▪ **Model of a Convertible Bond**

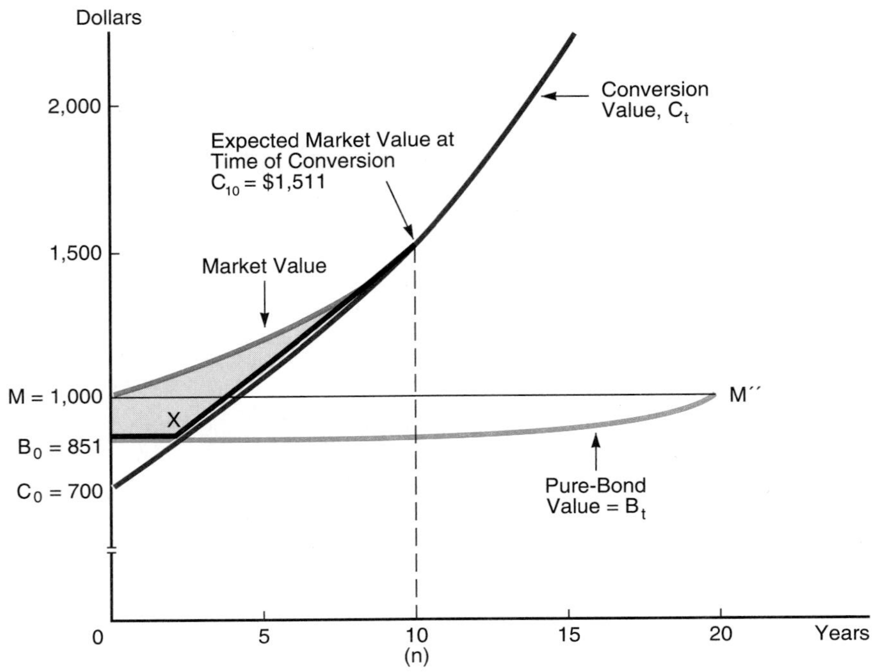

Year	Pure-Bond Value, B_t	Conversion Value, C_t	Maturity Value, M	Market Value	Floor Value	Premium
0	$ 851	$ 700	$1,000	$1,000	$ 851	$149
1	853	756	1,000	1,042	853	189
2	855	816	1,000	1,086	855	231
3	858	882	1,000	1,132	882	250
4	861	952	1,000	1,180	952	228
5	864	1,029	1,000	1,229	1,029	200
6	867	1,111	1,000	1,281	1,111	170
7	872	1,200	1,000	1,335	1,200	135
8	876	1,296	1,000	1,391	1,296	95
9	881	1,399	1,000	1,450	1,399	51
10	887	1,511	1,000	1,511	1,511	0
11	893	1,632	1,000	1,632	1,632	0
.	.	.	.	.	.	.
.	.	.	.	.	.	.
.	.	.	.	.	.	.
20	1,000	3,263	1,000	3,263	3,263	0

vertible is safer than the stock, for even if profits decline and the stock price drops, the bond's value will never fall below its pure-debt value.[15]

6. The gap between the market price of the convertible and the floor, or the premium investors are willing to pay, declines over time and is zero in Year 10. This decline occurs for two reasons. First, the dividends received on the stock presumably are growing at 8 percent a year, whereas the interest on the bond is fixed at $100 annually. After 8 years, the dividends which would be received from 20 shares of stock, $2.80(1.08)^8(20) = $103.65, would exceed the $100 of interest paid by the bond; beyond that point the opportunity cost of holding the bond rather than converting it would become increasingly heavy. Second, after 10 years the bond would become callable at a price of $1,000. If Jackson called the issue, the bondholder could either convert the bond to common stock worth $C_{10} = $1,511 or receive $1,000 in cash. The holder would, of course, choose the $1,511 of stock. Note, however, that if the convertible were selling at a price greater than $C_{10} = $1,511 when the call occurred, the holder would suffer an immediate loss equal to the difference between the bond's price and $1,511. Therefore, because of the call provision, the market value of the bond cannot logically exceed the higher of the call price or the conversion price after the bond becomes callable.

7. If investors purchased Jackson's stock, they would expect a return of $k_s = D_1/P_0 + g = $2.80/$35 + 8\% = 16\%$. If they bought a pure bond, they would earn 12 percent. The convertible has some guaranteed interest plus the expectation of some capital gains, so its risk and therefore its expected rate of return should lie between $k_d = 12\%$ and $k_s = 16\%$. We can find the expected return on the convertible by solving for k_c in the following equation:

$$\text{Initial price} = \sum_{t=1}^{n} \frac{\text{Interest}}{(1 + k_c)^t} + \frac{\text{Conversion value}}{(1 + k_c)^n} \qquad \text{(21-7)}$$

$$\$1,000 = \sum_{t=1}^{10} \frac{\$100}{(1 + k_c)^t} + \frac{\$1,511}{(1 + k_c)^{10}} .$$

Using a financial calculator, if we input N = 10, PV = −1000, PMT = 100, and FV = 1511, then we could find I = k_c = 12.8%. Therefore, under the assumptions of this example, an investor who purchased the convertible at its initial $1,000 offering price could expect to earn a rate of return of 12.8 percent.

Use of Convertibles in Financing

Convertibles offer three important advantages from the issuer's standpoint. First, convertibles, like bonds with warrants, permit a company to sell debt with a lower interest rate and with less restrictive covenants than straight bonds. Sec-

---

[15]Note, however, that the bond value line B_0M'' would fall if interest rates rose in the economy or if the company's credit risk deteriorated, both of which would cause k_d to rise.

ond, convertibles are generally subordinated to mortgage bonds, bank loans, and other senior debt, so financing with convertibles leaves the company's access to "regular" debt unimpaired. Third, convertibles provide a way of selling common stock at prices higher than those currently prevailing. Many companies actually want to sell common stock and not debt, but they believe that the price of their stock is temporarily depressed. The financial manager may know, for example, that earnings are depressed because of start-up costs associated with a new project, but he or she may expect earnings to rise sharply during the next year or so, pulling the price of the stock along. In this case, if the company sold stock now it would be giving up too many shares to raise a given amount of money. However, if it sets the conversion price at 20 to 30 percent above the present market price of the stock, then 20 to 30 percent fewer shares will have to be given up when the bonds are converted. Notice, however, that management is counting on the stock price's rising sufficiently above the conversion price to make the bonds attractive in conversion. If earnings do not rise and pull the stock price up, and hence if conversion does not occur, the company could be saddled with debt in the face of low earnings, which could be disastrous.

How can the company be sure that conversion will occur if the price of the stock rises above the conversion price? Typically, convertibles contain a call provision that enables the issuing firm to force bondholders to convert. Suppose the conversion price is $50, the conversion ratio is 20, the market price of the common stock has risen to $60, and the call price on the convertible bond is $1,050. If the company calls the bond, bondholders could either convert into common stock with a market value of $1,200 or allow the company to redeem the bond for $1,050. Naturally, bondholders prefer $1,200 to $1,050, so conversion will occur. The call provision therefore gives the company a means of forcing conversion, but only if the market price of the stock is greater than the conversion price.

Convertibles are useful, but they do have three important disadvantages. (1) The use of a convertible security may in effect give the issuer the opportunity to sell common stock at a price higher than it could sell stock otherwise. However, if the common stock increases greatly in price, the company would probably have been better off if it had used straight debt in spite of its higher interest rate and then later sold common stock to refund the debt. (2) If the company truly wants to raise equity capital, and if the price of the stock does not rise sufficiently after the bond is issued, then the firm will be stuck with debt. (3) Convertibles typically have a low coupon interest rate, an advantage that will be lost when conversion occurs. Warrant financings, on the other hand, permit the company to continue to use the low-coupon debt for a longer period.

Self-Test Questions

Does the exchange of convertible securities for common stock bring in additional funds to the firm? Explain.

How do you calculate (1) the conversion price, P_c, and (2) the conversion ratio, CR?

How is a convertible bond's initial conversion value, C_t, calculated? How does this value change over time?

Why does the premium (the excess of the market value of a convertible over either the conversion value or the straight bond value) decline over time and eventually go to zero?

What are the key advantages and disadvantages of convertibles?

REPORTING EARNINGS WHEN WARRANTS OR CONVERTIBLES ARE OUTSTANDING

If warrants or convertibles are outstanding, a firm can theoretically report earnings per share in one of three ways:

1. **Simple EPS.** The earnings available to common stockholders are divided by the average number of shares actually outstanding during the period.

2. **Primary EPS.** The earnings available are divided by the average number of shares that would have been outstanding if warrants and convertibles likely to be converted in the near future had actually been exercised or converted.

3. **Fully diluted EPS.** This is similar to primary EPS except that *all* warrants and convertibles are assumed to be exercised or converted, regardless of the likelihood of either occurring.

Simple EPS is virtually never reported by firms which have warrants or convertibles likely to be exercised or converted; the SEC prohibits use of this figure, and it requires that primary and fully diluted earnings be shown on the income statement.

  Self-Test Question

Differentiate between simple EPS, primary EPS, and fully diluted EPS.

SMALL BUSINESS Lease Financing for Small Businesses

Earlier in this chapter we saw that, under certain conditions, leasing an asset can be less costly than borrowing to purchase the asset. For the small firm, leasing often offers three additional advantages: it (1) conserves cash, (2) makes better use of managers' time, and (3) provides financing quickly.

Conserving Cash. Small firms often have limited cash resources. Because many leasing companies do not require the lessee to make even a small down payment, and because leases are often for longer terms and thus require lower payments than bank loans, leasing can help the small firm conserve its

cash. Leasing companies also may be willing to work with a company to design a flexible leasing package that will help the lessee preserve its cash during critical times. For example, when Surgicare of Central Jersey opened its first surgical center, the firm did not have sufficient cash to pay for the necessary equipment. Surgicare's options were to borrow at a high interest rate, to sell stock to the public (which is difficult for a start-up firm), or to lease the equipment. Surgicare's financial vice president, John Rutzel, decided to lease the needed equipment from Copelco Financial Services, a leasing company which specializes in health care equipment. Copelco allowed Surgicare to make very low payments for the first 6 months, slightly higher payments during the second 6 months, and level payments thereafter. These unique lease terms "got Surgicare through the start-up phase, when cash flow was the critical consideration."

Freeing Managers for Other Tasks. Most small business owners find that they never have enough time to get everything done—being in charge of sales, operations, budgeting, and everything else, they are simply spread too thin. If an asset is owned, the firm must maintain it in good working condition and also keep records on its use for tax depreciation purposes. However, leasing assets frees the business's owner of these duties. First, paperwork is reduced because maintenance records, depreciation schedules, and other records do not have to be maintained on leased assets. Second, less time may have to be spent "shopping around" for the right equipment because leasing companies, which generally specialize in a particular industry, can often provide the manager with the information necessary to select the needed assets. Third, since the assets can be traded in if they become obsolete, the initial choice of equipment is

less critical. And fourth, the burden of servicing and repairing the equipment can be passed on to the lessor.

Obtaining Assets Quickly and Inexpensively. Many new, small firms find that banks are unwilling to lend them money at a reasonable cost. However, because leasing companies retain the ownership of the equipment, they may be more willing to take chances with start-up firms. When Ed Lavin started Offset Printing Company, his bank would not lend him the money to purchase the necessary printing presses— the bank wanted to lend only to firms with proven track records. Lavin arranged to lease the needed presses from Eaton Financial, which also advised him on the best type of equipment to meet his needs. Recently, Lavin's firm achieved sales of $250,000, and as his company grew, he expanded by leasing additional equipment. Thus, (1) leasing allowed Lavin to go into business when his bank was unwilling to help, (2) his leasing company provided him with help in selecting equipment, and (3) the leasing company also provided additional capital to meet his expansion needs.

SUMMARY

This chapter discussed three hybrid forms of long-term financing: (1) preferred stock, (2) leasing, and (3) option securities. The key concepts covered are listed below.

▪ **Preferred stock** is a hybrid security having some characteristics of debt and some of equity. Equity holders view preferred stock as being similar to debt because it has a claim on the firm's earnings ahead of the claim of the common stockholders. Bondholders, however, view preferred as equity because debtholders have a prior claim on the firm's income and assets.

▪ The primary **advantages of preferred stock** to the issuer are (1) that preferred dividends are limited and (2) that failure to pay them will not bankrupt the firm. The primary disadvantage to the issuer is that the cost of preferred is higher than that of debt because preferred dividend payments are not tax deductible.

▪ To the investor, preferred stock offers the advantage of **more dependable income** than common stock, and, to a corporate investor, **70 percent of such dividends are not taxable.** The principal disadvantages to the investor are that the **returns are limited** and the investor has **no legally enforceable right to a dividend.**

▪ **Leasing** is a means of obtaining the use of an asset without purchasing that asset. The three most important forms of leasing are (1) **sale-and-leaseback** arrangements, under which a firm sells an asset to another party and leases the asset back for a specified period under specific terms; (2) **operating leases,** under which the lessor both maintains and finances the asset; and (3) **financial leases,** under which the asset is fully amortized over the life of the lease, the lessor does not normally provide maintenance, and the lease is not cancelable.

▌ The **decision whether to lease or to buy an asset** is made by comparing the financing costs of the two alternatives and choosing the financing method with the lower cost. All cash flows should be discounted at the **after-tax cost of debt** because lease analysis cash flows are relatively certain and are on an after-tax basis.

▌ An **option** is a contract that gives its holder the right to buy (or sell) an asset at some predetermined price within a specified period of time. Options features are used by firms to "sweeten" debt offerings.

▌ A **warrant** is an option issued by a firm which gives the holder the right to purchase a stated number of shares of stock at a specified price within a given period. A warrant will be exercised if it is about to expire and the stock price is above the exercise price.

▌ A **convertible security** is a bond or preferred stock which can be exchanged for common stock. When conversion occurs, debt or preferred stock is replaced with common stock, but no money changes hands.

▌ The **conversion of bonds or preferred stock** by their holders **does not provide additional funds** to the company, but it does result in a lower debt ratio. The **exercise of warrants does provide additional funds,** which strengthens the firm's equity position, but it still leaves the debt or preferred stock on the balance sheet. Thus, low interest rate debt remains outstanding when warrants are exercised, but the firm loses this advantage when convertibles are converted.

▌ For the small firm, leasing offers three advantages: (1) **cash is conserved,** (2) **managers' time is freed** for other tasks, and (3) **financing can often be obtained quickly** and at a **relatively low cost.**

Questions

21-1 For purposes of measuring a firm's leverage, should preferred stock be classified as debt or equity? Does it matter if the classification is being made (a) by the firm's management, (b) by creditors, or (c) by equity investors?

21-2 You are told that one corporation just issued $100 million of preferred stock and another purchased $100 million of preferred stock as an investment. You are also told that one firm has an effective tax rate of 20 percent whereas the other is in the 34 percent bracket. Which firm is more likely to have bought the preferred? Explain.

21-3 One often finds that a company's bonds have a higher yield than its preferred stock, even though the bonds are considered to be less risky than the preferred to an investor. What causes this yield differential?

21-4 Why would a company choose to issue floating rate as opposed to fixed rate preferred stock?

21-5 Distinguish between operating leases and financial leases. Would a firm be more likely to finance a fleet of trucks or a manufacturing plant with an operating lease?

21-6   One alleged advantage of leasing voiced in the past was that it kept liabilities off the balance sheet, thus making it possible for a firm to obtain more leverage than it otherwise could have. This raised the question of whether or not both the lease obligation and the asset involved should be capitalized and shown on the balance sheet. Discuss the pros and cons of capitalizing leases and related assets.

21-7   Suppose there were no IRS restrictions on what constitutes a valid lease. Explain in a manner that a legislator might understand why some restrictions should be imposed.

21-8   Suppose Congress changed the tax laws in a way that (1) permitted equipment to be depreciated over a shorter period, (2) lowered corporate tax rates, and (3) reinstated the investment tax credit. Discuss how each of these changes would affect the relative use of leasing versus conventional debt in the U.S. economy.

21-9   Why do options typically sell at prices higher than their formula values?

21-10   What effect does the expected growth rate of a firm's stock price (subsequent to issue) have on its ability to raise additional funds through (a) convertibles and (b) warrants?

21-11   a. How would a firm's decision to pay out a higher percentage of its earnings as dividends affect each of the following?
         (1) The value of its long-term warrants.
         (2) The likelihood that its convertible bonds will be converted.
         (3) The likelihood that its warrants will be exercised.
      b. If you owned the warrants or convertibles of a company, would you be pleased or displeased if it raised its payout rate from 20 percent to 80 percent? Why?

21-12   Evaluate the following statement: "Issuing convertible securities represents a means by which a firm can sell common stock at a price above the existing market price."

21-13   Suppose a company simultaneously issues $50 million of convertible bonds with a coupon rate of 9 percent and $50 million of pure bonds with a coupon rate of 12 percent. Both bonds have the same maturity. Does the fact that the convertible issue has the lower coupon rate suggest that it is less risky than the pure bond? Would you regard its cost of capital as being lower on the convertible than on the pure bond? Explain. (Hint: Although it might appear at first glance that the convertible's cost of capital is lower, this is not necessarily the case because the interest rate on the convertible understates its cost. Think about this.)

Self-Test Problems   *(Solutions Appear in Appendix B)*

ST-1   Define each of the following terms:
Key terms   a. Cumulative dividends; floating rate preferred stock
         b. Call premium
         c. Lessee; lessor
         d. Sale and leaseback; operating lease; financial lease
         e. Off balance sheet financing
         f. FASB #13
         g. Residual value
         h. Option; striking, or exercise, price; call option; put option
         i. Formula value; warrant; detachable warrant; stepped-up exercise price
         j. Convertible security; conversion ratio, CR; conversion price, P_c; conversion value, C_t; pure-debt value, B_t
         k. Simple EPS; primary EPS; fully diluted EPS

ST-2   The Olsen Company has decided to acquire a new truck. One alternative is to lease the
Lease analysis   truck on a 4-year contract for a lease payment of $10,000 per year, with payments to

be made at the *beginning* of each year. The lease would include maintenance. Alternatively, Olsen could purchase the truck outright for $40,000, financing with a bank loan for the net purchase price, amortized over a 4-year period at an interest rate of 10 percent per year, payments to be made at the *end* of each year. Under the borrow-to-purchase arrangement, Olsen would have to maintain the truck at a cost of $1,000 per year, payable at year-end. The truck falls into the MACRS 3-year class. It has a salvage value of $10,000, which is the expected market value after 4 years, at which time Olsen plans to replace the truck irrespective of whether it leases or buys. Olsen has a federal-plus-state tax rate of 40 percent.

a. What is Olsen's PV cost of leasing?

b. What is Olsen's PV cost of owning? Should the truck be leased or purchased?

c. The appropriate discount rate for use in Olsen's analysis is the firm's after-tax cost of debt. Why?

d. The salvage value is the least certain cash flow in the analysis. How might Olsen incorporate the higher riskiness of this cash flow into the analysis?

Problems

21-1
Balance sheet effects of leasing

Two textile companies, Meyer Manufacturing and Haugen Mills, began operations with identical balance sheets. A year later, both required additional manufacturing capacity at a cost of $200,000. Meyer obtained a 5-year, $200,000 loan at an 8 percent interest rate from its bank. Haugen, on the other hand, decided to lease the required $200,000 capacity from American Leasing for 5 years; an 8 percent return was built into the lease. The balance sheet for each company, before the asset increases, is as follows:

		Debt	$200,000
		Equity	200,000
Total assets	$400,000	Total liabilities and equity	$400,000

a. Show the balance sheet of each firm after the asset increase, and calculate each firm's new debt ratio. (Assume Haugen's lease is kept off the balance sheet.)

b. Show how Haugen's balance sheet would have looked immediately after the financing if it had capitalized the lease.

c. Would the rate of return (1) on assets and (2) on equity be affected by the choice of financing? How?

21-2
Lease analysis

As part of its overall plant modernization and cost reduction program, the management of Teweles Textile Mills has decided to install a new automated weaving loom. In the capital budgeting analysis of this equipment, the IRR of the project was found to be 20 percent versus a project required return of 12 percent.

The loom has an invoice price of $250,000, including delivery and installation charges. The funds needed could be borrowed from the bank through a 4-year amortized loan at a 10 percent interest rate, with payments to be made at the end of each year. In the event that the loom is purchased, the manufacturer will contract to maintain and service it for a fee of $20,000 per year paid at the end of each year. The loom falls in the MACRS 5-year class, and Teweles's marginal federal-plus-state tax rate is 40 percent.

Apilado Automation Inc., maker of the loom, has offered to lease the loom to Teweles for $70,000 upon delivery and installation (at t = 0) plus 4 additional annual lease payments of $70,000 to be made at the ends of Years 1 through 4. (Note that there are 5 lease payments in total.) The lease agreement includes maintenance and servicing. Actually, the loom has an expected life of 8 years, at which time its expected salvage value is zero; however, after 4 years, its market value is expected to equal its book value of $42,500. Teweles plans to build an entirely new plant in 4 years, so it has no interest in either leasing or owning the proposed loom for more than that period.

a. Should the loom be leased or purchased?

b. The salvage value is clearly the most uncertain cash flow in the analysis. Assume that the appropriate salvage value pretax discount rate is 15 percent. What would be the effect of a salvage value risk adjustment on the decision?

c. The original analysis assumed that Teweles would not need the loom after 4 years. Now assume that the firm will continue to use it after the lease expires. Thus, if it leased, Teweles would have to buy the asset after 4 years at the then existing market value, which is assumed to equal the book value. What effect would this requirement have on the basic analysis? (No numerical analysis is required; just verbalize.)

21-3
Convertibles

The Swift Company was planning to finance an expansion in the summer of 1993. The principal executives of the company agreed that an industrial company like theirs should finance growth by means of common stock rather than by debt. However, they believed that the price of the company's common stock did not reflect its true worth, so they decided to sell a convertible security. They considered a convertible debenture but feared the burden of fixed interest charges if the common stock did not rise enough to make conversion attractive. They decided on an issue of convertible preferred stock, which would pay a dividend of $1.05 per share.

The common stock was selling for $21 a share at the time. Management projected earnings for 1993 at $1.50 a share and expected a future growth rate of 10 percent a year in 1994 and beyond. It was agreed by the investment bankers and management that the common stock would continue to sell at 14 times earnings, the current price/earnings ratio.

a. What conversion price should be set by the issuer? The conversion rate will be 1.0; that is, each share of convertible preferred can be converted into one share of common. Therefore, the convertible's par value (as well as the issue price) will be equal to the conversion price, which in turn will be determined as a percentage over the current market price of the common. Your answer will be a guess, but make it a reasonable one.

b. Should the preferred stock include a call provision? Why or why not?

21-4
Financing alternatives

The Cox Computer Company has grown rapidly during the past 5 years. Recently its commercial bank urged the company to consider increasing its permanent financing. Its bank loan under a line of credit has risen to $150,000, carrying a 10 percent interest rate, and Cox has been 30 to 60 days late in paying trade creditors.

Discussions with an investment banker have resulted in the decision to raise $250,000 at this time. Investment bankers have assured Cox that the following alternatives are feasible (flotation costs will be ignored):

- *Alternative 1:* Sell common stock at $10 per share.

- *Alternative 2:* Sell convertible bonds at a 10 percent coupon, convertible into 80 shares of common stock for each $1,000 bond (that is, the conversion price is $12.50 per share).

- *Alternative 3:* Sell debentures with a 10 percent coupon; each $1,000 bond will have 80 warrants to buy one share of common stock at $12.50.

Charles Cox, the president, owns 80 percent of Cox's common stock and wishes to maintain control of the company; 50,000 shares are outstanding. The following are summaries of Cox's latest financial statements:

Balance Sheet

		Current liabilities	$200,000
		Common stock, $1 par	50,000
		Retained earnings	25,000
Total assets	$275,000	Total liabilities and equity	$275,000

Income Statement

Sales	$550,000
All costs except interest	495,000
EBIT	$ 55,000
Interest	15,000
EBT	$ 40,000
Taxes at 40%	16,000
Net income	$ 24,000
Shares outstanding	50,000
Earnings per share	$0.48
Price/earnings ratio	$18 \times$
Market price of stock	$8.64

a. Show the new balance sheet under each alternative. For Alternatives 2 and 3, show the balance sheet after conversion of the debentures or exercise of the warrants. Assume that $150,000 of the funds raised will be used to pay off the bank loan and the rest to increase total assets.

b. Show Charles Cox's control position under each alternative, assuming that he does not purchase additional shares.

c. What is the effect on earnings per share of each alternative if it is assumed that earnings before interest and taxes will be 20 percent of total assets?

d. What will be the debt ratio under each alternative?

e. Which of the three alternatives would you recommend to Charles Cox, and why?

21-5
Convertibles

Rentz Computers Inc. needs to raise $35 million to begin producing a new microcomputer. Rentz's straight, nonconvertible debentures currently yield 12 percent. Its stock sells for $38 per share, the last dividend was $2.46, and the expected growth rate is a constant 8 percent. Investment bankers have tentatively proposed that Rentz raise the $35 million by issuing convertible debentures. These convertibles would have a $1,000 par value, carry a coupon rate of 10 percent, have a 20-year maturity, and be convertible into 20 shares of stock. The bonds would be noncallable for 5 years, after which they would be callable at a price of $1,075; this call price would decline by $5 per year in Year 6 and each year thereafter. Management has called convertibles in the past (and presumably will call them again in the future), once they were eligible for call, as soon as their conversion value was about 20 percent above their par value (not their call price).

a. Draw an accurate graph similar to Figure 21-2 representing the expectations set forth in the problem.

b. Suppose the previously outlined projects work out on schedule for 2 years, but then Rentz begins to experience extremely strong competition from Japanese firms. As a result, Rentz's expected growth rate drops from 8 percent to zero. Assume that the dividend at the time of the drop is $2.87. The company's credit strength is not impaired, and its value of k_s is also unchanged. What would happen (1) to the stock price and (2) to the convertible bond's price? Be as precise as you can.

EXAM-TYPE PROBLEMS

The problems included in this section are set up in such a way that they could be used as multiple-choice exam problems.

21-6

Lease versus buy

Malitz Mining Company must install $1.5 million of new machinery in its Nevada mine. It can obtain a bank loan for 100 percent of the required amount. Alternatively, a Nevada investment banking firm which represents a group of investors believes that it can arrange for a lease financing plan. Assume that the following facts apply:

(1) The equipment falls in the MACRS 3-year class.
(2) Estimated maintenance expenses are $75,000 per year.
(3) Malitz's federal-plus-state tax rate is 40 percent.
(4) If the money is borrowed, the bank loan will be at a rate of 15 percent, amortized in 4 equal installments to be paid at the end of each year.
(5) The tentative lease terms call for end-of-year payments of $400,000 per year for 4 years.
(6) Under the proposed lease terms, the lessee must pay for insurance, property taxes, and maintenance.
(7) Malitz must use the equipment if it is to continue in business, so it will almost certainly want to acquire the property at the end of the lease. If it does, then under the lease terms it can purchase the machinery at its fair market value at that time. The best estimate of this market value is the $250,000 salvage value, but it could be much higher or lower under certain circumstances.

To assist management in making the proper lease-versus-buy decision, you are asked to answer the following questions.

a. Assuming that the lease can be arranged, should Malitz lease, or should it borrow and buy the equipment? Explain.
b. Consider the $250,000 estimated salvage value. Is it appropriate to discount it at the same rate as the other cash flows? What about the other cash flows—are they all equally risky? (Hint: Riskier cash flows are normally discounted at higher rates, but when the cash flows are *costs* rather than *inflows,* the normal procedure must be reversed.)

21-7

Warrants

Hawke Industries Inc. has warrants outstanding that permit its holders to purchase one share of stock per warrant at a price of $21.

a. Calculate the formula value of Hawke's warrants if the common stock sells at each of the following prices: $18, $21, $25, and $70.
b. At what approximate price do you think the warrants would actually sell under each condition indicated in Part a? What premium is implied in your price? Your answer will be a guess, but your prices and premiums should bear reasonable relationships to each other.
c. How would each of the following factors affect your estimates of the warrants' prices and premiums in Part b?
   (1) The life of the warrant is lengthened.
   (2) The expected variability (σ_p) in the stock's price decreases.
   (3) The expected growth rate in the stock's EPS increases.
   (4) The company announces the following change in dividend policy: whereas it formerly paid no dividends, henceforth it will pay out *all* earnings as dividends.
d. Assume Hawke's stock now sells for $18 per share. The company wants to sell some 20-year, annual interest, $1,000 par value bonds. Each bond will have 50 warrants, each exercisable into one share of stock at an exercise price of $21. Hawke's pure bonds yield 10 percent. Regardless of your answer to Part b, assume that the warrants will have a market value of $1.50 when the stock sells at $18. What coupon interest rate and dollar coupon must the company set on the bonds with warrants if they are to clear the market? Round to the nearest dollar or percentage point.

INTEGRATIVE PROBLEMS

21-8
Lease analysis

Martha Millon, capital acquisitions manager for Heath Financial Services Inc., has been asked to perform a lease-versus-buy analysis on a new stock price quotation system for Heath's Sarasota branch office. The system would receive current prices, record the information for retrieval by the branch's brokers, and display current prices in the lobby.

The equipment costs $1,200,000, and, if it is purchased, Heath could obtain a term loan for the full amount at a 10 percent cost. The loan would be amortized over the 4-year life of the equipment, with payments made at the end of each year. The equipment is classified as special purpose, and hence it falls into the MACRS 3-year class. If the equipment is purchased, a maintenance contract must be obtained at a cost of $25,000, payable at the beginning of each year.

After 4 years the equipment will be sold, and Millon's best estimate of its residual value at that time is $125,000. Because technology is changing rapidly in real-time display systems, however, the residual value is very uncertain.

As an alternative, National Leasing is willing to write a 4-year lease on the equipment, including maintenance, for payments of $340,000 at the *beginning* of each year. Heath's marginal federal-plus-state tax rate is 40 percent. Help Millon conduct her analysis by answering the following questions.

a. (1) Why is leasing sometimes referred to as "off balance sheet" financing?
   (2) What is the difference between a capital lease and an operating lease?
   (3) What effect does leasing have on a firm's capital structure?
b. (1) What is Heath's present value cost of owning the equipment? (Hint: Set up a table whose bottom line is a "time line" which shows the net cash flows over the period t = 0 to t = 4, and then find the PV of these net cash flows, or the PV cost of owning.)
   (2) Explain the rationale for the discount rate you used to find the PV.
c. (1) What is Heath's present value cost of leasing the equipment? (Hint: Again, construct a time line.)
   (2) What is the net advantage to leasing? Does your analysis indicate that Heath should buy or lease the equipment? Explain.
d. Now assume that Millon believes the equipment's residual value could be as low as $0 or as high as $250,000, but she stands by $125,000 as her expected value. She concludes that the residual value is riskier than the other cash flows in the analysis, and she wants to incorporate this differential risk into her analysis. Describe how this could be accomplished. What effect would it have on Heath's lease decision?
e. Millon knows that her firm has been considering moving to a new downtown location for some time, and she is concerned that these plans may come to fruition prior to the expiration of the lease. If the move occurs, the company would obtain completely new equipment, and hence Millon would like to include a cancellation clause in the lease contract. What effect would a cancellation clause have on the riskiness of the lease?

21-9
Warrants and convertibles

Kathy Allen, financial manager of MicroEd Inc., is facing a dilemma. The firm was founded 5 years ago to develop educational software for the rapidly expanding primary and secondary school markets. Although MicroEd has done well, the firm's founder and chairman believes that an industry shake-out is imminent. To survive, the firm must capture market share now, and this requires a large infusion of new capital.

Because the stock price may rise rapidly, Allen does not want to issue new common stock. On the other hand, interest rates are currently very high by historical standards, and, with the firm's B rating, the interest payments on a new debt issue would be too much to handle if sales took a downturn. Thus, Allen has narrowed her choice to bonds with warrants or convertible bonds. She has asked you to help in the decision process by answering the following questions.

a. What is a call option? How can a knowledge of call options help one understand warrants and convertibles?

b. A MicroEd competitor, Computerized Teaching Aids (CTA), has options listed on the Chicago Board Options Exchange. The following table gives the option price for its 6-month, $10 call option at 3 different stock prices:

Stock Price	Option Price
$10	$ 2
15	6
20	10

(1) What is the option's formula value and its premium at each stock price? Why do call options sell for more than their formula value?

(2) Assume that CTA's stock price increased from $10 to $15. What rate of return would this provide to a stock investor? To an option investor? What is the loss potential on the stock and on the option if the stock price remains at $10?

(3) Now assume that CTA's stock price increased from $15 to $20. What would be the rate of return to a stock investor? To an option investor? What is the loss potential on the stock? On the option? Why does the premium over the formula value decline as the stock price increases?

c. One of Allen's alternatives is to issue a bond with warrants attached. MicroEd's current stock price is $10, and its cost of 20-year, annual coupon debt without warrants is estimated by its investment bankers to be 12 percent. The bankers suggest attaching 50 warrants per bond, with each having an exercise price of $12.50. It is estimated that each warrant, when detached and traded separately, will have a value of $1.50.

(1) What coupon rate should be set on the bond with warrants if the total package is to sell for $1,000?

(2) Suppose the bonds are issued and the warrants immediately trade for $2.50 each. What does this imply about the terms of the issue? Did the company "win" or "lose"?

(3) When would you expect the warrants to be exercised?

(4) Will the warrants bring in additional capital when exercised? If so, how much and what type of capital?

(5) Because warrants lower the cost of the accompanying debt, shouldn't all debt be issued with warrants? What is the expected cost of the bond with warrants if the warrants are expected to be exercised in 5 years, when MicroEd's stock price is expected to be $17.50? How would you expect the cost of the bond with warrants to compare with the cost of straight debt? With the cost of common stock?

d. As an alternative to the bond with warrants, Allen is considering convertible bonds. The firm's investment bankers estimate that MicroEd could sell a 20-year, 10 percent annual coupon, callable convertible bond for its $1,000 par value, whereas a straight debt issue would require a 12 percent coupon. MicroEd's current stock price is $10, its last dividend was $0.74, and the dividend is expected to grow at a constant rate of 8 percent. The convertible could be converted into 80 shares of MicroEd stock at the owner's option.

(1) What conversion price, P_c, is implied in the convertible's terms?

(2) What is the straight debt value of the convertible? What is the implied value of the convertibility feature?

(3) What is the formula for the bond's conversion value in any year? Its value at Year 0? At Year 10?

(4) What is meant by the "floor value" of a convertible? What is the convertible's expected floor value in Year 0? In Year 10?

(5) Assume that MicroEd intends to force conversion by calling the bond when its conversion value is 20 percent above its par value, or at 1.2($1,000) = $1,200. When is the issue expected to be called? Answer to the closest year.

(6) What is the expected cost of the convertible to MicroEd? Does this cost appear consistent with the riskiness of the issue? Assume conversion in Year 5 at a conversion value of $1,200.

e. Allen believes that the costs of both the bond with warrants and the convertible bond are essentially equal, so her decision must be based on other factors. What are some of the factors that she should consider in making her decision?

COMPUTER-RELATED PROBLEM

Work the problem in this section only if you are using the computer problem diskette.

21-10

Lease versus buy

Use the model in the File C21 to work this problem.

a. Refer back to Problem 21-6. Determine the lease payment at which Malitz would be indifferent to buying or leasing; that is, find the lease payment which equates the NPV of leasing to that of buying. (Hint: Use trial-and-error.)

b. Using the $400,000 lease payment, what would be the effect if Malitz's tax rate fell to 20 percent? What would be the effect if the tax rate fell to zero percent? What do these results suggest?

Mergers, Divestitures, Holding Companies, and LBOs

Business is becoming increasingly global. In the manufacturing sector, de-velopment costs for products such as microchips, new drugs, autos, and planes are so high that companies must serve worldwide markets to cover fixed costs, while economies of scale in production add to the need for worldwide operations. Thus, IBM, Ford, and many other U.S. companies now generate over half of their sales and profits overseas. Further, as man-ufacturing and trade have "gone global," this has forced service industries to globalize, for if their clients are operating worldwide, so must banks, accounting firms, and advertising agencies. This, in turn, has led to the need for increased size, which has stimulated mergers.

Two years ago, Ford Motor Company won the battle for Jaguar PLC. By agreeing to pay a whopping $2.6 billion for Britain's leading luxury automaker, Ford beat out its arch-rival, General Motors, which had ear-lier announced its own hopes of buying a minority stake in Jaguar. The face-off was expected to be a drawn-out battle of the titans, but it ended before it even began. The Ford/Jaguar announcement, which followed marathon negotiations, occurred before GM had bought even a single share of stock. (GM eventually purchased 50 percent of Saab for $600 million.)

But Ford's victory may be costly, leaving GM with the last laugh. Jag-uar's earlier talks with GM, amid Ford's unwelcome pursuit of a 15 per-cent stake in Jaguar, turned the British company's shares into a feverish takeover stock. The share price more than doubled, and Ford was forced to pay over half a billion dollars more than it had expected to pay.

Ford bought a money-losing company which at the time manufac-tured a mere 50,000 cars a year at an outmoded former aircraft parts plant in Britain's ailing industrial heartland. Its biggest challenge has *been determining how to take an upscale label, valued for its exclusivity, and sell it to more people without diluting the distinctive Jaguar image. To reap a significant payoff from the Jaguar deal, Ford has had to spend an additional $1.5 billion to help Jaguar launch a less expensive range of so-called "executive cars." This move puts Ford into head-on competition with BMW and with the savvy Japanese automakers, whose luxury cars have been flooding Europe and the United States.*

Two years later, Ford is still trying to salvage its investment in Jaguar. Jaguar's sales have declined by 50 percent, and from the time Ford acquired it, the company has done nothing but lose money. Ford needs to reverse this trend (1) by convincing consumers that Jaguar's quality has improved and (2) by introducing new products. When Ford took over Jaguar, no new products were on the drawing board, but after the acquisition, Ford quickly launched a major design program. The first updated model should be out in 1994, with two others expected in 1996 and 1998.

However, not all news is bad for Ford. After two years of reinforcing Ford's quality message, assembly-line defects have been reduced by 80 percent. Because of its quality improvements, Jaguar has finally been able to enter the fast-growing leasing business, which now accounts for 25 percent of its U.S. business. In addition, assembly-line improvements have helped boost productivity by 35 percent, and by uniting with Ford to buy parts, Jaguar's purchasing costs have been reduced by 12 percent. Also, labor relations have improved, and the work force now understands that customer satisfaction begins on the factory floor.

On the other hand, Jaguar has a long way to go. It still takes three times longer to assemble a Jaguar than a deluxe-model Ford. Jaguar's production is forecasted to rebound from 23,000 cars in 1991 to 27,500 cars in 1992, but its breakeven point is still about 35,000 cars—a production point that will not be reached until 1994 at the earliest. The crucial test will come with the rollout of the new models.

Sources: "These Repair Jobs Are Taking a Little Longer Than Expected," *The Wall Street Journal,* April 27, 1992, and other related articles.

Mergers and leveraged buyouts have been taking place at a feverish pace. This chapter will help you understand the motivations behind all this activity, the procedures that make mergers work, and the importance of making a thorough analysis before finalizing merger arrangements.

Thus far we have discussed some of the operating and financing decisions financial managers must make. Firms also occasionally undertake massive restructuring programs in which major new businesses are acquired, large segments of the firm are sold off, or the capital structure is changed radically. Such events can occur either separately or in combination, and they can be decided by management or be forced on management by outsiders. We discuss such restructurings in this chapter, examining mergers, divestitures, the holding company form of organization, and leveraged buyouts (LBOs).

RATIONALE FOR MERGERS

merger
The combination of two firms to form a single firm.

In this section we present some of the motives which account for the high level of **merger** activity.[1]

Synergy

synergy
The condition wherein the whole is greater than the sum of its parts; in a synergistic merger, the postmerger value exceeds the sum of the separate companies' premerger values.

The primary motivation for most mergers is to increase the value of the combined enterprise. If Companies A and B merge to form Company C, and if C's value exceeds that of A and B taken separately, then **synergy** is said to exist.[2] Synergistic effects can arise from four sources: (1) *operating economies of scale*, generally from cost reductions when two companies are combined; (2) *financial economies,* which could include a higher price/earnings ratio, a lower cost of debt, or a greater debt capacity; (3) *differential management efficiency,* which implies that the management of one firm is relatively inefficient, so the profitability of the acquired assets can be improved by merger; and (4) *increased market power* resulting from reduced competition. Operating and financial economies are socially desirable, as are mergers that increase managerial efficiency, but mergers that reduce competition are both undesirable and illegal.[3]

Tax Considerations

Tax considerations have stimulated a number of mergers. For example, a firm which is highly profitable and in the highest corporate tax bracket could acquire a company with large accumulated tax losses, then use those losses to shelter its own income.[4] Similarly, a company with large losses could acquire a profita-

[1]As we use the term, *merger* means any combination that forms one firm from two or more existing firms. For legal purposes, there are distinctions among the various ways these combinations can occur, but our emphasis is on the fundamental business and financial aspects of mergers.

[2]If synergy exists, the whole is greater than the sum of the parts. Synergy is also called the "2 plus 2 equals 5 effect." The distribution of the synergistic gain between A's and B's stockholders is determined by negotiation, a point discussed later in the chapter.

[3]In the 1880s and 1890s, many mergers occurred in the United States, and some of them were clearly directed toward gaining market power rather than increasing operating efficiency. As a result, Congress passed a series of acts designed to insure that mergers are not used as a method of reducing competition. The principal acts include the Sherman Act (1890), the Clayton Act (1914), and the Celler Act (1950). These acts make it illegal for firms to combine in any manner if the combination will lessen competition. They are administered by the antitrust division of the Justice Department and by the Federal Trade Commission.

[4]Mergers undertaken only to use accumulated tax losses would probably be challenged by the IRS. However, because many factors are present in any given merger, it is hard to prove that a merger was motivated only, or even primarily, by tax considerations.

ble firm. Also, tax considerations could cause mergers to be a desirable use for excess cash. For example, if a firm has a shortage of internal investment opportunities compared to its cash flows, it will have excess cash, and its options for disposing of this excess cash are (1) paying an extra dividend, (2) investing in marketable securities, (3) repurchasing its own stock, or (4) purchasing another firm. If the firm pays an extra dividend, its stockholders will have to pay taxes on the distribution. Marketable securities such as Treasury bonds provide a good temporary parking place for money, but the rate of return on such securities is less than that required by stockholders. A stock repurchase might result in a capital gain for the remaining stockholders, but it could be disadvantageous if the company had to pay a high price to acquire the stock, and, if the repurchase was designed solely to avoid paying dividends, it might be challenged by the IRS. However, using surplus cash to acquire another firm has no immediate tax consequences for either the acquiring firm or its stockholders, and this fact has motivated a number of mergers.

Purchase of Assets below Their Replacement Cost

Sometimes a firm will become an acquisition candidate because the replacement value of its assets is considerably higher than its market value. For example, in the 1980s oil companies could acquire reserves more cheaply by buying out other oil companies than by exploratory drilling. This factor was a motive in Chevron's acquisition of Gulf Oil.

The acquisition of Republic Steel (the sixth largest steel company) by LTV (the fourth largest) provides another example of a firm's being purchased because its purchase price was less than the replacement value of its assets. LTV found that it was less costly to purchase Republic Steel for $700 million than it would have been to construct a new steel mill. At the time, Republic's stock was selling for less than one-third of its book value.

The acquisition of Federated Department Stores by Campeau Corporation, a Toronto-based real estate development firm, is yet another illustration of an acquisition that took place because the price of the stock of the company being acquired (Federated) did not reflect its true market value. Federated at the time was the largest department store chain in the United States, but its performance had been lackluster in recent years, and its stock price had fallen by more than 50 percent. However, steps taken by Federated were finally beginning to pay off, and earnings were rising. Federated had some of the best-known names in retailing, and its buildings had been acquired years ago at low prices. Thus, the company was an attractive takeover target. As a result, Campeau Corporation and R. H. Macy & Company (a long-time rival of Federated) made separate bids for control of Federated. Campeau was primarily interested in acquiring Federated's undervalued real estate assets, while Macy saw the situation as an opportunity to merge the operations of the two retailing chains to gain economies of scale in purchasing and operations. Eventually, Campeau and Macy joined forces, and their plan was to acquire Federated and then split up the company. Robert Campeau became the new king of American department stores; however, he had to pay top dollar to do it, and the takeover was financed with high-cost junk bonds. The win was costly, for Campeau was unable to meet his debt payments when the economy slowed. As a result, Campeau declared bankruptcy in 1990. R. H. Macy & Company declared bankruptcy in February 1992.

Diversification

Managers often claim that diversification helps to stabilize the firm's earnings and thus reduce corporate risk. Therefore, diversification is often given as a reason for mergers. Stabilization of earnings is certainly beneficial to a firm's employees, suppliers, and customers, but its value to stockholders and debtholders is less clear. If an investor is worried about earnings variability, he or she could probably diversify through stock purchases more easily than the firm could through acquisitions. Therefore, why should Firms A and B merge to stabilize earnings when a stockholder in Firm A could sell half of his or her stock in A and use the proceeds to purchase stock in Firm B, especially since the stockholder could take this action at a much lower cost than would be involved if the firms merged?

Of course, if you were the owner-manager of a closely held firm, it might be virtually impossible for you to sell part of your stock to diversify because this would dilute your ownership and also generate a large tax liability. For such a firm, a merger might well be the best way to achieve personal diversification. However, for publicly held firms, diversification to reduce stockholder risk is generally not a valid motive for a merger.

Maintaining Control

defensive merger
A merger designed to make a company less vulnerable to a takeover.

As we discuss in a later section, in recent years many hostile mergers and takeovers have occurred. The managers of the acquired companies generally lose their jobs, or at least their autonomy. Therefore, managers who own less than 51 percent of the stock in their firms look to devices that will lessen the chances of their firms' being taken over. Mergers can serve as such a device. For example, when Enron was under attack, it arranged to buy Houston Natural Gas Company, paying for Houston primarily with debt. That merger made Enron much larger and hence harder for any potential acquirer to "digest." Also, the much higher debt level resulting from the merger made it hard for any acquiring company to use debt to buy Enron. Such **defensive mergers** are difficult to defend on economic grounds. The managers involved invariably argue that synergy, not a desire to protect their own jobs, motivated the acquisition, but there can be no question that many mergers have been designed more for the benefit of managers than for stockholders.

❓ Self-Test Questions

What are the four primary motives behind most mergers?

From what sources do synergistic effects arise?

How have tax considerations stimulated mergers?

Is diversification to reduce stockholder risk a valid motive for mergers? Explain.

TYPES OF MERGERS

horizontal merger

A combination of two firms that produce the same type of good or service.

vertical merger

A merger between a firm and one of its suppliers or customers.

congeneric merger

A merger of firms in the same general industry, but for which no customer or supplier relationship exists.

conglomerate merger

A merger of companies in totally different industries.

Economists classify mergers into four groups: (1) horizontal, (2) vertical, (3) congeneric, and (4) conglomerate. A **horizontal merger** occurs when one firm combines with another in its same line of business—for example, the merger of Shearson Lehman and E. F. Hutton was a horizontal merger because both firms were brokerage houses. An example of a **vertical merger** is a steel producer's acquisition of one of its own suppliers, such as an iron or coal mining firm, or an oil producer's acquisition of a company which uses its products, such as a petrochemical firm. *Congeneric* means "allied in nature or action"; hence, a **congeneric merger** involves related enterprises but not producers of the same product (horizontal) or firms in a producer-supplier relationship (vertical). Examples of congeneric mergers include Unilever's takeover of Chesebrough-Ponds, a toiletry maker, and Philip Morris's acquisitions of General Foods and Kraft. A **conglomerate merger** occurs when unrelated enterprises combine, as illustrated by Mobil Oil's acquisition of Montgomery Ward.

Operating economies (and also anticompetitive effects) are dependent on the type of merger involved. Vertical and horizontal mergers generally provide the greatest synergistic operating benefits, but they are also the ones most likely to be attacked by the U.S. Department of Justice. In any event, it is useful to think of these economic classifications when analyzing the feasibility of a prospective merger.

 Self-Test Question

Explain briefly the four economic classifications of mergers.

LEVEL OF MERGER ACTIVITY

Four major "merger waves" have occurred in the United States. The first was in the late 1800s, when consolidations occurred in the oil, steel, tobacco, and other basic industries. The second was in the 1920s, when the stock market boom helped financial promoters consolidate firms in a number of industries, including utilities, communications, and autos. The third was in the 1960s, when conglomerate mergers were the rage, while the fourth began in the early 1980s, and it is still going strong.

The current "merger mania" has been sparked by seven factors: (1) the depressed level of the dollar relative to Japanese and European currencies, which made U.S. companies look cheap to foreign buyers; (2) the unprecedented level of inflation that existed during the 1970s and early 1980s, which increased the replacement value of firms' assets even while a weak stock market reduced their market values; (3) the Reagan and Bush administrations' stated view that "bigness is not necessarily badness," which has resulted in a more tolerant attitude toward large mergers; (4) the general belief among the major natural resource companies that it is cheaper to "buy reserves on Wall Street" through mergers than to explore and find them in the field; (5) attempts to ward off raiders by use of defensive mergers; (6) the development of the junk bond market, which made it possible to use far more debt in acquisitions than had been possible

Table 22-1   ∎   **The Five Biggest Mergers (Billions of Dollars)**

Companies	Year	Value	Percent of Book Value	Type of Transaction
Time-Warner	1989	$14.0	350%	Acquisition for cash, stock, and debt
Chevron-Gulf	1984	13.3	136	
Philip Morris-Kraft	1988	12.9	609	Acquisition for cash
Bristol Myers-Squibb	1989	11.5	250	Acquisition for stock
Texaco-Getty	1984	10.1	191	Acquisition for stock
				Acquisition for cash and notes

Note: KKR's acquisition of RJR Nabisco exceeded $25 billion, but that transaction was an LBO, not a merger.

earlier; and (7) the increased globalization of business, which has led to increased economies of scale and to the formation of worldwide corporations. Financial historians have not yet compiled the statistics and done the analysis necessary to compare the latest merger wave with the earlier ones, but it is virtually certain that the current wave will rank as the largest. Table 22-1 lists the top five mergers of all time, and they all occurred in the 1980s.

We present the highlights of seven recent mergers to give you a flavor of how actual mergers occur.

1. Getty Oil, the fourteenth largest U.S. oil company, was acquired by Texaco, the fourth largest, at a cost of $10.1 billion. Prior to the merger activity, Getty's shares were selling at around $65, and the descendants of J. Paul Getty, the founder and richest man in the world, were complaining of inefficient management. Then the controlling trustees of the Sarah C. Getty Trust, together with Pennzoil, announced plans to take the firm private by buying the shares which they did not already control at a price of $112.50 per share. Texaco then jumped in with an offer of $125 per share.

    The merger doubled Texaco's domestic oil and gas reserves, and, with Getty's retail outlets, gave Texaco a larger share of the gasoline market. Some analysts claimed that Texaco, with its sprawling network of refineries and rapidly dwindling reserves, made the correct decision by acquiring Getty, with its large reserves and minimal refining operations. Other analysts contended that Texaco paid too much for Getty. Acquiring Getty's reserves may have been cheaper for Texaco than finding new oil, but the value of these reserves will depend on the price of oil.

    Two side issues arose during the Getty merger. The first concerned the Bass Brothers of Texas, an immensely wealthy family that had acquired over $1 billion of Texaco stock during all the action. Texaco's management was afraid the Basses would try to take over Texaco, so they bought out the Bass interests at a premium of about 20 percent over the market value. Some of Texaco's stockholders argued that the payment amounted to "greenmail," or a payoff made with stockholders' money just to insure that Texaco's managers could keep their jobs. This situation, along with several similar ones, has led to the introduction of bills in Congress to limit the actions that a management group can take in its efforts to avoid being taken over. However, Congress has not actually passed such a law to date. The second side issue was a suit by Pennzoil, which charged that Texaco caused Getty to breach its contract with Pennzoil. Pennzoil won a $12 billion judgment, but Texaco appealed, and Pennzoil eventually settled for $3 billion, of which Pennzoil's lawyers will get $400 million.

2. Conoco, which had assets with a book value of $11 billion and which was, based on sales, the thirteenth largest company in the United States, was the target of three other giants: Mobil (the second largest U.S. corporation), Du Pont (the fifteenth largest U.S. corporation), and Seagram (a large Canadian company). This merger alone almost equaled in dollar amount the previous record for all mergers in any one year. Conoco's stock sold for about $50 just before the bidding started, but the bid price got up to over $100 per share before it was over because Conoco's oil and coal reserves, plus its plant and equipment, were worth far more than the company's initial stock market value.

     If Mobil had won, this would have been a horizontal merger. If Seagram had won, it would have been a conglomerate merger. Yet Du Pont won, and it was classified as a vertical merger because Du Pont uses petroleum in its production processes. The Justice Department would have fought a merger with Mobil, but it indicated that it would not do so in the case of Seagram or Du Pont. For this reason, even though Mobil made the highest bid of $115 per share, Du Pont ended up the winner with a bid of $98. Stockholders chose the Du Pont bid over that of Mobil because they were afraid a Mobil merger would be blocked, causing Conoco's stock to fall below the level of the Du Pont bid.

     This was a *hostile merger* — Conoco's management would rather have had the company remain an independent entity. Obviously, though, that was not to be, and Conoco's top managers found themselves working for someone else (or out of a job). This is a good illustration of a point made in Chapter 1, namely, that managers have a strong motivation to operate in a manner that will maximize the value of their firms' stock, for otherwise they can find themselves in the same boat as Conoco's managers.

3. Marathon Oil, a company only slightly smaller than Conoco, was the object of an attempted acquisition by Mobil after that company lost its bid for Conoco. Marathon's management resisted strongly, and again other bidders entered the picture. In the end, U.S. Steel picked up Marathon for about $6 billion, making this the fourth largest merger up to that time. U.S. Steel's bid for Marathon was unusual in that the firm offered to pay cash for only 51 percent of the stock and to exchange bonds for the remainder, with cash going to those stockholders who agreed to the merger at the earliest date. This is called a **two-tier offer,** and it prompted many stockholders to tender their stock to U.S. Steel out of fear of having to accept bonds if they waited to see if the bid might go higher.

4. Schlitz, once the largest U.S. brewer, had been losing both money and market share. By the 1980s it had become only the fourth largest brewer, with a market share of 8.5 percent, and it seemed to be on a collision course with bankruptcy. Schlitz's troubles arose from its poor marketing strategy, a problem that it was unable to conquer. G. Heileman, the sixth largest

two-tier offer

A merger offer which provides different (better) terms to those who tender their stock earliest.

brewer, with a market share of 7.5 percent, was better managed, and its sales were growing rapidly. (Heileman's ROE was 27.3 percent; Schlitz's was negative.) Because of its successful marketing programs, Heileman needed more brewing capacity, whereas because of its poor sales performance, Schlitz had 50 percent excess capacity. Heileman offered to buy Schlitz's common stock for $494 million. If the takeover attempt had been successful, Heileman would have acquired capacity at an effective cost of $19 per barrel versus a construction cost of about $50 per barrel. The merger would also have made Heileman the third largest brewer in the nation. Although the Justice Department under the Reagan administration had previously taken the position that "bigness is not necessarily badness," it opposed this merger because in its judgment the resulting concentration would substantially reduce competition in the brewing industry. Therefore, Heileman abandoned the merger effort. However, Schlitz was still in trouble, and it was later acquired by Stroh Brewery, another good marketer, which was smaller than G. Heileman.

5. General Motors acquired Electronics Data Systems (EDS), the world's largest data processing company, for $2.2 billion. GM had excess cash, and it wanted to diversify outside the auto industry to stabilize earnings. Also, its management believed that EDS could help GM set up better internal management control systems and help with the company's planned automation of manufacturing operations. Ross Perot, the founder and a 50 percent owner of EDS, was offered more than $1 billion plus a seat on the GM board for his stock, as well as a chance to continue running EDS. After the merger, Perot clashed with Roger Smith, GM's chairman at the time, and GM bought Perot's stock at a substantial premium over the market price to get him off the board. Shortly thereafter, Perot started a new company which will compete with EDS.

6. GM also acquired Hughes Aircraft, a privately held company that was started by the late Howard Hughes in the 1930s, for $4.7 billion. Hughes was one of the largest defense contractors and was highly profitable, but what GM really wanted was its expertise in high-tech electronic controls. GM must utilize such technology in its autos if it is to compete effectively with the Japanese. Investment analysts believe that there are tremendous potential synergistic benefits to GM from both the Hughes and the EDS mergers, but at this point one can only wait and see if the $6.9 billion spent on the mergers will really pay off.

7. In the early 1990s, the hottest area for mergers is in the banking and S&L industries. In both cases, the primary motive is a quest for synergies. Both banks and S&Ls are plagued with problem loans, and both industries suffer from excess capacity. Therefore, mergers, which can cut costs and thus boost profits, are desperately needed. In December 1991, NCNB, a North Carolina–based bank which, through a merger, had recently become the largest bank in Texas, acquired C&S/Sovran, a bank holding company which operated through the Southeast and which had serious problems with bad real estate loans. The acquisition was for $4.6 billion in stock. Also, in December 1991, Chemical Banking acquired Manufacturers Hanover for $1.8 billion in stock. The Chemical–Manny Hanny combination

beat out the NationsBank merger as the second largest U.S. bank (second to Citibank of New York). Both of these mergers will greatly reduce costs and thus raise profits, but many jobs will be lost. For example, when Chemical's managers announced their merger, they also announced that some 6,000 to 8,000 jobs will be eliminated in the New York City area.

? Self-Test Question

What are the seven factors that sparked the most recent "merger mania"?

PROCEDURES FOR COMBINING FIRMS

In the vast majority of mergers, one firm (generally the larger of the two) simply decides to buy another company, negotiates a price, and then acquires the target company. Occasionally, the acquired firm will initiate the action, but it is much more common for a firm to seek acquisitions than to seek to be acquired.[5] Following convention, we shall call a company that seeks to acquire another the **acquiring company** and the one it seeks to acquire the **target company.**

acquiring company
A company that seeks to acquire another.

target company
A firm that another company seeks to acquire.

Once an acquiring company has identified a possible target, it must establish the price, or range of prices, that it is willing to pay. With this in mind, its managers will then approach the target company's managers. If the acquiring firm has reason to believe that the target's management will approve the merger, it will propose the merger and try to work out suitable terms. If an agreement can be reached, the two management groups will issue statements to their stockholders recommending that they approve the merger. Assuming the stockholders do approve, the acquiring firm will then buy the target company's shares from its stockholders, paying for them either with its own shares (in which case the target company's stockholders become stockholders of the acquiring company), with cash, or with bonds. Such a transaction is defined as a **friendly merger.** Examples of friendly mergers include Time's merger with Warner Communications, General Electric's acquisition of RCA, and Federal Express's acquisition of Tiger International.

friendly merger
A merger whose terms are approved by the managements of both companies.

hostile merger
A merger in which the target firm's management resists acquisition.

Under other circumstances, the target company's management may resist the merger. Perhaps the managers believe that the price offered for the stock is too low, or perhaps they simply want to keep their jobs. In either case, the target firm's management is said to be *hostile* rather than friendly, and in a **hostile merger,** the acquiring firm must make a direct appeal to the target firm's stockholders. In a hostile merger, the acquiring company generally makes a **tender offer,** in which it asks the stockholders of the firm it is seeking to control to submit, or "tender," their shares in exchange for a specified price. The price is generally stated as so many dollars per share of the stock to be acquired, although it can be stated in terms of shares of stock of the acquiring

tender offer
The offer of one firm to buy the stock of another by going directly to the stockholders, frequently (but not always) over the opposition of the target company's management.

---

[5]However, if a firm is in financial difficulty, if its managers are elderly and do not think that suitable replacements are on hand, or if it needs the support (often the capital) of a larger company, then it may seek to be acquired. Thus, when a number of Texas banks were in trouble in the late 1980s, they lobbied to get the state legislature to pass a law that made it easier for them to be acquired. Out-of-state banks then moved in to help salvage the situation and minimize depositor losses.

firm. Because the tender offer is a direct appeal to stockholders, it need not be approved by the target firm's management. Tender offers are not new, but their frequency has increased greatly in recent years.[6]

 Self-Test Question

Differentiate between an acquiring company and a target company.

MERGER ANALYSIS

In theory, merger analysis is quite simple. The acquiring firm simply performs a capital budgeting analysis to determine whether the present value of the cash flows expected to result from the merger exceeds the price that must be paid for the target company, and if the net present value is positive, the acquiring firm should proceed with the acquisition. The target company's stockholders should accept the proposal if the price offered exceeds the present value of the cash flows they expect to receive in the future if the firm continues to operate independently. Theory aside, however, some difficult issues are involved: (1) The acquiring company must estimate the cash flows that will result from the acquisition; (2) it must also determine what effect, if any, the merger will have on its own required rate of return on equity; (3) it must decide how to pay for the merger—with cash, with its own stock, or with some other type or package of securities; and (4) having estimated the benefits of the merger, the acquiring and target firms' managers and stockholders must bargain (or fight) over how to share these benefits. The required analysis can be extremely complex.

Operating Mergers versus Financial Mergers

From the standpoint of financial analysis, there are two basic types of mergers: *operating mergers* and *financial mergers*.

operating merger
A merger in which operations of the firms involved are integrated in hope of achieving synergistic benefits.

1. An **operating merger** is one in which the operations of two companies are integrated with the expectation of obtaining synergistic effects. The Chemical–Manufacturers Hanover and the NCNB-C&S/Sovran deals are good examples of operating mergers.

financial merger
A merger in which the firms involved will not be operated as a single unit and from which no operating economies are expected.

2. A **financial merger** is one in which the merged companies will not be operated as a single unit and from which no significant operating economies are expected. Coca-Cola's acquisition of Columbia Pictures is an example of a financial merger.

Of course, mergers may actually combine these two features. Thus, if Mobil had acquired Marathon Oil, the merger would have been primarily an operating one. However, with U.S. Steel emerging as the victor, the merger was more financial than operating in nature.

---

[6]Tender offers can be friendly, with the target firm's management recommending that stockholders go ahead and tender their stock.

Estimating Future Operating Income

In a financial merger, the postmerger cash flows are simply the sum of the expected cash flows of the two companies if they continued to operate independently. However, if the two firms' operations are to be integrated, or if the acquiring firm plans to change the target firm's management to get better results, then accurate estimates of future cash flows, which are difficult to obtain but absolutely essential to sound merger decisions, will be required.

The basic rationale for any operating merger is synergy. Del Monte Corporation provides a good example of a series of well-thought-out, favorable operating mergers. Del Monte successfully merged and integrated numerous small canning companies into a highly efficient, profitable organization. It used standardized production techniques to increase the efficiency of all of its plants, a national brand name and national advertising to develop customer brand loyalty, a consolidated distribution system, and a centralized purchasing office to obtain substantial discounts due to volume purchases. Because of these economies, Del Monte became the most efficient and profitable U.S. canning company, and its merger activities helped make possible the size that produced these economies. Consumers also benefited, because Del Monte's efficiency enabled the company to sell high-quality products at relatively low prices.

An example of a poor pro forma analysis that resulted in a disastrous merger was the consolidation of the Pennsylvania and New York Central railroads. The premerger analysis suggested that large cost savings would result, but the analysis was grossly misleading because it failed to recognize that certain key elements in the two rail systems were incompatible and hence could not be meshed together. Thus, rather than gaining synergistic benefits, the combined system actually incurred additional overhead costs which led to bankruptcy. *In planning operating mergers, the development of accurate pro forma cash flows is the single most important aspect of the analysis.*[7]

Merger Terms

The terms of a merger include answers to two important questions: (1) Who will control the combined enterprise? (2) How much will the acquiring firm pay for the acquired company? These points are discussed next.

Postmerger Control.   The employment/control situation is often of vital interest. First, consider the situation in which a small, owner-managed firm sells out to a larger concern. The owner-manager may be anxious to retain a high-status position, and he or she may also have developed a camaraderie with the employees and thus be concerned about keeping operating control of the organization after the merger. If so, these points are likely to be stressed during

---

[7]Firms heavily engaged in mergers have "acquisition departments" whose functions include (1) seeking suitable merger candidates and (2) taking over and integrating acquired firms into the parent corporation. The first step involves the estimation of future cash flows and a plan for making the projections materialize. The second step involves streamlining the operations of the acquired firm and instituting a system of controls that will permit the parent to effectively manage the new division and to coordinate its operations with those of other units.

the merger negotiations.[8] When a publicly owned firm not controlled by its managers is merged into another company, the acquired firm's management also is worried about its postmerger position. If the acquiring firm agrees to retain the old management, then management may be willing to support the merger and to recommend its acceptance to the stockholders. If the old management is to be removed, it will probably resist the merger.[9]

The Price Paid.   The second key element in a merger is the price to be paid for the target company — the cash or securities to be given to the target firm's stockholders. The analysis is similar to a regular capital budgeting analysis: The incremental earnings are estimated; a discount rate is applied to find the present value of those earnings; and, if the present value of the future incremental earnings exceeds the price to be paid for the target firm, the merger is approved. Thus, only if the target firm is worth more to the acquiring firm than its market value as a separate entity will the merger be feasible. Obviously, the acquiring firm tries to buy at as low a price as possible, whereas the target firm tries to sell out at the highest possible price. The final price is determined by negotiations, with the party that negotiates best capturing most of the incremental value. *The larger the synergistic benefits, the more room there is for bargaining, and the higher the probability that the merger actually will be consummated.*[10]

Self-Test Questions

What is the essential difference between an operating merger and a pure financial merger?

---

[8]The acquiring firm may also be concerned about this point, especially if the acquired firm's management is quite good. A condition of the merger may be that the management team agree to stay on for a period, such as five years, after the merger. Also, the price paid may be contingent on the acquired firm's performance subsequent to the merger. For example, when International Holdings acquired Walker Products, the price paid was 200,000 shares of International Holdings stock (which sold for $63 per share) at the time the deal was closed plus an additional 30,000 shares each year for the next three years, provided Walker Products earned at least $2 million during each of these years. Since Walker's managers owned the stock and would receive the bonus, they had a strong incentive to stay on and help the firm meet its targets.

If the managers of the target company are highly competent but do not wish to remain on after the merger, the acquiring firm may build into the merger contract a noncompetitive agreement with the old management. Thus, Walker Products' principal officers had to agree not to affiliate with a new business which is competitive with the one they sold for a period of five years. Such agreements are especially important with service-oriented businesses.

[9]Managements of firms that are thought to be attractive merger candidates occasionally arrange "golden parachutes" for themselves. Golden parachutes are extremely lucrative retirement plans which take effect if a merger is consummated. Thus, when Bendix was acquired by Allied, Bill Agee, Bendix's chairman, "pulled the ripcord of his golden parachute" and walked away with $4 million. Congress is currently considering controls on golden parachutes as a part of its takeover legislative proposals.

[10]It has been estimated that of all merger negotiations seriously begun, fewer than one-third actually result in mergers. Also, in contested merger situations, the company that offers the most will usually make the acquisition, and the company that stands to gain the greatest synergistic benefits can generally bid the most.

In analyzing a proposed operating merger, what is the single most important factor?

When negotiating a friendly merger, what are the two most important considerations?

VALUING THE TARGET FIRM

To determine the value of the target firm, two key items are needed: (1) a set of pro forma financial statements which develop the expected cash flows and (2) a discount rate, or cost of capital, to use in finding the present value of the projected cash flows.

Pro Forma Income Statements

Table 22-2 contains the projected income statements for CompuEd Corporation, which is being considered for acquisition by American Technologies, a large high-tech company. The projected data are postmerger, so all synergistic effects are included. CompuEd currently uses 30 percent debt, but if it were acquired, American would increase CompuEd's debt ratio to 50 percent. Both American and CompuEd have a 40 percent marginal federal-plus-state tax rate.

The net cash flows shown in Table 22-2 are the flows that would be available to American's stockholders, and they provide the basis of the valuation.[11] Of course, the postmerger cash flows attributable to the target firm are extremely difficult to estimate. In a complete merger valuation, just as in a complete capital budgeting analysis, the component cash flow probability distributions would be specified, and sensitivity, scenario, and simulation analyses would be conducted. Indeed, in a friendly merger, the acquiring firm would send a team, consisting of literally dozens of accountants, engineers, and finance people, to the target firm's headquarters to go over its books, to estimate required maintenance expenditures, to set values on assets such as petroleum reserves, and the like.

Estimating the Discount Rate

Because the bottom line net cash flows shown in Table 22-2 are equity flows, they should be discounted at the cost of equity rather than at the overall cost of capital. Further, the cost of equity used must reflect the riskiness of the net cash flows in the table; thus, the appropriate discount rate is CompuEd's cost of

---

[11]We purposely kept the cash flows simple to help focus on the key issues of the valuation process. In an actual merger valuation, the cash flows would be much more complex, normally including such items as additional capital furnished by the acquiring firm, tax loss carry-forwards, tax effects of plant and equipment valuation adjustments, and inflows expected from planned asset sales.

Table 22-2 ▪ **CompuEd Corporation: Projected Postmerger Income Statements as of December 31 (Millions of Dollars)**

	1993	1994	1995	1996	1997
Net sales	$105.0	$126.0	$151.0	$174.0	$191.0
Cost of goods sold	80.0	94.0	111.0	127.0	137.0
Selling and administrative expenses	10.0	12.0	13.0	15.0	16.0
Depreciation	8.0	8.0	9.0	9.0	10.0
EBIT	$ 7.0	$ 12.0	$ 18.0	$ 23.0	$ 28.0
Interest[a]	3.0	4.0	5.0	6.0	6.0
EBT	$ 4.0	$ 8.0	$ 13.0	$ 17.0	$ 22.0
Taxes (40.0%)[b]	1.6	3.2	5.2	6.8	8.8
Net income	$ 2.4	$ 4.8	$ 7.8	$ 10.2	$ 13.2
Plus depreciation	8.0	8.0	9.0	9.0	10.0
Cash flow	$ 10.4	$ 12.8	$ 16.8	$ 19.2	$ 23.2
Less retentions for growth[c]	4.0	4.0	7.0	9.0	12.0
Plus terminal value[d]					151.2
Net cash flows to American[e]	$ 6.4	$ 8.8	$ 9.8	$ 10.2	$162.4

[a]Interest payment estimates are based on CompuEd's existing debt plus additional debt to increase the debt ratio to 50 percent, plus additional debt after the merger to finance asset expansion but subject to the 50 percent target capital structure.

[b]American will file a consolidated tax return after the merger. Thus, the taxes shown here are the full corporate taxes attributable to CompuEd's operations; there will be no additional taxes on the cash flowing from CompuEd to American.

[c]Some of the net income generated by CompuEd after the merger will be retained to finance its own asset growth, and some will be transferred to American to pay dividends on its stock or for redeployment within the corporation.

[d]CompuEd's available cash flows are expected to grow at a constant 10 percent rate after 1997. The value of all post-1997 cash flows to American, as of December 31, 1997, is estimated by use of the constant growth model to be $151.2 million:

$$V_{1997} = (\$23.2 - \$12.0)(1.10)/(0.1815 - 0.10) = \$151.2 \text{ million.}$$

In the next section, we discuss the estimation of the 18.15 percent cost of equity.

[e]These are the net cash flows which are available to American due to the acquisition of CompuEd. They may be used for dividend payments to American's stockholders or for financing asset expansion in American's other divisions and subsidiaries.

equity, not that of American or the consolidated postmerger firm. CompuEd's market-determined premerger beta was 1.30; however, this reflects its premerger 30 percent debt ratio, whereas its postmerger debt ratio will increase to 50 percent. American's investment bankers estimate that CompuEd's beta will rise to 1.63 if its debt ratio is increased to 50 percent.

We can use the Security Market Line to determine CompuEd's approximate cost of equity. If the risk-free rate is 10 percent and the market risk premium is

5 percent, then CompuEd's cost of equity after the merger would be $k_s = 18.15$ percent:[12]

$$k_s = k_{RF} + (RP_M)b$$
$$= 10\% + (5\%)1.63$$
$$= 18.15\%.$$

Valuing the Cash Flows

The value of CompuEd to American is the present value of the cash flows expected to accrue to American, discounted at 18.15 percent (in millions of dollars):

$$\text{Value} = \frac{\$6.4}{(1.1815)^1} + \frac{\$8.8}{(1.1815)^2} + \frac{\$9.8}{(1.1815)^3} + \frac{\$10.2}{(1.1815)^4} + \frac{\$162.4}{(1.1815)^5} = \$93.4.$$

Alternatively, using a financial calculator you would input the cash flows for each year in the cash flow register, input I $=$ 18.15, and then press the NPV button to arrive at the value of $93.4. Thus, if American can acquire CompuEd for $93.4 million or less, the merger appears to be acceptable from American's standpoint.

? Self-Test Questions

How are the cash flows required in a merger analysis determined?

How is the discount rate that is used to evaluate the postmerger cash flows of the target firm obtained? Should this be an equity return or an overall cost of capital? Why?

THE ROLE OF INVESTMENT BANKERS

The investment banking community is involved with mergers in a number of ways: (1) helping to arrange mergers, (2) aiding target companies in developing and implementing defensive tactics, and (3) helping to value target companies. These merger-related activities have been quite profitable. For example, Paramount Communications incurred fees and related costs of about $50 million in its failed attempt to acquire Time, and Time's costs to fend off Paramount and

---

[12]In actual merger situations, the companies often hire investment banking firms to help develop valuation estimates. For example, when General Electric acquired Utah International in the largest merger up to that time, it hired Morgan Stanley to determine Utah's value. The authors discussed the valuation process with the Morgan Stanley analyst in charge of the appraisal. Morgan Stanley considered using the CAPM but chose instead to base the discount rate on DCF methodology. However, other analysts, and Morgan Stanley people in other situations, have used CAPM analysis as described here. Merger analysis, like the analysis of any other complex issue, requires judgment, and people's judgments differ as to which method is most appropriate for any given situation.

to acquire Warner were over $100 million. No wonder investment banking houses are able to make top offers to finance graduates!

Arranging Mergers

The major investment banking firms have merger and acquisition groups which operate within their corporate finance departments. (Corporate finance departments offer advice, as opposed to underwriting or brokerage services, to business firms.) Members of these groups strive to identify firms with excess cash that might want to buy other firms, companies that might be willing to be bought, and firms that might, for a number of reasons, be attractive to others. If an oil company, for instance, decided to expand into coal mining, it might enlist the aid of an investment banker to help it locate and then negotiate with a target coal company. Similarly, dissident stockholders of firms with poor track records may work with investment bankers to oust management by helping to arrange a merger. Drexel Burnham Lambert, the investment banking house that developed junk bond financing, offered packages of financing to corporate raiders, with the package including both designing the securities used in the tender offer and getting people and firms to buy the target firm's stock now and then to tender it once the final offer was made.

Developing Defense Tactics

Target firms that do not want to be acquired generally enlist the help of an investment banking firm, along with a law firm that specializes in helping to block mergers. Defenses include such tactics as (1) changing the by-laws so that only one-third of the directors are elected each year and/or so that a 75 percent approval (a "supermajority") versus a simple majority is required to approve a merger, (2) trying to convince stockholders that the price offered by the potential acquirer is too low, (3) raising antitrust issues in the hope that the Justice Department will intervene, (4) issuing debt and using the proceeds to repurchase stock in the open market in an effort to push the price above that being offered by the potential acquirer, (5) persuading a **white knight** more acceptable to the target firm's management that it should compete with the potential acquirer, and (6) taking a "poison pill," as described below.

white knight

A company that is more acceptable to the management of a firm under attack in a hostile takeover attempt.

poison pill

An action which will seriously hurt a company if it is acquired by another.

golden parachutes

Large payments made to the managers of a firm if it is acquired.

Some examples of **poison pills** — some of which really do amount to virtually committing suicide to avoid a takeover — are such tactics as borrowing on terms that require immediate repayment of all loans if the firm is acquired, selling off at bargain prices the assets that originally made the firm a desirable target, granting such lucrative **golden parachutes** to the firm's executives that the cash drain from these payments would render the merger infeasible, and planning defensive mergers which would leave the firm with new assets of questionable value plus a huge amount of debt to service. Companies are even giving their stockholders the right to buy at half price the stock of an acquiring firm should the firm be acquired. The blatant use of poison pills is constrained by directors' awareness that such use could trigger personal suits by stockholders against directors who voted for them, and, perhaps in the near future, bylaws that would limit management's use of these tactics. Still, investment bankers are busy thinking up new poison pill formulas, and others are just as actively trying to come up with antidotes.[13]

Establishing a Fair Value

If a friendly merger is being worked out between two firms' managements, it is important to be able to document that the agreed-upon price is a fair one; otherwise, the stockholders of either company could sue to block the merger. Therefore, in most large mergers, each side will hire an investment banking firm to evaluate the target company and to help establish the fair price. For example, General Electric employed Morgan Stanley to determine a fair price for Utah International, as did Royal Dutch to help establish the price it paid for Shell Oil. Even if the merger is not friendly, investment bankers may still be asked to help establish a price. If a surprise tender offer is to be made, the acquiring firm will want to know the lowest price at which it might be able to acquire the stock, whereas the target firm may seek help in proving that the price being offered is too low.[14]

? Self-Test Questions

How is the investment banking community involved with mergers?

List some defense tactics that can be used by target firms to block mergers.

List some examples of poison pills.

CORPORATE ALLIANCES

corporate alliance
A cooperative deal that falls short of a merger.

Mergers are not the only way in which the resources of two firms can be combined. In fact, many companies are striking cooperative deals which fall far short of merging. Such cooperative deals are called **corporate alliances,** and they take many forms, from marketing agreements to joint ownership of world-scale

---

[13]In large part because of shareholder suits arising out of poison pills, greenmail, or other attempts to block mergers that would be profitable to stockholders, it is becoming both harder and more expensive for companies to buy insurance which protects directors from stockholder suits. This, in turn, is forcing directors to be more careful about approving management's proposals, and the whole situation is making it harder for companies to get good people to serve as directors. The final result, however, will probably be less "rubber stamping" by directors and more concern for stockholder as opposed to management interests. As an example, GM's board refused to go along with former Chairman Roger Smith's request that three GM senior vice presidents be added to the board. The existing board wanted to keep a majority of "outside" as opposed to "inside" (that is, officer) directors.

[14]Such investigations must obviously be done in secret, for if someone knew that Company A was thinking of offering, say, $50 per share for Company T, which was currently selling at $35 per share, huge profits could be made. The biggest scandal to hit Wall Street in the 1980s was the disclosure that Ivan Boesky, a well-known investor, was buying from Dennis Levine, a senior member of the investment banking house of Drexel Burnham Lambert, information about prospective takeovers of companies that Drexel Burnham was analyzing for others. Boesky's purchases, of course, raised the prices of the stocks and thus forced Drexel's clients to pay more than they otherwise would have had to pay. Incidentally, Boesky and Levine both went to jail for improper use of inside information, as did others involved in the scheme.

operations. For example, IBM and Apple Computer recently announced a deal whereby IBM will get access to some of Apple's software, and Apple will be given some of IBM's microchip technology. Another form of corporate alliance is the **joint venture,** which involves the joining together of parts of two or more companies to accomplish a specific, limited objective. Joint ventures are controlled by the combined management of the two (or more) parent companies.

joint venture

A corporate alliance in which two or more independent companies combine their resources to achieve a specific, limited objective.

Joint ventures have been used often by U.S., Japanese, and European firms to share technology and marketing expertise. For example, Whirlpool recently announced a joint venture with the Dutch electronics giant Philips that will produce appliances under the Philips brand names in five European countries. By joining with their foreign counterparts, U.S. firms are trying to establish a strong foothold in Europe before the European community becomes one unified market.

 Self-Test Question

What is the difference between a merger and a joint venture?

DIVESTITURES

Although corporations do more buying than selling of operating assets, quite a bit of selling does occur. In this section we briefly discuss the major types of divestitures, and then we present some recent examples of and rationales for divestitures.

Types of Divestitures

divestiture

The sale of some of a company's operating assets.

There are four types of **divestitures:** (1) sale of an operating unit to another firm, (2) sale to the managers of the unit being divested, (3) setting up the business to be divested as a separate corporation and then giving (or "spinning off") its stock on a pro rata basis to the divesting firm's stockholders, and (4) outright liquidation of assets.

Sale to another firm generally involves the sale of an entire division or unit, usually for cash but sometimes for stock of the acquiring firm. In a *managerial buyout,* the managers of the division purchase the division themselves, usually for cash plus notes. Then, as owners-managers, they reorganize it as a closely held firm. In a **spin-off,** the firm's existing stockholders are given new stock representing separate ownership rights in the company that was divested. The new company establishes its own board of directors and officers, and it operates as a separate company. The stockholders end up owning shares of two firms instead of one, but no cash has been transferred. Finally, in a *liquidation,* the assets of a division are sold off piecemeal rather than as a single entity. We present some recent examples of the different types of divestitures in the next section.

spin-off

A divestiture in which the stock of a subsidiary is given to the parent company's stockholders.

Divestiture Illustrations

1. Esmark Inc., a holding company which owned such consumer products companies as Swift Meats and Playtex, sold off several of its nonconsumer-oriented divisions, including petroleum properties for which Mobil and

some other oil companies paid $1.1 billion. Investors had generally thought of Esmark as a meat packing and consumer products company, and its stock price had reflected this image rather than that of a company with huge holdings of valuable oil reserves carried at low balance sheet values. Thus, Esmark's stock was undervalued, according to its managers, and the company was in danger of a takeover bid. Selling the oil properties helped Esmark raise its stock price from $19 to $45.

2. IU International, a multimillion-dollar conglomerate listed on the NYSE, spun off three major subsidiaries—Gotaas-Larson, an ocean shipping company which owned Carnival Cruise Lines; Canadian Utilities, an electric utility; and Echo Bay Mines, a gold mining company. IU also owned (and retained) some major trucking companies (Ryder and PIE), several manufacturing businesses, and some large agribusiness operations. IU's management originally had acquired and combined highly cyclical businesses such as ocean shipping and gold mining with stable ones such as utilities in order to gain overall corporate stability through diversification. The strategy worked reasonably well from an operating standpoint, but it failed in the financial markets. According to its management, IU's very diversity kept it from being assigned to any particular industrial classification, so security analysts tended not to follow the company and therefore did not understand it or recommend it to investors. (Analysts tend to concentrate on an industry, and they do not like to recommend—and investors do not like to invest in—a company they do not understand.) As a result, IU had a low P/E ratio and a low market price. After the spin-offs, IU's stock price plus those of the spun-off companies rose from $10 to over $75.

leveraged buyout (LBO)
A situation in which a firm's managers borrow heavily against the firm's assets and purchase the company themselves.

3. The managers of Beatrice Companies and some private investors borrowed $6.9 billion from a group of banks and used this money to buy all of the firm's stock. This type of debt-financed transaction is called a **leveraged buyout (LBO),** and Beatrice was said to have "gone private" because the public stockholders were bought out, and all of the stock went into the hands of the management group. We will look at LBOs in more detail in a later section. The new Beatrice has been busily selling off divisions to raise money to reduce its bank loans; its loan agreements required it to sell off at least $1.45 billion in assets within a year, but Beatrice beat that schedule. The company sold Avis for $250 million just 12 days after it went private, and it later sold off its Coca-Cola bottling operations for about $1 billion. Beatrice also sold its refrigerated warehouse network, its Max Factor cosmetic line, its dairy products line, and other operations, raising another $2.4 billion in total.

4. In 1984 AT&T was broken up to settle a Justice Department antitrust suit filed in the 1970s. For almost 100 years AT&T had operated as a holding company which owned Western Electric (its manufacturing subsidiary), Bell Labs (its research arm), a huge long-distance network system, and 22 Bell operating companies, such as Pacific Telephone, New York Telephone, Southern Bell, and Southwestern Bell. In preparation for the breakup, AT&T was divided into eight separate companies: a slimmed-down AT&T, which kept Western Electric, Bell Labs, and all interstate long-distance operations, and seven new regional telephone holding companies that were

created from the 22 old operating telephone companies. The stock of the seven new telephone companies was then spun off to the old AT&T's stockholders. Thus, a person who held 100 shares of old AT&T stock owned, after the divestiture, 100 shares of the "new" AT&T plus 10 shares of each of the seven new operating companies. These 170 shares were backed by the same assets that had previously backed 100 shares of AT&T common.

The AT&T divestiture occurred as a result of a suit by the Justice Department, which wanted to break up the Bell System into a regulated monopoly segment (the seven regional telephone companies) and a manufacturing/long-distance segment which would be subjected to competition. The breakup was designed to strengthen competition in those parts of the telecommunications industry which are not natural monopolies.[15]

5. Woolworth recently liquidated every one of its 336 Woolco discount stores. This made the company, which had had sales of $7.2 billion before the liquidation, 30 percent smaller. Woolco had posted operating losses of $19 million in the year before the liquidation, and its losses in the six months preceding it had climbed to an alarming $21 million. Woolworth's CEO, Edward F. Gibbons, was quoted as saying: "How many losses can you take?" Woolco's demise necessitated an after-tax write-off of $325 million, but management believed that it was better to go ahead and "bite the bullet" than to let the losing stores bleed the company to death.

6. As a result of some imprudent loans to oil companies and to developing nations, Continental Illinois, one of the largest U.S. bank holding companies, was recently threatened with bankruptcy. Continental then sold off several profitable divisions, such as its leasing and credit card operations, to raise funds to cover bad-loan losses and deposit withdrawals. In effect, Continental sold assets in order to stay alive. Ultimately, Continental was bailed out by the Federal Deposit Insurance Corporation and the Federal Reserve, which (1) arranged a $7.5 billion rescue package and (2) provided a blanket guarantee for all of Continental's $40 billion of deposits, which kept deposits larger than $100,000 from fleeing the bank because of their uninsured status.

The preceding examples illustrate the varied reasons for divestitures. Sometimes the market does not appear to properly recognize the value of a firm's assets when they are held as part of a conglomerate; the Esmark oil properties case was an example. Similarly, IU International had become so complex and diverse that analysts and investors did not understand it and consequently ignored it. Other companies need cash either to finance expansion in their primary business lines or to reduce a large debt burden, and divestitures can be used to raise this cash. Running a business is a dynamic process — conditions change, corporate strategies change in response, and, as a result, firms alter their

---

[15]Another forced divestiture involved Du Pont and General Motors. In 1921, GM was in serious financial trouble, and Du Pont supplied capital plus managerial talent in exchange for 23 percent of GM's stock. Many years later, the Justice Department won an antitrust suit which required Du Pont to spin off (to Du Pont stockholders) its GM stock.

asset portfolios by acquisitions, divestitures, or both. Some divestitures, such as Woolworth's liquidation of its Woolco stores, occur in order to unload losing assets that would otherwise drag the company down, while the AT&T example is one of the many instances in which a divestiture is the result of an antitrust settlement. Finally, Continental's actions represented a desperate effort to get the cash needed to stay alive.

Self-Test Questions

What are the four types of divestitures?

What are some reasons for divestitures?

HOLDING COMPANIES

holding company

A corporation that owns sufficient common stock of another firm to achieve working control of it.

parent company

A holding company; a firm which controls another firm by owning a large block of its stock.

operating company

A subsidiary of a holding company; a separate legal entity.

Strictly defined, any company that owns stock in another firm could be called a holding company. However, as the term is generally used, a **holding company** is a firm that holds large blocks of stock in other companies and exercises control over those firms. The holding company is often called the **parent company,** and the controlled companies are known as *subsidiaries* or **operating companies.** The parent can own 100 percent of the subsidiaries' stock, but control can generally be exercised with far fewer shares.

Many of the advantages and disadvantages of holding companies are identical to those of large-scale operations already discussed in connection with mergers and consolidations. However, as we show next, the holding company form of large-scale operations has some distinct advantages (as well as a few disadvantages) over those of completely integrated, divisionalized operations.

Advantages of Holding Companies

Holding companies have three potential advantages: (1) control with fractional ownership, (2) isolation of risks, and (3) legal and accounting separation when regulations make such separation desirable.

1. **Control with fractional ownership.** Through a holding company operation, a firm may buy 5, 10, 50, or any other percentage of another corporation's stock. Such fractional ownership may be sufficient to give the acquiring company effective working control over the operations of the firm in which it has acquired stock ownership. Working control is often considered to require more than 25 percent of the common stock, but it can be as low as 10 percent if the stock is widely distributed. One financier recently made this statement: "The attitude of management is more important than the number of shares you own. If they think you can control the company, then you do."

2. **Isolation of risks.** Because the various operating companies in a holding company system are separate legal entities, the obligations of any one unit are separate from those of the others. Therefore, catastrophic losses incurred by one unit might not be transmitted as claims on the assets of the other units. However, although this is a customary generalization, it is not

always valid. First, the parent company may feel obligated to make good on the subsidiary's debts, even though it may not be legally bound to do so, to keep its good name and thus retain customers. Examples of this would include American Express's payment of more than $100 million in connection with a swindle that was the responsibility of one of its subsidiaries, and United California Bank's coverage of a multimillion-dollar fraud loss incurred by its Swiss affiliate. Second, a parent company may feel obligated to supply capital to an affiliate to protect its initial investment; General Public Utilities' continued support of its subsidiaries' Three Mile Island nuclear plant is an example. Third, when lending to one of the units of a holding company system, an astute loan officer may require a guarantee by the parent holding company. Finally, an accident such as the one at Union Carbide's Bhopal, India, plant may be deemed the responsibility of the parent company, voiding the limited liability rules that would otherwise apply. Still, holding companies can at times be used to prevent losses in one unit from bringing down other units in the system.

3. **Legal separation.** Certain regulated companies such as utilities and financial institutions find it easier to operate as holding companies than as divisional corporations. For example, an electric utility such as The Southern Company, which operates in and is regulated by several states, found it most practical to set up a holding company (Southern) which in turn owns a set of subsidiaries (Georgia Power, Alabama Power, Mississippi Power, Gulf Power, and Savannah Electric). All of the Bell telephone companies are parts of holding company systems, and even utilities which operate only within a single state often find it beneficial to operate within a holding company format in order to separate those assets under the control of regulators from those not subject to utility commission regulation. Thus, Florida Power & Light reorganized as a holding company called FPL Group, which owns a utility (Florida Power & Light) plus subsidiaries engaged in insurance, real estate development, orange groves, and the like.

   Banks, insurance companies, and other financial service corporations have also found it convenient to be organized as holding companies. Thus, Citicorp is a holding company which owns Citibank of New York, a leasing company, a mortgage service company, and so on. Transamerica is a holding company which owns insurance companies, small loan companies, title companies, auto rental companies, and an airline.

Disadvantages of Holding Companies

Holding companies have two disadvantages: (1) partial multiple taxation and (2) ease of enforced dissolution.

1. **Partial multiple taxation.** Provided the holding company owns at least 80 percent of a subsidiary's voting stock, the Tax Code permits the filing of consolidated returns, in which case dividends received by the parent are not taxed. However, if less than 80 percent of the stock is owned, returns cannot be consolidated, and taxes must be paid on 30 percent of the dividends received by the holding company. With a tax rate of 34 percent, this means that the effective tax rate on intercorporate dividends is

$0.30 \times 34\% = 10.2\%$. This partial double taxation somewhat offsets the benefits of holding company control with limited ownership, but whether or not the penalty of 10.2 percent of dividends received is sufficient to offset other possible advantages is a matter that must be decided in individual situations.

2. **Ease of enforced dissolution.** It is relatively easy for the Justice Department to require dissolution by disposal of stock ownership of a holding company operation that it finds unacceptable. Thus, Du Pont was required to dispose of its 23 percent stock interest in General Motors Corporation, an interest that had been acquired back in the early 1920s. Because there had been no fusion between the two corporations, there were no difficulties, from an operating standpoint, in requiring their separation. If complete amalgamation had taken place, however, it would have been much more difficult to break up the company after so many years, and the likelihood of forced divestiture would have been reduced. Still, the forced breakup of AT&T shows that even fully integrated companies can be broken up.

Holding Companies as a Leveraging Device

The holding company vehicle has been used to obtain huge amounts of financial leverage. In the 1920s, several tiers of holding companies were established in the electric utility and other industries. In those days, an operating company at the bottom of the pyramid might have had $100 million of assets, financed by $50 million of debt and $50 million of equity. A first-tier holding company might have owned the stock of the operating firm as its only asset and then been financed with $25 million of debt and $25 million of equity. A second-tier holding company, which owned the $25 million of stock of the first-tier company as its only asset, might have been financed with $12.5 million of debt and $12.5 million of equity. Such systems were extended to four or more levels, but even with only two holding companies, we see that $100 million of operating assets could be controlled at the top by only $12.5 million of second-tier equity, and the $100 million of operating assets would have had to provide enough cash flow to support $87.5 million of debt. Such a holding company system is highly leveraged, even though the individual components each report 50 percent debt/assets ratios. Because of this *consolidated leverage*, even a small decline in profits at the operating company level could bring the whole system down like a house of cards.

Self-Test Questions

Differentiate between holding companies and operating companies.

What are the major advantages and disadvantages of holding companies?

Explain how holding companies can be used to obtain huge amounts of financial leverage.

| INDUSTRY PRACTICE | Are LBOs on Their Way Out? |

Investment bankers argue that although there has been a push to put more equity on corporations' balance sheets, leveraged buyouts will continue to appeal to firms in the 1990s. However, companies will be more cautious when taking on debt. One financial consultant states that using debt to purchase stock still makes sense for mature, low-debt companies with limited growth opportunities because money can be put into shareholders' hands for reinvestment in companies with better growth opportunities. In addition, these mature companies may be motivated to shed unproductive assets and to improve productivity by the need to meet their interest payments. Finally, a corporation's interest expense remains tax deductible, while dividends paid on its stock are not. Industries where leveraged buyouts and stock buybacks are forecasted include supermarkets, food, oil, and retailing.

Kohlberg, Kravis & Roberts, the largest leveraged buyout firm, expects to see fewer LBOs whose success is dependent on asset sales. The firm also expects future deals to call for between 25 and 30 percent of equity to capitalization, in contrast to the 1980s, when LBOs were completed with less than 10 percent equity.

One investment banker states that when leverage is added and equity is reduced, slow-growth equity often can be turned into "high octane" because the number of common shares have been reduced and each remaining share will get more income than before — as long as interest payments are not overwhelming. Merton Miller, who won the 1990 Nobel Prize for his work on capital structures, states that debt levels often look more burdensome than they actually are. Because equity book values are generally lower than market values, debt-to-book-equity ratios are greater than debt-to-market-equity ratios. In addition, Miller believes that the financial markets are self-correcting, and if corporations issue more debt than the public wants, interest rates will rise to discourage additional debt usage.

According to Standard & Poor's (S&P), bond raters have developed better tools for analyzing a company's financial position, and today there is less emphasis on the debt ratio per se. An S&P managing director stated that if a company has a strong cash flow, and if it can demonstrate financial liquidity, S&P may be forgiving even if its leverage is higher than the "normal" level.

Source: "Leveraged Buy-Outs May Be Down, But They Definitely Are Not Out," *The Wall Street Journal,* December 16, 1991.

LEVERAGED BUYOUTS (LBOs)

The 1980s witnessed a huge increase in the number and size of leveraged buyouts, or LBOs. This development occurred for the same reasons that mergers and divestitures occurred — the existence of potential bargains, situations in which companies were using insufficient leverage, and the development of the junk bond market, which facilitated the use of leverage in takeovers.

LBOs can be initiated in one of two ways: (1) The firm's own managers can set up a new company whose equity comes from the managers themselves, plus some equity from pension funds and other institutions. This new company then arranges to borrow a large amount of money by selling junk bonds through an investment banking firm. With the financing arranged, the management group then makes an offer to purchase all the publicly owned shares through a tender offer. (2) A specialized LBO firm, with Kohlberg, Kravis, & Roberts (KKR) being the largest and best known, will identify a potential target company, go to the management, and suggest that an LBO deal be done. KKR and other LBO firms have billions of dollars of equity, most put up by pension funds and other large investors, available for the equity portion of the deals, and they arrange junk bond financing just as would a management-led group. Generally, the newly formed company will have at least 80 percent debt, and sometimes the debt ratio is as high as 98 percent. Thus, the term "leveraged" is most appropriate.

To illustrate an LBO, consider the $25 billion leveraged buyout of RJR Nabisco by KKR. RJR, a leading producer of tobacco and food products with brands such as Winston, Camel, Planters, Ritz, and Oreo, was trading at about $55 a share. Then F. Ross Johnson, the company's president and CEO, announced a $75 per share, or $17.6 billion, offer to take the firm private. The day after the announcement, RJR's stock soared to $77.25, which indicated that investors thought that the final price would be even higher than Johnson's opening bid. A few days later, KKR offered $90 per share, or $20.6 billion, for the firm. The battle between the two bidders continued until late November, when RJR's board accepted a revised KKR bid of cash and securities worth about $106 per share, for a total value of about $25.1 billion.

Is RJR worth $25 billion, or did Henry Kravis and his partners let their egos govern their judgment? It will take several years before the answer is known, but at the time, analysts believed that the deal was workable—barely. To meet an estimated $2.5 billion in annual debt payments, KKR is expected to sell off a chunk of Nabisco's food businesses, lay off employees, cut advertising and marketing expenses, and slash spending on new plants. However, either a recession or soaring interest rates could jeopardize this strategy. In the highly leveraged world of LBOs, KKR insists that its buyout is relatively conservative. The new RJR owes banks and bondholders $22.8 billion, while stockholders' equity totals $7.4 billion. That's a 3-to-1 ratio, compared with the 9-to-1 ratio that is prevalent in most LBOs. Still, even the enormous annual cash flows produced by RJR's cigarettes and cookies probably will fall about $400 million short of meeting the annual interest payments over the next few years. On the plus side, RJR will no longer have to pay out $450 million annually in common dividends. Further, the new management team will be highly motivated to make a success of the venture.

It is not clear if LBOs are, on balance, a good or a bad idea. Some government officials, and others, have stated a belief that the leverage involved might destabilize the economy. On the other hand, LBOs have certainly stimulated some lethargic managements, and that is good. Good or bad, though, LBOs are helping to reshape the face of corporate America.

? Self-Test Questions

Identify and briefly explain the two ways in which an LBO may be initiated.

How has the development of the junk bond market affected the use of LBOs?

SUMMARY

This chapter discussed mergers, divestitures, holding companies, and LBOs. The key concepts covered are listed below.

▪ A **merger** occurs when two firms combine to form a single company. The primary motives for mergers are (1) synergy, (2) tax considerations,

(3) purchase of assets below their replacement costs, (4) diversification, and (5) gaining control over a larger enterprise.

▪ Mergers can provide economic benefits through **economies of scale** or through the **concentration of assets** in the hands of more efficient managers—these mergers reduce operating costs. However, mergers also have the potential for reducing competition, and for this reason they are carefully regulated by governmental agencies.

▪ In most mergers, one company **(the acquiring firm)** initiates action to take over another **(the target firm).**

▪ A **horizontal merger** occurs when two firms in the same line of business combine.

▪ A **vertical merger** is the combination of a firm with one of its customers or suppliers.

▪ A **congeneric merger** involves firms in related industries, but for which no customer-supplier relationship exists.

▪ A **conglomerate merger** occurs when firms in totally different industries combine.

▪ In a **friendly merger,** the managements of both firms approve the merger, while in a **hostile merger** the target firm's management opposes the merger.

▪ An **operating merger** is one in which the operations of the two firms are combined. A **financial merger** is one in which the firms continue to operate separately, and hence no operating economies are expected.

▪ In a **merger analysis,** (1) the price to be paid for the target firm and (2) the employment/control situation are the key issues to be resolved.

▪ To determine the **value of the target firm,** the acquiring firm must (1) forecast the cash flows that will result after the merger and (2) develop a discount rate to apply to the projected cash flows.

▪ **Poison pills** are actions a firm can take that will make the firm less valuable if it is acquired in a hostile takeover. **Golden parachutes** are a form of poison pill in which large payments are to be made to a firm's managers if it is acquired.

▪ A **joint venture** is a **corporate alliance** in which two or more companies combine some of their resources to achieve a specific, limited objective.

▪ A **divestiture** is the sale of some of a company's operating assets. A divestiture may involve (1) selling an operating unit to another firm, (2) selling a unit to that unit's managers, (3) **spinning off** a unit as a separate company, or (4) the outright **liquidation** of a unit's assets.

▪ The **reasons for divestitures** include antitrust, the clarification of what a company actually does, and the raising of capital needed to strengthen the corporation's core business.

▪ A **holding company** is a corporation which owns sufficient stock in another firm to achieve working control of it. The holding company is also known as the **parent company,** and the companies which it controls are called subsidiaries, or **operating companies.**

- Advantages to holding company operations include the following: (1) control can often be obtained for a smaller cash outlay, (2) risks may be segregated, and (3) regulated companies can separate regulated from unregulated assets.

- Disadvantages to holding company operations include (1) tax penalties and (2) the fact that incomplete ownership, if it exists, can lead to control problems.

- A **leveraged buyout (LBO)** is a transaction in which a firm's publicly owned stock is bought up in a mostly debt-financed tender offer, and a privately owned, highly leveraged firm results. Often, the firm's own management initiates the LBO.

Questions

22-1   Four economic classifications of mergers are (1) horizontal, (2) vertical, (3) conglomerate, and (4) congeneric. Explain the significance of these terms in merger analysis with regard to (a) the likelihood of governmental intervention and (b) possibilities for operating synergy.

22-2   Firm A wants to acquire Firm B. Firm B's management agrees that the merger is a good idea. Might a tender offer be used?

22-3   Distinguish between operating mergers and financial mergers.

22-4   In the spring of 1984, Disney Productions' stock was selling for about $12.50 per share (all prices have been adjusted for a 4:1 split in March 1986). Then Saul Steinberg, a New York financier, began acquiring it, and after he had 12 percent he announced a tender offer for another 37 percent of the stock—which would bring his holdings up to 49 percent—at a price of $16.88 per share. Disney's management then announced plans to buy Gibson Greeting Cards and Arvida Corporation, paying for them with stock. It also lined up bank credit and (according to Steinberg) was prepared to borrow up to $2 billion and use the funds to repurchase shares at a higher price than Steinberg was offering. All of these efforts were designed to keep Steinberg from taking control. In June, Disney's management agreed to pay Steinberg $19.36 per share, which gave him a gain of about $60 million on a two-month investment of about $26.5 million.

When Disney's buyback of Steinberg's shares was announced, the stock price fell almost instantly from $17 to $11.50. Many Disney stockholders were irate, and they sued to block the buyout. Also, the Disney affair added fuel to the fire in a Congressional committee that was holding hearings on proposed legislation that would (1) prohibit someone from acquiring more than 10 percent of a firm's stock without making a tender offer for all the remaining shares, (2) prohibit poison pill tactics such as those Disney's management had used to fight off Steinberg, (3) prohibit buybacks such as the deal eventually offered to Steinberg (greenmail) unless there was an approving vote by stockholders, and (4) prohibit (or substantially curtail) the use of golden parachutes (the one thing Disney's management did not try).

Set forth the arguments for and against this type of legislation. What provisions, if any, should it contain? Also, look up Disney's current stock price to see how its stockholders have actually fared.

22-5   Two large, publicly owned firms are contemplating a merger. No operating synergy is expected. However, since returns on the two firms are not perfectly positively correlated, the standard deviation of earnings would be reduced for the combined corporation. One group of consultants argues that this risk reduction is sufficient grounds for the merger. Another group thinks this type of risk reduction is irrelevant because stockholders can themselves hold the stock of both companies and thus gain the risk reduction benefits without all the hassles and expenses of the merger. Whose position is correct?

Self-Test Problem

ST-1

Key terms

Define each of the following terms:

a. Synergy; merger
b. Horizontal merger; vertical merger; congeneric merger; conglomerate merger
c. Friendly merger; hostile merger; defensive merger; tender offer; two-tier offer; target company
d. Operating merger; financial merger
e. White knight; poison pill; golden parachute
f. Joint venture; corporate alliance
g. Divestiture; spin-off; leveraged buyout (LBO)
h. Holding company; operating company; parent company

Problems

22-1

Capital budgeting analysis

Gentry Gifts & Stationery Shoppe wishes to acquire Celec's Card Gallery for $400,000. Gentry expects the merger to provide incremental earnings of about $64,000 a year for 10 years. Jim Gentry has calculated the marginal cost of capital for this investment to be 10 percent. Conduct a capital budgeting analysis for Gentry to determine whether or not he should purchase Celec's Card Gallery.

22-2

Merger analysis

TransWorld Products Inc., a large conglomerate, is evaluating the possible acquisition of Georgia Siding Company (GSC), a small aluminum siding manufacturer. TransWorld's analysts project the following postmerger data for GSC (in thousands of dollars):

	1993	1994	1995	1996
Net sales	$450	$518	$555	$600
Selling and administrative expense	45	53	60	68
Interest	18	21	24	27

Tax rate after merger	34%
Cost of goods sold as a percent of sales	65%
Beta after merger	1.50
Risk-free rate	8%
Market risk premium	4%
Terminal growth rate of cash flow available to TransWorld	7%

If the acquisition is made, it will occur on January 1, 1993. All cash flows shown in the income statements are assumed to occur at the end of the year. GSC currently has a capital structure of 40 percent debt, but TransWorld would increase that to 50 percent if the acquisition were made. GSC, if independent, would pay taxes at 20 percent, but its income would be taxed at 34 percent if it were consolidated. GSC's current market-determined beta is 1.40, and its investment bankers think that its beta would rise to 1.50 if the debt ratio were increased to 50 percent. The cost of goods sold is expected to be 65 percent of sales, but it could vary somewhat. Depreciation-generated funds would be used to replace worn-out equipment, so they would not be available to TransWorld's shareholders. The risk-free rate is 8 percent, and the market risk premium is 4 percent.

a. What is the appropriate discount rate for valuing the acquisition?

b. What is the terminal value? What is the value of GSC to TransWorld?

EXAM-TYPE PROBLEM

The problem included in this section is set up in such a way that it could be used as a multiple-choice exam problem.

22-3
Merger analysis

Anderson Appliance Corporation is considering a merger with the Vincent Vacuum Company. Vincent is a publicly traded company, and its current beta is 1.30. Vincent has been barely profitable, so it has paid an average of only 20 percent in taxes during the last several years. In addition, it uses little debt, having a debt ratio of just 25 percent.

If the acquisition were made, Anderson would operate Vincent as a separate, wholly owned subsidiary. Anderson would pay taxes on a consolidated basis, and the tax rate would therefore increase to 34 percent. Anderson also would increase the debt capitalization in the Vincent subsidiary to 40 percent of assets, which would increase its beta to 1.50. Anderson's acquisition department estimates that Vincent, if acquired, would produce the following net cash flows to Anderson's shareholders (in millions of dollars):

Year	Net Cash Flows
1	$1.30
2	1.50
3	1.75
4	2.00
5 and beyond	Constant growth at 6%

These cash flows include all acquisition effects. Anderson's cost of equity is 14 percent, its beta is 1.0, and its cost of debt is 10 percent. The risk-free rate is 8 percent.

a. What discount rate should be used to discount the estimated cash flows? (Hint: Use Anderson's k_s to determine the market risk premium.)

b. What is the dollar value of Vincent to Anderson?

c. Vincent has 1.2 million common shares outstanding. What is the maximum price per share that Anderson should offer for Vincent? If the tender offer is accepted at this price, what will happen to Anderson's stock price?

INTEGRATIVE PROBLEM

22-4
Merger analysis

Smitty's Home Repair Company, a regional hardware chain which specializes in "do-it-yourself" materials and equipment rentals, is cash rich because of several consecutive good years. One of the alternative uses for the excess funds is an acquisition. Linda Wade, Smitty's treasurer and your boss, has been asked to place a value on a potential target, Hill's Hardware, a small chain which operates in an adjacent state, and she has enlisted your help.

The following are Wade's estimates of Hill's earnings potential if it came under Smitty's management (in millions of dollars):

	1993	**1994**	**1995**	**1996**
Net sales	$60.0	$90.0	$112.5	$127.5
Cost of goods sold (60%)	36.0	54.0	67.5	76.5
Selling/administrative expense	4.5	6.0	7.5	9.0
Interest expense	3.0	4.5	4.5	6.0
Necessary earnings retentions	0.0	7.5	6.0	4.5

The interest expense listed here includes the interest (1) on Hill's existing debt, (2) on new debt that Smitty's would issue to help finance the acquisition, and (3) on new debt expected to be issued over time to help finance expansion within the new "H division," the code name given to the target firm. The retentions represent earnings that will be reinvested within the H division to help finance its growth.

Hill's Hardware currently uses 40 percent debt financing, and it pays taxes at a 30 percent rate. Security analysts estimate Hill's beta to be 1.2. If the acquisition were to take place, Smitty's would increase Hill's debt ratio to 50 percent, which would increase its beta to 1.3. Further, because Smitty's is highly profitable, taxes on the consolidated firm would be 40 percent. Wade realizes that Hill's Hardware also generates depreciation cash flows, but she believes that these funds would have to be reinvested within the division to replace worn-out equipment.

Wade estimates the risk-free rate to be 9 percent and the market risk premium to be 4 percent. She also estimates that net cash flows after 1996 will grow at a constant rate of 6 percent. Smitty's management is new to the merger game, so Wade has been asked to answer some basic questions about mergers as well as to perform the merger analysis. To structure the task, Wade has developed the following questions, which you must answer and then defend to Smitty's board.

a. Several reasons have been proposed to justify mergers. Among the more prominent are (1) tax considerations, (2) risk reduction, (3) control, (4) purchase of assets at below replacement cost, (5) synergy, and (6) globalization. In general, which of the reasons are economically justifiable? Which are not? Explain.

b. Briefly describe the differences between a hostile merger and a friendly merger.

c. Use the data developed in the table to construct the H division's cash flow statements for 1993 through 1996. Why is interest expense deducted in merger cash flow statements, whereas it is not normally deducted in a capital budgeting cash flow analysis? Why are retentions deducted in the cash flow statement?

d. Conceptually, what is the appropriate discount rate to apply to the cash flows developed in Part c? What is your actual estimate of this discount rate?

e. What is the estimated terminal value of the acquisition; that is, what is the estimated value of the H division's cash flows beyond 1996? What is Hill's value to Smitty's? Suppose another firm were evaluating Hill's as an acquisition candidate. Would they obtain the same value? Explain.

f. Assume that Hill's has 10 million shares outstanding. These shares are traded relatively infrequently, but the last trade, made several weeks ago, was at a price of $9 per share. Should Smitty's make an offer for Hill's? If so, how much should it offer per share?

g. What merger-related activities are undertaken by investment bankers?

Work the problem in this section only if you are using the computer problem diskette.

22-5

Merger analysis

Use the model in the File C22 to work this problem.

a. Refer back to Problem 22-2. Rework the problem assuming that sales in each year were $100,000 higher than the base case amounts and that the cost of goods sold/sales ratio was 60 percent rather than 65 percent. What would be the value of GSC to TransWorld under these assumptions?

b. With sales and the cost of goods sold ratio at the levels specified in Part a, what would be GSC's value if its beta were 1.60, if k_{RF} rose to 9 percent, and if RP_M rose to 5 percent?

c. Leaving all values at their Part b levels, what would be the value of the acquisition if the terminal growth rate rose to 12 percent or dropped to 3 percent?

Multinational Managerial Finance

In the 1960s and 1970s, the major players in international markets were the U.S. multinational corporations such as IBM, which obtained about 20 percent of its revenues from abroad. These giants treated foreign operations as distant appendages for producing products designed and engineered back home. The chain of command and nationality of the company were clear.

Today, however, the situation has changed dramatically. The United States no longer dominates the world economy, and innovation, new technologies, and capital flow in many different directions. The most sophisticated companies are making breakthroughs in foreign labs, obtaining capital from foreign investors, and putting foreign employees on the fast track to the top. Now, dozens of America's top manufacturers, including Dow Chemical, Colgate-Palmolive, Gillette, Hewlett-Packard, and Xerox sell more of their products outside the United States than they do at home. Service firms are not far behind, as Citicorp, Disney, McDonald's, and Time Warner all receive over 20 percent of their revenues from foreign sales.

The trend is even more pronounced in profits. In the past several years, Coca-Cola made more money in both the Pacific and Western Europe than it did in the United States. As companies begin to reap half or more of their sales and profits from abroad, they are blending into the foreign landscape to win acceptance and avoid political hassles. "IBM, to some degree, has successfully lost its American identity," said C. Michael Armstrong, senior vice-president in charge of IBM World Trade Corporation.

This chapter was coauthored by Professor Roy L. Crum of the University of Florida.

At the same time, foreign-based multinationals are arriving on American shores in greater numbers than ever before. Sweden's ABB, the Netherlands' Philips, France's Thomson, and Japan's Fujitsu are all waging campaigns to be identified as American companies that employ Americans, transfer technology to America, and help the U.S. trade balance and overall economic health. Few Americans know, or likely care, that Thomson owns the RCA and General Electric names in consumer electronics and that Philips owns Magnavox.

These new "world companies" raise a host of new questions for governments seeking to shape their nations' economic destinies. For example, does it make any difference what a company's nationality is as long as it provides jobs? What nation controls the technology developed by multinational corporations? What obligations do these companies have to adhere to rules imposed by Washington, Paris, or Tokyo on their foreign operations? And if a U.S. firm makes copiers in Japan and exports them to the United States, should they be counted in the trade deficit in the same way as Toyotas imported from Japan?

Managers of multinational companies face a wide range of issues that are not present when a company operates in a single country. In this chapter, we highlight the key differences between multinational and domestic corporations, and we discuss the impact of these differences on managerial finance for U.S. businesses.

MULTINATIONAL CORPORATIONS

multinational corporation

A firm that operates in two or more countries.

The term **multinational corporation** is used to describe a firm that operates in two or more countries. During the period since World War II, a new and fundamentally different form of international commercial activity has developed, and it has greatly increased worldwide economic and political interdependence. Rather than merely buying resources from foreign concerns, multinational firms now make direct investments in fully integrated operations, with worldwide entities controlling all phases of the production process—from extraction of raw materials, through the manufacturing process, to distribution to consumers throughout the world. Today, multinational corporate networks control a large and growing share of the world's technological, marketing, and productive resources.

Companies, both U.S. and foreign, go "international" for five primary reasons.

1. **To seek new markets.** After a company has saturated its home market, growth opportunities are often better in foreign markets. Thus, such home-grown firms as Coca-Cola and McDonald's have aggressively expanded into

overseas markets, and foreign firms such as Sony and Toshiba now dominate the U.S. consumer electronics market.

2. **To seek raw materials.** It is not surprising that many U.S. oil companies, such as Exxon, have major subsidiaries around the world to insure access to the basic resources needed to sustain the company's primary business line.

3. **To seek new technology.** No single nation holds a commanding advantage in all technologies, so companies are scouring the globe for leading scientific and design ideas. For example, Xerox has introduced over 80 different office copiers in the United States that were engineered and built by its Japanese joint venture, Fuji Xerox. Similarly, versions of the superconcentrated detergent that Procter & Gamble first formulated in Japan in response to a rival's product are now being marketed under the Ariel name in Europe and tested under the Cheer and Tide labels in the United States.

4. **To seek production efficiency.** Companies in high production cost countries are shifting production to low-cost countries. For example, GE has production and assembly plants in Mexico, South Korea, and Singapore, and even Japanese manufacturers are shifting some of their production to lower cost countries in the Pacific rim. The ability to shift production from country to country has important implications for labor costs in all countries. For example, when Xerox threatened to move its copier rebuilding work to Mexico, its union in Rochester, New York, agreed to work rule and productivity improvements that kept the operation in the United States. Some multinational companies make almost daily decisions on where to shift production. When Dow Chemical saw European demand for a certain solvent declining, the company scaled back production at a German plant and shifted it to another chemical which had previously been imported from the United States. Relying on complex computer models for making such decisions, Dow runs its plants at higher capacity and thus keeps capital costs down.

5. **To avoid political and regulatory hurdles.** The primary reason for Japanese auto companies to move production to the United States was to get around U.S. import quotas. Now, Honda, Nissan, Toyota, Mazda, and Mitsubishi are all assembling automobiles or trucks in the United States. One of the factors that prompted U.S. pharmaceutical maker SmithKline and Britain's Beecham to merge was that they wanted to avoid licensing and regulatory delays in their largest markets, Western Europe and the United States. Now, SmithKline Beecham can identify itself as an inside player in both Europe and the United States. Finally, when Germany's BASF launched biotechnology research at home, it confronted legal and political challenges from the environmentally conscious Green movement. Recently, BASF shifted its cancer and immune system research to two laboratories in Boston suburbs. This location is attractive not only because of its large number of engineers and scientists but also because the Boston area has better resolved controversies involving safety, animal rights, and the environment. "We decided it would be better to have the laboratories located where we have fewer insecurities about what will happen in the future," said Rolf-Dieter Acker, BASF's director of biotechnology research.

The past decade has seen an increasing amount of investment in the United States by foreign corporations. This "reverse" investment, which is of increasing concern to U.S. government officials, has actually been growing at a higher rate in the past few years than has U.S. investment abroad. These trends are important because of their implications for eroding the traditional doctrine of independence and self-reliance that has always been a hallmark of U.S. policy. Just as U.S. corporations with extensive overseas operations are said to use their economic power to exert substantial economic and political influence over host governments in many parts of the world, it is feared that foreign corporations are gaining similar sway over U.S. policy. However, these developments suggest an increasing degree of mutual influence and interdependence among business enterprises and nations, to which the United States is not immune.

In the past several years, some dramatic international changes have taken place, including the breakup, both politically and economically, of the former Soviet Union, the collapse of communism in many Eastern European countries, and the reunification of Germany. Future events will include the establishment of the European Economic Community with one Eurocurrency and the determination of how to help the cash-starved Eastern Bloc nations. Also, there has been a war with Iraq and continuing turbulence in the Middle East. These events, and others which will surely occur, will have an impact on the world economy.

Significant issues were discussed at the July 1991 Economic Summit, held in London. The "Group of Seven" (United States, Japan, Great Britain, France, Italy, Canada, and West Germany) discussed the major changes in East-West relations taking place, as well as ways to help improve the economies of the countries that emerged from the breakup of the former Soviet Union. (The new alliance formed by these countries often is referred to as the Commonwealth of Independent States.) Of critical importance were the discussions of how to prepare for this "new world order" where trade, rather than politics, will define relationships among nations.

? *Self-Test Questions*

What is a multinational corporation?

Why do companies "go international"?

MULTINATIONAL VERSUS DOMESTIC MANAGERIAL FINANCE

In theory, the concepts and procedures discussed in the first 22 chapters of the text are valid for both domestic and multinational operations. However, several problems uniquely associated with the international environment increase the complexity of the manager's task in a multinational corporation, and they often force the manager to alter the way alternative courses of action are evaluated and compared. Six major factors distinguish managerial finance as practiced by firms operating entirely within a single country from management by firms that operate in several different countries:

1. **Different currency denominations.** Cash flows in various parts of a multinational corporate system will be denominated in different currencies. Hence, an analysis of exchange rates, and the effects of fluctuating currency values, must be included in all financial analyses.

2. **Economic and legal ramifications.** Each country in which the firm operates will have its own unique political and economic institutions, and institutional differences among countries can cause significant problems when the corporation tries to coordinate and control the worldwide operations of its subsidiaries. For example, differences in tax laws among countries can cause a given economic transaction to have strikingly dissimilar after-tax consequences, depending on where the transaction occurred. Similarly, differences in legal systems of host nations, such as the Common Law of Great Britain versus the French Civil Law, complicate many matters, from the simple recording of a business transaction to the role played by the judiciary in resolving conflicts. Such differences can restrict multinational corporations' flexibility to deploy resources as they wish, and can even make procedures illegal in one part of the company that are required in another part. These differences also make it difficult for executives trained in one country to operate effectively in another.

3. **Language differences.** The ability to communicate is critical in all business transactions, and here U.S. citizens are often at a disadvantage because we are generally fluent only in English, while European and Japanese businesspeople are usually fluent in several languages, including English. Thus, they can invade our markets more easily than we can penetrate theirs. The importance of this factor cannot be stressed too strongly.

4. **Cultural differences.** Even within geographic regions that have long been considered relatively homogeneous, different countries have unique cultural heritages that shape values and influence the role of business in the society. Multinational corporations find that such matters as defining the appropriate goals of the firm, attitudes toward risk taking, dealings with employees, the ability to curtail unprofitable operations, and so on, can vary dramatically from one country to the next.

5. **Role of governments.** Most traditional models in finance assume the existence of a competitive marketplace in which the terms of trade are determined by the participants. The government, through its power to establish basic ground rules, is involved in this process, but its participation is minimal. Thus, the market provides both the primary barometer of success and the indicator of the actions that must be taken to remain competitive. This view of the process is reasonably correct for the United States and a few other major Western industrialized nations, but it does not accurately describe the situation in most of the world. Frequently, the terms under which companies compete, the actions that must be taken or avoided, and the terms of trade on various transactions are determined not in the marketplace, but by direct negotiation between the host government and the multinational corporation. This is essentially a political process, and it must be treated as such. Thus, our traditional financial models have to be recast to include political and other noneconomic facets of the decision.

INDUSTRY PRACTICE   Learning a New Vocabulary

Does your vocabulary include the word "globality"? How about "glocalism"? If neither word sounds familiar, you may be thinking "globaloney" and hoping the newspeak will somehow "glo" away. This, however, is unlikely. Many major companies realize that their very survival depends on their ability to see that "all the world is a stage" and to understand the "script" so well that they can "quickly step into the roles" that new opportunities offer them.

Currently, the traditional "triad" — the major markets of North America, Western Europe, and Japan — retains its world dominance. With only 15 percent of the world's population, the triad accounts for more than 50 percent of world output. Eastern Europe and the Third World countries of Indonesia, Mexico, Korea, and India are quickly growing, however, and together, the newly liberated countries of Hungary, Czechoslovakia, and what was once East Germany have a higher gross national product (GNP) than does China. With their well-trained and low-paid workers ready to enter the European Community market, they could be Europe's challengers to the Asian giants.

Indonesia is eagerly seeking foreign investors, making life easier for foreigners by cutting out 67 percent of the previously required paperwork. The government of this fifth-most-populous nation approved more than $4 billion in new projects in 1988 and 1989. Mexico had only one-third as many state-owned industries in 1990 as it did in 1984, and it is also welcoming foreign corporations. India, where the government has loosened its grip on the economy, has 150,000,000 middle-class citizens shopping for consumer products, plus millions of additional poorer people.

One U.S. product that is popular around the world is soft drinks. PepsiCo has 70 bottling franchises in Eastern Europe alone, and its management thinks sales there can increase by another 50 percent by 1995.

Capital goods should also find a ready global market since developing countries need new roads, bridges, electrical and telephone systems, and agricultural equipment. Many of these countries also need these goods to replace the infrastructure that is wearing out. The possibilities for worldwide sales of fiber-optic cable have impressed Corning Chairman James R. Houghton: "It's the only technology I know of that's even better for a developing country than for a developed one — because in a developing country you have no old copper to rip out."

Service industries may have even better opportunities, as evidenced by American Express, whose travel-related business in Eastern Europe rose 20 percent in 1989. American Express practices so-called "glocalism" — making global decisions on strategic questions about products, capital, and research, but letting local units decide tactical questions about packaging, marketing, and advertising. It hires local agencies to create ads for specific countries, even sometimes for specific cities, and this tactic has appealed to varying cultures so successfully that American Express's foreign customers provide 31 percent more revenue per card than its U.S. customers. As central planning gives way to capitalism in the Eastern Bloc, other opportunities are presenting themselves. A Washington consultant said, "With more investment in retail and wholesale trade, large improvements in efficiency — and consequently in profits — could be made."

If companies are profitable and growing already in their home areas, why should they take the difficult road to globalism? Says a Wharton School of Business professor, "Domestic markets have become too small. Even the biggest companies in the biggest countries cannot survive on their domestic markets if they are in global industries. They have to be in all major markets." A Wharton colleague identified 136 industries that must be world-class, including accounting, automobile manufacturing, banking, consumer electronics, entertainment, pharmaceuticals, publishing, travel services, and making washing machines.

Though no company is truly global yet, many have made huge strides in that direction. The key, say experts, is to visualize the world as a single market. Managers must set aside nationalism and go wherever necessary to raise capital, make products, buy supplies, and operate their headquarters. In a world without walls, a company without a country has an undeniable edge.

Another requirement for global success is to organize according to product lines rather than geography. Said one CEO, "For some products, you may find you need a plant on every continent, but not in every country." In global competition, market share is more important than short-term profits. When U.S. companies relied primarily on their large home markets, they could afford to be wary of foreign investment. Today, says the business dean at Columbia University, "When we walk away from a market, we're creating an opportunity for a European or Japanese company

—and they then use that muscle to come into *our* market."

Global managers also have to think "alliance." Combining one company's product with another's distribution system, for instance, could bring new opportunities to both. Making alliances is often quicker than expanding a business overseas and cheaper than buying a new one.

The corporation that may be closest to the global ideal is Imperial Chemical Industries (ICI), formerly of Great Britain, with 49 major operations scattered from Canada to Argentina, Scotland to South Africa, and Malaysia to New Zealand. Some of the units are factories, some are division headquarters, and some are research and development centers. ICI began going global in 1983, when it abandoned country-by-country organizations. The giant firm has annual sales of $21 billion in film, pharmaceuticals, explosives, agricultural chemicals, and other products. In moving toward globalization, ICI's management had to be tough. For example, 10,000 manufacturing jobs were abolished in Britain alone. "It's hard on people who have built national empires and [who] now don't have such freedom," says American Hugh Miller, head of ICI's advanced materials and electronics group, "We are asking people to be less nationalistic and more concerned with what happens outside their country." The advantage, says Miller, is better decision making. "Before, each territory would work up projects and you'd have warring factions competing in London for the same

money. Now, with one person responsible for a global product line, it becomes immaterial where a project is located. The profits will be the same. When you start operating in this manner, it takes a lot of steam out of the defense of fiefdoms."

ICI also has an international board of directors— 2 are Americans, 1 is Canadian, 1 is Japanese, 1 is German, and 11 are British. More than one-third of the company's 180 top executives are not British. Regardless of their nationalities, they may be assigned to work anywhere in the world.

One of the greatest hardships involved in going global is the ideal of giving up preference for one's own nation and compatriots in making business and residency decisions. This does not always come easily —especially when workers in the home country must be laid off and factories must be closed to relocate production elsewhere. Aside from unhappiness among its people, companies attempting to become global also risk difficulty in overcoming the barriers in other countries of entrenched bureaucracies, hyperinflation, and currency exchange rates. Most knowledgeable observers, however, agree that the biggest risk lies in not being ready to move quickly as global opportunities arise.

Sources: Jeremy Main, "How to Go Global—and Why," *Fortune,* August 28, 1989, and "How to Manage in the New Era," *Fortune,* January 15, 1990.

6. **Political risk.** The distinguishing characteristic of a nation that differentiates it from a multinational corporation is that the nation exercises sovereignty over the people and property in its territory. Hence, a nation is free to place constraints on the transfer of corporate resources and even to expropriate the assets of a firm without compensation. This is *political risk,* and it tends to be largely a given rather than a variable that can be changed by negotiation. Political risk varies from country to country, and it must be addressed explicitly in any financial analysis. Another aspect of political risk is terrorism against U.S. firms or executives abroad. For example, U.S. executives have been captured and held for ransom in several South American countries.

These six factors complicate managerial finance within multinational firms, and they increase the risks faced by the firms involved. However, prospects for high profits often make it worthwhile for firms to accept these risks, and to learn how to minimize or at least live with them.

Self-Test Question

Identify and briefly explain six major factors that complicate managerial finance within multinational firms.

EXCHANGE RATES

exchange rate

The number of units of a given currency that can be purchased for one unit of another currency.

An **exchange rate** specifies the number of units of a given currency that can be purchased for one unit of another currency. Exchange rates appear in the financial sections of newspapers each day. Selected rates from the April 21, 1992, issue of *The Wall Street Journal* are given in Table 23-1. The values shown in Column 1 are the number of U.S. dollars required to purchase one unit of foreign currency on April 20, 1992; this is called a *direct quotation*. Thus, the direct U.S. dollar quotation on April 20, 1992, for the German mark is $0.6006 because one German mark could be bought for 60.06 cents. The exchange rates given in Column 2 represent the number of units of foreign currency that can be purchased for one U.S. dollar; these are called *indirect quotations*. The indirect quotation for the German mark is DM1.6650. (The "DM" stands for *deutsche mark*; it is equivalent to the symbol "$.") Normal practice in the United States is to use indirect quotations (Column 2) for all currencies other than British pounds, for which direct quotations are given. Thus, we speak of the pound as "selling at $1.75" but of the German mark as "being at 1.67."

It is also a universal convention on the world's foreign currency exchanges to state all exchange rates except British pounds on a "dollar basis" — that is, as the foreign currency price of one U.S. dollar as reported in Table 23-1, Column 2. Thus, in all currency trading centers, whether in New York, Frankfurt, London, Tokyo, or anywhere else, the exchange rate for the German mark on April 20, 1992, would be displayed as DM1.6650. This convention eliminates confusion when comparing quotations from one trading center with those from another.

We can use the rates in Table 23-1 to show how one figures exchange rates. Suppose a U.S. tourist on holiday flies from New York to London, then to Paris, then on to Munich, and finally back to New York. When she arrives at London's Heathrow Airport on April 20, 1992, she goes to the bank to check the foreign exchange listing. The rate she observes for U.S. dollars is $1.7515; this means that 1 pound will cost her $1.7515. Assume that she exchanges $2,000 for $2,000/$1.7515 = £1,141.88 and enjoys a week's vacation in London, spending £641.88 while there.

At the end of the week she travels to Dover to catch the Hovercraft to Calais on the coast of France and realizes that she needs to exchange her 500 remaining British pounds for French francs. However, what she sees on the board is the direct quotation between pounds and dollars ($1.7515) and the indirect quotation between francs and dollars (FF5.6275). (For our purposes, we assume that the exchange rates in effect on April 20 remain in effect throughout our example. This is very unrealistic for reasons explained later in

Table 23-1   ▪   **Illustrative Exchange Rates, April 20, 1992**

	Direct Quotation: U.S. Dollars Required to Buy One Unit of Foreign Currency (1)	Indirect Quotation: Number of Units of Foreign Currency per U.S. Dollar (2)
British pound	$1.7515	0.5709
Canadian dollar	0.8464	1.1815
Dutch guilder	0.5336	1.8742
French franc	0.17770	5.6275
German mark	0.6006	1.6650
Greek drachma	0.005141	194.50
Indian rupee	0.03493	28.63
Italian lira	0.0007991	1,251.35
Japanese yen	0.007450	134.23
Mexican peso	0.0003265	3,062.51
Norwegian krone	0.1535	6.5155
Saudi Arabian riyal	0.26738	3.7400
Singaporean dollar	0.6033	1.6575
South African rand	0.2976	3.3602
Spanish peseta	0.009562	104.58
Swedish krona	0.1662	6.0180
Swiss franc	0.6506	1.5370

Note: Column 2 equals 1.0 divided by Column 1. However, rounding differences do occur.

Source: *The Wall Street Journal*, April 21, 1992.

this chapter.) The exchange rate between pounds and francs is called a *cross rate,* and it is computed as follows:

$$\text{Cross rate} = \frac{\text{Dollars}}{\text{Pound}} \times \frac{\text{Francs}}{\text{Dollar}} = \frac{\text{Francs}}{\text{Pound}}$$

$$= \$1.7515 \text{ per pound} \times 5.6275 \text{ francs per dollar}$$

$$= 9.8566 \text{ francs per pound.}$$

Therefore, for every British pound she would receive 9.8566 French francs, so she would receive $9.8566 \times 500 = 4{,}928.30 \approx 4{,}928$ francs.

When she finishes touring in France and arrives in Germany, the American tourist again needs to determine a cross rate, this time between French francs and German marks. The dollar-basis quotes she sees, as shown in Table 23-1, are FF5.6275 per dollar and DM1.6650 per dollar. To find the cross rate, she must divide the two dollar-basis rates:

$$\text{Cross rate} = \frac{\dfrac{\text{Marks}}{\text{Dollar}}}{\dfrac{\text{Francs}}{\text{Dollar}}} = \frac{\text{Marks}}{\text{Franc}}$$

$$= \frac{\text{DM1.6650 per } \$}{\text{FF5.6275 per } \$} = \text{DM0.2959 marks per franc.}$$

Then, if she had FF3,000 remaining, she could exchange them for 0.2959 × 3,000 = DM887.70, or about 888 marks.

Finally, when her vacation ends and she returns to New York, the quotation she sees is DM1.6650, which tells her that she can buy 1.6650 marks for a dollar. She now holds 50 marks, so she wants to know how many U.S. dollars she will receive for her marks. First, she must find the reciprocal of the quoted indirect rate,

$$\frac{1}{DM1.6650} = \$0.6006,$$

which is the direct quote shown in Table 23-1, Column 1. Then she will end up with

$$\$0.6006 \times 50 = \$30.03.$$

In this example, we made two very strong and generally incorrect assumptions. First, we assumed that our traveler had to calculate the appropriate cross rates. For retail transactions, it is customary to display the cross rates directly instead of a series of dollar rates. Second, we assumed that exchange rates remain constant over time. Actually, exchange rates vary every day, often dramatically. We will have more to say about exchange rate fluctuations in the next section.

 Self-Test Questions

What is an exchange rate?

Explain the difference between direct and indirect quotations.

What is a cross rate?

THE INTERNATIONAL MONETARY SYSTEM

fixed exchange rate system

The world monetary system in existence after World War II until 1971, under which the value of the U.S. dollar was tied to gold, and the values of the other currencies were pegged to the U.S. dollar.

From the end of World War II until August 1971, the world was on a **fixed exchange rate system** administered by the International Monetary Fund (IMF). Under this system the U.S. dollar was linked to gold ($35 per ounce), and other currencies were then tied to the dollar. Exchange rates between other currencies and the dollar were controlled within narrow limits but then adjusted periodically. For example, in 1964 the British pound was adjusted to $2.80 for 1 pound, with a 1 percent permissible fluctuation about this rate.

Fluctuations in exchange rates occur because of changes in the supply of and demand for dollars, pounds, and other currencies. These supply and demand changes have two primary sources. First, changes in the demand for currencies depend on changes in imports and exports of goods and services. For example, U.S. importers must buy British pounds to pay for British goods, whereas British importers must buy U.S. dollars to pay for U.S. goods. If U.S. imports from Great Britain exceeded U.S. exports to Great Britain, there would be a greater demand for pounds than for dollars; this would drive up the price of the pound relative to that of the dollar. In terms of Table 23-1, the dollar cost of a pound might rise from $1.7515 to $2.0000. The U.S. dollar would be

deficit trade balance

The situation where a country imports more than it exports.

said to be *depreciating,* whereas the pound would be *appreciating.* In this example, the primary cause of the change would be the U.S. **deficit trade balance** with Great Britain. Of course, if U.S. exports to Great Britain were greater than U.S. imports from Great Britain, Great Britain would have a deficit trade balance with the United States.[1]

Changes in the demand for a currency, and hence exchange rate fluctuations, also depend on capital movements. For example, suppose interest rates in Great Britain were higher than those in the United States. To take advantage of the high British interest rates, U.S. banks, corporations, and even sophisticated individuals could buy pounds with dollars and then use those pounds to purchase high-yielding British securities. These purchases would tend to drive up the price of pounds.[2]

Before August 1971 exchange rate fluctuations were kept within the narrow 1 percent limit by regular intervention of the British government in the market. When the value of the pound was falling, the Bank of England would step in and buy pounds, offering gold or foreign currencies in exchange. These government purchases would push up the pound rate. Conversely, when the pound rate was too high, the Bank of England would sell pounds. The central banks of other countries operated similarly.

devaluation

The process of officially reducing the value of a country's currency relative to other currencies.

Of course, a central bank's ability to control its exchange rate was limited by its supply of gold and foreign currencies. With the approval of the IMF, a country could **devalue** its currency — which means to officially lower its value relative to other currencies — if it experienced persistent difficulty over a long period in preventing its exchange rate from falling below the lower limit, and if its central bank was running out of the gold and other currencies that could be used to buy its own currency and thus prop up its price. For just these reasons the British pound was devalued from $2.80 per pound to $2.50 per pound in 1967. This lowered the price of British goods in the United States and elsewhere and raised the prices of foreign goods in Britain, thus stopping the British deficit trade balance that had been putting pressure on the pound in the first place.

---

[1] If the dollar value of the pound moved up from $1.7515 to $2.00, this increase in the value of the pound would mean that British goods would now be more expensive in the U.S. market. For example, a box of candy costing 1 pound in England would rise in price in the United States from $1.7515 to $2.00. Conversely, U.S. goods would become cheaper in England. For example, the British could now buy goods worth $2.00 for 1 pound, whereas before the exchange rate change, 1 pound would buy merchandise worth only $1.7515. These price changes would, of course, tend to *reduce* British exports and *increase* imports, and this, in turn, would lower the exchange rate, because people in the United States and other nations would be buying fewer pounds to pay for English goods. However, before 1971 the 1 percent limit severely constrained the market's ability to reach an equilibrium between trade balances and exchange rates.

[2] Such capital inflows would also tend to drive down British interest rates. If rates were high in the first place because of efforts by the British monetary authorities to curb inflation, the international currency flows would tend to thwart that effort. This is one of the reasons why domestic and international economics are so closely linked.

A good example of this occurred during the summer of 1981. In an effort to curb inflation, the Federal Reserve Board helped push U.S. interest rates to record levels. This, in turn, caused an outflow of capital from European nations to the United States. The Europeans were suffering from a severe recession and wanted to keep interest rates down in order to stimulate investment, but U.S. policy made this difficult because of international capital flows.

revaluation

The process of officially increasing the value of a country's currency relative to other currencies.

Conversely, a nation with an export surplus and a strong currency might **revalue** its currency upward, as West Germany did twice in the 1960s.

Devaluations and revaluations occurred only rarely before 1971. They were usually accompanied by severe international financial repercussions, partly because nations tended to postpone these needed measures until economic pressures had built up to explosive proportions. For this and other reasons the old international monetary system came to a dramatic end in the early 1970s, when the U.S. dollar, the foundation upon which all other currencies were anchored, was cut loose from the gold standard and, in effect, allowed to "float."

floating exchange rates

The system whereby exchange rates are for the most part not fixed by government policy but are allowed to float up or down in accordance with supply and demand.

The United States and the other major nations currently operate under a system of **floating exchange rates,** whereby currency prices are allowed to seek their own levels without much governmental intervention. The central bank of each country does still intervene in the foreign exchange market, buying and selling its currency to smooth out exchange rate fluctuations to some extent, and there have been agreements by groups of countries to keep the relative values of their currencies within a predetermined range. Such an agreement by the "Group of Seven" at the Seoul Economic Summit in October 1985 caused the U.S. dollar to fall substantially against most major currencies. This action was endorsed as appropriate at the Washington Economic Summit in September 1987. The "Group of Seven" was also responsible for helping to stabilize the falling dollar in early 1988.

Each central bank also tries to keep its average exchange rate at a level deemed desirable by its government's economic policy. This is important because exchange rates have a profound effect on the levels of imports and exports, which in turn influence the level of domestic employment. For example, if a country is having a problem with unemployment, its central bank might encourage a *decline* in the value of its currency. This would cause its goods to be cheaper in world markets and thus stimulate exports, production, and domestic employment. Conversely, the central bank of a country that is operating at full capacity and experiencing inflation might try to raise the value of its currency to reduce exports and increase imports. Under the current floating rate system, however, such intervention can affect the situation only temporarily, because market forces will prevail in the long run.

Figure 23-1 shows how the values of German marks and Japanese yen moved in comparison with the dollar from 1981 to 1991. The dollar strengthened, or appreciated, against the mark from 1981 to 1985 but then weakened, or depreciated, from 1985 to 1990, with slight reversals in 1989 and 1991. The Japanese yen was relatively stable against the dollar in the first half of the decade, but then it appreciated from 1985 to 1988 (fewer yen were required to buy a dollar), depreciated during the last two years of the decade, and then appreciated again in 1991.

Exchange rate fluctuations can have a profound impact on international monetary transactions. For example, in 1985 it cost Honda Motors 2,380,000 yen to build a particular model in Japan and ship it to the United States. The model carried a U.S. sticker price of $12,000. Since the $12,000 sales price was the equivalent of (238 yen per dollar)($12,000) = 2,856,000 yen, the automaker had built a 20 percent markup into the U.S. sales price. However, three years later, the dollar had depreciated to 128 yen. Now, if the model still sold for $12,000, the yen return to Honda would be only (128 yen per dol-

Figure 23-1 ▪ Yen and Mark Exchange Rates

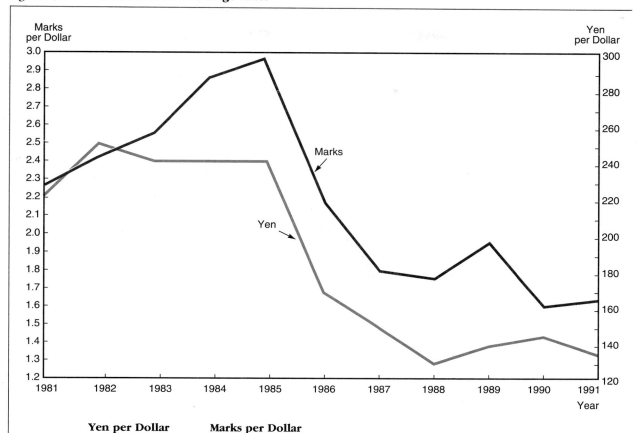

	Yen per Dollar	Marks per Dollar
1981	221	2.26
1982	249	2.43
1983	238	2.55
1984	237	2.85
1985	238	2.94
1986	168	2.17
1987	145	1.80
1988	128	1.76
1989	138	1.88
1990	145	1.62
1991	135	1.66

Note: The exchange rates listed above are annual averages.

lar)($12,000) = 1,536,000 yen, and the automaker would be losing about 35 percent on each auto sold. Even though U.S. prices held firm, the 46 percent depreciation of the dollar against the yen turned a healthy profit into a loss. In fact, for Honda to maintain its 20 percent markup, the model would have to sell in the United States for 2,856,000 yen/128 yen per dollar = $22,312.50. No wonder Honda now builds its most popular model, the Accord, in Marysville, Ohio!

You might be thinking that it takes years for major fluctuations in exchange rates to occur. However, major changes can occur in much shorter periods. Suppose, on January 1, 1986, a German investor wanted to take advantage of the comparatively high interest rates on U.S. Treasury securities, so he bought a 6-month T-Bill for $9,700 that would be worth $10,000 at the end of June. This works out to about a 6 percent annual return. In January, the exchange rate was 2.44 marks per dollar, so the T-bill cost the investor 2.44($9,700) = 23,668 marks. At the end of June, the exchange rate was only 2.23 marks per dollar, so the investor's mark return was 2.23($10,000) = 22,300 marks. Thus, exchange rate fluctuations turned the 6 percent expected return into a loss of about 12 percent.

The inherent volatility of exchange rates under a floating system increases the uncertainty of the cash flows for a multinational corporation. Because these cash flows are generated in many parts of the world, they are denominated in many different currencies. Since exchange rates change, the dollar-equivalent value of the consolidated cash flows can fluctuate. This is known as **exchange rate risk,** and it is a major factor differentiating the multinational corporation from a purely domestic one. However, there are numerous ways for a multinational corporation to manage and limit its exchange rate risk, and several of them are discussed in the next section.

Before closing our discussion of the international monetary system, we should note that not all currencies are **convertible.** A currency is convertible when the issuing nation allows it to be traded in the currency markets and is willing to redeem the currency at market rates. This means that, except for limited central bank influence, the issuing government loses control over the value of its currency. Lack of convertibility creates major problems for international trade.

For example, consider the situation faced by Pepsico when it wanted to open a chain of Pizza Hut restaurants in the Soviet Union. The Russian ruble was not convertible, so Pepsico could not take the profits from its restaurants out of the Soviet Union in the form of rubles. If it took rubles out, no mechanism existed to exchange the rubles for dollars, so the investment in the Soviet Union seemingly was worthless to a U.S. company. But, Pepsico arranged to use the ruble profits from the restaurants to buy Russian vodka, which it then shipped to the United States and sold. The profits on the vodka sales, which were in dollars, contained the profits from the Russian restaurants, as well as any added profits made on the vodka import business.

exchange rate risk
The risk that the value of a cash flow will decline due to a change in exchange rates.

convertible currency
A currency that may be readily exchanged for other currencies.

? Self-Test Questions

What is the difference between a fixed exchange rate system and a floating rate system? Which system is better? Explain.

What does it mean to say that the dollar is depreciating with respect to the British pound? For a U.S. consumer of British goods, would this be good or bad? How could consumption changes arrest the decline of the dollar?

What is a convertible currency?

TRADING IN FOREIGN EXCHANGE

Importers, exporters, and tourists, as well as governments, buy and sell currencies in the foreign exchange market. For example, when a U.S. trader imports automobiles from Germany, payment will probably be made in German marks. The importer buys marks (through its bank) in the foreign exchange market, much as one buys common stocks on the New York Stock Exchange or pork bellies on the Chicago Mercantile Exchange. However, whereas stock and commodity exchanges have organized trading floors, the foreign exchange market consists of a network of brokers and banks based in New York, London, Tokyo, and other financial centers. Most buy-and-sell orders are conducted by computer and telephone.[3]

Spot Rates and Forward Rates

spot rate

The effective exchange rate for a foreign currency for delivery on (approximately) the current day.

forward exchange rate

An agreed-upon price at which two currencies will be exchanged at some future date.

The exchange rates shown earlier in Table 23-1 are known as **spot rates,** which means the rate paid for delivery of the currency "on the spot" or, in reality, two days after the day of the trade. For most of the world's major currencies, it is also possible to buy (or sell) currencies for delivery at some agreed-upon future date, usually 30, 90, or 180 days from the day the transaction is negotiated. This rate is known as the **forward exchange rate.** For example, if a U.S. firm must make payment to a Swiss firm in 90 days, as Table 23-2 shows, the U.S. firm's treasurer can buy Swiss francs today for delivery in 90 days, paying the 90-day forward rate of $0.6433 per Swiss franc (which equals 1.5546 SF per dollar). Forward rates are exactly analogous to futures prices on commodity exchanges, where contracts are drawn up for wheat or corn to be delivered at agreed-upon prices at some future date. The contract is signed today, and the dollar cost of the Swiss francs is then known with certainty. Purchase of a forward contract is one technique for eliminating the volatility of future cash flows caused by fluctuations in exchange rates. This technique, which is called "hedging," will be discussed in more detail shortly.

discount on forward rate

The situation when the spot rate is less than the forward rate.

premium on forward rate

The situation when the spot rate is greater than the forward rate.

Forward rates for 30-, 90-, and 180-day delivery, along with the spot rates for April 20, 1992, for the more commonly traded currencies are given in Table 23-2. If one can obtain *more* of the foreign currency for a dollar in the forward than in the spot market, the forward currency is less valuable than the spot currency, and the forward currency is said to be selling at a **discount.** Thus, because 1 dollar could buy 0.5709 British pounds in the spot market but 0.5880 pounds in the 180-day forward market, forward pounds sell at a discount as compared with spot pounds. Conversely, if a dollar would buy *fewer* units of a currency in the forward than in the spot market, the forward currency is worth more dollars than the spot currency, and the forward currency is said to be selling at a **premium.** We see in Table 23-2 that on April 20, 1992, all the listed currencies were selling at a discount.

If the dollar is expected to *appreciate* against a particular foreign currency, then in the future $1 should buy *more* units of the foreign currency, and in that

[3]For a more detailed explanation of exchange rate determination and operations of the foreign exchange market, see Steven Bell and Bryan Kettell, *Foreign Exchange Handbook* (Westport, Conn.: Quorum Books, 1983).

Table 23-2   ▪   **Selected Spot and Forward Exchange Rates, April 20, 1992**
(Number of Units of Foreign Currency per U.S. Dollar)

| | | Forward Rates | | | Forward Rate at a |
	Spot Rate	30 Days	90 Days	180 Days	Premium or Discount
British pound	0.5709	0.5740	0.5798	0.5880	Discount
French franc	5.6275	5.6553	5.7112	5.7905	Discount
Japanese yen	134.23	134.26	134.41	134.46	Discount
Swiss franc	1.5370	1.5431	1.5546	1.5703	Discount
German mark	1.6650	1.6729	1.6884	1.7103	Discount

Notes:

a. These are representative quotes as provided by a sample of New York banks. Forward rates for other currencies and for other lengths of time can often be negotiated.

b. When it takes more units of a foreign currency to buy one dollar in the future, the value of the foreign currency is less in the forward market than in the spot market. Thus, the forward rate is at a *discount* to the spot rate.

Source: *The Wall Street Journal,* April 21,1992.

case, the forward rate will sell at a *discount* to the spot rate. Thus, based on Table 23-2, in April 1992, the dollar was expected to appreciate against the British, French, Japanese, Swiss, and German currencies. These expectations, in turn, were influenced by trade balances, relative interest rates, and all the other factors which lead to changing exchange rates.

Hedging in the Foreign Exchange Markets

hedging exchange rate exposure

The process whereby a firm protects itself against loss due to future exchange rate fluctuations.

Individuals and corporations can buy or sell forward currencies as a means of **hedging exchange rate exposure.** For example, suppose that on April 20, 1992, a U.S. firm buys televisions from a Japanese manufacturer for 100 million Japanese yen. Payment is to be made in Japanese yen 90 days after the goods are shipped, or on July 19, so the Japanese firm is extending trade credit for 90 days. The U.S. company is apprehensive that the dollar will depreciate relative to the Japanese yen because of large trade deficits. If the Japanese yen appreciates rapidly, more dollars will be required to buy the 100 million yen, and the profits on the television sets will be lost. Still, the U.S. firm does not want to forgo 90 days of free trade credit by paying cash. It can take the trade credit and protect itself by purchasing 100 million Japanese yen for delivery in 90 days. The 90-day rate is 134.41 yen, so the dollar cost is 100,000,000/134.41 = $743,992. When payment comes due on July 19, 1992, regardless of the spot rate on that day, the U.S. firm can obtain the needed Japanese yen at the agreed-upon price of $743,992. The U.S. firm is said to have *covered* its trade payables with a *forward market hedge.*

Note that it would cost the firm 100,000,000/134.23 = $744,990 to buy the yen on the spot market on April 20, and, since the forward contract is selling at a discount, the firm will save $744,990 − $743,992 = $998 by buying the forward contract. Thus, the firm not only reduces risk, but also saves money over the spot price. However, there are costs involved in the hedging transaction. First, there are commissions that must be paid to purchase the forward contract. Second, if the yen weakens against the dollar over the next 90 days, the firm would have been better off had it waited and bought the yen in the spot market when the payment becomes due.

The forward market permits multinational firms to transfer exchange rate risk to professional risk takers, for a price. Forward contracts can be written in any amount, for any length of time, and between any two currencies as long as the two parties to the contract are in agreement. Some forward contracts are entered into directly by individuals or firms without going through an intermediary. Usually, however, forward contracts are negotiated between banks and their clients and are tailored to the specific needs of the client.

To supplement forward contracts, which tend to be specialized, the Chicago Mercantile Exchange opened its International Monetary Market (IMM) currency futures market in 1972. The IMM currently offers contracts on the British pound, Canadian dollar, German mark, Japanese yen, Swiss franc, and Australian dollar. Because an organized market exists for futures contracts, they can be executed more rapidly than forward contracts can be negotiated. However, futures contracts are limited to a few currencies, and only a limited number of fixed maturity dates are available.

Firms engaged in international trade can hedge with futures or with forward contracts. When used for hedging purposes, both instruments produce the same end result, even though each differs with respect to when the profit or loss associated with the contract is recognized. With a futures contract, the profit or loss is recognized daily (called marking to the market), while the profit or loss associated with a forward contract is not recognized until the actual delivery date (the end of the contract). If the purpose is to hedge, both the futures and the forward contracts will have the same profit or loss at the date the required currency is delivered, and that profit or loss will be sufficient to offset the change in exchange rates that might have occurred during the contract period. Currently, dollar volume in the forward market exceeds volume in the futures market for foreign exchange because most large contracts take place in the forward market. However, more and more small firms that do not have transactions large enough for the forward market are now using the currency futures market to reduce exchange rate risk.

Self-Test Questions

Differentiate between spot and forward exchange rates.

Briefly explain what it means for a forward currency to sell at a discount, or at a premium.

What does "hedging exchange rate exposure" mean? Explain why a firm might wish to do this and how it might be done.

INFLATION, INTEREST RATES, AND EXCHANGE RATES

Relative inflation rates, or the rates of inflation in foreign countries compared with that in the home country, have many implications for multinational financial decisions. Obviously, relative inflation rates will greatly influence future production costs at home and abroad. Equally important, they have a dominant influence on relative interest rates as well as exchange rates. Both of these factors influence the methods chosen by multinational corporations for financing their foreign investments, and both have a notable effect on the profitability of foreign investments.

The currencies of countries with higher inflation rates than that of the United States tend to depreciate over time against the dollar. Some countries for which this has been the case include France, Italy, Mexico, and all the South American nations. On the other hand, the currencies of Germany, Switzerland, and Japan, which have had less inflation than the United States, have appreciated relative to the dollar. *In fact, a foreign currency will, on average, depreciate (or appreciate) at a percentage rate approximately equal to the amount by which its inflation rate exceeds (or is less than) our own.*

Relative inflation rates are also reflected in interest rates. The interest rate in any country is largely determined by its inflation rate; this point was discussed in Chapter 3. Therefore, countries currently experiencing higher rates of inflation than the United States also tend to have higher interest rates, whereas the reverse is true for countries with lower inflation rates.

It is tempting for the treasurer of a multinational corporation to borrow in the countries with the lowest interest rates. However, this is not always the best strategy. Suppose, for example, that interest rates in Germany are lower than those in the United States because of Germany's lower inflation rate. A U.S. multinational firm could save interest by borrowing in Germany. However, because of relative inflation rates, the mark can be expected to appreciate in the future, causing the dollar cost of annual interest and principal payments on this debt to rise over time. Thus, *the lower interest rate could be more than offset by losses from currency appreciation.* Similarly, one should not expect multinational corporations to avoid borrowing in a country like Brazil, where interest rates are very high, because future depreciation of the Brazilian cruzeiro could make such borrowing relatively inexpensive.

? *Self-Test Questions*

What effects do relative inflation rates have on relative interest rates?

What happens over time to the currencies of countries with higher inflation rates than that of the United States? To those with lower inflation rates?

Why might a multinational corporation decide to borrow in a country like Brazil, where interest rates are high, rather than in a country like Germany, where interest rates are low?

INTERNATIONAL CAPITAL MARKETS

Direct foreign investment by U.S. multinational corporations is one way for U.S. citizens to invest in world markets. Another way is to purchase stocks, bonds, or various money market instruments issued in foreign countries. U.S. citizens actually do invest substantial amounts in the stocks and bonds of large corporations headquartered in Europe, and to a lesser extent in firms headquartered in the Far East and South America. They also buy securities issued by foreign governments. Such investments in foreign corporations are known as *portfolio investments,* and they are distinguished from *direct investments* in physical assets by U.S. corporations.

Eurodollar Market

Eurodollar

A U.S. dollar deposited in a bank outside the United States.

A **Eurodollar** is a U.S. dollar deposited in a bank outside the United States. (Although they are called Eurodollars because they originated in Europe, Eurodollars are really any dollars deposited in any part of the world, other than the United States.) The bank in which the deposit is made may be a host country institution, such as Barclay's Bank in London; the foreign branch of a U.S. bank, such as Citibank's Paris branch; or even a foreign branch of a third-country bank, such as Barclay's Munich branch. Most Eurodollar deposits are for $500,000 or more, and they have maturities ranging from overnight to about 5 years.

The major difference between Eurodollar deposits and regular U.S. time deposits is their geographic locations. The two types of deposits do not involve different currencies—in both cases, dollars are on deposit. However, Eurodollars are outside the direct control of the U.S. monetary authorities, so U.S. banking regulations, such as fractional reserves and FDIC insurance premiums, do not apply. The absence of these costs means that the interest rate paid on Eurodollar deposits tends to be higher than domestic U.S. rates on equivalent instruments.

Although the dollar is the leading international currency, German marks, Swiss francs, Japanese yen, and other currencies are also deposited outside their home countries; these *Eurocurrencies* are handled in exactly the same way as Eurodollars.

Eurodollars are borrowed by U.S. and foreign corporations and governments, which need dollars for various purposes, especially to pay for goods exported from the United States and to invest in the U.S. stock market. Also, U.S. dollars are used as an international currency, or international medium of exchange, and many Eurodollars are used for this purpose. It is interesting to note that Eurodollars were actually "invented" by the Soviets in 1946. International merchants did not trust the Soviets or their rubles, so the Soviets bought some dollars (for gold), deposited them in a Paris bank, and then used these dollars to buy goods in the world markets. Others soon found it convenient to use dollars this same way, and soon the Eurodollar market was in full swing.

Eurodollars are always held in interest-bearing accounts. The interest rate paid on these deposits depends (1) on the bank's lending rate, as the interest a bank earns on loans determines its willingness and ability to pay interest on deposits, and (2) on rates of return available on U.S. money market instruments. If rates in the United States were above Eurodollar deposit rates, these funds would be sent back and invested in the United States, whereas if Eurodollar deposit rates were significantly above U.S. rates, which is more often the case, more dollars would be sent out of the United States to become Eurodollars. Given the existence of the Eurodollar market, and the easy flow of dollars to and from the United States, it is easy to see why interest rates in the United States cannot be insulated from those in other parts of the world.

Interest rates on Eurodollar deposits (and loans) are tied to a standard rate known by the acronym *LIBOR,* which stands for *London InterBank Offer Rate.* LIBOR is the rate of interest offered by the largest and strongest London banks on deposits of other large banks of the highest credit standing. In April 1992, LIBOR rates were about half a percentage point above domestic U.S. bank rates on time deposits of the same maturity — 3.55 percent for 3-month CDs versus 4.13 percent for LIBOR CDs. The Eurodollar market is essentially a short-term market; most loans and deposits are for less than one year.

International Bond Markets

foreign bond

A bond sold by a foreign borrower but denominated in the currency of the country in which it is sold.

Eurobond

A bond sold in a country other than the one in whose currency the bond is denominated.

Any bond sold outside the country of the borrower is called an international bond. However, there are two important types of international bonds: foreign bonds and Eurobonds. **Foreign bonds** are bonds sold by a foreign borrower but denominated in the currency of the country in which the issue is sold. For instance, Bell Canada may need U.S. dollars to finance the operations of its subsidiaries in the United States. If it decides to raise the needed capital in the domestic U.S. bond market, the bond will be underwritten by a syndicate of U.S. investment bankers, denominated in U.S. dollars, and sold to U.S. investors in accordance with SEC and applicable state regulations. Except for the foreign origin of the borrower (Canada), this bond will be indistinguishable from those issued by equivalent U.S. corporations. Since Bell Canada is a foreign corporation, however, the bond will be called a foreign bond.

The term **Eurobonds** is used to designate any bond sold in some country *other than* the one in whose currency the bond is denominated. Examples include a British firm's issue of pound bonds sold in France, a Ford Motor Company issue denominated in dollars and sold in Germany, or a German firm's sale of mark-denominated bonds in Switzerland. The institutional arrangements by which Eurobonds are marketed are different than those for most other bond issues, with the most important distinction being a far lower level of required disclosure than is usually found for bonds issued in domestic markets, particularly in the United States. Governments tend to be less strict when regulating securities denominated in foreign currencies than they are on home-currency securities because the bonds' purchasers are generally more "sophisticated." The lower disclosure requirements result in lower total transaction costs for Eurobonds.

Eurobonds appeal to investors for several reasons. Generally, they are issued in bearer form rather than as registered bonds, so the names and nationalities of investors are not recorded. Individuals who desire anonymity, whether for privacy reasons or for tax avoidance, find Eurobonds to their liking. Similarly, most governments do not withhold taxes on interest payments associated with Eurobonds. If the investor requires an effective yield of 10 percent, a Eurobond that is exempt from tax withholding would need a coupon rate of 10 percent. Another type of bond — for instance, a domestic issue subject to a 30 percent withholding tax on interest paid to foreigners — would need a coupon rate of 14.3 percent to yield an after-withholding rate of 10 percent. Investors who desire secrecy would not want to file for a refund of the tax, so they would prefer to hold the Eurobond.

More than half of all Eurobonds are denominated in dollars; bonds in Japanese yen, German marks, and Dutch guilders account for most of the rest. Although centered in Europe, Eurobonds are truly international. Their underwriting syndicates include investment bankers from all parts of the world, and the bonds are sold to investors not only in Europe but also in such faraway places as Bahrain and Singapore. Up to a few years ago, Eurobonds were issued solely by multinational firms, by international financial institutions, or by national governments. Today, however, the Eurobond market is also being tapped by purely domestic U.S. firms such as electric utilities, which find that by borrowing overseas they can lower their debt costs.

Self-Test Questions

Differentiate between foreign portfolio investments and direct foreign investments.

What are Eurodollars?

Has the development of the Eurodollar market made it easier or more difficult for the Federal Reserve to control U.S. interest rates?

Differentiate between *foreign bonds* and *Eurobonds.*

Why do Eurobonds appeal to investors?

MULTINATIONAL CAPITAL BUDGETING

Up to now we have discussed the general environment in which multinational firms operate. In the remainder of the chapter we will see how international factors affect key corporate decisions, beginning in this section with capital budgeting.

Although the same basic principles of capital budgeting analysis apply to both foreign and domestic operations, there are some key differences. First, cash flow estimation is generally much more complex for overseas investments. Most multinational firms set up a separate subsidiary in each foreign country in which they operate, and the relevant cash flows for these subsidiaries are the dividends and royalties repatriated to the parent company. Second, these cash flows must be converted to the currency of the parent company and thus are subject to future exchange rate changes. For example, General Motors' German subsidiary may make a profit of 100 million marks in 1992, but the value of these profits to GM will depend on the dollar/mark exchange rate. How many *dollars* is 100 million marks worth? This is the relevant issue for GM's managers and stockholders.

repatriation of earnings
The process of sending cash flows from a foreign subsidiary back to the parent company.

Third, dividends and royalties are normally taxed by both foreign and home-country governments. Furthermore, a foreign government may restrict the amount of the cash flows that may be **repatriated** to the parent company. For example, some governments place a ceiling, stated as a percentage of the company's net worth, on the amount of cash dividends that may be paid by a subsidiary to its parent company. Such restrictions are normally intended to force multinational firms to reinvest earnings in the foreign country, although restrictions are sometimes imposed to prevent large currency outflows, which might affect the exchange rate.

Whatever the host country's motivation, the result is that the parent corporation cannot use cash flows blocked in the foreign country to pay current dividends to its shareholders, nor does it have the flexibility to reinvest cash flows elsewhere in the world, where expected returns may be higher. Hence, from the perspective of the parent organization, *the cash flows relevant for the analysis of a foreign investment are the financial cash flows that the subsidiary can legally send back to the parent.* The present value of these cash flows is found by applying an appropriate discount rate, and this present value is then compared to the parent's required investment in the project to determine the project's NPV.

In addition to the complexities of the cash flow analysis, *the cost of capital may be different for a foreign project than for an equivalent domestic project because foreign projects may be more or less risky.* A higher risk could arise from two primary sources — (1) exchange rate risk and (2) political risk — while a lower risk might result from international diversification.

Exchange rate risk reflects the inherent uncertainty about the home currency value of cash flows sent back to the parent. In other words, foreign projects have an added risk element that relates to what the basic cash flows will be worth in the parent company's home currency. The foreign currency cash flows to be turned over to the parent must be converted into U.S. dollars by translating them at expected future exchange rates. An analysis should be conducted to ascertain the effects of exchange rate variations, and, on the basis of this analysis, an exchange rate risk premium should be added to the domestic cost of capital to reflect the *exchange rate risk* inherent in the investment. As we have seen, it is sometimes possible to hedge against exchange rate fluctuations, but it may not be possible to hedge completely, especially on long-term projects, and, in addition, the costs of hedging must be subtracted from the project's cash flows.

political risk

The risk of expropriation of a foreign subsidiary's assets by the host country, or of unanticipated restrictions on cash flows to the parent company.

Political risk refers to any action (or the probability of such action) by a host government which reduces the value of a company's investment. It includes at one extreme the expropriation without compensation of the subsidiary's assets, but it also includes less drastic actions that reduce the value of the parent firm's investment in the foreign subsidiary such as higher taxes, tighter repatriation or currency controls, and restrictions on prices charged. The risk of expropriation of U.S. assets abroad is small in traditionally friendly and stable countries such as Great Britain or Switzerland. However, in Latin America, Africa, the Far East, and Eastern Europe, the risk may be substantial. Past expropriations include those of ITT and Anaconda Copper in Chile, Gulf Oil in Bolivia, Occidental Petroleum in Libya, Enron Corporation in Peru, and the assets of many companies in Iraq, Iran, and Cuba.

Generally, political risk premiums are not added to the cost of capital to adjust for this risk. If a company's management has a serious concern that a given country might expropriate foreign assets, it simply will not make significant investments in that country. Expropriation is viewed as a catastrophic or ruinous event, and managers have been shown to be extraordinarily risk averse when faced with ruinous loss possibilities. However, companies can take steps to reduce the potential loss from expropriation in three major ways: (1) by financing the subsidiary with local capital, (2) by structuring operations so that the subsidiary has value only as a part of the integrated corporate system, and (3) by obtaining insurance against economic losses from expropriation from a source such as the Overseas Private Investment Corporation (OPIC). In the latter case, insurance premiums would have to be added to the project's cost.

⁇ *Self-Test Questions*

List some key differences in capital budgeting as applied to foreign versus domestic operations.

What are the relevant cash flows for an international investment?

Why might the cost of capital for a foreign project differ from that of an equivalent domestic project? Could it be lower?

What adjustments might be made to the domestic cost of capital for a foreign investment due to exchange rate risk and political risk?

INTERNATIONAL CAPITAL STRUCTURES

Significant differences have been observed in the capital structures of U.S. corporations in comparison to their German and Japanese counterparts. For example, the Organization for Economic Cooperation and Development (OECD) recently reported that, on average, Japanese firms use 85 percent debt to total assets (in book value terms), German firms use 64 percent, and U.S. firms use 55 percent. Of course, different countries use somewhat different accounting conventions with regard to (1) reporting assets on a historical versus a replacement cost basis, (2) the treatment of leased assets, (3) pension plan funding, and (4) capitalizing versus expensing R&D costs, and these differences make comparisons difficult. Still, even after adjusting for accounting differences, researchers find that Japanese and German firms use considerably more financial leverage than U.S. companies.

Why do international differences in financial leverage exist? Since taxes are thought to be a major reason for using debt, the effects of differential tax structures in the three countries have been examined. The interest on corporate debt is deductible in each country, and individuals must pay taxes on dividends and interest received. However, capital gains are not taxed in either Germany or Japan. The conclusions from this analysis are as follows: (1) From a tax standpoint, corporations should be equally inclined to use debt in all three countries. (2) Since capital gains are not taxed in Germany or Japan, but are taxed in the United States, and since capital gains are associated more with stocks than with bonds, investors in Germany and Japan should show a preference for stocks as compared with U.S. investors. (3) Investor preferences should lead to relatively low equity capital costs in Germany and Japan, and this, in turn, should cause German and Japanese firms to use more equity capital than their U.S. counterparts. Of course, this is exactly the opposite of the actual capital structures, so differential tax laws cannot explain the observed capital structure differences.

If tax rates cannot explain the different capital structures, what else might explain the observed differences? Another possibility relates to bankruptcy costs. Actual bankruptcy, and even the threat of potential bankruptcy, imposes a costly burden on firms with large amounts of debt. Note, though, that the threat of bankruptcy is dependent on the *probability* of bankruptcy. In the United States, equity monitoring costs are comparatively low—corporations produce quarterly reports, pay quarterly dividends, and must comply with relatively stringent audit requirements. These conditions are less prevalent in the other countries. Conversely, debt monitoring costs are probably lower in Germany and Japan than in the United States. In Germany and Japan, the bulk of corporate debt consists of bank loans as opposed to publicly issued bonds, but, more important, the banks are closely linked to the corporations which borrow from them. German and Japanese banks often (1) hold major equity positions in their debtor corporations, (2) vote the shares of individual shareholders for whom banks hold shares in trust, and (3) have bank officers sit on the boards of debtor corporations. Given these close relationships, the banks are much more directly involved with the debtor firms' affairs, and as a result they are also more accommodating in the event of financial distress than U.S. bondholders would be. This, in turn, suggests that any given amount of debt gives rise to a lower threat of bankruptcy for a German or a Japanese firm than for a U.S. firm with the same amount of business risk. Thus, an analysis of both bankruptcy costs and equity monitoring costs leads to the conclusion that U.S. firms ought to have more equity and less debt than firms in Japan and Germany.

We cannot state that one financial system is better or worse than another in the sense of making the firms in one country more efficient than those in another. However, as U.S. firms become increasingly involved in worldwide operations, they must become increasingly aware of worldwide conditions, and they must be prepared to adapt to conditions in the various countries in which they do business.

 Self-Test Question

Why do international differences in financial leverage exist?

MULTINATIONAL WORKING CAPITAL MANAGEMENT

Cash Management

The objectives of cash management in a multinational corporation are similar to those in a purely domestic corporation: (1) to speed up collections and to slow down disbursements as much as is feasible, and hence to maximize net float; (2) to shift cash as rapidly as possible from those parts of the business where it is not needed to those parts where it is needed; and (3) to obtain the highest possible risk-adjusted, after-tax rate of return on temporary cash balances. Multinational companies use the same general procedures for achieving these goals as domestic firms, but because of longer distances and more serious mail delays, lockbox systems and electronic funds transfers are even more important.

Although multinational and domestic corporations have the same objectives and use similar procedures, the multinational corporation faces a far more complex task. As was mentioned earlier in our discussion of political risk, foreign governments often place restrictions on transfers of funds out of the country, so although IBM can transfer money from its Salt Lake City office to its New York concentration bank just by pressing a few buttons, a similar transfer from its Buenos Aires office is far more complex. Buenos Aires funds are denominated in australs (Argentina's equivalent of the dollar), so the australs must be converted to dollars before the transfer. If there is a shortage of dollars in Argentina, or if the Argentinean government wants to conserve the dollars in the country to use for the purchase of strategic materials, then conversion, and hence the transfer, may be blocked. Even if no dollar shortage exists in Argentina, the government may still restrict funds outflows if those funds represent profits or depreciation rather than payments for purchased materials or equipment because many countries, especially the less developed countries, want profits reinvested in the country in order to stimulate economic growth.

Once it has been determined what funds can be transferred out of the various nations in which a multinational corporation operates, it is important to get those funds to locations where they will earn the highest returns. Whereas domestic corporations tend to think in terms of domestic securities, multinationals are more likely to be aware of investment opportunities all around the world. Most multinational corporations use one or more global concentration banks, located in money centers such as London, New York, Tokyo, Zurich, or Singapore, and their staffs in those cities, working with international bankers, know of and are able to take advantage of the best rates available anywhere in the world.

Credit Management

Like most other aspects of finance, credit management in the multinational corporation is similar to but more complex than that in a purely domestic business. First, granting credit is riskier in an international context because, in addition to the normal risks of default, the multinational corporation must also worry about exchange rate changes between the time a sale is made and the time a receivable is collected. For example, if IBM sold a computer to a Japanese customer for 147.85 million yen when the exchange rate was 147.85 yen per $1, IBM would obtain $147,850,000/147.85 = \$1,000,000$ for the computer. However, if it sold the computer on terms of net/6 months, and if the yen fell against the dollar so that one dollar would now buy 184.8125 yen, IBM would end up realizing only $147,850,000/184.8125 = \$800,000$ when it collected the receivable. As we discussed earlier, hedging can reduce this type of risk, but at a cost.

Credit policy is generally more important for a multinational corporation than for a purely domestic firm for two reasons. First, much U.S. trade is with poorer, less-developed nations, and in such situations granting credit is generally a necessary condition for doing business. Second, and in large part as a result of the first point, developed nations whose economic health depends upon exports often help their manufacturing firms compete internationally by granting credit to foreign countries. In Japan, for example, the major manufacturing firms have direct ownership ties with large "trading companies" engaged in international trade, as well as with giant commercial banks. In addition, a government agency, the Ministry of International Trade and Industry (MITI), helps Japanese firms identify potential export markets and also helps potential customers arrange credit for purchases from Japanese firms. In effect, the huge Japanese trade surpluses are used to finance Japanese exports, thus helping to perpetuate their favorable trade balance. The United States has attempted to counter with the Export-Import Bank, which is funded by Congress, but the fact that the United States has a large balance of payments deficit is clear evidence that we have been less successful than others in world markets in recent years.

The huge debt which countries such as Brazil, Mexico, and Argentina owe the international banks, including many U.S. banks, is well known, and this situation illustrates how credit policy (by banks in this case) can go astray. The banks face a particularly sticky problem with these loans because if a sovereign nation defaults, the banks cannot lay claim to the assets of the country as they could if a corporate customer defaulted. Note too that although the banks' loans to foreign governments are getting most of the headlines, many U.S. multinational corporations are also in trouble as a result of granting credit to business customers in the same countries in which the banks' loans to the government are on shaky ground.

By pointing out the risks in granting credit internationally, we are not suggesting that such credit is bad. Quite the contrary, for the potential gains from international operations far outweigh the risks, at least for companies (and banks) that have the necessary expertise.

Inventory Management

As in most other aspects of finance, inventory management in a multinational setting is similar to but more complex than that in a purely domestic one. First, there is the matter of the physical location of inventories. For example, where should Exxon keep its stockpiles of crude oil and refined products? It has refineries and marketing centers located worldwide, and one alternative is to keep items concentrated in a few strategic spots, from which they can then be shipped to the locations where they will be used as needs arise. Such a strategy may minimize the total amount of inventories needed to operate the global business and thus may minimize the firm's total investment in inventories. Note, though, that consideration will have to be given to potential delays in getting goods from central storage locations to user locations all around the world. Both working stocks and safety stocks will have to be maintained at each user location, as well as at the strategic storage centers. Problems like the Iraqi conflict in early 1991 complicate matters even more because, even though the United States drove Iraq out of Kuwait, Iraq destroyed most of the Kuwaiti oil fields in its retreat. Consequently, the world was cut off from a large portion of its oil supply (perhaps 20 percent) for an extended period of time.

Exchange rates also influence inventory policy. If a local currency, say the Danish krone, were expected to rise in value against the dollar, a U.S. company operating in Denmark would want to increase stocks of local products before the rise in the krone, and vice versa if the krone were expected to fall.

Another factor that must be considered is the possibility of import or export quotas or tariffs. For example, recently Apple Computer Company obtained 256k memory chips from Japanese suppliers at bargain prices—U.S. chipmakers had just charged the Japanese with dumping chips in the U.S. market at prices below cost and were seeking to force the Japanese to raise prices, so Apple decided to increase its chip inventory.[4] Then computer sales slacked off, and Apple ended up having an oversupply of expensive computer chips. As a result, Apple's profits were hurt, and its stock price fell, demonstrating once more the importance of careful inventory management.

As mentioned earlier, another danger in certain countries is the threat of expropriation. If that threat is large, inventory holdings will be minimized, and goods will be brought in only as needed. Similarly, if the operation involves extraction of raw material such as oil or bauxite, processing plants may be moved offshore rather than located close to the production site.

Taxes must also be considered, and they have two effects on multinational inventory management. First, countries often impose property taxes on assets, including inventories, and when this is done, the tax is based on holdings as of a specific date, say January 1 or March 1. Such rules make it advantageous for a multinational firm (1) to schedule production so that inventories are low on the assessment date, and (2) if assessment dates vary among countries in a region, to hold safety stocks in different countries at different times during the year.

Finally, multinational firms may consider the possibility of at-sea storage. Oil, chemical, grain, and other companies that deal in a bulk commodity that must be stored in some type of tank can often buy tankers at a cost not much greater—or perhaps even less, considering land cost—than land-based facilities. Loaded tankers can then be kept at sea or at anchor in some strategic location. This eliminates the danger of expropriation, minimizes the property tax problem, and maximizes flexibility with regard to shipping to areas where needs are greatest or prices highest.

This discussion has only scratched the surface of inventory management in the multinational corporation. As we noted at the outset, the task is much more complex than for a purely domestic firm. However, the greater the degree of complexity, the greater the rewards from superior performance, so if you want challenge along with potentially high rewards, look to the international arena.

---

[4]The term "dumping" warrants explanation, because the practice is so potentially important in international markets. Suppose Japanese chipmakers have excess capacity. A particular chip has a variable cost of $25, and its "fully allocated cost," which is the $25 plus total fixed cost per unit of output, is $40. Now suppose the Japanese firm can sell chips in the United States at $35 per unit, but if it charges $40 it will not make any sales because U.S. chipmakers sell for $35.50. If the Japanese firm sells at $35, it will cover variable cost plus make a contribution to fixed overhead, so selling at $35 makes sense. Continuing, if the Japanese firm can sell in Japan at $40, but U.S. firms are excluded from Japanese markets by import duties or other barriers, the Japanese will have a huge advantage over U.S. manufacturers. This practice of selling goods at lower prices in foreign markets than at home is called "dumping." U.S. firms are required by antitrust laws to offer the same price to all customers and, therefore, cannot engage in dumping.

Self-Test Questions

What are some factors that make cash management especially complicated in a multinational corporation?

Why is granting credit especially risky in an international context?

Why is credit policy especially important for a multinational firm?

SUMMARY

This chapter discusses the differences between multinational and domestic managerial finance. The key concepts covered are listed below.

- **International operations** are becoming increasingly important to individual firms and to the national economy. A **multinational corporation** is a firm that operates in two or more nations.

- Companies go "international" for five primary reasons: (1) **to seek new markets**, (2) **to seek raw materials**, (3) **to seek new technology**, (4) **to seek production efficiency**, and (5) **to avoid trade barriers.**

- Six major factors distinguish managerial finance as practiced by domestic firms from that of multinational corporations: (1) **different currency denominations**, (2) **economic and legal ramifications**, (3) **languages**, (4) **cultural differences**, (5) **role of governments**, and (6) **political risk.**

- The number of U.S. dollars required to purchase one unit of foreign currency is called a **direct quotation**, while the number of units of foreign currency that can be purchased for one U.S. dollar is an **indirect quotation.**

- Financial forecasting is especially difficult for multinational firms because **exchange rate fluctuations** make it difficult to estimate the dollars that overseas operations will produce.

- Prior to August 1971, the world was on a **fixed exchange rate system** whereby the U.S. dollar was linked to gold, and other currencies were then tied to the dollar. After August 1971, the world monetary system changed to a **floating system** whereby major world currency rates float with market forces, largely unrestricted by any internationally agreed-upon limits. The central bank of each country does intervene in the foreign exchange market, buying and selling its currency to smooth out exchange rate fluctuations, but only to a limited extent.

- **Spot rates** are the rates paid for delivery of currency "on the spot," while the **forward exchange rate** is the rate paid for delivery of currency at some agreed-upon future date, usually 30, 90, or 180 days from the day the transaction is negotiated. The forward rate can be at either a **premium** or a **discount** to the spot rate.

- Granting credit is more risky in an international context because, in addition to the normal risks of default, the multinational firm must worry about **exchange rate changes** between the time a sale is made and the time a receivable is collected.

▮ Credit policy is especially important for a multinational firm for two reasons: (1) Much of the U.S. trade is with less-developed nations, and in such situations granting credit is a necessary condition for doing business. (2) The governments of nations such as Japan whose economic health depends upon exports often help their manufacturing firms compete internationally by granting credit to foreign customers.

▮ Foreign investments are similar to domestic investments, but political risk and exchange rate risk must be considered. **Political risk** is the risk that the foreign government will take some action which will decrease the value of the investment, while **exchange rate risk** is the risk of losses due to fluctuations in the value of the dollar relative to the values of foreign currencies.

▮ Investments in **international capital projects** expose the investing firm to **exchange rate risk** and **political risk.** The relevant cash flows in international capital budgeting are the dollar cash flows which can be turned over to the parent company.

▮ **Eurodollars** are U.S. dollars deposited in banks outside the United States. Interest rates on Eurodollars are tied to **LIBOR,** the London InterBank Offer Rate.

▮ U.S. firms often find that they can raise long-term capital at a lower cost outside the United States by selling bonds in the **international capital markets.** International bonds may be either **foreign bonds,** which are exactly like regular domestic bonds except that the issuer is a foreign company, or **Eurobonds,** which are bonds sold in a foreign country but denominated in the currency of the issuing company's home country.

Questions

23-1 Under the fixed exchange rate system, what was the currency against which all other currency values were defined? Why?

23-2 Exchange rates fluctuate under both the fixed exchange rate and floating exchange rate systems. What, then, is the difference between the two systems?

23-3 If the French franc depreciates against the U.S. dollar, can a dollar buy more or fewer French francs as a result?

23-4 If the United States imports more goods from abroad than it exports, foreigners will tend to have a surplus of U.S. dollars. What will this do to the value of the dollar with respect to foreign currencies? What is the corresponding effect on foreign investments in the United States?

23-5 Why do U.S. corporations build manufacturing plants abroad when they could build them at home?

23-6 Most firms require higher rates of return on foreign projects than on identical projects located at home. Why?

23-7 What is a Eurodollar? If a French citizen deposits $10,000 in Chase Manhattan Bank in New York, have Eurodollars been created? What if the deposit is made in Barclay's Bank in London? Chase Manhattan's Paris branch? Does the existence of the Eurodollar market make the Federal Reserve's job of controlling U.S. interest rates easier or more difficult? Explain.

Self-Test Problem

ST-1
Key terms

Define each of the following terms:
a. Multinational corporation
b. Exchange rate
c. Fixed exchange rate system; floating exchange rates
d. Deficit trade balance
e. Devaluation; revaluation
f. Exchange rate risk; convertible currency
g. Spot rate; forward exchange rate
h. Discount on forward rate; premium on forward rate
i. Hedging exchange rate exposure
j. Repatriation of earnings; political risk
k. Eurodollar; Eurobond; international bond; foreign bond

Problems

23-1
Exchange rates

Table 23-1 lists foreign exchange rates for April 20, 1992. On that day how many dollars would be required to purchase 1,000 units of each of the following: Indian rupees, Italian lira, Japanese yen, Mexican pesos, and Saudi Arabian riyals?

23-2
Exchange rates

Look up the 5 currencies in Problem 23-1 in the foreign exchange section of a current issue of *The Wall Street Journal*.
a. What is the current exchange rate for changing dollars into 1,000 units of rupees, lira, yen, pesos, and riyals?
b. What is the percentage gain or loss between the April 20, 1992, exchange rate and the current exchange rate for each of the currencies in Part a?

23-3
Results of exchange rate changes

Early in September 1983, it took 245 Japanese yen to equal $1. Almost nine years later, in April 1992, that exchange rate had fallen to 134 yen to $1. Assume the price of a Japanese-manufactured automobile was $8,000 in September 1983 and that its price changes were in direct relation to exchange rates.
a. Has the price, in dollars, of the automobile increased or decreased during the 9-year period because of changes in the exchange rate?
b. What would the dollar price of the automobile be on April 20, 1992, again assuming that the car's price changes only with exchange rates?

23-4
Hedging

Chavalier French Imports has agreed to purchase 15,000 cases of French wine for 16 million francs at today's spot rate. The firm's financial manager, George Racette, has noted the following current spot and forward rates:

	U.S. Dollar/Franc	**Franc/U.S. Dollar**
Spot	0.17770	5.6275
30-day forward	0.17683	5.6553
90-day forward	0.17509	5.7112
180-day forward	0.17270	5.7905

On the same day Mr. Racette agrees to purchase 15,000 more cases of wine in 3 months at the same price of 16 million francs.
a. What is the price of the wine, in U.S. dollars, if it is purchased at today's spot rate?
b. What is the cost, in dollars, of the second 15,000 cases if payment is made in 90 days and the spot rate at that time equals today's 90-day forward rate?
c. If Mr. Racette is concerned about the dollar losing value relative to the franc in the next 90 days, what can he do to reduce his exposure to exchange rate risk?

d. If he does not hedge his exposure to exchange rate risk, and the exchange rate for the French franc is 5.00 to $1 in 90 days, how much will he have to pay for the wine (in dollars)?

EXAM-TYPE PROBLEMS

The problems included in this section are set up in such a way that they could be used as multiple-choice exam problems.

23-5
Exchange rate

If British pounds sell for $1.75 (U.S.) per pound, what should dollars sell for in pounds per dollar?

23-6
Currency appreciation

Suppose that 1 French franc could be purchased in the foreign exchange market for 18 U.S. cents today. If the franc appreciated 10 percent tomorrow against the dollar, how many francs would a dollar buy tomorrow?

23-7
Cross exchange rates

Recently the exchange rate between U.S. dollars and the French franc was FF5.6 = $1, and the exchange rate between the dollar and the British pound was £1 = $1.75. What was the exchange rate between francs and pounds?

23-8
Cross exchange rates

Look up the 3 currencies in Problem 23-7 in the foreign exchange section of a current issue of *The Wall Street Journal*. What is the current exchange rate between francs and pounds?

23-9
Foreign investment analysis

After all foreign and U.S. taxes, a U.S. corporation expects to receive 3 pounds of dividends per share from a British subsidiary this year. The exchange rate at the end of the year is expected to be $1.76 per pound, and the pound is expected to depreciate 5 percent against the dollar each year for an indefinite period. The dividend (in pounds) is expected to grow at 10 percent a year indefinitely. The parent U.S. corporation owns 10 million shares of the subsidiary. What is the present value in dollars of its equity ownership of the subsidiary? Assume a cost of equity capital of 14 percent for the subsidiary.

23-10
Exchange gains and losses

You are the vice president of International InfoXchange, headquartered in Chicago, Illinois. All shareholders of the firm live in the United States. Earlier this month you obtained a loan of 5 million Canadian dollars from a bank in Toronto to finance the construction of a new plant in Montreal. At the time the loan was received, the exchange rate was 85 U.S. cents to the Canadian dollar. By the end of the month it has unexpectedly dropped to 80 cents. Has your company made a gain or loss as a result, and by how much?

INTEGRATIVE PROBLEM

23-11
Multinational managerial finance

Citrus Products Inc. is a medium-sized producer of citrus juice drinks with groves in Indian River County, Florida. Until now, the company has confined its operations and sales to the United States, but its CEO, George Gaynor, wants to expand into Europe. The first step would be to set up sales subsidiaries in Spain and Portugal, then set up a production plant in Spain, and, finally, distribute the product throughout the European common market. The firm's financial manager, Ruth Schmidt, is enthusiastic about the plan, but she is worried about the implications of the foreign expansion on the firm's managerial finance process. She has asked you, the firm's most recently hired financial analyst, to develop a 1-hour tutorial package that explains the basics of multinational managerial finance. The tutorial will be presented at the next board of director's meeting. To get you started, Ms. Schmidt has supplied you with the following list of questions.
a. What is a multinational corporation? Why do firms expand into other countries?

b. What are the six major factors which distinguish multinational managerial finance from managerial finance as practiced by a purely domestic firm?

c. Consider the following illustrative exchange rates.

	U.S. Dollars Required to Buy One Unit of Foreign Currency
Spanish peseta	0.0093
Portuguese escudo	0.0067

(1) Are these currency prices direct quotations or indirect quotations?

(2) Calculate the indirect quotations for pesetas and escudos.

(3) What is a cross rate? Calculate the two cross rates between pesetas and escudos.

(4) Assume Citrus Products can produce a liter of orange juice and ship it to Spain for $1.75. If the firm wants a 50 percent markup on the product, what should the orange juice sell for in Spain?

(5) Now assume Citrus Products begins producing the same liter of orange juice in Spain. The product costs 200 pesetas to produce and ship to Portugal, where it can be sold for 400 escudos. What is the dollar profit on the sale?

(6) What is exchange rate risk?

d. Briefly describe the current international monetary system. How does the current system differ from the system that was in place prior to August 1971?

e. What is a convertible currency? What problems arise when a multinational company operates in a country whose currency is not convertible?

f. What is the difference between spot rates and forward rates? When is the forward rate at a premium to the spot rate? At a discount? How can a firm use the forward markets to hedge a future currency transaction?

g. What impact does relative inflation have on interest rates and exchange rates?

h. Briefly discuss the international capital markets.

i. What is the impact of multinational operations on each of the following managerial finance topics?

(1) Cash management.

(2) Capital budgeting decisions.

(3) Credit management.

(4) Inventory management.

Mathematical Tables

Table A-1 ▪ Present Value of $1 Due at the End of n Periods:

Equation: Financial Calculator Keys:

$$PVIF_{i,n} = \frac{1}{(1+i)^n}$$

n   i   0   1.0

[N] [I] [PV] [PMT] [FV]

TABLE
VALUE

Period	1%	2%	3%	4%	5%	6%	7%	8%	9%	10%
1	.9901	.9804	.9709	.9615	.9524	.9434	.9346	.9259	.9174	.9091
2	.9803	.9612	.9426	.9246	.9070	.8900	.8734	.8573	.8417	.8264
3	.9706	.9423	.9151	.8890	.8638	.8396	.8163	.7938	.7722	.7513
4	.9610	.9238	.8885	.8548	.8227	.7921	.7629	.7350	.7084	.6830
5	.9515	.9057	.8626	.8219	.7835	.7473	.7130	.6806	.6499	.6209
6	.9420	.8880	.8375	.7903	.7462	.7050	.6663	.6302	.5963	.5645
7	.9327	.8706	.8131	.7599	.7107	.6651	.6227	.5835	.5470	.5132
8	.9235	.8535	.7894	.7307	.6768	.6274	.5820	.5403	.5019	.4665
9	.9143	.8368	.7664	.7026	.6446	.5919	.5439	.5002	.4604	.4241
10	.9053	.8203	.7441	.6756	.6139	.5584	.5083	.4632	.4224	.3855
11	.8963	.8043	.7224	.6496	.5847	.5268	.4751	.4289	.3875	.3505
12	.8874	.7885	.7014	.6246	.5568	.4970	.4440	.3971	.3555	.3186
13	.8787	.7730	.6810	.6006	.5303	.4688	.4150	.3677	.3262	.2897
14	.8700	.7579	.6611	.5775	.5051	.4423	.3878	.3405	.2992	.2633
15	.8613	.7430	.6419	.5553	.4810	.4173	.3624	.3152	.2745	.2394
16	.8528	.7284	.6232	.5339	.4581	.3936	.3387	.2919	.2519	.2176
17	.8444	.7142	.6050	.5134	.4363	.3714	.3166	.2703	.2311	.1978
18	.8360	.7002	.5874	.4936	.4155	.3503	.2959	.2502	.2120	.1799
19	.8277	.6864	.5703	.4746	.3957	.3305	.2765	.2317	.1945	.1635
20	.8195	.6730	.5537	.4564	.3769	.3118	.2584	.2145	.1784	.1486
21	.8114	.6598	.5375	.4388	.3589	.2942	.2415	.1987	.1637	.1351
22	.8034	.6468	.5219	.4220	.3418	.2775	.2257	.1839	.1502	.1228
23	.7954	.6342	.5067	.4057	.3256	.2618	.2109	.1703	.1378	.1117
24	.7876	.6217	.4919	.3901	.3101	.2470	.1971	.1577	.1264	.1015
25	.7798	.6095	.4776	.3751	.2953	.2330	.1842	.1460	.1160	.0923
26	.7720	.5976	.4637	.3607	.2812	.2198	.1722	.1352	.1064	.0839
27	.7644	.5859	.4502	.3468	.2678	.2074	.1609	.1252	.0976	.0763
28	.7568	.5744	.4371	.3335	.2551	.1956	.1504	.1159	.0895	.0693
29	.7493	.5631	.4243	.3207	.2429	.1846	.1406	.1073	.0822	.0630
30	.7419	.5521	.4120	.3083	.2314	.1741	.1314	.0994	.0754	.0573
35	.7059	.5000	.3554	.2534	.1813	.1301	.0937	.0676	.0490	.0356
40	.6717	.4529	.3066	.2083	.1420	.0972	.0668	.0460	.0318	.0221
45	.6391	.4102	.2644	.1712	.1113	.0727	.0476	.0313	.0207	.0137
50	.6080	.3715	.2281	.1407	.0872	.0543	.0339	.0213	.0134	.0085
55	.5785	.3365	.1968	.1157	.0683	.0406	.0242	.0145	.0087	.0053

Table A-1 ▮   *(continued)*

Period	12%	14%	15%	16%	18%	20%	24%	28%	32%	36%
1	.8929	.8772	.8696	.8621	.8475	.8333	.8065	.7813	.7576	.7353
2	.7972	.7695	.7561	.7432	.7182	.6944	.6504	.6104	.5739	.5407
3	.7118	.6750	.6575	.6407	.6086	.5787	.5245	.4768	.4348	.3975
4	.6355	.5921	.5718	.5523	.5158	.4823	.4230	.3725	.3294	.2923
5	.5674	.5194	.4972	.4761	.4371	.4019	.3411	.2910	.2495	.2149
6	.5066	.4556	.4323	.4104	.3704	.3349	.2751	.2274	.1890	.1580
7	.4523	.3996	.3759	.3538	.3139	.2791	.2218	.1776	.1432	.1162
8	.4039	.3506	.3269	.3050	.2660	.2326	.1789	.1388	.1085	.0854
9	.3606	.3075	.2843	.2630	.2255	.1938	.1443	.1084	.0822	.0628
10	.3220	.2697	.2472	.2267	.1911	.1615	.1164	.0847	.0623	.0462
11	.2875	.2366	.2149	.1954	.1619	.1346	.0938	.0662	.0472	.0340
12	.2567	.2076	.1869	.1685	.1372	.1122	.0757	.0517	.0357	.0250
13	.2292	.1821	.1625	.1452	.1163	.0935	.0610	.0404	.0271	.0184
14	.2046	.1597	.1413	.1252	.0985	.0779	.0492	.0316	.0205	.0135
15	.1827	.1401	.1229	.1079	.0835	.0649	.0397	.0247	.0155	.0099
16	.1631	.1229	.1069	.0930	.0708	.0541	.0320	.0193	.0118	.0073
17	.1456	.1078	.0929	.0802	.0600	.0451	.0258	.0150	.0089	.0054
18	.1300	.0946	.0808	.0691	.0508	.0376	.0208	.0118	.0068	.0039
19	.1161	.0829	.0703	.0596	.0431	.0313	.0168	.0092	.0051	.0029
20	.1037	.0728	.0611	.0514	.0365	.0261	.0135	.0072	.0039	.0021
21	.0926	.0638	.0531	.0443	.0309	.0217	.0109	.0056	.0029	.0016
22	.0826	.0560	.0462	.0382	.0262	.0181	.0088	.0044	.0022	.0012
23	.0738	.0491	.0402	.0329	.0222	.0151	.0071	.0034	.0017	.0008
24	.0659	.0431	.0349	.0284	.0188	.0126	.0057	.0027	.0013	.0006
25	.0588	.0378	.0304	.0245	.0160	.0105	.0046	.0021	.0010	.0005
26	.0525	.0331	.0264	.0211	.0135	.0087	.0037	.0016	.0007	.0003
27	.0469	.0291	.0230	.0182	.0115	.0073	.0030	.0013	.0006	.0002
28	.0419	.0255	.0200	.0157	.0097	.0061	.0024	.0010	.0004	.0002
29	.0374	.0224	.0174	.0135	.0082	.0051	.0020	.0008	.0003	.0001
30	.0334	.0196	.0151	.0116	.0070	.0042	.0016	.0006	.0002	.0001
35	.0189	.0102	.0075	.0055	.0030	.0017	.0005	.0002	.0001	*
40	.0107	.0053	.0037	.0026	.0013	.0007	.0002	.0001	*	*
45	.0061	.0027	.0019	.0013	.0006	.0003	.0001	*	*	*
50	.0035	.0014	.0009	.0006	.0003	.0001	*	*	*	*
55	.0020	.0007	.0005	.0003	.0001	*	*	*	*	*

*The factor is zero to four decimal places.

Table A-2 ▪ Present Value of an Annuity of $1 per Period for n Periods:

Equation:

$$PVIFA_{i,n} = \sum_{t=1}^{n}\frac{1}{(1+i)^t} = \frac{1 - \dfrac{1}{(1+i)^n}}{i} = \frac{1}{i} - \frac{1}{i(1+i)^n}$$

Financial Calculator Keys:

| n | i | 1.0 | 0 |

| N | I | PV | PMT | FV |

TABLE VALUE

Number of Periods	1%	2%	3%	4%	5%	6%	7%	8%	9%
1	0.9901	0.9804	0.9709	0.9615	0.9524	0.9434	0.9346	0.9259	0.9174
2	1.9704	1.9416	1.9135	1.8861	1.8594	1.8334	1.8080	1.7833	1.7591
3	2.9410	2.8839	2.8286	2.7751	2.7232	2.6730	2.6243	2.5771	2.5313
4	3.9020	3.8077	3.7171	3.6299	3.5460	3.4651	3.3872	3.3121	3.2397
5	4.8534	4.7135	4.5797	4.4518	4.3295	4.2124	4.1002	3.9927	3.8897
6	5.7955	5.6014	5.4172	5.2421	5.0757	4.9173	4.7665	4.6229	4.4859
7	6.7282	6.4720	6.2303	6.0021	5.7864	5.5824	5.3893	5.2064	5.0330
8	7.6517	7.3255	7.0197	6.7327	6.4632	6.2098	5.9713	5.7466	5.5348
9	8.5660	8.1622	7.7861	7.4353	7.1078	6.8017	6.5152	6.2469	5.9952
10	9.4713	8.9826	8.5302	8.1109	7.7217	7.3601	7.0236	6.7101	6.4177
11	10.3676	9.7868	9.2526	8.7605	8.3064	7.8869	7.4987	7.1390	6.8052
12	11.2551	10.5753	9.9540	9.3851	8.8633	8.3838	7.9427	7.5361	7.1607
13	12.1337	11.3484	10.6350	9.9856	9.3936	8.8527	8.3577	7.9038	7.4869
14	13.0037	12.1062	11.2961	10.5631	9.8986	9.2950	8.7455	8.2442	7.7862
15	13.8651	12.8493	11.9379	11.1184	10.3797	9.7122	9.1079	8.5595	8.0607
16	14.7179	13.5777	12.5611	11.6523	10.8378	10.1059	9.4466	8.8514	8.3126
17	15.5623	14.2919	13.1661	12.1657	11.2741	10.4773	9.7632	9.1216	8.5436
18	16.3983	14.9920	13.7535	12.6593	11.6896	10.8276	10.0591	9.3719	8.7556
19	17.2260	15.6785	14.3238	13.1339	12.0853	11.1581	10.3356	9.6036	8.9501
20	18.0456	16.3514	14.8775	13.5903	12.4622	11.4699	10.5940	9.8181	9.1285
21	18.8570	17.0112	15.4150	14.0292	12.8212	11.7641	10.8355	10.0168	9.2922
22	19.6604	17.6580	15.9369	14.4511	13.1630	12.0416	11.0612	10.2007	9.4424
23	20.4558	18.2922	16.4436	14.8568	13.4886	12.3034	11.2722	10.3711	9.5802
24	21.2434	18.9139	16.9355	15.2470	13.7986	12.5504	11.4693	10.5288	9.7066
25	22.0232	19.5235	17.4131	15.6221	14.0939	12.7834	11.6536	10.6748	9.8226
26	22.7952	20.1210	17.8768	15.9828	14.3752	13.0032	11.8258	10.8100	9.9290
27	23.5596	20.7069	18.3270	16.3296	14.6430	13.2105	11.9867	10.9352	10.0266
28	24.3164	21.2813	18.7641	16.6631	14.8981	13.4062	12.1371	11.0511	10.1161
29	25.0658	21.8444	19.1885	16.9837	15.1411	13.5907	12.2777	11.1584	10.1983
30	25.8077	22.3965	19.6004	17.2920	15.3725	13.7648	12.4090	11.2578	10.2737
35	29.4086	24.9986	21.4872	18.6646	16.3742	14.4982	12.9477	11.6546	10.5668
40	32.8347	27.3555	23.1148	19.7928	17.1591	15.0463	13.3317	11.9246	10.7574
45	36.0945	29.4902	24.5187	20.7200	17.7741	15.4558	13.6055	12.1084	10.8812
50	39.1961	31.4236	25.7298	21.4822	18.2559	15.7619	13.8007	12.2335	10.9617
55	42.1472	33.1748	26.7744	22.1086	18.6335	15.9905	13.9399	12.3186	11.0140

Table A-2   ▪   *(continued)*

Number of Periods	10%	12%	14%	15%	16%	18%	20%	24%	28%	32%
1	0.9091	0.8929	0.8772	0.8696	0.8621	0.8475	0.8333	0.8065	0.7813	0.7576
2	1.7355	1.6901	1.6467	1.6257	1.6052	1.5656	1.5278	1.4568	1.3916	1.3315
3	2.4869	2.4018	2.3216	2.2832	2.2459	2.1743	2.1065	1.9813	1.8684	1.7663
4	3.1699	3.0373	2.9137	2.8550	2.7982	2.6901	2.5887	2.4043	2.2410	2.0957
5	3.7908	3.6048	3.4331	3.3522	3.2743	3.1272	2.9906	2.7454	2.5320	2.3452
6	4.3553	4.1114	3.8887	3.7845	3.6847	3.4976	3.3255	3.0205	2.7594	2.5342
7	4.8684	4.5638	4.2883	4.1604	4.0386	3.8115	3.6046	3.2423	2.9370	2.6775
8	5.3349	4.9676	4.6389	4.4873	4.3436	4.0776	3.8372	3.4212	3.0758	2.7860
9	5.7590	5.3282	4.9464	4.7716	4.6065	4.3030	4.0310	3.5655	3.1842	2.8681
10	6.1446	5.6502	5.2161	5.0188	4.8332	4.4941	4.1925	3.6819	3.2689	2.9304
11	6.4951	5.9377	5.4527	5.2337	5.0286	4.6560	4.3271	3.7757	3.3351	2.9776
12	6.8137	6.1944	5.6603	5.4206	5.1971	4.7932	4.4392	3.8514	3.3868	3.0133
13	7.1034	6.4235	5.8424	5.5831	5.3423	4.9095	4.5327	3.9124	3.4272	3.0404
14	7.3667	6.6282	6.0021	5.7245	5.4675	5.0081	4.6106	3.9616	3.4587	3.0609
15	7.6061	6.8109	6.1422	5.8474	5.5755	5.0916	4.6755	4.0013	3.4834	3.0764
16	7.8237	6.9740	6.2651	5.9542	5.6685	5.1624	4.7296	4.0333	3.5026	3.0882
17	8.0216	7.1196	6.3729	6.0472	5.7487	5.2223	4.7746	4.0591	3.5177	3.0971
18	8.2014	7.2497	6.4674	6.1280	5.8178	5.2732	4.8122	4.0799	3.5294	3.1039
19	8.3649	7.3658	6.5504	6.1982	5.8775	5.3162	4.8435	4.0967	3.5386	3.1090
20	8.5136	7.4694	6.6231	6.2593	5.9288	5.3527	4.8696	4.1103	3.5458	3.1129
21	8.6487	7.5620	6.6870	6.3125	5.9731	5.3837	4.8913	4.1212	3.5514	3.1158
22	8.7715	7.6446	6.7429	6.3587	6.0113	5.4099	4.9094	4.1300	3.5558	3.1180
23	8.8832	7.7184	6.7921	6.3988	6.0442	5.4321	4.9245	4.1371	3.5592	3.1197
24	8.9847	7.7843	6.8351	6.4338	6.0726	5.4509	4.9371	4.1428	3.5619	3.1210
25	9.0770	7.8431	6.8729	6.4641	6.0971	5.4669	4.9476	4.1474	3.5640	3.1220
26	9.1609	7.8957	6.9061	6.4906	6.1182	5.4804	4.9563	4.1511	3.5656	3.1227
27	9.2372	7.9426	6.9352	6.5135	6.1364	5.4919	4.9636	4.1542	3.5669	3.1233
28	9.3066	7.9844	6.9607	6.5335	6.1520	5.5016	4.9697	4.1566	3.5679	3.1237
29	9.3696	8.0218	6.9830	6.5509	6.1656	5.5098	4.9747	4.1585	3.5687	3.1240
30	9.4269	8.0552	7.0027	6.5660	6.1772	5.5168	4.9789	4.1601	3.5693	3.1242
35	9.6442	8.1755	7.0700	6.6166	6.2153	5.5386	4.9915	4.1644	3.5708	3.1248
40	9.7791	8.2438	7.1050	6.6418	6.2335	5.5482	4.9966	4.1659	3.5712	3.1250
45	9.8628	8.2825	7.1232	6.6543	6.2421	5.5523	4.9986	4.1664	3.5714	3.1250
50	9.9148	8.3045	7.1327	6.6605	6.2463	5.5541	4.9995	4.1666	3.5714	3.1250
55	9.9471	8.3170	7.1376	6.6636	6.2482	5.5549	4.9998	4.1666	3.5714	3.1250

Table A-3 ▪ Future Value of $1 at the End of n Periods:

Equation:

$FVIF_{i,n} = (1 + i)^n$

Financial Calculator Keys:

n	i	1.0	0	
N	I	PV	PMT	FV
				TABLE VALUE

Period	1%	2%	3%	4%	5%	6%	7%	8%	9%	10%
1	1.0100	1.0200	1.0300	1.0400	1.0500	1.0600	1.0700	1.0800	1.0900	1.1000
2	1.0201	1.0404	1.0609	1.0816	1.1025	1.1236	1.1449	1.1664	1.1881	1.2100
3	1.0303	1.0612	1.0927	1.1249	1.1576	1.1910	1.2250	1.2597	1.2950	1.3310
4	1.0406	1.0824	1.1255	1.1699	1.2155	1.2625	1.3108	1.3605	1.4116	1.4641
5	1.0510	1.1041	1.1593	1.2167	1.2763	1.3382	1.4026	1.4693	1.5386	1.6105
6	1.0615	1.1262	1.1941	1.2653	1.3401	1.4185	1.5007	1.5869	1.6771	1.7716
7	1.0721	1.1487	1.2299	1.3159	1.4071	1.5036	1.6058	1.7138	1.8280	1.9487
8	1.0829	1.1717	1.2668	1.3686	1.4775	1.5938	1.7182	1.8509	1.9926	2.1436
9	1.0937	1.1951	1.3048	1.4233	1.5513	1.6895	1.8385	1.9990	2.1719	2.3579
10	1.1046	1.2190	1.3439	1.4802	1.6289	1.7908	1.9672	2.1589	2.3674	2.5937
11	1.1157	1.2434	1.3842	1.5395	1.7103	1.8983	2.1049	2.3316	2.5804	2.8531
12	1.1268	1.2682	1.4258	1.6010	1.7959	2.0122	2.2522	2.5182	2.8127	3.1384
13	1.1381	1.2936	1.4685	1.6651	1.8856	2.1329	2.4098	2.7196	3.0658	3.4523
14	1.1495	1.3195	1.5126	1.7317	1.9799	2.2609	2.5785	2.9372	3.3417	3.7975
15	1.1610	1.3459	1.5580	1.8009	2.0789	2.3966	2.7590	3.1722	3.6425	4.1772
16	1.1726	1.3728	1.6047	1.8730	2.1829	2.5404	2.9522	3.4259	3.9703	4.5950
17	1.1843	1.4002	1.6528	1.9479	2.2920	2.6928	3.1588	3.7000	4.3276	5.0545
18	1.1961	1.4282	1.7024	2.0258	2.4066	2.8543	3.3799	3.9960	4.7171	5.5599
19	1.2081	1.4568	1.7535	2.1068	2.5270	3.0256	3.6165	4.3157	5.1417	6.1159
20	1.2202	1.4859	1.8061	2.1911	2.6533	3.2071	3.8697	4.6610	5.6044	6.7275
21	1.2324	1.5157	1.8603	2.2788	2.7860	3.3996	4.1406	5.0338	6.1088	7.4002
22	1.2447	1.5460	1.9161	2.3699	2.9253	3.6035	4.4304	5.4365	6.6586	8.1403
23	1.2572	1.5769	1.9736	2.4647	3.0715	3.8197	4.7405	5.8715	7.2579	8.9543
24	1.2697	1.6084	2.0328	2.5633	3.2251	4.0489	5.0724	6.3412	7.9111	9.8497
25	1.2824	1.6406	2.0938	2.6658	3.3864	4.2919	5.4274	6.8485	8.6231	10.835
26	1.2953	1.6734	2.1566	2.7725	3.5557	4.5494	5.8074	7.3964	9.3992	11.918
27	1.3082	1.7069	2.2213	2.8834	3.7335	4.8223	6.2139	7.9881	10.245	13.110
28	1.3213	1.7410	2.2879	2.9987	3.9201	5.1117	6.6488	8.6271	11.167	14.421
29	1.3345	1.7758	2.3566	3.1187	4.1161	5.4184	7.1143	9.3173	12.172	15.863
30	1.3478	1.8114	2.4273	3.2434	4.3219	5.7435	7.6123	10.063	13.268	17.449
40	1.4889	2.2080	3.2620	4.8010	7.0400	10.286	14.974	21.725	31.409	45.259
50	1.6446	2.6916	4.3839	7.1067	11.467	18.420	29.457	46.902	74.358	117.39
60	1.8167	3.2810	5.8916	10.520	18.679	32.988	57.946	101.26	176.03	304.48

Table A-3 ▪ *(continued)*

Period	12%	14%	15%	16%	18%	20%	24%	28%	32%	36%
1	1.1200	1.1400	1.1500	1.1600	1.1800	1.2000	1.2400	1.2800	1.3200	1.3600
2	1.2544	1.2996	1.3225	1.3456	1.3924	1.4400	1.5376	1.6384	1.7424	1.8496
3	1.4049	1.4815	1.5209	1.5609	1.6430	1.7280	1.9066	2.0972	2.3000	2.5155
4	1.5735	1.6890	1.7490	1.8106	1.9388	2.0736	2.3642	2.6844	3.0360	3.4210
5	1.7623	1.9254	2.0114	2.1003	2.2878	2.4883	2.9316	3.4360	4.0075	4.6526
6	1.9738	2.1950	2.3131	2.4364	2.6996	2.9860	3.6352	4.3980	5.2899	6.3275
7	2.2107	2.5023	2.6600	2.8262	3.1855	3.5832	4.5077	5.6295	6.9826	8.6054
8	2.4760	2.8526	3.0590	3.2784	3.7589	4.2998	5.5895	7.2058	9.2170	11.703
9	2.7731	3.2519	3.5179	3.8030	4.4355	5.1598	6.9310	9.2234	12.166	15.917
10	3.1058	3.7072	4.0456	4.4114	5.2338	6.1917	8.5944	11.806	16.060	21.647
11	3.4785	4.2262	4.6524	5.1173	6.1759	7.4301	10.657	15.112	21.199	29.439
12	3.8960	4.8179	5.3503	5.9360	7.2876	8.9161	13.215	19.343	27.983	40.037
13	4.3635	5.4924	6.1528	6.8858	8.5994	10.699	16.386	24.759	36.937	54.451
14	4.8871	6.2613	7.0757	7.9875	10.147	12.839	20.319	31.691	48.757	74.053
15	5.4736	7.1379	8.1371	9.2655	11.974	15.407	25.196	40.565	64.359	100.71
16	6.1304	8.1372	9.3576	10.748	14.129	18.488	31.243	51.923	84.954	136.97
17	6.8660	9.2765	10.761	12.468	16.672	22.186	38.741	66.461	112.14	186.28
18	7.6900	10.575	12.375	14.463	19.673	26.623	48.039	85.071	148.02	253.34
19	8.6128	12.056	14.232	16.777	23.214	31.948	59.568	108.89	195.39	344.54
20	9.6463	13.743	16.367	19.461	27.393	38.338	73.864	139.38	257.92	468.57
21	10.804	15.668	18.822	22.574	32.324	46.005	91.592	178.41	340.45	637.26
22	12.100	17.861	21.645	26.186	38.142	55.206	113.57	228.36	449.39	866.67
23	13.552	20.362	24.891	30.376	45.008	66.247	140.83	292.30	593.20	1178.7
24	15.179	23.212	28.625	35.236	53.109	79.497	174.63	374.14	783.02	1603.0
25	17.000	26.462	32.919	40.874	62.669	95.396	216.54	478.90	1033.6	2180.1
26	19.040	30.167	37.857	47.414	73.949	114.48	268.51	613.00	1364.3	2964.9
27	21.325	34.390	43.535	55.000	87.260	137.37	332.95	784.64	1800.9	4032.3
28	23.884	39.204	50.066	63.800	102.97	164.84	412.86	1004.3	2377.2	5483.9
29	26.750	44.693	57.575	74.009	121.50	197.81	511.95	1285.6	3137.9	7458.1
30	29.960	50.950	66.212	85.850	143.37	237.38	634.82	1645.5	4142.1	10143.
40	93.051	188.88	267.86	378.72	750.38	1469.8	5455.9	19427.	66521.	*
50	289.00	700.23	1083.7	1670.7	3927.4	9100.4	46890.	*	*	*
60	897.60	2595.9	4384.0	7370.2	20555.	56348.	*	*	*	*

*FVIF > 99,999.

Table A-4 ▪ Future Value of an Annuity of $1 per Period for n Periods:

Equation:

Financial Calculator Keys:

$$FVIFA_{i,n} = \sum_{t=1}^{n} (1 + i)^{n-t} = \frac{(1 + i)^n - 1}{i}$$

n	i	0	1.0	
N	**I**	**PV**	**PMT**	**FV**

TABLE
VALUE

Number of Periods	1%	2%	3%	4%	5%	6%	7%	8%	9%	10%
1	1.0000	1.0000	1.0000	1.0000	1.0000	1.0000	1.0000	1.0000	1.0000	1.0000
2	2.0100	2.0200	2.0300	2.0400	2.0500	2.0600	2.0700	2.0800	2.0900	2.1000
3	3.0301	3.0604	3.0909	3.1216	3.1525	3.1836	3.2149	3.2464	3.2781	3.3100
4	4.0604	4.1216	4.1836	4.2465	4.3101	4.3746	4.4399	4.5061	4.5731	4.6410
5	5.1010	5.2040	5.3091	5.4163	5.5256	5.6371	5.7507	5.8666	5.9847	6.1051
6	6.1520	6.3081	6.4684	6.6330	6.8019	6.9753	7.1533	7.3359	7.5233	7.7156
7	7.2135	7.4343	7.6625	7.8983	8.1420	8.3938	8.6540	8.9228	9.2004	9.4872
8	8.2857	8.5830	8.8923	9.2142	9.5491	9.8975	10.260	10.637	11.028	11.436
9	9.3685	9.7546	10.159	10.583	11.027	11.491	11.978	12.488	13.021	13.579
10	10.462	10.950	11.464	12.006	12.578	13.181	13.816	14.487	15.193	15.937
11	11.567	12.169	12.808	13.486	14.207	14.972	15.784	16.645	17.560	18.531
12	12.683	13.412	14.192	15.026	15.917	16.870	17.888	18.977	20.141	21.384
13	13.809	14.680	15.618	16.627	17.713	18.882	20.141	21.495	22.953	24.523
14	14.947	15.974	17.086	18.292	19.599	21.015	22.550	24.215	26.019	27.975
15	16.097	17.293	18.599	20.024	21.579	23.276	25.129	27.152	29.361	31.772
16	17.258	18.639	20.157	21.825	23.657	25.673	27.888	30.324	33.003	35.950
17	18.430	20.012	21.762	23.698	25.840	28.213	30.840	33.750	36.974	40.545
18	19.615	21.412	23.414	25.645	28.132	30.906	33.999	37.450	41.301	45.599
19	20.811	22.841	25.117	27.671	30.539	33.760	37.379	41.446	46.018	51.159
20	22.019	24.297	26.870	29.778	33.066	36.786	40.995	45.762	51.160	57.275
21	23.239	25.783	28.676	31.969	35.719	39.993	44.865	50.423	56.765	64.002
22	24.472	27.299	30.537	34.248	38.505	43.392	49.006	55.457	62.873	71.403
23	25.716	28.845	32.453	36.618	41.430	46.996	53.436	60.893	69.532	79.543
24	26.973	30.422	34.426	39.083	44.502	50.816	58.177	66.765	76.790	88.497
25	28.243	32.030	36.459	41.646	47.727	54.865	63.249	73.106	84.701	98.347
26	29.526	33.671	38.553	44.312	51.113	59.156	68.676	79.954	93.324	109.18
27	30.821	35.344	40.710	47.084	54.669	63.706	74.484	87.351	102.72	121.10
28	32.129	37.051	42.931	49.968	58.403	68.528	80.698	95.339	112.97	134.21
29	33.450	38.792	45.219	52.966	62.323	73.640	87.347	103.97	124.14	148.63
30	34.785	40.568	47.575	56.085	66.439	79.058	94.461	113.28	136.31	164.49
40	48.886	60.402	75.401	95.026	120.80	154.76	199.64	259.06	337.88	442.59
50	64.463	84.579	112.80	152.67	209.35	290.34	406.53	573.77	815.08	1163.9
60	81.670	114.05	163.05	237.99	353.58	533.13	813.52	1253.2	1944.8	3034.8

Table A-4 ▪ *(continued)*

Number of Periods	12%	14%	15%	16%	18%	20%	24%	28%	32%	36%
1	1.0000	1.0000	1.0000	1.0000	1.0000	1.0000	1.0000	1.0000	1.0000	1.0000
2	2.1200	2.1400	2.1500	2.1600	2.1800	2.2000	2.2400	2.2800	2.3200	2.3600
3	3.3744	3.4396	3.4725	3.5056	3.5724	3.6400	3.7776	3.9184	4.0624	4.2096
4	4.7793	4.9211	4.9934	5.0665	5.2154	5.3680	5.6842	6.0156	6.3624	6.7251
5	6.3528	6.6101	6.7424	6.8771	7.1542	7.4416	8.0484	8.6999	9.3983	10.146
6	8.1152	8.5355	8.7537	8.9775	9.4420	9.9299	10.980	12.136	13.406	14.799
7	10.089	10.730	11.067	11.414	12.142	12.916	14.615	16.534	18.696	21.126
8	12.300	13.233	13.727	14.240	15.327	16.499	19.123	22.163	25.678	29.732
9	14.776	16.085	16.786	17.519	19.086	20.799	24.712	29.369	34.895	41.435
10	17.549	19.337	20.304	21.321	23.521	25.959	31.643	38.593	47.062	57.352
11	20.655	23.045	24.349	25.733	28.755	32.150	40.238	50.398	63.122	78.998
12	24.133	27.271	29.002	30.850	34.931	39.581	50.895	65.510	84.320	108.44
13	28.029	32.089	34.352	36.786	42.219	48.497	64.110	84.853	112.30	148.47
14	32.393	37.581	40.505	43.672	50.818	59.196	80.496	109.61	149.24	202.93
15	37.280	43.842	47.580	51.660	60.965	72.035	100.82	141.30	198.00	276.98
16	42.753	50.980	55.717	60.925	72.939	87.442	126.01	181.87	262.36	377.69
17	48.884	59.118	65.075	71.673	87.068	105.93	157.25	233.79	347.31	514.66
18	55.750	68.394	75.836	84.141	103.74	128.12	195.99	300.25	459.45	700.94
19	63.440	78.969	88.212	98.603	123.41	154.74	244.03	385.32	607.47	954.28
20	72.052	91.025	102.44	115.38	146.63	186.69	303.60	494.21	802.86	1298.8
21	81.699	104.77	118.81	134.84	174.02	225.03	377.46	633.59	1060.8	1767.4
22	92.503	120.44	137.63	157.41	206.34	271.03	469.06	812.00	1401.2	2404.7
23	104.60	138.30	159.28	183.60	244.49	326.24	582.63	1040.4	1850.6	3271.3
24	118.16	158.66	184.17	213.98	289.49	392.48	723.46	1332.7	2443.8	4450.0
25	133.33	181.87	212.79	249.21	342.60	471.98	898.09	1706.8	3226.8	6053.0
26	150.33	208.33	245.71	290.09	405.27	567.38	1114.6	2185.7	4260.4	8233.1
27	169.37	238.50	283.57	337.50	479.22	681.85	1383.1	2798.7	5624.8	11198.0
28	190.70	272.89	327.10	392.50	566.48	819.22	1716.1	3583.3	7425.7	15230.3
29	214.58	312.09	377.17	456.30	669.45	984.07	2129.0	4587.7	9802.9	20714.2
30	241.33	356.79	434.75	530.31	790.95	1181.9	2640.9	5873.2	12941.	28172.3
40	767.09	1342.0	1779.1	2360.8	4163.2	7343.9	22729.	69377.	*	*
50	2400.0	4994.5	7217.7	10436.	21813.	45497.	*	*	*	*
60	7471.6	18535.	29220.	46058.	*	*	*	*	*	*

*FVIFA > 99,999.

Solutions to Self-Test Problems

Note: Except for Chapter 1, we do not show an answer for ST-1 problems because they are verbal rather than quantitative in nature.

Chapter 1

ST-1 Refer to the marginal glossary definitions or relevant chapter sections to check your responses.

Chapter 2

ST-2 Billingsworth paid $2 in dividends and retained $2 per share. Since total retained earnings rose by $12 million, there must be 6 million shares outstanding. With a book value of $40 per share, total common equity must be $40(6 million) = $240 million. Since Billingsworth has $120 million of debt, its debt ratio must be 33.3 percent:

$$\frac{\text{Debt}}{\text{Assets}} = \frac{\text{Debt}}{\text{Debt} + \text{Equity}} = \frac{\$120 \text{ million}}{\$120 \text{ million} + \$240 \text{ million}}$$
$$= 0.333 = 33.3\%.$$

ST-3 a. In answering questions such as this, always begin by writing down the relevant definitional equations, then start filling in numbers. Note that the extra zeros indicating millions have been deleted in the calculations below.

(1)
$$\text{DSO} = \frac{\text{Accounts receivable}}{\text{Sales}/360}$$

$$40 = \frac{\text{A/R}}{\$1,000/360}$$

$$\text{A/R} = 40(\$2.778) = \$111.1 \text{ million.}$$

(2)
$$\text{Quick ratio} = \frac{\text{Current assets} - \text{Inventories}}{\text{Current liabilities}} = 2.0$$

$$= \frac{\text{Cash and marketable securities} + \text{A/R}}{\text{Current liabilities}} = 2.0$$

$$2.0 = \frac{\$100 + \$111.1}{\text{Current liabilities}}$$

Current liabilities = ($100 + $111.1)/2 = $105.5 million.

(3)
$$\text{Current ratio} = \frac{\text{Current assets}}{\text{Current liabilities}} = 3.0$$
$$= \frac{\text{Current assets}}{\$105.5} = 3.0$$
$$\text{Current assets} = 3.0(\$105.5) = \$316.50 \text{ million.}$$

(4)
$$\text{Total assets} = \text{Current assets} + \text{Fixed assets}$$
$$= \$316.5 + \$283.5 = \$600 \text{ million.}$$

(5)
$$\text{ROA} = \text{Profit margin} \times \text{Total assets turnover}$$
$$= \frac{\text{Net income}}{\text{Sales}} \times \frac{\text{Sales}}{\text{Total assets}}$$
$$= \frac{\$50}{\$1,000} \times \frac{\$1,000}{\$600}$$
$$= 0.05 \times 1.667 = 0.0833 = 8.33\%.$$

(6)
$$\text{ROE} = \text{ROA} \times \frac{\text{Assets}}{\text{Equity}}$$
$$12.0\% = 8.33\% \times \frac{\$600}{\text{Equity}}$$
$$\text{Equity} = \frac{(8.33\%)(\$600)}{12.0\%}$$
$$= \$416.50 \text{ million.}$$

(7)
$$\text{Total assets} = \text{Total claims} = \$600 \text{ million}$$
$$\text{Current liabilities} + \text{Long-term debt} + \text{Equity} = \$600 \text{ million}$$
$$\$105.5 + \text{Long-term debt} + \$416.5 = \$600 \text{ million}$$
$$\text{Long-term debt} = \$600 - \$105.5 - \$416.5 = \$78 \text{ million.}$$

Note: We could have found equity as follows:

$$\text{ROE} = \frac{\text{Net income}}{\text{Equity}}$$
$$12.0\% = \frac{\$50}{\text{Equity}}$$
$$\text{Equity} = \$50/0.12$$
$$= \$416.67 \text{ million (rounding error difference).}$$

Then we could have gone on to find current liabilities and long-term debt.

b. Kaiser's average sales per day were $\$1,000/360 = \$2.8$ million. Its DSO was 40, so $\text{A/R} = 40(\$2.8) = \$111.1$ million. Its new DSO of 30 would cause $\text{A/R} = 30(\$2.8) = \$83.3$ million. The reduction in receivables would be $\$111.1 - \$83.3 = \$27.8$ million, which would equal the amount of cash generated.

(1)
$$\text{New equity} = \text{Old equity} - \text{Stock bought back}$$
$$= \$416.5 - \$27.8$$
$$= \$388.7 \text{ million.}$$

Thus,

$$\text{New ROE} = \frac{\text{Net income}}{\text{New equity}}$$

$$= \frac{\$50}{\$388.7}$$

$$= 12.86\% \text{ (versus old ROE of 12.0\%).}$$

$$(2) \qquad \text{New ROA} = \frac{\text{Net income}}{\text{Total assets} - \text{Reduction in A/R}}$$

$$= \frac{\$50}{\$600 - \$27.8}$$

$$= 8.74\% \text{ (versus old ROA of 8.33\%).}$$

(3) The old debt is the same as the new debt:

$$\text{Debt} = \text{Total claims} - \text{Equity}$$

$$= \$600 - \$416.5 = \$183.5 \text{ million.}$$

$$\text{Old total assets} = \$600 \text{ million.}$$

$$\text{New total assets} = \text{Old total assets} - \text{Reduction in A/R}$$

$$= \$600 - \$27.8$$

$$= \$572.2 \text{ million.}$$

Therefore,

$$\frac{\text{Debt}}{\text{Old total assets}} = \frac{\$183.5}{\$600} = 30.6\%,$$

while

$$\frac{\text{New debt}}{\text{New total assets}} = \frac{\$183.5}{\$572.2} = 32.1\%.$$

Chapter 3

ST-2   a. Average $= (6\% + 7\% + 8\% + 9\%)/4 = 30\%/4 = 7.5\%$.
b. $k_{\text{T-bond}} = k^* + \text{IP} = 3.0\% + 7.5\% = 10.5\%$.
c. If the 5-year T-bond rate is 11 percent, the inflation rate is expected to average approximately $11\% - 3\% = 8\%$ during the next 5 years. Thus, the implied Year 5 inflation rate is 10 percent:

$$8\% = (6\% + 7\% + 8\% + 9\% + I_5)/5$$

$$40\% = 30\% + I_5$$

$$I_5 = 10\%.$$

ST-3

Thompson's Taxes as a Corporation	1993	1994	1995
Income before salary and taxes	$60,000	$90,000	$110,000
Less: salary	(40,000)	(40,000)	(40,000)
Taxable income, corporate	$20,000	$50,000	$ 70,000
Total corporate tax	3,000[a]	7,500	12,500
Salary	$40,000	$40,000	$ 40,000
Less exemptions and deductions	(15,650)	(15,650)	(15,650)
Taxable personal income	$24,350	$24,350	$ 24,350
Total personal tax	3,653[b]	3,653	3,653
Combined corporate and personal tax:	$ 6,653	$11,153	$ 16,153

(continued)

Thompson's Taxes as a Proprietorship	1993	1994	1995
Total income	$60,000	$90,000	$110,000
Less: exemptions and deductions	(15,650)	(15,650)	(15,650)
Taxable personal income	$44,350	$74,350	$ 94,350
Tax liability of proprietorship	$ 7,764[c]	$16,164	$ 22,000
Advantage to being a corporation:	$ 1,111	$ 5,011	$ 5,847

[a]Corporate tax in 1993 = (0.15)($20,000) = $3,000.

[b]Personal tax (if Thompson incorporates) in 1993 = (0.15)($24,350) = $3,653.

[c]Proprietorship tax in 1993 = $5,370 + (0.28)($44,350 − $35,800)
$$= \$5,370 + \$2,394$$
$$= \$7,764.$$

The corporate form of organization allows Thompson to pay the lowest taxes in each year; therefore, on the basis of taxes over the 3-year period, Thompson should incorporate his business. However, note that to get money out of the corporation so he can spend it, Thompson will have to have the corporation pay dividends, which will be taxed to Thompson, and thus he will, sometime in the future, have to pay additional taxes.

Chapter 4

ST-2   a. The average rate of return for each stock is calculated by simply averaging the returns over the five-year period. The average return for each stock is 18.90 percent, calculated for Stock A as follows:

$$k_{Avg} = (-10.00\% + 18.50\% + 38.67\% + 14.33\% + 33.00\%)/5$$
$$= 18.90\%.$$

The realized rate of return on a portfolio made up of Stock A and Stock B would be calculated by finding the average return in each year as k_A(% of Stock A) + k_B(% of Stock B) and then averaging these yearly returns:

Year	Portfolio AB's Return, k_{AB}
1988	(6.50%)
1989	19.90
1990	41.46
1991	9.00
1992	30.65
k_{Avg} =	18.90%

b. The standard deviation of returns is estimated, using Equation 4-3a, as follows (see Footnote 4):

$$\text{Estimated } \sigma = S = \sqrt{\frac{\sum_{t=1}^{n}(\bar{k}_t - \bar{k}_{Avg})^2}{n-1}}. \tag{4-3a}$$

For Stock A, the estimated σ is 19.0 percent:

$$\sigma_A = \sqrt{\frac{(-10.00 - 18.9)^2 + (18.50 - 18.9)^2 + \ldots + (33.00 - 18.9)^2}{5 - 1}}$$

$$= \sqrt{\frac{1,445.92}{4}} = 19.0\%.$$

The standard deviation of returns for Stock B and for the portfolio are similarly determined, and they are as follows:

	Stock A	Stock B	Portfolio AB
Standard deviation	19.0	19.0	18.6

c. Since the risk reduction from diversification is small (σ_{AB} falls only from 19.0 to 18.6 percent), the most likely value of the correlation coefficient is 0.9. If the correlation coefficient were -0.9, the risk reduction would be much larger. In fact, the correlation coefficient between Stocks A and B is 0.92.

d. If more randomly selected stocks were added to the portfolio, σ_p would decline to somewhere in the vicinity of 15 percent; see Figure 4-8. σ_p would remain constant only if the correlation coefficient were $+1.0$, which is most unlikely. σ_p would decline to zero only if the correlation coefficient, r, were equal to zero and a large number of stocks were added to the portfolio, or if the proper proportions were held in a two-stock portfolio with $r = -1.0$.

Chapter 5

ST-2   a.

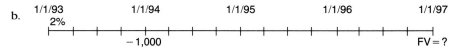

$1,000 is being compounded for 3 years, so your balance on January 1, 1997, is $1,259.71:

$$FV_n = PV(1 + i)^n = \$1,000(1 + 0.08)^3 = \$1,259.71.$$

Alternatively, using a financial calculator, input N = 3, I = 8, PV = -1000, PMT = 0, and FV = ? FV = $1,259.71.

b.

```
1/1/93            1/1/94            1/1/95            1/1/96            1/1/97
 2%
├──┼──┼──┼──┼──┼──┼──┼──┼──┼──┼──┼──┤
       -1,000                                                  FV = ?
```

The effective annual rate for 8 percent, compounded quarterly, is

$$\begin{array}{c}\text{Effective} \\ \text{annual} \\ \text{rate}\end{array} = \left(1 + \frac{0.08}{4}\right)^4 - 1.0$$

$$= (1.02)^4 - 1.0 = 0.0824 = 8.24\%.$$

Therefore, FV = $1,000(1.0824)^3 = \$1,000(1.2681) = \$1,268.10$. Alternatively, use FVIF for 2%, $3 \times 4 = 12$ periods:

$$FV_{12} = \$1,000(FVIF_{2\%,12}) = \$1,000(1.2682) = \$1,268.20.$$

Alternatively, using a financial calculator, input N = 12, I = 2, PV = -1000, PMT = 0, and FV = ? FV = $1,268.24.

Note that since the interest factors are carried to only four decimal places, rounding errors occur. Rounding errors also occur between calculator and tabular solutions.

c.

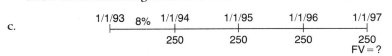

1/1/93	8%	1/1/94	1/1/95	1/1/96	1/1/97
		250	250	250	250
					FV = ?

As you work this problem, keep in mind that the tables assume that payments are made at the end of each period. Therefore, you may solve this problem by finding the future value of an annuity of $250 for 4 years at 8 percent:

$$FVA_4 = PMT(FVIFA_{i,n}) = \$250(4.5061) = \$1,126.53.$$

Alternatively, using a financial calculator, input $N = 4$, $I = 8$, $PV = 0$, $PMT = -250$, and $FV = ?$ $FV = \$1,126.53$.

d.

1/1/93	8%	1/1/94	1/1/95	1/1/96	1/1/97
		?	?	?	?
					FV = 1,259.71

$N = 4$; $I = 8\%$; $PV = 0$; $FV = \$1,259.71$; $PMT = ?$; $PMT = \$279.56$.

$$PMT(FVIFA_{8\%,4}) = FVA_4$$
$$PMT(4.5061) = \$1,259.71$$
$$PMT = \$1,259.71/4.5061 = \$279.56.$$

Therefore, you would have to make 4 payments of $279.56 each to have a balance of $1,259.71 on January 1, 1997.

ST-3   a.   Set up a time line like the one in the preceding problem:

1/1/93	8%	1/1/94	1/1/95	1/1/96	1/1/97
		PV = ?			1,000

Note that your deposit will grow for 3 years at 8 percent. The fact that it is now January 1, 1993, is irrelevant. The deposit on January 1, 1994, is the PV, and the FV is $1,000. Here is the solution:

$$N = 3; I = 8\%; PMT = 0; FV = \$1,000; PV = ?; PV = \$793.83.$$
$$FV_3(PVIF_{8\%,3}) = PV$$
$$PV = \$1,000(0.7938) = \$793.80 = \text{Initial deposit to accumulate}$$
$$\$1,000.$$

(Difference due to rounding error.)

b.

1/1/93	8%	1/1/94	1/1/95	1/1/96	1/1/97
		?	?	?	?
					FV = 1,000

Here we are dealing with a 4-year annuity whose first payment occurs one year from today, on 1/1/94, and whose future value must equal $1,000. You should modify the time line to help visualize the situation. Here is the solution:

$$N = 4; I = 8\%; PV = 0; FV = \$1,000; PMT = ?; PMT = \$221.92.$$
$$PMT(FVIFA_{8\%,4}) = FVA_4$$

$$PMT = \frac{FVA_4}{(FVIFA_{8\%,4})}$$

$$= \frac{\$1,000}{4.5061} = \$221.92 = \begin{array}{l} \text{Payment necessary} \\ \text{to accumulate } \$1,000. \end{array}$$

c. This problem can be approached in several ways. Perhaps the simplest is to ask this question: "If I received $750 on 1/1/94 and deposited it to earn 8 percent, would I have the required $1,000 on 1/1/97?" The answer is no:

```
1/1/93  8%  1/1/94      1/1/95      1/1/96      1/1/97
 |----------+-----------+-----------+-----------|
              -750                              FV = ?
```

$$FV_3 = \$750(1.08)(1.08)(1.08) = \$944.78.$$

This indicates that you should let your father make the payments rather than accept the lump sum of $750.

You could also compare the $750 with the PV of the payments:

```
1/1/93  8%  1/1/94      1/1/95      1/1/96      1/1/97
 |----------+-----------+-----------+-----------|
            221.92      221.92      221.92      221.92
            PV = ?
```

$$N = 4; I = 8\%; PMT = -\$221.92; FV = 0; PV = ?; PV = \$735.03.$$

$$PMT(PVIFA_{8\%,4}) = PVA_4$$

$$\$221.92(3.3121) = \$735.02 = \begin{array}{l} \text{Present value} \\ \text{of the required payments.} \end{array}$$

(Difference due to rounding error.)

This is less than the $750 lump sum offer, so your initial reaction might be to accept the lump sum of $750. However, this would be a mistake. The problem is that when you found the $735.02 PV of the annuity, you were finding the value of the annuity *today*, on January 1, 1993. You were comparing $735.02 today with the lump sum of $750 one year from now. This is, of course, invalid. What you should have done was take the $735.02, recognize that this is the PV of an annuity as of January 1, 1993, multiply $735.02 by 1.08 to get $793.82, and compare $793.82 with the lump sum of $750. You would then take your father's offer to make the payments rather than take the lump sum on January 1, 1994.

d.
```
1/1/93  i = ?  1/1/94      1/1/95      1/1/96      1/1/97
 |-------------+-----------+-----------+-----------|
    -750                                         1,000
```

$$N = 3; PV = -\$750; PMT = 0; FV = \$1,000; I = ?; I = 10.0642\%.$$

$$PV(FVIF_{i,3}) = FV$$

$$FVIF_{i,3} = \frac{FV}{PV}$$

$$= \frac{\$1,000}{\$750} = 1.3333.$$

Use the Future Value of $1 table (Table A-3 in Appendix A) for 3 periods to find the interest rate corresponding to an FVIF of 1.3333. Look across the Period 3 row of the table until you come to 1.3333. The closest value is 1.3310, in the 10 percent column. Therefore, you would require an interest rate of approximately 10 percent to achieve your $1,000 goal. The exact rate required, found with a financial calculator, is 10.0642 percent.

e.

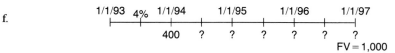

$N = 4; PV = 0; PMT = -\$186.29; FV = \$1,000; I = ?; I = 19.9997\%.$

$$PMT(FVIFA_{i,4}) = FVA_4$$
$$\$186.29(FVIFA_{i,4}) = \$1,000$$
$$FVIFA_{i,4} = \frac{\$1,000}{\$186.29} = 5.3680.$$

Using Table A-4 at the end of the book, we find that 5.3680 corresponds to a 20 percent interest rate. You might be able to find a borrower willing to offer you a 20 percent interest rate, but there would be some risk involved—he or she might not actually pay you your $1,000!

f.

Find the future value of the original $400 deposit:

$$FV_6 = PV(FVIF_{4\%,6}) = \$400(1.2653) = \$506.12.$$

This means that on January 1, 1997, you need an additional sum of $493.88:

$$\$1,000.00 - \$506.12 = \$493.88.$$

This will be accumulated by making 6 equal payments which earn 8 percent compounded semiannually, or 4 percent each 6 months:

$$N = 6; I = 4\%; PV = 0; FV = \$493.88; PMT = ?; PMT = 74.46.$$
$$PMT(FVIFA_{4\%,6}) = FVA_6$$
$$PMT = \frac{FVA_6}{(FVIFA_{4\%,6})}$$
$$= \frac{\$493.88}{6.6330} = \$74.46.$$

Alternatively, using a financial calculator, input $N = 6, I = 4, PV = -400,$ $FV = 1000,$ and $PMT = ?$ $PMT = \$74.46.$

g.

$$\text{Effective annual rate} = \left(1 + \frac{i_{Nom}}{m}\right)^m - 1.0$$

$$= \left(1 + \frac{0.08}{2}\right)^2 - 1 = (1.04)^2 - 1$$

$$= 1.0816 - 1 = 0.0816 = 8.16\%.$$

h. There is a reinvestment rate risk here because we assumed that funds will earn an 8 percent return in the bank. In fact, if interest rates in the economy fall, the bank will lower its deposit rate because it will be earning less when it lends out the funds you deposited with it. If you buy certificates of deposit (CDs) that mature on the date you need the money (1/1/97), you will avoid the reinvestment risk, but that would work only if you were making the deposit today. Other ways of reducing reinvestment rate risk will be discussed later in the text.

ST-4   Bank A's effective annual rate is 8.24 percent:

$$\text{Effective annual rate} = \left(1 + \frac{0.08}{4}\right)^4 - 1.0$$

$$= (1.02)^4 - 1 = 1.0824 - 1$$

$$= 0.0824 = 8.24\%.$$

Now Bank B must have the same effective annual rate:

$$\left(1 + \frac{i}{12}\right)^{12} - 1.0 = 0.0824$$

$$\left(1 + \frac{i}{12}\right)^{12} = 1.0824$$

$$1 + \frac{i}{12} = (1.0824)^{1/12}$$

$$1 + \frac{i}{12} = 1.00662$$

$$\frac{i}{12} = 0.00662$$

$$i = 0.07944 = 7.94\%.$$

Thus, the two banks have different quoted rates—Bank A's quoted rate is 8 percent, while Bank B's quoted rate is 7.94 percent; however, both banks have the same effective annual rate of 8.24 percent. The difference in their quoted rates is due to the difference in compounding frequency.

Chapter 6

ST-2   a. This is not necessarily true. Because G plows back two-thirds of its earnings, its growth rate should exceed that of D, but D pays higher dividends ($6 versus $2). We cannot say which stock should have the higher price.

b. Again, we just do not know which price would be higher.

c. This is false. The changes in k_d and k_s would have a greater effect on G—its price would decline more.

d. The total expected return for D is $\hat{k}_D = D_1/P_0 + g = 15\% + 0\% = 15\%$. The total expected return for G will have D_1/P_0 less than 15 percent and g greater than 0 percent, but $\hat{k}_G$ should be neither greater nor smaller than D's total expected return, 15 percent, because the two stocks are stated to be equally risky.

e. We have eliminated a, b, c, and d, so e should be correct. On the basis of the available information, D and G should sell at about the same price, $40; thus, $\hat{k}_s = 15\%$ for both D and G. G's current dividend yield is $2/\$40 = 5\%$. Therefore, $g = 15\% - 5\% = 10\%$.

ST-3   a. Pennington's bonds were sold at par; therefore, the original YTM equaled the coupon rate of 12%.

b. $$V_B = \sum_{t=1}^{50} \frac{\$120/2}{\left(1 + \frac{0.10}{2}\right)^t} + \frac{\$1,000}{\left(1 + \frac{0.10}{2}\right)^{50}}$$

$$= \$60(\text{PVIFA}_{5\%,50}) + \$1,000(\text{PVIF}_{5\%,50})$$
$$= \$60(18.2559) + \$1,000(0.0872)$$
$$= \$1,095.35 + \$87.20 = \$1,182.55.$$

Alternatively, with a financial calculator, input the following: N = 50, I = 5, PMT = 60, FV = 1000, and PV = ? PV = $1,182.56.

c.
$$\text{Current yield} = \text{Annual coupon payment/Price}$$
$$= \$120/\$1,182.55$$
$$= 0.1015 = 10.15\%.$$
$$\text{Capital gains yield} = \text{Total yield} - \text{Current yield}$$
$$= 10\% - 10.15\% = -0.15\%.$$

d.
$$\$916.42 = \sum_{t=1}^{13} \frac{\$60}{(1 + k_d/2)^t} + \frac{\$1,000}{(1 + k_d/2)^{13}}.$$

Try $k_d = 14\%$:

$$V_B = \text{INT}(\text{PVIFA}_{7\%,13}) + M(\text{PVIF}_{7\%,13})$$
$$\$916.42 = \$60(8.3577) + \$1,000(0.4150)$$
$$= \$501.46 + \$415.00 = \$916.46.$$

Therefore, the YTM on July 1, 1993, was 14 percent. Alternatively, with a financial calculator, input the following: N = 13, PV = −916.42, PMT = 60, FV = 1000, and $k_{d/2}$ = I = ? Calculator solution = $k_{d/2}$ = 7.00%; therefore, k_d = 14.00%.

e.
$$\text{Current yield} = \$120/\$916.42 = 13.09\%.$$
$$\text{Capital gains yield} = 14\% - 13.09\% = 0.91\%.$$

f. The following time line illustrates the years to maturity of the bond:

```
1/1/93      7/1/93    1/1/94    7/1/94    1/1/95    12/31/99
├──┼────────┼─────────┼─────────┼─────────┼── · · · ──┤
   3/1/93
```

Thus, on March 1, 1993, there were 13⅔ periods left before the bond matures. Bond traders actually use the following procedure to determine the price of the bond:
(1) Find the price of the bond on the next coupon date, July 1, 1993.

$$V_{B \ 7/1/93} = \$60(\text{PVIFA}_{7.75\%,13}) + \$1,000(\text{PVIF}_{7.75\%,13})$$
$$= \$60(8.0136) + \$1,000(0.3789)$$
$$= \$859.72.$$

Note that we could use a calculator to solve for $V_{B \ 7/1/93}$ or we could substitute i = 7.75% and n = 13 periods into the equations for PVIFA and PVIF:

$$\text{PVIFA} = \frac{1 - \dfrac{1}{(1 + i)^n}}{i} = \frac{1 - \dfrac{1}{(1 + 0.0775)^{13}}}{0.0775} = 8.0136.$$

$$\text{PVIF} = \frac{1}{(1 + k)^n} = \frac{1}{(1 + 0.0775)^{13}} = 0.3789.$$

(2) Add the coupon, $60, to the bond price to get the total value, TV, of the bond on the next interest payment date: TV = $859.72 + $60.00 = $919.72.

(3) Discount this total value back to the purchase date:

$$\text{Value at purchase date (March 1, 1993)} = \$919.72(\text{PVIF}_{7.75\%,4/6})$$
$$= \$919.72(0.9515)$$
$$= \$875.11.$$

Here

$$\text{PVIF}_{7.75\%,2/3} = \frac{1}{(1 + 0.0775)^{2/3}} = \frac{1}{1.0510} = 0.9515.$$

(4) Therefore, you would have written a check for $875.11 to complete the transaction. Of this amount, $20 = (⅓)($60) would represent accrued interest and $855.11 would represent the bond's basic value. This breakdown would affect both your taxes and those of the seller.

(5) This problem could be solved *very* easily using a financial calculator with a bond valuation function, such as the HP-12C or the HP-17B. This is explained in the calculator manual under the heading, "Bond Calculations."

ST-4 The first step is to solve for g, the unknown variable, in the constant growth equation. Since D_1 is unknown but D_0 is known, substitute $D_0(1 + g)$ as follows:

$$\hat{P}_0 = P_0 = \frac{D_1}{k_s - g} = \frac{D_0(1 + g)}{k_s - g}$$
$$\$36 = \frac{\$2.40(1 + g)}{0.12 - g}.$$

Solving for g, we find the growth rate to be 5 percent:

$$\$4.32 - \$36g = \$2.40 + \$2.40g$$
$$\$38.4g = \$1.92$$
$$g = 0.05 = 5\%.$$

The next step is to use the growth rate to project the stock price 5 years hence:

$$\hat{P}_5 = \frac{D_0(1 + g)^6}{k_s - g}$$
$$= \frac{\$2.40(1.05)^6}{0.12 - 0.05}$$
$$= \$45.95.$$

[Alternatively, $\hat{P}_5 = \$36(1.05)^5 = \$45.95.$]

Therefore, Ewald Company's expected stock price 5 years from now, $\hat{P}_5$, is $45.95.

ST-5 a. (1) Calculate the PV of the dividends paid during the supernormal growth period:

$$D_1 = \$1.1500(1.15) = \$1.3225.$$
$$D_2 = \$1.3225(1.15) = \$1.5209.$$
$$D_3 = \$1.5209(1.13) = \$1.7186.$$

$$\text{PV D} = \$1.3225(0.8929) + \$1.5209(0.7972) + \$1.7186(0.7118)$$
$$= \$1.1809 + \$1.2125 + \$1.2233$$
$$= \$3.6167 \approx \$3.62.$$

(2) Find the PV of Snyder's stock price at the end of Year 3:

$$\hat{P}_3 = \frac{D_4}{k_s - g} = \frac{D_3(1 + g)}{k_s - g}$$

$$= \frac{\$1.7186(1.06)}{0.12 - 0.06}$$

$$= \$30.36.$$

$$PV \; \hat{P}_3 = \$30.36(0.7118) = \$21.61.$$

(3) Sum the two components to find the value of the stock today:

$$\hat{P}_0 = \$3.62 + \$21.61 = \$25.23.$$

Alternatively, the cash flows can be placed on a time line as follows:

```
0        12%     1          2          3          4
├────────────────┼──────────┼──────────┼──────────┤
   g=15%                g=13%    g=6%
           1.3225    1.5209    1.7186         1.8217
                                                 ↓
                               30.3617    =   $1.8217
                               32.0803       0.12 − 0.06
```

Enter the cash flows into the cash flow register, I = 12, and press the NPV key to obtain P_0 = $25.23.

b. $$\hat{P}_1 = \$1.5209(0.8929) + \$1.7186(0.7972) + \$30.36(0.7972)$$

$$= \$1.3580 + \$1.3701 + \$24.2030$$

$$= \$26.9311 \approx \$26.93.$$

(Calculator solution: $26.93.)

$$\hat{P}_2 = \$1.7186(0.8929) + \$30.36(0.8929)$$

$$= \$1.5345 + \$27.1084$$

$$= \$28.6429 \approx \$28.64.$$

(Calculator solution: $28.64.)

c.

Year	Dividend Yield	+	Capital Gains Yield	=	Total Return
1	$\frac{\$1.3225}{\$25.23} \approx 5.24\%$		$\frac{\$26.93 - \$25.23}{\$25.23} \approx 6.74\%$		$\approx 12\%$
2	$\frac{\$1.5209}{\$26.93} \approx 5.65\%$		$\frac{\$28.64 - \$26.93}{\$26.93} \approx 6.35\%$		$\approx 12\%$
3	$\frac{\$1.7186}{\$28.64} \approx 6.00\%$		$\frac{\$30.36 - \$28.64}{\$28.64} \approx 6.00\%$		$\approx 12\%$

Chapter 7

ST-2   To solve this problem, we will define ΔS as the change in sales and g as the growth rate in sales, and then we use the three following equations:

$$\Delta S = S_0 g.$$

$$S_1 = S_0(1 + g).$$

$$AFN = (A^*/S)(\Delta S) - (L^*/S)(\Delta S) - MS_1(1 - d).$$

Set AFN = 0, substitute in known values for A*/S, L*/S, M, d, and S, and then solve for g:

$$0 = 1.6(\$100g) - 0.4(\$100g) - 0.10[\$100(1 + g)](0.55)$$
$$= \$160g - \$40g - 0.055(\$100 + \$100g)$$
$$= \$160g - \$40g - \$5.5 - \$5.5g$$
$$\$114.5g = \$5.5$$
$$g = \$5.5/\$114.5 = 0.048 = 4.8\%$$
$$= \text{Maximum growth rate without external financing.}$$

ST-3   Assets consist of cash, marketable securities, receivables, inventories, and fixed assets. Therefore, we can break the A*/S ratio into its components—cash/sales, inventories/sales, and so forth. Then,

$$\frac{A^*}{S} = \frac{A^* - \text{Inventories}}{S} + \frac{\text{Inventories}}{S} = 1.6.$$

We know that the inventory turnover ratio is sales/inventories = 3 times, so inventories/sales = 1/3 = 0.3333. Further, if the inventory turnover ratio can be increased to 4 times, then the inventory/sales ratio will fall to 1/4 = 0.25, a difference of 0.3333 − 0.2500 = 0.0833. This, in turn, causes the A*/S ratio to fall from A*/S = 1.6 to A*/S = 1.6 − 0.0833 = 1.5167.

This change has two effects: First, it changes the AFN equation, and second, it means that Weatherford currently has excessive inventories. Because it is costly to hold excess inventories, Weatherford will want to reduce its inventory holdings by not replacing inventories until the excess amounts have been used. We can account for this by setting up the revised AFN equation (using the new A*/S ratio), estimating the funds that will be needed next year if no excess inventories are currently on hand, and then subtracting out the excess inventories which are currently on hand:

Present conditions:

$$\frac{\text{Sales}}{\text{Inventories}} = \frac{\$100}{\text{Inventories}} = 3,$$

so

$$\text{Inventories} = \$100/3 = \$33.3 \text{ million at present.}$$

New conditions:

$$\frac{\text{Sales}}{\text{Inventories}} = \frac{\$100}{\text{Inventories}} = 4,$$

so

$$\text{New level of inventories} = \$100/4 = \$25 \text{ million.}$$

Therefore,

$$\text{Excess inventories} = \$33.3 - \$25 = \$8.3 \text{ million.}$$

Forecast of funds needed, first year:

$$\Delta S \text{ in first year} = 0.2(\$100 \text{ million}) = \$20 \text{ million.}$$
$$\text{AFN} = 1.5167(\$20) - 0.4(\$20) - 0.1(0.55)(\$120) - \$8.3$$
$$= \$30.3 - \$8 - \$6.6 - \$8.3$$
$$= \$7.4 \text{ million.}$$

Forecast of funds needed, second year:

$$\Delta S \text{ in second year} = gS_1 = 0.2(\$120 \text{ million}) = \$24 \text{ million.}$$

$$AFN = 1.5167(\$24) - 0.4(\$24) - 0.1(0.55)(\$144)$$

$$= \$36.4 - \$9.6 - \$7.9$$

$$= \$18.9 \text{ million.}$$

ST-4   Allied Food Products:
Pro Forma Income Statement
(Millions of Dollars)

	Second Pass	Feedback Effects	Third Pass
EBIT	$312		$312
Interest	93		93
EBT	$219		$219
Taxes (40%)	88		88
Net income before preferred dividends	$131		$131
Dividends to preferred	4		4
Net income available to common	$127		$127
Common dividends	$66		$66
Addition to retained earnings	$61		$61

$$\text{Change in interest expense} = (\$2 \times 0.08) + (\$2 \times 0.10)$$

$$= 0.36 \approx \$0.$$

Allied Food Products:
Pro Forma Balance Sheet
(Millions of Dollars)

	Second Pass	Feedback Effects	Third Pass
Total assets	$2,200		$2,200
Accounts payable	$ 66		$ 66
Notes payable	138	+2	140
Accruals	154		154
Total current liabilities	$ 358		$ 360
Long-term bonds	782	+2	784
Total debt	$1,140		$1,144
Preferred stock	40		40
Common stock	186	+3	189
Retained earnings	827		827
Total common equity	$1,013		$1,016
Total liabilities and equity	$2,193		$2,200
Additional funds needed	$ 7		$ 0

Chapter 8

ST-2   a.   (1) Determine the variable cost per unit at present, using the following definitions and equations:

$$Q = \text{units of output (sales)} = 5,000.$$
$$P = \text{average sales price per unit of output} = \$100.$$
$$F = \text{fixed operating costs} = \$200,000.$$
$$V = \text{variable costs per unit.}$$

$$\text{EBIT} = P(Q) - F - V(Q)$$
$$\$50,000 = \$100(5,000) - \$200,000 - V(5,000)$$
$$5,000V = \$250,000$$
$$V = \$50.$$

(2) Determine the new EBIT level if the change is made:

$$\text{New EBIT} = P_2(Q_2) - F_2 - V_2(Q_2)$$
$$= \$95(7,000) - \$250,000 - \$40(7,000)$$
$$= \$135,000.$$

(3) Determine the incremental EBIT:

$$\Delta\text{EBIT} = \$135,000 - \$50,000 = \$85,000.$$

(4) Estimate the approximate rate of return on the new investment:

$$\Delta\text{ROA} = \frac{\Delta\text{EBIT}}{\text{Investment}} = \frac{\$85,000}{\$400,000} = 21.25\%.$$

Since the ROA exceeds Olinde's average cost of capital, this analysis suggests that Olinde should go ahead and make the investment.

b.
$$\text{DOL} = \frac{Q(P - V)}{Q(P - V) - F}$$

$$\text{DOL}_{\text{Old}} = \frac{5,000(\$100 - \$50)}{5,000(\$100 - \$50) - \$200,000} = 5.00.$$

$$\text{DOL}_{\text{New}} = \frac{7,000(\$95 - \$40)}{7,000(\$95 - \$40) - \$250,000} = 2.85.$$

This indicates that operating income will be less sensitive to changes in sales if the production process is changed; thus the change would reduce risks. However, the change would increase the breakeven point. Still, with a lower sales price, it might be easier to achieve the higher new breakeven volume.

$$Old: Q_{\text{BE}} = \frac{F}{P - V} = \frac{\$200,000}{\$100 - \$50} = 4,000 \text{ units.}$$

$$New: Q_{\text{BE}} = \frac{F}{P_2 - V_2} = \frac{\$250,000}{\$95 - \$40} = 4,545 \text{ units.}$$

c.   The incremental ROA is:

$$\text{ROA} = \frac{\Delta\text{Profit}}{\Delta\text{Sales}} \times \frac{\Delta\text{Sales}}{\Delta\text{Assets}}.$$

Using debt financing, the incremental profit associated with the investment is equal to the incremental profit found in Part a minus the interest expense incurred as a result of the investment:

$$\Delta\text{Profit} = \text{New profit} - \text{Old profit} - \text{Interest}$$
$$= \$135,000 - \$50,000 - 0.10(\$400,000)$$
$$= \$45,000.$$

The incremental sales is calculated as:

$$\Delta\text{Sales} = P_2 Q_2 - P_1 Q_1$$
$$= \$95(7,000) - \$100(5,000)$$
$$= \$665,000 - \$500,000$$
$$= \$165,000.$$
$$\text{ROA} = \frac{\$45,000}{\$165,000} \times \frac{\$165,000}{\$400,000} = 11.25\%.$$

The return on the new equity investment still exceeds the average cost of capital, so Olinde should make the investment.

Chapter 9

ST-2   a. and b.

Income Statements for Year Ended December 31, 1992
(Thousands of Dollars)

	Vanderheiden Press		Herrenhouse Publishing	
	a	b	a	b
EBIT	$ 30,000	$ 30,000	$ 30,000	$ 30,000
Interest	12,400	14,400	10,600	18,600
Taxable income	$ 17,600	$ 15,600	$ 19,400	$ 11,400
Taxes (40%)	7,040	6,240	7,760	4,560
Net income	$ 10,560	$ 9,360	$ 11,640	$ 6,840
Equity	$100,000	$100,000	$100,000	$100,000
Return on equity	10.56%	9.36%	11.64%	6.84%

The Vanderheiden Press has a higher ROE when short-term interest rates are high, whereas Herrenhouse Publishing does better when rates are lower.

c. Herrenhouse's position is riskier. First, its profits and return on equity are much more volatile than Vanderheiden's. Second, Herrenhouse must renew its large short-term loan every year, and if the renewal comes up at a time when money is very tight, when its business is depressed, or both, then Herrenhouse could be denied credit, which could put it out of business.

ST-3   The Calgary Company: Alternative Balance Sheets

	Restricted (40%)	Moderate (50%)	Relaxed (60%)
Current assets	$1,200,000	$1,500,000	$1,800,000
Fixed assets	600,000	600,000	600,000
Total assets	$1,800,000	$2,100,000	$2,400,000
Debt	$ 900,000	$1,050,000	$1,200,000
Equity	900,000	1,050,000	1,200,000
Total liabilities and equity	$1,800,000	$2,100,000	$2,400,000

The Calgary Company: Alternative Income Statements

	Restricted	Moderate	Relaxed
Sales	$3,000,000	$3,000,000	$3,000,000
EBIT	450,000	450,000	450,000
Interest (10%)	90,000	105,000	120,000
Earnings before taxes (EBT)	$ 360,000	$ 345,000	$ 330,000
Taxes (40%)	144,000	138,000	132,000
Net income	$ 216,000	$ 207,000	$ 198,000
ROE	24.0%	19.7%	16.5%

Chapter 10

ST-2   a. First determine the balance on the firm's checkbook and the bank's records as follows:

	Firm's Checkbook	Bank's Records
Day 1: Deposit $500,000; write check for $1,000,000	($500,000)	$500,000
Day 2: Write check for $1,000,000	($1,500,000)	$500,000
Day 3: Write check for $1,000,000	($2,500,000)	$500,000
Day 4: Write check for $1,000,000; deposit $1,000,000	($2,500,000)	$500,000

After Upton has reached a steady state, it must deposit $1,000,000 each day to cover the checks written three days earlier.

   b. The firm has 3 days of float; not until Day 4 does the firm have to make any additional deposits.

   c. As shown above, Upton should try to maintain a balance on the bank's records of $500,000. On its own books it will have a balance of *minus* $2,500,000.

ST-3   First, determine the annual benefit to Kroncke from the reduction in cash balances under each plan:

$$\text{Average daily collections} = (30)(\$30,000) = \$900,000.$$

DTC:

Current collection float: $900,000 per day $\times$ 5 days = $4,500,000

New collection float: $900,000 per day $\times$ 3 days   =   2,700,000

Float reduction: $1,800,000

Kroncke can reduce its average cash balances by $1,800,000 by using DTCs, and it can earn 11 percent, which will provide $198,000 of additional income:

Additional income = ($1,800,000)(0.11) = $198,000.

Wire transfer:

Current collection float: $900,000 per day $\times$ 5 days = $4,500,000

New collection float: $900,000 per day $\times$ 1 day   =   900,000

Float reduction: $3,600,000

Kroncke can reduce its cash balances by $3,600,000 by using wire transfers, which will increase income by $396,000:

Additional income = ($3,600,000)(0.11) = $396,000.

Next, compute the annual cost of each transfer method:

Number of transfers = 30 $\times$ 260 = 7,800 per year.

Fixed lockbox cost = $14,000 $\times$ 12 = $168,000 per year.

DTC:

Total costs = (7,800)($0.75) + $168,000 = $173,850.

Wire transfer:

Total costs = (7,800)($11) + $168,000 = $253,800.

Finally, calculate the net additional income resulting from each transfer method:

DTC:

$198,000 − $173,850 = $24,150.

Wire transfer:

$396,000 − $253,800 = $142,200.

Therefore, Kroncke should adopt the lockbox system and transfer funds from the lockbox operators to the regional concentration banks using wire transfers.

Chapter 11

ST-2   Under the current credit policy, the Boca Grande Company has no discounts, has collection expenses of $50,000, has bad debt losses of (0.02)($10,000,000) = $200,000, and has average accounts receivable of (DSO)(Average sales per day) = (30)($10,000,000/360) = $833,333. The firm's cost of carrying these receivables is (Variable cost ratio)(A/R)(Cost of capital) = (0.80)($833,333)(0.16) = $106,667. It is necessary to multiply by the variable cost ratio because the actual *investment* in receivables is less than the dollar amount of the receivables.

Proposal 1: Lengthen the credit period to net 30 so that

1. Sales increase by $1 million.
2. Discounts = $0.
3. Bad debt losses = (0.02)($10,000,000) + (0.04)($1,000,000)
    = $200,000 + $40,000
    = $240,000.
4. DSO = 45 days on all sales.
5. New average receivables = (45)($11,000,000/360) = $1,375,000.
6. Cost of carrying receivables = (v)(k)(Average accounts receivable)
    = (0.80)(0.16)($1,375,000)
    = $176,000.
7. Collection expenses = $50,000.

Analysis of proposed change:

	Income Statement under Current Policy	Effect of Change	Income Statement under New Policy
Gross sales	$10,000,000	+ $1,000,000	$11,000,000
Less discounts	0	+ 0	0
Net sales	$10,000,000	+ $1,000,000	$11,000,000
Production costs (80%)	8,000,000	+ 800,000	8,800,000
Profit before credit costs and taxes	$ 2,000,000	+ $ 200,000	$ 2,200,000
Credit-related costs			
Cost of carrying receivables	106,667	+ 69,333	176,000
Collection expenses	50,000	+ 0	50,000
Bad debt losses	200,000	+ 40,000	240,000
Profit before taxes	$ 1,643,333	+ $ 90,667	$ 1,734,000
Federal-plus-state taxes (40%)	657,333	+ 36,267	693,600
Net income	$ 986,000	+ $ 54,400	$ 1,040,400

The proposed change appears to be a good one, assuming the assumptions are correct.

Proposal 2: Shorten the credit period to net 20 so that

1. Sales decrease by $1 million.
2. Discount = $0.
3. Bad debt losses = (0.01)($9,000,000) = $90,000.
4. DSO = 22 days.
5. New average receivables = (22)($9,000,000/360) = $550,000.
6. Cost of carrying receivables = (v)(k)(Average accounts receivable)
    = (0.80)(0.16)($550,000)
    = $70,400.
7. Collection expenses = $50,000.

Analysis of proposed change:

	Income Statement under Current Policy	Effect of Change	Income Statement under New Policy
Gross sales	$10,000,000	($1,000,000)	$9,000,000
Less discounts	0	0	0
Net sales	$10,000,000	($1,000,000)	$9,000,000
Production costs (80%)	8,000,000	(800,000)	7,200,000
Profit before credit costs and taxes	$ 2,000,000	($ 200,000)	$1,800,000
Credit-related costs			
Cost of carrying receivables	106,667	(36,267)	70,400
Collection expenses	50,000	0	50,000
Bad debt losses	200,000	(110,000)	90,000
Profit before taxes	$ 1,643,333	($ 53,733)	$1,589,600
Federal-plus-state taxes (40%)	657,333	(21,493)	635,840
Net income	$ 986,000	($ 32,240)	$ 953,760

This change reduces net income, so it should be rejected. Boca Grande will increase profits by accepting Proposal 1 to lengthen the credit period from 25 days to 30 days, assuming all assumptions are correct. This may or may not be the *optimal*, or profit-maximizing, credit policy, but it does appear to be a movement in the right direction.

Chapter 12

ST-2   a.

$$EOQ = \sqrt{\frac{2(F)(S)}{(C)(P)}}$$

$$= \sqrt{\frac{(2)(\$5,000)(2,600,000)}{(0.02)(\$5.00)}}$$

$$= 509,902 \text{ bushels.}$$

Because the firm must order in multiples of 2,000 bushels, it should order in quantities of 510,000 bushels.

b.

$$\text{Average weekly sales} = 2,600,000/52$$
$$= 50,000 \text{ bushels.}$$

$$\text{Reorder point} = 6 \text{ weeks' sales} + \text{Safety stock}$$
$$= 6(50,000) + 200,000$$
$$= 300,000 + 200,000$$
$$= 500,000 \text{ bushels.}$$

c. Total inventory costs:

$$TIC = CP\left(\frac{Q}{2}\right) + F\left(\frac{S}{Q}\right) + CP(\text{Safety stock})$$

$$= (0.02)(\$5)\left(\frac{510,000}{2}\right) + (\$5,000)\left(\frac{2,600,000}{510,000}\right) + (0.02)(\$5)(200,000)$$

$$= \$25,500 + \$25,490.20 + \$20,000$$

$$= \$70,990.20.$$

d. Ordering costs would be reduced by $3,500 to $1,500. By ordering 650,000 bushels at a time, the firm can bring its total inventory cost to $58,500:

$$\text{TIC} = (0.02)(\$5)\left(\frac{650,000}{2}\right) + (\$1,500)\left(\frac{2,600,000}{650,000}\right) + (0.02)(\$5)(200,000)$$

$$= \$32,500 + \$6,000 + \$20,000$$

$$= \$58,500.$$

Because the firm can reduce its total inventory costs by ordering 650,000 bushels at a time, it should accept the offer and place larger orders. (Incidentally, this same type of analysis is used to consider any quantity discount offer.)

Chapter 13

ST-2   a. **Commercial bank loan**

Amount loaned	= (0.75)($250,000)	= $187,500
Discount	= (0.09/12)($187,500) =	(1,406)
Compensating balance	= (0.20)($187,500)	(37,500)
Amount received		= $148,594

Interest expense	= (0.09)($187,500)	= $ 16,875
Credit department*	= ($4,000)(12)	= 48,000
Bad debts*	= (0.02)($250,000)(12)=	60,000
Total annual costs		= $124,875

*The costs of the credit department and bad debts are expenses that will be incurred if a bank loan is used, but these costs will be avoided if the firm accepts the factoring arrangement.

Factoring

Amount loaned	= (0.85)($250,000)	= $212,500
Commission for period	= (0.035)($250,000)	(8,750)
Prepaid interest	= (0.09/12)($203,750) =	(1,528)
Amount received		= $202,222

Annual commission	= ($8,750)(12)	= $105,000
Annual interest	= (0.09)($203,750)	= 18,338
Total annual costs		= $123,338

b. The factoring costs are slightly lower than the cost of the bank loan, and the factor is willing to advance a significantly greater amount. On the other hand, the elimination of the credit department could reduce the firm's options in the future.

Chapter 14

ST-2 a. *Payback:*

To determine the payback, construct the cumulative cash flows for each project:

	Cumulative Cash Flows	
Year	**Project X**	**Project Y**
0	($10,000)	($10,000)
1	(3,500)	(6,500)
2	(500)	(3,000)
3	2,500	500
4	3,500	4,000

$$\text{Payback}_X = 2 + \frac{\$500}{\$3,000} = 2.17 \text{ years.}$$

$$\text{Payback}_Y = 2 + \frac{\$3,000}{\$3,500} = 2.86 \text{ years.}$$

Net present value (NPV):

$$NPV_X = -\$10,000 + \frac{\$6,500}{(1.12)^1} + \frac{\$3,000}{(1.12)^2} + \frac{\$3,000}{(1.12)^3} + \frac{\$1,000}{(1.12)^4}$$

$$= \$966.01.$$

$$NPV_Y = -\$10,000 + \frac{\$3,500}{(1.12)^1} + \frac{\$3,500}{(1.12)^2} + \frac{\$3,500}{(1.12)^3} + \frac{\$3,500}{(1.12)^4}$$

$$= \$630.72.$$

Alternatively, using a financial calculator, input the cash flows into the cash flow register, enter I = 12, and then press the NPV key to obtain $NPV_X = \$966.01$ and $NPV_Y = \$630.72$.

Internal rate of return (IRR):

To solve for each project's IRR, find the discount rates which equate each NPV to zero:

$$IRR_X = 18.0\%.$$

$$IRR_Y = 15.0\%.$$

Modified internal rate of return (MIRR):

To obtain each project's MIRR, begin by finding each project's terminal value (TV) of cash inflows:

$$TV_X = \$6,500(1.12)^3 + \$3,000(1.12)^2$$
$$+ \$3,000(1.12)^1 + \$1,000 = \$17,255.23.$$
$$TV_Y = \$3,500(1.12)^3 + \$3,500(1.12)^2$$
$$+ \$3,500(1.12)^1 + \$3,500 = \$16,727.65.$$

Now, each project's MIRR is that discount rate which equates the PV of the TV to each project's cost, $10,000:

$$MIRR_X = 14.61\%.$$

$$MIRR_Y = 13.73\%.$$

b. The following table summarizes the project rankings by each method:

	Project Which Ranks Higher
Payback	X
NPV	X
IRR	X
MIRR	X

Note that all methods rank Project X over Project Y. In addition, both projects are acceptable under the NPV, IRR, and MIRR criteria. Thus, both projects should be accepted if they are independent.

c. In this case, we would choose the project with the higher NPV at k = 12%, or Project X.

d. To determine the effects of changing the cost of capital, plot the NPV profiles of each project. The crossover rate occurs at about 6 to 7 percent (6.2%).

NPV Profiles for Projects X and Y

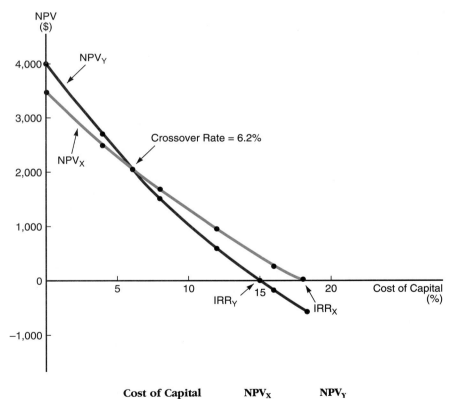

Cost of Capital	**NPV$_X$**	**NPV$_Y$**
0%	$3,500	$4,000
4	2,545	2,705
8	1,707	1,592
12	966	631
16	307	(206)
18	5	(585)

If the firm's cost of capital is less than 6 percent, a conflict exists because $NPV_Y > NPV_X$, but $IRR_X > IRR_Y$. Therefore, if k were 5 percent, a conflict would exist. Note, however, that when k = 5.0%, $MIRR_X$ = 10.64% and $MIRR_Y$ = 10.83%; hence the modified IRR ranks the projects correctly, even if k is to the left of the crossover point.

e. The basic cause of the conflict is differing reinvestment rate assumptions between NPV and IRR. NPV assumes that cash flows can be reinvested at the cost of capital, while IRR assumes reinvestment at the (generally) higher IRR. The high reinvestment rate assumption under IRR makes early cash flows especially valuable, and hence short-term projects look better under IRR.

Chapter 15

ST-2   a. *Estimated investment requirements:*

Price	($50,000)
Modification	(10,000)
Change in net working capital	(2,000)
Total investment	($62,000)

b. *Operating cash flows:*

	Year 1	Year 2	Year 3
1. After-tax cost savings[a]	$12,000	$12,000	$12,000
2. Depreciation[b]	19,800	27,000	9,000
3. Depreciation tax savings[c]	7,920	10,800	3,600
Net cash flow (1 + 3)	$19,920	$22,800	$15,600

[a]$20,000 (1 − T).

[b]Depreciable basis = $60,000; the MACRS percentage allowances are 0.33, 0.45, and 0.15 in Years 1, 2, and 3, respectively; hence, depreciation in Year 1 = 0.33($60,000) = $19,800, and so on. There will remain $4,200, or 7 percent, undepreciated after Year 3; it would normally be taken in Year 4.

[c]Depreciation tax savings = T(Depreciation) = 0.4($19,800) = $7,920 in Year 1, and so on.

c. *End-of-project cash flows:*

Salvage value	$20,000
Tax on salvage value[a]	(6,320)
Net working capital recovery	2,000
	$15,680

[a]Sales price	$20,000
Less book value	4,200
Taxable income	$15,800
Tax at 40%	$ 6,320

Book value = Depreciable basis − Accumulated depreciation
        = $60,000 − $55,800 = $4,200.

d. *Project NPV:*

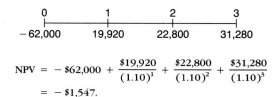

$$NPV = -\$62,000 + \frac{\$19,920}{(1.10)^1} + \frac{\$22,800}{(1.10)^2} + \frac{\$31,280}{(1.10)^3}$$

$$= -\$1,547.$$

Alternatively, using a financial calculator, input the cash flows into the cash flow register, enter I = 10, and then press the NPV key to obtain NPV = − $1,547. Because the earthmover has a negative NPV, it should not be purchased.

ST-3   *First determine the net cash flow at t = 0:*

Purchase price	($8,000)
Sale of old machine	3,000
Tax on sale of old machine	(160)[a]
Change in net working capital	(1,500)[b]
Total investment	($6,660)

[a]The market value is $3,000 − $2,600 = $400 above the book value. Thus, there is a $400 recapture of depreciation, and Dauten would have to pay 0.40($400) = $160 in taxes.

[b]The change in net working capital is a $2,000 increase in current assets minus a $500 increase in current liabilities, which totals to $1,500.

Now, examine the operating cash inflows:

Sales increase	$1,000
Cost decrease	1,500
Increase in pretax operating revenues	$2,500

After-tax operating revenue increase:

$$\$2,500(1 - T) = \$2,500(0.60) = \underline{\$1,500}.$$

Depreciation:

Year	1	2	3	4	5	6
New[a]	$1,600	$2,560	$1,520	$ 960	$ 880	$ 480
Old	350	350	350	350	350	350
Change	$1,250	$2,210	$1,170	$ 610	$ 530	$ 130
Depreciation Tax savings[b]	$ 500	$ 884	$ 468	$ 244	$ 212	$ 52

[a]Depreciable basis = $8,000. Depreciation expense in each year equals depreciable basis times the MACRS percentage allowances of 0.20, 0.32, 0.19, 0.12, 0.11, and 0.06 in Years 1–6, respectively.

[b]Depreciation tax savings = T(Δ Depreciation) = 0.4(Δ Depreciation).

Now recognize that at the end of Year 6 Dauten would recover its net working capital investment of $1,500, and it would also receive $800 from the sale of the replacement machine. However, since the machine would be fully depreciated, the firm must pay $0.40(\$800) = \$320$ in taxes on the sale. Also, by undertaking the replacement now, the firm forgoes the right to sell the old machine for $500 in Year 6; thus, this $500 in Year 6 must be considered an opportunity cost in that year. No tax would be due because the $500 salvage value would equal the old machine's Year 6 book value.

Finally, place all the cash flows on a time line:

	0	1	2	3	4	5	6
Net investment	(6,660)						
After-tax revenue increase		1,500	1,500	1,500	1,500	1,500	1,500
Depreciation tax savings		500	884	468	244	212	52
Working capital recovery							1,500
Salvage value on new machine							800
Tax on salvage value of new machine							(320)
Opportunity cost of old machine							(500)
Net cash flows	(6,660)	2,000	2,384	1,968	1,744	1,712	3,032

The net present value of this incremental cash flow stream, when discounted at 15 percent, is $1,335. Thus, the replacement should be made.

ST-4   a. First, find the expected cash flows:

Year	Expected Cash Flows		
0	$0.2(-\$100,000) + 0.6(-\$100,000) + 0.2(-\$100,000) =$		$(\$100,000)$
1	$0.2(\$20,000)\quad + 0.6(\$30,000)\quad + 0.2(\$40,000)\quad =$		$\$30,000$
2			$\$30,000$
3			$\$30,000$
4			$\$30,000$
5			$\$30,000$
5*	$0.2(\$0)\qquad + 0.6(\$20,000)\quad + 0.2(\$30,000)\quad =$		$\$18,000$

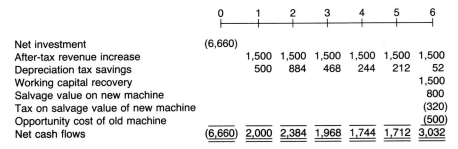

Next, determine the NPV based on the expected cash flows:

$$\text{NPV} = -\$100,000 + \frac{\$30,000}{(1.10)^1} + \frac{\$30,000}{(1.10)^2} + \frac{\$30,000}{(1.10)^3}$$
$$+ \frac{\$30,000}{(1.10)^4} + \frac{\$48,000}{(1.10)^5} = \$24,900.$$

Alternatively, using a financial calculator, input the cash flows in the cash flow register, enter I = 10, and then press the NPV key to obtain NPV = $24,900.

b. For the worst case, the cash flow values from the cash flow column farthest on the left are used to calculate NPV:

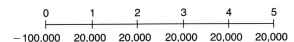

$$NPV = -\$100,000 + \frac{\$20,000}{(1.10)^1} + \frac{\$20,000}{(1.10)^2} + \frac{\$20,000}{(1.10)^3}$$
$$+ \frac{\$20,000}{(1.10)^4} + \frac{\$20,000}{(1.10)^5} = -\$24,184.$$

Similarly, for the best case, use the values from the column farthest on the right. Here the NPV is $70,259.

If the cash flows are perfectly dependent, then the low cash flow in the first year will mean a low cash flow in every year. Thus, the probability of the worst case occurring is the probability of getting the $20,000 net cash flow in Year 1, or 20 percent. If the cash flows are independent, the cash flow in each year can be low, high, or average, and the probability of getting all low cash flows will be

$$0.2(0.2)(0.2)(0.2)(0.2) = 0.2^5 = 0.00032 = 0.032\%.$$

c. The base case NPV is found using the most likely cash flows and is equal to $26,142. This value differs from the expected NPV of $24,900 because the Year 5 cash flows are not symmetric. Under these conditions, the NPV distribution is as follows:

P	NPV
0.2	($24,184)
0.6	26,142
0.2	70,259

Thus, the expected NPV is $0.2(-\$24,184) + 0.6(\$26,142) + 0.2(\$70,259) = \$24,900$. As is generally the case, the expected NPV is the same as the NPV of the expected cash flows found in Part a. The standard deviation is $29,904:

$$\sigma^2_{NPV} = 0.2(-\$24,184 - \$24,900)^2 + 0.6(\$26,142 - \$24,900)^2$$
$$+ 0.2(\$70,259 - \$24,900)^2$$
$$= \$894,261,126.$$
$$\sigma_{NPV} = \sqrt{\$894,261,126} = \$29,904.$$

The coefficient of variation, CV, is $\$29,904/\$24,900 = 1.20$.

d. Since the project's coefficient of variation is 1.20, the project is riskier than average, and hence the project's risk-adjusted cost of capital is $10\% + 2\% = 12\%$. The project now should be evaluated by finding the NPV of the expected cash flows, as in Part a, but using a 12 percent discount rate. The risk-adjusted NPV is $18,357, and therefore the project should be accepted.

Chapter 16

ST-2 a. A break point will occur each time a low-cost type of capital is used up. We establish the break points as follows, after first noting that LEI has $24,000 of retained earnings:

$$\text{Retained earnings} = (\text{Total earnings})(1.0 - \text{Payout})$$
$$= \$34,285.72(0.7)$$
$$= \$24,000.$$

$$\text{Break point} = \frac{\text{Total amount of low-cost capital of a given type}}{\text{Fraction of this type of capital in the capital structure}}.$$

Capital Used Up	Break Point Calculation		Break Number
Retained earnings	$BP_{RE} = \dfrac{\$24,000}{0.60}$	$= \$40,000$	2
10% flotation common	$BP_{10\%E} = \dfrac{\$24,000 + \$12,000}{0.60}$	$= \$60,000$	4
5% flotation preferred	$BP_{5\%P} = \dfrac{\$7,500}{0.15}$	$= \$50,000$	3
12% debt	$BP_{12\%D} = \dfrac{\$5,000}{0.25}$	$= \$20,000$	1
14% debt	$BP_{14\%D} = \dfrac{\$5,000 + \$5,000}{0.25}$	$= \$40,000$	2

Summary of break points

(1) There are three common equity costs and hence two changes and, therefore, two equity-induced breaks in the MCC. There are two preferred costs and hence one preferred break. There are three debt costs and hence two debt breaks.

(2) The numbers in the third column of the table designate the sequential order of the breaks, determined after all the break points were calculated. Note that the second debt break and the break for retained earnings both occur at $40,000.

(3) The first break point occurs at $20,000, when the 12 percent debt is used up. The second break point, $40,000, results from using up both retained earnings and the 14 percent debt. The MCC curve also rises at $50,000 and $60,000, as preferred stock with a 5 percent flotation cost and common stock with a 10 percent flotation cost, respectively, are used up.

b. Component costs within indicated total capital intervals are as follows: Retained earnings (used in interval $0 to $40,000):

$$k_s = \frac{D_1}{P_0} + g = \frac{D_0(1 + g)}{P_0} + g$$

$$= \frac{\$3.60(1.09)}{\$60} + 0.09$$

$$= 0.0654 + 0.09 \qquad\qquad = 15.54\%.$$

Common with F = 10% ($40,001 to $60,000):

$$k_e = \frac{D_1}{P_0(1.0 - F)} + g = \frac{\$3.924}{\$60(0.9)} + 9\% \qquad\qquad = 16.27\%.$$

Common with F = 20% (over $60,000):

$$k_e = \frac{\$3.924}{\$60(0.8)} + 9\% \qquad\qquad = 17.18\%.$$

Preferred with F $=$ 5% ($0 to $50,000):

$$k_p = \frac{\text{Preferred dividend}}{P_n} = \frac{\$11}{\$100(0.95)} \qquad = 11.58\%.$$

Preferred with F $=$ 10% (over $50,000):

$$k_p = \frac{\$11}{\$100(0.9)} \qquad = 12.22\%.$$

Debt at k_d $=$ 12% ($0 to $20,000):

$$k_d(1 - T) = 12\%(0.6) \qquad = 7.20\%.$$

Debt at k_d $=$ 14% ($20,001 to $40,000):

$$k_d(1 - T) = 14\%(0.6) \qquad = 8.40\%.$$

Debt at k_d $=$ 16% (over $40,000):

$$k_d(1 - T) = 16\%(0.6) \qquad = 9.60\%.$$

c. WACC calculations within indicated total capital intervals:
   (1) $0 to $20,000 (debt $=$ 7.2%, preferred $=$ 11.58%, and retained earnings [RE] $=$ 15.54%):

   $$\begin{aligned} \text{WACC}_1 &= w_d k_d(1 - T) + w_p k_p + w_s k_s \\ &= 0.25(7.2\%) + 0.15(11.58\%) + 0.60(15.54\%) = 12.86\%. \end{aligned}$$

   (2) $20,001 to $40,000 (debt $=$ 8.4%, preferred $=$ 11.58%, and RE $=$ 15.54%):

   $$\text{WACC}_2 = 0.25(8.4\%) + 0.15(11.58\%) + 0.60(15.54\%) = 13.16\%.$$

   (3) $40,001 to $50,000 (debt $=$ 9.6%, preferred $=$ 11.58%, and equity $=$ 16.27%):

   $$\text{WACC}_3 = 0.25(9.6\%) + 0.15(11.58\%) + 0.60(16.27\%) = 13.90\%.$$

   (4) $50,001 to $60,000 (debt $=$ 9.6%, preferred $=$ 12.22%, and equity $=$ 16.27%):

   $$\text{WACC}_4 = 0.25(9.6\%) + 0.15(12.22\%) + 0.60(16.27\%) = 14.00\%.$$

   (5) Over $60,000 (debt $=$ 9.6%, preferred $=$ 12.22%, and equity $=$ 17.18%):

   $$\text{WACC}_5 = 0.25(9.6\%) + 0.15(12.22\%) + 0.60(17.18\%) = 14.54\%.$$

d. IRR calculation for Project E:

$$\text{PVIFA}_{k,6} = \frac{\$20,000}{\$5,427.84} = 3.6847.$$

This is the factor for 16 percent, so $\text{IRR}_E = 16\%$.
Alternatively, N $=$ 6, PV $=$ -20000, PMT $=$ 5427.84, and I $=$? I $=$ 16.00%.
e. See the graph of the MCC and IOS schedules for LEI at the top of the next page.

LEI: MCC and IOS Schedules

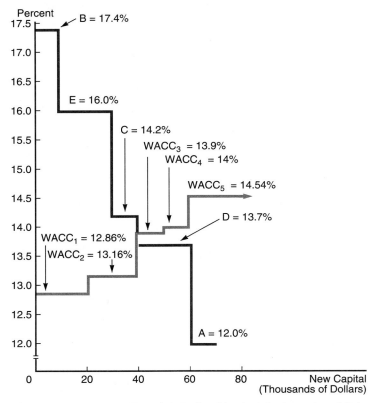

f. LEI should accept Projects B, E, and C. It should reject Projects A and D because their IRRs do not exceed the marginal costs of funds needed to finance them. The firm's capital budget would total $40,000.

Chapter 17

ST-2   a.

EBIT	$4,000,000
Interest ($2,000,000 × 0.10)	200,000
Earnings before taxes (EBT)	$3,800,000
Taxes (35%)	1,330,000
Net income	$2,470,000

$$EPS = \$2,470,000/600,000 = \$4.12.$$
$$P_0 = \$4.12/0.15 = \$27.47.$$

b.

$$Equity = 600,000 \times (\$10) = \$6,000,000.$$
$$Debt = \$2,000,000.$$
$$Total\ capital = \$8,000,000.$$

$$WACC = w_d k_d(1 - T) + w_s k_s$$
$$= (2/8)(10\%)(1 - 0.35) + (6/8)(15\%)$$
$$= 1.63\% + 11.25\%$$
$$= 12.88\%.$$

c.

EBIT	$4,000,000
Interest ($10,000,000 $\times$ 0.12)	1,200,000
Earnings before taxes (EBT)	$2,800,000
Taxes (35%)	980,000
Net income	$1,820,000

Shares bought and retired:

$$\Delta N = \Delta Debt/P_0 = \$8,000,000/\$27.47 = 291,227.$$

New outstanding shares:

$$N_1 = N_0 - \Delta N = 600,000 - 291,227 = 308,773.$$

New EPS:

$$EPS = \$1,820,000/308,773 = \$5.89.$$

New price per share:

$$P_0 = \$5.89/0.17 = \$34.65 \text{ versus } \$27.47.$$

Therefore, Gentry should change its capital structure.

d. In this case, the company's net income would be higher by $(0.12 - 0.10)$ $(\$2,000,000)(1 - 0.35) = \$26,000$ because its interest charges would be lower. The new price would be

$$P_0 = \frac{(\$1,820,000 + \$26,000)/308,773}{0.17} = \$35.18.$$

In the first case, in which debt had to be refunded, the bondholders were compensated for the increased risk of the higher debt position. In the second case, the old bondholders were not compensated; their 10 percent coupon perpetual bonds would now be worth

$$\$100/0.12 = \$833.33,$$

or $1,666,667 in total, down from the old $2 million, or a loss of $333,333. The stockholders would have a gain of

$$(\$35.18 - \$34.65)(308,773) = \$163,650.$$

This gain would, of course, be at the expense of the old bondholders. (There is no reason to think that bondholders' losses would exactly offset stockholders' gains.)

e.

$$TIE = \frac{EBIT}{I}.$$

$$\text{Original TIE} = \frac{\$4,000,000}{\$200,000} = 20 \text{ times.}$$

$$\text{New TIE} = \frac{\$4,000,000}{\$1,200,000} = 3.33 \text{ times.}$$

Chapter 18

ST-2 a.

Projected net income	$2,000,000
Less projected capital investments	800,000
Available residual	$1,200,000
Shares outstanding	200,000

$$DPS = \$1,200,000/200,000 \text{ shares} = \$6 = D_1.$$

b.

$$EPS = \$2,000,000/200,000 \text{ shares} = \$10.$$
$$\text{Payout ratio} = DPS/EPS = \$6/\$10 = 60\%, \text{ or}$$
$$\text{Total dividends/NI} = \$1,200,000/\$2,000,000 = 60\%.$$

c.

$$\text{Currently, } P_0 = \frac{D_1}{k_s - g} = \frac{\$6}{0.14 - 0.05} = \frac{\$6}{0.09} = \$66.67.$$

Under the former circumstances, D_1 would be based on a 20 percent payout on $10 EPS, or $2. With $k_s = 14\%$ and $g = 12\%$, we solve for P_0:

$$P_0 = \frac{D_1}{k_s - g} = \frac{\$2}{0.14 - 0.12} = \frac{\$2}{0.02} = \$100.$$

Although CMC has suffered a severe setback, its existing assets will continue to provide a good income stream. More of these earnings should now be passed on to the shareholders, as the slowed internal growth has reduced the need for funds. However, the net result is a 33 percent decrease in the value of the shares.

d. If the payout ratio were continued at 20 percent, even after internal investment opportunities had declined, the price of the stock would drop to $2/(0.14 − 0.06) = $25 rather than to $66.67. Thus, an increase in the dividend payout is consistent with maximizing shareholder wealth.

Because of the downward-sloping IOS curve (see Figure 18-4), the greater the firm's level of investment, the lower the average ROE. Thus, the more money CMC retains and invests, the lower its average ROE will be. We can determine the average ROE under different conditions as follows:

Old situation (with founder active and a 20 percent payout):

$$g = (1.0 - \text{Payout ratio})(\text{Average ROE})$$
$$12\% = (1.0 - 0.2)(\text{Average ROE})$$
$$\text{Average ROE} = 12\%/0.8 = 15\% > k_s = 14\%.$$

Note that the *average* ROE is 15 percent, whereas the *marginal* ROE is presumably equal to 14 percent. In terms of a graph like Figure 18-4, the intersection of the MCC and IOS curves would be 14 percent, and the average of the IOS curve above the intersection would be 15 percent.

New situation (with founder retired and a 60 percent payout):

$$g = 6\% = (1.0 - 0.6)(\text{ROE})$$
$$\text{ROE} = 6\%/0.4 = 15\% > k_s = 14\%.$$

This suggests that the new payout is appropriate and that the firm is taking on investments down to the point at which marginal returns are equal to the cost of capital. In terms of a graph like Figure 18-4, the IOS curve shifted to the left after the founder retired. Note that if the 20 percent payout was maintained, the *average* ROE would be only 7.5 percent, which would imply a marginal ROE far below the 14 percent cost of capital.

Chapter 20

ST-2 a. $100,000,000/10 = $10,000,000 per year, or $5 million each 6 months. Since the $5 million will be used to retire bonds immediately, no interest will be earned on it.

b. The debt service requirements will decline. As the amount of bonds outstanding declines, so will the interest requirements (amounts given in millions of dollars):

Semiannual Payment Period (1)	Sinking Fund Payment (2)	Outstanding Bonds on Which Interest Is Paid (3)	Interest Payment[a] (4)	Total Bond Service (2) + (4) = (5)
1	$5	$100	$6.0	$11.0
2	5	95	5.7	10.7
3	5	90	5.4	10.4
.	.	.	.	.
.	.	.	.	.
.	.	.	.	.
20	5	5	0.3	5.3

[a]Interest is calculated as $(0.5)(0.12)(\text{Column 3})$; for example: interest in Period 2 = $(0.5)(0.12)($95) = 5.7.

The company's total cash bond service requirement will be $21.7 million per year for the first year. The requirement will decline by $0.12($10,000,000) = $1,200,000$ per year for the remaining years.

c. Here we have a 10-year, 9 percent annuity whose compound value is $100 million, and we are seeking the annual payment, PMT. The solution can be obtained with a financial calculator. Input N = 10, I = 9, PV = 0, and FV = 100000000, and press the PMT key to obtain $6,582,009.

We could also find the solution using this equation:

$$\$100,000,000 = \sum_{t=1}^{10} PMT(1 + k)^t$$

$$= PMT(FVIFA_{9\%,10})$$

$$= PMT(15.193)$$

$$PMT = \$6,581,979 = \text{sinking fund payment.}$$

The difference is due to rounding the FVIFA to 3 decimal places.

d. Annual debt service costs will be $100,000,000(0.12) + $6,582,009 = $18,582,009.

e. If interest rates rose, causing the bond's price to fall, the company would use open market purchases. This would reduce its debt service requirements.

Chapter 21

ST-2 a. *Cost of leasing:*

	Beginning of Year			
	0	1	2	3
Lease payment (AT)[a]	($ 6,000)	($6,000)	($6,000)	($6,000)
PVIFs (6%)[b]	1.000	0.9434	0.8900	0.8396
PV of leasing	($ 6,000)	($5,660)	($5,340)	($5,038)
Total PV cost of leasing =	($22,038)			

[a]After-tax payment = $10,000(1 − T) = $10,000(0.60) = $6,000.
[b]This is the after-tax cost of debt: 10%(1 − T) = 10%(0.60) = 6.0%.

Alternatively, using a financial calculator, input the following data after switching your calculator to "BEG" mode: N = 4, I = 6, PMT = −6000, and FV = 0. Then press the PV key to arrive at the answer of ($22,038). Now switch your calculator back to "END" mode.

b. *Cost of owning:*

Depreciable basis = $40,000.

Here are the cash flows under the borrow-and-buy alternative:

	End of Year				
	0	1	2	3	4
1. Depreciation schedule					
(a) Depreciable basis		$40,000	$40,000	$40,000	$40,000
(b) Allowance		0.33	0.45	0.15	0.07
(c) Depreciation		13,200	18,000	6,000	2,800
2. Cash outflows					
(d) Net purchase price	($40,000)				
(e) Depreciation tax savings		5,280[a]	7,200	2,400	1,120
(f) Maintenance (AT)		(600)	(600)	(600)	(600)
(g) Salvage value (AT)					6,000
(h) Total cash outflows	($40,000)	$ 4,680	$ 6,600	$ 1,800	$ 6,520
PVIFs	1.000	0.9434	0.8900	0.8396	0.7921
PV of owning	($40,000)	$ 4,415	$ 5,874	$ 1,511	$ 5,164

Total PV cost of owning = ($23,036)

[a]Depreciation(T) = $13,200(0.40) = $5,280.

Alternatively, input the cash flows for the individual years in the cash flow register and input I = 6, then press the NPV button to arrive at the answer of ($23,036). Because the present value of the cost of leasing is less than that of owning, the truck should be leased: $23,036 − $22,038 = $998, net advantage to leasing.

c. The discount rate is based on the cost of debt because most cash flows are fixed by contract and, consequently, are relatively certain. Thus, the lease cash flows have about the same risk as the firm's debt. Also, leasing is considered to be a substitute for debt. We use an after-tax cost rate because the cash flows are stated net of taxes.

d. Olsen could increase the discount rate on the salvage value cash flow. This would increase the PV cost of owning and make leasing even more advantageous.

Answers to End-of-Chapter Problems

We present here some intermediate steps and final answers to selected end-of-chapter problems. Please note that your answer may differ slightly from ours due to rounding errors. Also, although we hope not, some of the problems may have more than one correct solution, depending upon what assumptions are made in working the problem. Finally, many of the problems involve some verbal discussion as well as numerical calculations; this verbal material is not presented here.

2-1 a. Current ratio = $1.98\times$; DSO = 75 days; Total assets turnover = $1.7\times$; Debt ratio = 61.9%.

2-2 A/P = \$90,000; Inv = \$90,000; FA = \$138,000.

2-4 a. Quick ratio = $0.85\times$; DSO = 37 days; ROE = 13.1%; Debt ratio = 54.8%.

2-5 $\dfrac{\text{NI}}{\text{S}}$ = 2%; $\dfrac{\text{D}}{\text{A}}$ = 40%.

2-6 \$262,500; $1.19\times$.

2-7 Sales = \$2,592,000; DSO = 36 days.

2-8 TIE = $3.5\times$.

2-9 ROE = 24.5%.

2-10 7.2%.

2-11 a.

2-12 a. $+5.54\%$.
b(2). $+3.21\%$.
(3). $+2.50\%$.

2A-1 Total sources = \$102; Net increase in cash and marketable securities = \$19.

3-1 a. k_1 = 9.20%; k_5 = 7.20%.

3-3 a. 8.20%.
b. 10.20%.
c. k_5 = 10.70%.

3-5 Tax_{1993} = \$0; Final tax_{1995} = \$0; Final tax_{1996} = \$15,450.

3-6 a. 1993 advantage as a corporation = \$1,820; 1994 advantage = \$4,420; 1995 advantage = \$5,720.

3-7 a. Personal tax = \$20,592.
c. IBM yield = 7.59%; choose FLA bonds.
d. 18.18%.

3-8 a. k_1 in Year 2 = 13%.

3-9 k_1 in Year 2 = 15%; Year 2 inflation = 11%.

3-10 Tax = \$107,855; NI = \$222,145; Marginal tax rate = 39%; Average tax rate = 33.8%.

3-11 a. Tax = $61,250.
b. Tax = $15,600.
c. Tax = $4,680.

3-12 1.5%.

3-13 AT&T bonds = 8.8%.

3-14 6.0%.

4-1 a. $0.5 million.

4-2 a. $k_i = 8\% + (5.5\%)b_i$.
b. 17.90%.
c. Indifference rate = 19.0%.

4-3 a. $\bar{k}_A = 11.30\%$.
c. $\sigma_A = 20.8\%; \sigma_P = 20.1\%$.

4-4 a. $\hat{k}_M = 13.5\%; \hat{k}_j = 11.6\%$.
b. $\sigma_M = 3.85\%; \sigma_j = 6.22\%$.
c. $CV_M = 0.29; CV_j = 0.54$.

4-5 a. $\hat{k}_Y = 14\%$.
b. $\sigma_X = 12.20\%$.

4-6 a. $b_A = 2$.
b. $k_A = 12.5\%$.

4-7 a. $k_i = 15.5\%$.
b(1). $k_M = 15\%; k_i = 16.5\%$.
c(1). $k_i = 18.1\%$.

4-8 $b_N = 1.16$.

4-9 $b_p = 0.7625; k_p = 12.1\%$.

4-10 4.5%.

4A-1 a. b = 0.62.

4A-2 a. $b_A = 1.0; b_B = 0.5$.
c. $k_A = 14\%; k_B = 11.5\%$.

5-1 a. $530.
d. $445.

5-2 a. $895.40.
b. $1,552.90.
c. $279.20.
d. $500.03; $867.14.

5-3 a. ≈ 10 years.
c. ≈ 4 years.

5-4 a. $6,374.96.
d(1). $7,012.46.

5-5 a. $2,457.84.
c. $2,000.
d(1). $2,703.62.

5-6 a. Stream A: $1,251.21.

5-7 b. 7%.
c. 9%.
d. 15%.

5-8 a. $881.15.
b. $895.40.
c. $903.05.
d. $908.35.

5-9 a. $279.20.
b. $276.85.
c. $443.70.

5-10 a. $5,272.40.
b. $5,374.00.

5-11 a. 1st City = 7%; 2nd City = 6.14%.

5-12 a. PMT = $6,594.94.

5-13 a. Z = 9%; B = 8%.
b. Z = $558.39; $135.98; 32.2%; B = $1,147.20; $147.20; 14.72%.

5-14 a. $61,203.
b. $11,020.
c. $6,841.

5-15 $1,000 today is worth more.

5-16 a. 15% (or 14.87%).

5-17 7.18%.

5-18 12%.

5-19 9%.

5-20 a. $33,872.
b. $26,243.04 and $0.

5-21 ≈ 15 years.

5-22 6 years; $1,106.01.

5-23 $PV_{7\%} = \$1,428.57; PV_{14\%} = \$714.29$.

5-24 $893.26.

5-25 $984.88 ≈ $985.

5-26 57.18%.

5-27 a. FV = $1,432.02.
b. PMT = $93.07.

5-28 $k_{Nom} = 15.19\%$.

5-29 PMT = $36,948.95 or $36,949.61.

6-1 a. $1,251.26.
b. $898.90.

6-2 a. $1,250.
b. $833.33.
d. At 8%, V = $1,196.31.

6-3 b. PV = $5.29.
d. $30.01.

6-4 a. 7%.
b. 5%.
c. 12%.

6-5 a(1). $9.50.
(2). $13.33.
b(1). Undefined.

6-7 a. YTM = 3.4%.
b. YTM ≈ 7%.
c. $878.06.

6-8 a. Dividend 1995 = $2.66.
b. P_0 = $39.42.
c. Dividend yield 1993 = 5.10%; 1997 = 7.00%.

6-9 a. P_0 = $54.11.

6-10 a. YTM = 8%; YTC = 6.1%.

6-11 a. P_0 = $21.43.
b. P_0 = $26.47.
d. P_0 = $40.54.

6-12 a. New price = $31.34.
b. beta = 0.49865.

6-13 a. V_L at 5 percent = $1,518.97; V_L at 8 percent = $1,171.15; V_L at 12 percent = $863.79.

6-14 a. YTM at $829 ≈ 15%.

6-15 a. 13.3%.
b. 10%.
c. 8%.
d. 5.7%.

6-16 $23.75.

6-17 a. k_C = 10.6%; k_D = 7%.

6-18 $25.03.

6-19 IBM bond = 9.33%.

6-20 YTC = 6.47%.

6-21 P_0 = $19.89.

7-1 a. $13.44 million.
b. Notes payable = $31.44 million.
c. Current ratio = 2.00×; ROE = 14.2%.
d(1). − $14.28 million.
(2). Total assets = $147 million; Notes payable = $3.72 million.
(3). Current ratio = 4.25×; ROE = 10.84%.

7-2 a. Total assets = $33,534; AFN = $2,128.
b. Notes payable = $4,228; AFN = $70; ΔInterest = $213.

7-3 a. 33%.
b. AFN = $2,549.
c. ΔInterest = $306; AFN = $73.
d. ROE = 13.4%.

7-4 a. AFN = $128,783.
b. Notes payable = $220,392; ΔInterest = $8,371; AFN = $8,028.
c. 3.45%.

7-5 a. AFN = $667.
b. Increase in notes payable = $51; Increase in C/S = $368.

7-6 a. $480,000.
b. $18,750.

7-7 AFN = $360.

8-1 a(1). − $60,000.
b. Q_{BE} = 14,000.
c(1). − 1.33.

8-2 a(2). $125,000.
b. Q_{BE} = 7,000.
c. Q_{CBE} = 2,600.

8-3 a. Feb. surplus = $2,000.

8-4 a. Oct. loan = $22,800.

8-6 a(1). − $75,000.
(2). $175,000.
b. Q_{BE} = 140,000.
c(1). − 8.3.
(2). 15.0.
(3). 5.0.

8-7 a. FC_A = $80,000; VC_A = $4.80/unit; P_A = $8.00/unit.

9-1 a(1). 67.
(2). 101.
d(1). 95.
(2). 142.

9-2 a. 32.
b. $288,000.
c. $45,000.
d(1). 30.
(2). $378,000.

9-3 a. ROE_T = 11.75%; ROE_M = 10.80%; ROE_R = 9.16%.

9-4 a. 83.
b. $356,250.
c. 4.8.

9-5 a. 56.
b(1). 1.875.
(2). 11.25%.
c(1). 41.
(2). 2.03.
(3). 12.2%.

10-1 a. $1,600,000.
c. Bank = $1,200,000;
Books = $-5,200,000$.

10-2 b. $420,000.
c. $35,000.

10-3 a. Wire transfer.
b. $7,250.

10-4 a. $C^* = \$45,000$.
b. $22,500.
c. 100.

10-5 a. $103,350.
b. $97,500.

11-1 a. $DSO_O = 27$ days; $DSO_N = 22.5$ days.
b. $D_O = \$15,680$; $D_N = \$38,220$.
c. $C_O = \$10,125$; $C_N = \$10,969$.
e. $NI_\Delta = +\$68,770$.

11-2 $NI_3 = \$59,700$; $NI_4 = \$22,344$; $NI_5 = \$15,708$.

11-3 $NI_\Delta = +\$13,350$.

11-4 a. DSO = 28 days.
b. $70,000.

11-5 $NI_\Delta = -\$60,578$.

11-6 $70.

12-1 EOQ = 110.

12-2 a. EOQ = 100,000.
b. $156,250.
c. TIC = $56,250.
d. 60,577.

12-3 a. EOQ = 5,200.
b. 65.
c. 14,600.
d(3). TIC = $20,704.

12-4 a. EOQ = 13,200.
b. 42.
c. 20,769.
d. 41%.

12-5 a. EOQ = 3,873.
b. 5,073 bags.
c. 3,137 bags.
d. Every 6 days.

13-1 a. $100,000.
c(1). $300,000.
(2). Approximate cost = 36.73%; Effective cost = 43.86%.

13-3 a. $300,000.

13-4 a. 11.73%.
b. 12.09%.
c. 18%.

13-5 b. $384,615.
c. Cash = $126.90; NP = $434.60.

13-6 a(1). $27,500.
(3). $25,833.

13-7 b. Total dollar cost = $160,800; 15.12%.

13-8 a. $515,464.

13-9 a. $46,167.
b. $40,667.

13-10 b. 14.69%.
d. 20.99%.

13-11 a. 44.54%.

13-12 $k_{d_a} = 12\%$; $k_{d_b} = 11.25\%$; $k_{d_c} = 11.48\%$; $k_{d_d} = 16\%$; Alternative b.

13-13 Approximate cost = 14.69%; Effective cost = 15.65%.

13-14 N/P = 13.64%.

13-15 d. 8.3723%.

14-1 b. NPV = $7,486.20.
d. DPP = 6.51 yrs.
e. MIRR = 13.89%.

14-2 b. $IRR_A = 18.1\%$; $IRR_B = 24.0\%$.
d(1). $MIRR_A = 15.10\%$;
$MIRR_B = 17.03\%$.
(2). $MIRR_A = 18.05\%$;
$MIRR_B = 20.49\%$.

14-3 a. $IRR_A = 20\%$; $IRR_B = 16.7\%$; Crossover rate $\approx 16\%$.

14-4 a. $NPV_A = \$14,486,808$; $NPV_B = \$11,156,893$; $IRR_A = 15.03\%$; $IRR_B = 22.26\%$.

14-5 d. 9.54%; 22.87%.

14-6 $NPV_T = \$409$; $IRR_T = 15\%$; $MIRR_T = 14.54\%$; Accept; $NPV_P = \$3,318$; $IRR_P = 20\%$; $MIRR_P = 17.19\%$; Accept.

14-7 $NPV_E = \$3,861$; $IRR_E = 18\%$; $NPV_G = \$3,057$; $IRR_G = 18\%$; Purchase electric-powered forklift; it has a higher NPV.

14-8 $NPV_S = \$448.86$; $NPV_L = \$607.20$; $IRR_S = 15.24\%$; $IRR_L = 14.67\%$; $MIRR_S = 14.67\%$; $MIRR_L = 14.37\%$.

14-9   b. $PV_C = -\$556,717$; $PV_F = -\$493,407$; Forklift should be chosen.

14-10 $MIRR_X = 13.59\%$.

14-11 $IRR_L = 11.74\%$.

14-12 $MIRR = 10.93\%$.

15-1   a. $-\$178,000$.
　　　b. $\$52,440$; $\$60,600$; $\$40,200$.
　　　c. $\$48,760$.
　　　d. NPV $= -\$19,549$; Do not purchase.

15-2   a. $-\$126,000$.
　　　b. $\$42,560$; $\$47,477$; $\$35,186$.
　　　c. $\$51,268$.
　　　d. NPV $= \$11,384$; Purchase.

15-3   a. $-\$88,400$.
　　　b. $\$46,770$; $\$52,890$; $\$37,590$; $\$33,510$; $\$29,940$.
　　　c. $-\$10,000$.
　　　d. NPV $= \$43,308$; Replace the old machine.

15-4   a. $-\$796,100$.
　　　c. $\$207,400$; $\$255,340$; $\$203,405$; $\$175,440$; $\$171,445$.
　　　d. $\$119,670$.
　　　e. NPV $= \$14,095$; Purchase the new machine.

15-5   a. Expected $CF_A = \$6,750$; Expected $CF_B = \$7,650$; $CV_A = 0.0703$.
　　　b. $NPV_A = \$10,037$; $NPV_B = \$11,624$.

15-6   a. 14%.

15-7 $NPV_5 = \$2,212$; $NPV_4 = -\$2,081$; $NPV_8 = \$13,329$.

15-8   NPV $= \$15,301$; Buy the new machine.

15-9   NPV $= \$22,329$; Replace the old machine.

15-10   a. $NPV_{190-3} = \$20,070$; $NPV_{360-6} = \$22,256$.

15-11   a. 16%.
　　　b. NPV $= \$411$; Accept.

15-12   a. 15%.
　　　b. 1.48; 15.4%; 17%.

15-13 $NPV_A = \$12.76$ million.

15A-1   PV $= \$1,273,389$.

16-1   a. 16.3%.
　　　b. 15.4%.
　　　c. 16%.

16-2   a. 8%.
　　　b. $\$2.81$.
　　　c. 15.81%.

16-3   a. $\$18$ million.
　　　b. BP $= \$45$ million.
　　　c. $BP_1 = \$20$ million; $BP_2 = \$40$ million.

16-4   a. $g = 3\%$.
　　　b. EPS $= \$5.562$.

16-5   a. $\$67,500,000$.
　　　c. $k_s = 12\%$; $k_e = 12.4\%$.
　　　d. $\$27,000,000$.
　　　e. $WACC_1 = 9\%$; $WACC_2 = 9.2\%$.

16-6   a. $k_d(1 - T) = 5.4\%$; $k_s = 14.6\%$.
　　　b. WACC $= 10.92\%$.
　　　d. WACC $= 11.36\%$.

16-7   a. 3 breaks; $BP_{D_1} = \$1,111,111$; $BP_{RE} = \$1,818,182$; $BP_{D_2} = \$2,000,000$.
　　　b. $WACC_1 = 10.96\%$; $WACC_2 = 11.50\%$; $WACC_3 = 12.14\%$; $WACC_4 = 12.68\%$.
　　　c. $IRR_1 = 16\%$; $IRR_3 = 14\%$.

16-8   a. 13%.
　　　b. 10.4%.
　　　c. 8.58%.

16-9 7.92%.

16-10 11.94%.

16-11   a. $F = 10\%$.
　　　b. $k_e = 15.8\%$.

16-12   WACC $= 12.72\%$.

16-13 $\$10$ million.

16-14 $\$42,000$.

16-15 $\$62,000$.

16-16   a. 14.40%.
　　　b. 10.62%.

16-17 7.2%.

16-18 $k_e = 16.51\%$.

17-1   a. $\$5.10$.

17-2 a. $DOL_A = 2.80$; $DOL_B = 2.15$; Method A.
b. $DFL_A = 1.32$; $DFL_B = 1.35$; Method B.
d. Debt = \$129,310; D/A = 5.75%.

17-3 a. $EPS_{Old} = \$2.04$; New: $EPS_D = \$4.74$;
$EPS_S = \$3.27$.
b. $DOL_{Old} = 2.30$; $DOL_{New} = 1.60$;
$DFL_{Old} = 1.47$; $DFL_{New, Stock} = 1.15$;
$DTL_{New, Debt} = 2.53$.
c. 33,975 units.
d. $Q_{New, Debt} = 27,225$ units.

17-4 Debt used: $E(EPS) = \$5.78$; $\sigma_{EPS} = \$1.05$;
$E(TIE) = 3.49\times$.
Stock used: $E(EPS) = \$5.51$; $\sigma_{EPS} = \$0.85$;
$E(TIE) = 6.00\times$.

17-5 a. $ROE_{LL} = 14.6\%$; $ROE_{HL} = 16.8\%$.
b. $ROE_{LL} = 16.5\%$.

17-6 No leverage: ROE = 10.5%; σ = 5.4%;
CV = 0.51; 60% leverage: ROE = 13.7%;
σ = 13.5%; CV = 0.99.

18-1 CS = \$79.50; PIC = \$464.25; RE = \$884.70.

18-2 a(1). \$3,960,000.
   (2). \$4,800,000.
   (3). \$9,360,000.
   (4). Regular = \$3,960,000;
         Extra = \$5,400,000.
c. 15%.
d. 15%.

18-3 a. PO = 63.16%; BP = \$9.55 million;
$WACC_1 = 10.67\%$; $WACC_2 = 10.96\%$.
b. \$15 million.

18-4 \$3,250,000.

18-5 Payout = 52%.

18-6 $D_0 = \$3.44$.

18-7 Payout = 31.39%.

19-1 a. \$1,050,000.
b. \$5,550,000.
c. $-\$3,450,000$.

19-2 a. $EPS_{1992} = \$9,600$; $DPS_{1992} = \$4,800$;
$BV_{1992} = \$72,000$/share.
b. g_{EPS}: HH = 8.4%; L = 6.4%; U = 8%;
g_{DPS}: HH = 8.4%; L = 6.4%; U = 7.4%.
e. $EPS_{1992} = \$2.40$; $DPS_{1992} = \$1.20$;
$BV_{1992} = \$18$/share.
f. $ROE_{HH} = 15.00\%$; $ROE_L = 13.64\%$;
$ROE_U = 13.33\%$.

i. $P/E_{HH} = 8\times$; $P/E_L = 8.65\times$.
k. $k_{HH} = 15.2\%$; $k_L = 12.5\%$; U-Fix-It's price:
$P_0(HH) = \$17.23$; $P_0(L) = \$26.93$.

19-3 a. \$35.00.
b. \$34.18.

19-4 600,000 shares.

20-1 PMT = \$395,053.92 or \$395,054.76.

20-2 d. at $k_d = 6.1\%$, V = \$49.18;
at $k_d = 2\%$, V = \$150.

20-3 a. 7,930 bonds.
b(1). 12%.
   (2). 8.28%.
c. 7.2%.

20-4 a. \$2,504,571 or \$2,504,565.
b. \$1,490,291 or \$1,490,295.
c. \$2,912,819 or \$2,912,835.
d. \$1,917,141 or \$1,917,135.

20-5 15.03%.

20-6 12.37%.

20-7 \$30,463.

20A-1 A/P = \$816; First mortgage = \$900;
Subordinated debentures = \$684, P/S = \$0.

20A-2 a. Trustee = \$281,250; N/P = \$750,000;
A/P = \$375,000; Subordinated debentures =
\$750,000; Equity = \$343,750.
b. Trustee = \$281,250; N/P = \$750,000;
A/P = \$318,750; Subordinated debentures =
\$525,000; Equity = \$0.

20B-1 h. NPV = \$2,119,718.

20B-2 a. NPV = \$960,607.

21-1 a. $D/A_H = 50\%$; $D/A_M = 67\%$.

21-2 a. PV cost of owning = $-\$185,112$; PV cost of
leasing = $-\$187,534$; Purchase loom.

21-4 b. Percent ownership: Original = 80%;
Plan 1 = 53%; Plans 2 and 3 = 57%.
c. $EPS_0 = \$0.48$; $EPS_1 = \$0.60$; $EPS_2 = \$0.64$;
$EPS_3 = \$0.86$.
d. $D/A_1 = 13\%$; $D/A_2 = 13\%$; $D/A_3 = 48\%$.

21-6 a. PV cost of leasing = $-\$954,639$; Lease
equipment.

21-7 a. FV = $-\$3$; FV = \$0; FV = \$4; FV = \$49.
d. 9%; \$90.

22-1   NPV = − $6,746; Do not purchase.

22-2   a. 14%.
b. T.V. = $1,160.2; V = $890.2.

22-3   a. 17%.
b. V = $14.65 million.

23-1

Dollars per 1,000 Units of:

Rupees	Lira	Yen	Pesos	Riyals
$34.93	$0.80	$7.45	$0.33	$267.38

23-3   b. $14,627.20.

23-4   a. $2,843,181.
b. $2,801,513.
d. $3,200,000.

23-5   0.5714 pounds per dollar.

23-6   5.0505 francs per dollar.

23-7   9.80 francs per pound.

23-9 $58.67/share or Total value = $586,666,667.

23-10 $250,000 gain.

Selected Equations and Data

Chapter 2

$$\text{Current ratio} = \frac{\text{Current assets}}{\text{Current liabilities}}.$$

$$\text{Quick, or acid test, ratio} = \frac{\text{Current assets} - \text{Inventories}}{\text{Current liabilities}}.$$

$$\text{Inventory turnover ratio} = \frac{\text{Sales}}{\text{Inventories}}.$$

$$\text{DSO} = \begin{matrix}\text{Days} \\ \text{sales} \\ \text{outstanding}\end{matrix} = \frac{\text{Receivables}}{\text{Average sales per day}} = \frac{\text{Receivables}}{\text{Annual sales}/360}.$$

$$\text{Fixed assets turnover ratio} = \frac{\text{Sales}}{\text{Net fixed assets}}.$$

$$\text{Total assets turnover ratio} = \frac{\text{Sales}}{\text{Total assets}}.$$

$$\text{Debt ratio} = \frac{\text{Total debt}}{\text{Total assets}}.$$

$$\text{D/E} = \frac{\text{D/A}}{1 - \text{D/A}}, \text{ and D/A} = \frac{\text{D/E}}{1 + \text{D/E}}.$$

$$\text{Times-interest-earned (TIE) ratio} = \frac{\text{EBIT}}{\text{Interest charges}}.$$

$$\begin{matrix}\text{Fixed charge} \\ \text{coverage ratio}\end{matrix} = \frac{\text{EBIT} + \text{Lease payments}}{\text{Interest charges} + \text{Lease payments} + \dfrac{\text{Sinking fund payments}}{(1 - \text{Tax rate})}}.$$

$$\text{Profit margin on sales} = \frac{\begin{matrix}\text{Net income available to} \\ \text{common stockholders}\end{matrix}}{\text{Sales}}.$$

$$\text{Basic earning power ratio} = \frac{\text{EBIT}}{\text{Total assets}}.$$

$$\text{Return on total assets (ROA)} = \frac{\text{Net income available to common stockholders}}{\text{Total assets}}.$$

$$\text{ROA} = \left(\frac{\text{Profit}}{\text{margin}}\right)(\text{Total assets turnover}).$$

$$\text{Return on common equity (ROE)} = \frac{\text{Net income available to common stockholders}}{\text{Common equity}}.$$

$$\text{Price/earnings (P/E) ratio} = \frac{\text{Price per share}}{\text{Earnings per share}}.$$

$$\text{Book value per share} = \frac{\text{Common equity}}{\text{Shares outstanding}}.$$

$$\text{Market/book (M/B) ratio} = \frac{\text{Market price per share}}{\text{Book value per share}}.$$

$$\text{ROE} = \left(\frac{\text{Profit}}{\text{margin}}\right)\left(\frac{\text{Total assets}}{\text{turnover}}\right)\left(\frac{\text{Equity}}{\text{multiplier}}\right)$$

$$= \left(\frac{\text{Net income}}{\text{Sales}}\right)\left(\frac{\text{Sales}}{\text{Total assets}}\right)\left(\frac{\text{Total assets}}{\text{Common equity}}\right)$$

$$= \frac{\text{Net income}}{\text{Common equity}}.$$

Chapter 3

$$k = k^* + IP + DRP + LP + MRP.$$

$$k_{RF} = k^* + IP.$$

$$IP_n = \frac{I_1 + I_2 + \ldots I_n}{n}.$$

$$\frac{\text{Equivalent pretax yield}}{\text{on taxable bond}} = \frac{\text{Muni yield}}{1 - T}.$$

Chapter 4

$$\text{Expected rate of return} = \hat{k} = \sum_{i=1}^{n} P_i k_i.$$

$$\text{Variance} = \sigma^2 = \sum_{i=1}^{n} (k_i - \hat{k})^2 P_i.$$

$$\text{Standard deviation} = \sigma = \sqrt{\sum_{i=1}^{n} (k_i - \hat{k})^2 P_i}.$$

$$CV = \frac{\sigma}{\hat{k}}.$$

$$\hat{k}_p = \sum_{i=1}^{n} w_i \hat{k}_i.$$

$$\sigma_p = \sqrt{\sum_{i=j}^{n} (k_{pj} - \hat{k}_p)^2 P_j}.$$

$$b_p = \sum_{i=1}^{n} w_i b_i.$$

$$SML = k_i = k_{RF} + (k_M - k_{RF})b_i.$$

$$RP_i = (RP_M)b_i.$$

$$b = \frac{Y_2 - Y_1}{X_2 - X_1} = \text{slope coefficient in } \bar{k}_{it} = a + b\,\bar{k}_{Mt} + e_t.$$

Chapter 5

$$FV_n = PV(1 + i)^n = PV(FVIF_{i,n}).$$

$$PV = FV_n \left(\frac{1}{1 + i}\right)^n = FV_n(1 + i)^{-n} = FV_n(PVIF_{i,n}).$$

$$PVIF_{i,n} = \frac{1}{FVIF_{i,n}}.$$

$$FVIFA_{i,n} = [(1 + i)^n - 1]/i.$$

$$PVIFA_{i,n} = [1 - (1/(1 + i)^n)]/i.$$

$$FVA_n = PMT(FVIFA_{i,n}).$$

$$FVA_n \text{ (Annuity due)} = PMT(FVIFA_{i,n})(1 + i).$$

$$PVA_n = PMT(PVIFA_{i,n}).$$

$$PVA_n \text{ (Annuity due)} = PMT(PVIFA_{i,n})(1 + i).$$

$$PV \text{ (Perpetuity)} = \frac{\text{Payment}}{\text{Interest rate}} = \frac{PMT}{i}.$$

$$PV_{\text{Uneven stream}} = \sum_{t=1}^{n} CF_t \left(\frac{1}{1 + i}\right)^t = \sum_{t=1}^{n} CF_t(PVIF_{i,t}).$$

$$FV_{\text{Uneven stream}} = \sum_{t=1}^{n} CF_t (1 + i)^{n-t} = \sum_{t=1}^{n} CF_t(FVIF_{i,n-t}).$$

$$FV_n = PV \left(1 + \frac{i_{Nom}}{m}\right)^{mn}.$$

$$\text{Effective annual rate} = \left(1 + \frac{i_{Nom}}{m}\right)^m - 1.0.$$

$$\text{Periodic rate} = i_{Nom}/m.$$

$$i_{Nom} = APR = (\text{Periodic rate})(m).$$

$$FV_n = PVe^{in}.$$

$$PV = FV_n e^{-in}.$$

Chapter 6

$$V_B = \sum_{t=1}^{N} \frac{INT}{(1 + k_d)^t} + \frac{M}{(1 + k_d)^N}$$
$$= INT(PVIFA_{k_d,N}) + M(PVIF_{k_d,N}).$$

$$V_B = \sum_{t=1}^{2N} \frac{INT/2}{(1 + k_{d/2})^t} + \frac{M}{(1 + k_{d/2})^{2N}} = \frac{INT}{2}(PVIFA_{k_{d/2},2N}) + M(PVIF_{k_{d/2},2N}).$$

$$\text{Price of callable bond} = \sum_{t=1}^{N} \frac{INT}{(1 + k_d)^t} + \frac{\text{Call price}}{(1 + k_d)^N}.$$

$$V_{ps} = \frac{D_{ps}}{k_{ps}}.$$

$$\hat{P}_0 = \text{PV of expected future dividends} = \sum_{t=1}^{\infty} \frac{D_t}{(1 + k_s)^t}.$$

$$\hat{P}_0 = \frac{D_0(1 + g)}{k_s - g} = \frac{D_1}{k_s - g}.$$

$$\hat{k}_s = \frac{D_1}{P_0} + g.$$

Chapter 7

$$AFN = (A^*/S)\Delta S - (L^*/S)\Delta S - MS_1(1 - d).$$

$$\text{Full capacity sales} = \frac{\text{Actual sales}}{\text{Percentage of capacity at which fixed assets were operated}}.$$

$$\text{Target FA/Sales ratio} = \frac{\text{Current fixed assets}}{\text{Full capacity sales}}.$$

$$\text{Required level of FA} = \text{Target FA/Sales ratio (Projected sales)}.$$

Chapter 8

$$TC = F + VQ.$$

$$Q_{BE} = \frac{F}{P - V}.$$

$$S_{BE} = PQ_{BE}.$$

$$S_{BE} = \frac{FC}{1 - \dfrac{VC}{\text{Sales}}}.$$

$$DOL = \frac{\dfrac{\Delta EBIT}{EBIT}}{\dfrac{\Delta Q}{Q}}.$$

$$DOL = \frac{Q(P - V)}{Q(P - V) - F}.$$

$$DOL_S = \frac{S - VC}{S - VC - F}.$$

$$EBIT = PQ - VQ - F.$$

$$Q_{CBE} = \frac{F - \text{Noncash outlays}}{P - V}.$$

Chapter 9

$$\text{Inventory conversion period} = \frac{\text{Inventory}}{\text{Sales}/360}.$$

$$\frac{\text{Receivables collection}}{\text{period}} = \text{DSO}.$$

$$\frac{\text{Inventory}}{\text{conversion}} + \frac{\text{Receivables}}{\text{collection}} - \frac{\text{Payables}}{\text{deferral}} = \frac{\text{Cash}}{\text{conversion}}.$$
$$\text{period} \qquad \text{period} \qquad \text{period} \qquad \text{cycle}$$

Chapter 10

Total costs = Holding costs + Transactions costs

$$= \frac{C}{2}(k) + \frac{T}{C}(F).$$

$$C^* = \sqrt{\frac{2(F)(T)}{k}}.$$

Chapter 11

$$\text{A/R} = \frac{\text{Credit sales}}{\text{per day}} \times \frac{\text{Length of}}{\text{collection period}}.$$

$$\text{ADS} = \text{Annual sales}/360 = \frac{(\text{Units sold})(\text{Sales price})}{360}.$$

Receivables = (ADS)(DSO).

Cost of carrying receivables = (DSO)(Sales/360)(v)(k).

Opportunity cost = (Old sales/360)(ΔDSO)(1 − v)(k).

Chapter 12

$$A = \frac{\text{Units per order}}{2} = \frac{S/N}{2}.$$

TCC = (C)(P)(A).

$$\text{TOC} = F\left(\frac{S}{2A}\right) = (F)(N).$$

TIC = TCC + TOC

$$= (C)(P)(A) + F\left(\frac{S}{2A}\right)$$

$$= (C)(P)\left(\frac{Q}{2}\right) + F\left(\frac{S}{Q}\right).$$

$$\text{EOQ} = \sqrt{\frac{2(F)(S)}{(C)(P)}}.$$

Reorder point = (Lead time in weeks × Weekly usage) − Goods in transit.

Chapter 13

$$\frac{\text{Approximate percentage}}{\text{cost of payables}} = \frac{\text{Discount percent}}{100 - \text{Discount}} \times \frac{360}{\text{Days credit is} - \text{Discount}}.$$
$$\text{percent} \qquad \text{outstanding} \qquad \text{period}$$

$$EAR_{Simple} = \frac{Interest}{Amount\ received} = \left(1 + \frac{k_{Nom}}{m}\right)^m - 1.0.$$

$$EAR_{Discount} = \frac{Interest}{Amount\ received} = \frac{Nominal\ rate\ (\%)}{1.0 - Nominal\ rate\ (fraction)}.$$

$$Face\ value_{Discount} = \frac{Funds\ received}{1.0 - Nominal\ rate\ (fraction)}.$$

$$EAR_{Simple/CB} = \frac{Interest}{Amount\ received} = \frac{Nominal\ rate\ (\%)}{1.0 - CB\ (fraction)}.$$

$$Face\ value_{Simple/CB} = \frac{Funds\ required}{1.0 - CB\ (fraction)}.$$

$$EAR_{Discount/CB} = \frac{Nominal\ rate\ (\%)}{1 - Nominal\ rate(fraction) - CB(fraction)}.$$

$$Face\ value_{Discount/CB} = \frac{Funds\ required}{1.0 - Nominal\ rate(fraction) - CB(fraction)}.$$

$$Approximate\ rate_{Add\text{-}on} = \frac{Interest}{Amount\ received/2}.$$

$$\begin{array}{l}\text{Additional funds needed} \\ \text{to meet CB requirement}\end{array} = \left(CB\% \times Loan\right) - \frac{Cash\ available}{for\ CB}.$$

$$Loan = Funds\ needed + (CB\% \times Loan) - Available\ cash.$$

$$EAR_{\text{With cash balances}} = \frac{Nominal\ rate\ (\%) \times Loan}{Funds\ needed}.$$

Chapter 14

$$NPV = CF_0 + \frac{CF_1}{(1+k)^1} + \frac{CF_2}{(1+k)^2} + \cdots + \frac{CF_n}{(1+k)^n}$$
$$= \sum_{t=0}^{n} \frac{CF_t}{(1+k)^t}.$$

$$IRR: CF_0 + \frac{CF_1}{(1+IRR)^1} + \frac{CF_2}{(1+IRR)^2} + \cdots + \frac{CF_n}{(1+IRR)^n} = 0$$
$$\sum_{t=0}^{n} \frac{CF_t}{(1+IRR)^t} = 0.$$

$$MIRR: PV\ costs = \sum_{t=0}^{n} \frac{COF_t}{(1+k)^t} = \frac{\sum_{t=0}^{n} CIF_t(1+k)^{n-t}}{(1+MIRR)^n} = \frac{TV}{(1+MIRR)^n}.$$

Chapter 15

$$Net\ cash\ flow = Net\ income + Depreciation.$$

$$\sigma_{NPV} = \sqrt{\sum_{i=1}^{n} P_i[NPV_i - E(NPV)]^2}.$$

$$CV_{NPV} = \frac{\sigma_{NPV}}{E(NPV)}.$$

$$k_p = k_{RF} + (k_M - k_{RF})b_p.$$

Chapter 16

After-tax component cost of debt $= k_d(1 - T)$.

$$\text{Component cost of preferred stock} = k_p = \frac{D_p}{P_n}.$$

$k_s = \hat{k}_s = k_{RF} + RP = D_1/P_0 + g$.

$k_s = k_{RF} + (k_M - k_{RF})b_i$.

$k_s = $ Bond yield + Risk premium.

$$k_e = \frac{D_1}{P_0(1 - F)} + g.$$

$WACC = w_d k_d(1 - T) + w_p k_p + w_s(k_s \text{ or } k_e)$.

$$BP = \frac{\text{Total amount of lower cost-of-capital of a given type}}{\text{Fraction of this type of capital in the capital structure}}.$$

Chapter 17

$$EPS = \frac{(S - FC - VC - I)(1 - T)}{\text{Shares outstanding}} = \frac{(EBIT - I)(1 - T)}{\text{Shares outstanding}}.$$

$$V = \frac{EBIT(1 - T)}{WACC}.$$

$$DOL_Q = \frac{Q(P - V)}{Q(P - V) - F}.$$

$$DOL_S = \frac{S - VC}{S - VC - F}.$$

$$DFL = \frac{EBIT}{EBIT - I}.$$

$$DTL = \frac{Q(P - V)}{Q(P - V) - F - I} = \frac{S - VC}{S - VC - F - I} = (DOL)(DFL).$$

$EPS_1 = EPS_0[1 + (DTL)(\% \Delta Sales)]$.

Chapter 18

$$\text{Dollars transferred from retained earnings due to stock dividend} = \left(\begin{array}{c}\text{Number of} \\ \text{shares} \\ \text{outstanding}\end{array}\right)\left(\begin{array}{c}\text{Percentage} \\ \text{of the stock} \\ \text{dividend}\end{array}\right)\left(\begin{array}{c}\text{Stock} \\ \text{market} \\ \text{price}\end{array}\right).$$

Chapter 21

$$\text{Formula value} = \frac{\text{Current price}}{\text{of the stock}} - \frac{\text{Striking}}{\text{price}}.$$

$$\frac{\text{Price paid for}}{\text{bond with warrants}} = \frac{\text{Straight-debt}}{\text{value of bond}} + \frac{\text{Value of}}{\text{warrants}}.$$

$$\text{Conversion price} = P_c = \frac{\text{Par value of bond}}{CR}.$$

$$CR = \frac{\text{Par value of bond}}{P_c}.$$

$$\begin{array}{l}\text{Price paid for} \\ \text{convertible bond}\end{array} = \sum_{t=1}^{n} \frac{INT}{(1 + k_c)^t} + \frac{\begin{array}{c}\text{Expected market value at} \\ \text{time of conversion}\end{array}}{(1 + k_c)^n}.$$

Conversion value $= C_t =$ Initial stock price $(1 + g)^t(CR)$.

Index

Accounting beta method, 559
Accounting profit, 39
Accounts payable (*See also* Short-term financing), 457–463
    trade credit, 457–463
Accounts receivable (*See also* Credit management), **410**
    factoring, 476
    financing, 476–479
    monitoring, 412–414
    pledging, 476
    recourse, 476
Accruals, 457
Acid test ratio, 49–50
Actual (realized) rate of return ($\bar{k}_s$), 256
Additional funds needed (AFN), 293
Additional paid-in capital, 717
Add-on interest, 468
Agency problem, 18
Agency relationships, 17
Agent, 17
Aging schedule, 413–414
Alternative forms of business organization, 10
American Stock Exchange (AMEX), 96
Amortization schedule, 216
Amortized loans, 215–217
Annual compounding, 210
Annual percentage rate (APR), 213
Annual report, 35
Annuity, 200
    annuity due, 200, 202–203
    ordinary, 200–202
Asked price, 97
Asset management ratios (*See also* Financial ratios), **50**–53
    days sales outstanding, 51
    fixed assets turnover ratio, 51–52
    inventory turnover ratio, 50–51
    total assets turnover ratio, 52–53
Asymmetric information, 648
Average collection period (ACP), 51
Average-risk stock, 162
Average tax rate, 120

Balance sheet (*See also* Financial statements), 33, **37**–40
Banking, investment (*See also* Investment markets), 721–730
Bank loans, 436–474
    add-on interest, 468
    annual percentage rate (APR), 213
    choosing, 472–474
    compensating balance, 463
    cost, 465–472
    discount interest, 466
    line of credit, 464
    prime rate, 465
    promissory note, 463

    revolving credit agreement, 464
    simple interest, 465
Bankruptcy (*See also* Reorganization), 764–765, 773–779
    Chapter 11, 774
    laws, 773–774
    liquidation, 775–779
    priority of claims, 775–776
Basic earning power ratio, 53, 57
Baumol model, 400–**402**, 403
Best efforts arrangement, 722
Beta coefficient (*See also* Capital Asset Pricing Model), **162**–166
    calculating, 182–185
    changes in a company's, 172
    graph, 183
    historic, 182
    portfolio, 166
    project betas, 557
    risk, 555–558
    techniques for measuring risk, 559–560
Bid price, 97
Bird-in-the-hand theory, 668
Blanket inventory lien, 479
Blue sky laws, 719
Bond issue refunding, 747, 765–766, 780–785
Bond ratings, 754–758
Bonds (*See also* Long-term debt), **236**, 742–745
    call provision, 237, 746–747
    convertible, 744
    coupon interest rate, 236
    coupon payment, 236
    current yield, 242, 252
    debenture, 744
    discount bond, 242, 244
    Eurobonds, 880
    floating rates, 752
    income, 744
    indenture, 743
    indexed (purchasing power), 745
    interest rate determinants, 104–108
    interest rate price risk, 247
    interest rate reinvestment risk, 248
    investment grade, 754
    junk, 753
    markets, 250–253
    maturity date, 237
    mortgage, 743–744
    municipal, 121
    original maturity, 237
    par value, 236
    premium bond, 241, 244
    putable, 744
    restrictive covenants, 746
    sinking fund, 747–748
    subordinated debenture, 744

    trustee, 746
    valuation, 236–253
    warrant, 744
    yield to call, 245
    yield to maturity, 244
    zero coupon, 748–752
Bond valuation model (*See also* Valuation), 238–247
    semiannual compounding, 246–247
Bond-yield-plus-risk-premium approach, 590–591
Bond yield to call, 245
Bond yield to maturity, 244
Book value per share, 59, 707
Bracket creep, 120
Breakeven analysis, 326–331
Breakeven point, 328
Break point, 600–603
Budget, 325
Building a banking relationship, 127–129
Business activity, 115
Business ethics, 16
Business organization, 10–12
Business risk (*See also* Risk), 623, **624**–626
Bylaws, 12

Call, 803
Call premium, 746, 791
Call protection, 747
Call provision, 746–747
Capital, 497, 585
Capital assets, 121
Capital Asset Pricing Model (CAPM), 154
    beta coefficients, 162–166
    market risk premium, 167
    portfolio beta coefficients, 166
    required rate of return (k_s), 256
    risk-free rate, 105
    Security Market Line, **168**–172
    summary, 165
Capital budgeting, 497–520, 532–547
    beta risk, 548, 555–558
    capital rationing, 563
    cash flow estimation, 532–533
    changes in net working capital, 536
    comparison of NPV and IRR methods, 509–515
    conclusions on decision methods, 518–519
    crossover rate, 511
    dealing with inflation, 547
    depreciation, 576–579
    discounted cash flow (DCF) techniques, 505
    discounted payback period, 503
    equivalent annual annuity (EAA) method, 545–546
    evaluation techniques, 501–517

Capital budgeting (continued)
  expansion project, 536–539
  externalities, 535
  generating ideas for, 498–499
  hurdle rate, 508
  importance of, 497–498
  incorporating project risk and capital
      structure into capital budgeting, 561–
      562
  incremental cash flows, 534
  independent projects, 503
  internal rate of return (IRR) method, 507
  IRR, 507
  modified IRR, 516–517
  multiple IRRs, 513
  mutually exclusive projects, 503
  net present value (NPV) method, 505
  normal project, 513
  NPV profiles, 509
  opportunity cost, 535
  optimal capital budget, 622
  payback period, 502
  post-audit, 519–520
  project classifications, 499–500
  project evaluation, 536–543
  reinvestment rate assumption, 513
  relevant cash flows, 533
  replacement analysis, 539–543
  **replacement chain (common life)
      approach, 544–545**
  risk analysis, 547–563
  salvage value, 578
  sensitivity analysis, 550–551
  similarities with security valuation, 500–
      501
  small firm, 520–521
  strategic business plan, 498
  sunk cost, 535
  unequal lives, 543–547
Capital component, 585
Capital formation process, 91
Capital gain or loss, 121
Capital gains yield, 256
Capital intensity ratio, 303
Capital lease, 795
Capital markets, 88
Capital rationing, 563
Capital structure, 622–656
  business risk, 623, 624–626
  checklist for decisions, 651–653
  degree of financial leverage, 640–641
  degree of leverage, 638–643
  degree of operating leverage, 639–640
  degree of total leverage, 642–643
  determining optimal, 628–638
  effect on stock price and cost of capital,
      635–637
  EPS indifference point, 632
  financial flexibility, 623
  financial leverage, 626
  financial risk, 624, 626–628
  liquidity and cash flow analysis, 644–646
  mergers, 651
  operating leverage, 639–640
  optimal, 595, 622–623, 760–761
  target, 595, 622–623, 760–761
  theory, 646–650
  times-interest-earned (TIE) ratio, 645
  variation among firms, 654
Career opportunities in finance, 5
Carrying costs, 435–436
Cash breakeven analysis, 336–338
  point, 336

Cash budget, 338–343
Cash conversion cycle, 361–362, 363–364
Cash flow (See also Capital budgeting), 38,
    207, **532**
  depreciation, 39
  estimation, 532–533
  incremental cash flows, 534
  operating cash flows, 40
  project evaluation, 536–543
  relevant cash flows, 533
Cash flow analysis, 644–646
Cash flow cycle, 40–42
Cash flow statement, 33, 41–42, 81–84
Cash flows versus accounting income, 38–41
Cash management, 382–403
  bank relationships, 392–393
  Baumol model, 400–402, 403
  check clearing, 385
  collections float, 387
  compensating balance, 383, 392–393
  compensating banks for services, 392–393
  concentration bank, 389
  controlled disbursement accounts, 390
  depository transfer check, 389
  disbursement float, 386
  discount, 383
  electronic depository transfer, 389
  float, 386–387
  kiting, 387
  lockbox plan, 388
  matching costs and benefits, 393–394
  multi-divisional firm, 390
  net float, 387
  overdraft systems, 393
  pre-authorized debit, 388
  precautionary balance, 383
  rationale for holding cash, 383
  speculative balance, 383
  synchronized cash flows, 385
  techniques, 384–390
  transactions balance, 383
  zero-balance account, 389
Change in net working capital, 536
Charter, 12
Check clearing, 385
Classified stock, 711
Clientele effect, 673
Closely held corporation, 714
Coefficient of variation (CV), 150
Collateral, 475
Collections float, 387
Commercial bank loans (See also Bank
    loans), 457, 463–474
  cost, 465–472
Commercial banks, 92
Commercial paper, 457, 474
Common equity, 36, 707
Common life approach, 544–545
Common stock, 254–266, 707–720
  actual (realized) rate of return ($\bar{k}_s$), 256
  additional paid-in capital, 707
  balance sheet accounts and definitions,
      707–709
  book value per share, 707
  capital gains yield, 256
  classified, 711
  closely held corporation, 714
  constant growth model, 260
  constant growth stock, 260
  cost of newly issued, 593–595
  dividend yield, 256
  evaluation as a source of funds, 711–713
  expected rate of return ($\hat{k}_s$), 256

  expected total return, 256
  flotation costs, 723
  founders' shares, 711
  going public, 715
  growth rate (g), 255
  initial public offering (IPO) market, 715
  intrinsic value ($\hat{P}_0$), 255
  legal rights and privileges, 709–710
  listing, 717
  market for, 714–720
  market price (P_0), 255
  normal (constant) growth, 259–261
  offering price, 723
  organized security exchange, 96, 714
  over-the-counter market, 97, 714
  par value, 707
  perpetuity, 206, 258
  preemptive right, 710
  primary markets, 88, 714
  proxy, 709
  proxy fight, 709
  publicly owned corporation, 714
  required rate of return (k_s), 256
  reserve borrowing capacity, 712
  retained earnings, 707
  secondary markets, 88, 714
  small business offering, 732–733
  **supernormal (nonconstant) growth,
      263–266**
  takeover, 710
  types, 711
  valuation, 254–266
  voting rights, 709
  zero growth stock, 258–259
Common stockholders' equity, 36
Company-specific risk (See also Risk),
    161
Comparative ratio analysis, 64
Comparison of types of interest rates, 217–
    220
Compensating balances, 383, 463
Compounding, 189
  continuous, 232
  semiannual, 210
Computerized financial planning models,
    309–310
Concentration bank, 389
Consol, 206
Constant growth model, 260
Consumer credit markets, 88
Continuous compounding, 232
Continuous compounding and discounting,
    232–233
Continuous discounting, 233
Convertibles, 744, 811–816
  advantages, 815–816
  bond analysis, 812–815
  conversion price (P_c), 811
  conversion ratio (CR), 811
  conversion value (C_t), 813
  disadvantages, 816
  effect on reported earnings, 817
Corporate alliance, 846
Corporate risk, 548
Corporation, 11–12
Correlation coefficient, 157
Cost of capital, 583–609
  **after-tax cost of debt, $k_d(1 − T)$, 586–
      587**
  basic definitions, 585–586
  bond-yield-plus-risk-premium approach,
      590–591
  break point (BP), 600–603

Cost of capital *(continued)*
  capital component, 585
  CAPM approach, 589–590
  combining the MCC and IOS schedules, 604–607
  cost of new common equity (k_e), 593–595
  cost of preferred stock (k_p), 588
  cost of retained earnings (k_s), 588–593
  DCF approach, 591–592
  divisional, 562
  flotation cost (F), 593
  investment opportunity schedule (IOS), 605
  logic of the weighted average cost of capital, 584–585
  marginal cost of capital, 596–603
  marginal cost of capital (MCC) schedule, 597
  newly issued common stock, 593–595
  opportunity cost, 588–589
  problem areas in cost of capital, 607–608
  project, k_p, 557
  small firms, 608–609
  target (optimal) capital structure, 595
  weighted average cost of capital (WACC), 595–596
Cost of money, 98–100
Coupon interest rate, 236
Coupon payment, 236
Coverage ratios, 56–57
Credit *(See also* Trade credit), 457–458
  line of, 464
  revolving, 464
  short-term versus long-term, 370
Credit associations, 419
Credit instruments, 422–423
  banker's acceptance, 422
  commercial draft, 422
  conditional sales contract, 422–423
  open account, 422
  promissory note, 422
  sight draft, 422
  time draft (trade acceptance), 422
Credit management *(See also* Receivables management; Credit instruments), 409–425
  analyzing proposed changes, 423–425
  carrying charges, 424
  cash discount, 420
  collection policy, 420
  factors influencing, 421–423
  five Cs of credit, 418
  legal considerations, 421
  period, 416
  policy, 416
  scoring systems, 417
  seasonal dating, 420
  standards, 416
  terms, 416
Credit reporting agencies, 419
Credit unions, 93
Crossover rate, 511
Cumulative dividends, 790
Current assets, 26, 365
  permanent, 365
  temporary, 366
Current liabilities, 26
Current ratio, 48–49
Current yield, 242, 252

Days sales outstanding, 51, 412
Debentures, 744

Debt *(See also* Bonds; Long-term debt; Short-term financing), 739–779
  after-tax cost of, 586–587
  floating rate debt, 752
  long-term, 739–779
  ratio, 55
  short-term, 455–482
  types, 741–745
Debt management ratios *(See also* Financial ratios), 53–57
  debt ratio, 55
  fixed charge coverage ratio, 56–57
  times-interest-earned (TIE) ratio, 55–56
Declaration date, 681
Default risk premium, 104, 106–**107**, 396
Deferred call, 747
Degree of financial leverage, 640–641
Degree of leverage, 638–643
Degree of operating leverage, 333–336, **639–**640
Degree of total leverage, 642–643
Depreciable basis, 578
Depreciation, 127, 576–579
  effect on cash flows, 38–39
  tax depreciation calculations, 127, 576–579
  tax depreciation life, 576–579
Deregulation of financial institutions, 7
Direct transfers, 91
Disbursement float, 386
Discount, 383
Discount bond, 242, 244
Discounted cash flow analysis *(See also* Time value of money), 188–220
Discounted cash flow techniques, 505
Discounted payback period, 503
Discounting, 196
  continuous, 233
Discount interest, 466
Diversifiable risk, 143
Divestitures, 847–850
  spin-off, 847
  types, 847
Dividend irrelevance theory, 667–668
Dividend payout ratio, 44, 301
Dividend policy, 667–686
  alternative sources of capital, 685–686
  bird-in-the-hand theory, 668
  clientele effect, 673
  constant, or steadily increasing, dividend, 679–680
  constant payout ratio, 681
  constraints, 685
  decision, 24
  declaration date, 681
  dividend reinvestment plans, 683
  effects, on k_s, 686
  ex-dividend date, 682
  extra dividend, 681
  holder-of-record date, 682
  information content (or signaling) hypothesis, 672
  in practice, 675–684
  investment opportunities, 685
  irrelevance theory, 667–668
  low regular dividend plus extras, 681
  optimal, 667
  other issues, 672–673
  payment date, 683
  payment procedures, 681–683
  residual dividend policy, 675–679
  small business, 693
  stock dividends and stock splits, 686–689

  summary of factors influencing, 684–686
  tax preference theory, 668
  tests of dividend theories, 671–672
  theories, 667–671
Dividend reinvestment plans, 683
Dividends, 47, 256–257
  basis for stock values, 256–257
  payout ratio, 44
  stock dividends, 687
  stock repurchases, 689–690, 691–692
  stock splits, 687
Dividend yield, 256
Double taxation, 120
Du Pont analysis, 343–345
Du Pont chart, 60
Du Pont equation, 60

Earnings per share (EPS), 23, 261
  effects of financial leverage, 24
  fully diluted, 817
  indifference point, 632
  primary, 817
  simple, 817
  timing, 23
Economic environment, 25
Economic ordering quantity (EOQ), 438
Economies of scale, 304–305
Effective annual rate (EAR), 212, 219–220, 466–471
Efficient Markets Hypothesis (EMH), 269
EOQ model, 439
Equilibrium, 267
Equilibrium price, 727
Equity *(See also* Common stock), 36, 38, 254–266
  common, 36, 707
  cost of common, 593–595
Equity multiplier, 62–63
Equivalent annual annuity (EAA) method, 545–546
Ethics, 16
Eurobond, 880
Eurodollar, 879
Event risk, 397
Exchange rate, 868–870
  direct quotation, 868
  indirect quotation, 868
Ex-dividend date, 682
Executive stock options, 20
Expansion project, 536–539
Expectations theory, 111–112
Expected rate of return, 146, 256
Expected return on a portfolio (k_p), 154
Expected total return, 256
Externalities, 535

Factoring, 476
Factors affecting stock prices, 24–25
Factors influencing long-term financing decisions, 759–764
Federal bankruptcy laws *(See also* Bankruptcy; Reorganization), 773–774
Federal income tax system, 118–127
Federal Reserve policy, 114
  margin requirements, 719
Finance in the organizational structure of the firm, 13
Financial analysis in the small firm, 68–69
Financial asset markets, 87
Financial control, 324

Financial forecasting, 289–310
  computerized model, 309–310
  excess capacity adjustments, 308–309
  formula method for forecasting AFN, 301–304
  other techniques, 307–308
  projected balance sheet method, 293–300
  sales forecast, 290–292
  simple linear regression, 307–308
  when balance sheet ratios change, 304–306
Financial institutions, 91–94
Financial intermediaries, 92
Financial lease (*See also* Lease financing), **795**
Financial leverage, 53, 640–641
Financial manager's responsibilities, 9
Financial markets, 87–90
Financial planning, 324
Financial planning and control, 323–345
  processes, 324–326
  budget, 325
  breakeven analysis, 325–331
  cash breakeven analysis, 336–338
  cash budget, 338–343
  control in multidivisional companies, 343
  operating leverage, 331–336
Financial ratios (*See also the specific type of ratios*), 53–68
  asset management, 50–53
  debt management, 53–57
  liquidity, 48–50
  market value, 58–59
  profitability, 57–58
  summary of, 61
Financial risk (*See also* Risk), 624, **626**–628
Financial service corporation, 94
Financial statements, 33–46
  analysis, 33–67
  annual report, 33
  balance sheet, 33, **35**–37
  cash flow cycle, 40–41
  depreciation, 38–39
  Du Pont chart, 61–64
  income statement, 33, **34**
  pro forma, 293
  projected, 293
  ratio analysis, 48–66
  statement of cash flows, 33, **41**–42, 81–84
  statement of retained earnings, 33, **37**–38
Financing feedbacks, 297
Financing policies (working capital), 365–369
  aggressive approach, 368
  conservative approach, 368–369
  maturity matching approach, 366
Fixed assets turnover ratio, 51–52
Fixed charge coverage ratio, 56–57
Fixed exchange rate system, 870
Float, 386–387
  collections, 387
  disbursement, 386
  net, 387
Floating rate bond, 752
Floating rate debt, 752
Floating rate preferred stock, 793
Flotation cost, 593, 723
Foreign trade balance, 114–115
Founders' shares, 711
Fractional time periods, 215
Funded debt, 741

Futures markets, 87
Future value (*See also* Time value of money), 189–**190**, 191–194
  annuity, 200–203
  interest factor, 191
  interest factor for an annuity, 201
  uneven cash flow stream, 209–210
FVA$_n$, 201

Global markets, 7
Goals and resources in the small firm, 27–28
Goals of the corporation, 14
Going public, 715
Golden parachutes, 19, 845
Gordon/Lintner, 668
Greenmail, 19
Growth, 255
  constant, 259–263
  nonconstant, 263–266
  zero, 258–259
Growth rate (g), 255

Half-year convention, 577
Holder-of-record date, 682
Holding company, 850–852
  leverage device, 852
  operating company, 850
  parent company, 850
  subsidiaries, 850
Hostile takeover, 14
Hurdle rate, 508
Hybrid, 253
Hybrid financing, 789–819

Improper accumulation, 125–126
Income bond, 744
Income statement (*See also* Financial statements), 33, **34**
Increasing importance of managerial finance, 8
Incremental cash flows, 534
Indenture, 743
Independent projects, 503
Indexed (purchasing power) bond, 745
Inflation, 7, **99**, 170
  effects on inventory management, 445
Inflation premium, 104, 105–**106**, 170
Inflation risk, 397
Inflow, 188
Information content (signaling) hypothesis, 672
Initial public offering (IPO) market, 715
Insiders, 719
Insolvency (*See also* Bankruptcy), 764
Installment loans, 468–469
Interest (*See also* Bank loans), 465–472
  add-on, 468–469
  discount, 466–468
  simple, 465–466
Interest rates, 98–118
  business decisions affected by, 116–118
  comparison of types, 217–220
  default risk premium, 104, 106–**107**
  determinants of market, 104–108
  effective annual (EAR), 212, 219–220
  effects on stock prices, 116
  federal deficits, 114
  Federal Reserve policy, 114
  foreign trade balance, 114–115
  inflation premium, 104, 105–**106**
  levels, 100–103
  liquidity premium, 104, 107
  maturity risk premium, 104, 107–**108**
  nominal, 104

nominal risk-free rate, 104, 105
  other factors that influence, 113–115
  price risk, 247, 397
  real risk-free rate, 104, 105
  reinvestment rate risk, 248
  risk, 108
  solving for, 198–199
  term structure, 109–113
  yield curve, 109
Internal rate of return (IRR) method, 507–515
  comparison with NPV, 509–515
  IRR, 507
  modified IRR, 516–517
  multiple, 513
  rationale, 509
  reinvestment rate assumption, 513
International (*See also* Multinational), 861–888
Intrinsic value ($\hat{P}_0$), 255
Inventory conversion period, 362
Inventory management, 431–448
  ABC system, 448
  carrying costs, 435–436
  computerized control systems, 446
  conversion period, 362
  control systems, 445–448
  costs, 434–437
  economic ordering quantity (EOQ), 438
  effects of inflation, 445
  EOQ model, 439
  financing, 479–482
  finished goods, 432
  goods in transit, 442
  just-in-time system, 446
  monitoring levels, 448
  ordering costs, 436
  out-sourcing, 447
  quantity discounts, 443–444
  raw materials, 432
  red-line method, 446
  reorder point, 441
  safety stocks, 442
  total inventory costs, 437
  turnover ratio, 50–51
  two-bin method, 446
  work-in-process, 432
Inverted (abnormal) yield curve, 110
Investment banking, 721–730, 844–846
  best efforts arrangement, 722
  competitive bid, 721
  flotation costs, 723
  house, 92
  IBM case study, 728–730
  lead, or managing, underwriter, 727
  mergers and, 844–846
  negotiated deal, 721
  offering price, 723
  selling group, 727
  selling procedures, 727
  shelf registrations, 728
  small business, 732–733
  spread, 97, 723
  trends, 730–731
  underwriting syndicate, 727
  underwritten arrangement, 722
Investment grade bonds, 754
Investment opportunity schedule (IOS), 605

Joint ventures, 847
Junk bonds, 753
Just-in-time system, 446

Kiting, 387

Lead underwriter, 727
Lease financing, 794–802
 cancellation clause, 795
 capitalizing a lease, 796
 effects on financial statements, 795–797
 FASB #13, 796
 financial (or capital) leases, 795
 lessee, 794
 lessor, 794
 NPV analysis, 799–801
 off balance sheet financing, 795
 operating leases, 794
 residual value, 802
 sale and leaseback, 794
 use by small businesses, 817–818
Leverage, 331
 degree of, 638–643
 financial, 53, 626
 financial flexibility, 623
 operating, 331–336
 total, 642–643
Leveraged buyout (LBO), 18, 848, 853–854
Life insurance companies, 93
Line of credit, 464
Liquid asset, 48
Liquidation, 775–778
Liquidity, 12
Liquidity and cash flow analysis, 644–646
Liquidity preference theory, 111
Liquidity premium, 104, **107**
Liquidity ratios (*See also* Financial ratios),
 48–50
 current ratio, 48–49
 quick, or acid test, ratio, 49–50
Loans (*See also* Bank loans), 457, 463–474
 bank, 457, 463–474
 secured, 475
 term, 741–742
Lockbox plan, 388
Long-term debt (*See also* Bonds), 739–779
 amortization, 215–217
 bankruptcy and reorganization, 764–765
 bond ratings, 754–758
 bonds, 742–745
 call premium, 746
 call provision, 746–747
 convertible bonds, 744
 debentures, 744
 factors influencing decisions, 759–764
 floating rate bond, 752
 funded debt, 741
 income bonds, 744
 indenture, 743
 indexed (purchasing power) bond, 745
 interest rate levels, 762
 investment grade bonds, 754
 junk bonds, 753
 maturity matching, 761–762
 mortgage bonds, 743–744
 putable bond, 744
 rationale for using different types, 759
 recent innovations, 748–754
 refunding operations, 765–766
 restrictive covenants, 746
 sinking fund, 747–748
 specific debt contract features, 745
 subordinated debenture, 744
 target capital structure, 595, 622–623,
 760–761
 term loans, 741–742
 traditional debt instruments, 741–745

 trustee, 746
 warrants, 744
 zero coupon bonds, 748–752
Lumpy assets, 305–306

Managerial actions to maximize shareholder
 wealth, 23
Managerial finance in the 1990s, 6
Managerial incentives, 14, 19
Marginal cost of capital (MCC) (*See also*
 Cost of capital), **596**–603
 break, 600
 schedule, 597
Marginal investor, 725
Marginal tax rate, 120
Margin call, 719
Margin requirements, 719
Marketability risk, 397
Marketable securities, 394–403
 default risk, 396
 event risk, 397
 factors influencing choice, 396–398
 inflation risk, 397
 interest rate price risk, 397
 marketability risk, 397
 near-cash reserves, 398
 rationale for holding, 394–395
 types, 398–399
Market/book ratio, 59
 Book value per share, 59
Market portfolio, 160
Market price (P₀), 255
Market risk (*See also* Risk), **161, 548, 555**–
 558
Market risk premium, 167
Market segmentation theory, 111–112
Market value, 708
Market value ratios, 58–59
 market/book ratio, 59
 price/earnings ratio, 58–59
Maturity date, 237
Maturity matching approach, 366
Maturity risk premium, 104, 107–**108**
Mergers, 831–846
 activity level, 834–838
 acquiring company, 838
 analysis, 839
 capital structure, 651
 congeneric, 834
 conglomerate, 834
 control, 833
 corporate alliance, 846
 defensive, 833
 discount rate, 842–844
 diversification, 833
 financial, 839
 friendly, 838
 golden parachutes, 19, **845**
 holding company, 850–852
 horizontal, 834
 hostile, 838
 investment bankers' role, 844–846
 joint venture, 847
 operating, 839
 operating company, 850
 operating versus financial, 839
 parent company, 850
 poison pill, 845
 postmerger control, 840–841
 price paid, 841
 procedures for combining, 838–839
 rationale for, 831–833
 replacement value of assets, 832–833

 synergy, 831
 target company, 838
 tax considerations, 831–832
 tender offer, 18, 838
 terms, 840–841
 two-tier offer, 836
 types, 834
 valuing the target firm, 842–844
 vertical, 834
 white knight, 845
**Moderate current asset investment policy,
 365**
Modified Accelerated Cost Recovery System
 (MACRS), 576–579
 class lives, 577
 illustration, 579
 recovery allowance percentages, 578
**Modified internal rate of return (MIRR),
 516**–517
Modigliani-Miller model, 646–648, 667–668
 capital structure, 646–648
 dividends, 667–668
Money market fund, 94
Money markets, 88
Monte Carlo simulation, 553–555
Mortgage bonds, 743–744
Mortgage markets, 88
Multinational, 861–888
 capital budgeting, 881–883
 capital structures, 883–884
 cash management, 884–885
 convertible currency, 874
 corporation, 862–864
 credit management, 885–886
 deficit trade balance, 871
 devaluation, 871
 discount on forward rate, 875
 Eurobond, 880
 Eurodollar, 879
 exchange rate, 868-870
 exchange rate risk, 874
 fixed exchange rate system, 870
 floating exchange rates, 872
 foreign bond, 880
 forward exchange rate, 875
 forward market hedge, 876
 hedging exchange rate exposure, 876
 inflation, interest rates, and exchange
 rates, 877–878
 international capital markets, 878–881
 international monetary system, 870–874
 inventory management, 886–888
 London Inter-Bank Offered Rate (LIBOR),
 880
 managerial finance, 861–888
 political risk, 882
 premium on forward rate, 875
 repatriation of earnings, 881
 revaluation, 872
 spot rate, 875
 trading in foreign exchange, 875–877
 versus domestic managerial finance, 864–
 868
 working capital management, 884–888
Multiple internal rates of return, 513
Municipal bonds or "munis," 121
Mutual funds, 93
Mutually exclusive projects, 503
Mutual savings banks, 93

National Association of Securities Dealers,
 98, **719**
Near-cash reserves, 398

Net float, 387
Net present value, 505–507
    comparison with IRR, 509–515
    method, 505–507
    profiles, 509
    reinvestment rate assumption, 513
Net working capital, 358
    change in, 536
Net worth, 36
New York Stock Exchange (NYSE), 96
Nominal (quoted) interest rate, 212, 217
Nominal risk-free interest rate, 104, 105
Nonconstant growth, 263–266
Nondiversifiable risk, 143
Normal, or constant, growth, 259–261
Normal profits/rates of return, 15
Normal yield curve, 110

Offering price, 723
Operating cash flows, 40
Operating lease, 794
Operating leverage, 331–336, 639–640
Opportunity cost, 195, 535
Optimal capital budget, 622
Optimal dividend policy, 667
Options (See also Convertibles; Warrants),
    802–806
    call, 803
    covered, 803
    formula value, 804
    naked, 803
    put, 803
    striking price, 803
    writer, 803
Ordering costs, 436
Ordinary (deferred) annuity, 200–202
Organized security exchanges, 96, 714
Original maturity, 237
Outflow, 188
Outsourcing, 447
Overdraft system, 393
Over-the-counter (OTC) market, 97

Paid-in capital, 717
Partnership, 10–11
Par value, 236, 707
Payables deferral period, 362–364
Payback period, 502
    discounted payback period, 503
Payment (PMT), 207
Payment date, 683
Payoff matrix, 146
Pension funds, 93
Performance shares, 20
Periodic interest rate, 218–219
Permanent current assets, 365
Perpetuities, 206
Physical asset markets, 87
Physical assets versus securities, 87, 173
Pledging receivables, 476
Poison pill, 19, 845
Poison puts, 22
Portfolio, 154
Portfolio beta coefficients, 166
Portfolio risk (See also Risk), 154–166
    correlation coefficient, 157
    expected return on a portfolio, ($\hat{k}_p$), 154
    negative correlation, 157
    positive correlation, 157
    realized rate of return ($\bar{k}$), 155
    relevant risk, 162
Post-audit, 519–520

Precautionary balance, 383
Preemptive right, 710
Preferred stock, 253, 789–793
    call premium, 791
    convertibility, 790
    cost of, 588
    cumulative dividends, 790
    floating rate, 793
    par value, 790
    priority, 790
    pros and cons, 791–792
    recent trends, 792–793
    valuation, 253–254
Premium bond, 241–244
Present value (See also Time value of
    money), 195–197
    annuity, 203–206
    annuity due, 205
    interest factor, 196
    interest factor for an annuity, 204
    opportunity cost rate, 195
    uneven cash flow stream, 207–210
Price/earnings ratio, 58-59
Primary markets, 88
Prime rate, 465
Principal, 17
Probability distributions, 144–145
    continuous, 147–148
Production opportunities, 99
Profitability ratios (See also Financial
    ratios), 57–58
    basic earning power ratio, 57
    profit margin on sales, 57
    return on common equity (ROE), 58
    return on total assets (ROA), 58
Profit margin on sales, 57
    effect on need for external funds, 303
Profit maximization, 23
Pro forma statements, 293
Progressive tax, 119
Projected balance sheet method, 293–300
Projects with unequal lives, 543–547
Promissory note, 422, 463
Proprietorship, 10
Prospectus, 718
Proxy, 709
Proxy fight, 14, 709
Publicly owned corporation, 714
Pure play method, 559
Put, 22, 803
Putable bond, 744
PVA_n, 204–205

Quick ratio, 49–50, 358

Rate of return on common equity (ROE),
    58, 63
Rate of return on total assets (ROA), 58,
    60–61
Ratio analysis (See also Financial ratios),
    48–66
    uses and limitations of, 66–68
    projected, 299–300
Realized rate of return ($\bar{k}$), 155
Real risk-free rate of interest (k^*), 104, 105
Receivables collection period, 362, 410
Receivables management (See also Credit
    policy), 410–415
    account receivable, 410
    accumulation, 410–412
    aging schedule, 413–414
    collection period, 362, 410

credit policy, 416
    days sales outstanding, 412
    financing accounts receivable, 410–411
Recovery allowance percentages, 578–579
Red-herring prospectus, 718
Red-line method, 446
Refunding operations, 747, 765–766, 780–
    785
Registration statement, 718
Regression analysis, 182–185, 307–308
Regression line or equation, 164, 182
Reinvestment rate assumption, 513
Reinvestment rate risk, 108
Relaxed current asset investment policy,
    365
Relevant cash flows, 533
Relevant risk, 162
Reorder point, 441
Reorganization (See also Bankruptcy), 764–
    765, 773–779
    standards of fairness, 775
    standards of feasibility, 775
Replacement analysis, 539–543
Replacement chain approach, 544–545
Required rate of return on equity (k_s), 256
Reserve borrowing capacity, 649
Residual policy of dividends, 675–679
Residual value, 802
Restricted current asset investment
    policy, 365
Restrictive covenant, 746
Retained earnings, 38, 707
    balance sheet, 37–40
    cost of, 588–593
Return on assets control, 343
Return on common equity (ROE), 58, 63
Return on total assets (ROA), 58, 60–61
Revolving credit agreement, 464
Rise over run method, 182
Risk, 99, 143, 547–563
    accounting beta method, 559
    adjusted discount rates, 562
    analysis for capital budgeting, 547–563
    aversion, 153
    beta, 548, 555–558
    business, 623, 624–626
    Capital Asset Pricing Model (CAPM), 154
    coefficient of variation, 150
    company-specific, 161
    conclusions on project risk, 560–561
    corporate, or within-firm, 548
    default, 104, 107
    defining and measuring, 143–145
    diversifying to reduce risk, 560
    financial, 624, 626–628
    global context, 174
    inflation, 104, 105–106
    interest rate, 108
    interest rate price, 247, 397
    introduction to project risk analysis, 547–
    548
    market, 161
    marketability, 397
    measuring risk, 148–152
    Monte Carlo simulation, 553–555
    portfolio, and the CAPM, 154–166
    premium, 101, 153, 168
    probability distributions, 144–145
    pure play method, 559
    reinvestment rate, 108, 248
    relationship between, and rates of return,
    167–172

Risk (continued)
  relevant, 162
  scenario analysis, 551–553
  sensitivity analysis, 550–551
  stand-alone risk, 547
  standard deviation, 149
  techniques for measuring beta risk, 558–559
  techniques for measuring stand-alone risk, 549–555
  variance, 149
  within-firm risk, 548

Safety stocks, 442
Sale and leaseback, 794
Sales forecasts, 290–292
  errors, 306
Salvage value, 578
Savings and loan associations (S&Ls), 93
Scatter diagram, 182
Scenario analysis, 551–553
  base case, 551
  best case, 551
  worst case, 551
S corporation, 126–127
Secondary markets, 88, 714
Section 179 expensing, 577
Secured loans, 475
Securities and Exchange Commission (SEC), 718–720
  insiders, 719
  margin call, 719
  margin requirements, 719
  prospectus, 718
  red herring prospectus, 718
  registration statement, 718
Security Market Line (SML), 168–172
  impact of inflation, 170
  risk aversion, 170
Security markets (See also Investment banking), 87–88, 714
  efficient markets hypothesis, 269
  equilibrium, 267
  regulation, 718–720
  transactions, 714–715
  trends in trading procedures, 98
Self-liquidating approach, 366
Selling group, 727
Semiannual compounding, 210–214
Sensitivity analysis, 550–551
Shareholder wealth maximization, 14
Shelf registration, 728
Short-term bank loans (See also Bank loans), 463–474
Short-term credit, 457
Short-term financing (See also Bank loans), 455–482
  accounts payable, 457
  accounts receivable financing, 476–479
  accruals, 457
  advantages and disadvantages, 369–370
  blanket lien, 479
  commercial paper, 457, 474
  compensating balances, 463
  factoring, 476
  inventory financing, 479–482
  line of credit, 464
  pledging receivables, 476
  promissory note, 463
  recourse, 476
  revolving credit agreement, 464
  secured, 479

  secured loans, 475
  small firm, 482–483
  sources, 457
  trade credit, 457-463
  trust receipt, 479
  use of security, 475–482
  warehouse receipt, 480
Signal, 649–650
Signaling theory, 648
Simple interest, 465
Simulation analysis, 553–555
  limitations of, 554–555
Sinking fund, 747–748
Small Business Administration, 27
Small businesses, 27–28, 68–69, 127–129, 275, 371–372, 482–483, 520–521, 608–609, 693, 732–733, 817–818
  building a banking relationship, 127–129
  capital budgeting, 520–521
  cost of equity capital, 608–609
  dividend policy, 693
  financial analysis, 68–69
  goals and resources, 27–28
  growth and working capital needs, 371–372
  lease financing, 817–818
  public stock offerings, 732–733
  receivables financing, 482–483
  taxation, 126–127
  valuation, 275
Social responsibility, 15
Sole proprietorship, 10
Solving for time and interest rates, 198–200
Speculative balances, 383
Spin-off, 847
Spontaneously generated funds, 295
Spot markets, 87
Stakeholders, 23
Standard deviation, 149
Statement of cash flows, 33, 41–42, 81–84
Statement of retained earnings, 33, 37–38
Stock dividends, 687
Stock exchanges, 96–97
Stockholders' equity, 36
Stockholder wealth maximization, 14
Stock market, 94–98
Stock market equilibrium, 266–274
Stock market reporting, 271–274
Stock options, 20
Stock price maximization, 14, 16
Stock repurchases, 689–690, 691–692
Stocks (See individual entries, such as Common stock; Preferred stock)
Stock splits, 687
Stock values with zero growth, 258–259
Straight line depreciation method, 576
Strategic business plan, 498
Striking price, 803
Subordinated debentures, 744
Sunk costs, 535
Supernormal growth, 263–266
Symmetric information, 648
Synchronized cash flows, 385
Synergy, 831
Systematic risk, 160

Takeover, 710
Target capital structure, 595, 622–623, 760–761
Target cash balance, 339
Taxable income, 120

Taxes, 118–127
  after-tax cost of debt, 586–587
  corporate, 122–123
  depreciation, 127
  individual, 119–120
  on dividend and interest income paid, 124
  on dividend and interest income received, 120–121, 123–124
  progressive, 119
  small business, 126–127
Tax loss carry-back and carry-forward, 125
Temporary current assets, 366
Tender offer, 18, 838
Terminal value, 209
Term loans, 741–742
Term structure of interest rates, 109–113
  expectations theory, 111–112
  liquidity preference theory, 111
  market segmentation theory, 111
Time lines, 188
Time preferences for consumption, 99
Times-interest-earned (TIE) ratio, 55–56, 645
Time value of money, 187–220
  amortization schedule, 216
  amortized loans, 215–217
  annuity, 200
  annuity due, 200
  comparison of different types of interest rates, 217–220
  compounding, 189
  compounding periods, 210–214
  consol, 206
  continuous compounding, 232
  continuous discounting, 233
  discounting, 196
  effective annual rate (EAR), 212, 219–220
  fractional time periods, 215
  future value (FV), 189–190, 191–194
  future value interest factor, 191
  future value interest factor for an annuity, 201
  future value of an annuity, 200–203
  nominal interest rate, 212, 217
  ordinary (deferred) annuity, 200
  periodic interest rate, 218
  perpetuities, 206
  present value (PV), 195–197
  present value interest factor, 196
  present value interest factor for an annuity, 204
  present value of an annuity, 203–206
  solving for time and interest rates, 198–200
  uneven cash flow streams, 207–210
Total assets turnover ratio, 52–53
Total leverage, 642–643
Total risk, 143
Trade credit, 457–463
  components, 462
  cost, 458–460
  costly, 462
  credit policy, 458
  effects on financial statements, 460–462
  free, 462
  stretching accounts payable, 460
  terms of credit, 458
Tradeoff theory, 646–648
Transactions balance, 383
Transfer price, 345

Treasury stock, 690
Trend analysis, 60
Trust receipts, 479
Trustee, 746
Two bin method, 446
Two-tier offer, 836

Underwriting syndicate, 727
Uneven cash flow streams, 207–210
Uniform Commercial Code, 476
Unsystematic risk, 160

Valuation, 236–266
    bond valuation, 236–253
    common stock valuation, 254–266
    convertibles, 811–816
    nonconstant growth, 263–266
    normal, or constant growth, 259–261
    options, 802–806
    preferred stock, 253–254
    small firms, 275
    warrants, 808–810
    yield to call, 245

    yield to maturity, 244
    zero growth, 258–259
Variance, 149
Volatility, 173

Warehouse receipts, 480
    field warehouse, 480
    public warehouse, 480
Warrants, 744, 808–810
    actual price, 808–809
    detachable, 809
    effect on reported earnings, 817
    stepped-up exercise price, 810
    value, 809
**Weighted average cost of capital (WACC),
    595**
    logic of, 584–585
White knight, 845
Window dressing techniques, 67
Within-firm risk, 548
Working capital, 358
    advantages and disadvantages of short
        term financing, 369–370

    cash conversion cycle, 361–**362**, 363–
        364
    changes in, 536
    investment and financing policies, 364
    loans, 359
    management, 26, 357–371
    net, 358
    permanent current assets, 365
    policy, 359
    requirement for external financing, 360–
        361
    small business growth, 371–372
    temporary current assets, 366
    terminology, 358–359

Yield curve, 109
Yield to call, 245
Yield to maturity, 244

Zero coupon bonds, 748–752
Zero growth stock, 258–259